AUTHOR

Philip Briggs (e *philip.briggs@bradtguides.com*) has been exploring the highways, byways and backwaters of Africa since 1986, when he spent several months backpacking on a shoestring from Nairobi to Cape Town. In 1991, he wrote the Bradt guide to South Africa, the first such guidebook to be published internationally after the release of Nelson Mandela. Over the rest of the 1990s, Philip wrote a series of pioneering Bradt travel guides to destinations that were then – and in some cases still are – otherwise
practically uncharted by the travel publishing industry. These included the first dedicated guidebooks to Tanzania, Uganda, Ethiopia, Malawi, Mozambique, Ghana and Rwanda, new editions of which have been published regularly ever since. More recently, he authored the first dedicated English-language guidebooks to Somaliland and Suriname, as well as a new guide to The Gambia, all published by Bradt. He spends at least four months on the road every year, usually accompanied by his wife, the travel photographer Ariadne Van Zandbergen, and spends the rest of his time battering away at a keyboard in the sleepy coastal village of Wilderness in South Africa's Western Cape.

MAJOR CONTRIBUTORS

Andrew Roberts has lived in Uganda since 1993. Born in Britain, he first visited the country with a backpack in 1990 and returned three years later to help the Ugandan Forest Department set up ecotourism projects. Nearly 25 years later he's still there, now with a wife and two daughters. Andrew considers himself lucky to have worked in every national park in Uganda, settings which he greatly prefers to his office in Kampala. He has updated several previous editions of Bradt's *Uganda* and also
covered Kampala and Entebbe for this edition. He also produces tourist maps of Uganda and East Africa.

Ariadne Van Zandbergen, who took most of the photographs for this book and contributed to the research, is a freelance photographer and tour guide. Born and raised in Belgium, she travelled through Africa from Morocco to South Africa in 1994/95 and is now resident in Wilderness, South Africa. She has visited 25 African countries and her photographs have appeared in numerous books, magazines, newspapers, maps, periodicals and pamphlets. She has her own online photo library (*www.africaimagelibrary.com; see ad, page 98*).

Uganda is a fairy tale. You climb up a railway instead of a bean-stalk and at the top there is a wonderful new world. The scenery is different, and most of all the people are different from anywhere else in Africa.

Winston Churchill, 1908

On our trip north from Cape Town to Cairo in 1976, George and I liked Uganda more than any other country – and that despite being arrested during the aftermath of the Entebbe Raid. It wasn't necessarily the most interesting, but the people, landscape and wildlife were superb. For overlanders backpacking through Africa, the welcome (or otherwise) you get at the border post can colour your impressions for the rest of your stay. It took us three days to walk and hitch to the Ugandan border post from what was then Zaire, and, in the politically turbulent Amin era, we were afraid that we would be refused entry. George wrote: 'A Ugandan border guard walked towards us, starched khaki shorts, crisply ironed shirt, bright boots, and said, "Welcome to Uganda!" We were completely overwhelmed … After he'd finished stamping us in he said, "But there is one problem …" Our hearts sank. "… about transport. But some men are driving into Kasese tonight if you'd care to wait for them."'

I have not had the opportunity to return to Uganda since that memorable trip, but reading Andy's excellent update to Philip's ground-breaking Uganda guide convinces me that I must not leave it much longer.

Eighth edition published November 2016   First published in 1994

Bradt Travel Guides Ltd
IDC House, The Vale, Chalfont St Peter, Bucks SL9 9RZ, England
www.bradtguides.com
Print edition published in the USA by The Globe Pequot Press Inc, PO Box 480, Guilford, Connecticut 06437-0480

Text copyright © 2016 Philip Briggs
Maps copyright © 2016 Bradt Travel Guides Ltd
Illustrations/photographs copyright © 2016 Individual photographers and artists
Cover image research: Pepi Bluck
Project manager: Laura Pidgley

ISBN: 978 1 78477 022 8 (print)
e-ISBN: 978 1 78477 167 6 (e-pub)
e-ISBN: 978 1 78477 267 3 (mobi)

British Library Cataloguing in Publication Data
A catalogue record for this book is available from the British Library

Photographs and illustrations See page 572 for details.
Maps David McCutcheon FBCart.S; colour map bases by Nick Rowland FRGS; additional map content supplied by Andrew Roberts/Uganda Maps

Typeset by Ian Spick, Bradt Travel Guides
Production managed by Jellyfish Print Solutions; printed in India
Digital conversion by www.dataworks.co.in

Acknowledgements

FROM PHILIP BRIGGS So many people have contributed towards putting together the eighth edition of this guidebook – not to mention earlier versions – that it is difficult to know where to start! First up, immense thanks to Andrew Roberts for his efforts updating the previous three editions, his work on Kampala and Entebbe for this edition, and his excellent company on a road trip to Kidepo Valley National Park. On the home front, I'm grateful as ever to my wife Ariadne Van Zandbergen for her support, and to the Bradt production team – in particular Laura Pidgley and cartographer David McCutcheon – for pulling it all together. Also, ongoing thanks to the many readers whose contributions are acknowledged on the Bradt Uganda update website, and the drivers Alex Gabito and Anatoli Ndeberetse, each of whom accompanied and assisted me for a significant stretch of the research trip.

I am also grateful in various ways and in no particular order to the many readers and people in the tourist industry who helped support this project in various ways. These include Alleyn Kiwana, Amos Wekesa, Angie and Johan Genade, Anil Ghei, Axel Rieke, Boniface Ng'ang'a, Daphne Murungi, David and Francesco Del Lago, Douglas Katumba, Dr Andrew Ggunga Seguya, Emmy Gongo, Felex Musinguzi, Gavin Parnaby, Grace Akiki, Helen Reynolds, Ilse van Agtmaal, Ineke Jongerius, Irene Namatovu, Isaiah Weboya, Ivan Mbabazi Batuma, Jane and Paul Goldring, John Hunwick, Jozef Serneels, Lydia Nakkazi, Lyn Jordaan, Magdalena Sadkowska, Merryde Loosemore, Miha Logar, Phillip Kiboneka, Polly Plica, Praveen Moman, Purity Wakibiru, Ralph Shenk, Raymond Engena, Robin Zaal, Rukia Mwai, Sarah Nandi, Steve Williams, Tamara Segal, Veronica Otter and Wim Kok.

Contents

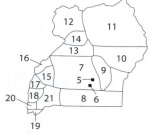

UGANDA UPDATES WEBSITE

For the latest travel news about Uganda, please visit the new interactive Bradt Uganda update website: www.bradtupdates.com/uganda. Administered by author Philip Briggs, it is an online forum where travellers can post and read the latest travel news, trip reports and factual updates from Uganda. The website is a free service to readers, or to anybody else who cares to drop by, and travellers to Uganda and people in the tourist industry are encouraged to use it to share their comments, grumbles, insights, news or other feedback. These can be posted directly on the website, or emailed to Philip (e *philip. briggs@bradtguides.com*).

It's easy to keep up to date with the latest posts by following Philip on Twitter (*@philipbriggs*) and/or liking his Facebook page: fb.me/pb.travel.updates. You can also add a review of the book to www.bradtguides.com or Amazon.

Introduction

Over 20 years ago, in the introduction to the first edition of this guide, I wrote that Uganda's attractions 'tend towards the low-key'. Many years later, when I re-read this assertion for the first time in years, my initial reaction was – well – bemusement, unease, even embarrassment.

Meeting the eyes of a mountain gorilla on the bamboo-clumped slopes of the Virungas? Rafting Grade 5 rapids on the Nile? Following a narrow rainforest trail awhirl with the heart-stopping pant-hoot chorusing of chimpanzees? Cruising the Kazinga Channel in the shadow of the Rwenzoris while elephants drink from the nearby shore? Watching a prehistoric shoebill swoop down on a lungfish in the brooding reed beds of Mabamba Swamp? The roaring, spraying sensory overload that is standing on the tall rocks above Murchison Falls ... Low-key? Goodness me – short of landing on the moon, what exactly would I have classified as a must-do or must-see attraction when I wrote that line?

But as I flicked through that yellowing first edition, all 150 pages of it, my unease slowly dissipated. It had not, I realised, been a reflection of any significant change in my own perceptions during the intervening decade, but rather of the remarkable strides made by Uganda in general, and its tourist industry specifically.

Uganda has changed. And how! When I first visited in 1988, Uganda's economy, infrastructure and human spirit – every aspect of the country, really – were still tangibly shattered in the aftermath of a 15-year cycle of dictatorship and civil conflict that had claimed an estimated one million human lives. Come 1992, when I researched the first edition of this guide, Uganda was visibly on the mend, but, a steady trickle of backpackers aside, its tourist industry remained in the doldrums. Incredible as it seems today, there was no facility to track gorillas within Uganda in 1992, no white-water rafting, no realistic opportunity to get close to chimpanzees, and the likes of Queen Elizabeth and Murchison Falls national parks were practically void of game. Many other tourist sites that today seem well established either didn't exist in their present form, were off-limits or unknown to travellers, or were far less accessible than they are now.

Uganda today does not lack for accessible travel highlights. There is the opportunity to trek within metres of one of the world's last few hundred mountain gorillas, arguably the most exciting wildlife encounter Africa has to offer – though observing chimps in the Kibale or Budongo runs it a damn close second. There is the staggering recovery made by Uganda's premier savannah reserves, where these days one can be almost certain of encountering lions, elephants and buffaloes, etc. There are the Rwenzoris and Mount Elgon, where one can explore East Africa's bizarre montane vegetation without the goal-oriented approach associated with ascents of mounts Kilimanjaro or Kenya. And there is Bujagali Falls, which – with its white-water rafting, kayaking and recently introduced bungee jump – is rapidly emerging as East Africa's answer to that more southerly 'adrenalin capital', Victoria Falls.

Nor does Uganda lack for tourist facilities. As recently as ten years ago, international-class hotels and restaurants were all but non-existent outside the

capital. Today, by contrast, practically every major attraction along the main tourist circuits is serviced by at least one luxury lodge and/or tented camp. Trunk roads have improved beyond recognition, as has the overall standard of local tour operators, public transport, budget accommodation, restaurants and service in general.

It should be noted, too, that the country's natural attractions far exceed the opportunity to see gorillas and lions and so on. Somebody once said that if you planted a walking stick overnight in the soil of Uganda, it would take root before the morning dawned. And it is certainly true that of all Africa's reasonably established safari destinations, Uganda is the most green, the most fertile – the most overwhelmingly tropical!

Uganda, in an ecological nutshell, is where the eastern savannah meets the west African jungle – and it really does offer visitors the best of both these fantastic worlds. In no other African destination can one see a comparable variety of primates with so little effort – not just the great apes, but also more than ten monkey species, as well as the tiny wide-eyed bushbaby and peculiar potto. And if Uganda will have primate enthusiasts wandering around with imbecile grins, it will have birdwatchers doing cartwheels. Uganda is by far the smallest of the four African countries in which more than 1,000 bird species have been recorded, and it is particularly rich in western rainforest specialists – in practical terms, undoubtedly the finest birdwatching destination in Africa.

And yet for all that, Uganda does feel like a more intimate, unspoilt and – dare I say it? – low-key destination than its obvious peers. For starters, it has no semblance of a package tourist industry: group tours seldom exceed eight in number, and even the most popular game-viewing circuits retain a relatively untrammelled atmosphere. The country's plethora of forested national parks and reserves remain highly accessible to independent travellers and relatively affordable to those on a limited budget, as do such off-the-beaten-track gems as the Ssese Islands, Katonga Wildlife Reserve, Sipi Falls and Ndali-Kasenda Crater Lakes.

Uganda has changed. Almost 40 years after Idi Amin was booted into exile, and over three decades from when President Museveni took power, the country bears few obvious scars of what came before. Today, Uganda enjoys one of the healthiest reputations of any African country when it comes to crime directed at tourists. The level of day-to-day hassle faced by independent travellers is negligible. And Ugandans as a whole – both those working within the tourist industry and the ordinary man or woman on the street – genuinely do come across as the most warm, friendly and relaxed hosts imaginable.

It's been with growing pleasure that I've documented Uganda's progress, as a country and as a tourist destination, over the course of eight editions of this guidebook. And this progress is, I hope, reflected in the evolution of the book – from its backpacker-oriented earliest incarnation into this totally reworked and vastly expanded eighth edition, which provides thorough coverage of all aspects of the country for all tastes and budgets. But progress begets progress, and doubtless the next few years will see a host of new and exciting tourist developments in Uganda.

My first visit to Uganda, in late 1988, was decidedly lacking in premeditation. I'd flown from London to Nairobi with broad thoughts of travelling through Tanzania to South Africa over a few months. But on my first night in town, I had a couple of beers with an enthused Canadian who'd just bussed back from Uganda, and was persuaded to revise my plans.

My memories of that first trip to Uganda reflect the decades of war and deprivation that had culminated in the coup of 1986. Bananas, bananas everywhere and nothing else to eat. Buses that took a day to cover 100km of violently pot-holed road. Heaped toilet bowls whose flush mechanism was habitually disused after years without running water. Buildings scarred with bullet holes. The pitiful war orphans who accosted me at every turn.

But there was also much to enjoy. I was enchanted by the verdant landscapes of the west, thrilled by a semi-successful gorilla track in what was then the Impenetrable Forest Reserve (heard them, could see where they were, never actually saw them – all in all, a reasonable return for an investment of US$1), and felt a growing empathy with the guarded optimism, expressed by most of the Ugandans to whom I spoke, that the dark days just might be in the past.

And, with the notable exception of the civil war in the far north, so they were. By 1992, Uganda, once a byword for the worst malaises associated with post-independence Africa, was sufficiently stable for Bradt to commission me to research and write a guidebook to the country. Since then, it's been my privilege to watch and document Uganda as it embarked on one of the most staggering economic and political transformations of our time, to become, in the words of a recent Oxfam report, 'an inspirational economic success story, and a symbol of a more vibrant, successful Africa'.

HOW TO USE THIS GUIDE

AUTHORS' FAVOURITES Finding genuinely characterful accommodation or that unmissable off-the-beaten-track café can be difficult, so the author has chosen a few of his favourite places throughout the country to point you in the right direction. These 'author's favourites' are marked with a ✳.

MAPS
Keys and symbols Maps include alphabetical keys covering the locations of those places to stay, eat or drink that are featured in the book. Note that regional maps may not show all hotels and restaurants in the area: other establishments may be located in towns shown on the map.

On occasion, hotels or restaurants that are not listed in the guide (but which might serve as alternative options if required or serve as useful landmarks to aid navigation) are also included on the maps; these are marked with accommodation (⌂) or restaurant (✗) symbols.

Grids and grid references Several maps use gridlines to allow easy location of sites. Map grid references are listed in square brackets after the name of the place or site of interest in the text, with page number followed by grid number, eg: [103 C3].

Shortly before going to print, the Directorate of Citizenship and Immigration Control announced the implementation of a new online e-visa system, stating that 'all persons intending to travel, study or work in Uganda must apply at least five working days before their intended dates of travel, and permits and passes are approved within 2–3 working days'. The e-visa can be applied for at visas.immigration.go.ug and the procedure is described in detail at immigration.go.ug/media/e-immigration-system.

This e-visa system came online on 1 July 2016, but it is unclear when it will completely replace the existing visa on arrival system. The directorate's most recent word on the subject (dated 28 July 2016) affirms that 'manual application of visas on arrival are being processed alongside the electronic visas and the strict date when we shall stop airlines from carrying passengers without travel authorisations (e-visa approval) or accept applications made at the point of entry shall be communicated to the airlines and tour operators'.

Readers are urged to check immigration.go.ug to monitor developments, and we'll also post news at www.bradtupdates.com/uganda as we become aware of it. For the time being, however, our advice to all prospective visitors is to complete the online e-visa application rather than risk the possibility of being refused boarding or discovering that the visa on arrival facility has been withdrawn at short notice.

Part One

GENERAL INFORMATION

UGANDA AT A GLANCE

Area 235,796km² (91,041 square miles), similar to Great Britain or the US state of Oregon

Location Equatorial Africa between latitudes 4°12′N and 1°29′S and longitudes 29°35′W and 25°E. Bordered by Rwanda (169km) and Tanzania (396km) to the south, Kenya (933km) to the east, South Sudan (435km) to the north and the Democratic Republic of Congo (DRC) for 765km to the west.

Altitude 85% of the country lies between 900m and 1,500m above sea level. The lowest region is the Lake Albert basin (612m) and the Albert Nile. The highest point is Mount Stanley (Rwenzori) at 5,109m.

Population 34.9 million (2014 census), 17% urban. Previously 28 million (2002), 16.7 million (1991), 12.6 million (1980), 9.5 million (1969), 6.5 million (1959), 5 million (1940), 3.5 million (1931), 2.9 million (1921) and 2.5 million (1911).

Capital Kampala (population 1.5 million in the 2014 census)

Other major towns Towns with populations of more than 100,000, in descending order, are Kira, Mbarara, Mukono, Gulu, Hoima, Masaka, Kasese, Lira and Mbale.

Language English, the official language, is spoken by most reasonably educated Ugandans. Among the country's 33 indigenous languages, Luganda is the closest to being a lingua franca.

Religion Christian (85%), Islam (12%), also some Hindu and Jewish, while tribes such as the Karamojong adhere to a traditional animist faith.

Currency Uganda shilling; exchange rates in August 2016 are US$1= Ush3,383, GB£1 = Ush4,415, €1= Ush3,752.

Head of State President Yoweri Museveni (since 1986)

Time zone GMT+3

International dial code +256 (Kampala: 414)

Electricity 240 volts at 50Hz

Mineral resources Copper, cobalt, limestone, salt, alluvial gold, oil.

Major exports Coffee (55%), fish (7.5%), tea (5%), tobacco (4%)

Other crops Bananas, maize, millet, sorghum, cotton, rice, cassava, groundnuts, potatoes

GDP US$27 billion in 2014, with a recent annual growth rate of around 6%.

Human development Average life expectancy 58.5 years; under-five mortality rate 5.7%; adult (age 15–49) HIV/AIDS prevalence 7.3% (estimate); primary school completion 56%; secondary school enrolment 27%; adult literacy 65%; access to safe water 66%; access to electricity 15%

Land use Arable land 25%; agriculture 9%; pasture 9%; forest and woodland 28%; open water 18%; marsh 4%; other 7%

National flag Two sets of black, yellow and red horizontal stripes, with a white central circle around the national bird, the grey crowned crane

National anthem

Oh! Uganda, May God uphold thee, We lay our future in thy hand,
United, free, for liberty, Together, We always stand.
Oh! Uganda the land of freedom, Our love and labour we give,
And with neighbours all at our country's call, In peace and friendship we'll live.
Oh! Uganda the land that feeds us, By sun and fertile soil grown,
For our own dear land we'll always stand, The Pearl of Africa's crown.

1

History and Background

HISTORY

Africa is frequently portrayed as a continent without history. Strictly speaking, this is true, as history by definition relies upon written records, which don't exist for much of the continent prior to the mid 19th century. All the same, the absence of documentation is not the same thing as the absence of incident implied within the many historical accounts that leap in the space of a paragraph from the human evolution to the advent of colonialism. Even without written records, scholars of pre-colonial African history have two main resources in the form of archaeological evidence and oral tradition, both of which tend to be patchy and riddled with contradictions, making them open to a diversity of interpretations. All the same, the ancient legends associated with the various Ugandan kingdoms and the more objective evidence unearthed by modern archaeologists display a high level of mutual corroboration when it comes to certain key events in Uganda between AD1100 and the present, suggesting that many local oral traditions, when stripped of overt mythologising, amount to a reasonably accurate account of actual events.

EARLY PREHISTORY It is widely agreed that the entire drama of human evolution was enacted in the Rift Valley and plains of East Africa. Although the fossil record is patchy, the combination of DNA evidence and various hominid bones unearthed in the region suggest that the ancestors of modern humans and modern chimpanzees diverged in the Ethiopian and Kenyan Rift Valley roughly five to six million years ago. Uganda has presumably supported hominid life for as long as any other part of East Africa, an assertion supported by the recent discovery of several fossils belonging to the semi-bipedal proto-hominid *Ugandapithecus major* in the vicinity of Moroto. These include a complete 20-million-year-old fossil skull unearthed on the slopes of Mount Napak in 2011, and now on display in the Uganda Museum in Kampala.

Stone Age implements dating to more than a million years ago have been discovered throughout East Africa, and it is highly probable that this earliest of human technologies arose in the region. For a quarter of a million years prior to around 8000BC, Stone Age technology was spread throughout Africa, Europe and Asia, and the design of common implements such as the stone axe was identical throughout this area. The oldest Stone Age sites in Uganda, Nsongezi on the Kigezi River and Sango Bay on Lake Victoria, were occupied between 150,000 and 50,000 years ago.

The absence of written records means that the origin and classification of the modern peoples of east and southern Africa are a subject of some academic debate. Broadly speaking, it is probable that East Africa has incurred two major human influxes since 1000BC, on both occasions, by people from West Africa.

Most Bantu languages use a variety of prefixes to form words so that several similar words are made from a common root. When discussing the various peoples and kingdoms of Uganda, this can be somewhat confusing.

The most common prefixes are *mu-*, *ba-* and *bu-*, the first referring to an individual, the second to the people collectively, and the third to the land they occupy. In other words, a Muganda is a member of the Baganda, the people who live in Buganda. The language of the Baganda is Luganda and their religion and customs are Kiganda. To use another example, the Banyoro live in Bunyoro, where they speak Runyoro and follow Kinyoro customs.

There is not a great deal of consistency in the use of these terms in the English-language books. Some use the adjective *Ganda* to describe, for instance, the *Ganda kabaka* (King of Buganda). Others will call him the Muganda or Baganda kabaka. Standards are more flexible when dealing with ethnic groups other than the Baganda: the Ankole people are usually referred to as the Banyankole but I've never seen the kingdom referred to as Bunyankole; the people of Toro are often referred to as the Batoro but I've not come across the term Butoro. In this following historical account, I've generally stuck with what seems to be the most common usage: prefixes for -ganda, -nyoro and -soga; no prefixes for Ankole and Toro.

The name Uganda of course derives from the word *Buganda*. The reason why the British protectorate came to be known by this abbreviated name is probably that most Europeans had their initial contact with Buganda through KiSwahili-speaking guides and translators. In KiSwahili, the prefix *u-* is the equivalent of the Luganda *bu-*, so that the Swahili speakers would almost certainly have referred to the Ganda kingdom as Uganda. Although many Baganda writers evidently find it annoying that their country has been misnamed in this way, it does simplify my task that there is a clear distinction between the name of Uganda the country and that of Buganda the kingdom.

When referring to the leaders of the various Ugandan groups, the title *kabaka* is bestowed on the Baganda king, the title *omukama* on the Banyoro king, and *omugabe* on the Ankole king.

The first of these influxes probably originated somewhere in modern-day DRC about 3,000 years ago. The descendants of these invaders, known locally as the Bambuti or Batwa, were slightly built hunter-gatherers similar in culture and physique to the Khoisan-speaking peoples of southern Africa and the Pygmoid people who still live in certain rainforests near the Congolese border. The rock paintings on several shelters near Mbale in eastern Uganda show strong affinities with rock art associated with Khoisan-speaking hunter-gatherers elsewhere in the continent, suggesting that at one time these people occupied most of Uganda, as did they most of east and southern Africa at the beginning of the 1st millennium AD.

The second human influx, which reached the Lake Victoria hinterland in roughly 200BC, apparently coincided with the spread of Iron Age technology in the region. There is good reason to suppose that the people who brought iron-working techniques into the region were the ancestors of the Bantu speakers who probably occupied most of sub-equatorial Africa by AD500. Few conclusive facts are known about the political and social structures of the early Bantu-speaking peoples who inhabited Uganda, but it is reasonable to assume that they lived in

loosely assembled chiefdoms similar to the pre-colonial *ntemi* structures which existed in the Tanzanian interior until colonial times.

It has been established beyond doubt that relatively centralised political systems made an early appearance in Uganda. The origin of the first of these kingdoms, Bunyoro-Kitara, is shrouded in legend, and the rough date of its foundation has yet to be determined by scholars. Nevertheless, a number of archaeological sites in the Mubende and Ntusi districts of central Uganda suggest that Bunyoro-Kitara was established long before AD1500.

THE BATEMBUZI AND BACHWEZI (AD1100–1500) A creation myth common to Kiganda, Kinyoro and several other Ugandan oral traditions asserts that the first man on earth was Kintu, a divinely-created being who lived in the vicinity of Wanseko and went on to marry Nambi, the daughter of his creator Ggulu (see box, page 174). Traditions are vague on how long ago this event occurred, but they do assert that the first dynasty to rule over Bunyoro-Kitara, the Batembuzi, lived between AD 1100 and AD 1350, and ample physical evidence at Ntusi would seem to confirm that a highly centralised society existed in this area as early as the 11th century.

The origin of the Batembuzi is obscured by legend and myth, but they must have ruled for several generations, as various local traditions list between ten and 22 dynastic kings. Oral traditions name Ruhanga, the King of the Underworld, as the founder of the dynasty (the Kinyoro Underworld is evidently closer to the Christian notion of heaven than to that of hell) and they consider the Batembuzi to have been deities with supernatural powers. Descriptions of the Batembuzi's physical appearance suggest that they may have migrated to the area from modern-day Sudan or Ethiopia. Whatever their origins, they evidently became culturally and linguistically integrated into the established Bantu-speaking culture of Bunyoro-Kitara.

Most traditions identify Isuza as the last Batembuzi ruler. Isuza is said to have fallen in love with a princess of the Underworld, and to have followed her into her homeland, from where he couldn't find his way back to Bunyoro-Kitara. Years later, Isuza's son Isimbwa visited Bunyoro-Kitara, and he impregnated the only daughter of the unpopular stand-in king, Bukuku. Their child, Ndahura, was thrown into a river shortly after his birth at the order of Bukuku, who had been told by diviners that he should fear any child born by his daughter; but his umbilical cord stuck in a tree, keeping him afloat, and he was rescued by a royal porter. Ndahura was raised by the porter and, after he reached adulthood, he drove Bukuku's cattle from his home, stabbed the king in the back, and claimed the throne as his own. His claim was supported by the people of Bunyoro-Kitara, who accepted that the true royal lineage was being restored because of Ndahura's striking physical resemblance to his grandfather Isuza.

Ndahura – 'the uprooter' – is remembered as the founder of the Bachwezi dynasty. The Bachwezi were most probably migrants from Ethiopia or Sudan (hence the physical resemblance between Ndahura and Isuza?), who, like the Batembuzi before them, adopted the language and culture of the local Bantu speakers over whom they assumed rule. Ndahura was almost certainly a genuine historical figure, and he probably came to power in the second half of the 14th century. In addition to having supernatural powers, Ndahura is traditionally credited with introducing Ankole cattle and coffee cultivation to Uganda.

The Mubende and Ntusi areas are identified by all traditional accounts as lying at the heart of Bunyoro-Kitara during the Bachwezi era, an assertion which is supported by a mass of archaeological evidence, notably the extensive earthworks at Bigo bya Mugyenyi and Munsa. This suggests that the Bachwezi Empire covered

most of Uganda south and west of the Nile River. Traditional accounts claim that it covered a much larger area, and that Ndahura was a militant expansionist who led successful raids into parts of western Kenya, northern Tanzania and Rwanda.

Ndahura was captured during a raid into what is now northern Tanzania. He eventually escaped, but he refused to reclaim the throne, instead abdicating in favour of his son Wamala. Ndahura then disappeared, some claim to the Fort Portal region. He abandoned his capital at Mubende Hill to his senior wife, Nakayima, who founded a hereditary matriarchy that survived into the colonial era. Wamala moved his capital to an unidentified site before eventually relocating it to Bigo bya Mugyenyi.

Considering the immense Bachwezi influence over modern Uganda – almost all the royal dynasties in the region claim to be of direct or indirect Bachwezi descent – it is remarkable that they ruled for only two generations. Tradition has it that Wamala simply disappeared, just like his father before him, thereby reinforcing the claim that the Bachwezi were immortal. It is more likely that the collapse of the dynasty was linked to the arrival of the Luo in Bunyoro-Kitara towards the end of the 15th century. Whatever their fate, the Bachwezi remain the focus of several religious cults, and places like the Nakayima Tree on Mubende Hill and the vast earthworks at Bigo bya Mugyenyi near Ntusi are active sites of Bachwezi worship to this day.

BUNYORO, BUGANDA AND ANKOLE (1500–1650)

In the second half of the 15th century, the Nilotic-speaking Luo left their homeland on the plains of southeastern Sudan, and migrated southwards along the course of the Nile River into what is now Uganda. After settling for a period on the northern verge of Bunyoro-Kitara at a place remembered as Pubungu (probably near modern-day Pakwach), they evidently splintered into three groups. The first of these groups remained at Pubungu, the second colonised the part of Uganda west of the Nile, and the third continued southwards into the heart of Bunyoro-Kitara.

It was probably the Luo invasion which ended Bachwezi rule over Bunyoro-Kitara. The Bachwezi were succeeded by the Babiito dynasty, whose founder Rukidi came to Bunyoro from Bukidi (a Runyoro name for anywhere north of Bunyoro). The tradition is that Rukidi was the son of Ndahura and a Mukidi woman, and that he was invited to rule Bunyoro by the Bachwezi nobles before they disappeared. Many modern scholars feel that the Luo captured Bunyoro by force, and that they integrated themselves into the local culture by claiming a genetic link with the Bachwezi, adopting several Bachwezi customs and rapidly learning the local Runyoro tongue.

The arrival of the Luo coincided with the emergence of several other kingdoms to the south and east of Bunyoro, notably Buganda and Ankole in modern-day Uganda, as well as Rwanda, Burundi and the Karagwe kingdom in what is now northwest Tanzania. All these kingdoms share a common Bachwezi heritage. Kinyoro and Kiganda traditions agree that Buganda was founded by an offshoot of the Babiito dynasty, while Ankole traditions claim that Ruhinda, the founder of their kingdom, was yet another son of Ndahura. Ankole retained the strongest Bachwezi traditions, and its most important symbol of national unity was a royal drum or Bagyendwaza said to have been owned by Wamala.

Bunyoro was the largest and most influential of these kingdoms until the end of the 17th century. It had a mixed economy, a loose political structure, and a central trade position on account of its exclusive control of the region's salt mines. Bunyoro was presided over by an *omukama*, who was advised by a group of special counsellors. The omukama was supported at a local level by several grades of semi-autonomous chiefs, most of whom were royally appointed loyalists of aristocratic descent.

Prior to 1650, Buganda was a small kingdom ruled over by a *kabaka*. Unlike those in Bunyoro, the local chiefs in Buganda were hereditary clan leaders and not normally of aristocratic descent. Buganda was the most fertile of the Ugandan kingdoms, for which reason its economy was primarily agricultural. Ankole, by contrast, placed great importance on cattle, and its citizens were stratified into two classes: the cattle-owning Bahima, who claimed to be descendants of Ruhinda, and the agriculturist Bairu. Ankole was ruled by an *omugabe*. As with the Omukama of Bunyoro and the Kabaka of Buganda, this was a hereditary title normally reserved for the eldest son of the previous ruler. Positions of local importance were generally reserved for Bahima aristocrats.

Another identifiable polity to take shape at around this time was the Busoga, which lies to the east of Buganda and is bordered by Lake Kyoga to the north and Lake Victoria to the south. The Basoga show strong linguistic and cultural affiliations to the Baganda, but their oral traditions suggest that their founder, remembered by the name of Mukama, came from the Mount Elgon region and had no Bachwezi or Babiito links. Busoga has apparently assimilated a large number of cultural influences over the centuries, and it seems to have remained curiously detached from the mainstream of Ugandan history, probably by allying itself to the dominant power of the time.

An indication of Bunyoro's regional dominance in the 16th century comes from the traditional accounts of the wars fought by Olimi I, the fifth omukama. Olimi is said to have attacked Buganda and killed the kabaka in battle, but he declined to occupy the conquered territory, opting instead to attack Ankole (of the several explanations put forward for this superficially peculiar course of action, the only one that rings true is that Olimi was after cattle, which were scarce in Buganda but plentiful in Ankole). Olimi occupied Ankole for some years, and according to Kinyoro traditions he withdrew only because of a full solar eclipse, an event which Banyoro traditionalists still consider to be portentous. If this tradition is true (and there is no reason to doubt it), Olimi must have been ruling Bunyoro at the time of the solar eclipse of 1520. Assuming that the four Babiito rulers who preceded Olimi would together have ruled for at least 30 or 40 years, this suggests that the Babiito dynasty and the Buganda and Ankole kingdoms were founded between 1450 and 1500.

BUNYORO, BUGANDA AND ANKOLE (1650–1850)
At its peak in the 17th century, Bunyoro covered an area of roughly 80,000km² south and west of the Nile and Lake Victoria. Buganda was at this time no more than 15,000km² in area, and Ankole covered a mere 2,500km² north of the Kagera River. Similar in size to Buganda, the relatively short-lived Kingdom of Mpororo, founded in about 1650, covered much of the Kigezi region of Uganda, as well as parts of what is now northern Rwanda, until its dissolution in the mid 17th century.

The period between 1650 and 1850 saw Bunyoro shrink to a fraction of its former area and relinquish its regional dominance to Buganda. The start of this decline can be traced to the rule of Omukama Cwa I (or Cwamali) in the late 17th or early 18th century. During Cwa's reign, Bunyoro suffered an epidemic of cattle disease. Cwa ordered all the cattle in the kingdom to be killed, and he then raided Ankole to seize replacements. Cwa occupied Ankole for three years, after which he attempted to extend his kingdom into Rwanda. He was killed in Rwanda and his returning troops were evicted from Ankole by Omugabe Ntare IV, who thereby earned himself the nickname Kitabunyoro – 'the scourge of Bunyoro'. After chasing out the Banyoro, Ntare IV extended Ankole's territory north to the Karonga River.

Bunyoro descended into temporary disarray as the aristocracy tried to cover up the omukama's death, and the empty throne was seized by one of his sisters,

1

stimulating a succession war that lasted for several years. Buganda took advantage of Bunyoro's weakness by taking control of several of its allied territories, so that in the years following Cwa's death it doubled in area. It is unclear whether Buganda acquired these territories by conquest or merely by exploiting the faltering loyalty of chiefs who were traditionally allied with Bunyoro.

Also linked to the upheavals following Cwa's death was the migration of the Palwo, the name given to the Luo speakers who had settled in the north of Bunyoro two centuries earlier. Some of the Palwo settled in Acholi, the part of northern Uganda east of the Albert Nile, where they founded several small Luo-speaking kingdoms modelled along the traditions of Bunyoro. Others migrated through Busoga in eastern Uganda to the Kisumu region of what is now western Kenya, where they are still the dominant group. A few groups settled in Busoga, south of modern-day Tororo, to found a group of small kingdoms known collectively as Jopadhola.

In 1731, Omukama Duhaga took the Banyoro throne. Kinyoro traditions remember him as being small, light-skinned, hairy and difficult, and as having had the second-greatest number of children of any omukama (the third omukama, Oyo I, reputedly had 2,000 children, a record which will take some beating). During Duhaga's 50-year reign, Buganda annexed the area around Lake Wamala, as well as the land immediately west of the Victoria Nile, from where it plundered large parts of Busoga. Duhaga died in battle along with 70 of his sons, attempting to protect Bunyoro from Baganda expansionists.

By the reign of Omukama Kyebambe III (1786–1835), Buganda was firmly entrenched as the major regional power. During the late 17th century, Kabaka Mutebi consolidated his power by dismissing some traditional clan leaders and replacing them with confirmed loyalists; by the end of the 18th century, practically every local chief in Buganda was one of the so-called 'king's men'. Buganda forged loose allegiances with Busoga and Karagwe (in northern Tanzania), and they maintained a peaceful equilibrium with Ankole, which had in the meantime further expanded its territory by absorbing several parts of the former Mpororo kingdom. Towards the end of Kyebambe III's rule, Bunyoro was dealt a further blow as several local princes decided to rebel against the ageing omukama. The most significant rebellion was in Toro, where a prince called Kaboyo declared autonomous rule in 1830, depriving Bunyoro of its important salt resources at Katwe.

By the mid 19th century, Buganda stretched west from the Victoria Nile almost as far as Mubende and over the entire Lake Victoria hinterland as far south as the Kagera River. Ankole covered an area of roughly 10,000km^2 between the Karonga and Kagera rivers, and the newly founded Toro kingdom occupied a similar area north of the Karonga. Bunyoro had been reduced to a quarter of its former size; although it had retained the Nile as its northern boundary, there was now no point at which it stretched further than 50km south of the Kafu River.

BUNYORO AND EGYPT (1850–89)

The death of Omukama Kyebambe III was followed by a period of internal instability in Bunyoro, during which two weak omukamas ruled in succession. In 1852, the throne was seized by Kamurasi, who did much to stop the rot, notably by killing a number of rebellious princes at the Battle of Kokoitwa. Kamurasi's rule coincided with the arrival of Arab traders from the north, who were admitted into Bunyoro in the recognition that their support could only strengthen the ailing kingdom. The Arabs based themselves at Gondoroko, from where they led many brutal raids into the small and relatively defenceless Luo kingdoms of Acholi.

In 1862, Kamurasi's court welcomed John Speke and James Grant, the first Europeans to reach Bunyoro. Two years later, Bunyoro was entered from the north by Samuel Baker, a wealthy big-game hunter and incidental explorer who travelled everywhere with his wife. The Bakers spent a year in Bunyoro, during which time they became the first Europeans to see Lake Mwatanzige, which they renamed Lake Albert. Baker also developed an apparently irrational antipathy towards his royal host, which almost certainly clouded his judgement when he returned to the region eight years later.

The years following the Bakers' departure from Bunyoro saw radical changes in the kingdom. Omukama Kamurasi died in 1869, prompting a six-month succession battle that resulted in the populist Kabalega ascending to the throne. Omukama Kabalega is regarded by many as the greatest of all Banyoro rulers who, were it not for British intervention, would surely have achieved his goal of restoring the kingdom to its full former glory. Kabalega introduced a set of military and political reforms which have been compared to those of Shaka in Zululand: he divided the army into battalions of 1,500 men, each of which was led by a trained soldier chosen on merit as opposed to birth, and he minimised the influence of the eternally squabbling Banyoro aristocracy by deposing them as local chiefs in favour of capable commoners with a sound military background.

In 1871, the imperialist Khedive Ismail of Egypt appointed the recently knighted Sir Samuel Baker to the newly created post of Governor General of Equatoria, a loosely defined province in the south of Egyptian-ruled Sudan. When Baker assumed his post in 1872, he almost immediately overstepped his instructions by declaring Bunyoro to be an annexe of Equatoria. Kabalega responded to Baker's pettiness by attacking the Egyptian garrison at Masindi. Baker was forced to retreat to Patiko in Acholi, and he defended his humiliating defeat by characterising Kabalega as a treacherous coward, thereby poisoning the omukama's name in Europe in a way that was to have deep repercussions on future events in Uganda.

The second Governor General of Equatoria, General Gordon, knew of Kabalega only what his biased predecessor had told him. Gordon further antagonised the omukama by erecting several forts in northern Bunyoro without first asking permission. Kabalega refrained from attacking the forts, but relations between Bunyoro and the Egyptian representative became increasingly uneasy. Outright war was probably averted only by the appointment of Emin Pasha as governor general in 1878. Sensibly, Emin Pasha withdrew from Bunyoro; and, instead of using his position to enact a petty vendetta against Kabalega, he focused his energy on the altogether more significant task of wresting control of the West Nile and Acholi regions from Arab slave traders. In 1883, following the Mahdist rebellion in Sudan, Emin Pasha and his troops were stranded in Wadelai. In 1889, they withdrew to the East African coast, effectively ending foreign attempts to control Uganda from the north.

The combined efforts of Baker and Gordon did little to curb Kabalega's empire-building efforts. In 1875, the Banyoro army overthrew Nyaika, the King of Toro, and the breakaway kingdom was reunited with Bunyoro. Kabalega also reclaimed several former parts of Bunyoro which had been annexed to Buganda, so that Bunyoro doubled in area under the first 20 years of his rule. Even more remarkably, Kabalega's was the first lengthy reign in centuries during which Bunyoro was free of internal rebellions. Following the Emin Pasha's withdrawal from Equatoria in 1889, the continued expansion, stability and sovereignty of Bunyoro under Kabalega must have seemed assured.

EUROPEANS IN BUGANDA (1884–92) In the mid 19th century, when the first Swahili slave traders arrived in central Africa from the east coast, the dominant regional power was Buganda, ruled over by Kabaka Mutesa from his capital at

In 1862, John Speke spent weeks kicking his heels in the royal capital of Buganda, awaiting permission to travel to the river he suspected might be the source of the Nile. His sojourn is described in four long and fascinating chapters in *Journal of the Discovery of the Source of the Nile*, the earliest and most copious document of courtly life in the kingdom.

The following extracts provide some idea of the everyday life of the subjects of Kabaka Mutesa – who is remembered as a more benevolent ruler than his predecessor Suuna or successor Mwanga. The quotes are edited to modernise spellings and cut extraneous detail.

A more theatrical sight I never saw. The king, a good-looking, well-figured, tall young man of 25, was sitting on a red blanket spread upon a platform of royal grass, scrupulously well dressed in a new *mbugu*. His hair was cut short, excepting on the top, where it was combed up into a high ridge, running from stem to stern like a cockscomb. On his neck was a large ring of beautifully worked small beads, forming elegant patterns by their various colours. On one arm was another bead ornament, prettily devised; and on the other a wooden charm, tied by a string covered with snakeskin. On every finger and every toe, he had alternate brass and copper rings; and above the ankles, halfway up to the calf, a stocking of very pretty beads. Everything was light, neat, and elegant in its way; not a fault could be found with the taste of his 'getting up'.

Both men, as is the custom in Uganda, thanked Mutesa in a very enthusiastic manner, kneeling on the ground – for no-one can stand in the presence of his majesty – in an attitude of prayer, and throwing out their hands as they repeated the words N'yanzig, N'yanzig, ai N'yanzig Mkahma wangi, etc, etc, for a considerable time; when, thinking they had done enough of this, and heated with the exertion, they threw themselves flat upon their stomachs, and, floundering about like fish on land, repeated the same words over again and again, and rose doing the same, with their faces covered with earth; for majesty in Uganda is never satisfied till subjects have grovelled before it like the most abject worms …

The king loaded one of the carbines I had given him with his own hands, and giving it full-cock to a page, told him to go out and shoot a man in the outer court; which was no sooner accomplished than the little urchin returned to announce his success, with a look of glee such as one would see in the face of a boy who had robbed a bird's nest, caught a trout, or done any other boyish trick. I never heard, and there appeared no curiosity to know, what individual human being the urchin had deprived of life …

The Namasole entered on a long explanation, to the following effect. There are no such things as marriages in Uganda; there are no ceremonies attached to it. If any man possessed of a pretty daughter committed an offence, he might give her to the king as a peace offering; if any neighbouring king had a pretty daughter, and the King of Uganda wanted her, she might be demanded as a fitting tribute. The men in Uganda are supplied with women by the king, according to their merits, from seizures in battle abroad, or seizures from refractory officers at home. The women are not regarded as property, though many exchange their daughters;

Kampala. Mutesa allowed the slave traders to operate from his capital, and he collaborated in slave-raiding parties into neighbouring territories. The Swahili converted several Baganda clan chiefs to their Islamic faith, and later, when Kampala was descended upon by the rival French Catholics and British Protestants,

and some women, for misdemeanours, are sold into slavery; whilst others are flogged, or are degraded to do all the menial services of the house …

Congow was much delighted with my coming, produced *pombe*, and asked me what I thought of his women, stripping them to the waist. I asked him what use he had for so many women? To which he replied, 'None whatever; the king gives them to us to keep up our rank, sometimes as many as one hundred together, and we either turn them into wives, or make servants of them, as we please …'

The king was giving appointments, plantations, and women, according to merit, to his officers. As one officer, to whom only one woman was given, asked for more, the king called him an ingrate, and ordered him to be cut to pieces on the spot; and the sentence was carried into effect – not with knives, for they are prohibited, but with strips of sharp-edged grass, after the executioners had first dislocated his neck by a blow delivered behind the head …

Nearly every day, I have seen one, two, or three of the wretched palace women led away to execution, tied by the hand, and dragged along by one of the body-guard, crying out, as she went to premature death, at the top of her voice, in the utmost despair and lamentation; and yet there was not a soul who dared lift hand to save any of them, though many might be heard privately commenting on their beauty … One day, one of the king's favourite women overtook us, walking, with her hands clasped at the back of her head, to execution, crying in the most pitiful manner. A man was preceding her, but did not touch her; for she loved to obey the orders of her king voluntarily, and in consequence of previous attachment, was permitted, as a mark of distinction, to walk free. Wondrous world! …

A large body of officers came in with an old man, with his two ears shorn off for having been too handsome in his youth, and a young woman who had been discovered in his house. Nothing was listened to but the plaintiff's statement, who said he had lost the woman for four days, and, after considerable search, had found her concealed by the old man. Voices in defence were never heard. The king instantly sentenced both to death; and, to make the example more severe, decreed that, being fed to preserve life as long as possible, they were to be dismembered bit by bit, as rations for the vultures, every day, until life was extinct. The dismayed criminals, struggling to be heard, in utter despair, were dragged away boisterously in the most barbarous manner, to the drowning music of drums …

A boy, finding the king alone, threatened to kill him, because he took the lives of men unjustly. The king showed us, holding the pistol to his cheek, how he had presented the muzzle to the boy, which so frightened him that he ran away … The culprit, a good-looking young fellow of 16 or 17, brought in a goat, made his *n'yanzigs*, stroked the goat and his own face with his hands, *n'yanzigged* again with prostrations, and retired … There must have been some special reason why, in a court where trifling breaches of etiquette were punished with a cruel death, so grave a crime should have been so leniently dealt with; but I could not get at the bottom of the affair.

even more chiefs were attracted away from traditional Kiganda beliefs. Mutesa's court rapidly descended into a hotbed of religious rivalry.

Mutesa died in 1884. His son and successor, Mwanga, was a volatile and headstrong teenager who took the throne as religious rivalries in Buganda were

building to a climax. Mwanga attempted to play off the various factions; he succeeded in alienating them all. In 1885, under the influence of a Muslim adviser, Mwanga ordered the execution of Bishop Hannington and 50 Christian converts (many of whom were roasted to death on a spit). In 1887, Mwanga switched allegiance to the traditionalist Kiganda chiefs, who in return offered to help him expel converts of all persuasions from Buganda. Threatened with expulsion, Muslims and Christians combined forces to launch an attack on the throne. Mwanga was overthrown in 1888. His Muslim-backed replacement, Kiwewa, persecuted Christians with even greater fervour than Mwanga had in 1885–86, but when Kiwewa's Kiganda leanings became apparent the Muslims rebelled and installed yet another leader. Events came to a head in 1889, when a civil war erupted between the Christian and Muslim factions, the result of which was that all Muslims were driven from the capital, later to join forces with Kabalega in Bunyoro. Mwanga was re-installed as kabaka.

The rival European powers were all eager to get their hands on the well-watered and fertile kingdom of Buganda, where, with the Muslims safely out of the way, rivalry between Francophile Catholics and Anglophile Protestants was increasingly open. In February 1890, Carl Peters arrived at Mengo clutching a treaty with the German East Africa Company. Mwanga signed it readily, possibly in the hope that German involvement would put an end to the Anglo–French religious intrigues which had persistently undermined his throne. Unfortunately for Mwanga, German deliverance was not to be: a few months after Peters's arrival, Germany handed Buganda and several other African territories to Britain in exchange for Heligoland, a tiny but strategic North Sea island.

In December 1890, Captain Frederick Lugard, the representative of the British East Africa Company, arrived at Kampala hoping to sign a treaty with an unimpressed Mwanga. The ensuing religious and political tensions sparked a crisis in January 1892, when a Catholic accused of killing a Protestant was acquitted by Mwanga on a plea of self-defence. Lugard demanded that the freed man be handed to him for a retrial and possible execution. Mwanga refused, on the rightful grounds that he was still the kabaka. Lugard decided it was time for a show of strength, and with the support of the Protestants he drove Mwanga and his Catholic supporters to an island on Lake Victoria. He then sent troops to rout Mwanga from the island; the kabaka fled to Bukoba in Karagwe (northern Tanzania) before returning in March to his kingdom, which was by then on the verge of civil war. Mwanga was left with no real option but to sign a treaty recognising the Company's authority in Buganda.

Lugard returned to Britain in October 1892, where he rallied public support for the colonisation of Buganda, and was instrumental in swaying a Liberal government which under Gladstone was opposed to the acquisition of further territories. In November, the British government appointed Sir Gerald Portal as the commissioner to advise on future policy towards Buganda. Portal arrived in Kampala in March 1893, to be greeted by a flood of petitions from all quarters. Swayed by the fact that missionaries of both persuasions felt colonisation would further their goals in the kingdom, Portal raised the Union Jack over Kampala in April; a month later he signed a formal treaty with the unwilling but resigned Mwanga, offering British protectorateship over Buganda in exchange for the right to collect and spend taxes.

THE CREATION OF UGANDA (1892–99) The protectorate of Uganda initially had rather vague boundaries, mimicking those of the indigenous kingdom to which it nominally offered protection. It is not at all clear to what extent the early British administrators conceived of their protectorate extending beyond the boundaries of

the kingdom, but all accounts suggest that Uganda was as chaotic an assemblage as can be imagined.

Captain Lugard had done a fair bit of tentative territorial expansion even before he signed a treaty with Buganda. It was evidently his intention to quell Bunyoro's rampant Omukama Kabalega, against whom he had been prejudiced by the combination of Baker's poisonous reports, and the not entirely unpredictable antipathy held for the Banyoro in Buganda. In August 1891, Lugard signed a treaty with the Omugabe of Ankole in a vain attempt to block arms reaching Bunyoro from the south. Lugard drove the Banyoro army out of Toro and installed Kasagama, an exiled prince of Toro, to the throne. He then built a line of forts along the southern boundary of Bunyoro, effectively preventing Kabalega from invading Toro. The grateful Kasagama was happy enough to reward Lugard's efforts by signing a treaty of friendship between Britain and Toro.

Britain's predisposition to regard Kabalega as a villain became something close to a legal obligation following the treaty of protectorateship over Buganda, and it was certainly paralleled by the residual suspicion of foreigners held by Kabalega after the Equatoria debacle. Elements opposing British rule over Buganda fled to Kabalega's court at Mparo (near Hoima), notably a group of Muslim Baganda and Sudanese soldiers whose leader Selim Bey was deported in 1893 following a skirmish with the imperial authorities in Entebbe. With the assistance of the Baganda exiles, Kabalega re-invaded Toro in late 1893, driving Kasagama into the Rwenzori Mountains and the only British officer present back to Buganda.

In December 1893, Colonel Colville led a party of eight British officers, 450 Sudanese troops and at least 20,000 Baganda infantrymen on to Mparo. Kabalega was too crafty to risk confrontation with this impressive force: he burnt his capital and fled with his troops to the Budongo Forest. During 1894, Kabalega led several successful attacks on British forts, but as he lost more men and his supplies ran low, his guerrilla tactics became increasingly ineffective. In August 1894, on the very same day that the formal protectorateship of Uganda was announced by Colville, Kabalega launched his biggest assault yet on the fort at Hoima. The fort was razed, but Kabalega lost thousands of men. He was forced to leave Bunyoro to go into hiding in Acholi and Lango, from where he continued a sporadic and increasingly unsuccessful series of attacks on British targets. Kabalega's kingdom was unilaterally appended to the British protectorate on 30 June 1896; the first formal agreement between Britain and Bunyoro was signed only in 1933.

Meanwhile, back in Kampala, Kabaka Mwanga and his traditionalist chiefs were becoming frustrated at the power which the British had invested in Christian converts in general and Protestants in particular. In July 1897, Mwanga left Kampala and raised a few loyalist troops to launch a feeble attack on the British forces. Swiftly defeated, Mwanga fled to Bukoba where he was captured by the German authorities. The British administration officially deposed Mwanga and they installed his one-year-old son Chwa as kabaka under the regency of three Protestant chiefs led by Apollo Kaggwa. The administration adopted the same tactic in Bunyoro, where a blameless 12-year-old son of Kabalega was installed as omukama in 1898 – only to be removed four years later for what the administration termed incompetence!

Mwanga escaped from his German captors in late 1897, after which he joined forces with his former rival Kabalega. After two years on the run, Mwanga and Kabalega were cornered in a swamp in Lango. Following a long battle, Kabalega was shot (a wound which later necessitated the amputation of his arm) and the two former kings were captured and exiled to the Seychelles, where Mwanga died in 1903 and Kabalega died 20 years later. Kabalega remained the spiritual leader of Bunyoro until his death: it is widely held that the unpopular Omukama Duhaga II,

installed by Britain in place of his 'incompetent' teenage brother, was tolerated by the Banyoro only because he was Kabalega's son.

Ankole succumbed more easily to British rule. Weakened by smallpox and rinderpest epidemics in the 1870s, the kingdom then suffered epidemics of tetanus and jiggers in the early 1890s, and it only just managed to repel a Rwandan invasion in 1895. Omugabe Ntare died later in the same year, by which time all the natural heirs to the throne had died in one or other epidemic. Following a brief succession war, a youthful nephew of the Ntare was installed on the throne. In 1898, Britain occupied the Ankole capital at Mbarara; the battered kingdom offered no resistance.

The southeast also fell under British rule without great fuss, because of the lack of cohesive political systems in the region. Much of the area was brought into the protectorate through the efforts of a Muganda collaborator called Semei Kakungulu who, incidentally, had assisted in the capture of Kabalega and Mwanga in Lango. Kakungulu set up a fiefdom in the Lake Kyoga region, where he installed a rudimentary administrative system over much of the area west of what is now the Kenyan border and south of Mount Elgon. Characteristically, the British administration eventually demoted Kakungulu to a subordinate role in the very system which he had implemented for them. Kakungulu's life story, as recounted in Michael Twaddle's excellent biography (see page 559), is as illuminating an account as any of the formative days of the protectorate.

By the end of the 19th century, the Uganda protectorate formally included the kingdoms of Buganda, Bunyoro, Ankole and Toro. Three of them were ruled by juveniles, while Toro was under the rule of the British-installed Kasagama. Whether through incompetence or malicious intent, the British administration was in the process of creating a nation divided against itself: firstly by favouring Protestants over Baganda of Catholic, Muslim or traditionalist persuasion, and secondly by replacing traditional clan leaders in other kingdoms with Baganda officials.

It is often asked whether colonialism was a good or a bad thing for Africa. There is no straightforward answer to this question. When writing about Malawi in 1995, I was forced to the conclusion that British intervention was the best thing to happen to that country in the troubled 19th century. By contrast, the arrogant, myopic and partial British administrators who were imposed on Uganda in the late 19th century unwittingly but surely sowed the seeds of future tragedy.

BRITISH RULE (1900–52) Ironically, the first governor of Uganda was none other than Sir Harry Johnston, whose vigorous anti-slaving campaign in the 1890s was as much as anything responsible for Britain's largely positive influence over Malawi. Johnston's instructions were to place the administration of the haphazardly assembled Uganda protectorate under what the Marquis of Salisbury termed 'a permanently satisfactory footing'. In March 1900, the newly appointed governor of Uganda signed the so-called Buganda Agreement with the four-year-old kabaka. This document formally made Buganda a federal province of the protectorate, and it recognised the kabaka and his federal government conditional upon their loyalty to Britain. It divided Buganda into 20 counties, each of which had to pass the hut and gun taxes collected in their region to the central administration, and it forbade further attempts to extend the kingdom, a clause inserted mostly to protect neighbouring Busoga.

The Buganda Agreement also formalised a deal which had been made in 1898, in recognition of Buganda's aid in quelling Kabalega. Six former counties of Bunyoro were transferred to Buganda and placed under the federal rule of the kabaka, a decision described by a later district commissioner of Bunyoro as 'one of the

greatest blunders' ever made by the administration of the protectorate. For lying within the Lost Counties (as the six annexed territories came to be called) were the burial sites of several former omukamas, as well as Mubende, a town which is steeped in Kinyoro traditions and the normal coronation site of an incoming omukama. In 1921, the Banyoro who lived in the Lost Counties formed the Mubende Bunyoro Committee to petition for their return to Bunyoro. This, and at least three subsequent petitions, as well as five petitions made by the omukama between 1943 and 1955, were all refused by the British administration on the basis that 'the boundaries laid down in 1900 could not be changed in favour of Bunyoro'. The issue of the Lost Counties caused Banyoro resentment throughout the colonial era, and it is arguably the trigger which set in motion the tragic events that followed Uganda's independence.

When Johnston arrived in Kampala in 1900, Uganda's borders were ill-defined. The first 15 years of the 20th century saw the protectorate expand further to incorporate yet more disparate cultural and linguistic groups, a growth which was motivated as much as anything by the desire to prevent previously unclaimed territories from falling into the hands of other European powers. The Kigezi region, a mishmash of small kingdoms which bordered German and Belgian territories to the south and west, was formally appended to Uganda in 1911. Baganda chiefs were installed throughout Kigezi, causing several uprisings and riots until the traditional chiefs were restored in 1929.

In the first decade of protectorateship, Britain had an inconsistent and ambiguous policy towards the territories north of the Nile. In 1906, it was decided not to incorporate them into Uganda, since they were not considered to be appropriate for the Kiganda system of government which was being imposed on other appended territories. More probably the administration was daunted by the cost and effort that would be required to subdue the dispersed and decentralised northern societies on an individual basis. In any event, the policy on the north was reversed in 1911, when the acting governor extended the protectorate to include Lango, and again in 1913, when Acholi and Karamoja were placed under British administration. The final piece in the Ugandan jigsaw was West Nile province: leased to the Belgian Congo until 1910, after which it was placed under the administration of the Sudan, West Nile was found a permanent home as part of Uganda in 1914.

Obsessed with the idea of running the protectorate along what it termed a Kiganda system of indirect rule, the British administration insisted not only on exporting its bastardised Kiganda system throughout the country, but also on placing its implementation in the hands of Baganda officials. In effect, Britain ruled Uganda by deploying the Baganda in a sub-imperialistic role; as a reward for their doing the administration's dirty work, Buganda was run as a privileged state within a state, a status it enjoyed right through to independence, when it was the only former kingdom to be granted full federality.

This divisive arrangement worked only because the administration had the legal and military clout to enforce it – even then, following regular uprisings in Bunyoro and Kigezi, traditional chiefs were gradually reinstated in most parts of the country. The 1919 Native Authority Ordinance delineated the powers of local chiefs, which were wide-ranging but subject always to the intervention of British officials. The Kiganda system was inappropriate to anywhere but Buganda, and it was absolutely absurd in somewhere like Karamoja, where there were no traditional chiefs, and decisions were made on a consensual basis by committees of recognised elders.

For all its flaws, the administrative system which was imposed on Uganda probably gave indigenous Ugandans far greater autonomy than was found

elsewhere in British-ruled Africa. The administration discouraged alien settlement and, with the introduction of cotton, it helped many regions attain a high degree of economic self-sufficiency. Remarkably, cotton growing was left almost entirely to indigenous farmers – in 1920, a mere 500km^2 of Uganda was covered in European-run plantations, most of which collapsed following the global economic slump of the 1920s and the resultant drop in cotton prices. Political decentralisation was increased by the Local Government Ordinance of 1949, which divided Uganda along largely ethnic lines into 18 districts, each of which had a district council with a high degree of federal autonomy. This ordinance gave even greater power to African administrators, but it also contributed to the climate of regional unity and national disunity which characterised the decades immediately preceding and following Uganda's independence.

The area that suffered most from this federalist policy was the 'backward' north. Neglected in terms of education, and never provided with reliable transport links whereby farmers could export their product to other parts of the country, the people of the north were forced to send their youngsters south to find work. There is some reason to suppose it was deliberate British policy to underdevelop an area which had become a reliable source of cheap labour and of recruits to the police and army. This impression is reinforced by the fact that when Africans were first admitted to the Central Legislative Council, only Buganda, the east and the west were allowed representation – the administrative systems which had been imposed on the north were 'not yet in all districts advanced to the stage requiring the creation of centralised native executives'. In other words, instead of trying to develop the north and bring it in line with other regions in Uganda, the British administration chose to neglect it.

Writing before Idi Amin ascended to power, the Ugandan historian Samwiri Karugire commented that 'the full cost of this neglect has yet to be paid, not by the colonial officials, but by Ugandans themselves'. More recent writers have suggested that it is no coincidence that Milton Obote and Idi Amin both hailed from north of the Nile.

THE BUILD-UP TO INDEPENDENCE (1952–62)
The cries for independence which prevailed in most African colonies following World War II were somewhat muted in Uganda. This can be attributed to several factors: the lack of widespread alien settlement, the high degree of African involvement in public affairs prior to independence, the strongly regional character of the protectorate's politics, and the strong probability that the status quo rather suited Uganda's Protestant Baganda elite. Remarkably, Uganda's first anti-colonial party, the Uganda National Congress (UNC), was founded as late as 1952, and it was some years before it gained any marked support, except, significantly, in parts of the underdeveloped north.

The first serious call for independence came from the most unlikely of sources. In 1953, the unpopular Kabaka Mutesa II defied the British administration by vociferously opposing the mooted federation of Uganda with Kenya and Tanzania. When the Governor of Uganda refused to give Mutesa any guarantees regarding federation, Mutesa demanded that Buganda – alone – be granted independence. The governor declared Mutesa to be disloyal to Britain, deposed him from the throne, and exiled him to Britain. This won Mutesa immense support, and not only in Buganda, so that when he was returned to his palace in 1955, it was as something of a national hero. Sadly, Mutesa chose not to use his popularity to help unify Uganda, but concentrated instead on parochial Kiganda affairs. A new Buganda Agreement was signed on 18 October 1955, giving the kabaka and his government even greater federal powers – and generating mild alarm among the non-Baganda.

Uganda's first indigenous party of consequence, the Democratic Party (DP), was founded in 1956 by Matayo Mugwanya after Mutesa had rejected him as a candidate for the Prime Minister of Buganda on the grounds of his Catholicism. The party formed a platform for the legitimate grievances of Catholics, who had always been treated as second-class citizens in Uganda, and it rose to some prominence after party leadership was handed to the lawyer Benedicto Kiwanuka in 1958. However, the DP was rightly or wrongly perceived by most Ugandans as an essentially Catholic party, which meant it was unlikely ever to win mass support.

The formation of the Uganda People's Union (UPU) came in the wake of the 1958 election, when for the first time a quota of Africans was elected to national government. The UPU was the first public alliance of non-Buganda leaders, and as such it represented an important step in the polarisation of Ugandan politics: in essence, the Baganda versus everybody else. In 1959, the UNC split along ethnic lines, with the non-Baganda faction combining with the UPU to form the Uganda People's Congress (UPC), led by Milton Obote. In 1961, the Baganda element of the UNC combined with members of the federal government of Buganda to form the overtly pro-Protestant and pro-Baganda Kabaka Yekka (KY) – which literally means 'The Kabaka Forever' (and was nicknamed 'Kill Yourselves' by opponents).

As the election of October 1961 approached, the DP, UPC and KY were clearly the main contenders. The DP won, largely through a Baganda boycott which gave them 19 of the seats within the kingdom – in East Kyaggwe, for instance, only 188 voters registered out of an estimated constituency of 90,000. The DP's Benedicto Kiwanuka thus became the first Prime Minister of Uganda when self-government was granted on 1 March 1962 – the first time ever that Catholics had any real say in public matters. Another general election was held in April of that year, in the build-up to the granting of full independence. As a result of the DP's success the year before, the UPC and KY formed an unlikely coalition, based on nothing but their mutual non-Catholicism. The UPC won 43 seats, the DP 24 seats, and the KY 24 (of which all but three were in Buganda), giving the UPC–KY alliance a clear majority and allowing Milton Obote to lead Uganda to independence on 9 October 1962.

THE FIRST OBOTE GOVERNMENT (1962–71)
Obote, perhaps more than any other Commonwealth leader, inherited a nation fragmented along religious and ethnic lines to the point of ungovernability. He was also handed an Independence Constitution of singular peculiarity: Buganda was recognised as having full federal status, the other kingdoms were granted semi-federal status, and the remainder of the country was linked directly to central government. His parliamentary majority was dependent on a marriage of convenience based solely on religious grounds, and he was compelled to recognise Kabaka Mutesa II as head of state. Something, inevitably, was going to have to give.

The Lost Counties of Bunyoro became the pivotal issue almost immediately after independence. In April 1964, Obote decided to settle the question by holding a referendum in the relevant counties, thereby allowing their inhabitants to decide whether they wanted to remain part of Buganda or be reincorporated into Bunyoro. The result of the referendum, almost 80% in favour of the counties being reincorporated into Bunyoro, caused a serious rift between Obote and Mutesa. It also caused the fragile UPC–KY alliance to split; no great loss to Obote since enough DP and KY parliamentarians had already defected to the UPC for him to retain a clear majority.

Tensions between Obote and Mutesa culminated in the so-called Constitutional Crisis of 1966. On 22 February, Obote scrapped the Independence Constitution,

thereby stripping Mutesa of his presidency. Mutesa appealed to the UN to intervene. Obote sent the army to the royal palace. Mutesa was forced to jump over the palace walls and into exile in London, where he died, impecunious, three years later. Ominously, an estimated 2,000 of the Baganda who had rallied around their king's palace were loaded on to trucks and driven away. Some were thrown over Murchison Falls. Others were buried in mass graves. Most of them had been alive when they were taken from the palace.

In April 1966, Obote unveiled a new constitution in which he abolished the role of prime minister and made himself 'Life President of Uganda'. In September 1967, he introduced another new constitution wherein he made Uganda a republic, abolished the kingdoms, divided Buganda into four new districts, and gave the army unlimited powers of detention without trial. In sole control of the country, but faced with smouldering Baganda resentment, Obote became increasingly reliant on force to maintain a semblance of stability. In September 1969, he banned the DP and other political parties. A spate of detentions followed: the DP leader Benedicto Kiwanuka, perceived dissidents within the UPC, the Baganda royal family, Muslim leaders, and any number of lawyers, students, journalists and doctors.

On 11 January 1971, Obote flew out of Entebbe for the Commonwealth Conference in Singapore. He left behind a memorandum to the commander of the Ugandan army, demanding an explanation not only for the disappearance of four million US dollars out of the military coffers, but also for the commander's alleged role in the murder of a brigadier and his wife in Gulu a year earlier, a dual murder for which he was due to be brought to trial. The commander decided his only option was to strike in Obote's absence. On 25 January 1971, Kampala was rocked by the news of a military coup, and Uganda had a new president – a killer with the demeanour of a buffoon, and charisma enough to ensure that he would become one of the handful of African presidents who have achieved household-name status in the West.

THE AMIN YEARS (1971–79) Idi Amin was born in January 1928 of a Muslim father and Christian mother at Koboko near the border with the DRC and Sudan. As a child, he moved with his mother to Lugazi in Buganda. Poorly educated and barely literate, Amin joined the King's African Rifles in 1946. He fought for Britain against the Mau-Mau in Kenya, after which he attended a training school in Nakuru. In 1958, he became one of the first two Africans in Uganda to be promoted to the rank of lieutenant. In 1962, he showed something of his true colours when he destroyed a village near Lake Turkana in Kenya, killing three people without provocation; a misdeed for which he only narrowly escaped trial, largely through the intervention of Obote.

By 1966, Amin was second in command of the Ugandan army, and, following the 1966 Constitution Crisis, Obote promoted him to the top spot. It was Amin who led the raid that forced Mutesa into exile, Amin who gave the orders when 2,000 of the kabaka's Baganda supporters were loaded into trucks and killed, and Amin who co-ordinated the mass detentions that followed the banning of the DP in 1969. For years, Amin was the instrument with which Obote kept a grip on power, yet, for reasons that are unclear, by 1970 the two most powerful men in Uganda were barely talking to each other. It is a measure of Obote's arrogance that when he wrote that fateful memorandum before flying to Singapore, he failed to grasp not only that its recipient would be better equipped than anybody else to see the real message, but also that Amin was one of the few men in Uganda with the power to react.

Given the role that Amin had played under Obote, it is a little surprising that the reaction to his military takeover was incautious jubilation. Amin's praises were sung by everybody from the man in the street to the foreign press and the Baganda royals whose leader Amin had helped drive into exile. This, quite simply, was a reflection less of Amin's popularity than of Obote's singular unpopularity. Nevertheless, Amin certainly played out the role of a 'man of peace', promising a rapid return to civilian rule, and he sealed his popularity in Buganda by allowing the preserved body of Mutesa to be returned for burial.

On the face of it, the first 18 months of Amin's rule were innocuous enough. Arguably the first public omen of things to come occurred in mid-1972, when Amin expelled all Asians from the country, 'Africanised' their businesses, and commandeered their money and possessions for 'state' use. In the long term, this action proved to be an economic disaster, but the sad truth is that it won Amin further support from the majority of Ugandans, who had long resented Asian dominance in business circles. Even as Amin consolidated his public popularity, behind the scenes he was reverting to type; this was, after all, a man who had escaped being tried for murder not once but twice. Amin quietly purged the army of its Acholi and Lango majority: by the end of 1973, 13 of the 23 officers who had held a rank of lieutenant colonel or higher at the time of Amin's coup had been murdered. By the end of 1972, eight of the 20 members of Obote's 1971 cabinet were dead, and four more were in exile. Public attention was drawn to Amin's actions in 1973, when the former prime minister, Benedicto Kiwanuka, was detained and murdered by Amin, as was the Vice Chancellor of Makerere University.

By 1974, Amin was fully engaged in a reign of terror. During the eight years he was in power, an estimated 300,000 Ugandans were killed by him or his agents (under the guise of the State Research Bureau), many of them tortured to death in horrific ways. His main targets were the northern tribes, intellectuals and rival politicians, but any person or group that he perceived as a threat was dealt with mercilessly. Despite this, African leaders united behind Uganda's despotic ruler: incredibly, Amin was made President of the Organisation of African Unity (OAU) in 1975. Practically the sole voice of dissent within Africa came from Tanzania's Julius Nyerere, who asserted that it was hypocritical for African leaders to criticise the white racist regimes of southern Africa while ignoring similarly cruel regimes in 'black' Africa. Nyerere granted exile to several of Amin's opponents, notably Milton Obote and Yoweri Museveni, and he refused to attend the 1975 OAU summit in Kampala.

As Amin's unpopularity with his own countrymen grew, he attempted to forge national unity by declaring war on Tanzania in 1978. Amin had finally overreached himself; after his troops entered northwest Tanzania, where they bombed the towns of Bukoba and Musoma, Tanzania and a number of Ugandan exiles retaliated by invading Uganda. In April 1979, Amin was driven out of Kampala into an exile from which he would never return prior to his death of multiple organ failure in a Saudi Arabian hospital in August 2003.

UGANDA AFTER AMIN (1979–86)
When Amin departed from Ugandan politics in 1979, it was seen as a fresh start by a brutalised nation. As it transpired, it was Uganda's third false dawn in 17 years – most Ugandans now regard the seven years which followed Amin's exile to have been worse even than the years which preceded it.

In the climate of high political intrigue which followed Amin's exile, Uganda's affairs were stage managed by exiled UPC leaders in Arusha (Tanzania), most probably because the UPC's leader Milton Obote was understandably cautious about announcing his return to Ugandan politics. The semi-exiled UPC installed

Professor Lule as a stand-in president, a position which he retained for 68 days. His successor, Godfrey Binaisa, fared little better, lasting eight months before he was bundled out of office in May 1980. The stand-in presidency was then assumed by two UPC loyalists, Paulo Muwanga and David Oyite-Ojik, who set an election date in December 1980.

The main rivals for the election were the DP, led by Paul Ssemogerere, and the UPC, still led by Milton Obote. A new party, the Uganda Patriotic Movement (UPM), led by Yoweri Museveni, was formed a few months prior to the election. Uganda's first election since 1962 took place in an atmosphere of corruption and intimidation. Muwanga and Oyite-Ojik used trumped-up charges to prevent several DP candidates from standing, so that the UPC went into the polling with 17 uncontested seats. On the morning of 11 December, it was announced that the DP were on the brink of victory with 63 seats certain, a surprising result that probably reflected a strong anti-Obote vote from the Baganda. In response, Muwanga and Oyite-Ojik quickly drafted a decree ensuring that all results had to be passed to them before they could be announced. The edited result of the election saw the DP take 51 seats, the UPM one seat, and the UPC a triumphant 74. After some debate, the DP decided to claim their seats, despite the overwhelming evidence that the election had been rigged.

Yoweri Museveni felt that people had been cheated by the election, and that under Obote's UPC the past was doomed to repeat itself. In 1982, Museveni formed the National Resistance Movement (NRM), an army largely made up of orphans left behind by the excesses of Amin and Obote. The NRM operated from the Luwero Triangle in Buganda north of Kampala, where they waged a guerrilla war against Obote's government. Obote's response was characteristically brutal: his troops waded into the Luwero Triangle killing civilians by their thousands, an ongoing massacre which exceeded even Amin's. The world turned a blind eye to the atrocities in Luwero, and so it was left to 'dissident' members of the UPC and the commander of the army, Tito Okello, to suggest that Obote might negotiate with the NRM in order to stop the slaughter. Obote refused. On 27 July 1985, he was deposed in a bloodless military coup led by Tito Okello. For the second time in his career, Obote was forced into exile by the commander of his own army.

Okello assumed the role of head of state and he appointed as his prime minister Paulo Muwanga, whose role in the 1980 election gave him little credibility. With some misgivings, the DP allied itself with Okello, largely because Ssemogerere hoped he might use his influence to stop the killing in Luwero. In a statement made in Nairobi in August 1985, Museveni announced that the NRM was prepared to co-operate with Okello, provided that the army and the other instruments of oppression used by previous regimes were brought under check. The NRM entered into negotiations with Okello, but after these broke down in December 1985, Museveni returned to the bush. On 26 January 1986, the NRM entered Kampala, Okello surrendered tamely, and Museveni was sworn in as president – Uganda's seventh head of state in as many years.

THE NRM GOVERNMENT (1986–PRESENT) In 1986, Museveni took charge of a country that had been beaten and brutalised as have few others. There must have been many Ugandans who felt this was yet another false dawn, as they waited for the cycle of killings and detentions to start all over again. Certainly, to the outside world, Uganda's politics had become so confusing in all but their consistent brutality that the NRM takeover appeared to be merely another instalment in an apparently endless succession of coups and civil wars.

But Museveni was far from being another Amin or Obote. He shied away from the retributive actions which had destroyed the credibility of previous takeovers; he appointed a broad-based government which swept across party and ethnic lines, re-established the rule of law, appointed a much-needed Human Rights Commission, increased the freedom of the press, and encouraged the return of Asians and other exiles. On the economic front, he adopted pragmatic policies and encouraged foreign investment and tourism, the result of which was an average growth rate of 10% in his first decade of rule. Museveni has also tried to tackle corruption, albeit with limited success, by gradually cutting the civil service. Most significantly, Uganda under Museveni has visibly moved away from being a society obsessed with its ethnic and religious divisions. From the most unpromising material, Museveni has, miraculously, forged a real nation.

In 1993, Museveni greatly boosted his popularity (especially with the influential Baganda) by his decision to grant legal recognition to the old kingdoms of Uganda. In July 1993, the Cambridge-educated son of Mutesa II, Ronald Mutebi, returned to Uganda after having spent over 20 years in Britain; in a much-publicised coronation near Kampala, he was made the 36th Kabaka of Buganda. The traditional monarchies of Bunyoro and Toro have also been restored, but not that of Ankole.

In the 1990s, the most widespread criticism of Museveni and the NRM was their tardiness in moving towards a genuine multi-party democracy. At the time, Museveni argued rather convincingly that Uganda needed stability offered by a 'no party' system more than it needed a potentially divisive multi-party system that risked igniting the ethnic passions that had caused the country so much misery in its first two decades of independence. As a result, the NRM remained the only legal political party until as recently as 2005, though the country's first open presidential elections were held in 1996, slightly more than ten years after Museveni had first assumed power. Museveni won with an overwhelming 74% of the vote, as compared with the 23% polled by his main rival, Paul Ssemogerere, a former DP leader who once served as prime minister under Museveni. A similar pattern was registered in the 2001 presidential elections, which returned Museveni to power with 70% of the vote, as compared with the 20% registered by his main rival Kizza Besigye. At the time, and for several years afterwards, Museveni reiterated his commitment to stand down from the presidency in 2006, in accordance with the maximum of two presidential terms specified by a national constitution drawn up years earlier by the NRM constitution.

During the course of 2004, Museveni made two crucial political about-turns. Firstly, he advocated a return to multi-party politics and held a national referendum that demonstrated the move was supported by 92.5% of voters. Only weeks after this political landmark, he pushed a constitutional amendment through parliament to scrap presidential term limits, clearing the way for him to seek a third term in the looming elections. In November, barely three months before the election was due, the main opposition leader Kizza Besigye, having recently returned from exile, was imprisoned and charged with terrorism, only to be released on bail in January 2006. A month later, Uganda's first multi-party election in 25 years was largely held to be free and fair by international observers, though this verdict was loudly disputed by Besigye, who polled 37% of the vote as compared with Museveni's 59%. Once again, this result can be viewed as ambiguous – the gap between the two primary candidates, though by no means insubstantial, had halved since the 2001 presidential election, and it is difficult to say to what extent the vote for Museveni represented overt support for his presidency and to what extent it simply reflected a fear of change.

Alexander Calder and Dr Joseph Kivubiro

Since its foundation in 1937, the School of Fine Art at Kampala's Makerere University has been the nucleus for East Africa's most influential and widespread contemporary art movement. While indigenous arts have flourished and evolved for centuries throughout East Africa, Makerere provided the region's first formal instruction in modern fine-art techniques, including drawing, painting and modern sculpture. Over the years, many students and graduates of this school became recognised innovators of striking new techniques and original styles.

During the particularly active 1950s and 1960s, artists held solo and group exhibitions at numerous locations. Growing interest in exhibitions by local artists led to the establishment of sizeable art collections by public museums, corporations and government institutions throughout the country. Further stimulating Uganda's environment for advancing local art during this time, Esso and Caltex held widely publicised annual art competitions, publishing work by awarded artists on calendars distributed locally and abroad.

Until 1961, Makerere generally emphasised representative art, using drawing, perspective and shading in compositions inspired by local imagery. Following independence, however, a cadre of leading artists embraced a new role as visual cultural historians, producing interpretative works that document the early post-independence era – often using representative forms and figures to symbolise uncertainties and ideals within a rapidly changing society.

In 1966, artist Norbert Kaggwa underscored the importance of representational art in Uganda's rapidly evolving culture: 'Wedged into a single generation, my own, is a double vision; we are the beginning of an industrialised, urban society and we are probably – to be realistic – the end of the nomadic and village ways of life. The two eras are usually separated by hundreds of years. Here they are separated by a few dozen miles. I am personally very moved by this phenomenon and feel some special responsibility towards it. This is at least one of the reasons why I am a realistic and not an abstract painter. In one way, I suppose, I consider myself as much a cultural historian as an artist … or rather, in my case, they are one and the same thing.'

Artists debated their perceived role and the purpose of their works against the backdrop of independence. Art of this period consequently benefited from rich cross-fertilisation: several artists embraced both idioms to find unique and expressive visual forms that drew from abstract as well as representational influences. The late Henry Lumu, Augustine Mugalula Mukiibi, Teresa Musoke and Elly Kyeyune were early leaders of Uganda's emerging Modernist school, spawning the distinctive semi-abstract styles that characterised much art of this era.

In 1968, Makerere graduate Henry Lumu was hired as art director by Uganda National Television, initiating regular broadcasts of televised art instruction classes. Exposure through this new medium further stimulated Kampala's burgeoning art community, which by that time extended well beyond the campus. The Uganda Art Club organised exhibitions throughout Kampala in the early to mid-1970s, prompting prominent hotels, banks and commercial buildings to amass and display collections of outstanding original works. During this period, artists attained unprecedented standing within Kampala's thriving cosmopolitan circles and among the country's elite.

By the late 1970s, political unrest had taken a dreadful toll among Uganda's artistic community. Professionals and intellectuals were targeted by the Obote and Amin regimes, and museums and galleries were looted or reoccupied – destroying numerous significant art collections. Forced to choose between seclusion, alternative occupations or self-imposed exile, many Ugandan artists emigrated to Kenya, South Africa, Europe or North America. The expatriate artists incorporated visual elements from their new surroundings into mediums, styles and colour palettes that still remained faithful to their Ugandan experience.

A large number of artists, including Henry Lumu, Joseph Mungaya, Dan Sekanwagi, Emmy Lubega, David Kibuuka, Jak Kitarikawe, David Wasswa Katongole and James Kitamirike, left for neighbouring Kenya. The colourful, innovative and uniquely stylised works of the Ugandan painters transformed Nairobi's art scene. Kenyan artist Nuwa Nnyanzi reflected recently: 'The impact of Ugandan artists in Kenya in the seventies and eighties was so great that it is still felt and highly visible today.'

Restored political stability in the late 1980s encouraged the homecoming or resurfacing of many Ugandan artists. Expressing rediscovered peacetime ideals through their art, many artists also reminded their audience of struggles and horrors endured during the troubled years. Exhibitions by Ugandan artists were held regularly at London's Commonwealth Institute, while other shows opened in Paris and Vienna. In 1992, President Museveni marked the opening of a Vienna show featuring Geoffrey Mukasa and Fabian Mpagi with these remarks:

As those destructive years have regrettably shown, art cannot flourish in a situation plagued with terror and human indifference. Peace and security has returned to our country. We have gone a long way to encourage the revival of arts. The fine works exhibited are a vivid testimony that art has come to life again in Uganda. Certainly, both the public and the critics will recognise that Uganda has taken up her place in the world of modern art. It is an opportune moment for us to portray through these paintings a promising new picture of the 'New Uganda'.

Exhibitions by and for Ugandan artists have also been held in Stockholm, Amsterdam, Berlin, Frankfurt, Rome, Johannesburg and seven cities in the USA. In North America, expatriate artists such as James Kitamirike, David Kibuuka, Dan Sekanwagi and Fred Makubuya have united to spearhead renewed interest in their art through the Fine Arts Center for East Africa, which opened in San Francisco in 1998. Organising group exhibitions in the USA and Canada, this active contingent of artists continues to garner recognition for their innovative styles, mediums and potent individual voices within Uganda's art movement.

In Kampala today, Uganda's renewed art scene embodies a vibrant and vital country redefining its past yet also reaching for a hopeful future. Sharing their unique visual arts legacy, Uganda's fine-art pioneers have become the country's cultural ambassadors, creating global awareness of their homeland's unique colours, cultures, peoples and art.

Locations to view art in Kampala are listed on page 152.

Reprinted with minor edits from the website of the Fine Arts Center for East Africa in San Francisco, with permission from Alexander Calder (415 333 9363; e gadart@ aol.com)

There is no doubt that Uganda has made fantastic progress under Museveni's rule. Kampala today is unrecognisable from the shattered capital that the NRM took control of in 1986, while most smaller towns have been visibly bolstered by the consistent economic growth of the past three decades. Tragically, however, while most of the country thrived during the first 20 years of the Museveni era, the north suffered terribly at the hands of the Lord's Resistance Army (LRA; see box, pages 300–1), an ostensible rebel organisation whose primary manifesto appeared to be the sadistic slaughter of unarmed civilians. Although protracted negotiations between the LRA and the government failed to result in a formal peace agreement, the former withdrew from Uganda into the Congo in 2005, and the north has been at peace – and enjoying a considerable economic revival of its own – ever since. The progress of Uganda post-1986 was showcased to the world in November 2007 when Uganda hosted Queen Elizabeth II and 57 heads of state for the Commonwealth Heads of Government Meeting (CHOGM). All the same, while popular support for the NRM remains strong, it is consistently undermined by corruption scandals and accusations of skulduggery which serve to fuel the sense senior government officials consider themselves to be above the law and accountable to themselves rather than their electorate.

Museveni, predictably, won a fourth term in the 2011 elections. This coincided with a period of massive inflation – at times reaching 25% – which led to price rises and widespread hardship. Though in part due to instability in the global financial markets, the situation was made worse by a shortfall in hard currency as the NRM siphoned off a large chunk of the annual budget to bankroll its re-election. This led to the post-election, opposition-led 'Walk to Work' protests which were firmly quashed by the police. In 2013, it emerged that senior officials in the Office of the Prime Minister appeared unable to account for billions of shillings of donor money meant to rebuild northern Uganda, a blip that led to the withholding of aid by several donor countries. Uganda's international profile and credibility among donor nations was further damaged by a draconian Anti-Homosexuality Act (originally threatening anyone found guilty of what was loosely termed 'aggravated homosexuality' with the death sentence, though this was later moderated to life imprisonment) that passed on to law on 14 February 2014. The act was overturned by the Supreme Court six months later, and it seems the government has declined to appeal this court ruling presumably due to concerns about foreign reaction.

Even within the NRM, a growing number of MPs were starting to hint that the 2016 election might be the right time for President Museveni to retire to his farm at Rwakitura and make way for fresh blood. Popular support for the septuagenarian president also wavered in the build up to 2016, particularly among the more educated and urbanised members of the electorate. Still, with no heir groomed to take up the reins within the NRM, nor any opposition candidate perceived to be of comparable calibre, it came as no surprise that the president of 30 years decided to stand for a fifth term in the presidential election of February 2016, nor that he took 60.8% of the vote (a drop of 8% since 2011) as opposed to Kizza Besigye's 35.4%. As with previous recent elections, Museveni's victory was overshadowed by widespread charges of vote-rigging. Besigye, who was arrested three times during election week, described the poll as 'the most fraudulent' ever in Uganda, and demanded an independent audit, while the chief observer for the EU Mission Eduard Kukan said the election was undermined by a 'lack of transparency [and] intimidating atmosphere'. Despite this, it seems unlikely that a recount would demonstrate a set of discrepancies so great as to reverse the result, but one can't help suspect the next election – due in 2021, by which time Museveni will be 76 – might finally result in a changing of the guard.

GOVERNMENT

Uganda is a republic presided over by a president who serves as the head of state and head of government. The ruling party is the National Resistance Movement (NRM), which seized power in 1986 to end the 15-year era of despotic rule and civil war initiated by a coup led by Idi Amin in 1971. President Yoweri Museveni of the NRM has served as president since 1986, having won his fifth presidential election in 2016. The post of prime minister, abolished under Milton Obote in 1966 but reinstated in 1980, has been held by six different NRM members since 1986. The incumbent since September 2014 is Ruhakana Rugunda, a Museveni loyalist who has held several cabinet posts since 1986, as as well as serving as Permanent Representative to the United Nations from 2009 to 2011. The cabinet currently comprises another 19 ministers, all of whom are members of the NRM.

Uganda is a democracy, and it has held elections every five years since 1996, However, the 'no party' system once espoused by the NRM, ostensibly to reduce sectarian violence, put a curb on multi-party activity until 2005, when the ban was cancelled by a constitutional referendum. The main opposition party is the Forum for Democratic Change (FDC), which was founded in the build-up to the 2005 referendum, and has since been led by Kizza Besigye. Since 2006, Besigye has lost three successive presidential elections to his former ally President Museveni, albeit amidst charges of vote rigging and other questionable electoral practices by the NRM.

Uganda has undergone several internal administrative reforms since the early 20th century. In the colonial era, the protectorate was divided into 14 administrative regions, including the Kingdoms of Buganda, Ankole, Bunyoro and Toro. Today, the country is divided into Central, Eastern, Northern and Western administrative regions, and these are further subdivided into 111 districts (most named after their main town) as well as the city of Kampala. The districts are clustered into 14 subregions: Acholi, Ankole, Buganda, Bugisu, Bukedi, Bunyoro, Busoga, Karamoja, Kigezi, Lango, Sebei, Teso, Toro and West Nile. Although these subregions seem to possess a limited significance as administrative entities, they closely resemble the original kingdoms and other ethnically defined divisions delineated by the British government in the early 20th century, and their names are still in wide vernacular use a century later.

ECONOMY

Uganda's free-market economy has experienced a steady per-annum growth of around 7% over the last 30 years, largely due to the atmosphere of political stability fostered by the NRM and economic reforms implemented by President Museveni in the early years of his rule. As a result, the national GDP (based on purchasing-power-parity) has soared from around US$7 million in 1986 to US$77 million in 2014, and a 2014 report compiled by Harvard University's respected Centre for International Development (CID) predicts it will join India as the world's fastest-growing economy in the coming decade. An important impetus for this growth has been the expansion of the service and industrial sectors since Museveni took power in 1986. Back then, the agricultural sector – despite having been undermined by the long years of civil strife under his predecessor – accounted for about 60% of the national GDP, and more than 90% of Ugandans were subsistence farmers or employed in agriculture-related fields. Today, by contrast, the industrial and service sectors contribute 27% and 50% of the GDP, while the agricultural sector's input has dropped to 23% (though it still employs around 80% of the work force of 16

million). Fertile soils and high rainfall have ensured that Uganda has been self-sufficient in food ever since independence. The major export crop is coffee, which generated US$425 million in foreign revenue in 2014, followed by tea, cut flowers and tobacco. Notable industries include sugar refinement, textiles, and cement and steel production. Historically, mining has not played a large role in the Ugandan economy, not unless you count salt extraction in the west, at sites such as Lake Katwe, but this is set to change with the reopening of the Kilembe copper mine near Kasese and discovery of oil in the vicinity of Lake Albert in the Rift Valley. As might be expected, most economic and social indicators have improved greatly in recent years, though it is estimated that 25% of the population still lives below the poverty line.

PEOPLE

The 2014 census showed Uganda to have a population of 34.9 million, which represents an increase of almost 50% on the 2002 figure of 28 million, a fivefold increase since independence (when the population stood at about seven million) and an annual growth rate of around 4%. The majority of Uganda's people are concentrated in the south and west. The most populous ethnic group are the Bantu-speaking Baganda, who account for about 18% of the population and are centred on Kampala. Other numerically significant Bantu-speaking groups are the Busoga (10%), Banyankole (8%) and Bakiga (8%). The east and north of the country are populated by several Nilotic- or Cushitic-speaking groups, including the Teso, Karamojong, Acholi and Lango.

The table below shows data for Uganda's ten largest urban centres in 2014, as well as in previous censuses, and provides a good indicator of the dramatic post-independence shifts in urban growth around the country. Kampala remains,

POPULATION TRENDS

	1959		1991		2002		2014	
1	Kampala	46,000	Kampala	775,000	Kampala	1,200,000	Kampala	1,568,900
2	Gulu	30,000	Jinja	65,000	Gulu	113,000	Kira	353,400
3	Lira	14,000	Mbale	54,000	Lira	89,500	Mbarara	202,800
4	Jinja	11,500	Masaka	49,500	Jinja	86,500	Mukono	170,200
5	Mbale	11,000	Entebbe	42,700	Mbale	70,000	Nansan	162,700
6	Mbarara	8,500	Mbarara	41,000	Mbarara	69,000	Gulu	161,200
7	Masaka	8,000	Soroti	40,900	Masaka	61,000	Hoima	108,700
8	Entebbe	7,000	Gulu	38,300	Entebbe	57,000	Masaka	107,700
9	Kasese	6,000	Njeru	37,000	Kasese	53,000	Kasese	106,300
10	Njeru	5,000	Fort Portal	32,800	Mukono	47,000	Lira	104,200

obviously, the most populous city by far with 2012 estimates putting the figure at 1.6–1.8m. The most striking increases recorded by the 2002 census concern Gulu and Lira, both of which experienced huge rural–urban migration as a result of the LRA war and continued to do so until 2006.

LANGUAGE

The official language, English, is spoken as a second language by most educated Ugandans. More than 33 local languages are spoken in different parts of the country. Most of these belong to the Bantu language group: for instance, Luganda, Lusoga and Lutoro. Several Nilotic and Cushitic languages are spoken in the north and east, some of them by only a few thousand people. Many Ugandans speak a limited amount of Swahili, a coastal language which spread into the East African interior via the 19th-century Arab slave traders.

RELIGION

Religion plays a far larger role in day-to-day life in Uganda than it does in most Western countries, with fewer than 1% of the population claiming to be atheist or agnostic. Freedom of religion is a constitutional right, though the activities of certain groups classified as cults is restricted. Christianity dominates. The Roman Catholic Church can claim around 42% of the total population, while the Church of Uganda (an offshoot of the Church of England) accounts for another another 36%, and 7% are Jehovah's Witnesses or belong to a Pentecostal church. Partially as a legacy of the Arab trade with Buganda in the late 19th century, roughly 12% of Ugandans are Muslim (mostly Sunni), with the majority living in the eastern half of the country. Today, there is little or no friction between Christian and Muslim, though post-independence political conflict did follow Catholic-Protestant lines. In most rural areas, these exotic faiths have not entirely displaced traditional beliefs, so that an estimated 25% of the Christian and Islam population might still partake in traditional religious practices such as making sacrifices to clan ancestors or other spirits. Other minority religions are Hindu, Bahai and a unique variant on Judaism practised by the Abayudaya of Mbale. The main centre of animism is the northeast, where the Karamoja – like the affiliated Maasai and other Rift Valley pastoralists – largely shun any exotic faith in favour of their own traditional beliefs.

EDUCATION

Uganda has a high standard of education by African standards, but is rather less impressive by global ones. Since independence, the schooling system has comprised seven years of primary education followed by six years of secondary education. Attendance rates were very low in the 1970s and 1980s, as reflected in a low adult literacy rate (just under 75%) but have soared since the introduction of a Universal Primary Education (UPE) system in 1997. UPE allows for free primary education for up to four children per family, and it resulted in a threefold increase in primary school attendance from two million in 1986 to more than six million at the turn of the millennium. By 2012, primary school attendance stood at almost 95% (as compared to 68% in 1995), and the literacy rate of young adults (aged 15–24) had improved to 87.5%. Fewer than 20% of Ugandans, however, continue on to secondary school, which follows the old British system of four years of O-Levels followed by two years of A-Levels. Fewer than 4% of Ugandans complete tertiary education.

Uganda Wildlife Authority

Come to Uganda and bring your holiday dreams to life.

Visit the serene, scenic and accessible National Parks where you can enjoy various activities and attractions including:-

- **Gorilla Tracking**
- **Chimpanzee tracking**
- **Game drives**
- **Boat Launch**
- **Hiking**
- **Mountain Climbing**
- **Camping**
- **Bird Watching**
- **Balloon Safaris**
- **Fishing**

Uganda Wildlife Authority
Plot 7 Kira Road Kamwokya,
P.O.Box 3530, Kampala Uganda.
📞+256 414 355 000
✉️ info@ugandawildlife.org
f ugandawildlifeauthority
🐦 ugwildlife

www.ugandawildlife.org

UWA
*Conserving
for Generations*

2

Natural History

Uganda differs from any other recognised African safari destination in that it has a relatively high proportion of closed canopy forest. This embraces Afro-montane forest such as that found on Mount Elgon, which has strong affinities to similar habitats on mounts Kilimanjaro and Kenya, as well as the likes of Semliki National Park, which is effectively an easterly extension of the lowland rainforest that blankets the Congo Basin and West Africa. Uganda thus harbours a wide variety of vertebrate and other species absent elsewhere in East and southern Africa, and the accessibility of its major forests by comparison to those in West Africa makes it an unbeatable destination for viewing African forest creatures – from gorillas and chimps to a colourful array of butterflies and birds – in their natural habitat.

When it comes to more conventional plains wildlife, Uganda doesn't quite bear comparison to top-ranking safari destinations such as Tanzania or Kenya. Nevertheless, the savannah wildlife of Queen Elizabeth, Murchison Falls and Kidepo Valley national parks is now largely recovered from the heavy poaching that took place during the civil war and political unrest of 1970–86. Perennial safari favourites such as lion, elephant, buffalo, giraffe and even leopard are now quite easily seen in Uganda's savannah parks, but with the added bonus that they form part of a circuit that offers the best forest primate viewing in Africa, as well as some matchless birdwatching.

A striking feature of the Ugandan landscape, with the exception of the semi-desert and dry acacia woodland of the northeast, is its relatively moist climate. A high precipitation level makes the countryside far greener and more fertile than elsewhere in East Africa, while lakes, rivers and other wetland habitats account for almost 25% of the country's surface area. The most extensive freshwater bodies that lie within Uganda or along its borders are, in descending order, lakes Victoria, Albert, Kyoga, Edward, Kwania and George. Lesser expanses include Lake Wamala near Mityana, lakes Bunyonyi and Mutanda in Kigezi, lakes Bisina and Opeta in the east, and more than 100 crater lakes dotted around the Rwenzori foothills. Of particular interest to birdwatchers are the half-dozen species associated exclusively with papyrus swamps – most notably the exquisite papyrus gonolek and eagerly sought-after shoebill, the latter seen more easily in Uganda than anywhere else.

Although most of Uganda is topographically relatively undramatic – essentially an undulating plateau perched at altitudes of 1,000–1,200m between the eastern and western arms of the Rift Valley – it is bordered by some of the continent's most impressive mountains. Foremost among these is the Rwenzori, which runs along the Congolese border and is topped by the third-highest point in Africa, the 5,109m Margherita Peak on Mount Stanley. Other major mountains include Elgon (4,321m) on the Kenyan border, the Virungas on the Rwanda/Congo border

(of which Muhabura is at 4,127m the highest of the Ugandan peaks), and Moroto (3,084m), Kadam (3,068m) and Morungole (2,750m) on the Kenyan border north of Elgon. Rising in solitude from the surrounding plains, these high mountains all support isolated microhabitats of forest and high grassland. The higher reaches of the Rwenzori, Elgon and to a lesser extent the Virungas, are covered in Afro-alpine moorland, a fascinating and somewhat other-worldly habitat noted for gigantism among plants such as lobelias, heather and groundsel, as well as habitat-specific creatures such as the dazzling scarlet-tufted malachite sunbird.

GEOGRAPHY

Uganda lies in the east-central African interior more than 500km inland of the Indian Ocean, and is one of only 13 countries worldwide run through by the equator. It stands on an elevated basin that separates the eastern branch of the Great Rift Valley, running through Kenya and Tanzania, from the western branch, which is also known as the Albertine Rift (after Lake Albert) and forms the border between Uganda and the Democratic Republic of the Congo (DRC). Most of Uganda is set at altitudes of greater than 1,000m, the main exception being parts of the Albertine Rift floor, where Lake Albert, at an elevation of 620m above sea level, is the lowest point in the country.

Topographically, much of Uganda is gently undulating or flat. The most mountainous area is the far southwest, where the steep slopes of Kigezi subregion are mostly covered in terraced cultivation, though patches of natural cover remain, most famously the rainforest protected within Bwindi Impenetrable National Park. The Congolese border immediately north of Kigezi is formed by Africa's third-highest massif, the 70km-long and 30km-wide Rwenzori, whose 5,190m summit is topped only by Mount Kilimanjaro and Kenya. Several other large mountains are associated with Uganda's border regions. The Virunga is a string of freestanding volcanic peaks that runs along the border with Rwanda and the DRC, while Mount Elgon on the Kenya border has the largest base of any of the world's volcanically formed massifs. Several other smaller volcanic mountains can be found in the north and east, while a field of more than 100 crater lakes set below the Rwenzori foothills from Fort Portal south to Kichwamba provides further evidence of the country's geologically volatile past.

With the exception of the semi-arid northeast, Uganda is characterised by high precipitation and fertile soils. Indeed, close on 25% of the country's surface comprises water. In the southeast, Lake Victoria, the largest lake in Africa and second-largest freshwater body in the world, is shared between Uganda, Tanzania and Kenya. In the west, lakes Albert, Edward and George lie on the Albertine Rift floor straddling or close to the Congolese border. At Jinja, on the Lake Victoria shore, Owen Falls (now submerged by the Owen Falls Dam) is the primary source of the White Nile, the world's longest river, which passes through the marshy and ill-defined Lake Kyoga in central Uganda, then through the northeast corner of Lake Albert, before crossing into Sudan and on to the Mediterranean.

CLIMATE

Uganda's equatorial climate is significantly tempered by its elevated altitude. In most parts of the country, the daily maximum is between 20°C and 27°C and the minimum is between 12°C and 18°C. The highest temperatures in Uganda occur on the plains immediately east of Lake Albert, while the lowest have been recorded on the glacial peaks of the Rwenzori. Except in the dry north, where in some areas the average annual rainfall is as low as 100mm, most parts of Uganda receive an

CLIMATE CHART

KAMPALA (1,155m)	Jan	Feb	Mar	Apr	May	Jun	Jul	Aug	Sep	Oct	Nov	Dec
Ave max (°C)	28	28	27	26	26	25	25	26	27	27	27	27
Ave min (°C)	18	18	18	18	17	17	17	16	17	17	17	17
Rainfall (mm)	45	60	125	170	135	75	50	85	90	100	125	105

ENTEBBE (1,145m)	Jan	Feb	Mar	Apr	May	Jun	Jul	Aug	Sep	Oct	Nov	Dec
Ave max (°C)	27	26	26	25	25	25	25	25	26	26	26	26
Ave min (°C)	17	18	18	18	17	16	16	16	16	17	17	17
Rainfall (mm)	75	95	155	250	240	115	75	75	75	80	130	115

FORT PORTAL (1,540m)	Jan	Feb	Mar	Apr	May	Jun	Jul	Aug	Sep	Oct	Nov	Dec
Ave max (°C)	27	27	26	26	25	25	25	25	25	25	25	26
Ave min (°C)	12	13	14	14	14	13	13	13	13	14	14	12
Rainfall (mm)	20	75	125	190	130	85	60	110	195	210	165	75

KABALE (1,950m)	Jan	Feb	Mar	Apr	May	Jun	Jul	Aug	Sep	Oct	Nov	Dec
Ave max (°C)	24	24	23	22	22	23	23	24	24	24	23	23
Ave min (°C)	10	10	11	12	11	10	9	10	11	11	11	10
Rainfall (mm)	50	100	125	120	95	25	20	45	95	100	115	90

GULU (1,110m)	Jan	Feb	Mar	Apr	May	Jun	Jul	Aug	Sep	Oct	Nov	Dec
Ave max (°C)	32	32	31	29	28	28	26	27	28	29	29	31
Ave min (°C)	17	18	18	18	18	17	17	17	17	17	17	16
Rainfall (mm)	10	35	85	160	200	140	155	215	165	140	95	30

MASINDI (1,145m)	Jan	Feb	Mar	Apr	May	Jun	Jul	Aug	Sep	Oct	Nov	Dec
Ave max (°C)	31	31	30	29	29	28	27	27	28	29	30	30
Ave min (°C)	12	12	13	13	13	12	12	12	12	12	13	12
Rainfall (mm)	20	50	10	140	135	95	100	45	120	125	110	45

MBALE (1,150m)	Jan	Feb	Mar	Apr	May	Jun	Jul	Aug	Sep	Oct	Nov	Dec
Ave max (°C)	32	32	31	29	28	28	27	28	28	29	30	3
Ave min (°C)	16	17	17	17	17	16	16	15	15	16	16	1
Rainfall (mm)	25	60	90	160	175	130	110	135	105	80	65	4

JINJA (1,145m)	Jan	Feb	Mar	Apr	May	Jun	Jul	Aug	Sep	Oct	Nov	Dec
Ave max (°C)	29	30	29	28	27	27	27	28	28	29	30	29
Ave min (°C)	15	15	15	15	15	14	14	15	15	15	15	14
Rainfall (mm)	50	70	120	170	130	65	50	105	80	95	100	85

The Uganda Wildlife Authority or UWA (pronounced ooh-er!) is the body responsible for Uganda's national parks and wildlife reserves. See page 61.

Visiting fees for UWA's protected areas fall into three categories. Murchison Falls, Queen Elizabeth, Bwindi Impenetrable, Mgahinga Gorilla, Lake Mburo, Kibale and Kidepo Valley national parks are classed as Category A. Semliki, Mount Elgon and Rwenzori Mountains national parks and Toro-Semliki Wildlife Reserve are classed as Category B. All other wildlife reserves are Category C.

Different prices apply to foreign non-residents, essentially visiting tourists and other foreign non-residents (FNR), foreign residents living in East Africa (FR) and Ugandan citizens. The prices given below will apply until a new two-year tariff comes into operation on 1 January 2018. For prevailing rates visit UWA's website, www.ugandawildlife.org and click on the link *Visitor Tariffs*.

Entrance to **Category A** reserves currently costs US$40/30 FNR/FR. Entrance to **Category B** protected areas is US$35/25 FNR/FR, and to **Category C** US$10/5 FNR/FR. Children under five enter all protected areas for free, and those aged 5 to 15 years pay US$10 for Category A parks and US$5 for others. Permits are valid for 24 hours from time of entrance. In addition, 4x4 vehicles registered in Uganda or elsewhere in East Africa pay an entrance fee of Ush30,000 (around US$10) while a rather stiffer US$150 applies to foreign vehicles. Ugandan saloon cars pay Ush20,000 (US$7), and foreign ones US$50. Motorcycles (bodas), which can be used to enter some parks, pay Ush10,000 (US$3) unless foreign registered, in which case the fee is US$10. Vehicle fees do not apply to forested parks such as Kibale and Mgahinga. Fees are currently payable in shillings or dollars but an electronic system using preloaded entry cards now applies to Lake Mburo, Bwindi Impenetrable, Queen Elizabeth, Kibale, and Murchison Falls, though at the time of writing cash is still accepted at all these parks.

Additional rates apply for park activities and are listed under the relevant sections in the regional parts of the guide.

annual rainfall of between 1,000mm and 2,000mm. There is wide regional variation in rainfall patterns. In western Uganda and the Lake Victoria region it can rain at almost any time of year. As a rough guide, however, the wet seasons are from mid-September to November and from March to May (see box, page 31).

CONSERVATION AREAS

Uganda's list of gazetted conservation areas embraces ten national parks and several other wildlife reserves and forest reserves. National parks are accorded a higher status and conservation priority than other reserves, and from the visitor's point of view they are generally better developed for tourism. Although several other wildlife reserves exist, most are merely adjuncts to one of the savannah national parks. The only ones that have any tourist facilities at present are Toro-Semliki, Katonga, Bugungu, Pian Upe, Kabwoya and Kyambura wildlife reserves. Also of interest to tourists are forest reserves such as Budongo, Kalinzu, Mpanga and Mabira. Chimp tracking in Budongo and Kalinzu is significantly cheaper than in the national parks.

NATIONAL PARKS

	Area	Habitat	Special attractions
Bwindi Impenetrable	310km²	forest	mountain gorillas, forest birds
Kibale	766km²	forest	chimpanzees, monkeys, forest birds
Kidepo Valley	1,344km²	savannah	dry-country antelopes, predators & birds
Lake Mburo	256km²	savannah	wide variety of antelope & waterbirds
Mgahinga Gorilla	33km²	montane	mountain gorillas, hiking, volcanic peaks
Mount Elgon	1,145km²	montane	hiking, forest birds
Murchison Falls	3,900km²	savannah	Murchison Falls, big game, waterbirds
Queen Elizabeth	1,978km²	savannah	big game, chimps, 612 bird species
Rwenzori	996km²	montane	hiking, forest birds, Afro-montane plants
Semliki	220km²	forest	hot springs, Rift Valley setting, 45 birds found nowhere else in Uganda

Several other sites are also of interest for their natural history. These include Lake Nkuruba and Bigodi Wetland near Fort Portal, Lake Bunyonyi and the Echuya Forest in Kigezi, and the Sipi Falls near Mbale. For birders in particular, it is easy to view Uganda, with its lush natural vegetation and dense tropical cultivation, as nothing less than one giant nature sanctuary. Even around the capital, the small relict forest protected in the Entebbe Botanical Garden offers an excellent introduction to Uganda's forest birds, while gardens in suburban Kampala offer the opportunity to see such colourful species as Ross's turaco, woodland kingfisher, white-throated bee-eater and a variety of robin-chats and weavers.

MAMMALS

The official Ugandan mammal checklist of 342 species comprises 132 larger mammals, 94 bats, 70 rats and mice, 33 shrews and otter shrews, eight gerbils, four elephant shrews and a solitary golden mole. Several useful field guides to African mammals are available for the purpose of identification (pages 559–60), but since they tend to lack specific distribution details for individual countries, the following notes emphasise local distribution and habitat, and are intended to serve as a Uganda-specific supplement to such a proper field guide.

PRIMATES Primates are exceptionally well represented, with 15 diurnal and seven nocturnal species listed, though the taxonomic status of many is controversial, and some go by several different common names.

Apes The great apes of the family Pongidae are so closely related to humans that a less partial observer might well place them in the same family as us (it is thought that the chimpanzee is more closely related to humans than it is to any other ape). There are four ape species, of which two are found in Uganda (for further details see below and pages 34–5).

Mountain gorilla (*Gorilla b. beringei*) This high-altitude subspecies of the eastern gorilla is the bulkiest member of the primate family, standing up to 1.8m high and weighing up to 210kg. An Albertine Rift Endemic, it is found in only two localities, namely the Virunga Mountains (shared between Uganda, DRC and Rwanda) and Uganda's Bwindi Impenetrable National Park, and the global

In this chapter, I've made widespread use of taxonomic terms such as genus, species and race. Some readers may not be familiar with these terms, so a brief explanation follows.

Taxonomy is the branch of biology concerned with classifying living organisms. It uses a hierarchical system to represent the relationships between different animals. At the top of the hierarchy are kingdoms, phyla, subphyla and classes. All vertebrates belong to the animal kingdom, phylum Chordata, subphylum Vertebrata. There are five vertebrate classes: Mammalia (mammals), Aves (birds), Reptilia (reptiles), Amphibia (amphibians) and Pisces (fish). Within any class, several orders might be divided in turn into families and, depending on the complexity of the order and family, various suborders and subfamilies. All baboons, for instance, belong to the Primate order, suborder Catarrhini (monkeys and apes), family Cercopithecoidea (Old World Monkeys) and subfamily Cercopithecidae (cheek-pouch monkeys, ie: guenons, baboons and mangabeys).

The Linnaean scheme of nomenclature, devised in the 18th century by the Swedish botanist Carolus Linnaeus, assigns every living organism a scientific binomial, which is a two-part name that indicates both its genus and species. Thus *Papio cynocephalus* is the yellow baboon and *Papio anubis* the olive baboon. These names are derived from Greek, Latin or a combination of the two, and it is conventional to italicise them.

Taxonomic constructs are designed to approximate the real genetic and evolutionary relationships between various living creatures, and on the whole they succeed. But equally the science exists to help humans understand a reality that is likely to be more complex and less absolute than any conceptual structure used to contain it. This is particularly the case with speciation – the evolution of two or more distinct species from a common ancestor – which might occur over many thousands of generations, and like many gradual processes may lack for any absolute landmarks.

Simplistically, the process of speciation begins when a single population splits into two mutually exclusive breeding units. This can happen as a result of geographic isolation (for instance mountain and lowland gorillas), habitat differences (forest and savannah elephants) or varied migratory patterns (the six races of yellow wagtail intermingle as non-breeding migrants to Africa during the northern winter, but they all have a discrete Palaearctic breeding ground). Whatever the reason, the two breeding communities will share an identical gene pool when first they split, but as generations pass they will accumulate a number of small genetic differences and eventually marked racial characteristics. Given

population is estimated at around 900. More detailed information on gorilla behaviour can be found on pages 514–15.

Mountain gorilla

Common chimpanzee (*Pan troglodytes*) This distinctive black-coated ape, more closely related to man than to any other living creature, lives in large, loosely bonded communities based around a core of related males with an internal hierarchy

long enough, the two populations might even deviate to the point where they wouldn't or couldn't interbreed, even if the barrier that originally divided them was removed.

The taxonomic distinction between a full species and a subspecies or race of that species rests not on how similar the two taxa are in appearance or habit, but on the final point above. Should it be known that two distinct taxa freely interbreed and produce fertile hybrids where their ranges overlap, or it is believed that they would in the event that their ranges did overlap, then they are classified as races of the same species. If not, they are regarded as full species. The six races of yellow wagtail referred to above are all very different in appearance, far more so, for instance, than the several dozen warbler species of the genus *Cisticola*, but clearly they are able to interbreed, and they must thus be regarded as belonging to the same species. And while this may seem a strange distinction on the face of things, it does make sense when you recall that humans rely mostly on visual recognition, whereas many other creatures are more dependent on other senses. Those pesky cisticolas all look much the same to human observers, but each species has a highly distinctive call and in some cases a display flight that would preclude crossbreeding whether or not it is genetically possible.

The gradual nature of speciation creates grey areas that no arbitrary distinction can cover – at any given moment in time there might exist separate breeding populations of a certain species that have not yet evolved distinct racial characters, or distinct races that are on their way to becoming full species. Furthermore, where no conclusive evidence exists, some taxonomists tend to be habitual 'lumpers' and others eager 'splitters' – respectively inclined to designate any controversial taxa racial or full specific status. For this reason, various field guides often differ in their designation of controversial taxa.

Among African mammals, this is particularly the case with primates, where in some cases up to 20 described taxa are sometimes lumped together as one species and sometimes split into several specific clusters of similar races. Our earlier baboon example is a case in point: some taxonomists regard olive and yellow baboon to represent a single species (conspecific) on the basis that they often interbreed where their ranges overlap. These taxonomists thus assign them trinomials, in this case *P. c. cynocephalus* and *P. c. anubis*, whose third part indicates the race. Such ambiguities can be a source of genuine frustration, particularly for birdwatchers obsessed with ticking 'new' species, but they also serve as a valid reminder that the natural world is and will always be a more complex, mysterious and dynamic entity than any taxonomic construct designed to label it.

topped by a benevolent alpha male. Chimpanzees are typical animals of the rainforest and woodlands from Guinea to western Uganda, which supports a population estimated at around 5,000 across a dozen sites. Chimps have been habituated to tourists in Kibale National Park, Kyambura Gorge (Queen Elizabeth National Park), Kaniyo Pabidi (near Murchison Falls National Park) and Kalinzu Forest Reserve. For more details about chimp behaviour and ecology, see box above.

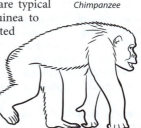

Chimpanzee

Monkeys All the monkeys found in Uganda are members of the family Cercopithecidae (Old World Monkeys), and they break up into two subfamilies, the leaf-eating colobus monkeys of the Colobinae and more generalised cheek-pouched monkeys of the Cercopithecinae.

Black-and-white colobus (*Colobus guereza*) Also known as the guereza, this beautifully marked and distinctive monkey has a black body, white facial markings, long white tail and, in some races, a white side-stripe.

Black-and-white colobus

It lives in small groups and is almost exclusively arboreal. An adult is capable of jumping up to 30m, a spectacular sight with its white tail streaming behind. It is probably the most common and widespread forest monkey in Uganda, occurring in most sizeable forest patches and even in well-developed riparian woodland.

Angola colobus (*Colobus angolensis*) Closely related and similar in appearance to the black-and-white colobus, the Angola colobus is represented in Uganda by the race *C. a. ruwenzorii*, which inhabits montane forests along the Albertine Rift.

Uganda red colobus (*Procolobus tephrosceles*) Split from the western red colobus (*P. badius*) in 2001, this relatively large red-grey monkey has few distinguishing features other than its slightly tufted crown. It is highly sociable and normally lives in scattered troops of 50 or more animals. Confined to a few localities along the Albertine Rift in Uganda and Tanzania, it is IUCN red-listed as Endangered, but is quite common in Kibale National Park, and is often seen on the swamp walk through the neighbouring Bigodi Wetland Sanctuary.

Anubis baboon (*Papio anubis*) Also known as the olive baboon, this heavily built and mainly terrestrial baboon can be distinguished from any other Ugandan monkey by its larger size and distinctive dog-like head. It lives in large troops with a complex and rigid social structure held together by matriarchal lineages. Males frequently move between troops in their search for social dominance. Omnivorous and highly adaptable, the Anubis is widespread and common in Uganda, where it is frequently seen on the fringes of forest reserves and even along the roadside.

Patas monkey (*Erythrocebus patas*) Another terrestrial primate, restricted to the dry savannah of north-central Africa, the patas (also known as the hussar monkey) could be confused with the vervet monkey, but it has a lankier build, a light reddish-brown coat, and a black stripe above the eyes (the vervet is greyer and has a black face mask). In Uganda, the patas monkey is restricted to the extreme north, where it can be seen in Kidepo

Patas monkey

and Murchison Falls national parks, as well as the Pian Upe Wildlife Reserve. The race found in Uganda is the Nile patas or nisras (*E. p. pyrrhonotus*).

Vervet monkey (*Chlorocebus pygerythrus*) This light-grey monkey is readily identified by its black face and the male's distinctive blue genitals. Associated with

Vervet monkey

a wide variety of habitats, it's the only guenon you're likely to see outside of forests and it is thought to be the most numerous monkey species in the world. It is sometimes listed a subspecies of the grivet monkey (*C. aethiops*). Vervet monkeys are widespread and common in Uganda, even outside of national parks, but they are absent from forest interiors and Afro-alpine habitats.

Blue monkey (*Cercopithecus mitis*) The blue monkey is the most widespread forest guenon in East Africa – uniform dark blue-grey in colour except for its white throat and chest patch, with thick fur and backward-projecting hair on its forehead. The blue monkey is common in most Ugandan forests, where it lives in troops of between four and 12 animals and frequently associates with other primates. It is also known as the diademed guenon, samango monkey, Sykes's monkey and gentle monkey, and several races are recognised.

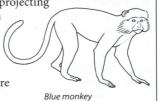
Blue monkey

Golden monkey (*Cercopithecus kandti*) Formerly treated as a subspecies of blue monkey, this bamboo-associated species is an endangered Albertine Rift Endemic named for the orange-gold patch on its upper flanks and back. Formerly more widespread, it is now effectively endemic to the Virunga Volcanoes, where it is the most common primate. A habituated troop can be visited in Mgahinga Gorilla National Park.

Silver monkey (*Cercopithecus doggetti*) Also recently split from the blue monkey, this forest-dwelling species has a rather uniform silver-grey coat. It is unclear which Ugandan populations still listed as blue monkey actually belong to this species.

Red-tailed monkey (*Cercopithecus ascinius*) A widespread forest guenon, the red-tailed monkey is brownish in appearance with white cheek whiskers, a coppery tail and a distinctive heart-shaped white patch on its nose, giving rise to the more descriptive alternative name white-nosed monkey. It is normally seen singly, in pairs or in small family groups, but it also associates with other monkeys and has been known to accumulate in groups of up to 200. It regularly interbreeds with blue monkeys in Kibale Forest. It also occurs in Semliki and Queen Elizabeth national parks, as well as in Budongo, Mpanga and several other forest reserves.

De Brazza's monkey (*Cercopithecus neglectus*) This spectacular thickset guenon has a relatively short tail, a hairy face with a reddish-brown patch around its eyes, a white band across its brow and a distinctive white moustache and beard. Primarily a West African species, De Brazza's monkey is very localised in East Africa, most likely to be seen in the vicinity of Mount Elgon and Semliki national parks.

L'Hoest's monkey (*Cercopithecus lhoesti*) This handsome Albertine Rift Endemic is often more difficult to see than most of its relatives, largely because of its terrestrial habits and a preference for dense secondary forest. It has a black face and backward-projecting white whiskers that partially cover its ears, and is the only guenon which habitually carries its tail in an upright position. L'Hoest's monkey is

very common in Bwindi Impenetrable National Park, but it also occurs in Kibale Forest and Queen Elizabeth national parks.

Uganda mangabey (*Lephocebus ugandae*) Endemic to Uganda, this heavy greyish-black monkey was split from the grey-cheeked mangabey (*L. albigena*) in 2007. It has few distinguishing features, but can be determined from other forest monkeys by its baboon-like mannerisms, shaggier appearance, light-grey cheeks and slight mane. A resident of lowland and mid-altitude forests, it is most likely to be seen in Mabira Forest or Kibale National Park.

Nocturnal primates Seldom observed on account of their nocturnal habits, the prosimians are a relict group of primitive primates more closely related to the lemurs of Madagascar than to the diurnal monkeys and apes of the African mainland.

Lesser bushbaby

Galagos Also called bushbabies, these small nocturnal primates are widespread in wooded habitats in sub-Saharan Africa and their piercing cry is one of the region's most distinctive night sounds. If you want to see a bushbaby, trace the cry to a tree, then shine a torch into it and you should easily pick out its large round eyes. Six galago species are found in Uganda, of which the lesser galago (*Galago senegalensis*) is the most common. An insectivorous creature, only 17cm long excluding its tail, the lesser bushbaby is a creature of woodland as opposed to true forest, and it has been recorded in all of Uganda's savannah reserves. The much larger and rather catlike silvery greater galago (*Otolemur monteiri argentatus*), though restricted to woodland habitats in the Lake Victoria basin, commonly visits Mihingo Lodge in Lake Mburo National Park shortly after dark.

Potto (*Perodicticus potto*) This medium-sized sloth-like creature inhabits forest interiors, where it spends the nights foraging upside down from tree branches. It can sometimes be located at night by shining a spotlight into the canopy. The potto occurs in Kibale, Bwindi and Queen Elizabeth national parks, as well as most other major rainforests, and it is most likely to be seen on guided night walks in Kibale Forest.

CARNIVORES A total of 38 carnivores have been recorded in Uganda: five canid species; seven felines; three hyenas; ten mongooses; six mustelids (otters, badgers and weasels); and seven viverrids (civets and genets).

Felines

Lion (*Panthera leo*) The largest African carnivore, and the one animal that everybody wants to see on safari, the lion is the most sociable of the large cats, living in loosely structured prides of typically five to 15 animals. Primarily a nocturnal hunter, its favoured prey are buffalo and medium-to-large antelope such as Ugandan kob. Females, working in teams of up to eight animals, are responsible for most hunts. Rivalry between male lions is intense: prides may have more than one dominant male working in collaboration to prevent a takeover and young males are forced out of their home pride at about three years of age. Pride takeovers are often fought to the death; after a successful one, it is not unusual for all the male cubs to be killed. Lions are not very active by day: they are most often seen lying

in the shade looking the picture of regal indolence. They occur naturally in most woodland and grassland habitats, and are now fairly common in Murchison Falls, Queen Elizabeth and Kidepo national parks, but are scarce or absent elsewhere.

Leopard (*Panthera pardus*) The most common of Africa's large felines, the leopard often lives in close proximity to humans, but it is rarely seen because of its secretive, solitary nature. Leopards hunt using stealth and power, often getting to within 5m of their intended prey before pouncing, and they habitually store their kill in a tree to keep it from being poached by other large predators. They can be distinguished from cheetahs by their rosette-shaped spots and more powerful build, as well as by their preference for wooded or rocky habitats. Leopards are found in virtually all habitats which offer adequate cover, and are present in most Ugandan national parks and forest reserves. The only place in Uganda where they are seen with regularity is along the Channel Drive in Queen Elizabeth National Park.

Leopard

Cheetah (*Acinonyx jubatus*) Superficially similar to the leopard, the cheetah is the most diurnal of Africa's cat species, and it hunts using speed as opposed to stealth. Cheetahs are the fastest land mammals, capable of running at up to 70km/h in short bursts. Male cheetahs are strongly territorial and in some areas they commonly defend their territory in pairs or trios. Cheetahs are the least powerful of the large predators: they are chased from a high percentage of their kills and 50% of cheetah cubs are killed by other predators before they reach three months of age. Like leopards, cheetahs are heavily spotted and solitary in their habits, but their greyhound-like build, distinctive black tear-marks and preference for grassland and savannah habitats preclude confusion. In Uganda, cheetahs are traditionally present only in the vicinity of Kidepo National Park, though several sightings in the north of Murchison Falls suggest that they might yet re-colonise this park.

Cheetah

Smaller cats The lynx-like **caracal** (*Caracal caraca*) is a medium-sized cat found in open habitats, and easily identified by its uniform reddish-brown coat and tufted ears. In Uganda, it occurs only in Kidepo National Park. The **African golden cat** (*Caracal aurata*) is a rarely seen creature of the West African forest: it is widespread in western Uganda, where it has been recorded in every forested national park except Semliki. The slightly larger **serval** (*Leptailurus serval*) has a pale spotted coat, making it possible to confuse it with some genet species. It favours moister habitats than the caracal, ranging from woodland to forest, and it is widespread in Uganda. The **African wild cat** (*Felis silvestris*), reminiscent of the domestic tabby, to which it is thought to be ancestral, is found in most savannah habitats in Uganda.

Canids The Canidae is a family of medium-sized carnivores of which the most familiar is the domestic dog. Five species – all recognisably dog-like in appearance and habits – are present in Uganda, though none is very common.

Black-backed jackal

Jackals (*Canis* spp) Jackals are small to medium-sized dogs associated with most savannah habitats. Although often portrayed as carrion-eaters, they are in fact opportunistic omnivores, hunting a variety of small mammals and birds with some regularity and also eating a substantial amount of fruit and bulbs. The most widespread canid in Uganda is the **side-striped jackal** (*C. adustus*), which occurs in all four savannah national parks as well as in Bwindi and Mgahinga, and is most likely to be seen in the north of Murchison Falls. Within Uganda, the similar **black-backed jackal** (*C. mesomelas*) is restricted to Kidepo National Park, Pian Upe and environs, while the **golden jackal** (*C. aureus*), though it appears on the national checklist, has been recorded in no national park and is presumably a vagrant. The three species are very similar in appearance, but recent DNA testing revealed that the side-striped jackal is more closely related to the coyote, grey wolf and Ethiopian wolf than to other jackals. It has thus been proposed that the black-backed and golden jackal be placed in a separate genus, *Lupulella*.

Bat-eared fox (*Otocyon megalotis*) This small but striking silver-grey insectivore, rendered unmistakable by its huge ears and black eye-mask, is most often seen in pairs or small family groups during the cooler hours of the day. Associated with dry open country, the bat-eared fox is quite common in the Kidepo and Pian Upe, but absent elsewhere in Uganda.

Bat-eared fox

African hunting dog (*Lycaon pictus*) The largest African canid, and the most endangered after the rare Ethiopian wolf, the African hunting dog (also known as the wild or painted dog) lives in packs of five to 50 animals and is distinguished by its cryptic black, brown and cream coat. Hunting dogs are highly effective pack hunters and were once widely distributed and common throughout sub-Saharan Africa. Hunted as vermin and highly susceptible to epidemics spread by domestic dogs, hunting dogs today have a very localised and scattered distribution pattern, with perhaps 25% of the estimated wild population of 5,000 confined to the Selous ecosystem in southern Tanzania. The African hunting dog is locally extinct in roughly half the countries it once inhabited, Uganda included. Re-colonisation, though unlikely, is not impossible, since hunting dogs are great wanderers and small populations do survive in parts of northern Tanzania and Kenya.

African hunting dog

Other carnivores

Spotted hyena (*Crocuta crocuta*) In Uganda, as elsewhere in Africa, the spotted hyena is by far the most common member of a family of large, hunchbacked carnivores whose somewhat canid appearance belies a closer evolutionary relationship to mongooses and cats. Often portrayed as an exclusive scavenger, the spotted hyena is an adept hunter capable of killing an animal as large as a wildebeest. In ancient times, the spotted hyena was thought to be hermaphroditic: the female's vagina is blocked by a false but remarkably realistic-looking scrotum

and penis. Most hyena species live in loosely structured clans of around ten animals, and their social interaction is fascinating to observe. Clans are led by females, which are stronger and larger than males. The spotted hyena is bulky with a sloping back, a light-brown coat marked with dark-brown spots and an exceptionally powerful jaw which enables it to crack open bones and slice through the thickest hide. The spotted hyena is found in all of Uganda's savannah national parks, as well as in Mgahinga, but is only seen with great regularity in Queen Elizabeth. Note that the secretive **striped hyena** (*Hyaena hyaena*) and the insectivorous **aardwolf** (*Proteles cristatus*) are present but uncommon in Kidepo National Park and environs.

Spotted hyena

African civet

African civet (*Civetticus civetta*) This bulky, long-haired, cat-like viverrid has been kept in captivity for thousands of years (its anal secretions were used in making perfumes until a synthetic replacement was found). Surprisingly, little is known about their habits in the wild. Civets are widespread and common in most wooded habitats, and they have been recorded in most of Uganda's national parks, but they are seen very rarely on account of their secretive, nocturnal habits.

Genets (*Genetta* spp) Closely related to civets, but often referred to mistakenly as cats because of various superficial similarities in appearance, the genets are slender, low-slung viverrids characterised by beautiful spotted coats and extraordinarily long tails. Secretive except when habituated, and subject to some taxonomic debate, genets are attracted to human waste and are occasionally seen slinking around campsites and lodges after dark. The **servaline genet** (*G. servalina*), **large-spotted genet** (*G. tigrina*) and **small-spotted genet** (*G. genetta*) are all widespread in Uganda, with the latter two generally occurring in more lightly wooded areas than the former, and sometimes observed on night drives in the Toro-Semliki Wildlife Reserve. A West African species, the **giant forest genet** (*G. victiriae*), has been recorded in Maramagambo Forest in Queen Elizabeth National Park.

Otters Three species of these familiar aquatic predators occur in sub-Saharan Africa, and their ranges overlap in western Uganda, where all three have been recorded in certain areas such as Lake Mburo National Park. The **Cape clawless otter** (*Aonyx capensis*) and **Western clawless otter** (*A. congica*), regarded to be conspecific by some authorities, are the largest African otters, growing up to 1.6m long, with a rich brown coat and pale chin and belly. Associated with most wetland habitats, the clawless otters are most active between dusk and dawn, and are hence less likely to be observed than the smaller and darker **spotted-necked otter** (*Lutra maculicollisi*), a diurnal species that is unusually common and visible on Lake Bunyonyi in Kigezi.

Ratel (honey badger) (*Mellivora capensis*) The ratel is a medium-sized mustelid with a puppy-like head, black sides and underparts and a grey-white back. It is an adaptable creature, eating whatever comes its way – it's said that they've been known to kill buffaloes by running underneath them and biting off their testicles which, if true, is certainly taking opportunism to a wasteful extreme. When not Bobbing bovines, the ratel occasionally indulges in a symbiotic relationship with a bird called the greater honeyguide: the honeyguide takes the ratel to a beehive,

which the ratel then tears open, allowing the honeyguide to feed on the scraps. Ratels are widespread in Uganda, but uncommon and rarely seen. Other mustelids found in Uganda include the **zorilla** (or striped polecat) and the **striped weasel**.

Mongooses Ten mongoose species have been recorded in Uganda, none of which – as is commonly assumed – feeds predominantly on snakes. Five species are widespread and common enough to have been recorded in at least half the national parks. They are the **marsh mongoose** (*Atilax paludinosus*), **Egyptian mongoose** (*Herpestes ichneumon*), **slender mongoose** (*Herpestes sanguineus*), **white-tailed mongoose** (*Ichneumia albicauda*) and **banded mongoose** (*Mungos mungo*). Of these the banded mongoose is the most regularly observed, particularly on the Mweya Peninsula in Queen Elizabeth National Park.

Banded mongoose

ANTELOPE Some 29 antelope species – about one-third of the African total – are included on the checklist for Uganda, a figure that fails to acknowledge a recent rash of near or complete local extinctions. There are probably no more than ten roan antelope remaining in Uganda, for example, while no oryx are left at all. Of the species that do still occur, five fall into the category of large antelope, having a shoulder height of above 120cm (roughly the height of a zebra); eight are in the category of medium-sized antelope, having a shoulder height of between 75cm and 90cm; and the remainder are small antelope, with a shoulder height of between 30cm and 60cm.

Large antelope

Common eland (*Taurotragus oryx*) The world's largest antelope is the common or Cape eland which measures over 1.8m in height, and which can be bulkier than a buffalo. The eland has a rather bovine appearance: fawn-brown colour, with a large dewlap and short, spiralled horns, and in some cases light-white stripes on its sides. The common eland occurs in open habitats throughout eastern and southern Africa. In Uganda, it is most likely to be seen in Lake Mburo National Park, but also occurs in Kidepo Valley and Pian Upe Wildlife Reserve.

Eland

Greater kudu

Greater kudu (*Tragelaphus strepsiceros*) This is another very large antelope, measuring up to 1.5m high, and it is also strikingly handsome, with a grey-brown coat marked by thin white side-stripes. The male has a small dewlap and large spiralling horns. The greater kudu lives in small groups in woodland habitats. In Uganda, it occurs only in small numbers in Kidepo.

Hartebeest (*Alcelaphus buselaphus*) This large and ungainly looking, tan-coloured antelope – a relative of the wildebeest, which is absent from Uganda – has large shoulders, a sloping back and relatively small horns. It lives in small herds in lightly wooded and open savannah habitats. The typical hartebeest of

Hartebeest

Uganda is **Jackson's hartebeest** (*A. b. jacksoni*), though it is replaced by the **Lelwel hartebeest** (*A. b. lelweli*) west of the Nile. The closely related and similarly built **topi** (*Damaliscus lunatus*) has a much darker coat than the hartebeest, and distinctive blue-black markings above its knees. Jackson's hartebeest is most frequently seen in Murchison Falls, though it also occurs in Kidepo Valley.

Common
waterbuck

Defassa waterbuck (*Kobus ellipsyprymnus defassa*) Shaggy-looking, with a grey-brown coat, white rump and large curved horns, the Defassa waterbuck is considered by some authorities to be a distinct species, *K. defassa* (the common waterbuck found east of the Rift Valley has a white ring on its rump), but the two races interbreed where they overlap. Defassa waterbuck live in small herds and are most often seen grazing near water. They are found in suitable habitats in all four of Uganda's savannah national parks.

Roan antelope (*Hippotragus equinus*) This handsome animal has a light red-brown coat, short backward-curving horns and a small mane on the back of the neck. It is present only in small numbers in Pian Upe having become locally extinct in Kidepo Valley and Lake Mburo national parks.

Roan
antelope

Medium-sized antelope

Ugandan kob (*Kobus kob thomasi*) Uganda's national antelope is a race of the West African kob confined to grassy floodplains and open vegetation near water in Uganda and South Sudan. Although closely related to waterbuck and reedbuck, the kob is reddish-brown in colour and similar to the impala, but bulkier in appearance and lacking the impala's black side-stripe. Ugandan kob live in herds of up to 100 animals in Queen Elizabeth and Murchison Falls and neighbouring conservation areas, as well as in Semliki and Katonga wildlife reserves.

Ugandan kob

Bushbuck (*Tragelaphus scriptus*) Probably the most widespread antelope in Uganda is the bushbuck, which lives in forest, riverine woodland and other thicketed habitats. The male bushbuck has a dark chestnut coat marked with white spots and stripes. The female is lighter in colour and vaguely resembles a large duiker. Although secretive and elusive, the bushbuck is very common in suitable habitats in most forests and national parks in Uganda.

Sitatunga (*Tragelaphus spekei*) This semi-aquatic antelope is similar in appearance to the closely related bushbuck, but the male is larger with a shaggier coat, both sexes are striped, and it has uniquely splayed hooves adapted to its favoured habitat of papyrus and other swamps. It is found in suitable habitats throughout Uganda, including six national parks, but is likely to be seen only in the Katonga Wildlife Reserve.

Sitatunga

Lesser kudu (*Tragelaphus imberbis*) This pretty, dry-country antelope is similar in appearance to the greater kudu, but much smaller and more heavily striped (greater kudu have between six and ten stripes; lesser kudu have 11 or more). Lesser kudu are present in Pian Upe and environs.

Grant's gazelle (*Gazella granti*) Yet another dry-country antelope which in Uganda has been reduced to 100 animals roaming the contiguous Pian Upe, Matheniko and Bokora wildlife reserves in Karamoja. This typical gazelle is lightly built, tan in colour, and lives in herds.

Reedbuck (*Redunca* spp) Also restricted to Kidepo is the **mountain reedbuck** (*R. fulvorufula*), a grey-brown antelope with small crescent-shaped horns. The very similar **Bohor reedbuck** (*R. redunca*) is more widespread, occurring in all four savannah national parks. Both reedbuck species are usually seen in pairs in open country near water, with the mountain reedbuck occurring at higher altitudes.

Reedbuck

Impala (*Aepyceros melampus*) This slender, handsome antelope, though superficially similar to the gazelles, belongs to a separate subfamily that is more closely related to hartebeest and oryx. The impala can be distinguished from any gazelle by its chestnut colouring, sleek appearance and the male's distinctive lyre-shaped horns. An adult impala can jump up to 3m high and has been known to broad-jump for over 10m. Impala live in herds of between 20 and a few hundred animals. They favour well-wooded savannah and woodland fringes, and are often abundant in such habitats. In Uganda, impalas are found only in Lake Mburo National Park and Katonga Wildlife Reserve.

Impala

Small antelope Nine of the small antelope species present in Uganda are duikers, a family of closely related antelopes which are generally characterised by their small size, sloping back, and preference for thickly forested habitats. Between 16 and 19 duiker species are recognised, many of them extremely localised in their distribution.

Grey duiker (*Sylvicapra grimmia*) Also known as the common or bush duiker, this is an atypical member of its family in that it generally occurs in woodland and savannah habitats. It has a grey-brown coat with a vaguely speckled appearance. The grey duiker is widespread in east and southern Africa, and it occurs in all four of Uganda's savannah national parks as well as in Mount Elgon.

Common duiker

Forest duiker (*Cephalophus* spp) The striking **yellow-backed duiker** (*C. sylviculter*) is also atypical of the family, owing to its relatively large size – heavier than a bushbuck – rather than any habitat preference. It is a West African species, but has been recorded in several forests in western Uganda, including those in Bwindi, Mgahinga, Rwenzori and Queen Elizabeth national parks; it's sometimes encountered fleetingly along the forest track leading uphill from the Buhoma headquarters at Bwindi. Of the more typical duiker species, **Harvey's red duiker** (*C. harveyi*) is a tiny chestnut-brown antelope found

in forested parts of Queen Elizabeth National Park and in the Kibale Forest. The **blue duiker** (*C. monticola*), even smaller and with a grey-blue coat, is known to occur in Queen Elizabeth, Murchison Falls, Kibale and Bwindi national parks. **Peter's duiker** (*C. callipygus*) has been recorded in Bwindi, Kibale and Queen Elizabeth; the **black-fronted duiker** (*C. nigrifrons*) in Mgahinga and Bwindi; and there have been unconfirmed sightings of the **white-bellied duiker** (*C. leucogaster*) for Bwindi and Semliki. The **red-flanked duiker** (*C. rufilatus*) and **Weyn's duiker** (*C. weynsi*) have not been recorded in any national park, but they most probably occur in the Budongo Forest.

Bates's pygmy antelope (*Neofragus batesi*) Not a duiker, but similar both in size and its favoured habitat, this diminutive antelope – the second-smallest African ungulate – is a Congolese rainforest species that has been recorded in Semliki National Park and in forests within and bordering the southern half of Queen Elizabeth National Park.

Klipspringer (*Oreotragus oreotragus*) This distinctive antelope has a dark-grey bristly coat and an almost speckled appearance. It has goat-like habits and is invariably found in the vicinity of koppies or cliffs (the name 'klipspringer' means 'rock-jumper' in Afrikaans). It lives in pairs in suitable habitats in Kidepo Valley and Lake Mburo national parks.

Oribi (*Ourebia ourebi*) This endearing gazelle-like antelope has a light red-brown back, white underparts, and a diagnostic black scent gland under its ears. It is one of the largest 'small' antelopes in Africa, not much smaller than a Thomson's gazelle. When disturbed, the oribi emits a high-pitched sneezing sound, then bounds off in a manner mildly reminiscent of a pronking springbok. The oribi favours tall grassland, and it occurs in all of the savannah national parks except for Queen Elizabeth. It is remarkably common in the Borassus grassland in the northern part of Murchison Falls National Park, most often seen in pairs or groups of up to five animals, consisting of one male and his 'harem', but also sometimes in larger groups.

Guenther's dik-dik (*Modoqua guentheri*) This pretty, small antelope has a dark red-brown coat and distinctive white eye markings. It is found in the dry savannah in and around Kidepo Valley.

OTHER HERBIVORES
African elephant (*Loxodonta africana*) The world's largest land animal is also one of the most intelligent and entertaining to watch. A fully grown elephant is about 3.5m high and weighs around 6,000kg. Female elephants live in closely knit clans in which the eldest female takes a matriarchal role over her sisters, daughters and granddaughters. Mother–daughter bonds are strong and may exist for up to 50 years. Males generally leave the family group at around 12 years, after which they either roam around on their own or form bachelor herds. Under normal circumstances, elephants range widely in search of food and water but, when concentrated populations are forced to live in conservation areas, their habit of uprooting trees can cause serious environmental damage. Two races of elephant are recognised: the **savannah elephant** of east and southern Africa (*L. a. africana*) and the smaller and slightly hairier **forest elephant** of the West African rainforest (*L. a. cyclotis*). The two races are thought to interbreed in parts of western Uganda. Despite severe poaching in the past, elephants occur in all national parks except for Lake Mburo. They are most likely to be seen in Murchison Falls, Queen Elizabeth and Kidepo national parks.

Black rhinoceros

Rhinoceros The **black rhinoceros** (*Diceros bicornis*) and **northern white rhinoceros** (*Ceratotherium simum cottoni*) both occur naturally in Uganda, but they have been poached to local extinction. A population of southern white rhino, originating from South Africa but relocated from introduced populations in Kenya and the USA, can be tracked on foot in Ziwa Rhino Sanctuary north of Kampala.

ALBERTINE RIFT ENDEMICS

Most of Uganda's forest inhabitants have a wide distribution in the Democratic Republic of Congo (DRC) and/or West Africa, while a smaller proportion comprises eastern species that might as easily be observed in forested habitats in Kenya, Tanzania and in some instances Ethiopia. A significant number, however, are endemic to the Albertine Rift: in other words, their range is more-or-less confined to montane habitats associated with the Rift Valley Escarpment running between Lake Albert and the north of Lake Tanganyika. The most celebrated of these regional endemics is of course the mountain gorilla, confined to the Virungas and Bwindi Mountains near the eastern Rift Valley Escarpment. Other primate species endemic to the Albertine Rift include golden monkey and Rwenzori colobus. Eight endemic butterflies have been described, and are regarded as flagship species for the many hundreds of invertebrate taxa that occur nowhere else in the world.

Of the remarkable tally of 38 range-restricted bird species listed as Albertine Rift Endemics, roughly half are regarded to be of global conservation concern. All 38 of these species have been recorded in the DRC, and nine are endemic to that country, since their range is confined to the western escarpment forests. More than 20 Albertine Rift Endemics are resident in each of Uganda, Rwanda and Burundi, while two extend their range southward into western Tanzania. All 25 of the Albertine Rift endemics recorded in Uganda occur in Bwindi National Park, including the highly sought African green broadbill, which is elsewhere known only from the Itombwe Mountains and Kahuzi-Biega National Park in the DRC. Other important sites in Uganda are the Rwenzori Mountains with 17 Albertine Rift Endemics, the Virungas with 14 and the Echuya Forest with 12.

Outside Uganda, all but one of the 29 endemics that occur on the eastern escarpment have been recorded in Rwanda's Nyungwe Forest, a readily accessible site that is highly recommended for the opportunity to observe several species absent from, or not as easily located in, Uganda. Inaccessible to tourists at the time of writing, the Itombwe Mountains, which rise from the Congolese shore of northern Lake Tanganyika, support the largest contiguous block of montane forest in East Africa. This range is also regarded to be the most important site for montane forest birds in the region, with a checklist of 565 species including 31 Albertine Rift Endemics, three of which are known from nowhere else in the world. The most elusive of these birds is the enigmatic Congo bay owl, first collected in 1952, and yet to be seen again, though its presence is suspected in Rwanda's Nyungwe Forest.

Several Albertine Rift forest endemics share stronger affinities with extant or extinct Asian genera than they do with any other living African species, affirming the great age of these forests, which are thought to have flourished during prehistoric climatic changes that caused temporary deforestation in lower-lying areas such as the Congo Basin. The Congo bay owl, African green broadbill and Grauer's cuckoo-shrike, for instance, might all be classed as living fossils – isolated

Hippopotamus (*Hippopotamus amphibius*) This large, lumbering aquatic animal occurs naturally on most African lakes and waterways, where it spends most of the day submerged, but emerges from the water to graze at night. Hippos are strongly territorial, with herds of ten or more animals being presided over by a dominant male. The best places to see them are in Murchison Falls, Queen Elizabeth and Lake Mburo national parks, where they are abundant in suitable habitats. Hippos are still

relics of a migrant Asian stock that has been superseded elsewhere on the continent by indigenous genera evolved from a common ancestor.

Among the other mammal species endemic to the Albertine Rift, the Rwenzori dwarf otter-shrew is one of three highly localised African mainland species belonging to a family of aquatic insectivores that flourished some 50 million years ago and is elsewhere survived only by the related tenrecs of Madagascar. A relict horseshoe bat species restricted to the Rwenzori and Lake Kivu is anatomically closer to extant Asian forms of horseshoe bat and to ancient migrant stock than it is to any of the 20-odd more modern and widespread African horseshoe bat species, while a shrew specimen collected only once in the Itombwe Mountains is probably the most primitive and ancient of all 150 described African species.

A full list of the Albertine Rift Endemic birds that occur in Uganda follows, with species regarded to be of global conservation concern marked with an asterisk. All are present in Bwindi National Park; those present elsewhere are indicated as M (Mgahinga), E (Echuya), R (Rwenzori) and/or K (Kibale Forest).

Handsome francolin	*Francolinus nobilis*	M E R
Rwenzori turaco	*Tauraco johnstoni*	M E R
Rwenzori nightjar	*Caprimulgus rwenzori*	R
Dwarf honeyguide	*Indicator pumilio* *	
African green broadbill	*Pseudocalyptomena grauri* *	
Kivu ground thrush	*Zoothera tanganjicae* *	
Red-throated alethe	*Alethe poliophrys*	E R
Archer's robin-chat	*Cossypha archeri*	M E R
Collared apalis	*Apalis rwenzori*	M E R K
Mountain masked apalis	*Apalis personata*	M R
Grauer's scrub warbler	*Bradypterus grauri* *	M R
Grauer's warbler	*Graueria vittata*	
Neumann's warbler	*Hemetisia neumanni*	
Red-faced woodland warbler	*Phylloscopus laetus*	M E R K
Yellow-eyed black flycatcher	*Melaeornis ardesiascus*	
Chapin's flycatcher	*Musicapa lendu* *	
Rwenzori batis	*Batis diops*	M E R
Stripe-breasted tit	*Parus fasciiventer*	M R
Blue-headed sunbird	*Nectarinia alinae*	R K
Regal sunbird	*Nectarinia regia*	M E R
Stuhlmann's double-collared sunbird	*Cinnyris stuhlmanni*	R
Purple-breasted sunbird	*Nectarinia purpureiventris*	R K
Dusky crimsonwing	*Cryptospiza jacksoni*	M E R K
Shelley's crimsonwing	*Cryptospiza shelleyi* *	M R
Strange weaver	*Ploceus alienus*	M E R

quite common outside of reserves, and they are responsible for killing more people than any other African mammal.

African buffalo (*Syncerus caffer*) Africa's only wild ox species is an adaptable and widespread creature that lives in large herds on the savannah and smaller herds in forested areas. Herds are mixed-sex and normally comprise several loosely related family clans and bachelor groups. Buffaloes can be seen in just about all of Uganda's national parks and large forests. In Queen Elizabeth and Murchison Falls national parks, you may see hybrids of the **savannah buffalo** (*S. c. caffer*) of East Africa and the **red buffalo** (*S. c. nanus*) of the West African forest.

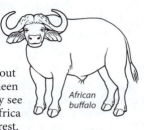
African buffalo

Giraffe (*Giraffa camelopardus*) The world's tallest animal (up to 5.5m) lives in loosely structured mixed-sex herds, typically numbering between five and 15 animals. As herd members may be dispersed over an area of up to 1km, they are frequently seen singly or in smaller groups, though unusually large aggregations are often seen in Uganda. The long neck of the giraffe gives it a slightly ungainly appearance when it ambles; giraffes look decidedly absurd when they adopt a semi-crouching position in order to drink. The race found in Uganda is **Rothschild's giraffe**, rare elsewhere in its former range but very common in the northern part of Murchison Falls National Park. A small herd is present in Kidepo Valley. Giraffes from northern Murchison Falls were recently relocated to Lake Mburo National Park and the southern half of Murchison Falls.

Burchell's zebra (*Equus burchelli*) This unmistakable striped horse is common and widespread throughout east and southern Africa. Zebras are often seen in large herds but their basic social unit is the small, relatively stable family group, which typically consists of a stallion, up to five mares, and their collective offspring. In Uganda, zebras are present only in Lake Mburo and Kidepo Valley national parks.

Swine The most visible pig species in Uganda is the **warthog** (*Phacochoerus africanus*), a common resident of the savannah national parks. Warthogs are uniform grey in colour and both sexes have impressive tusks. They are normally seen in family groups, trotting away briskly in the opposite direction with their tails raised stiffly and a determinedly nonchalant air. The bulkier and hairier **bushpig** (*Potamochoerus porcus*) is found mainly in thickets and dense woodland. Although bushpigs occur in all national parks except for Rwenzori, they are not often seen because of their nocturnal habits and the cover afforded by their favoured habitat. The **giant forest hog** (*Hylochoerus meinertzhageni*) is the largest African pig species. It is a nocturnal creature of the forest interior, and so very rarely seen, but it probably occurs in all national parks in western Uganda, and is often seen by day along Channel Drive in Queen Elizabeth National Park.

Hyraxes and other oddities Uganda's five hyrax species are guinea pig-like animals, often associated with rocky habitats, and related more closely to elephants than to any other living creatures – difficult to credit until you've heard a tree hyrax shrieking with pachydermal abandon through the night. Four types of

pangolin (similar in appearance to the South American scaly anteaters) occur in Uganda, as does the **aardvark**, a bizarre, long-snouted insectivore which is widespread in savannah habitats but very seldom seen because of its nocturnal habits. Also regarded as large mammals by the official checklist are 12 squirrel species, three flying squirrels (anomalures), three porcupines, three hares, two cane-rats, a hedgehog and the peculiar chevrotain.

Rock hyrax

BIRDS

Uganda is arguably the most attractive country in Africa to birdwatchers, not only because of the unusually high number of species recorded within its borders, but also because it offers easy access to several bird-rich habitats that are difficult to reach elsewhere. Uganda's remarkable avian diversity – 1,075 species recorded in an area similar to that of Great Britain – can be attributed to its location at a transitional point between the East African savannah, the West African rainforest and the semi-desert of the north.

Indicative of Uganda's transitional location is the fact that only one or two bird species are endemic to the country: Fox's weaver (associated with waterside vegetation in the southeast) and possibly Stuhlmann's double-collared sunbird (an Albertine Rift Endemic whose range might now be limited to the Ugandan slopes of the Rwenzori as a result of habitat loss). However, if you take only East Africa into consideration, then approximately 150 bird species (more than 10% of the regional checklist) are found only in Uganda. This list includes seven of the 20 hornbill species recorded in the region, five out of 14 honeyguides, seven out of 21 woodpeckers, 11 out of 36 bulbuls and greenbuls, five out of 20 bush shrikes, as well as 13 members of the thrush family, 11 warblers, ten flycatchers, eight sunbirds, eight weavers, eight finches, four tinkerbirds, four pigeons or doves, three kingfishers, three sparrowhawks, three cuckoos and three nightjars.

Most of these 'Uganda specials' are West African and Congolese forest birds that would be very difficult to see elsewhere, for the simple reason that the other countries in which they occur are poorly developed for tourism. The rainforests of western Uganda must be seen as the country's most important bird habitat, and the one that is of greatest interest to birdwatchers, particularly if they are already reasonably familiar with typical East African birds. The most alluring forest in terms of localised species is probably Semliki, closely rivalled by Budongo, Kibale and Bwindi. However, in practical terms, Kibale Forest is probably Uganda's best single stop for forest birds, because of the proficiency of the guides who take tourists into the forest and the nearby Bigodi Swamp Walk. That said, just about any forest in Uganda will be rewarding; even the relatively tame botanical garden in Entebbe will throw up several interesting species.

Unfortunately, most forest birds are very secretive, and it can be difficult to get even a glimpse of them in the dense undergrowth, let alone a clear enough look to make a positive identification. You would probably identify more bird species in ten minutes at the Backpackers' Hostel in Kampala than you would in an afternoon walking through the Semliki Forest. For this reason, first-time visitors to Africa might do better concentrating on locations other than forests – if you want to see a wide range of Ugandan birds, try to visit Entebbe (water and forest birds), Lake Mburo (water- and acacia-associated birds), Queen Elizabeth (a wide variety of habitats; over 600 species recorded), Murchison Falls (a wide variety of habitats; the best place in East Africa to see the papyrus-associated shoebill) and Kidepo (northern semi-desert specials; over 50 raptors recorded).

With its distinctive tall green stem topped by a luxuriant clump of thick, wide leaves, the banana (or plantain) is such an integral feature of the Ugandan landscape that it may come as a surprise to learn that it is not indigenous to the country. Kiganda folklore claims that the first banana plant was brought to the kingdom by Kintu, whose shrine lies on a hill called Magonga (almost certainly a derivative of a local name for the banana) alongside a tree said to have grown from the root of the plant he originally imported. If this legend is true, it would place the banana's arrival in Uganda in perhaps the 13th–15th century, probably from the Ethiopian Highlands. Most botanists argue, however, that the immense number of distinct varieties grown in modern Uganda could not have been cultivated within so short a period – a time span of at least 1,000 years would be required.

Only one species of banana (*Musa ensete*) is indigenous to Africa, and it doesn't bear edible fruit. The more familiar cultivated varieties have all been propagated from two wild Asian species (*M. acuminata* and *M. balbisiana*), and hybrids thereof. Wild bananas are almost inedible and riddled with hard pits, and it is thought that the first edible variety was cultivated from a rare mutant of one of the above species about 10,000 years ago – making the banana one of the oldest cultivated plants in existence. Edible bananas were most likely cultivated in Egypt before the time of Christ, presumably having arrived there via Arabia or the Indian Ocean. The Greek sailor and explorer Cosmas Indicopleustes recorded that edible bananas grew around the port of Adulis, in present-day Eritrea, CAD525 – describing them as 'moza, the wild-date of India'.

The route via which the banana reached modern-day Uganda is open to conjecture. The most obvious point of origin is Ethiopia, the source of several southward migrations in the past two millennia. But it is intriguing that while the banana is known by a name approximating to the generic Latin *musa* throughout Asia, Arabia and northeast Africa – *moz* in Arabic and Persian, for instance, or *mus* or *musa* in various Ethiopian languages and Somali – no such linguistic resemblance occurs in East Africa, where it is known variously as *ndizi*, *gonja*, *matoke*, etc. This peculiarity has been cited to support a hypothesis that the banana first travelled between Asia and the East African coast either as a result of direct trade or else via Madagascar, and that it was entrenched there before regular trade was established with Arabia. A third possibility is that the banana reached Uganda via the Congolese Basin, possibly in association with the arrival of Bantu speakers from West Africa.

However it arrived in Uganda, the banana has certainly flourished there, forming the main subsistence crop for an estimated 40% of the population. Some 50 varieties are grown in the country, divided into four broad categories based on their primary use – *matoke* for boiling, *gonja* for roasting, *mbide* for distillation into banana beer (*mwenge*) or wine (*mubisi*), and the more familiar sweet *menvu* eaten raw for a snack or dessert. Within these broad categories, many subtleties of nomenclature and cultivation are applied to different varieties. And first-time visitors to Uganda might take note of the above names when they shop for bananas in the market – or sooner or later you'll bite into what looks to be a large, juicy sweet banana, but is in fact a foul and floury uncooked *matoke* or *gonja*!

The banana's uses are not restricted to feeding bellies. The juice from the stem is traditionally regarded to have several medicinal applications, for instance as a cure for snakebite and for childish behaviour. Pulped or scraped

sections from the stem also form very effective cloths for cleaning. The outer stem can be plaited to make a strong rope known as *byai* in Luganda, while the cleaned central rib of the leaf is used to weave fish traps and other items of basketry. The leaf itself forms a useful makeshift umbrella, and was traditionally worn by young Buganda girls as an apron. The dried leaf is a popular bedding and roofing material, and also used to manufacture the head pads on which Ugandan women generally carry their loads.

The banana as we know it is a cultigen – modified by humans to their own ends and totally dependent on them for its propagation. The domestic fruit is the result of a freak mutation that gives the cells an extra copy of each chromosome, preventing the normal development of seeds, thereby rendering the plant edible, but also sterile. Every cultivated banana tree on the planet is effectively a clone, propagated by the planting of suckers or corms cut from 'parent' plants. This means that, unlike sexually reproductive crops, which experience new genetic configurations in every generation, the banana is unable to evolve mechanisms to fight off new diseases.

In early 2003, a report in the *New Scientist* warned that cultivated bananas could become extinct, because of their lack of defence against a pair of fungal diseases rampant in most of the world's banana-producing countries. These are black sigatoka, an airborne disease first identified in Fiji in 1963, and the soil-borne Panama disease, also known as fusarium wilt. Black sigatoka can be kept at bay by regular spraying – every ten days or so – but it is swiftly developing resistance to all known fungicides, which in any case are not affordable to the average subsistence farmers. There is no known cure for Panama disease.

So far as can be ascertained, Panama disease does not affect any banana variety indigenous to Uganda, but it has already resulted in the disappearance of several introduced varieties. Black sigatoka, by contrast, poses a threat to every banana variety in the world, and is present throughout Uganda. Buganda has been especially hard hit – a progressive reduction exceeding 50% has been experienced in the annual yield of the most seriously affected areas. In addition to reducing the yield of a single plant by up to 75%, black sigatoka can also cut its fruit-bearing life from more than 30 years to less than five. By 2014, actual banana production in some parts of Uganda amounted to just 10% of the potential crop.

International attempts to clone a banana tree resistant to both diseases have met with limited success – agricultural researchers in Honduras have managed to produce one such variety, but it reputedly doesn't taste much like a banana. Another area of solution is genetic modification (GMO), for instance by introducing a gene from a wild species to create a disease-resistant edible banana. The first trials of GMO bananas took place in Uganda in 2007, and met with some success, as four of the six new strains tested proved to be 100% resistant to black sigatoka. However, these strains have yet to be planted commercially, since the farming of GMO crops remains illegal in Uganda, and it also remains a highly emotive and controversial subject among ecologists. A more recent and less controversial development, funded by a US$13 million grant from the Bill and Melinda Gates Foundation in 2014, is the International Institute of Tropical Agriculture's ongoing project to create and distribute high-yield disease-resistant varieties of banana through hybridisation.

Placed by some authorities in the same family as the closely related sparrows, the weavers of the family Ploceidae are a quintessential part of Africa's natural landscape, common and highly visible in virtually every habitat from rainforest to desert. The name of the family derives from the intricate and elaborate nests – typically but not always a roughly oval ball of dried grass, reeds and twigs – that are built by the dextrous males of most species.

It can be fascinating to watch a male weaver at work. First, a nest site is chosen, usually at the end of a thin hanging branch or frond, which is immediately stripped of leaves to protect against snakes. The weaver then flies back and forth to the site, carrying the building material blade by blade in its heavy beak, first using a few thick strands to hang a skeletal nest from the end of a branch, then gradually completing the structure by interweaving numerous thinner blades of grass into the main frame. Once completed, the nest is subjected to the attention of his chosen partner, who will tear it apart if the result is less than satisfactory, and so the process starts all over again.

All but 12 of the 113 described weaver species are resident on the African mainland or associated islands, with some 40 represented within Uganda alone. A full 25 of the Ugandan species are placed in the genus *Ploceus* (true weavers), which is surely the most characteristic of all African bird genera. Most of the *Ploceus* weavers are slightly larger than a sparrow, and display a strong sexual dimorphism. Females are with few exceptions drab buff or olive-brown birds, with some streaking on the back, and perhaps a hint of yellow on the belly.

Most male *Ploceus* weavers conform to the basic colour pattern of the 'masked weaver' – predominantly yellow, with streaky back and wings, and a distinct black facial mask, often bordered orange. Eight Ugandan weaver species fit this masked weaver prototype more or less absolutely, and a similar number approximate it rather less exactly, for instance by having a chestnut-brown mask, or a full black head, or a black back, or being more chestnut than yellow on the belly. Identification of the masked weavers can be tricky without experience – useful clues are the exact shape of the mask, the presence and extent of the fringing orange, and the colour of the eye and the back.

The golden weavers, of which only two species are present in Uganda, are also brilliant yellow and/or light orange with some light streaking on the back, but they lack a mask or any other strong distinguishing features. The handful of forest-associated *Ploceus* weavers, by contrast, tend to have quite different and very striking colour patterns, and although sexually dimorphic, the female is often as boldly marked as the male. The most aberrant among these are Vieillot's and Maxwell's black weavers, the males of which are totally black except for their eyes, while the black-billed weaver reverses the prototype by being all black with a yellow facemask.

Few visitors to Uganda will depart totally unmoved by its avian wealth, but different people arrive in the country with a wide variety of expectations. Those European visitors for whom birdwatching ranks as a pursuit on a perversity level with stamp collecting might well revise that opinion when first confronted by a majestic fish eagle calling high from a riverine perch, or a flock of Abyssinian ground hornbills marching with comic intent through the savannah. First-time African visitors with a stated interest in birds are more likely to be blown away

Among the more conspicuous *Ploceus* species in Uganda are the black-headed, yellow-backed, slender-billed, northern brown-throated, orange and Vieillot's black weavers – for the most part gregarious breeders forming single or mixed species colonies of hundreds, sometimes thousands, of pairs. The most extensive weaver colonies are often found in reed beds and waterside vegetation – the mixed species colonies in Entebbe Botanical Garden or Ngamba Island are as impressive as any in Uganda. Most weavers don't have a distinctive song, but they compensate with a rowdy jumble of harsh swizzles, rattles and nasal notes that can reach deafening proportions near large colonies. One of the more cohesive songs you will often hear seasonally around weaver colonies is a cyclic 'dee-dee-dee-Diederik', often accelerating to a hysterical crescendo when several birds call at once. This is the call of the Diederik cuckoo, a handsome green-and-white cuckoo that lays its eggs in weaver nests.

Oddly, while most East African *Ploceus* weavers are common, even abundant, in suitable habitats, seven highly localised species are listed as range-restricted, and three of these – one Kenyan endemic and two Tanzanian endemics – are regarded to be of global conservation concern. Of the other four, Fox's weaver (*Ploceus spekeoides*) is the only bird species endemic to Uganda: a larger-than-average yellow-masked weaver with an olive back, yellow eyes and orange-fringed black facemask, confined to acacia woodland near swamps and lakes east of Lake Kyoga. The strange weaver (*Ploceus alienus*) – black head, plain olive back, yellow belly with chestnut bib – is an Albertine Rift endemic restricted to four sites in Uganda.

Most of the colonial weavers, perhaps relying on safety in numbers, build relatively plain nests with a roughly oval shape and an unadorned entrance hole. The nests of certain more solitary weavers, by contrast, are far more elaborate. Several weavers, for instance, protect their nests from egg-eating invaders by attaching tubular entrance tunnels to the base – in the case of the spectacled weaver, sometimes twice as long as the nest itself. The Grosbeak weaver (a peculiar, larger-than-average brown-and-white weaver of reed beds, distinguished by its outsized bill and placed in the monospecific genus *Amblyospiza*) constructs a large and distinctive domed nest, which is supported by a pair of reeds, and woven as precisely as the finest basketwork, with a neat raised entrance hole at the front. By contrast, the scruffiest nests are built by the various species of sparrow- and buffalo-weaver, relatively drab but highly gregarious dry-country birds, poorly represented in Uganda except for in the vicinity of Kidepo.

by their first sighting of a lilac-breasted roller or Goliath heron than by most of the country's long list of western forest specials. Birdwatchers based in Africa's savannah belt will generally want to focus more on forest birds, but mostly on such common and iconic species as great blue turaco or black-and-white casqued hornbill rather than on glimpsing a selection of more localised but duller forest greenbuls. The more experienced the individual birdwatcher in African conditions, the greater the priority they will place on the pursuit of Albertine

Uganda's wealth of invertebrate life – more than 100,000 species have been identified countrywide – is largely overlooked by visitors, but is perhaps most easily appreciated in the form of butterflies and moths of the order **Lepidoptera**. An astonishing 1,200 butterfly species, including almost 50 endemics, have been recorded in Uganda, as compared with fewer than 1,000 in Kenya, roughly 650 in the whole of North America, and a mere 56 in the British Isles. Several forests in Uganda harbour 300 or more butterfly species, and one might easily see a greater selection in the course of a day than one could in a lifetime of exploring the English countryside. Indeed, I've often sat at one roadside pool in the like of Kibale or Budongo forests and watched ten to 20 clearly different species converge there over the space of 20 minutes.

The Lepidoptera are placed in the class Insecta, which includes ants, beetles and locusts among others. All insects are distinguished from other invertebrates, such as arachnids (spiders) and crustaceans, by their combination of six legs, a pair of frontal antennae, and a body divided into a distinct head, thorax and abdomen. Insects are the only winged invertebrates, though some primitive orders have never evolved them, and other more recently evolved orders have discarded them. Most flying insects have two pairs of wings, one of which, as in the case of flies, might have been modified beyond immediate recognition. The butterflies and moths of the order Lepidoptera have two sets of wings and are distinguished from all other insect orders by the tiny ridged wing scales that create their characteristic bright colours.

The most spectacular of all butterflies are the swallowtails of the family **Papilionidae**, of which roughly 100 species have been identified in Africa, and 32 in Uganda. Named for the streamers that trail from the base of their wings, swallowtails are typically large and colourful, and relatively easy to observe when they feed on mammal dung deposited on forest trails and roads. Sadly, this last generalisation doesn't apply to the African giant swallowtail (*Papilio antimachus*), a powerful flier that tends to stick at canopy levels and seldom alights on the ground, but the first two generalisations certainly do. With a wingspan known to exceed 20cm, this black, orange and green gem, an endangered West African species whose range extends into Bwindi, Kibale, Semliki, Budongo and Kalinzu forests, is certainly the largest butterfly on the continent, and possibly the largest in the world. One of the most common large swallowtails in Uganda is *Papilio nobilis*, which has golden or orange wings, and occurs in suburban gardens in Kampala, Entebbe, Jinja and elsewhere.

The **Pieridae** is a family of medium-sized butterflies, generally smaller than the swallowtails and with wider wings, of which almost 100 species are present in Uganda, several as seasonal intra-African migrants. Most species are predominantly white in colour, with some yellow, orange, black or even red and blue markings on the wings. One widespread member of this family is the oddly named angled grass yellow (*Eurema desjardini*), which has yellow wings marked by a broad black band, and is likely to be seen in any savannah or forest-fringe habitat in southern Uganda. The orange-and-lemon *Eronia leda* also has yellow wings, but with an orange upper tip, and it occurs in open grassland and savannah countrywide.

The most diverse family of butterflies within Uganda is the **Lycaenidae**, with almost 500 of the 1,500 African species recorded. Known also as gossamer wings,

this varied family consists mostly of small to medium-sized butterflies, with a wingspan of 1–5cm, dull underwings, and brilliant violet blue, copper or rufous-orange upper wings. The larvae of many Lycaenidae species have a symbiotic relationship with ants – they secrete a fluid that is milked by the ants and are thus permitted to shelter in their nests. A striking member of this family is *Hypolycaena hatita*, a small bluish butterfly with long tail streamers, often seen on forest paths throughout Uganda.

Another well-represented family in Uganda, with 370 species present, is the **Nymphalidae**, a diversely coloured group of small to large butterflies, generally associated with forest edges or interiors. The Nymphalidae are also known as brush-footed butterflies, because their forelegs have evolved into non-functional brush-like structures. One of the more common and distinctive species is the African blue tiger (*Tirumala petiverana*), a large black butterfly with about two dozen blue-white wing spots, often observed in forest paths near puddles or feeding from animal droppings. Another large member of this family is the African queen (*Danaus chrysippus*), which has a slow, deliberate flight pattern, orange or brown wings, and is as common in forest-edge habitats as it is in cultivated fields or suburbia. Also often recorded in Kampala gardens is the African mother of pearl (*Salamis parhassus*), a lovely light-green butterfly with black wing dots and tips.

The family **Charaxidae**, regarded by some authorities to be a subfamily of the Nymphalidae, is represented in Uganda by 70 of the roughly 200 African species. Typically large, robust, strong fliers with one or two short tails on each wing, the butterflies in this family vary greatly in coloration, and several species appear to be scarce and localised since they inhabit forest canopies and are seldom observed. Bwindi is a particularly good site for this family, with almost 40 species recorded, ranging from the regal dark-blue charaxes (*Charaxes tiridates*) (black wings with deep-blue spots) to the rather leaf-like green-veined charaxes (*Charaxes candiope*).

Rather less spectacular are the 200 grass-skipper species of the family **Hersperiidae** recorded in Uganda, most of which are small and rather drably coloured, though some are more attractively marked in black, white and/or yellow. The grass-skippers are regarded as the evolutionary link between butterflies and the generally more nocturnal moths, represented in Uganda by several families of which the most impressive are the boldly patterned giant silk-moths of the family **Saturniidae**.

An obstacle to developing a serious interest in Uganda's butterflies has been the absence of useful literature and field guides to aid identification. The publication of Nanny Carter and Laura Tindimubona's *Butterflies of Uganda* (Uganda Society, 2002) has gone a long way to rectifying this situation, illustrating and describing roughly 200 of the more common and striking species, with basic information about distribution and habitat. It's not quite the same as a comprehensive field guide, since many allied butterfly species are very similar to each other in appearance, while other species are highly localised or endemic to one specific forest. But certainly this book does pave the way for a greater appreciation of Uganda's most colourful invertebrate order, and as such it is highly recommended to anybody with even a passing interest in butterflies. Another very useful resource is www.ugandabutterflies.com.

Rift Endemics and Semliki 'specials'. At the extreme end of the scale, there are those whose life's mission is to tick every bird species in the world, in which case dedicating several days to seeking out the endemic Fox's weaver might rank above all other considerations in planning a Ugandan itinerary.

Uganda's appeal as a birding destination has been enhanced in recent years by improving avian knowledge, and general guiding practices, on the part of local guides. The best of these are capable of identifying most species by call, and even calling up the more responsive species. In the parks and reserves you'll meet some ranger guides whose knowledge compares favourably with their counterparts in any part of Africa. Birding capabilities do vary from one guide to the next, however, so specify your interest when you ask for a guide. Better still, to secure the services of a guide for a nationwide tour of birding hotspots, contact the Uganda Bird Guides Club (℡ 041 4222737; m 0777 912938; e ugandabirdguides@ hotmail.com; www.ugandabirdguides.org), an organisation whose membership includes most of the country's best privately operating bird guides. Their website also contains plenty of useful information including a national checklist and lists for different regions and Important Bird Areas. An essential purchase is Stevenson and Fanshawe's *Birds of East Africa*, which includes accurate depictions, descriptions and distribution details for every species recorded in the country. Harder to obtain, but worth locating for its detailed site descriptions, is the out-of-print *Where to Watch Birds in Uganda* by Russouw and Sacchi. Finally, a PDF containing two annotated lists of Uganda's top birds, one aimed at beginners and the other at twitchers, can be downloaded from our update website www.bradtupdates.com/uganda.

REPTILES

NILE CROCODILE The order Crocodilia dates back at least 150 million years, and fossil forms that lived contemporaneously with dinosaurs are remarkably unchanged from their modern ancestors. The largest species are the Australian saltwater and the African Nile crocodiles which regularly attain lengths of up to 6m. Widespread throughout Africa, the Nile crocodile was once common in most large rivers and lakes, but it has been exterminated in many areas in the past century – hunted professionally for its skin as well as by vengeful local villagers. Contrary to popular legend, Nile crocodiles generally feed mostly on fish, at least where densities are sufficient. They will also prey on drinking or swimming mammals where the opportunity presents itself, dragging their victim underwater until it drowns, then storing it under a submerged log or tree until it has decomposed sufficiently for them to eat. A large crocodile is capable of killing a lion or wildebeest, or an adult human for that matter, and in certain areas such as the Mara or Grumeti rivers in the Serengeti, large mammals do form their main prey. Today, large crocodiles are mostly confined to protected areas. The gargantuan specimens that lurk on the sandbanks along the Nile below Murchison Falls National Park are a truly primeval sight, silent and sinister, vanishing under the water when the launch approaches too closely. Other reliable sites for crocs are Lake Mburo and increasingly the Kazinga Channel in Queen Elizabeth National Park.

SNAKES A wide variety of snakes is found in Uganda, though – fortunately, most would agree – they are typically very shy and unlikely to be seen unless actively sought. One of the snakes most likely to be seen on safari is Africa's largest, the **rock python**, which has a gold-on-black mottled skin and regularly grows to lengths

exceeding 5m. Non-venomous, pythons kill their prey by strangulation, wrapping their muscular bodies around it until it cannot breathe, then swallowing it whole and dozing off for a couple of months while it is digested. Pythons feed mainly on small antelopes, large rodents and similar. They are harmless to adult humans, but could conceivably kill a small child. A slumbering python might be encountered almost anywhere in East Africa, and one reasonably relaxed individual is often present at the bat cave near the visitors' centre in Maramagambo Forest, Queen Elizabeth National Park.

Of the venomous snakes, one of the most commonly encountered is the **puff adder**, a large, thick resident of savannah and rocky habitats. Although it feeds mainly on rodents, the puff adder will strike when threatened, and it is rightly considered the most dangerous of African snakes, not because it is especially venomous or aggressive, but because its notoriously sluggish disposition means it is more often disturbed than other snakes. The related **Gabon viper** is possibly the largest African viper, growing up to 2m long, very heavily built, and with a beautiful cryptic geometric gold, black-and-brown skin pattern that blends perfectly into the rainforest litter it inhabits. Although highly venomous, it is more placid and less likely to be encountered than the puff adder.

Several **cobra** species, including the spitting cobra, are present in Uganda, most with characteristic hoods that they raise when about to strike, though they are all very seldom seen. Another widespread family is the **mambas**, of which the black mamba – which will only attack when cornered, despite an unfounded reputation for unprovoked aggression – is the largest venomous snake in Africa, measuring up to 3.5m long. While the dangers from these snakes are well documented, those of two of Africa's most toxic species – the variably coloured, arboreal **boomslang** and its relative, the twig-coloured **twig snake** – were long underrated. In fact both were long considered harmless to humans, being back-fanged (meaning that they have to work at biting humans) and characteristically inoffensive. Nevertheless, their venom, if injected effectively, is deadly. Even so, African records contain just one confirmed fatality for each snake, both involving herpetologists subscribing to the 'harmless' theory.

Most snakes are in fact non-venomous and not even potentially harmful to any other living creature much bigger than a rat. One of the more non-venomous snakes in the region is the **green tree snake** (sometimes mistaken for a boomslang, though the latter is never as green and more often than not brown), which feeds mostly on amphibians. The **mole snake** is a common and widespread grey-brown savannah resident that grows up to 2m long, and feeds on moles and other rodents. Unusually, its fangs protrude as frontal spikes in order to spear prey in tunnels. The remarkable **egg-eating snakes** live exclusively on birds' eggs, dislocating their jaws to swallow the egg whole, then eventually regurgitating the crushed shell in a neat little package. Many snakes will take eggs opportunistically, for which reason large-scale agitation among birds in a tree is often a good indication that a snake (or small bird of prey) is around.

LIZARDS All African lizards are harmless to humans, with the arguable exception of the **giant monitor lizards**, which could in theory inflict a nasty bite if cornered. Two species of monitor occur in East Africa, the **water** and the **savannah**, the latter growing up to 2.2m long and occasionally seen in the vicinity of termite mounds, the former slightly smaller but far more regularly observed by tourists, particularly along the Kazinga Channel in Queen Elizabeth National Park (QENP). Their size alone might make it possible to fleetingly mistake a monitor for a small crocodile,

Common and widespread in Uganda, but not easily seen unless they are actively searched for, chameleons are arguably the most intriguing of African reptiles. True chameleons of the family Chamaeleontidae are confined to the Old World, with the most important centre of speciation being the island of Madagascar, to which about half of the world's 120 recognised species are endemic. Aside from two species of chameleon apiece in Asia and Europe, the remainder are distributed across mainland Africa.

Chameleons are best known for their capacity to change colour, a trait that has often been exaggerated in popular literature, and which is generally influenced by mood more than the colour of the background. Some chameleons are more adept at changing colour than others, with the most variable being the **common chameleon** (*Chamaeleo chamaeleon*) of the Mediterranean region, with more than 100 colour and pattern variations recorded. Many African chameleons are typically green in colour but will gradually take on a browner hue when they descend from the foliage in more exposed terrain, for instance while crossing a road. Several change colour and pattern far more dramatically when they feel threatened or are confronted by a rival of the same species. Different chameleon species also vary greatly in size, with the largest being **Oustalet's chameleon** of Madagascar, known to reach a length of almost 80cm.

A remarkable physiological feature common to all true chameleons is their protuberant round eyes, which offer a potential 180° degree vision on both sides and are able to swivel around independently of each other. Only when one of them isolates a suitably juicy-looking insect will the two eyes focus in the same direction as the chameleon stalks slowly forward until it is close enough to use the other unique weapon in its armoury. This is its sticky-tipped tongue, which is typically about the same length as its body and remains coiled up within its mouth most of the time, to be unleashed in a sudden,

but their more colourful yellow-dappled skin precludes sustained confusion. Both species are predatorial, feeding on anything from birds' eggs to smaller reptiles and mammals, but will also eat carrion opportunistically.

Visitors to East Africa will soon become familiar with the **common house gecko**, an endearing bug-eyed, translucent white lizard, which as its name suggests reliably inhabits most houses as well as lodge rooms, scampering up walls and upside down on the ceiling in pursuit of pesky insects attracted to the lights. Also very common in some lodge grounds are various **agama** species, distinguished from other common lizards by their relatively large size of around 20–25cm, basking habits, and almost plastic-looking scaling – depending on the species, a combination of blue, purple, orange or red, with the flattened head generally a different colour from the torso. Another common family are the **skinks**: small, long-tailed lizards, most of which are quite dark and have a few thin black stripes running from head to tail.

TORTOISES AND TERRAPINS These peculiar reptiles are unique in being protected by a prototypal suit of armour formed by their heavy exoskeleton. The most common of the terrestrial tortoises in the region is the **leopard tortoise**, which is named after its gold-and-black mottled shell, can weigh up to 30kg, and has been known to live for more than 50 years in captivity. It is often seen motoring

blink-and-you'll-miss-it lunge to zap a selected item of prey. In addition to their unique eyes and tongues, many chameleons are adorned with an array of facial casques, flaps, horns and crests that enhance their already somewhat fearsome prehistoric appearance.

In Uganda, you're most likely to come across a chameleon by chance when it is crossing a road, in which case it should be easy to take a closer look at it, since most chameleons move painfully slowly and deliberately. Chameleons are also often seen on night game drives, when their ghostly nocturnal colouring shows up clearly under a spotlight – as well as making it pretty clear why these strange creatures are regarded with both fear and awe in many local African cultures. More actively, you could ask your guide if they know where to find a chameleon – a few individuals will be resident in most lodge grounds.

The **flap-necked chameleon** (*Chamaeleo delepis*) is probably the most regularly observed species of savannah and woodland habitats in East Africa. Often observed crossing roads, the flap-necked chameleon is generally around 15cm long and bright green in colour with few distinctive markings, but individuals might be up to 30cm in length and will turn tan or brown under the right conditions. Another closely related and widespread savannah and woodland species is the similarly sized **graceful chameleon** (*Chamaeleo gracilis*), which is generally yellow-green in colour and often has a white horizontal stripe along its flanks.

Characteristic of East African montane forests, **three-horned chameleons** form a closely allied species cluster of some taxonomic uncertainty. Darker and much larger than the savannah chameleons, the males of all taxa within this cluster are distinguished by a trio of long nasal horns that project forward from their face. Within Uganda, the spectacular Rwenzori three-horned chameleon (*Trioceros johnstoni*), which grows up to 30cm long, is often seen in and around Bwindi National Park.

along in the slow lane of game reserve roads in Uganda. Four species of terrapin – essentially the freshwater equivalent of turtles – are resident in East Africa, all somewhat flatter in shape than the tortoises, and generally with a plainer brown shell. They might be seen sunning on rocks close to water or peering out from roadside puddles. The largest is the **Nile soft-shelled terrapin**, which has a wide, flat shell and in rare instances might reach a length of almost 1m.

3

Practical Information

WHEN AND WHERE TO VISIT

Equator-straddling Uganda has a warm to hot climate all year through with limited temperature variations but a strongly seasonal rainfall pattern. The wettest months in most parts of the country are April, May, October and November, when camping can be unpleasant and hiking on the Rwenzori is particularly miserable. Abundant rainfall also means that large wildlife tends not to congregate conveniently around water sources in the national parks. On the other hand, landscape photographers will revel in the haze-free skies of the rainy season.

The highlight and focal point of a many a visit to Uganda is tracking mountain gorillas in Bwindi Impenetrable National Park in the extreme southwest. Consequently, most formal itineraries follow an established circuit between Kampala and the southwest, an area blessed with a high density of natural attractions and a good tourist infrastructure. A typical tour heads west from Kampala (or the international airport at nearby Entebbe) to the scenic Fort Portal area, where the main attraction is chimpanzee tracking in forested Kibale National Park, followed by a two- to three-night visit to Queen Elizabeth National Park (QENP) at the foot of the Rwenzori Mountains. South of QENP, Bwindi now offers no fewer than four separate gorilla tracking locations. It's a long haul from Bwindi back to Kampala/Entebbe and many tour operators now offer their clients an overnight break at Lake Mburo National Park. It is possible to cover this itinerary in seven days (ten would be better) and many people do. However, those with time and flexibility to delay and detour will discover much more. Days can be spent exploring the Fort Portal and Rwenzori area, while Lake Bunyonyi and the Virunga volcanoes are worthwhile diversions near Bwindi. Visitors intent on reaching true East African wilderness (a rare commodity in the densely populated south of Uganda) will want to head north to the Murchison Falls and Kidepo Valley national parks. These experiences do, however, incur a cost of increased travel time and expenditure. Visitors with time for a day trip at the end of their visit invariably head east from Kampala to visit the famed source of the Nile at Jinja. If this event represents a tick on a list rather than a life-affirming experience, the same cannot be said for Jinja's other main attraction: the menu of adventure sports offered along the Nile corridor north of the town. Activities such as white-water rafting, kayaking, bungee jumping and quad biking attract a steady flow of the young and young at heart.

TOURIST INFORMATION

Useful websites include those operated by the **Uganda Tourist Board** (*www.visituganda. com*) and **Uganda Wildlife Authority** (*www.ugandawildlife.org; see ad, page 28*), along with the privately run www.traveluganda.co.ug, www.i-uganda.com and www. africatravelresource.com/uganda-gorilla-safari. The website for the car-hire company

Roadtrip Uganda (*www.roadtripuganda.com; see ads, pages 60, 85 & 3rd colour section*) has a selection of practical itineraries with an emphasis on camping, while comprehensive coverage of the southwest, including a fun new video map, can be found on www.gorillahighlands.com. For updates to this book, visit www.bradtupdates.com/uganda.

TOUR OPERATORS

An ever-growing number of local and international tour operators offer a range of standard and customised private safaris to Uganda. Two-week itineraries typically cover the full western circuit from Murchison Falls to Lake Mburo via Kibale Forest, Queen Elizabeth and Bwindi or Mgahinga national parks, sometimes nipping across the border to Rwanda to go gorilla tracking when no permits are available within Uganda. Shorter itineraries generally omit the long drive to and from Murchison Falls, and one-stop gorilla tours of three days' duration are also available out of Kampala. Several other variations are available, depending on the individual's interests and how much time they have available. The high cost of vehicle maintenance, fuel and upmarket accommodation in Uganda is reflected in the price of private safaris, but this can be reduced by using cheaper accommodation, such as the Red Chilli Rest Camp at Paraa at Murchison Falls or Mweya Hostel in QENP, or by camping.

Uganda, mercifully, shows no signs of trying to establish itself as a package destination, nor is it likely to for as long as its premier attraction remains the relatively exclusive experience of tracking mountain gorillas in Bwindi or the Virungas. The country is, however, well suited to small group tours that offer the same standard of accommodation and service as private safaris, but generally at a reduced individual price because transport and related costs are divided between several passengers. In addition to general group tours, packages are also available for special-interest groups such as birdwatchers, primate enthusiasts and photographers.

The following locally based and international operators can all be recommended as experienced and reliable. Note that contacts for companies that operate offices in Uganda and abroad are combined in the *Uganda* section below.

UGANDA These companies are reliable high-end outfits.

Classic Africa Safaris *Uganda*: ☏0414 320121; m 0772 642527; e classic@classicafricasafaris. travel; www.classicuganda.com; *US*: ☏+1 304 876 1315; m + 1 304 268 0033; e phil@classicuganda. com. Fully escorted safaris. You'll probably never see Classic's superb vehicle workshop in Entebbe but it's reassuring to know it exists.

Kagera Safaris m 0782 477992; e info@ kagerasafaris.com; www.kagerasafaris.com. Tailor-made gorilla, primate & birding safaris, plus hiking trips to Mount Elgon. See ad, page 369.

Wild Frontiers (Johannesburg & Entebbe) *Uganda*: ☏0414 321479; m 0772 502155; e info@wildfrontiers.co.ug; www.wildfrontiers. co.ug; *South Africa*: ☏+27 11 702 2035; e reservations@wildfrontiers.com; www. wildfrontiers.com. One of Uganda's oldest tour operators, Wild Frontiers offers a range of custom

& fixed-departure photographic, birdwatching, primate & other interest tours led by experts in their fields. Its Ugandan partner, G&C Tours, operates Ishasha Wilderness Camp (Queen Elizabeth National Park), Buhoma Lodge (Bwindi), Baker's Lodge & Nile river boat trips (Murchison Falls National Park). See ads, page 369 & 407.

Wildplaces ☏0414 251182; m 0772 489497; e info@wildplacesafrica.com; www.wildplacesafrica. com. Guided safaris countrywide. Wildplaces operates lodges in the Semliki Valley, Kidepo Valley & Bwindi.

Volcanoes Safaris *Uganda*: ☏0414 346464/5; m 0772 741718; e salesug@volcanoessafaris. com; www.volcanoessafaris.com; *UK*: ☏+44 0870 870 8480; e salesuk@volcanoessafaris.com; *US*: ☏+1 866 599 2737; e salesus@volcanoessafaris. com. High-end company with 15 years' experience specialising in gorilla- & chimp-tracking safaris.

RELIABLE ALTERNATIVES The following tour operators are also listed alphabetically but otherwise in no particular order. They are also considered reliable but a little easier on the pocket.

See also **Yebo Tours** in Masindi (page 341) and **Kabarole Tours** in Fort Portal (page 385). All of those listed are (we believe) members of AUTO (*Association of Ugandan Tour Operators; www.auto.or.ug*), an accreditation that implies a certain standard of operation, experience and integrity. This is worth bearing in mind if you intend to make advance payments by credit card – one company, Volvo Tours, was blacklisted for making off with advances from clients. Visit the AUTO website for a full list of members. By the way, be wary if your chosen tour company suddenly asks for payment details to be sent to an alternative email address. We recently heard of an incident where the email was bogus, the address having been hacked, and the money, sent by Western Union, was collected by a third party.

Across Africa m 0701 630684; e manager@across-africa.de; www.acrossafrica.travel. See ad, 3rd colour section.

Access Uganda e accessug@utonline.co.ug. Safari company run by Hassan Mutebi, one of Uganda's most experienced bird guides.

Adventure Trails 0312 261 930; m 0712 723191; e info@gorilla-safari.com

Africa's Great Exploration Safaris *Uganda*: Acacia Mall, Kampala; 0414 662300; m 0776 723274; e info@agesafaris.com; www.agesafaris.com; *US*: Toll free 1 800 349 9930, ext 1122; e age@ugandatravelnetwork.com

Around Africa Safaris 0414 693576; m 0773 599507; e reservations@aroundafricasafari.com; www.aroundafricasafari.com. Small company, headed by redoubtable driver-guide, Oketch Obur. See ad, 4th colour section.

Bird Uganda Safaris m 0777 912938; e info@birduganda.com; www.birduganda.com. One for the birders, BUS is run by Herbert Byarahanga, one of Uganda's foremost bird guides.

BIC Safaris 0312 111513; e info@bic-tours.com; www.bic-tours.com. English, Japanese & Rukiga spoken.

Cheetah Safaris m 0772 413766/0702 413766; e info@cheetahsafaris.com; www.cheetahafricasafaris.com

Churchill Safaris *Uganda*: + 256 0414 341815; m 0705 111943; e info@churchillsafaris.com; www.churchillsafaris.com. *UK*: 01844 290000; m 07516 409335; e gcarr@churchillsafaris.com. *US*: + 1 56 2434 0352; e henryk@churchillsafaris.com. See ad, 3rd colour section.

Destination Jungle m 0712 385446; e d.jungle@safaritoeastafrica.com; www.safaritoeastafrica.com. See ads, pages 85 & 418.

Gorilla Tours 0414 200221; m 0777 820071; www.gorillatours.com. Busy, Dutch-owned company.

Great Lakes Safaris 0414 267153; m 0772 426 368; e info@safari-uganda.com; www.safari-uganda.com. This large (by Ugandan standards) mid-range company also runs Primate Lodge in Kibale Forest, Simba Safari Camp close to Queen Elizabeth National Park & Budongo Eco Lodge in Murchison Falls National Park. See ad, 4th colour section.

Kazinga Tours Ltd 0414 274457; m 0772 552819; e mail@kazingatours.com; www.kazingatours.com. Middle-market tour company with offices in Kabale & Kampala. See ad, 4th colour section.

Kombi Nation Tours m 0792 933773; e info@kombitours.com; www.kombitours.com. As well as the usual Land Cruiser safari vehicles, this friendly bunch runs a fleet of vintage VW camper vans.

Let's Go Travel/BCD Travel 0414 346667; e letsgo@bcdtravel.co.ug; www.bcdtravel.co.ug. Nationwide safaris & regional package holidays.

Matoke Tours *Uganda*: 0390 202907; www.matoketours.com; *Netherlands*: +31 (0) 73 612 3364; e info@matoketours.com. Uganda's largest mid-market safari outfit. See ad, 4th colour section & page 169.

Moses Uganda Tours & Taxis (Motours) m 0772 422825/0752 422825; e moses.tours@live.com; www.traveluganda.co.ug/motours. Mbarara-based company.

Prime Uganda Safaris 0414 232730; e info@primeuganda.com; www.primeugandasafaris.com

NatureTrack Expeditions m 0774 132967; e safari@naturetrack-expeditions.com; www.naturetrack-expeditions.com

Oribi Tours & Safaris www.oribitours.com. Wildlife & activity tours led by local guides. See ad, page 472.

Pearlafric ☎0414 232730; e info@pearlafric.com; www.pearlafric.com. Small, Kampala-based outfit plugged by happy readers.
Primate Watch Safaris Ltd ☎0414 266 824; www.primatewatchsafaris.com. See ad, page 98.
Ranger Africa Safaris m 0772 853372; e enquiries@rangerafricasafaris.com; www.rangerafricasafaris.com. See ad, page 532.
Stebar Safaris ☎0414 323123; m 0785 754434; e advice@stebar-safaris.com; www.stebar-safaris.com
TIA m 0789 476328; e bookings@tia-adventures.com; www.tia-adventures.com
Uganda Trails m 0793 382481; e info@uganda-trails.com; www.uganda-trails.com. Explore Uganda by car, bike, canoe & on foot.

Safari Talk ☎0392 174723; m 0751 465020; e info@safaritalkuganda.com; www.safaritalkuganda.com.
Yoga Uganda m 0789 476328; e leyla@yogauganda.com; www.yogauganda.com. Yoga retreats in relaxed up-country & national park settings.
Uganda Travel Bureau ☎0312 232555; e deo.lubega@ug.fcm.travel; www.travelutb.com
What's Wild ☎0784 461368; e safaris@whatswildsafaris.com; www.whatswildsafaris.com
White Nile Walking Safaris m 0783 129 738; e enquiries@whitenilewalkingsafaris.com; www.whitenilewalkingsafaris.com. This new outfit, headed by the only UWA-accredited walking safari guide, operates short & extended wilderness hikes in Murchison & Kidepo national parks.

LOCAL OPERATORS A growing choice of smaller operators is also emerging, often Ugandan safari guides setting up on their own with a vehicle. These are invariably not AUTO members and may not offer the same 'fully comprehensive' service as the operators listed above. Nevertheless, they may represent an affordable compromise between a fully fledged safari and the bus. Ask around or check noticeboards at the backpacker hangouts. If booking a freelance tour guide, check his (or her) status with the Uganda Safari Guides Association (USAGA) (*www.ugasaf.org*) or the Uganda Bird Guides Club (*www.ugandabirdguides.org*).

All of the companies and individuals listed below can provide you with tailor-made itineraries. Another option is to sign up for a fixed-itinerary camping tour to a specific destination. Kampala Backpackers (page 137) and Red Chilli (pages 141–2) run trips from their Kampala hostels to Murchison Falls National Park. Another cost-saving strategy is to hire a car yourself and travel where and when the fancy takes you. The companies listed on page 62 typically offer self-drive or provide drivers if required. Worth singling out is the innovative car and camping gear service provided by Road Trip Uganda. Check their website for possible itineraries (*www.roadtripuganda.com*). Since you are most likely to need a private vehicle to visit a national park, the most economical strategy would be to take the bus to the closest town and engage a local tour or vehicle hire operator.

Robert Joseph Mugerwa m 0772 866700; e info@customsafarisafrica.com. Reliable, punctual & a very decent birder, too.
Eco-Specialists Tours m 0712 955671/0714 871145; e info@ecotoursuganda.com; www.ecotoursuganda.com. With 15 years' birding experience behind them, the Mabira Forest guides have formed their own company. Recommended to birders.

Emmy Gongo m 0772 853372; e emmygongo@yahoo.com. Born on the edge of Bwindi Forest, Emmy is one of Uganda's best-known birding guides.
Farouk Busulwa ☎0392 813391; m 0701 858025; e moroukprod@yahoo.co.uk. Freelance safari/birding guide.

INTERNATIONAL OPERATORS
UK
Aardvark Safaris RBL Hse; ☎01980 849160; e mail@aardvarksafaris.com; www.aardvarksafaris.co.uk. Private & small-group tailored itineraries.

Africa Travel Resource ☎01306 880770; e info@africatravelresource.com; www.africatravelresource.com. Leading tailor-made safari company with a remarkably comprehensive

website containing thousands of images of hotels & lodges across the region.

Bailey Robinson ☏01488 689700; e travel@baileyrobinson.com; www.baileyrobinson.com. Top-end safari specialists in east & southern Africa.

Cox & Kings Travel ☏020 3813 9460; e info@coxandkings.co.uk; www.coxandkings.co.uk. Group & individual tours.

Explore Worldwide ☏01252 888781; e hello@explore.co.uk; www.explore.co.uk. Market leader in small-group, escorted trips worldwide.

Gane & Marshall ☏01822 600600; e info@ganeandmarshall.com; www.ganeandmarshall.com. Long-established Africa specialist. See ad, page 60.

Hartley's Safaris ☏01673 861600; e info@hartleys-safaris.co.uk; www.hartleys-safaris.co.uk. Reliable safaris to east & southern Africa, as well as diving & island holidays in the region.

Imagine Africa ☏020 3468 0785; e info@imagineafrica.co.uk; www.imagineafrica.co.uk. Award-winning luxury tours.

Journeys by Design ☏01273 623790; e info@journeysbydesign.com; www.journeysbydesign.com. Experienced operator offering stylish, tailor-made safaris across southern & east Africa including helicopter.

Journeys Discovering Africa ☏0800 088 5470; e enquiries@journeysdiscoveringafrica.com; www.journeysdiscoveringafrica.com. High-end company specialising in tailor-made private & small group tours with fully owned ground operations in Uganda & Rwanda.

Natural World Safaris ☏01273 691642; e sales@naturalworldsafaris.com; www.naturalworldsafaris.com. NWS specialise in tailor-made safaris to Uganda to track mountain gorillas.

Rainbow Tours ☏020 3131 4927; e info@rainbowtours.co.uk; www.rainbowtours.co.uk. Independent Africa & Latin America specialists.

Royle Safaris ☏0845 226 8259; e info@royle-safaris.co.uk; www.royle-safaris.co.uk. Small, specialist tours led by expert zoologists in search of rare & elusive wildlife.

Safari Consultants ☏01787 888590; e info@safariconsultantuk.com; www.safari-consultants.co.uk. Specialists in African safari holidays.

Steppes Travel ☏01285 601629; e enquiry@steppestravel.co.uk; www.steppestravel.co.uk.

Worldwide tailor-made specialists with a long Africa history.

Theobald Barber ☏020 7724 6521; e info@theobaldbarber.com; www.theobaldbarber.com. High-end operator specialising in highly individual holidays to east & southern Africa in remote wilderness areas far from any madding crowds.

Tribes Travel ☏01473 890499; e info@tribes.co.uk; www.tribes.co.uk. ATOL-protected tailor-made holidays in Uganda & elsewhere.

Wildlife & Wilderness ☏01625 838225; e info@wildlifewilderness.com; www.wildlifewilderness.com. Tailor-made & small group trips across Africa & worldwide.

Wildlife Worldwide ☏01962 302 086; e reservations@wildlifeworldwide.com; www.wildlifeworldwide.com. Tailor-made & small group trips worldwide.

World Odyssey ☏01905 731373; e info@world-odyssey.com; www.world-odyssey.com. Tailor-made trips across the globe (a different company from Africa Odyssey).

US

Aardvark Safaris ☏+1 858 523 9000; www.aardvarksafaris.com

eTrip Africa ☏+1 302 722 6226; www.etripafrica.co.uk. Custom-built itineraries.

The African Adventure Company ☏+1 800 882 9453; e safari@africanadventure.com; www.africanadventure.com

Germany

Abendsonneafrika www.abendsonneafrika.de. German safari company which engages some of Uganda's most experienced local guides.

Hauser Exkursionen International ☏+49 89 235 0060; e info@hauser-exkursionen.de; www.hauser-exkursionen.de

Safari Uganda ☏+49 06 207 7378; e kontakt@safariuganda.de; www.safariuganda.de. Reliable outfit run by the owners of Lagoon Resort near Kampala.

Wigwam ☏+49 83 799 2060; e info@wigwam-tours.de; www.wigwam-tours.de

South Africa

Pulse Africa PO Box 2417, Parklands 2121, Johannesburg; ☏+27 11 325 2290; e info@pulseafrica.com; www.pulseafrica.com. See ad, page 60.

RED TAPE

A valid passport is required to enter Uganda. Entry may be refused if it is set to expire within six months of your intended departure date. Should your passport be lost or stolen while you are on the road, it will be easier to get a replacement if you have a photocopy or scan of the important pages.

Nationals of most countries require a **visa** in order to enter Uganda. Previously, this could be bought in advance at any Ugandan embassy or high commission, but as of July 2016 a new system has been rolled out in which it is mandatory for all visitors to apply for an e-visa online before travelling (see box, page xi, for more details). However, if necessary you might still be able to buy a visa upon arrival at any overland border or at Entebbe International Airport until the system is properly implemented, a straightforward procedure that usually takes a few minutes, except perhaps when a couple of major airlines arrive within an hour of each other.

A standard single-entry visa, valid for 90 days, costs US$50. A 90-day East African Tourist Visa, valid for Uganda, Rwanda and Kenya, is also available on arrival for US$100. Check the current visa situation with your travel agent, or at a Ugandan diplomatic mission, or keep an eye on our updates site (*www.bradtupdates.com/uganda*).

Don't overstay your visa or the date of the immigration stamp in your passport, or you'll be liable for a hefty fine. And note that even though you hold a three-month visa, immigration authorities may only stamp your passport for a period of one month or less. This can be extended to three months at any immigration office in Kampala or upcountry. Irrespective of what they might tell you, there is no charge for this. In Kampala, you may be asked to provide an official letter from a sponsor or the hotel where you are staying.

If there is any possibility you'll drive in Uganda, bring a valid driving licence. Your domestic (home country) driving licence is okay for up to three months. If you spend longer in Uganda, you must either obtain a local licence or (cheaper and simpler) carry an international driving licence along with your domestic licence. Rather than carrying the originals, photocopies will suffice. The situation with yellow fever shots changes regularly, but as things stand you must produce an international health certificate showing you've had a vaccination when you enter Uganda or upload it when you apply for an e-visa.

For **security** reasons, it's advisable to detail all your important information in one document, which you can then print out and distribute in your luggage, and/or store on a smartphone, and/or email to your webmail address and a reliable contact at home. The sort of things you want to include on this are travel insurance policy details and 24-hour emergency contact number, passport number, details of relatives or friends to be contacted in an emergency, bank and credit card details, camera and lens serial numbers, etc.

CUSTOMS The following items may be imported into Uganda without incurring customs duty: 400 cigarettes or 500g of tobacco; one bottle of spirits and wine and 2.5 litres of beer; 1oz bottle of perfume. Souvenirs may be exported without restriction but game trophies such as tooth, bone, horn, shell, claw, skin, hair, feather or other durable items are subject to export permits.

GETTING THERE AND AWAY

BY AIR For obvious reasons, the most convenient means of reaching Uganda from Europe and North America is by air. An established specialist UK operator

is Africa Travel (📞 *020 7387 1211; www.africatravel.co.uk*). Reputable agents specialising in round-the-world tickets rather than Africa specifically are **Trailfinders** (📞 *020 7368 1200; www.trailfinders.com*) and **STA** (📞 *0333 321 0099; www.statravel.co.uk*). A full list of international airlines that fly to Uganda is included under the Kampala listings on page 115.

Arriving (and leaving)

Arriving (and leaving) The main entry point for flights into Uganda is **Entebbe International Airport**, on the outskirts of Entebbe 40km from Kampala. International charter flights can also land, usually by arrangement with immigration, at some airstrips around the country such as Pakuba (Murchison Falls NP), Kakira (Jinja) and Apoka (Kidepo Valley NP). Customs and immigration at Entebbe is usually a straightforward procedure, and there are 24-hour foreign-exchange facilities and ATMs at the airport.

A private taxi from the airport to Entebbe costs up to US$10 and one to Kampala should cost no more than US$30. The alternative is to take a shared taxi between the airport and Entebbe, where you can pick up a matutu to the old taxi park in Kampala for next to nothing.

OVERLAND

OVERLAND Uganda borders five countries: Kenya, Tanzania, Rwanda, DRC and South Sudan. A high proportion of visitors to Uganda enter and leave the country overland at the borders with Kenya or Tanzania. Few people enter or leave Uganda from Rwanda, though a fair number cross briefly from Uganda to see mountain gorillas. The DRC is still largely off-limits to casual travel. International NGOs and other organisations are now active in South Sudan, the world's youngest nation, excised from the Republic of the Sudan in 2011. Plenty of Ugandan commercial traffic crosses the borders near Nimule, Oraba and Moyo and a growing number of foreign travellers are headed that way to explore. Uganda's land borders are generally very relaxed, provided that your papers are in order. It may be necessary to exchange money at any overland border in or out of Uganda.

To/from Kenya

To/from Kenya Crossing between Kenya and Uganda couldn't be more straightforward. The pick of a few direct coach services between Kampala and Nairobi is **Easy Coach** (📱 *0776 727273; www.easycoach.co.ke; US$14*), which depart from Kampala's Oasis Mall three times daily and dock at the rough (River Road) end of the Nairobi city centre from which, rather than walk, it's safer to take a taxi to your next destination. You can also do the trip in hops, stopping at the likes of Jinja and Busia in Uganda, and Kisumu and Nakuru in Kenya. The direct rail service between Nairobi and Kampala foundered years ago, but it is possible to take a **train** from Nairobi as far as Kisumu. Plenty of **public transport** runs on from Kisumu to the Ugandan border at Busia, where buses to Kampala tend to pass through in the early morning, but matatus run throughout the day.

To/from Tanzania

To/from Tanzania Following the suspension of the ferry service between Mwanza and Port Bell, the best way to cross between Uganda and Tanzania depends on which part of Tanzania you want to visit. The only direct road between the two countries connects Masaka to the port of Bukoba, crossing at the Mutukula border post. It is possible to travel between Kampala and Bukoba in hops, but far easier to take the direct **Friends Safaris** bus from their office in Old Kampala. These leave at 05.00 and 13.00 and tickets cost Ush30,000. Friends Bus also runs to Mwanza (*Ush60,000*) (though it is more interesting to leave the bus in Bukoba and take the thrice weekly ferry across Lake Victoria) and a marathon ride all the way down to

Dar (*Ush160,000*). If heading from Kampala to Arusha and Moshi it's quicker and more comfortable to travel via Nairobi. Regular shuttle buses run between Nairobi and Arusha and take around 5 hours.

To/from South Sudan The 'Nile Route' via Juba was very popular with travellers before it was closed for years by a long-running civil war in Sudan and northern Uganda. There were hopes, when the independent Republic of South Sudan was excised from the Republic of the Sudan in 2011, that this might once again be possible but these quickly evaporated. Initially, strained relations between the two Sudans stifled travel across the shared border before the South Sudanese became embroiled in their very own civil war in 2014. You can still fly to Juba from Entebbe or travel by bus from Kampala to Juba though right now we wouldn't recommend doing so without a good reason.

LOL buses depart the Old Kampala Bus Terminal at 21.30, reaching Nimule at 08.00 and arriving in Juba around noon. Don't travel without seeking current information regarding availability of visas on arrival at Nimule border crossing or Juba Airport. The best source of tourist information (though published prior to the current war) is Sophie Ibbotson and Max Lovell-Hoare's Bradt guide to South Sudan (*www.bradtguides.com*).

To/from Rwanda Two main border crossings connect Uganda and Rwanda. Cyanikia lies 15km south of Kisoro while Katuna is 21km south of Kabale. There's also a minor crossing at Mirama Hills, 30km from Ntungamo. It's perfectly straightforward to drive yourself so long as you remember that the Rwandan authorities expect vehicles to drive on the right, have appropriate insurance and carry breakdown warning triangles. **Jaguar** buses run from Kampala to Kigali from their stage on Namirembe Road, 500m uphill from the main cluster of bus and taxi parks around Nakivubu Stadium. Visas, if required, can be obtained at the border. See page 66 for additional information.

To/from DRC There are several routes between Uganda and the Democratic Republic of Congo. From north to south, the main ones are Arua–Aru, Ntoroko–Kasenyi (a boat crossing on Lake Albert), Bwera–Kasindi, Ishasha, and Bunagana. Of these, only the last sees much in the way of tourist traffic, this being the most convenient crossing for tracking mountain gorillas in the Virunga National Park, and visiting other locations such as Nyiragongo Volcano. Bunagana is 8km from Kisoro and served by daily buses from Kampala. However (and this happens every time we update this section), travel to eastern Congo is frequently complicated by some form of instability so travellers should seek reliable and up-to-date information before considering crossing into the DRC.

WHAT TO TAKE

The key to packing for a country like Uganda is finding the right balance between bringing everything you might possibly need and carrying as little luggage as possible, something that depends on your own priorities and experience as much as anything. Worth stressing is that most genuine necessities are surprisingly easy to get hold of in main centres, and that most of the ingenious gadgets you can buy in camping shops are unlikely to amount to much more than dead weight on the road. If it came to it, a hardy backpacker could easily travel in Uganda with little more than a change of clothes, a few basic toiletries and a medical kit.

CARRYING YOUR LUGGAGE A normal suitcase is ideal for organised tours, or for those who are travelling mostly by air or private transport. Ideally, buy a suitcase that easily slings across your back, or that rolls, or both. Travellers using public transport should either use a backpack or a suitcase that converts into one. Make sure your luggage is designed in such a manner that it can easily be padlocked. This won't prevent a determined thief from slashing it open, but it is a real deterrent to casual theft.

CAMPING EQUIPMENT Travellers on a tight budget might want to bring a lightweight but mosquito-proof tent to Uganda, along with a sleeping bag and roll-mat. There is no real need to carry a stove, as firewood is available at most campsites where meals cannot be bought. Cheap cutlery, plastic cups and plates, and lightweight metal pans (*suferias*) are the norm for most Ugandans and are available everywhere.

CLOTHES Uganda has a warm climate so bring plenty of light clothing, ideally made from natural fabrics, such as cotton, though people prefer quick-dry synthetic trousers designed specifically for tropical travel. Western Uganda has a wet climate, and showers are normal even during the supposed dry seasons, so a light waterproof jacket is close to essential. At higher altitudes (for instance in Fort Portal) it can cool down in the evening, so bring at least one warm sweater, fleece jacket or sweatshirt. If you intend to hike on Mount Elgon or the Rwenzori, you will need very warm clothing. As for footwear, genuine hiking boots are worth considering only if you're a serious off-road hiker, rather go for a good pair of walking shoes with solid ankle support. It's also useful to carry sandals, flip-flops or other light semi-open shoes – just watch out for irregular pavements! Rather than spending a fortune outfitting yourself for Africa before leaving home, you might follow the lead of informed travellers and volunteers who pack a minimum of clothes and buy the remainder in Kampala's superb Owino Market, where secondhand clothes bought in bulk from charity shops for export to Uganda sell for a fraction of what they would in Europe or North America.

OTHER USEFUL ITEMS Bring a universal electric socket adaptor for charging your batteries in hotel rooms. A torch will be useful during power cuts. Some people wouldn't travel without a good pair of earplugs to help them sleep through traffic noise or mosque calls, while a travel pillow might make long bus journeys that bit easier to endure. Carry a small medical kit, the contents of which are discussed in *Chapter 4*. A pack of wet or facial cleansing wipes can help maintain a semblance of cleanliness on long, dusty journeys, and anti-bacterial gel is a good way of making sure you don't make yourself sick with your own grime if you're eating on the move.

All the toilet bag basics (soap, shampoo, conditioner, toothpaste, toothbrush, deodorant, basic razors) are very easy to replace as you go along, so there's no need to bring family-sized packs. If you wear contact lenses, be aware that the various cleansing and storing fluids are not readily available, and, since many people find the intense sun irritates their eyes, you might consider reverting to glasses. Disposable contact lenses are another option. Most budget hotels provide toilet paper and many also provide towels, but if you are travelling on the cheap, it is worth taking your own.

If you're interested in wildlife, nothing will give you such value-for-weight entertainment as a pair of light binoculars, which allow you to get a good look at the colourful local birds, and to watch distant mammals in game reserves. For most

purposes, 7x21 compact binoculars will be fine, though some might prefer 7x35 traditional binoculars for their larger field of vision. Serious birdwatchers will find a 10x magnification more useful.

Novels are difficult to get hold of outside Kampala. Your best bet is to carry an e-book tablet loaded with reading material. If you prefer the real thing, bring a supply of books with you or visit Kampala's excellent Aristoc bookshop in Garden City Mall.

These days it seems to be standard practice to move around with either a tablet or notebook computer. If entertainment and internet access are your priorities, and your typing requirements are limited to the odd email, a tablet (fitted with a full-body protective casing) is ideal. If your surfing requirements can await the increasingly frequent occasions when you reach a Wi-Fi hotspot, then all well and good. If not, bring a model with 3G capability, fit it with a local SIM card loaded with data credit, and you can access the internet anywhere your chosen network provides a signal. MTN provides the most comprehensive service.

MONEY

The local currency is the Uganda shilling, which traded at around Ush2,500 to the US dollar in early 2013. Notes are printed in denominations of Ush50,000, 20,000, 10,000, 5,000 and 1,000. Ush500, 200, 100, and 50 notes have been replaced by coins and are no longer legal tender. Ush1,000 notes are in the process of being phased out in favour of coins. Foreign exchange used to be a bureaucratic headache in Uganda but these days it is very straightforward. Most visitors rely primarily on a credit or debit card, which can be used to draw local currency at ATMs countrywide, and supplement it with some hard currency cash as a fall back (travellers' cheques are no longer accepted).

CASH The most widely recognised currencies in Uganda are the US dollar, pound sterling and euro, which can be changed into local currency in a matter of minutes at any bank or foreign exchange (forex) bureau. With US dollars specifically, bills issued before 2007 are not accepted. Nor are torn or blemished notes of any currency, no matter how insignificant the damage. Large-denomination hard currency bills attract a better exchange rate than denominations of 20 or less, though the latter can be useful in some situations. In Kampala, ubiquitous forex bureaux tend to offer better exchange rates than banks, and are less bureaucratic (no ID required and the receipt serves only as a souvenir). Outside Kampala, there are fewer forex bureaux, so you'll mostly depend on banks. Banks are open from 09.00 to 15.00 on weekdays (though some banks in Kampala stay open later) and from 09.00 to 12.00 on Saturdays. Forex offices may open earlier and typically close at 17.00 Monday to Saturday. You'll struggle to find anywhere to change money on a Sunday. If you have shillings left over at the end of the trip, it's perfectly straightforward to convert them back to foreign currency in a matter of minutes at any forex bureau, albeit at a slight loss.

CREDIT AND DEBIT CARDS A radical advance in Ugandan travel over the past few years has been a proliferation of 24-hour ATMs where local currency can be drawn against any international PIN-protected credit/debit card with a Visa or MasterCard logo. All Ugandan towns of any substance now have at least one such ATM, most usually associated with a branch of Stanbic, which operates more than 150 machines nationwide, and allows for daily withdrawals of up to Ush700,000

(around US$230). Larger towns also usually have branches of Barclays and/or Standard Chartered with ATMs where you can draw up to Ush2,000,000 (around US$650). Other banks with expanding upcountry networks with viable ATMs are Crane Bank and Kenya Commercial Bank. Charges are levied for withdrawals, but it tends to more-or-less balance out against the charges on cash forex transactions. If you'll be dependent on a card, alert your bank in advance to the dates you will be travelling so they will not be concerned about unusual foreign transactions. It might also be prudent to contact them to check your card's compatibility with East African systems and find out what they will charge in addition to locally levied fees. Other than using ATM machines, there is little scope to use your credit card for direct payments and a levy of 5% will often be added to the bill.

MOBILE MONEY If you're going to be in Uganda for a while think about signing up for an 'electronic wallet service' with a local mobile phone company. There are several options but MTN's MobileMoney is the most widespread. You'll need an MTN SIM card for your mobile phone and a copy of your ID. You can then load money on to your account, and later withdraw funds to the equivalent from any of 20,000-plus MobileMoney Agents nationwide (assuming that they have sufficient cash to oblige), or pay for services by sending money directly to another registered number. Visit www.mtn.co.ug for further details.

MONEY TRANSFERS Transferring funds between banks in Europe/North America and Uganda remains surprisingly slow, taking several days. It's much quicker to have a friend or relative to send you money using Western Union or MoneyGram. You'll be able to collect Ugandan shillings converted from a sum paid to an agent in your home country as little as ten minutes earlier. It will take you at least this long to receive – by phone, email or text message – a code word registered by your Good Samaritan which you must quote to obtain your money. The service is not cheap but it's convenient in an emergency, and branches are found in most Ugandan towns.

PRICES QUOTED IN THIS BOOK Practically everything in Uganda can be paid for using the Uganda shilling, irrespective of the currency in which a price is quoted. For example, Ugandan Wildlife Authority (UWA) tariffs for entrance fees and activities are quoted in US dollars, but can be paid either in US dollars or in Uganda shillings (though gorilla-tracking permits must be paid in dollars). However, in order to pre-empt an ever sliding exchange rate, and to help readers at the planning stage of the trip, all prices in this book are quoted in US dollars, using a rate of around US$1 = Ush3,000, often rounded upwards to the nearest dollar. As always, be assured that the prices given in this book will most likely change during the lifetime of this edition. These may be minor or they may be quite spectacular. During the lifespan of the sixth edition of this book, changes were even more significant than usual owing to the global economic squeeze, fluctuating fuel prices, highs and lows in the US dollar exchange rate and the considerable expense of a general election. By contrast, US dollar prices quoted in the seventh edition were often practically unchanged when we came to research the eighth edition, thanks largely to a consistently plunging exchange rate.

BUDGETING Independent travel in Uganda is inexpensive by most standards, but your budget will depend greatly on how and where you travel. The following guidelines may be useful to people trying to keep costs to a minimum.

In most parts of the country, it will be difficult to keep your basic travel expenses (food, transport and accommodation) to much below US$30 per day. You could spend as little as US$20 per day by camping everywhere and by staying put for a few days at somewhere cheap like the Ssese Islands or Lake Nkuruba. Typically, a room in the most basic sort of local hotel will cost close to US$10, camping around US$4–5 per person, and a meal US$2–7 depending on whether you are content to stick to the predictable local fare or want to eat a more varied menu. A treat in one of Kampala's best restaurants won't cost more than US$10–12 for a main course. Bus fares cost around Ush15,000–25,000 so transport costs will probably work out at around US$6–10 daily, assuming that you're on the move every other day or thereabouts. If you don't want *always* to stay in the most basic room and *always* to go for the cheapest item on the menu, I would bank on spending around US$35–40 per day on basic travel costs. You could travel very comfortably for US$50–60 per day.

Unless you go on an organised safari, the only expenses over and above your basic travel costs will be incurred in national parks where you can expect to spend around US$75 per day for every 24-hour period in entrance and activity fees, as well as inflated meal prices. Gorilla tracking in Uganda will cost US$600.

If funds are tight, it is often a useful idea to separate your daily budget from one-off expenses. At current prices, a daily budget of around US$40–50 with US$500 set aside for expensive one-off activities (excluding gorilla tracking) would be comfortable for most travellers.

GETTING AROUND

BY AIR Since few major urban centres lie more than 5–6 hours' drive from the capital, flying has never been an option for most people, though some more upmarket safaris now use flights to cut the driving time between Murchison Falls National Park and Queen Elizabeth or Bwindi Impenetrable national parks. The only destination in Uganda which is reached by air almost as often as it is by road is Kidepo Valley National Park, since the drive up from Kampala takes two days. Three operators, Fly Uganda (*www.flyuganda.com*), Aerolink (*www.aerolinkuganda.com*) and Eagle Air (*www.eagleair-ug.com*) offer scheduled and charter flights to various tourist destinations. The scheduled flights are subject to a minimum number of passengers and are often diversions to other destinations.

SELF-DRIVE By African standards, Uganda's major roads are in good condition. Decent surfaced roads radiate out from Kampala, running east to Jinja, Busia, Malaba, Tororo, Mbale and Soroti, south to Entebbe, southwest to Masaka, Mbarara and Kabale, west to Fort Portal, northwest to Hoima, north to Gulu, northeast to Gayaza and Kayunga (and on to Jinja). Other surfaced roads connect Karuma Falls to Arua, Mbale to Sipi Falls, Masaka to the Tanzanian border, Mbarara to Ibanda, and Ntungamo to Rukungiri. Most other roads are unsurfaced and tend to be variable in condition from one season to the next, with surfaces being trickiest during the rains. Road conditions described in this guide are of necessity a snapshot of conditions in late 2015 and should not be taken as gospel. When in doubt, ask local advice – if matatus are getting through, then so should any 4x4, so the taxi park is always a good place to seek current information.

The main hazard on Ugandan roads is the road hog mentality of, and risks taken by, other drivers. Matatus in particular are given to overtaking on blind corners, while coaches routinely bully their way along trunk routes at up to 120km/h, forcing drivers of smaller vehicles to keep an eye on their rear-view mirror and

pull off the road to let them pass. Bearing the above in mind, a coasting speed of 80km/h in the open road is comfortable without being over cautious, and it's not a bad idea to slow down and cover the brake in the face of oncoming traffic. In urban situations, particularly downtown Kampala, right of way essentially belongs to he who is prepared to force the issue – a considered blend of defensive driving tempered by outright assertiveness is required to get through safely without becoming too bogged down in the traffic.

A peculiarly African road hazard – one frequently taken to unnecessary extremes in Uganda – is the giant sleeping policeman, or 'speed bump' as it's known locally. A lethal bump might be signposted in advance, it might be painted in black-and-white stripes, or it might simply rear up without warning above the road like a macadamised wave. Other regular obstacles include weaving bicycles laden with banana clusters, as well as livestock and pedestrians blithely wandering around in the middle of the road. Piles of foliage placed in the road at a few metres interval warn of a broken-down vehicle. Note too that indicator lights are not used to signal an intent to turn, but are switched on when approaching oncoming traffic to suggest that following drivers should not overtake. Ugandans also display a strong aversion to switching on their headlights except in genuine darkness. In rainy, misty or twilight conditions, don't expect to be alerted to oncoming traffic by headlights, or for that matter to expect drivers to avoid overtaking or speeding simply because they cannot see more than 10m ahead. It's strongly recommended that you avoid driving at night on main highways altogether, but if you do, be warned that a significant proportion of vehicles lack a full complement of functional headlights, so never assume a single glow indicates a motorcycle! Another very real danger is unlit trucks that have broken down in the middle of the road.

If you decide to rent a self-drive vehicle, check it over carefully and ask to take it for a test drive. Even if you're not knowledgeable about the working of engines, a few minutes on the road should be sufficient to establish whether it has any seriously disturbing creaks, rattles or other noises. Check the condition of the tyres (bald is beautiful might be the national motto in this regard) and that there is at least one spare, better two, both in a condition to be used should the need present itself. If the tyres are tubeless, an inner tube of the correct size can be useful in the event of a repair being required upcountry. Ask to be shown the wheel spanner, jack and the thing for raising the jack. If the vehicle is a high-clearance 4x4 make sure that the jack is capable of raising the wheel high enough to change it. Ask also to be shown filling points for oil, water and petrol and check that all the keys do what they are supposed to do – we've left Kampala before with a car we later discovered could not be locked! Once on the road, check oil and water regularly in the early stages of the trip to ensure that there are no existing leaks.

Ugandans follow the British custom of driving on the left side of the road, albeit somewhat loosely on occasions. The following documentation is required at all times: vehicle registration book (a photocopy is acceptable); vehicle certificate of insurance, and driving licence. Your own domestic licence is acceptable for up to three months. If you're nicked for speeding (the limit is 100km/h on the open road and 50km/h in built-up areas, unless otherwise indicated), not having a valid insurance sticker, or any other transgression, the worst case scenario is that you'll be presented with a charge sheet to clear at a bank within 28 days. As often as not, however, after a few minutes or so of friendly back and forth (remain polite, admit guilt, plead stupidity), you'll be let on your way. Still, safest to show the officer a photocopy of your licence or an expendable international licence, just in case they decide to retain it until you pay the fine.

Filling stations charge around US$1.10 per litre for petrol and slightly less for diesel. Stick with branded filling stations, specifically Shell or Total, both of which have at least one outlet in larger towns, as shown on town maps where applicable. Most Ugandan towns also have numerous filling stations of more parochial affiliations, and while many of these are fine to use, others might stock watered down or dirty fuel, and it is difficult to know which can be relied upon (though any station selling fuel more cheaply than its branded peers should be assumed to be suspect). Uganda being quite a small country by African standards, you're unlikely to drive too long without an opportunity to refuel, but there are a few stretches – notably the Gulu and Arua roads north of Luwero, or the drive from Bwindi to Mweya/Kasese via Ishasha, and Karamoja in general – where branded filling stations are few and far between, so plan ahead. It is also always worth filling up before you enter any national park where you expect to do a few game drives (i.e. Murchison Falls, Queen Elizabeth, Lake Mburo or Kidepo Valley). In more remote areas, filling stations may be absent altogether and self-drivers who forgot to fill up in advance will be reliant on buying fuel in jerry cans. This tends to be both pricey and highly suspect (even if the fuel is pure, the container may be dirty) so it would be prudent to use nylon stockings or a similar material to filter the fuel as you empty it into the tank.

A PDF of self-driving tips for Uganda, compiled a few years back by Dr Fritz Esch, can be downloaded at www.bradtupdates.com/uganda.

MOUNTAIN BIKING Uganda is relatively compact and flat, making it ideal for travel by mountain bike. New-quality bikes are not available in Uganda so you should try to bring one with you (some airlines are more flexible than others about carrying bicycles; you should discuss this with your airline in advance). However, if you are prepared to look around Kampala, some decent secondhand bikes can be bought from a few private importers for as little as US$75: check the shop opposite Old Kampala Police Station. Main roads in Uganda are generally in good condition and buses will allow you to take your bike on the roof, though you should expect to be charged extra for this. Minor roads are variable in condition, but in the dry season you're unlikely to encounter any problems. Several of the more far-flung destinations mentioned in this book would be within easy reach of cyclists.

Before you pack that bicycle, do consider that cyclists – far more than motorists – are exposed to an estimable set of hazards on African roads. The 'might-is-right' mentality referred to in the section about self-drive is doubly concerning to cyclists, who must expect to be treated as second-class road users, and to display constant vigilance against speeding buses, etc. It is routine for motorised vehicles to bear down on a bicycle as if it simply didn't exist, hooting at the very last minute, and enforcing the panicked cyclist to veer off the road abruptly, sometimes resulting in a nasty fall. Should this not put you off, do at least ensure that your bicycle is fitted with good rear-view mirrors, a loud horn and luminous strips, and that you bring a helmet and whatever protective gear might lessen the risks. Cycling at night is emphatically not recommended.

The **International Bicycle Fund** (*www.ibike.org*) produces a useful publication called *Bicycling in Africa*, as well as several regional supplements including one about Malawi, Tanzania and Uganda.

PUBLIC TRANSPORT Following the permanent suspension of most passenger rail and ferry services over the past few years, public transport in Uganda essentially boils down to buses and other forms of motorised road transport. The only exceptions are the new passenger/vehicle ferry between Entebbe and the Ssese Islands and

local boat services connecting fishing villages on lakes Victoria, Albert and Kyoga. Details of these services are given under the appropriate sections in the regional part of the guide, but it's worth noting here that overloading small passenger boats is customary in Uganda, and fatal accidents are commonplace, often linked to the violent storms that can sweep in from nowhere during the rainy season.

Buses   Coach and bus services cover all major routes, and are probably the safest form of public transport in Uganda. On all trunk routes, the battered old buses of a few years back have been replaced or supplemented by large modern coaches that typically maintain a speed of 100km/h or faster, allowing them to travel between the capital and any of the main urban centres in western Uganda in less than 5 hours, generally at a cost of less than US$10. Details of individual operators and routes are included in the Kampala and relevant regional chapters.

A **word of warning**: there have been a few incidents in East Africa in recent years whereby travellers have accepted drugged food from fellow passengers – and they awake much later to find themselves relieved of their belongings. Though 99 times out of 100 offers of refreshment will be made from genuine courtesy, a polite refusal may be the safest option.

Matatus   In addition to buses, most major routes are covered by a regular stream of white minibuses referred to locally as matatus or (rather confusingly) taxis. Generally, these have no set departure times, but simply leave when they are full. Matatus tend to charge slightly higher fares than buses, and the drivers tend to be more reckless, but they allow more flexibility, especially for short hops. It's customary on most routes to pay shortly before arriving rather than on departure, so there is little risk of being overcharged provided that you look and see what other passengers are paying. A law enforcing a maximum of three passengers per row is stringently enforced in most parts of Uganda, and seat belts are now mandatory. All minibus-taxis by law now have to have a distinctive blue-and-white band round the middle, and special hire cars have to have a black-and-white band. Throughout this book, we use the term matatu (as opposed to taxi) to describe this form of transport, but we follow the local custom of referring to the terminal from where they depart as the 'taxi park'.

Shared taxis   Shared taxis, generally light saloon cars that carry four to six passengers, come into their own on routes that attract insufficient human traffic for minibuses, for instance between Katunguru and Mweya in Queen Elizabeth National Park. They tend to be crowded and slow in comparison with minibuses, and on routes where no other public transport exists, fares are often highly inflated. The drivers habitually overcharge tourists, so establish the price in advance.

Special hire   You won't spend long in Uganda before you come across the term special hire – which means hiring a vehicle privately to take you somewhere. There are situations where it is useful to go for a special hire, but beware of people at matatu stations who tell you there are no vehicles going to where you want, but that they can fix you up a special hire. Nine times out of ten they are trying their luck. If you organise a special hire vehicle, bargain hard. Urban taxis are also known locally as special hires.

Boda   One of the most popular ways of getting around in Uganda is the bicycle-taxi or boda (or *boda-boda* in full, since they originated as a means of smuggling goods from border to border along rural footpaths). Now fitted with

pillions instead of panniers, and powered by foot or by 100cc engines, they are a convenient form of suburban transport and also great for short side trips where no public transport exists. Fares are negotiable and affordable – a fraction of a US dollar in most towns. If you're reliant on public transport it's inevitable that you'll use a boda at some stage, but before hopping aboard you should be aware of their poor safety record. Boda riders are invariably lacking in formal training, road safety awareness and, it is frequently suggested, much between the ears. Back in December 2005, 1,383 vehicles were involved in accidents sufficiently serious to be reported. Of these, 22% involved matatus and 15% bodas. Bodas and their passengers are of course far more vulnerable than the occupants of larger vehicles, and in the same month 15 boda drivers were killed. More recently, the 2011 annual traffic report showed a monthly average of almost 150 serious accidents involving motorbikes occurred in Kampala, while a 2012 survey carried out by the Ministry of Works and Transport indicated that an average of 10 to 20 victims of boda accidents were received daily at the city's Mulago Hospital.

By all means use bodas, but do try to identify a relatively sensible-looking operator, ideally of mature years. Older riders are generally better than 16-year-old village kids with no comprehension of traffic. Tell your driver to go slowly and carefully and don't be afraid to tell him to slow down (or even stop for you to get off) if you don't feel safe. Officially, helmets for boda-boda drivers and their passengers have been mandatory since 2005 but the law is rarely enforced.

Though boda muggings are largely confined to Kampala (see warning on page 81), we have heard reports of similar incidents at night in Fort Portal. Presumably it could happen elsewhere, too, so just be sure to keep your wits about you and keep personal belongings with you at all times.

ACCOMMODATION

The number of hotels in Uganda has grown enormously in recent years. Indeed, wherever you travel, and whatever your budget, you'll seldom have a problem finding suitable accommodation. Most towns have a good variety of moderately priced and budget hotels, and even the smallest villages will usually have somewhere you can stay for a couple of dollars. Upmarket accommodation, on the other hand, is centred on major towns and tourist centres such as national parks. All accommodation entries in this travel guide are placed in one of six categories: luxury/exclusive, upmarket, moderate, budget, shoestring and camping. The purpose of this categorisation is twofold: to break up long hotel listings that span a wide price range, and to help readers isolate the range of hotels that will best suit their budget and taste. Any given hotel is categorised on its overall feel as much as its actual prices (rack rates are quoted anyway) and in the context of general accommodation standards in the town or reserve where it is situated. Comments relating to the value for money represented by any given hotel should also be read in the context of the individual town and of the stated category. In other words, a hotel that seems to be good value in one town might not be such a bargain were it situated in a place where rates are generally cheaper. Likewise, a hotel that we describe as good value in the upmarket category will almost certainly feel madly expensive to a traveller using budget hotels.

Broadly speaking, hotels, lodges and tented camps placed in the exclusive or luxury bracket are truly world-class institutions that meet the highest standards and have a strong individual flair. Upmarket hotels often have all the facilities you'd expect of a three- to four-star hotel, making them top-drawer for Uganda,

but are not quite so outstanding by global standards. Moderate hotels are more middling in quality but would still come across as very comfortable to tourists used to developing world standards. Budget accommodation mostly consists of ungraded accommodation that is aimed primarily at the local market but would still be considered reasonably comfortable by hardened backpackers, often with facilities such as en-suite hot showers, satellite TV and good netting. Shoestring accommodation consists of the cheapest rooms around, usually unpretentious local guesthouses, often with shared bathrooms. Camping generally refers to sites where you would pitch your own tent (as opposed to camps with standing tents).

Note that most East African hotels in all price ranges refer to a room that has en-suite shower and toilet facilities as self-contained. Several hotels offer accommodation in *bandas*, a term used widely to designate detached rooms or cottages. Be aware that Ugandan usage of the terms single, double and twin is inconsistent with Western conventions. A room with one double bed is often referred to as a single room, while one with two beds is termed a double rather than a twin. For this reason, couples should make a habit of looking at a 'single' room before assuming they need to pay extra for a double or twin. (And do note that in this guidebook, we reflect what a room actually is, rather than what the hotel calls it, so if it has a double bed, we call it a double, and if it has two beds, we call it a twin).

Hotels assigned as author's favourites (indicated by a ✳ before the listing) stand out as being unusually characterful, service-orientated, or good value – often, all three! As an easy visual reference, all hotels are assigned a price band, based on the price of a standard room with double or twin occupancy, as follows:

$	under US$15
$$	US$15–50
$$$	US$50–120
$$$$	US$120–250
$$$$$	over US$250

EATING AND DRINKING

EATING OUT If you are not too fussy and don't mind a lack of variety, you can eat cheaply almost anywhere in Uganda. In most towns numerous local restaurants (often called *hotelis*) serve unimaginative but filling meals for under US$2. Typically, local food is based around a meat or chicken stew eaten with one of four staples: rice, chapati, ugali or matoke. *Ugali* is a stiff maize porridge eaten throughout sub-Saharan Africa. *Matoke* is a cooked plantain dish, served boiled or in a mushy heap, and the staple diet in many parts of Uganda. Another Ugandan special is groundnut sauce. *Mandazi*, the local equivalent of doughnuts, are tasty when they are freshly cooked, but rather less appetising when they are a day old. *Mandazi* are served at *hotelis* and sold at markets. You can often eat very cheaply at stalls around markets and bus stations.

Cheap it may be, but for most travellers the appeal of this sort of fare soon palls. In larger towns, you'll usually find a couple of better restaurants (sometimes attached to upmarket or moderate hotels) serving Western or Indian food for around US$5–8. There is considerably more variety in Kampala, where for US$10–12 per head you can eat very well indeed. Upmarket lodges and hotels generally serve high-quality food. Vegetarians are often poorly catered for in Uganda (the exception being Indian restaurants), and people on organised tours should ensure that the operator is informed in advance about this or any other dietary preference.

COOKING FOR YOURSELF The alternative to eating at restaurants is to put together your own meals at markets and supermarkets. The variety of foodstuffs you can buy varies from season to season and from town to town, but in most major centres you can rely on finding a supermarket that stocks frozen meat, a few tinned goods, biscuits, pasta, rice and chocolate bars. Fruit and vegetables are best bought at markets, where they are very cheap. Potatoes, sweet potatoes, onions, tomatoes, bananas, sugarcane, avocados, paw-paws, mangoes, coconuts, oranges and pineapples are available in most towns. For hikers, packet soups and noodles are about the only dehydrated meals that are available throughout Uganda. If you have specialised requirements, you're best off doing your shopping in Kampala, where a wider selection of goods is available in the supermarkets.

DRINKS Brand-name soft drinks such as Coca-Cola and Fanta are widely available in Uganda and cheap by international standards. If the fizzy stuff doesn't appeal, you can buy imported South African fruit juices at supermarkets in Kampala and other large towns. Tap water is reasonably safe to drink in larger towns, but bottled mineral water is widely available if you prefer not to take the risk.

Locally, the most widely drunk hot beverage is *chai*, a sweet tea where all ingredients are boiled together in a pot. In some parts of the country *chai* is often flavoured with spices such as ginger (an acquired taste, in the author's opinion). Coffee is one of Uganda's major cash crops, but you'll be lucky if you ever meet a Ugandan who knows how to brew a decent cup – coffee in Uganda almost invariably tastes insipid and watery except at upmarket hotels and quality restaurants.

The main alcoholic drink is lager beer. Jinja's Nile Breweries (a subsidiary of South African Breweries) brews Nile Special, Nile Gold and Club whilst Uganda Breweries at Port Bell near Kampala brews Bell, Pilsner, Tusker, Tusker Malt Export and Guinness. All local beers come in 500ml bottles, which cost around US$1.50 in local bars and up to US$4 in some upmarket hotels. Nile Special is probably the most popular tipple with locals and travellers alike, though after a few experiments, many opt for the milder Club and Bell. If you've never been to Africa before, you might want to try the local millet beer. It's not bad, though for most people once is enough.

A selection of superior plonk-quality South African wines is available in most tourist-class hotels and bars, as well as in some supermarkets, generally starting at around US$10–20 per bottle. Local gins can be bought very cheaply in a variety of bottle sizes or in 60ml sachets – very convenient for hiking in remote areas or taking with you to upmarket hotels for an inexpensive nightcap in your room. These are known by the rather endearing term 'tot pack', though the African fondness for tacking an additional vowel to the end of a noun has actually resulted in 'totter pack'; you may appreciate this inadvertent irony if you overindulge.

PUBLIC HOLIDAYS

In addition to the following fixed public holidays, Uganda recognises as holidays the Christian Good Friday and Easter Monday and the Muslim Eid-el-Fitr and Eid-el-Adha. Expect any institutions that would be closed on a Sunday – banks and forex bureaux, for instance, or government and other offices – to also be closed on any public holiday, but most shops and other local services will function as normal. Public transport is typically more intermittent than normal on public holidays, but it still operates.

1 January	New Year's Day
26 January	NRM Liberation Day
16 February	Janan Luwum Day
8 March	International Women's Day
1 May	Labour Day
3 June	Martyrs' Day
9 June	National Heroes' Day
9 October	Independence Day
25 December	Christmas Day
26 December	Boxing Day

SHOPPING

A good range of imported goods is available in Kampala, though prices are often inflated. Most upcountry towns, especially those with significant expatriate communities or tourist flow, have at least one well-stocked supermarket, along with any number of smaller shops selling toilet rolls, soap, toothpaste, pens, batteries and locally produced foodstuffs. Normal shopping hours are between 08.30 and 18.00.

CURIOS Typical curios include carvings, batiks, musical instruments, wooden spoons and various soapstone and malachite knick-knacks. There are several curio shops in Kampala, and there are good craft markets next to the National Theatre and on Buganda Road. Antique shops are found in the Sheraton Hotel and in the city centre on Portal Avenue.

MEDIA AND COMMUNICATIONS

NEWSPAPERS Uganda has a good English-language press, with the daily *New Vision* and *Monitor* offering the best international coverage as well as local news. The *East African*, a Kenyan weekly, has excellent regional coverage and comment. *Time* and *Newsweek* can be bought at street stalls in Kampala. The bi-weekly *Independent* magazine, produced by independent journalist Andrew Mwenda, provides insightful coverage of current controversies.

RADIO AND TELEVISION A varied selection of local and national radio stations service Uganda, most of them privately run, offering listeners a lively mix of talk, hard and soft news, local and other current music – not to mention a litany of dodgy 1970s disco anthems you'd probably forgotten about! For entertainment from the outside world, BBC World Service relays through a number of regional stations (in Kampala, Capital Radio on 91.3 FM) while Touch FM (95.9 FM) gives regular airtime to classic rock staples. The national television channels aren't up to much, but most international hotels and many smaller ones subscribe to DSTV and GTV, multi-channel satellite services featuring the likes of CNN or Sky News as well as movie and sports channels. Bars and restaurants with DSTV and GTV tend to be packed on Saturday afternoons during the English football season, and for all other major football events.

TELEPHONE Uganda's land telephone system is reasonably efficient, but mobile phones rule. If you bring your mobile from home, you'll enjoy international roaming – albeit at a significant cost – through a local network. Far cheaper,

however, especially if you also want to make use of data services, is to bring a compatible phone with you and insert a local SIM card, which costs next to nothing. MTN (*www.mtn.co.ug*) is the provider best suited to travellers due to its excellent countrywide network. Airtime cards are available everywhere, and both calls and data bundles are cheap!

Both land and mobile numbers are included in this guidebook. All numbers are ten digits. Land line numbers start with 03 or 04 and are listed in the format nnn nnnnnnn. Mobile numbers start with 07 and are listed in the format nnnn nnnnn. Generally you're more likely to get through to mobile phones more quickly than to land lines. Note, however, that many of the mobile numbers listed in this book belong to somebody's personal device, so they are far more likely to become obsolete than land lines. Calling from overseas, the international code is +256, and you need to drop the leading zero from the local number.

INTERNET AND EMAIL Inexpensive internet cafés are dotted around all large towns, while many tourist hotels and restaurants now offer free Wi-Fi to their guests. Better still, buy a local MTN SIM card for your smart phone, load it up with a data bundle, and you'll have more-or-less permanent access to the internet, email and various apps for next to no cost. That said, access may be slow or erratic in national parks and other remote areas, so best to warn anxious loved ones at home or business associates that contact may be intermittent.

Email and internet are not really a standard medium of communication in Uganda. Except at the very top end of the price scale, few hotels and other institutions have websites or email addresses, and even if they do in theory, the URLs and email addresses printed boldly on business cards or signposts are often misspelt or non-existent. We have done our best to validate all URLs and any improbable-looking email addresses before including them in this book, but even this can be problematic, as domains we discover to be expired or suspended might yet be reactivated, and email addresses whose inbox is so full that new emails sent to them bounce back might one day be emptied. Furthermore, even where addresses are valid, a great many Ugandans are not in the habit of replying to emails, so you are far more likely to get somewhere by phoning instead.

CRIME AND SECURITY

Uganda has been an acceptably safe travel destination since Museveni took power in 1986. The only region that subsequently experienced long-term instability is the north, which was practically off-limits to travel prior to 2007 due to a rebellion led by the Lord's Resistance Army (see box, pages 300–1). The north is now widely regarded as safe for travel, though government security advisories still apply to the northeast because of banditry related to Karamojong cattle rustlers. Elsewhere, Kampala, like most cities around the world, is vulnerable to terrorist attacks, as demonstrated in 2010 when 74 people were killed in twin blasts at two venues showing World Cup matches on television. Despite that, however, the most significant threat to life and limb in Uganda comes not from banditry or terrorism, but rather from the malaria parasite and car or boat accidents.

Violence associated with the DRC and Rwanda occasionally spilt over into border regions of southwest Uganda between 1986 and the turn of the millennium. The most notorious incident was the killing of six tourists and two rangers abducted from Bwindi in 1999. A more sustained outbreak of violence was orchestrated by the somewhat mysterious Allied Democratic Forces (ADF), a small and 'rebel' army – thought to consist solely of Congolese thugs – responsible for several brutal attacks in the Rwenzori border area in the late 1990s. The activities of the ADF forced the closure of Semliki and Rwenzori national parks in 1997, but there have been no incidents of concern since the two parks reopened in 1999 and 2002 respectively. Almost 20 years later, there seems little cause for serious concern in the southwest, and the authorities would be unlikely to allow tourists to visit reserves and national parks with a known security problem.

THEFT Uganda is widely and rightly regarded as one of the most crime-free countries in Africa, certainly as far as visitors need be concerned. Muggings are comparatively rare, even in Kampala, and it is largely free of the sort of con tricks that abound in places like Nairobi. Even petty theft such as pickpocketing and bag snatching is relatively unusual, though it does happen from time to time. Walking around large towns at night is reputedly safe, though it would be tempting fate to wander alone along unlit streets. On the basis that it is preferable to err on the side of caution, a few tips that apply to travelling anywhere in east and southern Africa:

- Most casual thieves operate in busy markets and bus stations. Keep a close watch on your possessions in such places, and avoid having valuables or large amounts of money loose in your daypack or pocket.
- Keep all your valuables and the bulk of your money in a moneybelt that can be hidden beneath your clothing. A belt made of cotton or another natural fabric is most pleasant on the skin, but such fabrics tend to soak up sweat, so wrap everything inside in plastic. Never show this moneybelt in public, and keep any spare cash you need elsewhere on your person.
- Where the choice exists between carrying valuables on your person or leaving them in a locked room, we would generally favour the latter option, though you need to use your judgement and be sure the room is absolutely secure.
- Leave any jewellery of financial or sentimental value at home.

BRIBERY AND BUREAUCRACY For all you read about the subject, bribery is not a major issue for travellers in Africa, especially if you are travelling on public transport or

as part of a tour. Travellers driving themselves are vulnerable to being asked for a bribe by traffic police, but less so in Uganda than in the likes of Mozambique and Kenya.

When dealing with African bureaucrats, a big factor in determining how you are treated will be your own attitude. If you come across as friendly and patient, and accept that the person to whom you are talking does not speak English as a first language and may have difficulty following everything you say, it should all go smoothly. By contrast, if you enter an encounter with officialdom with a confrontational approach, you are quite likely to kindle the feeling held by many Africans that Europeans are arrogant and offhand in their dealings with other races.

WOMEN TRAVELLERS Women generally regard sub-equatorial Africa as one of the safest places in the world to travel alone. Uganda in particular poses few if any risks specific to female travellers. It is reasonable to expect a fair bit of flirting and the odd direct proposition, especially if you mingle with Ugandans in bars, but a firm 'no' should be enough to defuse any potential situation. And, to be fair to Ugandan men, you can expect the same sort of thing in any country, and for that matter from many male travellers. Ugandan women tend to dress conservatively. It will not increase the amount of hassle you receive if you avoid wearing clothes that, however unfairly, may be perceived to be provocative, and it may even go some way to decreasing it.

More mundanely, tampons are not readily available in smaller towns, though you can easily locate them in Kampala, Entebbe and Jinja, and in game lodge and hotel gift shops. When travelling in out-of-the-way places, carry enough tampons to see you through to the next time you'll be in a large city, bearing in mind that travelling in the tropics can sometimes cause heavier or more irregular periods than normal. Sanitary pads are available in most towns of any size.

GAY AND LESBIAN TRAVELLERS All homosexual activity is illegal in Uganda, and has been since colonial times. However, the issue came to the fore in 2009, with the submission to parliament of a draconian and so-called 'Kill the Gays' bill, and the international furore that greeted it. The Anti-Homosexuality Act (AHA) was eventually passed in February 2014, albeit in a moderated form (with life imprisonment replacing the death sentence), only to be overturned by the Supreme Court six months later. Since then the government has gone quiet on the subject and, perhaps as an indication that the issue has blown over, on 8 August 2015, a gay pride rally was held outside Kampala to commemorate the first anniversary of the court ruling. It is also interesting to note that the despite international outrage, the AHA contained little that was not already tackled under Ugandan law; its content being little more than a re-packaging of existing legislation imposed during an era when British attitudes to gay activity were considerably less liberal than today.

The bottom line, however, is that visiting gays and lesbians should recognise that the AHA saga reflected a deep-held and often vociferous anti-gay sentiment among the general populace (96% of which believes that homosexual lifestyles are immoral and should not be socially acceptable, according to the Pew Global Attitudes Project of 2007). This prejudice has been fuelled partly by the vitriolic outpourings of right-wing American evangelists, but it also reflects a widespread perception throughout Africa that homosexuality (unlike American evangelism, or more conventional Christianity for that matter) is an un-African activity introduced by foreigners to fulfil a Western agenda. None of which should provide a practical obstacle to gay and lesbian travellers visiting Uganda, provided they are willing to be discreet about their sexuality. Some, however, might well regard it to be an ethical stumbling block.

Ugandans are generally relaxed, friendly and tolerant in their dealings with tourists, and you would have to do something pretty outrageous to commit a serious faux pas there. But, like any country, it does have its rules of etiquette, and while allowances will always be made for tourists, there is some value in ensuring that they are not made too frequently!

GENERAL CONDUCT Perhaps the single most important point of etiquette to be grasped by visitors to Africa is the social importance of formal greetings. Rural Africans tend to greet each other elaborately, and if you want to make a good impression on somebody who speaks English, whether they be a waiter or a shop assistant (and especially if they work in a government department), you would do well to follow suit. When you need to ask directions, it is rude to blunder straight into interrogative mode without first exchanging greetings. Most Ugandans speak some English, but for those who don't the Swahili greeting '*Jambo*' delivered with a smile and a nod of the head will be adequate.

Among Ugandans, it is considered to be in poor taste to display certain emotions publicly. Affection is one such emotion: it is frowned upon for members of the opposite sex to hold hands publicly, and kissing or embracing would be seriously offensive. Oddly, it is quite normal for friends of the same sex to walk around hand in hand. Male travellers who get into a long discussion with a male Ugandan shouldn't be surprised if that person clasps them by the hand and retains a firm grip on their hand for several minutes. This is a warm gesture, one particularly appropriate when the person wants to make a point with which you might disagree.

Visitors should be aware of the Islamic element in Ugandan society, particularly in Kampala. In Muslim society, it is insulting to use your left hand to pass or receive something or when shaking hands (a custom adhered to in many parts of Africa that aren't Muslim). If you eat with your fingers, it is also customary to use the right hand only. Even those of us who are naturally right-handed will occasionally need to remind ourselves of this (it may happen, for instance, that you are carrying something in your right hand and so hand money to a shopkeeper with your left). For left-handed travellers, it will require a constant effort.

TIPPING AND GUIDES The question of where and when not to tip can be difficult in a foreign country. In Uganda, it is customary to tip your driver/guide at the end of a safari or hike, as well as any cook or porter who accompanies you. A figure of roughly US$5–US$10 per day would be a fair benchmark, though do check this with your safari company in advance. It is not essential to tip the guides who take you around in national parks and other reserves, but it is recommended. A similar sum in shillings would be appreciated, especially if the guide has found you that lion, leopard or shoebill. In both cases, feel free to give a bigger or smaller tip based on the quality of service.

In some African countries, it is difficult to travel anywhere without being latched on to by a self-appointed guide, who will often expect a tip over and above any agreed fee. This sort of thing is unusual in Uganda, but if you do take on a freelance guide, then it is advisable to clarify in advance that whatever price you agree is final and inclusive of a tip.

It is not customary to tip for service in local bars and eateries, but if you feel like doing so, it will be appreciated. A 5% tip would be acceptable and 10% generous. Generally, any restaurant that caters primarily to tourists and to wealthy Ugandan

residents will automatically add a service charge to the bill, but since there's no telling where that service charge ends up, it would still be reasonable to reward good service with a 10% tip.

BARGAINING AND OVERCHARGING Prices in hotels, restaurants and shops are generally fixed, and overcharging in such places is very unusual. For this reason, the need to bargain generally exists only in reasonably predictable circumstances, for instance when chartering a private taxi, organising a guide, or buying curios and to a lesser extent other market produce.

The main instance where bargaining is essential is when buying curios. However, the fact a curio seller is open to negotiation does not mean that you were initially being overcharged or ripped off. Curio sellers will generally quote a price knowing full well that you are going to bargain it down (they'd probably be startled if you didn't) and it is not necessary to respond aggressively or in an accusatory manner. To get a feel for prices, check a few similar items at different stalls before you actually buy anything.

At markets and stalls, bargaining is the norm, even between locals, and the healthiest approach is to view it as an enjoyable part of the African experience. There will normally be an accepted price band for any particular commodity. To find out what it is, listen to what other people pay and try a few stalls. A ludicrously inflated price will always drop the moment you walk away. It's simpler when buying fruit and vegetables which are generally piled in heaps for a set price. You'll elicit a smile and a few extra items thrown in if you ask '*Yongela ko*' meaning 'addition'. Above all, bear in mind that when somebody is reluctant to bargain, it may be because they asked a fair price in the first place.

Matatu conductors often try to overcharge tourists, so check the correct ticket price in advance, and try to book your ticket the day before you travel. Failing that, you will have to judge for yourself whether the price is right, and if you have reason to think it isn't, then question the conductor. In such circumstances, it can be difficult to find the right balance between standing up for your rights and becoming overtly obnoxious.

A final point to consider on the subject of overcharging and bargaining is that it is the fact of being overcharged that annoys; the amount itself is generally of little consequence in the wider context of a trip to Uganda. So while travellers shouldn't allow themselves to be routinely overcharged, there are occasions when it helps to retain some perspective with respect to relative incomes. If you find yourself quibbling over a pittance with an old lady selling a few piles of fruit by the roadside, you might perhaps bear in mind that the notion of a fixed price is a very Western one. When somebody is desperate enough for money, or afraid that their perishable goods might not last another day, it may well be possible to push them down to a price lower than they would normally accept. In such circumstances, it might be kinder to err on the side of generosity.

GETTING INVOLVED

It goes without saying, or it ought to, that you'll observe a vast difference in Uganda between your standard of living and that of many local people, and many visitors are moved to help. To do so effectively and appropriately can, however, be difficult; there are plenty of tricksters looking to fleece well-meaning donors with school-fee scams, as well as the odd dodgy pastor using bogus community campsites/volunteer schemes to line their own pockets. Rather than handing out

cash, a good way to be certain of making a difference is to stuff empty spaces in your rucksack with items that are hugely useful but which are costly or unavailable in Uganda. Check out the website of **Sanyu Babies Home** (*0414 274032;* m *0712 370950;* e *barbara@sanyubabies.com; www.sanyubabies.com*) before you travel, a charitable foundation that cares for orphaned, destitute and abandoned babies until they are adopted or graduate to orphanages. An annual needs list on the website includes 24 large tubs of Sudocrem, 21,900 disposable nappies and 2,160 tins of formula milk – all items easily bought in Europe or North America and stuffed into an empty corner in a suitcase or rucksack. Sanyu Babies Home also welcomes volunteers and paying guests; accommodation on site is provided in a pleasantly homely guesthouse (*US$25 shared facilities*). The home is found on the side of Namirembe Hill on Natete Road just before Mengo Hospital. It's a particularly convenient place to visit: many budget and independent travellers stay in this area, while tourists staying in central hotels will invariably pass the gate on their way to/from destinations in western Uganda.

Volunteers for Sustainable Development (*VFSD;* m *0782 808257;* e *salim@ vfsdafrica.org; www.vfsdafrica.org*), a small organisation established by local residents, is doing its best to provide a life for a handful of orphans in Bwaise, Kampala's largest slum. It's a truly humbling initiative, tackling overwhelming odds and every little helps. Assistance can take the form of volunteering, simply spending time with the kids to help them practise their English, donating funds (supporters in the US have set up a 501C facility) or taking the VFSD slum tour (pages 130–1) to better understand the reality of life in Bwaise.

If you're moved to support the Uganda Wildlife Authority's struggle to protect Uganda's wildlife, visit www.ugandacf.org to learn about the work of the **Uganda Conservation Foundation** (see ad, page 346). UCF helps UWA with much-needed infrastructure, equipment, training and support for research. Recent activities include the construction of ranger posts in Queen Elizabeth and Murchison Falls national parks, donation of bicycles and patrol boats, training of boat coxwains, a hippo survey in Queen Elizabeth and the refurbishment of a veterinary vehicle for Murchison Falls. Administration costs are kept to a minimum and 90% of funding is channelled directly into conservation action. If you would like to support UCF in the US, a 501C facility can be accessed on the website.

4

Health

With Dr Felicity Nicholson

Uganda, like most parts of Africa, is home to several tropical diseases unfamiliar to people living in more temperate and sanitary climates. However, with adequate preparation, and a sensible attitude to malaria prevention, the chances of serious mishap are small. To put this in perspective, your greatest concern after malaria should not be the combined exotica of venomous snakes, stampeding wildlife, gun-happy soldiers or the Ebola virus, but something altogether more mundane: a road accident.

Private clinics, hospitals and pharmacies can be found in most large towns, and doctors generally speak good English. The main private hospital is the International Hospital Kampala (*St Barnabas Road, Namuwongo;* \ *031 2200400; http://ihk. img.co.ug*). Private clinics include The Surgery in Kampala (\ *0414 256003;* m *0752 756003; www.thesurgeryuganda.org*).

Consultation fees and laboratory tests are inexpensive when compared with most Western countries, so if you do fall sick, don't allow financial considerations to dissuade you from seeking medical help. Commonly required medicines such as broad-spectrum antibiotics, painkillers, asthma inhalers and various antimalarial treatments are widely available. If you are on any short-term medication prior to departure, or you have specific needs relating to a less common medical condition (for instance if you are allergic to bee stings or nuts), then bring necessary treatment with you.

PREPARATIONS

Sensible preparation will go a long way to ensuring your trip goes smoothly. Particularly for first-time visitors to Africa, this includes a visit to a travel clinic to discuss matters such as vaccinations and malaria prevention. A list of recommended travel clinic websites worldwide is available at www.itsm.org, and other useful websites for prospective travellers include www.travelhealthpro.org.uk and www. netdoctor.co.uk/travel. The Bradt website now carries a health section online (*www. bradtguides.com/africahealth*) to help travellers prepare for their African trip, elaborating on most points raised below, but the following summary points are worth emphasising:

- Don't travel without comprehensive medical **travel insurance** that will fly you home in an emergency.
- Make sure all your **immunisations** are up to date. A yellow fever certificate is not required unless you are coming from a yellow fever endemic zone; however, you are advised to have the yellow fever vaccine for health reasons. If the vaccine is not suitable for you then you may need to discuss how safe it is to travel to Uganda without vaccination with a travel health expert.

If your onward travel from Uganda is to a country that requires a yellow fever certificate for entry (eg: South Africa), then make sure you either have a valid yellow fever certificate or yellow fever exemption where appropriate. It's also reckless to travel in the tropics without being up to date on tetanus, polio and diphtheria (now given as an all-in-one vaccine, Revaxis) and hepatitis A. Immunisation against meningitis, typhoid, hepatitis B, TB and rabies may also be recommended.

- The biggest health threat is **malaria**. There is no vaccine against this mosquito-borne disease, but a variety of preventative drugs is available, including mefloquine, malarone and the antibiotic doxycycline. The most suitable choice of drug varies depending on the individual and the country they are visiting, so visit your GP or a travel clinic for medical advice. If you will be spending a long time in Africa, and expect to visit remote areas, be aware that no preventative drug is 100% effective, so carry a cure too. It is also worth noting that no homeopathic prophylactic for malaria exists, nor can any traveller acquire effective resistance to malaria. Those who don't make use of preventative drugs risk their life in a manner that is both foolish and unnecessary.
- Though advised for everyone, a **pre-exposure rabies vaccination**, involving three doses taken over a minimum of 21 days, is particularly important if you intend to have contact with animals, or are likely to be 24 hours away from medical help.
- Anybody travelling away from major centres should carry a **personal first-aid kit**. Contents might include a good drying antiseptic (eg: iodine or potassium permanganate), Band-Aids, suncream, insect repellent, aspirin or paracetamol, antifungal cream (eg: Canesten), ciprofloxacin or norfloxacin (for severe diarrhoea), antibiotic eye drops, tweezers, condoms or femidoms, a digital thermometer and a needle-and-syringe kit with an accompanying letter from a healthcare professional.
- Bring any **drugs or devices relating to known medical conditions** with you. That applies both to those who are on medication prior to departure, and those who are, for instance, allergic to bee stings, or are prone to attacks of asthma.
- Prolonged immobility on long-haul flights can result in **deep vein thrombosis** (DVT), which can be dangerous if the clot travels to the lungs to cause pulmonary embolus. The risk increases with age, and is higher in obese or pregnant travellers, heavy smokers, those taller than 6ft/1.8m or shorter than 5ft/1.5m, and anybody with a history of clots, recent major operation or varicose veins surgery, cancer, a stroke or heart disease. If any of these criteria apply, consult a doctor before you travel.

COMMON MEDICAL PROBLEMS

MALARIA This potentially fatal disease is widespread in tropical Africa. Within Uganda, it is possible to catch malaria almost anywhere below the 2,000m contour (everywhere, that is, except the upper slopes of high mountains such as the Rwenzori, Virunga and Elgon). In mid-altitude locations, malaria is largely but not entirely seasonal, with the highest risk occurring during the rainy season (March to May and October to December). Moist and low-lying areas such as the Nile at Murchison Falls are high risk throughout the year, but the risk is greatest during the rainy season. This localised breakdown might influence what foreigners living in Uganda do about malaria prevention, but all travellers to Uganda must assume that they will be exposed to malaria and should take suitable preventative drugs and other precautions throughout their trip.

Since no malaria prophylactic is 100% effective, it makes sense to take all reasonable precautions against being bitten by the nocturnal *Anopheles* mosquitoes that transmit the disease (see box, page 91). Malaria usually manifests within two weeks of transmission (though it can be as short as seven days), but it can take months, which means that short-stay visitors are most likely to experience symptoms after they return home. These typically include a rapid rise in temperature (over 38°C), and any combination of a headache, flu-like aches and pains, a general sense of disorientation, and possibly even nausea and diarrhoea. The earlier malaria is detected, the better it usually responds to treatment. So if you display possible symptoms, *get to a doctor or clinic immediately*. A simple test, available at even the most rural clinic in Africa, is usually adequate to determine whether you have malaria. And while experts differ on the question of self-diagnosis and self-treatment, the reality is that if you think you have malaria and are not within easy reach of a doctor, it would be wisest to start treatment.

TRAVELLERS' DIARRHOEA Many visitors to unfamiliar destinations suffer a dose of travellers' diarrhoea, usually as a result of imbibing contaminated food or water, and Uganda seems to be particularly bad in this respect. Rule one in avoiding diarrhoea and other sanitation-related diseases is arguably to wash your hands regularly, particularly before snacks and meals, and after handling money (one birr notes in particular are often engrained with filth). As for what food you can safely eat, a useful maxim is: PEEL IT, BOIL IT, COOK IT OR FORGET IT. This means that fruit you have washed and peeled yourself should be safe, as should hot cooked foods. However, raw foods, cold cooked foods, salads, fruit salads prepared by others, ice cream and ice are all risky. It is rarer to get sick from drinking contaminated water but it happens, so stick to bottled water, which is widely available.

If you suffer a bout of diarrhoea, it is dehydration that makes you feel awful, so drink lots of water and other clear fluids. These can be infused with sachets of oral rehydration salts, though any dilute mixture of sugar and salt in water will do you good, for instance a bottled soda with a pinch of salt. If diarrhoea persists beyond a couple of days, it is possible it is a symptom of a more serious sanitation-related illness (typhoid, cholera, hepatitis, dysentery, worms, etc), so get to a doctor. If the diarrhoea is greasy and bulky, and is accompanied by sulphurous (eggy) burps, one likely cause is giardia, which is best treated with tinidazole (four x 500mg in one dose, repeated seven days later if symptoms persist).

BILHARZIA Also known as schistosomiasis, bilharzia is an unpleasant parasitic disease transmitted by freshwater snails most often associated with reedy shores where there is lots of water weed. It cannot be caught in hotel swimming pools, but should be assumed to be present in any freshwater river, pond, lake or similar habitat, probably even those advertised as 'bilharzia free'. The riskiest shores will be within 200m of villages or other places where infected people use water, wash clothes, etc. Ideally, however, you should avoid swimming in any fresh water other than an artificial pool. If you do swim, you'll reduce the risk by applying DEET insect repellent first, staying in the water for under ten minutes, and drying off vigorously with a towel. Bilharzia is often asymptomatic in its early stages, but some people experience an intense immune reaction, including fever, cough, abdominal pain and an itching rash, around four to six weeks after infection. Later symptoms vary but often include a general feeling of tiredness and lethargy. Bilharzia is difficult to diagnose, but it can be tested for at specialist travel clinics, ideally at least six weeks after likely exposure. Fortunately, it is easy to treat at present.

MENINGITIS This nasty disease can kill within hours of the appearance of initial symptoms, typically a combination of a blinding headache (light sensitivity), blotchy rash, and high fever. Outbreaks tend to be localised and are usually reported in newspapers. Fortunately, immunisation protects against the most serious bacterial form of meningitis. Nevertheless, other less serious forms exist, and a severe headache and fever – possibly also symptomatic of typhoid or malaria – should be sufficient cause to visit a doctor immediately.

RABIES This deadly disease can be carried by any mammal and is usually transmitted to humans via a bite or deep scratch. Beware village dogs and habituated monkeys, but assume that *any* mammal that bites or scratches you (or even licks your skin) might be rabid. First, scrub the wound with soap under a running tap, or while pouring water from a jug, then pour on a strong iodine or alcohol solution, which will guard against infections and might reduce the risk of the rabies virus entering the body. Whether or not you underwent pre-exposure vaccination, it is vital to obtain post-exposure prophylaxis as soon as possible after the incident. However, if you have had the vaccine before exposure treatment is very much easier. It removes the need for a human blood product (Rabies Immunoglobulin (RIG)) which is not pleasant to have, expensive and often hard to find. Death from rabies is probably one of the worst ways to go, and once you show symptoms it is too late to do anything – the mortality rate is 100%.

TETANUS Tetanus is caught through deep dirty wounds, including animal bites, so ensure that such wounds are thoroughly cleaned. Immunisation protects for ten years, provided you don't have an overwhelming number of tetanus bacteria on board. If you haven't had a tetanus shot in ten years, or you are unsure, get a booster immediately.

HIV/AIDS Rates of HIV/AIDS infection are high in most parts of Africa, and other sexually transmitted diseases are rife. Condoms (or femidoms) greatly reduce the risk of transmission.

TICK BITES Ticks in Africa are not the rampant disease transmitters that they are in the Americas, but they may spread tickbite fever along with a few dangerous rarities. They should ideally be removed complete as soon as possible to reduce the chance of infection. The best way to do this is to grasp the tick with your finger nails as close to your body as possible, and pull it away steadily and firmly at right angles to your skin (do not jerk or twist it). If possible douse the wound with alcohol (any spirit will do) or iodine. If you are travelling with small children, remember to check their heads, and particularly behind the ears, for ticks. Spreading redness around the bite and/or fever and/or aching joints after a tick bite implies that you have an infection that requires antibiotic treatment, so seek advice.

SKIN INFECTIONS Any mosquito bite or small nick is an opportunity for a skin infection in warm humid climates, so clean and cover the slightest wound in a good drying antiseptic such as dilute iodine, potassium permanganate or crystal (or gentian) violet. Prickly heat, most likely to be contracted at the humid coast, is a fine pimply rash that can be alleviated by cool showers, dabbing (not rubbing) dry and talc, and sleeping naked under a fan or in an air-conditioned room. Fungal infections also get a hold easily in hot moist climates, so wear 100% cotton socks and underwear and shower frequently.

AVOIDING MOSQUITO AND INSECT BITES

The *Anopheles* mosquitoes that spread malaria are active at dusk and after dark. Most bites can thus be avoided by covering up at night. This means donning a long-sleeved shirt, trousers and socks from around 30 minutes before dusk until you retire to bed, and applying a DEET-based insect repellent (around 50% DEET) to any exposed flesh. It is best to sleep under a net, or in an air-conditioned room, though burning a mosquito coil and/or sleeping under a fan will also reduce (though not entirely eliminate) bites. Travel clinics usually sell a good range of nets and repellents, as well as Permethrin treatment kits, which will render even the tattiest net a lot more protective, and helps prevent mosquitoes from biting through a net when you roll against it. These measures will also do much to reduce exposure to other nocturnal biters. Bear in mind, too, that most flying insects are attracted to light: leaving a lamp standing near a tent opening or a light on in a poorly screened hotel room will greatly increase the insect presence in your sleeping quarters.

It is also advisable to think about avoiding bites when walking in the countryside by day, especially in wetland habitats, which often teem with diurnal mosquitoes. Wear a long loose shirt and trousers, preferably 100% cotton, as well as proper walking or hiking shoes with heavy socks (the ankle is particularly vulnerable to bites), and apply a DEET-based insect repellent to any exposed skin.

EYE PROBLEMS Bacterial conjunctivitis (pink eye) is a common infection in Africa, particularly for contact-lens wearers. Symptoms are sore, gritty eyelids that often stick closed in the morning. They will need treatment with antibiotic drops or ointment. Lesser eye irritation should settle with bathing in salt water and keeping the eyes shaded. If an insect flies into your eye, extract it with great care, ensuring you do not crush or damage it, otherwise you may get a nastily inflamed eye from toxins secreted by the creature.

SUNSTROKE AND DEHYDRATION Overexposure to the sun can lead to short-term sunburn or sunstroke, and increases the long-term risk of skin cancer. Wear a T-shirt and waterproof sunscreen when swimming. When visiting outdoor historical sites or walking in the direct sun, cover up with long, loose clothes, wear a hat, and use sunscreen. The glare and the dust can be hard on the eyes, so bring UV-protecting sunglasses. A less direct effect of the tropical heat is dehydration, so drink more fluids than you would at home.

UNUSUAL MEDICAL PROBLEMS

SNAKE AND OTHER BITES Snakes are very secretive and bites are a genuine rarity, but certain spiders and scorpions can also deliver nasty bites. In all cases, the risk is minimised by wearing closed shoes and trousers when walking in the bush, and watching where you put your hands and feet, especially in rocky areas or when gathering firewood. Only a small fraction of snakebites deliver enough venom to be life-threatening, but it is important to keep the victim calm and inactive, and to seek urgent medical attention.

OTHER INSECT-BORNE DISEASES Although malaria is the insect-borne disease that attracts the most attention in Africa, and rightly so, there are others, most too uncommon to be a significant concern to short-stay travellers. These include dengue

fever and other arboviruses (spread by diurnal mosquitoes), sleeping sickness (tsetse flies), and river blindness (blackflies). Bearing this in mind, however, it is clearly sensible, and makes for a more pleasant trip, to avoid insect bites as far as possible (see box on page 91). Two nasty (though ultimately relatively harmless) flesh-eating insects associated with tropical Africa are *tumbu* or *putsi* flies, which lay eggs, often on drying laundry, that hatch and bury themselves under the skin when they come into contact with humans, and jiggers, which latch on to bare feet and set up home, usually at the side of a toenail, where they cause a painful boil-like swelling. Drying laundry indoors and wearing shoes are the best way to deter this pair of flesh-eaters. Symptoms and treatment of all these afflictions are described in greater detail on Bradt's website (*www.bradtguides.com/africahealth*).

OTHER SAFETY CONCERNS

WILD ANIMALS Don't confuse habituation with domestication. Most wildlife in Africa is genuinely wild, and might attack a person given the right set of circumstances. Fortunately, however, most wild animals fear people far more than we fear them, and their normal response to any human encounter is to leg it as quickly as possible, which means such attacks are rare, and they almost always stem from a combination of poor judgement and poorer luck.

The need for caution is greatest near water, particularly around dusk and dawn, when hippos are out grazing. Responsible for more human fatalities than any other large mammal, hippos are not actively aggressive to humans, but they do panic easily and tend to mow down any person that comes between them and the safety of the water, usually with fatal consequences. Never cross deliberately between a hippo and water, and avoid well-vegetated riverbanks and lakeshores in overcast weather or low light unless you are certain no hippos are present. Be aware, too, that any path leading through thick vegetation to an aquatic hippo habitat was most probably created by grazing hippos, so there's a real risk of a heads-on confrontation in a confined channel at times of day when hippos might be on land.

Crocodiles are more dangerous to locals but represent less of a threat to travellers, since they are unlikely to attack outside of their aquatic hunting environment. So don't bathe in any potential crocodile habitat unless you have reliable local information that it is safe. It's also wise to keep a berth of a metre or so from the shore, since a large and hungry individual might occasionally drag in an animal or person from the water's edge.

There are parts of Uganda where hikers might stumble across an elephant or a buffalo, the most dangerous of Africa's terrestrial herbivores. Elephants almost invariably mock charge and indulge in some hair-raising trumpeting before they attack in earnest. Provided that you back off at the first sign of unease, they seldom take further notice of you. If you see them before they see you, give them a wide berth, bearing in mind they are most likely to attack if surprised at close proximity. If an animal charges you, the safest course of action is to head for the nearest tree and climb it. And should an elephant or buffalo stray close to your campsite or lodge, do suppress any urge to wander closer on foot – it may well react aggressively if surprised!

An elephant is large enough to hurt the occupants of a vehicle, so if it doesn't want your vehicle to pass, back off and wait until it has crossed the road or moved off. Never switch off the engine around elephants until you're certain they are relaxed, and avoid allowing your car to be boxed in between an elephant and another vehicle (or boxing in another vehicle yourself). If an elephant does threaten

a vehicle in earnest and backing off isn't an option, then revving the engine hard will generally dissuade it from pursuing the contest.

Monkeys, especially vervets and baboons, can become aggressive where they associate people with food. For this reason, feeding monkeys is highly irresponsible, especially as it may ultimately lead to their being shot as vermin. If you join a guided tour where the driver or guide feeds any primate, tell him not to. Although most monkeys are too small to be more than a nuisance, baboons have killed children and maimed adults with their vicious teeth. Unless trapped, however, their interest will be food, not people, so in the event of a genuine confrontation, throw down the food before the baboon gets too close. If you leave food (especially fruit) in your tent, monkeys might well tear it down. Chimps and gorillas are potentially dangerous, but they are only likely to be encountered on a guided forest walk, where you should obey your guide's instructions at all times.

Despite their fierce reputation, large predators generally avoid humans and are only likely to kill accidentally or in self-defence. Lions are arguably the exception, though they seldom attack unprovoked. Should you encounter any large predator on foot, be aware that running away might well trigger its 'chase' instinct, and that it will win the race. Better to stand still and/or back off very slowly, preferably without making eye contact. If (and only if) the animal looks really menacing, then noisy confrontation is probably a better tactic than fleeing. Sleeping in a sealed tent practically guarantees your safety – but don't sleep with your head sticking out or you risk being decapitated through predatorial curiosity. Never store meat in the tent.

As for the smaller stuff, venomous snakes and scorpions are present but unobtrusive, though you should be wary when picking up the wood or stones under which they often hide. Snakes generally slither away when they sense the seismic vibrations made by footfall, though be aware that rocky slopes and cliffs are a favoured habitat of the slothful puff adder, which may not move off in such circumstances. Good walking boots protect against the 50% of snakebites that occur below the ankle, and long trousers help deflect bites higher on the leg. But lethal bites are a rarity – in South Africa, which boasts its fair share of venomous snakes, more people are killed by lightning!

When all's said and done, Africa's most dangerous non-bipedal creature, and exponentially so, is the malaria-carrying mosquito. Humans, particularly when behind a steering wheel, come in a close second!

CAR ACCIDENTS Dangerous driving is probably the biggest threat to life and limb in most parts of Africa. On a self-drive visit, drive defensively, being especially wary of stray livestock, gaping pot-holes, and imbecilic or bullying overtaking manoeuvres. Many vehicles lack headlights and most local drivers are reluctant headlight-users, so avoid driving at night and pull over in heavy storms. On a chauffeured tour, don't be afraid to tell the driver to slow or calm down if you think he is driving too fast or being reckless.

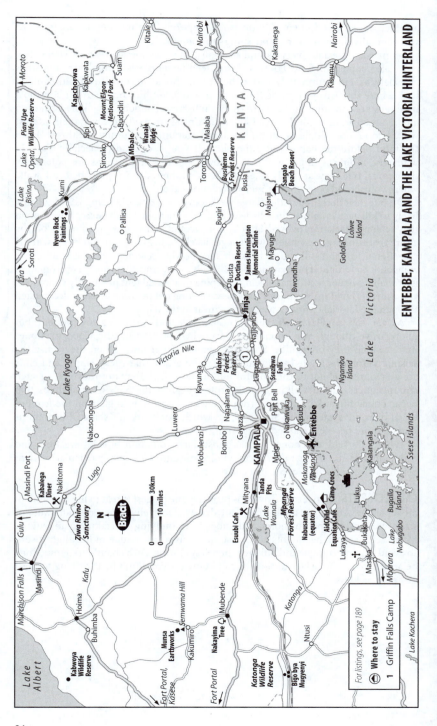

ENTEBBE, KAMPALA AND THE LAKE VICTORIA HINTERLAND

For listings, see page 189
ⓘ **Where to stay**
1 Griffin Falls Camp

Part Two

ENTEBBE, KAMPALA AND THE SOUTHEAST

OVERVIEW

The main port of entry to Uganda, Kampala – or more accurately nearby Entebbe, where the country's only international airport is lapped by the waters of Lake Victoria – is often perceived by tourists to be nothing more than a springboard to the legendary national parks of the southwest. But Kampala also lies at the hub of a varied and readily accessible set of attractions associated with the fertile lake hinterland and slopes of Mount Elgon on the border with Kenya. These include the Kasubi Tombs, Nakayima Tree, Tanda Pits and other sites associated with the Buganda Kingdom and its ancient Bachwezi forebears, as well as bird-rich jungle-like forests such as Mabira and Mpanga, and the self-evident attractions of Ziwa Rhino Sanctuary and Ngamba Island Chimpanzee Sanctuary. At the heart of it all, however, lies the vast island-studded expanse of Lake Victoria, and its primary outlet, the White Nile, whose long journey to the Mediterranean starts at Jinja, and is shortly afterwards punctuated by a succession of rapids renowned as one of the top two white-water rafting sites in Africa.

This section of the book is divided into six chapters. It starts, as do most trips to Uganda, with Entebbe, in a chapter that also covers Murchison Bay to the south of Kampala. The second chapter is dedicated to Kampala itself, while the third details a wide variety of standalone sites situated within easy day-tripping or overnight distance of the capital. The next three chapters respectively cover Masaka and the Ssese Islands to the southwest of Kampala, Jinja and the upper waters of the White Nile to its immediate east, and the more remote and relatively little-visited Kenya border region centred on Mount Elgon.

HIGHLIGHTS

KAMPALA It may not rank as one of the world's most compelling capitals, but perennially gridlocked Kampala – Uganda's only genuine city – has a lively nightlife and restaurant scene, while sightseeing highlights include the national museum and UNESCO-protected Kasubi Tombs. Pages 114–68.

ENTEBBE BOTANICAL GARDENS Forest birds and monkeys galore inhabit this lush century-old botanical garden running down to the Lake Victoria shore, 10 minutes' drive from the international airport. Page 110.

TANDA PITS This revered sacrificial site an hour's drive west of Kampala ranks as probably the most important traditional shrine in Buganda, with strong links to the creation legend associated with the medieval Bachwezi cult. Page 173.

ZIWA RHINO SANCTUARY One of East Africa's most exciting wildlife experiences is tracking white rhinos on foot at this well-wooded sanctuary *en route* to Murchison Falls and Kidepo Valley. Also a good site for shoebills. Pages 181–2.

MABIRA FOREST RESERVE The most important biodiversity hotspot within day-tripping distance of Kampala is home to 300 bird species, the endemic Uganda mangabey, and a thrilling new canopy zip line connecting six platforms. Pages 184–90.

SSESE ISLANDS Accessible by ferry from Entebbe or Masaka, these lushly forested islands in the heart of Lake Victoria arguably rank as Uganda's most underrated chill-out venue. Pages 209–15.

JINJA No longer the second-largest town in Uganda, sleepy but well-equipped Jinja retains a historic architectural flavour befitting its geographically poignant location overlooking the White Nile as it exits Lake Victoria. Pages 216–34.

BUJAGALI Overlooking the former Bujagali Falls (which are now submerged below an artificial lake), this village on the Upper Nile remains the heart of Uganda's white-water rafting and adrenalin tourism industry. Pages 234–46.

MOUNT ELGON Towering to a lofty 4,321m, this massive extinct volcano is a hiker's paradise, whether you ascend slowly to the caldera or just potter about in the vicinity of Sipi Falls on the western footslopes. Pages 259–67.

NYERO ROCK PAINTINGS Uganda's finest prehistoric rock art site was painted by unknown hunter-gatherers many hundreds – possibly thousands – of years ago. Pages 273–77.

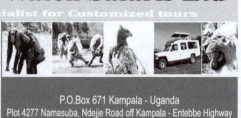

5

Entebbe

Tropical and verdant Entebbe, capital of Uganda during the colonial era, stands on the Lake Victoria shore a few hundred metres north of the equator and only 40km south of the modern capital Kampala. Though modestly proportioned by comparison to Kampala, Entebbe has long been the main port of entry to Uganda, thanks to the presence of the country's only international airport on the adjacent lakeshore. Yet for all its logistical significance, Entebbe is a remarkably unfocused and green town, carved haphazardly into the lakeshore jungle in such a manner that one might reasonably wonder whether most of its 70,000 residents haven't packed up their tents and gone on holiday.

Back in 1913, Sir Frederick Treves arrived at Entebbe fresh from the ports of Mwanza and Kisumu, and described it as 'the prettiest and most charming town of the lake … a summer lake resort where no more business is undertaken than is absolutely necessary. The town spreads in a languid careless way to the lake … the golf links are more conspicuous than the capital.' Almost a century later, as Entebbe entered the new millennium, it remained much as Treves had described it: surely the only former or extant African capital whose tallest buildings were dwarfed by the antiquated trees of the botanical garden, and whose golf course was more expansive than the nominal town centre.

Even today, Entebbe retains an unusually green feel, not least because its main roads divert around the market suburb of Kitoro, which shelters a sizeable proportion of our missing 70,000 residents. But, make no mistake, business is booming, much of it on the back of a service industry catering to a steady influx of UN personnel, tourists and other newly arrived air passengers. Indeed, unlike its soporific turn-of-the-millennium incarnation, Entebbe today is home to a quite extraordinary number of hotels and guesthouses, not to mention an excellent selection of eateries, banks, bars and shops (including a spanking new mall).

Entebbe's hotels vary widely in standard and character, but all have this much in common: they tend to be very expensive by comparison to other towns in Uganda. This situation presents many visitors with a dilemma: pay through the nose to stay in Entebbe, or head to Kampala for better value for money. Our advice, assuming you're just there for a night or two, and that natural history is your priority, is to stay in Entebbe. Any financial saving made by heading to Kampala will be offset by the tedium of sitting in the capital's appalling traffic. Better to use that time ticking off birds in Entebbe Botanical Garden, exploring the neighbouring Uganda Wildlife Education Centre, or relaxing on the beach before heading directly upcountry the following day. Similarly, a night in Entebbe prior to departure will (depending on the time of your flight) eliminate the possibility of missing your flight due to congestion in or *en route* from Kampala.

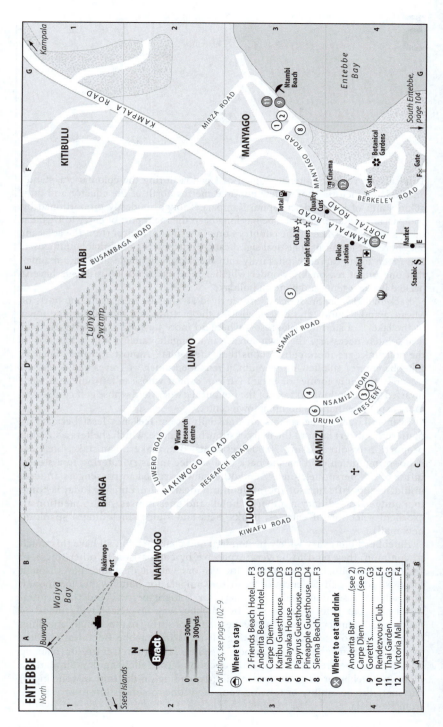

ENTEBBE
North

Kampala

KAMPALA ROAD

KITIBULU

KATABI

Lunyo Swamp

BUSAMBAGA ROAD

LUWERO ROAD

NAKIWOGO ROAD

RESEARCH ROAD

BANGA

NAKIWOGO

Nakiwogo Port

Waiya Bay

Buwaya

Ssese Islands

N

Brad

0   300m
0   300yds

LUGONJO

KIWAFU ROAD

LUNYO

NSAMIZI ROAD

Virus Research Centre

5

4

6   URUNGI

NSAMIZI

NSAMIZI ROAD

CRESCENT

3   7

MIRZA ROAD

MANYAGO

Ntambi Beach

Entebbe Bay

11   9

1   2

8

MANYAGO ROAD

Cinema

12

Gate

BERKELEY ROAD

Botanical Gardens

Gate

Total

Quality Cuts

Club XS

Knight Riders

KAMPALA ROAD

PORTAL ROAD

Police station

Hospital

Stanbic

Market

South Entebbe, page 104

Entebbe has been the main point of arrival for international arrivals to Uganda for about as long as the country has been receiving international visitors. The first such newbies consisted of a boatload of French missionaries who landed there in 1879 following a 300km lake crossing from Mwanza in present-day Tanzania. Theirs was a stormy and dangerous journey (legend has it that their boat disintegrated as soon as they made landfall) but the journey to Uganda soon became more comfortable with the completion of the Uganda Railway in 1901. A two-day train ride brought travellers from Mombasa to the Lake Victoria port of Kisumu for an overnight steamer voyage to Entebbe pier. Conveniently for arriving civil servants, Entebbe was the capital of the Uganda Protectorate with the offices of the British administration 5 minutes' walk uphill from the pier.

During the 1930s, Entebbe surrendered its mantle as Uganda's *entrepôt* to Kampala, firstly when the railway was extended there, leaving the lake steamers high and dry, and secondly with the introduction of the Empire flying boat service from the UK which landed in the relatively sheltered bay off Kampala's Port Bell rather than on Entebbe's choppy waters. Entebbe regained its status after technological advances made during World War II enabled non-stop flights from Europe to land there. Entebbe's bumpy airstrip was upgraded to create Uganda's first international airport in 1951. This first terminal (which was the site of the 1976 Entebbe Raid described below) is now the UN Regional Service Centre (which coordinates UN activities in Uganda's more temperamental neighbours), while passenger traffic passes through a second terminal. Entebbe served as the seat of government for much of the colonial era, but relinquished this status to Kampala – traditionally the head of the Buganda Kingdom – following independence in 1962.

Entebbe achieved instant immortality in June 1976 when an Air France airbus flying from Israel was hijacked by Palestinian terrorists and forced to land there. Non-Jewish passengers were released and the remainder held hostage against the demand that certain terrorists be freed from Israeli jails. In response, on 4 July 1976, a group of Israeli paratroopers stormed the airport in a daring surprise raid that resulted in all the hostages being freed. During the hijack, Amin pretended to play a mediating role between the Israeli government and the hijackers, but his complicity soon became apparent. A 75-year-old Israeli woman called Dora Bloch, who had been rushed into a Ugandan hospital after choking on her food, was killed by Amin's agents. Afterwards, incensed that the Israelis had been allowed to refuel in Nairobi before flying to Entebbe, Amin killed some hundreds of Kenyans resident in Uganda and broke off relations with his eastern neighbour, effectively ending the already tenuous East African community.

GETTING THERE AND AWAY

Entebbe lies at the end of a peninsula from which there are three main exits; the 40km Kampala Road; a cross-country route to join Masaka Road at Mpigi (for Bwindi and Lake Mburo); and lake transport. For details of **flights**, and getting between Kampala and the airport, see page 115.

BY PUBLIC TRANSPORT The road to Kampala is well served by matutus. These leave the capital every few minutes from the old taxi park and also from the junction of Entebbe and Nasser roads. Another park for Entebbe recently opened in the shabby

Katwe suburb but it's 15 minutes walk out beyond the old park and is not in an area you'd want to head for after dark. If travelling in the opposite direction, you'll find Entebbe's taxi park [104 D1] tucked away in the warts-and-all suburb of Kitoro, 1km south out of the town centre, off the Airport Road. You can also board matutus to Kampala opposite the Municipal Council office next to the Golf Club. If you're using public transport to travel from Entebbe to southwestern Uganda (or vice versa), you can dodge Kampala's central taxi/bus parks. Take a matatu to Natete taxi park on the southern edge of the city and transfer to a vehicle headed to your destination.

BY CAR   If self-driving to/from Entebbe, try to avoid peak traffic hours when the drive is a slow bumper-to-bumper crawl and the queues to enter or leave Kampala extend for some kilometres. Plan accordingly if heading to Entebbe to catch a plane. The appalling congestion should enjoy some respite in 2017 with the completion of a new dual carriageway from between Entebbe and the western end of Kampala's northern bypass.

If driving yourself, you can avoid the chaos of the capital entirely by heading north for 10km to Kisubi, where you can turn left and zig zag across country to Mpigi on the Kampala–Masaka–Mbarara Road.

BY FERRY   Entebbe's Nakiwogo port [100 B1] offers a free vehicle ferry across Waiya Bay to Buwaya, 20km from Mpigi. The ferry shuttles across the bay throughout the day from around 07.30. This option is less convenient for pedestrians; you'll probably have to take a boda to Mpigi where you'll be unlikely to find public transport going further west than Masaka. It is, however (if you're happy with a 16km boda ride), a useful route from Entebbe to Mabamba Swamp (pages 191–2). If the ferry schedule doesn't match yours, you can hire a boat to cross the bay for about US$3.

Nakiwogo is also the site of the daily passenger/vehicle ferry (dep 14.00) to Buggala Island in the Ssese archipelago (page 212).

WHERE TO STAY

Proximity to Uganda's primary airport – and primary international gateway – means that there is no shortage of accommodation in Entebbe for arriving and departing travellers. However, prices are considerably higher than Kampala and if you're on a budget, or looking for value for money, head north to the capital. Most of the listings below range from bland internationalism to decidedly ordinary. If your criteria include character as well as comfort, Lake Heights, The Boma, Gately in Entebbe, Carpe Diem, Karibu Guesthouse, Airport Guesthouse, Oasis, Skyway and Entebbe Backpackers stand out from the crowds in their respective categories. When booking, check whether your hotel offers a complimentary airport transfer (usually one transfer per guest, either arriving or leaving). If you're looking for the usual cluster of cheap lodges around the local taxi park (which in the case of Entebbe, is in the scruffy but bustling suburb of Kitoro, to the west of Airport Road, 1km from the official town centre) you're out of luck. Though suitably basic places exist, their prices (with the single exception of the Shade Guesthouse) are so inflated that better value for money is to be found in the budget listings.

UPMARKET

Lake Heights [104 D2] (33 rooms) Church Rd; \0312 208000; e info@lakeheightshotel. com; www.lakeheightshotel.com. The latest

addition to Entebbe's upmarket listings, Lake Heights occupies a modern, 3-storeyed building set in a delightful garden shaded by some spectacular mature trees. The highlight is a

The name Entebbe derives from the Luganda phrase 'Entebe za Mugala' ('Headquarters of Mugala', head of the lungfish clan) and thus literally means 'Headquarters' – somewhat prescient, given that it would later serve as the British administrative capital of Uganda. Entebbe's prominence as a harbour is essentially a modern phenomenon: even into the 1890s, it was too remote from the centre of Baganda political activity to be of comparable significance to Munyonyo and Kaazi on Murchison Bay. But Entebbe's potential was hinted at as early as 1879 by the French missionaries Lourdel and Amans, who noted that 'the port … is large and very well sheltered; on the shore there are no more than three or four houses for travellers'.

Entebbe's potential was first realised in 1896, with the arrival of a European steamship on Lake Victoria – shipped from Scotland to Mombasa, from where it was transported to Port Florence (Kisumu) in pieces by a caravan of porters! And it was sealed in 1901, when the railway line from Mombasa finally reached Port Florence, allowing travellers to and from the coast to reach Entebbe directly by the combination of train and ferry. Within two years, Entebbe had replaced Kampala as the colonial administrative capital – though Kampala would remain capital of the Buganda kingdom throughout the colonial era.

W E Hoyle, who arrived in Uganda in 1903, would later recall that Entebbe, not Kampala, 'was then regarded as the "metropolis" of Uganda'. This switch evidently occurred in 1901, judging by a lamentation published in the *Mengo Notes* late that year: 'The traders in Uganda are not very numerous … we know of … only two Germans [who] have both left Kampala and now appear to be doing chiefly wholesale business in Entebbe.' By 1903, certainly, Entebbe had a greater population of European residents than Kampala, most prominently the commissioner of Uganda and his administrative officers, who were 'mostly living in houses with thatched roofs'. By 1904, Entebbe even boasted a hotel, the Equatorial, evidently the precursor of the present-day Lake Victoria Hotel, owned by an Italian couple whose 'charming daughter,' according to Hoyle, 'became engaged to the first English postmaster …'. Neither knew the other's language, but both knew Swahili, so that little problem was solved.

Entebbe served as administrative capital of Uganda into the 1960s, and still houses a few government departments to this day, but its claims to outrank Kampala in the metropolitan stakes were rather more short-lived. Sir Frederick Treves wrote in 1913 that Entebbe 'is as unlike a capital as any place can well be, while as for administration it must be of that kind which is associated with a deck-chair, a shady veranda, the chink of ice on glass, and the curling smoke of a cigar'. Norma Lorimer, who visited 'gay little' Entebbe in the same year, paints a more pastoral picture: 'very tidy and clean and civilised … its gardens by the lake, full of gorgeous flowering trees and ferns, its red roads with no dust, and its enchanting views of the islands … Baganda moving about in their white *kanzus* on the red roads, silhouetted against a background of deep blue sky and tropical vegetation'.

rooftop bar/dining terrace that looks across the garden towards State House, the golf course & Lake Victoria. The en-suite rooms have AC & DSTV, & facilities include a swimming pool & gym. Good value for this category. *US$165/195 sgl/dbl B&B.* **$$$$**

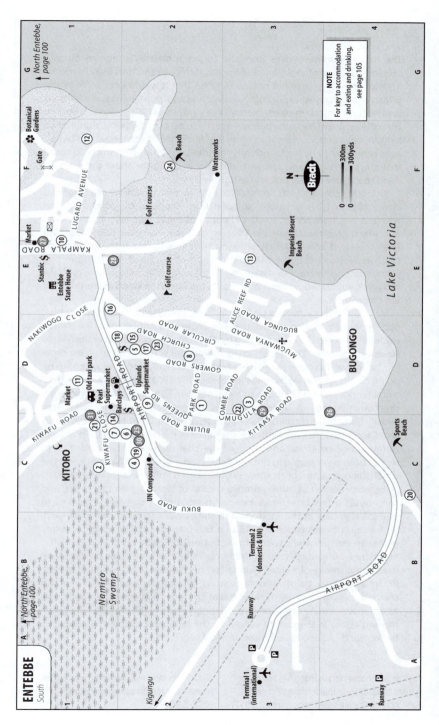

ENTEBBE
South

A ← *North Entebbe,* B
page 100

G ← *North Entebbe,*
page 100

Botanical
Gardens

Gate

Golf course

Beach

Waterworks

Imperial Resort
Beach

LUGARD AVENUE

Market

Stanbic $

Entebbe
State House

KAMPALA ROAD

NAKIWOGO CLOSE

Golf course

KITORO

Market

Old taxi park

Pearl
Supermarket

Barclays $

KIWAFU ROAD

KIWAFU CLOSE

Uplands
Supermarket

CHURCH ROAD

CIRCULAR ROAD

GOWERS ROAD

ALICE REEF RD

MUGWANYA ROAD

BUGUNGA ROAD

BUGONGO

PARK ROAD

COMBE ROAD

QUEENS RD

BULIME ROAD

CMUGULA ROAD

KITAASA ROAD

AIRPORT ROAD

UN Compound

BUKU ROAD

Namiro
Swamp

Kigungu

Terminal 2
(domestic & UN)

Runway

Terminal 1
(international)

AIRPORT ROAD

Runway

Sports
Beach

Lake Victoria

N

Bradt

0   300m
0   300yds

NOTE
For key to accommodation
and eating and drinking,
see page 105

104

⊖ **Where to stay**

1	Airport Guesthouse	D2	13	Imperial Resort Beach	E3
2	Airport View	C1	14	Kidepo Guesthouse	C1
3	Askay Suites	D3	15	Lake Heights	D2
4	Betty's	C2	16	Lake Victoria	E1
5	The Boma	D2	17	New Haven Guesthouse	D2
6	Camp Entebbe	C2	18	Oasis	D1
7	Capital Cave Garden	C1	19	Prestige Resort	C2
8	Entebbe Backpackers	D2	20	Protea	C4
9	Entebbe Flight Motel	D2	21	Shade Guesthouse	C1
10	Gately in Entebbe	E1	22	Skyway	D3
11	Glory Guesthouse	D1	23	Sunset Motel	D2
12	Imperial Botanical Beach	F1	24	Wildlife Education Centre	F2

✕ **Where to eat and drink**

25	4 Point	C2	29	Maanzo	D3
26	Faze 3	D4	30	Pulickal Hotel	C2
27	Four Turkeys	E1		The Red Rooster	(see 18)
	Gately in Entebbe	(see 10)	31	Smokie's Cantina	C1
28	Golf Club	E1			

Entebbe WHERE TO STAY

5

🏠 **The Boma** [104 D2] (16 rooms) Plot 20a, Gowers Rd; m 0772 467929; e boma@infocom. co.ug; www.boma.co.ug. In the quiet suburb behind the Lake Victoria Hotel, this welcoming, family-run guesthouse is so popular with inbound/ outbound tourists & expats that it's often full so be sure to book ahead. The Boma occupies a tastefully restored colonial homestead, which is well placed for the airport. A swimming pool is welcome on hot equatorial afternoons. *US$142/165/212 sgl/dbl/trpl inc full English b/fast on a lovely veranda.* **$$$$**

🏠 **Protea Hotel** [104 C4] (73 rooms) Airport Rd; 🕾 0414 323132; 0312 207500; e res1@ proteaebb.co.ug; www.protea.com/entebbe. If your priority is no-expense-spared comfort combined with good airport access, you'll appreciate the lakeshore Protea Hotel directly across the road from the end of Runway 2. The rooms are every bit as smart & well appointed (Wi-Fi, AC, hairdryer, etc) as you'd expect from this established South African hotel chain. Private balconies attached to the south-facing suites view Lake Victoria beyond a neat garden provided with a bar & lovely swimming pool. The cheaper rooms on the northern side face the car park, a dual carriageway & Runway 2. *US$235/275 sgl/ dbl for std rooms; US$235/315 deluxe sg/dbl & US$380/420 sgl/dbl for exec suites. B&B.* **$$$$$**

🏠 **Imperial Resort Beach Hotel** [104 E3] (more than 100 rooms) 🕾 0414 303000; e information@irbhcom; www.imperialhotels. co.ug. Known locally as the 'Blue Hotel', the interior

of this smart hotel is dominated by an imposing central atrium, 6 floors high, capped by a glass roof. Glass-sided lifts scale the walls to access 4.5m-wide carpeted corridors & internal balconies that lead to the truly sumptuous rooms. Glazed entirely in blue & sinuous in plan, the building's lengthy façade has been designed to suggest a wave, which is unfortunate since waves don't have balconies & neither does this hotel, making it a bit of an AC prison. *US$150/180 deluxe sgl/dbl, US$236/250 club rooms B&B.* **$$$$**

🏠 **Lake Victoria Hotel** [104 E1] 🕾 0414 351600/0312 310100; e ronnie.matovu@ laicohotels.com; www.laicohotels.com. This former government hotel exudes an atmosphere of tropical grandeur within smallish but immaculate grounds close to the golf course. Once the obvious choice for safari-goers & other travellers, the Lake Vic's dominance has been dented by consistently poor service, optimistic pricing & growing competition. The b/fast buffet remains excellent but other meals are rather ordinary (*US$8*). The lovely setting & swimming pool make the Lake Vic a smashing location for a day visit but given the alternatives, the prices seem a bit steep. *US$180/230 sgl/dbl B&B.* **$$$$**

MODERATE

🏠 **Carpe Diem** [100 D4] m 0793 396832; e carpediem.uganda@gmail.com; www. carpediemuganda.com. This smart new guesthouse overlooking Waiya Bay from the quiet Urungi

Crescent on the hillside above Kitoro has gained a reputation for consistently high standards of hospitality & food. The pristine lawn is a marvellous place to end the day with a drink as the sun sets over the lake. *US$100/124 sgl/dbl. B&B.* **$$$$**

🏠 **Karibu Guesthouse** [100 D3] (7 rooms) 84 Nsamizi Rd; m 0777 044984; e night@ karibuguesthouse.com; www.karibuguesthouse. com. This boutique guesthouse on the western side of town has quickly become a favourite with travellers using the airport. The en-suite rooms are individually furnished & colour-themed, & the rooftop dining terrace (just about with a lake view beyond a verdant tropical garden) is a fine setting for the beautifully presented meals. *US$125/135 sgl/dbl B&B.* **$$$$**

🏠 **Gately in Entebbe** [104 E1] (10 rooms) Portal Rd (the main road to the airport near the concrete rhino); ☎0414 321313; e stay@gatelyinn. com; www.gatelyinn.com. The en-suite rooms & cottages at this deservedly popular guesthouse are constructed & furnished using natural materials: stone, reed, wood, rough plaster & traditional fabrics. Though light sleepers may notice some traffic noise from the main road, the central dining/ lounging terrace, sheltered from elements above & enclosed by foliage, is a delightful spot to spend time. Continental meals US$10. An excellent gift shop is attached. *US$142/189 sgl/dbl B&B.* **$$$**

🏠 **Pineapple Guesthouse** [100 D4] (5 rooms) Nsamizi Rd; m 0782 460840; e pineappleguesthouse@gmail.com. This attractive new establishment occupies a refurbished villa with a quiet hillside location on the west side of town. Pineapple has 4 en-suite rooms, 2 with lake/sunset views & 2 facing the colourful garden, plus a garden cottage facing the swimming pool. Rates are B&B. Additional meals available on request. *US$70/90 sgl/dbl room, Garden cottage US$120.* **$$$**

🏠 **Sienna Beach** [100 F3] (16 rooms) Ntambi Dr; ☎0414 323363. The 1st-floor communal balcony & en-suite rooms at the front of this new lakeside hotel enjoy a terrific view over Lake Victoria & the adjacent Botanical Garden. Dodge the drab ground-floor bar/restaurant & eat out at one of the numerous lakeshore eateries on Ntambi Drive. *US$62/82/100/120 sgl/dbl/twn/trpl B&B.* **$$$**

🏠 **2 Friends Beach Hotel** [100 F3] (16 rooms) m 0772 236608, e stay@2friends.info, www.2friendshotel.com. Conveniently located close to the lakeshore & the town centre, this popular owner-managed lodge stands in small but green

gardens with a swimming pool & outdoor dining area & bar. The stylish, individually-decorated smoke-free rooms all come with wooden 4-poster bed, fitted nets, en-suite hot shower, fan, flatscreen DSTV & Wi-Fi. It has good left luggage facilities, while mountain bikes & kayaks are available free of charge. *US$150/180 sgl/dbl B&B.* **$$$$**

🏠 **Papyrus Guesthouse** [100 D3] (9 rooms) Uringi Crescent Rd; m 0787 778424; e info@papyrusguesthouse.com; www. papyrusguesthouse.com. This intimate new owner-managed guesthouse has a quiet but rather isolated suburban location in a renovated 1940s' building, about 10 mins' drive from the airport & 1km north of the town centre. The spacious en-suite rooms have fitted nets, & a terrace looks out over a large garden. Decent value. *US$85/120 sgl/dbl B&B.* **$$$$**

🏠 **Airport View Hotel** [104 C1] Off Airport Rd, Kitoro; ☎0312 261754. This smart hotel offers a friendly welcome & spacious, tiled rooms. A pleasant in-house restaurant serves good dinners for around US$11.50. *US$150/180 sgl/dbl B&B.* **$$$$**

🏠 **Imperial Botanical Beach Hotel** [104 F1] ☎0414 320800; e ibbhotel@afsat.com. Back in '98, the sparkling new Botanical Beach was the obvious choice to accommodate President Bill Clinton when he brought his circus into town. These days, sidelined by competition & changing tastes, it hosts conference delegates rather than heads of state – though the glory days may well return if internal fibreglass rock walls come back into vogue. A large, covered swimming pool & sandy lakeshore are redeeming features. *US$120/140/ sgl/dbl B&B for new wing rooms (old wing US$20 cheaper). US$130/150 sgl/dbl exec room.* **$$$$**

BUDGET

🏠 **Askay Suites** [104 D3] (25 rooms) Park Rd. Set in a green garden & with comfortable rooms provided with AC & DSTV, this new, 3-storey hotel is the smartest option in this category. Good value, too. *US$50/60/80.* **$$$**

🏠 **Entebbe Flight Motel** [104 D2] (88 rooms) Airport Rd; ☎0414 320812; e entebbeflighthotel@ gmail.com; www.entebbeflightmotel.net. The 60-room extension of this long-serving facility has been a long time coming & it's now so close to completion that they've opened it for business anyway. The rates are so reasonable that you'll be inclined to overlook any minor finishing touches awaiting attention. *US$35/45 en-suite sgl/dbl B&B.* **$$**

🏠 **Betty's** [104 C2] (4 rooms) Old Airport Rd opp the UN compound; m 0759 253251. Betty's popular Ethiopian Restaurant has a small number of affordable rooms upstairs. *US$25/30 & 30/40 en-suite sgl/dbl US$20 small en-suite sgl. All rates B&B.* **$$**

🏠 **New Haven Guesthouse** [104 D2] (10 rooms) Gower Rd; m 0772 586710; e info@ newhavenuganda.com; www.newhavenuganda. com. This smart villa is the converted family residence of a hospitable Ugandan couple who offer clean, tiled en-suite rooms at a reasonable rate. *US$40/50 B&B.* **$$**

🏠 **Airport Guesthouse** [104 D2] (8 rooms) Mugula Rd; ☎ 0414 370932; m 0777 086877; e postmaster@gorillatours.com. This deservedly popular little guesthouse is found off Park Rd in a quiet suburb where smart & comfortable en-suite rooms face a pretty garden. Conveniently located for the airport & very reasonably priced. *US$70/82/112 sgl/dbl/trpl B&B.* **$$$**

🏠 **Sunset Motel** [104 D2] (13 rooms) Church Rd; ☎ 0414 323502; m 0776 323501; e enquiries@sunsetentebbe.com; www. sunsetentebbe.com. Housed in a colonial bungalow in a pretty garden, this guesthouse offers comfortable tiled en-suite rooms plus some small but adequate rooms at the rear. *US$50/70/70 sgl/dbl/twin standard rooms, US$95 trpl/family room, US$40 sgl, budget rooms B&B.* **$$$**

🏠 **Camp Entebbe** [104 C2] (11 rooms) m 0783 414877. Off Airport Rd, behind the 4 Point (page 108). A small site contains a cluster of clean, tiled en-suite 2-unit cottages surrounding a pleasant thatched dining shelter. *US$30/40 sgl/dbl B&B.* **$$**

🏠 **Oasis** [104 D1] (8 rooms) Church Rd (corner of Airport Rd); m 0785 224475; e oasiscampsite@ gmail.com. This appendage to the Red Rooster sports bar (page 109) is good value. *US$40/50 sgl/ dbl, US$10 for smaller twin/dbl rooms sharing a spotless communal bathroom.* **$$**

🏠 **Wildlife Education Centre** [104 F2] (5 cottages) ☎ 0414 322169; e info@uwec.ug; www.uwec.ug. Have you ever wondered what happens in a zoo when the visitors go home? Try the basic but roomy en-suite bandas at UWEC. Twin beds are provided downstairs & on a mezzanine platform. Meals are available in the UWEC café. The cottages are several hundred metres inside the zoo; hire a boda-boda if you've got luggage & no vehicle. *US$50/70 sgl/family occupancy inc the zoo entrance fee.* **$$$**

🏠 **Capital Cave Garden** [104 C1] (12 rooms) Off Airport Rd behind 4 Point; m 0772 869774. You'll get better value for money in Kampala, but if you're in Entebbe for a night on a budget, this'll do fine. Eat snacks from the restaurant or wander up to 4 Point (page 108) for greater choice. *US$30/35 sgl/dbl B&B.* **$$**

🏠 **Entebbe Backpackers** [104 D2] (10 rooms) Church Rd; ☎ 0414 320432; m 0712 849973; e stay@entebbebackpackers.com; www. entebbebackpackers.com. This popular hostel fills a much-needed niche for affordable accommodation in Entebbe. Food is available & the lounge has DSTV. A selection of rooms including en-suite dorm cottages, each with a bunk bed of 2 sgl+ units. *US$14/27 sgl/dbl en suite; US$8/10 sgl/dbl shared facilities. Garden Cottages en-suite sgl US$16; Garden Cottage w/bathroom 2x sgl & bunk beds US$13pp; camping US$4. Rates excl b/fast.* **$$**

🏠 **Prestige Resort** [104 C2] (5 rooms) Old Airport Rd opp UN compound; ☎ 0414 320668. Basic guesthouse with clean, tiled en-suite rooms with own DSTV. *US$30 sgl, US$40–50 dbl B&B.* **$$**

🏠 **Anderita Beach Hotel** [100 G3] (40 rooms) ☎ 0414 322435; e anderitahotel@yahoo.com. Attractively located on the palm-lined Ntambi Rd, rooms at the front of the hotel enjoy lake views. A restaurant is attached plus a bar on the beach across the road. Guests have a choice of rooms based on prices rather than occupancy needs. *US$50/60/70 en-suite rooms.* **$$$**

SHOESTRING

Though Entebbe has a few hotels of shoestring standard the rates are anything but basic. With the exception of the authentic Shade Guesthouse, you'll find more attractive deals at comparable prices in the budget category above.

🏠 **Shade Guesthouse** [104 C1] (8 rooms) Kinyarwanda Rd, Kitoro. This basic lodge is the only place we found in Entebbe that combines shoestring facilities (perfectly acceptable rooms with nets & clean communal facilities) with appropriate rates. Snacks available on the premises or there are plenty of bars & BBQ joints close by. *US$8/9 dbl/twin.* **$**

🏠 **Skyway** [104 D3] (24 rooms) Mugula Rd; m 0700 951317. A dash of style, imagination & expense could transform this superb, 3-storey period building into Entebbe's most appealing hotel. As it is, the adequate rooms, pleasant upstairs bar/restaurant, spacious lawns & fair

prices make this a popular choice with budget travellers. *US$25/30 sgl/dbl en-suite B&B.* **$$**

🏠 **Kidepo Guesthouse** [104 C1] (20 rooms) Kitoro; ✆ 0414 322722. Though the rooms are now tiled & ensuite, the layout, with courtyard rooms behind a plain restaurant/bar, is classic shoestring. *US$35/35/53 sgl/dbl/twin.* **$$**

🏠 **Glory Guesthouse** [104 D1] (8 rooms with an extension under construction) Fulu Rd, Kitoro; ✆ 0414 321563; e gloryhouse@yahoo.com. Everything about this lodge close to the market & taxi park is distinctly ordinary – except the prices. *US$30/35 sgl/dbl en-suite B&B.* **$$**

✘ WHERE TO EAT AND DRINK

Entebbe is a great place in which to eat out, thanks to a broad choice of international cuisine (continental, Thai, Indian, Chinese and even a KFC) and the fact that everywhere is nice and easy to get to – unlike in Kampala where the appeal of going out for a meal is diminished by the bother of getting there. Entebbe's eateries are scattered widely throughout the town and the only location to vaguely resemble an entertainment hub is the lakeside Ntambi Road. This has a selection of bars and restaurants that include basic beer 'n' barbecue snack joints, the pleasantly rustic Goretti's pizzeria and the genteel Thai Gardens.

RESTAURANTS

✘ **4 Point** [104 C2] Airport Rd beside the Pulickal Hotel. This popular eating & drinking joint just past Barclays offers Entebbe's most extensive Indian & Chinese menu. Though the curries are sufficiently authentic to be a uniform brown, 'medium spiced' tends towards 'rather mild'. A bakery on the premises sells good bread and pastries. *US$8.*

✘ **Carpe Diem** [100 D4] 33 Urungi Crescent; m 0793 396832 Hillside guesthouse (pages 105–6) with a pleasant lawn facing Waiya Bay & a panoramic sunset (around 19.00 daily). Sandwiches, shakes, smoothies, consistently good 4-course dinners & reasonably priced daily specials. *US$8.*

✘ **Faze 3** [104 D4] Circular Rd at end of Airport Rd. Best steaks in town, so I'm told. Eat indoors if lake flies abound, or outside on a covered deck overlooking the lake. *Meals US$8–12.*

✘ **Gately in Entebbe** [104 E1] The covered terrace at this guesthouse is a particularly pleasant setting for a meal. Gately offers grills, salads, Thai dishes & an impressive selection of smoothies, juices, teas & coffees. *Main courses US$12.*

✘ **Maanzo** [104 D3] Park Rd. Rambling restaurant complex serving a wide-ranging but possibly over ambitious 'global menu' (grills, pastas, fish, Caribbean, etc). *Mains US$8.*

✘ **Golf Club** [104 E1] The veranda restaurant at the golf club offers grills, stews & burgers. Whole grilled tilapia is a speciality. *Meals US$6–10.*

✘ **Pulickal Hotel** [104 C2] The rooftop bar of this new, 4-floor hotel (still under construction when we visited) looks to be a great place to enjoy a meal & a drink with a 360° view.

✘ **Victoria Mall** [100 F4] Entebbe's brand new shopping mall offers branches of Café Javas & KFC. Though the choice in the food hall upstairs is still rather limited, a wall of foliage provided by the forest trees in the adjacent Botanical Garden creates a marvellous backdrop.

✘ **Thai Garden** [100 G3] Ntambi Rd; m 0786 572001; ⊕ closed Sun. Entebbe's best Thai cuisine is served in a pretty bungalow facing a tropical garden with the lake beyond. *US$9 excl rice.*

✘ **Goretti's** [100 G3] Ntambi Rd; m 0772 308887. This pizzeria has a smashing location right beside the lake. Service can be slow so this is not the place to spend your last couple of hours before a flight. Don't leave your passports & tickets in the car either while you dine. Cheaper meals are available in the adjacent lakefront bar run by the Anderita Beach Hotel (pages 107 & 109). *Meals US$8–13.*

✘ **Malayka House Orphanage** [100 E3] m 0790 554509 for directions. The Tue & Thu pizza nights (⊕ 06.00–22.00) at this children's home are popular with Entebbe residents & others in the know. Head down Nakiwogo Rd from the town centre towards Nakiwogo port but turn right at the sign for Entebbe Christian School. *Pizzas US$8, chocolate mousse US$3.*

BARS

The following listings all serve food but are primarily places to enjoy a drink or two.

Four Turkeys [104 E1] Kampala Rd. The town centre's liveliest hangout is an English-style pub full of prostitutes & UN operatives. Filling & inexpensive snacks such as burgers & toasted sandwiches are served. *Meals US$8.*

The Red Rooster [104 D1] Church Rd, on corner of Airport Rd. The place to watch live football events on DSTV. The pub's owner played for Watford during the Elton John era & the pub's large collection of sporting memorabilia includes a hilarious black & white picture of the be-wigged & bespectacled songster leading the team on to the pitch.

Rendezvous Club [100 E4] Kampala Rd. One of a cluster of open-air bars at the northern end of the town centre where you can drink inexpensive beer & nibble on meat (*US$1*) grilled on roadside BBQs.

Smokie's Cantina [104 C1] Opp taxi park, Kitoro. By far the most pleasant place to enjoy a drink & a game of pool in downmarket Kitoro. Roasted snacks have largely replaced the Tex-Mex menu but you'll still get a taco.

Anderita Bar [100 G3] Ntambi Rd. This basic waterfront bar is right on the lakeshore directly across the road from the related Anderita Hotel. This is a pleasant spot to enjoy a drink & snacks.

ENTERTAINMENT AND NIGHTLIFE

NIGHTLIFE The town's two main nightclubs, **Club XS** [100 F3] and **Knight Riders** [100 E3], are located on Kampala Road, 500m downhill from the town centre. A casino has recently opened on the Airport Road next to Red Rooster.

SHOPPING In the new Victoria Mall [100 F4], a Nakumatt supermarket is the town's best one-stop source of fresh meats, vegetables and bakery products. Elsewhere, you'll find **Pearl Supermarket** [100 D1] at the turning off Airport Road into Kitoro, and the perennial **Uplands Supermarket** [100 D1], aka 'John's shop' 100m further down the same road. The main market for fresh produce is also in Kitoro. **Quality Cuts** butchers/deli [100 F4] on Portal Road will provide you with the raw materials (or a ready-made sub sandwich) for a picnic in the botanical garden; gift shops are found at the Wildlife Education Centre, Gately in Entebbe guesthouse (page 106) and on Lugard Avenue near Golf View Hotel. **Lifestyle Tactical Training** [104 C2], a shop at the front of the Pulickal Hotel, sells rucksacks, hiking boots, multitools and torches from the US.

CINEMA The 2-screen Nu Max cinema (✆ *0392 176315*) in the new Victoria Mall shows recent international releases. Afternoon and evening screenings.

HAIRDRESSING Aisha Salon in the Victoria Mall keeps the UN crowd looking neat and tidy.

SWIMMING POOL The pool at the Lake Victoria Hotel is open to non-residents on payment of US$6.50. The Imperial Botanical Beach Hotel has a huge covered pool which you can use, also for US$6.50.

OTHER PRACTICALITIES

FOREIGN EXCHANGE Stanbic [104 E1] (*Kampala Rd*) and Barclays [104 D2] (*Kitoro junction on Airport Rd*) will change money, but expect long queues. Service at the forex next to Uplands supermarket (50m from Barclays) is quicker. Out of banking hours, hop on a matutu to the airport, where a number of private forex bureaux offer rates that are reasonable, though somewhat lower than you'd get in Kampala.

INTERNET Most guesthouses offer internet facilities and there are a couple of internet cafés on Kampala Road in the town centre.

MEDICAL The Kenyan AAR hospital chain has a branch in the Victoria Mall (☏ *0414 560900*). Pharmacies are prevalent throughout the town.

LUGGAGE STORAGE Rather than risk sitting in Kampala traffic when you should be checking in for your outbound flight at Entebbe Airport, it's more relaxing to leave the city early to spend a relaxed afternoon in Entebbe town. Both the Lake Victoria and Imperial Botanical Beach hotels (pages 105 and 106) are happy to store luggage for day visitors using the swimming pool or taking lunch. The Lake Vic has the nicer setting but the Botanical is more convenient if you want to wander down to the botanical garden or Wildlife Education Centre.

WHAT TO SEE AND DO

ENTEBBE BOTANICAL GARDEN [100 F4] (⊕ *daily; admission US$3.50, vehicle US$0.50 & a camera US$0.50*) Established in 1902, Entebbe's botanical garden is an attractively laid-out mix of indigenous forest, cultivation and horticulture, and a highly attractive destination to birdwatchers. The botanical garden offers an excellent introduction to Uganda's birds, ranging from Lake Victoria specials such as grey kestrel, yellow-throated leaflove, slender-billed weaver and Jackson's golden-backed weaver to the more widespread but nonetheless striking black-headed gonolek, red-chested sunbird, grey-capped warbler and common wattle-eye. In addition to various shorebirds, the impressive palmnut vulture and fish eagle are both common, and a pair of giant eagle owls is resident. Forest birds include the splendid Ross's and great blue turaco, as well as the noisy black-and-white casqued hornbill.

It is said that some of the early *Tarzan* films were shot on location in Entebbe – a thus-far unverifiable legend that gains some plausibility when you compare the giggling of the plantain-eaters that frequent the botanical garden with the chimp noises that punctuate the old movies. There are some mammals around – no chimps, of course, nor even the sitatunga and hippos that frequented the lakeshore swamps into the 1960s – but you can be confident of seeing vervet and black-and-white colobus monkeys, as well as tree squirrels.

On a less agreeable note, the botanical garden is a popular haunt for young men lacking funds for college fees and/or with ambitions to visit your home country. If you engage in casual conversation with people matching this description, don't be surprised if these topics crop up.

UGANDA WILDLIFE EDUCATION CENTRE [104 F2] (⊕ *daily; admission US$6.50/10 FR/FNR*) ☏ *0414 322169;* e *info@uwec.ug; www.uwec.ug*) The animal orphanage near the former Game Department headquarters was established as a sanctuary for animals which would be unable to fend for themselves in the wild, and it has played an important role in the protection of rare and threatened animals. Residents include a few lions (whose nocturnal vocalisations add a distinct sense of place to a night in any nearby hotel), a pair of reintroduced black rhinos, and a variety of smaller predators that are seldom seen in the wild. The aviary provides the most reliable opportunity in Uganda of getting a close-up shot of the renowned shoebill. In addition to a standard visit, there are also a couple of alternative scenerios. The popular half-day 'Behind the Scenes' tour does exactly what it says on the tin; indeed rather more since this particular tin is filled with pythons, giraffes, rhinos, crocodiles, etc (*US$70pp*). The new Chimpanzee Close Up (*US$290pp*) allows you to assist zoo staff in the on-site

chimpanzee sanctuary. Book through UWEC or (more reliably) the Entebbe-based Wild Frontiers (e *reservations@wildfrontiers.co.ug; www.wildfrontiers. co.ug*).

GOLF [104 E2] (f *fb.me/Entebbegolfclub; Non-members US$10, club hire costs US$6.50*) The open expanse of the 18-hole golf course sloping towards Lake Victoria is Entebbe's most distinctive feature on the drive towards the airport. It's one of few clubs worldwide where a hooked drive on the third might hit a rhino (in the neighbouring Wildlife Education Centre). Golfers should try for early morning or late afternoon starts to avoid the heat of the day.

UGANDA REPTILES VILLAGE (m *0782 349583; www.reptiles.ug; tourists pay US$5 & residents US$3.50; a boda from Entebbe costs about US$1.50*) Established to encourage Ugandans to respect reptiles, rather than automatically banging them on the head, this worthwhile destination lies on the northwestern edge of Entebbe, 3km off the main road. You'll find a variety of snakes, chameleons, monitor lizards and a couple of crocodiles. It's a pretty site on the edge of the extensive Waiya Swamp; boat and birding voyages are available on a channel cut through to the open lake. Bottled refreshments but no food is available.

THE KAMPALA ROAD AND MURCHISON BAY

As far as most visitors to Uganda are concerned, the 40km Entebbe–Kampala peninsula is nothing more than a transit route between the capital and the airport. It does, however, provide access to a few low-key attractions, some decent scenery and some worthwhile accommodation. While the road corridor itself is mostly a ribbon of suburban development, it runs parallel to the scenic Murchison Bay which extends north from Entebbe for 40km before terminating at Kampala's Port Bell. A number of side roads, indicated on the 'Uganda Maps' Sheet No 3, *Beyond Kampala*, run east to the shores of Murchison Bay leaving the suburban sprawl behind to explore some still-unspoiled countryside.

WHERE TO STAY AND EAT These listings include accommodation in Murchison Bay (extending south to Bulago Island) and along its western margin. For accommodation on the eastern side (accessed from Kampala's Ggaba port), see pages 142–4 in the Kampala chapter.

Upmarket

Pineapple Bay Resort (8 rooms) Bulago Island; 0414 251182; e info@wildplacesafrica. com; www.wildplacesafrica.com. This luxurious resort lies on the privately owned Bulago Island, 16km east of Entebbe & 2° south of the equator. It's a terrific place to relax with lakeside lawns, airy, open-sided lounges & spacious beachfront cottages. Massages, great fishing & long walks with picnics are on offer. Use the pool, not the lake – bilharzia risk is low but a large crocodile likes to sunbathe on an offshore rock. *US$300/460 sgl/dbl FB, boat from Munyonyo or Entebbe included for 2+ nights.* **$$$$$**

2 degrees south (6 rooms) Bulago Island; m 0776 709970; e stay@oneminutesouth.com; www.oneminutesouth.com. This gorgeous private house & swimming pool occupies a terrific clifftop site overlooking the lake. It's a self-catering setup, though meals can be provided. *Rates for up to 14 guests are US$850 for 1st night; US$650 2nd & 3rd nights. Further discounts for additional nights. Meals (FP) US$25pp/day. Rates inc boat transfer for up to 8 guests from Entebbe or Ggaba.* **$$$$**

Lake Victoria Serena (120 rooms) 5km off Entebbe Rd at Lweza; 0417 121000; e lakevictoria@serena.co.ug; www.serenahotels. com. This monumental development extends

across a 100ha lakeshore site, 5km from Kajjansi town on the Entebbe Road. The dirt road to the complex is pretty grim, but access from Entebbe and Kampala will become infinitely smoother when the Munyonyo spur of the new Entebbe Expressway opens in 2018. The interior of the main hotel is truly striking with a high, airy atrium inspired by Zanzibari architecture. If the connection seems slightly irrelevant, then you haven't seen the surrounding accommodation blocks; these are modelled on Roman insulae complete with classical arches, pastel-toned walls & terracotta roofs. Recreational options include a beautiful swimming pool, gym/sauna (*free for guests; day visitors pay US$10*), a daunting 9-hole lakeside golf course rippling with water hazards (*US$25/35 guests/visitors*), & lake excursions. For sheer style, the veranda of the golf clubhouse, which faces a tiny island containing the 9th green beyond a small but extremely exclusive marina, is difficult to beat in Uganda. A smashing location for a meal (*US$8–12*) or drink. *Weekday rates for the spacious & luxurious rooms are US$275/325 sgl/dbl & US$ 365/390 exec suites B&B. Significant discounts are offered at weekends.* **$$$$**

Moderate

🏠 **Country Lake Resort** (5 cottages) Garuga Rd; ☎ 0312 106482; www.countrylakeresort.com. Located beside the lake, this 2ha site is by far the smartest & most attractive of the cheaper lakeside resorts on Murchison Bay. It's also rather more appealing than a few other lakeside hotels on the same road. To get there, turn off Entebbe Rd on to

Garuga Rd at Kitala Trading Centre. *US$83/100 sgl/dbl cottage B&B.* **$$$**

Budget

🏠 **Banana Village** (10 cottages) Off Garuga Rd; **m** 0772 509692; www.bananavillageuganda.com. An appealingly rustic alternative to a night in Kampala or Entebbe, Banana Village offers a selection of cottages in a garden site adjoining remnant forest. Birders will enjoy looking for the 150+ resident bird species while others relax around the swimming pool & garden bar. Banana Village is a short distance down the Garuga Rd, 10km north of Entebbe. *Standard en-suite cottages US$45/85/85/120 sgl/dbl/twn/trpl, storeyed en-suite forest cottages (sleep 4) US$150, dorm US$20. All rates B&B.* **$$$**

Shoestring & camping

🏠 **Nabinoonya Resort Beach** (13 rooms, 5 dorm bandas) About 10km north of Entebbe; **m** 0774 972027; **e** ficnabinonya@yahoo.co.uk. A shady 30mins' walk from the Kampala Rd at Kisubi, this secluded lakeshore resort is a peaceful w/day retreat, though w/ends are crowded & noisy. The accommodation, though ordinary, is a cheap alternative to budget options in Entebbe. The large grounds are genuinely lovely, with remnant forest trees inhabited by red-tailed monkeys & plenty of birdlife. Also does food (*fish & chips US$5–6.50*). *US$8/13/13 en-suite sgl/dbl/twin, US$15 twins using common showers, US$8 bed in a 4-berth banda, US$2.50pp camping.* **$**

WHAT TO SEE AND DO

Kampala Snake Park This low-key attraction is signposted off the east side of the main Kampala–Entebbe Road, about 3km south of Kajjansi. It's then another 2km or so on dirt roads, also signed. It's not such a pretty site as that of Uganda Reptiles Village (page 111) but there is a greater selection of snakes displayed in glass-windowed bandas dotted around the site. A reasonable entrance fee is charged for a guided tour.

Zika Forest Officially a research site for the Entebbe-based Uganda Virus Research Institute (UVRI), this small (25ha) patch of remnant forest lies a couple of hundred metres off the Kampala–Entebbe Road at Kisubi, 23km from Kampala. If you've insufficient time to visit larger and better-known forests, or are short of money, a visit to Zika provides a cheap and convenient taste of a tropical forest. A small trail network explores the forest at ground level while a 36m-high metal tower (once used to ascertain what sort of bugs inhabit which strata of forest vegetation) provides a bird's- and monkey's-eye view across the top of the forest canopy (though the ascent, using a narrow metal ladder, may not be for everyone).

ZIKA FOREST

A research site for the Uganda Virus Research Institute, Zika Forest was thrust into the international limelight in 2016, thanks to the spread, across South and Central America, of a mosquito-borne virus first identified there in 1947. But before you run a mile from the place, there is no record of humans ever contracting the now famous Zika virus inside Zika Forest. The site of its discovery is less to do with Zika being a fetid reservoir for obscure diseases and more to do with the efficiency of UVRI methodologies. The first recorded Zika carrier was actually a sentinel monkey caged on a research tower during yellow fever studies. The only confirmed human victim in Uganda was a British UVRI student who was messing around with Zika strains isolated from infected mosquitoes in 1964. He described the fever as 'mild' and lived to write reams of literature on the subject. The next case, ten years later, also involved a lab assistant, this time in Mozambique, while the first outbreak, of 330 cases confirmed and 19,000 suspected, was in distant French Polynesia.

If using public transport from Kampala or Entebbe, ask to disembark at the entrance to Kisubi University. The turning to Zika is 200m north on the west side of the road, distinguished only by a sculpted concrete sign for 'Nook Gardens'. Finding the turning to Zika Forest when driving along the fast Entebbe Road is a little trickier. From Entebbe, follow the directions above. Coming from Kampala, your first landmarks are likely to be roadworks for the new Entebbe–Kampala Expressway, just beyond Kisubu village and then a Petro fuel station. It's then simplest and safest to overshoot the Zika junction and make a U-turn using the entrance to Kisubi University to find the Nook Gardens junction described above. The tin uniports that serve as the Zika offices are 200m down this track. Zika is geared towards school visits rather than tourists and the dour caretaker/guide commands only sufficient English to request and receive a visitation fee of US$6.50.

Lutembe Bay Ramsar Site This small (just 98ha) wetland on the eastern side of the Kampala–Entebbe Road is notable for seasonal Palaearctic (26 species) and Afro-tropical (15) migrants. Regular surveys by Nature Uganda have recorded an average of 1,429,829 wetland birds. These include an average of 1,048,602 white-winged black terns, a figure representing more than half of the global population. The 108 species of waterbird recorded at the site include the globally vulnerable shoebill, Madagascar squacco heron, and the papyrus yellow warbler, the near-threatened papyrus gonolek, great snipe, African skimmer and pallid harrier, and 24 regionally threatened species such as the northern brown-throated weaver, greater cormorant, slender-billed gull and (as mentioned above) quite a lot of white-winged black terns. As far as getting there is concerned, contact one of the specialist bird guides (pages 63–4) and arrange an excursion to get the best out of your visit.

Garuga Motocross Circuit Uganda MotoX Club puts on regular, weekend events at its lakeside circuit, 10km off the Entebbe–Kampala Road on Garuga Peninsula. Competitions, which include club, national and regional-level events, make for a fun afternoon out. For details contact club director Arthur Blick (m *0772 506380*; e *ablickjr@hotmail.com*).

6

Kampala

Situated on rolling hills some 10km inland of the lake, Kampala, the economic and social hub of Uganda, is the archetypal African capital – more verdant than many of its counterparts, not quite so populous or chaotic as others – but essentially the familiar juxtaposition of a bustling compact high-rise city centre rising from a leafy suburban sprawl, increasingly organic in appearance as one reaches its rustic periphery.

As a city, Kampala's history dates back to the arrival of Captain Frederick Lugard, who established his camp on the stumpy Kampala Hill in 1890. However, the more prominent of the surrounding hills had already been used by the Bugandan *kabakas* for their *kibugas* (citadels). Kasubi Hill, only 2.5km northwest of the modern city centre, served briefly as the capital of Kabaka Suuna II in the 1850s, and it also housed the palace of Kabaka Mutesa I from 1882–84, while Mengo Hill formed the capital of Mutesa's successor Mwanga, as it has every subsequent kabaka. The name Kampala derives from the Luganda expression Kosozi Kampala – Hill of Antelope – a reference to the domestic impala that cropped the lawns of Mengo during Mutesa's reign.

In the first decade of the post-independence era, Kampala was widely regarded to be the showpiece of the East African community: a spacious garden city with a cosmopolitan atmosphere and bustling trade. It was also a cultural and educational centre of note, with Makerere University regarded as the academic heart of East Africa. Under Idi Amin, however, Kampala's status started to deteriorate, especially after the Asian community was forced to leave Uganda. By 1986, when the civil war ended, Kampala was in complete chaos: skeletal buildings scarred with bullet holes dotted the city centre, shops and hotels were boarded up after widespread looting, and public services had ground to a halt, swamped by the huge influx of migrants from war-torn parts of the country.

Thirty years later, Kampala is practically unrecognisable from the dire incarnation of the mid 1980s. The main shopping area along Kampala Road might be that of any African capital, while the edge of the city centre has seen the development of a clutch of bright, modern supermarkets and shopping malls. The area immediately north of Kampala Road, where foreign embassies and government departments rub shoulders with renovated tourist hotels, is as smart as any part of Nairobi or Dar es Salaam. Admittedly it's a different story downhill of Kampala Road where overcrowded backstreets, congested with hooting matutus and swerving boda drivers, reveal a more representative face of Kampala – the city as most of its residents see it.

Kampala is not only smarter than it used to be but considerably larger. These days it covers almost 200km² as the population has risen from 330,000 in 1969 to at least 1.8 million inhabitants today if one includes the contiguous Kira town council – a figure easily ten times greater than any other town in Uganda.

If you're looking for a smart, international-standard hotel (or indeed a good value budget hotel), a splendid choice of cuisine, shopping opportunities, live music and

the latest movie – or just a taste of urban African life – you'll probably love Kampala. Compared with the likes of Nairobi or Dar es Salaam, it's a remarkably safe city to explore. If, however, your main reason for visiting Uganda is its natural history, then you'll be much better off staying a night in Entebbe and then pushing on upcountry. Sightseeing options in and around Kampala are in any case pretty limited (pages 156–66), but the main reason for giving the capital a wide berth is the horrendous traffic that results as the resident population, swollen by daily commuters from surrounding districts, attempts to move around in a motley assortment of private vehicles, buses, matatus and boda. If you *do* stay in Kampala, establish what you want to do and find lodgings in that part of town. Spending the evening sitting in 'the jam' instead of a selected restaurant or cinema is no fun at all. Of course, if you're at home on a boda and happy for the lunatic of your choice to whizz you through the gridlock, then ignore this paragraph and have fun!

GETTING THERE AND AWAY

BY AIR Fly-in visitors will arrive in Uganda at **Entebbe International Airport**, which lies on the Lake Victoria shore about 3km from Entebbe Town. If you arrive outside banking hours, there are 24-hour foreign-exchange facilities at the airport. Historically, these used to offer dreadful rates compared with private forex bureaux in Kampala, and while their rates have improved of late, it's still worth waiting until you get into town for larger sums. Special hire taxis licensed to operate within the airport are marked 'Airport Taxi' and identified by their yellow stripe. Pick a driver from the throng outside the arrivals door or visit the adjacent Taxi Office (0414 321292) inside the building. Expect to pay US$6 to Entebbe and US$30 to Kampala. Airport collection can also be arranged in advance through most tour operators and upmarket hotels in Kampala and Entebbe. Several of the latter send their buses along to pick pre-booked clients and hopefully some additional trade.

There are no buses between Kampala and Entebbe, but matutus leave from both the old and the new taxi parks and from the Entebbe Road end of Nasser Road. The cheapest option is to take a shared taxi from the airport to the taxi park in Entebbe's Kitoro suburb, 4km away, where you can hop on a matutu to Kampala. Subject to the usual misgivings about local driving standards, this is safe enough during daylight hours, but a pretty scary introduction to Uganda after dark. If you do arrive in Kampala (or any major African city) after dark with all your luggage, it's best to find a reasonable bed quickly and wait for the morning to locate more comfortable/affordable/quieter lodgings if this proves necessary.

Airlines The following international airlines fly into/out of Entebbe:

✈ **Brussels Airlines** [127 E2] 0414 234200–2; http://uganda.brusselsairlines.com
✈ **EgyptAir** [127 F3] 0414 233960; m 0772 200119; www.egyptair.com
✈ **Emirates** [127 H3] 0414 349941–4; www.emirates.com
✈ **Ethiopian Airways** [127 H3] 0414 345577/8; www.flyethiopian.com
✈ **Etihad Airways** 0312 314438; www.etihad.com
✈ **Fast Jet** m 0750 080190; www.fastjet.com

✈ **Kenya Airways** [104 B4] 0312 236000/0414 233068; www.kenya-airways.com
✈ **KLM Royal Dutch Airlines** [104 B4] 0414 338000/1; www.klm.com
✈ **Rwandair** [127 F2] 0414 344851; www.rwandair.com
✈ **South Africa Airways** [127 G4] 0414 255501/2; www.saa.co.za
✈ **Turkish Airlines** [104 B2] m 0788 006296; www.turkishairlines.com

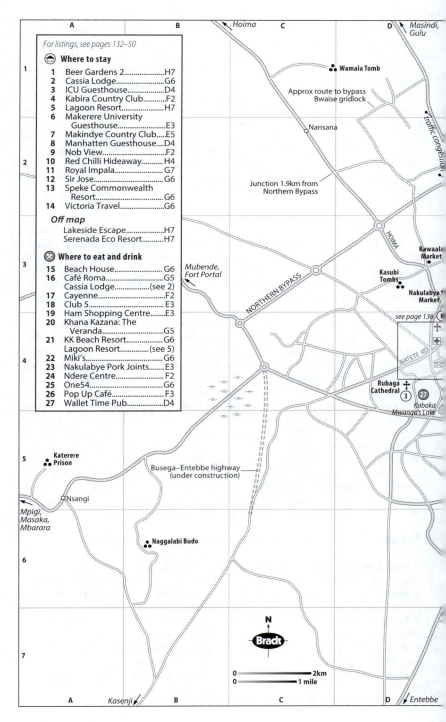

For listings, see pages 132–50

Where to stay
1   Beer Gardens 2....................H7
2   Cassia Lodge..........................G6
3   ICU Guesthouse...................D4
4   Kabira Country Club............F2
5   Lagoon Resort.......................H7
6   Makerere University
        Guesthouse.........................E3
7   Makindye Country Club.....E5
8   Manhatten Guesthouse....D4
9   Nob View................................F2
10   Red Chilli Hideaway...........H4
11   Royal Impala.........................G7
12   Sir Jose..................................G6
13   Speke Commonwealth
        Resort.................................G6
14   Victoria Travel......................G6

Off map
     Lakeside Escape....................H7
     Serenada Eco Resort...........H7

Where to eat and drink
15   Beach House..........................G6
16   Café Roma...............................G5
     Cassia Lodge..................(see 2)
17   Cayenne....................................F2
18   Club 5..E3
19   Ham Shopping Centre........E3
20   Khana Kazana: The
        Veranda..............................G5
21   KK Beach Resort...................G6
     Lagoon Resort..............(see 5)
22   Miki's.......................................G6
23   Nakulabye Pork Joints........G6
24   Ndere Centre.........................F2
25   One54.......................................G6
26   Pop Up Café............................F3
27   Wallet Time Pub..................D4

Hoima

Masindi,
Gulu

Wamala Tomb

Approx route to bypass
Bwaise gridlock

Nansana

Traffic congestion

Junction 1.9km from
Northern Bypass

HOIMA

Kawaala
Market

Mubende,
Fort Portal

Kasubi
Tombs

NORTHERN BYPASS

Nakulabye
Market

see page 136

NATETE RD

Rubaga
Cathedral

Kabaka
Mwanga's Lake

Katerere
Prison

Busega–Entebbe highway
(under construction)

Nsangi

Mpigi,
Masaka,
Mbarara

Naggalabi Budo

N

Bradt

0 ————————— 2km
0 ————————— 1 mile

Kasenji

Entebbe

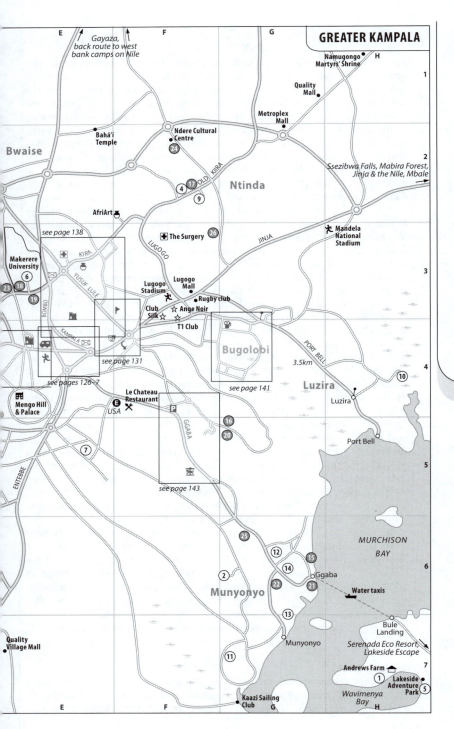

GREATER KAMPALA

Gayaza,
back route to west
bank camps on Nile

Namugongo
Martyrs' Shrine

Quality
Mall

Metroplex
Mall

Bahá'í
Temple

Bwaise

Ndere Cultural
Centre 24

OLD KIRA

Ntinda

4 17
9

Ssezibwa Falls, Mabira Forest,
Jinja & the Nile, Mbale

AfriArt

see page 138

The Surgery 26

Mandela
National
Stadium

JINJA

LUGOGO

Makerere
University 6

KIRA

23 18

19

YUSUF LULE

BOMBO

Lugogo
Stadium

Lugogo
Mall

Rugby club

Club
Silk ☆ ☆ Ange Noir

T1 Club

see page 131

Bugolobi

PORT BELL

3.5km

Luzira

see pages 126~7

KAMPALA

10

Luzira

Mengo Hill
& Palace

Le Chateau
Restaurant

E
USA ✗

P

GGABA

see page 141

16

20

Port Bell

see page 143

7

ENTEBBE

25

*MURCHISON
BAY*

12

14

15

2

Munyonyo

22

Ggaba

21

Water taxis

13

Bule
Landing

Quality
Village Mall

Munyonyo

*Serenada Eco Resort,
Lakeside Escape*

11

Andrews Farm

1

Lakeside
Adventure
Park 5

*Wavimenya
Bay*

Kaazi Sailing
Club

Kampala lies at the political and geographical heart of the Kingdom of Buganda, home to the Baganda (singular Muganda), who form the largest single ethnic group in Uganda, comprising more than 20% of the national population. The kingdom originally consisted of four counties: Kyadondo, Busiro, Busujju and Mawokota. It expanded greatly during the early to mid 18th century, mainly at the expense of Bunyoro, to extend over 20 counties, as well as the semi-autonomous Ssese Islands. During the colonial era, Buganda remained a kingdom with unique privileges, but it was relegated to provincial status after Obote abolished the monarchy in 1966. Today, Buganda is divided across nine administrative districts: Kampala, Mpigi, Mukono, Masaka, Kalangala, Kiboga, Rakai, Sembabule and Mubende.

Buganda is ruled by a kabaka, an autocratic monarch whose position, though hereditary, is confined to no single clan. Traditionally, the kabaka would marry into as many clans as possible – Stanley estimated Mutesa's female entourage to number 5,000, of which at least one-tenth were members of the royal harem – and his heir would take the clan of his mother, a custom that encouraged loyalty to the throne insofar as each of the 52 clans could hope that it would one day produce a king. Mutesa, who held the throne when Speke arrived in Buganda in 1862, is listed by tradition as the 30th kabaka. Although the dates of Mutesa's predecessors' reigns are a matter for conjecture, an average duration of a decade would place the foundation of Buganda in the mid 16th century, while 20 years would push it back into the 13th century.

The founding kabaka of Buganda was Kintu, who, it is widely agreed, came to power after defeating a despotic local ruler called Bemba. Kintu is otherwise the subject of several conflicting traditions. Some say that he descended from the heavens via Bunyoro, others that he originated from the Ssese Islands, or was indigenous to the area, or – most credible perhaps – that he arrived in Buganda from beyond Mount Elgon, suggesting an origin in Sudan or Ethiopia. The identity of Kintu is further confused by the Kiganda creation legend asserting that the first man on earth, though presumably a totally different person, was also called Kintu (see box *In the Beginning*, page 174, and *The Two Kintus,* page 120). A common tradition holds that Kintu, having defeated the unpopular Bemba, took over his house at Nagalabi Buddo, about 20km west of present-day Kampala, as a spoil of victory. The house was called Buganda, a name that was later transferred to all the territory ruled by Kintu. Nagalabi Buddo remains the coronation site of the kabaka to this day.

Traditional Buganda society allowed for some upward and downward mobility – any talented person could rise to social prominence – but it was nevertheless strongly stratified, with three distinct classes recognised. The highest class was the hereditary Balangira (aristocracy), which based its right to rule on royal blood. In addition to the kabaka, several aristocratic figureheads were recognised, including the *namasole* (queen mother), *lubuga* (king's sister) and *katikiro* (prime minister). Other persons who occupied positions of political and social importance were the *gabunga* and *mujasi*, the respective commanders of the royal navy and army.

Travel companies

BCD Travel Bandali Rise behind Village Mall, Bugolobi; ☏04142 346667; www.bcdtravel.co.ug
Global Interlink Travel Services [127 F3]

Grand Imperial Hotel; ☏04142 35233; e global@global-interlink.org; www.global-interlink.org
Intek Travel Balikuddembe Rd, Naguru; ☏0414

The middle class in Baganda society consisted of chiefs or *baami*. Initially, the status of the baami was hereditary, enjoyed solely by the *bataka* (clan heads). After 1750, however, *bakopi* men could be promoted by royal appointment to baami status, on the basis of distinguished service and/or ability. A hierarchic system of chieftaincy existed, corresponding with the importance of the political unit over which any given chief held sway. The most important administrative division was the Saza (county), each of which was ruled by a Saza chief. These were further subdivided into Gombolola (sub-counties), then into parishes and sub-parishes, and finally Bukungu, which were more or less village units. The kabaka had the power to appoint or dismiss any chief at will, and all levels of baami were directly responsible to him.

At the bottom of the social strata was the serf class known as the *bakopi*: literally, the people who don't matter. The bakopi were subsistence farmers, whose labour (as tends to be the case with those who matter not to their more socially elevated masters) formed the base of Buganda's agricultural economy. Many bakopi kept chickens and larger livestock, but they were primarily occupied with agriculture – the local staple of bananas, supplemented by sweet potatoes, cassava, beans and green vegetables. The bakopi were dependent on land to farm, but they had no right to it. All land in Buganda was the property of the kabaka, who could allocate (or rescind) the right of usage to any subsidiary chief at whim. The chiefs, in turn, allocated their designated quota of land as they deemed fit – a scenario that encouraged the bakopi to obedience. Peasant men and women were regularly sacrificed by the aristocracy – Kabaka Suuna, during one bout of illness, is said to have ordered 100 bakopi to be slaughtered daily until he was fully recovered.

Kiganda, the traditional religion of Buganda (discussed more fully in the box on pages 186–7), is essentially animist, in thrall not to a supreme being but rather a variety of ancestral and other spirits. Temples dedicated to the most powerful spirits were each served by a medium and a hereditary priest, who would liaise between the spirit and the people. The priests occupied a place of high religious and political importance – even the most powerful kabaka would consult with appropriate spirit mediums before making an important decision or going into battle. The kabaka appointed at least one female slave or relative to tend each shrine and provide food and drink to its priest and medium.

The traditions of Buganda are enormously complex, and the kingdom's history is packed with incident and anecdote. The above is intended as a basic overview, to be supplemented by more specific information on various places, events, characters and crafts elsewhere in this book. Readers whose interest is whetted rather than sated by this coverage are pointed to the informative website www.buganda.com, and to Richard Reid's excellent *Political Power in Pre-Colonial Buganda* (James Currey, 2002), a comprehensive source of information about most aspects of traditional Baganda society. Many old and out-of-print editions of the *Uganda Journal* also contain useful essays on pre-colonial Buganda – they can be viewed at the Uganda Society Library in the National Museum of Uganda in Kampala (page 155).

342907; e fly@intektravel.com; www.intektravel.com
Travelcare [117 F3] Unit 16, Lugogo Mall;
m 0754 222600; e declan@travelcare.co.ug;
www.travelcare.co.ug

Uganda Travel Bureau [127 H3] ✆ 0312 223255/0414 335335 (emergency 24hr line: m 0772 232555); e info@utb.co.ug; www.utb.co.ug

Intriguingly, Kiganda tradition holds that Kintu, the founding Kabaka of Buganda, shares his name with Kintu, the first man on earth (see box *In the Beginning*, page 174). As result, outsiders tend to assume that these two seminal personages are one and the same figure, a more-or-less mythical embodiment of the creation both of mankind and of Buganda. Muganda traditionalists, however, tend to assert otherwise. Yes, many would concede that Kintu and his wife Nambi, the first people on earth, are allegorical 'Adam and Eve'-like figures whose story has little basis in historical fact. But not so Kintu, the founder of Baganda, who is both a wholly separate person, and a genuine historical figure.

The 'two Kintus' claim is legitimised by the contrast between the unambiguous absence of other humans in the creation myth, and the presence of humanity explicit in any foundation legend in which one king defeats another king and rules over his former subjects. There is a popular Kiganda saying, derived from the mythical Kintu's last words, that translates as 'Kintu's children will never be removed from the face of the earth.' And if this saying does pre-date the foundation of Buganda, then it is plausible – even likely – that the founder of Buganda would have adopted Kintu as his throne name, with the deliberate intention of legitimising his rule by association with the mythical father of mankind.

BY RAIL Travelling by train is not an option at present. There used to be two slow and unreliable internal rail services in Uganda, one connecting Kampala to Kasese in the west, and the other connecting Kampala to Pakwach via Tororo and Gulu. A third, regional, service ran between Kampala and Nairobi and was once the most attractive means of transport between these cities. However, all three routes shut down during the 1990s. Rebel attacks forced the closure of the Gulu line while the other services were cancelled due to the poor state of the tracks. The Tororo–Pakwach track is currently being reconstructed and we're told that the Kasese line will also reopen. In the meantime, passenger services in Uganda are limited to a commuter shuttle, initiated in 2015, between Kampala Railway Station and Namboole Industrial Park on the eastern edge of the city.

BY BOAT Despite the obvious potential of the world's second-largest freshwater body for regional navigation, it's been years since any official passenger boats ran out of Port Bell, Uganda's main ferry port, 10km southeast of Kampala. The ferry service linking Port Bell and Mwanza (Tanzania) was aborted following the sinking of the MV *Bukoba* in 1996 (in which as many as 1,000 people are thought to have drowned). Cargo boats between Port Bell and Mwanza will sometimes take passengers, however. Otherwise, the only lake service relevant to travellers crossing between Tanzania and Uganda is a thrice-weekly overnight ferry from Mwanza to Bukoba, which connects with a direct bus service to Kampala via Masaka

ROAD TRANSPORT

Buses Most bus services from Kampala to upcountry destinations operate out of, or from sites close to, the central bus station. Officially titled the Qualicell Bus Terminal, it is more commonly known as the Buganda bus park [126 B4]. This lies

Kampala might have long outgrown its initial seven hills but it remains a simple matter to stay orientated within the urban sprawl. Uganda's capital covers a landscape of distinct hills separated by swampy valleys draining into Lake Victoria. Many of these hills, both the historic seven (those included here are marked *) and others settled more recently, bear landmarks that mean that you need never get completely lost in Greater Kampala. This happy situation contrasts starkly with, say, Nairobi and Dar es Salaam, where geography is less helpful.

The city's most obvious reference point is the modern multi-storeyed city centre on Nakasero Hill. This is ringed by more discreet, but no less identifiable, landmarks on neighbouring summits. These are described here moving clockwise around Nakasero, starting with **Old Kampala Hill***, just a few hundred metres southwest of the city centre. This stumpy knoll attained initial significance as the site of Lugard's 1899 encampment, but since the 1970s has provided central Kampala with its most dramatic reference point. Initially, this was the shell of an unfeasibly tall tower, noted for a distinct list halfway up, rising above an incomplete mosque initiated by Idi Amin. This well-loved folly was demolished around 2001 to make way for the magnificent new Old Kampala National Mosque (pages 157–8) with its more practically proportioned tower. Due south of Old Kampala, the kabaka's palace stands on the broad, low hill of **Lubiri*** (page 160). This circular area, a full kilometre in diameter, remains mostly undeveloped and is conspicuous as a green expanse, enclosed within a crumbling brick wall in an area of low-rent housing and workshops. Lubiri is neighboured by **Namirembe*** and **Rubaga*** hills, topped by the Anglican and Catholic cathedrals respectively. St Paul's on Namirembe is identified by its dome (more modest than that of its London namesake but still striking) and Rubaga Cathedral by two bell towers. Moving northeast from Namirembe, the white bell tower of Uganda's oldest university is visible on the leafy ridge of Makerere. Looking north from Kisementi and Kiira Road, the striking Bahá'í temple is conspicuous on a grassy hill off the Gayaza road. Immediately behind Kisementi is leafy Kololo, the city's highest hill and the site of many embassies and diplomatic residences. South of Jinja Road, a cluster of white minarets and palm trees mark **Kibuli*** Mosque, where Uganda's first Islamic visitors settled in the mid 19th century. Just south of Kibuli is the upmarket Muyenga Hill, on which posh homes mushroomed during Kampala's 1990s renaissance. Popularly known as 'Tank Hill' after the conspicuous municipal water reservoirs on its summit, Muyenga is an effective beacon for the nightspots of Kabalagala and Ggaba Road at its base.

between the two taxi parks, enhancing the general aura of chaos in this astonishingly congested part of town – even bodas avoid the 200m section between Namirembe Road and Luwum Street. There are regular departures – every 1–2 hours from around 07.00 until early afternoon – to most regional centres (the exception being more distant towns such as Kitgum, Soroti and Kisoro which are usually limited to an early morning and evening departure). It's worth checking out departure times in advance to limit the chance of delays on the day. Note that public transport fares are hiked immediately before holiday periods such as Easter and Christmas when

Kampala's multi-tribal society moves out en masse to their home areas. These increases are only partially due to opportunistic profiteering; they also compensate for vehicles returning almost empty to Kampala at these times.

Details of buses plying the route between Kampala and upcountry destinations are given on pages 120–1 and in relevant chapters. The fastest means of travel is with private bus companies who have an obvious interest in getting from A to B

EARLY DAYS IN KAMPALA

The original city centre – little more than a fort and a few mud houses – stood on the hill known today as Old Kampala. Its early expansion and urbanisation from 1897 onwards is best catalogued in the memoirs of two early settlers, the medical pioneer Sir Albert Cook (arrived 1897) and W E Hoyle (arrived 1903), both of which were published in early (and long out of print) editions of the *Uganda Journal*, the main sources of what follows. Unattributed quotes relating to before 1903 are from Cook.

Conditions for the few settlers in Kampala in 1897 were rudimentary. Imported provisions were scarce, and when available at the town's two English stores they were very expensive. Most settlers suffered ongoing health problems, often related to malaria, which had not yet been connected to mosquito bites. The settlers lived in simple abodes made of reeds, elephant grass and thatch, with a stamped mud floor 'cow-dunged once a week to keep out jiggers'. Cook, a doctor, performed his first operations 'on a camp bedstead, the instruments sterilised in our cooking saucepans, and laid out in vegetable dishes filled with antiseptics'. A 12-bed hospital, built in the local style, opened in May 1897, and a larger one was constructed three years later, only to be destroyed in a lightning strike in 1902. Still, Cook 'introduced the natives to the advantages of anaesthetics and antiseptics' and also started a programme of vaccinations after a chief warned him that a smallpox epidemic was approaching the capital.

The arrival of the telegraph line in April 1900 was a major boon to the remote community, allowing it regular contact with the coast and to keep abreast of world affairs. Cook notes that: 'this happy condition of affairs did not last long, however, for where the line passed through the Nandi country it was constantly being cut down. On one occasion no less than sixty miles [100km] of wire were removed and coiled into bracelets or cut into pieces and used as slugs for their muzzle-loading guns.' More significant still was the arrival of the Mombasa Railway at Kisumu, in December 1901, connected by a steamer service to Entebbe. Not only did this facilitate personal travel between Kampala and the coast, but it also allowed for the freight of imported goods on an unprecedented scale.

Prior to the arrival of the railway, most buildings in Kampala had been thatched firetraps, routinely destroyed by lightning strikes – not only Cook's hospital, but also the first cathedral at Namirembe, the telegraph office, a trading store and several private homesteads. Now, permanent brick buildings could be erected, with corrugated-iron roofing, proper guttering and cement floors, all of which made for more hygienic living, as well as reducing the risk of destruction by fire. The railway also improved the quality of life for the small European community by attracting 'a flood of Indian shopkeepers' and associated 'influx of European trade goods'.

The original European settlement, as already mentioned, stood atop Old Kampala Hill. To its east, an ever-growing local township sprawled downhill to where Nakivubo Stadium [126 B5] and Owino Market [126 B6] stand today.

as fast as possible. If safety is your priority however, it's generally accepted that the slower **Post Bus** [127 F4] is the best option (see below). For details of **international bus services** to and from Kampala, see pages 120–1.

Post Bus The Post Bus service (📞 *0414 255511-5 ex: 303 or 239; www.ugapost. co.ug*) operates from Kampala's main post office [127 F4]. Each morning five buses

The present-day city centre took shape as an indirect result of the improved transportation to the coast via Kisumu. It was, Hoyle writes: 'realised by the government that the space below Kampala Fort was inadequate to meet growing trade, and they decided to start a new township on the more expansive hill named Nakasero, half a mile [0.8km] to the east. Already by 1903 a new fort had been built there [and] by 1905 practically all government offices and staff and traders' shops had been moved to Nakasero.' Over the next few years, writes Cook, the government had 'good roads cut and well laid out in the new town … bordered with trees' – essentially the nascent modern city centre, which slopes across the valley dividing Old Kampala from Nakasero Hill.

The Mombasa Railway also facilitated the export trade out of Uganda, which until 1906 consisted primarily of wild animal produce such as hide, skins and ivory, controlled by an Italian and an American firm, as well as the Indian storekeeper Allidina Visram. Hoyle writes: 'It was a memorable sight to see frequent safaris laden with ivory tusks filing towards Kampala from the strip of country between the Congo Free State and Uganda Protectorate, which at that point was in dispute, a kind of no-man's-land and therefore the elephant-hunters' paradise.' Hoyle writes elsewhere of Allidina Visram's store that in 1903 it was 'to Europeans, the most important … existence almost entirely depended on [it], for his firm not only supplied the necessities of life, but in the absence of any bank it provided ready money in exchange for a cheque'.

Oddly, perhaps, English money held no currency in Kampala's early days. The Indian rupee was effectively the official currency, equivalent to one English shilling and four pence. But Hoyle writes that: 'the most generally used currency among the Baganda was cowrie shells … one thousand to the rupee … through which a hole had been made for threading … using banana fibre. The Baganda were very adept at counting shells, usually strung in hundreds … It was amusing, having paid a porter … five thousand shells, to see him sit down and count them … report that he was one, two, or maybe up to five short, and it was easier to throw these to him from a quantity of loose shells kept in a bag for that purpose.' Cowries continued in general use until about 1905, and were still employed in petty trade until 1922, when the shilling was introduced.

Last word to Hoyle, and an improbable anecdote relating to Sir Hesketh Bell, Governor of Uganda from 1905–09: 'Bell conceived the idea that elephants might be trained to do the many useful jobs they do in India. The experiment was made of bringing a trained elephant from India. It was a great business getting the elephant aboard the [ferry] at Kisumu and landing it in Entebbe. [Bell] came to Kampala to make a triumphant entry riding the elephant, mounting it two miles outside the township. He was greeted by a large crowd of Europeans and Baganda. Some young elephants were caught, but the experiment of training them was not successful, and eventually the Indian elephant was sold to a menagerie in Europe.'

The life of a *mumbeja* – a Muganda princess – wasn't quite as romantic as it might sound. The sisters of the kabaka generally lived a life close to bondage, as ladies-in-waiting to the king, at risk of being put to death for any perceived breach of conduct. Marriage was forbidden to the king's sisters and daughters, as was casual sex or becoming pregnant – and the punishment for transgressing any of these taboos was death by cremation.

The first princess to break the mould was Clara Nalumansi, a daughter of Mutesa I. Nalumansi angered Mwanga by converting to Islam during the first year of his reign, and further aggravated him by publicly reconverting to Catholicism in May 1886. Then, in early 1887, Princess Clara capitalised on her rights as a Christian – in the process scandalising the whole of Buganda – by tying the marital knot with another convert, a former page of Mwanga named Yosef Kadu.

The admirable princess didn't stop there. Shortly after her marriage, Clara was appointed to succeed the recently deceased *namasole* of Kabaka Junju, a charge that, traditionally, would have entailed her moving permanently to a house alongside Junju's tomb and tending the royal shrine in solitude for the rest of her days. Instead, Clara and Yosef arrived at the tomb, chased away the attendant spirit medium, then cleared the previous namasole's house of every last fetish and charm, and dumped the lot on a bonfire.

Clara's next move? Well, it's customary for the umbilical cord of a Muganda princess – and all other royals for that matter – to be removed with care and preserved until they die, when it is buried with the rest of the body. So Clara dug out her umbilical cord from wherever it was stored, cut it into little pieces, and chucked it out – leading to further public outcry and a call for both her and her husband to be executed.

The general mood of unrest in Buganda in late 1887 diverted attention from the Christian couple and gave them temporary respite. But not for long. In December, Clara placed herself back in the spotlight when she arranged for an immense elephant tusk, placed by her grandfather Kabaka Suuna at a shrine dedicated to the water god Mukasa, to be removed from its sacred resting place.

The errant princess's luck ran out in August 1888, a month before Mwanga was forced into exile, when she was killed by a gunshot fired by a person or persons unknown. Not entirely incredibly, her relatives claimed that the assassination was arranged by Mwanga, who – characteristically paranoid – feared that the English Christians might follow the British example and name the princess as the new ruler of Buganda.

More than a century after her death, it's impossible to know what to make of Princess Clara Nalumansi's singular story. Quite possibly she was just a religious crank, recently converted to Christianity and set on a self-destructive collision course with martyrdom. But it's more tempting, and I think credible, to remember her as a true rebel: a proto-feminist whose adoption of Christianity was not a matter of blind faith, but rather a deliberately chosen escape route from the frigid birthright of a *mumbeja*.

depart for Kisoro (*07.00; US$10*), Lira (*07.00; US$10*), Kitgum (*07.00; US$10*), Gulu (*08.00; US$8*) and Kabale (*08.00; US$9*). Along the way, they stop in numerous towns (22 in the case of the Gulu bus) to drop off and collect mail and passengers. Fares to towns along the way are accordingly cheaper.

Pineapple Express The daily Pineapple Express (m *0787 992277/0753 794030;* e *pineappleexpressuganda@gmail.com; www.entebbejinjashuttle.com;* f *fb.me/entebbejinjashuttle*) is a popular, punctual and reliable option connecting Kampala to Jinja (*US$10 one-way*) or Entebbe. It leaves Jinja at 07.30, arrives in Kampala between 09.30 and 10.30, then reaches Entebbe at around 12.00. In the opposite direction, it leaves from Entebbe at 14.45, arrives in Kampala at 16.30, and usually gets to Jinja at around 19.00. The bus will collect or drop you at any hotel or backpackers in Entebbe, Jinja or Bujagali. Drop-off points in Kampala are Nakumatt Oasis Mall and Fat Cat Backpackers.

Private bus companies The better private bus services all have reasonably fixed or regular departure times, with one or another coach leaving in either direction between Kampala and the likes of Mbale, Mbarara, Kabale, Kasese, Fort Portal and Masindi every hour or so from around 07.00 to mid afternoon. The two main departure points are Qualicell Terminal (also known Buganda Bus Park), located off Namirembe Road behind the new taxi park [126 A3], and the Kasenyi Bus Terminal [126 A5], located just off Namirembe Road and accessed from the road passing along the side of Nakivubo Stadium. Other buses run from a number of locations on or close to the floor of the Nakivubo Valley near the Nakivubo Stadium.

Bismarken Bus Reliable operator to Kabale (*05.30/07.00/10.00; 5–6hrs; US$10*) & Kisoro (*8–9hrs; US$10*), as well as Butogota (20km from Buhoma) (*19.30; 8hrs*). Leaves from Qualicell Bus Terminal [126 B4].

Courier Bus Daily to Lira (*US$10*) via Soroti (*US$7*). Leaves from Kasenyi Bus Terminal [126 A5].

Gateway Bus Though usually best avoided, this operator runs a useful daily service to Kaabong (for Kidepo National Park) via Soroti & Kotido. Leave from Kasenyi Bus Terminal [126 A5].

Gaagaa Coaches m 0772 198988/465104. The best operator to West Nile runs 3 buses daily (*8–10hrs; US$12*) to Arua via Pakwach. Buses leave from Arua Stage on Johnston St [126 B2].

Highway Bus m 0774 608325/0705 144119. Slightly battered buses running directly to the Buhoma Gate of Bwindi Impenetrable National Park (*08.00; US$13*). Leave from Kasenyi Bus Terminal [126 A5].

Homeland Northern Express m 0791 805841/0794 805843; www.homeland.co.ug. Well-regarded operator running 5 coaches daily in either direction between Kampala & Kitgum via Gulu. Leave from Kasenyi Bus Terminal [126 A5].

Jaguar Executive Coaches m 0782 811128. The top operator for Kabale or Kisoro (or indeed on to the Rwandan capital Kigali) runs 5 executive buses daily to Kisoro or Kigali via Kabale, leaving from a terminal on Namirembe Rd 500m west of the Qualicell Bus Park [136 E2]. Also recommended is the Rwandan company Trinity Coaches, whose buses to Kigali via Kabale leave from close by.

Kalita Coaches ☎048 3422959; m 0756 897930. Long-serving operator with its own park on Namirembe Rd in front of Nakivubo Stadium [126 B4]. It serves Mubende (*2hrs; US$5*), Fort Portal (*4hrs; US$8*) & Kasese (*5–6hrs; US$10*).

Link Bus ☎041 4255426; e info@link.co.ug; www.link.co.ug. Dominating Qualicell Terminal [126 B4], this large & reasonably reliable operator runs several times daily to the following destinations: Hoima (*3hrs; US$4*); Masindi (*3hrs; US$4*); Kasese (*5–6hrs; US$10*), Fort Portal (*4hrs; US$10*); Bundibugyo (*5–6hrs; US$10*); & Mutukula (Tanzanian border) (*4hrs; US$5*) via Masaka.

Savanna Buses Useful service to Kihihi (between Bwindi & Ishasha) via Ntungamo (*05.30; 7hrs; US$8*). Leaves from the Kasenyi Bus Terminal.

Swift Safaris m 0702 529663/230160; f fb.me/swift.safaris.1. Recommended operator running a comfortable service to Mbarara via Masaka leaving from Kasenyi Terminal every 30mins in either direction between 05.30 & 20.30.

YY Coach m 0706 614040/0703 115259; f fb.me/yycoaches. Daily coaches to Mbale (*4hrs; US$8*) from Qualicell [126 B4].

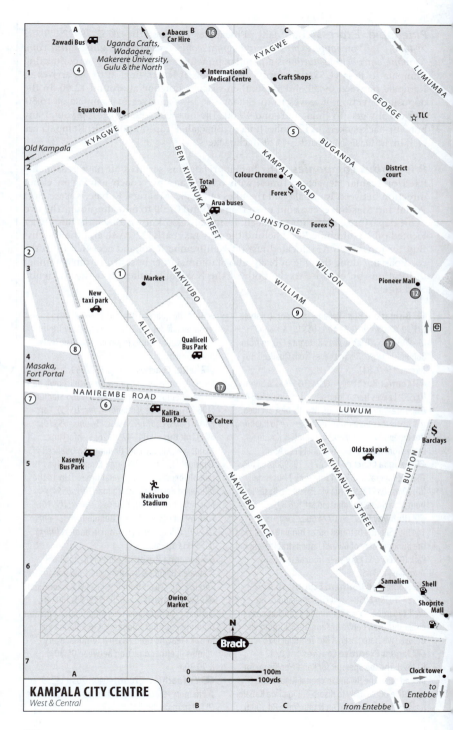

KAMPALA CITY CENTRE
West & Central

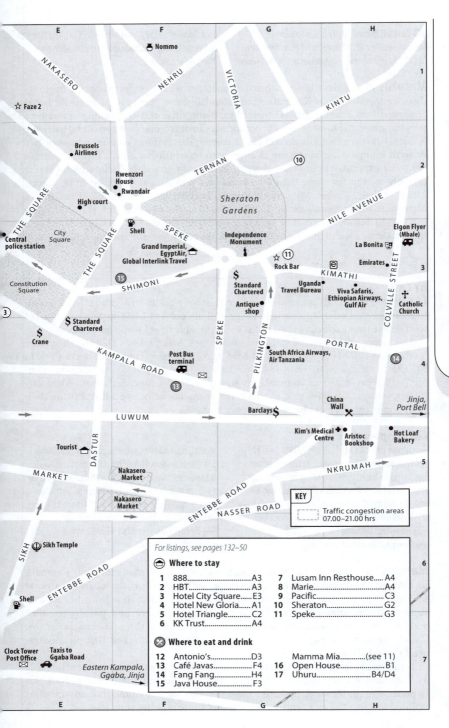

KEY

Traffic congestion areas
07.00–21.00 hrs

For listings, see pages 132–50

Where to stay

1	888	A3
2	HBT	A3
3	Hotel City Square	E3
4	Hotel New Gloria	A1
5	Hotel Triangle	C2
6	KK Trust	A4
7	Lusam Inn Resthouse	A4
8	Marie	A4
9	Pacific	C3
10	Sheraton	G2
11	Speke	G3

Where to eat and drink

12	Antonio's	D3
13	Café Javas	F4
14	Fang Fang	H4
15	Java House	F3
	Mamma Mia	(see 11)
16	Open House	B1
17	Uhuru	B4/D4

Eastern Kampala, Ggaba, Jinja

Zawadi Buses Daily buses to Gulu (*US$8*) from their office at the Bombo Rd end of William St [126 A1]. The service continues north from Gulu to Adjumani (*US$12*) and Moyo (*US$13*), the latter stage including a memorable ferry crossing over the Nile at Laropi.

Matutus These days, buses rather than matutus are the preferred option for long-distance travel to/from Kampala. Understandably, few people want to spend hours crammed into a hot, cramped metal box being driven at frightening speed by a person lacking the most basic of precautionary instincts and (very possibly) a driving licence. However, matutus do still play a role for destinations within an hour or two or so of Kampala and if you are in a hurry to travel further afield. Though matutus are more expensive than buses, departures are more regular – before noon, you're unlikely to wait for more than 30 minutes for a matutu to leave for Jinja, Tororo, Mbale, Kabale, Kasese, Mityana, Mubende, Fort Portal, Masindi, Gulu or Hoima. Matutus to destinations west of the city leave from the **new taxi park** [126 A3], while matutus to destinations east of Kampala leave from the **old taxi park** [126 D5]. Local matutus leave for Entebbe from both taxi parks every few minutes.

GETTING AROUND

BY CAR
Car hire Poor roads make vehicle hire relatively costly in Uganda. Most expat/tourist-oriented safari companies charge well in excess of US$100 per day for a 4x4 with driver (but excluding fuel) but it's still possible to get some good deals.

The major international car-hire companies **Avis** (\ *0414 320516; freephone* \ *0870 606 0100 (UK), +1 800 230 4898 (US); www.avis.com*) and **Hertz** (\ *0414 347191; freephone* \ *0870 848 4848 (UK), +1 800 654 3131 (US);* e *www.hertz.com*) are both represented in Kampala, though you'll get better deals from local car-hire operators. It is advisable to make arrangements before you travel using their freephone central reservations services or websites.

Local operators
Alpha Rent A Car [138 A5] \ 0414 344332; www.alpharentals.co.ug; see ad, 3rd colour section. This Kampala-based company offers excellent rates. A 4x4 for upcountry use with a driver excluding fuel costs US$95/day. A saloon used around Kampala costs US$50 with a driver & fuel, or US$35 without fuel.

Roadtrip Uganda m 0773 363012; e info@roadtripuganda.com; www.

roadtripuganda.com; see ads, pages 60, 85, 168 & 3rd colour section. This Dutch outfit provides Rav4 & Landcruiser vehicles with everything you need for a self-drive safari in Uganda & Tanzania. Attractive rates between US$59–89/day inc 24/7 road support. The website is a good source of information.

Safari Talk m 0751 465020; www. safaritalkuganda.com

Matutus A steady stream of matutus plies most trunk roads through Kampala, picking up and dropping off passengers more or less at whim, and charging around US$0.30–1.50 per person depending on the routing. Unlike in many other African capitals, the minibuses are seldom overcrowded – police and passengers alike actively ensure that conductors adhere to the maximum of three passengers per row – and I've neither experienced nor heard of anything to suggest that pickpockets are a cause for concern.

It can be confusing coming to terms with matutu routes in Kampala, particularly as the routes are unnumbered. Heading from the suburbs into central Kampala is pretty straightforward, however, since you can safely assume that any minibus pointed towards the city centre along a trunk route is going your way.

Heading out from the city centre is rather more daunting (though, increasingly, taxis have boards on the dash stating the destination). If you're heading to anywhere along the Natete and Hoima roads (for instance Kampala Backpackers, Namirembe Guesthouse, Kasubi Tombs) you'll find a vehicle going your way in the new taxi park. Matutus to most other parts of the city leave from the old taxi park.

There is, however, no avoiding the fact that sitting in a taxi crawling into or out of a central taxi park is hot, slow and uncomfortable so you may prefer to avoid these locations altogether. If arriving in town, follow the example of incoming passengers who pile out of the vehicle when it reaches the end of the queue to enter the terminus. If heading out of the city centre, it's simpler and more pleasant to walk a short distance to an alternative taxi stage. On Kampala Road, taxis parked around the Total fuel station (100m east of the junction with Entebbe Road) run to Red Chilli Hideaway and other places along Port Bell Road, while those at the junctions with Burton Street will take you to Bombo Road, Makerere University, the National Museum and Kisementi. Taxis to Ggaba Road go from a stop beside the Clock Tower Post Office [127 E7]. When in doubt, the conductors are normally pretty helpful, assuming that they can speak English, or you can ask one of your fellow passengers.

There are drawbacks to simply walking out of town along your route to catch a taxi along the way. Firstly, taxis only leave the park when full and won't stop to pick you up until a passenger disembarks and vacates a seat. This can be a problem if headed to Mengo and the Kampala Backpackers; you may find yourself walking all the way up the long hill to the taxi stage in Mengo before getting a ride.

Secondly, and more seriously, following a couple of incidents involving commuters, Red Chilli Backpackers warns that you should only board a taxi at a recognised stage rather than one that slows to a speculative crawl beside you. If you must do the latter, do check that the vehicle contains an acceptable number and mixture of male/female/old/young passengers. If the demographics are limited to a clutch of feral-looking young men, decline the invitation. Forewarned is forearmed.

Taxis (special hire) Conventional taxis – generally referred to as special hires – are usually easy to locate within the city centre and normally charge a negotiable US$3–5 or so for short trips and up to US$16.50 for longer rides or travel during congested hours. Taxi stands can be found outside most of the upmarket hotels, on Dastur Street close to the intersection with Kampala Road, on Ben Kiwanuka Street opposite the old taxi park, near the junction of Navibuko and Kyagwe streets behind the new taxi park, and at the roundabout at the junction of Bombo and Makerere Hill roads. Any hotel or decent restaurant will be able to call a special hire taxi for you.

Boda The easiest way to get around Kampala's increasingly congested traffic system is by boda (moped taxi). However, you shouldn't hop aboard without reading about their poor road safety record on page 76. Fares start at Ush1,000.

Given that bodas represent the main source of employment for young men in Kampala, it is inevitable that they now also provide opportunities for crime. If walking after dark, be alert for the possibility of bag snatching by a boda rider's accomplice; such incidents are on the rise. Also, before you leave a bar or restaurant late at night and hop on a motorcycle with an unknown male, ask yourself, 'Would I do this at home?' Probably not. Have the management of the establishment recommend a boda rider or (preferably) a special hire driver who is known to them (see above). The backpacker hostels will update you and suggest sensible strategies to avoid problems.

Vehicle congestion in Kampala means that despite their poor record, bodas have an important role to play and there are now initiatives to help commuters get around safely. One such is Safe Boda, which provides trained drivers, identifiable by orange helmets and reflective vests. You can hail one on the street, call ☎ 0800 300200 (toll free) or use the Google or Apple app. If further endorsement is needed, the website (*www.safeboda.com*) suggests, the organisation enjoys an impressive range of expatriate as well as local expertise, plus support from USAID and the Global Innovation Fund.

EMBASSIES

More than 50 embassies, high commissions and other diplomatic missions can be found in Kampala. Visit www.i-uganda.com/embassies-in-uganda.html for a regularly updated list of embassies with full contact details and opening hours, etc.

TOURIST INFORMATION

Kampala has no tourist information offices, or at least none worthy of the name. The closest thing is the booking office at the Uganda Wildlife Authority where the staff is generally well informed, at least about UWA's area of operations (eg: the parks and reserves). The best sources of current information for budget travellers are the staff and fellow guests at the city's backpacker haunts such as Kampala Backpackers, Bushpig Backpackers, Fat Cat, Red Chilli Hideaway and City Annex Hotel. In addition, pick up a copy of the locally produced *The Eye* magazine (☎ 0312 251117; e *theeye@theprinthouse.co.ug; www.theeye.co.ug*) – you'll find current issues at most upmarket hotels, selected booksellers and tour agents. Essentially a privately run Yellow Pages, this A5 booklet contains useful and regularly updated nationwide listings for hotels, national park fees, buses, airlines, rafting companies, safari companies, etc, plus a few general articles including lodge and restaurant reviews and plenty of ads.

TOURS AND TOUR OPERATORS

Full details of international and local tour operators servicing Uganda are listed on pages 62–5.

※ **Kampala Walking Tours** m 0774 596222; www.kampalawalktour.com. You could easily wander around the sights of central Kampala on your own with the aid of this book. However, your day will be infinitely more enjoyable in the company of the personable & informed Zulaika Birungi, founder of Kampala Walking Tours. From the main post office, Zulaika will take you downhill into the chaotic taxi parks & labyrinthine markets on the floor of the Nakivubo Valley. Then, if you're up for more, she'll lead you up the opposite hillside to the vantage points provided by the National Mosque & Namirembe Cathedral before concluding with the tour of the Twekobe Palace in Mengo.

A 3hr tour of Nakivubo costs US$20pp; 6hr tour, continuing to Mengo, is US$30pp. Cost excludes nominal entrance fees at the mosque and palace. Highly recommended.
Bwaise Slum Tour m 0782 808257; e salim@ vfsdafrica.org; www.vsfdafrica.org. Every large African city has its slums & Bwaise, which spans the Gulu Rd just outside the Northern Bypass, is Kampala's primary contribution to the genre. Most people's experience of Bwaise is limited to its notorious traffic congestion on the way to/ from Murchison Falls. What goes unseen are the difficulties faced by Bwaise's 50,000 residents to secure basic needs such as water, nutrition,

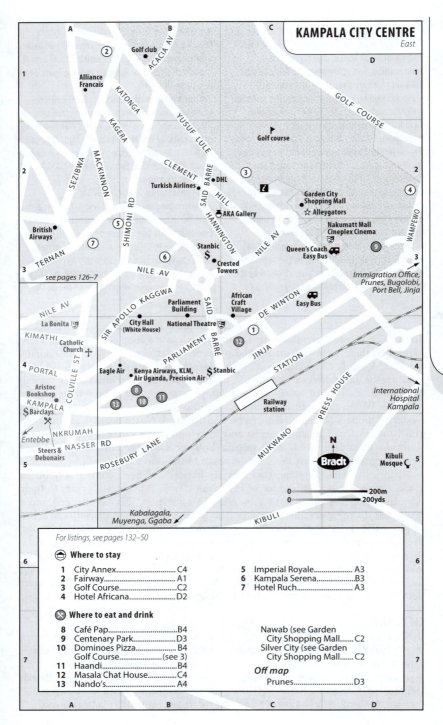

KAMPALA CITY CENTRE

Golf club

Alliance Francais

ACACIA AV

KATONGA

KAGERA

SEZIBWA

MACKINNON

YUSUF LULE

CLEMENT

HILL

SAID BARRE

DHL

Turkish Airlines

Golf course

GOLF COURSE

SHIMONI RD

British Airways

HANNINGTON

AKA Gallery

Stanbic

Crested Towers

TERNAN

NILE AV

NILE AV

Garden City Shopping Mall

☆ Alleygators

Nakumatt Mall
Cineplex Cinema

Queen's Coach
Easy Bus

WAMPEWO

Immigration Office,
Prunes, Bugolobi,
Port Bell, Jinja

see pages 126–7

NILE AV

La Bonita

KIMATHI

Catholic
Church

PORTAL

Aristoc
Bookshop

KAMPALA

Barclays

Entebbe

Steers &
Debonairs

NKRUMAH

NASSER RD

ROSEBURY LANE

COLVILLE ST

SIR APOLLO KAGGWA

City Hall
(White House)

Parliament
Building

National Theatre

PARLIAMENT

SAID BARRE

African
Craft
Village

DE WINTON

Easy Bus

JINJA

STATION

Railway
station

MUKWANO

PRESS HOUSE

International
Hospital
Kampala

Eagle Air

Kenya Airways, KLM,
Air Uganda, Precision Air

Stanbic

Kabalagala,
Muyenga, Ggaba

KIBULI

N

Bradt

Kibuli
Mosque

| 0 | | 200m |
| 0 | | 200yds |

For listings, see pages 132–50

🛏 **Where to stay**

1	City Annex	C4
2	Fairway	A1
3	Golf Course	C2
4	Hotel Africana	D2
5	Imperial Royale	A3
6	Kampala Serena	B3
7	Hotel Ruch	A3

✖ **Where to eat and drink**

8	Café Pap	B4
9	Centenary Park	D3
10	Dominoes Pizza	B4
	Golf Course	(see 3)
11	Haandi	B4
12	Masala Chat House	C4
13	Nando's	A4

Nawab (see Garden
  City Shopping Mall | C2
Silver City (see Garden
  City Shopping Mall | C2

Off map
  Prunes | D3

sanitation, education, housing & some sort of income. For most, this daily quest is complicated by a daunting cocktail of challenges such as overcrowding, unemployment, HIV-AIDS, alcohol/drug abuse, an unsympathetic city council, seasonal flooding & cholera, & crime. The statistics are grim; to state but one, 30% of women over 14 in Bwaise are involved in the sex trade with an encounter costing as little as Ush500. Lifelong Bwaise resident Salim Semambo has set up a small organisation, Volunteers for Sustainable Development (VFSD), to tackle these problems, primarily by providing a very basic home for 26 orphaned or abandoned kids, many of them HIV positive. Their main source of income is a slum tour that shows visitors this little-known side of Kampala. It is an extraordinary experience in which harsh reality is countered by the optimism, friendliness & resilience of local residents, & by the determination of VFSD to make a tiny difference

in the face of monumental odds. The tour costs US$25 & the proceeds, as you'll see, really do make a difference. Salim also offers walking tours similar to those described for Kampala Walking Tours. See also page 85.

Walter's boda-boda tours m 0791 880106; www.walterstours.com. Rather than crawling through traffic in a safari car, Walter Wandera & his mates can take you around the city sights by boda. He & his team are exceedingly safety conscious & helmets are provided. Excursions cost US$30–40pp depending on group size.

Go Free Uganda m 0779 76737; e gofreeuganda@gmail.com; www.gofreeuganda.com; fb.me/Gofreebicycletoursandhires. Go Free offers cycle hire & guided cycle tours. While we'd hesitate to suggest you explore Kampala traffic on a push bike, we can highly recommend the excursion across Murchison Bay from Ggaba to explore the unspoiled countryside on the far side.

WHERE TO STAY

The choice of accommodation in Kampala has come a long way since the early '90s when there were two established options; backpackers slept on the floor of the YMCA, while NGO and business travellers stayed in the Sheraton. Also long gone are the days when we were able to list most reasonable facilities in the capital. With an abundance of hotels in every budget category, we're now forced to be selective. We've also split accommodation into geographical areas: city centre, western Kampala (Mengo, Namirembe and Rubaga), Ggaba Road and Muyenga Hill (southeastern Kampala) Ggaba and Munyono (Lake Victoria shore), eastern Kampala (mostly Bugolobi) and Kampala–Entebbe Road. The Entebbe chapter lists developments out of town along the shores of Murchison Bay.

Historically, most of Kampala's smarter hotels have been comfortably bland places that one might encounter in any major city worldwide, with clues to their African setting being limited to a few crafts in a gift shop. This has changed, and a few hotels do enjoy genuine character (though not exclusively African) and sense of place. Check out the Speke and Emin Pasha in refurbished colonial buildings, the palatial excesses of the Serena in central Kampala, the safari-chic luxury of Le Petit Village on Ggaba Road, the panoramic setting of Cassia Lodge in Munyonyo and the Mediterranean-style Bougainviller in Bugolobi. The central shoestring listings are becoming rather depleted, as several classic dives have recently been demolished and replaced by downmarket shopping malls.

CITY CENTRE
Upmarket

✱ 🏠 **Emin Pasha Hotel** [138 B3] (20 rooms) 27 Akii Bua Rd, Nakasero; 0414 236977–9; e info@eminpasha.com; www.eminpasha.com. Located on leafy Nakasero Hill, 1km north of the city centre, the Emin Pasha is far & away the most

attractive & atmospheric of central Kampala's hotels. Set in a carefully restored 2-storey 1930s town house, the place bristles with taste & character. Terraces, balconies & courtyards abound above a landscaped garden & swimming pool. The brasserie has gained a reputation for good

food. Rooms contain large & comfortable beds, gorgeous antique-finish hardwood furniture & framed artwork. *US$250/270 sgl/dbl garden rooms & superior rooms, US$350/370 garden suites & superior suites B&B.* **$$$$$**

🏠 **Kampala Serena** [104 B3] (150 rooms) Nile Av; 📞 0414 309000; www.kampala@serena. co.ug. The former Nile Hotel, a facility remembered for its gruesome associations with Idi Amin's secret service, was reborn as the Kampala Serena in 2006, courtesy of a US$12 million facelift funded by the Serena Hotel chain & the Aga Khan Foundation. The doors reopened in Aug 2006 to mark a major quantum leap in Ugandan hotel standards. Outside are beautifully landscaped grounds, a 6ha site replete with cliffs, lakes & waterfalls. The interior of this once tasteless 1960s 3-storey block is equally grand, having been infused with a Moroccan flavour, seasoned by a dash of explorers-era nostalgia. Expect to dig deep into your pocket for the experience; you'll pay US$3 for a beer in the Explorers Bar, US$20 for the lavish lunch buffet in the Lakes Restaurant & US$43 for the Fri-night seafood extravaganza. *US$425/497 std/exec rooms sgl/dbl B&B.* **$$$$$**

🏠 **Kampala Sheraton** [127 G2] (200 rooms) Between Nile & Ternan avs; 📞 041 420000/7; ✉ reservation.kampala@sheraton.com. This 15-storey skyscraper stands in lush, manicured gardens bordering the city centre. Back in the '90s, 'Sheraton' was the local synonym for 'smart, luxurious & expensive.' Nowadays however, the 'classic' rooms seem small & ordinary, the internal spaces bland & the in-house Rhino Pub a hive of prostitutes. On the positive side, the garden terrace is a delightful place to enjoy a drink, a meal & live music by local artists while the environs of the large, round, '70s-style pool provide a private setting for working on your tan. *US$267/326 sgl/dbl 'classic' rooms, US$291/350 'superior' rooms B&B.* **$$$$$**

🏠 **Imperial Royale Hotel** [104 A3] (275 rooms) Shimoni Rd; 📞 0417 111001 ✉ information@irh.co.ug; www.imperialhotels. co.ug. Despite a fading, monolithic exterior, the en-suite rooms in this modern, centrally located hotel are still seriously smart, spacious, attractively furnished & with terrific views south across the city sprawl & north to the green & exclusive Kololo Hill. The site is too small for a garden, but there's a 3rd-floor terrace with swimming pool. The rates seem

excellent value. *US$177/236/236 deluxe sgl/dbl/twin; US$224/236 sgl/dbl exec suite. B&B* **$$$$$**

Moderate

🏠 **Speke Hotel** [127 G3] (50 rooms) Nile Av; 📞 0414 235332/5; ✉ spekehotel@spekehotel.com; www.spekehotel.com. The last of the central hotels to retain any period character, the Speke enjoys a prime location & has a selection of restaurants on the premises. The long veranda facing Speke Av is Kampala's answer to the frontages of Nairobi's historic Norfolk & New Stanley hotels, & is a popular spot for a reunion/business meeting/crossword/doze/drink/meal. The peaceful atmosphere is dispelled at night by the adjacent Rock Bar, a nightspot famous for the city centre's most persistent prostitutes, so ask for a room at the rear of the hotel. All rooms are en suite & are spacious & well appointed. *US$138 sgl & dbl B&B.* **$$$$**

🏠 **Golf Course Hotel** [104 C2] (100 rooms) Kitante Rd; 📞 0312 302280; ✉ reservation@golfcoursehotel.com; www.golfcoursehotel.com. At the upper end of the mid-market section, this attractive & luxurious hotel is conveniently located on the edge of the city centre next to Garden City Shopping Mall. There's a revolving restaurant, a serpentine swimming pool & Wi-Fi in the en-suite rooms. If you're too lazy to walk to the gym, exercise machines are provided in the corridors. *US$183/213 deluxe sgl/dbl, US$213/243 exec.* **$$$$**

🏠 **Humura Resort** [138 C3] (18 rooms) Off Kitante Rd; 📞 0414 700402; ✉ reservations@humura.or.ug. Humura means 'peaceful' or 'calm' in the Lukiga language of southwest Uganda & this hotel near the golf course is certainly that. The rooms face a central garden area with a terraced restaurant, a gym & swimming pool. *US$148/165 sgl/dbl B&B.* **$$$$**

🏠 **Hotel Africana** [104 D2] (115 rooms) Wampewo Av; 📞 0414 348080/6; ✉ hotelafricana@hotelafricana.com; www.hotelafricana.com. Situated opposite the golf course, immediately east of the city centre, this modern hotel offers similar facilities & standard of accommodation to its competitors, but in prettier surrounds & at a more realistic price. Facilities include a vast swimming pool, huge & very popular gym/health club, a forex bureau, shops & hair salons, 2 restaurants, business & internet services & 24hr room service. The garden can be noisy with

parties at w/ends. Rates inc use of health club. *US$120/150 sgl/dbl B&B.* **$$$$**

🏠 **Urban by City Blue** [138 B3] (16 rooms) Akii Bua Rd; 📞 0312 563000. This currently small (a 21 room extension is under construction) & stylish retreat focuses on a central lawn, pool & veranda restaurant, Café Mamba (main courses on the tempting Italian & continental menu cost US$10). *US$140–60/170 sgl/dbl B&B.* **$$$$**

🏠 **Hotel Triangle** [126 C2] (60 rooms) Buganda Rd; 📞 0414 231747. The action in this new, street-front hotel is on the ground-floor atrium where a circular swimming pool is plonked (rather curiously & hardly invitingly) right in front of the main dining area. Underground parking is available for guests. Upstairs, the en-suite & AC rooms are attractively furnished at the expense of the Malaysian rainforests. Good value for the location. *US$100/120/140 sgl/dbl/twin.* **$$$**

🏠 **Fairway Hotel** [104 A1] (72 rooms) Kitante Rd; 📞 0414 257171; www.fairwayhotel.co.ug. If you last visited Kampala in 1969, you might well have stayed in the brand new Fairway Hotel, Kampala's first international-standard hotel, & 47 years on, its doors are still open. While new & more polished pretenders now tussle for the 'international' mantle, in most respects, the Fairway (though inevitably rather dated now) still delivers the goods. Facilities include a gym, an antique swimming pool & conference centres. The 2 outside restaurants & bar are preferable to the alternatives inside. The refurbished rooms have AC & DSTV; those in Block A are superior. *US$115/135 sgl/dbl B&B.* **$$$$**

Budget

* 🏠 **Pacific Hotel** [126 C3] (53 rooms) William St; 📞 0414 340920; e info@ thepacifichotel. A number of readers have written to commend this unexpectedly smart entry on William St, 2 blocks downmarket from Kampala Rd. It is indeed extraordinary value, particularly as the rooms provide a level of taste & comfort not otherwise associated with central Kampala's budget listings. A street-facing balcony of a 1st-floor bar keeps you in touch with the insalubrious setting. *US$13–17/18–22 sgl/dbl excl b/fast.* **$$**

🏠 **Makerere University Guesthouse** [117 E3] 📞 0414 534169; e guesthouse@projects.mak.ac.uk.

Simply as a place to sleep, the MUG is both ordinary & overpriced but its setting beats everything else in this category hands down. Instead of a plot in the concrete jungle, the MUG stands within Kampala's last remnant patch of real jungle, the pleasantly green & well-wooded university campus (page 158). Perfectly placed for an early morning or evening stroll/jog/bout of birdwatching. The rooms vary, so ask to see a section before you decide. *US$33/40/60 sgl/dbl/twin.* **$$**

🏠 **Hotel Ruch** [104 A3] (63 rooms) Ternan Av; 📞 0312 210110 www.hotelruch.com Occupying the former premises of the Uganda Wildlife Authority, the Ruch does give the impression of a hotel-shaped peg being hammered into an office-shaped hole. However, the en-suite rooms are spacious & comfortable while the location, between the Sheraton & the Imperial Royale, is conveniently central. Compared to its upmarket neighbours, the prices are refreshingly low. *US$70/80–100 sgl/dbl B&B.* **$$**

🏠 **College Inn** [138 A2] Bombo Rd (Wandegere end); 📞 0414 533835. Situated close to Makerere University on the northern side of the city centre & recently refurbished. Plenty of public transport runs past it. En-suite rooms are comfortable & have DSTV. *US$24/28 sgl/dbl.* **$$**

🏠 **Hotel City Square** [127 E3] (23 rooms) Kampala Rd; 📞 0414 256257/251451. Overlooking City Square, this acceptable budget option is only 200m from the post office – ideal for the 08.00 departure of the Post Buses to upcountry destinations. The balcony restaurant is nothing special but a good vantage point from which to watch city life go by. *US$25/32/32 sgl/dbl/twin B&B.* **$$**

Shoestring

* 🏠 **City Annex** [104 C4] (31 rooms) De Winton Rd; 📞 0414 254132; e ncahotel@gmail. com. This rambling & rather dated hotel is located opposite the National Theatre. It's a favourite with backpackers & volunteers due to its proximity to the popular Masala Chaat House restaurant, the Garden City & Oasis shopping malls, and the terminal for the Nairobi-bound Easy Bus, & evening events at the theatre. There's a wide selection of rooms to choose from (those with shared facilities are a particularly good deal) & the thatched courtyard restaurant at the back is

a bonus. Continental menu (*US$5–6.50*) & local meals served. *US$6/8/9 sgl & 14 twin with spotless shared bathrooms, US$20/23 dbl & US$25/35 en-suite dbl/twin. Rates excl b/fast.* **$$**

🏠 **Hotel New Gloria** [126 A1] (25 rooms) William St, behind Equatoria Mall; opposite the Zawadi bus office serving northern Uganda. Secure parking. Rooms are clean & en suite. *US$12/20 sgl/dbl.* **$$**

NAKIVUBO (BUS AND TAXI PARKS) The hotels listed here are centrally located but presented separately due to their proximity to the main bus and taxi parks around Nakivubo Stadium. These options are strictly for those using public transport; permanent traffic congestion means that this is not an area to bring a vehicle. Most of Nakivubo's 'classic' shoestring hotels have been replaced by shop premises in recent years, so what we have listed instead are the cheapest acceptable options. If you really are strapped for cash, you'll find the dreadful Samalien, Mukwano and ABC guesthouses on the back road behind Nakivubo Place [126 D6].

Budget

✳ 🏠 **HBT** [126 A3] [143 G2] (77 rooms) Rhashid Khamis Rd (off Kyagwe Rd intersection); 📞0414 252361.This excellent modern hotel lies 5mins' walk from Kasenyi Bus Park & 10mins from the Qualicell Bus Park. As the pick of the Nakivubo bunch, the HBT is often full so phone ahead. *US$17–20/23 sgl/dbl B&B.* **$$**

🏠 **KK Trust** [126 A4] (40 rooms) Namirembe Rd; 📞0312 516861. This decent option lies at the bottom of Namirembe Rd opposite the Nakivubo Stadium (you can see 2/3 of the Saturday match action from the restaurant), & is accessed through 2 floors of shops. It's ideal for Bwindi-bound travellers, being just around the corner from the Kasenyi Bus Park. *US$20/24 sgl/dbl B&B.* **$$**

🏠 **Tuhende Safari Lodge** [154 F2] (10 rooms) Martin Rd; 📱 0772 468360; www.tuhendesafarilodge.com. This popular lodge occupies a 1940s building of Asian design on the edge of the city centre in Old Kampala. Before closing for a couple of years, it was a favourite with backpackers & upcountry volunteers thanks to its location & pavement restaurant serving tasty & affordable BBQ meals. The accommodation recently reopened & we hope the BBQ will soon follow suit. Room are basic but spacious: 3-bed dorms, suites & semi-en-suite rooms (1 bathroom per 2 rooms). *US$12 dorm bed with bedding & nets in large 3-bed room, US$33 twin & dbl.* **$$**

Shoestring

🏠 **888 Hotel** [126 A3] (23 rooms) Off Nakivuko Rd; 📱 0776 728888. Backpackers appreciate the location of this labyrinthine Chinese-owned hotel rather more than its rooms. Close to the Buganda/Qualicell Bus Park & the new taxi park it's a safe bet if you bus into town after dark or want an early start. A Chinese restaurant is attached. *US$13/15/17 sgl/dbl/twin with common showers, US$9/12/14 en-suite sgl/dbl/twin.* **$**

🏠 **Lusam Inn Resthouse** [126 A4] (47 rooms) Namirembe Rd; 📱 0772 514773. This decent, no-frills lodge is conveniently located a few hundred metres uphill from the main bus & taxi parks & a short distance down from the Jaguar buses to Rwanda. A renovation is getting underway so expect changes. *US$10/12/14 en-suite sgl/dbl/twin.* **$**

🏠 **Marie Hotel** [126 A4] (18 rooms) Cnr of Martin Rd, just off Namirembe Rd; 📞0392 961139. This clean & surprisingly cheap hotel overlooking the new taxi park is rather better than its shoestring listing deserves & there's a decent restaurant attached. *US$12/15 en-suite sgl/dbl.* **$**

WESTERN KAMPALA See also box, page 139.

Moderate

🏠 **Kenron Hotel** [136 A4] (25 rooms) Natete Rd; 📞0414 272638. This smart & very reasonably priced new hotel stands on the busy road between the city centre & destinations west. The rooms (en-suite with AC) are very nice indeed; the ones at the front have balconies & a view of the expanding metropolis. There's a decent bar while the restaurant includes excellent wraps (*US$6*) & burgers (*US$5*) with great chips. *US$41/53 sgl/dbl B&B.* **$$$**

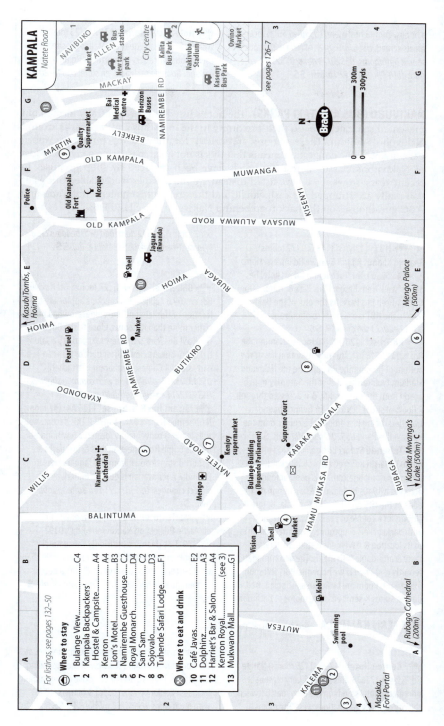

KAMPALA
Natete Road

For listings, see pages 132–50

Where to stay
1 Bulange View..................C4
2 Kampala Backpackers'
   Hostel & Campsite.........A4
3 Kenron...........................A4
4 Lion's Motel...................B3
5 Namirembe Guesthouse...C2
6 Royal Monarch...............D4
7 Sam Sam.......................C2
8 Sojovalo........................D3
9 Tuhende Safari Lodge......F1

Where to eat and drink
10 Café Javas....................E2
11 Dolphinz.......................A3
12 Harriet's Bar & Salon......A4
   Kenron Royal...........(see 3)
13 Mukwano Mall...............G1

see pages 126–7

0   300m
0   300yds

N Bradt

⌂ **Sojovalo Hotel** [136 D3] (35 rooms) Rubaga Rd; ☎0414 271879. It's good to know that there is a bona fide mid-range hotel in Mengo, though the rates & the spacious, attractively furnished rooms are at variance with its position on the less attractive section of Rubaga Rd. Secure parking. *US$72/95 sgl/dbl.* **$$$**

Budget

⌂ **Kampala Backpackers' Hostel & Campsite** [136 A4] (15 rooms) Natete Rd, Lungujja, about 3km from the city centre; m 0772 430587/502758; e backpackers@infocom.co.ug; www.backpackers.co.ug. Kampala's first backpacker hostel has been in business for over 20 years now. Though plenty of other backpacker options now exist, it remains well placed for the bus & taxi parks (to get there, go to the new taxi park & ask for a matutu to 'Backpackers') & a quick route out of town to destinations west in your own vehicle. Services include gorilla-tracking information & permit bookings (US$50 commission), free luggage storage & internet, clean ablution blocks with hot water, a good bar, craft shop & a restaurant serving pizzas, burgers, salads, juices, smoothies, & daily 'specials' (main courses US$5–9). A wide range of accommodation is offered in dorms, thatched bandas, garden cottages & a 4-room flat. *US$7pp camping, US$10–12 dorm bed, US$15/25/30 sgl/dbl/twn shared facilities. US$30 dbl en suite.* **$$**

⌂ **Royal Monarch** [136 D4] (11 rooms) Kabakanjagala; ☎0312 109843; m 0752 482806. The majestic name refers to the location close to the Kabaka's Mengo Palace rather than the facilities, but it's a good deal nevertheless especially if you choose an upstairs dbl beside the balcony facing the palace gates – an appropriate place to read up on the game-changing events of February 1996 (page 21). Eat in, or pop next door to the gardens of the Kenlon Royal for a more tempting menu. *US$12/17 sgl/dbl en-suite B&B.* **$$**

⌂ **ICU Guesthouse** [116 D4] (10 rooms) m 0774 338 708/0701 100486; e sander@icuganda.org; www.icuganda.org/guesthouse. This Dutch–Ugandan venture is located in a large residential house in a maze of roads behind Rubaga Cathedral. Dorms, rooms & a kitchen for guests' use are proving popular with students & volunteers seeking a slightly more homely base than the usual backpacker haunts. Safaris arranged (www.grassrootzuganda.com). *US$16/22/34/48 dorm/sgl/dbl/trpl.* **$$**

⌂ **Sam Sam Hotel** [136 C2] (25 rooms) Natete Rd; ☎0414 274211; m 0773 291351. Modern hotel on the side of Namirembe Hill close to the shops in Mengo. A sauna is provided. Steep driveway to the main road. Good value. *US$14 rather small sgls, US$18/27 more spacious dbls.* **$$**

⌂ **Manhatten Guesthouse** [116 D4] (10 rooms) Balintuma Rd; m 0788 169841. Readers unimpressed by the Namirembe Guesthouse have praised this small & welcoming church-oriented guesthouse on the northern side of Namirembe Hill. Meals (*US$5*) & beer are served. *US$21/24/24/36 en-suite sgl/dbl/twin/suite B&B.* **$$**

⌂ **Bulange View Hotel** [136 C4] (10 rooms) Kivebulaya Rd. The grandiose foyer ceiling suggests equal vulgarity upstairs but the rooms are actually plain, simple and reasonably priced. There's no view of the Bulange (Buganda Parliament), 200m up the road, but there is underground parking. *US$20 sgl/dbl.* **$$**

⌂ **Namirembe Guesthouse** [136 C2] (40 rooms) ☎0414 237981/273778; e ngh@utlonline.co.ug; www.namirembe-guesthouse.com. The Church of Uganda's sprawling guesthouse just below the Namirembe Cathedral has long provided a secure & convenient choice for a respectable & invariably church-oriented clientele, & its reputation as such seems sufficiently secure to justify the immodest rates. The 2nd-floor rooms in the new block enjoy a fabulous view of the metropolis (as does the thatched Coffee & Juice Bar). *New block US$55/70/80/100 en-suite sgl/dbl/twin/exec dbl, old block US$25 per bed family rooms (4–9 people), US$30 sgl with shared facilities, US$45/56 en-suite sgl/twin, US$72 3-bed rooms. All rates B&B.* **$$$**

Shoestring

⌂ **Lion's Motel** [136 B3] (30 rooms) Kivebulaya Rd; m 0778 774991. This perfectly acceptable hotel is the cheapest deal in Mengo for a dbl room. Good value. *US$13 sgl & dbl.* **$**

NORTHEAST KAMPALA Kololo, Kampala's most affluent residential district, covers the hill immediately east of the city centre beyond the golf course. Historically

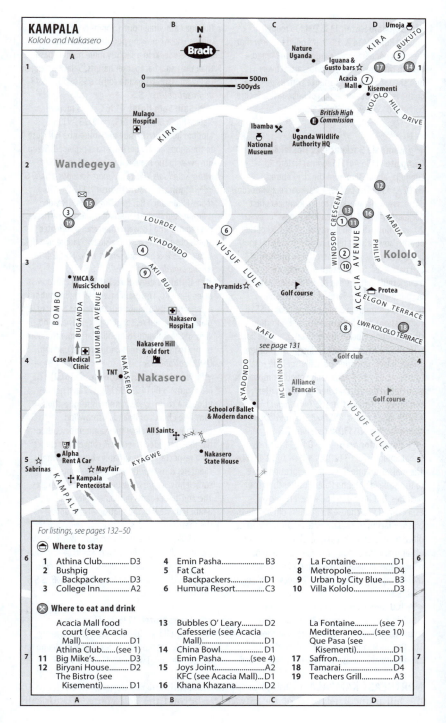

KAMPALA
Kololo and Nakasero

Bradt

0 ————————— 500m
0 ————————— 500yds

Wandegeya

Mulago Hospital

KIRA

Nature Uganda

Iguana & Gusto bars ☆

Acacia Mall

⑰ ⑤ ⑭

Kisementi

KOLOLO HILL DRIVE

BUKUTO

Umoja

British High Commission

Ibamba ✗

National Museum

Uganda Wildlife Authority HQ

⑫

WINDSOR CRESCENT

⑬ ⑯

① ⑪

② ⑩

Kololo

MABUA

PHILIP

ACACIA AVENUE

LOURDEL

KYADONDO

AKII BUA

⑥

YUSUF LULE

⑨

The Pyramids ☆

Golf course

YMCA & Music School

BOMBO

BUGANDA

LUMUMBA AVENUE

Nakasero Hospital

Case Medical Clinic

TNT

NAKASERO

Nakasero Hill & old fort

Nakasero

KAFU

ELGON TERRACE

Protea

⑧

LWR KOLOLO TERRACE

⑱

see page 131

MCKINNON

Golf club

Alliance Francais

Golf course

YUSUF LULE

KYADONDO

School of Ballet & Modern dance

All Saints ✝

Alpha Rent A Car

☆ Sabrinas

☆ Mayfair

✝ Kampala Pentecostal

KAMPALA

KYAGWE

Nakasero State House

For listings, see pages 132–50

🛏 **Where to stay**

1	Athina Club..............D3	**4**	Emin Pasha.................B3	**7**	La Fontaine...................D1
2	Bushpig	**5**	Fat Cat	**8**	Metropole......................D4
	Backpackers..........D3		Backpackers.................D1	**9**	Urban by City Blue......B3
3	College Inn...............A2	**6**	Humura Resort..............C3	**10**	Villa Kololo...................D3

✗ **Where to eat and drink**

Acacia Mall food court (see Acacia Mall)..................D1	**13** Bubbles O' Leary...........D2	La Fontaine............(see 7)
	Cafesserie (see Acacia Mall)...........................D1	Meditteraneo......(see 10)
Athina Club.......(see 1)	**14** China Bowl.....................D1	Que Pasa (see Kisementi)...................D1
11 Big Mike's..................D3	Emin Pasha.............(see 4)	**17** Saffron............................D1
12 Biryani House..........D2	**15** Joys Joint.......................A2	**18** Tamarai..........................D4
The Bistro (see Kisementi).............D1	KFC (see Acacia Mall)...D1	**19** Teachers Grill.................A3
	16 Khana Khazana...........D2	

The Natete Road, which runs between the cathedral-capped hills of Mengo/Namirembe and Rubaga, is a popular area for budget travellers: a broad category that in this case includes backpackers, budget safari clients, independently mobile travellers (ie: with their own wheels) and church- and project-oriented groups. Part of the appeal lies in the easy escape from Kampala that the area offers. The main bus parks lie at the eastern, city end of this corridor, while travel in the opposite direction (towards Natete) leads out of town towards western Uganda. I'll therefore note a few useful locations which I'll describe in relation to the Backpackers' Hostel (page 137).

Firstly, there's a 20m **swimming pool** [136 A4] 200m from the hostel opposite Lyna Day Care kindergarten on the steep road leading to Rubaga Cathedral. This gets very crowded at weekends but it's quiet enough during the week (US$1). It's a stiff climb up the hill past the pool to the **Catholic cathedral** but worth it for the superb view across the city. A less precipitous route to this viewpoint turns right out of the Backpackers' gate, left at the nearby crossroads and then uphill at successive junctions. A less crowded pool (US$1.50) and a gym/sauna and bar/restaurant can be found at the storeyed **Pacify Guesthouse**, 500m down the main road from Backpackers towards Natete. Along the way, you'll pass the new **Kenron Hotel** which provides the smartest accommodation and bar/restaurant on Natete Road.

On the tarmac Lungujja road just behind the hostel, **Harriet's** [136 A4] bar/hairdresser's offers budget beer and manicures while an adjacent row of shops sells basic provisions. The large green grounds of **Dolpinz** [136 A4], 50m up the road, is Mengo's most pleasant spot for outdoor refreshments.

Back on the main road, heading from the hostel towards Kampala, market produce and cheap local food is available halfway up Mengo Hill in **Mengo Market** [136 B4]. Some small supermarkets and eateries (of the liver/sausage/deep-fried object with chips ilk) can be found further up the hill in **Mengo trading centre**. From Mengo trading centre it's a pleasant stroll up to the **Anglican cathedral** on Namirembe Hill, which has good city views. For those with an interest in history, the gravestones in the small, iron-fenced area and plaques inside the cathedral read like a Who's Who of early Kampala.

associated with embassies and the diplomatic residences, options for affordable accommodation in this part of the city have always been thin on the ground. Though the higher slopes of the hill remain as exclusive as ever, there are now a number of budget options on the periphery, temptingly close to the entertainment hotspots of Kisementi and Acacia Avenue (pages 150–1). Further east, the more affordable suburbs of Ntinda and Naguru are the stronghold of Uganda's emergent middle class. Proximity to the Northern Bypass and the Ndere Centre (pages 151–2) are the main reasons for seeking a hotel in this part of town.

Kololo
Upmarket

🏠 **Metropole Hotel** [138 D4] (60 rooms) Acacia Av; ☎ 0312 391000/5/6/7/8; e reservations@metropolekampala.com. The pick of the CHOGM 2007 club (page 24), this attractively priced hotel has been shoe-horned into a small plot beside the golf course. Full marks to the architect who has created a feeling of space using an open-plan central reception/café & 1st-floor balcony, taking full advantage of the outlook across the fairways towards the greenery of

Nakasero Hill. Book a room at the front of the hotel for a private view. Facilities include Thai & grill restaurants, beauty spa & Wi-Fi. Excellent value! *US$120/145 exec sgl/dbl. US$145/170 business sgl/ dbl. B&B.* **$$$$**

🏠 **Villa Kololo** [138 D3] (8 rooms) 31 Acacia Av; ☎ 0414 500533; e villakololo@gmail. com. Located at the rear of the atmospheric Mediterraneo restaurant (page 148), the intimate Villa Kololo injects a dash of romantic escapism to Kampala's mostly bland upmarket menu. As in the restaurant, the appeal is a product of contrasting spaces & an eclectic array of antique furniture & fittings. A private 1st-floor balcony enjoys a terrific view towards Nakasero Hill. *US$130/180/250 sgl/ dbl/ste en-suite B&B.* **$$$$$**

Budget

✴ 🏠 **Bushpig Backpackers** [138 D3] Acacia Av; m 07772 285243; e bookings@ bushpigkampala.com; www.bushpigkampala. com. Kampala's first boutique backpacker hostel occupies a converted, 3-storey apt block at the bottom half of leafy Acacia Av. Though a little further out from the Acacia Mall entertainment hub than Fat Cat (see below), it lies within its own cluster of bars & restaurants on Acacia Av, & has its own restaurant/pizzeria on site. Where Bushpig really scores over its rivals is for the considerably broader (& smarter) choice of rooms. Given the location next to the upmarket locations listed immediately above, it really is extraordinary value for the location. *US$15/25/35/40/54 dorm bed/ small/dbl/twin/trpl (shared bathrooms), US$45/55 sgl/dbl ensuite.* **$$**

🏠 **Athina Club** [138 D3] (6 rooms) Windsor Crescent. The Greek-owned Athina Club has provided a home from home (with copious quantites of moussaka & alcohol) for visitors & upcountry expats for longer than even we can remember. True to the Mediterranean tradition of *manyana*, a makeover is still pending & though the prevailing décor isn't quite Ancient Greece, it is uncompromisingly retro. Great fun! *US$50/60 sgl/dbl B&B.* **$$$**

Shoestring

🏠 **Fat Cat Backpackers** [138 D1] (30 beds) Cnr of Bukoto St & Kanyokya St; m 0771 393892. This terrific new set up opened in 2013 to pioneer the unlikely concept of backpacker accommodation in upmarket Kololo. Housed in a rambling period

town house in the old Asian quarter of Kamwokya, it's 2mins' walk from all the indulgences that Kisementi & Acacia Mall can throw at the treat-starved traveller or volunteer. The downside is that accommodation is pretty much limited to dorm beds, & food is not really available after b/fast time but that's really no hardship with Kampala's densest concentration of quality eateries just outside the gate. *Dorm bed US$15; US$30/40 sgl/ dbl (2 rooms) all shared facilities, US$50 dbl en suite (1 room). B&B.* **$$**

🏠 **La Fontaine** [138 D1] Sturrock Rd, opp Kisementi; m 0772 406197. La Fontaine restaurant is known for terrific steaks prepared at glacial speed but they also have a few basic rooms upstairs. An Acacia Av night-owl recommends them to us as a cheap alternative to a special hire taxi home. *US$11/22 sgl/dbl shared facilities.* **$$**

Ntinda & Bukoto
Upmarket

🏠 **Kabira Country Club** [117 F2] (95 rooms) Old Kiira Rd; ☎ 0312 227222; e info@ kabiracountryclub.com; www.kabiracountryclub. com. Though the KCC, set in the ever-expanding suburbs of northeast Kampala, can hardly claim to be a 'country club' it is a calm & luxurious retreat from the busy commuter corridor of Kira Rd. Amenities include a large, palm-fringed swimming pool, tennis courts, a well-equipped gym & a restaurant. *US$218 sgl/dbl, US$277/411 1/2-bedroom suites.* **$$$$$**

Budget

🏠 **Nob View** [117 F2] (80 rooms) Kira Rd; ☎ 0312 515302; www.nobviewhotel.com. Should you need a decent budget hotel with a swimming pool & strange name in northeast Kampala, look no further. Upper rooms on the south side have balconies with a view. Turn off Kira Rd between the Shell & Total fuel stations in Ntinda. *US$33/40/50 sgl/dbl/twin.* **$$**

BUGOLOBI AND LUZIRA
Map, page 141, unless otherwise stated
Moderate

🏠 **Royal Suites** (80 units) Binayoba Rd, off Luthuli Av; ☎ 0312 263816; e royal@royalsuites. co.ug; www.royalsuites.co.ug. Tucked away at the back of Bugolobi on the margins of the Nakivubo wetland, this sprawling apartment complex caters

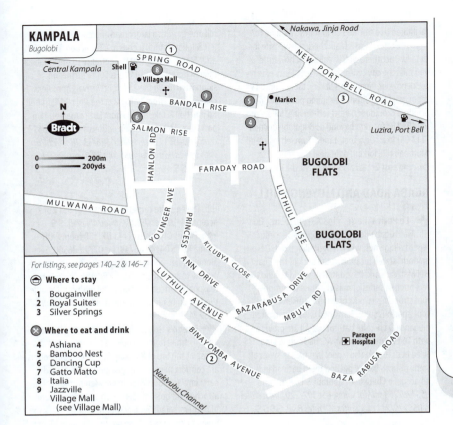

KAMPALA
Bugolobi

← Central Kampala

For listings, see pages 140–2 & 146–7

🛏 **Where to stay**
1 Bougainviller
2 Royal Suites
3 Silver Springs

✴ **Where to eat and drink**
4 Ashiana
5 Bamboo Nest
6 Dancing Cup
7 Gatto Matto
8 Italia
9 Jazzville
   Village Mall
   (see Village Mall)

for everyone. Though mainly aimed at visiting consultants & business travellers (some stay for a year or more), the spacious en-suite studio apts are equally attractive to tourists. The green grounds to the rear contain a swimming pool & a well-equipped gym. *US$154 sgl/dbl studio suite & US$236/295/383 1/2/3 bed apts B&B.* **$$$$**

🛏 **Hotel Bougainviller** (24 rooms) Port Bell Rd, opposite Shell; ☏0414 220966; e bougainviller@utlonline.co.ug; www. bougainviller.com. Inspired by classic Mediterranean villa architecture, this delightful French-owned hotel surrounds a terraced & landscaped courtyard with a small swimming pool. The airy, spacious rooms have stone-tiled floors & glass doors lead out to the patio & central garden. The suites are provided with a fitted kitchen & gas stove, & a large bed elevated on a small mezzanine floor. A restaurant for residents is provided. *US$116/136 sgl/dbl standard, US$126/146 suites & 136/156 duplex rooms B&B.* **$$$$**

🛏 **Silver Springs** (92 units) Port Bell Rd; ☏0414 505976. Silver Springs Hotel was established in the 1930s to accommodate transit passengers using the flying-boat service to South Africa (planes landed on the lake at nearby Port Bell). The original structure has been long overlain by a series of renovations & it's currently a smart, modern hotel offering rooms & cottages, conference facilities, a swimming pool, & pizzeria. *US$100/120 sgl/dbl B&B.* **$$$**

Budget
🛏 **Red Chilli Hideaway** [117 H4] (30 rooms) Butabika Rd, near Luzira; ☏0312 202903 (office); m 0772 509150; e reservations@redchillihideaway. com; www.redchillihideaway.com. This excellent backpackers' hostel occupies new, purpose-built premises on a 2ha site in Butabika in southeast Kampala. It really is a hideaway, on the city's farthest extremity overlooking wetland with Lake Victoria beyond. It's a bit of a way out of town but access is

facilitated by a free Red Chilli shuttle running to/ from the central Oasis Mall; check the website for details. Once there, you'll realise just how little you miss the city centre & there are plenty of ways to spend your time with a library, table tennis, TV room, pool table, 16m swimming pool, free Wi-Fi & indoor & outdoor bars. If self-driving, follow the Port Bell Rd for 2km beyond its Bugolobi junction [117 G4] to an Oryx fuel station. Turn left & ascend Mutungo Hill, forking right near the summit to descend past Great Lakes Safaris. At the foot of the

hill, merge with a larger road approaching from the left & follow it until it ends at a T-junction. Turn left & after 500m veer right at the entrance to the Butabika Mental Hospital. The hostel is 500m further on, signposted down the 2nd right. Arrivals from Jinja can take a taxi from Nakawa at the Jinja Rd/Port Bell Rd junction & take a boda from Luzira market, 1km past Oryx. Accommodation options are varied. *US$7 camping, US$11 dorm bed, US$28/33/38 sgl/dbl/trpl with shared bathroom, US$40/45/50 en-suite sgl/ dbl/trpl.* **$$**

GGABA ROAD AND MUYENGA HILL
Upmarket

🏠 **Le Petit Village** [143 A3] (10 rooms) Quality Hill Mall, Ggaba Rd; 📞 0312 265530–3; e info@ lepetitvillage.net; www.lepetitvillage.net. Despite an understated location at the back of the Quality Hill Mall car park, it's a different world behind the reception. A series of massive grass & gumpole roof structures (works of art in themselves) shelter cool, spacious suites furnished with understated elegance & en-suite bathrooms. All are provided with DSTV, Wi-Fi, minibar, AC, bathtub, & king-sized bed. There's also a pool in which to swim off some pounds before putting them back on in the adjacent Le Chateau Restaurant & La Patisserie. *US$179/203 sgl/dbl suites, US$197/220 junior suites & US$220/244 exec suites. All rates B&B.* **$$$$**

Budget

🏠 **Hotel Diplomate** [143 D4] (30 rooms) Tank Hill; 📞 0414 267655/572828; e diplomatekampala@hotmail.com. The service & facilities at this long-serving listing come in for a bit of stick, but it remains famous for the fabulous city view from its position near the top of Tank

Hill. The en-suite carpeted rooms with DSTV are acceptable value. *US$28/36 sgl/dbl B&B.* **$$**

🏠 **Hotel Olympia** [143 D7] (30 rooms) Off Ggaba Rd; 📞 0414 266743; m 0772 686300. Set along a quiet side road beyond the main cluster of pubs & restaurants on Ggaba Rd, the Olympia is a reasonably priced 4-storey hotel with comfortable tiled en-suite rooms. Excellent value. *US$17 sgl & US$20/23 dbl B&B.* **$$**

🏠 **Fuego's Hotel** [143 C2] (8 rooms) Tank Hill Rd. This small hotel occupies a converted town house at the top of Kabalagala. The en-suite rooms are comfortable yet unpretentious with glazed earthenware floors & plain wooden furniture. The attached Fuego's Café serves an appetising menu of burgers, salads & daily specials but do check the menu prices match those on the computer billing system. *US$40/70 sgl/dbl B&B.* **$$**

🏠 **Rwizi Arch** [143 D6] Kiwafu Rd, Kansanga; 📞 0414 501081; e info@rwizihotels.com; www. rwizihotels.com. This new listing is distinguished by pleasant public spaces softened by greenery & ochre stonework, plus smart en-suite rooms (some with AC). *US$40/50 sgl/dbl.* **$$**

GGABA AND MUNYONYO An extension of the Ggaba Road listings above, this section covers the lakeside suburbs of Ggaba and Munyonyo at the eastern end of Ggaba Road.

Upmarket

🏠 **Speke Commonwealth Resort** [117 G6] (449 rooms) Munyonyo; 📞 0414 227111; e spekeresort@spekeresort.com; www. spekeresort.com. This top-quality resort offers sumptuous rooms & suites set in expansive & gorgeously landscaped grounds on the Lake Victoria waterfront. Those in the Commonwealth wing are furnished & decorated with impeccable taste in brown & copper tones, & fitted with

everything you'd require; indeed the executive suites contain rather more (bathtub, shower, 2 hand basins, 2 loos, 2 flatscreen TVs . . .). The complex contains a large swimming pool, marina & stables. Horseriding, fishing & boat excursions are available. The restaurant serves continental meals for US$8 upwards. *US$182/201 sgl/dbl deluxe rooms, US$225 for 1-bedroom apt (sleeps 2) & US$312 for 2-bedroom apt (sleeps up to 4).* **$$$**

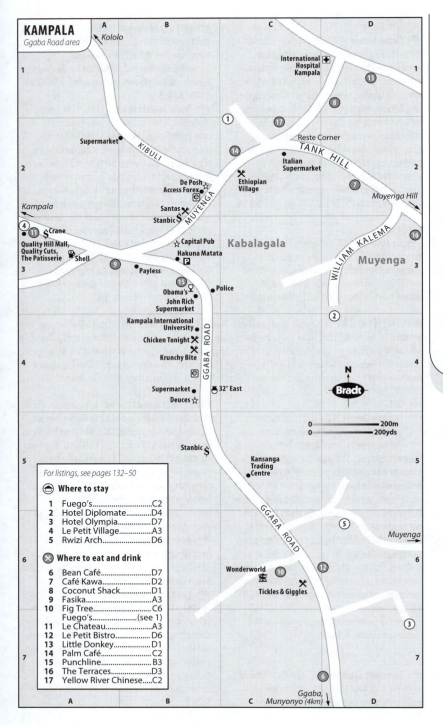

KAMPALA
Ggaba Road area

↑ *Kololo*

← *Kampala*

Supermarket

KIBULI

De Posh
Access Forex ☆
MUYENGA

Santos ✕
Stanbic $

④ ⑪ ↕ **Crane**
Quality Hill Mall,
Quality Cuts,
The Patisserie **Shell**

☆ **Capital Pub**
Hakuna Matata 🅿

⑨ ● **Payless**

Ethiopian
Village ✕

Kabalagala

International
Hospital
Kampala ✚

⑬

⑧

① ⑰

⑭

Reste Corner
TANK HILL

Italian
Supermarket ●

⑦

Muyenga Hill

WILLIAM KALEMA

⑯

Muyenga

Obama's ☕
John Rich
Supermarket

⑮ ● **Police**

Kampala International
University ●

Chicken Tonight ✕
Krunchy Bite ✕

GGABA ROAD

②

Supermarket ●
Deuces ☆

● **32° East**

N
Bradt

0 ━━━ 200m
0 ━━━ 200yds

Stanbic $

Kansanga
Trading
Centre ●

GGABA ROAD

⑤

Muyenga

Wonderworld
⑩
🀄

✕
Tickles & Giggles

⑫

③

⑥

Ggaba,
Munyonyo (4km) ↓

A   B   C   D

For listings, see pages 132–50

🛏 Where to stay

1	Fuego's	C2
2	Hotel Diplomate	D4
3	Hotel Olympia	D7
4	Le Petit Village	A3
5	Rwizi Arch	D6

✕ Where to eat and drink

6	Bean Café	D7
7	Café Kawa	D2
8	Coconut Shack	D1
9	Fasika	A3
10	Fig Tree	C6
	Fuego's	(see 1)
11	Le Chateau	A3
12	Le Petit Bistro	D6
13	Little Donkey	D1
14	Palm Café	C2
15	Punchline	B3
16	The Terraces	D3
17	Yellow River Chinese	C2

Moderate

Cassia Lodge [117 G6] (30 rooms) Buziga Hill; m 0755 777004; e info@cassialodge.com; www.cassialodge.com. This deservedly popular lodge is found high on affluent Buziga Hill where it enjoys a fabulous view of southern Kampala, the lake, & its adjoining wetlands. The main buildings are a curiosity, being a pair of 2-storey blocks softened by gumpole cladding in the fashion of an upcountry safari lodge. A swimming pool, an excellent 1st-floor restaurant (page 150) & Wi-Fi are provided. The comfortable, tiled en-suite rooms have fan, walk-in nets & a veranda or balcony, & are reasonably priced. *US$140/160 sgl/dbl B&B.* **$$$$**

Budget

Sir Jose [117 G6] (20 rooms) Ggaba Rd, Bunga; 0414 667008; m 0772 500332; e sirjosehotel@hotmail.com; www.sirjosehotel.com. This smart modern hotel is the best of the budget hotels along Ggaba Rd. Outside, a green garden is tucked away to the side of the hotel while upstairs the en-suite tiled, glass-fronted rooms open on to balconies overlooking the lake & upmarket Buziga Hill. Watch out for functions at the w/ends but otherwise a good deal. *US$30/50 sgl/dbl B&B.* **$$**

Royal Impala Hotel [117 G7] (31 rooms) Munyonyo; 0414 577413; royalimpalahotel.com. Tucked away behind the Speke Resort, this hotel occupies a slightly eccentric but nonetheless attractive garden. Outside the hotel is a shrine to St Andrew Kaggwa, a Baganda Christian who fell victim to the murderous 19th-century Kabaka Mwanga. The tiled, en-suite rooms seem good value for money – though some are smarter & more spacious than others. *US$33/43/50 sgl/dbl/exec dbl B&B.* **$$**

Victoria Travel Hotel [117 G6] (35 rooms) Ggaba Rd, Ggaba; 0414 501084. This pleasant hotel between Bunga & Ggaba has decent en-suite rooms & view of the lake & Buziga Hill. *US$27/33/40 sgl/dbl/twin.* **$$**

WAVIMENYA BAY Though the resorts below are located in countryside on the eastern side of Murchison Bay, they appear here as a continuation of the Ggaba and Munyonyo listings above since they are accessed from Ggaba port and/or the Speke Commonwealth Resort. Indeed, most of them are actually closer – and quicker to reach – to Munyonyo than to the city centre. Unless stated, rates exclude boat transfers.

Moderate

Lagoon Resort [117 H7] (8 cottages) 0777 511339; www.ug-lagoonresort.com. This offshore resort is popular with both tourists & Kampala residents (the wealthier ones anyway). A thatched lodge building & external viewing decks overlook a lovely garden sloping towards the sandy beach, while the accommodation is provided in elevated en-suite chalets, discreetly positioned in a nearby patch of forest. A swimming pool is provided while other diversions include mountain biking, kayaking, a sunset cruise & a cultural walk. Also has a reputation as a good out-of-town eatery. Boats to Lagoon (*25mins*) run from Speke Commonwealth Resort at Munyonyo (page 142). Advance booking is essential. *US$140/220 sgl/dbl FB inc. boat transfers. Low season & resident discounts available.* **$$$$$**

Budget

Serenada Eco Resort [117 H7] (14 rooms/tents) m 0772 428456; e serenadakyaggwe@gmail.com; www.serenadaecoresort.com. This pretty resort occupies a series of clearings around an attractive, forest-shaded beach in Wavimenya Bay, 30mins' boat ride from Ggaba. Chill by the lake or go kayaking, walk in the forest, tick off birds (the resort list stands at 200 species) & climb nearby Kyasa Hill. A variety of basic accommodation includes some cramped en-suite rooms (*US$60/80 B&B*); Dream Cottage, a cosy & privately positioned en-suite timber cabin (*US$80/120*) & a row of standing tents (*shared facilities; US$25/40 B&B*). **$$**

Beer Gardens 2 [117 H7] 0392 964474. Basic en-suite banda accommodation in a pretty lakeside plot, 30mins by boat from Ggaba. See also Beach House, page 150. *US$40.* **$$**

Lakeside Escape [117 H7] m 0792 760351; lakesideescapeug.com. Located beside Gobero Bay, just south of Wavimenya Bay 45mins from Munyonyo, this new resort offers spacious cottages with a rustic flavour. Diversions include a swimming pool, boat rides, guided walks & cycling. *En-suite cottages US$130 dbl, small en-suite sgl rooms at rear US$50. All rates B&B.* **$$$$**

MAKINDYE An amorphous overlap of Kampala's haves and have-nots, the suburb of Makindye follows a ridge running southeast from Kibuye roundabout where the Masaka and Entebbe roads intersect. It centres on a tiny trading centre containing a supermarket, coffee shop and the Makindye Country Club (see below). It's well placed for a quick escape to Entebbe and for the Ggaba Road nightspots.

✳ 🏠 **Makindye Country Club** [117 E5] (12 rooms) \041 4510290; e info@ makindyecountryclub.com; www. makindyecountryclub.com. Recently privatised & renamed, the former American Recreation Association is a family-friendly lodge set in large green gardens graced by a swimming pool, tennis court, table tennis, children's playground & gym. Rooms are variable in size & shape, but all are en suite with walk-in nets & TV. A likeable terrace restaurant serves a varied selection of Western-style meals for US$4–7, & rates include temporary club membership & use of all amenities. *From US$75/85 sgl/dbl.* $$

✖ WHERE TO EAT AND DRINK

Over the past 15 years, Kampala has transformed into a diner's paradise. Hundreds of new eateries have sprung up all over the city offering a variety of cuisine for all tastes and budgets. There are also, of course, numerous small take-aways, pork joints, roadside chicken grills and market stalls which offer cheap and reasonable local food.

During the troubled late 1970s and 80s, people headed directly out of the city before dark and drank (Ugandans like to drink) close to home in the suburbs. For many years after, the city centre was a dead zone while nightlife shifted to suburbs such as Kansanga and Kabalagala (3km down Ggaba Road), and Wandegeya. Things have changed since those dark days, and the central district of Nakasero once again hosts numerous good restaurants and bars. However, this central renaissance complements rather than replaces the suburban action and the theme of satellite entertainment is still going strong. While numerous low-key centres exist, there are three main hubs. The oldest of these is the red light area of **Kabalagala-Kansanga** on Ggaba Road while newer, smarter centres have developed around **Kisementi and Acacia Avenue**, 1.5km north of the city centre and **Bugolobi**, 3km to the east.

In addition to the restaurants listed below, **Red Chilli Hideaway** (pages 141–2), **Kampala Backpackers** (page 137) and most other hotels in the upmarket and moderate ranges have restaurants serving international cuisine to guests and outsiders. The list below is only a small selection of what's on offer. For a fuller picture (at least of Kampala's smarter eateries) get hold of the free monthly ad-mag *The Eye* or check www.theeye.co.ug. Each edition includes updated listings and a restaurant review.

CITY CENTRE

These listings are presented as a geographical tour of the city's central restaurants. Starting at Uhuru next to the Qualicell Bus Park, this is an anticlockwise tour of a selection of the (mostly) smart restaurants mushrooming across the slopes of Nakasero Hill.

✖ **Uhuru Restaurant** [126 B4] Namirembe Rd. Uhuru's solid reputation is built on pilau rice with meat & spicy sauce. The 2nd-floor location beside the bus park offers great views over the gridlocked streets below. There's another branch on Wilson Rd [126 D4]. *Meals US$2.*

✖ **Antonio's** [126 D3] Pioneer Mall, Kampala Rd; ⏲ 06.30–late. Kampala Rd's best budget eatery serves good b/fasts, lunch specials & juices at bargain prices. *B/fast US$1–1.50, local food US$2–3, burgers US$2.*

✖ **Café Javas** [127 F4] Kampala Rd, opposite the post office; [136 E2] Oasis Mall. This popular Kenyan restaurant chain has two branches in the

city centre & others in Kisementi, Namirembe & on Bombo Rd. The menu includes pies, burgers, steaks, wraps, quesadillas, salads, a superb 'English style' battered fish 'n' chips & a range of cakes for afters. The prices aren't cheap but the main courses will often feed 2. *Mains around US$8–10.*

🖳 **Java House** [127 F3] Grand Imperial Hotel. Nairobi's Java House has followed its Kenyan rival, Café Javas, up to Kampala to compete for the middle-class shilling & expat dollar. Their menu is similar in price & content but distinguished by its selection of coffees. Additional branches in Bugolobi, Lugogo Mall & Acacia Av. *Mains around US$8–10.*

✖ **Nando's** [104 A4] Cnr of Kampala Rd/ Parliament Av; ☎0414 340840/3. This fast-food complex offers ice creams, pizzas, BBQ chicken, as well as good bread, pies & pastries.

✖ **Dominoes Pizza** [104 B4] Kampala Rd; ☎0414 251513. Dominoes, next to Nandos, offers excellent pizzas & burgers to eat in or take away. Food can also be delivered.

🖳 **Café Pap** [104 B4] 13 Parliament Av; ☎0414 254647; m 0772 652443. The place for coffee connoisseurs. Excellent coffee, good food, early opening times & internet access make it a popular stop for laptop owners & office workers.

✖ **Haandi Restaurant** [104 B4] 1st Fl, Commercial Plaza, Kampala Rd; ☎0414 346283. Odd setting for the city centre's best Indian food. *Meals US$10 excl rice/naan.*

✖ **Fang Fang Restaurant** [127 H4] 1st Fl, Communications Hse, Colville St; ☎0414 344806. Enjoy Kampala's best Chinese food either inside or on the airy roof terrace. *Meals US$12*

✖ **Mamma Mia** [127 G3] Speke Hotel; ☎0414 346340; m 0772 630211. The corner plot of Nile/ Kimathi avs has served Italian food since the mid 1960s (with a few excusable interruptions in service). Handily located within the Speke Hotel complex this restaurant is popular for lunch & dinner alike. *Meals US$8.*

✖ **Masala Chat House** [104 C4] De Winton Rd; ☎0414 236487. Popular with travellers as an informal, good-value Indian restaurant, this place is located just opposite the National Theatre. The food is not as good as the more upmarket Indian restaurants, but significantly cheaper. *Main course US$5–7.*

✖ **Centenary Park** [104 D3] Jinja Rd. This historic public green space has become

controversially cluttered with a tacky cluster of bars & eating places – Turkish, Indian, *nyama choma* (roast meat) & Chinese.

✖ **Nawab** [104 C2] Rooftop, Garden City; ☎0414 263333. Indian restaurant with sister branches in Dubai. Very good food, though it looks nothing like the pictures on the menu. *Main course excl rice/ naan around US$7.*

✖ **Silver City** [104 C2] Garden City. Smart South African chain serving American-style fast food. Popular for family outings. Kids' play area provided. *Meals US$5–12.*

✖ **Golf Course Hotel** [104 C2] ☎0414 563500. Watch the world go by (once every 90mins) from Uganda's 1st revolving restaurant. *Main courses US$10 & over.*

✖ **Emin Pasha Hotel** [138 B3] Akii Bua Rd; ☎0414 236977. The terraced Brasserie restaurant at Kampala's 1st boutique hotel is a delightful setting for a special occasion, especially if someone else is paying! *Starters US$5–10, main course US$14, desserts US$6.*

✖ **Open House** [126 B1] Buganda Rd. Located on the premises of the Uganda Institute, this (mostly) outdoor restaurant/bar serves brilliant Indian food at reasonable prices. *Main course excl rice/naan US$6.*

BUGOLOBI
Map, page 141
With heavy traffic complicating excursions to Kabalagala & the city centre, the residents of Bugolobi & Mbuya were, until recently, all dressed up, with no place to go. Local entrepreneurs have responded by providing a range of opportunities to dine and party.

✖ **Dancing Cup** Luthuli Av. The centrepiece of the D-Cup is a covered wooden deck; a relaxed setting for a drink &/or a meal chosen from a diverse menu supplemented by daily specials. As an added bonus, the prices are carefully pitched to keep the riff raff out. *US$8–12.*

✖ **Gatto Matto** Bandali Rise, behind Village Mall. With cosy seating & warm night-time illuminations, this garden bar-restaurant is a deservedly popular spot for an evening drink. Live music on Tue.

🍷 **Jazzville** Bandali Rise. Popular & classy bar offering *muchomo* (roast meat) & with live music every evening until 23.00.

THE HUMBLE ROLEX

A welcome, if humble, addition to Kampala's edible offerings is the 'rolex'. This is nothing more (or less) than a freshly cooked *chapati* enhanced by a fresh omelette, chopped onions, tomatoes, green peppers and finely sliced cabbage. The latter items are rolled up inside the former, hence the name, and popped into a polythene bag. You'll find rolex street vendors armed with metal hot plates, a charcoal stove and a chopping board in all popular nightspots of 'local' flavour. It's exactly the sort of street food your mother warned you against eating in Africa, so rolexes are obviously a firm favourite with backpackers, gap-year students and volunteers. Expect to pay around US$0.50.

Bamboo Nest This popular bar occupies the rambling, storeyed thatched structure opposite Bugolobi Market. Roasted meat a speciality.

Italia Behind Shell Bugolobi; m 0772 956882. Genuine Italian food in relaxed garden atmosphere. *US$7–10.*

Ashiana Directly across the road from Bugolobi Market & the conspicuous Bamboo Nest, this Indian restaurant is worth seeking out for a top-quality curry. *Main course excl rice/naan US$7.*

Village Mall Dining options include Java Coffee & the ubiquitous KFC.

WESTERN KAMPALA (RUBAGA & MENGO)

Café Javas [154 E2] Namirembe Rd, near Bakuli crossroads. Eating out on the Mengo side of town is now an option with the opening of this Café Javas outlet (though no alcohol is served). Huge portions & free Wi-Fi. *Meals US$6–10.*

Wallet Time Pub [116 D5] Kabusu Rd, beyond Rubaga Cathedral. Excellent roast pork in shady thatch shelters. A few similar setups are to be found in the vicinity.

Kenron Royal [136 A4] Opposite the entrance to the Mengo Palace, this efficient set up offers an indoor menu of burgers, wraps & grills & roasted meat on the lawn behind.

Harriet's Bar & Salon [136 A4] Kalema Rd, just behind the Backpackers' Hostel. Harriet, aka Mama Salooni, will provide you with a beer & a hairdo.

Dolphinz [136 A3] Kalema Rd. Large thatched bar complex set in an expansive garden, 5mins' walk from Kampala Backpackers'. Excellent performances of traditional music & dance some evenings.

Mukwano Mall [136 G1] Kyagwe Rd/Rhashid Khamis Rd. In terms of shopping opportunities, this 3-storey mall on the western edge of the city centre fails to excite. However, the roof level is notable for a few budget restaurants that serve tasty Indian & Chinese dishes that local Indians & Chinese clearly enjoy & at prices they seem happy to pay. A good choice if staying at budget hotels around the bus/taxi parks or in Old Kampala. Access the 3rd-storey/roof level directly from Rhashid Khamis Rd to find the restaurants on the right. *Moderately sized main portions cost US$4 excl. rice/naan.*

MAKERERE/WANDEGERE

As you might expect, entertainment options on Makerere University campus & its immediate environs target students on a budget. Smarter options in the vicinity are Café Javas on Bombo Rd & Emin Pasha on the other side of Wandegere crossroads.

Ham Shopping Centre [117 E3] Opp the main gate to Makerere University. Though Kampala's ugliest mall exists mainly to provide students with basic staples, the Dine & Dash café serves surprisingly good coffee.

Joys Joint [138 A2] Next to post office. A pork feast awaits!

Teachers Grill [138 A2] Bombo Rd, Wandegere. Downstairs behind the College Inn, the 1970s' interior must surely be in a scene in *The Last King of Scotland* movie. A trendy hangout for university students.

Club 5 [117 E3] Makerere University. This café is worth a visit if you're on campus. Affordable local & international staples plus some good Indian

specials are served in a semi-open setting. The complex includes a bar with DSTV, a gym, sauna, & an internet café. Take the 1st left inside the main gate.

✕ **Nakulabye Pork Joints** [117 E3] A kilometre west of the university, Makerere Hill Rd is lined with pork joints/bars offering roast pork with 'accompaniments' (tomato, avocado, onion, cassava...). Strictly dining-with-fingers.

KOLOLO

The western side of the upmarket Kololo Hill has become Kampala's main destination for eating out. So great is the choice that we're obliged to spread the options over three sections; Kisementi & Acacia Mall; Acacia Av; & Kololo.

Kisementi

✴ ✕ **La Fontaine** [138 D1] Sturrock Rd. Located in the shadow of the looming Acacia Mall & next door to the pumping Iguana Bar, the long-serving La Fontaine is an overlooked gem. If you want a quality steak/salad/burger/stir fry, this really is the best deal in town. The reason why it is not better known or busier is the extremely slow service in the evenings (lunchtimes are OK). If it comes to it, there are cheap rooms upstairs. *Mains US$5–7.*

✕ **Que Pasa** [138 D1] m 0783 874469. Further evidence in support of Kisementi's claim as home to Uganda's most varied selection of international menus is provided by this new cantina in the corner plot next to Crane Bank. The popularity of the Tex Mex menu is boosted by a daily happy hour for beers & cocktails. *Snack items US$4; meals US$9.*

✕ **The Bistro** [138 D1] Hidden from the touts, peddlars & hawkers of the Kisementi car park (& other members of the budget dining classes) by a screen of greenery, this posh eatery offers diners a choice between a shady, stone-flagged terrace & a cool, AC interior. A wide-ranging selection of burgers, pastas, salads, grills & curries keeps everyone happy. *Main courses US$8–12.*

✕ **Saffron** [138 D1] Sturrock Rd; m 0750 999555. Beyond a bland, motel-style foyer, a thatch-shaded compound is the setting for some very decent Indian grub. The folk at the Fat Cat Backpackers (immediately outside a rickety back entrance) rave about the veg thali (*US$7*). *Main courses excl rice/naan US$6.*

✕ **China Bowl** [138 D1] Cnr of Prince Charles Drive & Sturrock Rd. Excellent Chinese food served by Indians. In a bold break with convention, the 'authentically Chinese' dining arena draws on communist principles of scale & utilitarianism. *Main courses excl rice US$6–7.*

✕ **Cafesserie** [138 D1] Acacia Mall. The terrace at the entrance to Kampala's most fashionable mall is currently the place to be seen at lunchtime. Scan the prices before you get too comfortable though; if you blanch at the price of a burger (*US$9*), best not to check the steaks. Though you might consider a little treat from Kampala's best selection of freshly made ice cream.

✕ **KFC** [138 D1] Acacia Mall. Love him or hate him, Col Sanders is finally in town with his unique blend of herbs & spices.

✕ **Acacia Mall food court** [138 D1] As well as the usual range of curry, shawarma & burger vendors, this 1st-floor food hall also enjoys a great view towards the hills of Makerere, Mulago & Nakasero.

Acacia Avenue

✴ ✕ **Khana Khazana** [138 D2] Acacia Av; ☎ 0414 233049/347346; ⊕ closed Mon. One of Kampala's most atmospheric restaurants, KK serves rich & creamy dishes from across India. Splash out! *Main excl rice & naan US$10.*

✕ **Mediterraneo** [138 D3] 31 Acacia Av; ☎ 0414 500533. Kampala's most distinctive Italian restaurant comprises a mélange of decks, shades & shelters decorated with antique fittings & furniture. A lovely lunch spot, it is altogether more magical as an evening venue. If you think yourself immune to an involuntary 'oooh' of appreciation, arrive after dark when the place is illuminated by the glow from antique paraffin lanterns. *Main course US$10–20.*

✕ **Big Mike's** [138 D3] Acacia Av; m 0778 360001. Kololo's deservedly popular one-stop entertainment centre provides a swish cocktail bar, an outside beer terrace, sports events on large screen TV, live music on Thu (⊕ 20.00–22.00) & a stylish compact nightclub (⊕ Thu–Sat; free entrance).

✕ **Biryani House** [138 D2] Acacia Av. The thatched barn premises lack the ambience of nearby Khana Khazana but the comprehensive Mughlai menu is a little cheaper. *Main courses US$7–8 excl rice/naan.*

top	**Red-throated bee-eater colony** (AVZ)
above left	**Shoebill** (AVZ) pages 366–7
above	**Verreaux's eagle owl** (AVZ)
left	**Grey-crowned cranes** (AVZ)
below	**African fish eagle** (AVZ)

above   The zig-zag outline of the Virunga volcanoes provides a dramatic backdrop to the placid waters of Lake Mutanda (NP/AWL) pages 493–6

below left   On its way downhill from Mount Elgon's central caldera, the Sipi River plunges over ochre basalt cliffs to create the massif's emblematic waterfall (S/P) pages 268–70

below right   Bwindi Impenetrable National Park was not named lightly – as you'll appreciate as you traverse its steep, soggy and densely vegetated slopes in search of gorillas (S/KB) pages 504–32

above Ringed by distant mountains in Uganda, Kenya and South Sudan, the plains of Kidepo Valley National Park are one of Africa's great wildernesses (AVZ) pages 308–12

right In the shadow of the Kijura Escarpment, Ugandan kob graze the Rift Valley plains in Toro-Semliki Wildlife Reserve (AVZ) pages 409–13

below The trails to the snow peaks of the Rwenzori Mountains follow the floors of glacier-carved chasms inhabited by surreal groves of giant groundsel (SS) pages 424–37

above   The king of the jungle waits for his meal while the females in his pride do the hunting (AVZ) pages 38–9

left   The side-striped jackal is the most widespread canid in Uganda (AVZ) page 40

below   Elephants commonly roam the slopes of the Katwe volcanic craters in Queen Elizabeth National Park (S/MEH) page 45

above   A crocodile basks on the banks of the Nile below the Murchison Falls (FLPA) page 56

right   The hippo's characteristic gape may look like a yawn but it is a warning sign other creatures do well to heed (S/SU) pages 47–8

below   Buffalo tolerate oxpeckers, which rid their hides of ticks (AVZ) page 48

above   The graceful Ugandan kob appears on the national coat of arms along with the crowned crane (AVZ) page 43

above left   Jackson's hartebeest is the typical hartebeest of Uganda (AVZ) page 43

below   Rothschild's giraffe are common in the Buligi grasslands of Murchison Falls National Park (AVZ) page 48

above Warthogs reverse into their burrows at night in order to present predators with a faceful of tusks rather than the desired rump of pork (AVZ) page 48

right The gazelle-like oribi is usually seen in pairs or small groups in tall grassland (AVZ) page 45

below Ankole pastoralists take great pride in their cattle's progeny and colouration, as well as the size and spread of the horns (AVZ) pages 546–7

top   Some chimpanzees use sticks to 'fish' for termites (AVZ) pages 402–3

above left   The distinctive red-tailed monkey can be located by its cheerful, chirruping call and identified by its long, russet tail (AVZ) page 37

above right   Though it rarely comes to ground level, the black-and-white colobus is readily located thanks to a loud croaking call and distinctive coat (S/MR) page 36

left   While most other Ugandan primates inhabit forest, the patas monkey is a creature of the open savannah (AVZ) page 36

✕ Athina Club [138 D3] Windsor Crescent. Tucked away at the back of Acacia Av & hidden within a jungle of potted foliage, Kololo's longest serving restaurant serves up a big, fat, Greek buffet (*US$7*). The content changes from day to day (tasty meatballs, moussaka…) which is nice, since little else has in 20+ years (including its status as unofficial HQ of the Mountain Club of Uganda). See also page 153.

♀ Bubbles O' Leary [138 D2] Acacia Av. Authentic Irish pub (fittings imported from a bankrupt bar in Eire) but without the authentic Guinness. Popular expat pub.

Kololo

✕ Tamarai Restaurant [138 D4] 14 Lower Kololo Terr. Thai food in a pleasant environment.

☕ Prunes [104 D3] Wampewo Av, opposite IHK clinic. Stylish coffee shop & café in a garden setting between Kololo airstrip & Jinja Rd. Ugandan Arabica coffee, juices, smoothies, sandwiches, salads.

NTINDA

✕ Cayenne [117 F2] Kira Rd, near Kabira Country Club. Restaurant complex with something for everyone: a broad menu to keep families happy, evening music, dancing til late at w/ends, a hairdresser's, a lovely poolside terrace, & an enticing pool that for some reason you're not allowed to swim in. *Meals US$7–10.*

✕ Pop Up Café [117 F3] Small community café close to Ntinda New Market created to support young Ugandans with special needs.

✕ Ndere Centre [117 F2] Kampala's focus for traditional entertainment is a great place to combine a meal with a lively evening of music and dance. See also pages 151–2.

KABALAGALA

Kabalagala (or 'Kabs' to those in the know) contains Kampala's densest concentration of bars, restaurants & roadside grills. It's *the* place to enjoy a meal & party until late without moving too far. The traditional hotspot is the first few hundred metres of Muyenga Rd above its junction with Ggaba Rd. Evening parking here is all but impossible so take a matatu or a special hire taxi. Two secondary hubs also exist. One is located 500m further down Ggaba Rd & exploits its proximity to Kampala International University & Deuce's

(previously the notorious Al's Bar). The second is centred on a new line of bars & cafés at the top of Muyenga Rd near the landmark Reste Corner junction.

✕ Fasika [143 A3] Ggaba Rd, opp Tank Hill Rd; ☎0414 510441. This good-value Ethiopian restaurant next to Payless supermarket offers tasty & authentic Ethiopian dishes – pancake-like *injera* with spicy *wat* sauces – in a small garden. A good option for combining eating with a night out at the nearby Kabalagala bars. *Meals US$7.*

♀ Fuego's [143 C2] Zimwe Rd. Turn left off Tank Hill Rd at Reste Corner junction at the very top of Kabalagala. Extremely popular bar in a converted storeyed residential house & garden. *Meals US$8–10.*

✕ Khana Kazana: The Veranda [117 G5] Sister to the legendary Khana Khazana restaurant in Kololo (page 148), the Veranda allows Muyenga residents to enjoy excellent Indian food in a pleasant setting without first doing battle in city traffic. *Main excl rice & naan US$10.*

✕ The Terraces [143 D3] Tank Hill Rd. Hillside garden restaurant on the steepest bit of Tank Hill Rd. The Mongolian BBQ is a popular speciality. *BBQ US$10.*

✕ Café Kawa [143 D2] Tank Hill Rd. Terrific coffee (one of the best places in Kampala) & a good range of light lunches & more substantial meals. Free Wi-Fi. *US$8–10.*

✕ Little Donkey [143 D1] This great little restaurant has a cool atmosphere & good Mexican food. Proceeds support an organisation called S7 (ie: the year after S6, the final year in a Ugandan school) to increase options for school leavers. *US$4–8.*

✕ Yellow River Chinese Restaurant [143 C2] Reste Corner Jn, Muyenga Rd. In a city where a stomach upset is always a possibility, this Chinese restaurant doesn't have the most appealing name. Nor is it the smartest (though the 1st-floor balcony is pleasantly airy) or significantly cheaper than the competition. The food is good however, & the place is clearly a favourite with the local Chinese community who come to hoover down the noodles & stir-fries at weekends. *US$7 excl rice/naan.*

✕ Punchline [143 B3] Ggaba Rd. Pub & pork joint frequented by students from nearby Kampala International University.

✕ Le Chateau [143 A3] Quality Hill Shopping Mall, Ggaba Rd; ☎0414 510404; e sales@

qualitycuts.net. There's plenty of choice at this small but smart mall, such as this excellent & long-established Belgian restaurant in airy, thatched premises that serves a wide variety of food – from steaks to snails & guineafowl, not forgetting the essential Belgian *frites*. It's a venue worthy of a special occasion. The adjacent Quality Cuts butchery does good ham/beef/chicken baguettes while La Patisserie is a popular spot for pastries, cakes & coffee. *US$8–14*.

✖ **Café Roma** [117 G5] As you might guess, this popular restaurant at the back of Muyenga Hill is renowned primarily for its excellent pizzas & pasta dishes. Good grills & salads are also served. Expat prices. US$8–12.

✖ **Palm Café** [143 C2] Near Reste Corner junction; m 0779 674727; ⊕ closed Tue. This small roadside joint is our favourite for excellent pizzas at an affordable price. A reliable option for delivery. *US$5–7*.

✖ **Coconut Shack** [143 D1] On the road linking Reste Corner junction & the International Hospital. This decent Indian restaurant lacks the splendid setting of the nearby Khana Veranda but is slightly cheaper. *Main excl rice/naan US$7*.

KANSANGA

✖ **Le Petit Bistro** [143 D6] Ggaba Rd; ☎0393 513371; m 0772 403080. This long-serving roadside eatery is known for slow service & excellent steak dishes cooked to French prescriptions. It's a good idea to phone your order through in advance. *Meals US$8*.

✖ **Fig Tree** [143 C6] Soweto Rd; m 0772 407670. The largest public green space on Ggaba Rd, this beer garden serves roasted meats plus daily specials *(US$6)*.

✖ **Bean Café** [143 D7] This deservedly popular little café serves good coffee & some tasty wraps & sandwiches with thoughtful trimmings. If you're headed down Ggaba Rd, it's the Last Chance Saloon before the culinary wastelands of Bunga & Ggaba. The adjacent Flock of Birds craft shop is also worth a diversion. *US$5–7*.

GGABA & MUNYONYO

✖ **Cassia Lodge** [117 G6] Buziga Hill. Kampala's most spectacularly placed dining terrace overlooks Lake Victoria's Murchison Bay from the upper slopes of Buziga Hill. *Continental meals US$12*.

♀ **Miki's** [117 G6] Munyonyo Rd, off Ggaba Rd. There's more to Munyonyo than the posh Speke Resort. This roadside bar is popular with locals & expats.

✖ **Beach House** [117 G6] ☎0392 964474; m 0772 448617. A downsized & downmarket version of the sprawling Speke Resort, the Beach House is a pleasant spot to enjoy a lake view & platter of tilapia & chips (*US$10–12*). Beach House runs boat trips across the bay to a pretty sand beach called Beer Gardens 2 where BBQs & basic en-suite bandas can be arranged (page 144).

✖ **KK Beach Resort** [117 G6] On a sunny Sun afternoon, this small lakeside resort is the most hectic spot in town, thanks to hundreds of punters drawn by the prospect of beer, fish & chips & boat rides.

✖ **Lagoon Resort** [117 H7] m 0777 511339. On the other side of the bay from Munyonyo. It has quite a reputation as an out-of-town eatery. Return boat transfer (1–12 people) from Speke Resort costs US$50. *Tasty 3-course meals, cooked to exacting German prescriptions, US$20pp*.

NIGHTLIFE AND ENTERTAINMENT

NIGHTCLUBS It's perfectly possible to visit any of the places mentioned above for a meal and a couple of drinks and retire happily before midnight. If that doesn't appeal, the locations listed below will keep you entertained until very late. You can simplify things by taking a **Club Popping Tour** (m *0700 885246;* e *clubpopping@ gmail.com; www.kampalaclubpopping.yolasite.com*). Tours cost US$13 per person for a minimum six people. You're collected from Kampala Backpackers or Red Chilli on Friday and Saturday nights at 21.30 to spend about 90 minutes at each of three clubs, before being returned at 03.30.

A **word of warning**. If you're out late on a Friday night (or theoretically at any time) carry a copy of your passport and visa page. We've heard of police asking tourists for copies of ID and charging those unable to oblige with immigration

offences. On a Friday, this either means a weekend in the cells or an off-the-record contribution to the police welfare fund.

City centre

☆ **Alleygators** [104 C2] Garden City Complex. Karaoke bar & bowling alley.

☆ **Rock Bar** [127 G3] Next to the Speke Hotel (page 133). The city centre's liveliest hangout.

☆ **Sabrinas** [138 A5] Bombo Rd; ☏ 0414 250174. The original karaoke pub in Kampala with tasty buffet lunches & a good atmosphere.

☆ **Faze 2** [127 E1] Lumumba Av. Great bar/club with good music.

☆ **Iguana & Gusto bars** [138 D1] Directly behind the new Acacia Mall facing Kisementi plaza. Get in the mood with cold beers & decent blend of rock favourites in the ground floor Gusto until you feel ready to climb the wooden staircase to the heaving Iguana on the floor above.

Kabalagala/Kansanga

☆ **Deuces** [143 B4] Ggaba Rd. Deuces occupies the premises of the famous Al's Bar, an institution that rocked Gaba Rd into the small hours for over 20 years. Less intense than its predecessor but still popular.

☆ **Capital Pub** [143 B3] Kabalagala. This noisy, sprawling & crowded bar in the heart of the Kabalagala cluster still rocks after all these years. First-time male visitors will be surprised at the attention they receive from the ladies. They might be attracted by your wit & good looks, but your money is a more likely draw.

☆ **De Posh** [143 B2] Kabalagala. One of a couple of dozen nightspots lining the main drag in Kabalagala, De Posh can be distinguished by its multi-coloured illuminations.

☆ **One54** [117 G6] Ggaba Rd. Popular bar in Bunga, 2km beyond the Kansanga cluster around Deuces.

Industrial area off Jinja Road

☆ **Club Silk** [117 F3] 15–17 1st St; ☏ 0414 250907. Cheap drinks & expensive admission.

☆ **Ange Noir** [117 F3] Off Jinja Rd, between 1st & 3rd streets. Good DJs, cheap drinks, & a guaranteed lively crowd. Check out Ange Mystique upstairs for a more sophisticated clientele.

☆ **T1 Club** [117 F3] 2nd St near Ange Noir & Silk. Popular new offering.

ENTERTAINMENT

Cinema Century Cinemax's 3-screen cinema in Acacia Mall shows brand-new international releases opening within a day or so of their premieres in London and New York (and at a fraction of the cost). Pick up a copy of the *New Vision* or *Monitor* to find out what's showing when you're in town. Other cinemas are found in Metroplex, Ntinda and Ham shopping centres.

Theatres and live performances
Kampala has an active English-language theatre community, which mainly stages locally written plays in English. The **National Theatre** [104 C4] (☏ *0414 254567*), which opened in 1959 on the corner of Said Barre Avenue and De Winton Road, puts on productions most weekends. Tickets cost around US$5–6.50. Regular events during the week include the Monday night jam session when local musicians gather. There's no charge and if you play an instrument, you'll be welcome to join in. On Tuesdays at 20.00 there's a cultural performance (*US$3.50 entrance*), on Wednesdays youthful acrobats perform (⊕ *20.00; US$1.50*) and on Thursdays there's comedy (⊕ *20.00; US$3.50*). Performances take place inside the theatre, in the driveway just in front and in the bar/restaurant around the back.

Rather smarter than the National Theatre is the **La Bonita** [127 H3] theatre on Colville Street, home to The Ebonies, Kampala's most popular performing group. A plush restaurant is attached.

The **Ndere Centre** [117 F2] (☏ *0414 288123*), a purpose-built venue, set in large lawns on the outskirts of the city at Ntinda, is home to the well-known Ndere

Troupe. Performances of traditional dance and music from all corners of Uganda are given every Sunday between 18.00 and 21.00 (US$5). Additional performances include an excellent Afro-jazz night each Thursday and a talent show on Fridays for up-and-coming artists (*free entrance*). Contact the centre for other one-off plays and performances. The Ndere Centre includes an outdoor auditorium, an indoor theatre, a restaurant and even some limited accommodation. To get there, head up Kiira Road to Ntinda trading centre in northeastern Kampala, turn left at the crossroads and then head north for about 2km.

Art scene (*with thanks here to Rocca Gutteridge*) Kampala has a vibrant art scene with several good art galleries and other venues scattered around the city. Highly recommended locations are the **AfriArt Gallery** [117 F2] (*www.afriartgallery.org*) off Kiira Road in Kamwokya; **AKA Gallery** [104 B2] (*www.akagalleryuganda.com*) and **Umoja Art Gallery** [138 D1] (*www.umojaartgallery.com*) on Hannington Road and **Nommo Gallery** [127 F1] on Victoria Street, on the edge of the city centre in Nakasero. The Faculty of Fine Arts in **Makerere University** [117 E3] has some impressive resources and displays works by several of the country's leading or most promising talents. Down on the Ggaba Road opposite Deuces, **32˚ East: Ugandan Arts Trust** [143 B4] (*www.ugandanartstrust.org*) has studios, an art library, and supports new and upcoming talent through workshops and public art events.

SHOPPING

SHOPPING MALLS Several shopping malls have sprung up in Kampala in recent years though the choice and appeal of the goods available varies wildly.

The newest and smartest of Kampala's shopping centres is **Acacia Mall** [138 D1] beside Kisementi Plaza. Offerings include Aristoc bookshop, a Nakumatt supermarket, KFC, and the fashionable Cafesserie restuarant. The food hall is the best of any Kampala mall and enjoys a great view of the city, Out in Bugolobi suburb, **Village Mall** is another smart new mall, again with a Nakumatt and a bookshop, plus a branch of Javas Coffee.

On the periphery of the city centre, the pioneering **Garden City** [104 C2] and **Oasis Mall** [104 D3] are dying slowly; a consequence of competition and an ill-conceived location on Kampala's most congested roundabout. To their credit, Oasis still has Uganda's largest supermarket, a two-floor Nakumatt, while Garden City hosts the city's largest branch of Aristoc bookshop and the excellent Nawab Indian restaurant on the rooftop.

Lugogo Mall [117 F3] on the east side of the city contains two South African 'megastores', a Shoprite supermarket and an equally extensive Game store. If you're using public transport, the rather limited **Shoprite Mall** [126 D7] by the old taxi park will be most convenient (avoid this if you're driving; this congested area is virtually impossible to reach in a vehicle). On the eastern side of the expanding metropolis, you'll find a couple of average malls at Naalya: **Metroplex Mall** [117 G2] is right beside the Northern Bypass while **Quality Mall** [143 A3] is 1km towards Namugongo. If you're on the southern, Entebbe side of town, the related **Quality Village** [117 E7] at Lubowa is the most convenient (see below).

SUPERMARKETS You'll find most of your day-to-day requirements in small supermarkets in suburbs such as Mengo, Bugolobi, Kabalagala/Ggaba Road and Kisementi. Two international supermarket chains are present in Kampala. The best – though not the cheapest – is the Kenyan megastore chain, **Nakumatt**. In addition

to its flagship branch in Oasis Mall [104 D3], Nakumatt has smaller outlets in Bugolobi, Naguru and Katwe. Otherwise the South African **Shoprite** [126 D7] is represented at Lugogo Mall, Metroplex Mall and the Shoprite Mall near the old taxi park. Better value than all the above is the local **Quality Supermarket** chain found in Old Kampala [143 A3] and inside the Quality Malls at Lubowa and Naalya (near Metroplex Mall). Capital Shoppers has branches in Garden City, beside Nakasero Market, and in Ntinda's Capital Mall.

If you're stocking up for a safari and hope to avoid the usual packaged or frozen foodstuffs, the Chinese-owned Italian Supermarket in Kabalagala's Tank Hill Parade [143 C2] has a decent selection of cold meats and cheese. For years, the leader in this field was the **Quality Cuts** [143 A3] deli/butchery in Quality Hill Mall but the standard has dropped under new management.

BAKERIES Salt bread, as well as the locally preferred sweet variety, is available from most supermarkets these days. For basic loaves, the **Shoprite** supermarkets will do nicely but for buns, baguettes, croissants, French sticks, etc, head down the Ggaba Road to **The Patisserie** in the tiny Quality Hill Mall [143 A3]. The Dutch **Brood** operates from Nando's on Kampala Road.

BOOKSHOPS There are several bookshops in Kampala, though most focus exclusively on religious texts. The main exception is **Aristoc Bookshop** [127 H5] which has branches on Kampala Road and in Garden City and Acacia malls. These stock an impressive selection of current novels, travel guides, field guides, tourist maps and publications about Ugandan history. The closest competition is **Bookpoint** in the Village Mall in Bugolobi. Prunes restaurant on Wampewo Avenue has a good selection of second hand texts.

HANDICRAFTS AND CURIOS Though home-produced crafts are increasing and improving, most local craft shops are still dominated by ubiquitous Kenyan carvings of animals and Maasai warriors. For the greatest choice of vendors (rather than choice of items), visit the **African Craft Village** [104 C3] behind the National Theatre and the **Exposure Africa** [126 C1] collective on Buganda Road. The small but long-established **Uganda Crafts** [126 B1] on Bombo Road is pretty good and benefits disabled people. For less obvious items, try the lower section of **Nakasero Market** [127 F5].

The best source of quality crafts is the **'Banana Boat'** (✆ *0414 252190;* e *crafts@ bananaboat.co.ug; see ad, 4th colour section*) shops at Kisementi, Garden City and Lugogo Mall. These contain an excellent variety of items produced by over 90 small Ugandan artisans and workshops, many of them exclusively for Banana Boat. Bespoke items include jewellery, leather trunks and boxes, tribal art, handmade paper products as well as guidebooks and maps.

OTHER PRACTICALITIES

CLUBS AND SOCIETIES Travellers with special interests may want to contact the following clubs and societies. A fuller list is contained in Kampala's free monthly ad-mag, *The Eye*.

International Women's Organisation
e ugandaiwo@yahoo.com. Regular meetings on the 1st Thu of the month at the National Museum on Kiira Rd. Special events.

Mountain Club of Uganda m 0772 200745/ 0757 107330; www.mcu.org. Meets at 17.30 on the 1st Thu of each month at the Athina Club on Windsor Crescent (page 149).

Nature Uganda ⦚0414 540719. Ring for details of free monthly nature walks around Kampala. **Uganda Bird Guides Club** m 0777 912938; e ugandabirdguides@hotmail.com. www. ugandabirdguides.org. The country's top bird guides all belong to this club, which is well worth contacting if you're looking for a reliable freelance guide with local knowledge.

COMMUNICATIONS

Post and courier services The main **post office** [127 F4] on the corner of Kampala and Speke roads has a poste restante service as well as selling stamps, etc. Post into and out of Kampala is fairly reliable, but it is extremely slow and should be avoided for valuable or urgent dispatches. It is more expensive but safer to use a major international courier service such as **DHL** [104 B2] (*Clement Hill Rd;* ⦚ *0312 210006*) or **TNT** [138 A4] (*behind Clock Tower;* ⦚ *0414 343942*).

Internet and email The advent of smartphones has drastically reduced the number of internet cafés in Kampala. However, most suburbs still contain a couple of basic setups in which kids surf for porn on Trojan-riddled computers. For more serious research, an internet café survives at Club 5 on the Makerere University campus. Most hotels offer free Wi-Fi for guests as does the Café Javas restaurant (though offset by pricey food).

Telephone Mobile phones have rendered the parastatal landline services all but obsolete when it comes to international calls. All over the city centre you'll see shops and kiosks offering domestic and international calls. Calls within Uganda cost around Ush300 per minute and Ush500 (a quarter US dollar) to most of the rest of the world. An international payphone is available at the Kampala Backpackers, and most upmarket hotels can book international calls at inflated rates.

Useful telephone numbers See pages 155–6 for clinics with 24-hour emergency and ambulance services.

Emergencies (ambulance, fire or police assistance) ⦚ 999 or 0414 342222/3

Central Police Station ⦚ 0414 254561/2

GORILLA-TRACKING PERMITS Permits for reserves in Uganda can be bought directly from the **Uganda Wildlife Authority (UWA) headquarters** on Kiira Road [138 C2] (⦚ *0414 355000;* e *info@ugandawildlife.org; www.ugandawildlife.org; information office* ⊕ *08.00–13.00 & 14.00–17.00 Mon–Fri, 09.00–13.00 Sat*) between the Uganda Museum and the British High Commission or through any major tour operator. The **Kampala Backpackers' Hostel** (page 137) can usually arrange permits for reserves in Uganda, Rwanda and (if operational at the time) the Democratic Republic of Congo (DRC). If in Jinja, contact Nile River Explorers (page 242).

HAIR AND BEAUTY SALONS Though men and women around the world prioritise haircare differently, the distinction is most marked in Africa and Uganda is no exception. While Ugandan men simply offer their heads for a quick shave and polish, their female counterparts demand all manner of perms, straightenings, highlights, weaves, wigs and braids – exercises that can involve teams of attendants and can take a day or more.

As you would expect, therefore, ladies have plenty of places to choose from in Kampala, including several recommended locations that cater for both African and Caucasian hair. Recommended salons include 5enses [sic] at **Cayenne** in Ntinda (m *0772 587603*), **Aisha** at Kisementi (⦚ *0414 344366*) and **Sparkles** in the Lugogo,

Forest, Garden City and Oasis malls (m *0783 926871*). Several of the upmarket hotels in the city centre also have in-house salons. While you're at it, a nail makeover is an additional and affordable treat. Even the most basic of local salons have an in-house specialist. It's also perfectly normal procedure, while sitting at a roadside bar or café, to hail a roaming mani/pedi-curist with his basket of files and nail polish.

Gents' haircuts are more complicated unless you fancy a US$1 crew cut with an electric shaver. Any local barber will provide this (let's hope your trip doesn't coincide with a power cut) but it's considerably harder to find one who has mastered the use of scissors. The most reliable place is **Aisha** (*US$8.50*) while at other locations, such as **Sparkles** (page 154) and the **Indian barber** (*US$3*) in Old Kampala it's pot luck. You may emerge as a fashion icon or an apparition from which babies cringe and adults politely avert their eyes.

LIBRARIES   The **Uganda Society** (☏ *0414 234964;* e *ugsociety@bushnet.net* ⊕ *08.00– 12.30 Mon–Fri, closed public holidays; a nominal daily membership fee is charged to casual visitors*), in the National Museum Building on Kiira Road, houses what is probably the most comprehensive public collection of current and out of print books about Uganda in existence. Serious readers and researchers may hear about the magnificent Africana collection in the otherwise useless Makerere University library. However, its valuable contents are securely (and very sensibly) segregated within a caged section and access requires one to jump through a number of bureaucratic hoops.

MEDIA
Newspapers   The main local English-language newspapers are *New Vision* and *Monitor*, both of which include reasonable coverage of African and international affairs and are widely available in Kampala, as is the excellent Nairobi-published weekly *East African*. Current and old issues of the American *Time* and *Newsweek* magazines can be bought from street vendors. You'll find UK and US newspapers in the Sheraton Bookshop.

Medical services   The standard of health care in Kampala has improved greatly in recent years and while not up to Western standards for serious medical attention, you'll find the city's better hospitals and clinics superior in terms of speed of service, referrals and cost. Though those listed below are generally considered competent by expats and travellers, your hotel may be able to suggest other options in your vicinity.

✚ **The Surgery** [117 F3] Naggulu Dr; ⊕ 0.341490, 32.6020; ☏ 0312 256001, 24hr emergency & ambulance service: m 0752 756003. Previously the clinic in the British High Commission, this is the choice of many expats. Many travellers have also found the website a useful resource (*www.thesurgeryuganda.org*).
✚ **Case Medical Centre** [138 A4] 69–71 Buganda Rd; ☏ 0414 250362, 24hr emergency line: ☏ 0312 250362. Modern, well-equipped clinic close to the city centre.
✚ **Bai Medical Centre** [136 G2] Rashid Khamis Rd, Old Kampala; ☏ 0414 345326/34/0312 261551,

emergency line: 0414 255700. This hospital is conveniently located if you're staying in budget lodgings in the Natete Road area.
✚ **International Hospital Kampala (IHK)** [143 D1] Namuwongo/Kisugu; ☏ 0312 200400; e ihk@africaonline.co.ug. This modern hospital (allied to the IMC clinic below) can be approached either from Kabalagala (off Ggaba Road), heading behind the Reste Corner junction or from the junction just west of the 'Mukwano' roundabout railway crossing junction on Mukwano Rd.

✚ **International Medical Centre (IMC)** [126 B1] KPC Bldg, Bombo Rd; ☎ 0312 200400, or Kitgum Hse, Jinja Rd; ☎ 0312 341291; 24hr emergency line: m 0772 741291; 24hr ambulance service: m 0772 200400/1. IMC also has several branches upcountry.

Dental services Kampala has a small clique of competent dentists including **Jubilee Dental Practice** (☎ *0414 344647*) and **Doctors A & G Madan** (m *0772 433058/9*). The well-equipped dental clinic at **Mengo Hospital** [136 C2] is equally efficient and very reasonably priced.

MONEY

Credit cards Most upmarket hotels in Kampala accept major international credit and debit cards, as do some of the smarter restaurants, but you will need to pay cash for most services and purchases. Visa and MasterCard can be used to draw cash from ATM machines (pages 70–1).

Foreign exchange (cash) Private forex bureaux are dotted all over the city, with the main concentration along Kampala Road, and will readily exchange US dollars and other hard currencies into Uganda shillings. Most bureaux are open from 09.00 to 17.00 on weekdays and a few are also open on Saturday mornings. Exchange rates at the major forex bureaux are pretty uniform, and better than at the banks, though you might want to shop around before you change large sums of money. If you need to change money on Sundays or outside normal office hours, try the forex in Speke Hotel. This will also exchange travellers' cheques but at an extremely poor rate. You could also try the upmarket hotels, but generally they change money only for hotel residents.

NATIONAL PARKS AND RESERVES The **UWA** (see box, page 32) is in charge of all of Uganda's national parks and game reserves. Their headquarters is on Kiira Road between the Uganda Museum and the British High Commission. Gorilla-viewing permits for Bwindi and Mgahinga can be booked and paid for here (see also page 154), as can *banda* accommodation in the various national parks and game reserves, and you can also pick up some informative brochures. For information about Budongo, Mpanga, Mabira, Kalinzu and other forest reserves, contact the **National Forest Authority** (☎ *0414 230365*).

PHOTOGRAPHY Most visitors to Uganda now use digital cameras and are spared the disappointment that can result from poor-quality film and developing processes available in Uganda. If you are still using slide or photographic film, be sure to bring a sufficient supply with you and take it home to be developed. If you do need photographic services your first port of call should be **Colour Chrome** [126 C2] which has a branch on Kampala Road (☎ *0414 230556*) and another in Acacia Mall at Kisementi [138 D1]. Photographic, digital photographic and slide-processing services are offered.

WHAT TO SEE AND DO

The National Museum, Kasubi Tombs and other sites of interest situated more-or-less within the city limits of Kampala are covered on the following pages. As with any city, however, just strolling around can be illuminating; the contrast between the posh part of town north of Kampala Road and the sleazier area near the bus and taxi parks is striking. It is also possible to take a boda-boda tour – see page 132. Sites

of interest in Entebbe are covered in the next chapter, while those further afield from Kampala are covered under *Day trips out of Kampala*, pages 166–8.

CITY CENTRE Kampala's modern city centre – which sprawls across a valley about 2.5km east of Kabaka Mwanga's former capital on Kasubi Hill, immediately east of Lugard's original **fort** [136 F1] on Old Kampala Hill – boasts little in the way of compelling sightseeing. The most important cluster of architecturally noteworthy buildings is centred on the acacia-lined **Parliament Avenue** [104 B4] on the east side of the city centre. On Parliament Avenue itself, the imposing though not exactly inspiring **Parliament Building**, built during the colonial era and still the seat of national government today, is a vast white monolith entered via an angular and some might say rather ugly concrete arch, built to commemorate independence in 1962. On the same block lies the so-called **White House**, occupied by the Kampala City Council, while immediately to its east, on De Winton Road, stand the **National Theatre** [104 C4] and attached **African Crafts Village**. Arguably more attractive than any of the above is the **railway station** [104 C4], which lies on Jinja Road about 200m further south, and was built in the 1920s but has fallen into virtual disuse since passenger services out of Kampala were suspended a few years ago.

The **Independence Monument** [127 G3] on Nile Avenue, just outside the fenced gardens, is worth a minor diversion – a tall, attractively proportioned neo-traditional statue of a mother and child emerging from mummy-like bandages of colonial bondage. The attractive gardens behind the statue were originally created to commemorate the jubilee of King George VI and now form the grounds of the Kampala Sheraton. Once a popular lunchtime space, today they are closed to the general public, security reasons being the rather lame excuse.

OLD KAMPALA NATIONAL MOSQUE [136 F1] (☉ *09.00–18.00 Mon–Thu & Sat–Sun, 09.00–11.00 & 14.30–18.00 Fri; tour US$3.50*) Old Kampala Hill, which rises gently to the immediate west of the city centre, 10 minutes' walk from the new taxi park, was the site of the original fort and capital founded by Captain Frederick Lugard in 1890. Enclosed within the oval Old Kampala Road, the hill is dotted with a few fine colonial-era buildings of Asian design, now generally rather rundown though some have been strikingly renovated. Old Kampala is most notable today as the focal point for Kampala's Islamic community and an imposing new mosque. It was initiated by Idi Amin in the 1970s, but the project stalled after the dictator's overthrow and was only completed in 2006 with funds provided by the late Libyan leader, Colonel Gadaffi. When work on the mosque restarted after a 25-year delay, Amin's concrete monolith was demolished to make way for today's magnificent copper-domed structure.

Given the dearth of sightseeing highlights in Kampala, a visit to the mosque is an increasingly popular – and genuinely worthwhile – diversion. Visitors are welcomed and you'll find a tented tourism office (m *0772 502037*) just inside the main gate. There is no need to book a daytime tour but a sunrise visit must be booked in advance: starting at 06.30, this enables you to climb the tower and watch dawn break over the city. Girls will be provided with shawls to wear. Men may wear shorts that extend below the knee. If they are deemed too short, a kanzu will be provided.

The highlights are the main hall and the ascent of the minaret. The former is an imposing space which, carpeted but otherwise unfurnished, is dominated by a forest of massive columns that support the roof and copper dome. European, Arab and African influences meld with Italian stained-glass windows, Ugandan timber and an Arabian mosaic on the underside of the dome above a massive and magnificent

metal chandelier. Inside the minaret, 306 steps spiral upwards to provide a superbly giddy 360° view over the city.

Part of the complex, but accessed from Old Kampala Road, is a period building with a vaguely Arcadian frontage. This is an approximation of a historic building that was unfortunately demolished to make way for the mosque car park. Though widely known as the Old Fort, it was built some years after Lugard's occupation in 1908 and was actually Kampala's first museum.

MAKERERE UNIVERSITY [117 E3] The main campus of Uganda's respected Makerere University, which was founded in 1922, lies about 1km north of the city centre and can be entered via the main gate on Makerere Hill Road, some 200m west of Wandegeyre traffic lights on Bombo Road. The **university library** has an extensive Africana section, the **campus bookshop** stocks a selection of local-interest academic works, and the gallery in the **Faculty of Fine Arts** has regular exhibitions. The spacious green grounds possess an aura of academic gentility at odds with the hustle and bustle of downtown Kampala, while the older buildings – in particular the whitewashed **Main Hall** with its handsome bell tower – will be of interest to students of colonial architecture. Students of contemporary architecture can also learn a thing or two (mainly the sort of thing they can expect to get away with these days) from recent additions to the campus.

NATIONAL MUSEUM OF UGANDA [138 C2] (*Kiira Rd, about 2km from the city centre;* ◷ *08.00–17.00 daily; a small admission fee is charged*) The National Museum of Uganda is the oldest in East Africa, and perhaps the best, rooted in an ethnographic collection first exhibited in 1905 in a small Greek temple near Lugard's fort on Old Kampala Hill. Formally established in 1908, the museum was initially known by the local Baganda as Enyumba ya Mayembe (House of Fetishes) and its exhibits were believed to bestow supernatural powers on the colonial administration. In 1954, the museum relocated to its present site on Kiira Road. For those with an interest in pre-colonial African history, there are stimulating displays on the Nakayima Tree, Ntusi and Bigo bya Mugenyi, as well as other aspects of Ugandan history. Of more general interest is a fantastic collection of traditional musical instruments from all over the continent, and the ethnographic gallery, which houses a variety of exhibits relating to traditional Ugandan lifestyles. On foot or in a private vehicle, follow Kampala/Bombo Road north out of the city centre, turning right at the traffic lights at Wandegeyre into Haji Kasule Road, crossing straight across another roundabout after 400m into Kiira Road. The museum is clearly signposted to the right, 600m past this roundabout. Matutus between the new taxi park and Kamwokya will drop passengers roughly opposite the museum entrance, and can be picked up at taxi ranks along Kampala/Bombo road north of the junction with Burton Road. The **Uganda Society Library** in the main museum building (◷ *08.00–noon Mon–Fri*) has a comprehensive collection of published works relating to Uganda.

NATETE ROAD A number of minor historical sites lie within 1km of the Natete Road, which runs east out of central Kampala, past the popular Namirembe Guesthouse and Kampala Backpackers, in the direction of Masaka.

Namirembe Cathedral [136 C1] The Anglican (now Church of Uganda) cathedral perched atop Namirembe Hill, roughly 1.5km west of the city centre off Natete Road, is one of the most impressive colonial-era constructions in Kampala, and it

JAWBONE SHRINES

The Baganda traditionally believe that the spirit of a dead man resides in his jawbone, for which reason it is customary for the jawbone of a deceased king to be removed and preserved in a separate shrine before the rest of the body is buried. The jawbone shrine is normally located at the last capital site used by the dead ruler and is housed within a miniature reproduction of his palace. Jawbone shrines associated with almost all of the kabakas who preceded Mutesa I lie scattered across an area of less than 500km² northwest of present-day Kampala. Most are now untended and have suffered from serious neglect over the past century, but their location remains well known to locals.

According to the historian Roland Oliver: 'after the dislocation of the jawbone, the body of the king was handed over to the chief executioner, Senkaba, who took it away … to the royal cemetery. There, the body was placed on a bed and certain friends and officials of the dead kabaka were killed and their bodies were thrown upon the heap. These sites did not, like the jawbone shrines, become places of pilgrimage. Nevertheless they were guarded by Senkaba and his representatives.' While jawbone shrines are associated with one specific king, the royal burial grounds are more centralised entities. At least ten tombs of the earlier kings are situated within a 1km² area at Gombe, 20km north of Kampala, while a similar number of more recent kings are buried at Merera along the Hoima Road.

The last ruler of Buganda to receive a traditional royal burial was Kabaka Suuna II, whose jawbone shrine is preserved in a large traditional structure at the site of his last *kibuga* (capital) at Wamala. Suuna's successors – influenced by Islam and Christianity – were buried at Kasubi with their jawbones intact. There is some ambiguity about where the rest of Suuna's remains are located: one tradition asserts that he was the last king to be buried at Merera, while others claim that he was buried at Wamala. The most likely explanation is that Suuna was originally buried at Merera, but his body was later exhumed by his son Mutesa I to be buried alongside the jawbone at Wamala.

also offers superb views over the city centre and suburbs. The original cathedral, completed in 1903 and consecrated a year later (see box, page 164), was built entirely by Baganda artisans, albeit under the supervision of a British missionary, and could hold a congregation of 3,000 people. It was described contemporaneously by W E Hoyle as 'a remarkable building with walls of sun-dried bricks, and brick columns supporting the thatch roof, containing 120 tonnes of thatch [and a] ceiling covered with washed reeds of elephant grass'. This building was destroyed by lightning in 1910 and the present cathedral, a more conventional red-brick structure, built to vast dimensions and graced by some attractive stained-glass windows, was completed in 1919. The cemetery contains the grave of Bishop Hannington, murdered near Jinja in 1885, as well as that of Sir Albert Cook, a pioneering medical doctor who arrived in Kampala in 1896 and whose extensive writings about the early colonial era are quoted elsewhere in this guide. Brass memorial plaques on the wall testify to the often short lives of Europeans in those early days.

Bulange Building [136 C3] Less than 500m past the turn-off to Namirembe, the Bulange Building – traditional seat of the Buganda Parliament – stands on

the south side of Natete Road, directly opposite the junction with Sentema Road. It is one of the most impressive colonial-era buildings in Uganda. Though its high roof, capped with a trio of spires, is visible from the main road, to see the building properly you'll have to leave Natete Road to find the main entrance at the head of a straight, tree-lined avenue known as Kabaka Njagala ('the king is coming') which runs for a mile to Mengo Palace (see below) on the facing hill. Entrance to the Bulange is allowed unless the building is in official use. About 100m downhill from the Bulange, two exotic giant tortoises dawdle around the gardens of an impressive old building, once the home of Stanley Kisingire, one of the regents of the infant king, Daudi Chwa. Local wisdom is that the tortoises are around 500 years old, but they apparently came to Mengo as recently as 1945.

A 'Buganda Tourism Center' [sic] stands beside the Bulange gate. It's still early days for this worthy initiative, but as things stand, you'll be better informed by reading this book.

Kabaka Mwanga's Lake, Rubaga Cathedral and Mengo Palace In 1885, Mwanga settled on the ultimately overambitious scheme of digging a large lake near his capital and linking it with Lake Victoria. The lake was completed in 1888, but the intended link was abandoned when Muslim dissenters drove the kabaka from his capital.

The lake was at one time more of a health hazard than it was a tourist attraction, but the surrounding area has been cleared and there are some interesting birds to be seen on its fringes – notably large colonies of cattle egrets and weavers. Follow the Natete Road out of the city centre for about 2km then turn left just beyond the spired Bulange Building. As you descend the hill, you'll see the lake. The shore can be reached about 1km further on, by taking a steep dirt road on your left towards the Miracle Church where the deep pockets of born-again Christians – or *savedees* as they are known – have funded a massive auditorium.

The lake can easily be visited in conjunction with the Catholic cathedral on Rubaga Hill, which lies about 500m south of Natete Road along Mutesa Road, but is neither as old nor as impressive as its Church of Uganda equivalent at Namirembe. Also close to the lake is the kabaka's Twekobe Palace on the low Lubiri Hill, the site chosen by Mwanga after his coronation in 1884. The ill-fated Kabaka Edward Mutesa was driven from this palace in 1966 by Idi Amin on Obote's orders. The army subsequently occupied the site until 1993, gaining a reputation for terror. Hundreds were taken through its gates by the agents of Amin and Obote, never to be seen again, while ill-paid and ill-disciplined troops terrorised the leafy suburbs of Rubaga and Mengo. The Buganda Kingdom is once more in possession of Lubiri Hill and you'll find an informed guide to show you round at the tourism office just inside the main gate (*US$3.50pp*). The restored Twekobe Palace is closed to the public and the 'attractions' mostly relate to the Amin era. The centrepiece is a complex of underground cells and execution chambers decorated by movingly defiant graffiti scrawled in charcoal by the doomed inmates (you'll need a translator). It's a grim hark back to dark days and it's a relief to emerge into Mengo's picturesque environs and be thankful that those days are past.

HOIMA ROAD Two important sets of royal tombs, collectively housing the bodies of the four kabakas of Buganda to have died since the 1850s, lie within walking distance of the road running northwest from central Kampala towards Hoima. The Kasubi Tombs are the more publicised of the two sites, but the Wamala Tomb is no less worthwhile (its caretakers are less accustomed to tourist visits).

Kasubi Tombs [116 D3] (**m** *0773 747319*; ⊕ *08.00–18.00 daily; admission US$3.50, inc the services of a knowledgeable guide*) In 1882, Kabaka Mutesa relocated his *kibuga* (palace) to Nabulagala Hill, briefly the capital of his father Suuna II some 30 years earlier, and renamed it Kasubi Hill after his birthplace some 50km further east. Mutesa constructed a large hilltop palace called Muziba Azala Mpanga (roughly translating as 'a king is born of a king'), where he died in 1884 following a prolonged illness. As was the custom, Kasubi Hill was abandoned after the king's death – his successor Mwanga established a new capital at Mengo Hill – but rather less conventionally Mutesa was the first kabaka to be buried with his jawbone intact, in a casket built by the Anglican missionary Alexander Mackay. In a further break with tradition, Kasubi rather than Mengo was chosen as the burial place of Kabaka Mwanga in 1910, seven years after his death in exile (see box, pages 162–3). It also houses the tombs of his successor Daudi Chwa II, who ruled from 1897 to 1939, and of Edward Mutesa II, whose body was returned to Uganda in 1971, two years after his death in exile.

Until 2010, the tombs were housed within the original palace built by Mutesa, a fantastic domed structure of poles, reeds and thatch, which – aside from the addition of a concrete base – seemed to have changed little in appearance over the intervening 130 years. Unfortunately on the night of 16 March 2010, the building, for causes still unknown, burned down. The structure, reduced to an arching framework of hitherto unsuspected (or at least unmentioned) metal beams, remained under a patchwork of gaudy orange tarpaulins for almost three years before a Ush10 billion reconstruction programme started in January 2013. When complete, it should then be business as usual. Fifty-two giant reed rings in the roof of the new hut will once more represent each of the clans of Buganda while a giant veil – created from countless pieces of barkcloth – will screen the four tombs from the vulgar gaze of the public. Unfortunately, a fascinating collection of irreplaceable royal artefacts that stood in front of the curtain – including portraits of the four monarchs, traditional musical instruments, weapons, shields, fetishes, gifts donated by Queen Victoria and a stuffed leopard once kept as a pet by Mutesa I – were destroyed in the fire.

Interestingly, the restoration is providing the Baganda with the opportunity to reconstruct the tombs using their original design. Historically, it has transpired, the tomb of a kabaka was a massive cone resembling a huge, thatched wigwam, some 16m tall. The significantly lower, dome-like structure destroyed in 2010 was a British imposition dating back to 1938 when the introduction of load bearing concrete beams enabled the overall height of the structure to be reduced by 6m. Whether this was (as some academics claim) a colonial attempt to hijack Baganda tradition and anchor it in the shadow of British authority, or an attempt to reduce the building's vulnerability to lightning, the new Kasubi Tombs is rising upwards in its original – and even more imposing – form. It should be completed by the middle of 2017.

The tombs are maintained by the wives of the various kings – or more accurately by female descendants of their long-deceased wives – some of whom live on the property, while others do a one-month shift there twice every year. Many of the kings' wives, sisters and other female relations are also buried at Kasubi, not in the main palace but in the series of smaller buildings that flank the driveway. The complex is entered via a large traditional reception hut known as a *bujjabukula*. This is tended by the chief gateman, known as Mulamba (a hereditary title), who customarily dresses in a brilliant yellow barkcloth robe, as do his assistants.

An excellent booklet on the tombs is sometimes on sale at the site, and well worth buying for its background information on Baganda culture. To get there from the city centre, follow Makerere Hill Road west from Wandegere crossroads

Edited from the Uganda Notes *of September 1910*

Mwanga was deported in the year 1899 [and] moved to the Seychelles, where he died in May 1903 ... Nothing can be more distressing to the Baganda mind than that a near relative should not be buried in his own Butaka [home] ... So the leading chiefs and the descendants of Mwanga have been agitating to exhume the body and have it transferred to Uganda, and at last permission was obtained.

2 August [1910] was a day of great excitement, and business, as far as natives was [sic] concerned, was suspended. A large crowd proceeded to meet the steamer at Kampala Port to bring up the large packing case in which was enclosed the leaden coffin containing the body of the deceased king [Mwanga], and at 15.00 an enormous concourse followed the body to Namirembe Cathedral ... The funeral cortège entered the church, filling it from end to end, and part of the Burial Service was read ... The body was then removed to Kasubi, the burial place of King Mutesa ... [where] a vault had been carefully prepared of brick and cement, and a double coffin was in readiness.

On the morning of Wednesday [3 August], everyone of any importance in or near Mengo was present at the tomb and the gruesome process of opening the leaden shell in order to examine the remains was gone through. Repugnant though it seems to open a coffin so many years after a death has taken place, it was insisted that as King Daudi had never seen his father in the flesh he must on no account miss seeing his corpse, and to the surprise of everyone concerned the features were quite recognisable ... Daudi took hold of a barkcloth together with Mugemo and Kago and covered up the corpse, this being the custom of a son whose father is dead, and then the body was buried ... In the afternoon the concluding part of the Burial Service was read; Bishop Tucker and a very large number of Europeans were present, together with a crowd of natives, to perform the last rites.

To follow old custom, Mwanga should really have been buried inside his own court [on Mengo Hill], and many of the natives were inclined to follow precedent; but it was finally decided that if he were to be buried in Mengo, the Kabaka Daudi would have to turn out [of his] comfortable and permanent residence, [which] seemed inadvisable, especially when there is the difficulty of securing a suitable site for the new court in the Capital. On the morning of Thursday 4 August, a very

(passing the main gate of Makerere University) for almost 2km to Nakulabye roundabout. Turn right and 2km further on you'll reach Kasubi Market at the junction with Kimera Road, from where the tombs – signposted to the left – lie about 500m uphill along Masiro Road. Plenty of matutus run from the city centre to Kasubi Market.

Wamala Tomb [116 C1] Situated on the crest of a low hill some 12km northwest of central Kampala, Wamala Tomb is housed in an attractive, traditional, thatched domed building, slightly smaller and older than its counterpart at Kasubi. The hill is the former palace and sacred resting place of Kabaka Mutesa I's father and predecessor Kabaka Suuna, who ascended the throne c1830 and died in 1856. Suuna is remembered as a despotic ruler and keen hunter. The menagerie he maintained at Wamala – said to have included lions, leopards, elephants and various smaller creatures – sufficiently impressed the first Arab traders to reach Buganda that word of it reached Sir Richard Burton at the Swahili Coast.

interesting ceremony took place, which had been deemed impossible until such time as Mwanga should be buried in his own country.

The following is a translation of an account of the ceremony, written by the Rev Henry Wright Duta:

[King Daudi] came and stood outside his court [on] the coronation chair … Mugema opened proceedings by bringing a barkcloth and hanging it about the king from his shoulders … He then put on a calfskin to remind [Daudi] that his first forefather was thus dressed … Then came Kasuju, who brought a second barkcloth and also a leopard skin, with which he also proceeded to dress the king … the meaning of the leopard skin is that it separates him from all other princes and makes him into the king … The reason why he is dressed in two barkcloths is because he is called the 'father of twins', that is to say he gives birth to many people and he rules over many people.

[Kasuju] brought the king a sword … saying 'take this sword and with it cut judgement in truth (distribute justice equally and fairly), anyone who rebels against you, you shall kill with this sword'. Then they brought before him the drum which is called Mujagazo which is very old indeed and which has carved on it a python (once sacred to the Baganda) … this is supposed to be the drum which Kimera had with him when he came from Bunyoro … A shield was then presented to the king and … two spears … [and] a bow and arrows … the weapons with which Kimera first came to Uganda … Then came a long string of people bringing offerings too numerous to mention.

After that the king was placed on the shoulders of Namutwe so that the crowd might all have a good look at him, saying 'This is your king' and the crowd set up a loud yell beating their hands with their mouths to produce a tremulant effect. Then the king together with the Lubuga (queen sister) and an old woman to represent the head of the king's wives were all carried on the shoulders of their attendants back into the [royal] Court … Then came the whole of the visitors to the king to congratulate him on his accession, he sitting down on the seat called Mubanga, which resembles a drum, and old Prince Mbogo, the brother of [the late king] Mutesa, came and wrapped some cents around his wrist in place of the cowrie shells which used to obtain here. Every member of the king's tribe – princes, princesses and everyone else who could be present – brought him presents of money … and for days afterwards all his relatives came in batches and went through the same ceremony.

Wamala is neither as well known as Kasubi, nor as carefully tended, but it is just as interesting in its comparatively low-key way. A diverse array of royal artefacts – spears, shields, drums and other musical instruments – is displayed in front of the barkcloth drape that veils the tomb itself. Opposite the main building stands the former palace and tomb of Suuna's mother, Namasole Kanyange, according to tradition a very beautiful woman and also highly influential – it's said that Suuna insisted the namasole live alongside him so that he could keep an eye on her doings. In keeping with Kiganda royal custom, Kanyange appointed a successor as namasole before her death. The lineage survives to this day: the fourth namasole to Suuna is resident at Wamala and still performs traditional duties such as tending the royal tomb.

To reach Wamala, follow the Hoima Road out of Kampala, passing the junction for Kisubi, then after another 6km the trading centre of Nansana. Right at the end of the elongated and congested corridor of Nansana, a small faded purple signpost indicates a right turn to Wamala (200m before a swamp hinders Nansana's further extension). From this junction, a rough 1.5km dirt track marked with wooden signs

The consecration of Namirembe Cathedral on 21 July 1904 was described vividly in the Mengo Notes *a month after the event:*

A great crowd began to assemble at 06.00, and … the crush at the doors [was] so great that they had to be opened to prevent people being crushed to death. There was a considerable amount of struggling and good-natured fighting among the Baganda desirous of gaining admission, for not more than 3,000 could get in, and the crowd must have numbered nearly 10,000 … Numbers climbed through the windows and jumped down on to those seated inside … Mr Savile had a bone in the hand broken in trying to repress a rush. To while away the time of waiting Mr Hattersley gave half an hour's organ recital … The European and native clergy, over 40 in number, assembled at the west door, and all in procession marched up to the Church, repeating the opening sentences of the Consecration Service … in English and Luganda … Then came morning prayer … and the wonderful way in which the congregation responded, and joined in the hymns and chants, will long be remembered.

Instead of dispersing, the vast crowd unable to gain admission to the service had filled all the school rooms around the church, and still enough remained to nearly fill the yard. [They] contributed to the collection just as though they had taken part in the service. This considerably delayed matters, and it seemed as though the bringing in of offerings would never cease … The collection consisted of rupees, rice, and cowrie shells … in bundles more than enough to fill a whole collecting bag. Then came goats led up by ropes to the communion rails … fowls in a coop and singly; one, trussed feet and wings, was solemnly handed by the sideman to the Bishop along with his bag of shells … More than 30 head of cattle had been sent in by chiefs, but it was wisely decided that it would not be well to admit these to the church. The proceeds of the collection thus totalled up to over £80, the exact amount we cannot give, as the cattle have not all been sold at the time of writing.

leads to the hilltop tomb, which, though now surrounded by surburban growth, is still visible from some distance away.

GGABA AND MUNYONYO The twin ports of Ggaba and Munyonyo lie about 2km apart near the southwest of Murchison Bay on Lake Victoria, some 10km southeast of central Kampala. Both are worthwhile goals for a day's outing. Ggaba is a compact, bustling settlement with a busy market that spills down to a waterfront that used to consist of a grim and muddy littoral. This was tidied up a few years ago with the construction of a number of stone quays. While the vegetable market, fish auction, and fish smoking activities remain as sensory as ever, the quays have become a popular spot for residents and visitors to take the lake air and perhaps a drink at a makeshift bar. Folk do much the same, but in greener and more spacious surroundings, at the historically more significant port of Munyonyo, 2km south. This was (and technically still is) the royal port to which the Bagandan kabakas led their entourages in periodical exoduses from their Kampala palaces. During the 19th century it was home to a large canoe fleet reserved for the kabaka – mainly for pleasure cruises and hunting expeditions, but also on standby to evacuate the king in times of emergency.

Speke and Stanley both accompanied Kabaka Mutesa to the lakeshore where the former considered 'the royal yachting establishment' at Munyonyo to be 'the Cowes of Uganda'. Today however, the title would go to the plush marina stocked with modern speedboats and cabin cruisers at the neighbouring **Speke Commonwealth Resort** (page 142). This sprawling development is set in beautifully landscaped gardens with a magnificent tropical lakeshore setting opposite the forested Buliguwe Island. A US$6.50 day entrance fee allows access to the swimming pool and restaurant – a great place to chill out should you have a spare day in the capital. For those using public transport, a steady stream of matutus connects the old taxi park in Kampala to Ggaba and Munyonyo.

NAMUGONGO MARTYRS' SHRINE [117 H1] Situated about 12km from central Kampala along the Jinja Road, Namugongo, an established place of execution in pre-colonial Buganda, is remembered today for the massacre that took place there on 3 June 1886 at the order of Kabaka Mwanga (see box, pages 194–5). In the last week of May, an unknown number of Baganda men and women, suspected or known to have been baptised, were detained near Mengo and forced to march, by some accounts naked, to Namugongo, where they were imprisoned for several days while a large pyre was prepared. On the morning of 3 June, those prisoners who had not already done so were given one final opportunity to renounce their recently adopted faith. Whether any of the neophyte Christians accepted this offer goes unrecorded, but 26 known individuals, divided evenly between Catholic and Protestant, declined. Charles Lwanga, the leader of the Catholic contingent, was hacked apart and burnt alive on the spot. Later in the day, the remaining individuals were bound in reed mats, thrown on to the pyre, and roasted alive. The 26 remembered victims of the massacre were all baptised, and thus known to one or other mission by name, but contemporary reports indicate that more than 30 people were thrown on to the fire.

In 1920, Pope Benedict XV paved the way for future canonisation by declaring blessed the 13 known Catholic martyrs at Namugongo, together with another nine Catholic victims of separate killings in May 1886. The 22 Catholic martyrs were finally canonised by Pope Paul VI on 18 October 1964 during the Vatican II Conference. In July 1969, Pope Paul VI visited Uganda – the first reigning pope to set foot in sub-Saharan Africa – to make a pilgrimage to Namugongo, where he instructed that a shrine and church be built on the spot where Lwanga had been killed. The **Church of the Namugongo Martyrs**, dedicated in 1975 and subsequently named a basilica church, is an unusual and imposing structure, modernistic and metallic in appearance, but based on the traditional Kasiisira style (epitomised, ironically, by the tombs of Mwanga and three other kabakas at Kasubi). The site of the massacre was visited by Archbishop Robert Runcie of Canterbury in 1984, by Pope John Paul II in 1993 and Pope Francis in November 2015. The 3 June massacre remains a public holiday in Uganda and is marked worldwide on the church calendar in honour of the Uganda Martyrs.

BAHÁ'Í TEMPLE [117 E2] Opened on 15 January 1962, the Bahá'í Temple on Kikaya Hill, 6km from Kampala on the Gayaza Road, is the only place of worship of its kind in Africa. It is the spiritual home to the continent's Bahá'í, adherents to a rather obscure faith founded by the Persian mystic Bahá'u'lláh in the 1850s. Born in Tehran in 1812, Bahá'u'lláh was the privileged son of a wealthy government minister, but he declined to follow his father into the ministerial service, instead devoting his life to philanthropy.

6

In 1844, Bahá'u'lláh abandoned his Islamic roots to join the Bábí cult, whose short-lived popularity led to the execution of its founder and several other leading figures by the religious establishment – a fate escaped by Bahá'u'lláh only because of the high social status of his family. Bahá'u'lláh was nevertheless imprisoned, with his feet in stocks and a 50kg metal chain around his neck in Tehran's notoriously unsanitary and gloomy Black Pit. It was whilst imprisoned that Bahá'u'lláh received the Godly vision that led to the foundation of Bahá'í. Upon his release, Bahá'u'lláh dedicated the remaining 40 years of his life to writing the books, tracts and letters that collectively outlined the Bahá'í framework for the spiritual, moral, economic, political and philosophical reconstruction of human society.

Bahá'í teaches that heaven and hell are not places, but states of being defined by the presence or absence of spirituality. It is an inclusive faith, informed by all other religions – Hindu, Christian, Jewish, Zoroastrian, Buddhist and Islamic holy texts are displayed in the temple – which it regards to be stepping stones to a broader, less doctrinal spiritual and meditative awareness. It is also admirably egalitarian: it regards all humankind to be of equal worth, and any member of the congregation is free to lead prayers and meditations. Although not a didactic religion, Bahá'í does evidently equate spiritual well-being with asceticism: the consumption of alcohol and intoxicating drugs is discouraged in Bahá'í writings, and forbidden in the temple grounds, along with loud music, picking flowers and 'immoral behaviour'.

The Bahá'í Temple in Kampala, visible for miles around and open to all, is set in neatly manicured gardens extending over some 30ha atop Kikaya Hill. The lower part of the building consists of a white nonagon roughly 15m in diameter, with one door on each of its nine shaded faces. This is topped by an immense green dome, covered with glazed mosaic Italian tiles, and a turret that towers 40m above the ground. The interior, which can seat up to 800 people, is illuminated by ambient light filtered through coloured glass windows, and decorated with lush Persian carpets. Otherwise, it is plainly decorated, in keeping with the Bahá'í belief that it would belittle the glory of God to place pictures or statues inside His temple. A solitary line of Arabic text repeated on the wall at regular intervals approximately translates to the familiar Christian text Glory of Glories.

DAY TRIPS OUT OF KAMPALA

If sightseeing within the city is rather limited, day trips beyond Kampala also tend towards the low key – unless you're a keen birdwatcher in which case you'll be spoilt for choice by a menu that includes Mpanga Forest (pages 193–6), Mabira Forest (pages 184–90), Mabamba Swamp (pages 191–2), Zika Forest (pages 112–13) and Entebbe Botanical Garden (page 110). If you simply want to get out into the countryside, visit the eastern shores of Murchison Bay (see below). Further afield – and far from low key – is the Nile corridor at Jinja where activities include horseriding and white-water rafting (pages 242–6), Though technically feasible as a day trip from Kampala, the 4–5-hour return drive means that an overnight excursion is more enjoyable. The same applies to a visit to Ziwa Rhino Sanctuary (pages 181–3).

EAST MURCHISON BAY [117 H7] In most points of the compass, the distinction between Kampala and the surrounding countryside is blurred by suburban sprawl. To the southeast, however, the conurbation stops abruptly on the shores of Lake Victoria and Kyagwe County, on the opposite side of Murchison Bay, which remains as rustic as any corner of central Uganda. With lake viewpoints,

The centre of political power in Buganda for several centuries prior to the colonial era was the kibuga (capital) of the kabaka (king), generally situated on a hilltop for ease of defence. Based on the knowledge that at least ten different kibuga sites were used by three kabakas between 1854 and 1894, it would appear that the capital was regularly relocated, possibly for security reasons. It was also customary for a kibuga to be abandoned upon the death of its founder, at least until 1894, when Kabaka Mwanga founded a new capital on Mengo Hill, one that remained in use until the Baganda monarchy was abolished in 1966. Mengo Palace, damaged by the military during the Amin era, remains in poor shape, but following the reinstitution of the monarchy in 1993, a new kibuga was established 10km east of Kampala at Banda.

Banda was also the site of the first capital of Kabaka Mutesa, visited in 1862 by Speke, who wrote: 'the palace or entrance quite surprised me by its extraordinary dimensions, and the neatness with which it was kept. The whole brow and sides of the hill on which we stood were covered with gigantic grass huts, thatched as neatly as so many heads dressed by a London barber, and fenced all round with the tall yellow reeds of the common Uganda tiger-grass; whilst within the enclosure, the lines of huts were joined together, or partitioned off into courts, with walls of the same grass.' The next European visitor to Mutesa's capital – by then relocated to Rubaga – was Stanley, in 1875, who was equally impressed: 'Broad avenues [of] reddish clay, strongly mixed with the detritus of hematite … led by a gradual ascent to the circular road which made the circuit of the hill outside the palace enclosure … his house is an African palace, spacious and lofty.' Visitors to Kabaka Mwanga's kibuga some ten years later were less complimentary – Gedge, for instance, described it as a 'miserable collection of huts [where] dirt and filth reign supreme' – but this was probably a temporary decline linked to the instability that characterised Mwanga's early rule.

The most detailed description of a kibuga was published by the Rev John Roscoe in 1911:

> The king lived upon a hill situated in the neighbourhood of the lake. The summit of the hill was levelled, and the most commanding site overlooking the country was chosen for the king's dwelling houses, court houses, and shrine for fetishes, and for the special reception room … The whole of the royal enclosure was divided up into small courtyards with groups of huts in them; each group was enclosed by a high fence and was under the supervision of a responsible wife. Wide paths between high fences connected each group of houses with the king's royal enclosure. In the reign of the famous King Mutesa, there were several thousand residents in the royal enclosure; he had five hundred wives, each of whom had her maids and female slaves; and in addition to the wives there were fully two hundred pages and hundreds of retainers and slaves. A high fence of elephant grass surrounded the royal residence, so that it was impossible for an enemy with the ordinary primitive weapons to enter … There was one plan followed, which has been used by the kings for years without variation. The [royal] enclosure was oval shaped, a mile in length and half a mile wide, and the capital extended five or six miles in front and two miles on either side.

wetlands and forests, the peninsulas that separate the satellite bays of Wavimenya and Gobero are great to explore by pushbike, boda or on foot. Go Free Uganda (page 132) offers guided cycle tours of the area. We've also seen expat motorbikes being ferried across the bay from Ggaba. Attractive circuits are possible by heading down Gobero Peninsula to one of several landing sites from where you can cross to the far side of either bay by boat to continue on your way. Of passing interest in Gobero are a couple of Bagandan shrines. If a day trip doesn't suffice, there is a choice of accommodation in the area (page 144).

If you're up for greater distances, you could spend a delightful couple of days exploring the area between Murchison Bay and Jinja. See 'Uganda Maps' Sheet 3: *Beyond Kampala* for inspiration and location of shoestring lodgings. Kyagwe is accessed from Kampala's Ggaba Port where the 15-minute trip by 'special hire' boat to Bule or Kisinsi landings should cost US$3.50, or US$6.50 per person on a public boat. The latter are most numerous on Ggaba market days (Monday and Thursday) while boda-bodas are most numerous at Bule landing.

LAKESIDE ADVENTURE PARK [117 H7] (m *0771 676880; www.lakeside.ug.info@ lakeside.ug; high ropes course US$20pp; dorm bed US$12; tents US$8; costs excl boat transfers from KK Beach in Ggaba*) Located next to Lagoon Resort at the head of Wavimenya Bay, Kampala's first obstacle course offers the chance to test yourself on lofty rope walks, cable runways, climbing walls and the like.

MATOKE TOURS

7

Around Entebbe and Kampala

This chapter covers a mixed bag of natural and cultural attractions that lie close enough to the capital to make for feasible self-standing day and/or overnight trips for residents of Entebbe or Kampala, or visitors with a spare day or two at the start or end of a business trip or longer safari. For wildlife enthusiasts, these include a few genuine highlights – tracking rhinos on foot at Ziwa, watching Ngamba Island's orphaned chimps at play, or taking a wobbly dugout in search of shoebills at Mabamba Swamp – to more-low key forest reserves such as Mabira and Mpanga. The area around Kampala and Entebbe also houses several important traditional Kiganda shrines, most accessibly the Tanda Pits, Nakayima Tree and Ssezibwa Falls, while the newly installed Canopy Skyway Zipline at Griffin Falls provides an adrenalin-charged taster for the type of activity on offer at nearby Bujagali outside Jinja (pages 242–6). Although the destinations included in this chapter can all be visited as round trips out of the capital, most lie *en route* to other popular attractions further afield – Ziwa, for instance, could easily be visited on the way to the far north, while Mabamba Swamp makes for a great diversion coming to or from the southwest – so they have been structured to follow the main roads out of the capital: west towards Fort Portal; north towards Murchison Falls and Gulu; east towards Jinja; and southwest towards Masaka.

NGAMBA ISLAND CHIMPANZEE SANCTUARY

Situated 23km southeast of Entebbe, Ngamba is a formerly uninhabited 50ha island in the Kome Archipelago, which is separated from the northern shore of Lake Victoria by the 10km-wide Damba Channel. Supporting a rainforest environment that includes 50-plus plant species utilised by free-ranging chimps, Ngamba was established as a sanctuary in 1998, when 19 orphaned chimps, all of which had been saved from a life in captivity or a laboratory, were relocated there. Today, 48 orphaned chimpanzees, many captured illegally in the forests of the DRC and smuggled across Uganda for trade, are resident on Ngamba.

The island is divided into two unequal parts, separated by an electric fence. On one side of the fence, a tented camp, visitors' centre and staff quarters extend over an area of about 1ha on a partially cleared stretch of northwestern shore notable for its immense weaver colonies. The rest of the island is reserved more-or-less exclusively for the chimps and their attendants. There's also a small tented camp sleeping up to eight on the island.

The fenced-off part of the island offers plenty of room for the chimps to roam, but it isn't large enough to sustain the entire community – indeed, its area corresponds roughly to the natural range of one chimpanzee – so the chimps are fed a porridge-like mixture for breakfast, and then fruits and vegetables twice during the day. The fruits are given to the chimps from a viewing platform, which provides an opportunity for visitors to observe and photograph them through a fence.

The sanctuary aims to provide the best facilities and care to the captive chimpanzees, who are given the choice of staying in the forest overnight or returning to a holding facility built to enhance social integration and veterinary management. The management has elected not to allow the chimps to breed, so all sexually mature females are given a contraceptive implant, which doesn't disrupt the community's normal sexual behaviour, but does prevent pregnancy.

Ngamba Island is the flagship project of the Chimpanzee Sanctuary and Wildlife Conservation Trust, jointly established in 1997 by the Born Free Foundation, the International Fund for Animal Welfare, the Jane Goodall Institute, UWEC and the Zoological Board of New South Wales (Australia). It is part of an integrated chimpanzee conservation programme that also includes an ongoing census study of wild chimpanzee populations in Uganda, two snare-removal programmes, chimpanzee habituation for ecotourism, and education and outreach initiatives in local communities. Proceeds from tourist visits go directly back into the maintenance of the sanctuary and the organisation's other chimpanzee-related projects.

ENTRANCE FEES Entrance to day/overnight visitors is US$35/40/10/15 FNR adults/children, US$15/20/5/10 for FR adults/children. This fee includes an introductory lecture and the opportunity to watch the chimpanzees from a viewing platform at feeding time. Other activities are extra.

HEALTH People doing the Caregiver-for-a-Day (see below) activity are required to show proof of a current vaccination against hepatitis A and B, measles, meningococcal meningitis, polio, tetanus, yellow fever and seasonal flu. It also requires visitors to have tested negative for TB and HIV within the previous six months. A form listing all current medical requirements, to be signed by your doctor, is downloadable from www.ngambaisland.org.

GETTING THERE AND AWAY Access is by boat or helicopter only, and can be arranged directly with the booking office or through any operator in Kampala or Entebbe. Motorboat crossings from Entebbe take 45 minutes and cost US$407–440 per party, depending on group size. Motorised traditional canoes take 90 minutes and cost the same for groups of up to five, but more for larger groups. Make sure your boat leaves Entebbe in time for the twice-daily supplementary feeding session. Helicopter transfers from Entebbe cost around US$780 per party (up to four people).

WHERE TO STAY AND EAT

Ngamba Island Tented Camp (4 units) ✿ -0.10013, 32.65224; ✆ 041 4320662; m 0758 221880; e reservations@ngambaisland.org. This small camp next to the landing jetty comprises classic stilted safari tents with twin beds, solar lighting & en-suite hot showers. Buffet lunches are served to day visitors for US$15 per head. Cheaper off-season & resident rates are available, while a number of pricier packages including transport & activities are detailed on the website. *US$318/536 sgl/dbl FB.* **$$$$$**

ACTIVITIES Day trips to the island are timed to coincide with the pre-arranged supplementary feeding times of 11.00 and 14.30, when the chimpanzees come to within metres of a raised walkway, offering an excellent opportunity to observe and photograph one of our closest animal relatives. This is included in the entrance fee, but visitors who want a more hands-on experience (and who've arranged the required vaccines in advance) can opt for the Caregiver-for-a-Day programme, which aims at creating an understanding of what it takes to look after the orphans

of Ngamba. This is available only as part of an all-inclusive overnight package that costs US$918 for one person, or US$668 per person for groups of two or more. Kayaks are available to explore the island bays and go searching for monitor lizards, otters and some of the 154 recorded bird species, while other optional activities for overnight visitors include a visit to a local fishing village, a sunset cruise, and fishing, all of which can be arranged through the camp.

WEST TOWARDS FORT PORTAL

The 300km surfaced road from Kampala to Fort Portal can be covered in a solid half-day, if – as is the case with most tourists – you're concerned solely with getting from A to B. It passes through a lush and densely populated part of Buganda and Bunyoro punctuated by a trio of bustling medium-sized towns, namely Mityana, Mubende and Kyenjojo. Recognised tourist attractions are practically non-existent, but this is arguably compensated for by a number of little-known archaeological sites and sacrificial shrines associated with the medieval Bachwezi Kingdom. These include the Tanda Pits and Lake Wamala near Mityana, set within easy day tripping distance of the capital, as well as the Nakayima Tree and Munsa Earthworks near Mubende, which lies in the far west of Buganda almost exactly halfway to Fort Portal.

MITYANA AND SURROUNDS Sprawling along the Fort Portal Road about 60km west of Kampala, Mityana is a substantial and fast-growing town of 50,000 set in an area steeped in Bachwezi and Kiganda legend. Though inherently unremarkable and arguably too close to Kampala for a rest or an overnight stay, there's some interesting sightseeing in the area, most notably the ancient shrine at the Tanda Pits, but also to a lesser extent the little-visited Lake Wamala. For those seeking a quick break before driving on further west, the new Esuubi Café is a pleasant spot for a hot or cold drink, and it also has clean toilets.

Getting there and away Mityana should in theory be only an hour's drive from Kampala, but the congested city traffic means the drive usually takes at least twice as long. If you plan on stopping at Tanda, note that the junction is 9km before Mityana coming from Kampala. Inexpensive matatus connect Mityana to Kampala's new taxi park and Mubende throughout the day.

Where to stay

Budget

Enro Hotel (62 rooms) ✆ 0.39808, 32.05926; m 0772 442227; e enrohotellimited@ yahoo.com; www.enrohotel.com. Prominently signposted to the right as you enter town coming from Kampala, this long-serving hotel remains Mityana's finest. All rooms are en suite with nets, fan, DSTV & hot shower, but those in the new wing are smarter & correspondingly pricier. A restaurant & bar is attached. *US$10/22 sgl/dbl old wing, US$17/28 executive sgl/twin in new wing. All rates B&B.* **$$**

Shoestring

Kolping Hotel (16 rooms) ✆ 0.3999, 32.04259; ✆ 043 4132820. Situated on the old high street about 1km south of the Kampala–Fort Portal Rd & only 100m from the bus station, this is another well-established & well-priced set-up. The clean rooms all come with net, DSTV & en-suite cold shower, while a terrace restaurant serves local fare in the US$2–3 range. *US$7/9/10 sgl/dbl/ twin.* **$**

✕ Where to eat and drink The hotels above both serve decent food but the out-of-town Esuubi Café listed on the next page is better suited to passing traffic.

✗ Esuubi Café ⊕ 0.4107, 32.02015; m 0704 956349; www.esuubicafe.com; ⊕ 09.30–17.30 Mon–Sat. Set on the north side of the Fort Portal Road 2.5km west of Mityana, this clean & pleasant café serves great coffee, cakes, pancakes & other snacks, as well as a small selection of mains (chilli con carne, vegetable stir-fry, fish fillet). A good craft shop is attached & all profits go to support an orphanage. *Snacks under US$2, mains in the US$3–5 range.*

What to see and do

Tanda Pits (m *0751 777370/0772 870689;* ⊕ *24hrs daily; entry US$5*) An intriguing goal for a day trip out of Kampala or diversion *en route* to Fort Portal, Tanda comprises a field of around 240 pits scattered in a 10ha rectangle of ancient forest whose undergrowth has been cleared, though its canopy remains intact. Some of the pits are quite shallow, but others are narrow, deep and, according to Kiganda tradition, bottomless. Legend holds that this shady enclave served as the stage for much of the formative earthly action described in the box on page 174. Indeed, a rock shelter only 500m from Tanda is supposedly where Kintu, the first man on earth, settled down with his wife Nambi. As for the pits, they were excavated by Nambi's brother Kayikuzi (literally, 'Digger of Holes') in an unsuccessful attempt to capture their third sibling Walumbe, the spirit of death and disease, and rid the world of his malevolent presence.

Today, Tanda ranks as probably the most important Bachwezi shrine in Buganda. Eighteen of the pits at Tanda are revered as sacrificial sites, each one dedicated to a different Bachwezi spirit. The largest pit and most important shrine, covered in several layers of barkcloth and surrounded by massive clusters of five-fingered spears and gourds, is the one associated with Walumbe, who is said to return there from time to time. Elsewhere, sacrifices are tailored to appease the particular spirit for which they were left. Carved wooden boats and fish skins are littered around the shrine for Mukasa, the spirit of lakes and rivers; bottled alcohol and other addictive substances have been sacrificed to Bamweyana, the spirit of madness; while electric sockets, light bulbs and other such appliances are draped from a tree overhanging the shrine to Kiwanuka, the spirit of thunder and lightning.

A truly fascinating (and in some respects quite surreal) repository of Bachwezi tradition, Tanda is far more active than might be expected of an ancient animist shrine in 21st-century Uganda. Tourists are welcome, provided they stick to photographing the actual shrines rather than the (often distraught, bereaved or suffering) locals who come to place sacrifices at them. Unpaid English-speaking guides are available, and highly recommended both for the insight they'll provide into the Kiganda traditions associated with Tanda, and to ensure that you avoid any cultural *faux pas*, but a fair tip will be expected.

Getting to Tanda could hardly be more straightforward. The junction (⊕ *0.39488, 32.13146*), signposted 'Ttanda Archaeological Archives and Walumbe Tombs', lies on the south side of the Fort Portal Road about 48km west of Kampala's Busega Roundabout and 9km east of the Enro Hotel in Mityana. It's almost 2km from the junction to the entrance gate (⊕ *0.3852, 32.12795*). Those without private transport could either catch a matatu between Kampala and Mityana and walk from the junction, or else charter a boda in Mityana.

Lake Wamala Extending over 180km² southwest of Mityana, Lake Wamala was submerged by Lake Victoria until about 4,000 years ago, and it still drains into the larger lake via the rivers Kibimba and Katonga. The lake is named after the last Bachwezi leader Wamala and, as with so many other sites in this part of Uganda, it has strong associations with traditional religions. One legend has it that the lake

Once upon a time, Ggulu, the creator, sent his daughter Nambi and her siblings on a day trip to earth, where they chanced upon its only human inhabitant: poor lonely Kintu, who lived in the vicinity of Lake Wamala, near present-day Mityana, his sole companion a beloved cow. Nambi was at once attracted to Kintu and upset at his enforced solitude, and she determined there and then to marry and keep him company on earth. Nambi's brothers were appalled at her reckless decision and attempted to dissuade her, eventually reaching the compromise that she and Kintu would return to heaven to ask Ggulu's permission to marry. Ggulu reluctantly blessed the union, but he did advise the couple to descend to earth lightly packed and in secret, to avoid being noticed and followed by Nambi's brother Walumbe, the spirit of disease and death.

The next morning, before dawn, the delighted newly weds set off for earth, carrying little other than Nambi's favourite chicken. When they arrived, however, Nambi realised that she had forgotten to bring millet to feed the chicken and decided to return to heaven to fetch it. Kintu implored Nambi to stay, fearing that she might encounter Walumbe and suggesting that a substitute chicken feed would surely be available on earth. But Nambi ignored Kintu's pleadings and returned to heaven, where sure enough she bumped into Walumbe, who – curious as to where his sister might be headed so early in the morning – followed her all the way back to join Kintu.

A few years later, Kintu, by then the head of a happy family, received a visit from Walumbe, who insisted that he be given one of their children to help with his household chores. Heedful of his father-in-law's warning, Kintu refused Walumbe, who was deeply angered and avenged himself by killing Kintu's eldest son. When Kintu returned to heaven to ask for assistance, Ggulu chastised him for ignoring the warning, but he agreed nevertheless to send another son Kayikuzi to bring Walumbe back to heaven. Walumbe refused to leave earth, however, so that Kayikuzi was forced to try and evict him against his will. The brothers fought violently, but the moment Kayikuzi gained an upper hand, Walumbe vanished underground. Kayikuzi dug several large holes, found Walumbe's hiding place, and the two resumed their fight, but soon Walumbe fled into the ground once again, and so the pattern repeated itself.

After several days, Kayikuzi, now nearing exhaustion, told Kintu and Nambi he would try one last time to catch Walumbe, at the same time instructing them to ensure that their children stayed indoors and remained silent until his task was done. Kayikuzi chased Walumbe out of hiding, but some of Kintu's children, who had disobeyed the instruction, saw the sparring brothers emerge from underground and they started screaming, giving Walumbe the opportunity to duck back into his subterranean refuge. Kayikuzi, angry that his earthly charges had ignored his instructions, told them he was giving up the chase, and the embarrassed Kintu did not argue. He told Kayikuzi to return to heaven and said: 'If Walumbe wishes to kill my children, so be it. I will keep having more, and the more he kills, the more I will have. He will not be able remove them all from the face of the earth.'

… and so ends the Kiganda creation myth, one whose association between human disobedience and the arrival of death and disease on earth has an oddly Old Testament ring.

was formed by water leaked from a skin-carrier that belonged to King Wamala, while another states that its Bachwezi namesake disappeared into it at a site called Nakyegalika and that his spirit still resides there today. Despite its size and historical associations, Lake Wamala is virtually unknown as a tourist destination. If you want to explore, the best point of access is the village of Naama, which lies on the Fort Portal Road about 6km west of Mityana. From there it's a 20-minute walk to the lakeshore, along footpaths that weave between mud huts, coffee trees and patches of indigenous bush. You should be able to organise a dugout canoe to take you across to one of the lake's larger islands or to look for the water birds (and reputedly hippos) that frequent the shallows and well-vegetated shore.

MUBENDE AND SURROUNDS Roughly midway along the main road between Kampala and Fort Portal, Mubende (population 50,000) ranks among Uganda's prettier small towns, set below and named after a 1,573m-high hill that reputedly served as the 15th-century capital of King Ndahura. More recently, the breezy climate, fertile soil and clear springs of Mubende Hill so impressed the early colonials that it was chosen as the site of a sanatorium where weary Entebbe-based administrators could, according to a contemporary issue of the *Mengo Notes*, 'repair thither for a period of change and invigoration'. These days, Mubende – or rather the bustling stretch of main road 1km south of the more sedate town centre – visibly revels in its status as a halfway house where Kampala- or Fort Portal-bound travellers can pause to enjoy a chilled drink, a barbecued chicken-on-a-stick, or whatever other refreshments take their fancy. And while most passers-by decline to explore any further, the Mubende area is of some interest for its wealth of important Bachwezi-related sites. The most accessible of these, set atop Mubende Hill perhaps 10 minutes' drive from the town centre, is the splendid Nakayima Tree, an active centuries-old sacrificial shrine whose immense buttresses house the spirit of Ndahura and several other traditional spirits.

History The hill known as Mubende, literally 'Place of Disaster', earned that name in the 16th century, when its summit served as the capital of a notorious king whose reign was characterised by several massacres. But both oral tradition and archaeological evidence suggest the sacred hilltop plateau formerly called Kisozi supported a substantial and important settlement for some centuries before that. In pre-Bachwezi times, Kisozi is said to have been settled by Kamwenge, a sorceress from present-day Ankole. Kamwenge's two sons established themselves as important local rulers, and their hilltop capital became one of the region's largest settlements. Kisozi was later usurped by the Bachwezi ruler Ndahura, who resided there for several years before he abdicated in favour of his son Wamala, and retired to his birthplace near Fort Portal

Perhaps a century after Ndahura's vanishing act, Kisozi became the capital of the murderous king whose reign is alluded to in the name Mubende. According to tradition, the only person able to persuade this despot to mend his ways was a powerful sorceress of the cow clan whose heroism earned her the soubriquet Nakayima – literally, 'Advocator'. Eventually, however, the king lost patience with all the advocacy, and he attempted to capture Nakayima, who spirited herself away inside a large tree planted many decades earlier in memory of Ndahura. This was the Nakayima Tree: believed ever since to harbour the spirit of Ndahura, who is deified by both the Banyoro and Baganda as the god of smallpox, as well as the spirit of Nakayima, as manifested in an oddly shaped branch that resembles her clan animal, the cow.

Ever since the spirit took refuge in the Nakayima Tree, a hereditary line of priestesses, also known by the title Nakayima, and said by some to descend from the eponymous wife of Ndahura, have maintained it as a sacrificial shrine. The Nakayima priestess is also regularly possessed by the spirit of Ndahura, and her alleged powers include the ability to cure infertility and smallpox. She was probably the most important single spiritual leader in pre-colonial Buganda and Bunyoro, and received regular tributes from the kings of both polities, as well as overseeing various ritual ceremonies that involved the sacrifice of livestock and more occasionally teenage boys and girls.

The decline of the Nakayima lineage started in 1888, when the religious conflict that rocked Buganda forced the incumbent priestess, named Nyanjara, to flee Mubende. Nyanjara returned to Mubende a year later, only to find six of the seven huts traditionally inhabited by the Nakayima had been razed, the sacred drums they held had vanished, and the graves of her predecessors had been defaced. This attack had no immediate impact on the Nyanjara's influence in Bunyoro, which was then relatively unexposed to exotic religions – indeed, King Kabalega visited Mubende Hill to pay her tribute in 1899. But as foreign missionaries persuaded the Baganda elite to turn away from traditional beliefs, so the Nakayima's spiritual importance in Buganda diminished.

The last blow came in 1902, when the British administration placed Mubende Hill under the indirect colonial rule of a Muganda chief. Nyanjara retired to Bugogo, where she died five years later, and became the first Nakayima not to be interred in a traditional cemetery near the sacred tree (though eventually she was buried in isolation at the base of Mubende Hill). Her fantastic regalia, confiscated by the colonial authorities, now forms one of the most impressive displays in Kampala's National Museum – together with two large and ancient pots, probably used in Bachwezi-related religious rituals, unearthed during excavations on Mubende Hill.

The present-day status of the Nakayima is unclear. After the death of Nyanjara, no successor to the title emerged until 1926, when a Muhima sorceress took up brief residence on Mubende Hill only to vanish a short while later. Ten years later, another short-lived candidate showed up in the form of a young Ankole girl, dressed in full priestly regalia, who spent several nights screeching at the base of the Nakayima Tree before she too disappeared. All written sources agree that that the spirit of Nakayima has been unclaimed ever since. On site, by contrast, an elderly woman living below the tree claims to have served as the Nakayima priestess since the 1960s, and seems to be accepted as such by the many Baganda and Banyoro traditionalist who still come to make sacrifices below there.

Getting there and away Mubende lies about 150km west of Kampala and a similar distance east of Fort Portal, a drive of 2½–3 hours in either direction in a private vehicle, though traffic congestion around the capital often slows down the easterly leg. All buses between Kampala and Fort Portal stop at Mubende, and regular matatus connect Mubende to Kampala's new taxi park (*US$3.50; 3–4hrs*), Mityana (*US$1.50; 1½hrs*), Kyenjojo (*US$2.50; 2hrs*) and Fort Portal (*US$3.50; 3–4hrs*) throughout the day.

Where to stay and eat

Budget

 Prime Rose Hotel (38 rooms)
⊕ 0.54712, 31.39713; ☏ 039 2613407;
🅵 fb.me/PrimeRoseHotel. Situated 200m south

of the Kampala Road & clearly signposted as you enter town from that side, this blandly modern high-rise has comfortable en-suite rooms with nets, DSTV & hot shower, as well as a well-stocked

restaurant/bar, gardens seating, & free Wi-Fi. *US$24/35 B&B sgl/dbl.* **$$**

🏠 **Town View Hotel** (21 rooms) ✪ 0.56523, 31.38705; 📞 039 2612567; 📱 0706 761407; 📧 trudy@trudysdiner.com; www.trudysdiner.com/TownviewHotel.html. Situated 500m north of the high street off the road to the top of Mubende Hill, this aptly named hotel offers a range of en-suite double rooms that vary in size & décor but all have nets, DSTV & hot shower. The attached Trudy's Diner serves reasonably priced local dishes. *From US$14 B&B dbl.* **$**

What to see and do

Nakayima Tree (✪ 0.57355, 31.37761; 🔲 *fb.me/nakayima.tree;* ⏰ *24hrs daily; entry US$1.50*) The best-known Bachwezi-associated sacrificial site in Buganda is the Nakayima Tree, which stands on the plateau-like summit of Mubende Hill close to a sanatorium built by the British in 1908. It isn't difficult to see why this particular tree – estimated by various scientific teams to be between 500 and 1,000 years old – has acquired such a revered status. It is a compelling piece of natural engineering, towering almost 40m above its park-like surrounds like an oversized surrealist sculpture whose fin-shaped buttresses fan out from the base to create around a dozen cavernous hollows, each of which is dedicated to one particular spirit. The most popular spirits associated with the tree are of course Nakayima (fertility and various illness) and Ndahura (smallpox), but others with their buttressed 'rooms' include Nabuzana (marriage), Walumbe (death and disease), Mukasa (lakes and rivers) and Bamweyana (madness). As with nearby Tanda, the Nakayima Tree remains an active shrine, visited by Bachwezi cultists from all around Buganda and Bunyoro to pay homage or leave sacrifices (coins, cowrie shells, gourds, food, et al) to the relevant spirit. Every so often, a group of cultists will spend a night by the tree, where they might roast a goat or pig in honour of the incumbent priestess, who claims to have lived below the tree and served in that role since the 1960s (though sceptics might note that she wasn't present on any of our several visits prior to 2015). Other points of interest include some old grinding stones said to date to Bachwezi times.

From central Mubende, the Nakayima Tree can be reached along a dirt road leading uphill from the large four-way junction 100m west of the taxi park. The road is fairly steep and possibly too rough for anything but a 4x4 vehicle. If you're walking, you should make it up in an hour, depending on how often you stop to enjoy the prolific birdlife and views south to Masaka Hill. Once there, an optional guide asks a flat fee of US$1.50 for one person or US$3 for two or more; if the articulate and friendly lady who showed us around is anything to go by, it's well worth the minor investment.

Munsa Earthworks (✪ 0.8228, 31.31308) Situated 38km north of Mubende, Munsa comprises a maze of deep but silted-up trenches enclosing Bikekete Hill, a prominent granite outcrop riddled with tunnels and caves. Oral tradition links Bikekete and Munsa – derived from the Runyoro 'Mu-ensa', or 'place of ditches' – with the Bachwezi prince Kateboha, who reputedly lived in a cave large enough to seat 50 people. This tradition is supported by archaeological evidence that indicates Bikekete was inhabited in the 14th century, and that the 7m-wide, 3m-deep V-shaped earthworks were excavated to protect his rocky stronghold. Significant discoveries at Bikekete include a clay iron-smelting furnace, innumerable pot shards, glass trade beads from the Swahili Coast, and a small cemetery where one skeleton lay beneath a second inverted one, suggestive of the grisly royal custom that a servant should be buried alive above the king, in order to attend his dead master.

Long-standing talk of developing Munsa for tourism has yet to translate into action. All the same, the earthworks are easy enough to visit. With a torch and a

local guide, you can crawl through a tight tunnel into the cave once inhabited by Kateboha, while the outline of the silted-up earthworks is clearly visible from the top of the hill. Look out too for a pair of deep, narrow artificial holes in a slab of flat granite 150m south of the hill's base – according to local tradition, these were receptacles from where Kateboha drank beer offerings from his subjects at the start of the harvest season. On the way to or from Munsa, you might also want to investigate Semwama Hill, a massive granite whaleback renowned as the site of a venerable Bachwezi sacrificial shrine set in the twin-chambered cave where Kateboha of Munsa reputedly used to hold council with his elders and advisors.

Munsa Earthworks makes for a feasible day trip out of Mubende, even for those dependent on public transport. It is reached via Kakumiro, a junction village 32km north of Mubende, and no more than an hour's drive, whether in a private vehicle or a matatu. From Kakumiro, follow the Hoima road 1km north then turn left at the junction (⊕ *0.79047, 31.32474*) signposted for Munsa Primary School. The primary school lies about 3.5km along this road, and the inconspicuous track to the earthworks (⊕ *0.81742, 31.32004*) runs left from practically opposite it. Roughly 700m down this track, and only 100m before the earthworks, lies the home of the local priest, who is also the official caretaker. If you also want to visit Semwama Hill (⊕ *0.79949, 31.32179*), an overgrown 200m track (⊕ *0.79725, 31.32045*) to the base of this conspicuous outcrop leads right from the road to Munsa Primary School about 1km past the junction with the Hoima Road. There is no public transport beyond Kakumiro, but you could walk from there to either site in an hour, or charter a boda.

Bigo bya Mugyenyi and the Ntusi Mounds

These two archaeologically important but relatively inaccessible sites, neither of which is likely to convey much to a day visitor, lie in the vicinity of Ntusi, a small town situated 75km south of Mubende along a little-used back route to Masaka and Lyantonde. The 15th-century Bigo bya Mugyenyi (literally 'Fort of the Stranger'), situated at the confluence of the Katonga and Kakinga rivers, is the largest of several earthworks excavated by the Bachwezi, but the site has never been cleared and it lacks the impact of Munsa. Older still are the Ntusi Mounds, a pair of immense trash heaps containing bones, pottery shards and other waste material deposited over a 300-year period by the inhabitants of what was probably the largest medieval settlement in the East African interior. The Ntusi Mounds lie within 1km of Ntusi district headquarters, and can be visited on foot over a couple of hours, but Bigo bya Mugyenyi is a long hour's drive from Ntusi along poor unmarked roads that shouldn't be attempted without a local guide.

KATONGA WILDLIFE RESERVE (*entry US$10/5 FNR/FR*)

The closest wildlife reserve to Kampala as the crow flies, little-known Katonga comprises 207km² of mixed savannah, papyrus swamp and rainforest along the northern edge of the river for which it is named. Geologically, it lies within one of Africa's oldest river valleys – one that once flowed all the way from western Kenya to the Atlantic, and that pre-dates the formation of the Rift Valley, Lake Victoria and even the Nile by many millions of years. Gazetted in 1964, the reserve originally supported large resident herds of zebra, elephant and buffalo, whilst doubling as part of a game migration corridor between western Uganda, Tanzania and South Sudan. Poaching and cattle encroachment took a heavy toll on the environment and wildlife in the 1970s and 1980s, but improved protection in recent years has ensured that populations are now on the increase. A low-key but worthwhile ecotourism site

offers several activities led by guides who are extremely knowledgeable about the local fauna and flora.

Fauna The current mammal checklist stands at 40 species, including black-and-white colobus, olive baboon, Ugandan kob and small numbers of elephant and buffalo. Waterbuck, reedbuck and bushbuck are common and sufficiently habituated to approach on foot. Katonga is one of perhaps three places in East Africa where the secretive sitatunga antelope is likely to be seen by a casual visitor. Recent reintroductions include a herd of 11 zebras and more than 50 impalas from Lake Mburo National Park. Katonga is also of great interest for its varied birdlife – over 338 species have been recorded – and among the more interesting likely to be seen are green- and blue-headed coucal, Ross's and great blue turaco, crested malimbe and papyrus gonolek.

Getting there and away The signposted junction for Katonga is Kyegegwa, which lies on the Fort Portal Road, 42km west of Mubende. From here, a 40km dirt road heads south to the entrance gate via Mparo and Kalwreni. It's easy enough to find public transport to Kyegegwa and on to Kalwreni, possibly changing vehicles at Mparo. Kalwreni lies 7km from the entrance gate, so if you can't find transport, you could walk or hire a boda.

It is also possible to approach Katonga from Kibale National Park via Kamwenge, Ibanda and Kabagole. Public transport is plentiful on all legs of this route.

Where to stay The Katonga Visitors' Centre, which overlooks the valley 1km from the entrance gate, is basically a campsite with a covered dining area and ablutions. Water and firewood are provided, but you should bring everything else you require with you. Camping costs US$5 per person. Basic lodgings are available in the village of Kabagole, which lies on the southern edge of the valley, about 1km from the reserve entrance gate.

What to see and do The main attraction at Katonga used to be a canoe trip through the wetland, but this activity has been discontinued for safety reasons following the colonisation of the channel by hippos. Three guided half-day **walking trails** can be arranged on the spot for US$30 per person. The Sitatunga Trail runs through a mixture of grassland and wetland habitats, offering a better than even chance of spotting the elusive antelope for which it is named. The Kisharara Trail passes through all the main habitats protected within the park – grassland, savannah and swamp fringes – and is also good for sitatunga, as well as monkeys and birds. The Kyeibale Trail loops away from the water into an area of drier scrub dotted with tall rock formations as well as forested valleys and caves.

NORTH TOWARDS MASINDI AND GULU

The 170km trunk road running from Kampala to Kafu Bridge via Bombo and Luwero is traversed by practically all tourists heading further north, whether they intend to branch left for Masindi or Murchison Falls National Park immediately after crossing the Kafu River, or to continue straight ahead for Pakwach, Gulu, Lira or Kidepo Valley National Park. Despite the strategic importance of this road, it carries a relatively low volume of traffic, at least once you've cleared Luwero, and is rather short on tourist attractions. The one rather thrilling exception, signposted to the left 8km before Kafu Bridge, is Ziwa Rhino Sanctuary, which offers northbound

travellers the opportunity to track an introduced population of white rhinos on foot, and also makes for a great day or overnight bush break from the capital. Another important landmark only 2km past the junction for Ziwa is the excellent Kabalega Diner, now entrenched as *the* place to break for a bite, drink or leg stretch before crossing the Kafu River, which effectively marks the boundary between southern Uganda and the north.

RHINOS IN UGANDA

Historically, Uganda's main white rhino stronghold is West Nile, which supported a population estimated at 350 individuals in 1955. Back then, Murchison Falls and Kidepo Valley National Park were home to a similar number of black rhino. By the mid-1960s, however, the country's white rhino population had plummeted to 80, split between West Nile's Ajai Wildlife Reserve and a herd of 15 introduced to Murchison Falls. No figures for black rhino are available, but they had also become scarce by the late 1960s. Today, both species are naturally extinct in Uganda, with the last documented sightings of white and black rhino being in 1982 and 1983 respectively. The main cause of this rapid decline was commercial poaching – rhino horns, used as dagger handles in the Middle East and as an aphrodisiac in parts of Asia, fetch up to US$1 million on the black market – exacerbated by the lawlessness that prevailed during and after the rule of Idi Amin.

In 2001, the NGO Rhino Fund Uganda bought a pair of 2½-year-old white rhinos from Kenya's Solio Ranch, flew them to Entebbe to a festive reception, then interred them in the Uganda Wildlife Education Centre, a respected zoo-like facility where they remain to this day. This led to the initiation of a longer-term reintroduction programme centred on Ziwa Rhino Sanctuary, a former cattle ranch, now sealed off within a 2m-high electric fence, in Nakasongola District. In 2005, four southern white rhinos from Kenya were introduced to Ziwa, supplemented a year later by two more individuals from Disney Animal Kingdom USA. In 2009, a rhino was born on Ugandan soil for the first time in almost three decades, and named Obama, on account of its half-Kenyan, half-American ancestry. Today, following nine more births, the sanctuary supports a total of 16 white rhinos, whose every move is monitored by a team of 40 rangers. Once numbers have grown sufficiently, the long-term intention is to release a few individuals into Murchison Falls and possibly a few other national parks.

Admirable as the programme at Ziwa may be, it is arguably of greater symbolic and touristic value than ecological worth. This is because the imported white rhinos all belong to the southern race *Ceratotherium s. simum*, whose natural range extends little further north than the Zambezi River (though it has since been introduced to Kenya). Unfortunately, the northern white rhino (*C. s. cottoni*) – which once ranged across northwest Uganda, northeast DRC, southeast CAR and southwest South Sudan – is now practically extinct. The world's last wild population of northern white rhinos, a herd of six living in DRC's Garamba National Park, were shot dead by poachers in 2006. True, three individual northern white rhinos still survive in captivity, housed in a large pen in Kenya's Ol Pejeta Conservancy, but since the two females are incapable of natural reproduction, and the male has a very low sperm count, the likelihood of them ever breeding is negligible.

KIGOMAN MIXED FARM (m *0782 793750;* e *kigomanud@hotmail.com*) On your way north of Kampala (or indeed south, west or east for that matter), you'll pass numerous makeshift markets and lone ramshackle stalls groaning beneath abundant quantities of fresh fruit and veg. If you're curious to see how all this stuff is produced, take a half-day tour of the Ugandan–Dutch Kigoman Mixed Farm, which lies 4km off the Gulu Road some 80km north of Kampala (look out for the signposted junction 17.5km north of Luwero town). The tour costs US$12 per person and includes water and fresh-fruit snacks. Advance booking is essential and traditional meals are available by arrangement.

ZIWA RHINO SANCTUARY (m *0772 713410/0778 933490;* e *administration@ rhinofund.org; www.rhinofund.org;* ◷ *main gate 07.30–18.30 daily; free entry)* A 70km² tract of tangled woodland situated a short way south of the Kafu River, Ziwa Rhino Sanctuary is the only place in Uganda where rhinos can be seen in a more-or-less wild state, thanks to an ongoing introduction programme overseen by the NGO Rhino Fund Uganda (see box opposite). The sanctuary's main attraction is its population of 16 white rhinos, which can be tracked on foot by day or overnight visitors in the company of an experienced ranger. It is also home to around 20 other large mammal species, most conspicuously warthog, vervet monkey, bushbuck and waterbuck, while an impressive checklist of 300-plus bird species include the shoebill, which can be tracked on canoe or on foot in Lugogo Swamp. Offering accommodation to suit all budgets, the sanctuary makes for a great overnight bush break out of Kampala, but it is also conveniently located for a day visit or overnight stop *en route* from the capital to Murchison Falls, Gulu or elsewhere in the north.

Getting there and away The junction (✪ *1.5076, 32.09613*) for Ziwa Rhino Sanctuary is clearly signposted on the west side of the Gulu Road as it passes through the small trading centre of Nakitoma (pronounced 'Nachitoma') about 170km north of Kampala and 8km before Kafu Bridge. From the junction, it's about 2.5km to the entrance gate (✪ *1.48583, 32.09564*), then another 5km to the sanctuary headquarters (✪ *1.44783, 32.07738*), which is also the also the site of Ziwa Rhino Lodge and the departure point for all activities. For Amuka Lodge, which lies 6km from the entrance, follow the road towards the headquarters for 2.5km, then turn right at the signposted junction (✪ *1.46671, 32.08745*).

Using public transport, your best bet is to catch a Link Bus towards Masindi from Kampala Qualicell and hop off at Nakitoma (*US$3; 3–4hrs*). Failing that, or coming from another direction, any bus or matatu running in either direction between Kampala and Masindi, Gulu, Arua or Lira could drop you at Nakitoma. Once at Nakitoma, a boda to the sanctuary headquarters shouldn't cost more than US$2.

Where to stay and eat In addition to the restaurant at Ziwa Rhino Lodge, day visitors might take note that the far superior Kabalega Diner (pages 182–3) is only 2km from the junction to Ziwa.

Upmarket

🏠 **Amuka Lodge** (9 rooms) ✪ 1.46991, 32.06558; m 0771 600812/0785 457202; e info@amukalodgeuganda.com; www. amukalodgeuganda.com. This isolated family-run lodge is carved into the bush about 6km by road from the sanctuary headquarters. The widely spaced-out rooms all have a tiled floor, earthy décor, double bed with net, en-suite hot shower & private balcony, & there are also 3 family rooms with 2 additional sgl beds. Amenities include a small swimming pool on the deck & campfires at night. The 3-course meals come highly praised. *US$144/250 sgl/dbl FB.* **$$$$**

Moderate, budget & camping

🏠 **Ziwa Rhino Lodge & Backpackers** (10 guesthouse rooms, 12 budget rooms) ✪ 1.44783, 32.07738; m 0775 621035/0782 819777; e info@ziwarhino.com; www.ziwarhino.com. Situated alongside the sanctuary headquarters, this unpretentious lodge is set in shady park-like gardens frequented by warthog, waterbuck, bushbuck & plentiful birds. For accommodation, 2 guesthouses have a selection of dbl, twin & trpl rooms with nets, en-suite hot showers & shared balconies, & there is also a backpacker hostel where twin rooms use common showers. A thatched restaurant, also open to day visitors, offers terrace or indoor seating, an adequately stocked bar & a limited selection of mains in the US$6–7 range. *US$40pp B&B in the guesthouse; US$15pp bed only for a backpacker room, US$10pp camping.* **$$$**

🏠 **Kafu River Lodge** (10 rooms) ✪ 1.52033, 32.05698; ☎ 041 4322140; m 0752 747333/0772 986509; e neul@neul.co.ug; www.neul.co.ug. This seemingly underutilised facility occupies grounds excised from ranch land beside the Kampala–Gulu Road between the turnings to Ziwa Rhino Sanctuary & Masindi. En-suite rooms are simple & clean. *US$35 dbl or twin.* **$$**

What to see and do Those who arrive with their own transport can use it as required for any of the activities described below. Those without can rent a 4x4 from the sanctuary headquarters at US$25 per group per activity. Note also that those who want to track rhinos and shoebills get a US$10 discount on the package deal. Closed shoes and long trousers are mandatory for all excursions, and insect repellent is recommended in the swamp.

Rhino tracking (*2hrs; US$40/30/10 FNR/FR/Ugandan citizen, discounts for children*) One of the most exciting wildlife activities on offer anywhere in Uganda, tracking the white rhinos of Ziwa usually takes place on foot, though you may need to drive a short way from the headquarters first, depending on the location of the nearest individuals. Because they are solitary animals, the rhinos are usually seen singly, though youngsters tend to stick close to their mother until they are almost fully grown. The rhinos are very habituated, since they are protected by armed rangers 24/7, so it is often possible to approach them to within 30m. White rhinos are not generally aggressive towards people (certainly not by comparison to their notoriously grouchy black counterparts), but like any wild animal, they can be unpredictable, so it is vital you stick close to the ranger, listen to his instructions, and avoid sudden movements. There are no fixed departure times, but early morning and late afternoon tend to be cooler for walking, and better for photography.

Shoebill canoe safari (*4hrs; US$30/25/15 FNR/FR/Ugandan citizen*) Best undertaken in the early morning (departing from your lodge at 06.00), the shoebill-tracking excursion involves driving to the edge of Lugogo Swamp, then canoeing or walking – or both – in search of one of the resident shoebills. The activity enjoys a high success rate, but you will seldom get as close to the shoebills as you might in Murchison Falls. Even if you dip on shoebills, plenty of other water-associated birds can be seen in the swamp.

Bird and nature walks (*2hrs; US$25/20/15 FNR/FR/Ugandan citizen*) The best way to see a selection of the sanctuary's non-aquatic birds and larger mammals is a guided bird or general nature walk using one of four trails that emanate from the headquarters. These are best undertaken from 08.00–10.00 or 16.00–18.00, when wildlife tends to be most active.

KABALEGA DINER (✪ *1.51305, 32.07661;* ☎ *041 4691910;* e *kabalegadinerug@ gmail.com; www.kabalegadiner.com;* ⊕ *07.00–19.00 daily; see ad, 3rd colour section*).

Probably the best roadside eatery in Uganda, Kabalega Diner stands on the left side of the Gulu Road 2km past the junction for Ziwa and 6km before the turn-off for Masindi, making it an ideal place for northbound travellers to stop for a snack, meal or drink. Breakfasts, soups, salads and sandwiches are in the US$2.50–3.50 range, while pizzas, curries, stir-fries, burgers and grills cost US$5–7. Good coffee and juices are available, as are flush toilets. Large groups and those special with dietary requests or allergies might want to phone ahead.

EAST TOWARDS JINJA

The surfaced 85km road between Kampala and Jinja usually takes around 2 hours to cover, though as with all escape routes from the capital, this depends greatly on traffic. The main attraction along this road, easily visited as a day trip from Kampala or Jinja, is the Mabira Forest Reserve, which offers excellent birding and monkey viewing as well as a good selection of overnight accommodation and – a recent addition for adrenalin junkies – the country's first canopy zipline. Lesser or more esoteric attractions are the legend-steeped Ssezibwa Falls only 40km east of Kampala, and the superb Mehta Golf Course outside Lugazi.

SSEZIBWA FALLS RESORT (⊕ *0.35867, 32.8659;* ⊕ *08.30–18.00 daily; entry US$3/1.50 FNR/FR*) A notable beauty spot and focal point of Kiganda legendeering, the Ssezibwa Falls Resort is a private ecotourism venture offering a variety of guided nature and cultural walks, as well as an attractive terrace restaurant and campsite. In the 19th century, the waterfall, which lies on the Ssezibwa River, was a favourite spot of Kabaka Mwanga and Kabaka Mutesa II, both of whom planted trees there that still flourish today (an act emulated by Kabaka Ronald Mutebi II in 2002). According to legend, the Ssezibwa River is not a natural phenomenon, but the progeny of a woman called Nakangu, who lived many hundreds of years ago and belonged to the Achibe (ox) clan. The heavily pregnant Nakangu was expected to give birth to twin children, but instead what poured from her womb was a twin river, one that split into two distinct streams around an island immediately below the waterfall. The spirits of Nakangu's unborn children – Ssezibwa and Mobeya – each inhabit one of these streams, for which reason it used to be customary for any Muganda passing the river's source at Namukono, some 20km further east, to throw a handful of grass or stones into it for good luck. Even today, a thanksgiving sacrifice of barkcloth, beer and a cockerel is made at the river's source every year, usually led by a Ssalongo (father of twins).

Given the supernatural significance that many Ugandan societies attach to twins, it is unsurprising that a number of shrines are maintained among the colourful quartzite rocks over which the river tumbles for perhaps 15m before it divides into two. Various gaps in the rock are dedicated to specific lubaale, among them the river spirit Mukasa, the hunting spirit Ddunga and the rainbow spirit Musoke. A fertility shrine in the rocks adjacent to the falls is associated with the thunder spirit Kiwanuka, and generally used for individual rather than communal sacrifices. Women who have been blessed with twins, one of which is human, the other a benevolent spirit manifested in a python or leopard, often visit this shrine to leave eggs for their python spirit or a cock for its feline counterpart. Communal ceremonies, in which nine pieces of meat are sacrificed at the appropriate spirit's shrine, are also still held at the waterfall. Tourists are welcome to visit on such occasions, but unfortunately their timing is difficult to predict – ceremonies are not held every year, and the date is usually announced at short notice when a medium

7

is consulted by a hungry spirit. Certain spirits, after having accepted a sacrifice and taken the requested action, appreciate having a live sheep or cock – white for Mukasa, brown for Kiwanuka – thrown over the waterfall itself, and they always ensure that the animal survives.

Getting there and away Ssezibwa Falls Resort lies 40km east of Kampala. It can be reached by following the Jinja road as far as Kayanja trading centre, where a green, tea-covered hill comes into view. At the signposted junction (⊕ *0.37256, 32.87338*), turn right and continue south for almost 2km, then turn right again on to a signposted track that brings you to the entrance gate after 350m. Using public transport, any eastbound matatu out of Kampala old taxi park can drop you at Kayanja, from where it is a 30-minute walk to the resort.

✗ Where to eat and drink

✗ **Ssezibwa Falls Restaurant & Campsite**
m 0704 022096/0756 677768;
e ssezibwafallsresort@yahoo.com; ⏲ 08.30–18.00 daily, but the restaurant will close later if the campsite is in use. Offering a pretty view over the Ssezibwa River from its shady terrace, this thatched restaurant serves a selection of grills, curries, sandwiches & salads in the US$4–7 range. There's no accommodation, nor any sign of any under construction, but camping is permitted for US$3pp.

What to see and do Ssezibwa Falls is a very pretty spot and there would be worse ways to spend an afternoon than chilling on the restaurant terrace enjoying the scenery, passing birdlife and a cold drink. For more energetic visitors, a variety of guided walks is offered for US$7–10 per person. The most interesting is a cultural walk that provides extensive background to the waterfall's history and associated legends. Bird walks don't really compare to what's on offer at nearby Mabira Forest, but they do offer Uganda newbies a good opportunity to seek out such charismatic species as great blue turaco and black-and-white casqued hornbill. Also available are longer (up to 3-hour) forest walks and hikes outside the resort.

MEHTA GOLF CLUB A contender for the most scenic golf course in Uganda, this compact nine-holer on the northeastern outskirts of Lugazi town, midway between Kampala and Jinja, has to be seen to be believed! The creation of the Asian owners of the town's sugar factory, it is an utterly surreal golfing paradise set in a lush valley hidden from the vulgar gaze of the masses toiling in the factory and in the surrounding cane plantations. Good curry lunches can be arranged, and there are a few simple hotels in town. To get there coming from Kampala, turn left at the main traffic circle in Lugazi (⊕ *0.36938, 32.94089*) and continue north for about 1.8km to the clubhouse. For further details, contact the factory management at m 0703 666308/0772 748211.

MABIRA FOREST RESERVE The 306km² Mabira Forest Reserve, whose southern extremities are skirted by the main Kampala–Jinja Road as it runs between Lugazi and Njeru, ranks as the largest remaining block of moist semi-deciduous forest in central or eastern Uganda. Although it suffered from heavy logging in the colonial era and substantial encroachment in the 1980s, Mabira remains the most important biodiversity hotspot within easy day-tripping distance of Kampala, with a bird checklist of more than 300 species and a varied mammalian fauna that includes the endemic Uganda mangabey. Highly accessible, whether as a round trip from Kampala or *en route* to Jinja, Mabira is now serviced by a decent selection of accommodation, while the lovely forest interior can be explored

along a network of walking trails, making it a highly attractive goal for jaded city dwellers and freshly arrived travellers alike. And if tranquil isn't your thing, then the Mabira Canopy Super Skyway surely will be: recently installed near Griffin Falls, this underpublicised zipline system connecting six lofty canopy platforms offers an adrenalin surge to match the white-water rafting and bungee jump at nearby Bujagali!

History The first attempt to exploit Mabira was initiated in 1900, when the colonial administration leased the forest to the Mabira Forest Rubber Company, which intended to reap an annual harvest of around 250,000kg from the estimated half-a-million *Funtuma elastica* (African silk rubber) trees that grow wild there. This plan was quickly scrapped as uneconomic, due to the high cost of clearing around these low yield trees, but the forest was heavily exploited for timber, even after it was gazetted as the Mabira Forest Reserve in 1932. After independence, Mabira's proximity to Kampala and Jinja led to an estimated 1,500 tonnes of charcoal being extracted from it annually throughout the 1960s. Less reversible was the damage done during the civil war of the early 1980s, when roughly 25% of the forest was cleared or otherwise degraded by subsistence farmers, who were eventually evicted in 1988. Since then, much of the degraded forest has recovered through the replanting of indigenous trees, and illegal felling has practically ceased. A more recent, and more serious, threat to the integrity of Mabira was a 2007 government proposal to degazette one-third of the forest reserve and transfer ownership to the Lugazi-based Sugar Corporation of Uganda for conversion to sugarcane plantations. This proposal sparked widespread and unexpectedly passionate public protest, ranging from reasoned letters to the press and the vociferous intervention of Kabaka Ronald Mutebi II of Buganda to a nasty riot in the middle of Kampala that led to three fatalities. Possibly because the furore exploded during the build-up to the prestigious Commonwealth Heads of Government Meeting (CHOGM) held in Kampala in November 2007, the proposal was quickly scrapped. It was briefly resurrected and then shelved again in 2011, since when the government has been silent on the issue. The short-term future of the forest reserve thus looks reasonably secure, but many environmentalists fear that it is only a matter of time before the proposal is revived.

Flora and fauna The reserve is primarily composed of moist semi-deciduous forest, with some 202 tree species identified to date, including the only known Ugandan specimens of *Diphasia angolensis*. The forest is interspersed with patches of open grassland, while several of the valleys support extensive papyrus swamps. Large mammals are relatively scarce in Mabira today, though a small population of elephant was present as recently as the 1950s. Primates include red-tailed monkey and black-and-white colobus, but Mabira is particularly important as a stronghold for the Uganda mangabey, a national endemic first recognised in 2007. More than 300 species of moth and butterfly have been identified in the forest.

Mabira ranks as one of the most important ornithological sites in Uganda, with a checklist of 315 (mostly forest-associated) species, including several rarities. Conspicuous larger birds include the stunning great blue turaco and more familiar African grey parrot, while three forest hornbill species and a variety of colourful sunbirds are often seen around the camp. Mabira is one of only two places in East Africa where the pretty tit-hylia has been recorded, and this rare bird is seen here with surprising regularity. It is also one of the few places in Uganda where the localised forest wood-hoopoe, African pitta, purple-throated cuckoo-shrike, leaf-love, Weyn's weaver and Nahan's francolin are regular. Note, however, that the

The spirit of Kiganda, the traditional religion of Buganda, 'is not so much adoration of a being supreme and beneficent', wrote John Speke, 'as a tax to certain malignant furies … to prevent them bringing evil on the land, and to insure a fruitful harvest'. Certainly, like many traditional African religions, Kiganda does revolve largely around the appeasing and petitioning of ancestral and animist spirits both benign and malevolent. But Kiganda is unusual in that it has a core of monotheism. The supreme being of the Baganda is Katonda – literally, Creator – who is not of human form, and has neither parents nor children, but who brought into being the heavens, the earth, and all they contain. Katonda is the most powerful denizen of the spiritual world, but somewhat detached from human affairs, which means he requires little attention by comparison to various subordinate spirits with a more hands-on approach.

Ranking below Katonda, the *balubaale* (singular *lubaale*) are semi-deities who play a central role in day-to-day affairs affecting Buganda. At least 30 balubaale are recognised (some sources claim a total of 70), and many are strongly associated with specific aspects or attributes of life. The balubaale have no equivalent in the Judaic branch of religions. Certainly not gods, they are more akin perhaps to a cross between a saint and a guardian angel – the spirits of real men (or more occasionally women) whose exceptional attributes in life have been carried over in to death. Traditionally, the balubaale form the pivot of organised religion in Buganda: prior to the introduction of exotic religions they were universally venerated, even above the Kabaka (king), who in all other respects was an absolute ruler.

The most popular lubaale is Mukasa, a spirit of lakes and rivers honoured at many temples around Buganda. Mukasa is strongly associated with Lake Victoria, so it's no surprise that the most important shrine to his spirit is located in the Ssese Archipelago, on Bubembe Island, to where the Kabaka would send an annual offering of cows and a request for prosperity and good harvests. Mukasa is also associated with fertility: barren women would regularly visit an adjacent shrine on Bubembe, dedicated to his wife Nalwanga, to ask her to seek her husband's blessing. Another important lubaale, Wanga is the guardian of the sun and moon, and as such has no earthly shrine. Wanga is the father of Muwanga, literally 'the most powerful'. Other prominent male balubaale with specific areas of interest include Musoke (rainbows), Kawumpuli (plagues), Ndahura (smallpox), Kitinda (prosperity), Musisi (earthquakes), Wamala (Lake Wamala) and Ddunga (hunting).

Female balubaale are fewer, and in most cases their elevated status is linked to kinship with a male lubaale, but they include Kiwanuka's wife Nakayage (fertility) and Kibuuka's mother Nagaddya (harvests). Nabuzaana, the female lubaale of obstetrics, is possibly unique in having no kin among the other balubaale, furthermore in that she is tended by priestesses of Banyoro rather than Baganda origin. The male lubaale Ggulu, guardian of the sky, is a confusing figure. Listed in some traditions as the creator, his existence, in common with that of Katonda, pre-dated that of humanity, and he has no earthly shrine, furthering the suggestion that unlike other balubaale he is not the spirit of a dead person. Ggulu's children include the lightning spirit Kiwanuka as well as Walumbe, the spirit of sickness and death.

The balubaale are expected to intercede favourably in national affairs related to their speciality when petitioned with sacrifices and praise. Sacrifices to the water spirit Mukasa might be made during periods of drought, in case he has forgotten that the people need rain. The rainbow spirit Musoke, by contrast, might be placated with sacrifices after extended rains that prevent harvesting or ploughing, and he will

signal his assent to stop the rain with a rainbow. In past times, all the major temples would be consulted and offerings made before any major national undertaking – a coronation, for instance, or a war – and any Kabaka who ignored this custom was inviting disaster. One main shrine or *ekiggwa* is dedicated to each lubaale, though many are also venerated at a number of lesser shrines scattered around Buganda. Every shrine is tended by a *mandwa*: a priest or medium who is on occasion possessed by the shrine's spirit and acts as its oracle. The mandwa for any given temple might be male or female, but will usually come from a specific clan associated with that temple. The three main shrines dedicated to Katonda – all situated in Kyagwe, near the Mabira Forest – are, for instance, tended by priests of the Njovu (elephant) clan. Sacred drums, ceremonial objects and sometimes body parts of the deceased are stored in the temple, the upkeep of which is governed by elaborate customs.

While a relatively small cast of balubaale is concerned with national affairs, the day-to-day affairs of local communities and of individual Muganda are governed by innumerable lesser spirits. These are divided into two main categories: *mizimu* (singular *omuzimu*) are the spirits of departed ancestors, while *misambwa* (singular *omusambwa*) are spirits associated with specific physical objects such as mountains, rivers, forests or caves. Dealings with the ancestral spirits are a family matter, undertaken at a household shrine where small items, such as cowries or beans, are offered on a regular basis, while a living sacrifice of a chicken or goat might be offered before an important event or ceremony. Appeasing the misambwa, by contrast, is a community affair, with communal offerings made on a regular basis. Unlike balubaale or mizimu, misambwa are generally cantankerous spirits: one's main obligation to an omusambwa is to keep out of its way and uphold any taboos associated with it.

The place of Kiganda in modern Buganda is difficult to isolate. In the latter half of the 19th century, when the kingdom was first infiltrated by evangelical foreigners – initially just Arabs, later also Europeans – a significant number of Muganda, especially the elite, converted to an exotic religion. Thereafter, the converts tended to regard their indigenous spiritual traditions as backward and superstitious, a stance that caused considerable friction within the kingdom during the 1880s. The trend against traditionalism continued throughout the 20th century. Today, most if not all Baganda profess to be either Christian or Muslim, and certainly very few educated and urbanised Baganda take Kiganda traditions very seriously, if they consider them at all.

In rural Buganda, by contrast, many people still adhere partially or concurrently to two apparently contradictory religious doctrines. In other words, they might be dedicated Christians or Muslims, but in times of trouble they will as likely consult a traditional oracle or healer as they will a priest or imam or a Western doctor. This dualism in Buganda is perhaps less conspicuous to outsiders than it would be in many other parts of Africa. But its existence is confirmed by the fact that sacrificial shrines such as Ssezibwa Falls, Tanda Pits and the Nakayima Tree remain active focal points for traditionalist cults – far more so perhaps in 2015 than they did ten or 20 years before that. Outside of Buganda, post-1986 Christian cults centred on the Acholi and Bakiga mediums Alice Lakwena and Credonia Mwerinde; though very different, both possessed undeniable traditionalist undertones. And so, it is out of respect for Kiganda traditions, rather than any wish to offend the many Baganda who reject them, that this box has been written not in the past tense but in the present.

The first European survey of Mabira Forest referred to it as Mabira Nakalanga, which translates as Nakalanga Forest, since Mabira is simply a generic Luganda term used to denote any large forest. In reality, then, the local Baganda would have known the forest as Nakalanga, which is also the name of a mischievous spirit said to inhabit it. According to folklore, Nakalanga is associated with one specific stream that runs through Mabira Forest, the source of which was until recent times the site of an important sacrificial shrine consisting of several huts.

Several early colonial writers reported that Mabira harboured a Pygmy tribe called the Banakalanga (people of Nakalanga) and assumed that these people were related to the Batwa Pygmies of the Congolese border area. Local Luganda legend, however, doesn't regard the Banakalanga as a tribe, but rather as spirits of nature. The belief is that the forest spirit punishes families that have fallen out of favour by cursing one of its children to be a puny and often mildly deformed dwarf.

In the 1950s, Rapper and Ladkin of the Uganda Medical Service investigated the Nakalanga phenomenon and determined that the dwarfish sufferers did indeed appear to be born randomly to physiologically normal parents with other healthy offspring. They concluded that the Banakalanga were affected by a form of infantilism linked to a pituitary defect, one that generally first showed itself when the afflicted person was about three years of age. The disease, Rapper and Ladkin believed, was pathological rather than genetic in origin, but its precise cause was indeterminate, as was its apparent restriction to one small area around Mabira Forest. Subsequent studies confirmed that Nakalanga dwarfism is a complication of a pituitary malfunction caused by onchocerciasis (a disease spread by the *Simulium* blackfly) and note that the condition also occurs in the Kabarole District of western Uganda.

Interestingly, the first written references to the Banakalanga interchangeably calls them the Bateemba (people of the nets), evidently in reference to a hunting method used by Pygmoid peoples elsewhere in Africa. Furthermore, according to Rapper and Ladkin, a local Saza chief interviewed back in the early 20th century told his interrogators that a tribe of true Pygmies did once live in the forest, but it vanished sometime before Europeans arrived in the area. It seems probable, then, that both Nakalanga and the medical condition attributed to the spirit's mischief-making derive their name from that of a Pygmoid tribe which once inhabited Mabira Forest.

forest's reputation as a good place to see the rare blue swallow is based on one vagrant sighting many years ago.

Fees The fee structure is rather quirky, and seems to be subject to an element of on-the-ground interpretation. If you base yourself or do activities out of the Mabira Forest Eco-Tours Camp, entrance costs US$7, while guided forest walks cost US$12 per person and birding with an expert guide costs US$30/40 per person half/full-day. At Griffin Falls, the rates quoted are US$5 per person entrance, with an additional US$5 per person for a guided walk, or US$22/33 per person half/full-day birding. Two activities offered at Griffin Falls but not at Mabira Forest Eco-Tours Camp are the canopy skyway zipline tour and mangabey tracking, which

cost US$50 and US$17 per person respectively, *inclusive* of the entrance fee. The above fees apply to all foreigners, whether resident or non-resident, but fees are significantly discounted for Ugandan citizens.

Getting there and away Mabira Forest Reserve is easily accessible by private vehicle or public transport since the surfaced Kampala–Jinja Road runs right through it. There are two main access points. The small town of Lugazi 50km east of Kampala and 35km west of Jinja is the springboard for Griffin Falls Camp and the Canopy Skyline, which both lie a few kilometres north of the main road, while Najjembe, 10km closer to Jinja, is the junction village for Mabira Forest Eco-Tours, Rainforest Lodge and Little Kingston.

To get to Griffin Falls Camp, first head to Lugazi, then branch to the north at a large junction (✪ *0.3687, 32.93636*) immediately west of the taxi park. Follow this road for 800m, passing a small market to your left, until you reach a T-junction (✪ *0.37558, 32.93623*) in front of a sugarcane plantation where you need to turn left. From here, it's a fairly straightforward 9km drive, with all junctions signposted, to the village of Wuswa (✪ *0.42936, 32.95182*), then another 1km to the camp. Using public transport, plenty of matatus run to Lugazi from Kampala or Jinja throughout the day, and a boda on to Griffin Falls Camp should cost around US$1.50–2.

Any public transport heading between Kampala and Jinja can drop you at the forest-enclave village of Najjembe. From the main crossroads in Najjembe (✪ *0.39558, 33.00888*), the road heading north leads to Mabira Forest Eco-Tours after 500m, while the one south runs past Little Kingston after 100m and terminates at Rainforest Lodge after another 2km.

Where to stay and eat *Map, page 241, unless otherwise stated*

Upmarket

✱ 🏠 **Rainforest Lodge** (12 cottages) ✪ 0.38191, 33.01703; 📞 0414 258273/0312 260758; m 0774 898611; e info@geolodgesafrica. com; www.geolodgesafrica.com. This attractive lodge, set on the forested Gangu Hill 2km south of Najjembe, offers accommodation in beautifully furnished stilted timber dbl or twin cottages with wooden furniture, wrought iron fittings, en-suite hot shower & elevated private balcony looking into the canopy where hornbills, turacos & red-tailed monkeys abound. An elevated restaurant building & swimming pool-sauna area enjoy similar views. *US$210/330 sgl/dbl FB, discounts available for Ugandan residents.* **$$$$$**

Budget
Rates at both the places listed below exclude reserve entrance fees.

✱ 🏠 **Griffin Falls Camp** [map, page 94] (6 rooms & dorms) ✪ 0.43685, 32.95416; m 0751 949368/0781 858919; e info@mabiraforestcamp. com; www.mabiraforestcamp.com. Owned & managed by the Mabira Forest Integrated Community

Organisation (MAFICO), this bona fide ecotourism camp is set in a forest clearing near the village of Wuswa & far from any possibility of traffic noise. It offers a good selection of budget accommodation, including twin bandas, 4-bed dorms & camping. The bandas are simple but well ventilated & come with nets, electricity & private balcony. A restaurant serves a reasonably varied menu, with most mains priced at around US$8, & beers & sodas are sold. Activities include guided forest walks, birding, mangabey tracking & the canopy skyway zipline. The staff prefer prospective visitors to phone in advance, but it isn't compulsory. *US$23/33 twin with common/en-suite showers, US$10pp per dorm bed, US$1.50pp.* **$$**

🏠 **Mabira Forest Eco-Tours Camp** (3 bandas & 1 dorm) ✪ 0.39967, 33.01033; m 0752 353098; e angelie_muge@yahoo.com; www.nfa.org.ug. Established back in 1995, this inherently attractive but rather rundown rest camp suffers from the noise associated with the high volume of road haulage traffic on the nearby Kampala–Jinja Road & has been superseded in all respects other than accessibility by the newer Griffin Falls Camp. The staff will prepare reasonable meals for around US$4 by advance order, beers & sodas are available,

& Najjembe 500m away is renowned for a truck stop selling cheap & succulent grilled chicken, as well as fruits & vegetables. *US$10/17 sgl/dbl banda, US$3pp dorm bed, US$3pp camping, US$10 tent hire (sleeping up to 5).* **$$**

Shoestring
🏠 **Little Kingston da Global Village**
(4 rooms & 1 dorm) 📱 0772 615618;
✉ flandersrazaka@yahoo.com; 📘 fb.me/

FRasNpolanGoma. This cosy Belgian–Ugandan lodge in Najjembe has clean & affordable en-suite rooms with net, a 4-bed dorm, a campsite, & a bar/restaurant with pool table serving meals for around US$2. Activities include mountain biking & village/forest walks. Secure parking is available in the compound. The only downside is the rather noisy location practically adjacent to the main road. Otherwise, very good value. *US$7 dbl, US$3pp dorm bed, US$5pp camping.* **$**

What to see and do

Forest walks It is possible to explore motorable tracks through the forest unaccompanied, but you'll benefit greatly from taking a guide to discover the excellent network of forest trails that emanates from both Mabira Forest Eco-Tours Camp and Griffin Falls Camp. Non-specialised walks are cheaper than dedicated birding walks, but the latter increase your chance of seeing rare birds, as you'll be allocated a guide with a good knowledge of bird calls, which can be invaluable when it comes to locating more elusive species in the dense forest. One of the best individual birding sites in Mabira is a forest-fringed pond that can be reached by following the Jinja Road east for 5km past Najjembe, then turning left and following a small dirt road for a few hundred metres. The main attraction at Griffin Falls Camp is the 30-minute forest walk to the pretty Griffin Falls, where all three type of monkey might be seen – though be prepared for the water to have a slight whiff of molasses, thanks to effluent dumped into the Musamya River from the Sugar Corporation of Uganda's factory at Lugazi.

Canopy Super Skyway (*3hrs; US$50/20 for foreigners/Ugandans, inc entry fee & guides, & irrespective of group size (it will run even if only 1 person wants to go)*) Opened in 2014, this thrilling 250m canopy zipline, the first of its kind in Uganda, connects six canopy platforms, the tallest being 40m above the ground, alongside the Musamya River 15 minutes' walk from Griffin Falls Campsite. The excursion leaves from Griffin Falls Camp at 08.00 and 14.00 daily, and can also be booked as a day trip out of Jinja/Kampala, inclusive of transport, lunch and nature walk, for US$80/100 per person, with a minimum group size of three – contact Griffin Falls Camp for details.

Mangabey tracking (*US$17pp, inc entry fee & guides*) Mabira is an important stronghold for the Uganda mangabey (*Lophocebus ugandae*), a recently described species that was split from the more widespread grey-cheeked mangabey in 2007. The only primate species endemic to Uganda, it is significantly smaller than other mangabeys – a group of monkeys closely related to baboons – and easily distinguished from other monkeys in Mabira by its overall dark coloration with a pale ruff. Several troops living in the vicinity of Griffin Falls Camp have been habituated, and can be tracked, ideally leaving first thing in the morning, when sightings are almost certain, though nothing is guaranteed. The excursion normally takes 3–4 hours, but might take longer if the monkeys prove difficult to locate.

Mountain biking Mountain bike trails have been cut in the vicinity of Griffin Falls Camp, but no bicycles are available to hire there, so you need your own. It may be possible to rent a bike for US$7 at Mabira Forest Eco-Tours Camp.

SOUTHWEST TOWARDS MASAKA

The Lake Victoria hinterland west of Kampala and Entebbe is dotted with low-key attractions. The most alluring of these, often visited as destinations in their own right, are the Mabamba Swamp, which is the most reliable site for shoebills in the immediate vicinity of Kampala, and the underpublicised Mpanga Forest, which abuts the main road to Masaka 35km from the capital. Other attractions in the region – most notably perhaps the equator crossing at Nabusanke – are more often visited *en route* between Kampala and points further southwest, such as Masaka, Lake Mburo National Park or Bwindi Impenetrable National Park.

MABAMBA SWAMP Only 12km west of Entebbe as the crow flies, the 100km² Mabamba Swamp is a Ramsar Site and Important Bird Area that extends across a shallow marshy bay on the northern shore of Lake Victoria. Some 300 bird species have been recorded in the swamp, including an alluring selection of water-associated species, and it is also home to a relict population of sitatunga antelope and more than 200 varieties of butterfly. The prime attraction of Mabamba, however, is that it is the most reliable place in the vicinity of Kampala – indeed, perhaps anywhere in the country – to look for the charismatic shoebill. Dugout trips into the swamp run out of the tiny village of Mabamba, where the local boaters have organised themselves into a community-based ecotourism project that has also played an important role in conserving the few shoebills left in the area. A boat capable of carrying one to three people costs around US$35, and the enthusiastic guides are usually able to locate a shoebill within a few minutes. Even if you're out of luck on that score, it's a lovely, mellow boat trip, and the general birdlife is fantastic, with a good chance of spotting localised species such as pygmy goose, lesser jacana, gull-billed tern, blue-breasted bee-eater and the papyrus-specific Carruthers's cisticola, papyrus gonolek and white-winged warbler.

Getting there and away Mabamba is easily visited as a day trip from Kampala or Entebbe, but it also makes a straightforward and popular diversion for those travelling to or from destinations further southwest, such as Lake Mburo or Bwindi Impenetrable national parks.

Organised tours The easiest way to visit Mabamba is on a day tour, which can be organised through any operator in Kampala or Entebbe. A highly regarded specialist operator, based out of the Sunset Entebbe Hotel, is Mabamba Shoebill Tours (m *0786 710050/0755 778790*; e *enquiries@shoebillmabamba.com; www.shoebillmabamba.com*), which has good links to the local community and offers daily departures at 07.30 by demand. Mabamba Shoebill charges US$160 per party for up to three people, plus US$33 for every additional person, for a half-day trip inclusive of hotel pick-up within Entebbe, road transport to the swamp and guided dugout trip.

Self-drive Despite their close geographical proximity, Entebbe and Mabamba lie at least 40km apart by road, and the drive takes about 1 hour. The most direct route out of Entebbe involves following the surfaced Kampala Road north for about 12km to Kisubi (✪ *0.13031, 32.53293*), then following a good dirt road northwest for about 15km to Nakawuka (✪ *0.18858, 32.46215*), where another left turn leads after 6km to the small town of Kasanje (✪ *0.15295, 32.39934*). Turn left again at an outsized roundabout and after 3.5km, you'll reach a minor road on the right

by a large tree (⌖ *0.12569, 32.41031*). Follow this for 9km to reach Mabamba (⌖ *0.07591, 32.35071*). Coming from Kampala or Masaka, follow the main road to Mpigi, then turn south at a junction a short way further east (⌖ *0.21926, 32.33349*) and follow it for 12km to Kasanje, where you need to go straight across the roundabout mentioned above, then continue as if coming from Entebbe.

Public transport Mabamba is quite easily reached by public transport. Coming from Kampala, catch a matatu from the new taxi park to Mpigi, then on to Kasanje, from where you can hire a boda to Mabamba village. If you're in Entebbe, take a boat from Nakiwogo port to Buwaya landing on the western side of Waiya Bay. It's 5km from Buwaya to the large tree junction mentioned above (approaching from the opposite direction).

KATEREKE PRISON (☏ *041 4501866;* ☉ *08.00–17.00 daily; entry US$2*) The extensive prison ditch at Katereke is a relic of the instability that characterised Buganda in the late 1880s (see box, pages 194–5). It was constructed by Kabaka Kalema, an Islamic sympathiser who was controversially placed on the throne in October 1888, less than two months after Kabaka Mwanga had been forced into exile. Kalema ordered that every potential or imagined rival to his throne be rounded up and sent to Katereke – which, given the fragility of his position in the divided kingdom, added up to an estimated 40 personages.

One of the first to be imprisoned at Katereke was Kiwewa, who had ruled Buganda for the brief period between Mwanga's exile and Kalema's ascent to the throne. Kiwewa was soon joined by a bevy of his wives, as well as the two infant sons of the exiled Mwanga, and the last two surviving sons of the late Kabaka Suuna. Kalema also feared a secession bid from his own brothers, and even his sisters – like Mwanga before him, Kalema was unsettled by the fact that a woman sat on the English throne – and most of them were imprisoned, too.

Six months into his reign, sensing a growing threat from the budding alliance between the Christian faction in Buganda and its former persecutor Mwanga – the latter by this time openly resident on an island in Murchison Bay, only 10km from the capital – Kalema decided to wipe out the potential opposition once and for all. Most of the occupants of the prison were slaughtered without mercy. Other less significant figures, for instance some of the princesses and one elderly son of Kabaka Suuna, were spared when they agreed to embrace Islam. The massacre wasn't confined to the prison's occupants either: Mukasa, the traditionalist Katikiro who had served under Mwanga, was shot outside his house, which was then set on fire with the body inside. The wives of the former Kabaka Kiwewa, according to Sir John Milner Gray, were 'put to death in circumstances of disgusting brutality'.

Ultimately, this massacre probably hastened Kalema's downfall by strengthening the alliance between Buganda's Christians, who suffered several casualties, and the island-bound Mwanga, left mourning several brothers and sisters as well as his two sons. And the lingering death that Kalema had reserved for his predecessor set many formerly neutral chiefs and other dignitaries against him. Kiwewa was starved of food and water for seven days, then a bullet was put through his weakened body, and finally his remains were burnt unceremoniously in his prison cell – not, in the words of Sir Apollo Kaggwa, 'a fit manner in which to kill a king'.

Katereke Prison lies to the west of Kampala, and can be reached by following the Masaka Road out of town for about 15km, passing through Nsangi trading centre, then about 2km later turning right at a left-hand bend in the road marked by a series of speed bumps. The 2km track to Katereke is marked by a fading mauve signpost

(ignore a similar but premature sign 1km back down the road towards Nsangi). It's a surprisingly peaceful and leafy spot, considering its bloody historical associations, and guides are available to show you around what remains of the prison trench.

A visit to Katereke could be combined with a side trip to **Nagalabi Buddo**, which lies about 5km south of Nsangi trading centre and has reputedly served as the coronation site for the Kabaka since Buganda was founded.

MPANGA FOREST RESERVE Gazetted in the 1950s, the 45km² Mpanga Forest Reserve, situated 36km from Kampala near the small town of Mpigi, makes for an agreeably rustic (and affordable) short trip out of the capital, or first stop *en route* to further flung destinations. It protects an extensive patch of medium-altitude rainforest characteristic of the vegetation that extended over much of the northern Lake Victoria hinterland prior to the early 20th century. Although Mpanga harbours a less diverse fauna than the larger forests in the far west of Uganda, its accessibility and proximity to Kampala more than justify a visit. The most readily observed mammal is the red-tailed monkey, though bushpig, bushbuck and flying squirrels are also present. Blue-breasted kingfisher, black-and-white casqued hornbill, African pied hornbill, African grey parrot and great blue turaco are among the more striking and conspicuous of the 180-plus bird species recorded. Resident birds with a rather localised distribution elsewhere in Uganda include shining blue kingfisher, spotted greenbul, Uganda woodland warbler, green crombec, Frazer's ant-thrush, grey-green bush shrike, pink-footed puff-back and Weyn's weaver. Mpanga Forest is also noted for its butterflies, which are abundant wherever you walk.

Fees Fees are refreshingly low. Entrance costs US$1.50 per person, while an additional US$1.50 per person is charged for an unguided forest walk. Optional guides cost US$3 per party.

Getting there and away Coming from Kampala, about 3km past the turn-off to Mpigi, the road passes through a dip flanked by the southernmost tip of the forest. Immediately past the dip, a signposted turn-off to the right (⊕ *0.20265, 32.30618*) leads to the ecotourism centre after about 500m. Matatus to Mpigi leave Kampala from the new taxi park and cost around US$2. From Mpigi, a boda to the forest will cost less than US$1. Alternatively, any minibus or bus heading between Kampala and Masaka can drop you at the turn-off 500m from the ecotourism centre.

Where to stay and eat

 **Mpanga Ecotourism Site** (5 rooms & 1 dorm) ⊕ 0.2061, 32.30189; ☎ 039 2736030; ▥ 0789 400123/0706 123891. This pretty camp centres on a grassy picnic area overlooked by the southern edge of the forest & resounding with the calls of hornbills & other forest birds. Accommodation options include a 4-bedroom cottage with communal shower, a fabulous en-suite stilted wooden banda set in a private forest clearing, a rather dour 2-bed dorm & camping at a clearing 100m deeper in the forest. It is all a bit rundown, but great shoestring value & the setting is marvellous. With a few hours' notice, simple meals can be arranged. *US$13 dbl en-suite banda, US$10 dbl or twin room in cottage, US$3pp dorm bed, US$1.50pp camping.* **$**

What to see and do A network of wide footpaths initially cut by researchers is now the basis of a selection of forest walks emanating from the Mpanga Ecotourism Centre. You can wander along the footpaths alone if you wish, or take a guide. The undemanding 3km **Base Line Trail** is the main route through the forest,

The succession of Kabaka Mwanga in October 1884 was an unusually smooth affair, accepted by his brothers and kin without serious infighting, and supported by the majority of Saza chiefs as well as the foreign factions that had by then settled around the royal capital. The five years that followed Mwanga's coronation were, by contrast, the most tumultuous in Buganda's 400-plus years of existence, culminating in three changes of Kabaka within 12 months, and paving the way for the kingdom to relinquish its autonomy to a colonial power in 1890.

Mwanga's career comes across as the antithesis of the epithet 'come the moment, come the man'. In 1884, the missionary Alexander Mackay, who had witnessed Mwanga develop from 'a little boy … into manhood' described Mwanga as an 'amiable … young fellow' but 'fitful and fickle, and, I fear, revengeful', noting that 'under the influence of [marijuana] he is capable of the wildest unpremeditated actions'. These misgivings were echoed by other contemporary commentators: Robert Walker, for instance, dismissed Mwanga as 'frivolous … weak and easily led; passionate and if provoked petulant … possessed of very little courage or self-control'.

Whatever his personal failings, Mwanga was also forced to contend with a daunting miscellany of natural disasters, religious tensions and real or imagined political threats. Three months into his reign, he lost several wives and trusted chiefs to an epidemic that swept through his first capital at Nubulagala, while his second capital on Mengo Hill was destroyed by fire in February 1886 and again in 1887. Politically, Mwanga was threatened to the west by a resurgent Bunyoro, whose charismatic leader Kabalega inflicted several defeats on the Kiganda army in the 1880s. From the east, meanwhile, Buganda faced a more nebulous and less quantifiable threat, as news filtered through of the growing number and influence of European colonial agents on the coast.

Buganda (c1884) was riddled with religious factionalism. Kiganda traditionalists had for some time co-existed uneasily with a growing volume of Islamic converts influenced by Arab traders. And both of these relatively established factions faced further rivalry from the late 1870s onwards, following the establishment of Catholic and Anglican missions near the capital. The divisions between these religious factions were not limited to matters purely ecclesiastical. Many established Kiganda and Islamic customs, notably polygamy, were anathema to the Christian missionaries, who also spoke out against participation in the slave trade – the lifeblood of the Arab settlers, and profitable to several prominent Kiganda traditionalists.

Mwanga's personal religious persuasions were evidently dictated by pragmatic concerns. During the early years of his rule, his views were strongly shaped by his *katikiro*, an influential Kiganda traditionalist who distrusted all exotic religions, but was relatively sympathetic to Islam as the lesser – or more tolerant towards Kiganda customs – of the two evils. It also seems likely that the traditionalist faction, not unreasonably, perceived a connection between the European missionaries and threat of European imperialism, and thus reckoned it had less to fear from the Arabs.

Three months after he took the throne, Mwanga signalled his hostility to Christianity by executing three young Anglican converts. Then, in October 1885, the king received news of Bishop Hannington's attempt to become the first European through the 'back door' of Busoga. In Kiganda tradition, the back door is used only by close friends or plotting enemies, and Hannington – a stranger to Mwanga – was clearly not the former. Motivated by fear more perhaps than any religious factor, Mwanga ordered the execution of Hannington (see box,

page 234). Weeks after the bishop's death, Joseph Mukasa, a Catholic advisor to the king, criticised Mwanga for having Hannington killed without first giving him an opportunity to defend himself, and was also executed for his efforts. These two deaths led to an increasing estrangement between the Kabaka and the missionaries – Mackay included – who resided around his court, fuelled partially by Mwanga's fear of a European reprisal for the attack on Hannington.

Mwanga's distrust of Christianity exploded into blind rage on 25 May 1886. The catalyst for this was probably the subversive actions of his sister Princess Clara Nalumansi (see box, page 124), though it has been suggested by some writers that Mwanga was a homosexual paedophile whose temporary hatred of Christians stemmed from his rejection by a favoured page, recently baptised. Exactly how many Baganda Christians were speared, beheaded, cremated, castrated and/ or bludgeoned to death over the next ten days is an open question – 45 deaths are recorded by name, but the actual tally was probably several hundred. The persecution culminated at Namugongo on 3 June 1886, when at least 26 Catholic and Anglican converts, having rejected the opportunity to renounce their new faith, were roasted alive (see box, page 124).

His rage evidently spent, Mwanga set about repairing his relationship with the European missionaries, who had been not been directly victimised by the persecution, and who depended on the Kabaka's tolerance to continue their work in the kingdom. Tensions resurfaced in June 1887 when, according to Mackay, Stanley's non-military expedition to Equatoria was described to Mwanga by an Arab trader as 'a Mazungu coming here with a thousand guns' – a ploy designed to reawaken the king's concern that Hannington's death would be avenged by his countrymen. In December 1887, Hannington's successor wrote Mwanga a letter, delivered by Rev E C Gordon, stating that: 'we do not desire to take vengeance for this action of yours, we are teachers of the religion of Christ, not soldiers … We believe that you must see now that you were deceived as to the object for which [Hannington] had come.' The increasingly paranoid Mwanga interpreted this as a declaration of war, and Gordon was imprisoned for two months.

During 1888, Mwanga's concerns about a foreign invasion were diverted by the domestic chaos induced by years of vacillation between the religious factions. On 10 September, Mwanga was forced to flee into exile. His successor, a Muslim convert called Kiwewa, enjoyed a six-week reign, marked by violence between the opposing religious factions, before he was ousted by another Muslim convert called Kalema. Under Kalema, Buganda descended into full civil war, with an unexpected reversal of alliances in which the Christian and traditionalist Baganda lent their support to Mwanga, who was restored to power in February 1890. Three months later, Captain Lugard arrived in Kampala waving a treaty of protectorateship with England.

E B Fletcher, who knew Mwanga in his later years, regarded him to be 'nervous, suspicious, fickle, passionate … with no idea whatever of self-discipline, without regard for life or property, as long as he achieved his own end'. Yet in 1936 Fletcher also wrote an essay exonerating many of the king's excesses and flaws as symptomatic of the troubled times through which he'd lived. 'To steer a straight course through a time when such radical changes were taking place', Fletcher concluded, 'needed a man of a strong character, a firm will and wide vision. Those characteristics Mwanga did not possess.'

crossing two streams before it emerges on the western margin at Nakyetema Swamp, where sitatunga and shoebill are resident, though seldom seen. The 5km **Hornbill Loop** covers more undulating terrain, and involves fording several streams along minor footpaths, passing a striking tree-root arch along the way. For those with limited time, the 1km **Butterfly Loop** offers a good chance of seeing monkeys and common forest birds, as well as myriad colourful butterflies, and can be completed in less than an hour.

In addition to forest walks, guided visits can also be arranged to two important Kiganda shrines that lie within walking distance of the forest. Less than 1km from the ecotourism centre, **Nakibinge Shrine**, dedicated to the eponymous 16th-century king, is housed in a small thatched building in the style of the Kasubi Tombs. The **Kibuuka Shrine** near Mpigi, 3–4km back along the Kampala Road, is dedicated to a god of war who hailed from the Ssese Islands. Beyond the forest, the **flat-topped hill** south of the main road is worth climbing for the attractive grassland environment and views over the forest and surrounding swamp valleys.

FROM MPANGA TO MASAKA

Mpambire and Kabira About 1km beyond Mpanga Forest, the small village of **Mpambire**, traditional home of the Buganda royal drum-makers, is lined with stalls selling drums (US$10 upwards, depending on size) and other musical instruments. Even if you're not interested in buying drums, it's fascinating to watch the craftsmen at work, and there's no hassle attached to wandering around. At **Kabira**, another 5km further towards Masaka, a row of stalls sells distinctive and colourful baskets and stools. Between these two locations, the road fords an extensive papyrus swamp – stretching all the way to Lake Victoria – in which the shoebill is resident and reportedly sometimes observed from the road.

Makanaga Wetland Effectively a western extension of the better-known Mabamba Swamp, Makanaga is a mosaic of shallow open water and papyrus swamps extending across a vast bay on the northern shore of Lake Victoria. As with Mabamba, the wetland's principal attraction is shoebill, which are regularly seen on dugout trips into the swamps. But a profusion of other water-associated birds is present, particularly on the open shallows, which often hosts seething flocks of white-winged black tern and various ducks and waders. The rare blue swallow is often observed over fringing grassland between November and January, while the forested verges of the Namugobo boat landing host the likes of great blue turaco, Ross's turaco, pied hornbill and Weyn's weaver. Namugobo Landing, the best place to arrange a boat into the wetland, lies only 6km from the Masaka Road along a fair dirt road branching south at Kamengo (✪ *0.14675, 32.22413*), about 13km west of Mpanga Forest.

Camp Crocs Established on Lake Victoria shore south of Buwawa in 1991, Uganda Crocs (m *0792 844944; info@ugandacrocs.com; www.ugandacrocs.com;* ⊕ *08.00–18.00 daily; entry US$1.50*) is a long-serving Nile crocodile farm whose main products are crocodile meat (most of which is consumed locally) and crocodile skin for the lucrative export market. Activities include guided tours of the farm, where you'll see a vast array of farmed Nile crocodiles, from hatchlings to some that are five years old, along with a few venerable man-eaters who were relocated here by UWA from other parts of Uganda where they were harassing the surrounding population. An open-air restaurant facing the lake serves crocodile meat along with more mainstream Ugandan dishes in the US$4–7 range, and accommodation in

four spacious clean hillside cabins costs US$24/40 single/double. Coming from Kampala, Camp Crocs lies 10km south of the Masaka Road along a dirt turn-off signposted at Buwama (⊕ *0.06231, 32.10593*). If you miss that turn-off, or are coming in the opposite direction, a second (slightly shorter) road branches south to the camp about 4km southwest of this (⊕ *0.0387, 32.07963*).

Nabusanke The most popular stop on the Masaka Road, 75km from Kampala, Nabusanke (literally 'Small Parts') is an otherwise unremarkable location shunted into the limelight by the fact that the equator happens to cross the road here. A pair of much-photographed white concrete hoops attest to the fact, while a local entrepreneur has set up buckets and jugs between these unprepossessing landmarks. For a small fee he will demonstrate (or at least intimate) that water swirls in opposite directions in the northern and southern hemispheres.

A long line of roadside craft stalls with the usual mundane offerings lines the equator, as do half a dozen small cafés. The most professional of these places is the AidChild Equation Café (⊕ *-0.00093, 32.03901; www.aidchild.org/aidchild-businesses;* ⊕ *05.00–19.00 daily*), which sells a variety of high-quality local crafts and artwork, and serves tasty coffee and muffins, as well a wraps and light meals in the US$2–5 range. There are flushing toilets, too. It's not the cheapest option, but it's good value, and all money raised by AidChild goes to a self-explanatory good cause.

Lukaya If you're travelling by bus, expect to have a potential buffet of barbecue snacks and bottled drinks thrust up to your window at Lukaya, which lies about 30km before Masaka, on the western edge of a 14km-wide swamp close to the shore of Lake Victoria. Look out for colonies of pelicans, and occasionally herons or storks, roosting on roadside trees.

7

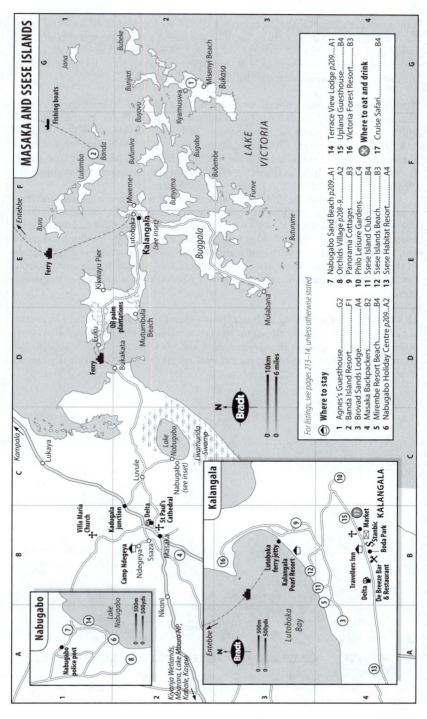

MASAKA AND SSESE ISLANDS

For listings, see pages 213–14, unless otherwise stated

Where to stay
1 Agnes's Guesthouse................G2
2 Banda Island Resort..............F1
3 Brovad Sands Lodge..............A4
4 Masaka Backpackers..............B2
5 Mirembe Resort Beach...........B4
6 Nabugabo Holiday Centre p209..A2
7 Nabugabo Sand Beach p209...A1
8 Orchids Village p208-9...........A2
9 Panorama Cottages................B3
10 Philo Leisure Gardens...........C4
11 Ssese Island Club.................B4
12 Ssese Islands Beach..............B3
13 Ssese Habitat Resort.............A4
14 Terrace View Lodge p209.......A1
15 Upland Guesthouse...............B4
16 Victoria Forest Resort...........B3

Where to eat and drink
17 Cruise Safari.......................B4

Nabugabo

Kalangala

8

Masaka, Ssese Islands and Environs

The Lake Victoria hinterland southwest of Kampala and Entebbe is traversed by almost all tours heading to Bwindi or Queen Elizabeth national parks, but not many bother to explore on their way through. It is a region of few highlights, with its main focal point being the large and well equipped but unexciting town of Masaka, which is bypassed by the Mbarara Road 2 hours south of the capital. Altogether more compelling is the pretty Lake Nabugabo, a Ramsar wetland whose reputedly bilharzia-free waters and plentiful birdlife can be enjoyed from a quartet of inexpensive resorts. The region's main attraction, however, is the lovely Ssese Archipelago, whose largest and most developed island, Buggala, is readily accessible by ferry from Entebbe or Masaka.

MASAKA

Uganda's eighth-largest town (population 108,000), Masaka has an attractive location amidst the fertile green hills of the northwestern Lake Victoria hinterland. It was founded as an Indian trading post in the first decade of the 20th century, and its name is said variously to have derived from that of a tree which once grew profusely in the area, or to be a Luganda mispronunciation of an Ankole word for millet. With an economy based largely on agriculture and fishing in the nearby lake, it had grown to become the country's third-largest town prior to 1979, when it was invaded by the Tanzanian forces that ousted Idi Amin (see box, page 200). Masaka experienced further destruction during the civil war of 1981–86, and the town centre retained an aura of economic stagnation for many years after that. Things have perked up in recent years as a result of extensive post-millennial construction and the agricultural wealth of the surrounding countryside, though the southern end of the town centre retains a rather down-at-heel appearance.

Masaka offers little to excite travellers, but it is a popular base with NGOs and volunteers, and some good hostelries and restaurants cater to that market. It also forms a minor route focus, sitting at the junction of the main road between Kampala and Mbarara, the main overland route south to the border with Tanzania, and a side road running east to Lake Nabugabo and the Ssese Islands.

GETTING THERE AND AWAY Masaka lies roughly 140km from Kampala along the surfaced Mbarara Road, which bypasses it at Nyendo, some 3km north of the town centre. In a private vehicle, the drive takes about 2 hours depending on how quickly you clear Kampala. Coming from Entebbe, you can bypass Kampala and spare yourself the worst of the traffic by branching left from the Old Entebbe–Kampala Road at Kisubi, then following a good dirt road northwest for about 15km to Nakawuka (crossing below the currently-under-construction Entebbe–Kampala Expressway after about 5km). At Nakawuka, you can either drive straight along the

THE SACKING OF MASAKA

In October 1978, Idi Amin ordered his Masaka-based Suicide Battalion and Mbarara-based Simba Battalion to invade Tanzania, under the pretext of pursuing 200 mutineers from his army. In the event, the Ugandan battalions occupied Tanzania's northwestern province of Kagera, and ravaged the countryside in an orgy of rape, theft and destruction that forced about 40,000 peasants to flee from the area.

In retaliation, Tanzania's Julius Nyerere ordered 45,000 Tanzanian troops, supported by the UNLA (a 1,000-strong army of exiled Ugandans), to drive Amin's army out of Kagera, then to create a military buffer zone by capturing the largest Ugandan towns close to the Tanzanian border, Masaka and Mbarara. Masaka was taken with little resistance on 24 February 1979. The outnumbered Suicide Battalion fled to a nearby hilltop, from where they watched helplessly as first the governor's mansion and several other government buildings collapsed under missile fire, and then shops and houses were ransacked as the Tanzanian soldiers poured into the town centre.

Two days later, Nyerere achieved his stated aims for the campaign with the capture of Mbarara. But in early March it was announced that Amin would be enlisting the help of 2,500 Libyan and PLO soldiers to recapture Masaka and Mbarara, and possibly launch a counterattack on Tanzanian territory. Nyerere decided to retain the offensive, ordering his troops to prepare to march northeast towards the capital. Meanwhile, Radio Tanzania broadcast details of the fall of Masaka and Mbarara across Uganda, demoralising the troops, and prompting several garrisons to mutiny or desert as it became clear their leader's rule was highly tenuous. On 10 April 1979, the combined Tanzanian and UNLA army marched into Kampala, meeting little resistance along the way. Amin, together with at least 8,000 of his soldiers, was forced into exile.

15km road to Ketene, which straddles the main Kampala–Masaka Road 6km east of Mpigi, or divert left to Mabamba Swamp (see pages 191–2), reaching the main road at Mpigi itself.

Using public transport, the best option coming to/from Kampala are the regular Swift Safaris buses to Mbarara that leave from Kasenyi Terminal every 30 minutes between 05.30 and 20.30. These and most other coaches drop off and pick up passengers at the Masaka bypass 3km north of the town centre. In addition, regular matatus run between Masaka's central taxi park and Kampala's new taxi park (*US$4; 2–3hrs*), Masaka (*US$3; 2–3hrs*) and the Mutukula border post (*US$3; 2hrs*). Those heading further west, for instance to Kasese or Kabale, will need to change vehicles at Mbarara.

The small town of Nyendo, which lies 2km from central Masaka close to the Kampala–Mbarara bypass, is an important road junction and its taxi park is the best place to pick up matatus heading towards Ntusi, Lake Nabugabo and the Ssese Islands.

WHERE TO STAY Distinctly lacking when it comes to genuinely upmarket accommodation, Masaka nevertheless offers a great selection of very well-priced options in the moderate to shoestring ranges. Simple accommodation and camping is also offered at the out-of-town Camp Ndegeya (page 204).

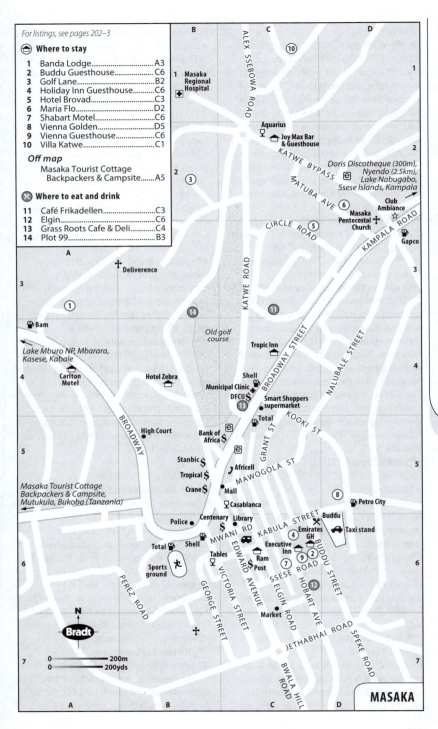

For listings, see pages 202–3

Where to stay

1 Banda Lodge.................................A3
2 Buddu Guesthouse.....................C6
3 Golf Lane.....................................B2
4 Holiday Inn Guesthouse............C6
5 Hotel Brovad...............................C3
6 Maria Flo.....................................D2
7 Shabart Motel.............................C6
8 Vienna Golden............................D5
9 Vienna Guesthouse....................C6
10 Villa Katwe..................................C1

Off map
    Masaka Tourist Cottage
      Backpackers & Campsite.......A5

Where to eat and drink

11 Café Frikadellen..........................C3
12 Elgin..C6
13 Grass Roots Cafe & Deli.............C4
14 Plot 99...B3

MASAKA

Moderate

✳ 🏠 **Villa Katwe** [201 C1] (6 rooms) Somero Road, m 0791 000637; e info@villakatwe.com; www.villakatwe.com. Set in palm-shaded hilltop gardens full of tame rabbits about 1.5km north of the town centre, this popular Dutch-owned lodge has the relaxed & sociable feel of a backpackers', but the en-suite accommodation is far superior. Amenities include a self-catering kitchen, nightly campfires, book swap service, cosy lounge & in-house operator offering local tours. An excellent b/fast is included in the bed price, & other meals can be ordered & delivered from Plot 99. A boda from the town centre costs less than US$1. *US$25/40/48 en-suite sgl/dbl/trpl room. US$40/60/80/100 for 1/2/3/4 people in a 4-bed apartment. US$14pp dorm bed. US$12pp camping. All rates B&B.* **$$$**

✳ 🏠 **Banda Lodge** [201 A3] (5 rooms & 2 dorms) off Birch Close; m 0791 000679; e bandalodge@gmail.com; www.banda.dk. Set in terraced gardens off the Mbarara Rd 1km northwest of the town centre, this small but very pleasant lodge is under the same Danish management as the more established Café Frikadellen. Thatched bandas come with modern décor, fitted nets, writing desk, fan & en-suite hot shower, while the dorms each contain 2 bunk beds with net & shared bathroom. Amenities include a residents-only swimming pool & a garden restaurant with the same menu as Café Frikadellen. *US$30/50 sgl/dbl or US$12pp dorm. All rates B&B.* **$$$**

🏠 **Hotel Brovad** [201 C3] (250 rooms) Circular Rd; m 0772 425666/0752 425666; e hotelbrovad@utlonline.co.ug; www.hotelbrovad.com. First & foremost a conference venue, Masaka's smartest city hotel sprawls across pleasant green suburban gardens centred on a large swimming pool that give it an edge over other similarly bland competitors. The carpeted rooms wouldn't win any décor awards, but they are pleasant enough & come with net, balcony, DSTV & writing desk. A restaurant & gym are attached. Fair value. *US$35/52/83/120 b&b sgl/dbl/deluxe/suite.* **$$$**

🏠 **Golf Lane Hotel** [201 B2] (84 rooms) Kinanina Rd (off Katwe Rd); m 0700 868956; e info@golflanehotel.com; www.golflanehotel.com. This smart & modern multi-storey doesn't quite do justice to its hilltop site's potential 360° panorama with its solitary ground floor terrace.

Otherwise, it seems like good value, & the spacious rooms all have wood furniture, dbl bed with net, DSTV, plenty of cupboard space, en-suite hot showers & large private balconies. *US$31/41 B&B sgl/dbl.* **$$**

Budget

🏠 **Maria Flo Hotel** [201 D2] (49 rooms) Mutuba Av; m 0752 643456/800329; e mariaflohotel@gmail.com or mariaflo_hotel@yahoo.com; 📘 fb.me/MariaFloHotelMasaka. Though nothing special in itself, this pleasant set-up is far cheaper than other hotels of comparable standard, making it very good value for money. The bright, modern rooms come with nets, DSTV & en-suite hot shower, & a restaurant is attached. *US$17/23 sgl/dbl.* **$$**

🏠 **Shabart Motel** [201 C6] (27 rooms) Hobart St; m 0701 973616/0778 594721. Outstanding value in a town that's generally well-endowed with good cheapies, this multi-storey hotel has clean en-suite tiled rooms with fitted net, DSTV & hot shower. *US$10 dbl.* **$**

🏠 **Vienna Golden Hotel** [201 D5] (47 rooms) Kabula St; m 0702493369; e viennagoldenhotel@yahoo.com; www.viennagoldenhotel.com. Newly opened on a quiet side opposite the taxi park but overlooking cultivated fields, this attractively priced multi-storey gem has brightly decorated & spacious modern rooms with net, optional flatscreen TV & en-suite hot shower. *US$12/17 dbl without/with TV.* **$**

Shoestring & camping

✳ 🏠 **Masaka Tourist Cottage Backpackers & Campsite** [201 B2] (10 rooms & 2 dorms) ✪ -0.3634, 31.71463; m 0752 619389; e masakabackpackers@gmail.com; http://masakabackpackers.webklik.nl. Situated on a rural hilltop 4km out of town off the Mutukula Rd, this long-serving owner-managed retreat offers the option of en-suite rooms, a bed in a 4- or 10-bed dorm, or camping (with your own tent). It also serves tasty meals in the US$3–6 range & has a well-stocked drinks fridge. *US$9/13 sgl/dbl, US$6pp dorm, US$3pp camping.* **$**

🏠 **Holiday Inn Guesthouse** [201 C6] (22 rooms) Hobart St; ✆ 048 1420395; m 0773 403794. The best of several decent shoestring options clustered in & around Hobart St, this has large tiled rooms with nets, writing desk & en-

suite hot showers. *US$4.50/5.50/7.50 sgl/dbl/twin, or US$10 twin with DSTV.* **$**

🏠 **Buddu Guesthouse** [201 C6] (41 rooms) Ssese Rd; m 0772 482579. The clean en-suite rooms at this central hotel around the corner from the taxi park come with carpets, nets & cold showers. Great value. *US$4/7/10 sgl/dbl/twin.* **$**

🏠 **Vienna Guesthouse** [201 C6] (40 rooms) Hobart St; m 0782 457450. This long-serving cheapie, though a bit frayed at the edges, has cool en-suite rooms housed in a characterful old building with a convenient central location near the taxi park. Facilities include a fan-cooled ground-floor restaurant/bar. *US$6/7/10 sgl/dbl/twin.* **$**

✗ **WHERE TO EAT AND DRINK** In addition to the bespoke eateries described below, most of the hotels listed above have decent restaurants, though none really stand out as justifying a special trip.

✳ ✗ **Café Frikadellen** [201 C3] Mutuba Gardens; m 0792 081010; ⨍ fb.me/ CafeFrikadellen; ⏰ 07.30–19.30 Sat–Thu, 07.30–22.00 Fri. Affiliated to an NGO called Childcare, this stylish Danish-run eatery has the choice of indoor, terrace or garden seating, & an extensive & varied menu including salads, sandwiches, filled pancakes & Greek & Italian cuisine, with most mains in the US$6–9 range. It also serves great coffee & desserts, & a good selection of alcoholic & other beverages. The Fri night BBQ buffet (*US$13 per head*) is a highlight of Masaka's expat calendar, so best book ahead. Wi-Fi available.

✳ ✗ **Plot 99** [201 B3] Hill Rd; m 0700 151649; e info@ugogreen.eu; www.plot99.ugogreen.eu; ⏰ noon–22.00 Mon, Wed, Thu & 10.00–22.00 Fri–Sun. Popular with the younger volunteer crowd, this chilled restaurant, bar & coffee shop is housed in a bungalow & green gardens overlooking the former golf course. The menu includes burgers, pizzas, grills,

curries & salads in the US$4.50–8.50 range, as well as a good selection of coffees, smoothies, juices & cocktails. Other facilities include a gym, aerobics, massage & Wi-Fi.

✗ **Grass Roots Café & Deli** [201 C4] m 0779 14118; ⨍ fb.me/grassrootscafeanddeli; ⏰ 08.00–19.00 Mon–Sat. Launching shortly before we went to print, this new café with free Wi-Fi promises to be a great place to stop for a quick lunch *en route* between Kampala & the southwest. Fresh sandwiches, salads, wraps & other dishes are supplemented by juices, smoothies, wine & homemade produce. It also plans to host events such as educational workshops, quiz nights, movie screenings & live music. Mains cost around US$2.50.

✗ **Elgin Restaurant** [201 C6] Elgin Rd. Dropping down quite a few notches here, this decent local eatery serves a variety of local dishes for around US$3.

NIGHTLIFE

☆ **Club Ambiance** [201 D2] Broadway Rd; m 0756 603761/0752 935869; info@ clubambiance.net; www.clubambiance.net; ⏰ 18.00–late Tue–Sun. One of Uganda's best-known nightclubs, the original Ambiance – now also represented by branches in Kampala & Mityana – is a monumental glass-fronted building that uses 6 different DJs. Popular with locally based volunteers, the club peaks in popularity on Fri &

Sat nights, when the dancefloor action really only kicks in after midnight. Tue is ladies' night, Wed old school, Fri campus night, Sat variety night & Sun oldies' night.

☆ **Doris Discotheque** [201 D2] Broadway Rd. Situated 500m past Club Ambience, this well-established nightclub has a local reputation as a bit of a pick-up joint.

SHOPPING Several good supermarkets are dotted around the town centre, especially at the northern end of Eglin Road.

OTHER PRACTICALITIES
Foreign exchange Cash can be exchanged at Stanbic Bank [201 B5], which also has an ATM offering 24/7 withdrawals.

Internet There are good internet cafés on Broadway Road next to the Bank of Africa and in the new mall south of the junction with Elgin Road. Wi-Fi is available at Café Frikadellen and Plot 99.

Swimming pool The Hotel Brovad charges day visitors US$5 to use its swimming pool.

WHAT TO SEE AND DO

Nabajjuzi Wetland Listed as an Ramsar Wetland and Important Bird Area, the 17.5km² Nabajjuzi Wetland, which follows a tributary of the Katanga River as it flows west past Masaka, is also the town's sole source of drinking water. Though it incorporates some open water, the wetland is dominated by papyrus and reed swamps, which support large numbers of lungfish and mudfish. Otters and sitatunga antelope are still reputedly common in Nabajjuzi, as are a host of alluring birds, including shoebill, rufous-bellied heron, papyrus yellow warbler, papyrus gonolek and blue swallow. A few years back, the community-based Nabajjuzi Ecotourism Project was developed outside Masaka with funding from the UK's RSPB. So far as we can establish, the project no longer exists in any meaningful way, but its physical centrepiece – a raised wooden viewing deck offering a distance view to a small papyrus-fringed pool where shoebill, sitatunga and other rarities might be observed through binoculars – still stands on the outskirts of town, right opposite the Masaka Water Treatment Plant. Though unsignposted, the viewing platform (✪ -0.33695, 31.71873) is easy to locate, being situated only 50m along a dirt road that runs south from the Mbarara Road, 100m past the junction of the Masaka bypass and the feeder road into town.

Camp Ndegeya [198 B2] (✪ -0.29306, 31.72941; m 0778 092417/0792 417322; e carsonbuka@gmail.com; f fb.me/campndegeyauganda, entry US$1.50) Situated on a eucalyptus-covered hilltop near the village of Ndegeya (literally 'Place of Weaverbirds'), this arts collective 5km north of Masaka is dominated by an open-air sculpture garden displaying the work of six Ugandans, including founder Collin Sekajugo and artists-in-residence Carson Buka and Dennis Lubega. The grounds also offer great views over the Nabajjuzi Wetland 1.5km to the west, while amenities include three basic bandas (US$10 sgl) and a campsite (USA$7 per tent), all using common showers. A proper guesthouse is likely to open in Ndegeya village by the end of 2016.

Ndegeya Camp is most easily reached from Ssaza Junction (✪ -0.31916, 31.73998), on the Kampala–Mbarara Bypass about 3km from the junction with the eastern feeder road into Masaka and 3.3km from the junction with the western feeder. From the junction, head north for 3km to the village of Ndegeya, whose main traffic circle is adorned with a prominent sculpture. The proposed guesthouse lies about 200m before the circle, while Ndegeya Camp is another 1.2km past the circle along a road that winds uphill. A boda from Nyendo or Masaka shouldn't cost more than US$1. When arranging transport to Ndegeya, be warned that a better-known village of the same name straddles the Mbarara Road, 25km west of Masaka.

Villa Maria Church [198 B1] One of Uganda's most historic buildings, Villa Maria was established in 1892 in the wake of a religious civil war that resulted in the temporary exile from Kampala of Kabaka Mwanga and his fellow Catholics. The exiles briefly settled in Buddu, the most westerly country of Buganda, where Chief Alex Ssebbowa, a supporter of Mwanga, donated a tract of land north of present-

day Masaka to Henri Streicher, a French missionary of the White Father order, so that he could establish a church there. In 1897, when Streicher was appointed Bishop of Northern Victoria Nyanza, he made Villa Maria the headquarters of a vicariate that included 30,000 baptised Catholics. Uganda's first indigenous Catholic priests – Fathers Basil Lumu and Victor Mukasa – were ordained at Villa Maria in 1913, and it was also the diocese that produced Africa's first indigenous Catholic bishop, Doctor Joseph Kiwanuka, who was ordained into Kitovu Diocese in 1940. Henri Streicher, who died in 1952 aged 89, was interred in the church, along with several of the young African priests he trained.

The main point of interest at Villa Maria is the original cruciform church (✚ -0.22875, 31.74559) built by Streicher in the 1890s. It is one of the country's largest churches, with a floor area of 1,800m², and its 60cm-thick walls are comprised entirely of unbaked clay bricks and mud mortar. The roof was thatched up until the early 1930s, and the original wooden struts have been retained to support the modern topping of red-painted iron sheets. Still in active use, the church has recently undergone extensive restoration work, and part of the building is earmarked to become a museum documenting the mission's history. Also of historic interest, about 1km south of Villa Maria, Bwamba Convent (✚ -0.23722, 31.74941) is home to the Banna-Biikira ('Daughters of Mary'), Africa's oldest indigenous society of Catholic nuns, founded in 1910 at the urging of Bishop Streicher by Mother Mechtilde, a Dutch White Sister. The Banna-Biikira are now responsible for administering the 125-bed Villa Maria Hospital, which was established by Stretcher in 1902, primarily to assist victims of sleeping sickness.

To get to Villa Maria Church from central Masaka, follow the Kampala Road out of town for about 2.5km past Club Ambience to Nyendo, then turn left on to Villa Road, crossing the Kampala–Mbarara Bypass after about 1km, and keep going straight for another 12km. Coming directly from Kampala, follow the bypass past the main turn-off to Masaka for about 1km (✚ -0.30866, 31.75636), then turn right on to Villa Road.

Kiyanja Wetlands This readily accessible 3km² reed marsh, part of the drainage system that feeds Lake Kacheera on the eastern border of Lake Mburo National Park, lies immediately south of the Mbarara Road some 42km west of Masaka. Kiyanja is an important breeding and foraging site for the spectacular grey crowned crane (Uganda's national bird), with some 20 breeding pairs resident and much larger temporary aggregations often recorded. Other aquatic birds are exceptionally well represented: at least 30 species were noted during a recent 15-minute stop, among them saddle-billed and open-billed storks, African jacana, spur-winged goose, pink-backed pelican and long-toed lapwing. A 12km footpath used by local farmers encircles the wetland, and you'd doubtless see a great many more species if you followed it in part or full. Coming from Masaka, the 600m feeder road to the edge of the wetland runs south from the Mbarara Road at an inconspicuous junction (✚ -0.4043, 31.37248) about 1km past the small trading centre of Kyawagonya, which is passed through by all public transport along this trunk road.

LAKE NABUGABO

Lake Nabugabo, 20km east of Masaka, is a shallow 33km² freshwater body set within the 225km² Lwamunda Swamp on the western shore of Lake Victoria. Nabugabo was isolated from its larger neighbour around 4,000 years ago, when

Known to the Baganda as Nalubaale – Home of the Spirit – Lake Victoria is the world's second-largest freshwater body, set in a shallow basin with a diameter of roughly 250km on an elevated plateau separating the eastern and western forks of the Great Rift Valley, and shared between Tanzania, Uganda and Kenya. The environmental degradation of the lake began in the early colonial era, when the indigenous lakeshore vegetation was cleared and swamps were drained to make way for plantations of tea, coffee and sugar. This increased the amount of topsoil washed into the lake, with the result that its water became progressively muddier and murkier. A more serious effect was the wash-off of toxic pesticides and other agricultural chemicals whose nutrients promote algae growth, and as a result a decrease in oxygenation. The foundation of several lakeshore cities and plantations also attracted migrant labourers from around the region, leading to a rapid increase in population and – exacerbated by more sophisticated trapping tools introduced by the colonials – heavy overfishing.

By the early 1950s, the above factors had conspired to create a noticeable drop in yields of popular indigenous fish, in particular the Lake Victoria tilapia (*ngege*), which had been fished close to extinction. The colonial authorities introduced the similar Nile tilapia, which restored the diminishing yield without seriously affecting the ecological balance of the lake. More disastrous, however, was the gradual infiltration of the Nile perch, a voracious predator that feeds almost exclusively on smaller fish, and frequently reaches a length of 2m and a weight exceeding 100kg. How the perch initially ended up in Lake Victoria is a matter of conjecture, but they regularly turned up in fishermen's nets from the late 1950s onwards. The authorities, who favoured large eating fish over the smaller tilapia and cichlids, decided to ensure the survival of the alien predators with an active programme of introductions in the early 1960s.

It would be 20 years before the full impact of this misguided policy hit home. In a UN survey undertaken in 1971, indigenous cichlids belonging to the genus *Haplochromis* still constituted their traditional 80% of the lake's fish biomass, while the introduced fish had effectively displaced the indigenous tilapia without otherwise altering the ecology of the lake. A similar survey undertaken ten years later revealed that the perch population had exploded to constitute 80% of the lake's fish biomass, while *Haplochromis* cichlids – the favoured prey of the perch – now accounted for a mere 1%. Lake Victoria's estimated 150–300 endemic cichlid species, all of which have evolved from a mere five ancestral species since the lake dried out 10,000–15,000 years ago, are regarded to represent the most recent comparable explosion of vertebrate-adaptive radiation in the world. In simple terms, this is when a large number of species evolve from a limited ancestral stock in a short space of time, in this instance owing to the lake having formed rapidly to create all sorts of new niches. Ironically, at least 65% of these species are now thought to be extinct, and several others are headed that way, an ecological disaster described as 'the greatest vertebrate mass extinction in recorded history' by Les Kauffman of Boston University.

For all this, the introduction of perch could be considered a superficial success within its own terms. The perch now form the basis of the lake's thriving fishing industry, with up to 500 metric tonnes of fish meat being exported from the lake annually, at a value of more than US$300 million, by commercial fishing concerns in the three lakeshore countries. The tanned perch hide is used as a substitute for leather to make shoes, belts and purses, and the dried swim bladders, used to filter beer and make fish stock, are exported at a high profit too. The flip side of this

is that as fish exports increase, local fishing communities are forced to compete against large commercial companies with better equipment and more economic clout. Furthermore, since the perch is too large to roast on a fire and too fatty to dry in the sun, it does not really meet local needs.

The introduction of perch is not the only damaging factor to have affected Lake Victoria's ecology. It is estimated that the amount of agricultural chemicals being washed into the lake has more than doubled since the 1950s. Tanzania alone is currently pumping two million litres of untreated sewage and industrial waste into the lake daily, and while legal controls on industrial dumping are tighter in Kenya and Uganda, they are not effectively enforced. The agricultural wash-off and industrial dumping has led to a further increase in the volume of chemical nutrients in the lake, promoting the growth of plankton and algae. At the same time, the cichlids that once fed on these microscopic organisms have been severely depleted in number by the predatorial perch.

The lake's algae levels have increased fivefold in the last four decades, with a corresponding decrease in oxygen levels. The lower level of the lake now consists of dead water – lacking any oxygenation or fish activity below about 30m – and the quality of the water closer to the surface has deteriorated markedly since the 1960s. Long-term residents of the Mwanza area say that the water was once so clear that you could see the lake floor from the surface to depths of 6m or more. Today visibility near the surface is more like 1m.

A clear indicator of this deterioration has been the rapid spread of water hyacinth, which thrives in polluted conditions leading to high phosphate and nitrogen levels, and then tends to further deplete oxygen levels by forming an impenetrable mat over the water's surface. An exotic South American species, unknown on the lake prior to 1989, the water hyacinth has subsequently colonised vast tracts of the lake surface, and clogged up several harbours. To complete this grim vicious circle, Nile perch, arguably the main cause of the problem, are known to be vulnerable to the conditions created by hyacinth matting, high algae levels and decreased oxygenation in the water. On a positive note, hyacinth infestation on the Ugandan waters of Lake Victoria has decreased markedly since 2001, though it still requires careful management. But a new threat to the lake's welfare has emerged with the recent opening of a major Tanzanian gold mine less than 20km from the lakeshore, a location that carries a genuine risk of sodium cyanide, used in the processing of gold, finding its way into Lake Victoria.

As is so often the case with ecological issues, what might at first be dismissed by some as an esoteric concern for 'bunny-huggers' in fact has wider implications for the tens of millions of people resident in the Lake Victoria basin. The infestation of hyacinth and rapid decrease in indigenous snail-eating fish has led to a rapid growth in the number of bilharzia-carrying snails. The deterioration in water quality, exacerbated by the pumping of sewage, has increased the risk of sanitary-related diseases such as cholera spreading around the lake. The change in the fish biomass has encouraged commercial fishing for export outside the region, in the process depressing the local semi-subsistence fishing economy, leading to an increase in unemployment and protein deficiency. And the risk remains that Africa's largest lake will eventually be reduced to a vast expanse of dead water, with no fish in it at all – and ecological, economic and humanitarian ramifications that scarcely bear thinking about.

a narrow sand bar drifted across what was formerly a large shallow bay. Silt accumulation has subsequently reduced the extent of open water fourfold, and all but the western shore of Nabugabo are now lined by more-or-less impenetrable papyrus and reed swamps. Despite its relatively recent formation, Nabugabo has a substantially different mineral composition from the main lake: its calcium content, for instance, is insufficient for molluscs to form shells, hence the alleged absence of the freshwater snails that transmit bilharzia. Impressively, a full five of nine cichlid fish species indigenous to Nabugabo are endemics that evolved since it was separated from Lake Victoria, one of the most recent incidents of speciation known from anywhere in the world. Unfortunately, however, the introduction of the predatory Nile perch and red-belly tilapia in the 1950s has had a negative effect on indigenous fish populations, which are now most common in a few small satellite lakes. The lake and surrounding swamp are listed as an Important Bird Area and Ramsar Wetland.

More popular with Kampala weekenders than it is with foreign visitors, Nabugabo is nonetheless an excellent place to rest up for a day or two. Its largely marsh-free western shore is serviced by several tranquil and reasonably priced resorts, though be warned that these tend to transform into local party spots over the weekends. The forest patches that line the lakeshore, interspersed with grassy clearings and cultivated smallholdings, are rustling with small animals such as tree squirrels, vervet monkeys and monitor lizards, and can easily be explored along several roads and footpaths. Birdlife is prolific, too – look out for broad-billed roller, Ross's turaco, black-and-white casqued hornbill, African fish eagle and a variety of sunbirds and weavers. Lwamunda Swamp is an important stronghold for papyrus endemics such as shoebill, white-winged swamp warbler and papyrus canary, but these are unlikely to be seen from Nabugabo's western shore.

GETTING THERE AND AWAY In a private vehicle, there are two main routes to Nabugabo, neither surfaced but both in fair condition. Coming from Masaka, head along the Kampala feeder road to Nyendo, then turn right on to the Bukakata Road and follow it for 14km to a junction (✪ -0.31393, 31.85918) where the 5km feeder road to the lake resorts is signposted to the right. Coming from Kampala, you can avoid Nyendo and save a bit of driving time by taking an unsignposted 6km shortcut that branches south from the main Masaka Road at Kadugala (✪ -0.27903, 31.79795) and connects with the Nyendo–Bukakata Road at a junction (✪ -0.30983, 31.83881) 2.5km west of the signposted turning to the lake.

Using public transport, you have two broad options. The first is to catch a matatu (or any other transport) along the Nyendo–Bukakata Road, hop off at the junction for Nabugabo, then walk the last (very flat) 5km to the resort of your choice. Alternatively, take a bus or matatu to Kadugala, from where a boda to Nabugabo should cost around US$2–3, and a special hire in the ballpark of US$10–15.

 WHERE TO STAY AND EAT The three resorts listed below lie within a few hundred metres of each other on the lake's western shore. All of them allow camping, with the smart Orchids Village being by far the most attractive place to pitch a tent. The shabbier but far cheaper Nabugabo Holiday Centre has an equally nice location for camping, as well as the only dorm on the lake.

Moderate

✱ 🏠 **Orchids Village** [198 A2] (4 cottages, more under construction) ✪ -0.35615, 31.87343;

m 0755 166675/0777 512120; e info@orchidsvillage.com; www.orchidsvillage.com.
The newest & most southerly resort on Nabugabo,

owner-managed Orchids Village is also the smartest option, the most tranquil, & the least likely to become rowdy over weekends. Set in sprawling 6ha lakeshore grounds whose indigenous vegetation has been touched as little as possible in the process of transforming it into a resort, it has much to offer birders, while black-&-white colobus & vervet monkeys are easily seen in nearby forest patches. Accommodation is in brightly decorated self-catering 6- or 2-bed cottages with fitted nets, hot showers, private balconies & well-equipped kitchens. The large campsite runs right down to the lakeshore. A newly opened restaurant serves local & continental dishes in the US$8–12 range. *US$33/42 weekday/ weekend per unit 6-bed cottage; US$20pp B&B dbl cottage, US$7pp camping.* **$$**

Budget

✳ 🏠 **Nabugabo Sand Beach** [198 A1] (12 cottages) ✆ -0.34723, 31.87948; m 0702 416047; e sandbeachnabugabo@yahoo.com. This extensive resort with 200m of lake frontage is a lovely, peaceful spot during the week, but over weekends it transforms into Uganda's version of the good old British migration to the seaside – as reflected by a holiday camp-style row of glass-fronted chalets, boat & donkey rides, canoe hire, cheap beer & a fish 'n' chips menu with mains for around US$5. Despite the regimental layout, the tiled cottages are well-maintained, come with fitted net, en-suite hot shower & DSTV, making them great value at the price. Birders might also note that Forbes's

plover was spotted in the adjacent wetland in 2010 (only the 4th sighting in Uganda). *US$17 dbl.* **$$**
🏠 **Terrace View Lodge** [198 A1] (6 rooms) ✆ -0.34961, 31.87953; m 0755 136901; contact@ lake-nabugabo.net; www.lake-nabugabo.net. Whether the 'terrace' refers to the pleasant veranda of the thatched main building or the low cliff on which the resort stands is an open question, but the slight elevation does mean that this isn't the best resort for swimming. Accommodation is in a row of spacious & airy en-suite brick face rooms with net & hot shower. Facilities include a bar, pool table & restaurant. *US$17/20 B&B dbl/twin.* **$$**

Shoestring

🏠 **Nabugabo Holiday Centre** [198 A2] (5 cottages, 1 dorm) ✆ -0.35246, 31.8771; m 0752 539000/0772 433332; e info@nabugabo. com; www.nabugabo.com. This long-serving Church of Uganda resort has a friendly atmosphere & lovely setting in a shady glade sloping down to a good swimming beach. All but 1 of the 5 cottages have 2 dbl or twin rooms, shared bathroom & common lounge with DSTV, but they feel rather run-down & overpriced compared to the competition. More appealing for shoestring travellers are the options of camping by the lake or taking a bed in the dorm. Simple meals cost US$4 (b/fast) or US$6.50 (lunch or dinner). Soft drinks, tea & coffee are sold, but you must bring any alcohol you require with you. *From US$21 dbl or twin room; from US$42 4-bed cottage; US$5pp dorm, US$3.50pp camping.* **$$**

THE SSESE ISLANDS

Situated in the northwest of Lake Victoria, the Ssese Archipelago comprises 84 separate islands, some large and densely inhabited, others small and deserted, but all lushly forested thanks to an annual average rainfall in excess of 2,000mm. By far the largest island in the Ssese group is Buggala, which accounts for more than half the archipelago's land area, and lies around 40km southwest of Entebbe as the crow flies. Buggala's principal settlement is Kalangala, which lends its name to, and serves as the administrative centre of, a thinly populated district comprising a 468km^2 terrestrial component and 8,635km^2 of open water. Kalangala, or more accurately the tiny lakeshore village of Lutoboka 1km to its north, is also the archipelago's main tourist focus, supporting as it does around half-a-dozen low-key beach resorts, as well as being the landing point for a daily vehicle ferry from Entebbe.

The Ssese Islands have a chequered history as a tourist destination. In the mid-1990s, when tourism to Uganda was still dominated by backpackers, Buggala emerged as the country's most popular word-of-mouth chill-out destination. That changed later on in the decade, when the discontinuation of the Port Bell Ferry

limited safe access to Buggala to a more roundabout approach via Masaka and Bukakata, and opened the way for the more accessible Lake Bunyonyi to capture the hearts of independent travellers. In recent years, the introduction of a daily passenger ferry from Entebbe has initiated a renaissance in tourism activity on Buggala, though facilities are now geared towards Kampala weekenders more than to backpackers. That said, Buggala, with its scenic lake vistas and practically limitless opportunities for casual rambling along lush forest-fringed roads and footpaths, remains an utterly beguiling retreat, particularly on weekdays (when it tends to be very tranquil) and for those seeking a more off-the-beaten track and uncontrived alternative to the ever-busy Bunyonyi.

Although Buggala remains the main tourist focus on the Ssese Archipelago, a significant number of travellers also head to tiny Banda Island. Other islands that can be visited with varying degrees of ease are Bubeke, Bukasa and Bufumira.

GEOLOGY AND WILDLIFE The Ssese Islands came into being about 12,000 years ago when the then reduced Lake Victoria refilled at the end of the last Ice Age, forming the lake as we know it today. The archipelago supports a cover of mid-altitude rainforest, similar in composition to the forest that once swathed to the facing mainland, but far less affected by agriculture and other forms of encroachment. The most common large terrestrial mammal is the vervet monkey, which is often seen in the vicinity of Lutoboka and Kalangala. Bushbuck and black-and-white colobus are also present, but seldom observed. Since Buggala was separated from the mainland, one endemic creek rat and three endemic butterfly species have evolved on the island. Water and forest birds are prolific. Expect to see a variety of hornbills, barbets, turacos, robin-chats, flycatchers and weavers from the roads around Kalangala. Particularly common are the jewel-like pygmy kingfisher, the brown-throated wattle-eye and a stunning morph of the paradise flycatcher intermediate to the orange and white phases illustrated in most East African field guides. African fish eagles and palm-nut vultures are often seen near the lake, while immense breeding colonies of little egret and great cormorant occur on Lutoboka and other bays.

HISTORY Little is known about the earliest inhabitants of Ssese, but some oral traditions associated with the creation of Buganda claim that its founder Kintu hailed from the islands, or at least arrived in Buganda via them. The Baganda traditionally revere Ssese as the Islands of the Gods. In pre-colonial times it was customary for the kings of Buganda to visit the islands and pay tribute to the several balubaale whose main shrines are situated there. These include shrines to Musisi (spirit of earthquakes) and Wanema (physical handicaps) on Bukasa Island, as well as the shrine to Mukasa, spirit of the lake, on Bubembe. Some Baganda historical sources romanticise this relationship, claiming that in pre-colonial times Ssese, because of its exalted status, was never attacked by Buganda, nor was it formally incorporated into the mainland kingdom. In reality, while Ssese probably did enjoy a degree of autonomy, it was clearly a vassal of Buganda for at least a century prior to the colonial era. Furthermore, while the Baganda revered the islands' spirits, Stanley recorded that they looked down on their human inhabitants for their 'coal-black colour, timidity, superstition, and generally uncleanly life'.

The most popular legend associated with a deity from the Ssese Islands dates from the mid-16th-century war, when Buganda, led by King Nakibinge, was being overwhelmed in a war against Bunyoro. Nakibinge visited the islands in search of support, and was offered the assistance of the local king's youngest son, Kibuuka,

who leaped to the mainland in one mighty bound to join the war against Bunyoro. Tall and powerful though he was, Kibuuka – which means the flier – was also possessed of a somewhat more singular fighting skill. A deity in human form, he was able to fly high above the clouds and shower down spears on the enemy, who had no idea from where the deadly missiles emanated. Led by Kibuuka's aerial attacks, rout followed rout, and the tide of war reversed swiftly in Nakibinge's favour as the Baganda army proceeded deeper into Banyoro territory.

Although Buganda went on to win the war, Kibuuka didn't survive to enjoy the spoils of victory. After yet another successful battle, the Baganda soldiers captured several Banyoro maidens and gave one to Kibuuka as his mistress. Kibuuka told the Munyoro girl his secret, only to find that she had vanished overnight. The next day, Kibuuka sailed up into the sky as normal, and was greeted by a barrage of Banyoro spears and arrows projected up towards the clouds. Kibuuka fell wounded into a tall tree, where he was spotted the next morning by an elder, who attempted to rescue the wounded fighter, but instead accidentally let him drop to the ground, where he died on impact. The scrotum, testes, penis and certain other body parts of the great Ssese warrior – now regarded as the greatest lubaale of war – were preserved in a shrine, where his spirit could be called upon before important battles. The shrine, which lies close to the Mpanga Forest, can still be visited today, as can a nearby shrine to Nakibinge, also revered as a deity on account of his successful campaign against Bunyoro. The shrine to Kibuuka was desecrated by the British during the colonial era, and the contents, including his jawbone, are on display in a museum in Cambridge.

The Bassese people of the islands, who speak a distinct Bantu language closely related to Luganda, and were described by Stanley as 'the principal canoe builders and the greater number of the sailors' of Buganda, played a more verifiable – albeit less overtly aggressive – role in Baganda expansionism during the second half of the 19th century. At this time, Kabaka Suuna and his successor Mutesa dispatched regular military fleets of 300-plus fighting canoes across Lake Victoria to present-day northwestern Tanzania. These fleets consisted almost entirely of canoes built on Ssese, which – in comparison with the simple dugouts used on the mainland – were highly sophisticated in design, constructed with several pieces of interlocking timber, and boasted an extended prow that could be used to batter other boats. Speke described one such fleet as follows: 'some fifty large [boats]… all painted with red clay, and averaged from ten to thirty paddles, with long prows standing out like the neck of a siphon or swan, decorated on the head with the horns of the Nsunnu [kob] antelope, between which was stuck upright a tuft of feathers exactly like a grenadier's plume'. The islanders were also more skilled as oarsmen and navigators than their landlubber Baganda neighbours, and although they played no role in the fighting, it was they who generally powered and directed the war fleets.

In the late 19th century, the demands of the Buganda military became a heavy drain on the Ssese economy. So much so that in 1898 the islanders petitioned the British governor, complaining that they were 'regarded in Uganda as being inferior and subordinate to that country' and that the 'severe strain upon the island labour resources [was] so serious as to endanger the canoe service, now so essential with the increasing demands on the Victoria Nyanza lake transport'. In 1900, an agreement between Buganda and Britain placed Ssese and nine other formerly autonomous counties under the full jurisdiction of Buganda. Over the next ten years, Ssese was hit by a sleeping sickness epidemic that claimed thousands of lives annually, forcing the government to relocate 25,000 islanders to the mainland.

Resettlement of Ssese was gradual, and it is largely due to the sleeping sickness epidemic that the islands' total population was estimated at fewer than 20,000 as recently as the mid-1990s. Since then, however, the population has risen rapidly, doubling from around 35,000 in 2002 to an estimated 70,000 in 2015. Although much of the land remains uncultivated and supports a cover of natural forest, Buggala also supports a major palm oil industry, which until recently consisted mainly of local farmers who grew a few oil palm trees on their smallholding and sold the produce on to the Jinja-based processor Bidco Uganda. That changed in 2011 when Oil Palm Uganda Limited (OPUL), a subsidiary of Bidco Uganda, controversially razed 61km² of natural forest and smallholdings west of Kalangala to make way for new oil palm plantations. Displaced local community members, some of whom were effectively squatters but nevertheless lost their homes or livelihood in the land grab, have since taken OPUL to court, demanding compensation.

GETTING THERE AND AWAY There are two reliable options for Buggala, either using a direct daily ferry from Entebbe, or a more roundabout route via Masaka and Bukakata. When the Entebbe ferry is non-operational (as happens from time to time), you could also use a motorised lake-taxi from nearby Kasenyi, which comprise the only public transport to the other smaller islands. However, it is possible to charter a lake-taxi from Lutoboka (Buggala Island) to Banda Island for around US$50.

By ferry from Entebbe The MV *Kalangala* is a daily passenger/vehicle ferry service that connects Lutoboka Port on Buggala Island to Nakiwogo Port (✪ *0.08054, 32.44919*), which lies only 3km (and less than 10 minutes by boda) west of central Entebbe. The ferry leaves Nakiwogo at 14.00 daily and starts the return trip from Lutoboka at 08.00 the next morning, taking 4 hours in either direction. One-way fares are US$3/5 2nd/1st class (the latter with padded seating and tables). Vehicles are charged US$23 for a one-way crossing, but can also be parked in a compound at Nakiwogo for a small fee. Bottled drinks and snacks are available on board. The return trip to Entebbe can be busy at the end of holiday weekends, and drivers should park on the jetty the night before and have a quiet word with the captain.

By ferry via Bukakata A free vehicle ferry service connects the mainland port of Bukakata (40km east of Masaka) to Luko (30km west of Kalangala) several times daily. Two different ferries cross back and forth regularly between 08.00 and 18.00, taking 30 minutes in either direction, but the connection between their real-time movements and the complicated timetable posted at the port is tenuous in the extreme, so best to just pitch up when it suits you – you'll seldom wait more than an hour for the next boat. To get to Bukakata in a private vehicle, you can follow either of the routes to Lake Nabugabo detailed on page 208, but continue straight ahead at the final junction, from where it's another 22km to Bukakata (✪ *-0.27205, 32.02629*). Using public transport, a reliable daily bus service (*US$7; 7–8hrs*) to Kalangala via Bukakata leaves Kampala's new taxi park at 08.00, and starts the return trip from Kalangala at around 06.30. Coming from Masaka, a few matatus run daily between Nyendo and Kalangala via Bukakata (*US$5; 3hrs*).

By lake-taxi from Kasenyi The main port for motorised lake-taxis to Ssese, Kasenyi lies 5km east of Entebbe as the crow flies, but 11km away by road. Lake-taxis to Lutoboka (*US$3; 5hrs*) tend to be overloaded, and frequently capsize during stormy weather, killing up to 100 people annually, so cannot be recommended.

Lake-taxis from Kasenyi to Banda or Bukasa Island are no safer, but since they are the only direct option from the mainland, many travellers opt to use them. Kasenyi lies 7km south of the Abaita Abibiri (⊕ *0.09516, 32.50251*) junction on the Kampala Road, 4km out of Entebbe.

WHERE TO STAY Buggala Island offers a broad selection of accommodation. Options on Banda and Bukasa Islands are more limited.

Buggala

Accommodation on Buggala is concentrated along sandy Lutoboka Bay (the landing point for ferries from Nakiwogo) & around Kalangala, a short distance uphill. If you visit at weekends, pray that the neighbours from hell, the notoriously inconsiderate Pearl Gardens Beach Hotel (next to the ferry landing and not listed below) is not hosting an all-night party.

Upmarket

✳ 🏠 **Brovad Sands Lodge** [198 A4] (13 rooms) ⊕ -0.31893, 32.28068; m 0774 334655; e info@brovadsandslodge.com or brovadsandslodge@gmail.com; www. brovadsandslodge.com. Opened in 2013, the newest & by some way smartest lodge on the islands lies at the southwest end of Lutoboka Bay, 2km from the ferry jetty. The large stone-&-thatch cottages, which wouldn't look out of place in a game lodge, are spaced around well-wooded gardens running down to a sandy beach. The stylish contemporary wood-dominated décor is complemented by good amenities including a small reception with writing desk & dressing mirror, sitting area with sofas & flatscreen DSTV, a large bathroom with tub & shower, & a well-appointed private balcony. Very reasonably priced for a place of this quality. *US$67/83 B&B sgl/dbl. An additional US$17pp FB.* **$$$**

Moderate

✳ 🏠 **Ssese Islands Beach Hotel** [198 B3] (26 rooms) ⊕ -0.31431, 32.28735; ☎0414 220065; m 0772 408244/845905; e barbara@sseseislandsbeachhotel.com; http:// sseseislandsbeachhotel.com. This agreeable & sensibly priced resort 1km southwest of the ferry jetty offers a choice of lake-, forest- or golf course-view rooms, all with dbl bed, walk-in net, flatscreen DSTV, en-suite hot shower & private balcony. The large grounds run down to a sandy swimming beach overlooked by a terrace

restaurant, & incorporate a 9-hole golf course that should be operational (with clubs for rent) by the time you read this. *US$25/45 B&B sgl/dbl. Camping US$7 pp. Tent hire US$3pp.* **$$**

🏠 **Ssese Habitat Resort** [198 A4] (19 rooms) ⊕ -0.32395, 32.27344; m 0772 506605; e ssehab@gmail.com. This stylish new lodge has an isolated hilltop location off the Luko Road, 500m walk from the nearest swimming beach & 1.5km west of Kalangala. The en-suite rooms all have nets, lake views, DSTV & hot shower. An attractive restaurant serves Ugandan & Italian dishes, including with a good selection of salads & desserts. Amenities & activities include sauna, nature walks & boat rides. *US$40/60pp B&B/FB.* **$$$**

Budget

🏠 **Mirembe Resort Beach** [198 B4] (18 rooms) ⊕ -0.31701, 32.28314; ☎0392 772703; m 0782 528651; e info@miremberesort.co.ug; www.miremberesort.com. Set in a quiet location at the northern end of the beach almost 2km from the ferry jetty, this neatly laid-out resort offers a choice of standard rooms with DSTV & en-suite hot shower, or spacious cottages that also have a writing desk, walk-in netting & tub. A decent restaurant serves an unadventurous selection of Ugandan mains in the US$7–8 range. *US$32/40 standard sgl/dbl, or US60/80 sgl/dbl cottage. All rates B&B.* **$$**

🏠 **Victoria Forest Resort** [198 B3] (11 rooms, more under construction) ⊕ -0.30223, 32.28933; m 0701 922725/0704 285418; 🔲 fb.me/victoria.forest.resort. Probably the most peaceful & nature-oriented lodge at Lutoboka, this place has an isolated beachfront location 1.2km northwest of the ferry & a backdrop of dense forest alive with birdsong. Accommodation is in a rather regimental row of thatched circular cottages with dbl bed & net. A restaurant is attached & extensive renovations were underway in 2015. *US$27/37 B&B sgl/dbl.* **$$**

Panorama Cottages [198 B3] (13 rooms)
-0.3129, 32.29383; m 0772 406371/0782 310629. Stronger on the cottages than the panorama, this friendly owner-managed lodge lacks a beachfront location, but has an attractive garden setting in a forest clearing 500m inland from the ferry landing. A selection of spacious but rather tired-looking chalets all come with net, TV & en-suite hot shower. *US$27–40 dbl, depending on size & furnishing.* **$$**

Ssese Island Club [198 B4] (11 rooms)
-0.3159, 32.28494; m 0772 504027; e islandsclub@hotmail.com; www. sseseislandsclub.com. This place has a superb beachfront location about 1.5km southwest of the ferry jetty, but décor is rather fuddy-duddy & rates seem high for what it is. *US$23pp B&B.* **$$**

Shoestring & camping

Philo Leisure Gardens [198 C4] (5 rooms)
-0.31821, 32.30098; m 0774 006331/0792 585649; e reservations_philoleisuregardens@ yahoo.com; fb.me/philoleisuregardens. Set in tranquil fruiting gardens off the main road between Kalangala & Lutoboka, this new lodge is centred on a slate-terraced restaurant serving a good selection of grills, curries & other dishes in the US$5–7 range. The twin rooms with fitted nets use common showers, & camping is permitted. *US$17 dbl, US$7pp camping.* **$$**

Upland Guesthouse [198 B4] (25 rooms)
-0.31988, 32.2951; m 0773 310006. Tucked away behind the main road through Kalangala

opposite the prominent Cruise Safaris, this clean & friendly place is the pick of a few basic guesthouses dotted around the small town. All rooms are en suite & have nets. *US$8/10/13 sgl/dbl/twin.* **$**

Banda Island

Banda Island Resort [198 F1]
(4 cottages, 2 dorms) -0.25543, 32.39765; m 0772 222777; e banda.island@gmail.com. This marvellously idiosyncratic & laid-back island camp has survived the untimely death of its hedonist creator Dominic Symes, with family & friends making sure that his legend lives on. It remains on a different plane(t) to the beachfront resorts on Buggala Island, & a significant number of budget travellers forsake Lutoboka in search of the more authentic (a word covering all possible contingencies) experience on Banda. Bring your own tent or sleep in a dorm or a basic stone cottage. Rates include all meals & complimentary tea/coffee all day. Other attractions are the friendly dogs & amazing sunsets. *US$53pp en-suite beach cottage or safari tent, US$35 dorm bed or lazy camping, US$33pp camping in own tent. AI rates FB.* **$$$**

Bukasa Island

Agnes's Guesthouse [198 G2] -0.42022, 32.50854. A short walk from the ferry pier on Bukasa Island, this basic, rarely visited but friendly & relaxed guesthouse has a veranda overlooking the lake, which is spectacular at sunset. Meals are served, but it is a good idea to bring some food with you just in case. *US$4pp.* **$**

✕ WHERE TO EAT AND DRINK Most of the resorts on Buggala serve adequate to good meals, with the standouts being Brovad Sands, Ssese Habitat and Philo Leisure Gardens.

✕ Cruise Safari Restaurant [198 B4]
-0.32064, 32.29517; m 0771 913987/ 0758706108; 07.00–midnight daily. This stilted wooden restaurant set upstairs of Kalangala's only quad-biking set-up serves a varied & unexpectedly

cosmopolitan menu of b/fasts, fajitas, grills & other dishes in the US$5–8 range. It also has a good vegetarian & juice selection, & sells freshly baked bread over the counter.

OTHER PRACTICALITIES The Ssese Islands feel very undeveloped by comparison to the rest of Uganda, but even so Kalangala now has a Stanbic Bank with an ATM. Internet facilities are almost non-existent, though some of the smarter resorts may have Wi-Fi.

WHAT TO SEE AND DO The options below deal primarily with activities and excursions on the narrow and irregularly shaped Buggala Island, which is nowhere

much more than 10km wide, but extends for more than 25km to the west and the south from the town of Kalangala on its northeastern pivot. If you don't fancy exploring on foot, note that Cruise Safari in Kalangala (page 214) rents out quad bikes at US$17 per person per hour inclusive of a guide. Bicycles can be rented and local guides arranged through the Ssese Island Tour Guides Association (*SITGA; m 0771 291658*), which has an office next to Lutoboka ferry jetty.

Lutoboka There's more to this beautiful bay than a ferry jetty. Situated 1km downhill from Kalangala, the sandy forest-fringed bay offers a variety of beach activities, including swimming, though bilharzia is certainly a risk (see page 89 for more information). Canoeing is available at some resorts, and the new nine-hole golf course at Ssese Islands Beach Hotel was reputedly set to open in 2016. The forest encircling the bay hosts a wealth of birdlife, best seen from the dirt road running northwest of the jetty towards Victoria Forest Resort.

Further afield Strike out in any direction from Kalangala Town for pleasing views over forests and grassy clearings to the lakeshore and more distant islands, as well as the opportunity to see a variety of forest birds and vervet monkeys. One potentially interesting goal further afield is is the marshy southwestern shore, which harbours small numbers of hippo as well as a population of sitatunga antelope with larger horns than the mainland equivalent, regarded by some authorities to represent an endemic island race. Another popular cycling excursion is to Mutumbula swimming beach, which lies off the road towards Luko, and is reputedly but unverifiably free of bilharzia.

Other islands The second-largest island in Ssese is **Bukasa**, which lies on the eastern end of the archipelago and is widely regarded to be even more attractive than Buggala. Extensively forested, the island supports a profusion of birds and monkeys, and can be explored on foot along a network of fair roads, with the one to Rwanabatya being particularly recommended. Individual points of interest on Bukasa include an attractive beach at Misenyi Bay, 20 minutes' walk from Agnes's Guesthouse, and a plunge-pool ringed by forest and a waterfall, about an hour's walk from the guesthouse. Several other small, mostly uninhabited islands can be reached by fishing boat as day trips from Buggala.

8

9

Jinja and the Upper Nile

Set on the northern shore of Lake Victoria 80km east of Kampala, Jinja is a large and historic town whose main claim to fame is as the source of the Nile: the place where the world's longest river exits Africa's largest lake to commence an epic 6,500km journey to the Mediterranean via the deserts of Sudan and Egypt. It was here, back in 1862, that the explorer John Speke recognised Ripon Falls to be the geographic holy grail that had lured the obsessed, and hopelessly misdirected, Livingstone to a feverish death near Lake Bangweulu (in present-day Zambia) less than a decade earlier. These days, however, the Upper Nile's main touristic draw is not so much Jinja's poignant location as it is nearby Bujagali's status as East Africa's adventure tourism capital. For some years now, white-water rafting on the rapids upriver of Jinja has vied with gorilla tracking as Uganda's most popular tourist activity, and while its long-term future is in the process of being curtailed by the construction of a series of hydro-power dams – the first of which submerged the talismanic Bujagali Falls in 2011 – it is likely to remain viable throughout the lifespan of this present edition. Other activities on offer along the Upper Nile include kayaking, motorboat trips, bungee-jumping, horseback safaris and quad-biking.

JINJA

Uganda's second-largest settlement for most of the 20th century, Jinja (sometimes referred to in Lusoga as 'Idindha') occupies a lush wide peninsula flanked by Lake Victoria to the south and east, and the Nile and now-submerged Ripon Falls to the west. In colonial times and the early years of independence, Jinja was the industrial heart of Uganda, but its economy collapsed during the Amin years, and has never quite recovered. The town's years of economic torpor are reflected in what must surely be the tardiest population growth rate of any major town in East Africa. In 1991, Jinja was still Uganda's second-largest town, according to a census that recorded its population as 65,000. By 2014, it had dropped to 14th – a place behind the once insignificant village of Njeru directly across the river – with a population of 73,000.

Partly as a result of this slow growth, Jinja retains the spacious and attractive layout of its colonial-era incarnation, and its roads are lined with some some fine Asian architecture, giving it a sense of place that is further enhanced by the spread of thickly vegetated residential suburbs carved from the jungle between the town centre and the lake and river. Tourism is big business, though the main focal point of rafting and other adventure activities is further upriver at Bujagali, and most of Jinja's hotels cater primarily to the conference market. A significant contributor to the local economy is the plethora of NGO workers, voluntourists and missionaries who can be seen lunching in the unexpected glut of deli- and bistro-style eateries that dot the old town centre.

HISTORY Jinja, or rather the subsequently-submerged Ripon Falls, entered the history books on 28 July 1862, when the explorer John Hanning Speke first set sight on them and identified the site as the long sought-after headwaters of the Nile. As a result, the somewhat elegiac tone that informs the first written description of the locale probably has less to do perhaps with its inherent scenic qualities than its author's conviction that he had solved the greatest geographic mystery of his time:

> The 'stones', as the Waganda call the falls, was by far the most interesting sight I had seen in Africa … It attracted one to it for hours – the roar of the waters, the thousands of passenger-fish leaping at the falls with all their might; the Wasoga and Waganda fishermen coming out in boats and taking post on all the rocks with rod and hook, hippopotami and crocodiles lying sleepily on the water, the ferry at work above the falls, and cattle driven down to drink at the margin of the lake – made, in all, with the pretty nature of the country – small hills, grassy-topped, with trees in the folds, and gardens on the lower slopes – as interesting a picture as one could wish to see … I felt as if I only wanted a wife and family, garden and yacht, rifle and rod, to make me happy here for life, so charming was the place.

Speke named the waterfall after the Marquess of Ripon, a former president of the Royal Geographical Society, while a second set of rapids about 1km downriver subsequently became known as Owen Falls, after Major Roddy Owen, a member of Sir Gerald Portal's 1893 expedition to Uganda. But the local name for the site has survived, too, since Jinja is a corruption of Ejjinja (Stones), the original Luganda name for the Ripon Falls, as well as for a nearby village and associated sacrificial stone.

An informal European settlement was founded at Jinja in 1900, when the rocky waterfall was selected as the most suitable place for the telegraph line to Kampala to cross the Nile. At this time, the administrative centre for Busoga was at Iganga, regarded by Governor Sir Harry Johnston to be 'not a very healthy place, and, so to speak, "nowhere"'. In 1901, however, Johnston relocated the headquarters to Jinja, with its 'aggregation of European settlers' at the head of a potentially important riverine transport route north along the Nile and Lake Kyoga.

Jinja's rapid emergence as a pivotal commercial centre and international transport hub was further cemented by the completion of the railway line from Mombasa to the lake port of Kisumu, and the introduction of a connecting ferry service. The local economy was further boosted by the successful introduction of cotton as a cash crop for export, and by the construction of a railway line north to Namasagali in 1912. Even so, Sir Frederick Treves, writing in 1913, dismissed Jinja as 'a little tin town … a rough settlement of some size [but] purely utilitarian and without the least ambition to be beautiful'. Jinja's importance as a port undoubtedly diminished after the late 1920s, when the railway line was extended to Kampala, but by this time the town was firmly established as an administrative and retail centre servicing the local cotton industry.

Instrumental in Jinja's post-World War II emergence as Uganda's major industrial and manufacturing centre was the construction of a dam and an associated hydro-electric plant at Owen Falls. As early as 1904, the Uganda Company had mooted erecting 'an electric generating station to be worked by waterpower from the Ripon Falls'. Winston Churchill, who visited the falls three years later, supported this notion enthusiastically: 'So much power running to waste, such a coign of vantage unoccupied, such a lever to control the natural forces of Africa ungripped, cannot but vex and stimulate imagination. And what fun to make the immemorial Nile begin its journey by driving through a turbine!'

The Victoria Nile, running past Jinja, forms the boundary between the kingdoms of Buganda and Busoga, the latter being the home of the Basoga, Uganda's second most populous linguistic group. The Basoga speak a Bantu language very similar to Luganda – particularly close to the dialect of the Ssese Islands – but claim a different origin to the Baganda, and traditionally adhere to a far less centralised political structure. It is also the case that many traditional Basoga customs – for instance, the largely abandoned practice of extracting six teeth from the lower jaw of a boy as an initiation to adulthood – are influenced by the Nilotic-speaking Luo.

The Basoga have been subject to numerous migrations and a great deal of cultural intermingling over the past few centuries, leading to a more diverse and contradictory set of traditions than Uganda's other kingdoms. It is generally agreed, however, that the Basoga originate from the eastern side of Mount Elgon. A popular tradition has it that Busoga was founded by a hunter called Makuma, who crossed the western slopes of the mountain accompanied by his wives, dogs and other followers about 600 years ago to settle in the vicinity of present-day Iganga. Makuma had eight sons, each of whom was appointed ruler of a specific area of Busoga. Makuma was buried at Iganga, where it is said his tomb magically transformed into a rock now known as Buswikara, which forms an important ancestral shrine.

Uniquely, Busoga's status as a kingdom is rooted not in any pre-colonial political or social structure but in 20th-century developments. Pre-colonial Busoga was divided into about 70 autonomous principalities ruled by hereditary chiefs who had originally paid tribute to the King of Bunyoro, but had generally switched allegiance to the King of Buganda by the end of the 19th century. This traditional system of decentralised government was undermined in 1900 when Britain divided Busoga

Only in 1946, however, did the colonial administration look seriously at damming the lower Nile, initially as part of a proposed Equatorial Nile Project that involved Egypt, Sudan, Uganda and other indirectly affected nations. The broad idea behind this scheme was that Egypt would fund the construction of a large dam at the outlet of each of the two largest lakes along the Nile's course: Victoria and Albert. The advantage to Uganda was that the dams could be harnessed as a reliable source of hydro-electric power, not only for domestic use, but also to sell to neighbouring Kenya. At the same time, the dams would transform the lakes into vast semi-artificial reservoirs from where the flow of the Nile downriver to Sudan and Egypt could be regulated to prevent the sporadic flooding and droughts that had long been associated with annual fluctuations in the river's water level.

Protracted and often acrimonious negotiations between the various governments over the next two years eventually broke down as both Uganda and to a lesser extent Kenya objected to the significant loss of land that would result from the construction of the proposed dams. In 1949, Egypt reluctantly signed a treaty allowing Uganda to build a hydro-electric plant at Owen Falls, provided that it did not significantly disrupt the natural flow of the river and that an Egyptian engineer would regulate the water flow through the dam. The Owen Falls Dam cost £7 million to construct, and was formally opened in 1954.

Jinja's proximity to this reliable source of cheap electricity proved attractive to industry, and several textile and other manufacturing plants, including the country's major cigarette factory and brewery, were established. For two decades, the local economy boomed. The modern town centre – one of the few in East Africa to display much

into 14 larger principalities for administrative and tax purposes. It was shattered entirely six years later, when Busoga was amalgamated into one cohesive political entity, modelled on Buganda, and administered by a Muganda 'president', Semei Kakungulu. The office occupied by Kakungulu was abandoned after his retirement in 1913, but the traditional leaders of Basoga put pressure on the British authorities for it to be reinstated – and awarded to a prominent Musoga.

In 1919, Britain created the title of *kyabazinga*, transforming Busoga into a centralised monarchy that enjoyed a similar status within the Uganda protectorate to the ancient kingdoms of Bunyoro or Buganda. Ezekieri Wako Zibondo was crowned as the first kyabazinga, to be succeeded by Sir Wilberforce Nadiope II, whose active rule was terminated when Obote abolished the traditional kingdoms of Uganda in 1967. In 1996, when the kingdoms were reinstated, Henry Wako Muloki – the son of the first kyabazinga – was installed on the throne. Today, the kyabazinga is regarded as the overall leader of Basoga, but he is supported by a parliament of 11 semi-autonomous hereditary Saza chiefs. Five of these chiefs claim accession from Makuma, the founder of Busoga, and the kyabazinga is picked from one of these elite families using a system of rotating accession, to be succeeded only upon death, abdication or serious illness. Muloki ruled until his death in 2008. Perhaps not surprisingly, given the vague process set out for succession, the clans of Busoga took several years to identify an heir acceptable to all. The six-year deadlock was broken only in September 2014 when 26-year-old William Gabula Nadiope IV – the grandson of Sir Wilberforce Nadiope II – was instated as the fourth Kyabazinga of Busoga at a ceremony attended by President Museveni.

indication of considered urban planning – essentially dates to the early 1950s, when the population increased from 8,500 to more than 20,000 in the space of three years. This included a settler community of 800 Europeans and 5,000 Asians, reflected today in the ornate Indian façades of the town centre, as well as the sprawling double-storey mansions that languish in the suburbs. Other relics of this period are the impressive town hall and administrative buildings at the southern end of the town centre.

Jinja's fortunes slumped again following the expulsion of Asians from Uganda in 1972. Most of the town's leading industries had been under Asian management, and the cohorts of Amin who were installed in their place generally lacked any appropriate business experience or managerial skill, resulting in a total breakdown in the local economy. In the early 1990s, the town centre's boarded-up shops and deeply pot-holed roads epitomised a more general aura of lethargy and economic torpor. Today, however, while Jinja remains somewhat sleepy in comparison with Kampala, it no longer feels unhealthily so. Indeed, the freshly painted shopfronts that line the neatly tarred roads of the town centre seem emblematic of its urban rejuvenation, as do the once-rundown suburban mansions that have been restored as private houses or hotels. All the same, a 2014 census figure of 73,000 places Jinja well behind the faster-growing likes of Mbarara, Gulu, Masaka, Kasese and Hoima in terms of both population and – one suspects – economic vitality.

GETTING THERE AND AWAY Jinja lies along the surfaced Nairobi–Kampala Road, 82km east of Kampala, 130km west of Tororo, and 145km southwest of Mbale. Owing to congestion and slow trucks along the way, the journey in a

private vehicle now takes almost 2 hours, possibly longer if you get stuck in heavy traffic in Kampala. For this reason, there's a lot to be said for using the more northerly route via Gayaza and Kayunga, which is 30km longer but far mellower, except for the initial section leaving Kampala along Gayaza Road. This northern route is definitely the one to use if you are headed to any of the lodges or tourist sites around Kalagala Falls on the West Bank of the Nile. Either way, when you reach the outskirts of Jinja, the Kampala Road crosses Owen Falls Dam then arrives at a roundabout where a right turn leads to the town centre and a left turn to Bujagali.

For those without transport, all of the rafting companies offer a free transfer between Kampala and Jinja/Bujagali to anybody who rafts with them or stays at accommodation operated by them. Otherwise, a popular, punctual and reliable option to/from Kampala (*US$10 one-way*) or Entebbe (*US$12 one-way*) is the daily **Pineapple Express** (see page 125). At other times, the safest option from Kampala are the **coaster buses** (*US$2*) that run between the old taxi park and Jinja. Buses to Mbale, Tororo and Busia leave Jinja bus park between 06.00 and 08.00 and cost around US$3. Later in the day, you can either board one of the matatus that leave throughout the day, or head out to the police barracks roundabout on the Jinja bypass to catch a buses travelling from Kampala to locations further east.

 WHERE TO STAY There's no shortage of accommodation in Jinja. Indeed, the number of hotels seems to have doubled in the past few years, and the options now range from a quartet of upmarket boutique hotels to a trio of suburban backpacker hostels and campsites, and several simple central guesthouses.

Upmarket

✳ 🏠 **Source of the Smile Guesthouse**
[222 D3] (11 rooms) Kiira Rd; m 0783 842021/0756 078147; e info@sourceofthesmile.com; www.sourceofthesmile.com. Get past the cringeworthy name, & this Swedish-owned & managed guesthouse is easily the best-value upmarket option in Jinja, set in serene leafy gardens with a swimming pool & terrace bar hung with hammocks. The eclectically decorated common areas are adorned with contemporary African artworks, while comfortable en-suite rooms all have 4-poster beds, fitted nets, fans & hot shower. There's no restaurant but food can be ordered in from nearby restaurants. *US$78/88 sgl/dbl, or US$87/98 poolside room. Family rooms sleeping 4 cost US$125. All rates B&B.* **$$$**

✳ 🏠 **Surjio's Pizzeria and Guesthouse**
[223 E7] (23 rooms) Kisinja Rd; 📞 043 4122325; m 0772 500400; e bookings@surjios.com; www.surjios.com. This attractively renovated owner-managed colonial house is set in lush gardens centred on a sparkling swimming pool. Individually decorated in continental style, the rooms have wood or terracotta tile floors, 4-poster dbl or twin

bed & fitted net & en-suite hot tub or shower. An excellent pizzeria is attached. *US$80/125/145 B&B sgl/dbl/trpl.* **$$$$**

🏠 **2 Friends** [222 D3] (19 rooms) Jackson Crescent; m 0783 160804; e post@2friends. info; www.2friends.info. This pleasant suburban guesthouse is centred on a swimming pool & terrace softened by a border of tropical plants that separate it from the affiliated All Friends restaurant. The en-suite rooms, though on the small side, are attractively decorated in safari style, & well equipped with DSTV, safe, fridge, fan, Wi-Fi & hot shower. *US$107/124/159 sgl/dbl/trpl in main house, or US$136/154/189 poolside. All rates B&B.* **$$$$**

🏠 **Gately on Nile** [223 F7] (11 rooms) Nile Crescent; 📞 043 4122400; m 0772 469638; e stay@gatelyonnile.com; www.gatelyonnile. com. Jinja's longest-serving boutique hotel, this Australian-owned retreat, set in a lush tropical garden, comprises a restored colonial house decorated with colourful African fabrics & wood-&-bamboo furniture, as well as a trio of distinctive storeyed suites (each boasting a lounge, kitchenette & sofa bed below & a bedroom & balcony with lake

views). Facilities include Wi-Fi & a cosmopolitan menu known for its Thai specialties. *US$50/80 sgl/dbl budget room, US$80/105 standard room, US$120/160 lake view suite. All rates B&B.* **$$$**

🏠 **Living Waters Resort** [222 C6] (3 units) m 0793 845255, e info@sourceofthenile.org, www.sourceofthenile.org. Situated on the West Bank of the Nile opposite Jinja, this small & rather pricey new lodge boasts the finest view in town, overlooking the point where the Nile exits Lake Victoria. Accommodation is in luxury standing tents with fan, net, wooden deck with comfortable seating & en-suite hot shower. Facilities include an open-sided restaurant, 15-minute walking trail & boat trips at US$7pp. The resort is accessible by road from the West Bank, or you can charter a boat from Jinja. *US$130/220 b&b sgl/dbl or US$180/300 FB. Camping US$5pp.* **$$$$**

Moderate

🏠 **Source of the Nile Hotel** [222 D4] (44 rooms) Bridge St; 043 4123034; m 0718 660202; e sourceofthenilehotel@gmail.com; www.sourceofthenile.co.ug. The pick of several rather old-fashioned & institutional mid-range hotels on the leafy suburban roads west of the town centre, this well-priced set-up has a good river view & large modern rooms with tiled floor, king-sized bed, net, DSTV, fan & en-suite hot shower. *US$55/72 B&B sgl/dbl.* **$$$**

🏠 **Nile Village Hotel** [222 C2] (27 rooms) Kiira Rd; 043 4120879; m 0773 826420; e reservations@nilevillagehotel.com; www.nilevillagehotel.com. This smart, new service-oriented hotel is notable for its great swimming pool area & terrace restaurant serving Thai, Indian & continental dishes for around US$8. Walled in & lacking a view, it also scores highly on the security front: body search, bag search, mine-sweeper, etc. Set in 2-storey circular huts, the pleasantly furnished en-suite rooms come with flatscreen DSTV, dbl or twin bed, fridge, writing desk & private balcony. *US$61/67 B&B sgl/dbl.* **$$$**

🏠 **Al-Nisaa Hotel and Spa** [225 C3] (6 rooms, more under construction) Iganga Rd; 043 4122660; e reservations@jinjahotelandspa.com; www.jinjahotelandspa.com. The smartest hotel in the town centre, the recently opened Al-Nisaa is set in a colonial-style building with a wide terrace & clean en-suite tiled rooms with modern fittings

including dbl bed with fitted nets, fan, safe, flatscreen DSTV & hot water. Amenities include good restaurant & spa, with Wi-Fi throughout. Good value. *US$33/40 B&B sgl/dbl.* **$$**

🏠 **Nile Anchor Palace** [222 D3] (22 rooms) Wakoli Rd; m 0712 600223; e nileanchorpalace@yahoo.com; www.nileanchorpalace.com. Set in palm-shaded suburban gardens next to Explorers Backpackers, this well-maintained & sensibly priced 3-storey hotel has comfortable tiled rooms with fitted net, flatscreen DSTV, fan, writing table, fridge, modern African art on the walls & private balcony with seating. There's a restaurant & Wi-Fi throughout. *US$44/51 B&B sgl/dbl.* **$$$**

🏠 **Travel Hotel** [223 E2] (49 rooms) 043 4120837; m 0772 758081. This multi-storey business/NGO hotel is bland & distanced from any points of interest, but the en-suite rooms with hot baths are good value & a good wellness spa & reasonably priced garden restaurant are attached. *US$29/33/41 sgl/dbl/twin B&B.* **$$**

Budget

🏠 **Safari Hotel** [222 D2] (19 rooms) Nalufenya Rd; m 0704 629992/0751 224000; e booking@jinjasafarihotel.com; www.jinjasafarihotel.com. The 1st hotel on the right coming into town from Bujagali Roundabout, this long-serving & well-priced place stands in green grounds with a new swimming pool & bright, nicely furnished 1st-floor rooms with net, Wi-Fi, DSTV & en-suite hot shower. *US$18/30 B&B dbl.* **$$**

🏠 **Bilkon Hotel** [223 D3] (38 rooms) Nalufenya Rd; 043 4123944; m 0772 504452; e bilkonhotel@gmail.com; www.bilkon-hotel.com. Marred only by the noise from the main road running past, this characterless but friendly multi-storey hotel offers very reasonably priced en-suite rooms with fitted nets, DSTV, fan, private balcony & hot water. *US$21/24 B&B sgl/dbl.* **$$**

🏠 **Crested Crane Hotel** [222 D3] (35 rooms) Hannington Sq; m 0705 832378. Set in palatial green grounds bordering the town centre, this time-warped old government hotel seems to undergo regular but ineffective facelifts, & doubles as a training ground for the Uganda Hotel & Tourism Training Institute, creating plenty of scope for Fawlty Towers-style entertainment. Despite this, the en-suite rooms with hot water, nets, fan & DSTV are more than fair value. *US$21/27 B&B sgl/dbl.* **$$**

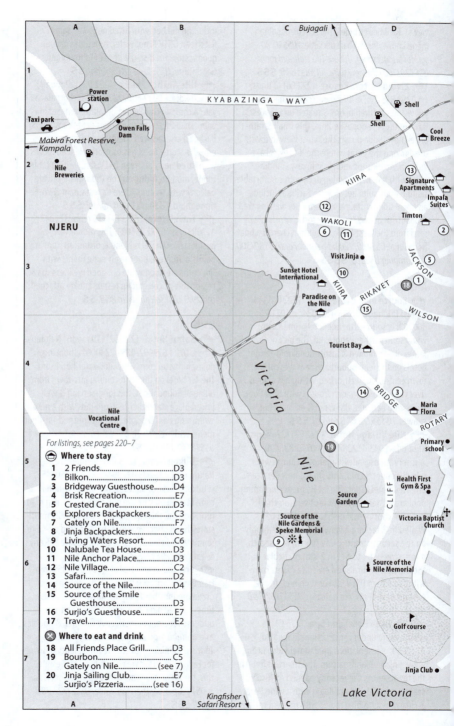

For listings, see pages 220–7

🛏 **Where to stay**
1	2 Friends	D3
2	Bilkon	D3
3	Bridgeway Guesthouse	D4
4	Brisk Recreation	E7
5	Crested Crane	D3
6	Explorers Backpackers	C3
7	Gately on Nile	F7
8	Jinja Backpackers	C5
9	Living Waters Resort	C6
10	Nalubale Tea House	D3
11	Nile Anchor Palace	D3
12	Nile Village	C2
13	Safari	D2
14	Source of the Nile	D4
15	Source of the Smile Guesthouse	D3
16	Surjio's Guesthouse	E7
17	Travel	E2

✖ **Where to eat and drink**
18	All Friends Place Grill	D3
19	Bourbon	C5
	Gately on Nile	(see 7)
20	Jinja Sailing Club	E7
	Surjio's Pizzeria	(see 16)

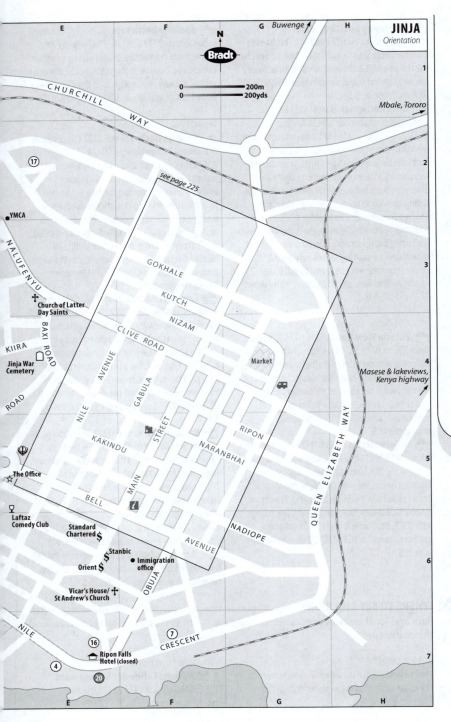

see page 225

JINJA
Orientation

Bradt

N

Buwenge

0 ———— 200m
0 ———— 200yds

CHURCHILL WAY

Mbale, Tororo

Masese & lakeviews,
Kenya highway

YMCA

NALUFENYU

Church of Latter
Day Saints

BAXI ROAD

KIIRA

Jinja War
Cemetery

ROAD

NILE

AVENUE

GABULA

CLIVE ROAD

GOKHALE

KUTCH

NIZAM

Market

STREET

RIPON

NARANBHAI

KAKINDU

The Office

MAIN

BELL

Laftaz
Comedy Club

Standard
Chartered $

$ Stanbic

Orient $

● Immigration
office

NADIOPE

AVENUE

OBUJA

QUEEN ELIZABETH WAY

Vicar's House/ ✝
St Andrew's Church

NILE

16

Ripon Falls
Hotel (closed)

4

20

7

CRESCENT

🏠 **Bridgeway Guesthouse** [222 D4] (13 rooms) Bridge Rd; m 0772 480142. This friendly 2-storey house set in a quiet suburban gardens has the feel of a B&B & the neat, tiled en-suite rooms are very comfortable & decent value. *US$22/26/29 B&B sgl/dbl/suite.* **$$**

🏠 **Brisk Recreation Hotel** [223 E7] (130 rooms) Nile Crescent Rd; ☎0434 122098; m 0772 501100; e info@briskhoteltriangle.co.ug; www.briskhoteltriangle.co.ug. Jinja's largest hotel, formerly the Triangle Annex, is a concrete monstrosity seemingly designed to uglify an otherwise superb shoreline location between the sailing club & golf course. The large swimming pool is adorned with a rock bridge & concrete sculpture of a crocodile, while the restaurant serves unexciting but reasonably priced meals. The en-suite rooms are starting to look very tired & the whole atmosphere is rather moribund. *US$21/25 sgl/dbl without view, or US$25/28 with lake view. All rates B&B.* **$$**

Shoestring

🏠 **Victoria View Hotel** [225 D1] (24 rooms) Kutch Rd; m 0772 582851. Although the implied outlook is restricted to the rooftop laundry area, this venerable high-rise is the closest hotel to the taxi park & the en-suite tiled rooms with cold shower are decent value following recent renovations. *US$6.70/8.30/12 sgl/old dbl/renovated dbl.* **$**

🏠 **Bellevue Hotel** [225 B1] (38 rooms) Kutch Rd; m 0712 578314; e info@bellevue.ug; www.bellevue.ug. This long-standing & well-priced favourite lies on the smarter side of the Main St, 5mins' walk from the bus & taxi parks. Rooms are clean & facilities include a restaurant, bar, lounge with DSTV, pool table & Wi-Fi. *US$5 sgl with common showers or US$14/17/23 en-suite sgl/dbl/twin.* **$$**

🏠 **Sparrow Resthouse** [225 C5] (15 rooms) Luba's Rd; m 0777 918120. This long-serving but recently refurbished cheapie has a quiet but convenient location at the south end of the town centre, & clean rooms with tiled floor, ¾ or twin beds & fitted nets. *US$6.30/13.30 sgl/twin.* **$**

Dorms & camping

✷ 🏠 **Jinja Backpackers** [222 C5] (2 rooms & 3 dorms) Bridge Close; m 0774 730659/0777 436433; info@jinjabackpackers.com; www. jinjabackpackers.com. Set in magnificent wooded grounds flanking the Nile & bisected by a tributary stream, this underpublicised backpackers' offers the choice of private rooms or 8-bed dorms, all with nets & towels provided, Wi-Fi access & power points. The idyllically located Bourbon Bar & Restaurant is in the same compound. *US$25/30 sgl/dbl, US$1pp dorm, US$5pp camping.* **$$**

🏠 **Explorers Backpackers** [222 C3] (1 room & 5 dorms) Wakoli Pl; m 0772 422373; e rafting@ raftafrica.com; www.raftafrica.com. Ideal for sociable solo travellers, Jinja's oldest backpackers', doubling as the base for the rafting company Nile River Explorers, has a lively bar/restaurant with pool table, DSTV, free Wi-Fi & power points, inexpensive meals, & free tea & coffee until 10.00. *US$30 dbl, US$12pp dorm bed, US$7pp camping.* **$$**

🏠 **Nalubale Tea House** [222 D3] (2 rooms & 1 dorm) Kiira Rd; m 0782 638938; e bookings@ nalubalerafting.com; 📘 fb.me/NalubaleTeaHouse. The home of Nalubale Rafting, this spruced-up 1950s house gives an idea of how lovely Jinja's suburbs must have been in their heyday. The light & airy lounge area, opening directly on to the large garden, is a pleasant place to hang out, while a diary of regular events include a weekly movie night. A restaurant offers a varied menu of meals & snacks. *US$25 dbl, US$10pp dorm bed, US$5pp camping, all with shared facilities.* **$$**

✗ **WHERE TO EAT AND DRINK** In addition to the places listed below, numerous small bars and local eateries are scattered along the south end of Main Street and around the market area.

Town centre

Most of Jinja's best eateries are in the town centre, but do be aware that many places close in the evenings &/or on Sun.

Moderate to expensive

✷ ✗ **Flavours Coffee Bar & Restaurant** [225 C5] Main St; m 0793 263333; www. enjoyflavours.com; 🕐 08.30–22.30 daily.

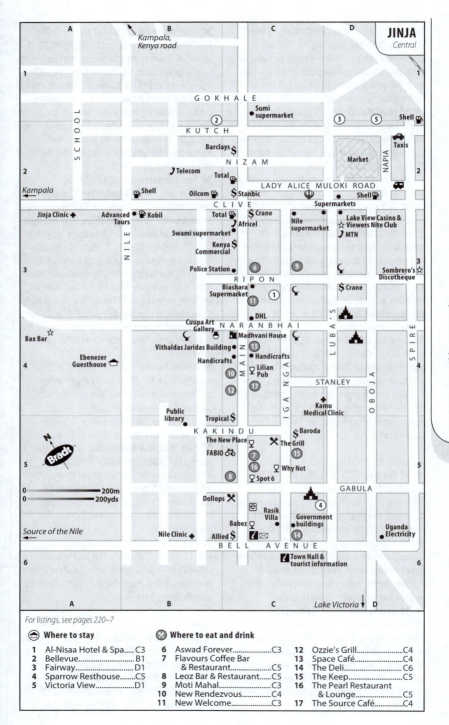

JINJA
Central

GOKHALE

Sumi supermarket

② ③ ⑤ Shell

KUTCH

Barclays $

Taxis

Telecom

Total

NIZAM

Market

NAPIA

Kampala ←

Shell

Oilcom $ Stanbic

LADY ALICE MULOKI ROAD

Shell

CLIVE

Supermarkets

Jinja Clinic ✚   Advanced Tours   Kobil

Total   Crane

Africel

Nile supermarket

Lake View Casino & Viewers Nite Club

NILE

Swami supermarket

Kenya Commercial $

MTN

Police Station

RIPON

⑥

⑨

Sombrero's Discotheque

Biashara Supermarket

① Crane

⑪ ①

DHL

Cuupa Art Gallery

NARANBHAI

Bax Bar ☆

Madhvani House

LUBA'S

Ebenezer Guesthouse

Vithaldas Jaridas Building

Handicrafts ⑬

SPIRE

Handicrafts

⑩   Lilian Pub

STANLEY

IGANGA

MAIN

⑫   ⑰

OBOJA

Kamu Medical Clinic

Public library

Tropical $

KAKINDU

Baroda $

The New Place   The Grill

FABIO   ⑦   ⑮

⑯   Why Not

⑧   Spot 6

GABULA

N

Bradt

0   200m
0   200yds

Dollops

④

Rasik Villa

Government buildings

Uganda Electricity

Source of the Nile

Babez

Nile Clinic ✚   Allied $ ⑭

BELL   AVENUE

Town Hall & tourist information

Kampala, Kenya road

SCHOOL

Lake Victoria ↓

For listings, see pages 220–7

225

This smart restaurant has a contemporary feel & cosmopolitan menu including stir fries, salads, imaginative curries (chicken & apple, pumpkin & chick pea) & couscous-based dishes. It has a good wine list, garden seating in the back, & serves coffee, juices & smoothies. *Mains US$6.50–8.50.*

✳ ✖ **Moti Mahal** [225 C3] Iganga Rd; ☎043 4121839; m 0718 357199; ⊕ 09.30–22.30 daily. Central Jinja's best Indian restaurant might not be much to look at from the outside, but the thalis & curries are truly superb, & it also offers plenty of choice to vegetarians. *Mains cost around US$6.50–8.*

✳ ✖ **The Keep** [225 C5] Iganga Rd; m 0788 073649; ◼ fb.me/thekeepuganda; ⊕ 08.00–21.00 Mon–Sat. This popular café, rather oddly designed to resemble a castle, owes its existence to a devout Christian couple, & profits fund various community projects. A lengthy menu of tasty salads, soups, sandwiches, snacks & pizzas (Fri & Sat only) can be washed down with herbal teas, milkshakes & various hot & iced coffees. Wi-Fi available. *Mains US$5–6.*

✖ **Leoz Bar & Restaurant** [225 C5] Main St; m 0712 622699; ⊕ 09.00–23.00 daily. This unpretentious pan-Asian restaurant serves an extensive selection of Manchurian, Nepali, Chinese & Indian meat & vegetarian dishes, with thalis & Chinese hotties being the main speciality. Drinks include lassis, juices & a full bar. *Mains in the US$5–9 range.*

Cheap to moderate

✳ ✖ **The Deli** [225 C6] Iganga Rd; m 0794 589400; e thedeliug@gmail.com; ◼ fb.me/thedeliug; ⊕ 09.00–16.00. Jinja's most happening lunch spot, this excellent new Finnish-owned & managed snack bar, with terrace seating facing the town hall gardens, specialises in DIY wraps & sandwiches using a wide choice of fresh ingredients, but also serves salads, fresh coffee & smoothies. For self-caterers, it also sells organic chicken, fresh veggies & other goodies. *Mains US$3–5.*

✳ ✖ **Ozzie's Grill** [225 C4] Main St; m 0712 755180; ⊕ 07.30–18.30 Mon–Sat. This long-serving & well-priced Australian-owned restaurant has been a 'home from home' for scores of volunteers over the years. Fillet steak is the speciality, but it also serves wraps, pasta, burgers, omelettes & other grills. Bread & cakes are baked fresh daily. *Mains US$4–6.*

✖ **The Source Café** [225 C4] Main St; ☎043 4120911; www.source.co.ug; ⊕ 08.00–18.30 Mon–Sat. A non-profit initiative supporting several local schools, this characterful café, set in a lovingly restored 1920s' warehouse, looks & smells like an old-time European coffee house, though the busily whirring fans place it firmly in the tropics. Freshly brewed coffee, juices, cakes & light meals can be imbibed indoors or on the terrace. An internet café, small library & craft shop are attached. *Meals up to US$5.*

✖ **New Rendezvous** [225 C4] Main St; ⊕ 08.00–late. The brick-fronted Rendezvous has been dishing out beer & tasty local food for more than 2 decades. *US$2.50 vegetarian dishes, US$3 with meat.*

✖ **The Pearl Restaurant & Lounge** [225 C5] Main St; m 0776 302798; ⊕ 10.00–01.00 daily. With its comfortable sofas, terrace seating & large screen TV, this friendly cocktail-meets-sport-bar tends to be very busy when big football matches are being screened. At all times it is a good place to try inexpensive Uganda-style goat, fish or chicken stew, though more sophisticated continental dishes are also offered. *Local dishes US$2, other mains US$6–7.*

✖ **Aswad Forever** [225 C3] Main St; m 0712 531024; ⊕ 08.30–22.00 daily. Panjabi dishes are the specialty at this new Indian eatery with pleasant & shady pavement seating, but the extensive menu also includes pizzas & burgers. Good vegetarian selection. *Mains US$4–6.*

✖ **New Welcome Restaurant** [225 C3] Main St; m 0711 280840; ⊕ 10.00–22.00 daily. Recognisably converted from an old filling station, this popular Indian restaurant serves a long & varied menu of curries & other Indian dishes, with vegetarians being particularly well catered for. *Mains around US$5.*

✖ **Space Café** [225 C4] Main St; m 0772 565131; 07.00–22.00 daily. This small modern café with Wi-Fi & leather-&-wood furniture serves smoothies, coffee, juices, Mexican dishes, grills & burgers. *Mains US$4–6.*

Suburban

✳ ✖ **Jinja Sailing Club** [223 E7] Nile Crescent; ☎043 4120222; m 0750 035901; e mgr@jinjasailingclub.com; www.jinjasailingclub.com; ⊕ 09.00–22.00 daily. Set in lovely lakeshore gardens complete with an incongruous statue of a dinosaur, Jinja's once-prestigious sailing

club recently reopened under the same name as arguably the town's best restaurant. The varied menu is longest on Indian dishes, but it also has a good selection of grills as well as a 'world cuisine' section & a wide choice of desserts & cakes. *Mains are mostly in the US$8.50–10 range.*

✳ ✖ **All Friends Place Grill** [222 D3] Jackson Crescent; m 0772 984821; e allfriendsplace2014@ gmail.com; www.allfriendsgrill.com; ⊕ 09.00– midnight daily. Affiliated to the neighbouring 2 Friends (page 220), this popular & chilled-out garden restaurant majors in steak, chops & other grills (the whole tilapia cooked in a banana leaf is something of a speciality) but it also has a selection of salads, pizzas & Indian dishes. *Mains in the US$7–12 range.*

✖ **Surjio's Pizzeria** [223 E7] Kisinja Rd; ✆043 4122325; www.surjios.com; ⊕ 11.00–21.30 daily.

BARS AND NIGHTLIFE

☆ **The Office** [223 E5] Grant Rd; m 0752 925371; ⊕ daily. This quirky 2-storey suburban venue is most popular on Fri & Sat nights, when there's usually a DJ & occasionally live music. On other nights it functions as a more relaxed bar with Tue being quiz night.

♉ **Laftaz Comedy Lounge** [223 E5] Nile Crescent; m 0776 541648; ⊕ 09.00–late daily. This colourful & attractive semi-outdoor bar hosts live comedy (in English & Luganda) on Thu nights, when there's an entrance fee of around US$1.50. On other nights its a relaxed place for a drink or *nyama choma* (grilled meat, US$4.50 per plate) in stylish surrounds.

♉ **Jinja Club** [222 D7] Nile Crescent; ⊕ 08.00–late daily. A pleasant location for a quiet drink in green surrounds, the members' clubhouse attached to the Jinja Golf Course is open to the public & serves the usual drinks as well as snacks for around US$3.

Quite simply the best pizzas in Jinja, supplemented by a few dishes of the day, served in a lovely old terraced colonial homestead with lush green gardens. *Mains US$7–9.*

✖ **Gately on Nile** [223 F7] Nile Crescent; m 0772 469638; www.gatelyonnile.com; ⊕ 08.00–21.00 daily. Specialising in Thai food & gourmet burgers, this well-established boutique hotel (pages 220–1) also has plenty of ambience & a selection of other dishes. *Mains US$7–10.*

✖ **Bourbon** [222 C5] Bridge Close; m 0750 356011; ⊕ 11.00–late daily. Located in the Jinja Backpackers' compound, Bourbon is perfectly situated for a riverside sundowner or some boozy aquatic birdwatching, but the food gets mixed feedback & it can get a bit rowdy late at night. Serves pizza, pasta, Mexican & grills. *Food in the US$6–9 range.*

☆ **Sombrero's Discotheque** [225 D3] Spire Rd; ⊕ 20.00–late Wed–Sat; entrance US$2/5 ordinary/executive. Currently Jinja's most popular full-on nightspot, this 2-storey disco has an executive dance floor upstairs.

☆ **Viewers Nite Club** [225 D3] Luba's Rd; m 0750 982734; ◰ fb.me/NileViewCasino; ⊕ 08.00–late Wed–Sat. Another very popular nightclub, set in the Nile View Casino, this caters to a more local clientele than other such clubs listed.

♉ **Bax Bar** [225 A4] Baxi Rd; m 0703 092807; ⊕ daily. Wed is comedy night here, but other nights focus on different styles of music.

♉ **Babez** [225 C6] Main St; https://babezuganda. wordpress.com; ⊕ 24hrs daily. Pronounced 'babes', this full-on drinking joint is the liveliest & loudest of perhaps half a dozen bars clustered at the south end of Main St.

SHOPPING Jinja is well supplied with supermarkets. The highest concentration lies along Clive Road, while **Biashara Supermarket** [225 C3] on Main Street is closer to the main cluster of craft shops and cafés frequented by tourists. If you're looking for fresh fruit and vegetables, visit the **main market** [225 D2] near the taxi park, which is now a covered multi-storey building. The market is worth a browse, too, if you're short of dried fish, door handles, traditional cloth, second-hand T-shirts, cow's stomachs, spanner sets or whatever.

The **Cuupa Arts Gallery** [225 B4] (*Naranbhai Rd*; m *0706 265287*; ⊕ *08.00–19.00 Mon–Sat*) sells a good selection of high-quality handicrafts including jewellery and coffee mugs, as well as original paintings and other artworks. A number of well-stocked craft shops line Main Street either side of The Source Café.

OTHER PRACTICALITIES

Bicycle hire   An well-organised NGO called First African Bicycle Information Organisation [225 C5] (*FABIO; 9 Main St;* 043 4122758; 0705 935030; *info@ fabio.or.ug; www.fabio.or.ug;* 09.00–17.00 Mon–Fri) can rent out single-speed bikes for US$5 per day without a guide, or US$17 with a guide who can show you various sites of interest around town.

Book swap   An excellent book exchange, charging less than US$1 per swap, and proceeds of which go to Soft Power (see box, page 243), operates out of Gately on Nile guesthouse (pages 220–1).

Foreign exchange   Foreign exchange is possible at **Barclays**, **Stanbic**, **Standard Chartered** and **Crane** banks, either over the counter or using your credit cards in the ATMs.

Immigration   If your three-month tourist visa is stamped for only one month on arrival in Uganda, you can get it extended with no hassle (and no charge) at the immigration office behind the town hall (opposite Stanbic bank).

Internet   There are plenty of internet cafés in the middle of Jinja and most hotels and many restaurants now have Wi-Fi.

Maps   A free map of Jinja, accurate but curiously short on landmarks, can be picked up at the tourist office. Far more detailed, the *Jinja and the Nile* title in the 'Uganda Maps' series includes a map of the Upper Nile on its reverse.

Spa   The Travel Hotel's **Wellness Spa** (0750 548180; *wellnessspajinja@gmail. com;* 06.30–22.30 Mon–Sat & 10.30–20.30 Sun) offers a full range of treatments at very reasonable prices by international standards. The more central spa in the **Al-Nisaa Hotel** (*Iganga Rd;* 043 4122660; *www.jinjahotelandspa.com*) has also been recommended.

Swimming   The Jinja Club charges US$1.50 daily for non-members to use its 25m swimming pool.

TOURIST INFORMATION AND OPERATORS   There is now an official tourist information centre [225 C6] (08.00–17.00 Mon–Fri) in the Town Hall on Bell Avenue. See also the rafting companies and operators listed under the Upper Nile on page 242.

Advanced Tours   [225 B2] Plot 28/30, Clive Rd West; 043 4120457; 0712 463474/0753 706271; advanced@advancedtours.ug; www.advancedtours.ug

The Tourist Centre   [225 C6] Post office bldng; 043 4122758; 0706 600001; info@jinjatouristcentre.co.ug; www.jinjatouristcentre.co.ug. Offer a ½-day tour of Jinja Town & a full-day tour of the town & the surrounding area on foot or by car. Also vehicle hire & safaris.

Visit Jinja   [222 D3] 41 Wilson Rd; 0794 789851; info@visitjinja.com; www.visitjinja.com. New 1-stop shop online booking agency for most activities & accommodation in Jinja & the Upper Nile.

WHAT TO SEE AND DO   Note that the many activities listed under the Upper Nile section on pages 242–6 can be (and frequently are) undertaken as day excursions

from Jinja. Any hotel, backpackers or local tour operator can book such excursions, or put you in touch with the right organisation.

Historic Jinja The roads of central Jinja are lined with several colonial-era British and Asian architectural gems, some now restored to their former glory, others in varying states of disrepair. Among the former, both on Main Street, are the handsome **Madhvani House** [225 C4], which dates to 1919, and **The Source Café** [225 C4], which occupies a warehouse built in 1924 by the Kampala Oriental Company. In poorer shape are **Rasik Villa** [225 C6] (built 1935) on Iganga Road, the **Police Station** [225 C3] (1928) on Main Street, and **Vithaldas Jaridas Building** [225 C4] (1919) on Naranbhai Road.

Southwest of the town centre, Nile Crescent, an erratically surfaced avenue lined by palm trees laden with fruit bats, leads past the attractive golf course and some fine old colonial homesteads. Probably the oldest building in this part of town is the 1914 Vicar's House behind St Andrew's Church on Busoga Road. Many other old houses between the town centre and Nile Crescent have been beautifully renovated as hotels or private residences. Sadly, however, no attempt has been made to restore and reopen the historic Ripon Falls Hotel, which stands semi-derelict opposite the Jinja Sailing Club.

Jinja War Cemetery [223 E4] (*Baxi Rd; www.cwgc.org;* ⊕ *06.00–18.00 Mon–Fri*) Tended by the Commonwealth War Graves Commission, this well-maintained cemetery comprises 178 graves of Ugandan and British soldiers killed in World War II, when Jinja was the Ugandan centre for the King's African Rifles. It also contains one World War I grave, and four of servicemen who died after 1945. Within the cemetery, the Jinja Memorial is a screen wall inscribed with the names of 127 East African servicemen who died during World War II but whose graves were too remotely located to be maintained properly. Every year, on the second Sunday of November, the British High Commissioner to Uganda and various other representatives of Commonwealth states visit the cemetery to pay their respects.

Jinja Club [222 D7] Also known as the golf club, this sports club is centred on a lovely nine-hole golf course that overlooks the Nile and was at one time famous for games being interrupted by a stray hippo. A day membership costs US$10, clubs can be hired at US$16 per day, and the caddie fee is US$3.30 per round. A fee of US$1.50 is charged to non-members who want to use the 25m swimming pool or squash or tennis courts.

Boat trips The most reliable place to arrange motorboat trips to the source of the Nile is the Jinja Sailing Club (pages 226–7), which charges from US$6.50 per person, with a minimum group size of three. These boat trips usually visit a few islands dotted around the Nile effluent, as well as a supposed underwater spring locally considered to be the true source of the Nile. Other possibilities for short boat trips are the riverside operators based at the source of the Nile (East Bank), and the boat operators at the fish landing by the Jinja Sailing Club. In both cases, be prepared to negotiate, and once a price is agreed, insist on a life jacket.

Source of the Nile (East Bank) [222 D6] (*Cliff Rd; entry US$3pp; parking fee US$3 per vehicle*). About 1km west of the town centre, Jinja Municipality maintains a landscaped park on the East Bank of the now-submerged Ripon Falls, the natural landmark associated with the source of the Nile prior to the construction of the

The first European to see Lake Victoria was John Hanning Speke, who marched from Tabora to the site of present-day Mwanza in 1858 following his joint 'discovery' of Lake Tanganyika with Richard Burton the previous year. Speke named the lake for Queen Victoria but, prior to that, Arab slave traders called it Ukerewe (still the name of its largest island). It is unclear what name was in local use, since the only one referred to by Speke was Nyanza, which simply means 'lake'.

A major goal of the Burton–Speke expedition had been to solve the great geographical enigma of the age, the source of the White Nile. Speke, based on his brief glimpse of the southeast corner of Lake Victoria, somewhat whimsically proclaimed his 'discovery' to be the answer to that riddle. Burton, with a comparable lack of compelling evidence, was convinced that the great river flowed out of Lake Tanganyika. The dispute between the former travelling companions erupted bitterly on their return to Britain, where Burton – the more persuasive writer and better respected traveller – gained the backing of the scientific establishment.

In 1862–63, Speke and Captain James Grant returned to Lake Victoria, hoping to prove Speke's theory correct. They looped inland around the western shore of the lake, arriving at the court of King Mutesa of Buganda, then continued east to the site of present-day Jinja, where a substantial river flowed out of the lake after tumbling over a cataract that Speke named Ripon Falls. From here, the two explorers headed north, sporadically crossing paths with the river until they reached Lake Albert, then continued following the Nile to Khartoum and Cairo.

Back home, Speke's declaration that 'The Nile is settled' met with mixed support. Burton and other sceptics pointed out that Speke had bypassed the entire western shore of his purported great lake, had visited only a couple of points on the northern shore, and had not attempted to explore the east. Nor, for that matter, had he followed the course of the Nile in its entirety. In other words, according to his detractors, Speke might have encountered several different lakes and rivers that were unconnected except in his deluded mind. But while the naysayers did have a point, equally true the geographical evidence gathered by Speke lent a great deal of credibility to his theories, which were also supported by anecdotal information gathered from local sources along the way.

Matters were scheduled to reach a head on 16 September 1864, when an eagerly awaited debate between Burton and Speke – in the words of the former, 'what silly tongues called the "Nile Duel"' – was due to take place at the Royal Geographic Society (RGS). And reach a head they did, but in circumstances more tragic than anybody could have anticipated. On the afternoon of the debate, Speke went out shooting with a cousin, only to stumble while crossing a wall, in the process discharging a barrel of his shotgun into his heart. The subsequent inquest recorded a verdict of accidental death, but it has often been suggested – purely on the basis of the curious timing – that Speke deliberately took his life rather than face up to Burton in public. Burton, who had seen Speke less than three hours earlier, was by all accounts deeply troubled by Speke's death, and years later he was quoted as stating 'the uncharitable [say] that I shot him' – an accusation that seems to have been aired only in Burton's imagination.

Speke was dead, but the 'Nile debate' would keep kicking for several years. In 1864, Sir Samuel and Lady Baker became the first Europeans to reach Lake Albert and nearby Murchison Falls in present-day Uganda. The Bakers, much to the delight of the anti-Speke lobby, were convinced that this newly named lake

was a source of the Nile, though they openly admitted it might not be the only one. Following the Bakers' announcement, Burton put forward a revised theory, namely that the most remote source of the Nile was the Rusizi River, which he believed flowed out of the northern head of Lake Tanganyika and emptied into Lake Albert.

In 1865, the RGS followed up on Burton's theory by sending Dr David Livingstone to Lake Tanganyika. Livingstone, however, was of the opinion that the Nile's source lay further south than Burton supposed, and so he struck out towards the lake along a previously unexplored route. Leaving from Mikindani in the far south of present-day Tanzania, Livingstone followed the Ruvuma River inland, continuing westward to the southern tip of Lake Tanganyika. From there, he ranged southward into present-day Zambia, where he came across a new candidate for the source of the Nile, the swampy Lake Bangweulu and its major outlet, the Lualaba River. It was only after his famous meeting with Henry Stanley at Ujiji, in November 1871, that Livingstone (in the company of Stanley) visited the north of Lake Tanganyika and Burton's cherished Rusizi River, which, it transpired, flowed into the lake. Burton, nevertheless, still regarded Lake Tanganyika as the most likely source of the Nile, while Livingstone was convinced that the answer lay with the Lualaba River. In August 1872, Livingstone headed back to the Lake Bangweulu region, where he fell ill and died six months later, the great question still unanswered.

In August 1874, ten years after Speke's death, Stanley embarked on a three-year expedition every bit as remarkable and arduous as those undertaken by his predecessors, yet one whose significance is often overlooked. Partly, this is because most histories have painted such an unsympathetic picture of Stanley: a grim caricature of the murderous, pre-colonial White Man blasting and blustering his way through territories where Burton, Speke and Livingstone had relied largely on diplomacy. It is also the case, however, that Stanley set out with no intention of seeking headline-making fresh discoveries. Instead, he determined to test methodically the theories advocated by Speke, Burton and Livingstone about the Nile's source. First, Stanley sailed around the circumference of Lake Victoria, establishing that it was indeed as vast as Speke had claimed. Stanley's next step was to circumnavigate Lake Tanganyika, which, contrary to Burton's long-held theories, clearly boasted no outlet sufficiently large to be the source of the Nile. Finally, and most remarkably, Stanley took a boat along Livingstone's Lualaba River to its confluence with an even larger river, which he followed for months with no idea as to where he might end up.

When, exactly 999 days after he left Zanzibar, Stanley emerged at the Congo mouth, the shortlist of plausible theories relating to the source of the Nile had been reduced to one. Clearly, the Nile did flow out of Lake Victoria at Ripon Falls, before entering and exiting Lake Albert at its northern tip to start its long course through the sands of the Sahara. Stanley's achievement in putting to rest decades of speculation about how the main rivers and lakes of East Africa linked together is estimable indeed. He was nevertheless generous enough to concede that: 'Speke now has the full glory of having discovered the largest inland sea on the continent of Africa, also its principal affluent as well as its outlet. I must also give him credit for having understood the geography of the countries we travelled through far better than any of us who so persistently opposed his hypothesis'.

The first plaque erected in the Source of the Nile Gardens read 'Speke discovered this source of the Nile on the 28th July 1862'. This was removed some years back on the basis that local people knew of the place long before any European arrived there, which is true enough, but somewhat misses the point. Of course, Speke didn't really 'discover' Lake Victoria or the Ripon Falls: people had been living there for millennia before any he arrived. But Speke *was* the first person to make a connection between this 13m-high waterfall and the life-bearing river that flows through the deserts of Egypt before emptying into the Mediterranean 6,500km further north.

Being nit-picky, the newer plaque that replaced the original is also somewhat contentious. For while Ripon Falls is unambiguously *a* source of the Nile, its semi-official status as *the* source of the Nile could be said to be arbitrary and sentimental – posthumous recognition of Speke's momentous but contemporarily controversial discovery – rather than being based on geographical logic.

Strictly speaking, the truest source of the Nile is the most remote headwater of the Kagera, which is the longest river to feed Lake Victoria. And the location of this landmark is open to debate. In 1892, the German explorer Oscar Baumann traced the Kagera to a source in Burundi's Kabera Forest, while 11 years later his countryman Richard Kandt located a possibly more remote spring in Rwanda's Nyungwe Forest. In 1937, however, the German explorer Burkhart Waldecker located what has since been recognised as the most remote of the Nile's headwaters, the source of the Kagera River, a hillside spring known as Kasumo (Gusher) and situated some 4° south of the Equator in Burundi. But the mantle was handed back to Rwanda in 2006, when a modern-day GPS-guided expedition following the Nile all the way from Alexandria hit on a 'new' source in Nyungwe Forest, 15km from the location identified by Kandt. One implication of this most recent discovery is that the Nile, if traced to its most remote source, is actually 6,718km long – a full 107km more than previously accepted.

There are other sources to consider. Before crossing into Sudan, the Victoria Nile flows through Lake Kyoga and into the northern tip of Lake Albert, from where it emerged as the Albert Nile. And Lake Albert is also fed by the Semliki River, several of whose tributaries rise on the Rwenzori Mountains, which count as the highest and most fabulous source of the Nile. In truth, depending on how you look at these things, Nyungwe Forest, the Rwenzori Mountains or even the point where the river exits Lake Albert all vie with Ripon Falls as the point where the Nile can be considered to start its long journey to the Mediterranean.

Owen Falls Dam a short distance upriver in the 1950s. It's a pleasant spot and deserving of a once-in-a-lifetime visit, and while its significance is less obvious than in Speke's day, a prominent plaque is there to remind you it 'marks the place where the Nile starts its long journey to the Mediterranean'. An additional plaque with a sculpted bust commemorates Mahatma Gandhi, some of whose ashes were scattered into the river here following his death in 1948. Also set within the park is an alley of craft shops and a concrete terrace serving refreshments beside the remnants of Ripon Falls. Greater choice of food and a nicer setting are provided by Rumours, a riverside bar/restaurant set in a patch of riverine woodland 100m distant.

Source of the Nile Gardens (West Bank) [222 C6] (⊕ *0.420531, 33.193013; entry US$3pp*) Now operated privately by Living Waters (see page 221), the Source of the Nile Gardens incorporates the spot from where Speke first viewed Ripon Falls in 1862, and is also altogether prettier and more enjoyable than its eastern counterpart. Furthermore, unlike the outlook from the Jinja side, the magnificent view from the West Bank puts the whole thing into context. As you behold the sight seen by Speke – of the river being funnelled towards you out of a broad bay of Lake Victoria – you'll appreciate his conviction that he had solved the age-old mystery. Speke's visit is remembered by an inscribed pillar-like **Speke Monument** which, erected in 1954, has thus far survived any attempt to replace it with something more politically correct. Other facilities include a decent open-sided restaurant and a 15-minute walking trail that offers much to birders. The gardens can be reached by canoe from the East Bank or by following the Kampala Road across Owen Falls Dam to Njeru, where you need to turn left (just before Nile Breweries) and keep heading south for about 3.5km.

James Hannington Memorial Site (⊕ *0.43389, 33.42887;* m *0757 992485/0701 500452;* e *info@bishophannington.org; www.bishophannington.org*) Situated in the village of Kyando (pronounced Chando) about 25km east of Jinja as the crow flies, this newly developed memorial site forms part of a church and health centre named after the Anglican missionary Bishop James Hannington, who was killed in 1885, together with 50 of his porters, by an emissary of Kabaka Mwanga (see box, pages 234–5). It is an important pilgrimage site that attracts thousands of Anglicans from all over East Africa on 29 October, the anniversary of the bishop's death. The stone where Hannington was speared to death is now a covered shrine, and the caretaker will also show you other sites associated with the bishop. These include a concreted-up spring of holy water once drunk from by the bishop, as well as a a pair of rocky shelters on a nearby hill, one of which is reputedly where he slept, and the other where he stored the books he was carrying. There is no entrance fee but a tip will be expected.

The memorial can easily be visited as a day trip from Jinja or Bujagali. The signposted dirt road there runs south from a junction in the small town of Busita (⊕ *0.5281, 33.38455*) on the Mbale Road about 21km east of Jinja. Follow this dirt road south for 8km to Bufululubi (⊕ *0.49543, 33.43143*), then turn right at the signpost for the memorial, passing through Nkombe after 7km, then continuing for another 2.5km to the prominent church and shrine. There is no public transport past Bufululubi, but bodas are available at Busita. A resthouse is under construction at the church and the caretaker reckons it will open before the end of 2016.

Lolwe Island Also known as Lolui or Dolwe, this substantial but remote island, extending over around 20km² some 30km by boat from the mainland landing at Bwondha, is strewn with giant granite outcrops that harbour some of the most intriguing archaeological sites anywhere in Uganda. Several prehistoric rock-art sites exist on the island, the best known being the Sanctuary, a chamber supported by four extensively painted granite boulders near the lakeside village of Golofa. Reminiscent of Nyero near Kumi, the artwork at Lolwe mostly comprises geometric patterns – sets of concentric circles, or sausage and dumbbell shapes – painted with ochre pigments. The island is also liberally scattered with ancient rock gongs, ceramics and cairns dating back more than 500 years, several rock shrines to important Luo deities, and literally thousands of artificial stone hollows whose purpose is unknown.

It is currently undeveloped for tourism, but adventurous travellers could think about travelling there by road and boat. The launch is the village of Bwondha

The Rev James Hannington first set foot in East Africa in June 1882 as the leader of a reinforcement party for the Victoria Nyanza Mission in Kampala, but he was forced to return to England before reaching Uganda owing to a debilitating case of dysentery. In June 1884, he was consecrated in London as the first bishop of Eastern Equatorial Africa. In November of the same year, he left England to assume his post, inspired by Joseph Thomson, who months earlier had become the first European to travel to Lake Victoria through Maasailand, rather than the longer but less perilous route pioneered by Speke around the south of the lake.

Thomson advised future travellers against attempting to reach Buganda through the territory occupied by the militant Maasai, but Bishop Hannington – attracted by its directness and better climatic conditions – paid him no heed. And, as it transpired, Hannington and his party of 200 porters negotiated the route without encountering any significant resistance from the Kikuyu or Maasai, to arrive at Mumias (in present-day western Kenya) on 8 October 1885. A few days later, accompanied by a reduced party of 50 porters, Hannington continued the march westward, obtaining his first view of Lake Victoria on 14 October.

Hannington had been fully aware of the risks involved in crossing Maasailand, but he had no way of knowing about the momentous change in mood that had marked Buganda since the death of King Mutesa a year earlier. Mutesa was succeeded by his son Mwanga, who became increasingly hostile towards outsiders in general and the Anglican Church in particular during the first year of his reign. Worse still, Mwanga was deeply affected by a vision that foretold the destruction of Buganda at the hands of strangers who entered the kingdom through the 'back door' – the east – as opposed to the more normal approach from the southwest.

On 21 October 1885, Hannington and his party entered the fort of Luba, an

($\oplus$ *0.17041, 33.56568*), a 50km drive or matatu ride southeast of Busita via Bufululubi (the junction for the James Hannington Memorial Site – page 233) and the modest district capital Muyage. An erratic public boat service links Bwondha to Golofa, the largest town on the island, and you should also be able to arrange a private charter. Be warned, however, that it is a long trip, and at least two boats travelling between between Bwondha and Golofa have vanished without trace in recent years, so avoid stormy weather and check the weather forecast.

BUJAGALI AND THE UPPER NILE

Set on the East Bank of the Nile 7km north of Jinja, Bujagali is East Africa's adventure tourism capital and one of the world's top white-water rafting venues. Its main attraction, at least for the time being, is a series of Grade V rapids every bit as exhilarating as the Zambezi Gorge below Victoria Falls. Sadly, however, this is set to change soon, following the construction of what will be the third hydroelectric dam on the Upper Nile, and consequent submersion of the rapids below a new reservoir. Almost certainly, this loss will spell the end of commercial white-water rafting at Bujagali, but hopefully it won't quell the multifaceted tourist industry that has gathered its own momentum at Bujagali in the rafters' wake.

Fortunately – both for tourists, and for the great many locals whose income is dependent on them – there's a great deal more to the Upper Nile than white-water rafting. Supplementary activities such as bungee jumping, horseriding

important Basoga chief with strong loyalties to the King of Buganda. Hours later, the bishop was attacked and imprisoned, and Luba sent a party of messengers to Mwanga to seek instructions. The messengers returned on 28 October accompanied by three Baganda soldiers. The next morning, Hannington wrote in his diary: 'I can hear no news. A hyena howled near me last night, smelling a sick man, but I hope it is not to have me yet.' On the afternoon of 29 October, Hannington was informed that he would be escorted to Buganda immediately. Instead, he was led to a nearby execution rock, stripped of his clothes and possessions, and speared to death. That night, Luba's soldiers massacred the bishop's entire party of 50 porters, with the exception of three men who managed to escape and one boy who was spared on account of his youth.

It is said locally that the murder of Bishop Hannington displeased the spirits and resulted in a long famine in Busoga. King Mwanga, not entirely plausibly, would subsequently claim that he had never ordered Hannington's death; instead, his instructions to release the bishop had been misinterpreted or disregarded by overzealous underlings. In 1890, the bishop's skull – identifiable by his gold fillings – and some of his clothes were brought to Sir Frederick Jackson in Mumias by the one member of Hannington's party who had been spared by Luba's soldiers. The mortal remains of Bishop Hannington were interred at Namirembe Cathedral on 31 December 1892 in a lavish ceremony attended by Mwanga. On 29 October 1939, the 54th anniversary of his death, a bronze memorial dedicated to James Hannington was erected on a boulder near the small port of Buluba (Place of Luba), some 20km east of Jinja as the crow flies. In 2013, a more lavish memorial was unveiled at the Bishop Hannington Church and Health Centre in Nkombe, the site of his death, some 7km south of Buluba (page 233).

and quad biking are not directly affect by the new dam. Meanwhile, the calm waters of Lake Bujagali, which was created in 2011 following the construction of another hydroelectric dam, have opened up opportunities for new and more serene recreational activities: birdwatching, fishing, sit-on-top kayaking, stand-up paddle boarding, wine-and-nibbles sunset voyages, and down-yer-neck booze cruises. Furthermore, Bujagali, set in lush riparian woodland that now overlooks the rather narrow and serpentine lake, is a very scenic spot, especially given a half-decent sunset and a suitable sundowner, and the area as whole is alive with birds and monkeys.

Although the East Bank around Bujagali remains the primary tourism hub on the Upper Nile, the West Bank now hosts a number of relaxed lodges aiming at a relatively sedate and upmarket clientele. The undoubted jewel of the West Bank, 28km north of Jinja, is the Kalagala and Itanda Falls, a set of stunning and unraftable rapids that thunder through the rocky channels flowing between the naturally forested islands that host the stunning Wildwaters Lodge. The West Bank Kalagala Falls Forest Reserve is a prominent Baganda cultural site: a massive tree beneath which visiting kabakas sat stands on the promontory near the falls, while a shrine, still of considerable importance to traditionalists, is found with a jumble of massive riverside boulders. The Kalagala and Ibanda Falls and Wildwaters will reputedly survive the flooding that will take place when Isimbi Dam is completed in the next year or so, but rapids further downstream, including the legendary Nile Special, will be submerged, as will the popular Hairy Lemon Camp.

HISTORY AND BACKGROUND Only 20 years ago, tourism activity on the Upper Nile immediately downstream of Jinja amounted to one peaceful and little-visited picnic site overlooking the Bujagali Falls. The region has undergone two major transformations since then. The first was initiated in 1996, when Adrift established a commercial white-water rafting operation on the East Bank overlooking Bujagali, thereby kickstarting an adventure tourism industry that soon grew to embrace a dozen riverside lodges and camps, along with numerous small operators offering a plethora of aquatic and terrestrial adventure activities. By the early 2000s, once-becalmed Bujagali had become entrenched as the undisputed adventure tourism capital of East Africa, attracting up to 50,000 rafters annually, and for several years outstripping the gorillas of Bwindi as Uganda's most important tourist draw.

The second transformation took place in 2011, when the construction of a 250MW hydroelectric dam at Dumbbell Island caused several sets of white water, including the Grade V rapids Total Gunga and Silverback/Big Brother, and the emblematic Bujagali Falls itself, to be submerged below the reservoir now known as Lake Bujagali. This forced the rafting companies to relocate their embarkation point from the East Bank below Bujagali to the West Bank at Overtime, 8km downriver. A third transformation is now on the cards, following the recently commenced construction of the 180MW Isimbi Hydroelectric Dam about 10km further downriver. The completion of this dam, which is scheduled for 2016, though a couple of years later seems more likely, will result in the submersion of most of the Upper Nile's other major rapids, and sound the death knell on the once thriving white-water rafting industry.

GETTING THERE AND AWAY Bujagali lies 7km from Jinja along a clearly signposted road running north from the main roundabout (⊕ *0.44523, 33.19784*) on the Kampala Road. The junction to Jinja Nile Resort and Adrift Riverbase and complex is about 2.5km along this road. If you don't have your own transport and can't arrange or don't qualify for a lift with a rafting company, the best option from Kampala or Entebbe is the daily Pineapple Express (see page 125). From Jinja, a boda to Bujagali, Jinja Nile Resort or Adrift Riverbase will cost around US$1.50, and a private hire will charge around US$7–8. Alternatively, you can pick up a matatu from the main roundabout to Bujagali for less than US$1.

West Bank lodges such as Holland Park, The Haven and Wildwaters are all accessed from a quiet tarmac road that follows the Nile north from Njeru on the West Bank opposite Jinja. The junction (⊕ *0.44033, 33.1783*) is on the Kampala Road about 750m west of Owen Falls Dam, opposite Nile Breweries. If you're driving directly from Kampala, this stretch of road forms the last part of the route via Gayaza and Kayunga recommended under *Getting there and away* for Jinja (see pages 219–20). Public transport on this road runs from Kampala's old taxi park or from Njeru taxi park opposite Nile Breweries.

WHERE TO STAY *Map, page 241*
Bujagali and the East Bank
Upmarket

✳ 🏠 **The Nile Porch** (8 tents, 2 family cottages) ⊕ 0.48361, 33.16386; m 0782 321541; e relax@nileporch.com; www.nileporch.com. Superbly located on an elevated plateau fringed by acacia trees, Nile Porch overlooks Lake Bujagali, a lovely sight in the misty dawn or at sunset.

The luxury tents are spacious yet marvellously cosy, with 1 sgl & 1 dbl bed, walk-in mosquito netting, solar-powered hot water & river-facing verandas. Facilities include a swimming pool & it is the site if the superb Black Lantern Restaurant. 2-bedroom cottages for families are also available. Highly recommended. *US$113/136/166 sgl/dbl/trpl. US$213 cottage (sleeps 6) B&B.* **$$$$**

Jinja Nile Resort (125 rooms) ✆ 0.45757, 33.17981; ☎ 0434 122190; e nileresort@source. co.ug; www.madahotels.com. Once one of the country's most sumptuous hotels but now starting to look a little ragged at the edges, this sole Ugandan component of the Kenyan chain overlooks a stretch of the Nile studded with forested islands, about 2km downriver of the Owen Falls Dam. The spacious split-level mini-suites all have 2 beds (1 dbl, 1 sgl) with walk-in netting, a small sitting area with DSTV, fan & private balcony. Facilities include a fabulous swimming pool & outdoor bar area, gym, massage parlour, business centre, & squash & tennis courts. Unfortunately, some refurbishment would be required to justify the hefty price tag. *US$190/212 B&B sgl/dbl, or US$212/255 with a river view.* **$$$$**

Budget & camping
Nile River Camp (10 standing tents, 8 dorms) ✆ 0.48243, 33.16457; m 0776 900450; e bookings@camponthenile.com; www. camponthenile.com. This popular budget-friendly camp is owned by the adjacent Nile Porch & enjoys the same great lake view. Facilities include a swimming pool, a sociable bar serving mains in the US$3–5 range & activities such as mountain biking, kayaking & birding cruises. Standing tents have lake views & use common showers. *US$45 dbl tent, US$12 dorm bed, US6pp camping.* **$$**

Explorers River Camp (31 rooms & tents, 8 dorms) ✆ 0.48432, 33.16346; m 0782 320552; e nrecamp@raftafrica.com; www.raftafrica. com. Superbly located on a high bluff above Lake Bujagali, this popular & sociable base for rafting & other activities has a lively bar serving good meals for around US$5. It's operated by Nile River Explorers (NRE), & facilities include a day spa, book swap service, common shower with a lake view, & a zip-line chute. *US$50 en-suite dbl room, US$30 tents with lake view using shared shower, US$10pp dorm bed, US$5pp camping.* **$$**

Eden Rock Bandas (14 rooms) ✆ 0.48453, 33.16219; m 0772 970181; e contact@edenrocknile.com; www.edenrocknile. com. Eden Rock centres on a large & spacious thatched restaurant/lounge building that lacks a river view but compensates with lovely flowering gardens & a good-sized swimming pool. The en-suite bandas are very clean & seem well priced compared to the competition in this range. It

lacks the sociable vibe of its competitors, but will be preferable to people seeking peace & quiet. *US$35/45 b&b dbl/twin banda, US$10pp dorm, US$5pp camping.* **$$**

Adrift Riverbase (12 rooms, & tents & dorms) ✆ 0.46114, 33.17611. Located on something of a limb 500m north of Jinja Nile Resort, this once popular resort, affiliated to the rafting company Adrift, seemed a touch run down, indifferently managed & overpriced on last inspection. *US$70 dbl cottage, US$60 dbl furnished tents, US$12 dorm bed, all using shared facilities.* **$$$**

Kalagala Falls and the West Bank
Exclusive/Luxury
✳ **Wildwaters Lodge** (10 cottages) ✆ 0.59432, 33.05497 (parking); m 0772 237400; e info@wild-uganda.com; www.wildwaterslodge. com. This magnificent lodge sprawls across a forested island between 2 raging channels of white water at Kalagala Falls, 28km upriver of Jinja. The huge thatch-&-canvas en-suite cottages are beautifully appointed, decorated with genuine flair & come with a private balcony provided with an outdoor bathtub. Each cottage is individually shaped to the terrain & the forest setting, & while 6 cottages look directly into the roaring rapids, the remainder enjoy peaceful outlooks across a more placid stretch of river. The main lodge building is accommodating to trees, which grow upwards through the thatch, & has a well-stocked library corner with cosy armchairs, & a natural rock swimming pool artfully isolated from the river. The 5-course dinners are superb. Access to Wildwaters is by boat from a landing upstream of the rapids. *US$345/460 FB sgl/ dbl. Rates increase by US$100pp in Dec. Discounts for residents.* **$$$$$**

Upmarket
✳ **The Haven** (9 cottages) ✆ 0.54195, 33.08996; m 0702 905959; e thehavenuganda@ yahoo.com; www.thehaven-uganda.com. This riverside lodge, 17km along the road from Njeru, boasts a great location overlooking the Grade 5 Overtime Rapid, now the embarkation point for a white-water rafting excursion on the Upper Nile. The spacious en-suite bungalows, constructed using natural materials & decorated in earthy tones, have nets, river-facing balcony & hot showers, & there's a Honeymoon Cottage with a floor-level bathtub in front of a picture window overlooking the rapids.

The Nile is the world's longest river, flowing for 6,718km (4,174 miles) from its most remote headwater in Rwanda to the delta formed as it enters the Mediterranean in Egypt. Its vast drainage basin occupies more than 10% of the African mainland and includes portions of ten countries: Tanzania, Burundi, Rwanda, the DRC, Kenya, Uganda, Ethiopia, South Sudan, Sudan and Egypt. While passing through South Sudan, the Nile also feeds the 5.5-million-hectare Sudd or Bar-el-Jebel, the world's most expansive wetland system.

A feature of the Nile Basin is a marked decrease in precipitation as it runs further northward. In the East African lakes region and Ethiopian Highlands, mean annual rainfall figures are typically in excess of 1,000mm. Rainfall in south and central Sudan varies from 250mm to 500mm annually, except in the Sudd (900mm), while in the deserts north of Khartoum the annual rainfall is little more than 100mm, dropping to 25mm in the south of Egypt, then increasing to around 200mm closer to the Mediterranean.

The Nile has served as the lifeblood of Egyptian agriculture for millennia, carrying not only water, but also silt, from the fertile tropics into the sandy expanses of the Sahara. Indeed, it is widely believed that the very first agricultural societies arose on the floodplain of the Egyptian Nile, and so, certainly, did the earliest and most enduring of all human civilisations. The antiquity of the name Nile, which simply means 'river valley', is reflected in the ancient Greek (Nelios), Semetic (Nahal) and Latin (Nilus).

Over the past 50 years, several hydro-electric dams have been built along the Nile, notably the Aswan Dam in Egypt and the Owen Falls Dam in Uganda. The Aswan Dam doesn't merely provide hydro-electric power; it also supplies water for various irrigation schemes, and protects crops downriver from destruction by heavy flooding. Built in 1963, the dam wall rises 110m above the river and is almost 4km long, producing up to 2,100MW and forming the 450km-long Lake Nasser. The construction of the Aswan Dam enforced the resettlement of 90,000 Nubians, whilst the Temple of Abu Simbel, built 3,200 years ago for the Pharaoh Ramesses II, had to be relocated 65m higher.

The waterway plays a major role in transportation, especially in parts of the Sudan between May and November, when transportation of goods and people is not possible by road owing to the floods. Like other rivers and lakes, the Nile provides a variety of fish as food. And its importance for conservation is difficult

Pitch-your-own & lazy camping are also available. Facilities include a swimming pool & restaurant serving European cuisine. Shoreline wildlife includes fish eagles & other birds, red-tailed monkeys, otters & monitor lizards. *US$290 FB dbl Honeymoon Cottage, US$150 dbl Family House, plus US$40 per child, bandas from US$140/230 sgl/dbl, US$70/130 sgl/dbl lazy camping, US$50pp camping. All rates FB.* **$$$$**

🏠 **Kipling Lodge** (5 cottages) ✪ 0.56583, 33.07305; m 0794 020342; e lodgekipling@gmail.com or info@thekiplinglodge.com; www.thekiplinglodge.com. About to open as we went

to print, this new lodge enjoys a super view of the oncoming Nile from its position on a bend in the river. Wallow in the swimming pool, cruise up to the Overtime Rapid or hire a 350cc vintage Royal Enfield motorbike to explore local highways & byways. Kipling is located off the Kayunga Rd, about 17km north of Njeru. Accommodation is in thatched en-suite cottages. *US$150 dbl HB.* **$$$$**

Moderate

✳ 🏠 **Holland Park** (3 cottages, 1 safari tent) ✪ 0.4749, 33.15711; m 0782 507788; e info@hollandpark.com; www.hollandparkuganda.com.

to overstate. The Sudd alone supports more than half the global populations of Nile lechwe and shoebill (more than 6,000), together with astonishing numbers of other water-associated birds – aerial surveys undertaken between 1979 and 1982 counted an estimated 1.7 million glossy ibis, 370,000 marabou stork, 350,000 open-billed stork, 175,000 cattle egret and 150,000 spur-winged goose.

The Nile has two major sources, often referred to as the White and Blue Nile, which flow respectively from Lake Victoria near Jinja and from Lake Tana in Ethiopia. The stretch of the White Nile that flows through southern Uganda is today known as the Victoria Nile (it was formerly called Kiira locally). From Jinja, it runs northward through the swampy Lake Kyoga, before veering west to descend into the Rift Valley over Murchison Falls and empty into Lake Albert. The Albert Nile flows from the northern tip of Lake Albert to enter the Sudan at Nimule, passing through the Sudd before it merges with the Blue Nile at the Sudanese capital of Khartoum, more than 3,000km from Lake Victoria.

The discovery of the source of the Blue Nile on Lake Tana is often accredited to the 18th-century Scots explorer James Bruce. In fact, its approximate (if not exact) location was almost certainly known to the ancients. The Old Testament mentions that the Ghion (Nile) 'compasseth the whole land of Ethiopia', evidently in reference to the arcing course followed by the river along the approximate southern boundary of Ethiopia's ancient Axumite Empire. There are, too, strong similarities in the design of the papyrus *tankwa* used on Lake Tana to this day and the papyrus boats depicted in ancient Egyptian paintings. Furthermore, the main river feeding Lake Tana rises at a spring known locally as Abay Minch (literally 'Nile Fountain'), a site held sacred by Ethiopian Christians, whose links with the Egyptian Coptic Church date to the 4th century AD. Bruce's claim is further undermined by the Portuguese stone bridge, built c1620, which crosses the Nile a few hundred metres downstream of the Blue Nile Falls and only 30km from the Lake Tana outlet.

By contrast, the source of the White Nile was for centuries one of the world's great, unsolved mysteries. The Roman emperor Nero once sent an expedition south from Khartoum to search for it, but it was forced to turn back at the edge of the Sudd. In 1862, Speke correctly identified Ripon Falls as the source of the Nile, a theory that would be confirmed by Stanley in 1875. Since then, the river has been traced to various headwaters of the Kagera – the largest river flowing into Lake Victoria – in Rwanda and Burundi (see box, page 232).

Spread across a lovely 4ha garden on the lofty plateau above Lake Bujagali 4.5km from Njeru, this strictly self-catering set-up is deservedly popular with Kampala residents. With thatched roofs, mezzanine bedrooms, beautiful Indonesian wooden furniture & fitted kitchens (solar fridge, gas stove & all utensils) the cottages are quite delightful, as indeed is a more modest safari tent (also en suite with kitchen). Though relaxing in these exquisite surroundings – a pool with Wi-Fi lounge is provided – would seem sufficiently time-consuming, some guests manage to squeeze in a lake cruise or a boat trip across to

the East Bank. Great value. *US$100/150 sgl/dbl.* **$$$$**

Bohemia Resort (16 rooms)
0.50891, 33.12765; m 0750 026869; e info@bohemiaresortuganda.com; www.bohemiaresortuganda.com. This new lodge, situated 9km along the road from Njeru, occupies large undeveloped gardens with a pleasant pool area sloping down to a restaurant set on the bank of the Nile. More institutional than bohemian in feel, the cottages are laid out in a large square & face each other across an unprepossessing swathe of bare lawn. En-suite rooms are uncluttered, light

Bujagali is named after a set of fast-flowing rapids long held sacred by the local community as the home of an eponymous river spirit that manifested in more than 30 human incarnations over several centuries. Traditionally, anybody who claimed to be the spirit's newest reincarnation was required to prove it by sitting on a magical piece of barkcloth and drifting across the rapids. Only if he succeeded in this risky venture would the local villagers accept him as their new spiritual leader.

The last uncontested Bujagali died without nominating an heir in the 1970s, and the identity of his successor became the subject of a heated dispute. Most villagers believed the spirit resided in a local called Ja-Ja, who reputedly crossed the rapids on the magical barkcloth while evading military arrest under Idi Amin. Ja-Ja's rival for the title was an outsider called Jackson, who dreamed that he was the reincarnation of Bujagali, travelled to the village with a companion to stake his claim, then ran off with the magic barkcloth in order to float over the rapids. Before Jackson could attempt the crossing, however, he was caught by the villagers, who killed his companion. Jackson was banished to live out his days on a nearby island. In 2011, both the rapids and the island were submerged below what is now known as Lake Bujagali, making it unlikely there will ever be another reincarnation of the spirit for which it is named.

& airy, with white tiles, dark-wood furniture, dbl or twin bed & hot shower. *Decent value at US$80/100 b&b sgl/dbl, or an additional US$20pp FB.* **$$$**

🏠 **Baobab Cottage** (2 rooms) ⊕ 0.54972, 33.08111; m 07522 00073; f fb.me/BaobabCottageontheNile. This grand A-framed thatched self-catering cottage is the centrepiece of a state-of-the-art riverside smallholding 2km off the Kayunga Rd between Kipling Lodge & The Haven. The elevated deck at the front provides a Nile panorama which, if you're not shy, you can enjoy from an al fresco claw-foot bathtub. If you can't all fit in the cottage's 2 bedrooms, there's plenty of camping space. *US$60 for 1st person plus US$40 per additional guest.* **$$$**

Budget

✳ 🏠 **The Hairy Lemon** (6 rooms) ⊕ 0.67751, 33.05468; ☎ 043 4130349; m 0752 828338; e hairylemonuganda@gmail.com; www.hairylemonuganda.com. This great little camp, accessed from the West Bank of the river, stands on an island close to the rafting takeout point about 15km upriver of Kalagala Falls. The forested island supports an abundance of birdlife, as well as red-tailed monkeys & otters. The nearby Nile Special rapid is one of the world's best rafting 'play-holes'

anywhere. It is not unusual for devotees to spend a month or more here following a laid-back daily progression between the tent/dorm, dining area, amply cushioned chill-out shelters, 'frisbee golf' course & river. All rates include filling communal fare thrice daily (& tea/coffee at any time) with both meat & vegetarian food. Advance booking is essential & day visitors are not catered for. The island is 10km from Nazigo trading centre on the Njeru-Kayunga road (a boda costs around US$2), where you bang on a tyre rim to alert a boatman to collect you for the 2min boat crossing. Secure parking is provided. It is possible the island will be submerged following the completion of the Isimbi Dam during the lifespan of this edition. *From US$69/108 sgl/dbl twin banda, US$45pp lazy camping, US$38 dorm bed, US$30pp camping. All rates FB & using shared facilities.* **$$$**

✳ 🏠 **Tulina Riverside Retreat** (8 rooms & 1 dorm) ⊕ 0.54076, 33.09108; m 0752 460354/0772 610831; e tulina@tulinariverside.com; www.tulinariverside.com. This new budget lodge next to The Haven has a fabulous riverside setting in large pretty gardens, & functional but comfortable & well-priced en-suite rooms, & an adequate restaurant with terrace seating. *US$31/42 B&B sgl/dbl, or US$67 for a 4-bed dorm.* **$$**

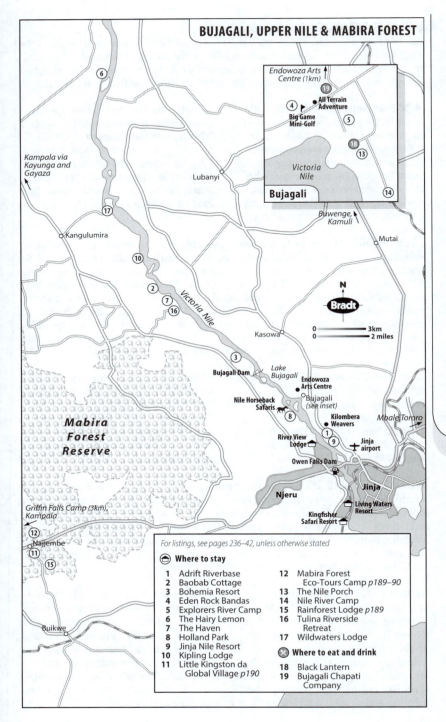

BUJAGALI, UPPER NILE & MABIRA FOREST

Endowoza Arts Centre (1km)

All Terrain Adventure

Big Game Mini-Golf

Victoria Nile

Bujagali

Kampala via Kayunga and Gayaza

Lubanyi

Buwenge, Kamuli

Mutai

Kangulumira

Victoria Nile

Kasowa

N

Bradt

| 0 | | 3km |
| 0 | | 2 miles |

Bujagali Dam

Lake Bujagali

Endowoza Arts Centre

Bujagali (see inset)

Nile Horseback Safaris

Kilombera Weavers

Mbale Tororo

River View Lodge

Jinja airport

Owen Falls Dam

Mabira Forest Reserve

Jinja

Njeru

Living Waters Resort

Griffin Falls Camp (3km), Kampala

Kingfisher Safari Resort

Najjembe

Buikwe

For listings, see pages 236–42, unless otherwise stated

⊖ **Where to stay**

1	Adrift Riverbase	12	Mabira Forest
2	Baobab Cottage		Eco-Tours Camp p189–90
3	Bohemia Resort	13	The Nile Porch
4	Eden Rock Bandas	14	Nile River Camp
5	Explorers River Camp	15	Rainforest Lodge p189
6	The Hairy Lemon	16	Tulina Riverside
7	The Haven		Retreat
8	Holland Park	17	Wildwaters Lodge
9	Jinja Nile Resort		
10	Kipling Lodge	⊗ **Where to eat and drink**
11	Little Kingston da		
	Global Village p190	18	Black Lantern
		19	Bujagali Chapati
			Company

✕ WHERE TO EAT AND DRINK *Map, page 241*

All the places listed under *Where to stay* serve food and the more isolated lodges on the West Bank generally include all meals in a full board package. Even on the East Bank, most travellers will end up eating at the same place they stay. There are, however, two bespoke eateries – at opposite ends of the quality and price spectrum – at Bujagali.

✳ ✕ **Black Lantern** ✆ 0.48361, 33.16386; m 0782 321541; e relax@nileporch.com; www. nileporch.com; ⏰ 07.00–21.30 daily. Attached to Nile Porch & under the same management, this stylish restaurant, with indoor & terrace seating facing Lake Bujagali, serves good salads & a cosmopolitan selection of mains including excellent steak, Mexican & Indian dishes, & various other grills. The house specialty is a full rack of spare ribs (*US$18*) but vegetarians are also well catered for. *Most dishes are in the US$8–10 range.*

✕ **Bujagali Chapati Company** ✆ 0.48494, 33.16316; m 0774 158346; ⏰ 05.00–23.00 daily. This cheap 'n' cheerful stall opposite the entrance to Explorers River Camp serves a great selection of filled chapatis – meat, vegetarian or sweet (eg: banana & Nutella). *Dishes around US$1.*

TOUR OPERATORS Nalubale and Nile River Explorers are well-established rafting operations that can boast of high safety standards and an excellent track record. So until recently was Adrift, but several reports suggest they have dropped the paddle following a recent change of ownership. White Nile Rafting is a promising new set-up established by Uganda's most experienced female kayaker and her Dutch husband. Feather & Fin is a newer subsidiary of Nalubale specialising in birding, fishing and other more sedate boating activities, and Kayak the Nile is a specialist kayaking operation based at Explorers River Camp. Other rafting companies do exist, but they have lower standards when it comes to safety and guiding.

Adrift ☎ 031 2237438; m 0772 237438; e raft@ adrift.ug; www.adrift.ug.
Feather & Fin m 0772 900451; ◼ fb.me/ featherandfinpursuits.
Kayak the Nile m 0772 880322; e info@ kayakthenile.com; www.kayakthenile.com.
Nalubale Rafting m 0782 638938;

e bookings@nalubalerafting.com; www. nalubalerafting.com; see ad, 3rd colour section.
Nile River Explorers (NRE) m 0772 422373; e rafting@raftafrica.com; www.raftafrica.com.
White Nile Rafting m 0782 836257/0787 508236; e info@whitenilerafting.com; www. whitenilerafting.com.

WHAT TO SEE AND DO White-water rafting is traditionally the most popular excursion on the Upper Nile, but a host of other activities are available and can be booked directly with the rafting operators listed above, or indirectly through any tour company in Jinja or backpacker hostel in Kampala. Should you be thinking of doing more than one activity, be aware that the rafting companies usually offer discounted packages combining rafting with other activities such as jet-boating, paddle-boarding, tandem kayaking and bungee-jumping.

White-water rafting
The rafting companies listed above offer similar one-day itineraries starting on the West Bank of the river above Overtime Rapid and finishing near Hairy Lemon Island, about 20km downriver. The route includes eight Grade III-or-higher rapids, including the Grade V Overtime and Bad Place, and it also offers an opportunity to see a lot of different birds, and to swim in calm stretches of water. All companies charge US$125 for a full-day excursion inclusive of return transportation from Kampala or Jinja, buffet lunch, and beers and sodas. Two-day rafting trips are also available at a cost of US$200–240, with day two offering fewer rapids but plenty of opportunity for paddle-boarding.

White-water and tandem kayaking The Upper Nile is a top spot for adventure kayaking, attracting experienced enthusiasts from across the world. Kayaking is a more testing activity than rafting, since it offers, in the words of an appreciative reader, 'the opportunity to develop your own skills, rather than just bouncing along in a raft controlled by the professionals'. Courses and expeditions are offered by Kayak the Nile, whose instructors are trained to the UK's BCU standard. Options start with a half/full-day introductory course (*US$85/115*) and progress to longer and more testing two-, three- or five-day courses. Full-on Grade V tandem kayaking (*US$140*) is also offered.

Flat-water kayaking The placid Lake Bujagali is ideal for short beginner or family kayaking trips, which are offered by Kayak the Nile (*US$20/hr, US$30 with a guide*) as well as by Nile River Camp, the home of Nalubale Rafting (*US$20/30 for 1/2 people for 2hrs, US$20 more for a guide*).

Lake cruises NRE now offers lunch and sunset cruises on Lake Bujagali in comfortable two-storeyed aluminium crafts (minimum group size five). The lunch

SOFT POWER

Bujagali Falls may be known as the adrenalin capital of East Africa, but it is also home to British charity Soft Power Education (SPE). In 1999 Hannah Small addressed a desire for visiting tourists to get involved in development for a day by offering tourists a unique one-day volunteering experience.

From humble beginnings of two pre-schools for 180 vulnerable children, which they continue to fund and run, SPE now runs a multitude of programmes ranging from conservation through to special needs.

An impressive education centre sits in the heart of Kyabirwa village, where Ugandan tutors instruct daily groups of visiting school children in topics either poorly represented in the local curriculum or lacking for materials, such as drama, art, library and computer use, as well as science and agriculture, all taught in a unique environment far removed from the classroom.

Today thanks to literally thousands of volunteers spending one day, a month or a year volunteering with SPE, over 80 schools in both Jinja and Buliisa have been lifted out of their dilapidated states with permanent classrooms, rainwater-collection tanks and safe latrines. Over 700 classrooms have been built, refurbished and painted thanks to the generosity of these volunteers. In 2015 SPE also began building teachers' houses in an effort to deepen their impact on the education system.

On average, Soft Power Education raises over £250,000 annually through the support of visiting overland passengers, independent long-term volunteers, groups of university students, standing orders, one-off donations and fundraising by ex-volunteers in their home countries.

The core of its success lies in creating innovative volunteer programmes to suit everyone's budget whilst ensuring donations reach their intended target. Its reputation for spending donations wisely has allowed SPE to expand beyond those early beginnings. SPE is a fabulous place to volunteer and we are happy to see that it has grown into a serious development organisation, now also working in conservation, special needs and livelihoods. Soft Power Education welcomes volunteers from one day through to 12 months. For more details contact e info@ softpowereducation.com or check out www.softpowereducation.com.

When Speke prepared for his first audience with King Mutesa of Baganda, he put on his finest clothes, but admitted that he 'cut a poor figure in comparison with the dressy Baganda [who] wore neat bark cloaks resembling the best yellow corduroy cloth, crimp and well set, as if stiffened with starch'.

The stiff, neat barkcloth cloak or *mbugu*, as described by Speke, was the conventional form of attire throughout Baganda for at least 100 years prior to the coronation of Mutesa. Exactly how and when the craft arose is unknown. One legend has it that Kintu, the founder of Baganda, brought the craft with him from the heavens, which would imply that it was introduced to the kingdom, possibly from Bunyoro. Another story is that the Bachwezi leader Wamala discovered barkcloth by accident on a hunting expedition, when he hammered a piece of bark to break it up, and instead found that it expanded laterally to form a durable material.

Whatever its origin, barkcloth has been worn in Baganda for several centuries, though oral tradition maintains that the cloth was originally worn only by the king and members of his court, while commoners draped themselves more skimpily in animal skins. In the late 18th century, however, King Semakokiro decreed that all his subjects should grow and wear barkcloth – men draped it over their shoulders, women tied it around their waist – or they would be fined or sentenced to death. At around the same time, barkcloth exported from Baganda grew in popularity in most neighbouring kingdoms, where it was generally reserved for the use of royalty and nobles.

Ironically, the historical association between barkcloth cloaks and social prestige was reversed in Baganda towards the end of the 19th century, when barkcloth remained the customary attire of the peasantry, but the king permitted his more favoured subjects to wear cotton fabrics imported by Arab traders. During the early decades of colonial rule, the trend away from barkcloth spread through all social strata. W E Hoyle, who arrived in Kampala in 1903, noted that barkcloth clothing was then 'so very common'. By 1930, when Hoyle departed from Uganda, it had been 'discarded in favour of "amerikani" (cotton sheeting); and later *kanzus* (of finer cotton material known as "bafta"), with a jacket of the cheaper imported cloth and a white round cap, the ideal "Sunday best"'. Hoyle also noted that while 'women kept to barkcloth much longer than men … by the 1920s many were attired in the finest cotton materials and silks'. In the early 1930s, Lucy Mair recorded that 'European [cloths] are popular and barkcloth is made for sale by not more than three or four men in each village'. By the time of independence, barkcloth had practically disappeared from everyday use.

Barkcloth – *olubugo* in Luganda – can be made from the inner bark lining of at least 20 tree species. The best-quality cloth derives from certain species in the genus *Ficus*, which were extensively cultivated in pre-colonial Baganda and regarded as the most valuable of trees after the plantain. Different species of tree yielded different

cruise costs US$30 inclusive of a buffet meal, and the sunset cruise US$45 inclusive of snacks, all the lager you can drink in two hours and, if you're paying attention, a sunset. Feather & Fin also offers more sober sunset cruises for US$25 per person (minimum group size is four).

Birding trips Lake Bujagali offers excellent opportunities for birding, with up to 150 species having been seen in one day. Local specialties include white-backed night heron, rock pratincole, papyrus gonolek and crimson-rumped

textures and colours, from yellow to sandy brown to dark red-brown. The finest-quality rusty brown cloth, called *kimote*, is generally worn on special occasions only. A specific type of tree that yielded a white cloth was reserved for the use of the king, who generally wore it only at his coronation ceremony.

The common barkcloth tree can be propagated simply by cutting a branch from a grown one and planting it in the ground – after about five years the new tree will be large enough to be used for making barkcloth. The bark will be stripped from any one given tree only once a year, when it is in full leaf. After the bark has been removed, the trunk is wrapped in green banana leaves for several days, and then plastered with wet cow dung and dry banana leaves, to help it heal. If a tree is looked after this way, it might survive 30 years of annual use.

The bark is removed from the tree in one long strip. A circular incision is made near the ground, another one below the lowest branches, and then a long line is cut from base to top, before finally a knife is worked underneath the bark to ease it carefully away from the trunk. The peeled bark is left out overnight before the hard outer layer is scraped off, and then it is soaked. It is then folded into two halves and laid out on a log to be beaten with a wooden mallet on alternating sides to become thinner. When it has spread sufficiently, the cloth is folded in four and the beating continues. The cloth is then unfolded before being left to dry in the sun.

There are several local variations in the preparation process, but the finest cloth reputedly results when the freshly stripped bark, instead of being soaked, is steamed for about an hour above a pot of boiling water, then beaten for an hour or so daily over the course of a week. The steaming and extended process of beating is said to improve the texture of the cloth and to enrich the natural red-brown or yellow colour of the bark.

Although it is used mostly for clothing, barkcloth can also serve as a blanket or a shroud, and is rare but valued as bookbinding. At one time, barkcloth strips patterned with the natural black Muzukizi dye became a popular house decoration in Kampala. Sadly, however, barkcloth production appears to be a dying craft, and today it would be remarkable to see anybody wandering around Kampala wrapped in a bark cloak. It is still customary to wear it in the presence of the king, and at funerals, when barkcloth is also often wrapped around the body of the deceased.

One place where you can be certain of seeing some impressive strips of red barkcloth is at the Kasubi Tombs in Kampala (pages 161–2). If you're interested in looking for barkcloth at source, the forests around Sango Bay in Buddu County, south of Masaka, are traditionally regarded as producing the highest-quality material in Baganda. The Ugandan artist Mugalula Mukiibi is dedicated to reviving the dying craft through his work, and a number of his abstracts painted on traditional barkcloth can be viewed online (*www.mugalulaarts.com*).

waxbill. Feather & Fin offers half-/full-day birding cruises with expert guides for US$40/90 per person. Minimum group size is four, and the full-day cruise includes lunch.

Fishing trips Yellow fish, Nile perch and catfish are among the more alluring fish that inhabit Lake Bujagali and the Nile, but densities are low due to netting. As a result, Feather & Fin no longer offers fishing trips on the lake, but it can arrange bespoke multi-day fishing excursions in the area.

Quad biking Based in Bujagali (next to Eden Rock), All Terrain Adventures (m *0772 377185;* e *info@atadventures.com; www.atadventures.com;* ⊕ *08.00–17.00 daily*) runs quad-biking trips following local footpaths and tracks that connect some stunning Nile viewpoints. Rates range from US$49 per person for an hour-long ride to US$195 per person for an 8-hour day with lunch. A two-day trip along the Nile Valley costs US$275 including overnight accommodation and meals.

Mountain biking Mountain bikes can be hired from several hotels and lodges on the Upper Nile. A recommended specialist, based at Nile River Camp, is Alex Dot Com (m *0782 063780/0776 900450;* e *alexdotcombiked260@gmail.com*), which charges US$30/45 per person for a 2-/4-hour guided trip. Rates for unguided bike usage are negotiable.

Horseriding All horseback excursions offered by various operators in and around Jinja are run by Nile Horseback Safaris (⊕ *0.47585, 33.15479;* m *0701 101196/0774 101196;* e *info@nilehorsebacksafaris.com; www.nilehorsebacksafaris.com*), whose stables, housing around 20 calm and well-cared-for horses, stand on the West Bank about 4.5km north of Njeru. Short safaris leave daily at 10.00 and 14.00, and sunset safaris leave on demand at 16.30 on Fridays and Saturdays. For more experienced riders, overnight and multi-day safaris using upmarket lodges on the Nile West Bank and in Mabira Forest are also available, as are kids' pony rides. Day rates range from US$40per person for 1 hour to US$80 per person for 3 hours.

Bungee jumping While most activities along the Jinja Nile explore water and terra firma, at Adrift's Nile High Camp (between Jinja and Bujagali) you can investigate (fleetingly) a 44m column of thin air – an experience enabled by a 12m cantilevered steel bungee tower atop a 32m riverside cliff. The cost is US$115, a second jump costs US$50, and the third is free. Discounts are available to East Africa residents and as part of a combo that also includes rafting.

Kilombera Weaving (⊕ *0.46951, 33.16979;* m *0793 439619/0772 824206;* e *kilomberaweaving@gmail.com;* f *fb.me/kilomberaweaving;* ⊕ *09.00–17.00 Mon–Fri, 09.00–13.00 Sat*) Named after a species of weaver bird that spends hours weaving its intricate nest in order to attract a mate, Kilombera Weaving specialises in colourful and lightweight handwoven cotton kikois, hammocks, bedspreads and other items made using traditional looms. Its new workshop and retail outlet, overlooking the Nile midway between Jinja Nile Resort and Bujagali, can provide a demonstration of the weaving process by arrangement.

Endowoza Arts Centre (⊕ *0.48883, 33.16212;* m *0774 162541;* ⊕ *08.30–16.30 Mon–Fri*) This centre forms part of Soft Power Education (SPE)'s programme with the Amagezi Education Centre (AEC), where pupils from primary schools within Jinja come for hands-on interactive lessons in art, drama, ICT, library and child protection. Although pupils visit during term time only, the AEC operates throughout the year and a small shop (proceeds to SPE) sells locally made crafts and knitted items created by its own knitting group. Endowoza and the AEC are located in Kyabirwa village just a 5-minute walk from Bujagali.

Mini-golf The Big Game Mini-Golf course complete with concrete hippos, tigers, buffalo, etc, is situated next to All Terrain Adventure's quad-biking compound and charges US$3 per person for a round.

10

Mbale and the Mount Elgon Region

Straddling the Kenyan border east of Kampala and Jinja, freestanding Mount Elgon, centrepiece of an eponymous national park on both sides of the border, is the second-highest massif in Uganda at 4,321m, and it boasts the largest base of any extinct volcano in the world. Although it is a worthwhile and relatively affordable hiking destination, the national park sees relatively little tourist traffic compared to the Rwenzori, though Sipi Falls, on its western footslopes, has long been popular with backpackers and volunteers looking for a relaxed rambling destination to settle into for a few days. The main town in the region, set at the base of the mountain, is Mbale, an agreeable but unremarkable place associated with the unusual Abayudaya, a Jewish community founded by a Ugandan in the early 20th century. Also of interest are Tororo, a small but rather pretty town set below a large volcanic plug, and the Nyero Rock Art Site and Pain Upe Wildlife Reserve north of Mount Elgon. Lake Bisina, also to the north of Elgon, is the best place to look for the endemic Fox's weaver.

BUSIA

The busiest border crossing between Kenya and Uganda is Busia (⊕ *0.46521, 34.09958*), which lies on the main highway between the Nairobi and Kampala. Busia is also the name of the similarly sized twin towns that flank the border post, both of which are significant trade and market centres with a population of around 55,000 apiece. Arriving from Kenya by bus, most travellers continue straight on through to Jinja or Kampala, but if you need to stop over, there are several banks with ATMs, including a Barclays only 100m from the border post.

GETTING THERE AND AWAY Busia lies about 450km west of Nairobi, 120km west of Kisumu, 120km east of Jinja and 200km east of Kampala. All coaches running between the two countries stop there to complete border formalities. There are also plenty of matatus from the taxi park to the likes of Tororo, Jinja, Mbale and Kampala.

WHERE TO STAY The pick of the lodgings are the friendly and comfortable **Jireh Christian Guesthouse** and the nearby **Rand Hotel**, which is ostensibly smarter but rather rundown, and has a good garden restaurant. Both lie alongside the main road to Kampala about 3km from the border post. On the Kenyan side, about 1.5km from the border post, is the superior **Farmland Hotel** (⊕ *0.45769, 34.10547;* ☏ *+254 (020) 2315443;* e *info@farmviewhotel.com; farmviewhotel.com*).

WHAT TO SEE AND DO
Majanji The closest thing to an established tourist attraction in the Busia District is Majanji, which lies on an attractive bay on the Lake Victoria shore about 30km to

the south. Here, the **Sangalo Beach Resort** (0.24081, 33.99119; 0772 503693/0701 503693; info@sangalosandbeach.com; www.sangalosandbeach.com) is a pleasant and low-key set-up with a stunning setting on a palm-lined peninsula facing the small Kenyan port of Sio. Rooms are a little rundown but decent value (*US$20/25 B&B sgl/ dbl or US$25/30 for a thatched banda*), and the restaurant serves decent enough meals. Beaten-up matatus run to Majanji from the Busia police station, but you may need to transfer to a boda for the last few kilometres to the resort.

Busitema Forest Reserve Bisected by the Kampala–Tororo Road as it runs northeast from the junction to Busia, this reserve protects 28km² of semi-deciduous woodland comprising more than 200 tree species depleted by recent encroachment and a voracious bush fire in 2015. Baboons and other monkeys are frequently seen from the roadside, and its birdlife reputedly includes the endemic Fox's weaver. No entrance fee is charged.

TORORO

Situated 10km west of the Malaba border post with Kenya, this backwater of around 42,000 people is best known as the site of the iconic Tororo Rock, an isolated volcanic plug that rises about 300m above the town centre to an altitude of 1,485m, where it is capped by a copse of radio and satellite masts. For much of the 20th century, Tororo was one of Uganda's important rail, road and trade hubs, but it has fallen off the travel map in recent years – partly because of the railway's closure, partly because Busia is now the more popular border crossing with Kenya, and partly because there is now a more direct and westerly surfaced road connecting Mbale to Kampala/Jinja. Still, Tororo's exaggeratedly wide pavements, lined with a straggle of flowering trees and colonial-era façades, pay testament to its former prosperity, as does a trio of impressive Hindu temples. The town's main attraction is the eminently climbable Tororo Rock, and the views offered from the top.

HISTORY Although little information is available about the early history of Tororo, the Catholic Apostolic Vicariate of Upper Nile was established immediately north of the present-day town centre in 1894. The original Uganda Railway terminated at Tororo when it started operation in 1926, and it remained an important rail hub after 1931 when it became the junction of new lines running west to Kampala and north to Soroti. Well located for cross-border trade and the site of Uganda's main cement factory from 1952 onwards, Tororo supported roughly 1,000 Asian and European settlers by the time of independence, when it ranked among Uganda's ten most populous and prosperous towns. Its economic significance has since diminished, partly because of the closure of the railway in the 1990s and associated ascent of more southerly Busia as the more important border crossing with Kenya. Two recent developments bode well for the future of Tororo. In 2010, a site near Malaba, 15km to the east, was designated for the construction of a US$120 million dry port where containers coming from the Kenyan coast will be stored for clearance prior to being transported to other parts of Uganda or to neighbouring Rwanda, Burundi, South Sudan and DR Congo. In July 2015, the Tororo Cement Company, which had been privatised in the 1990s, commenced on a US$25 million expansion to increase its annual production from 1.8 to 3.0 million metric tonnes.

GETTING THERE AND AWAY Tororo lies on the old surfaced road between Jinja (130km to the west) and Mbale (40km to the north), at the junction with the road

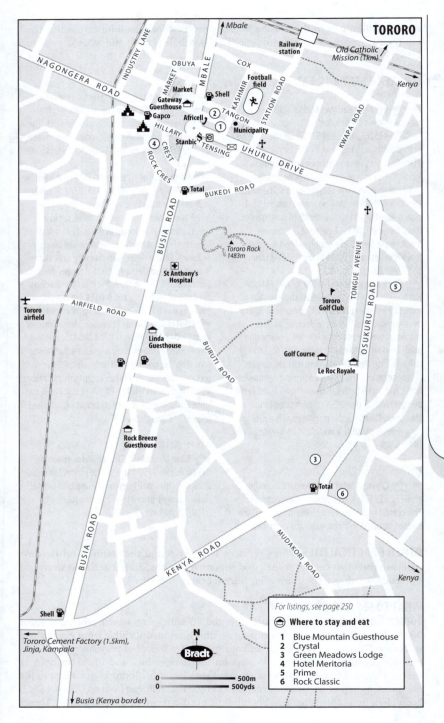

↑ Mbale

Railway station

Old Catholic Mission (1km) ↗

Kenya →

OBUYA

COX

Football field

Market

Gateway Guesthouse

Shell

Gapco

Africell

Municipality

Stanbic

KASHMIR

TANGON

STATION ROAD

KWAPA ROAD

NAGONGERA ROAD

INDUSTRY LANE

MARKET

MBALE

HILLARY

CREST

ROCK CRES

BUSIA ROAD

TENSING

UHURU DRIVE

Total

BUKEDI ROAD

Tororo Rock 1483m

St Anthony's Hospital

✈ Tororo airfield

AIRFIELD ROAD

Linda Guesthouse

BURUTI ROAD

Tororo Golf Club

Golf Course

Le Roc Royale

TONGUE AVENUE

OSUKURU ROAD

Rock Breeze Guesthouse

Shell

BUSIA ROAD

KENYA ROAD

MUDAKORI ROAD

Kenya →

Total

↓ Busia (Kenya border)

← Tororo Cement Factory (1.5km), Jinja, Kampala

N

Bradt

0 ————— 500m
0 ————— 500yds

For listings, see page 250

⌂ **Where to stay and eat**

1 Blue Mountain Guesthouse
2 Crystal
3 Green Meadows Lodge
4 Hotel Meritoria
5 Prime
6 Rock Classic

running 10km east to the Malaba border post. Few long-haul buses use this road, but regular matatus run to/from Jinja (*US$3*), Mbale (*US$1*) and Malaba (*less than US$1*).

WHERE TO STAY AND EAT   *Map, page 249*

Moderate

✳ 🏠 **Green Meadows Lodge**   (12 rooms) Buwesa Close (off Malaba Rd); m 0755 435063/0756 628877; e info@ greenmeadowslodge.com. By far the nicest place to stay in Tororo, this quiet out-of-town lodge stands in well-tended gardens on the slopes below the main cement quarry. The neat, spacious & modern-looking rooms come with 1 queen-sized or 2 ¾ beds with fitted nets, garden view, flatscreen DSTV & en-suite hot shower, & a restaurant serves a selection of fried & grilled meat & vegetarian dishes in the US$5–7 range. *US$33/40 B&B sgl/dbl.* **$$**

🏠 **Rock Classic Hotel**   (100 rooms) Malaba Rd; m 0775 024945; e rockclassichotel@yahoo. com. The imposing stone-clad frontage of Tororo's best-known hotel flatters to deceive, as does the attractive garden complete with swimming pool. Tired en-suite rooms come with AC, DSTV, balcony, fitted nets & terrifying maroon carpets, & service retains the feel of a former government hotel. Not much better than any hotel listed in the budget range & dismal value compared to Green Meadows. That said, the poolside bar is a nice spot for a drink & possibly a meal. *US$40/57/60 sgl/dbl/ twin.* **$$$**

Budget

✳ 🏠 **Crystal Hotel**   (14 rooms) Bazaar Rd; m 0772 555174; e crystalhoteltororo@gmail.com. This central multi-storeyed building has been the budget standout in Tororo since the early 1990s, &

it remains so today following recent renovations. Clean tiled en-suite rooms come with net, fan DSTV, & a private balcony facing Tororo Rock. The inexpensive ground-floor restaurant remains the best central option, too. *US$15/17/20 B&B sgl/dbl/ twin.* **$$**

🏠 **Prime Hotel**   (26 rooms) Off Malaba Rd; ☎0392 791862; m 0700 598828/0772 591862; e primehoteltororo@gmail.com; www.prime-hotel-tororo.com. This modern hotel, set in a green, garden compound in the leafy Malakasi suburb, seems to be the popular choice for visitors to Tororo. Staff members are friendly, articulate & seem efficient, & the restaurant serves good continental & Indian food. The rates for spacious tiled rooms with nets, fan & DSTV are extremely friendly, too. *US$27/29/39 B&B sgl/dbl/twin.* **$$**

🏠 **Hotel Meritoria**   (20 rooms) Rock Crescent West; ☎048 4437693; m 0774 005415; e info@ www.hotelmeritoria.com; www.hotelmeritoria. com. Another good central hotel, despite the preposterous name, this has acceptable but rather small tiled rooms with DSTV, Wi-Fi, balcony & en-suite hot shower. A decent restaurant is attached. *US$18/24 B&B sgl/dbl.* **$$**

Shoestring

🏠 **Blue Mountain Guesthouse**   (6 rooms) Bazaar Rd; m 0752 740935. The pick of Tororo's cheapies, this small guesthouse opposite Crystal Hotel has well-priced tiled en-suite rooms. *US$9/12 dbl/twin.* **$**

OTHER PRACTICALITIES Forex services are provided at the **Stanbic** and **Barclays** banks in the town centre. Some good **supermarkets** are located at the western end of Bazaar Road, and there are a few internet cafés.

WHAT TO SEE AND DO

Tororo Rock   This steep and partly forested volcanic plug, which protrudes about 300m above the town centre's southern skyline, is reputedly visible from everywhere in Tororo District. It takes about an hour to climb, a short but very steep hike using recently constructed steps and ladders on the trickier bits, and up to an hour to descend again. The peak offers panoramic views towards Mount Elgon 35km to the northeast, as well as across the border into Kenya. The trailhead (✪ 0.68375, 34.18743) is on High Road (off Tongue Av) behind the northern end of the golf course. There's

no entrance fee. Guides are optional but recommended, and can be arranged through the Rock Classic and most other hotels in town, and usually ask around US$5 per party. The best time to hike is in the relative cool of the early morning.

Tororo Golf Club
(*Tongue Av;* ✆ *0.67752, 34.18926;* ☎ *039 2965103;* m *0772 434018*) Visitors are welcome at this venerable club, whose nine-hole golf course, set at the southeast base of Tororo Rock, was constructed during the town's 1950s heyday and is still very well tended but rather undersubscribed to. Other facilities are a badminton court, snooker table, tennis court, the best swimming pool in town and a good restaurant/bar. A nominal fee is charged to outsiders for use of the pool or to play a round of golf.

MBALE

Perched at a temperate altitude of 1,200m on the western footslopes of Mount Elgon, Mbale is an agreeable and substantial town whose compact and rather hectic centre is surrounded by leafy suburbs, sprawling eastward to the foot of the dramatic Wanale Cliffs. The town was established at the start of the 20th century (see box, pages 252–3) and soon grew to become Uganda's third most populous settlement, a status it retained until the mid-1990s, since when it has slipped to 11th place, with population now estimated at about 98,000. Relatively few travellers visit Mbale, and those who do generally pass through briefly in transit to Mount Elgon or the Sipi Falls. Despite this, Mbale has a greater sense of place than most Ugandan towns east of the Nile, thanks largely to its striking cliff-base location below Mount Elgon, whose volcanic peaks are sometimes visible in clear weather. Also in its favour, Mbale was left relatively unscarred by the events of 1971–86, and its streets are lined with many well-preserved examples of colonial-era Asian and European architecture.

GETTING THERE AND AWAY Mbale lies about 230km from Kampala along an excellent surfaced road through Jinja and Iganga (turn left about 3km east of Iganga to avoid Tororo and follow the almost traffic-free new road to its west). Traffic congestion on the outskirts of Kampala, plus slow trailers and tankers on the Jinja Road, mean that the trip can take up to 4 hours. Other distances and estimated driving times are 144km/2 hours from Jinja, 55km/45 minutes from Tororo, 100km/90 minutes from Soroti, and 45km/45 minutes from Sipi.

There is plenty of public transport from Kampala to Mbale. A popular option is the **Post Bus**, which leaves Kampala from the main post office on Kampala Road at 08.00 daily except Sundays, and takes about 6 hours to reach Mbale *en route* to Lira. A faster and equally reliable option from Kampala is the **Elgon Flyer bus** (m *0200 900323*), which leaves from Colville Street. YY Coaches (f *fb.me/yycoaches*) has also been recommended. Regular **matatus** out of the old taxi park are quicker still, but driven with less care. These are the best option coming to or from Jinja (*US$3*), Tororo (*US$1*) or Soroti (*US$2*). Most local places of interest can be reached by matatu and details are given under the individual sites later in this chapter.

WHERE TO STAY
Upmarket
✷ 🏠 **Mount Elgon Hotel & Spa** [254 F3] (50+ rooms) Masaba Rd; ☎ 045 4433454; m 0773 008903; e sales@mountelgonhotel.com; www. mountelgonhotel.com. Built in 1958, this stalwart former government hotel, set in spacious grounds

In 1900, the narrow belt of no-man's-land that divided the cultivated footslopes of Nkokonjeru and its Bagisu inhabitants from the pastoralist people of the Kyoga Basin made a less than favourable impression on visitors. C J Phillips described the area as 'a long wilderness of scrub', William Grant deemed it 'a dreary waste', while one early Muganda visitor called it 'a small and fearsome place, swarming with wild animals'. Back then, certainly, it would have taken a bold soul to suggest this area would become the site of the third-largest town in Uganda! But then Mbale is possibly unique among comparably sized East African towns in that it isn't rooted in a pre-colonial settlement, nor is it truly a colonial creation, but was instead founded by the controversial Muganda administrator and soldier Semei Kakungulu.

Between 1889 and 1901, Kakungulu had single-handedly – or rather with the assistance of a private army of 5,000 Baganda soldiers – subjugated and administered the region of eastern Uganda known as Bukedi (a disparaging Luganda term meaning 'Land of Naked People') as an agent of the British Crown. By 1901, however, Kakungulu was perceived by his colonial paymasters to have developed into a tyrannical force – the self-appointed 'King of Bukedi' – that they could neither stem nor control. In the words of A L Hitching, Kakungulu had indeed 'first reduced [Bukedi] to order, cut the roads, and began to direct the local chiefs', but it was 'rather after the method of making desolation and calling it peace'. And bad enough, that Kakungulu and his army evidently regarded Bukedi 'as a sort of El Dorado', raiding the local cattle and crops at whim. Worse still, the authorities at Entebbe had every reason to believe that their employee was less than scrupulous when it came to declaring and returning the tax he had collected in his official capacity for the Crown.

The Entebbe administration decided that this untenable situation could be resolved only by retiring the self-styled King of Bukedi from the colonial service. But how to achieve this when any hint of force might prompt Kakungulu's army to stage a rebellion the authorities would find difficult to contain? A series of tense communications resulted in a mutually agreeable compromise: Kakungulu would resign his post and hand over his fort at Budoka (30km west of present-day Mbale). In exchange, he would be given 20 square miles (52km^2) of land at a site of his own choosing. Kakungulu selected the plains below Nkokonjeru, which, although practically unoccupied, were run through by several perennial streams and lay close to a reliable supply of the favoured Baganda diet of *matoke*.

Kakungulu and his Baganda followers relocated to Mbale in March 1902, and immediately set about building a new township, one that by several accounts bore strong similarities to the Buganda royal enclosure on Kampala's Mengo Hill. The first European visitors to trickle through Mbale in early 1903 were astonished at the transformation wrought by Kakungulu in one brief year. Bishop Tucker reported that 'on what was little better than a wilderness … we found ourselves surrounded by gardens, well cultivated and well kept; houses, too, had sprung up on every hand, most of them well built'. An equally gushing William Grant described Mbale as 'flourishing with gardens, teeming with life' and added that 'good wide roads have been cut, rivers have been bridged and embankments made through marshy ground, all at [Kakungulu's] expense and for public use'. A map of Mbale dating to 1904 indicates that the central market

was situated roughly where the clock tower stands today. Running southwest from the market, a wide road lined with shops and houses approximated the equivalent stretch of present-day Kumi Road. This road continued southwest for about 300m to Kakungulu's fortified compound, which consisted of a large rectangular stone building and seven smaller huts protected within a tall reed fence.

This rapid growth of Mbale was not solely due to its founder's estimable ambition and drive. One contemporary visitor, the missionary J J Willis, described the town's location as 'a natural centre' for trade, elaborating that: 'An excellent road connects Mbale with Jinja to the southwest. A caravan route, very far from excellent, connects it with Mumias to the south. Caravans [from Karamoja] pass through Mbale laden with ivory. And to the northwest a caravan route passes through Serere and Bululu to the Nile Province.' Mbale usurped nearby Mumias as the most important regional trading centre; indeed its market soon became the largest anywhere in the protectorate after Kampala and Entebbe. The permanent population of the nascent metropolis – estimated by Willis to stand at around 3,000 – comprised not only Kakungulu's Buganda followers, but also a substantial number of Greek, Arab, Indian and Swahili traders.

In hindsight, it might be said that when Kakungulu handed over Budoka Fort to Britain, he did not so much abandon his 'El Dorado' as relocate it (and expand it) at his personal estate of Mbale. That much was recognised by the new commissioner, James Sadler, when he made a tour of Bukedi in January 1904. Sadler characterised the established administrative centre at Budoka as consisting of 'two wattle and daub houses and some dilapidated police lines' on a 'bad' site that was 'neither liked by Europeans nor natives'. Mbale, by contrast, impressed him as 'the natural trade centre of the district [and] centre of a Baganda civilisation [of] flourishing plantations [and] substantially built grass-roofed houses'. Sadler decided that Mbale should forthwith replace Budoka as the administrative centre of Bukedi, and attempted to rein in Kakungulu by reappointing him to the regional administration. In 1906, the authorities realised that they would gain full control over Bukedi only in the physical absence of Kakungulu, which they achieved not by retiring him, but by tantalising him away to Jinja to serve as the official head of state of Busoga, a position he held until 1913.

Mbale's rise to prominence had its setbacks. In 1909, Cook described it as a 'thriving little place entered along a broad well-kept road, nearly a mile in length, bordered by thousands of *emsambya* trees and numerous native houses … crowded with the once-turbulent Bagisu engaged in the peaceful activity of bartering their native produce'. A year later, the colonial administration – for a variety of opaque reasons – banned the ivory trade from Karamoja, causing foreign traders to desert Mbale and the district commissioner to bemoan that 'a legacy of debts is about all that remains of what used to be a profitable and flourishing business'. A few years later, tentative plans to relocate the regional administration to Bugondo, a newly developed ferry port on Lake Kyoga and the site of two large ginneries, were shelved following the outbreak of World War I. As it transpired, Bugondo's brief heyday would be curtailed by a post-war drought that left it high and dry, while the strategic location chosen by Kakungulu took on fresh significance with the rise of the motor vehicle as the natural hub of the road network east of Lake Kyoga.

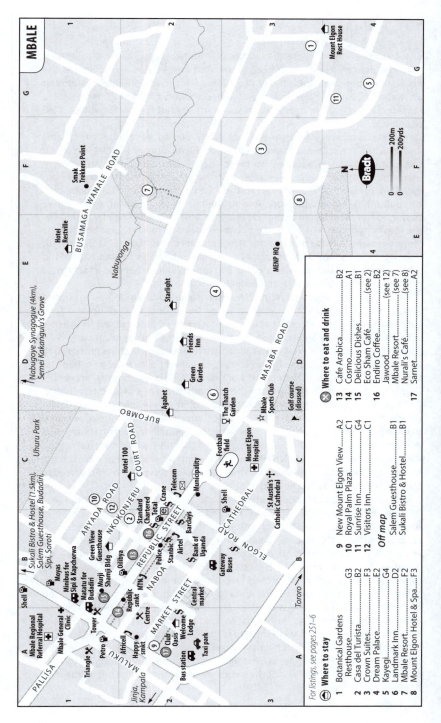

MBALE

BUSAMAGA WANALE ROAD

Nabuyonga

Uhuru Park

Nabugoye Synagogue (4km),
Semei Kakangulu's Grave

BUFOMBO

COURT ROAD

ARYADA ROAD

NKOKONJERU

NABOA STREET

REPUBLIC STREET

MARKET STREET

PALLISA

MALUKU

Jinja,
Kampala

Tororo

ELGON ROAD

CATHEDRAL

MASABA ROAD

N

Bradt

0 ▬▬▬ 200m
0 ▬▬▬ 200yds

Mount Elgon
Rest House

Hotel
Restville

Smak
Trekkers Point

Starlight

Friends
Inn

Green
Garden

Agabet

The Thatch
Garden

Mbale
Sports Club

Golf course
(disused)

Football
field

Mount Elgon
Hospital

MENP HQ

St Austin's ✝
Catholic Cathedral

Municipality

Telecom

Crane

Standard
Chartered Total

Bardays

Bank of
Uganda

Airtel

Stanbic

Police

MTN

Shanji Bldg

Oilibya

Murji

Green View
Guesthouse

Hotel 100

Matatu for
Budadiri

Moyas
Minibus for
Sipi & Kapchorwa

Mbale General
Clinic

Mbale Regional
Referral Hospital

Shell

Tower

Petro

Triangle

Afritell

Happy
smkt

Welcome
Lodge

Club
Oasis

Centre

Republic
smkt

Central
market

Bus station

Taxi park

Gateway
Buses

Shell

Sukali Bistro & Hostel (1.5km),
Salem Guesthouse, Budadiri

Sipi, Soroti

254

facing the Wanale Cliffs 1km from the town centre, is the most characterful & classy option in Mbale following a thorough refurbishment a few years back. Spacious & stylishly decorated en-suite rooms all come with queen-sized or twin beds, netting, AC, DSTV & hot shower, while the well-maintained gardens incorporate a swimming pool terrace, mini-golf course & luxurious spa. The restaurant serves a varied menu with most mains in the US$8.50–10 range. *From US$80/100 standard sgl/dbl to US$150/160 junior suite. All rates B&B.* **$$$**

✳ 🏠 **Mbale Resort Hotel** [254 F2] (94 rooms) Bungukho Rd; 📞045 4434485; e sales@ mbaleresorthotel.com; www.mbaleresorthotel. com. Situated 1.5km east of the town centre, this plush & professionally managed 3-storey hotel – briefly part of the South African Protea hotel chain – stands in large, leafy suburban gardens bisected by a stream & alive with birdsong. Facilities include a large swimming pool, a gym & spa, 3 restaurants & 2 bars. The smart & spacious carpeted rooms in the main building come with AC, DSTV, tea-/ coffee-making facilities & fast Wi-Fi. There are also a few cheaper, smaller & scruffier sgl rooms in the old wing. It lacks the character of the Mount Elgon Hotel, but has marginally better facilities & rates are significantly cheaper. *US$60/67 standard sgl/ dbl, US$90/107 sgl/dbl suite, US$30 sgl in old wing. All rates B&B.* **$$$**

Moderate

🏠 **Dream Palace Hotel** [254 E2] (15 rooms) Bwayo Crescent; 📞045 4432955; m 0754 780386; e info@dreampalace.co.ug; www.dreampalace. co.ug. Situated in peaceful gardens that juxtapose neat hedgerows with tropical palms & bamboo, this unexceptional but pleasant hotel ranks among the best of several mid-range places dotted around the eastern suburbs. The cool tiled rooms all have fitted nets, DSTV & en-suite hot shower, & facilities include Wi-Fi & a decent restaurant. *US$23/30 standard sgl/dbl, US$33/40 deluxe. All rates B&B.* **$$**

🏠 **Crown Suites Hotel** [254 F3] (15 rooms) Wanale Rd; m 0702 204727/0788 575503; e info@crownsuiteshotel.com; www. crownsuiteshotel.com. This bland new multi-storey hotel has a slightly unfinished feel & limited facilities, & the clean carpeted rooms with queen-sized bed, net, flatscreen DSTV & fan don't come

close to matching up to the similarly priced Mbale Resort Hotel. *From US$50/62 standard sgl/dbl to US$177 suite.* **$$$**

🏠 **Kayegi Hotel** [254 G4] (25 rooms) Masaba Rd; 📞039 2176499; m 0784 809278; e kayegihotelug@gmail.com. This uninspiring multi-storey hotel 2km east of the town centre ignores the potential view of the Wanale Cliffs in favour of the parking lot, but the en-suite rooms with nets, fan & DSTV are reasonably priced, & a restaurant serves a varied selection of local & Western dishes in the US$3–4 range. *US$28/30/40 B&B sgl/dbl/twin.* **$$**

Budget

✳ 🏠 **Casa del Turista** [254 B2] (8 rooms) Nkokonjeru Terrace; m 0772 328085/0702 328085; e salehnam@yahoo.com; http:// casadelturistauganda.webs.com. Mbale's hottest backpacker & volunteer hangout has a relaxed & friendly vibe, while comfortable rooms with stylish wood & iron furniture are supplemented by the brightly coloured Eco Sham Café, which serves great coffee & smoothies as well as a tempting menu of salads, stir-fries, wraps, sandwiches & pasta in the US$2–5 range. Wi-Fi throughout. *US$17/20/22 sgl/dbl/twin, or US$33 dbl for a quirky jungle-inspired eco-room.* **$$**

✳ 🏠 **Salem Guesthouse** [254 B1] (16 cottages) ⊕ 1.14213, 34.1493; 📞045 4436030; m 0772 505 595; e salem-uganda@salem-mail. net; www.salem-mbale.com. Situated in a wooded 10ha stand about 10km north of Mbale, this praiseworthy guesthouse is run by the Salem Brotherhood to help fund healthcare projects & orphan support. The large clean bandas have 1–3 beds & en-suite hot showers. A great vegetarian restaurant using locally sourced ingredients serves tasty pizzas, fresh bread & various stews & salads, as well as a selection of alcoholic & soft drinks. To get there, follow the Kumi Rd out of town (or catch a Kumi-bound matatu) to Nakaloke, then take a left turn on to the Kolonyi Rd & follow it for another 2km to the guesthouse. *US$12/17/25 B&B sgl/dbl/trpl.* **$$**

🏠 **Sukali Bistro & Hostel** [254 B1] (1 room & 2 dorms) Mukamba Rd; ⊕ 1.08709, 34.18264; 📞039 2178395; m 0750 617625; e sales@ sukaliuganda.com; www.sukaliuganda.com. Set in a small suburban garden with mountain views north of the town centre, this family-managed

hostel is still something of a work in progress, but the clean & brightly decorated rooms & dorms with nets & shared hot shower are already getting positive feedback from solo travellers. The 'bistro' serves a conventional selection of Ugandan grills with chips or rice for around US$4 per plate. To get there, follow the Kumi Rd north out of town for 1.2km past the main roundabout, then take the first right after the Livingstone International University, follow it for 500m, & you'll see Sukali on your left opposite the Primrose Guesthouse. *US$12 per person B&B.* **$$**

🏠 **Sunrise Inn** [254 G4] (14 rooms) Wanale Rd; ☏ 045 4433090; m 0772 438861; e snrsinn@ gmail.com/snrsinn@yahoo.com; 🄵 fb.me/ sunriseinnmbale. This quiet & cosy inn 2km east of the town centre has perfectly acceptable & reasonably priced carpeted rooms with nets, DSTV, Wi-Fi & en-suite hot tub/shower. A small garden restaurant serves good food but tends to be slow. *US$26/31/37 B&B sgl/dbl/twin.* **$$**

Shoestring

✳ 🏠 **Visitors Inn** [254 C1] (46 rooms) Nkokonjeru Rd; m 0700 470344/0789 639624. This high-rise above the Jawood Restaurant has small but clean en-suite tiled rooms with nets, DSTV & hot shower. Exceptional value. *US$7/10/17 sgl/dbl/twin.* **$**

🏠 **Royal Palm Plaza Hotel** [254 C1] (14 rooms) Aryada St. The former Little Princess Hotel, situated on the northern edge of the town centre & a favourite with volunteers, has bright, clean tiled

rooms with 4-poster bed, fitted net & en-suite hot shower. Good value. *US$10/12 sgl/twin.* **$**

🏠 **Landmark Inn** [254 D2] (3 rooms) Wanale Rd; m 0712 328333/0714 328333. Set in large overgrown gardens 500m east of the town centre, this grand but rundown colonial homestead, complete with red-tiled roof, wooden stairs & floor, & pillared veranda, won't be to everyone's taste, but it's good value for those who enjoy a little period character. The restaurant, effectively a branch of the central Delicious Dishes, serves excellent Indian food. *US$13 en-suite dbl.* **$**

🏠 **Botanical Gardens Resthouse** [254 G3] (19 rooms) Bungukho Rd; m 0788 269897. This unpretentious & sensibly priced guesthouse is set in a quiet & pleasant palm-shaded bird-filled garden, 2km east of the town centre. Basic en-suite rooms with nets are a little scruffy but clean, & there's a common lounge with DSTV. There's no restaurant, but it's only 500m to the Sunrise Inn & Kayegi Hotel. *US$10/12 sgl/dbl B&B.*

🏠 **New Mount Elgon View Hotel** [254 A2] (21 rooms) Cathedral Rd; m 0702 385273/0772 652629. New in name only, this long-serving backpackers' haunt is located conveniently (but noisily) close to the taxi park. Fans of Indian food will love the ground-floor Nurali's Café (see below). The rooms with nets are starting to show their age, making it poor value compared to the newer competition. *From US$7/10/15 sgl/dbl/trpl using common shower or US$18 en-suite twin.* **$$**

✗ **WHERE TO EAT AND DRINK** Of the hotels listed above, the suburban **Mount Elgon Hotel** and **Mbale Resort Hotel** both serve good Western food in agreeable surrounds, while the **Landmark Inn** has the same menu as Delicious Dishes but in a greener environment. The **Eco Sham Café** in Casa del Turista is a popular and affordable central option.

Moderate to expensive

✳ ✗ **Endiro Coffee** [254 B2] Republic St; ☏ 045 4437783; www.endirocoffee.com; 🕓 07.00–22.00 daily. Set in a converted warehouse tucked away below street level opposite the Stanbic Bank, this rustically funky restaurant serves an imaginative selection of gourmet burgers, wraps, salads & sandwiches, , with several vegetarian & health options, as well as cheaper tapas & cakes. There's also great coffee, a wonderful selection of fruit & vegetable juices, herbals teas & smoothies, but no

alcohol. Proceeds support various projects assisting vulnerable children. Free Wi-Fi. *Mostly in the US$6–7 range.*

✳ ✗ **Nurali's Café** [254 F3] Cathedral Rd; m 0772 455567; 🕓 08.30–22.30 daily. The ground floor of the New Mount Elgon View Hotel houses this excellent Indian restaurant, which also serves good pizzas & other non-Indian dishes. The menu caters to vegetarians & alcohol is served. *Main with rice & naan around US$5–6.*

✕ Delicious Dishes [254 B1] Republic St; 📱 0712 326333; ⏰ 10.30–22.20 daily. Daft name & bland décor notwithstanding, this central Indian restaurant is known for its tasty food & huge portions. Vegetarians have plenty of choice, while the drinks menu includes inexpensive fruit juices & alcoholic beverages. *Mains in the US$4–6 range.*

✕ Café Arabica [254 B2] Republic St; 📱 0757 072729; www.cafearabica.com; ⏰ 08.00–22.00 Mon-Sat & 09.00–20.30 Sun. This pleasant café serves a varied selection of sandwiches, salads, grills, curries & pizzas. It has a good internet café & free Wi-Fi, while the extensive drinks menu includes a tempting selection of liqueur coffees & cocktails. *Meals in the US$5–7 range.*

Cheap to moderate

❋ ✕ Cosmo Restaurant [254 A1] Republic St; 📱 0790 916393; 📘 fb.me/cosmo.mbale;

⏰ 08.00–21.30 daily. This simply but brightly decorated 1st-floor restaurant serves local dishes for around US$2, supplemented by a globetrotting selection of pricier mains – risottos, burritos, curries, goulash, pizza, etc. The vegetarian selection is unusually diverse, too. *Mains in the US$3–5 range.*

✕ Sarnet Restaurant [254 A2] Off Bishop Wasike Rd; ⏰ 08.00–22.00 daily. This is a good spot for unexciting but cheap & filling local fare. It tends to be packed on Sat & Sun afternoons during the English football season. *Mains around US$1.*

✕ Jawood Restaurant [254 C1] Nkokonjeru Rd; ⏰ 06.30–22.00 daily. This popular local eatery on the ground floor of the Visitors Inn serves filling portions of pilau & meat or beans with matok. *Mains around US$3–4.*

NIGHTLIFE

☆ Club Oasis [254 A2] Cathedral Rd; 📱 0772 552150. Mbale's top nightclub, situated next to Nurali's Café, hosts a disco most nights & live music on occasion.

♀ The Thatch Garden [254 C3] Masaba Rd; ☎ 039 2943405; 📱 0701 119299. This suburban garden complex a short walk east of the town

centre, dominated by a large thatched building, is a pleasant spot to enjoy music, drinks & grilled snacks.

☆ Mbale Sports Club [254 C3] Masaba Rd; 📱 0787 462100. Built in 1952 & attached to a defunct golf course, the old sports club in the eastern suburbs is now a popular dance venue with DJs most nights.

SHOPPING Good, centrally located **supermarkets** are found on the road to Tororo between the clock tower and the Mount Elgon View Hotel, and on Republic Road. The central **market** [254 B2] on Cathedral Road is usually overflowing with fresh produce from the surrounding agricultural lands.

OTHER PRACTICALITIES

Foreign exchange The Stanbic [254 B2], Crane [254 C2] and Standard Chartered [254 B2] banks on Republic Road can change foreign currency at Kampala rates, and have ATMs outside.

Internet The best internet café is in the Café Arabica, which also has fast Wi-Fi. Several other internet cafés are dotted around town, and Wi-Fi is available in the smarter hotels.

TOURIST INFORMATION All aspects of hikes on Mount Elgon, including equipment hire, can be arranged at the national park's helpful tourist information office [254 E3] (☎ 045 4433170/4435035; e *menpuwa@yahoo.ie*) on Masaba Road, 1km southeast of the town centre.

WHAT TO SEE AND DO The main tourist attractions in the Mbale area are Mount Elgon National Park and the Sipi Falls, both covered deeper into this chapter. The following sites also make for interesting excursions out of Mbale.

Wanale Cliffs The waterfall-streaked cliffs of Wanale Ridge dominate Mbale's eastern skyline, marking the end of the 2,348m Nkokonjeru 'Arm', a ridge of lava extruded through a parasitic vent on the western flank of Mount Elgon. A 20km road from Mbale climbs up on to the ridge through a cleft in the cliffs, meandering through superb mountain scenery before terminating at a cluster of radio masts that provide a map-like view of Mbale and vast panoramas towards distant horizons. The ridge is also accessible from Mbale using a steep footpath (find a guide in Mbale or at the UWA office) or on one of the few daily matutus. Mount Elgon National Park extends along Nkokonjeru to Wanale, and the UWA offers two guided walking trails of 3km and 6km in length through regenerating forest. An interesting geological feature along the trail is **Khauka Cave** (*US$25/35 FR/FNR per 24 hours, plus US$15/30*), which contains logs of petrified wood. However, the UWA entrance fee for a mandatory guide, is rather off-putting, since walking along the road or public lands is equally attractive.

Nabugoye Synagogue and Kakungulu's Grave Situated 4km northeast of central Mbale as the crow flies, Nabugoye Hill is the spiritual home to the Abayudaya, an isolated Jewish community established in 1920 under the Musoga politician Semei Kakungulu (see box, pages 260–1). The community's centrepiece is the Moses Synagogue, which is currently being reconstructed and expanded with foreign funding, but might reopen before the end of 2016. The most interesting time to visit Nabugoye, especially if you're prepared to stay overnight, is for the weekly Shabbat, which starts on Friday night and runs into Saturday morning, climaxing with a reading from the Torah by Rabbi Gershom Sizomu (the first indigenous black African rabbi, having been ordained in the USA in 2008). The synagogue has evidently become something of a pilgrimage site for curious Israeli and other Jewish visitors to Uganda, but it is open to people of all religious backgrounds, and the rabbi speaks good English. No fee is charged but donations are gratefully accepted, and do be aware that all forms of photography are forbidden between Friday sunset and Saturday sunset. Of minor interest, 10–15 minutes' walk east of the synagogue, is the covered grave of Semei Kakungulu (*entrance US$1.50*), marked with a Star of David and three spears, which lies alongside those of his brother and daughter.

Getting there and away Nabugoye Synagogue (✆ *1.09886, 34.20375*) lies 5.5km from Mbale by road, close to the village of Makadui. To get there from the town centre, follow Masaba Road east from the post office for 200m, then turn left into Bufombo Road and continue for 1.7km until you reach a fork where you need to branch right along the Namwanyi Road. Makadui lies about 3km along this road, and a sharp left turn there will take you to the parking area outside the synagogue compound after about 600m. Matatus from Mbale to Makadui cost less than US$1, a boda shouldn't cost a great deal more one-way, or you can phone the guesthouse and arrange to be collected for around US$6.50. A rough but motorable 1.5km track winds east from the car park to Semei Kakungulu's Grave (✆ *1.09654, 34.19443*).

🏠 ***Where to stay*** *Map, page 264*

🏠 **Abayudaya Guesthouse** (4 rooms & 4 dorms) ✆ 1.099, 34.20268; m 0773 902927/0778 063585. Situated 100m downhill from the synagogue, this quiet & comfortable resthouse offers the choice of en-suite twin rooms or a bed in a 4-berth dorm. All beds have nets. Simple meals cost around US$3. *US$10pp dorm bed or US$27 twin.* **$$**

MOUNT ELGON

An extinct shield volcano straddling the Kenya border east of Mbale, Mount Elgon is Africa's eighth-highest massif, rising to 4,321m at Wagagai Peak, and it has the broadest base of any free-standing mountain anywhere in the world. Two contiguous national parks share a 10km border on the massif's upper slopes. Kenya's 169km² Mount Elgon National Park was created in 1968, while its larger Uganda namesake, gazetted in 1993, extends over 1,145km² above the 2,000m contour. The highland moors and forests protected within these national parks harbour an impressively varied flora and fauna, while the lower slopes outside the national park are the site of Sipi Falls, the most popular tourist attraction in the Elgon region.

Elgon has enormous potential as a hiking destination, but it lacks the iconic status of Kilimanjaro, Mount Kenya or the Rwenzori, and sees far fewer visitors. Nevertheless, for budget travellers seeking a relatively affordable off-the-beaten-track opportunity to explore East Africa's weird and wonderful Afro-alpine vegetation, Elgon is a far less financially draining prospect than any other comparably lofty massif. The mountain can be climbed from either side of the border, but the Uganda trailheads are more accessible on public transport, and Wagagai, the tallest peak, falls on that side of the border. It is also now possible to do a cross-border traverse, ascending on the Ugandan side and descending in Kenya (ask at the national park office in Mbale for further details). For less serious walkers, the Mount Elgon foothills outside the national park offer plenty of alluring prospects, with Sipi Falls and to a lesser extent Kapchorwa being particularly popular bases in a coffee-growing area endowed with many scenic vistas.

FEES A park entrance fee of US$25/35 FR/FNR per 24 hours applies to all overnight hikes on the upper slopes protected within Mount Elgon National Park, as well as to overnight stays and/or day hikes in Kapkwai Forest Exploration Centre. Overnight hikers pay a daily hiking fee of US$75 inclusive of park entrance and a guide. Other fees applicable to overnight hikers are a camping fee of US$5 per night, while optional extras include US$6 per day per porter, and US$7 per party per day for a cook. No park fee is charged for visiting Sipi Falls or any other sites that are associated with the mountain but lie outside the national park boundaries.

GEOLOGICAL AND HISTORICAL BACKGROUND Like most other major East African massifs, Elgon is an extinct volcano whose formation was associated with the tectonic activity that created the Rift Valley several million years ago. It is the region's oldest extinct volcano, having first erupted 20–25 million years ago, and would have remained active for at least 14 million years, standing far higher than Kilimanjaro does today in its explosive prime. Today, Elgon's tallest peaks form a jagged circle around the more-or-less-intact caldera, which has a diameter of about 8km (making it one of the largest in the world) and is dotted with small crater lakes and hot springs created by Pleistocene glacial activity. The tallest peak, set on the Uganda side of the border, is Wagagai (4,321m), which lies on the southwestern rim. Of the next four tallest peaks, three fall within Uganda: Sudek (also known as Kiongo, 4,302m) in the south; Mubiyi (4,210m) in the north; and Jackson's Summit (also known as Masaba, 4,165m) in the east. Elgon is one of the region's most important watersheds, feeding rivers that empty into both Lake Victoria and Lake Turkana, and forming the main source of fresh water for more than two million people in Uganda alone.

Situated on the outskirts of Mbale, Nabugoye Hill is the site of the Moses Synagogue, spiritual home to a small, isolated community of Ugandan Jews known as Abayudaya. The Abayudaya are not formally accepted as Jews, nor will they be until they undergo an official conversion recognised by a court of rabbis, but this seems likely to change in the coming years. Either way, the Abayudaya are devout in their observance of Jewish customs and rituals, recognising the same holidays as other Jews, holding their Sabbath services on Friday evening and Saturday morning, and keeping kosher according to Talmudic law. They do not participate in local Basigu circumcision rituals, but instead circumcise males eight days after birth. And those who marry outside the community are no longer considered Abayudaya unless their spouses agree to convert.

Abayudaya is the Luganda word for Jews, coined in the late 19th century when missionaries attempted to dissociate their exotic religion from British colonialism by explaining to locals that the Bible was written not by Europeans but by Jews – the People of Judea or Ba-Judea. This ploy backfired somewhat when the first Luganda translation of the Bible appeared and literate Muganda started to question why, their local tradition of polygamy was condemned by the missionaries when many of the Abayudaya in the Old Testament unashamedly possessed more than one wife.

The most prominent of these religious dissidents was Malaki Musajakawa, whose Africanist Christian sect called the Malakites managed to attract up to 100,000 Ugandans away from more conventional denominations during its short-lived heyday. The Malakite doctrine was based on a fairly random selection of Old Testament verses: it was vehemently against the consumption of pork and the use of any medicine whatsoever, and – of course – it came out in strong support of polygamy. Not surprisingly, the British colonists were less than enamoured with this development and tensions between the authorities and the sect came to a head in 1926, when the plague swept through Uganda and the Malakites launched a violent protest against the use of inoculations to combat the disease. In the aftermath, Malaki Musajakawa was imprisoned and exiled to northern Uganda, where he died after a protracted hunger strike, and the sect gradually disbanded.

The main proponent of the spread of Malakitism in eastern Uganda was Semei Kakungulu, who – embittered with the colonial authorities after his retirement from the 'presidency' of Busoga in 1913 – heartily embraced the anti-establishmentarianism of the breakaway faith. Kakungulu withdrew from politics to focus his attention on spiritual matters, dedicating his life to reading the Bible and other Christian tracts. And, somewhat inevitably, he soon started to develop his own variations on the established Malakite doctrines, leading to a dispute that would eventually split the Mbale Malakites into two opposing factions. The key issue was male circumcision, which Kakungulu and his followers believed to be in line with Old Testament teachings, but which most other Malakites regarded as sacrilege. The true reason behind the widespread Malakite objection to circumcision was rooted in Kiganda tradition, which forbade bodily mutilation of any sort. But this was rationalised away by claiming that circumcision was the way of the Abayudaya, people who don't believe in Jesus Christ.

The present-day Abayudaya community was founded in 1920, when Kakungulu, fed up with the quarrelling, announced to the Malakites that 'because of your insults ... I have separated completely from you and stay with those who want to be circumcised: and we will be known as the Jews.' Kakungulu – at the age of 50 – was circumcised along with his first-born son. He circumcised all his subsequently

born sons eight days after their birth, and gave them all Old Testament names. In 1922, he published an idiosyncratic Luganda religious text steeped in the Jewish religion, demanding complete faith in the Old Testament and its commandments from himself and his followers.

In reality, Kakungulu's version of Judaism was a confused hotchpotch of Jewish and Christian customs. Neither he nor any of his followers had actually ever met a genuine Jew, and they knew little of real Jewish customs. As a result, the Abayudaya referred to their temple not as a synagogue but as a 'Jewish Church', and they placed as much emphasis on the Christian baptism of children as on the severing of their foreskins! That would change after 1926, however, when Kakungulu spent six months under the instruction of one Yusufu, the Jewish settler who effected the community's final conversion to Judaism. Under Yusufu's guidance, Kakungulu deleted all the Christian prayers from his book, and he instructed his followers to cease baptising their children, to observe the Saturday Sabbath, and to eat meat only if it had been slaughtered within the community according to Jewish custom. Ever the iconoclast, however, Kakungulu did remain vehement when it came to at least one pivotal Malakite doctrine that has no place in modern Judaism: the rejection of medicine. On 24 November 1928, Semei Kakungulu died of pneumonia, refusing to the last to touch the medication that might have saved his life.

By this time, a community of 2,000 Jewish converts lived on Kakungulu's estate at Nabugoye Hill, also known as Galiraya, a Luganda rendition of Galilee. After their founder's death, the Abayudaya had little contact with their neighbours and eschewed materialistic values: it is said that they could be recognised in a crowd by their 'backward' attire of animal hides and barkcloth. The Abayudaya suffered mild persecution during these early years, especially from neighbouring Christian communities who regarded Jews to be Christ killers. But essentially the community thrived until 1971, when Idi Amin banned Judaism, closed 32 synagogues and ordered the Abayudaya to convert to Christianity or Islam. During the Amin years, some 3,000 Abayudaya abandoned their faith rather than risk being beaten or tortured by the military, and some of the more stubborn among them – one group, for instance, who were beaten to death by Amin's thugs for collecting remnants of a synagogue roof that had blown away in a storm – did not survive. By the end of the Amin era, the total number of practising Abayudaya numbered a few hundred. Since then, the Abayudaya have been able to follow their faith without persecution, and the national community has grown to roughly 2,000 individuals, most of whom live around Nabugoye Hill, the site of Kakungulu's original 'Jewish Church'. A smaller community and synagogue exist at nearby Namanyoyi, and two others lie further afield in the town of Pallisa and in a village called Namatumba. There is still some debate within Jewish circles as to whether the Abayudaya should be fully accepted as members of the faith, but great strides towards integration have been made under the recent leadership of Gershom Sizomu, the Chief Rabbi of Uganda.

Under Kakungulu, the Abayudaya developed a distinct style of spiritual music, setting the text of recognised Jewish prayers to African melodies and rhythms. Several of these songs, sung in Hebrew or Luganda over a simple guitar backing, are collected on two CDs *Shalom Everybody Everywhere* and *Lecha Dodi*, available online (*www.kulanu.org/abayudaya/abayudayamusic.php*). The Moses Synagogue at Nabugoye Hill welcomes visitors with a genuine interest in its faith (see page 258). For more information, see www.kulanu.org.

The western slopes of Mount Elgon are home to the Bagisu, a Bantu-speaking people with few cultural or historical links to the linguistically affiliated kingdoms of western Uganda. The origin of the Bagisu is uncertain; their oral traditions assert simply that the founding ancestor Masaba emerged from a cave in the eponymous mountain perhaps 500 years ago. Masaba – also the local name for the mountain – is said to still inhabit Elgon's upper slopes, where he holds meetings with lesser deities at a place where stones have been laid out to form chairs and tables. Bagisu society recognises no central leadership and each autonomous clan is presided over by its own non-hereditary chief, appointed by a committee of elders. Traditionally, the judicial powers of the chief were, in many respects, subservient to those of sorcerers and witch-finders, who used to exert a steel grip on the social affairs and perceptions of the Bagisu.

The Bagisu, together with their Sabiny neighbours, are the only Ugandans to practise male circumcision (unlike the Sabiny, however, the Bagisu do not circumcise females – see box, pages 274–5). The origin of this custom is obscure, and several contradictory traditions have been recorded. One somewhat improbable legend has it that the first Bagisu man to be circumcised had a reputation for seducing the wives of his neighbours, and was taken before the committee of elders, who decreed that he should be semi-castrated as both punishment and deterrent. This plan backfired when, having recovered, the offender went back to his seductive ways, and – it was whispered – had become an even more proficient lover following the operation. After that, his rivals decided that they too would have to be circumcised in order to compete for sexual favours! Nice story, but all things considered it's more likely that the custom arose through contact with a neighbouring people who had an existing tradition of circumcision, for instance the Kalenjin of western Kenya.

Whatever its origin, the circumcision ceremony or *imbalu*, held on even-numbered years, is the pivotal occasion in Bagisu society, an individual rite of passage to manhood that involves the entire local community. Unusually among those African societies that practise circumcision, the year in which an individual will undergo the ritual is dictated not by strict convention nor by the council of elders, but by his own personal choice – any age between 16 and 26 is considered acceptable. Those who elect to be circumcised in any given year announce their intention in May or June, and spend the next few months preparing for the main ceremony. The most visible facet of the preparations involves the initiate, adorned in plantain fronds or animal skins and ash-plastered face, and accompanied by a band of cheering friends, parading and dancing through the streets to visit all his close relatives and seek their approval.

The climactic ceremony, according to certain historical sources, is traditionally held in August by the Bagisu and in December by the Sabiny, but these days it appears that both groups hold ceremonies during both of these months, though mainly in December. It normally takes place in the morning, well before 10.00, and involves all the initiates from a given clan – anything from one to several dozen young men – being marched by a whistling, cheering crowd to the circumcision

The local Bagisu know the mountain as Masaba, the name of their founding ancestor, who legendarily emerged from a cave on its slopes several centuries ago. Masaba's spirit is personified by Jackson's Summit, which appears to be the mountain's tallest peak from most vantage points, while Wagagai is named after

ground. The initiates have their faces plastered in ash, and they are stripped below the waist on the way to the circumcision ground, where they must line up in front of a crowd of family and friends of both sexes and all ages. Elsewhere in Africa, the circumcisions are normally performed indoors, with only a handful of associates in attendance. This was previously the case with the Bagisu, as only the initiates and the circumcisor were allowed into the special initiation enclosure. Today, however, the circumcision is a public event that anybody – including tourists – may attend.

The operation lasts for about one minute. The initiate holds both his arms rigid in front of him, clasping a stick in his hands, and staring forward expressionlessly. The circumcisor then makes three bold cuts around the foreskin to remove it from the penis. When the operation is complete, a whistle is blown and the initiate raises his hands triumphantly in the air, then starts dancing, proudly displaying his bloodied member to an ululating crowd. Any initiate who cries out during the painful procedure is branded a coward (as is any Bagisu man who is circumcised by a doctor under local anaesthetic). Once the crowd is satisfied of his bravery, the initiate is led away to a quiet place by a few friends, and seated on a stool and wrapped in cloth while he waits for the bleeding to cease. He is then taken to his father's house, where he will be hand fed by his relatives for three days. Finally, the initiate's hands are ritually washed, after which he is permitted to eat with his own hands, and his rite to manhood is completed.

While it is wholly acceptable for a Bagisu man to delay circumcision into his late 20s, he will not be considered a true man until he has undergone the rite, and will be forbidden from marrying or attending important clan meetings. A man who refuses to be circumcised past the accepted age parameters may be hunted down by his peers, and cut by force. Indeed, in one famous incident a few years ago, an uncut Bagisu man who had lived overseas for decades was abducted by his peers and taken away to be circumcised as soon as his plane home landed at Entebbe International Airport. These days, however, an increasing number of people are circumcised privately and unceremoniously at home or in a hospital, a surgical approach that carries a far lower risk of infection or other complications. Furthermore, while the traditional ceremony is still condoned by the government, President Museveni personally denounced it as retrogressive when he presided over the launch of the 2014 circumcision season, and used the occasion to call on the Bagisu elite to encourage their communities to discontinue the practice.

Travellers who visit Mbale, Sipi or Kapchorwa during the circumcision season are welcome to attend any local ceremonies that take place – they occur on practically a daily basis during December and to a lesser extent August, of all even-numbered years. The easiest way to find out about upcoming ceremonies is to ask local hotel staff. A small fee will usually be asked – particularly if you're thinking of taking pictures – but the Bagisu and Sabiny seem genuinely keen to have outsiders attend their most important ceremony. There is no taboo on women being present. Male visitors can expect a few (joking?) invitations to join the initiates as they line up to be cut!

and associated with Masaba's wife. It seems that Elgon was well known to the Arab slave traders who passed through the area throughout the 19th century, but the first person to document its existence was the explorer Henry Morton Stanley, who obtained a distant view of its peaks in 1875. The first European

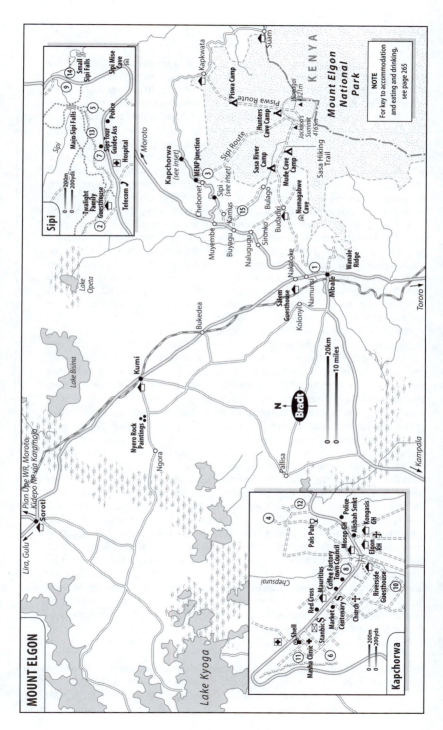

MOUNT ELGON

Sipi

- Small Sipi Falls
- Sipi Mise Cave
- Majo Sipi Falls
- Police
- Sipis Tour Guides Ass
- Hospital
- Twalight Family Guesthouse
- Telecom

0 200m
0 200yds

Mount Elgon National Park

NOTE
For key to accommodation and eating and drinking, see page 265

K E N Y A

Mount Elgon National Park

- Suam
- Kapkwata
- Piswa Camp
- Piswa Route
- Wagagai 4321m
- Hunters Cave Camp
- Jackson's Summit 4165m
- Sasa River Camp
- Kapchorwa (see inset)
- Chebonet
- MENP Junction
- Sipi Route
- Sipi (see inset)
- Sasa Hiking Trail
- Mude Cave Camp
- Sasa Hiking Trail
- Bulago
- Numagabwe Cave
- Budadiri
- Kamus
- Sironko
- Muyembe
- Buyagu
- Nalugugu
- Nakaloke
- Namunsi
- Mbale
- Wanale Ridge
- Salem Guesthouse
- Kolonyo
- Bukedea
- Moroto →
- Tororo →

Lake Opeta

Lake Bisina

- Kumi
- Nyero Rock Paintings
- Ngora
- Pallisa
- Kampala →

Pian Upe WR, Moroto, Kidepo NP via Karamoja →
Lira, Gulu →
- Soroti

Lake Kyoga

N Bradt

0 ————— 20km
0 ————— 10 miles

Kapchorwa

- Pals Pub
- Police
- Mosop GH
- Alishah Smkt
- Kongasis GH
- Elgon RH
- Coffee Factory
- Town Council
- Mauritius
- Red Cross
- Market
- Centenary
- Church
- Riverside Guesthouse
- Shell
- Stanbic
- Masha Clinic

Chepsurai

0 200m
0 200yds

MOUNT ELGON

Where to stay

1 Abayudaya Guesthouse *p258*
2 The Crow's Nest *p269*
3 Kapkwai Rest Camp *p271*
4 La Bamba Country Resort *p272*
5 Lacam Lodge *p269*
6 Masha *p272*
7 Moses's Campsite *p269*
8 Noah's Ark Motel *p272*
9 Noah's Ark Resort (Sipi Falls) *p269*
10 Noah's Ark Resort (Kapchorwa) *p272*
11 Pacific Sunset *p272*
12 Savannah Guesthouse *p272*
13 Sipi Falls Resort *p269*
14 Sipi River Lodge *p269*
15 Sisiyi Falls Camp & Resort *p268*

to reach the lower slopes was Joseph Thomson, who approached it from the direction of Maasailand in 1883, and named it Elgon, an anglicisation either of the Maasai name Ol Doinyo Ilgoon (literally 'Breast Mountain') or else of El Kony, the name of the tribe that inhabited the eastern footslopes. The first recorded summit took place in February 1890, when Frederick (later Sir Frederick) Jackson and Ernest Gedge ascended to the caldera from a base camp at modern-day Kapchorwa, and climbed one of the subsidiary peaks (long assumed to have been Jackson's Summit, but now more widely thought to have been Sudek).

FLORA AND FAUNA Elgon's vegetation zones are similar to those of other large East African mountains. Below the 3,000m contour, the mountain supports a contiguous belt of evergreen forest extending over roughly 750km² within Uganda. This forest belt can be divided into two broad strata: tall Afro-montane forest below 2,500m; and low canopy montane forest and bamboo between 2,500m and 3,000m. The slopes below the 2,000m contour, which lie outside the national park, also supported significant forest cover a century ago, but much of this has since been cleared for cultivation. Above 3,000m lies the heather belt, giving way at around 3,500m to other-worldly Afro-alpine vegetation studded with stands of giant lobelia and groundsel, including the endemic *Senecio barbatipes* and *S. elgonensis*.

The mammalian fauna of Mount Elgon is poorly known. The most common species, or at least the most visible to hikers, are blue monkey and black-and-white colobus. A small number of elephant are resident in the forests, as is the striking De Brazza's monkey, along with leopard, bushpig, buffalo, sitatunga and common duiker. The bird checklist stands at more than 300 species and includes a rich variety of forest birds, as well as several Afro-montane moorland endemics. Twelve of the species listed for Elgon occur in no other Ugandan national park, in many instances because Elgon lies at the most westerly extent of its range. Of particular interest are Jackson's francolin (recorded only once), moorland francolin (elsewhere common only in Ethiopia's Bale Mountains), moustached green tinker-bird, red-throated wryneck, black-collared apalis, Hunter's cisticola, alpine chat, marsh widow-bird and Weyn's weaver. The endangered bearded vulture or lammergeyer is regularly observed soaring at higher altitudes.

ACCESS AND ORIENTATION Mount Elgon National Park can be explored only on foot, but the three main trailheads are all accessible by road. The most established of these trailheads is Budadiri, which lies on the western slopes 38km by road from Mbale via Sironko, and forms the starting point of the perennially popular Sasa Route. Two more recently established and less frequently traversed trails can be accessed from the main road running around the northern footslopes to the Kenyan border town of the Suam. These are the Sipi Route, whose trailhead is at Kapkwai 60km from Mbale, and the Piswa Route, which starts at Kapkwata 100km from Mbale. Kapkwai is also the site of the national park's Forest Exploration Centre, an excellent goal for anyone who wants to do a day hike in the forest zone.

10

Other important landmarks along the road to Suam include Sipi Falls, 45km from Mbale, and the town of Kapchorwa another 20km past that. Information about public transport to each of these sites is given individually later in the chapter.

🏠 WHERE TO STAY
Accommodation of some sort exists at all three trailheads, as well as at Sipi and Kapchorwa, as listed under the header for the individual site. Once on the trail, there's only one hut for hikers, so you'll need a tent and sleeping bag. Porters will cut grass to make you a 'mattress' for comfort and warmth at higher altitudes. Tents (*US$3*) as well as sleeping bags and roll mats (*US$1.50 each*) can be hired from Rose's Last Chance in Budadiri (pages 267–8).

TOURIST INFORMATION
It's well worth dropping into the national park tourist office in Mbale (see page 257) before heading to the mountain or trailheads. The best map is 'Uganda Maps' No. 10 *Mount Elgon & Environs*, which also includes good coverage of Mbale town and the Sipi area.

OVERNIGHT HIKES ON MOUNT ELGON
Elgon is not a difficult mountain to climb. Aspirant hikers need to be reasonably fit, but no specialised equipment or skill are required to reach the peaks, and there's no serious risk of the altitude-related illnesses that regularly afflict hikers on the upper slopes of mounts Kilimanjaro or Kenya. Elgon can be climbed at any time of year, though the dry seasons (June to August and November to March) are best, in particular November and December when the highland flowers are in bloom. A noteworthy attraction of Elgon is the relatively low cost compared to other large East African mountains: allowing for one porter and allocating US$15 for food, you'll spend around US$130 a day.

All hikes must be arranged directly through the national park staff. This can be done at the Mount Elgon tourist office in Mbale, which lies about 100m from the Mount Elgon Hotel, or the equivalent office at the trailheads of Budadiri, Kapkwata or Kapkwai Forest Exploration Centre. It doesn't really matter where you make arrangements, but it probably does make sense to drop into the central office in Mbale to talk through route options before you decide on a trailhead. Porters (carrying a maximum of 18kg each) must also be arranged through the national park offices. Most hikers cater for themselves, but this can be talked through with the park staff.

Several hiking routes are available. Traditionally, the most popular has been a **four-day round trip** from Budadiri to Wagagai following the Sasa Route in both directions. Other possibilities include a **five-day round hike** from Budadiri, taking in Wagagai and the hot springs, and a **six-day hike** between Budadiri and Kapkwata via Wagagai and the hot springs. These days, however, it's probably best to ascend via the newer Piswa or Sipi routes, which start at much higher altitudes than Budadiri, making for a more gradual and far less strenuous ascent, then to return using the Sasa Route. The experienced national park staff can give more detailed advice on the various options.

On the first day out of Budadiri (1,250m), the Sasa Trail involves a stiff 6- to 8-hour walk via the village of Bumasifwa to Sasa River Camp (2,900m). This is followed on the second day by a 4- to 5-hour walk to the 16-berth hut at Mude Cave (3,500m). Many people use the spare afternoon at Mude Cave to ascend Jackson's Summit (4,165m), which is a round trip of around 5 hours. On the third day, you will ascend from Mude Cave to Wagagai (4,321m) and back, a long hike of 8–9 hours. Hikers doing the standard four-day route will descend from Mude Cave to Budadiri the following day.

Alternatively, day four will see hikers doing the full trek to Kapkwata proceed from Mude Cave to Hunters Cave Camp (3,870m) via the hot springs, a trek of at

least 10 hours. On the fifth day, they will descend to Piswa Camp, a 5-hour trek, and on the sixth day to Kapkwata, a further 4 hours. It is possible to combine the last two days into one, thereby cutting the duration of the trek to five days. As already noted, hikers who want to do the full route should consider starting at higher elevation at Kapkwata or Kapkwai rather than Budadiri.

The construction of a 16-bunk hut at Mude Cave means that a tent is no longer absolutely necessary. In theory, trekkers can hike up from Budadiri to Mude Cave Hut on the first day, make a round trip between Mude and the peak on the second, and descend to Budadiri on the third. These are long days though and you'll need to be a strong climber to appreciate them.

A few **warnings**: Elgon lies below the snow line, but it can be very cold at night or in windy weather. You must be sure to bring enough warm clothing. It is not high enough for altitude sickness to be a major cause of concern, but you may experience headaches and other altitude-related symptoms near the peaks. Water on the mountain should be purified or boiled before drinking. The ascent of the escarpment via a tricky path known as the Wall of Death on the Sasa Route is not recommended if you are afraid of heights. It is mandatory for trekkers visiting the hot springs area between Mude and Hunters caves to be escorted by an armed ranger.

In addition to the mandatory fees, guides, porters and cooks will expect to be tipped at the end of a successful hike. Rough guidelines are upwards of US$15 per party for the guide and US$10 per party for each cook or porter.

AROUND THE MOUNTAIN The main sites and trailheads in the Elgon foothills are covered below, clockwise from Mbale, starting at Budadiri and ending at the remote Kenya border town of Suam. Traditionally, the most popular destination in the area is **Sipi Falls**, which is readily accessible on public transport and has accommodation to suit all budgets, as well as offering several day-walking possibilities outside the national park. The **Kapkwai Forest Exploration Centre** on the northern slopes is a more worthwhile goal for those with a strong interest in natural history, but also more costly as park visitation fees must be paid.

Budadiri This small trading centre 10km west of the park boundary is the trailhead for the Sasa Route and best-established starting point for hikes on Mount Elgon. Although non-hikers seldom visit Budadiri, one interesting local attraction is the **Numagabwe Cave**, which lies about 7km to the southeast and is decorated with ancient rock paintings. Either of the hotels in Budadiri can organise a day trip to the caves, as well as longer caving expeditions for those with the necessary equipment.

Getting there and away Budadiri (✛ *1.17051, 34.33575*) lies about 38km from Mbale by road. The best route entails following the surfaced Kapchorwa Road out of town for 27km through Sironko to the village of Nalugungu (✛ *1.24814, 34.27223*), then turning right into a signposted 11km dirt road that can be dangerously slippery after rain. Matatus from Mbale to Budadiri cost around US$1.25, take 45–60 minutes, and leave from the Kumi Road about 100m north of the clock tower.

Where to stay and eat
☀ ⌂ **Rose's Last Chance** (7 rooms & 1 dorm) m 0772 623206/0752 203292; e lastchance. hotel@yahoo.com; http://roseslastchance.yolasite.

com. This long-serving & friendly set-up is split between a scruffy old house opposite the UWA office & newer but similarly rustic premises just

up the road. Inexpensive meals & day tours are offered, & it also rents out tents, sleeping bags, roll mats & hiking boots. *US$15/22 sgl/dbl, or US$10 dorm bed, US$7pp camping. All rates B&B.* **$$**

🏠 **Wagagai Hotel** (28 rooms) m 0776 613664. Appropriately, the number of rooms in this hotel equates to the number of years that elapsed between the start of construction in 1980 & eventual opening in 2008. The long-awaited product is clean, smart but otherwise unremarkable – save for a 1st-floor balcony with a stupendous view up the valley from Budadiri towards a montane amphitheatre crowded by Elgon's high peaks. A new campsite & dorm block make this the town's most attractive option for climbing groups. *US$10/18 en-suite sgl/dbl, US$8 dorm bed, US$4 camping.* **$$**

Bulago

An attractive detour on the way up to Sipi leads to the scenic village of Bulago (also known as Buluganya). Approaching from Mbale along the new surfaced Sipi Road, turn right on to the *old* Sipi Road at Kaserem (⊕ *1.32139, 34.33612*), 6.5km past the junction with the Moroto Road. After 3km you reach Kamus, where you need to turn left up the mountain. From here, a 15km road winds beneath some superb cliffs and passes through a small but pretty rock gorge before reaching Bulago, which stands on a cliff top above a lovely waterfall dropping into a pretty, grassy meadow. A rocky plateau beyond the village overlooks the Simu Valley to Butandiga Ridge, and a path climbs to the cliffs bordering the national park, over which a couple of streams fall. There is no formal accommodation in Bulago, and the steep road there deteriorates quickly after rain, so be ready to retreat if necessary.

Sisiyi Falls

This pretty waterfall is visible for miles around as it plunges over a lofty cliff from the direction of Bulago village. The base of the falls is occupied by the basic but beautifully located **Sisiyi Falls Camp & Resort** (m *0703 588284/0772 638516*; e *sisiyifalls@yahoo.com*; f *fb.me/sisiyi.falls*; *US$32 en-suite dbl cottage room B&B, US$20pp lazy camping, US$10pp own tent, all rates B&B; day visitors US$1.50 entrance; map, page 264*). Dotted with house-sized basalt boulders softened by lichen and surrounded by lush, tropical vegetation, the result is a delightful 'Lost World' feel. The falls are a couple of minutes' walk uphill but their constant sound permeates the gardens. In the middle of all this are a couple of cottages, each containing two self-contained rooms. Whilst crying out for a Sipi River Lodge-style facelift (see Sipi Falls, below) they are very fair value. The real jewel is a camping ground set among the boulders, which is one of the loveliest in the whole country. Sisiyi Falls lies 5km off the main tarmac road at Buyaga, about 7km north of Sironko town. A boda from Buyaga should cost around US$1.50.

Sipi Falls

Elgon's main tourist focus is the small trading centre of Sipi, which lies at an altitude of 1,775m on the mountain's northeastern footslopes, only 45km from Mbale along a good surfaced road. The village overlooks the 99m-high Sipi Falls, the last in a series of three pretty waterfalls formed by the Sipi River as it cascades downhill from the upper slopes of Mount Elgon into the Kyoga Basin. Serviced by half a dozen resorts and lodges that collectively cater to most tastes and budgets, Sipi is a very peaceful and pretty spot, and it makes a most agreeable base for gentle day walks in the surrounding hills, which offer spectacular views to the lowlands further west and – weather permitting – occasional glimpses of the Elgon peaks.

Getting there and away Sipi trading centre lies about 45km from Mbale along the surfaced road to Kapchorwa. Self-drivers must follow the Kumi Road

out of town for 5km to Namunsi (⊕ *1.12395, 34.16863*), where they need to turn right on to the Moroto Road and follow it for another 28km before turning right on to the Kapchorwa Road at a junction (⊕ *1.3357, 34.29741*) 1km past Muyembe. Sipi lies about 12km along this road. Matatus from Mbale to Sipi cost US$3, take 45–60 minutes, and leave from the Kumi Road about 100m north of the clock tower.

Where to stay and eat Map, page 264

Upmarket

✳ 🏠 **Sipi River Lodge** (4 cottages) ⊕ 1.33805, 34.38308; m 0751 796109; e info@ sipiriverlodge.com; www.sipiriverlodge.com. Set in lovely wooded grounds at the foot of the middle waterfall, this terrific little lodge is comfortably the best in the Mount Elgon region, & very reasonably priced by countrywide standards, making it a great place to rest up for a couple of days. There are 2 stylish en-suite cottages with dbl bed, 2 sgl beds, sitting area & large picture window facing the waterfall, but cheaper & simpler accommodation is also available. The main lodge occupies a transformed bungalow with a cosy lounge, bar & an excellent library but no Wi-Fi. Activities include Sipi walks, coffee tours, mountain biking, archery ascents of Mount Elgon & fly fishing in the river above the waterfall. *US$183/238/324/415 for 1/2/3/4 people in a cottage. US$107/132 sgl/dbl banda with shared facilities, US$56pp dorm banda. All rates HB; & US$12pp for lunch.* **$$$$**

Moderate

🏠 **Sipi Falls Resort** (6 cottages) ⊕ 1.33596, 34.3773; m 0753 153000; info@sipifallsresort. com; www.sipifallsresort.com. Sipi's oldest resort started life in the 1950s as a quaint retreat from where the Governor of the Uganda Protectorate could enjoy a splendid view over the main waterfall. The site has since been expanded with the addition of simple but attractive rustic cottages made of wood & bamboo thatch. The view is still great, the price is very fair, & the food is pretty good too. Activities include walks & coffee tours. *US$50/60/74 B&B sgl/dbl/trpl, plus US$7pp lunch & US$13 dinner.* **$$$**

🏠 **Lacam Lodge** (6 rooms) ⊕ 1.33598, 34.37989; e info@lacamlodge. co.uk; www.lacamlodge.co.uk. Lacam occupies a steep hillside provided with plenty of steps immediately beside the main Sipi Falls – so close that the waterfall is mostly heard rather than seen. Though the steep cliff below the site will give

parents with young kids the willies, the sudden drop makes the view down Sipi Valley to the Kyoga Basin particularly dramatic. En-suite cottages with hot showers & compost toilets are fashioned from log offcuts & topped with roofs thatched in the local style. *US$32/48/72 sgl/dbl/trpl en-suite cottages & US$24pp dorm bed B&B.* **$$**

Budget

🏠 **Noah's Ark Resort** (7 rooms) ⊕ 1.33832, 34.38198; m 0772 646364; e info@ noahsarkhotel.co.ug; www.noahsarkhotel.co.ug. This small & unremarkable guesthouse is set in grounds adorned with inept statues of animals, but it does boast a great stilted platform overlooking the Sipi River. Rooms are basic & serviceable but feel a touch overpriced. *US$40 dbl HB.* **$$**

Shoestring & camping

✳ 🏠 **Moses's Campsite** (5 rooms) ⊕ 1.33554, 34.37555; m 0752 208302; e mosescampsitesipi@yahoo.com. By far the simplest of Sipi's offerings, this friendly & long-serving family-run set-up has a wooded clifftop location with a terrific waterfall view (again, not one for parents with young kids) & accommodation in basic bandas using common showers. Camping permitted & meals cost around US$3. *US$6pp bandas, US$3pp camping.* **$**

🏠 **The Crow's Nest** (8 rooms) ⊕ 1.33519, 34.3693; m 0772 687924/0752 965815. This well-established shoestring resort, set on a small hill to the left as you enter Sipi trading centre, offers a wonderful grandstand view of all the waterfalls along the Sipi River as well as the peaks of Mount Elgon. Accommodation is in simple log cabins or dorms with 4–12 beds, & a simple restaurant/ bar serves a selection of stir-fry, spaghetti & local dishes for around US$4. A short nature trail encircles the hill above the camp, while longer guided walks can be arranged to the various waterfalls. *US$13 twin cabin, US$7pp dorm, US$3pp camping.* **$**

What to see and do
Guided walks The most popular walking trail, only 20 minutes in each direction, leads from behind the post office in Sipi trading centre to the base of the main waterfall. If you choose, you can continue along this trail for another 20 to 30 minutes to reach a cluster of caves on the cliff above the river. The largest of these caves extends for about 125m into the rock face, and contains rich mineral salt deposits that have clearly been worked extensively at sometime in the past, as well as traces of petrified wood. Walking back to the trading centre from the caves along the main road, you'll pass the top of the main waterfall, as well as Sipi Mise Cave, an important local shrine set within a small forest-fringed cavern.

More ambitiously, it is possible to undertake a day hike from the main waterfall to the three smaller falls that lie upstream, one of which has a tempting swimming pool at its base. Another interesting option is a coffee tour to local subsistence farms where you can learn about the coffee farming process from harvesting and drying the beans to roasting and grinding them for consumption.

It is more-or-less mandatory to take a guide on any walks to the waterfalls or on other local hikes and coffee tours. This is not only to help you locate some of the sites, but also because the flat guiding fees include a contribution to local landowners for access to each of the falls. A guide can be arranged through any of the lodges listed on the previous page, or through the Sipi Tour Guides Association (✪ *1.33527, 34.37639;* m *0781 831078/0753 331078*) at the entrance to the Sipi Falls Resort. The going rate is around US$5–10 per person depending on the duration of the walk and where you arrange it.

Abseiling Rob's Rolling Rock (m *0752 963078/0705 597496;* e *robsrollingrocks@ yahoo.com;* f *fb.me/RobsRollingRock*) arranges abseiling and rock climbing on the cliffs around the waterfall for US$50.

Fishing Rainbow trout imported from Kenya were released into a stretch of the Sipi River above the top waterfall near Kapkwai, about an hour's walk or 30 minutes' drive from Sipi trading centre. Fly-fishing is now very good, and permits can be bought and gear rented from Sipi River Lodge. The permit costs US$50 for 24 hours, and a rod and tackle cost US$30 per person.

Kapkwai forest exploration centre
Only 3km east of Sipi as the crow flies and easily accessed by foot or by road, the Kapkwai Forest Exploration Centre is an attractive destination for hikers and wildlife enthusiasts who don't want to overnight on the upper slopes of Mount Elgon, though some might balk at the hefty combined entrance and guided walk fee. Set at an altitude of 2,050m immediately inside the national park boundary, the centre was originally designed as an educational facility but now doubles as a base for tourism. Its main attraction is a network of day trails that offer access to the surrounding Afro-montane forest and offer a good opportunity to see associated monkeys and birds. Kapkwai is also the starting point for the overnight Sipi Trail, which leads to the Elgon peaks, and the site of a comfortable rest camp consisting of four log cottages offering affordable banda and dormitory accommodation as well as a good canteen.

Fees A park entrance fee of US$25/35 FR/FNR per 24 hours is payable even if you only stay overnight at the rest camp. Day walks cost an additional US$15/30 inclusive of a mandatory guide.

Getting there and away Kapkwai entrance gate (⊕ *1.33518, 34.41142*) lies 12km from Sipi by road. To drive there, follow the surfaced Kapchorwa Road out of Sipi for 6km, then turn right at a prominently signposted junction (⊕ *1.36778, 34.39141*) on to the 6km dirt feeder road, which may require 4x4 after heavy rain. For those without private transport, any vehicle running between Mbale or Sipi and Kapchorwa can drop you at the junction, from where the walk to Kapkwai shouldn't take longer than 90 minutes. Alternatively, the guides in Sipi can lead you along a more direct 90-minute walking trail for about US$5 per person. Another option is a boda out of Sipi or even Mbale.

Where to stay and eat Map, page 264

🏠 **Kapkwai Rest Camp** (3 bandas, 1 dorm) ⊕ 1.33479, 34.41462; 📞 0414 355000 (UWA Kampala HQ); m 0773 427679 (Mbale office, e menpuwa@yahoo.ie). Sprawling across forested slopes near the source of the Sipi River 500m east of the entrance gate, this attractive rest camp offers the choice of en-suite timber cabins, a dorm bed, or camping. The Bamboo Grove Canteen serves basic but decent meals for around US$3–4, as well as air-cooled beers & sodas. The national park entrance fee must be added to the otherwise very reasonable rates. *US$10/18 sgl/dbl, US$7 dorm bed, US$5pp camping.* **$$**

What to see and do

Hiking Three connecting, circular day trails run through the exploration centre. The **Mountain Bamboo Loop** (*7km; 4hrs*) leads past a cave before climbing to the main viewpoint (from where, on a clear day, the peaks of Mount Elgon can be seen), and then runs north along a ridge, through montane forest, to a large bamboo forest. The popular **Chebonet Falls Loop** (*5km; 3hrs*) passes the eponymous waterfalls, and also involves a climb up a rock chimney and passing through areas of montane and bamboo forest leading to the main viewpoint. The **Ridge View Loop** (*3km; 2hrs*) involves a relatively easy ascent of the ridge, where it connects with the other trails at the main viewpoint.

In addition to passing through areas of regenerating forest, fields of colourful wild flowers and extensive stands of bamboo, the day trails offer a good chance of sighting black-and-white colobus and blue monkeys.

Birding Kapkwai is highly rewarding to birders, since a high proportion of the 305 species recorded in the national park are present in the vicinity. The lovely cinnamon-chested bee-eater, Doherty's bush-shrike and golden-winged sunbird head a long list of highland species resident in the riverine scrub close to the rest camp. The Mountain Bamboo Loop is probably the most productive trail for true forest birds, including black-and-white casqued hornbill, Hartlaub's turaco, bar-tailed trogon, grey-throated barbet, montane oriole, mountain greenbul and black-collared apalis.

Kapchorwa Administrative headquarters of the eponymous district, Kapchorwa lies at the heart of Uganda's main Arabica coffee-production area, and its major development is a vast and recently rehabilitated coffee-processing plant. Kapchorwa is an odd little place: a vast but unfocused semi-urban sprawl of fewer than 15,000 inhabitants that somehow manages to straddle the Suam Road for more than 2km. An attractive and breezy montane setting goes some way to compensating for the town's rather scruffy appearance, but you could argue that the best thing about Kapchorwa is the scintillating ascent road from Sipi, which offers some wonderful views to Lake Kyoga and the isolated Mount Kadam. If you're up for some

exploration, Kapchorwa now has a decent selection of budget accommodation, and the surrounding slopes offer plenty of good walking, with one possible goal being a little-known series of caves on a cliff outside town.

Getting there and away Kapchorwa lies about 60km from Mbale along a good surfaced road that can be covered in under 1 hour. Directions are as for Sipi, which the road passes through 15km before it reaches Kapchorwa. Regular matatus to Kapchorwa (*US$3*) leave Mbale from a taxi park on the Kumi Road 100m north of the clock tower, stopping at Sipi on request.

Where to stay and eat *Map, page 264*

Moderate

Noah's Ark Resort (20 rooms)
⊕ 1.39367, 34.44718; m 0772 646364, e info@ noahsarkhotel.co.ug, www.noahsarkhotel.co.ug. Owned by the same people as its Sipi namesake (page 269), this rambling owner-managed 'For VIP use only' lodge 500m south of the main road has comfortable & well-equipped en-suite rooms with nets, hot water & flatscreen DSTV, but they are a bit frayed at the edges & seem quite pricey for what you get, even allowing that rates include all meals. *US$40/50 sgl/dbl room or US$50/60 suite, all rates FB.* **$$**

Budget

✴ **La Bamba Country Resort** (18 rooms)
⊕ 1.40368, 34.45239; m 0777 848560. Situated 500m north of the main road, this clifftop lodge offers wonderful views over green slopes to the wide open plains of Pian Upe. The en-suite rooms & cottages are small but clean, come with hot water & fitted nets, & rates are as attractive as the location. A dual purpose restaurant/lounge has DSTV & serves simple meals for around US$3, as well as the usual range of drinks. *US$12 en-suite dbl, or US$10 using common shower.* **$**

Savannah Guesthouse (6 rooms)
⊕ 1.40119, 34.45359; m 0772 350411. This quiet & unpretentious lodge at the east end of town has clean & well-priced en-suite rooms with fitted net & hot shower. *US$12 dbl.* **$**

Pacific Sunset Hotel (25 rooms)
⊕ 1.40106, 34.4415; ☎ 039 2175217; m 0775 981069. The views from this 5-storey hotel are splendid, but it is still unfinished despite having been open several years, & the entrenched construction-site feel isn't much fun. Spacious en-suite twin rooms come with 2 ¾ beds, fitted nets & hot shower. A semi-functional restaurant is attached. *US$17 B&B dbl.* **$$**

Masha Hotel (13 rooms) ⊕ 1.39891, 34.44148; m 0722 636868/0754 334044, e mashahotel@gmail.com. Neat green gardens with good views over the slopes south of the town centre, & a variety of rooms ranging from scruffy twins using common showers to nice but rather old-fashioned en-suite dbl rooms. Fair value. *US$7 twin (common shower) or US$13/17 en-suite twin/ dbl.* **$$**

Shoestring

Noah's Ark Motel (11 rooms)
⊕ 1.39726, 34.44802; m 0772 646364; e info@ noahsarkhotel.co.ug; www.noahsarkhotel.co.ug. Flanking the main road through town, this self-styled 'average' counterpart to the namesake resort is in fact a rock-bottom shoestring lodge with timeworn rooms using common cold showers, & a popular restaurant & bar serving local dishes in the sub-US$2.50 range. Good value. *US$3 B&B sgl.* **$**

Kapkwata The small trading centre of Kapkwata, some 35km from Kapchorwa along the dirt road to Suam, is of interest mainly as the trailhead for the **Piswa Trail** up Mount Elgon. Kapkwata also provides Suam-bound travellers with a good excuse to break up the journey in the form of UWA's **Kapkwata Resthouse** (*3 rooms;* m *0773 427679;* e *menpuwa@yahoo.ie; US$12/13 sgl/dbl using common showers, no park entrance fee charged;* **$**), which is situated at the rangers' post roughly 500m past the trading centre and serves meals for around US$4. There are several good day walks from the resthouse to local viewpoints. Any transport heading between Kapchorwa and Suam can drop you at Kapkwata.

Suam Set at an altitude of 2,070m on the Kenyan border, Suam is likely to be passed through only by travellers crossing between Mbale and its Kenyan counterpart Kitale. There are a couple of basic lodgings as well as a **UWA Suam Guesthouse** (*9 rooms;* m *0773 606340;* e *menpuwa@yahoo.ie; US$12/13 sgl/dbl en suite or using common showers;* **$**). Up to half-a-dozen trucks daily run along the 78km dirt road between Kapchorwa and Suam (US$8, 3-4 hours when dry, longer when wet) but transport should improve as and when plans to surface the road come to fruition. Heading on to Kenya, Suam is connected to Kitale by a reasonable surfaced road and regular matutus.

KUMI

Kumi, founded in 1904 by Semei Kakungulu as an administrative substation of Mbale, is named after the jackal-berry or African ebony (*Diospyros mespiliformis*), known locally as *ekum*, that proliferates in the vicinity. Kumi is today the headquarters of Kumi District, a full 35% of which comprises wetland habitats associated with Lake Kyoga and its drainage basin, while the remainder is covered in dry savannah studded with spectacular volcanic outcrops. A rather sleepy and nondescript small town (population 12,000), Kumi is of interest to travellers primarily as a springboard for visits to the impressive prehistoric rock art at Nyero 10km to the west. Kumi also provides access to Lake Bisina and its prolific populations of sitatunga antelope, shoebill and the endemic Fox's weaver.

GETTING THERE AND AWAY Kumi straddles the surfaced Mbale–Soroti Road roughly 55km north of Mbale and 45km south of Soroti. The drive from either of these towns should take less than an hour in a private vehicle. Plenty of matatus run along this road, stopping at Kumi.

WHERE TO STAY AND EAT Though the Nyero Rock Paintings are usually visited as a day trip from Mbale, Sipi or Soroti, Kumi's selection of budget and shoestring hotels might be useful for an early start to Lake Bisina.

Kumi Hotel (22 rooms) Malera Rd; 045 4471012; m 0772 490659; e kumihotel1@yahoo.com. Reasonably smart en-suite rooms & a decent hotel. *US$22/27/28 B&B sgl/dbl/twin en suite.* **$$**

Green Top Hotel (10 rooms) Soroti Rd; m 0772 542340. Shabby but reputedly soon-to-be-renovated lodge distinguished by a pleasant open-sided bar/dining area & a bit of a garden. *US$10/16/24 B&B sgl/dbl/twin en suite.* **$$**

WHAT TO SEE AND DO
Nyero Rock Paintings (✣ *1.47114, 33.84699; entrance US$1.50/3pp residents/ non-residents*) The finest of several rock-art sites scattered around eastern Uganda (see box, page 276), Nyero is also perhaps the most accessible, situated only 10km west of Kumi on a good dirt road. The site comprises six discrete painted panels set within a few hundred metres of each other on a prominent granite outcrop called Moru Ikara. Most impressive is **Panel Two**, a 6m-high rock face reached via a narrow cleft between two immense boulders. At least 40 sets of red concentric circles are partially or wholly visible on the face, as is one 'acacia pod' figure. At the top right is a (very faded) painting of three zebras. The most striking naturalistic figures on the panel are two large canoes, of which one is about 1.5m long and evidently carrying people. **Panel One** is far less elaborate, consisting of six sets of white concentric circles and a few 'acacia pod' figures. **Panel Three** consists of just

10

The Sabiny people of Kapchorwa District are the only ethnic group in Uganda to practise female genital mutilation (FGM) – often and somewhat euphemistically referred to as female circumcision. Traditionally, Sabiny girls are expected to succumb to the knife shortly after reaching puberty but before marriage, in the belief that having the clitoris removed reduces the temptation to indulge in promiscuity. Traditionally, should a female Sabiny refuse to be cut, she will forever be accorded the social status of a girl – forbidden from marrying, or from speaking publicly to circumcised women, or from undertaking women's tasks such as milking cows, collecting dung to plaster walls and drawing grain from the communal granary.

FGM is traditionally performed during the December of every even-numbered year. Several girls will participate in one communal ceremony, and the festivities last for several days before and after the actual operation, which takes only a few minutes to perform. One by one, the girls are instructed to lie down with their arms held aloft and their legs spread open. Cold water is poured on the vagina, and the clitoris is pulled and extended to its fullest possible length before it is sliced off, together with part of the labia minora. Should a girl cry out during the procedure, she will be branded a coward and bring shame and misfortune to her family. When all the participants have endured the operation, they are herded to a collective enclosure. Here, according to J P Barber, who witnessed a ceremony in the 1950s: 'they bend and kneel, they moan and whistle, in an attempt to lessen their extreme agony. Their faces … are drawn and contracted. They are too conscious of pain to notice or care about anything or anybody.'

No anaesthetic or disinfectant is used, and the operation is often performed on several girls in short succession using a non-sterilised knife or razor, or even a scrap of sharp metal or glass. Short-term complications that frequently follow on from the procedure include haemorrhaging, urinary retention and temporary lameness. In the years that follow, mutilated women often experience extreme pain during sexual intercourse, and bear an increased risk of complications related to childbirth. For some, circumcision will prove fatal. A small proportion of girls will die immediately or shortly after the operation from uncontrolled bleeding, shock or infection. Others face a lingering death sentence: the HIV virus is occasionally transmitted during mass operations, and mutilated women are often prone to vaginal tearing during intercourse, which makes them especially vulnerable to sexually transmitted diseases.

Public debate around the subject of FGM is traditionally taboo. The first local woman to come out strongly against the custom was Jane Frances Kuka, who served as head of a local teacher-training college in the 1970s. Herself defiantly uncircumcised, Kuka educated her students about the dangers of FGM, hoping they would act as ambassadors to the wider community. In 1986, encouraged by Museveni's strong commitment to women's rights, and assisted by the local representative of the WHO, Kuka launched a more open campaign, one that met strong opposition from community leaders who felt that outsiders were criticising and interfering with their culture. In response to this provocation, a district by-law was passed in 1988 requiring all Sabiny women to undergo FGM – any woman who did not submit to the knife voluntarily would do so by force. Kuka visited the cabinet minister for women in Kampala, and together they flew a helicopter to

Kapchorwa to rescue as many victims as they could. At the minister's insistence, the by-law was revoked shortly after it came into being, but still too late for the hundreds of women that had been seized, bound and forcibly circumcised by the district authorities.

Kuka's major breakthrough came in 1992, with the formation of the Sabiny Elders Association, which aimed to protect the Sabiny culture by preserving songs, dances and other positive customs, but also wanted to eliminate more harmful traditions, notably FGM. At the same time, Kuka consolidated her network of local women's groups to launch the UN-funded REACH programme, which adopted a culturally sensitive strategy, endorsing most Sabiny traditional values but highlighting the health risks associated with FGM. In 1996, coinciding with the start of the initiation season, the two organisations staged the first Sabiny Culture Day, which highlighted the positive aspects of local traditions while doubling as a substitute for the traditional female initiation ceremony. In place of a rusty knife, female initiates were given a symbolic gift, and counselled on subjects such as HIV prevention, family planning and economic empowerment. The number of girls who underwent FGM in 1996 was 36% lower than it had been in 1994. In 1996, Kuka swept to a landslide victory in local elections for a parliamentary representative, to be appointed Minister of State for Gender and Cultural Affairs, giving her a more prominent forum for her campaign. Her new appointment also ensured that she had the ear of President Museveni, who made a personal appearance at the 1998 Culture Day to deliver a speech about the dangers of FGM.

Many Sabiny traditionalists regard female circumcision as integral to their cultural identity: the rite of passage that transforms a girl into a woman. In more remote parts of the district, uncircumcised women still experience social discrimination, and their families stand to gain materially from the substantial gifts they customarily receive from friends and relatives on the day of initiation. One strongly reactionary element is the female elders who are paid to perform the operations – finance aside, these women are not eager to relinquish their elevated status as community advisors and custodians of tradition and magic.

In recent years, Museveni and his government have made great strides towards the total abolition of FGM in Uganda. In 2010, it was made illegal to carry out FGM, or to participate in any event leading to its practice, or to discriminate against a woman who hasn't undergone it. Clandestine ceremonies are still held in remote areas, but illegal practitioners of the operation now risk being arrested – indeed, five such individuals each received a four-year jail sentence in 2014 – and the number of women who undergo FGM today is a fraction of what it would have been in the 1990s. In the 2013 Tumaini Awards Programme, Jane Frances Kuka was named a Lifetime Achiever for her role as a heroine in the fight against FGM.

The remarkable progress made towards eradicating FGM locally within the space of one generation can be attributed partially to the Sabiny being culturally anomalous in Uganda – the rest of the population has never subscribed to the practice. It is sobering to realise that, according to WHO estimates, up to 140 million women across 28 countries elsewhere in Africa have suffered some form of genital mutilation, and every year another three million girls in Africa are at risk of being subjected to FGM.

A dozen discrete panels of prehistoric rock art are known from five different localities in Uganda's far southeast, namely Nyero, Kakoro, Obwin Rock, Ngora and Lolwe Island (Lake Victoria). Collectively added to the tentative list of UNESCO World Heritage Sites in 1997, these 'hunter-gatherer geometric rock art sites of eastern Uganda' are in most cases monochromatic – typically either red or white – and the predominant figures are sets of four or five concentric circles, and strange compartmentalised sausage-shaped figures reminiscent of acacia pods. It would be misleading to compare the impact of these geometric rock paintings, many of which are very faded, to their more naturalistic and better-preserved counterparts in central Tanzania or southern Africa. Nevertheless, a visit to one of the more accessible sites, in particular Nyero, is recommended to anybody with a passing interest in archaeology or human prehistory.

The limited palate drawn on by the artists of Kumi and Soroti was sourced from whatever natural materials were available to them. Red pigments were created by scraping the surface of a ferruginous rock, while white paint was derived from a combination of clay, dung and sap, and black from oxidised organic matter such as charcoal and burned fat. The raw ingredients would be ground finely then mixed into a thick liquid such as albumin to form an adhesive paste that was applied to the rock surface using a rudimentary brush of animal hair. Unless you assume that the artists had one eye focused on posterity, it is reasonable to think that the surviving paintings constitute a minute proportion of their work, much of which would have been painted on to exposed rocks or more ephemeral surfaces such as animal hide.

The age of the rock art is a matter for conjecture, as is the identity of the artists. The Iteso people who have inhabited the region for the last 300 years reckon that the art has always been there. Iteso tradition does relate that the region's rock shelters were formerly occupied by a short, light-skinned race of people, and excavations at Nyero have unearthed several microlithic tools of a type not used by the Iteso. Most likely, then, that the artists were hunter-gatherers with ethnic and cultural affiliations to the so-called Bushmen who were responsible for much of the rock art in southern Africa. The paintings must be at least 300 years old, and are possibly much older.

As for the intent of the artists, the field is wide open. The circle is a universal theme in prehistoric art and its use could be mythological, symbolic (for instance, a representation of the cycle of the seasons) or more literal (the sun or moon). A possible clue to interpreting the rock art of eastern Uganda comes from a style of house painting practised in northeast DRC in association with rainmaking ceremonies. Here, concentric circles represent the sun, while wavy lines symbolise the moon's feet, which – it is said – follow the rain (a reference to the link between the new moon and stormy weather). Could a similar purpose reasonably be attributed to the rock art of eastern Uganda? Quite possibly, since Nyero is known to have been the site of Iteso rainmaking ceremonies in historic times. But it is a considerable part of these ancient paintings' mystique that they pose more questions than there are answers forthcoming – the simple truth is that we'll never know.

one white set of concentric circles on the roof of a low rock shelter. The other three panels are very faded or damaged.

The springboard for visits to Nyero is Kumi, about halfway along the surfaced road between Mbale and Soroti. Head west from the main crossroads in Kumi (◈ *1.48913, 33.93674*) on to the Ngora Road for 8km, passing through the tiny trading centre of Nyero (somewhat incongruously, the site of a large private university), then 2km later you'll see the 100m side road to the rock-art site signposted clearly to the right. Any public transport between Kumi and Ngora can drop you here.

Lake Bisina Shaped like a wobbly smiley, this narrow and shallow freshwater body extends over roughly 190km² along an eastern arm of the Kyoga drainage system, some 12km northeast of Kumi as the crow flies. Bisina is an attractive lake, fringed by extensive swamps and towered over by the (normally obscured) peaks of Elgon to the south and the jagged outline of Mount Kadam to the east. More significantly, it is the largest component in the Lake Opeta–Bisina Wetland System, a vast mosaic of open lakes, permanent swamps and seasonal floodplains that submerge the eastern Kyoga Basin. In 2006, Lake Bisina and the smaller Lake Opeta, together with their soggy catchments, were recognised as a 550km² Ramsar Wetland Site due to their scientific importance. Both lakes harbour endemic cichlid fish species considered extinct in the more accessible lakes of Kyoga and Victoria. Lake Bisina and its enclosing swamps also support a number of localised bird species, including the legendary shoebill and localised papyrus gonolek, white-winged warbler, pygmy goose and lesser jacana. Bisina is also one of a handful of localities known to harbour Fox's weaver, a swamp fringe-associated bird endemic to this one small part of eastern Uganda.

Tourist development along the shores of Lake Bisina is all but non-existent. The most convenient way to get there from the south is to follow the surfaced Mbale–Soroti Road north of Kumi for 25km to the village of Kapiri, from where a 4km side road runs east to the western tip of Bisina. Once at the lakeshore, you'll need to negotiate for a local dugout to ferry you towards the reedy northwestern shore, where up to 50 pairs of Fox's weaver have been recorded breeding.

SOROTI

Soroti, with a population of almost 50,000, is the headquarters of an eponymous district mainly populated, like Kumi to the south, by Iteso people. Soroti is most relevant to tourist traffic as the springboard for the little-used but fascinating alternative northeastern route to Kidepo Valley National Park via Karamoja (see pages 302–3). This route to Kidepo was long discouraged by insecurity, and while it is a lot safer following the disarmament of the Karamoja warriors in 2011, it has now been superseded, at least in terms of convenience, by a shorter and easier route through Gulu and Kitgum

Strategic location aside, Soroti – unlike many other towns in Uganda – has retained much of its historical feel, as aging architectural gems such as street front verandas and rusting iron roofs have yet to be weeded out and replaced by storeyed concrete blocks, while a smattering of mosques and temples, some now converted to other purposes, testify to the former influence of Asian traders. The most prominent natural attraction in the immediate vicinity is Soroti Rock, a striking granite formation whose pinnacle towers above the town centre and offers good views across to Lake Kyoga. Further afield, Soroti is the closest town to Obwin Rock Art Site, which is similar but inferior in quality to Nyero, and the best jumping-off point for visits to Lake Opeta, which forms part of the same wetland complex as

the larger and more accessible Lake Bisina. Another possibility is to catch a matutu to Serere, 30km southwest of Soroti near Lake Kyoga, and arrange to take a dugout canoe on to the lake with one of the local fishermen.

GETTING THERE AND AWAY Soroti lies 100km northwest of Mbale along a surfaced road passing through Kumi and the marshy western fringes of Lake Bisina. There is plenty of bus and matatu traffic between Mbale and Soroti, while the direct Kakise bus from Kampala costs US$7.

A good surfaced road runs between Soroti and Lira to the west. Several buses and matutus cover this route each day. Transport north to Moroto is less regular, but at least one bus does the run daily, leaving Soroti at around noon and taking 5 hours. Heading towards Kidepo, the daily Gateway bus from Kampala passes through Soroti at around 10.00 and arrives at Kaabong at around 17.30.

WHERE TO STAY

Soroti Hotel (68 rooms) 0414 561269. A kilometre from the town centre on the Serere Rd, Soroti's inheritance from the defunct Uganda Hotels chain provides the standard combination of slightly run-down original infrastructure & modern 'bolt-on' additions. A small rock outcrop at the rear of the lawn provides a modest view over the outskirts of the town. *US$35/38/42 sgl/dbl/twin.* **$$**

Landmark Hotel (32 rooms) m 0704 408547. This centrally located hotel on the busy Market St offers clean, tiled en-suite rooms, secure parking at the rear & a particularly affordable restaurant serving main courses for around US$3. Good value. *US$22/25/32 sgl/dbl/twin.* **$$**

Golden Ark (45 rooms) m 0785 325700. This rambling establishment on the Mbale Rd offers a variety of basic en-suite rooms. *US12/17/30 sgl/dbl/twin.* **$$**

Garden Guesthouse Located at the eastern end of Market St, beyond the temple, this simple set-up offers basic rooms using common showers & a pleasant open-fronted bar. *US$5/7 sgl/dbl.* **$**

TOUR OPERATOR Soroti and Kumi are staging points for the range of rather low-key attractions described below. Though it's possible to locate them by yourself you'll get considerably more out from your exploration with a little local knowledge. Margaret Stevens of Loughborough, UK, suggests that the grassroots tour operator listed below provides the necessary spark.

Homestead Tours m 0784 685856; e homesteadtours@gmail.com. A community tourism project based on the main road at Kapir halfway between Soroti & Kumi. Activities offered include guided walks, cycle rides & boat trips; fishing; rock paintings on Kapir Hill; processing & eating traditional foods including peanut butter; ox ploughing; birdwatching (including wetland rarities); traditional musical instruments, singing, dancing & storytelling; & visiting local markets.

WHAT TO SEE AND DO

Obwin Rock About 7km south of Soroti along the surfaced road to Mbale stands this tall granite outcrop, whose name means 'place of hyenas' in the local Ateso tongue. You'd be fortunate to see any hyenas at Obwin today, but the formation is riddled with small caves and shelters, one of which is the site of an ancient red rock painting. There's just one pattern on the panel, a set of six concentric circles, but – unusually – the outer circle is decorated with eight rectangles, while what might be a pair of legs dangles from the circle's base.

Lake Opeta Part of the same Ramsar wetland as the larger and more accessible Bisina, Opeta comprises about 12km² of shallow open water enclosed by a much

larger area of papyrus swamp. The lake and its swampy environs support one of Africa's most prolific shoebill populations, as well as the marsh-dwelling sitatunga antelope, breeding colonies of the endemic Fox's weaver, and other localised bird species including rufous-bellied heron and papyrus gonolek. Lake Opeta cannot be reached on public transport. To get there in a private vehicle, follow the Moroto Road out of Soroti for 55km, turning right a few hundred metres past the village of Katakwi. From here, it's another 50km or so to the lakeshore village of Peta, passing *en route* through the villages of Toroma and Magoro. A trip to Lake Opeta could be combined with a diversion to the northern shore of Lake Bisina (page 277), which lies about 10km south of Toroma.

PIAN UPE WILDLIFE RESERVE

The little-known Pian Upe Wildlife Reserve extends over 2,788km² of semi-arid country to the north of Mount Elgon, making it the second-largest protected area in Uganda after Murchison Falls. The reserve protects a diverse selection of dry-country wildlife, ranging from patas monkey and cheetah to Burchell's zebra and roan antelope, but populations are very thin and scattered. Pian Upe is home to two pastoralist tribes: the Pian being a sub-group of the Karamoja, while the Upe are a Kalenjin-speaking people also known as the Pokot. The Pian and Upe have a history of armed conflict related to cattle rustling, having at times teamed up together to take on neighbouring tribes in Kenya or Uganda, and at other times have directed their violence towards each other. This insecurity is the main reason why the reserve has seen little tourist development to date, but this seems to have changed following the disarmament of the two tribes in 2011, making Pian Upe of interest both as a potential gateway to Karamoja/Kidepo and as an intriguing goal for a day safari out of the Elgon region.

FEES An entrance fee of US$10 per person per 24 hours is levied. No fee is charged for using the public road through the reserve.

FLORA AND FAUNA Pain Upe protects a tract of semi-arid country that usually receives some rain in April and more substantial showers from June to early September, but is also subject to regular rainfall failure. The predominant cover of mixed *Acacia-Commiphora* savannah is essentially the Ugandan extension of an eastern savannah belt encompassing much of northern Kenya and the Amboseli–Tsavo–Mkomazi complex of reserves on the border between Kenya and Tanzania.

No reliable wildlife population estimates exist for Pian Upe, and poaching has taken a heavy toll since the 1970s, but anecdotal information suggests that Pian Upe still harbours a wide variety of large mammals, and furthermore that populations have stabilised or even increased in recent years. Leopard, cheetah and spotted hyena are all seen quite regularly by ranger patrols, and a small population of lion is present. Among the ungulate species are Burchell's zebra, buffalo, eland, hartebeest, greater kudu, topi, oribi, dik-dik and Uganda's last population of roan antelope. In addition to the widespread vervet monkey and olive baboon, the far more localised patas monkey is quite common on the savannah.

Wildlife concentrations are highest in the vicinity of the Loporokocho Swamps, which lie near the eastern border and are inhabited by Upe pastoralists who (unlike the Pian) have no tradition of killing wild animals for food. Pian Upe is of some ornithological interest, since the dry plains harbour several dry-country species with a restricted distribution in Uganda, for instance ostrich, yellow-necked spurfowl, Hartlaub's bustard, Jackson's hornbill and white-headed buffalo weaver.

GETTING THERE AND AWAY The headquarters at Murujore is situated right alongside the direct Mbale–Moroto Road, roughly 90km north of Mbale (11km north of the reserve's southern boundary) and 50km south of Nakapiripirit. Coming from the south, the first 30km, as far as the junction for Sipi, this road is surfaced and in a good state of repair. However, the condition of the subsequent dirt road is erratic and can be pretty dire after rain. You'll know you've entered the reserve when, shortly after passing through the trading centre of Chepsikunya, the road crosses a bridge over the forest-fringed Kerim River. In theory, a couple of daily **buses** run right past the reserve headquarters on their way between Mbale and Moroto but in practice, because of the condition of the road between Pian Upe and Muyembe, public transport has ceased on this route.

 WHERE TO STAY AND EAT Four cheap bandas exist at the Murujore reserve headquarters, and a canteen serves a limited selection of drinks. Expect to bring anything else you need with you, unless advised to the contrary.

WHAT TO SEE AND DO Assuming that security is no longer an issue, the main problem concerning tourism in Pian Upe is now the restricted internal road network. Other than the main road between Mbale and Moroto, this is limited to a recently reopened track leading towards Loporokocho Swamp. Guided game walks can be arranged, accompanied by an armed ranger, as can informal visits to one of the Pian/Karamojong villages within the reserve. The UWA now runs the reserve in partnership with a private operator (Karamojong Overland Safaris), and improved facilities and an expanded game track network is planned. Current information can be obtained from the UWA offices in Kampala and Mbale.

Part Three

NORTHERN UGANDA

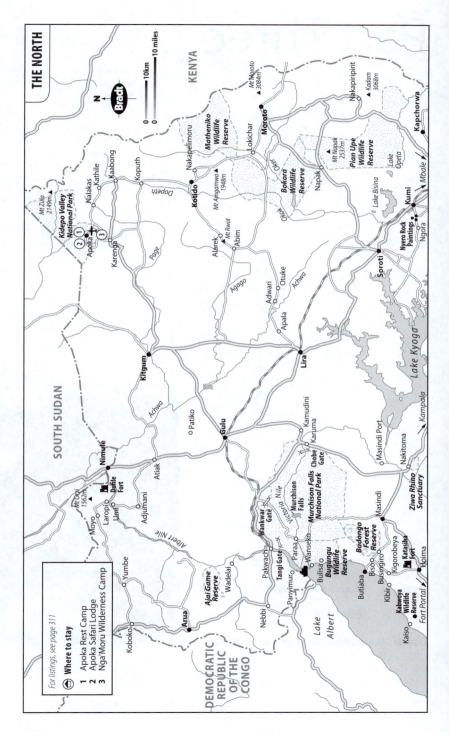

THE NORTH

KENYA

SOUTH SUDAN

DEMOCRATIC
REPUBLIC
OF THE
CONGO

For listings, see page 311
○ Where to stay
1 Apoka Rest Camp
2 Apoka Safari Lodge
3 Nga'Moru Wilderness Camp

Kidepo Valley
National Park

Mt Zilia
2149m▲

Malakas
Kathile
Kaabong
Koputh
Karenga

Mt Otzi
1562m▲

Duffle
Fort

Nimule

Moyo
Laropi
Umi
Adjumani

Yumbe

Koboko

Arua

Nebbi

Panyimuro

Wadelai

Pakwach
Tangi Gate
Paraa
Wanseko

Ajai Game
Reserve

Lake
Albert

Butiaba
Kibiro

Kaiso

Kabwoya
Wildlife
Reserve

Fort Portal

Hoima

Busingiiro
Bisoo
Kigorobeya

Katasiha
Fort

Bulisa

Bugungu
Wildlife
Reserve

Budongo
Forest
Reserve

Masindi

Ziwa Rhino
Sanctuary

Nakitoma

Masindi Port

Murchison Falls
National Park

Murchison
Falls

Wankwar
Gate

Victoria Nile

Albert Nile

Chobe
Gate

Karuma
Kamudini

Atiak

Patiko

Gulu

Kitgum

Achwa

Achwa

Lira

Apala
Otuke
Adwari
Agago

Alarek
Abim

Mt Ywot

Nakapelimoru

Kotido

Mt Angamwa ▲
1948m

Oket
Okok

Napak

Mt Napak
2537m

Bokora
Wildlife
Reserve

Matheniko
Wildlife
Reserve

Lokichar

Moroto

Mt Moroto
3084m ▲

Nakapiripirit

Mt Napak
2537m

Kadam
3068m ▲

Pian Upe
Wildlife
Reserve

Lake
Opeta

Kapchorwa

Mbale

Kumi

Ngora

Soroti

Nyero Rock
Paintings

Lake Bisina

Lake Kyoga

Kampala

Dopeth

Page

Apoka

N

Bradt

0   10km
0   10 miles

282

OVERVIEW

The north of Uganda, defined for the purposes of this book as pretty much everywhere north of Lake Kyoga and the rivers Kafu and Nkusi, accounts for roughly half the country's terrestrial surface area. When it comes to tourism, however, the north is relatively undeveloped, partly as a result of the decades-long civil war that embroiled much of the region until as recently as 2005, and partly because it lacks slightly when it comes to compelling places of interest. The top attraction is undoubtedly Murchison Falls National Park, which forms the focal point of almost all organised tours to the region. Less well known, but also highly rewarding, is the emergent Kidepo Valley in the far northeast, while other less-developed natural attractions include the bird-rich Budongo Forest Reserve, scenic Lake Albert, and the untrammelled Albert Nile as it courses north from Pakwach to the South Sudan border. Otherwise, much of northern Uganda falls into the category of 'travel for its own sake' – which is not to say that larger northern towns such as Gulu, Arua or Lira aren't enjoyable places to hang out, only that they offer little in the way of prescribed sightseeing.

This section on northern Uganda is divided into four chapters. The first and longest of these chapters deals with a vast swathe of north-central and northeast Uganda: towns such as Gulu, Lira and Kitgum, as well as the remote and rustic Karamoja subregion, all of which are likely to be visited by tourists only as part of a road safari from Kampala to Kidepo Valley National Park, the chapter's centrepiece. The next three chapters deal mainly with Murchison Falls and associated access routes northwest of Lake Kyoga. The second chapter in the section covers the town of Pakwach, an increasingly important gateway to Murchison Falls coming from Kampala, along with the remote and little-visited administrative subregion of West Nile. The next covers Bunyoro, an ancient kingdom whose major towns, Hoima and Masindi, are frequently passed through by tourists crossing between Murchison Falls and the southwest or Kampala. Finally, the last chapter in the section focuses tightly on Murchison Falls Conservation Area, which incorporates the eponymous national park as well as Kaniyo Pabidi Forest, a popular site for chimp tracking and forest birding.

HIGHLIGHTS

MPARO TOMBS The former capital of Bunyoro's King Kabalega, situated on the outskirts of Hoima, now houses a fantastic domed thatch construction where he and his successor are buried. Pages 332–3.

KIBIRO SALT GARDENS The goal of a truly off-the-beaten-track day hike down the Rift Escarpment to the shore of Lake Albert, Kibiro has been Bunyoro's most important source of salt since the 13th century. Pages 333–4.

KABWOYA WILDLIFE RESERVE This small and scenic reserve fringing Lake Albert offers a great range of activities including horseback safaris, mountain biking and day hikes. Pages 334–8.

BUDONGO FOREST RESERVE Superseded as a chimp-tracking destination by Kaniyo Pabidi, this vast forest east of Masindi remains a birding hotspot of note. Pages 341–4.

PAKWACH AND SURROUNDS The gateway to the little-visited West Nile, Pakwach is the only town to front the Nile on its meandering journey from Jinja to the South Sudan border, and is a useful budget base for day visits to Murchison Falls. Pages 314–18.

MURCHISON FALLS NATIONAL PARK Boat trips on a mesmerising stretch of the tropical Nile, game drives in search of elephants, lion and shoebills, and the mighty waterfall itself are among the myriad attractions of Uganda's largest national park. Pages 347–70.

KANIYO PABIDI FOREST Set within Murchison Falls Conservation Area but outside the national park, this forest offers the opportunity to track Uganda's densest chimpanzee population. Pages 359–60.

GULU A bustling hub of economic activity, northern Uganda's largest town is also notable for its friendly vibe and surprisingly cosmopolitan amenities. Pages 287–92.

KARAMOJA Uganda's remote 'Wild East' retains a genuine frontier feel underscored by the defiant traditional of its pastoralist Karamojong inhabitants. Pages 302–8.

KIDEPO VALLEY NATIONAL PARK Uganda's third-largest and most remote national park combines a spectacular submontane setting with plentiful wildlife, including elephant, lion and thousand-strong buffalo herds. Pages 308–12.

11

Gulu and the Northeast

Culturally, linguistically and economically, Uganda's far north has always been a land apart. Geographically, this sense of dislocation is largely attributable to Lake Kyoga, the 1,720km² centrepiece of a vast shallow sump, whose spidery swamp-lined fingers form a natural barrier between the predominantly Bantu-speaking south and the Nilotic-speaking north. Politically, the long-standing isolation of the north intensified after 1986, when – in stark contrast to the much-lauded economic and social recovery that characterised southern Uganda – the Lord's Resistance Army (LRA) subjected the region to a brutal and destructive civil war that endured for almost 20 years, leading early editions of this guidebook to characterise travel there as 'highly risky, if not downright suicidal'.

Security has improved dramatically since 2005, when the LRA ceased operating within Uganda. Indeed, of the three administrative subregions covered in this chapter, two – Acholi and Lango – are now regarded to be as safe as anywhere in the country. The third, Karamoja, though never greatly affected by LRA activity, has long been prone to sporadic tribal conflict, but this too has eased in recent years, although long-standing warnings against road travel there are still posted on certain government advisories. Despite the deprivation experienced during the 20-year civil war, the far north has also undergone a remarkable economic recovery, to the extent that larger towns such as Lira and Gulu now positively bustle with commercial activity.

Northern Uganda genuinely lies off any beaten tourist track, and is arguably worth visiting for that reason alone, but it would be disingenuous to pretend it overflows with tourist attractions. The region's one genuine highlight, set along the South Sudan border in the far northeast of Karamoja, is Kidepo Valley National Park, whose spectacular scenery and plentiful game is complemented by an excellent luxury lodge as well as a great little rest camp catering to budget travellers. Of cultural interest are the iconic Karamojong pastoralists who inhabit the semi-arid Karamoja plains and slopes running south from Kidepo. By contrast, northern towns such as Gulu, Lira and Kitgum offer limited scope for conventional tourism, though they do tend to offer unexpectedly good amenities – thanks largely to an ongoing post-conflict influx of NGO workers and volunteers – making them useful staging posts along the various routes to Kidepo.

HISTORY

Northern Uganda has a very different ethnic and historical identity to the south. Historically, the region is inhabited by a mosaic of politically-decentralised Nilotic-speaking tribes whose cultural and linguistic affiliations point north towards South Sudan rather than south towards the centralised Bantu-speaking areas of the south and west of Uganda. The most populous of these northern tribes are the Acholi

(a relatively recent confederation of chiefdoms created by the British and centred on Gulu), the Langi (centred on Lira) and the semi-nomadic Karamojong pastoralists of the far east. The Nilotic languages spoken by these people are quite distinct from the Bantu dialects spoken in the south, having as much in common as English has with, say, Chinese.

During the colonial era, it was northern cotton and tobacco rather than any southern produce that enabled the fledgling Uganda protectorate to turn a profit. Northerners earned a reputation as tough and hard-working that still persists today.

DRIVING IN NORTHERN UGANDA   *By Andrew Roberts*

Cultural differences between northern and southern Uganda extend to the use of vehicles, and anyone who has travelled any distance in the south will soon raise an eyebrow at one particular northern idiosyncrasy. The women ride bicycles! Indeed, some of the cheeky lasses even ride motorbikes! This sort of thing is simply not done south of Lake Kyoga. And that is not all! In Arua, a significant number of cyclists actually use lights at night, a precaution that would seem to remove much of the happy uncertainty of nocturnal bicycling.

Sadly, this cautious approach doesn't extend to other aspects of road use. In the south, large vehicles such as buses and trucks enforce the maxim of 'might is right'. Beyond the Nile, passage belongs to whoever is prepared to push hardest for it, and that includes bicycles and boda-bodas. Southern drivers work on the assumption that cyclists will get out of their way: rather than waiting for a gap in a stream of urban bicycle traffic, they are apt to create one with their vehicle. This is not acceptable up north. If inconvenienced, a rider will quickly inform you; and in the event of a knock, a vocal civil society, in the form of the town's considerable community of cyclists and bystanders, will flock to his (or indeed her) cause. This uncompromising approach is disconcerting enough in towns, but terrifying on rural roads where larger vehicles approach each other head on in the manner of medieval jousters, doubtless a legacy of the northern warrior tradition. That any vehicles remain on the roads means that one of a pair of drivers must give way, although the goodly amount of shattered glass on the roads suggests that this is not always so. In my own experience, the driver giving way was always me.

The need for a prudent approach to driving is underlined by the nature of the dirt roads in northern Uganda. Geology dictates that, instead of the compacted red laterite used down south, engineers must often work with more gravelly material that is less slippery in wet weather but all too easy to lose grip on in dry weather. It is also particularly prone to erosion, and deep gullies can develop parallel to or indeed across the road. Since you'll want to negotiate these additional hazards at your leisure, rather than driving into them to avoid a fellow road user, my advice is to slow down on sighting any approaching vehicle!

The north is more sparsely populated than the rest of the country when it comes both to people and to branded filling stations such as Shell or Total. Heading north from Kampala to Pakwach/Arua or Gulu/Kidepo, be aware that the only sources of brand-name fuel north of Luwero or south of Gulu and Arua are the Shell filling station at Byetale and Total at Kigumba. Brand-name fuel is also in short supply in Karamoja generally.

By 1959, Gulu had become Uganda's second-largest town with 30,000 residents, and Lira was placed third with 14,000 – a combined population not far short of the 46,000 that then lived in Kampala. Northerners formed the backbone of the protectorate army, and many, used to hard graft on plantations in their homeland, migrated south to work on sugar estates in Buganda. But if the north provided the raw materials and the manpower for Uganda's development, it was the south that tended to enjoy the rewards.

In the immediate post-independence era, this long-standing economic divide festered into tribal persecution and bloodshed. During Obote's two terms as president, the Acholi- and Langi-dominated army terrorised southerners. In between, Amin and his West Nile cronies (known as 'Sudanese') terrorised everyone; though curiously it was their fellow northerners, the Acholi and Langi, who were most heavily targeted on ethnicity grounds. Come 1986, when Museveni seized power, the north had good cause to fear, their menfolk having brutalised the Ugandan population over the best part of 20 years. They were right to be worried, for Museveni's southern-dominated army mounted a decidedly heavy-handed campaign to stamp their authority on northern Uganda. Amidst an atmosphere of fear, resentment and hatred of the National Resistance Movement (NRM) regime, the stage was set for Alice Lakwena's short-lived but almost successful rebellion, and the subsequent 20-year campaign waged by Joseph Kony and his LRA – see boxes pages 294–5 and 300–1.

Despite the NRM's failure to secure a formal agreement with Kony, the LRA ceased to be active in Uganda in 2005, and the north has been peaceful ever since. Nevertheless, the legacy of these long years is still apparent in the likes of Gulu, Lira and Kitgum. While the rest of the country has enjoyed the benefit of almost three decades of stability and economic growth, the north has lagged far behind. It will take years to achieve some sort of normality and the challenges are both numerous and daunting. Many of the abducted combatants have returned home where they must reintegrate into the society they were forced to terrorise. Collectively, this society also faces its own problems. For the best part of 18 years, most of the rural populace was forced to live under military guard in squalid and insanitary camps for Internally Displaced People (IDP), or to migrate into large towns. For up to 20 years, these IDPs were stuck in protected camps where they were fed by aid agencies and were unable to do any useful work. Then finally when they did return home, their houses had crumbled, termites had reduced their furniture to dust, once fertile fields had been reclaimed by the bush, and boundary lines with neighbouring proprieties had been lost. Indeed, with no other source of support, many old people, alcoholics, infirm, sick and other disadvantaged northerners are still dependent on charity today.

GULU

A name familiar to anyone who's taken the slightest interest in Uganda's recent history, Gulu was for many years a mysterious place of unhappy repute, a kind of sinister modern-day Timbuktu set at the heart of the territory terrorised by the LRA. Today, with northern Uganda having been safe for a full decade, Gulu is no longer a place of mystery, but an unexpectedly normal looking town, not that different in feel to Mbale, say, or Fort Portal. From a travel point of view, Gulu is of interest primarily as a potential stopover *en route* to Kidepo Valley National Park, but it also attracts a steady stream of NGO-associated visitors and volunteers, and has a surprisingly good selection of hotels and restaurants.

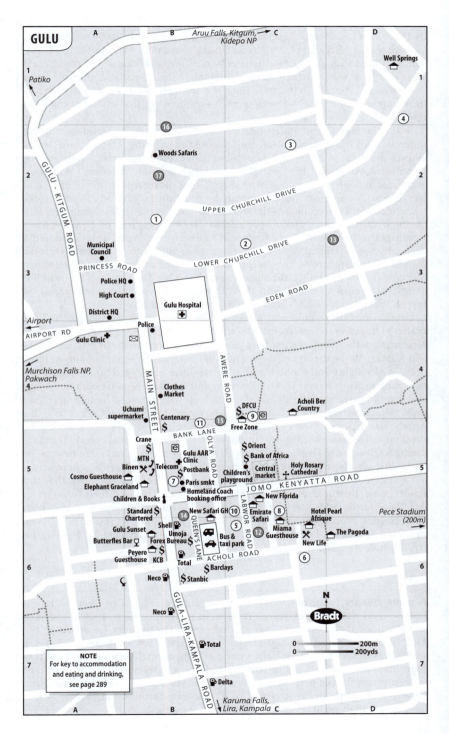

GULU

A   B   Aruu Falls, Kitgum, → C   D
Kidepo NP

Well Springs

Patiko

GULU - KITGUM ROAD

16

Woods Safaris

17

UPPER CHURCHILL DRIVE

1

Municipal Council

PRINCESS ROAD

LOWER CHURCHILL DRIVE

2

13

Police HQ

High Court

Gulu Hospital

EDEN ROAD

District HQ

Airport

AIRPORT RD

Police

Gulu Clinic

Murchison Falls NP, Pakwach

AWERE ROAD

Clothes Market

Acholi Ber Country

Uchumi supermarket

Centenary

DFCU

9

Free Zone

MAIN STREET

BANK LANE

11

15

OLYA ROAD

Crane

MTN

Gulu AAR Clinic

Orient

Bank of Africa

Binen

Telecom

Postbank

Children's playground

Central market

Holy Rosary Cathedral

Cosmo Guesthouse

7

Paris smkt

Elephant Graceland

Children & Books

Homeland Coach booking office

LABWOR ROAD

JOMO KENYATTA ROAD

Pece Stadium (200m)

New Florida

Standard Chartered

14

New Safari GH

10

Emirate Safari

8

Hotel Pearl Afrique

Gulu Sunset

Shell

QUEEN'S LANE

Bus & taxi park

5

Miama Guesthouse

New Life

The Pagoda

Butterfles Bar

Umoja

Forex Bureau

12

Peyero Guesthouse

KCB

Total

ACHOLI ROAD

6

Neco

Bardays

Stanbic

N

Neco

GULA-LIRA-KAMPALA ROAD

Bradt

NOTE
For key to accommodation and eating and drinking, see page 289

Total

0   200m
0   200yds

Delta

Karuma Falls, Lira, Kampala

A   B   C   D

GULU

For listings, see pages 290–1

Where to stay
1 Acholi Inn...............................B2
2 Bomah....................................C3
3 Churchill Courts...................C2
4 Dove's Nest..........................D1
5 Gulu Creamson
   Guesthouse........................C6
6 Gulu Crystal.........................C6
7 Franklin Guesthouse...........B5
8 The Iron Donkey..................C5
9 Jojo's Palace........................C4
10 Lexus Guesthouse...............C5
11 New Kakanyero.....................B5

Where to eat and drink
12 Abyssinia Ethiopian.............C6
13 BJ'z Bar & Grill.....................D3
14 The Coffee Hut....................B5
   The Iron Donkey..........(see 8)
15 The Kitchen..........................B5
16 Sankofa Café.......................B2
17 Through Art Keep
   Smiling (TAKS) Centre......B2

Gulu is a town of two distinct halves, separated by the gentle marshy valley alluded to in its name, which means 'pot' in the Acholi language. To the north of the valley lies a network of quiet curving avenues lined with government offices, smartish hotels and green gardens. To the south, the compact town centre is unexpectedly busy and prosperous-looking; roads choked with bicycle traffic, shops filled with goods and the central market with produce, and a rash of banks and other corporate concerns occupying freshly painted premises with smartly tiled verandas – the same buildings that once served as sleeping quarters for the 15,000-odd children who filed into town every evening to escape the clutches of the LRA.

It may not quite look the part, but Gulu is now Uganda's fifth-largest settlement, supporting a predominantly Acholi population that soared from below 15,000 in 1980 to more than 150,000 in 2015. In large part, this rapid population growth can be attributed to the many rural northerners who took refuge in Gulu's IDP camps in the 1990s, and stayed on afterwards. Gulu is also the main economic hub in northern Uganda, and an important centre of NGO operations, as well as being the site of the country's second-longest surfaced runway, and a recently refurbished railway linking it to Tororo and Pakwach.

GETTING THERE AND AWAY

By air Eagle Air (*http://eagleair-ug.com*) flies from Entebbe to Gulu on Mondays (departing 12.30, arriving 14.20), Wednesdays and Fridays (departing 12.30, arriving 13.30). The timetable is subject to change.

By road Gulu lies 335km north of Kampala, a 6-hour drive along a good surfaced road which crosses the Nile at Karuma Falls, then 13km further passes through Kamdini Corner, a nondescript junction town that enjoys almost legendary status as *the* place to stop for roasted roadside chicken. If **driving** yourself from Kampala, reliable opportunities to top up along the way are few and far between, especially on the 60km sections north and south of Karuma.

Regular **buses** run between Kampala Kasenyi Terminal and Gulu. The best service is the five-times daily Homeland Northern Express (*US$8*), which arrives in Gulu after 6 hours then continues on to Kitgum, arriving there 2 hours later. Also recommended at around the same price is the Zawadi Bus, which leaves Kampala from its William Street office behind Equatoria Mall. In the event that you're trying to reach Gulu from Masindi, you'll need to find some rustic form of public transport to cut across country to Kigumba on the Kampala–Gulu Road where you'll board a more conventional taxi. If you want to travel between Gulu and southeastern Uganda, a daily bus leaves Gulu at 07.00 and passes through Lira, Soroti and Mbale on its way to the Kenyan border crossing at Busia (and vice versa).

11

🏠 **WHERE TO STAY** The ongoing proliferation of NGOs means that Gulu is well provided with hotels for all budgets.

Upmarket

🏠 **Bomah Hotel** [288 C3] (90 rooms) Eden Rd; 📞 047 1432479; m 0779 945063; e bomahhotelltd@yahoo.com. Recently transformed into a smart 6-storey block, this is the only hotel in Gulu with pretensions to upmarket status, though it wouldn't quite make the grade in a more competitive environment. The fresh airy en-suite rooms come with nets, DSTV, AC & hot water, & the popular garden restaurant serves grills & curries in the US$5–8 range. Other facilities include free Wi-Fi, a pleasant swimming pool area, & health club with steam/sauna. *US$54/83 B&B sgl/dbl.* **$$$**

Moderate

🏠 **Churchill Courts Hotel** [288 C2] (38 rooms) Upper Churchill Drive; 📞 047 1432245; m 0777 764409; e gcchotel@gmail.com; www. churchillcourtshotel.com. The pick in this range is this friendly, secluded & comfortable hotel whose generously sized carpeted rooms are provided with nets, AC, DSTV & en-suite hot shower. Bland but good value. *US$35/45/64 B&B sgl/dbl/exec.* **$$**

🏠 **Dove's Nest Hotel** [288 D1] (26 rooms) Lower Churchill Drive; m 0790 912355, 🟦 fb.me/ guludovesnesthotel. This smart, family-run guesthouse is justifiably billed as an 'oasis of peace & quietude'. It has a pleasant ground-floor restaurant & the attractively furnished en-suite rooms with nets, DSTV, fan or AC, Wi-Fi & hot shower are good value. *US$29/36 sgl/dbl with fan, or US$49/54 with AC. All rates B&B.* **$$**

🏠 **New Kakanyero** [288 B5] (33 rooms) Bank Lane; m 0772 933077; e kakanyero@ yahoo.com. The entrance to this hotel serves as a portal between a hot, dusty & undistinguished central setting & a proximate dimension where comfortable bedrooms are provided with AC, DSTV & en-suite hot showers. The old wing next door has perfectly adequate rooms & much cheaper en-suite rooms with fan. The 1st-floor restaurant has a street-facing balcony. Courtyard parking. *US$25/47 B&B sgl/dbl (new wing) or US$15/20 (old wing).* **$$**

🏠 **Acholi Inn** [288 B2] (54 rooms) Churchill Drive; m 0701 367970/0772 367972; e stay@ acholiinn.com; www.acholiinn.com. Currently under renovation, Gulu's oldest hotel houses the once shabby bar in which MPs, army officers & retired rebels mingle in the book *Wizard of the Nile*. The spacious en-suite rooms come with nets, AC & DSTV, but seem overpriced compared to the above, even if rates include free internet & use of the swimming pool & health club. *US$49/60/80 B&B sgl/dbl/suite.* **$$$**

Budget

🏠 **Gulu Crystal Hotel** [288 C6] (21 rooms) Acholi Rd; m 0790 912182. This central 4-storey hotel has clean tiled rooms with fitted nets, fan, TV, Wi-Fi & plenty of cupboard space. Very good value. *US$13/20/23 sgl/dbl/twin.* **$$**

🏠 **The Iron Donkey** [288 C5] (10 rooms) Olya Rd; m 0793 719563; 🟦 fb.me/IronDonkeyGulu. Very popular with volunteers & NGO workers, the comfortable rooms at the back of this superb café have bunk beds, fitted nets & fan, but use common showers. They're a little overpriced for what you get, but the safe & sociable atmosphere compensates, & the food is great. Fast free Wi-Fi. *US$20/25 B&B sgl/dbl occupancy.* **$$**

🏠 **Jojo's Palace** [288 C4] (18 rooms) Bank Lane; m 0756 545378. This agreeable cheapie has bright, clean spacious rooms with TV & nets, some en suite. Try for a 1st-floor room as they're cooler than those situated in the courtyard. A decent ground-floor restaurant is attached. *US$10/13 sgl/dbl using common showers, US$14/20 en-suite sgl/dbl.* **$**

Shoestring

🏠 **Lexus Guesthouse** [288 C5] (13 rooms) Labwar Rd; m 0779 885467. The pick of several cheapies clustered in this part of town, the Lexus has very clean tiled rooms with fitted nets, fan & en-suite cold shower. A nice terrace restaurant is attached. *US$7.50/9.50 sgl/dbl.* **$**

🏠 **Gulu Creamson Guesthouse** [288 C6] (10 rooms) Labwar Rd; m 0777 488271. This quiet but central courtyard guesthouse has clean rooms with fitted nets, some en suite. A good fall-back if the nearby Lexus is full. A bakery & restaurant spills out on the pavement in front. *US$7 dbl using common shower or US$8.50 en-suite sgl.* **$**

🏠 **Franklin Guesthouse** [288 B5] (13 rooms) Gulu Av; m 0758 796197. This pocket-friendly, centrally located lodge with street-front veranda was good enough for the chap who wrote the *Wizard of the Nile* while he pieced together the story of Moses, the LRA escapee. *US$8.50 en-suite sgl, US$6/17 sgl/twin with shared facilities.* $

✕ WHERE TO EAT AND DRINK
Town centre
☀ 💻 **The Iron Donkey** [288 C5] Olya Rd; m 0793 719563, f fb.me/IronDonkeyGulu; ⏰ 09.00–19.00 Wed–Sat, 09.00–15.00 Sun. Opened in 2014 & already entrenched as the hangout of choice for 20-something NGOs & volunteers, this cosily decorated bakery-cum-café with blasting fans & free Wi-Fi serves a great selection of wraps, toasted sandwiches, filled pancakes, quiches & burritos, along with smoothies, fresh juices, iced & hot coffee & cupcakes. A selection of herbal teas, home roast coffee & fresh artisan bread. are sold over the counter. *Meals in the US$4–6 range.*

☀ ✕ **Abyssinia Ethiopian Restaurant** [288 C6] Labwar Rd; m 0774 423132. For something different, try this down-to-earth vegan-friendly eatery, which serves typical Ethiopian dishes such as *tibs* (fried meat), *shiro* (spicy chickpea stew), *kitfo* (minced beef) & *atkilt* (mixed vegetables) with rice or an injera 'pancake'. *Mains around US$9.*

💻 **The Coffee Hut** [288 B5] Awich Rd; m 0754 608728; [0] 07.00–20.00 daily. Situated opposite the bus station, this modern street-side café serves juices, smoothies & coffee, as well as an imaginative selection of salads, wraps & sandwiches. Free Wi-Fi. *Around US$5.*

✕ **The Kitchen Restaurant** [288 B5] Bank Lane; m 0777 004338/0779 825683; ⏰ 08.00–22.00 daily. This friendly local eatery does a great buffet lunch, as well as à la carte Ugandan dishes, plus good juices & shakes. *Buffet US$4 inc drink, mains from US$7.*

North of the centre
☀ 💻 **Sankofa Café** [288 B2] Samuel Doe Rd; m 0776 712198/0701 217198; f fb.me/ sankofagulu; ⏰ 08.00–22.00 daily. Set in pleasant gardens about 1km north of the town centre, this cheerful café dishes up a good selection of snacks, burgers, pizzas & salads, plus juices, smoothies, coffees or beers. *Meals in the US$2–7 range.*

✕ **Through Art Keep Smiling (TAKS) Centre** [288 B2] Upper Churchill Drive; ☎ 047 1433906; m 0471 433 906; e takscentre@gmail. com; http://takscentre.blogspot.co.za; ⏰ 08.00–22.00 Mon–Sat. Best known as an art gallery & installation, TAKS also has an internet café, a garden restaurant & bar & regular film evenings.

☆ **BJ'z Bar & Grill** [288 D3] Eden Rd; ☎ 047 1432235. More bar than grill, this lively venue near the Bomah Hotel has garden seating, big screens to lure in the punters during football matches, pool tables, quiz night (Thu) & themed music evenings. No food is served.

OTHER PRACTICALITIES
Foreign exchange Several banks, including Stanbic and Barclays, offer foreign exchange facilities and have 24-hour ATMs outside.

Internet Most of the moderate hotels listed have Wi-Fi or internet facilities, as do the central Coffee Hut and Iron Donkey. In the town centre, there are a cluster of internet cafés – though with extremely slow systems – towards the bottom of Queen's Road.

Swimming pool The best pool is at the Bomah Hotel. Day visitors pay US$3 to use it.

TOUR OPERATORS
Woods Safaris [288 B2] Upper Churchill Rd; m 0772 832430/0786 650477; e ronnie@ woodssafaris.com; www.woodssafaris.com. This new Gulu-based operator offers day trips to Fort Patiko, Aruu Falls, Chobe Safari Lodge & Ziwa Rhino Sanctuary, as well as longer trips to Kidepo & Murchison Falls National Park.

WHAT TO SEE AND DO

Baker's Fort, Patiko Remnants of the fort established in 1872 by Sir Samuel Baker (see box, page 293) can be found at Patiko, 25km north of Gulu. The fort centres on a large kopje consisting of several rock outcrops and a number of massive boulders. Three mortared stone structures still stand on the central plateau, but rather disappointingly they were all grain stores rather than part of the Bakers' residence. The mud houses that stood below the kopje are long gone, but an encircling defensive ditch, 100m in diameter, still curves into opposite ends of the kopje like the ring through a bull's nose. This ditch was reinforced with a wooden palisade with access through a small surviving gatehouse with a narrow doorway and rifle ports. Your guide, if you find one, will show you fissures between the rocks, the holding cells in which men and women were separately confined prior to 'sorting' on an adjacent rock plateau, and the passage between two boulders through which rejected wretches were led to be speared to death and tossed off the kopje for the hyenas. On a lighter note, the tour includes two massive boulders – separated by a gap and a drop slightly too wide for carefree leaping – between which Baker is said to have regularly jumped 'for exercise'; a feat which you'll be invited to emulate, but probably shouldn't!

The road to Patiko leads out of Gulu opposite the Bank of Uganda, just beyond the government offices. Bear right after 800m or you'll end up in Kitgum. The drive takes about 45 minutes. A special hire will cost around US$40–50 return, while boda riders quote US$5–8. Upon reaching Patiko, pass through the small trading centre and turn left immediately in front of a shiny row of police uniports. A visitors' book is kept in a caretaker's hut on the right of the access track but it's usually locked. Somebody purporting to be a guide will no doubt materialise; a tour of the site is more interesting with local interpretation, however skewed, so sign them up to show you around.

Aruu Falls (*Entry US$3*) This impressive 250m-wide waterfall comprises five different streams that cascade westwards down a series of moss-covered rocks on a tributary of the Aswa River called the Agogo or Aruu. Situated about 55km northeast of Gulu by road, it is easily visited as a day trip out of Gulu, or *en route* to Kidepo Valley National Park, provided that you have public transport. To get there, follow the Kitgum Road out of Gulu, crossing the Aswa River bridge after 40km, then continuing for another 7km further to Angagura trading centre. As you enter the trading centre (✪ *2.9661, 32.6399*) turn right on to an unsignposted dirt road and follow it for 8km, passing Aruu Falls Primary School on the way, to where the Agogo River effectively blocks the road (✪ *2.89664, 32.64884*). Walk west along the north bank of the fast-flowing river for about 300m, and you'll reach the top of the waterfall.

LIRA

The term 'backwater' might have been coined specially to describe the principal town of Langi subregion. Lake Kyoga provides the water, with all main roads between south and north diverting around its shores, and Lira lies behind it, on the road to nowhere of specific interest to tourists. Despite its isolation, Lira is a pleasant and bustling place, with unusually narrow streets for Uganda, and a rather crowded feel befitting its status as the country's tenth-largest town (population 100,000). As with Gulu, Lira suffered greatly at the hands of the LRA. The conflict's most notoriously heart-rending episode, the abduction of 139 schoolgirls in 1996,

Samuel and Florence Baker made repeated visits to Patiko (which they recorded as Fatiko). On the first two occasions, both in 1864, they were just passing through, firstly as explorers *en route* from Gondokoro (Sudan) to Lake Albert and Murchison Falls, then again on the return journey to Gondokoro. Patiko then was the southernmost outpost of a vast territory from which Egypt's Turkish rulers and their mercenaries plundered slaves, cattle and ivory.

The Bakers returned to Patiko in 1872 on a crusade to stamp out slavery. On this occasion they marched under a different flag; ironically, that of Egypt. The wind had changed in Cairo with the opening of the Suez Canal in 1869. Egypt's ruler, the Khedive Ismail, was aware that while this ultra-modern development had gained him recognition from the great powers, Egypt's international standing remained tempered by the ongoing medieval barbarism in Sudan and northern Uganda. Slavery, banned a full half century earlier by Britain and France, needed to be stopped or at any rate, a high-profile attempt to do so needed to be seen to be made. Samuel Baker, whose 1865 travelogue *The Albert N'yanza* had exposed the practice to the world, was the ideal candidate and in due course (after accepting the fabulous salary of £10,000 per year) Baker returned to central Africa with his wife and nephew to formalise Egypt's presence in southern Sudan and northern Uganda by officially annexing it as a province, to be named Equatoria. Specifically, he was to establish a chain of forts to pacify the region, and end the slave trade. He found the territory around Patiko so ravaged by the Egyptian Turks that they struggled to capture sufficient people or cattle to transport their vast hauls of ivory north to Khartoum. Baker headed south to Masindi in his vain attempt to include Bunyoro into the Egyptian Empire (see box, pages 328–9), before returning to Patiko where he established his headquarters around the kopje, from which he was able to banish the slavers and pacify local tribes made belligerent by their activities, at least in Gulu region. A long-running wrangle with a notorious slaver, Abu Saood, culminated in the slavers being routed in a battle at Patiko. When Baker finally returned to Britain, he felt able to write: 'The White Nile, for a distance of 1,600 miles from Khartoum to Central Africa was cleansed of an abomination of a traffic which had hitherto sullied its waters'. In truth, Baker had merely inconvenienced the slavers of Equatoria; he had lopped off their tentacles around Gulu – an area too despoiled to be of further interest – but more soon grew elsewhere. It was, for the time being, a hopeless cause anyway, for little real success could be achieved without the support of the Egyptian administration in Khartoum. By way of example, the defeated Abou Saood fled north to Gondokoro where, to Baker's outrage, Egyptian officials did not detain him but allowed him to return to Khartoum to regroup.

Baker's legacy in Uganda is interesting. Speke and Stanley are remembered simply as explorers who passed through and their achievements are cited as historical fact. Baker, however, was the first to spend any significant time in the region, in the process making both friends and enemies. Around Masindi, he is remembered with little warmth as the colonial aggressor who sought to conquer Bunyoro (and kick-started a history of poor relations between Britain and Bunyoro). It's a different story in Gulu though, where Baker is still remembered to this day with genuine warmth as the man who drove the Arabs from Patiko.

The civil war that consumed the Acholi districts of Kitgum and Gulu until 2005 has deep roots. They stretch to the beginning of the colonial era, when the culturally divergent northern territories were arbitrarily annexed to the Uganda protectorate and effectively placed under joint British–Baganda rule. And they reach back through 60 years of colonial underdevelopment: education in the northwest, and associated prospects of employment were deliberately stifled by the British, in order that the region might remain a ready source of military recruits and manual labourers. The roots of the present-day conflict are also embedded in the complex Jok system of spiritual belief, possession and sorcery that informs Acholi culture past and present. And they cannot easily be disentangled from the teachings of the early Christian missionaries who appropriated traditional Acholi spiritual concepts and icons into their biblical translations, in order that they might better hawk their exotic religious product to the locals.

As good a place to start as any, however, is June 1985 when Alice Auma, or Alice Lakwena as she had recently started calling herself, was introduced to General Tito Okello at Gulu's Acholi Inn. Auma was then a 29-year-old Acholi woman whose largely undistinguished life – divorced, childless and eking out a living as a fish-seller in Pakwach – had been transformed three months earlier when she was possessed by the spirit of an Italian soldier called Lakwena. Okello, by contrast, was the chief of the defence force (UPDF), slowly coming to the realisation that his troops would be unable to hold out indefinitely against the rebel National Resistance Army (NRA) and frustrated at President Obote's refusal to negotiate with NRA leader Yoweri Museveni. Lakwena was made aware of Okello's plans to oust Obote, and offered her services as his spiritual advisor, only to be passed over in favour of an established peer. Whether the general and the medium ever met again goes unrecorded, but both would play a leading role in national events over the next two years.

On 27 June 1985, the Obote regime was toppled by Okello and his Acholi supporters within the military. In the aftermath of this coup, the NRA captured Fort Portal, to eventually assume control over western Uganda as close to the capital as Masaka. Okello, who had no great personal ambition to power, formed a broad-based Military Council (MC) that included representatives of all political factions except the NRA. Museveni was invited to the party, and in December 1985, following protracted negotiations in Nairobi, a peace accord was signed leaving Okello as chairman of the MC and installing Museveni as vice-chairman. On 25 January 1986, less than two months after the accord had been signed, the NRA marched into Kampala to topple Okello.

Museveni's given reason for breaking the peace accord was the ineffectiveness of Okello's MC and in particular its inability to curb atrocities against civilians being perpetrated by its defence force. To the Acholi, the coup against Uganda's first Acholi head of state was betrayal pure and simple. And, whatever the rights and wrongs of the matter, Museveni's coup undeniably did represent a loss of power and prestige to the Acholi. It also prompted thousands of Acholi soldiers to flee north for fear of reprisal, while the subsequent NRA occupation of Acholi territory was allegedly accompanied by a spate of unprovoked civilian killings. Put simply, in 1986, when most Ugandans perceived or willed Museveni to be a national saviour, the Acholi viewed him as a liar and an oppressor – indeed, a full ten years later, Museveni would poll a mere 20% of the Acholi vote in the 1996 presidential election, as compared with 75% countrywide.

After being rebuffed by Okello, Alice Lakwena continued using her powers as a medium and healer to tend wounded Acholi soldiers. On 6 August 1986, however, the spirit Lakwena ordered his medium to abandon her healing to form the Holy Spirit Mobile Forces (HSMF) and lead a war against the forces of evil in Uganda. Alice assembled an initial force of 150 Acholi men, all of whom had served in the UPDF prior to the NRA coup, and made them undertake an elaborate purification ritual, laced with elements of both Christian and traditional Acholi ritual, as laid out to her by the spirit Lakwena. The newly inducted soldiers were also issued with a list of 20 commandments – the Holy Spirit Safety Precautions – ranging from the predictable 'Thou shalt not commit adultery' to the decidedly left-field 'Thou shalt have two testicles, neither more nor less'.

A compelling book could be – and indeed has been – written about the outwardly contradictory aims and beliefs of the HSMF. One central aim of the movement was the elimination of witchcraft (allegations of which were rife in the early days of the HIV pandemic) in favour of Christian values. Yet it could be argued that the movement's obsession with sorcery itself stood in contravention of biblical teachings, as certainly did some of its more obtuse beliefs, for instance that smearing a soldier's body with shea butter would make him immune to bullets. And even if Alice herself was sincere in her beliefs, it is difficult to say whether her mostly ex-UPDF followers – at least 3,000 at the movement's peak – were motivated primarily by spiritual considerations or simply by the prospect of exacting revenge on the hated NRA.

Whatever their motives, this improbable army came closer to ousting Museveni than anybody has before or since. Led by the spirit Lakwena and his earthly vessel Alice, the HSMF marched through Kitgum, Lira, Soroti, Kumi, Mbale and Tororo, inflicting significant defeats on the NRA and replacing the dead and wounded with new recruits along the way. Defeat came finally in November 1987, on the outskirts of Jinja, where the HSMF enjoyed little public support and its movements were relayed to the government forces by local villagers. After the defeat, the spirit of Lakwena abandoned Alice in favour of her father Severino Lukoya, who resuscitated the HSMF with some success, at least until March 1988, when 450 of his followers were killed in an attack on Kitgum. Six months later, Severino was captured and beaten up by the Uganda People's Democratic Army (UPDA – a rival anti-NRA army) and informed by a leading officer – an HSMF deserter – that there would be no more talk of spirits.

Following the defeat at Jinja, Alice fled into exile in Kenya, and spent the rest of her days in a refugee camp at Dabaab near Garissa, despite having been pardoned in January 2003 under an act granting amnesty to combatants who surrender voluntarily. She died of an unknown illness, possibly HIV/AIDS-related, in January 2007. Her father Severino escaped from the UPDA in May 1989, and was arrested by the NRA six months later, only to be released in 1992. Severino was later abandoned by the spirit of Lakwena, but – having renounced violence in favour of prayer and fasting – he remains active as a self-proclaimed prophet in Kitgum at the age of 94. The UPDA officer who so violently exhorted Severino against spiritual talk back in 1988 has subsequently stated that he is possessed by Lakwena, a claim publicly refuted by Severino, who describes his former tormentor as a 'devil'. And that former UPDA officer, whether spirit medium or devil, would go on to exert a murderously destabilising influence over the whole of northern Uganda for almost two decades. His name is Joseph Kony, and the chilling story of his subsequent career continues on pages 300–1.

took place at St Mary's School in Aboke, 28km to the northwest of Lira. By 2004, 39% of Lira District's total population had been displaced to the town, whose population increased from 27,568 to 89,781 between 1991 and 2002. Though many of these displaced people have returned to their rural homes, others have opted to remain in town.

GETTING THERE AND AWAY Lira lies about 340km from Kampala, a 5–7-hour drive. The most direct route entails following the Gulu Road north across the Nile, then turning right on to a 70km road running east from Kamdini Corner (✪ *2.24648, 32.33084*). Soroti lies 120km further southeast on a newly surfaced road. A 25km shorter (but not necessarily any quicker) murram alternative to the surfaced road through Kamdini Corner runs from Aboke (28km from Lira) and joins the Gulu road at Paranga (28km before Gulu). Driving from Kampala, ensure you have sufficient fuel, as there are no conventional opportunities to fill up on the last 110km or so, though expensive dirty jerry cans can usually be bought in Karuma trading centre.

Lira is well served by buses running to/from Kampala Qualicell (*5–6hrs; US$8*), Soroti (*2½hrs; US$5*), Gulu (*2hrs; US$4*) and Arua (*4hrs; US$6.50*). Buses between Soroti and Gulu stop in Lira to pick up and set down passengers, which avoids the customary early start and wait for the vehicle to fill.

Note that all conventional public transport to and from Kampala to Kitgum passes via Gulu rather than Lira. If intent on travelling direct, head to Kitgum stage on Oyam Road and be prepared for a bumpy ride on the back of a laden truck.

WHERE TO STAY *Map, opposite*

Moderate

✴ **Brownstone Country Home** (13 rooms) ✪ 2.21686, 32.85387; m 0772 480055, e brownstoneanai@gmail.com; www. brownstonecountryhome.com. Situated in large well-wooded grounds 6km southwest of town, this agreeable owner-managed lodge offers the choice of new but poorly ventilated tiled rooms with a walk-in net, solar-powered lighting, en-suite shower & small private balcony, or older & cheaper but better ventilated cottages with similar facilities. There's a TV lounge & small restaurant serving continental & local dishes in the US$6–8 range. To get there, follow the Apoch Rd south out of town for 3.5km to a signposted right junction (✪ 2.21399, 32.87287) from where it's another 2.5km on a dirt road. *US$35/40 B&B old/new dbl.* **$$**

St Lira Hotel (20 rooms) Erute Rd; m 0753 869891. This long-serving, slightly rundown & freshly canonised former government hotel is set in large quiet grounds near the former golf course. A restaurant serves decent meals in the US$5–6 range & opens on to a central tree-shaded courtyard, while the spacious rooms come with net, fan & en-suite hot shower. Strong on character & good value. *US$25/35/62 B&B sgl/dbl/suite.* **$$**

Lillian Towers Hotel (18 rooms) Inomo Rd; m 0774 192310; e lillian_towers_hotel@ hotmail.com; www.lilliantowershotel.com. Despite its rather tired-looking façade, this 2-storey hotel is the smartest central option, offering spacious tiled rooms with understated décor, nets, DSTV & (uniquely for Lira) AC. There's also a swimming pool on a separate property 1km away, a fair restaurant & Wi-Fi. *US$35/55/59 B&B sgl/dbl/ twin.* **$$$**

Budget

Kanberra Hotel (14 rooms) Oyam Rd; m 0790 915981; e reception@kanberrahotel.com; www.kanberrahotel.com. Far & away the best option in this category, this small 2-storey hotel lies in compact green gardens where a garden restaurant serves international cuisine in the US$4–5 range. Spacious tiled modern rooms have Wi-Fi, net, fan, DSTV & en-suite hot shower. *US$28 B&B dbl.* **$$**

Day's Inn Hotel (30 rooms) ✆ 0392 870514; m 0786 035995; e daysinnliralimited@gmail.com; www.daysinnhotellira.net. Set around the corner from the taxi park, this good-value hotel has a vivid salmon pink exterior & spacious carpeted

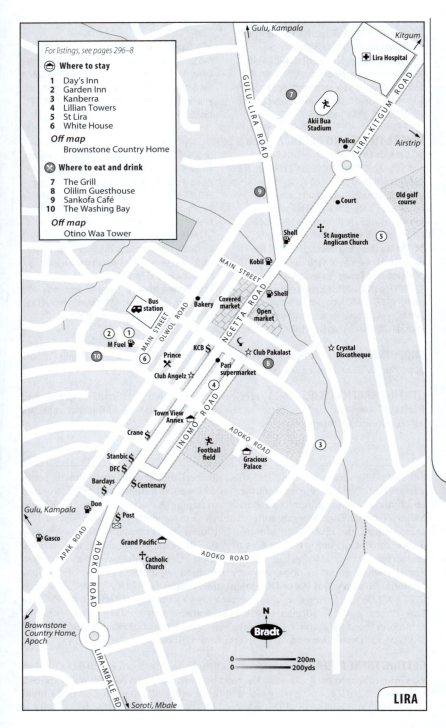

For listings, see pages 296–8

⌂ Where to stay
1 Day's Inn
2 Garden Inn
3 Kanberra
4 Lillian Towers
5 St Lira
6 White House

Off map
   Brownstone Country Home

✕ Where to eat and drink
7 The Grill
8 Olilim Guesthouse
9 Sankofa Café
10 The Washing Bay

Off map
   Otino Waa Tower

Gulu, Kampala
Kitgum
✚ Lira Hospital
GULU–LIRA ROAD
LIRA–KITGUM ROAD
7
Akii Bua Stadium
Police
Airstrip
Court
Old golf course
9
Shell
✝ St Augustine Anglican Church
5
Kobil
MAIN STREET
Shell
Bus station
Bakery
Covered market
Open market
NGETTA ROAD
2 1
M Fuel
6
10
Prince
Club Angelz ☆
KCB
Pari supermarket
☆ Club Pakalast
8
☆ Crystal Discotheque
4
Town View Annex
ADOKO ROAD
OLWOL ROAD
MAIN STREET
INOMO ROAD
Crane
Football field
Gracious Palace
3
Stanbic
DFC
Barclays
Centenary
Gulu, Kampala
Don
Gasco
APAK ROAD
Post
Grand Pacific
ADOKO ROAD
✝ Catholic Church
ADOKO ROAD
N
Bradt
0 ———— 200m
0 ———— 200yds
Brownstone Country Home, Apoch
LIRA–MBALE RD
Soroti, Mbale

11

LIRA

rooms with writing desk, net, fan, DSTV & en-suite hot shower. *US$18/22/33 sgl/dbl/suite.* **$$**

🏠 **White House** (29 rooms) m 0783 434667. Named for its white, tiled exterior, this central hotel has clean en-suite rooms with net, fan, DSTV & hot water. Close to the taxi park. Secure parking. *US$11/22/24 sgl/dbl/twin.* **$$**

🏠 **Garden Inn Hotel** (25 rooms) m 0706 645583. A notch up from the row of cheapies lining Oyam Rd, this offers adequate en-suite rooms with net & cold shower, set in large untended gardens around the corner from the bus station. *US$8/12 sgl/dbl.* **$**

✖ WHERE TO EAT AND DRINK *Map, page 297*

✖ **Sankofa Café** Gulu Rd; m 0704 712198; 🕐 08.00–22.00 Mon–Sat, 09.00–22.00 Sun. The standout non-hotel restaurant in Lira, this cousin of its Gulu namesake serves juices, smoothies, herbal teas & coffees, as well as burgers, pizza, sandwiches & salads. It's on the 3rd floor & has balcony seating. *Meals in the US$4–9 range.*

✖ **The Washing Bay** Kwania Rd. Excellent Indian food in a semi-open setting.

✖ **Otino Waa Tower** Kampala Rd; ✛ 2.29163, 32.78937; m 0751 260834; www.pathministries. net; 🕐 07.30–18.00 Mon–Sat. Well worth the 7km drive out of town for those with wheels, this roadside café & craft shop is a wholly unexpected treat with its small landscaped garden & excellent coffee, juices, muffins, pizzas, tortilla chips & ice cream. Proceeds support an orphanage housing 300 children. It now runs a second branch called Pathfinder on Ireda Rd, a couple of hundred metres beyond the Gracious Palace Hotel.

🍷 **The Grill** Teso Bar Rd; m 0773 099462; 🕐 09.00–midnight daily. This brightly decorated garden bar serves grilled port or chicken with chips. *Around US$3 per plate.*

🍷 **Olilim Guesthouse** Oyam Rd. Seemingly open 24/7, this down-at-heel drinking hole is Lira's equivalent of the bar scene in *Star Wars*.

SHOPPING The town's best supermarkets are **Pari** supermarket on Ngetta Road, opposite KCB, and **New Lira** on Olwol Road.

OTHER PRACTICALITIES Forex services are provided by Stanbic, Crane and Barclays banks. Most of the better hotels have Wi-Fi and several internet cafés are dotted around the town centre.

KITGUM

Situated 435km from Kampala, this most northerly of Uganda's major towns, set in a landscape only a sweet-potato farmer could love, has a substantial NGO presence and some strategic significance to tourists as a staging or stocking-up post for Kidepo Valley National Park. Kitgum suffered much deprivation and housed several IDP camps during the LRA's reign of terror, but today it is a pleasant little town whose 45,000 inhabitants enjoy the services of a Stanbic bank, a few reliable fuel stations, and an internet signal to keep in touch with global trends in the sweet potato market. Shortly before going to print, we were informed about the opening of the new **National Memory and Peace Documentation Center** *(NMPDC;* 🖀 *039 2592400;* m *0776 897117;* e *jackodong@refugeelawproject.org),* a joint project between the Refugee Law Project and the Kitgum District Government that contains a museum-like exhibition about the conflict in the north between 1986 and 2006, and features related artefacts such as old weapons and pictures from IDP camps.

GETTING THERE AND AWAY It takes about 8 hours to drive from Kampala to Kitgum via Gulu, 105km to the southwest. The road between Gulu and Kitgum is unsurfaced, but as of late 2015, it was in the process of being widened and graded, so that should change within the lifespan of this edition. Using public transport, the best service is

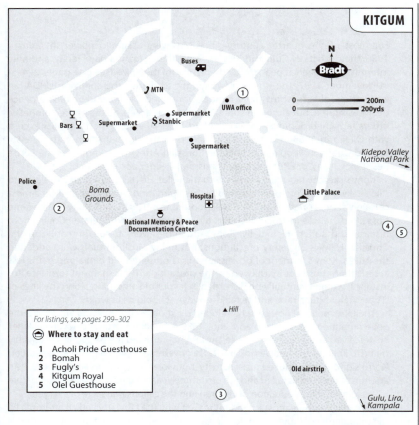

Bradt

N

0   200m
0   200yds

Buses

♪ MTN

① UWA office

● Supermarket

$ Stanbic

Bars ♀ Supermarket

● Supermarket

Kidepo Valley
National Park

Police ●

Boma
Grounds

②

Hospital ✚

● National Memory & Peace
Documentation Center

Little Palace

④ ⑤

▲ Hill

Old airstrip

③

Gulu, Lira,
↘ Kampala

For listings, see pages 299–302

Where to stay and eat

1	Acholi Pride Guesthouse
2	Bomah
3	Fugly's
4	Kitgum Royal
5	Olel Guesthouse

Homeland Northern Express (m *0791 805841/0794 805843; www.homeland.co.ug*), which operates five coaches daily in either direction between Kampala and Kitgum. These leave from Kampala's Kisenyi Bus Terminal at 08.00, 12.00, 15.30, 19.00 and 22.00, and from Kitgum at 06.00, 08.00, 12.00, 17.00 and 18.00. The 15.30 service out of Kampala and 18.00 service out of Kitgum comprise an executive coach with extra sitting room, Wi-Fi and charging sockets (*US$10*). Homeland can be used to travel between Gulu and Kitgum, a route also serviced by regular matatus.

TOURIST INFORMATION The **UWA** office in the town centre is a useful source of information, especially if looking for transport to Kidepo Valley National Park.

WHERE TO STAY AND EAT *Map, above*
Moderate

Fugly's (14 rooms) Church Crescent; ⊕ 3.28761, 32.88175; m 0785 551911; e fugls. limited@gmail.com. This converted residential building set in large gardens near the airfield & 1km south of the town centre comprises a bar, restaurant, small swimming pool & choice of accommodation ranging from spacious clay-tiled

en-suite garden suites to basic rooms using shared facilities. It's main attraction, however, is as *the* place to chill out with an evening beer or enjoy a tasty curry, burger or pizza (*mains around US$5–7*). US$50/60 en-suite sgl/dbl. US$13pp room with shared facilities. **$$**

Bomah Hotel (20 rooms) Uhuru Drive; ⊕ 3.293786, 32.876475; m 0775 593123;

For most of the quarter century since Museveni assumed power in January 1986, the districts of Gulu and Kitgum in northern Uganda have rarely, and only intermittently, been at peace. After the demise of the HSMF (see box, pages 294–5) in November 1987, the government sought to defuse the surviving UPDA, an army of ex-soldiers who'd served under Obote and Okello, and in 1988 a peace deal was signed. But although some 20,000 rebels accepted the offered amnesty, others remained dubious – Museveni had, after all, reneged on a similar accord with Okello in 1985 – and were persuaded to throw their lot in with a newly formed Ugandan People's Democratic Christian Army (now known as the Lord's Resistance Army, or LRA) and their charismatic leader, Joseph Kony.

Kony's sketchy biography varies with the teller. He has claimed to be related to Alice Lakwena, and to be possessed by her spirit (and by others), and he almost certainly served briefly with the HSMF. Sometime in 1987, when Kony first became possessed, he was instructed to start a new movement to 'liberate humans from disease and suffering'. Initially, Kony's doctrines were based primarily on the Christian HSMF's 20 'safety precautions', but many Muslim rituals were added in the 1990s. Kony's ferment of possessive spirits often guided him along paths less ascetic than those cut by Lakwena – the precaution 'Thou shalt not fornicate', for instance, would eventually be discarded in favour of something along the lines of 'Thou shalt abduct, rape and sexually enslave schoolgirls at whim'.

The LRA's political objective has eluded most observers. Attempts to topple the government ended long ago and since 1989, when Kony attacked several villages he perceived as disloyal to his cause, the LRA has targeted the people it is ostensibly trying to liberate: the rural Acholi. In 1991, a government campaign called Operation North significantly reduced rebel activity, but violence flared up again in 1993. An attempt at peace talks failed and the next three years saw suffering like never before in the form of mass abduction of children and the callous massacre of villagers.

Perhaps the single most important reason why the LRA survived all attempts by the Ugandan government to defeat it was the support it received from the National Islamic Front (NIF) government of Sudan. In a tit for tat scenario, the NIF aided Kony in retaliation for Ugandan support for the rebel Sudanese People's Liberation Army (SPLA) in southern Sudan. Between 1993 and early 2002, Kony and the LRA were based in Sudan, able to flee across the border whenever things heated up in Uganda.

This changed in March 2002, when Sudan signed a protocol allowing the Uganda People's Defence Force (UPDF) to follow LRA rebels into southern Sudan. Despite some victories, the ensuing Operation Iron Fist failed to destroy the rebels, and sparked off the LRA's most vicious civilian attacks yet. On 24 July, Kony's rebels killed 48 people in a village near Kitgum – the adults hacked apart with machetes and knives, the young children beaten against a tree until their skulls smashed open – before abducting an estimated 100 teenagers. On 24 October, *New Vision* printed a chilling picture of a singularly callous attack: the LRA executed 28 villagers, chopped off their heads and limbs, boiled them in a pot, and had been about to force the surviving villagers to eat the human stew when the government army arrived.

The LRA became more vulnerable following the signing of a peace accord between the Sudanese government and the SPLA in January 2005. The LRA moved outside Uganda and Sudan into the forests of Garamba in northeastern DRC. In October of that year, the outside world finally took a firm stance on the LRA when the International Criminal Court (ICC) in The Hague issued warrants against Kony and

four of his deputies for crimes against humanity. In June 2006, Interpol issued wanted persons' notices to 184 countries. The rebels let it be known that they were prepared to talk peace with the Ugandan government and in July 2006, negotiations began in the southern Sudanese town of Juba mediated by Riek Machar, Vice President of the Government of Southern Sudan. Once again, a definite end to the conflict proved elusive. Though an estimated 3,000 rebels massed in southern Sudan to be demobbed and returned to the Acholi society from which most of them had been abducted, Kony failed to turn up to to sign a peace agreement. Though many rebels did return home, others melted back into the bush. This period of uncertainty saw new divisions in the LRA's ranks. Kony's 59-year-old deputy, Vincent Otti, supposedly in favour of a peace deal, was executed in November 2007, casting doubt on Kony's own commitment to the peace process. The stumbling block remained – and, it would seem, still remains – the warrants issued by the ICC. Though Acholi people seemed content for returning rebels to be reabsorbed into society through traditional ceremonies of cleaning and forgiveness, and the Ugandan government was prepared to give amnesty, the ICC insisted that the warrants cannot be revoked.

By the end of 2008, the peace process was going nowhere. On 14 December, the forces of Uganda, the DRC and southern Sudan reacted to reports from the DRC that the LRA was rearming and abducting fresh recruits by attacking the rebel stronghold in Garamba. Operation Lightning Thunder was aptly named, with plenty of flashes and bangs, but no Kony, dead or alive. The rebels fled towards the Central African Republic (CAR), murdering hundreds of Congolese peasants living in their path. In January 2015, Dominic Ongwen, an LRA commander charged with seven counts of crimes against humanity and war crimes by the ICC, surrendered himself to US forces in the CAR. Kony himself remains at large, probably in the CAR, but possibly in South Sudan or indeed elsewhere.

Though efforts to formally end the war failed, it remains that the LRA has not operated in Uganda since 2005. As long as Kony remains at liberty, however, the big question remains: why did the war drag on for so long? The standard answer cites a lack of motivation in Kampala to end it. A more telling reason was a general feeling in northern Uganda that although Kony might be bad, Museveni is worse. Were Kony to return he would find a change of mood in Acholi; popular support for the LRA and antipathy towards the government have been overtaken by a desire to live in peace.

The legacy of the war is a brutal one. The civilian death toll in Gulu and Kitgum districts exceeded 10,000 while a similar number of schoolchildren were abducted and thousands more people maimed or disabled. However, some two million people – 90% of the rural population in the affected areas – were forced to take refuge in towns or protected IDP camps offering limited food and facilities, and appalling sanitation – for up to 18 years. Dozens of schools were destroyed, while lamentable medical facilities were highlighted by a 30% mortality rate among children under the age of five. Average annual per-capita household income (US$30) was just 10% of the national average, while the number of cattle in the region fell to only 2% of 1986 figures (compared with an increase of 100% countrywide). Since 2005, though, most people have left the camps and returned home to start rebuilding a normal existence. Inevitably, the process of achieving this will take time.

Joseph's Kony's story is well told in Matthew Greens's Wizard of the Nile *(page 558) and the 30-minute film* Kony 2012.

11

e bomahhotelktgm@yahoo.com. Set in pleasant grounds bordering the town centre, this private hotel has a rather institutional feel & isn't nearly as smart as its namesake in Gulu. Positives include the sparkling swimming pool, safe parking, free Wi-Fi & restaurant/bar serving decent curries & continental food. Rooms all come with nets, DSTV & en-suite hot shower, but the state of repair ranges from adequate to seriously dishevelled, so check them out before you check in. *US$21/33/36/48 B&B sgl/ dbl/twin/exec.* **$$**

Budget
🏠 **Kitgum Royal Hotel** (11 rooms) m 0753 189911. Behind the smart stone-clad façade, the

courtyard is softened by pot plants & a fountain, while the en-suite rooms are tiled with nets & fans. There's an indoor restaurant & an evening pork roast outside. Good value. *US$15/18/25 sgl/dbl/twin.* **$$**

🏠 **Acholi Pride Guesthouse** (12 rooms) m 0772 687793. This basic lodge next to the UWA office is conveniently close to the bus station & has a popular local restaurant. *US$9 en-suite dbl, US$4.50 sgl with shared facilities.* **$**
🏠 **Olel Guesthouse** (10 rooms) m 0772 301542. Very basic but clean twin rooms with nets right alongside the Kitgum Royal. *US$4/8 sgl/dbl occupancy.* **$**

SHOPPING The **A-One Supermarket** and **Women's Initiative** near the Stanbic bank are both well stocked with packaged goods.

OTHER PRACTICALITIES
Foreign exchange The Stanbic bank has forex and ATM services.

KARAMOJA

Extending over 27,900km² in the far northeast of Uganda, the relatively thinly-populated semi-arid administrative subregion of Karamoja is named after its Karamojong inhabitants, a group of Nilotic-speaking, semi-nomadic pastoralists whose traditionalist lifestyle revolves around their precious cows. For many years, this Kenya border region ranked among the most unsafe parts of East Africa due to the high prevalence of cattle raids and large number of guns in circulation, but it has been far more stable since the disarming campaign of 2011 (see box, pages 304–5). Karamoja remains one of the least touristed parts of Uganda, with a limited network of rough roads and few amenities, but it is a fascinating destination culturally, whether visited in its own right, or as an off-the-beaten-track alternative to the main Gulu–Kitgum route through to Kidepo Valley National Park, which lies in the far north of the subregion.

GETTING THERE AND AROUND Two main routes (with several minor variations) run to Kidepo Valley via Karamoja, both arriving at the park's Nataba Gate, 13km southeast of Apoka Rest Camp. Coming from Kampala, the more interesting but longer route entails skirting east of Lake Kyoga along the surfaced road to Mbale, then following a rougher 420km road north to Nataba Gate via Pian Upe Wildlife Reserve (pages 279–80), Nakapiripirit, Moroto, Kotido and Kaabong. The other route involves taking the Gulu Road as far as Kamdini Corner and branching right to Lira, from where a 300km road runs to Nataba Gate via Abim, Kotido and Kaabong. In a private vehicle, assuming a very early start, you could drive from Mbale or Lira to Apoka Rest Camp in a long dusty day, but it will be a push, and you'll get more from the experience by allowing for an overnight stop. You can also get through using public transport, possibly supplemented by the occasional boda, but assign two to three days for the trip, and be prepared for some bumpy travel.

The roads through Karamoja pass through wild country with some challenging conditions, so don't head there without contacting UWA or recent visitors to ask about the road surface. If driving yourself, you'll need a 4x4, recently serviced and checked over by a mechanic, and with good clearance. Pack something for digging yourself out and take a tow rope if you can. Keep plenty of drinking water and snacks in the car as a matter of routine. If you know where you are going within the park, tell someone at your lodge or hostel and get a phone number. With regards to phones, MTN and Airtel are both fine but Orange doesn't work anywhere in Karamoja. Fill your fuel tank when you can and don't bank on finding further supplies past Kitgum or Moroto. Once at Kidepo, you can top up at the UWA workshop at Apoka, assuming the pump is working. You'll also find a mechanic at Apoka if your vehicle is making strange noises.

SECURITY Karamoja has long had a reputation for instability, much of which is associated with armed domestic and cross-border cattle raids. Since 2011, the region has widely been regarded as safe for travel by locally based UWA officials, hoteliers and expatriates, though driving after dark should be avoided, as should off-road exploration in the direction of the Kenyan border. That said, the likes of the British foreign office (*www.gov.uk/foreign-travel-advice/uganda*) and US state department (*http://travel.state.gov/content/passports/en/country/uganda.html*) have yet to lift long-standing warnings against road travel in Karamoja, though both advisories do permit flying to Kidepo. Certainly, it would be prudent to ask around before heading overland through Karamoja, UWA staff in Kitgum, Mbale, Moroto, Kotido and Kidepo Valley National Park would be a good source of advice.

TOUR OPERATOR
Kara-Tunga Tours m 0781 079049; e info@kara-tunga.com; www.kara-tunga. com. This new Moroto-based operator offers a number of activities in Karamoja, all organised in collaboration with the local community & led by local Karamojong guides. These include day & overnight hikes on the region's highest 4 mountains (Kadam, Moroto, Napak and Murungole), each of which has its own characteristics, challenges & sights such as craters, caves, rainforests & rare monkeys. It also arranges visits to Kamion, where a small museum offers insight into the culture of the Ik people, & a campsite overlooks the rift valley around Kenya's Lake Turkana. Other possibilities are an overnight stay in a Karamoja *kraal* (homestead), visits to prehistoric rock art sites, & boda tours through the region.

NAKAPIRIPIRIT Situated about 130km north of Mbale along a road through Pian Up Wildlife Reserve, Nakapiripirit is a rambling Karamojong village (population 2,800) set at the northern base of Mount Kadam, an isolated range of spectacularly tortured turrets and bleak volcanic plugs whose forest-clad slopes rise to an altitude of 3,063m. If you have provisions and tents, it's possible to climb this 40km-long range. Plan for at least one night on the mountain, two if you want to reach the summit. Guides can be obtained in the village.

The road from Mbale to Nakapiripirit is surfaced for the first 40km, until the junction east for Sipi, but erratically maintained dirt thereafter, so self-drivers should allow at least 3 hours. Matatus between Mbale and Nakapiripirit (*US$10; 3–5hrs*) tend to fill up rather slowly, and breakdowns are commonplace, especially during the rains. The pick of Nakapiripirit's modest lodges, the Hill View Resort is set in large gardens facing Mount Kadam, and has en-suite cottages and rooms, as well as a fair restaurant and TV lounge (*US$12/16 B&B sgl/dbl*; **$$**).

MOROTO Nestled at the western base of an eponymous 3,084m volcanic massif, Moroto is Karamoja's largest urban centre (with a population of 15,000), and the obvious place for an overnight break driving between Mbale and Kidepo. Mount

Adapted from the draft of Uganda Safari *by Andrew Roberts*

The northeast is home to Uganda's most distinctive ethnic group, the Karamojong; nomadic agro-pastoralists known primarily for their love of cattle and cattle rustling and their resistance to the trappings of modern civilisation. The idea of 'the Karamojong people' is in fact an administrative invention, a convenient lumping together of several tribes. These do admittedly have plenty in common. The various Karamojong factions are all 16th- or 17th-century migrants from Ethiopia, all speak dialects of a common language, Akarimojong, and, most significantly, most are obsessively keen cattle keepers. This latter point is a dividing rather than a uniting factor, thanks to the fact that 'keeping thy neighbours' cattle', ideally after obtaining them by force, is equally central to Karamojong ideology. Without a patchwork of distinct tribes and clans to enable feuds, grudges, reprisals, alliances and understandings, cattle rustling would lose much of its appeal.

The so-called Karamojong people arose from a southerly migration by the Jie, an Abyssinian pastoralist tribe, 300–400 years ago. On reaching the Kenya–Uganda– Sudan border region, the Jie split to create the Toposa of Southern Sudan, the Turkana of Kenya and the Dodoth of northern Karamoja. Some of the Turkana Jie then crossed the mountains that line the present-day Kenyan border on to the plains of northeastern Uganda. Some groups remained around Kotido as the Uganda Jie. Others continued further until they were, quite literally, fed up with walking; the gist of the word 'Karamojong' means 'the old men sat down'. Some Jie groups reached southern Karamoja where they gave rise to the Matheniko (around Mount Moroto), the Bokora (on the plain to the west) and the Pian (on the plains below Mount Kadam) while others continued southwest to become the Iteso people around Soroti. The 'old men …' line is in fact attributed to a hardcore group of walkers who continued even further west before finally 'sitting down' as the Langi of Lira District.

The language of the Karamojong people is an interesting and apparently ancient curiosity. Scotsman John Wilson, who lived in and around Karamoja for 30 years, has identified numerous words and phrases of similar meaning in Akarimojong and Gaelic. Subsequent investigation has identified further similarities with other widely spaced languages including Hebrew, Spanish, Sumerian, Akkadian and Tibetan among others. To give just a few examples, we have *bot* (a house in Gaelic) and *eboot* (a temporary dwelling in Akarimojong); *cainnean* (live embers in Gaelic) and *ekeno* (a fireplace in Akarimojong); *oibirich* (ferment in Gaelic) and *aki-pirichiar* (to overflow as beer foam in Akarimojong); *cuidh* (an enclosure in Gaelic) and *aki-ud* (to drive cattle into an enclosure in Akarimojong).

Elsewhere, the Spanish word *corral*, for a circular stock enclosure, is uncannily close to the Akarimojong synonym *ekorr*, and the Spanish *ajorar* for 'theft of cattle' is not dissimilar to the Akarimojong *ajore* meaning 'cattle raid'. The thinking is that these various, far-flung modern languages are legacies of a common tongue spoken by an ancient human population, presumably before the Tower of Babel incident and perhaps as far back as the late Pleistocene. If corroborated, this would be of more than just a passing interest, for such linguistic evidence helps us to identify practices that fail to show up on the archaeological radar. From the commonalities

Moroto, which dominates the landscape for miles, is far more impressive than the small town, whose central business district consists of a 100m length of tarmac lined by shabby single-storey trading premises and interspersed with a few freshly

identified we might infer that, before they went their separate ways, the speakers of this mother tongue were (for example) cultivating land, harvesting ears of grain, creating simple reservoirs, getting drunk, plastering houses and pinching each other's cows (source: http://treasuresofafricamuseum.blogspot.com/).

More recently, the Karamojong have been something of an embarrassment to more Westernised Ugandans. The common view was that they were a backward lot who ran around naked and, half a century ago, the latter point was certainly true. Male attire consisted solely of an elaborately styled hairdo, a feathered headdress, a small, T-shaped stool and a spear, while female dress was represented by a heavy roll of neck beads and a bit of a skirt. These minimalist styles were driven underground in the 1970s when Idi Amin sent soldiers to force Western dress on the Karamojong at gunpoint. Men took to wearing, at the very least, a light blanket/cloak, usually of a striped or – interestingly given the suggestion of a Gaelic connection – tartan pattern. During the 1990s, this was frequently worn as a sole item of clothing but these days, some additional layers now seem mandatory, most obviously in the undercarriage department. Flashers – at least along the routes you're likely to explore – are now rare in Karamoja.

Despite expanding wardrobes and pressure from Kampala to join the modern world, most rural Karamojong remain true to their traditional way of life. Communities still commonly inhabit *manyattas*: traditional homesteads in which concentric, defensive rings of thorny brushwood surround a central compound containing huts, granaries and cattle pens. Unlike the rest of Uganda, some semblance of cultural dress remains part of everyday attire. For men this is epitomised by the cloak and some form of Western hat with ostrich feathers added to indicate status. Though the great beaded ruffs of yesteryear are less common, neck beads remain very much in vogue with the ladies.

The recent history of the region owes much to another, more sinister addition to the well-dressed warrior's kit. In 1979, when Amin's army fled north, leaving a well-stocked arsenal in Soroti barracks unattended, the Karamojong, who had suffered terribly at the hands of the dictator's soldiers, took the opportunity to arm themselves against future depredations. Thereafter, a warrior's personal effects consisted of an AK47 as well as a spear. This development transformed the nature of regional cattle raiding. Outgunned, the Pokot and Turkana sourced their own armaments from the perennial conflict in southern Sudan. Traditional cattle rustling escalated from a violent form of football hooliganism (with perhaps more spear wounds than usually recorded on the terraces) to intentionally murderous assaults. The possibility of being caught up in such events meant that few risked visiting the region and Karamoja's isolation deepened. Between 2006 and 2011 however, the Ugandan army managed to effectively disarm the Karamojong warriors, a process sometimes nastier than the violence it sought to suppress, but which has restored security to the region. That being said, the immediate border region remains subject to armed cattle raids since the Kenyan government has not disarmed its own pastoralists; now reduced to their traditional spears, the Karamojong in this area are at a distinct disadvantage.

painted and whitewashed bank façades. There's not much to see here, nor much choice regarding where to stay, so most visitors make a beeline for the unexpectedly agreeable Mount Moroto Hotel on the town's southern outskirts.

Getting there and away Moroto lies 105km north of Nakapiripirit along a variable dirt road. It can also be reached on a 170km road branching northeast from Soroti. Using public transport, a Gateway bus runs daily from Kampala to Moroto via Mbale and Soroti (*over 8hrs*) then on to Kotido (*over 10hrs*). Gateway is nobody's favourite bus company so you may want to travel as far as Mbale or Soroti with a more reputable outfit. Occasional matatus run to Moroto from Soroti (*US$8*) and Mbale via Nakapiripirit (*US$10*), but they tend to be very slow and crowded.

Where to stay and eat

Mount Moroto Hotel (40 rooms)
⊕ 2.523696, 34.670535; ☎ 039 2897300;
m 0751 493000; e info@morotohotel.com; www.
morotohotel.com. This slightly faded but very
pleasant former government hotel has a superb
setting in a grassy bowl in the Mount Moroto
foothills, 2km southeast of the town centre.
Acceptable meals are available, & the tiled en-suite
rooms & cottages have nets, flatscreen DSTV & hot
showers. Walks on Mount Moroto can be arranged.
From US$25/35 B&B sgl/dbl. **$$**

Hotel Leslona (20 rooms) ☎ 039 2943977;
e reservations@hotelleslona.com; www.
hotelleslona.com. This serviceable & friendly
modern hotel at the top end of the small town
centre lacks the charm of the Moroto Hotel, but the
more central location is useful for those without
private transport. *US$17/25 sgl/twin.* **$$**

Exclusive Royale (8 rooms) This basic
shoestring lodge is located in the town centre next
to Stanbic bank. *US$7/12 with shared facilities.* **$**

What to see and do A ramble on **Mount Moroto** is a popular Sunday afternoon activity for the local expats, and visitors are welcome to join in. Options range from the 10-hour round trip to one of several summits, to a 10-minute potter to a lesser viewpoint behind the Moroto Hotel. This grass- and scrub-covered mountain is home to the Tepeth people whose dwellings are concealed among jumbles of rocks. There's a waterfall up there, as well as cave paintings, while the 480km^2 Mount Moroto Forest Reserve harbours some 220 bird species, including Karamoja apalis, Boran cisticola and blue-capped cordon bleu, the latter previously unrecorded in Uganda.

Inaugurated in 2012, the French-funded **Karamoja Cultural Museum** contains several displays relating to Karamojong culture and history. Further out of town, the Mount Moroto and Leslona Hotels can both arrange a visit to a traditional **Karamojong *manyatta*** (see box, pages 304–5).

ABIM Situated 120km from Lira on the little-used road running northeast to Kotido, Abim is a junction town of 15,000 inhabitants set in a region characterised by wildly spectacular mountains and rock formations. The most impressive of these is Mount Rwot (⊕ *2.79088, 33.69215*), a massive volcanic outcrop whose name is the Acholi word for 'Chief', which towers several hundred metres above the west side of the Kotido Road some 10km north of Abim near the village of Alarek. If you feel like exploring, the Green Star Hotel (*8 rooms;* ☎ *039 2889420;* m *0772 641666;* e *greenstarhotel2010@gmail.com; US$12 dbl*) on the main junction has clean and comfortable en-suite rooms with net. All public transport between Lira or Soroti and Kotido stops at Abim.

KOTIDO Dusty Kotido, Karamoja's second-largest town (population 25,000), is an important local route hub, situated at the junction of the roads running southwest to

Abim and Lira, south to Moroto and Mbale, and north to Kaabong and Kidepo. It's an undistinguished but reasonably well-equipped town, hosting a few modest hotels, a Stanbic bank with ATM, a large market, and a couple of filling stations whose fuel supply is notoriously erratic. Karamoja Arts, a church-affiliated NGO that operates a shop and guesthouse in Kotido, can arrange visits to Nakipelemoru, a vast traditional manyatta 8km out of town, as well as to the so-called 'sliding rock' at nearby Kalikruk.

Getting there and away Kotido is about 110km northwest of Moroto, a slow 3-hour drive on a dirt road with some bad sections. It lies 190km northeast of Lira along a somewhat better road through Abim that takes up to 4 hours. Coming from the direction of Moroto, the best public transport option is a daily Gateway bus from Kampala via Soroti and Moroto (*US$12*). Coming from Lira, there's one daily bus via Abim (*US$8*). There are also two buses daily connecting Soroti to Kotido via Abim, one of which continues to Kaabong. If headed for Kidepo or Moroto, you could pop into the UWA office (just off the central roundabout) in case one of their pick-ups is going your way.

Where to stay and eat

Karamoja Arts Community Resthouse m 0788 335442; e karamoja.arts@ yahoo.com; www.karamojaarts.com. This Christian NGO, which promotes traditional Karamoja handicrafts as a source of revenue, operates a shop & simple guesthouse close to the vegetable market. Accommodation is in thatched traditional-style huts using common showers, or you can camp, while a kitchen serves a limited menu of vegetarian and meat dishes in the US$4–5 range. *US$10–12pp in rooms, US$2pp camping, plus US$1.50 b/fast.* **$$**

Kotido Resort (28 rooms) ⊕ 3.00881, 34.11707; m 0783 933700. The pick of a few local lodges scattered around Kotido, this self-styled resort set around a small courtyard is a little rundown but the dbl rooms with net & cold shower are pleasant enough. *US$8.50 dbl using common showers, US$12 en-suite dbl.* **$**

What to see and do The main attraction close to Kotido, about 10km to the east, is Nakipelemoru, a Karamojong manyatta whose population of 10,000 makes it the largest traditional settlement in East Africa. Nakapelimoru (literally Nakipel's Hill) is quite regularly visited by foreign NGO workers, missionaries and other concerned parties, but bona fide tourists are rare, and it's a very friendly and interesting place. Visits can be arranged through Karamoja Arts (*US$16/32/28 for groups of 1–3/4–6/7–10 people inclusive of a local guide/translator but exclusive of transport*). The best time to visit is Sunday afternoon, when the Karamojong of Nakapelimoru perform a traditional dance. Visits can also be arranged through the UWA office, just off the main roundabout. Karamoja Arts also arranges day outings to Kalikruk, a large boulder so smooth you can slide from the top to the base (*US$5.50pp*).

KAABONG Possibly the most remote town in Uganda, Kaabong (population 23,000) runs southward from the banks of the seasonal Dopeth River in a spectacular and somewhat surreal landscape of scattered volcanic plugs and giant standing boulders that look like an unintentional parody of the Easter Island statues. Its bustling daily market attracts plenty of rural Karamojong in traditional attire, while modern amenities include a Stanbic bank complete with Karamoja's most northerly ATM.

Getting there and away Kaabong lies 69km north of Kotido along a fair dirt road that can usually be covered in under 90 minutes. Though some maps suggest that the main road to Kaabong runs north directly out of central Kotido, you actually need

11

to follow the Soroti Road west out of town for about 5km to an obvious junction (⊕ *3.01017, 34.07817*) where you need to make a right turn to the north. Several matatus cover this road daily (*US$3; 2hrs*). Masochists could also travel directly from Kampala with the dreaded Gateway bus, which does a daily run up from the New Bus Park in Kasenyi, leaving Kampala at 03.00, passing through Soroti at around 10.00, then trundling into Kaabong at around 17.30.

Heading on to Kidepo from Kaabong in a private vehicle, the 53km drive to Nataba Gate takes about 1 hour. No public transport runs to Nataba, but one or two matatus daily trundle along the 70km road from Kaabong to Karenga (*US$5*).

Where to stay and eat

Sachavian Hotel (16 rooms) ⊕ 3.51544, 34.1286; m 0777 982984/0759 006273. Overlooking the river on the edge of town along a 400m road leading west through the market, Kaabong's smartest hotel has decent en-suite rooms with nets. No restaurant. *US$10 dbl.* **$**

Memano Hotel (11 rooms) ⊕ 3.51197, 34.13477; m 0780 593565. Located towards the southern end of town, this has rather pokey rooms with nets & adequate shared bathrooms. It also has a decent restaurant. *US$7/9 sgl/dbl.* **$**

KARENGA Situated just 8km south of Lokumoit Gate, tiny Karenga is the main urban gateway to Kidepo Valley National Park, especially for those without their own wheels. Karenga is most usually approached from Kitgum, a 2-hour and 115km drive in a private vehicle, but it might take twice that time in the occasional open-backed trucks (*US$3*) that serve as public transport along this road. It can also be reached from the direction of Moroto or Soroti, since one or two matatus cover the 70km road from Kaabong daily (*US$5*). Once in Karenga, the roadside Buffalo Base (*6 rooms;* ⊕ *3.57525, 33.69697;* m *0775 193270/0776 146548;* e *info@grassrootzuganda. com; www.buffalobase.com; US$12pp*), though not exactly glitzy, has bright little rooms, and it also serves decent food. A boda from Karenga to Apoka Rest Camp costs around US$7 exclusive of entrance fees for the cyclist and bike.

KIDEPO VALLEY NATIONAL PARK

Uganda's most remote and third-largest national park, Kidepo lies in the far northeast of Karamoja subregion, bordering South Sudan to the northwest and only 5km from the easterly border with Kenya. It's one of the country's most alluring safari destinations, combining rugged mountain scenery and a compelling wilderness atmosphere with some exceptionally good game viewing, particularly in the Narus Valley with its dense populations of lion, buffalo, elephant and many smaller ungulates. Until recently, the expense and difficulty of reaching Kidepo meant it attracted a low volume of tourists, but this is starting to change as a result of increased stability in northern Uganda, improved approach roads, and better amenities. Even so, it retains a genuinely off-the-beaten-track character by comparison to most other comparably wildlife-rich savannah reserves in East Africa – indeed, it was voted Africa's third-best wilderness park in the 2013 CNN Travel Awards.

FEES Entrance to Kidepo Valley National Park costs US$30/40 per FR/FNR per 24 hours. The standard vehicle entrance fees are also charged (see box, page 32), but only once per entry.

HISTORY AND GEOGRAPHY Kidepo was gazetted as a game reserve in 1958, with the dual purpose of clearing the bush in the name of tsetse-fly control, and protecting

Mihingo
Lodge

Africa at its most magical

Lake Mburo National Park

safari@mihingolodge.com   www.mihingolodge.com   075-2410509

Broadbill Forest Camp

Your home for the ultimate gorilla-tracking experience and endemic wildlife

Tel: +256 754 134 875
E-mail: enquiries@broadbillforestcamp.com
Web: www.broadbillforestcamp.com

CHALLENGE YOUR SPIRIT
CHOOSE YOUR ADVENTURE

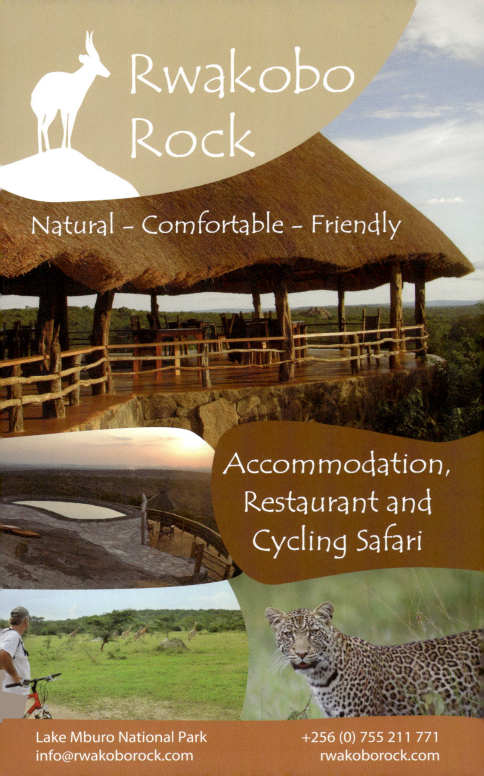

Rwakobo Rock

Natural - Comfortable - Friendly

Accommodation, Restaurant and Cycling Safari

Lake Mburo National Park
info@rwakoborock.com

+256 (0) 755 211 771
rwakoborock.com

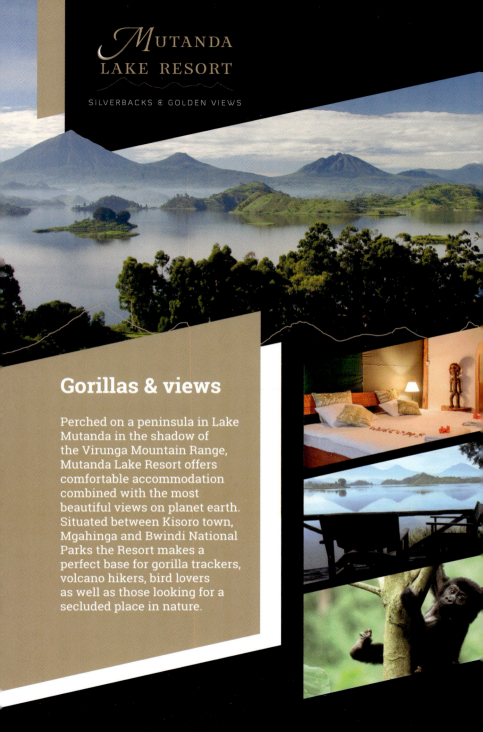

MUTANDA LAKE RESORT

SILVERBACKS & GOLDEN VIEWS

Gorillas & views

Perched on a peninsula in Lake Mutanda in the shadow of the Virunga Mountain Range, Mutanda Lake Resort offers comfortable accommodation combined with the most beautiful views on planet earth. Situated between Kisoro town, Mgahinga and Bwindi National Parks the Resort makes a perfect base for gorilla trackers, volcano hikers, bird lovers as well as those looking for a secluded place in nature.

mutandalakeresort.com • (+256) (0) 789951943
info@mutandalakeresort.com

its larger wild inhabitants from hunters. Prior to this, the area had been inhabited by two ethnic groups: the Dodoth Karamojong pastoralists who herded their cattle in the valleys, and the semi-nomadic Ik who eked out a hunter-gatherer existence on higher land. Tragically, the Ik, who speak a relict Nilo-Saharan language of uncertain affiliations, were evicted from the game reserve when it was gazetted in 1958, and forced to turn their hand to agriculture, resulting in the drought-related famine in the early 1960s, and the deaths of hundreds of elderly people and children.

The original 1,259km^2 reserve was upgraded to national park status following independence in 1962, and extended to its present size of 1,442km^2 seven years later. Altitudes range from 914m above sea level to the 2,750m peak of Mount Morungole, the highest point on an extinct volcanic range running along the park's southeastern border. The slightly taller Mount Lutoke (2,797m), which lies on the opposite side of a 50km border shared with South Sudan, is also visible from several points in the park. This ruggedly mountainous terrain is broken by the Narus Valley in the southwest and the Kidepo Valley in the northeast.

Kidepo has a moister climate than other parts of Karamoja, but almost all the average annual rainfall of 800mm falls between April and October, so the plains become very hot and parched towards the end of the dry season. The park is named after the river Kidepo, a derivative of the Karamojong 'akidep' which means 'to pick', and refers to the fruits of the borassus palms that line this seasonal waterway and formed an important source of nourishment in past times of drought. The only perennial river is the Narus, which flows through the eponymous valley, and attracts a profusion of game in the dry season.

FAUNA AND FLORA The dominant habitat in the Narus Valley is open grassland studded with tall sausage trees (*Kigelia africana*) and the massive elongated fruits for which they are named. The Kidepo Valley supports drier acacia woodland, though some significant stands of borassus palms line the watercourses. Elsewhere are patches of montane forest and riparian woodland. Kidepo protects one of the most exciting faunas of any Ugandan national park, although its total of 86 **mammal** species has been reduced to 77 after a rash of local extinctions in recent years. Predators are particularly well represented, with 20 resident species, including lion, leopard and spotted hyena, while black-backed jackal, bat-eared fox, aardwolf, cheetah and caracal are not to be found in any other Ugandan national park. Five primate species have been recorded, including the localised patas monkey.

Kidepo's elephant population has surged from around 200 in the mid-1990s to more than 650 today. The African buffalo is probably the most numerous ungulate, with the population now estimated at more than 10,000. Kidepo is an important refuge for the localised Rothschild's giraffe, which has bred up to around 50 individuals from a bottleneck mid-1990s population of three, supplemented by another three translocated from Kenya. Other conspicuous ungulates include Burchell's zebra, warthog, Jackson's hartebeest, Bohor reedbuck, oribi and, to a lesser extent, eland. Kidepo is the only park in Uganda to harbour populations of greater kudu, lesser kudu, Guenther's dik-dik and mountain reedbuck, none of which are all that common. The localised white-eared kob is an occasional vagrant from South Sudan.

The **bird** checklist of 470 species is second only to Queen Elizabeth National Park, and includes more than 60 birds recorded in no other Ugandan national park. It supports East Africa's only population of Clapperton's francolin and the spectacular rose-ringed parakeet. Raptors are particularly well represented: there are 56 species in total, of which the most commonly observed include

11

dark chanting goshawk, pygmy falcon, tawny eagle, bateleur and several types of vulture. Other birds that must be regarded as Kidepo specials in a Ugandan context include common ostrich, secretary-bird, fox kestrel, white-eyed kestrel, white-bellied go-away bird, carmine bee-eater, little green bee-eater, Abyssinian roller, Abyssinian scimitar-bill, red-and-yellow barbet, black-breasted barbet, red-billed hornbill, yellow-billed hornbill, Jackson's hornbill, Karamoja apalis, rufous chatterer and purple grenadier – to name only a few of the more colourful and/or visible species.

FURTHER READING Sheet 11 in the 'Uganda Maps' series covers Kidepo Valley National Park (*www.east-africa-maps.com*) and contains lists of bird and mammal highlights. The informative new 72-page Kidepo Valley National Park Information Guide, written by Mark Jordhal and published by UWA in 2014, can be bought at Apoka Rest Camp.

GETTING THERE AND AWAY Two entrance gates are regularly used by tourists. The main Lokumoit Gate (✿ *3.64032, 33.71571*), also sometimes referred to as Katarum Gate, lies about 8km north of Karenga and 16km south of Apoka Rest Camp, and is the normal point of entry coming from the direction of Kitgum. The more easterly Nataba Gate (✿ *3.69709, 33.80248*), 12km from Apoka, is likely to be used only by self-drivers coming from the direction of Kaabong in eastern Karamoja.

By air The quickest way to reach Kidepo is the quite costly 2-hour flight from Entebbe to Apoka Airstrip (✿ *3.71763, 33.74991*), 3km southeast of the eponymous safari lodge and rest camp. **Fly Uganda** (*www.flyuganda.com*) flies to Apoka daily, departing from Kajjansi Airstrip (40 minutes' drive from Entebbe Airport), usually departing at 09.30, subject to confirmation. It charges US$550 per person one-way, and a minimum of two passengers is required. **Aerolink** (www.*aerolinkuganda.com*) flies from Entebbe on Wednesday, Friday and Sunday only, departing at 12.30. It charges US$422/690 single/return per person, and requires a minimum of four passengers to make the journey. Assuming you are staying at Apoka Safari Lodge, flights are best booked in conjunction with your accommodation.

By road Driving to Kidepo is perfectly feasible, though it would be a push to try to get through from Kampala in a day. The best and most direct route, through Gulu and Kitgum to Lokumoit Gate, is covered piecemeal elsewhere in this chapter, but the total drive of around 565km (the last 230km all on dirt) will require around 10 hours to cover in full, though you can expect to cut an hour off that once the stretch from Gulu to Kitgum is finally surfaced. The trip can be broken up with an overnight stop at Ziwa Rhino Sanctuary, Chobe Safari Lodge (in the far east of Murchison Falls National Park), Gulu or Kitgum.

Two longer routes pass through Karamoja subregion, arriving at Nataba Gate. These are the 740km drive via Mbale and Moroto or 650km road through Lira/Abim, as outlined in the Karamoja section (pages 302–3).

Coming from Murchison Falls National Park, the 380km drive from Paraa via Pakwach, Gulu and Kitgum should be doable in a day, ideally with a very early start.

By public transport It is possible to reach Kidepo without your own vehicle. The most straightforward option is the bus to Kitgum, where the UWA office can let you know about any park vehicle headed up to Kidepo, or arrange a special hire there (around US$200 inclusive of one night in the park and a game drive). Failing that,

unless you luck a hitched lift, your only option is to board a truck to Karenga (US$3, opposite the Stanbic bank) and then catch a boda to Apoka Rest Camp. It is also possible to get to Karenga via Karamoja, as covered stage by stage in the Karamoja section, but allow at least three days coming from Kampala.

WHERE TO STAY   Map, page 282

Accommodation within and around the park is currently limited to the lodges and camps listed below. However, plans exist for a private investor to restore the stunningly located cliffside Katurum Lodge, which was constructed and abandoned during the Idi Amin era, to become a 110-room four-star facility complete with health club and a soundproof subterranean nightclub.

Exclusive/luxury

Apoka Safari Lodge (10 units)
✪ 3.73962, 33.72406; 📞041 4251182; m 0772 489497; e info@wildplacesafrica.com; www. wildplacesafrica.com. This stunning lodge stands on a rocky hillside in the heart of the park, & overlooks a close-by waterhole that attracts steady ungulate traffic, as well as the rolling plains of the Narus Valley & its mountainous backdrop. The thatched main building, set into the side of a kopje, comprises a large timber deck where all meals are served, & leads out to a magnificent swimming pool with a natural rock floor. The spacious & stylish canvas-walled en-suite cottages have walk-in nets & a private balcony facing the plains. *US$760/1170 sgl/dbl for non-residents in peak season (Jan, Feb, June, July, Aug, Sep, Dec), US$495/760 sgl/dbl for residents &/or during the low season. Rates are FB & inc drinks, game drives & walking but excl park entrance.* **$$$$$**

Moderate

Nga'Moru Wilderness Camp (6 cottages, 4 tents) ✪ 3.62903, 33.7425; m 0785 551911; e ngamoruwildernesscamp@gmail.com; www. ngamoru.com. Set on private land bordering the park 2km east of Lokumoit Gate, this owner-managed lodge overlooks the Narus Valley & is well positioned for game drives there. Simple but spacious cottages have large meshed windows

& en-suite hot showers. More basic en-suite furnished tents are also available. *US$160/240 FB. Discounts for East African residents.* **$$$$**

Budget

Apoka Rest Camp (21 bandas) ✪ 3.73516, 33.72839; 📞0392 899500; e info@ugandawildlife. org. Comprising renovated rondawels formerly occupied by park rangers, this rest camp doesn't offer many luxuries, but it has most things a budget traveller could ask for, & the price is right. The location close to the Narus Valley game tracks is also very convenient, & a newly installed observation tower with telescope allows you to scan the surrounding plains for wildlife. All bandas have fitted nets, & towels are supplied. A restaurant serves adequate meals in the US$1.50–3 range, & the usual drinks. Overall, an excellent no-frills set-up. *US$20/24 en-suite sgl/dbl, US$14/17 with shared facilities, US$5pp camping.* **$$**

Kakine & Nagusokopire Campsites UWA plans to open bandas similar to those at Apoka at these 2 splendid hilltop campsites, both of which overlook the Narus Valley, & have observation towers with telescopes as well as new ablution blocks with showers & flush toilets, which have basic shower/latrine blocks & shelters. You may need to fill water jerry cans at Apoka before heading out to pitch a tent. *US$5pp camping.* **$**

WHAT TO SEE AND DO

Self-drive game drives If you have your own 4x4 vehicle, you'll have no problem exploring the park, though it would be wise to enquire about road conditions. If you prefer to take a UWA guide, this costs US$20 per person per drive.

Narus Valley Apoka Safari Lodge and Rest Camp both lie in the prime game-viewing territory of the Narus Valley. Wildlife here is prolific throughout the year, but doubly so in the later dry season (January to March) when the Narus River is

the only reliable water source for miles around. The valley can be explored along two excellent road loops, both around 15–20km long, that run south from Apoka. These are the Kakine Circuit, whose centrepiece Kakine Rocks is often frequented by lions, and Katurum Circuit, named after a (currently disused) cliffside lodge built in the Amin era.

On either circuit, you should look out for the herds of 20 or 30 elephant that come to drink from the river in the mid-morning, before marching back to more remote grazing grounds mid-afternoon. They are usually quite relaxed around vehicles, but be warned that recent returnees from South Sudan, where poaching is still rife, can sometimes be wary or aggressive when approached too closely. A feature of Narus Valley is the spectacular thousand-strong herds of buffalo that are frequently encountered around Apoka, generally preferring wooded savannah to completely open grassland. These buffalo are the main prey of the park's 100-odd lion population, which currently includes two large prides of more than 20 individuals each. Kidepo's lions are often seen on top of the park's trademark granite outcrops, which they use as lookout points. Other large mammals likely to be seen along these circuits are Rothschild's giraffe, Burchell's zebra, warthog, Jackson's hartebeest, Bohor reedbuck and oribi.

For birders, Clapperton's francolin and rose-ringed parakeet are quite common around Apoka – the latter usually seen in small squawking flocks – while other conspicuous 'specials' include Abyssinian ground hornbill, bateleur, Meyer's parrot, black coucal (rainy season only) and superb starling.

Kidepo Valley Game is scarce in the Kidepo Valley, partly because it is drier than the Narus Valley, partly as a result of poaching by South Sudanese visitors. Worth a visit is the Kidepo River itself, which is beautiful in its unorthodox fashion. Lined by lovely borassus palm forest, it is completely dry for 95% of the year and its 50m-wide course is a swathe of white sand. The Kanatarok Hot Spring on the South Sudan border is a low-key event that doesn't compare to its counterpart in Semliki National Park. The thicker bush here looks promising for greater and lesser kudu, and it's the place to look for Uganda's only population of common ostrich, as well as secretary-bird, Jackson's hornbill, speckle-fronted weaver (look out for its conspicuous nests) and Karamoja apalis (often associated with the whistling-thorn acacia V*achellia drepanolobium*).

The road to the Kidepo Valley passes through a 10km^2 gated enclosure contained within a 2m-high electrified fence. This was created in 2001 as a secure location for the introduction of locally extinct or endangered species. Unfortunately, less than rigorous firebreak maintenance enabled flames to sweep through the compound in 2005, whereupon the herd of eland recently translocated from Lake Mburo crashed through the fence and dispersed. The compound has awaited new residents ever since.

Guided drives
Game drives led by highly knowledgeable driver/guides are part of the all-inclusive package offered by Apoka Safari Lodge. UWA also offers guided game drives at US$90 per vehicle for 1–3 people, plus US$30 per additional passenger.

Guided hikes
It is possible to arrange guided walks around the Apoka area in the hope of seeing more common species such as elephant, buffalo, zebra, waterbuck and hartebeest. UWA also now offers an exciting 15km hike across the ridges of the Narus Valley, which costs US$30 per person, with no minimum group size.

12

Pakwach and West Nile

The subregion of West Nile is a remote northwestern protrusion hemmed in on three sides by international borders, and bordered to the east by the Nile as it meanders northward from Lake Albert towards South Sudan. Integrated into the Uganda Protectorate as late as 1910, West Nile still feels somewhat isolated from the rest of the country, and its main ethnic groups (the Alur of Nebbi, Lugbara of Arua, Kaka of Koboko and Madi of Moyo) maintain strong cultural and trade links with their Congolese and South Sudanese neighbours. This isolation is emphasised by the fact that the only road between West Nile and the rest of Uganda is over a solitary bridge that spans the Albert Nile at Pakwach, though this is supplemented by ferry services linking Wanseko to Panyimur and Umi to Laropi.

West Nile holds one under-recognised touristic trump card in the form of Pakwach, a tropical river port and the only substantial town set alongside the Nile on its long journey from Jinja to the South Sudan border. Since the Lord's Resistance Army (LRA) left Uganda in 2005, Pakwach has also emerged as an increasingly popular base for exploring Murchison Falls National Park, whose northerly Tangi Gate lies just 3km out of town. A more remote attraction, 40km north of Pakwach, is Fort Wadelai, a long-neglected historical site that's currently being developed for tourism as part of an ongoing Emin Pasha Historical Fort Preservation and Development Project under the auspices of the German Embassy and Department of Museums and Monuments.

Elsewhere, West Nile ranks among the least-visited parts of Uganda, but it is known for the friendliness of its people, while its traditionalist character is reflected by the widespread use of thatch as opposed to iron sheet roofing. Adventurous travellers coming from Bunyoro might be tempted to make use of the ferry service linking Wanseko, on the Lake Albert shore immediately south of the Victoria Nile Delta, to Panyimur, on the West Bank of the Albert Nile close to where it leaves the lake. Arua, the subregion's largest town, is a pleasant enough place and an important NGO base, but situated as it is 130km north of Pakwach, it feels rather out of the way unless you have specific business there, or you plan to follow the thoroughly off-the-beaten-track northern road loop that connects it to Gulu via the Laropi–Umi ferry.

HISTORY

Remote though it is today, the far northwest was the first part of Uganda to attract the interest of the outside world. In 1839, Khedive Muhammad Ali Pasha, of Ottoman Egypt, instructed Captain Salim Kapudan to lead an expedition up the White Nile in search of its source. In 1842, following two failed attempts to cross the swampy Sudd, Salim made it past Gondokoro into what is now West Nile. This expedition led to a spate of mercantile activity, and by the late 1850s up to 80 Egyptian boats

were docking at Gondokoro annually to buy ivory and other goods. By the early 1860s, West Nile's once plentiful elephant population had been depleted, and slaves had replaced ivory as the main item of export.

In 1862, West Nile was traversed by Samuel and Florence Baker, who became the first Europeans to see Lake Albert. An ardent abolitionist, Baker returned to the region in 1869 to establish and serve as the first Governor-General of Egypt's Equatoria Province. Baker succeeded not only in suppressing the slave trade but also in opening up the area to legitimate trade. West Nile and the rest of Equatoria became part of the British Empire following the occupation of Egypt in 1862. However, a treaty signed with King Leopold only two years later led to the region – then known as the Lado Enclave – being administered by the Belgian Congo until 1910.

In the post-independence era, West Nile became known for spawning Uganda's most famous son: Idi Amin Dada. Oddly, it is not certain that Amin was actually born in West Nile, but with a mother from Arua and a father from Koboko, he strongly identified with the area. Under Amin, West Nile and its people enjoyed preferential treatment, and after his downfall in 1979, the region's isolation was exacerbated by memories of his brutal excesses elsewhere in the country. Over the next 25 years, while West Nile was not directly involved in the civil war with the LRA, the only road routes to the region passed through a conflict zone characterised by regular rebel ambushes. Agricultural production slumped, since nobody dared come to buy any produce, with revenue from cotton, for instance, dropping by 50% between the late 1970s and mid-1990s. Access has improved dramatically since the evacuation of the LRA, and the surfacing of the 500km road between Kampala and Arua means the journey can now be made in a single day. The railway line connecting Pakwach to Tororo, where it meets the line between Kampala and the Kenyan port of Mombasa, was also under rehabilitation in 2015, and is like to start carrying cargo during the lifespan of this edition. A further cause for economic optimism is that relative stability in South Sudan means West Nile is no longer a cul-de-sac but a trade corridor – indeed, plans to extend the railway line north from Pakwach to Juba are already in place.

PAKWACH

It may not rank among the country's 50 largest settlements, nor is it designated a district headquarters, but modest Pakwach (population 23,000) does claim boasting rights for having the most interesting location of any town in northern Uganda. Perched on the West Bank of the Albert Nile as it flows out of Murchison Falls National Park, Pakwach is also the only road gateway to West Nile, linked to the East Bank by a large modern bridge, as well as the northern railhead of a line running via Tororo to Nairobi and Mombasa.

Despite this, Pakwach, on first glance, comes across as little more than a broad main street lined with the usual motley collection of local shops, restaurant and guesthouses. Explore further, however, and you'll find that away from that main street, this is one of the most overtly traditional towns in Uganda, its side roads lined with a mix of circular and rectangular adobe huts distinguished by neatly-layered thatch roofs. The town's Alur inhabitants, who speak a sub-dialect called Jonam (literally, 'People of the River'), also come across as unusually friendly, though the woodcarving sellers who tend to lurk opposite the Sunrise Guesthouse can be rather persistent.

For self-drivers and those on organised safaris, Pakwach – or, more accurately, a cluster of new lodges set above the facing East Bank of the Nile – is rapidly

emerging as a popular base from which to explore Murchison Falls National Park, whose Tangi Gate lies only 3km out of town. Pakwach is also the closest town to the historic settlement of Wadelai, which is currently being developed for tourism after years of neglect.

For backpackers, this readily accessible small town has two main attractions. Remarkably, it is the only substantial riverside settlement anywhere along the Nile's lengthy northwesterly course from Jinja to the South Sudan border, and several footpaths and tracks run down from the main road to the lushly vegetated riverbank. Thanks to its proximity to Murchison Falls, Pakwach also has plenty of birding and wildlife potential: hippos and shoebills frequent the shallows and swamps close to town, while the Tangi River Wetland, only 1km from town, is often frequented by elephants and other large mammals.

HISTORY Local legend has it that Pakwach is where the Alur and Acholi peoples split into separate tribes circa 1450AD. The rift is said to have been initiated by an an argument between Labongo and Gipir, the elder and younger sons of a Luo ruler who then lived on the East Bank of the river, over the loss of their clan's ancestral hunting spear and the resultant death of Labongo's daughter. Several variations are in circulation, but the broad sequence of events is that Gipir came home to find an elephant raiding their crops and grabbed the nearest spear to hurl at it and chase it away. Unfortunately, he had inadvertently used the clan's sacred ancestral spear, and the elephant walked away with it embedded in his wounded body. Labongo, who had been charged with looking after the spear by his father, was furious with his younger brother, refused to accept his apologies, and chased him deep into the forest. Gipir returned several months later having retrieved the spear from the dead elephant, but still furious with his brother. A few months later, roles were reversed when Labongo's daughter swallowed one of the ancestral beads in Gipir's charge. Labongo pleaded with Gipir to wait until the bead passed out of his daughter's body naturally. Gipir refused, and had Labongo's daughter cut open with the ancestral spear in order to retrieve the bead. After that, the brothers went their separate ways, with Labongo remaining on the east side of the river to establish the Acholi people, while Gipir crossed the river with his people to found the Alur tribe of Nebbi District. It is said that the troublesome spear, or bead, can sometimes be seen floating in the river at certain places. You could ask locals to show you the site near Pakwach Bridge where the two reputedly parted ways.

GETTING THERE AND AWAY Pakwach lies 370km northwest of Kampala along an excellent surfaced road that continues north to Arua. Coming from Kampala, follow the Gulu road out of town for 260m to Karuma Bridge, then after another 2km turn left on to the new sealed Arua Road and follow it for 108km before crossing the impressive Pakwach Bridge at the eastern entrance to town.

Any bus headed between Arua stage in Kampala and Arua itself can drop passengers at Pakwach; Gaagaa Coaches, KKT Kampala and Nile Coach are recommended. These take 6–8 hours and you may be expected to pay the full US$12 fare to Arua. Plenty of matatus run between Pakwach and Arua via Nebbi, and between Pakwach and Gulu via Purongo.

A more off-the-beaten track route to Pakwach is to catch the daily (except Sunday) motor ferry connecting Wanseko on the East Bank of Lake Albert to Panyimur on the West Bank (page 319). Pakwach can also be reached via Masindi and Murchison Falls National Park, crossing the Victoria Nile by ferry at Paraa, and exiting the park through Tangi Gate.

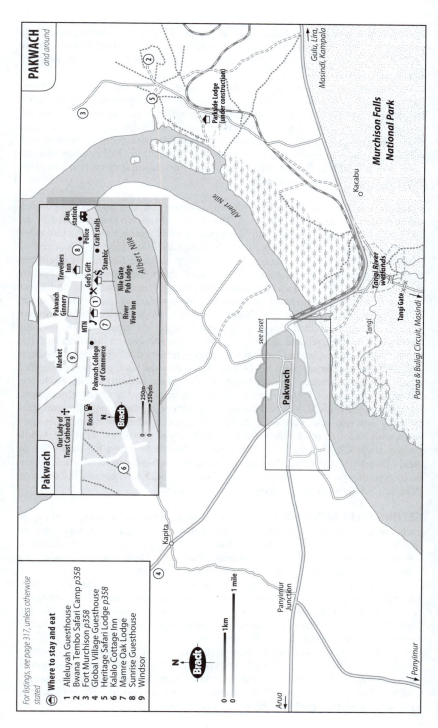

Murchison Falls
National Park

Gulu, Lira,
Masindi, Kampala

Paraa & Buligi Circuit, Masindi

Tangi Gate

Tangi River
wetlands

Tangi

Kacabu

Albert Nile

Parkside Lodge
(under construction)

Pakwach

see inset

Pakwach

Our Lady of
Trust Cathedral

Rock

Market

Pakwach College
of Commerce

MTN

Pakwach
Ginnery

Travellers
Inn

God's Gift

Nile Gate
Pub Lodge

River
View Inn

Stanbic

Bus
station

Police

Craft stalls

Albert Nile

0   250m
0   250yds

Bradt

Kapita

Panyimur
Junction

Panyimur

Arua

0   1km
0   1 mile

Bradt

N

For listings, see page 317, unless otherwise
stated

Where to stay and eat

1 Alleluyah Guesthouse
2 Bwana Tembo Safari Camp *p358*
3 Fort Murchison *p358*
4 Global Village Guesthouse
5 Heritage Safari Lodge *p358*
6 Kalalo Cottage Inn
7 Mamre Oak Lodge
8 Sunrise Guesthouse
9 Windsor

Transport options for visiting Murchison Falls National Park via the nearby Tangi Gate are described on pages 352–4.

WHERE TO STAY AND EAT   *Map, opposite*

In recent years, several mid-range to upmarket lodges have been constructed above the East Bank of the Albert Nile opposite Pakwach. These lodges all lie within 10km of town by road, but since they exist to service nearby Murchison Falls National Park rather than Pakwach, they are covered separately in that chapter, under the heading *The Albert Nile and Northwest* (pages 357–9).

Moderate

Global Village Guesthouse (9 rooms) 039 2300586; m 0782 797937. This modern guesthouse is set in quiet gardens off the Wadelai Rd, 3.5km northwest of the town. Spacious tiled en-suite rooms come with fan, net, DSTV & hot tub or shower, & there's a bar/restaurant serving simple meals by prior arrangement. It can rent out an open-sided 9-passenger game-viewing vehicle at US$150 half-day or US$185 full-day inclusive of driver/guide & fuel, but exclusive of park fees & food. *US$30/40 B&B sgl/dbl.* **$$**

Budget

Windsor Hotel (18 rooms) m 0772 482035; e windsorhotelpakwach@gmail.com; www.windsorhotelpakwach.com. This new 4-storey hotel on the main road has smart, spacious en-suite rooms with fitted nets, fan & cold shower. Facilities include a decent ground-floor restaurant serving grills, salads & stews in the US$3–4 range, a bar with DSTV, a craft shop, & community walks including visits to a traditional Jonam homestead (around US$7–13). *US$25/30 sgl/dbl.* **$$**

Kalalo Cottage Inn (8 rooms) 039 2903973; m 0785 290905; e parmuray@yahoo. com. Set alongside a dirt backroad 1km southwest of the town centre, this quiet & pleasant lodge has modern clean rooms with ¾ bed, fitted net, fan & en-suite cold shower. *US$17 sgl or dbl occupancy.* **$**

Alleluyah Guesthouse (10 rooms) This pleasant 2-storey hotel lies 150m from the river, 1 block south of the main road. All rooms are en suite & have a net, but those upstairs are larger & more airy. A garden restaurant serves chicken or fish with rice or chips for US$3. *US$9/10 ground floor sgl/dbl. US$17 upstairs dbl.* **$**

Sunrise Guesthouse (11 rooms) m 0777 469674. Located on the main road at the eastern end of town, this place has very clean & spacious en-suite rooms with fan & net. Meals can be prepared by advance order. Fair value. *US$9/12/17 sgl/twin/dbl.* **$**

Shoestring

Mamre Oak Lodge (12 rooms) m 0750 163150. Situated a block south of the main road, this has clean & simple rooms with ¾ bed & net. Common showers only. *US$3.50 sgl or dbl occupancy.* **$**

WHAT TO SEE AND DO The best-known attraction in the area is Murchison Falls National Park, whose Tangi Gate lies just 3km from Pakwach. The park is covered in detail in *Chapter 14*, but for those who don't have their own vehicle, the Global Village Guesthouse (see above) arranges affordable day safaris for small groups. For those who favour organised activities, community walks can be arranged through the Windsor Hotel.

Wildlife and birding
Any track or road leading south from the main road through Pakwach will bring you to the West Bank of the Nile, opposite the papyrus-lined confluence with the Tangi River on the northwest border of Murchison Falls National Park. Hippos are frequently seen here – indeed they sometimes wander into the town at night – and the birding can be very good. Better still, follow the Kampala Road southeast out of town across the Pakwach Bridge, which offers a great vantage point over the East Bank and an extensive papyrus swamp where

shoebill are seen with some regularity. About 750m south of the bridge, at the junction for the national park's Tanji Gate (✪ *2.45236, 31.51123*), the surfaced main road runs for about 1km along the northern flank of the Tanji River Wetland. This semi-seasonal mosaic of open pools, mudflats and vegetated marshland is home to Uganda kob, Defassa waterbuck and warthog, while elephant pass through on a regular basis, and a profusion of water birds (you might easily see 30 species in 15 minutes) includes various herons, egrets and smaller waders. Shoebills are also sometimes seen from the 1km feeder road to Tanji Gate, or from a second track that branches to its left then runs through the heart of the swamp for about 1km before rejoining the Kampala Road.

Fort Wadelai (*Entry US$7*) Named after a 7ha fort constructed by Emin Pasha in 1885, the fishing village of Fort Wadelai, set on the West Bank of the Nile 40km north of Pakwach, is locally infamous for having served as an Arab trade outpost and slave-holding pen earlier in the 19th century. By 1876, when the former slave trading post was visited by General Gordon's lieutenant Romolo Gessi, it had been adopted as the capital of one Chief Wadelai, the local vassal of Omukama Kabalega of Bunyoro. Three years later, the site by then known as Wadelai became headquarters of the Egyptian province of Equatoria under Emin Pasha. The fort was abandoned by him in December 1888, only to be captured by the Mahdists and held by them for several years. Wadelai resumed service as a British government post in 1894, but when Winston Churchill visited it in 1907, it was recently abandoned and already going to ruin. No trace of Emin Pasha's fort remains, and for many decades the only evidence of Wadelai's past significance was a plaque affixed to a 2m-tall concrete obelisk. That seems set to change, however, following the recent construction of an on-site information centre as part of the Emin Pasha Historical Fort Preservation and Development Project. Long-term plans include the opening of a campsite at Wadelai, and the implementation of boat trips upriver from Murchison Falls National Park. For the time being, Wadelai is most easily visited along a 40km road leading north from Pakwach at a signposted junction (✪ *2.4609, 31.49486*) 100m west of the Windsor Hotel.

Nebbi The capital of Nebbi District is a substantial but unremarkable town straddling the main surfaced road through West Nile, 50km west of Pakwach and 80km south of Arua. The only site of potential interest, some 2km west of the town centre along the road to Paidha, is the palace where Phillip Olarker Rauni III, the 34th Rwot (King) of Alur, was crowned on 30 October 2010. Logistically, Nebbi is where travellers using matatus between Pakwach and Arua might need to change, and the only reason you'd be likely to stay overnight is if you missed that connection. A few lodgings are strung along the main road, the pick being the surprisingly pleasant Leosim Hotel (*45 rooms;* ✪ *2.48051, 31.09471;* m *0791 787673; US$7/13 sgl/twin using common shower or US$18/22 en-suite sgl/dbl*), which serves meals from US$3.

PANYIMUR

This small fishing village, 35km southwest of Pakwach, has a fabulous location on the West Bank of the Albert Nile close to where it exits Lake Albert below the 1,618m Mount Erusi on the Rift Valley Escarpment. Though there are some hot springs in the vicinity, Panyimur is of interest mainly as the western terminus of a free vehicle ferry connecting West Nile to Wanseko on the eastern shore of Lake

Albert. Should you need to spend the night in Panyimur, facilities are few, but the optimistically named Quality Guesthouse is your best bet, charging less than US$10 for basic rooms using common showers.

GETTING THERE AND AWAY

By boat According to the (not entirely reliable) official timetable, the free vehicle ferry to Panyimur (*2hrs*) departs from Wanseko at noon on Monday, Wedesday and Friday, and 07.00 and at 16.00 on Tuesday, Thursday and Saturday. In the opposite direction, the boat leaves Panyimur at 07.00 and 16.00 on Monday, Wednesday and Friday, and at noon on Tuesday, Thursday and Saturday. There are no boats on Sundays. If you're not constrained by a vehicle, fishing boats travel between Wanseko and Panyimur throughout the day (*US$3; 1hr*), but they tend to be overloaded and regularly capsize with fatal results during the tempests for which Lake Albert is renowned, so stay put if there's any hint of an oncoming storm.

By road A 35km murram road runs southwest to Panyimur from the surfaced Arua Road; the junction (✢ *2.45991, 31.46844*) is only 2.5km west of Pakwach. A few matatus trundle back and forth between Pakwach and Panyimur daily.

For self-drivers arriving at Panyimur by ferry, a more adventurous onward option would be to follow the murram road that leads west out of the village to the northernmost stretch of the Rift Valley Escarpment. This steep climb provides good views of the higher Rift Valley wall as it follows Lake Albert's Congo shore south towards the 2,500m Mount Hoyo. The road then passes through a pretty, hilly and distinctly rural hinterland, reaching the small town of Parombo, about an hour from Panyimur. From Parombo, the most direct route to Arua runs north to meet the main road at Nyaravur 18km before Nebbi. Attractive pottery is sold by the roadside. Alternatively, a longer but considerably more scenic route passes around Mount Erusi before heading north to arrive at the main road a short distance east of Nebbi. Aside from being achievable in a private vehicle, this is potentially a great trip on a motorcycle, hot work on a bicycle, and a real adventure (or chore) using public transport, which consists mostly of pick-up trucks.

ARUA

The largest town in West Nile with a population of 63,000, Arua has an isolated location in an area of undistinguished scrubland only 10km east of the Congolese border. Despite its remoteness, Arua – whose name reputedly derives from the Lugbara word 'Aru', meaning 'prison' – has much in common with other similarly sized Uganda towns, with its tight central street grid, bustling open market and smarter 'senior quarters' centred on the golf course. Arua is also a significant centre of NGO activity and an important transport hub along the supply corridor to the South Sudanese towns of Yei and Juba.

Whilst Arua lacks for essential tourist attractions, it makes up for this with its friendly aura, economic vitality, and dense weave of bicycle traffic. There's no better way to explore this busy little town than to engage a boda to pedal you about Arua's excellent tarmac streets and point out such major landmarks as the hospital and police station, several mosques, and a market rated to be one of the biggest in Uganda, with a wide selection of Congolese *vitenge* (sarongs) on sale. Ediofe Cathedral, which was built by Catholic missionaries in 1917, and is currently being renovated in time to celebrate its centenary, lies 2km west of the town centre along Ediofe Road. Elsewhere, the hill above the main roundabout is worth climbing for

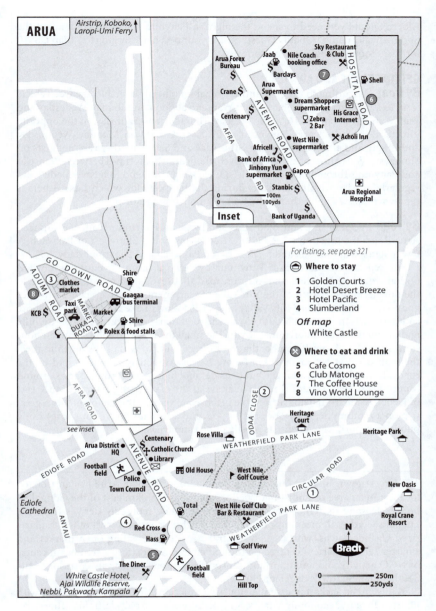

ARUA

Airstrip, Koboko,
Laropi-Umi Ferry

Inset

Sky Restaurant & Club
Nile Coach booking office
Jaab
Arua Forex Bureau
Barclays
Shell
Crane
Arua Supermarket
Dream Shoppers supermarket
Centenary
His Grace Internet
Zebra 2 Bar
Acholi Inn
Africell
West Nile supermarket
Bank of Africa
Jinhony Yun supermarket
Gapco
Stanbic
Arua Regional Hospital
Bank of Uganda

0   100m
0   100yds

For listings, see page 321

🛏 **Where to stay**
1 Golden Courts
2 Hotel Desert Breeze
3 Hotel Pacific
4 Slumberland

Off map
   White Castle

✖ **Where to eat and drink**
5 Cafe Cosmo
6 Club Matonge
7 The Coffee House
8 Vino World Lounge

GO DOWN ROAD
Shire
ADUMI ROAD
Clothes market
Gaagaa bus terminal
Taxi park
Market
KCB
Shire
Rolex & food stalls
MARKET ST
DUKAT ROAD

AFRA ROAD

see inset

Centenary
Catholic Church
Library
Arua District HQ
EDIOFE ROAD
AVENUE ROAD
Old House
Rose Villa
WEATHERFIELD PARK LANE
ODAA CLOSE
Heritage Court
Heritage Park

Football field
Police
Town Council
ANYAU
West Nile Golf Course
CIRCULAR ROAD
New Oasis

Ediofe Cathedral
Total
West Nile Golf Club Bar & Restaurant
WEATHERFIELD PARK LANE
Royal Crane Resort

Red Cross
Hass
Golf View
N
Bradt

The Diner
Football field
White Castle Hotel, Ajai Wildlife Reserve, Nebbi, Pakwach, Kampala
Hill Top

0   250m
0   250yds

views east towards the Nile and west into DRC, while the West Nile Golf Course is a pleasant setting for a stroll, a doze in the shade, or indeed a round of golf.

GETTING THERE AND AWAY

By air Eagle Air flies thrice weekly in either direction between Kampala and Arua. Their Arua office (*Arua Av;* m *0772 777331/400341; www.eagleair-ug.com*) is close to the Hotel Pacific. The airstrip is about 2km north of the town centre on the Kaya Road.

By road Arua is a 500km drive from Kampala via Karuma, Pakwach and Nebbi. This road is now surfaced in its entirety (bar the first 20km out of Pakwach, which was under construction in 2015) and should be doable in a private vehicle in 7–8 hours. The best bus service between Kampala and Arua is Gaagaa Coaches (m *0772 198988/465104; 3 buses daily; 8–10hrs; US$12*), but KKT Kampala and Nile Coach have also been recommended. Buses leave Kampala from Arua Stage on Johnston Street. Plenty of matatus run between Pakwach and Arua, though you might have to change vehicles at Nebbi.

WHERE TO STAY *Map, opposite*

Moderate

Hotel Desert Breeze (50 rooms) Odaa Close (off Weatherhead Lane); m 0781 620905/0754 900343; e desertbreezehotel@ gmail.com; www.desertbreezehotel.com. This characterless but efficiently-run 3-storey hotel, complete with shiny fittings from Dubai, has spacious rooms with fan or AC, flatscreen DSTV, nets & free Wi-Fi. A restaurant serves decent food & a swimming pool is planned. Good value. *US$31/34/40 B&B sgl/dbl/suite.* **$$**

Golden Courts Hotel (40 rooms) Circular Rd; 047 6420170; m 0711 560124; e info@ goldencourtsarua.com; www.goldencourtsarua. com. Better than the Desert Breeze, but less competitively priced, Golden Courts has an attractive green location next to the golf course & smart modern rooms with walk-in nets, flatscreen DSTV, telephone, AC, Wi-Fi & en-suite hot shower. A stylish restaurant is attached. *US$50/60/80 B&B sgl/dbl/suite.* **$$$**

Budget

White Castle Hotel (28 rooms) ⊕ 2.97555, 30.91885; 037 2260033; m 0772 880830; e info@whitecastlehotel.com; www. whitecastlehotel.com. Situated 4km south of Arua on the Pakwach Rd, Arua's most popular hotel provides decent en-suite rooms with TV, nets & fan in 4-unit cottage blocks in a garden of sorts. Other attractions include one of Arua's most reliable restaurants, serving continental, Indian & Italian dishes in the US$6–8 range, & a clean pear-shaped swimming pool. *US$26/36 B&B sgl/dbl.* **$$**

Slumberland Hotel (11 rooms) off Arua Av; m 0773 330999. This quiet & friendly brick-faced lodge, set in small but neat gardens, has comfortable & clean en-suite rooms with fan, fitted net, DSTV, balcony & hot shower, & a residents-only restaurant. *US$21/29 B&B sgl/ dbl.* **$$**

Shoestring

Hotel Pacific (28 rooms) Arua Av; m 0700 265546/0772 667314. This long-serving & suitably timeworn 3-storey hotel has a central location, clean rooms with net, polished floor & en-suite shower, & a characterful ground-floor bar & restaurant serving meals in the US$2–3 range. *US$7/9/11 sgl/twin/dbl.* **$**

WHERE TO EAT AND DRINK *Map, opposite*

Café Cosmo Off the Pakwach Rd; m 0794 116699/0756 335577; e info@cafecosmoug.com; www.cafescosmoug.com; ⊕ 11.00–23.00 daily. This superb Indian-owned restaurant at the south end of the town centre has a cosmopolitan menu dominated by Indian tandoors & curries, but also including salads, pizzas, wraps, burgers, Chinese sizzlers & plenty of vegetarian options. Coffee & a varied selection of alcoholic & non-alcoholic beverages are served indoors or in the large garden. Free Wi-Fi. *Mains mostly in the US$5–7 range.*

Vino World Lounge Arua Av; m 0772 928699; ⊕ 07.00–01.00 Mon–Fri, 24hrs over weekends. This 1st floor club-cum-restaurant diagonally opposite the Hotel Pacific serves a tasty selection of grills as well as salads, sandwiches & snacks. The bar has a good wine selection. *Grills in the US$6–8 range, snacks US$3.*

The Coffee House off Transport Road; m 0784 376093; ⊕ 08.00–23.00 daily. This pleasant café with indoor & outdoor seating serves local mains accompanied by matoke, potatoes or rice. There's freshly ground coffee but no alcohol. *Mains in the US$2–3 range.*

☆ **Club Matonge** Hospital Rd. This popular nightclub & bar hosts occasional live music & is often frequented by local Peace Corps & other volunteers.

SHOPPING The Jinhony Yun, Arua Supermarket and Dream Shoppers are among the best of several supermarkets to line Arua Avenue. The central market is one of the largest and busiest in Uganda, with stalls selling everything from Rolexes and fresh produce to colourful Congolese cloth and car spares.

OTHER PRACTICALITIES

Foreign exchange Stanbic, Barclays and several other banks offer forex services at Kampala rates, and have 24-hour ATMs outside. There is also the private Arua Forex Bureau, which should be able to buy/sell South Sudanese dollars in addition to the usual hard currencies.

Golf Founded in the 1950s, the West Nile Golf Course (*Circular Rd;* m *0772 620680/874384*) still boasts a playable nine holes – a commendable achievement up on the northwestern frontier. The green fees are around US$3. Willing caddies and ball spotters can be recruited for around US$1. Club hire is also available. The clubhouse is a pleasant spot for a beer in green surrounds.

Internet Several internet cafés are dotted around the town centre and the better hotels have free Wi-Fi, as does Café Cosmo (page 321).

Swimming The White Castle Hotel (page 321) has a swimming pool (*US$1.50 Mon–Fri, US$3 w/ends*).

WHAT TO SEE AND DO

Ajai Wildlife Reserve This 158km² reserve, which flanks the West Bank of the Nile east of Arua, was set aside in the 1960s to protect what was then the world's largest population of northern white rhino, estimated at 60 individuals. By 1975, only six survivors remained in Ajai, and today the northern race of white rhino is listed as extinct. The reserve still exists, despite considerable human encroachments, and it supports around 35km² of papyrus swamp, along with grassy floodplains and savannah woodland. Large mammals present include leopard, Uganda kob, sitatunga, hippo, black-and-white colobus and warthog, and there are reputedly long-term plans to introduce southern white rhinos. A limited ornithological survey undertaken in 1993 recorded 115 species. In 2008, UWA delegated management of the reserve to the Uganda Safari Company (*www.uganda-wildlife-safaris.com*), which runs hunting trips there from January to April, and also reputedly intends to develop it further for photographic safaris. To get to Ajai from Arua, follow the surfaced Pakwach Road south for 15km to Olevu (⊕ *2.94641, 30.96312*), then branch left on to a 40km dirt road running east to the reserve.

ARUA TO GULU VIA THE LAROPI–UMI FERRY

A contender for the most remote road in Uganda, the 320km northern loop from Arua to Gulu via Koboko, Laropi, Umi and Adjumani passes through a region whose main allure is its genuinely off-the-beaten-track feel rather than any must-see travel highlights. The only real scenic drama lies in the Moyo–Laropi Hills, which also provides opportunities to visit the site of Emin Pasha's fort at Dufile, go sport fishing or search for shoebills on the Nile, or climb Mount Otzi and watch birds in the Otzi Forest Reserve.

KOBOKO For many Ugandans, this small town in their country's northwestern corner close to the borders with Sudan and the DRC is the epitome of remoteness.

It's little more than a disproportionately wide main street with a roundabout at the northern end. Branch left for Yei in South Sudan (via the border crossing at Oraba) or right to Moyo. Amenities include a Stanbic Bank with an ATM and perhaps the most expensive fuel stations in Uganda.

The only potential tourist attraction in the vicinity of Koboko is the 250m long Lake Adomila, which despite its serpentine shape is claimed locally to sit in a volcanic crater. To get there, follow the Yei Road out of town for 12km, then turn right on to a dirt road that leads to Ludara after another 8km. The lake lies about 5km north of Ludara and you can drive to within a few hundred metres in a 4x4.

Getting there and away Koboko lies 55km north of Arua and 100km west of Moyo on a fair unsurfaced road. Buses and taxis pass through Koboko on their way between Arua and the Sudan border. Traffic headed east to Moyo is lighter but you should find a bus before resorting to a perch in the back of a truck.

Where to stay and eat

Hotel de L'Ambiance (7 rooms) Lurojo (Moyo) Rd. Smart, tiled en-suite rooms are contained within a terraced line. Dinner is served under a simple but shady thatch shelter. Relative luxury! *US$12/16 sgl/dbl.* **$$**

Hotel Pacific (24 rooms) Arua Rd; m 0777 466611. Only if L'Ambiance is full! Cheap & simple rooms have nets & use shared facilities. Cottages are provided with bucket showers. **$**

MOYO AND LAROPI–UMI FERRY Once a prosperous hub of cross-border trade, Moyo is an unassuming and rather pretty backwater of 25,000 people, perched on the edge of an elevated plateau 10km north of the Nile's West Bank, and 7km south of the South Sudan border. Though not much in itself, Moyo lies about 25km from the small and sleepy but strategically important villages of Laropi and Umi, which respectively form the West Bank and East Bank landings for the only vehicle ferry to cross the Albert Nile downriver of Pakwach. Though most through traffic is simply intent on crossing the river, this area has plenty to offer an interested visitor and, if you've taken the trouble to travel all the way up there, it's well worth taking a few days to explore. The Nile itself is an obvious attraction, flanked as it is by a 5km floodplain of papyrus swamps and open lakes that support a fantastic birdlife. The superb riverine scenery is complemented by Mount Otzi, which towers to an altitude of 1,562m towering above the West Bank. For all that, the area is only intermittently troubled by tourists, most of whom are are guests of the Arra Fishing Lodge near Umi.

Getting there and away The ferry between Laropi landing (⊕ 3.55175, 31.81256) and Umi landing (⊕ 3.54462, 31.81078) lies about 175km from Arua, 25km from Moyo, 20km from Adjumani and 140km from Gulu. Ferry crossings start daily at 06.30 and run throughout the day whenever full until 17.30. There is no charge. Buses run throughout the day to Moyo from Arua (*US$5*) and Adjumani (*US$3*). The Zawadi bus company runs to Moyo (*US$12*) via Adjumani from its Kampala office on William Street. A special hire between Moyo and Arra Fishing Lodge costs around US$40.

Where to stay and eat

Arra Fishing Lodge (7 rooms) Umi; ⊕ 3.53387, 31.80884; m 0752 212260/0772 975468; e holiday@uganda-fishing.com; www. uganda-fishing.com. Situated on the Nile's East Bank

2km south of Umi landing, this delightful camp, whose en-suite tents are supplemented by a couple of cottages, looks over the river, past a fringe of acacia trees & papyrus, to the hills of Moyo District.

12

Birdlife abounds, hippos grunt in the reeds, & a small swimming pool & the cool thatched veranda with fish-dominated menu provide relief from the heat. Activities include fishing, hiking, birding & historical excursions. Prices are extremely fair. *US$40pp B&B, or US$60 FB.* **$$**

Penthouse Inn Moyo; m 0772 962601; e penthouseinn@gmail.com. The pick of a few lodges in Moyo, has en-suite rooms & an adequate restaurant. *US$16–26 sgl, US$26 dbl B&B.* **$$**

Multipurpose Centre Moyo. This church-run facility has basic rooms. *US$6.* **$**

What to see and do The activities described below are operated by Arra Fishing Lodge at the prices quoted. It is possible to find local guides and boatmen to assist you at reduced cost, though you are unlikely to enjoy the same level of expertise.

Birdwatching boat cruises (*3hrs; US$40 for up to 4 passengers*) A variety of waterbirds can be sighted along the banks of the Nile. The prize is undoubtedly the shoebill, but other species often seen include open-billed and yellow-billed storks, African spoonbill, knob-billed duck, pygmy goose, giant kingfisher, and various herons. For those lacking ornithological intent, an early evening cruise to enjoy a cool beer and the terrific scenery is highly recommended.

Fishing (*US$15/hr for 2 fishermen; additional charges apply for hire of equipment & lost lures*) The Nile at Arra provides a good opportunity to catch sizeable Nile perch (the local record with rod and line is 75kg), catfish, and to battle with the aggressive tiger fish. Excursions use a motorised canoe with captain and guide.

Mount Otzi Northwest Uganda's most distinctive peak, the 1,562m Mount Otzi rises a full 960m above the Nile's banks on the South Sudan border 18km northeast of Moyo. Its slopes support the 188km² Otzi Forest Reserve, whose dominant cover of *Butyrospermum-Hyparrhenia* and *Combretum* savannah is interspersed with semi-deciduous thicket and riverine forest. More than 260 tree species are known from the reserve, which is identified as an Important Bird Area, with 168 bird species recorded. This checklist includes 14 of Uganda's 22 Sudan–Guinea savannah biome species: fox kestrel, white-crested turaco, red-throated bee-eater, Uganda spotted woodpecker, Emin's shrike, red-pate and foxy cisticolas, chestnut-crowned sparrow weaver, black-bellied firefinch, brown-rumped bunting, black-rumped waxbill, bronze-tailed glossy starling, purple glossy starling and piacpiac. A chimpanzee population estimated at 20–40 individuals was documented in the early 1990s, but surveys undertaken in 2009 and 2015 suggest it is either extinct or seasonal (crossing into South Sudan for part of the year). Other primates include Anubis baboon, patas and vervet monkey, and what might turn out to be East Africa's only population of the western black-and-white colobus (*C. g. occidentalis*).

Arra Fishing Lodge offers full day excursions to Otzi at US$100 for 4–5 people including transport to the trailhead. If you're driving yourself, a track into the mountains – mostly good but with some extremely steep and rocky 4x4 sections – leaves the main road midway between Moyo and Laropi.

Dufile Fort Perched on the northern bank of the Albert Nile 20km downstream of Laropi, Dufile was established by Emin Pasha in 1879 as a station of Equatoria, and housed some 4,000 people at its busiest. By 1885, however, most of its inhabitants had been relocated south to Wadelai, increasing their distance from the Mahdist insurgents in Sudan, though a reduced garrison remained to guard the northern limit of Emin's shrinking domain. In 1888, when Henry Stanley arrived to assist Emin's withdrawal from Equatoria, the soldiers ensconced at Dufile turned

mutinous and refused to follow their leader. Instead, Emin and another British officer were briefly imprisoned in the fort before the mutineers allowed them to return to Stanley's camp on Lake Albert. Shortly after this, Dufile was attacked by the Mahdist army, and while Emin's men won the battle, they recognised they were bound to lose the war, so they hotfooted it south to Lake Albert in January 1889, only to find that Emin and Stanley had already left for the coast. The mutineers remained near Lake Albert until 1890, when they were sought out and headhunted by Frederick Lugard to add some backbone to his understaffed fort in Old Kampala.

The future restoration of Dufile Fort is earmarked as part of the same Emin Pasha Historical Fort Preservation and Development Project currently being implemented at Wadelai. For the time being, however, the only obvious evidence of the former fortification is part of the perimeter ditch. Archaeological excavations over 2006/7 were able to ascertain the positions of a few buildings whose age and significance is uncertain, since the original fort was overlaid by Belgian structures during 1902–07, when West Nile was part of the Congo's Lado Enclave. Nevertheless, the site can be reached by 4x4 or boat, the latter being preferable as the river journey is a lot more rewarding than the actual destination. The return boat trip from Arra Fishing Lodge takes seven hours and costs US$130 for up to four people.

ADJUMANI Adjumani is a substantial town (population 43,000) with very little going for it touristically other than a location only 20km south of the Laropi–Umi ferry. Adjumani district has long been the site of a massive Sudanese refugee camp, and while many of its inhabitants returned home following the peace agreement that led to South Sudan's independence, recent events north of the border have led to a fresh influx and the total number of refugees had risen to almost 60,000 in mid 2015. Pekelle, 6km out of town along on the Atiak Road, is the site of the region's oldest Catholic Church, founded by missionaries who baptised their first 22 converts in November 1911.

Getting there and away Adjumani lies 117km north of Gulu on the murram road that branches off the main Sudan route at Atiak, 72km from Gulu. The town is well served by public transport. The Zawadi bus company's Moyo-bound buses run through Adjumani (*US$10*) from Kampala's William Street. Other services run to Gulu and Arua.

Where to stay and eat

Zawadi Hotel (27 rooms) Magni Rd; m 0755 899041. This unexpectedly smart Mediterranean-style hotel has a clay-tiled roof & white walls softened with climbing plants surrounding a courtyard. Clean en-suite rooms come with walk-in nets, fans & TV. A pleasant restaurant serves main courses for around US$6. Attractively priced. *US$10/18 sgl/dbl.* **$$**

ATIAK Situated 45km southeast of Adjumani and 72km north of Gulu, the small junction town of Atiak also lies on the main road north to Nimule on the South Sudan border. It is remembered as the site of one of the LRA's most notorious atrocities: the Atiak Massacre of 20 April 1995. After repulsing an enthusiastic but ill-advised attack by a newly trained home guard, the rebels drove the vigilantes back into the town, handpicked a number of young boys and girls to conscript into their ranks as child soldiers or sex slaves, then slaughtered the remaining 200 to 300 in a burst of gunfire. A memorial erected by the surviving townsfolk still stands in the town. Atiak can be reached directly from Adjumani in about an hour, or from Gulu in up to 2 hours, though coming from the latter, travellers might prefer to use the more-or-less equidistant alternative road via Baker's Fort at Patiko.

Bunyoro

Extending over 18,580km² of Rift Valley floor and escarpment immediately east of Lake Albert, the administrative subregion of Bunyoro is bounded by the Victoria Nile in the north and another of the lake's effluents, the Muzizi, to the south. The modern subregion approximates the late 19th-century shape of the Bunyoro Kingdom, which was founded in the 16th century, unwillingly incorporated into the Buganda Protectorate in 1894, disbanded under Milton Obote in 1967, then revived in 1994 with the coronation of the still incumbent Omukama (King) Gafabusa Iguru I. For much of the 20th century, Bunyoro's largest town was Masindi, an important trade centre set at the crossroads of three transport routes. In recent years, however, Hoima has superseded Masindi both in size and in terms of economic vibrancy.

From a touristic perspective, Bunyoro is of interest primarily as the southern gateway to Murchison Falls National Park (covered separately in *Chapter 14*), whose main Kichambanyobo Gate lies only 22km north of the town of Masindi, though the park can also be accessed from Masindi along a longer and rougher route via Wanseko on the Lake Albert shore. Those travelling between Murchison Falls and Fort Portal, or elsewhere in the southwest, will need to pass through Hoima as well as Masindi. Bunyoro hosts a few other worthwhile but underpublicised attractions, notably the impressive Mparo Tombs outside Hoima, the bird-rich Budongo Forest Reserve west of Masindi, and the Kabwoya Wildlife Reserve and Kibiro Salt Gardens on the shores of Lake Albert.

HOIMA

With a population now topping the 100,000 mark, the once rather pokey and moribund town of Hoima has recently emerged as something of an economic hub. This is partly due to it having superseded Masindi as the main political centre of Bunyoro under Omukama Gafabusa Iguru I, but it probably has more to do with the discovery of oilfields below nearby Lake Albert, and the earmarking of Hoima District as the inland terminus of the planned 1,500km Uganda-Kenya Crude Oil Pipeline (UKCOP) linking it to the Indian Ocean port of Lamu. For all that, Hoima is of limited interest to tourists, except as a potential overnight stop along the (mostly dirt) road connecting Murchison Falls and Masindi to Fort Portal and the southwest. Now connected to Kampala by a good surfaced 200km road, Hoima is also the gateway to the underpublicised Kabwoya Wildlife Reserve on the Lake Albert shore, while the thatched tomb of Omukama Kabalega at Mparo, 4km from the town centre, ranks among the most interesting cultural sites in Uganda.

GETTING THERE AND AWAY Hoima stands at a minor route junction. It is the only major town on the road between Fort Portal and Masindi, while additional

roads run southeast to Kampala, north to the Lake Albert port of Butiaba, and northwest to Kabwoya Wildlife Reserve, also on Lake Albert. The 200km journey on the surfaced Kampala Road shouldn't take more than 2½ hours, at least once you've cleared the city outskirts. Buses between Kampala's Qualicell bus terminal and Hoima run throughout the day and cost US$4.50.

Other roads out of Hoima are a mixed batch. The superb 80km road west to Kabwoya is surfaced and can easily be covered in an hour. By contrast, the first three-quarters of the 200km Fort Portal Road (as far as Kyenjojo) is very rough and demanding, and prone to deteriorate after heavy rain, so allow around 5 hours in a private vehicle. The 60km road to Masindi is better but might still take 90 minutes after rain. The 120km back route to Murchison Falls National Park or Wanseko via Butiaba and Bulisa is also very rough, and at least 4 hours should be allowed.

Regular matatus connect Hoima to Fort Portal (*US$8*), Masindi (*US$3*), Butiaba (*US$3*) and Bulisa/Wanseko (*US$5*). If there is no direct matatu to Fort Portal, you could hop in stages, possibly changing vehicles at Kitoke, Mabaale and Kyenjojo, all of which have at least one basic hotel.

WHERE TO STAY   *Map, page 331*

Hoima has witnessed a recent burgeoning of decent but unremarkable budget hotels catering to the conference market and other business travellers. The listings below are selective.

Upmarket

 **Hoima Cultural Lodge**   (12 rooms)
⊕ 1.43701, 31.34645; Hoima Lodges Dr;
✆ 039 2341815; m 0750 671281;
e reservations@churchillsafaris.com; www.
hoimaculturalsafarilodge.com. Set in large semi-rural grounds close to the palace a few hundred metres north of the town centre, this new lodge is easily the smartest in Hoima, offering en-suite accommodation in brightly coloured thatched cottages with funky ethnic décor, walk-in nets & modern bathrooms. A stylish restaurant with indoor & outdoor seating serves soups & salads for US$3–4, as well as a selection of stir-fries, curries & grills in the US$6.50–9.50 range. A sports bar, children's playground & swimming pool are planned. Quite overpriced for foreigners; the residents' rate seems more realistic. *Foreigners US$120pp/US$200pp B&B/FB, residents US$33/50 B&B sgl/dbl.* $$$$

Eco Gardens Tourist Hotel   ✆ 046 5442565. Currently under construction, this promising new hotel lies on the terraced & well-wooded riverside site of Fort Katasiha, 2km north of the town centre along the Butiaba Rd.

Moderate

✷ **Hotel KonTiki**   (25 rooms) ⊕ 1.41021, 31.37278; ✆ 046 5442890; m 0772 775005/0773 304752; e info@hoimakontikihotel.com; www.

hoimakontikihotel.com. Set in large landscaped gardens 3km out of town off the Kampala Rd, this peaceful & agreeable lodge offers accommodation in airy slate-floor, thatch-roof & stone-wall cottages set between tall trees that attract plenty of birds, including the spectacular Ross's turaco. There are also pokier rooms in a more nondescript modern building, evidently for the same price. All rooms come with walk-in nets & en-suite hot shower. Facilities include a swimming pool & charming terrace restaurant serving a varied selection of international dishes in the US$6–7 range. *US$40/50/60/75 B&B sgl/dbl/twin/trpl. Camping US$13pp B&B.* $$

Budget

Hoima Kolping Hotel   (22 rooms)
Butiaba Rd; ✆ 046 540167; m 0772 516421; e hoikolping@yahoo.com; www.kolpingguesthouses-africa.com/uganda/hoima. This clean & long-serving Catholic guesthouse lies in pleasant central grounds, where a shady garden restaurant serves excellent lunch & dinner buffets (*US$5*) as well as chilled beers & other drinks. The large rooms in the new wing come with queen-sized bed, fitted nets, DSTV & private balcony, & seem like very good value. The rather dated rooms in the old wing aren't a great deal cheaper but are greatly inferior in standard. *US$25 dbl or twin in new wing; US$22 dbl in old wing. All rates B&B.* $$

On 9 September 1862, Speke and Grant became the first Europeans to set foot in the Bunyoro capital of Mruli, near present-day Masindi Port. Grant described the site as 'bare and dreary'. Speke dismissed the royal palace as 'a dumpy, large hut, surrounded by a host of smaller ones … nothing could be more filthy', adding that 'it was well, perhaps, that we were never expected to go there, for without stilts and respirators it would have been impracticable'. Nor were Speke and Grant much taken with the reigning Omukama Kamurasi Kyebambe IV, who – understandably troubled by 'absurd stories which he had heard from the Baganda' about the cannibalistic, mountain-eating, river-drying powers of the white man – left his European visitors waiting for nine days before finally granting them an audience. When finally they met, Speke wrote:

'Kamurasi was enshrouded in his *mbugu* dress, for all the world like a pope in state – calm and actionless. One bracelet of fine-twisted brass wire adorned his left wrist, and his hair, half an inch long, was worked up into small peppercorn-like knobs by rubbing the hand circularly over the crown of the head … Kamurasi asked [Speke's translator] Bombay, 'Who governs England?' 'A woman.' 'Has she any children?' 'Yes', said Bombay, with ready impudence; 'these are two of them' (pointing to Grant and myself). That settled, Kamurasi wished to know if we had any speckled cows, or cows of any peculiar colour, and would we like to change four large cows for four small ones, as he coveted some of ours.'

Speke was clearly frustrated by the mixed reception accorded to him by Kamurasi, not to mention the king's endless demands for gifts, but he also regarded him to be more benevolent than the despotic Kabaka Mutesa of Buganda. 'Kamurasi conducts all business himself', Speke wrote: 'awarding punishments and seeing them carried out. The most severe instrument of chastisement is a knob-stick, sharpened at the back … for breaking a man's neck before he is thrown into the lake. But this severity is seldom resorted to, Kamurasi being of a mild disposition compared with Mutesa, whom he invariably alludes to when ordering men to be flogged, telling them that were they in Buganda, their heads would suffer instead of their backs.' The king's attitude towards his family, Speke explained, was somewhat dictatorial:

'Kamurasi's sisters are not allowed to wed; they live and die virgins in his palace. Their only occupation in life consisted of drinking milk, of which each one consumes the produce daily of from ten to twenty cows, and hence they become so inordinately fat that they cannot walk. Should they wish to see a relative, or go outside the hut for any purpose, it requires eight men to lift any of them on a litter. The brothers, too, are not allowed to go out of his reach. This confinement of the palace family is considered a state necessity, as a preventive to civil wars, in the same way as the destruction of the Baganda princes, after a certain season, is thought necessary for the preservation of peace there.'

The only other Europeans to visit Bunyoro during Kamurasi's rule were the Bakers (see box, page 362), who arrived at Mruli on 10 February 1864, remarking that it was a 'delightful change to find ourselves in comparative civilisation'. Baker waxed lyrical about 'the decency of the clothing' in the 'thickly populated and much cultivated' kingdom. 'The blacksmiths', he noted 'were exceedingly clever and used iron hammers instead of stones … they made a fine quality of jet black earthenware, producing excellent tobacco pipes, extremely pretty bowls and also

bottles. The huts are very large … made entirely of reeds and straw, and very lofty … like huge inverted baskets, beehive shaped.'

Kamurasi, once again, made a poor impression, badgering his guests with interminable demands for gifts, culminating in the suggestion that Baker leave his wife behind at Mruli as a royal consort. But after the Bakers left Mruli for Lake Albert, they received a message from Kamurasi requesting another meeting, at which it transpired that the 'king' they had met at Mruli was an impostor, installed by Kamurasi for reasons that remain unclear. The real Kamurasi impressed Baker as 'a remarkably fine man, tall and well-proportioned … beautifully clean', but still perturbed by the earlier deceit in Mruli, he also observed in Kamurasi a 'peculiarly sinister expression'. When the king started with the customarily outrageous requests for gifts, Baker 'rose to depart, telling him I had heard that Kamurasi was a great king, but that he was a mere beggar, and was doubtless [another] impostor'.

In April 1872, the recently knighted Sir Samuel Baker returned to Bunyoro as governor of Egypt's Equatoria Province, accompanied by a detachment of Egyptian troops, and charged with stopping the Arab slave trade out of the region. Kamurasi had died three years earlier, to be succeeded by his son Chwa II Kabalega. Baker was impressed by the physical attributes of the new king, describing him as 'excessively neat [and] very well clad, in a beautifully made bark-cloth striped with black … about twenty years of age … five feet ten inches in height, and of extremely light complexion'. Kabalega welcomed Baker's attempt to suppress the slave trade, but he also resented his kingdom being placed under Egyptian sovereignty, and relations between the two men swiftly deteriorated. On 8 June 1872, Kabalega led a surprise attack on Baker's Fort, expecting that resistance would be minimal, since he had craftily arranged for poisoned beer to be supplied to the Egyptian troops on the previous day. But Baker repulsed the attack, and having done so burned Kabalega's capital to the ground. Kabalega retreated southward to Mparo (close to modern-day Hoima), where he established a new capital. A decade earlier, Baker had written of Bunyoro that 'the deceit of this country was incredible'. The apparently unprovoked attack on Masindi only confirmed his earlier judgement.

Sir Samuel Baker, who left Equatoria in 1873, repeatedly expressed a strong antipathy towards Bunyoro's 'cowardly, treacherous, beggarly drunkard' of a ruler, one that went on to mould Britain's colonial policy towards the kingdom. Yet a very different impression is given in the writings of the first European to build a lasting relationship with Kabalega: Emin Pasha, who visited Mparo in 1877 to negotiate the peace between Equatoria and Bunyoro, and then served as Governor of Equatoria between 1878 and 1889. 'I have often visited Kabalega,' he wrote, 'and cannot say that I have ever heard him utter an improper word or make an indecent gesture, or that he was ever rude … Kabalega is cheerful, laughs readily and much, talks a great deal, and does not appear to be bound by ceremony, the exact opposite to Mutesa, the conceited ruler of Buganda. I certainly cannot charge Kabalega with begging; on the contrary he sent me daily, in the most hospitable manner, stores … which although they were intended to last one day, could easily have been made to last us a fortnight. I received a detailed account of all the events that happened during Baker's visit, a curiously different account from that given [by Baker]. I had to listen to a long account of the doings of the Danaglas [Egyptian soldiers] … the sum and substance of all being that [Kabalega] had been continually provoked and attacked by them, although he, as occupant on the throne, was entitled to rule over them.'

Crown Hotel (19 rooms) Kijungu Rd; ⊕ 1.4236, 31.35574; m 0783 160163. Though slightly past its prime, this comfortable suburban hotel is scheduled for renovations & it has the distinct bonus of boasting a large welcoming swimming pool & 1st-floor dining balcony with views. The sensibly-priced en-suite rooms have net, fan, DSTV & hot water. *US$20/23/27 B&B sgl/dbl/ trpl.* **$$**

Kijungu Hill Hotel (30 rooms) Circular Rd; ⊕ 1.42219, 31.35883; ☎ 036 2274218; m 0774 688402/0712 020477; e kinjuguhillhotel@yahoo. com. This popular suburban hotel, situated on Kijungu Hill a short distance south of the centre, has comfortable en-suite rooms with Wi-Fi, net, DSTV, fan & hot water. A bar & restaurant is attached. *US$27/30/33/50 B&B sgl/dbl/twin/trpl.* **$$**

Rosaline's Suites (20 rooms) Main St; m 0752 515433/0772 534111; rosalinesplace@ yahoo.com; www.rosalinessuiteshoima.com. The smartest hotel in the town centre, 4-storey Rosaline's has modern, attractively furnished rooms with chairs, writing desk, flatscreen DSTV, net, fan & en-suite shower. Some rooms also have AC. The ground-floor Rosaline's Place is an equally good spot for coffee, drinks & meals (page 332). *Website rates are unduly hefty at US$50/75/100 B&B sgl/dbl/suite, but walk-in rates are less than half for the same rooms & great value.* **$$**

Hoima Resort Hotel (45 rooms) Kijungu Rd; ⊕ 1.42472, 31.35955; ☎ 045 6440734; m 0782 929092; info@hoimaresorthotel.co.ug; www.hoimaresorthotel.co.ug. This modern 3-storey hotel on the southern town outskirts is rather lacking in character but well organised & good value. Clean en-suite rooms come with nets, fan, DSTV & hot water, & restaurant is attached. Rates include use of gym & sauna. *US$23/28 small/ large dbl, US$40-60 suites. All rates B&B.* **$$**

TWINS

Traditionally, within what is today Uganda, the birth of twins was seen as an event of great significance, though some cultures regarded it as a great blessing while others perceived it be an omen of ill. Speke, while stuck in Bunyoro in 1862, compared some of the customs he had come across on his travels:

A Munyoro woman, who bore twins that died, now keeps two small pots in her house, as effigies of the children, into which she milks herself every evening, and will continue to do so for five months, fulfilling the time appointed by nature for suckling children, lest the spirits of the dead should persecute her. The twins were not buried, as ordinary people are buried, under ground, but placed in an earthenware pot, such as the Banyoro use for holding pombe [beer]. They were taken to the jungle and placed by a tree, with the pot turned mouth downwards. Manua, one of my men, who is a twin, said, in Nguru, one of the sister provinces to Unyanyembe, twins are ordered to be killed and thrown into water the moment they are born, lest droughts and famines or floods should oppress the land. Should any one attempt to conceal twins, the whole family would be murdered by the chief; but, though a great traveller, this is the only instance of such brutality Manua had ever witnessed in any country.

In the province of Unyanyembe, if a twin or twins die, they are thrown into water for the same reason as in Nguru; but as their numbers increase the size of the family, their birth is hailed with delight. Still there is a source of fear there in connection with twins, as I have seen myself; for when one dies, the mother ties a little gourd to her neck as a proxy, and puts into it a trifle of everything which she gives the living child, lest the jealousy of the dead spirit should torment her. Further, on the death of the child, she smears herself with butter and ashes, and runs frantically about, tearing her hair and bewailing piteously; whilst the men of the place use towards her the foulest language, apparently as if in abuse of her person, but in reality to frighten away the demons who have robbed her nest.

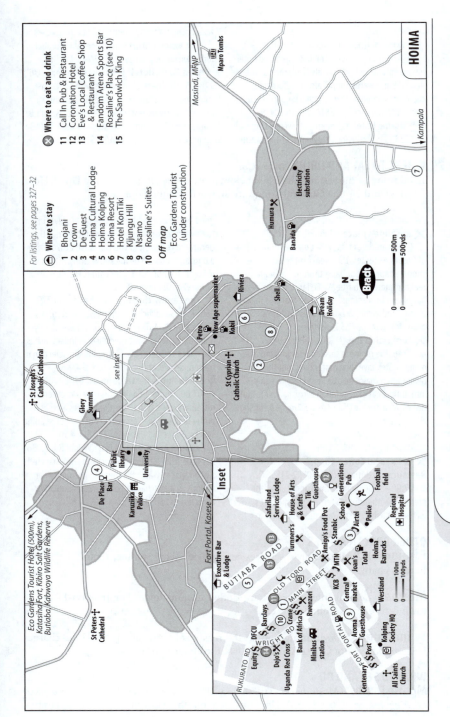

HOIMA

For listings, see pages 327–32

Where to stay
1 Bhojani
2 Crown
3 De Guest
4 Hoima Cultural Lodge
5 Hoima Kolping
6 Hoima Resort
7 Hotel KonTiki
8 Kijungu Hill
9 Nsamo
10 Rosaline's Suites

Off map
Eco Gardens Tourist
(under construction)

Where to eat and drink
11 Call In Pub & Restaurant
12 Coronation Hotel
13 Eve's Local Coffee Shop
& Restaurant
14 Fandom Arena Sports Bar
Rosaline's Place (see 10)
15 The Sandwich King

Shoestring

🏠 **Bhojani Hotel** (27 rooms) Main Rd; m 0712 737319. This central Indian-owned hotel has acceptable (albeit garishly tiled) rooms with net, TV & hot water. There's also an affordable, curry-dominated residents-only menu. *US$5 sgl using common shower, US$10 en-suite dbl.* **$**

🏠 **Nsamo Hotel** (25 rooms) Off Kyenjojo Rd; m 0754 134557. This long-serving hotel opposite the taxi park now stands 3-storeys tall, but the spotless en-suite rooms with net remain fine value. Alcohol forbidden on the premises. *US$12/14 sgl/dbl.* **$**

🏠 **De Guest Hotel** (9 rooms) Main Rd; 036 2280066. The neat, clean rooms with net & en-suite hot shower are good value but potentially noisy. A courtyard restaurant serves pizzas, salads, sandwiches & Uganda-style stews in the US$2–3 range. *US$11.50/13.50 sgl/dbl.* **$**

✗ WHERE TO EAT AND DRINK *Map, page 331*

In addition to the restaurants listed below, those at the Hoima Kolping Hotel, Hotel KonTiki and Hoima Cultural Lodge are all worth singling out.

Moderate to expensive

✗ **Rosaline's Place** Main Rd; m 0752 515433; ⏰ 07.00–midnight daily. Set on the ground floor of Rosaline's Suites, this well-ventilated coffee-shop/restaurant/bar has a thoroughly modern feel complete with free Wi-Fi, large screen TV & hardwood furnishings. The menu features pizzas, pasta, sandwiches & typical Ugandan stews & grills. *Meals in the US$3–6 range.*

✗ **Coronation Hotel** Rusaka Rd; 041 4693346. The rooms in this long-serving Indian-owned hotel have seen better days, but the restaurant remains an excellent place to enjoy authentic meat or vegetarian curry, paneer & thali dishes. *Meals in the US$6.50–8.50 range including rice or naan.*

Cheap to moderate

✗ **Eve's Local Coffee Shop & Restaurant** Butiaba Rd; m 0702 215567; ⏰ 07.00–23.00 daily. Comprising 2 adjacent premises with indoor & terrace seating, Eve's well-established restaurant puts together a good buffet at lunchtime & à la carte stews in the evening, while at her new & more brightly decorated coffee shop you can wash down a burger, sandwich or chicken & chips with inexpensive but good filter coffee. No alcohol. *Buffet & most mains US$4.*

✗ **The Sandwich King** Butiaba Rd; m 0779 086613; e sandwichrestaurant@gmail.com; ⏰ 06.15–23.15 daily. This small & misleadingly named new restaurant specialises in Indian dishes, but it also serves pizzas, local grills, & a selection of fresh cakes & pastries. *Mains US$2–4.*

🍷 **Call In Pub & Restaurant** m 0772 470047; ⏰ 07.00–midnight daily. This cheap 'n' cheerful restaurant-by-day/bar-by-night serves a great buffet lunch, as well as a variety of alcohol-sopping snacks. *Buffet US$4, snacks US$3.50–4.50.*

🍷 **Fandom Arena Sports Bar** Wright Rd; 036 2274206. This 1st-floor boozer with large screens is a good spot to watch Premier League football at w/ends, & it also has a decent snack menu. *Most items less than US$2.*

OTHER PRACTICALITIES

Foreign exchange Forex services are provided by Stanbic, Crane, KCB and Barclays banks.

Internet Several internet cafés are dotted around town. For free Wi-Fi in the town centre, try Rosaline's Place.

Swimming The swimming pool at the reasonably central Crown Hotel charges US$3 to day visitors. There's also a pool at the Hotel KonTiki.

WHAT TO SEE AND DO

Mparo Tombs (*Masindi Rd,* ✦ *1.42753, 31.3831;* m *0784 427662;* ⏰ *no fixed opening hours; entry US$3*) Now situated on the eastern outskirts of Hoima,

the village of Mparo was chosen as the capital of Omukama (King) Kabalega of Bunyoro in 1872, after Sir Samuel Baker forced his retreat out of Masindi. It was from Mparo that Kabalega led his raids into the neighbouring kingdoms of Toro and Buganda before the British drove him into hiding in 1891. After Kabalega's death at Jinja in 1923, his body was returned to Hoima and interred at Mparo. The burial ceremony was traditional in most respects, but certain customs were deemed obsolete. The most grisly of these discarded practices involved digging a 10m-deep hole, the floor of which would be covered in barkcloth on the morning of the burial. One of the late king's wives – usually the eldest or the favourite – would be seated in the hole, holding in her lap a parcel containing the dead man's jawbone. Onlookers were then seized randomly from the crowd, their limbs were amputated, and then they were thrown into the hole one by one until it was filled.

Today, the main tomb at Mparo is protected within a large domed construction made mostly from natural materials, and not dissimilar in appearance to the more famous Kasubi Tombs in Kampala, though considerably smaller. Kabalega's grave is covered with a type of white spotted brown cowhide called *entimba*, held in place by nine traditional hoes, and surrounded by many of his personal effects, including some spears and crowns said to be handed down from the Bachwezi dynasty. Kabalega's son and successor Omukama Tito Winyi is also buried at Mparo, while a plaque and monument outside the main enclosure marks the spot where Kabalega granted an audience to Emin Pasha in 1877 (see box, pages 328–9).

Coming from Hoima, Kabalega's grass-roofed tomb and the whitewashed Emin Pasha monument are visible about 100m south of the Masindi Road, 1.6km past the junction with the Kampala Road. If you don't have a vehicle, a return boda from Hoima shouldn't set you back more than a few US dollars. In theory, a 'community guide' will materialise as you arrive to unlock the compound and show you around. In practice, the site is often abandoned, so it might be safer to ring ahead.

Karuziika Palace (⊕ *1.43397, 31.34543*) The palace of the Omukama of Bunyoro lies 500m northwest of Hoima town centre just past the main university campus and library. Though the building itself is modern, a fierce sense of tradition is still evident in the Throne Room, which contains a wealth of ancient royal regalia, some said to date to the Bachwezi era. These include a stool-like nine-legged throne swathed in leopard skins and barkcloth, as well as an array of spears, royal headdresses and musical instruments. Visits should be arranged through the Omukama's private secretary (and respected historian) Yolamu Nsamba (m *0772 471251;* e *nsambay@yahoo.com*).

Katasiha Fort (⊕ *1.44922, 31.34092*) Situated 2km north of Hoima on the west side of the Butiaba Road, Katasiha was the largest of the forts built by General Colville after Kabalega abandoned his capital at Mparo in late 1893. All that remained of the fort a few years back was the 8m dry moat (now filled in) that surrounded it, and a small cave used as a hiding place by Kabalega and later as an arsenal by the British. The site of the fort now lies in the grounds of the Eco Gardens Tourist Hotel, which was still under construction and closed to visitors when this edition was researched.

Kibiro Salt Gardens and Hot Spring Inaccessible by road, the Lake Albert fishing village of Kibiro, 25km north of Hoima as the crow flies, is an appealing goal for travellers who enjoy a short but steep off-the-beaten-track hike. Kibiro stands on the narrow plain that divides the lake from the Rift Valley Escarpment, where it is distinguished from several other similarly inaccessible lakeside settlements by its

proximity to a saline hot spring that has supplied Bunyoro with salt for centuries. In 1885, Emin Pasha, probably the first foreign visitor to Kibiro, described the gardens and salt-making process, observing helpfully that 'when taken in large quantities, [the spring water] acts as a moderate purgative'. But the salt industry at Kibiro is much older than this: indeed, glass beads found by archaeologists indicate that salt was bartered for here in the 13th century, and most probably earlier.

The salt-gardeners of Kibiro employ a clever technique to obtain an unusually pure product. Their so-called gardens are patches of salty ground from which all grass and topsoil has been removed. These mineral-rich depressions are saturated with water diverted in earthen channels from a searingly hot stream fed by a spring hidden deep within a cleft in the Rift Escarpment. This already slightly salty water dissolves additional salts from the soil. Loose dry soil is then scattered across the 'garden' into which, over a week or so, the salty water is drawn up by capillary action. When the enriched earth changes colour it is scraped into jars to be repeatedly leached by a further quantity of spring water. The result is a concentrated solution of 14% salt which is boiled off to produce crystals of 97.6% pure sodium chloride. In contrast, the product at Lake Katwe, the region's other major salt supplier, is only 85% pure.

Salt gardens aside, the short but steep hike to Kibiro provides a rare opportunity to appreciate a dramatic out-of-the-way stretch of the Rift Valley on foot. And as you follow the footpath to Kibiro, you'll notice it becomes steeper as you approach the base. This is because the escarpment actually comprises three distinct planes, each corresponding to a different phase of uplift. The highest section is 4.5 million years old and has eroded into a relatively gentle slope, while the lowest section was heaved above the lake within the last 1.5 million years and remains much steeper.

To get to Kibiro from Hoima, follow the Butiaba Road north for 24km to Kigorobeya (✪ *1.61602, 31.30792*), where a left turn takes you on to a decent 8km track terminating at the escarpment edge. Here, for a small fee (around US$1), you can park safely at the Kato family compound, doubtless alongside a few other bodas and other vehicles associated with local traders carrying salt up or goods down the busy footpath to the escarpment base. The foot descent should take around 45 minutes, and it can be hot going, so take along plenty of water. Once there, no formal system is in place for escorting visitors around, so pop past the home of the village chairman to sign the ubiquitous visitors' book, make a quasi-official donation of around US$2, and be allocated a guide (who'll most likely expect a fee of around US$1).

KABWOYA WILDLIFE RESERVE

Uganda's newest protected area, the 87km² Kabwoya Wildlife Reserve has an isolated but superbly scenic location on the narrow plain sandwiched between the eastern shore of Lake Albert and the Rift Valley Escarpment. When it comes to viewing big game, Kabwoya cannot be mentioned in the same breath as the likes of Murchison Falls or Queen Elizabeth national parks, for which reason it is seldom a focal point on rushed tour itineraries. That said, it's a very scenic reserve, and the attractive lakeshore Lake Albert Lodge offers an unusual variety of outdoor activities, ranging from horseback excursions, guided walks, mountain biking and quad biking to night safaris, game fishing, birdwatching and even fossil hunting. Logistically, the recent completion of an excellent surfaced road from Hoima has made Kabwoya well worth considering as a one- or two-night detour to break up the long slog of largely unpaved road connecting Murchison Falls to Fort Portal. An entrance fee of US$10 per person per 24 hours is levied; payment can be made at the lodge.

HISTORY Kabwoya was originally set aside for conservation in 1963 as part of the 227km² Kaiso-Tonya Controlled Hunting Area (KTCHA), which then represented an important component in a migration route along the east shore of Lake Albert between Murchison Falls National Park and the Toro-Semliki Wildlife Reserve. Sadly, however, the large herds of buffalo, Defassa waterbuck, Ugandan kob and Jackson's hartebeest once associated with the KTCHA had all but vanished when a survey was undertaken there in 1982. Most of these animals were wiped out by poachers during the long years of civil war, while others dispersed elsewhere as a result of competition with cattle herders. At the turn of the millennium, a belated effort to protect the remnant wildlife led to an 87km² portion of KTCHA southwest of the river Hohwa being upgraded in status to form the Kabwoya Wildlife Reserve, while the northeast was rebranded as the Kaiso-Tonya Community Wildlife Area (KTCWA), the country's lowest and most meaningless category of protected area.

In 2002, Kabwoya and the KTCWA was leased to Lake Albert Safaris, a private concessionaire that works in partnership with UWA and the Hoima District administration to manage the reserve and develop it for tourism. Sadly, it was uphill all the way for the new management team, which ended up winching its Land Rovers over the escarpment into a reserve empty of large mammals (other than cattle) prior to finally opening a lodge overlooking the lakeshore in 2006. The opening of the lodge roughly coincided with the discovery of oil reserves beneath Kabwoya and the arrival of prominent and ecologically unfriendly exploratory rigs. Despite this, impressive progress has been made in Kabwoya. With the backing of local politicians and the Bunyoro royalty, most of the cattle have been relocated from the wildlife reserve to KTCWA, resulting in a rapid increase in wildlife. And while oil rigs are soon expected to open offshore, the significance of Kaiso (a fishing village 5km northeast of the lodge) to the pending Uganda-Kenya Crude Oil Pipeline (UKCOP) is not without a silver lining. The completion of a magnificent 82km surfaced road connecting Hoima to Kaiso in 2014 has suddenly made Kabwoya highly accessible to tourists and elevated it to be a potential weekend break from Kampala, which is now only 3–4 hours' drive distant on good surfaced roads.

FAUNA AND FLORA Wildlife populations in Kabwoya, though still recovering from years of poaching and encroachment, are steadily on the increase. Of the so-called Big Five, lion and elephant have not been seen regularly in decades, but buffalo and presumably leopard are still present in small numbers. The most common large mammals are Ugandan kob, oribi, Anubis baboon and warthog, but Jackson's hartebeest, Defassa waterbuck, bushbuck and common duiker are also present in significant numbers. More localised species include hippo, which have recolonised the lake close to the lodge, and the small numbers of giant forest hog, chimpanzee, black-and-white colobus and vervet monkey that dwell in the riparian forest along the rivers Hohwa and Wambabya. A full bird list has yet to be compiled, but a mix of habitats including grassland, wooded savannah, riverine forest and lakeshore suggests birders are unlikely to be disappointed – indeed, a survey undertaken in 2009 recorded 176 species, while the lodge itself claims an unofficial checklist of 460 species for Kabwoya and KTCWA.

GETTING THERE AND AWAY Kabwoya Wildlife Reserve lies about 80km west of Hoima by road. The best route there entails following the Butiaba Road north out of town for 6km then turning left at the Kyesiga traffic circle (✪ *1.4795, 31.3439*). After another 75km on what is quite possibly the best (and least trafficked) road

13

anywhere in Uganda, passing *en route* through the unmanned entrance gate (⊕ *1.41688, 30.96524*), which stands next to a dam that often hosts a few kob and baboon, you arrive at a T-junction (⊕ *1.52473, 30.96238*) where you'll see the Joy Max Hotel to your immediate left. A right turn at this junction leads to Kaiso fishing village after a few hundred metres, while a left turn takes you past the village of Kyahoro to Lake Albert Lodge, which is signposted to the right after 5.5km. From this junction (⊕ *1.493, 30.94296*), it's another 1.5km to the lodge itself.

An alternative route to the lodge runs northwest from Kabwoya trading centre on the Hoima–Fort Portal Road, but it is very rough and cannot be recommended, even if you are coming from the direction of Fort Portal.

So far as we can ascertain, no public transport runs to Lake Albert Lodge, but it would be surprising if the quality of the new road doesn't eventually stimulate sufficient traffic to justify a matatu service between Hoima and Kaiso.

WHERE TO STAY AND EAT
Upmarket
 Lake Albert Lodge (10 cottages)
⊕ 1.49543, 30.93253; m 0772 221003/0755 793657; e reservations@lodgelakealbert.com; www.lodgelakealbert.com. Built by the reserve concessionaire at a stunning location atop 60m cliffs rising from the lakeshore, this excellent lodge is the perfect place to watch the sun set over the Congolese Blue Mountains across 40km of water. Attractive canvas-sided, glass-fronted & immaculately thatched cottages come with a queen-sized bed, fitted nets, en-suite hot shower

PETROLEUM IN UGANDA

The presence of oil beneath the Albertine Rift Valley has long been suspected: the first report on the subject, *Petroleum in Uganda*, was completed by E J Wayland in 1927. Eighty-odd years later, it became official when, in 2006, test drilling programmes found significant reserves of oil in the Lake Albert–Edward basins along the Uganda–Congo border. These may contain in excess of a billion barrels of stuff suitable for diesel, paraffin and aviation fuel (but not petrol). Reaction to the news varies widely, from joy to deep concern. If effectively utilised, revenue from oil could do much for Uganda, improving the substandard services that hinder development and ushering in a new age of investment and economic activity. On the other hand, if clumsily implemented, Uganda's fistfuls of oil dollars could be gained at the expense of those generated by tourism (a useful US$800m in 2011). The catch is that the oil deposits are clustered beneath western Uganda's primary tourism destinations, most notably the Murchison Falls and Queen Elizabeth national parks. It is unfortunate, though perhaps understandable, that the Uganda government does not consider internationally recognised protected area status an insurmountable obstacle. The neatest but most drastic solution mooted involves excising the oil-rich sectors from the protected areas. This possibility has given rise to tremendous concern from the tourism industry as well as environmentalists – though interestingly it has failed to ignite public passion in the fashion of the Mabira Forest debacle of 2007 (see page 185). The supposed sanctity of protected areas apart, apprehension is founded on the fact that (within a conservation area exceeding 5,000km²!) Murchison's oilfields are found in the Paraa and Buligi areas where the park's wildlife, tourism activity and investment are also concentrated, while those in Queen Elizabeth National Park lie below the fabulous wilderness of Ishasha. UWA, fortunately, does not seem prepared

& private balcony. The small swimming pool is a welcome feature in the hot trough of the Albertine Rift Valley, & all the activities described below are arranged here. *US$80pp/US$105pp resident/non-resident, bed only. Camping US$20pp. B/fast, lunch or dinner & additional US$20pp per meal. Multi-day horseback, walking & other packages including activities are also offered.* **$$$$$**

Budget

🏠 **Joy Max Hotel** (11 rooms) ✆ 1.52405, 30.96241; **m** 0784 822241. Situated on the left side of the T-junction where the roads for Kaiso & Kabwoya split, this more-than-adequate guesthouse has small but clean en-suite rooms with fitted net & cold shower, as well as a restaurant/bar with terrace seating & pool table. *US$20/27 dbl/twin.* **$$**

WHAT TO SEE AND DO

Organised activities Lake Albert Lodge offers a wide variety of activities to both day and overnight visitors. These include day and night game drives, fossil hunting, guided walks and waterfall hikes, all of which cost around US$15–25 per person and require a minimum of four people. Horseback safaris starts at US$20 per person and require a minimum of two people. Game fishing excursions, which cost US$200/350 per person half/full day, with a minimum of three people, include a professional fishing guide, tackle, packed lunch and water. Mountain bikes and quad bikes are also available for rental.

Unguided walks Parts of the KTCWA could be explored on foot or in a private vehicle by day visitors or those using Joy Max Hotel as a base. Kaiso itself is a rather surreal

to allow an emergent oil industry to make free with, or within, its estate, and Moses Mapesa, UWA's executive director, assures me that 'degazettement' is not an option. Nevertheless, exploration will go ahead, with up to ten wells being sunk by Heritage Oil at the western end of Murchison Falls and six in and around Ishasha. UWA is insisting on stringent measures to limit impacts on the environment, wildlife and tourism. Environmental Impact Assessments stipulate that drilling in each location will be phased, a single vehicle-mounted rig (one-third the height of the usual 50m structure) being moved between sites and timed to limit activity during high tourist seasons. My own view has been that Murchison is quite large enough to absorb any adverse visual effects from the exploration programme (it is 30km from Paraa to the peninsula's extremity at Delta Point) and this was borne out on my most recent visit.

Of far greater concern than these short-lived drilling sites is what will happen in the long term. As yet, it's pointless to speculate on how oil will be extracted, transported and refined until the results of the exploration are known. In the meantime, there is fervent hope that future operations are also carried out by a company from North America or Europe, rather than a part of the world not renowned for environmental sensitivity or accountability.

There are also international issues to consider. The Rift Valley drains directly into the Nile, a river subject to international treaties and which Sudan and Egypt would not wish diluted with spilled oil. Secondly, since the Uganda–Congo border runs along the Rift Valley, some reservoirs beneath Murchison, Ishasha and also Lake Albert will certainly be shared between these two countries. Exploration in Uganda is keenly monitored by Congo which will certainly wish to share in the rewards from extraction along the common border.

lakeshore fishing village dominated by traditional reed-and-thatch huts encircled by a pristine loop of asphalt road associated with the soon-to-come oil drilling industry. Its busy fishing beach is lined with several dozen boats, and there's a large market where you can see fish being dried using traditional methods. A 20-minute walk along the Lake Albert shore northwest of the main fishing beach leads to the tip of the marshy arrow-shaped peninsula where a shallow 2km² lake is fed by the Hohwa River. In the opposite direction, where the road towards Lake Albert Lodge crosses the Hohwa floodplain about 1km southwest of the Joy Max, is a series of small swamps and pools where you are likely to see kob, baboon and a good variety of water-associated birds.

MASINDI

The second-largest town in Bunyoro with a population of 95,000, Masindi comes across as rather sleepy and economically subdued by comparison to Hoima, but it is of greater interest to tourists, since it serves as the main urban gateway to Murchison Falls National Park, whether coming from the direction of Kampala or the southwest. The compact town centre isn't much to look at: a tight grid of erratically surfaced roads, dusty or muddy depending on how recently it last rained, emanate from a central market, lined with the faded colonial-era shopfronts that characterise so many small Ugandan towns. Rather more appealing is the green, leafy stretch of suburbia that runs north from the town centre past the golf course. In 1924, Etta Close was charmed by Masindi and its 'European officials [who] live in trim little bungalows with little gardens full of European flowers placed in a circle around a golf course and two lawn tennis courts, the one and only hotel being not far off'. The European officials are long gone, but this description otherwise feels surprisingly apposite today, right down to the renovated Masindi Hotel, built in 1923 and once host to the writer and hunting enthusiast Ernest Hemingway.

HISTORY Masindi served as the capital of Bunyoro and a major centre of ivory trade prior to 1872, when Omukama Kabalega relocated his court to Mparo to distance himself from the military attentions of Sir Stanley Baker. In the early colonial era, Masindi re-emerged as a thriving hub of trade, thanks to its location at the pivot of three key international transport routes: from Butiaba across Lake Albert to what was then the Belgian Congo, north along the Nile to what is now South Sudan, and southeast across Lake Kyoga to the Busoga Railway (which connected the main line to the Kenyan port of Mombasa). Commerce declined after 1962, when the rising level of Lake Albert enforced the closure of Butiaba Port, and it was further undermined by the havoc wrought on the national economy and transport infrastructure under Idi Amin. Masindi's post-1986 recovery has been restricted by several factors, among them the effective closure of the Congolese and (until recently) South Sudanese borders, the long years of unrest in Uganda north of the Nile, and the collapse of the road-rail-steamer transport network that once linked lakes Albert, Kyoga and Victoria. Over recent years, Masindi has been superseded by Hoima, the fast-growing seat of the Omukama situated some 50km to its southwest, in terms of both population size and economic vibrancy.

GETTING THERE AND AWAY
From Kampala Masindi lies 215km north of Kampala, a drive of around 3 hours on good surfaced roads. To get there, follow the Gulu Road north for 170km before turning left at a conspicuous junction (✪ *1.54471, 32.04156*) about 200m north of Kafu Bridge. A popular overnight or afternoon stop between Kampala and Masindi,

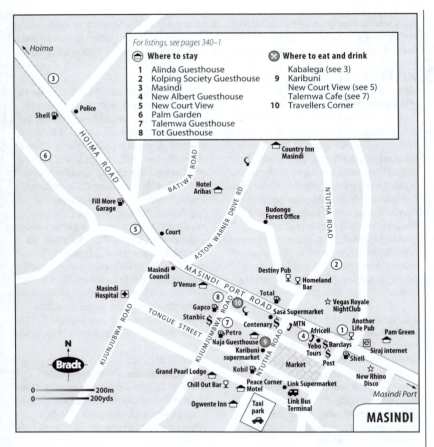

For listings, see pages 340–1

Where to stay
1 Alinda Guesthouse
2 Kolping Society Guesthouse
3 Masindi
4 New Albert Guesthouse
5 New Court View
6 Palm Garden
7 Talemwa Guesthouse
8 Tot Guesthouse

Where to eat and drink
Kabalega (see 3)
9 Karibuni
New Court View (see 5)
Talemwa Cafe (see 7)
10 Travellers Corner

Hoima

Shell
Police
Hoima Road
Batiwa Road
Fill More Garage
Court
Aston Warner Drive Rd
Country Inn Masindi
Hotel Aribas
Budongo Forest Office
Ntutha Road
Masindi Council
D'Venue
Masindi Hospital
Destiny Pub
Homeland Bar
Total
Masindi Port Road
Gapco
Stanbic
Petro
Naja Guesthouse
Karibuni supermarket
Kijunjimbwa Road
Tongue Street
Centenary
Sasa Supermarket
Vegas Royale NightClub
MTN
Africell
Another Life Pub
Pam Green
Yebo Tours
Barclays
Shell
Siraj internet
Market
Post
Grand Pearl Lodge
Kobil
New Rhino Disco
Chill Out Bar
Peace Corner Motel
Link Supermarket
Masindi Port
Ogwente Inn
Taxi park
Link Bus Terminal

N
Bradt
0   200m
0   200yds

MASINDI

the Ziwa Rhino Sanctuary (pages 181–2) lies immediately west of the main road about 8km before Kafu Bridge. Also worth a stop is the excellent Kabalega Diner 2km past the turning to Ziwa Rhino Sanctuary.

Regular buses run between Kampala Qualicell and Masindi (*US$3; 3hrs*), the most reliable being Link Bus (*041 4255426; e info@link.co.ug; www.link.co.ug*), which operates five scheduled departures daily in either direction, leaving Kampala at 09.00, 11.00, 14.30, 16.00 and 17.30, and Masindi at 08.00, 09.30, 11.00, 14.00 and 16.30. Matatus to Kampala cost US$4, and run back and forth throughout the day.

From Fort Portal Southwest of Masindi, the 260km road to Fort Portal via Hoima is erratically maintained dirt for the first 210km of its length (as far as Kyenjojo) and it tends to deteriorate after heavy rain. Allow 6–7 hours in a private vehicle. Plenty of matatus cover this road but you will need to change vehicles at Hoima and possibly elsewhere. A matatu to Hoima costs US$3.

Heading for Paraa (Murchison Falls) on the direct 85km route via Kaniyo Pabidi, you need to follow the Hoima Road 500m north from the town centre, then turn right opposite the Shell garage (the last opportunity to fill up at reasonable fuel prices), then to the left after another 6km. Using the longer and more scenic 135km route via Budongo Forest and Bulisa, you need to follow the Hoima Road as it loops

Bunyoro MASINDI

13

339

back south, then turn right after 2.5km. There is no public transport to Paraa along either of the routes described, but a daily bus does connect Kampala to Wanseko via Masindi, and matatus also run to Butiaba (*US$4*) and Bulisa/Wanseko (*US$6*).

🏠 WHERE TO STAY   *Map, page 339*
Upmarket

🏠 **Masindi Hotel** (28 rooms) Hoima Rd; ☏ 046 5420023; m 0772 420130. Located almost 1km northwest of the town centre, Masindi's oldest hotel was built in 1923 by the East Africa Railways & Harbours Company as a transit point between ferries on lakes Kyoga & Albert. Following an effective facelift, the long verandas, airy, tiled en-suite rooms & revamped public areas once again exude the charm of its salad days, when the hotel register read like a Who's Who of celebrity safari-goers (Hemingway, Bogart, Bacall, Hepburn . . .). En-suite twin & dbl rooms have red polished floors, 4-poster beds with fitted nets, DSTV & combined hot tub/shower. The Kabalega Restaurant is attached (see below). *US$95/115 B&B sgl/dbl occupancy.* **$$$**

Budget

❋ 🏠 **Kolping Society Guesthouse** (30 rooms) Ntuha Rd; ☏ 0465 420458; m 0782 394992; e masindikhotel@kolpingug.org; http://kolpingguesthouses-africa.com/uganda/masindi. Set in large green gardens only 200m north of the town centre, this Catholic guesthouse feels like a real retreat from the bustle of downtown Masindi. Older rooms in the main building are nothing special but come with king-sized bed, fitted net, DSTV & en-suite hot shower. The spacious & contemporarily decorated garden cottages have similar facilities, plus fans, fridge & private balcony, & seem like exceptional value at the price. A fair restaurant & bar is attached. *US$23/42 dbl room/cottage.* **$$**

❋ 🏠 **New Court View Hotel** (17 rooms) Hoima Rd; m 0752 446463; e info@newcourtviewhotel.com; www.newcourtviewhotel.com. A perennial favourite

en route to Murchison Falls, this well-run lodge has a cluster of small but brightly decorated bandas with net, fan & solar-heated en-suite shower. An excellent garden restaurant is attached. Early b/fasts can be served or packed for birdwatchers & other early risers. *US$27/32 B&B sgl/dbl.* **$$**

🏠 **Talemwa Guesthouse** (20 rooms) Market St; m 0772 406074; e talemwa232@gmail.com. This likeable central guesthouse has small but brightly decorated rooms with net, DSTV, fan & en-suite hot shower. An equally attractive coffee shop is attached. *US$17/24/27 sgl/dbl/twin.* **$$**

🏠 **Palm Garden Hotel** (11 rooms) Off Hoima Rd. Low-key family-run hotel, in a quiet location around the corner from the Masindi Hotel, is very literal about its singular palm, the most impressive feature of the small grassy garden. Clean tiled rooms have a fan, net & in some cases DSTV. *US$17 en-suite dbl, US$13 dbl using common showers.* **$$**

Shoestring

🏠 **Tot Guesthouse** (10 rooms) Market St; m 0777 912357. This above-par cheapie, tucked away on a quiet alley, has clean tiled en-suite rooms with ¾ or dbl bed, fitted net & writing desk. *US$8 dbl.* **$**

🏠 **New Albert Guesthouse** (20 rooms) Masindi Port Rd; m 0754 606036/0774 706236. This is a central & reasonably clean rock-bottom cheapie. Not all rooms have nets. Good value. *US$3/5 sgl/dbl using common showers, US$7 en-suite dbl.* **$**

🏠 **Alinda Guesthouse** (40 rooms) Masindi Port Rd; m 0782 640100. Now looking rather rundown, this long-serving 2-storey guesthouse has adequate rooms with fan & net. *US$10/17 en-suite sgl/dbl, US$6/12 sgl/dbl using common showers.* **$**

✕ WHERE TO EAT AND DRINK   *Map, page 339*
Moderate to expensive

✕ **Kabalega Restaurant** Hoima Rd; ☏ 046 5420023; ⊕ 07.00–23.00 daily. The restaurant at the venerable Masindi Hotel (see above) is the most stylish in town, offering the option of indoor or garden seating & a long menu of Indian, Chinese & continental dishes. *Mains around US$8.*

✕ **New Court View Hotel** Hoima Rd m 0752 446463; www.newcourtviewhotel.com, ⊕ 07.00–222.00 daily. The popular garden restaurant at this hotel (*US$27/32 B&B sgl/dbl*) boasts a varied menu specialising in Indian dishes & pizza, plus some tasty Chinese items & home-grown salads. *Most mains in the US$4–7 range.*

Cheap to moderate

✕ Talemwa Café Market St; m 0772 406074; ☉ 07.30–22.00 daily. The funky little coffee shop attached to the Talemwa Guesthouse serves the best coffee & fruit juice in town, as well as a selection of local dishes. *Mains around US$3.*

✕ Travellers Corner Masindi Port Rd; m 0776 251510; ☉ 07.00–23.00 daily. Though not quite the must-try it was a few years back, this stalwart bar & restaurant, located on a corner plot in a colonial-era building, has a wide balcony, pool table, notice board & varied menu (salads, pasta, fajitas, sandwiches). *Mains in the US$3–5 range.*

✕ Karibuni Restaurant Ntuha Rd; ☉ 07.30–22.00 daily. This busy local eatery opposite the market has indoor & outdoor seating. *Mains in the US$2–3 range.*

SHOPPING Several supermarkets are scattered around the market area. The Karibuni Supermarket opposite the market is a good place to stock up before heading to Murchison Falls, as are the Link Supermarket next to the Link Bus Terminal and Sasa Supermarket on Masindi Port Road.

OTHER PRACTICALITIES Forex services are provided by Stanbic and Barclays banks. Several internet cafés are scattered around town, the best being Siraj Internet on Masindi Port Road.

TOUR OPERATORS

Yebo Tours Masindi Port Rd; ☏ 046 520029; m 0772 637493; e yebotours2002@yahoo.com. This reliable Masindi-based operator can provide 4x4/minibus hire to Murchison Falls at around US$80/100 per day, inclusive of driver & unlimited kilometres, but exclusive of fuel. It also arranges all-inclusive camping tours to Murchison Falls.

WHAT TO SEE AND DO

Masindi Town Walking Trail If you have a spare afternoon, pick up this informative brochure (compiled by a group of Masindi-based VSO volunteers) from the New Court View Hotel, and follow the route described past several historical landmarks.

Masindi Port Masindi Port, almost 40km east of town, but only 7km from the main Kampala-Gulu Road, fringes the 500m-wide Victoria Nile a short distance downriver of the marshy area where it exits Lake Kyoga. The port peaked in importance during the colonial era, when it formed part of a trade network linking Lake Albert to the Kenyan coast, but no commercial boats sail from it today. The surrounding marshes are of potential interest to birdwatchers, and there are quite a few hippos around. You'd be unlikely to have any problems organising a dugout to explore Lake Kyoga, and the Nile River is navigable to the top of Karuma Falls, 70km downstream.

In a private vehicle, Masindi Port is only 10 minutes' drive east from a signposted junction at Rwekunye (✥ 1.70989, 32.02877) on the main Kampala–Gulu Road. Little formal public transport runs there, but you could wait at Rwekunye Junction for a lift or a boda, or even walk out from the main road. A free ferry service crosses the Nile between Masindi Port and Waitumba on the opposite bank. When it's not running, you can hire a dugout to take you across for a small consideration. From Waitumba, a road heads north to Lira.

BUDONGO FOREST RESERVE

One of East Africa's most extensive and ecologically diverse blocks of contiguous rainforest, the Budongo Forest Reserve extends over an area of 435km² west of Masindi, east of the Albertine Rift Escarpment and south of Murchison Falls Conservation

Area (MFCA). In pre-colonial times, Budongo, a Runyoro name meaning 'fertile soil', was accorded protection by the Omukama of Bunyoro, who used it as a royal hunting ground and forbade his subjects from hunting there without permission. In 1926, the colonial authorities opened a sawmill in the forest, which was producing 600 tonnes of hardwood timber per month by the 1960s. The sawmill closed in the 1980s, by which time an estimated 35 cubic metres of timber per hectare had been removed from Budongo, at least 65% of which comprised mahogany. The forest has recovered well since then, with *Ficus* and other fruiting trees having taken the place of many of the felled mahoganies and ironwoods, though some illegal logging still takes place.

Today, Budongo is renowned both for harbouring Uganda's largest population of chimpanzees and as one of its key ornithological destinations. Indeed, such is its avian wealth that the track nicknamed the 'Royal Mile', because it was once a favourite haunt of Omukama Kabalega, is widely regarded to be the country's single most rewarding birding hotspot. In 1992, an internationally-funded ecotourism project was established at Budongo and neighbouring Kaniyo Pabidi (the two were then jointly administered as a 793km² forest reserve but the latter is now part of the MFCA) to help conserve the forest through the implementation of tourist projects that benefited local communities. Two ecotourism sites were created: Busingiro, to the east of Masindi within Budongo proper; and Kaniyo Pabidi in what is now the MFCA (pages 354–5). Chimpanzee tracking, basic accommodation and camping were offered at Busingiro for several years, but these services have been discontinued and the site now offers only general forest walks and birding excursions.

FLORA AND FAUNA Classified as a moist semi-deciduous medium-altitude forest, Budongo supports at least 450 species of tree, the most impressive being those large buttressed giant mahoganies that have been left unfelled and now stand up to 60m tall. More than 250 butterfly and 360 bird species have been recorded in Budongo and/or Kaniyo Pabidi. The bird checklist includes 60 west or central African bird species known from fewer than five locations in East Africa. Yellow-footed flycatcher, often associated with ironwood trees, has not been recorded elsewhere in Uganda, while Ituri batis, lemon-bellied crombec, white-thighed hornbill, black-eared ground thrush and chestnut-capped flycatcher are known from only one other East African forest.

Together with Kaniyo Pabidi, Budongo supports an 800-strong chimpanzee population, the largest anywhere in Uganda. Budongo's chimpanzees were first studied in 1962 by Professor Vernon Reynolds, whose went on to publish a book *Budongo: An African Forest and its Chimpanzees* in 1965. In 1990, Reynolds established the Budongo Forest Project, subsequently renamed the Budongo Conservation Field Station (*www.budongo.org*), an ongoing research project dedicated to a habituated chimp community located near Busingiro. Other primates resident in Budongo include red-tailed monkey, blue monkey, black-and-white colobus, potto and various forest galago species. The forest is also occasionally visited by elephants and other large mammals associated with the adjacent UWA-managed Murchison Falls Conservation Area (MFCA).

GETTING THERE AND AWAY Budongo Forest is flanked by the Butiaba Road some 30km west of Masindi. To get to Nyabyeya Forestry College, the springboard for the Royal Mile, follow the Butiaba Road out of Masindi for about 30km to Nyamegita, then turn right into the signposted 2km feeder road. Busingiro Tourist Site lies along the left side of the Butiaba Road about 10km past Nyabyeya. The drive from Masindi will take up to an hour in a private vehicle.

Using public transport, any matatu heading from Masindi to Butiaba or Wanseko can drop you at Nyamegita or Busingiro, though you'll probably have to pay the full fare for Butiaba. A 4x4 with driver can be hired in Masindi through Yebo Tours (page 341).

For details of continuing from Budongo to Murchison Falls via Lake Albert, see pages 344–5.

WHAT TO SEE AND DO Though no longer used for chimp tracking, Busingiro's complex and extensive trail system remains open for forest walks. Some routes are of note, variously, for trees, birds or butterflies, so it is worth discussing any special interests and preferences with the guides, who will tailor your walks accordingly. A 3-hour forest walk costs US$50 per person, as does a bird walk with a specialised guide. Visitors may walk unaccompanied along the main road, but are permitted to enter the forest on either side only when accompanied by a guide.

The Royal Mile The best place to do a guided bird walk is along the Royal Mile, a 2.5km stretch of dirt road that runs north from Nyabyeya Forestry College to the Budongo Conservation Field Station. Unfortunately, the Royal Mile lies about 14km

HEMINGWAY AND BUTIABA

The American writer Ernest Hemingway and his fourth wife Mary Welsh arrived at Butiaba on 23 January 1954, somewhat the worse for wear after a bruising 24-hour trip to Murchison Falls. The day before, their chartered Cessna had dipped to avoid hitting a flock of birds, in the process clipping a wing on an abandoned telegraph wire, and forcing a crash landing in which Hemingway dislocated his right shoulder and Mary cracked several ribs. The injured passengers and their pilot spent the night huddled on the riverbank below Murchison Falls, to be rescued the next morning by a boat headed to Butiaba.

At Butiaba, Hemingway chartered a De Havilland to fly him and his wife back to Entebbe the next morning. On take-off, however, the plane lifted, bumped back down, crashed, and burst into flames. Mary and the pilot escaped through a window. Hemingway, too bulky to fit through the window and unable to use his dislocated arm, battered open the buckled door with his head, to emerge with bleeding skull and a rash of blistering burns. The battered couple were driven to Masindi to receive medical attention and spent a few days recuperating at the Masindi Hotel. On 25 January 1954, New York's *Daily News* broke the news of the accident under the headline 'Hemingway Feared Dead in Nile Air Crash'. A spate of premature obituaries followed before it was discovered that the writer had survived, if only just.

Hemingway had, in addition to the dislocated arm and several first-degree burns, limped out of the burning plane with a collapsed intestine, a ruptured liver and kidney, two crushed vertebrae, temporary loss of vision in one eye, impaired hearing, and a fractured skull. In October of that year, he was awarded the Nobel Prize in Literature, but was too battered to attend the ceremony. Nor did he have the energy to work the 200,000 words he wrote on safari into publishable shape – an edited version finally appeared in 1999 under the name *True at First Light*. It is widely asserted, too, that the injuries Hemingway sustained at Butiaba sparked the gradual decline in his mental well-being that led ultimately to his suicide in 1961.

from Busingiro, so it's not really a viable option for a day trip unless you have private transport. Generally regarded as being one of Uganda's best forest-birding sites, the Royal Mile supports a wide variety of localised species, with the sought-after African dwarf, blue-breasted and chocolate-backed kingfishers all very common. A long list of other local specials includes Cassin's hawk eagle, Nahan's francolin, white-thighed hornbill, yellow-billed barbet, lemon-billed crombec, black-capped apalis, forest flycatcher, yellow-footed flycatcher and Jameson's wattle-eye. Various monkeys are also likely to be seen, along with giant forest squirrels and the bizarre chequered elephant-shrew. Equally bizarre in this remote patch of forest is the Our Lady Queen of Poland Catholic Church, which was built during World War II by Polish refugees who were settled in the area and in some cases were buried in the adjacent cemetery.

Around Busingiro The alternative to visiting the Royal Mile is to walk along the main road past Busingiro. Though not on a par with the Royal Mile, the birding here is still excellent and it is generally easier to locate birds than it is in the forest proper. Among the species to look for on the road and around the campsite are brown-crowned eremomela, Ituri batis, chestnut-capped flycatcher, Cassin's and Sabine's spinetails, and grey and yellow longbills. The chocolate-backed kingfisher, common in the area, is most easily located by call. A small pool by the side of the road about 1km back towards Masindi is a reliable place to see the shining blue kingfisher and black-necked weaver. In addition to birds, you should also see at least three types of primate on this stretch of road. There's nothing to prevent you from walking along the road alone, but it's worth taking a guide from the tourism site – they are very knowledgeable, particularly with regard to bird calls, and they all carry binoculars and a field guide. With a vehicle and spotlight, the road could be worth exploring at night – a colony of gigantic hammerhead bats roosts along the road between Busingiro to the aforementioned pool, and the nocturnal potto and tree pangolin are also resident.

MASINDI TO WANSEKO VIA LAKE ALBERT

Although most organised tours to Murchison Falls National Park favour the direct route between Masindi and Paraa, the longer alternative via Lake Albert is one of the most scenic roads in Uganda, with a number of possible diversions along the way. Foremost among these, and covered under a separate heading above, is the Busingiro Tourist Site in Budongo Forest, which can easily be visited as a day trip out of Masindi, ideally with your own wheels. Other points of interest are the small but historic port of Butiaba, and the Victoria Nile Delta at Wanseko, a good site for spotting the rare shoebill.

GETTING AROUND The 135km road between Masindi and Murchison Falls via Lake Albert is unsurfaced in its entirety and the journey takes about 4 hours. Follow the Hoima Road out of Masindi for about 3km, then turn right on to the murram road to Bulisa. About 52km out of Masindi (10km past Busingiro) you arrive at Biso, where a secondary road branches south to Hoima via Kigorobeya (for Kibiro Salt Gardens). Past Biso, the road snakes down the Butiaba Escarpment to the Rift Valley floor, offering stunning views across Lake Albert to the Blue Mountains of the DRC. At the base of the escarpment a left turn leads west to the lakeshore port of Butiaba (see box, page 343) while the main road continues north, running roughly parallel to the Lake Albert shore for 40km before arriving at Bulisa, from

where it leads north for another 6km to terminate at the lakeshore port of Wanseko. Those heading for Murchison Falls, however, must turn right at Bulisa (clearly signposted), from where it's another 20km to Bugungu Entrance Gate and another 5km to the junction with the main road from Masindi, roughly 8km south of Paraa.

If you're using public transport, a daily bus does connects Kampala to Wanseko via Masindi, Busingiro and Bulisa, a journey that should keep you occupied for the best part of a day. Irregular matatus also run between Masindi and Butiaba (*US$4*) or Bulisa/Wanseko (*US$6*).

For those who aren't heading directly into Murchison Falls National Park, a possible onward option from Wanseko is to ferry across to Panyimur and drive on to Pakwach or Arua (page 319).

BUTIABA You'd scarcely credit it today, but the port of Butiaba, set on the lakeshore 8km west of Masindi–Wanseko Road, was a commercial centre of some significance back in the colonial era. In the 1920s, the colonial government earmarked the existing administrative station – contemporaneously described by Etta Close as 'a few native huts, an Indian store, and three little European houses by the edge of the water' – for a major harbour development. A regular steamer service was established out of Butiaba, effectively extending the existing import–export route between Masindi and Mombasa further west, to the Congolese port of Mahagi and to Nimule on the Sudanese border.

Butiaba's stock rose further in 1931, when it was selected as a landing site for the first seaplane flights between Cairo and East Africa. Over the subsequent decade, it also became something of a tourist focus, after a freshly dredged channel through the Victoria Nile Estuary allowed boats from Butiaba to divert to a landing point a short distance downstream of Murchison Falls. During the production of the classic Bogart/Hepburn movie *The African Queen*, a boat called the *Murchison* was chartered by director John Huston to carry supplies and run errands between Butiaba and the nearby filming location. Butiaba's celebrity connections don't end with Bogart and Hepburn – see box, *Hemingway and Butiaba*, page 343.

In 1962, coincidentally the same year that Uganda gained independence, unusually heavy rains caused Lake Albert to rise several metres overnight, sinking all of the ships in Butiaba harbour and leaving much of the town submerged. The port was officially abandoned in 1963, never to be redeveloped. Today it is little more than an overgrown fishing village. The airstrip where Hemingway so nearly died in 1954 reputedly still flies a windsock, but it sees little aerial traffic other than ducks and herons flapping overhead. There is now little other evidence of Butiaba's former significance. Until very recently, it made an interesting detour from the Masindi–Bulisa Road to walk between rusting iron derricks and other dockyard machinery on the weed-ravaged quay to the listing wreck of the SS *Robert Coryndon* (named after Sir Robert Coryndon, Governor of Uganda 1918–22), which foundered during the floods of 1962. Exactly 50 years later, the remains of this historic passenger boat, built in 1930 and later described by Hemingway as 'magnificence on water' and by Sir Winston Churchill as 'the best library afloat', were dismantled and removed for scrap metal. If you feel like making the diversion to Butiaba, the junction lies about 10km past Biso, shortly after the Wanseko Road reaches the Rift Valley floor.

BUGUNGU WILDLIFE RESERVE This small reserve protects an area of savannah and seasonal swamp lying at the base of the Rift Valley Escarpment to the west of Murchison Falls National Park. It supports many of the same species as the neighbouring national park, with an estimated 1,200 head of oribi and 600

Ugandan kob as well as substantial populations of leopard, buffalo, warthog, hippo, reedbuck, sitatunga, waterbuck, bushbuck, dik-dik, black-and-white colobus and baboon. Roughly 240 bird species have been recorded, including Abyssinian ground hornbill, shoebill and saddle-billed stork. Though the road between Butiaba junction and Wanseko flanks the reserve boundary for around 20km as far north as Waiga Bridge, there are are no tourism facilities at present.

WANSEKO End-of-the-road Wanseko is a hot, dusty fishing village whose Wild West feel is compensated for by some impressive views across the lake to the Blue Mountains, not to mention the proximity of the Nile Estuary, and the most estimable virtue of not being Bulisa, the depressing junction village 6km to its south. The papyrus-lined estuary, only a few minutes' walk from town, is home to the odd hippo or crocodile as well as a profusion of birds, notably crowned crane and, with a bit of luck, shoebill. The only reasonable place to stay, 200m before the ferry landing, is the Wanseko Deluxe, which asks around US$13 for a no-frills en-suite double. A possible but little-used onward option from Wanseko is the free vehicle ferry to Panyimur, then continue to the West Nile towns of Pakwach or Arua (page 319).

14

Murchison Falls Conservation Area

Flanking the 100km stretch of the Victoria Nile that arcs west from Karuma Bridge towards Lake Albert, the 3,840km² Murchison Falls National Park (MFNP) is the largest protected area in Uganda, and one of the most exciting. Its centrepiece Murchison Falls is the most electrifying sight of its type in East Africa, with the fast-flowing but wide Nile being transformed into an explosive froth of thunderous white water as it funnels through a narrow cleft in the Rift Valley Escarpment. MFNP offers some superb terrestrial and boat-based game viewing, with lion, elephant, hippo, buffalo and Rothschild's giraffe being particularly common along the north bank of the Nile. MFNP is the largest component in the greater Murchison Falls Conservation Area (MFCA), which also incorporates the collectively managed 750km² Bugungu and 720km² Karuma wildlife reserves to its south. From a visitor's perspective, the most important feature of Bugungu and Karuma is the Kaniyo Pabidi Forest, which harbours an 80-strong chimpanzee community habituated for tourists, as well as a number of localised forest birds. For most birders, however, the star attraction among the 550-plus species recorded in the MFCA is the shoebill, an elusive and bizarre waterbird frequently seen in the delta where the Nile empties into Lake Albert.

GENERAL INFORMATION

HISTORICAL BACKGROUND Gazetted in 1952, Murchison Falls National Park formerly fell within the Bunyoro Game Reserve, which was proclaimed in 1910 following a sleeping-sickness epidemic that forced the local human population to be evacuated. In its early days, Murchison Falls was universally regarded as one of East Africa's most compelling national parks, thanks to its spectacular waterfall, prolific game, and a clutch of outstanding lodges built in the 1950s and 1960s. A census undertaken in 1969 confirms the park then supported some quite incredible large mammal populations, including 14,500 elephant, 26,500 buffalo, 14,000 hippo, 16,000 Jackson's hartebeest, 30,000 Ugandan kob and 11,000 warthog, as well as substantial populations of Rothschild's giraffe, black rhinoceros, and northern white rhinoceros (introduced from the West Nile in the early 1960s). Ironically, the main conservation issue associated with Murchison Falls back then was environmental destruction caused by the overpopulation of elephant, some 3,500 of which were eventually culled, along with 4,000 hippos.

Murchison Falls remained a popular tourist draw in the early days of the Amin regime, but the gates closed in September 1972 when foreign visitors were banned from Uganda. It was at around this time that Amin rechristened both the waterfall and the national park as Kabalega Falls after the former king of Bunyoro (this name still appears on some maps of Uganda, though it fell into disuse in the 1980s). Following the ban on foreigners, conservation activities within the national park

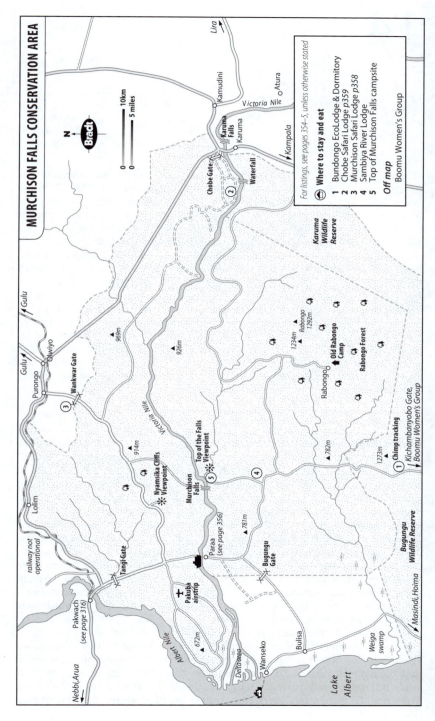

MURCHISON FALLS CONSERVATION AREA

For listings, see pages 354–5, unless otherwise stated

Where to stay and eat
1 Bundongo EcoLodge & Dormitory
2 Chobe Safari Lodge p359
3 Murchison Safari Lodge p358
4 Sambiya River Lodge
5 Top of Murchison Falls campsite

Off map
Boomu Women's Group

Lira

Kamudini

Victoria Nile

Kamwaar Gate

Karuma Falls

Karuma

Kampala

Chobe Gate

Waterfall

Karuma Wildlife Reserve

969m

926m

Rabongo 1292m

1234m

Old Rabongo Camp

Rabongo Forest

Rabongo

782m

1273m

Chimp tracking

Kichambanyobo Gate, Boomu Women's Group

Gulu

Gulu

Owiyo

Purongo

Wankwar Gate

Victoria Nile

Nyamsika Cliffs Viewpoint

914m

Top of the Falls Viewpoint

Murchison Falls

Lolim

Nebbi, Arua

Pakwach (see page 316)

railway not operational

Tangi Gate

672m

Pakuba airstrip

Paraa (see page 356)

781m

Bugungu Gate

Bugungu Wildlife Reserve

Masindi, Hoima

Wanseko

Delta area

Bulisa

Weiga swamp

Lake Albert

N

Bradt

0   10km
0   5 miles

348

also dwindled, and the wildlife became easy prey for commercial and subsistence poachers. An aerial survey undertaken in 1980, the year after Amin was ousted, indicated that the number of elephants and hippos had been reduced to around 10% of their 1969 levels, while populations of buffalo and most other large mammals had halved. The slaughter continued unabated during the turbulent early to mid 1980s, as a succession of military factions occupied the park and treated it as a moving larder. By 1990, the future of MFNP looked bleak in the extreme: rhinos and African hunting dogs had been hunted to local extinction, dwindling giraffe and lion populations seemed to be headed the same way, while elephant numbers stood at around 250, buffalo at 1,000, and the total head of Jackson's hartebeest and Ugandan kob had plummeted to around 3,000 and 6,000 respectively. Furthermore, declining tourist arrivals coupled with ongoing guerrilla activity had rendered all three of the park's lodges inoperative.

The downward trend was reversed in the early 1990s, and although wildlife populations have yet to re-approach their pre-Amin highs, the last 25 years have witnessed a steady and significant growth in the number of most of the park's large mammal species. The early 1990s also saw a revival of low-key tourism following the opening of a very basic rest camp (where Red Chilli now stands) on the south bank, and the subsequent construction of the more upmarket Nile Safari Lodge and reopening of Paraa Safari Lodge. Despite this, MFNP's proximity to Acholi enabled the Lord's Resistance Army (LRA) to launch sporadic attacks in the vicinity of Paraa and elsewhere north of the Nile until as recently as 2005, when it ceased operations within Uganda. Following the withdrawal of the LRA, Murchison Falls has been regarded to be as safe as anywhere in the country, and several new lodges have opened in the vicinity of Pakwach, Pakuba and Karuma Bridge – areas that were previously practically off-limits to tourists. Currently, the main threats to the park's future are ecological: an increase in poaching and snare setting on the banks of the Albert Nile outside the park, and the potential long-term consequences of ongoing oil exploration within Murchison's prime tourism and wildlife area (see box, pages 336–7).

GEOGRAPHY AND VEGETATION Although it spans altitudes of 619m to 1,292m, MFNP is mostly quite low-lying by Ugandan standards, and it often experiences stiflingly hot weather, with average daily highs peaking at 32–33°C through December to March. The average annual rainfall of 1,085mm, though significantly lower than in the forests of the southwest, compares favourably with most other East African savannah ecosystems. A long, steady rainy season runs from March to November, when average rainfall hovers at around 100mm per month, most of it falling in the form of short drenching storms. December to February is somewhat drier.

The park's most important geographical feature is the Victoria Nile, which bisects it for around 100km as it flows in a northwesterly then southwesterly direction between lakes Kyoga and Albert. The Nile drops 420m in altitude along this relatively short stretch, which incorporates many rapids and two major cataracts: Karuma Falls immediately east of the Kampala–Gulu Road where it skirts MFNP's eastern gate; and the more explosive Murchison Falls about 30km upriver of Lake Albert. The Nile divides MFNP into two parts of comparable area. North of the river, the vegetation broadly consists of tall, green grassland interspersed with isolated stands of borassus palms, acacia trees and riverine woodland. South of it, denser woodland gives way to closed canopy forest around Rabongo Hill (the park's highest peak) in the southwest, and Kaniyo Pabidi on the Masindi Road. In total, 755 plant species have been identified in the park.

14

WILDLIFE According to fresh survey results published in 2015, MFCA supports at least 144 mammal, 556 bird, 51 reptile and 51 amphibian species. As noted elsewhere, large mammal populations have yet to climb back to their pre-Amin highs, but they are impressive all the same. MFCA is one of the few areas where African elephants are increasing in number, based on aerial survey figures of 900 in 2010 and 1,330 in 2013. It also supports the world's largest population of the endangered Rothschild's giraffe, estimated at almost 1,000 based on aerial surveys undertaken in 2012. Historically, the giraffes exclusively inhabit the sector north of the Nile, but in January 2016 some 20 individuals were translocated to the southern sector, with the dual goal of creating a second viable free-ranging giraffe population in MFCA, and boosting tourism in the south. The buffalo population has increased from fewer than 4,000 in 1999 to more than 10,000 today, while Ugandan kob numbers have leaped from around 7,500 to more than 35,000 over the same period. The lion population is credibly estimated at a healthy 150–200 individuals split across 15–20 prides, and other large predators such as leopard and spotted hyena are present in significant numbers. Also common in varying degrees are Jackson's hartebeest, oribi, bushbuck, Defassa waterbuck, Bohor reedbuck and warthog. In the savannah and woodland areas, vervet monkey, Anubis baboon and the localised patas monkey are also present. The Rabongo and Kaniyo Pabidi forests harbour chimpanzees, black-and-white colobus and other forest primates.

The bird checklist is headed in desirability by the shoebill, which is most common along the stretch of river between Nile Safari Lodge and Lake Albert Delta. Many other water-associated birds are prolific along the river, while raptors make a strong showing on the checklist with 53 species recorded. MFNP is perhaps the best place in East Africa for sightings of the localised white-crested turaco, red-headed lovebird and red-winged grey warbler, all of which are associated with the riparian woodland in the vicinity of the south bank camps running west from Baker's Lodge to Nile Safari Lodge. Key birds of the northern plains include Abyssinian ground hornbill, Denham's bustard, black-headed lapwing and black-billed barbet, while Kaniyo Pabidi supports a wealth of localised forest birds including chocolate-backed kingfisher, green-breasted pitta and East Africa's only known population of the localised Puvel's illadopsis.

ORIENTATION The focal point of tourist activities is Paraa, which flanks the Nile about 15km downstream of Murchison Falls. The park headquarters lie on the south bank of the Nile at Paraa, as does the park reception/ticket office, the main launch site for boat trips operated by UWA and Wild Frontiers (page 62), and Red Chilli Rest Camp (page 357). Paraa Safari Lodge lies on the north bank at Paraa, as does the launch site for its boat trips, while the stretch of south bank a few kilometres further downriver, immediately outside the park's Mubako Gate, is lined with half a dozen tourist accommodations, starting with Bakers Lodge in the east and terminating with Nile Safari Lodge in the west. There is no bridge at Paraa, only a ferry (see box, page 353), but since this is the only place downstream of Karuma Bridge where vehicles can cross the Victoria Nile, almost all roads into the park converge there. Other important sites within or bordering MFCA are Kaniyo Pabidi Forest (alongside the road from Masindi about two hours' drive south of Paraa), the Top of the Falls Viewpoint (45 minutes' drive east of Paraa), the Delta Game-Viewing Circuit (on the north bank west of Paraa) and the small town of Pakwach (overlooking the Albert Nile a few kilometres outside the park's main northern entrance gate). Note that whereas all the above-mentioned sites are to some extent visitable from each other, this is not really true of Chobe Safari Lodge, which lies out on a limb in the

far east of the park close to Karuma Bridge. Though Chobe is a popular upmarket weekend retreat from Kampala, and a useful potential overnight staging point *en route* between the capital and Gulu/Kidepo, it cannot really be classed as a safari destination in its own right or as a base for exploring the rest of MFNP.

FEES Entrance to Murchison Falls National Park costs US$30/40 FR/FNR per 24 hours. The standard vehicle entrance fees are also charged (see box, page 32), but only once per entry. Note that although Kaniyo Pabidi Forest, which is split between Bugungu and Karuma wildlife reserves, technically falls outside MFNP, it does fall within the MFCA and full park fees are levied, even if you never actually cross into the national park. Since the introduction of the new card system (www.ugandawildlife.org/wildlife-card), the idea is that entrance fees for MFNP must be paid either at the UWA reservations office in Kampala, or else at the Kichambanyobo Gate. However, activity and ferry fees can be paid for at the ticket office on the south bank at Paraa, and it seems that most other more remote entrance gates also accept cash payments for entrance fees.

FURTHER READING The informative new *Murchison Falls National Park Information Guide*, written by Mark Jordhal and published by UWA in 2014, is well worth a look. Sheet 8 in the 'Uganda Maps' series contains maps of the national park and Buligi game tracks plus a wildlife checklist and general information.

GETTING THERE AND AWAY

For many years, the LRA presence in Acholi enforced a southern approach to MFNP via Masindi. Most safaris still do arrive from the south, but since the LRA withdrew in 2005, three new routes to the park have opened to the north of the Nile, all of them accessible from Kampala via Karuma Bridge on the Gulu Road. Note that all direct overland routes between Kampala and Murchison Falls follow the Gulu Road at least as far as Kafu Bridge (the junction for Masindi) and can thus be broken up with a day or overnight visit to Ziwa Rhino Sanctuary (pages 181–2), or a pit stop at the nearby Kabalega Diner.

TOURS Organised fly-in or overland tours to Murchison Falls can be organised through any operator in Kampala (pages 130–2). For budget travellers, a popular option is the three-day, two-night trips offered by Kampala-based **Red Chilli Hideaway** using its Red Chilli Rest Camp at Paraa; these start at US$380 per person inclusive of all transport, entrance fees and meals, and incorporate a game drive, a launch trip on the Nile, and a visit to the Top of the Falls viewpoint.

BY AIR Two airstrips are found close to Paraa: Bugungu on the south side of the river and Pakuba on the north. Another airstrip lies adjacent to Chobe Lodge in the northeast of the park. **Fly Uganda** (*www.flyuganda.com*) and **Aerolink** (*www. aerolinkuganda.com*) run scheduled flights from Entebbe or Kajjansi to Murchison. As well as dodging the dull drive from Kampala, flights also provides the thrilling prospect of viewing Murchison Falls from the air. Flights from Entebbe or Kajjansi cost around US$300 one-way and take about 90 minutes.

SELF-DRIVE
Southern approaches The main southern gateway to MFNP, Masindi (see above) lies 215km/3 hours northwest of Kampala on a surfaced road, or 260km/

14

7 hours northeast of Fort Portal via Hoima along a road that remains unsurfaced north of Kyenjojo. The roads through Masindi remain the best option for those travelling between Fort Portal (or elsewhere in southwest Uganda) and anywhere in MFNP. Coming from Kampala, the route through Masindi is also the most direct option to Paraa and all lodges south of the Nile. It is best to fill up with fuel at Masindi, though petrol and diesel are usually available at an inflated price from a filling station at Paraa Safari Lodge. Two routes run from Masindi to Paraa: one via Kichambanyobo Gate and the other via Mubako Gate. Both are unsurfaced and likely to require extra care after rain.

Kichambanyobo Gate (⊕ *1.85323, 31.70965*) The direct 85km route from Masindi to Paraa, passing through Kichambanyobo Gate after 22km, takes up to 3 hours. In practical terms, it is the best choice for those heading to Budongo EcoLodge (7km past Kichambanyobo), Sambiya Lodge (40km past Kichambanyobo), Red Chilli River Camp or Paraa Safari Lodge.

Mubako Gate (⊕ *2.25855, 31.53536*) The 135km route between Masindi and Paraa via Lake Albert (covered in detail on pages 344–5) offers spectacular views as you descend from Budongo Forest into the Rift Valley, but it's a long 5-hour drive. Should you be booked into any of the accommodations on the south bank west of Paraa, these all lie outside Mubako Gate, which means that unless you opt to explore MFNP on the same day, you won't need to pay entrance fees on your day of arrival/departure.

Northern and eastern approaches
Murchison Falls can be approached from three gates north of the Nile. These are Chobe Gate on the Kampala–Gulu Road, Wankwar Gate 10km south of Purongo, and Tangi Gate 3km from Pakwach.

Chobe Gate (⊕ *2.25505, 32.24194*) The most easterly entrance to MFNP, Chobe Gate, 2km north of Karuma Bridge on the surfaced Gulu Road, is also the quickest gate to reach from Kampala, a 260km drive that takes around 3 hours. It is aimed mainly at people overnighting at Chobe Safari Lodge, which lies 18km further into the park along a relatively well-maintained dirt road. From Chobe Safari Lodge it is possible to continue west all the way to Paraa following the 95km Chobe Track. Be warned, however, that the first 40km of the Chobe Track follows a poor road through dense tsetse-infested woodland that tends to be poor for game viewing.

Wankwar Gate (⊕ *2.47214, 31.81893*) Situated 10km south of Purongo, Wankwar Gate is particularly well suited to those travelling between Paraa and Gulu or Kidepo Valley National Park following the recent surfacing of the direct 65km Gulu–Olwiyo Road, which connects to the Karuma-Pakwach Road 4km east of Purongo. It is also a useful access point coming from Kampala: just following the Gulu Road for 200m past Chobe Gate, then turn left on to the new sealed Arua Road and follow it for 58km to Purongo. Once there, Wankwar Gate is only 45km northeast of Paraa along a reasonably well-maintained road that usually offers excellent game viewing, even though the first few kilometres pass through a wooded area that sporadically hosts large numbers of tsetse flies. Allow at least 5 hours to the gate driving directly from Kampala, and another hour to reach Paraa.

Tangi Gate (⊕ *2.44579, 31.51188*) This once little-used gate is situated only 3km from Pakwach, a small town set on the West Bank of the Albert Nile immediately

after it exits MFNP. Tangi Gate has become rather busy in recent years thanks to the opening of several nearby mid-range and upmarket lodges on the East Bank of the Albert Nile opposite Pakwach. Although the lodges lie outside the park, they are well situated for exploring it, since Tangi Gate is only an hour's drive from Paraa and the Buligi game-viewing circuit. Coming from Kampala or Gulu, follow directions for Wankwar Gate as far as Purongo, where instead of branching south on to a dirt road, you need to continue for another 50km west along the Arua Road towards Pakwach. Tangi Gate lies almost 1km south of the main road along a turn-off signposted 700m before the Pakwach Bridge crosses the Albert Nile. Allow 6 hours to the gate driving directly from Kampala.

PUBLIC TRANSPORT No public transport actually runs into MFNP, and all things considered, wheelless travellers who can afford it are probably best off joining a budget tour with Red Chilli. If you prefer to go it alone, the closest public transport access point is technically Chobe Gate, on the west side of the Kampala–Gulu Road 2km north of Karuma Bridge, but while any passing bus or matatu could drop you here, it would leave you somewhat stranded in terms of getting into the park. Slightly more promising springboards are Masindi, Wanseko and Pakwach.

From Masindi via Kichambanyobo Gate No public transport runs along the 85km road from Masindi to Paraa via Kichambanyobo Gate. It is possible, however, to arrange a special hire (expect to pay upwards of US$50 one-way) or to rent a

---

PARAA FERRY

The only place downstream of Karuma Bridge where cars can cross the Victoria Nile is Paraa (⊕ *2.28283, 31.56563*), where a motor ferry connects the south bank, close to the park headquarters, to the north bank, below Paraa Safari Lodge. All visitors coming from the south by road and staying at Paraa Safari Lodge will need to take the ferry across, while those sleeping on the south bank will need to cross in both directions every time they go on a game drive north of the river.

The 500m crossing takes less than 5 minutes. Official departure times in both directions are 07.00, 09.00, 11.00, 12.00, 14.00, 18.00 and 19.00, with the last of these crossings being reserved for visitors overnighting in the park. In practice, the ferry often leaves a few minutes late or early, so try to be waiting at the jetty 10 minutes ahead of schedule. If you plan on crossing northward at 07.00, be aware that this first trip often attracts long queues of safari vehicles heading out from the various south bank lodges to do a morning game drive north of the river, so aim to be at the jetty at least 30 minutes early to be sure of obtaining a berth. Having said that, don't race to get a particular ferry, as it is easy to lose control of your vehicle on the park's loose and gravelly road surfaces.

Daily tickets, valid for as many scheduled crossings as are made on the day of purchase, are sold at the reception office a few hundred metres before the jetty. The ticket cost depends on the size of the vehicle: US$1.50 for motorcycles; US$7 for light vehicles (under 2 tonnes); US$13 for medium vehicles (2–5 tonnes); and upwards of US$17 for heavier vehicles. Additional passengers and pedestrians pay US$1.50 per person. Unscheduled crossings can be arranged, but at a cost of around US$33 one-way.

vehicle from Yebo Tours from around US$80 per day. You could even think about trying to hitch from the junction opposite the Shell garage in Masindi, though do make sure that the vehicle will be going as far as Paraa to drop you at Red Chilli Rest Camp. A boda from Masindi to the chimp-tracking site at Kaniyo Pabidi will cost around US$7 one-way, but it is best to go with a UWA-sanctioned driver, which can be arranged by calling Budongo EcoLodge (see below). We've heard of people using bodas to cover the 85km from Masindi to Paraa, but this cannot be recommended on account of the risk of encountering buffalo and other potentially stroppy animals.

From Wanseko via Mubako Gate   A fair number of matatus run daily from Masindi to Wanseko (page 346), which lies about 30km west of Paraa via Mubako Gate. From Wanseko, you could try to hitch through to Paraa, or failing that organise a boda to Red Chilli, a far safer option than biking through Kichambanyobo Gate, since the area between Wanseko and the gate is well populated, while the final 5km or so to Red Chilli passes through the park headquarters and other areas where wildlife is relatively used to humans.

From Pakwach via Tangi Gate   The only substantial town fronting the Nile along its course from Jinja to the South Sudan border, Pakwach (see pages 314–18) lies only 3km from the Tangi Gate and an hour's drive from Paraa. The surrounding area can offer some rewarding game viewing even if you don't actually enter MFNP. For groups, Global Village Guesthouse (see page 317) rents out an open-sided game-viewing vehicle that seats up to nine. The cost is US$150 half-day (enough time to do a game drive on the Buligi circuit or the launch trip from Paraa) or US$185 full-day (enough time to do both) inclusive of driver/guide and fuel, but exclusive of park fees and fuel, which seems like great value for a small group.

WHERE TO STAY AND EAT

KANIYO PABIDI AND THE MASINDI ROAD   *Map, page 348*

The accommodation listed below all lie alongside the unsurfaced 85km main road between Masindi and Paraa. The lodges are all well situated for activities in Kaniyo Pabidi Forest, and make a viable base for the launch trip from Paraa, but are a bit too remote to be a realistic base for early-morning game drives north of the river.

Upmarket

 Sambiya River Lodge (26 cottages & 12 bandas) ✪ 2.1816, 31.69871; ✆ 041 4233596; e reservations@sambiyariverlodge.com; www. sambiyariverlodge.com. This long-serving & reasonably priced set-up sprawls across large wooded grounds off the main road between Masindi & Paraa, about 35km north of Kaniyo Pabidi. It suffers slightly from the lack of Nile frontage, but is only 20mins' drive from the Top of the Falls Viewpoint, a great place to be at sunset. It is also conveniently located for those who want to use one base to track chimps at Kaniyo Pabidi & do a launch trip out of Paraa. The stone-&-thatch en-suite bandas are colourfully decorated & come

with fan, net & screen door, & there are also simple budget bandas using shared facilities. A small swimming pool is provided. *US$162/240 FB sgl/dbl, with a small discount offered to residents. Budget bandas US$45/80 B&B sgl/dbl.* **$$$–$$$$**

Moderate/budget

Budongo EcoLodge & Dormitory (6 cottages & 1 dorm) ✪ 1.91791, 31.71934; ✆ 041 4267153; m 0701 426368; e info@ ugandalodges.com, www.ugandalodges.com. Aimed mainly at chimp-trackers & birders, this pleasant & unpretentious lodge 8km north of Kichambanyobo Gate oversees all tourist activities in the surrounding Kaniyo Pabidi Forest. The log

cabins are individually carved into the forest & come with fitted nets, private balcony, en-suite shower & long drop toilet, but the tin roofs absorb a lot of sunlight so they can be stinking hot during the day. Plenty of monkeys can be seen around the camp, while tree hyrax are often heard at night. The main building doubles as an information centre with informative wall-mounted exhibits & restaurant with terrace seating, while facilities include 24-hour solar electricity & Wi-Fi. There's also a 20-bed dorm, which you'll have to yourself as often as not. *US$81/134 sgl/dbl, US$26 dorm bed, all rates B&B, add US$32pp FB.* **$$$**

Shoestring

✳ 🏠 **Boomu Women's Group** (10 rooms) ✛ 1.8499, 31.70888; m 0772 448950; e boomuwomensgroup@yahoo.com; www.boomuwomensgroup.org. Traditional accommodation & experiences don't come any more authentic than at this small community

tourism project located immediately outside Kichambanyobo Gate. A traditional mango-shaded homestead brightened by flowers & shrubs, it provides accommodation in small, simple & spotless thatched bandas & an interesting variety of activities & demonstrations offering insights into rural Ugandan life. Among other things, it's a reassuring backup for backpackers trying to hitch to Paraa or Kaniyo Pabidi: if transport isn't forthcoming you can at least find a bed & learn how to weave a basket. *US$18.50pp B&B.* **$$**

Camping

⛺ **Top of Murchison Falls** ✛ 2.27618, 31.68962. Visitors with a private 4x4 vehicle can pitch a tent at this secluded & little-used campsite set a couple of hundred metres upstream from the waterfall. It is a beautiful location above a natural pool that's reputedly safe for swimming & there's great birding – look out for the localised bat hawk towards dusk. *US$5pp.* **$**

PARAA AND THE VICTORIA NILE *Map, page 356*

Of the accommodation listed below, Paraa Safari Lodge stands on the north bank overlooking Paraa Ferry, while Red Chilli is about 700m inland of the south bank jetty. The remainder all lie just outside the park close to the south bank of the Victoria Nile, clustered within 2km of Mubako Gate about 6km drive from Paraa. These lodges are all well placed for boat trips and within a feasible driving distance of the chimp-tracking site at Kaniyo Pabidi. They are also convenient for morning game drives north of the river, though Paraa Safari Lodge has the edge in this respect, because you don't need to wait for the ferry to make its first crossing at 07.00.

Exclusive/luxury

✳ 🏠 **Bakers Lodge** (8 rooms) ✛ 2.25923, 31.53129; ☎ 041 4321479; m 0772 721155; e reservations@ugandaexclusivecamps.com; www.ugandaexclusivecamps.com. Opened in 2015, the newest & most luxurious lodge in Murchison Falls lies immediately outside the national park boundary on a stretch of riverbank alive with hippos & birdlife. The spacious canvas-&-thatch rooms are the ultimate in bush chic, offering a king-sized bed with walk-in net, private balcony with river view & massive bathrooms with cobblestone showers & quirky touches like towel racks made with Ankole cattle horns. Excellent 3-course meals are served on a spacious communal wooden deck or on candlelit tables down by the river, & there's a swimming pool tucked away at the back behind a papyrus fence. It's managed by Wild Frontiers, which also operates its own

boat trips to the base of Murchison Falls & Lake Albert Delta (page 62). *US$360/560 FB sgl/dbl non-resident, US$200/350 East African resident.* **$$$$$**

Upmarket

🏠 **Paraa Safari Lodge** (54 rooms) ✛ 2.29013, 31.57286; ☎ 041 4259390/4/5; m 0772 788880; e reservations2@marasa.net; www.paraalodge.com. Overlooking the north bank of the Nile at Paraa, this double-storey monolith was reconstructed in 1997 using the shell of an original lodge built in 1959 but gutted during the civil war. A superior example of the 'hotel in the bush' architectural genre, its interiors are attractively decorated in colonial style, & a feel of solidity makes it a reassuring choice for nervous first time visitors to Africa, while children will enjoy the large swimming pool with its view over the Nile

NOTE
Due to oil exploration in this area, some existing tracks may be closed while new tracks may be opened

N

Bradt

(SKETCH MAP)
Not to scale

Pakwach,
Tangi Gate

Wankwar
Gate

Albert Nile

ALBERT NILE TRACK

QUEEN'S TRACK

VICTORIA NILE TRACK

LION

Pakuba
airstrip

5

5

1.8

10

16

13

20

BULIGI TRACK

7

Delta
Point

Kob
breeding
ground

Pool

Marsh
(elephant &
shoebill)

Delta

Lake
Albert

7

9

Victoria Nile

Wild Frontiers
Nile River Safaris

Booking
office

Mubaku
(UWA staff village)

Mubako Gate

Park
boundary

Masindi

2

1

4

3

5

9

10

11

8

7

6

For listings, see pages 355–9

Where to stay and eat

1	Bakers Lodge	**5**	Nile Safari Lodge	**9**	Shoebill Campsite
2	Delta Campsite	**6**	Pakuba Safari Lodge	**10**	Water View Rest Camp
3	Kabalega River Lodge	**7**	Paraa Safari Lodge	**11**	Yebo Safari Camp
4	Murchison River Lodge	**8**	Red Chilli Rest Camp		

to the low hills beyond. The large en-suite rooms have walk-in nets, AC, & private river-facing balcony (views are best from the upper floor). Some rooms are fitted for those with limited mobility, & there's also a trio of luxury standing tents, & a cottage that was occupied by the Queen Mother during a 1959 visit. Logistically, Paraa Lodge stands out as the most convenient accommodation to combine game drives in the north with boat trips on the river. *From US$196/301 sgl/dbl room, US$251/357 sgl/dbl tent, US$794 dbl cottage. All rates B&B. Add US$24pp for FB.* **$$$$$**

🏠 **Nile Safari Lodge** (10 rooms) ⊕ 2.25122, 31.52085; ☎041 4258273; e reservations@ geolodgesafrica.com; www.geolodgesafrica.com. The longest-serving of the south bank lodges has a wonderful location on a well-wooded rise,

2km west of the park boundary. Standing tents have recently been replaced by timber cottages with walk-in tents, en-suite hot shower & private balcony with river view. Hippos & crocodiles can be seen on the river, the facing northern bank & mid-river island is regularly visited by waterbuck, elephant & shoebill, & a 1km guided walk through the adjacent riparian forest often throws up the localised white-crested turaco, red-headed lovebird & red-winged grey warbler. A discreetly located swimming pool overlooks the river. A boat transfer can run you upriver to connect to the Paraa launches. *US$210/330 sgl/dbl FB.* **$$$$$**

🏠 **Kabalega River Lodge** (6 rooms) ⊕ 2.25431, 31.52486; m 0783 864900; e info@ kabalegalodge.com; www.kabalegalodge.com. Opened in 2014 but already looking in need

of some upkeep, this pleasant riverside lodge offers accommodation in earthy rooms that use a combination of wood, canvas, traditional mud plaster & thatch (rooms 1 & 2 have the best river view), & come with queen-sized bed, walk-in net & balcony with seating. Meals are served on a wooden deck right above the river, & there's 24/7 solar power. A touch overpriced. *US$150/250 B&B sgl/dbl or US$199/299 FB.* **$$$$$**

Moderate
☀ 🏠 **Murchison River Lodge** (20 units)
⊕ 2.24981, 31.52496; **m** 0714 000085/0782 007552; **e** bookings@murchisonriverlodge.com; www.murchisonriverlodge.com; see ad, 4th colour section. Offering a range of accommodation spanning the moderate & upmarket categories, this attractive riverside bush lodge 1.5km outside Mubako Gate is set in large wooded grounds & centred on a cool thatched restaurant/bar that's positioned to enjoy the view of the Nile & whatever might be lurking on the facing island. Spacious thatched family cottages have a ground floor dbl bed & a mezzanine dbl above. The en-suite safari tents are old-fashioned in the best possible way (tents 5, 6 or 7 have the advantage of river frontage but use chemical toilets), while simpler furnished tents at the rear use shared facilities in a palatial bathroom block. Facilities include Wi-Fi & a swimming pool. *US$175/280/380/480 cottage for 1/2/3/4 person, US$130/200 sgl/twin safari tents, US$85/140 tent using shared facilities. All rates FB.* **$$$$**

Budget
☀ 🏠 **Red Chilli Rest Camp** ⊕ 2.27702, 31.56434; ☏ 031 2202903; **m** 0772 509150; **e** reservations@redchillihideaway.com; www. redchillihideaway.com. This scion of Kampala's Red Chilli Hideaway has provided pocket-friendly bed & board in the heart of the park since it first opened in 2002. Chilled drinks & meals are served in the welcome shade of a thatch restaurant, while

accommodation is provided by a variety of bandas & tents boasting electricity, fans & mosquito nets. River views are rather distant, but it's only 10mins' walk from the launch & ferry jetties. The camp itself is frequented by warthog, bushbuck & a wide variety of birds. It's frequently booked solid so try to reserve accommodation well in advance. *US$55/90 en-suite twin/family banda (sleeping 5), US$38 twin banda with shared facilities, US$33 twin safari tents with shared facilities, US$7pp camping. All rates bed only.* **$$**

Shoestring
☀ 🏠 **Yebo Safari Camp** (7 rooms)
⊕ 2.24798, 31.52133; ☏ 046 5420029; **m** 0772 637493; **e** yebotours2002@yahoo.com. Run by Masindi-based Yebo Tours, this rustic lodge is set 500m back from the river 2km west of Mubako Gate, a location that minimises expenditure on park fees. The choice is between a simple but clean traditional en-suite mud-&-thatch bandas, or a bed in a 6-berth dorm. A dining shelter provides meals & much needed shade. Book in advance so they can turn on the fridge to cool the drinks. *US$20pp bed only, US$10 camping. Meals from US$5 per plate.* **$$**
🏠 **Water View Rest Camp** (3 rooms)
m 0777 605510/0757 605510. This no-frills option is located 200m from the river & 1km outside Mubako Gate, close to Kabalega River Lodge. The utilitarian rooms have fitted beds & use outside showers. *US$25pp B&B.* **$$**

Camping
☀ ⛺ **Shoebill Campsite** ⊕ 2.25091, 31.51708. Under the same management as Nile Safari Lodge 400m to the east, this fabulous forest-fringed campsite stands on a plateau overlooking the Nile. The camping fee allows access to the lodge's swimming pool & restaurant, where meals cost around US$10–15. Self-catering is permitted. *US$10pp.* **$$**

THE ALBERT NILE AND NORTHWEST *Map, page 356, unless otherwise stated*
Of the places listed below, only Pakuba Safari Lodge, set on the East Bank of the Albert Nile between the Buligi Circuit and Tangi Gate, actually lies within MFNP, though Murchison Safari Lodge, just outside Wankwar Gate, certainly feels like it does. The other lodges are all clustered on the east side of the Albert Nile opposite Pakwach, between 5km and 10km north of Tangi Gate. Any of the lodges listed on the following pages would make a good base for a day trip combining a game drive on the Buligi Circuit with a boat trip from Paraa. For budget-conscious travellers,

the lodges outside Tangi Gate are all very reasonably priced, and their location would allow you to get a good look at the park paying only one day's entrance fee. If they're too pricey, then the selection of inexpensive town lodges listed under Pakwach (page 317) are equally well positioned for day trips into MFNP.

Upmarket

⌂ Pakuba Safari Lodge (30 rooms) ✪ 2.38969, 31.48535; ☎ 041 4253597; e info@ pakubasafarilodge.com; www.pakubasafarilodge. com. Set in magnificent isolation on the East Bank of the Albert Nile 20km downstream of where it exits Lake Albert, the current incarnation of Pakuba Lodge opened in 2013 alongside the ruins of a long-abandoned 1960s government hotel that once served as the personal retreat of President Idi Amin. The location, alongside a scenic stretch of river fringed by park-like woodland teeming with kob & giraffe, is perfect, especially when you consider it's the closest lodge to the Buligi Circuit & only 45mins' drive from the launch site at Paraa. The spacious & modern but sparsely furnished en-suite rooms, with dbl or twin bed, fitted net & private balcony, are also fine at the price. Unfortunately, it's all let down by the unimaginative architecture, institutional feel & bland grassy lawns, which conspire to make it look less like the safari lodge it aspires to be than the staff quarters it actually once was when the original lodge was still a going concern. Still, a good choice for those who want to be in the thick of the wildlife action. Good value. *US$177/236 FB sgl/ dbl.* **$$$$**

Moderate

✳ ⌂ Fort Murchison [map, page 316] (12 rooms, 12 standing tents) ✪ 2.4891, 31.53613; ☎ 031 2294894; m 0700 283135; e booking@ naturelodges.biz; www.naturelodges.biz. Situated on a rise overlooking the Nile about 10km north of Tangi Gate, this architecturally innovative lodge place is inspired by the chain of riverside forts established by imperialists & traders along the Nile corridor, & looking out from the 1st-floor rooftop lounge, it doesn't take much imagination to picture General Gordon's exploratory flotillas of canoes & steamships coming into sight. A bold break from the usual safari style, the imposing storeyed gatehouse is a good take on a period etching of Dufile Fort, & it serves excellent meals in generous quantities. The only criticism that might be levelled at the brightly decorated en- suite rooms with fitted net & private river-facing

balcony is that they don't have a fan & can get a little muggy. The simple standing tents with twin bed, net & thatched roof are hard to fault at the price. *US$125/150 sgl/dbl room, US$35/60 sgl/dbl tent, US$15 camping. All rates B&B, add US$15 pp dinner & US$10pp lunch.* **$$$–$$$$**

⌂ Bwana Tembo Safari Camp [map, page 316] (10 units) ✪ 2.4799, 31.54309; m 0791 217028/0772 957850; e davide_francescotours@ yahoo.com; www.bwanatembosafaricamp.com. Owned & managed by a hands-on Italian family, this relaxed hilltop camp 7km north of Tangi Gate is named after the elephants that regularly pass through at night, & it also offers fabulous views for the papyrus-lined river 1km to its west. The circular en-suite cottages with net, fan & hot water are clean & comfortable, while en- suite standing tents offer a more canvas-soaked safari ambience. Set menus have a strong Italian flavour. *US$100/180/225 sgl/dbl/trpl cottages, US$90/155/190 sgl/dbl/trpl safari tents. All rates B&B. Lunch & dinner an extra US$10–15pp.* **$$$$**

Budget and camping

✳ ⌂ Heritage Safari Lodge [map, page 316] (11 rooms) ✪ 2.47969, 31.53773; m 0752 890009/0793 890009; e info@heritagesafarilodge. com; www.heritagesafarilodge.com. Perched right above the Albert Nile 6km from the Tangi Gate, this exceptionally well-priced lodge offers accommodation in spacious & airy bandas whose mud-&-thatch architecture is inspired by the traditional Jonam huts that are conspicuous in & around Pakwach. Although it lies outside the park, the lodge is regularly frequented by elephants & hippos, while early morning or late afternoon boat trips upriver (US$120 up to 6 people, US$20 per additional passenger) come with a fair chance of spotting both these large mammals as well as shoebill. There are hot springs in the property. *US$60/80 en-suite sgl/dbl. US$20pp using common shower. US$10pp camping. All rates B&B. 3-course lunch or dinners cost US$10 each.* **$$$**

⌂ Murchison Safari Lodge [map, page 348] (6 units) ☎ 041 274767; m 0772 430587; e backpackers@infocom.co.ug; www.backpackers.

co.ug/murchisontour.html. Allied to the Kampala Backpackers' Hostel, this basic but rather wonderfully isolated facility stands just outside Wankwar Gate, close to the park's greatest concentrations of herbivores & 10km from Purongo on the 110km tarmac highway between Karuma & Pakwach. *US$32 dbl bandas & US$16pp dorm tents B&B with shared facilities. US$27 dbl banda using common shower. US$14pp dorm.* **$$**

KARUMA FALLS   *Map, page 348*
Exclusive/luxury
🏠 **Chobe Safari Lodge**   (63 rooms)
⊕ 2.24243, 32.13573; ✆ 041 4259390/4/5; m 0772 788880; e reservations2@marasa.net; www.chobelodgeuganda.com. Situated in the far east of the park 18km from Chobe Gate & Karuma Bridge, Chobe Safari Lodge opened in 2010 on the site of an old 3-storey lodge built in the 1960s & trashed 2 decades later. It has a magnificent setting on a jungle-lined 500m-wide stretch of the Nile that rushes by audibly between dozens of islands & minor rapids. The multi-million dollar restoration of the lodge was undertaken by the same company that own Paraa & Mweya Safari Lodge, & the result surpasses both those lodges when it comes to the stylish decor, well-managed spa & restaurant, sumptuous accommodation (in

🏕 **Delta Campsite**   ⊕ 2.27413, 31.37866. Not for the faint of heart, this amenity-free campsite, set on the tip of the peninsula flanked by the Victoria Nile to the south & Albert Nile to the north, lies in prime game-viewing territory & plenty of noisy nocturnal wildlife activity is guaranteed. You need your own vehicle & camping gear. An armed ranger for protection must be arranged at Paraa. *US$5pp.* **$**

rooms or luxury standing tents) & quartet of tiered swimming pools that separate the dining veranda & river. Plenty of wildlife frequents the well-wooded grounds, notably giraffe, buffalo, hippo, warthog & black-&-white colobus, & the birdlife is legion. Unfortunately, however, the location is otherwise unpromising for wildlife viewing: this stretch of the Nile is too rough for boat trips, the surrounding road network is limited & passes through thick woodland where tsetse flies are rife, while Paraa & the Buligi Circuit are about 4 hours distant. Still, Chobe is a great place to break up the trip between Kampala & Kidepo, & it is also popular as an upmarket venue for weekend breaks & conferences. *From US$188/330 sgl/dbl room, US$234/358 sgl/dbl tent, US$600/811 dbl cottage. All rates B&B. Add US$24pp for FB.* **$$$$**

WHAT TO SEE AND DO

Murchison Falls Conservation Area offers a diverse selection of activities to visitors. Most popular, and best undertaken in the afternoon with the sun in the west, is the atmospheric and all-but-obligatory return boat trip that follows the Nile from Paraa to the base of Murchison Falls. This is closely followed in the must-do stakes by a morning game drive on the Buligi Circuit, a network of game-viewing tracks traversing the 10km-wide peninsula that separates the Victoria and Albert Niles as they course in and out of Lake Albert. For those with more time, other highlights include chimpanzee tracking or forest birding at Kaniyo Pabidi, the spectacular Top of the Falls Viewpoint on the south side of the river, the boat trip downriver from Paraa to the bird-rich Lake Albert Delta, and the oft-neglected game-viewing road running northeast of Paraa towards Wankwar Gate.

Those with their own vehicle are permitted to undertake game drives without an armed ranger, though safari novices might feel it is worth the investment of US$20 to have some assistance navigating the often poorly marked game-viewing tracks, and to help locate well-camouflaged animals such as lion and leopard. For those without their own transport, organised game drives are offered by Red Chilli Rest Camp or (more expensively) Paraa Safari Lodge.

KANIYO PABIDI FOREST   The 28km² Kaniyo Pabidi Forest, which lies in the south of MFCA, split between the Bugungu and Karuma wildlife reserves, is essentially

a northeastern extension of the larger Budongo Forest Reserve. It harbours similar (though not identical) fauna and flora to Budongo, and because it has never been logged it contains a far higher proportion of large buttressed mahogany and ironwood trees. Forest primates include black-and-white colobus and blue monkey, while large troops of olive baboon are a regular sight along the main road through the forest. It also supports Uganda's densest chimp population, recently estimated at around 6.5 individuals per square kilometre, along with an alluring selection of forest birds. The focal point for tourist activities in Kaniyo Pabidi is Budongo EcoLodge (pages 354–5), which lies on the east side of the main road to Paraa 29km north of Masindi (via Kichambanyobo Gate), and can easily be visited driving between the two, or as a day trip from either. Chimp tracking and other activities can be arranged here on the spot, unless all permits are sold out in advance.

Chimp tracking Kaniyo Pabidi supports two chimpanzee communities, each estimated to number around 90 individuals, and the one centred closest to Budongo EcoLodge has been habituated for tourist visits since the late 1990s. Up to 36 permits are issued by the lodge daily, with trackers set off in up to six guided groups, each comprising up to three people, at 08.00 then again at 14.00. Tracking at Kaniyo Pabidi is not quite as reliable as Kibale Forest, but the terrain is flatter and easier, and the success rate currently stands at around 80%, with most groups locating chimps within an hour of setting off, in which case the full activity should take around 3 hours. It may take longer if the chimps are more difficult to locate. Permits cost US$85 bought in advance or US$90 on the spot (assuming availability). A full-day habituation experience allowing up to two people to experience a full day of chimpanzee activity (minimum 6 hours, starting at 07.00) is also available at US$155 per person.

Bird walks One of the top forest birding sites in Uganda, Kaniyo Pabidi protects a similar range of species to Budongo Forest. The best place to look for birds is around the lodge, especially the gallery forest along the main road, which offers good views into the canopy and can be explored freely and without a guide if you so choose. Among the more interesting species we've observed here are common shrike-flycatcher, chestnut wattle-eye, Narina trogon, little greenbul, chestnut-winged starling, grey apalis, dwarf and pygmy kingfishers, and a great many forest sunbirds and hornbills. A local speciality is Puvel's illadopsis, which is quite common in Kaniyo Pabidi, but known from no other locality in East Africa. The extremely localised and magnificently garish green-breasted pitta has also been recorded. To stand a realistic chance of seeing these and other more elusive denizens of the forest interior, you're best off organising a formal bird walk with a specialised guide through the lodge. This costs US$20/35 half/full-day.

SOUTH OF THE NILE The main attraction south of the Nile is the spectacular Top of the Falls Viewpoint, which lies up to 90 minutes' drive from Paraa or 30 minutes from the junction with the main road from Masindi. A visit to this viewpoint can also be tagged on to the boat trip to the base of the falls by prior arrangement. Game drives south of the river are possible but relatively unrewarding due to the dense bush and local prevalence of tsetse flies.

Rabongo Forest Situated in the far southeast of the park, the little-visited Rabongo Forest is smaller and less ecologically interesting than Kaniyo Pabidi, and the 40km access road there – branching from the main Paraa road a few kilometres south of Sambiya Lodge – is both rough and tsetse-infested. General forest walks are

available on the spot, but are of interest mostly to birdwatchers, though black-and-white colobus and red-tailed monkeys are also likely to be seen, and the number and variety of butterflies is impressive.

Top of the Falls Viewpoint Murchison Falls is an impressive sight from the boat, but for sheer sensory overload, be sure to visit this spectacular south bank viewpoint, which is reached along a sporadically steep and rough 15km road that branches north from the main Paraa road at a signposted junction (⊕ 2.18259, 31.69194) about 500m past Sambiya Lodge. From the car park (⊕ 2.27718, 31.6872), a short footpath leads downhill to the waterfall's head and a fenced viewpoint from where one can truly appreciate the staggering power with which the Nile crashes through the narrow gap in the escarpment, not to mention the deafening roar and voluminous spray it generates.

From this main viewpoint, a longer footpath, perhaps 20 minutes' walking time, leads to Baker's View on a ridge looking directly towards Murchison Falls as well as the broader Uhuru Falls a hundred metres or so to the north. Historical records suggest that this latter falls was an impermanent (possibly seasonal) feature until the great floods of 1962, since when it has been more or less constant, though it is still subject to dramatic variations in volume. The face-on view of the two cataracts – separated by a lushly forested hillock – is truly inspiring, but surpassed perhaps by following another footpath down to the base of the short gorge below the two waterfalls. If you want to check out all the viewpoints, allow at least 2 hours – ideally in the afternoon, when the sun is better positioned for photography.

There is not much wildlife in the vicinity of the falls and it is considered safe to walk unaccompanied between the viewpoints, though you may encounter troops of baboons and black-and-white colobus. The so-called 'bat cliff' immediately south of the main waterfall (visible from Baker's View) is worth scanning with binoculars for raptors and swallows. Wait around until dusk and you should see some impressive flocks of bats emerging from the caves in this cliff, as well as a few bat hawks soaring around in search of a quick dinner. After dusk, the drive from the Top of the Falls back to the main road is particularly good for nocturnal birds, including spotted eagle owl and (seasonally) Africa's three most spectacular and distinctive nightjar species: long-tailed (Mar–Aug); pennant-winged (Mar–Sep); and standard-winged (Sep–Apr).

Although the Top of the Falls is easily visited by road, the most satisfying way to get there is to tag it on to a launch trip from Paraa. This entails disembarking from the boat at a landing point a few hundred metres below the falls, then ascending a tree-shaded footpath through the gorge to the viewpoints at its rim, where you will need to arrange for a vehicle to collect you. Alternatively, you could be driven to the viewpoint and then walk down in time to be collected by the launch, with the disadvantage that the boat's captain tends to stop less often to look at wildlife on the return leg to Paraa. In both cases, a hiking fee of US$10/15 FR/FNR must be paid in advance at the ticket office at Paraa, and a ranger will be allocated to escort you on foot between the landing point and Baker's View.

Southern Game Drive Circuit The combination of dense vegetation and low concentrations of wildlife mean that game viewing is generally poor south of the river. Tsetse flies are also an annoyance in many areas. Nevertheless, a newly cut game-viewing loop running to the east of the main road between Paraa and Masindi is particularly well suited to people staying at Sambiya River Lodge, and it would also make a useful extension to a visit to the Top of the Falls. The loop starts

Murchison Falls is first alluded to in the writings of Speke, who upon visiting Karuma Falls to the east in 1862 was told that a few other waterfalls lay downriver, mostly 'of minor importance' but 'one within ear-sound … said to be very grand'. Speke does not record the name by which this waterfall was known locally, but his guide did inform him that a few years earlier 'at the Grand Falls … the king had the heads of one hundred men, prisoners taken in war against Rionga, cut off and thrown into the river'. Two years later, partially to fulfil a promise they had made to Speke, Samuel and Florence Baker became the first Europeans to explore the stretch of river between Lake Albert and Karuma Falls. As they were paddling about 30km east of the estuary, Samuel Baker wrote:

> We could distinctly hear the roar of water [and] upon rounding the corner a magnificent site burst upon us. On either side of the river were beautifully wooded cliffs rising abruptly to a height of about 300 feet [100m]; rocks were jutting out from the intensely green foliage; and rushing through a gap that cleft exactly before us, the river, contracted from a grand stream, was pent up in a passage of scarcely 50 yards [46m] in width; roaring furiously through the rock-bound pass, it plunged in one leap of about 120 feet [36m] perpendicular into a large abyss below. The fall of water was snow white, which had a superb effect as it contrasted with the dark cliffs that walled the water, while the graceful palms of the tropics and wild plantains perfected the beauty of the view. This was the greatest waterfall of the Nile, and in honour of the distinguished president of the Royal Geographic Society, I named it the Murchison Falls, the most important object through the entire course of the river.

at a junction ($\oplus$ 2.24098, 31.69228) about 8km along the feeder road to the Top of the Falls, then runs east for about 20km before arriving at a three-way junction where you need to turn right. After another 15km you'll see reach the junction for Rabongo Forest, where you need to keep to the right, before reconnecting with the Masindi–Paraa Road after about 25km. This route passes through some lovely open areas where Ugandan kob, Jackson's hartebeest, waterbuck, baboon and oribi may be encountered as well as – more occasionally – elephant and lion. It also passes through tracts of dense woodland where you are advised to wind up your windows sharpish, before the tsetse flies pour in.

BOAT TRIPS FROM PARAA A highlight of any visit to MFNP is one of the boat trips that follow the Victoria Nile east or west from Paraa. For many years, these were operated on a monopolistic basis by UWA, which still runs twice-daily boat trips from Paraa to the base of Murchison Falls, bookable through the ticket office a few hundred metres south of the jetty. Two private operators now also run daily boat trips from Paraa to the base of the falls, charging a marginally lower price for what is generally regarded to be a better service. These are Paraa Safari Lodge (pages 355–6) on the north bank, and the more specialised Wild Frontiers Nile River Safaris ($\oplus$ 2.28301, 31.5648; ✆ 041 4321479; m 0773 897275/0702 152928; e murchisonboats@wildfrontiers.co.ug; www.wildfrontiers.co.ug/murchison-falls-boats) on the south bank immediately west of the Paraa ferry jetty. Where UWA and Paraa Safari Lodge focus mainly on trips to the base of the falls, Wild Frontiers also operates boat trips to the Lake Albert Delta and bespoke fishing and birding cruises.

Base of the Falls The 3-hour return launch trip to the base of Murchison Falls has been MFNP's most popular attraction since the Queen Mother made the inaugural voyage in a spanking-new boat back in 1959. Starting at Paraa, the boat cruises slowly eastward along an archetypically African stretch of the Nile, fringed by borassus palms, acacia woodland and mahogany stands, before finally docking in a small bay a few hundred metres away from the cashing waterfall.

Game viewing along the way is excellent. Expect to see hippos in their hundreds, along with some of Africa's largest surviving crocodiles, and small herds of buffalo, waterbuck and kob. Giraffe, bushbuck and black-and-white colobus are also regularly seen, while elephants are frequently observed playing in the water, often within a few metres of the launch. A bit more luck is required to see lion or leopard.

The birdlife is reliably stunning, though the exact species composition varies depending on season and sandbank exposure. Look out for African fish eagle, Goliath heron, saddle-billed stork, African jacana, pied and malachite kingfishers, African skimmer, piacpiac, rock pratincole, black-headed gonolek, black-winged red bishop, yellow-mantled widow-bird, yellow-backed weaver and, at the right time of year, a variety of migrant waders. The dazzlingly colourful red-throated bee-eater nests in sandbanks between Paraa and the falls, and is more likely to be seen here than anywhere in East Africa. The top avian prize is of course the shoebill, which is spotted here less frequently than it is around the delta, but remains a fair possibility in the dry season.

There's not a great to choose between the three operators offering daily trips to the base of the falls. All use double-decker boats, follow the same route, take 2–3 hours there and back, and charge a similar price (*US$28 with Paraa Safari Lodge, US$30 with UWA or US$32 with Wild Frontiers; children get a discount*). All operators can collect passengers from either side of the river, but it is advantageous to be on the boat early in order to take one of the better seats (the left side of the boat gives you the best view towards the wildlife-rich north bank on the slower outbound leg), which means passengers embarking on the north bank are best off booking with Paraa Safari Lodge, while those on the south bank should go with Wild Frontiers or UWA. It is also worth noting that the newer crafts used by Wild Frontiers are more comfortable and take the return trip from the falls to Paraa at a faster pace (a useful consideration if travelling with kids). All three operators usually offer morning and afternoon trips, with the former offering better birdwatching but the latter being better for photography, since the sun is behind you on the outbound leg and when you reach the falls. Morning departures are staggered between 08.00 and 09.00 and afternoon departures between 14.00 and 15.00. An advantage of being on the first morning or first afternoon boat is that it is quite likely to scare off shyer animals coming down to drink before the other boats come past. Keen photographers, however, would certainly want to take the last afternoon departure in order to capture the best light. On that note, Wild Frontiers also offers a daily Falls Sundowner Cruise leaving at 15.30 for US$45 per adult. All boats are provided with lifejackets and river guides.

Delta cruise The 20km voyage downriver from Paraa to the Lake Albert Delta is favoured by birdwatchers as one of the best opportunities anywhere in Africa to see the rare shoebill, particularly during the rainy season. More often than not, those who take the boat trip are rewarded with multiple shoebill sightings, but nothing is guaranteed and occasionally they dip totally. Without the shoebill as a motivating factor, the delta trip is not as worthwhile as the one to the falls, since there's less wildlife to be seen, and the general birding is more-or-less duplicated, though

14

other papyrus endemics are sometime observed. Wild Frontiers runs a daily delta cruise in a shaded 15-seater boat that leaves Paraa at 07.00 (*5hrs return; US$55pp, minimum two passengers*).

Fishing excursions There is good fishing along the Murchison Nile, with large Nile perch and tiger fish offering the main challenge. The record for rod and line in Murchison was established by Kevin Nicholson in 2013. His mammoth catch weighed 114kg, just eclipsing Tim Smith's 113kg catch in 2009, but far heavier than the previous official record of 73kg, set by C D Mardach in 1959. Local fishermen claim to have netted specimens weighing up to 160kg. Wild Frontiers offers half- (*US$190/170/116 for 1/2/3 people*) and full-day (*US$375/205/155 for 1/2/3 people*) fishing cruises. A sport-fishing permit must be bought from UWA at a cost of US$50 for one day or US$150 for four days.

NORTH OF THE NILE The northern half of MFNP is far more rewarding than the bushier south when it comes to game drives. The most popular and best game-viewing circuit is Buligi, which stretches west from the main road between Paraa and Tangi Gate to the Lake Albert Delta. However, the area to the east of the Paraa–Tangi Road, off-limits until 2005 or so due to the security concerns, can also be very worthwhile, and it attracts far less safari traffic.

Buligi and the Delta Circuit The bulk of Murchison Falls' wildlife is concentrated to the north of the Nile, and the established area for game drives is a circuit of tracks within the Buligi area, an extensive promontory of grassland running west from the Paraa–Tangi Road to the promontory flanked by the Victoria Nile and Albert Nile as they enter and exit Lake Albert. To reach the Buligi area from Paraa, follow the Pakwach Road north of the ferry crossing, then after 7km turn left at Te Bito Junction (✪ *2.34323, 31.56463*). About 3km from here, the road passes through a patch of whistling thorns, a type of acacia whose marble-sized round pods – aerated by insects – whistle softly when a wind comes up. About 3km further (✪ *2.33035, 31.51938*), the **Buligi Track** branches off to the left, then about 3km further on the road passes the fenced Pakuba Airstrip (✪ *2.32931, 31.49921*). The road between Te Bito and the airstrip passes through a scenic area of rolling grassland studded with tall borassus palms, where game concentrations are unpredictable, but generally highest in the rainy season.

About 2km past the airstrip, the road forks twice in the space of a kilometre, giving you the option of following three different tracks, all of which lead west towards the delta. For those with limited time, the central 10km **Queen's Track** is not only the shortest route, but also the smoothest, and generally the most productive for game viewing. The northerly 12km **Albert Nile Track**, branching right at the first junction (✪ *2.32316, 31.48511*), passes through patches of dense acacia woodland that will be as attractive to birdwatchers as they are, unfortunately, to tsetse flies. The southerly 25km **Victoria Nile Track**, branching left at the second junction (✪ *2.31765, 31.48123*), is far longer and game concentrations are generally low, except as it approaches the delta.

The three tracks converge on a grassy peninsula, flanked by the delta to the south and the Albert Nile to the north, and crossed by a network of interconnecting tracks that run through several kob breeding grounds. A good place to stop here is an unsignposted lookout we'll call Hippo Point (✪ *2.28352, 31.38682*), where the convention is to hop out of the vehicle and wander down to the shore to gawp at the profusion of hippos and birds in the reedy shallows. Large concentrations of

Ugandan kob are a certainty in this area, as are family parties of Defassa waterbuck and the rather doleful-looking Jackson's hartebeest, as well as small groups of the dainty oribi. A striking feature of the area is its giraffe herds, which often number 50 or more, something you seldom see elsewhere in Africa on a regular basis. Substantial buffalo herds are also common around the delta, usually containing a few individuals whose coloration indicates some genetic input from the smaller, redder forest buffalo of West Africa.

The limitless supply of kob has attracted several prides of lion to the delta area. The best place to look for these languid predators is along the series of short anonymous tracks that connect the Albert Nile and Queen's tracks. At least one pride maintains an almost permanent presence in this area, often lying out in the open in the early morning and late afternoon, but generally retreating deep into the thicket during the heat of the day. The most reliable way to locate the lions is by observing the behaviour of the male kobs that always stand sentry on the edge of a herd. If one or two kobs persistently emit their characteristic high wheezing alarm whistle, they are almost certainly conscious that lions are around, so follow their gaze towards the nearest thicket. Conversely, should you hang around a kob herd for a few minutes and not hear any alarm calls, you can be reasonably sure that no lions are to be found in the immediate vicinity. The area frequented by these lions is also a good place to look for the endearingly puppyish side-striped jackal, and troops of the localised and rather skittish patas monkey.

The delta area offers some great birdwatching. Noteworthy ground birds include the preposterous eye-fluttering Abyssinian ground hornbill, the majestic grey crowned crane and saddle-billed stork, the localised Denham's bustard, the handsome black-headed and spur-winged lapwings, and the Senegal thick-knee. The tall acacia stands that line the Albert Nile Track, immediately north of the junction with Queen's Track, harbour a host of good woodland birds, including the rare black-billed barbet and delightfully colourful swallow-tailed, northern Carmine, blue-breasted and red-throated bee-eaters. Herds of grazers – in particular buffalo – are often attended by flocks of insectivorous cattle egret, piacpiac and red-billed and yellow-billed oxpeckers. An abundance of aquatic habitats – not only the rivers and lake, but also numerous small pools – attracts a wide variety of waterfowl, waders, herons and egrets, while the mighty African fish eagle and both species of marsh harrier are often seen soaring above the water. All birders should take a slow drive along the extension of the Victoria Nile Track that branches southwest at an easily-missed junction (✪ 2.27576, 31.38234) about 1.5km south of Hippo Point, then runs adjacent to the papyrus lined Victoria Nile for 3km to a seasonal hippo pool only 200m from the riverbank. Shoebills are frequently observed in this area, flying over the delta or standing stock still in the papyrus beds, while a solitary osprey is often observed at the hippo pool itself.

The Buligi Circuit is also readily accessed from Pakwach and the Tangi Gate. To get there, turn right on to the Pakuba track at a signposted junction (✪ 2.40878, 31.51421) 5km south of Tangi Gate, and follow it for 15km (passing Pakuba Safari Lodge to your right) until you come to a T-junction with the Albert Nile Track (✪ 2.32503, 31.46849), where a right turn leads towards the delta.

Northeast of Paraa Although it doesn't quite compare with the Buligi Circuit for general game viewing or aquatic birds, the road running east from Te Bito junction (7km north of Paraa) towards Wankwar Gate can still be very rewarding and tends to carry far less tourist traffic. A recommended 2km diversion, branching south at a junction (✪ 2.34386, 31.64009) just some 10km east of Te Bito crossroads, leads to the

Perhaps the most eagerly sought of all African birds, the shoebill is also one of the few that is likely to make an impression on those travellers who regard pursuing rare birds to be about as diverting as hanging about in windswept railway stations scribbling down train numbers. Three factors combine to give the shoebill its bizarre and somewhat prehistoric appearance. The first is its enormous proportions: an adult might stand more than 150cm (5ft) tall and typically weighs around 6kg. The second is its unique uniform slate-grey coloration. Last but emphatically not least is its clog-shaped, hook-tipped bill – at 20cm long, and almost as wide, the largest among all living bird species. The bill is fixed in a permanent Cheshire-cat smirk that contrives to look at once sinister and somewhat inane, and when agitated the bird loudly claps together its upper and lower bill, rather like outsized castanets.

The first known allusions to the shoebill came from early European explorers to the Sudan, who wrote of a camel-sized flying creature known by the local Arabs as Abu Markub – Father of the Shoe. These reports were dismissed as pure fancy by Western biologists until 1851, when Gould came across a bizarre specimen amongst an avian collection shot on the Upper White Nile. Describing it as 'the most extraordinary bird I have seen', Gould placed his discovery in a monotypic family and named it *Balaeniceps Rex* – King Whale-Head! Gould believed the strange bird to be most closely allied to pelicans, but it also shares some anatomic and behavioural characteristics with herons, and until recently it was widely held to be an evolutionary offshoot of the stork family. Recent DNA studies support Gould's original theory, however, and the shoebill is now placed in a monotypic subfamily of Pelecanidae.

The life cycle of the shoebill is no less remarkable than its appearance. One of the few birds with an age span of up to 50 years, it is generally monogamous, with pairs coming together during the breeding season (April to June) to construct a grassy nest up to 3m wide on a mound of floating vegetation or a small island. Two eggs are laid, and the parents rotate incubation duties, in hot weather filling their bills with water to spray over the eggs to keep them cool. The chicks hatch after about a month, and will need to be fed by the parents for at least another two months until their beaks are fully developed. Usually only one nestling survives, probably as a result of sibling rivalry.

The shoebill is a true swamp specialist, but it avoids dense stands of papyrus and tall grass, which obstruct its take-off, preferring instead to forage from patches of low floating vegetation or along the edge of channels. It consumes up to half its weight in food daily, preying on whatever moderately sized aquatic creature might come its way, ranging from toads to baby crocodiles, though lungfish are especially favoured. Its method of hunting is exceptionally sedentary: the bird might stand semi-frozen for several hours before it lunges down with remarkable speed and power, heavy wings stretched backward, to grab an item of prey in its

Nyamsika Cliffs Viewpoint (✪ *2.33133, 31.64951*). Named for the sandy waterway it overlooks, this craggy cliff hosts seasonal colonies of several types of bee-eater, while lion and buffalo sometimes come to drink at the river below, which is also one of the few places in East Africa where the dashing Egyptian plover is frequently recorded. Another 2km past Nyamsika junction, a series of newly created roadside waterholes often attracts giraffe, elephant, buffalo, hartebeest, waterbuck, Ugandan kob, oribi, duiker and warthog. Another 4km past this, game viewing tends to dry up at about

large, inescapable bill. Although it is generally a solitary hunter, the shoebill has occasionally been observed hunting co-operatively in small flocks, which splash about flapping their wings to drive a school of fish into a confined area.

Although the shoebill is an elusive bird, this – as with the sitatunga antelope – is less a function of its inherent scarcity than of the inaccessibility of its swampy haunts. Nevertheless, BirdLife International has recently classified it as Vulnerable, and it is classed as CITES Appendix 2, which means that trade in shoebills, or their capture for any harmful activity, is forbidden by international law. Estimates of the global population vary wildly. In the 1970s, only 1,500 shoebills were thought to exist in the wild, but this estimate has subsequently been revised to 5,000–10,000 individuals concentrated in five countries – Sudan, Uganda, Tanzania, DRC and Zambia. Small breeding populations also survive in Rwanda and Ethiopia, and vagrants have been recorded in Malawi and Kenya.

The most important shoebill stronghold is the Sudd floodplain on the Sudanese Nile, where 6,400 individuals were counted during an aerial survey in 1979–82, a figure that dropped to 3,830 when a similar survey was undertaken in 2005. Another likely stronghold is western Tanzania's rather inaccessible Moyowosi-Kigosi Swamp, whose population was thought to amount to a few hundred prior to a 1990 survey that estimated it to be greater than 2,000, though recent reports suggest a maximum of 500. Ironically, although Uganda is the easiest place to see the shoebill in the wild, the national population probably amounts to no more than 250 adult birds, half of which are concentrated in the Kyoga–Bisina–Opeta complex of wetlands. For tourists, however, the most reliable locations for shoebill sightings are Murchison Falls National Park, Toro-Semliki Wildlife Reserve and the Mabamba Swamp near Entebbe – none of which is thought to hold more than a dozen pairs. Visitors to Uganda who fail to locate a shoebill in the wild might take consolation from the Wildlife Orphanage in Entebbe, where a few orphaned individuals are kept in a large aviary.

The major threat to the survival of the shoebill is habitat destruction. The construction of several dams along the lower Nile means that the water levels of the Sudd are open to artificial manipulation. Elsewhere, swamp clearance and rice farming pose a localised threat to suitable wetland habitats. Lake Opeta, an important shoebill stronghold in eastern Uganda, has been earmarked as a source of irrigation for a new agricultural scheme. A lesser concern is that shoebills are hunted for food or illegal trade in parts of Uganda. In the Lake Kyoga region, local fishermen often kill shoebill for cultural reasons – they believe that seeing a shoebill before a fishing expedition is a bad omen. As is so often the case, tourism can play a major role in preserving the shoebill and its habitat, particularly in areas such as the Mabamba Swamp, where the local community has already seen financial benefits from ornithological visits.

the same time as the road reaches a wooded area where tsetse flies are numerous and visitors on a short game drive would be well advised to turn back to Paraa.

Alternatively, continue for another 12km towards Wankwar to the signposted junction (✪ 2.41308, 31.75815) for the recently reopened **north bank viewpoint** over Murchison Falls. Be warned, however, that the reality of this northern viewpoint falls way short of expectations, with the main waterfall being identifiable only by a distant plume of spray. The theoretical prospect of eyeballing the comparably

voluminous Uhuru Falls is also thwarted, since the flight of concrete steps that descends from the parking area terminates at a nondescript riverside spot in sight of neither waterfall. All that might change should the vague plans to open a trail to Uhuru Falls and rebuild the bridge across the gorge ever come to fruition, Until that time, however, it's a poor incentive for a 3-hour, 110km round-trip from Paraa.

Shortly before reaching Wankwar Gate, a junction (⊕ 2.43465, 31.78508) to the right leads to Chobe Lodge, 53km away. Much of this route passes through woodland where little wildlife is seen and tsetse flies are numerous, so if you opt or need to head this way, best wind up your windows.

KARUMA FALLS Crossed by the Kampala–Gulu Road 2km south of MFNP's Chobe Gate, Karuma Bridge is the spot where, a few years ago, fearful tension gripped northbound travellers, while the mood on vehicles headed south lightened immeasurably. Today, it's a beautiful location: beneath the bridge, the river races down rapids between high, forested banks. On the north side these lie within Murchison Falls National Park, and on the southern, downstream side, in the Karuma Wildlife Reserve. Unfortunately, the soldiers posted to guard the bridge seem to view photography as an Eighth Deadly Sin, and simply pausing on the bridge is sufficient to stir them into activity.

Though the bridge crosses a lovely section of rapids, the main Karuma Falls lie about 2km upriver on an elevated promontory overlooking a broad forested gorge behind Karuma town. The first major plunge in an 80km-long stretch of rapids ending at Murchison Falls, Karuma represents the point where an older and larger incarnation of Lake Kyoga eventually burst its banks, allowing the Nile to scour its present-day course towards the Rift Valley. It's a worthwhile diversion, despite the curious fact that Speke, who visited in 1864, was sufficiently underwhelmed to record it by its local name rather than allocating it to a contemporary royal or sponsor. The north bank of the waterfall can easily be visited from the ground of the Heritage Garden, on the north side of the bridge opposite the junction to Pakwach, which charges US$1.50 per person entrance and US$1.50 per party for a guide. Visiting the south bank is complicated by the need to obtain permission at the office of the Karuma Falls power station.

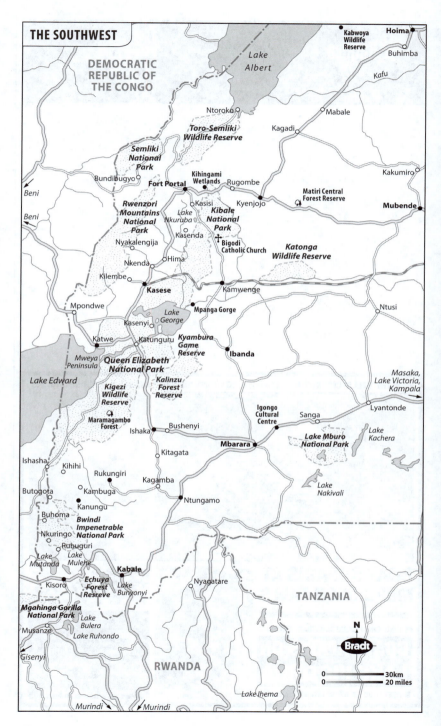

THE SOUTHWEST

DEMOCRATIC
REPUBLIC OF
THE CONGO

Lake
Albert

Kabwoya
Wildlife
Reserve

Hoima

Buhimba

Kafu

Mabale

Kagadi

Kakumiro

Ntoroko

Toro-Semliki
Wildlife Reserve

Semliki
National
Park

Bundibugyo

Fort Portal

Kihingami
Wetlands

Rugombe

Kyenjojo

Matiri Central
Forest Reserve

Mubende

Beni

Beni

Rwenzori
Mountains
National
Park

Kasisi

Lake
Nkuruba

Kibale
National
Park

Kasenda

Bigodi
Catholic Church

Katonga
Wildlife Reserve

Nyakalengija

Nkenda

Hima

Kilembe

Kasese

Kamwenge

Ntusi

Mpondwe

Kasenyi

Lake
George

Mpanga Gorge

Katwe

Katunguru

Kyambura
Game
Reserve

Ibanda

Mweya
Peninsula

Queen Elizabeth
National Park

Kalinzu
Forest
Reserve

Masaka,
Lake Victoria,
Kampala

Lake Edward

Kigezi
Wildlife
Reserve

Maramagambo
Forest

Ishaka

Bushenyi

Igongo
Cultural
Centre

Sanga

Lyantonde

Lake
Kachera

Ishasha

Kihihi

Rukungiri

Kitagata

Mbarara

Lake Mburo
National Park

Butogota

Kambuga

Kagamba

Buhoma

Kanungu

Ntungamo

Lake
Nakivali

Bwindi
Impenetrable
National Park

Nkuringo

Rubuguri

Kabale

Nyagatare

Lake
Mutanda

Lake
Mulehe

Kisoro

Echuya
Forest
Resreve

Lake
Bunyonyi

TANZANIA

Mgahinga Gorilla
National Park

Lake
Bulera

N

Bradt

Musanze

Lake Ruhondo

Gisenyi

0   30km
0   20 miles

RWANDA

Lake Ihema

Murindi

Murindi

Part Four

SOUTHWEST UGANDA

OVERVIEW

Hosting the most varied safari circuit anywhere in Africa, southwest Uganda is studded with national parks shielding a range of habitats that embraces everything from snow-capped glacial peaks and frosty Afro-alpine moorland to marsh-fringed Rift Valley lakes and forest-swathed volcanoes – not forgetting some vast tracts of archetypal African savannah. The highlight for most is tracking mountain gorillas in Bwindi or Mgahinga Gorilla national parks – one of the world's most thrilling wildlife encounters – but it is also a good place to see habituated chimpanzees, tree-climbing lions, furtive leopards, huge African elephants, not to mention a dazzling variety of monkeys, antelope and birds. Wildlife aside, the Rwenzori and Virunga mountains offer some utterly superb – albeit challenging – high-altitude hiking and climbing opportunities, while more sedentary visitors get to choose between an extraordinary range of upmarket lodges and low-key budget camps servicing pretty Lake Bunyonyi and the hundred-odd crater lakes that run south from Fort Portal (one of Uganda's most appealing towns) to the Kichwamba Escarpment.

Although it covers quite a small area in geographic terms, this section of the book breaks up into seven chapters. Starting in the north, the first chapter covers the town of Fort Portal along with the nearby Toro Crater Lakes and Kibale National Park, and the next two cover the remote Semliki Valley and hiker-orientated Rwenzori National Park. Biodiverse Queen Elizabeth National Park gets its own chapter, as does Bwindi Impenetrable National Park to its south, but the two are separated by a chapter dealing with the small towns of Kabale and Kisoro, both of which are near to the Rwandan border, and Mgahinga Gorilla National Park plus a cluster of lakes including Bunyonyi and Mutanda. Finally, the last chapter in the section covers Ankole on the road back towards Kampala, as well as its principal town Mbarara and the relatively low-key Lake Mburo National Park.

HIGHLIGHTS

TORO CRATER LAKES Studding the volcanically formed Rwenzori footslopes like a ribbon of green and blue gemstones, the 30-plus crater lakes of Toro provide the setting for some Uganda's most attractive upmarket lodges and budget camps. Pages 388–97.

KIBALE NATIONAL PARK Uganda's top chimpanzee-tracking site also protects the country's densest and most varied monkey population and a fabulous variety of forest birds is showcased at the community-run Bigodi Swamp Walk. Pages 397–407.

SEMLIKI VALLEY As scenically stunning as it is remote, the section of the Albertine Rift that divides the northern Rwenzori footslopes from Lake Albert supports two fine but little-visited conservation areas known for their ecological affinities to the Ituri Forest in the neighbouring Congo Basin. Pages 409–18.

RWENZORI MOUNTAINS NATIONAL PARK The montane forest, Afro-alpine moorland and craggy glacial peaks of the 5,109m-high Mountains of the Moon provide some of the most challenging and rewarding high-altitude hiking anywhere in Africa. Pages 424–37.

QUEEN ELIZABETH NATIONAL PARK Arguably the most biodiverse conservation area in East Africa with a bird checklist topping the 600 mark, QENP's variety embraces the elephant, hippos and giant forest hogs that haunt the Kazinga Channel

– serviced by several boat trips daily – as well as the chimps of Kyambura Gorge and celebrated tree-climbing lions of Ishasha. Pages 439–72.

KALINZU ECOTOURISM SITE This underpublicised forest reserve bordering QENP is second only to Kibale National Park when it comes to reliable chimp tracking, but at prices far better suited to budget-conscious backpackers. Pages 466–7.

LAKE BUNYONYI A flooded riverine valley set between the steep terraced slopes of Kigezi, lovely Lake Bunyonyi is entrenched as the place to chill out for a few days before or after gorilla tracking in nearby Bwindi. Pages 479–89.

MGAHINGA GORILLA NATIONAL PARK Protecting the upper slopes of the Ugandan portion of the Virunga Mountains, this small national park is home to one group of habituated mountain gorillas, but other attractions include the opportunity to visit habituated golden monkeys and day hikes to a trio of spectacular volcanic peaks including the the 4,127m Muhabura. Pages 498–502.

BWINDI IMPENETRABLE NATIONAL PARK Home to 12 habituated mountain gorilla groups, Bwindi's densely forested slopes also offer great monkey viewing, occasional elephant encounters, and the opportunity to tick two dozen bird species endemic to the Albertine Rift. Pages 504–32.

LAKE MBURO NATIONAL PARK A popular stopover between Bwindi and Kampala, this low-key acacia-dominated reserve supports a rich variety of ungulates, ranging from giraffe to half a dozen antelope species, while activities include day or overnight horseback excursions and night drives in search of leopards. Pages 542–51.

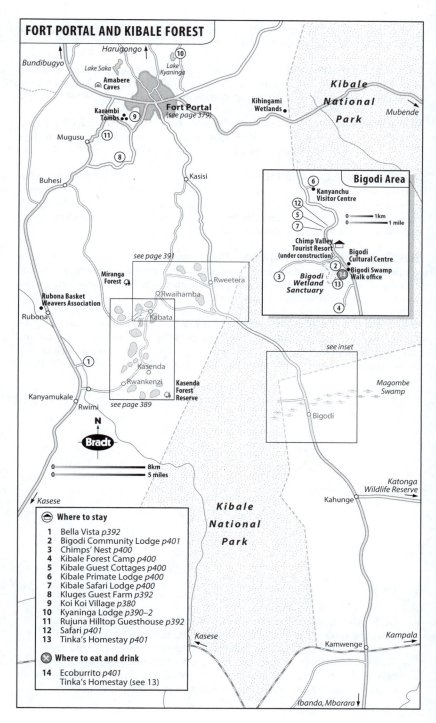

FORT PORTAL AND KIBALE FOREST

Harugongo

Bundibugyo

Lake Saka

Lake Kyaninga

(10)

Amabere Caves

Karambi Tombs (9)

Fort Portal *(see page 379)*

Kihingami Wetlands

Kibale National Park

Mubende

Mugusu (11)

(8)

Buhesi

Kasisi

Bigodi Area

(6)

Kanyanchu Visitor Centre

(12)

(5)

(7)

0   1km
0   1 mile

Chimp Valley Tourist Resort *(under construction)*

Bigodi Cultural Centre

(2)

(14)

Bigodi Swamp Walk office

(3)

Bigodi Wetland Sanctuary

(13)

(4)

see page 391

Miranga Forest

Rweetera

Rwaihamba

Rubona Basket Weavers Association

Rubona

Kabata

see inset

Magombe Swamp

(1)

Kasenda

Rwankenzi

Kasenda Forest Reserve

Bigodi

Kanyamukale

Rwimi

see page 389

N

Bradt

0   8km
0   5 miles

Kasese

Katonga Wildlife Reserve

Kahunge

Kibale National Park

Where to stay

1 Bella Vista *p392*
2 Bigodi Community Lodge *p401*
3 Chimps' Nest *p400*
4 Kibale Forest Camp *p400*
5 Kibale Guest Cottages *p400*
6 Kibale Primate Lodge *p400*
7 Kibale Safari Lodge *p400*
8 Kluges Guest Farm *p392*
9 Koi Koi Village *p380*
10 Kyaninga Lodge *p390–2*
11 Rujuna Hilltop Guesthouse *p392*
12 Safari *p401*
13 Tinka's Homestay *p401*

Where to eat and drink

14 Ecoburrito *p401*
Tinka's Homestay (see 13)

Kasese

Kamwenge

Kampala

Ibanda, Mbarara

15

Fort Portal, Kibale National Park and the Toro Crater Lakes

The principal town of Toro subregion, likeable Fort Portal forms the urban gateway to a circuit of magnificent natural attractions that includes one of the country's most biodiverse rainforests, several dozen lushly vegetated crater lakes, and the spectacular northern Rwenzori foothills. The top attraction, situated to the southeast of Fort Portal, is Kibale National Park, which forms Uganda's premier chimp-tracking destination, as well as supporting its greatest primate diversity and a thrilling variety of forest birds. Running Kibale a close second, the Toro Crater Lakes are nestled within a longitudinal band of volcanic calderas that run west of the national park border from Fort Portal south to Kasenda. The region's other main attraction, stretching west from Fort Portal to the Congolese border, is the more remote Semliki Valley, covered in *Chapter 16*.

Approximating the borders of the 19th-century kingdom of Toro, the area covered in this chapter is endowed with plenty of appealing accommodation. At the top end, you have the choice of intimate jungle-fringed bush camps or boutique-style lodges perched above aquamarine crater lakes, while budget travellers are catered for by an above-par selection of inexpensive hotels and simple banda/camping sites. The area also supports several budget-friendly community projects, notably the Bigodi Wetland Sanctuary bordering Kibale National Park, and Lake Nkuruba Nature Reserve near Rwaihamba. It is worth emphasising that, where accommodation is concerned, the division between Fort Portal, the Toro Crater Lakes and Kibale National Park is rather arbitrary. In reality, most places covered in this chapter lie within an easy hour's drive of each other, which means, for instance, that many tourists use a lodge in Fort Portal or at one of the crater lakes as a base for chimp tracking and other activities in Kibale National Park.

FORT PORTAL

The administrative centre of Kabarole District and seat of the Toro Kingdom, Fort Portal is perhaps the most attractive town in Uganda, situated amid lush rolling hillsides swathed in neat tea plantations and – clouds permitting – offering excellent views across to the glacial peaks of the Rwenzori Mountains to the west. Some 300km from Kampala along a good surfaced road, this well-equipped town is also a useful springboard for exploring Kibale National Park and the Toro Crater Lakes, though most organised tours literally just pass through *en route* to more of the many upmarket lodges around the forest and lakes. The town centre has seen a great deal of renovation since the early 1990s, making it barely recognisable from the rundown 'Fort Pothole' of a few years back. It is also rather short on noteworthy

Fort Portal lies at the physical and political heart of Toro, the youngest of Uganda's traditional kingdoms, ruled – aptly – by the world's most youthful monarch, not quite four years old when he took the throne in 1995. Toro started life as a southern principality within the Bunyoro kingdom, from which it broke away to become an independent kingdom in the late 1820s under Prince Kaboyo, the son of the Bunyoro king, Nyakamaturu. The original kingdom corresponded roughly with the present-day administrative districts of Kabarole (which includes Fort Portal), Kyenjojo, Kamwenge, Bundibugyo and Kasese, but the latter two are not considered to be part of Toro today.

In the mid-1820s, Nyakamaturu, reaching the end of his 50-year reign, was evidently regarded as a weak and unpopular ruler. As a result, Kaboyo, the king's favourite son and chosen heir to the throne, had become impatient to claim his inheritance. In part, Kaboyo's haste might have been linked to a perceived threat to his future status: Nyakamaturu had already survived at least one attempted overthrow by a less-favoured son, while the elders of Bunyoro openly supported his younger brother Mugenyi as the next candidate for the throne. While on a tour of Toro c1825, Kaboyo came to realise the full extent of his father's unpopularity in this southern part of Bunyoro, and he was persuaded by local chiefs to lead a rebellion that left Toro a sovereign state.

Nyakamaturu's army had the better of the rebels in the one full-scale battle that occurred between them, but the ageing king was not prepared for his favourite son to be killed, and he eventually decided to tolerate the breakaway state. It has even been suggested that Kaboyo was invited to succeed the Banyoro throne after Nyakamaturu's death in the early 1830s, but declined, leaving the way clear for Mugenyi to be crowned King of Bunyoro. By all accounts, Kaboyo's 30-year reign over Toro was marked by a high level of internal stability, as well as a reasonably amicable relationship with Bunyoro.

The death of Kaboyo c1860 sparked a long period of instability in Toro. Kaboyo's son and nominated successor Dahiga proved to be an unpopular leader, and was soon persuaded to abdicate in favour of his brother Nyaika, who was in turn overthrown, with the assistance of the Baganda army, by another brother called Kato Rukidi. Nyaika was exiled to the present-day DRC, where he rebuilt his army to eventually recapture Toro, killing Kato Rukidi and reclaiming the throne as his own. Toro enjoyed a brief period of stability after this, but Nyaika was not a popular ruler, and the long years of civil strife had left his state considerably weakened and open to attack.

The start of Nyaika's second term on the Toro throne roughly coincided with the rise of Bunyoro's King Kabalega, who avowed to expand his diminished sphere of influence by reintegrating Toro into the ancient kingdom, along with various other smaller breakaway states. In 1876, Kabalega led an attack on Toro that left its king dead. The Banyoro troops withdrew, and a new Toro king was crowned, but he too was captured by Kabalega and tortured to death, as was his immediate and short-lived successor. The remaining Toro princes fled to Ankole, where they were granted exile, and for the next decade Banyoro rule was effectively restored to Toro.

And that might have been that, had it not been for a fortuitous meeting between the prominent Toro prince Kasagama (also known as Kyebambe) and Captain Lugard in May 1891, at the small principality of Buddu in Buganda. Kasagama was eager for any assistance that might help him to restore the Toro throne, while Lugard quickly realised that the young prince might prove a useful ally in his plans to colonise Bunyoro – 'Inshallah, this may yet prove a trump card', he wrote of the meeting in his

diary. Kasagama and his entourage joined Lugard on the march to Ankole, where they gathered together a small army of exiled Toro royalists. They then proceeded to march towards Toro, recapturing one of its southern outposts and most important commercial centres, the salt mine at Lake Katwe, then continuing north to the vicinity of Fort Portal, where a treaty was signed in which Kasagama signed away Toro sovereignty in exchange for British protection.

When Lugard left for Kampala in late 1891, leaving behind a young British officer named De Winton, the Kingdom of Toro had to all intents and purposes been restored, albeit under a puppet leader. De Winton oversaw the construction of a string of small forts along the northwestern boundaries of Toro, designed to protect it from any further attacks by Kabalega, and manned by 6,000 Sudanese troops who had been abandoned by Emin Pasha on his withdrawal from Equatoria a few years earlier. In early 1892, however, De Winton succumbed to one or other tropical disease, leaving Toro at the mercy of the Sudanese troops, who plundered from communities living close to the forts, and rapidly established themselves as a more powerful force than Kasagama and his supporters. The withdrawal of the Sudanese troops to Buganda in mid-1893 proved to be a mixed blessing: in the absence of any direct colonial presence in Toro, Kasagama briefly enjoyed his first real taste of royal autonomy, but this ended abruptly when Kabalega attacked his capital in November of the same year. Kasagama retreated to the upper Rwenzori, where several of his loyal followers died of exposure, but was able to return to his capital in early 1894 following a successful British attack on Kabalega's capital at Mparo.

Toro functioned as a semi-autonomous kingdom throughout the British colonial era. Kasagama died in 1929, to be succeeded by King George Rukidi II, a well-educated former serviceman who is regarded as having done much to advance the infrastructure of his kingdom prior to his death in 1965. In February 1966, King Patrick Kaboyo Rukidi III ascended to the Toro throne, only eight months before the traditional monarchies of Uganda were abolished by Obote. The king lived in exile until the National Resistance Movement took power in 1986, after which he enjoyed a distinguished diplomatic career serving in Tanzania and Cuba.

In July 1993, the traditional monarchies were restored by Museveni, and two years later Patrick Rukidi returned to Fort Portal for a second coronation. He died a few days before this was scheduled to take place, to be succeeded by his son Prince Oyo Nyimba Kabamba Iguru Rukidi IV who was only three years old when he came to power. The first years of the restored monarchy were marked by controversy. The sudden death of the former king just before he would have been restored to power attracted allegations of foul play from certain quarters. The plot thickened when Toro prime minister John Kataramu (one of three regents appointed to assist the young Oyo) was convicted for ordering the murder of another prince in 1999.

Following his official coronation in 2010, King Oyo is now in his mid 20s and is doing what he can to develop Toro through various charitable organisations. Thus far, however, the young king is yet to match the fundraising prowess of his mother Best Kemigisha, a close associate of Muammar Gaddafi, whose munificence funded the restoration of the derelict Toro Palace on a hill outside Fort Portal as well the expensive educations enjoyed by Oyo and his sister Komuntale. As a result, King Oyo named Gaddafi the 'defender' of his kingdom, and the Libyan dictator's miserable end in 2011 was deeply mourned in Toro, at least by those who had benefited from his philanthropy.

15

landmarks, unless perhaps you count the hilltop Omukama's Palace built in the 1960s and restored more recently with Libyan funds, but it does offer a very good selection of hotels, restaurants and nightspots, making it an agreeable place to settle into for a few days.

HISTORY The area around Fort Portal has strong associations with the legendary Bachwezi Empire. It is said the Ndahura, the first Bachwezi king, retired from his capital in Mubende after he abdicated in favour of his son Wamala, and that the many crater lakes in the vicinity were his creation. It seems probable that the site of the modern-day town served as the capital of Toro prior to 1891, when a British fort was constructed there to protect it from guerrilla raids by Omukama Kabalega of Bunyoro. Situated where the golf club is today, Fort Gerry, as it was originally known, was named posthumously after the British Consul General of Zanzibar Sir Gerald Portal, who arrived in Buganda in late 1892 to formalise its protectorateship and died of malaria on Zanzibar a few months later. Norma Lorimer, who travelled to Fort Portal in 1913, referred to the settlement as 'Toro', adding that it then consisted of 'about six bungalows, the bank, the Boma, the huts for a few KARs (King's African Rifles), the Indian bazaar and the native settlement'. By 1980, it had grown to become the largest town in western Uganda, and fifth countrywide, with a population of 28,800. It has grown at a relatively modest rate since then, but the current population of 56,000 still places it just inside the country's 20 largest settlements.

GETTING THERE AND AWAY Coming directly from Kampala, the surfaced 300km road to Fort Portal via Mubende can be covered in 4–6 hours in a **private vehicle**, depending on how quickly you drive and how easily you clear the traffic around the capital. Using public transport, **buses** are the safest option and cost US$7 one-way. The reliable Post Bus leaves from Kampala's central post office at 07.00 daily except Sundays, arriving in Fort Portal 4–6 hours later. Two other reliable but faster and more regular services can be recommended: Link Bus (\ 041 4255426; www.link.co.ug) leaves Kampala Qualicell every hour on the hour in either direction between 06.00 and 19.00, and arrives at Fort Portal at a small station on Kahinju Road opposite Africana Bar; Kalita Coaches (\ 048 3422959; m 0756 897930) runs five vehicles a day in either direction, leaving Kampala from Nabungu Road when full and its Fort Portal Terminal on Lugard Road at 07.00, 09.30, 11.00, 13.00 and 16.00.

Fort Portal lies only 60km north of Kasese – less than an hour's drive – along an excellent surfaced road, and it can also be approached from Murchison Falls National Park via Masindi and Hoima, a full day's drive – or better two days – along a route covered more fully on pages 326–7. The main point of arrival and departures for **matatus** is the new Nyakaseke Taxi Park off Bwamba Road, where they depart regularly to Kasese (*US$2, 60–90mins*), Bundibugyo (*US$3; 2–3 hrs*), Mbarara (*US$7; 4–5hrs*), Kampala (*US$7; 4–6hrs*) and Hoima (*US$10; 5–7hrs*). Note that all transport for Kibale National Park, Bigodi and the nearby crater lakes leaves from a separate park close to the Manga Bridge.

 WHERE TO STAY *Map, page 382, unless otherwise stated*
A good selection of accommodation suited to most tastes and budgets can be found in Fort Portal. Note, however, that the most exclusive accommodation in the immediate vicinity of Fort Portal is the out-of-town Kyaninga Lodge (pages 390–2), set on the rim of the eponymous crater lake. At the other end of the price scale, Kibale National Park's Sebitoli Camp (see page 406) is an underutilised

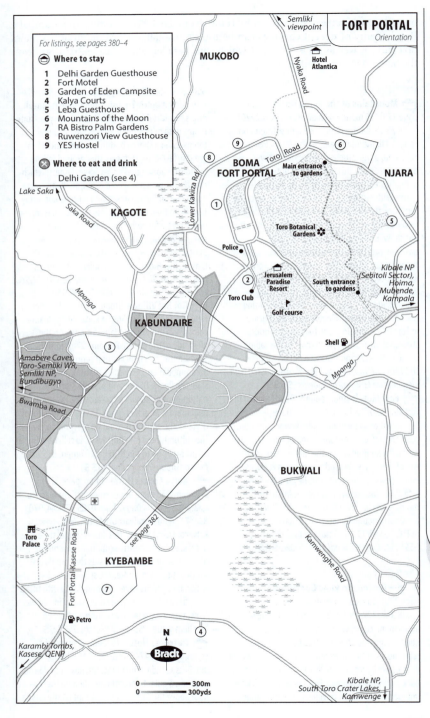

For listings, see pages 380–4

🛏 **Where to stay**

1 Delhi Garden Guesthouse
2 Fort Motel
3 Garden of Eden Campsite
4 Kalya Courts
5 Leba Guesthouse
6 Mountains of the Moon
7 RA Bistro Palm Gardens
8 Ruwenzori View Guesthouse
9 YES Hostel

✖ **Where to eat and drink**

Delhi Garden (see 4)

Semliki viewpoint

MUKOBO

Hotel Atlantica

Nyaka Road

BOMA
FORT PORTAL

Toro Road

Main entrance to gardens

NJARA

Lower Kakiiza Rd

Lake Saka

Saka Road

KAGOTE

Police

Toro Botanical Gardens

Kibale NP (Sebitoli Sector), Hoima, Mubende, Kampala

Mpanga

Jerusalem Paradise Resort

Toro Club

South entrance to gardens

Golf course

KABUNDAIRE

Shell

Amabere Caves, Toro-Semliki WR, Semliki NP, Bundibugyo

Mpanga

Bwamba Road

see page 382

BUKWALI

Toro Palace

Fort Portal–Kasese Road

Kamwenghe Road

KYEBAMBE

Petro

Karambi Tombs, Kasese, QENP

N

Bradt

Kibale NP, South Toro Crater Lakes, Kamwenge

0 ——— 300m
0 ——— 300yds

budget forest retreat situated only 16km from Fort Portal along the Kampala Road. Plenty of decent cheapies can be found on Malibo Road uphill of the main taxi park, as well as on Balya Road, which runs parallel to the Kasese Road. Some of the better ones are listed below.

Upmarket

Mountains of the Moon Hotel [map, page 379] (33 rooms) Nyaika Av; ✆ 048 3422201; m 0775 557840; e info@mountainsofthemoon. com; fb.me/Mountains.of.the.Moon.Hotel. Following a sumptuous & tasteful makeover a few years back, this colonial-era hotel set in manicured 7ha gardens offers comfortable rooms with terracotta floors & verandas, wooden furniture, flatscreen DSTV, tea-/coffee-making facilities, private balcony with seating & en-suite hot shower. The delightful veranda frontage has been provided with comfortable chairs & is the most attractive place in Fort Portal to enjoy a book/beer/meal, doze, watch the birdlife, or use the Wi-Fi. More active residents can enjoy a gym, sauna & a lovely stone-lined swimming pool. A comprehensive new menu, the priciest in Fort Portal, includes stir-fries, fajitas, grills, stews, salads & pizzas, with most mains falling in the US$8–13 range. Service can be variable. *US$120/140/160/230 B&B sgl/dbl/twin/suite, with discounts for East Africa residents.* **$$$$**

Fort Motel [map, page 379] (18 rooms) Off Toro Rd; m 0772 731307/0792 220259; e reservations@fortmotel.com; www.fortmotel. com. This restored 2-storey colonial bungalow lies in small neat grounds on the hilltop close to the site of Fort Gerry. Verandas, balconies & lawns enjoy views of the mountains beyond the town, & facilities include Wi-Fi & swimming pool. The rooms with clay-tiled floors, nets, DSTV & fridge are smart enough but starting to look in need of TLC. *US$90/110/115 standard sgl/dbl/twin, US$105/145/150 sgl/dbl/twin deluxe.* **$$$**

Moderate

✴ **Ruwenzori View Guesthouse** [map, page 379] (10 rooms) Lower Kakiiza Rd; ✆ 048 3422102; m 0772 722102; e ruwview@ africaonline.co.ug; www.ruwenzoriview.com. This outstanding guesthouse, set in the quiet back roads north of the town centre, has been showered with praise by readers since it first opened its doors back in 1997 & it remains Fort Portal's top pick for independent-minded travellers on a mid-range

budget. Owned & managed by the same friendly & hands-on Dutch-English couple all that time, it offers comfortable accommodation in airy en-suite rooms with nets & hot water, as well as a few rooms using a shared bathroom. Rates include a great b/fast, & most guests stick around for the wonderful home-cooked 4-course dinners, which cost US$11pp, & are served communally to create a sociable ambience in keeping with its homestay feel. More than 60 bird species have been recorded in the pretty flowering gardens, which face the glacial peaks of the Rwenzori. A selection of baskets & other local crafts is on sale. Wi-Fi is available. Highly recommended at the price. *US$22/33 sgl/dbl using common showers. US$42/60 en-suite sgl/dbl. All rates B&B.* **$$–$$$**

Koi Koi Village [map, page 374] (4 rooms) m 0751 744239/ 569569; e koikoivillage@gmail. com; fb.me/Koikoivillage. Situated on the west side of the Kasese Rd some 2km from the town centre, this new cultural centre also offers accommodation in stylish & spacious rooms with slate tile floors, DSTV, twin ¾ beds & private balconies offering views towards the Rwenzori. A restaurant is attached (page 383) & the location is quite idyllic, though it could be noisy on Sun when the cultural show is in full swing. Excellent value, & all proceeds go to the NGO Ensi Women. *US$50/58 twin on ground/upper floor.* **$$$**

Kalya Courts Hotel [map, page 379] (12 rooms, 30 more under construction) Maguru Itaara Rd; ✆ 039 2080321; m 0705 876044/0703 886471; e info@kalyacourtshotel.com; www. kalyacourtshotel.com. This smart single-storey hotel stands in extensive suburban grounds of hedge & lawn that look towards the Toro Palace south of the town centre. The spacious & airy white-tiled rooms have a modern look, with fitted nets, flatscreen DSTV, Wi-Fi & en-suite hot shower. A restaurant with terrace seating is attached. Excellent value. *US$39/69 B&B sgl/dbl.* **$$$**

Dutchess Hotel (5 rooms) Mugurusi St; m 0704 879474/0718 746211; e info@ dutchsuganda.com; www.dutchsuganda.com. Boasting a quiet but central location on the 1st-floor above the Dutchess Restaurant (& the town's

most varied & appetising menu), this small owner-managed hotel offers stylish & brightly coloured rooms with twin or dbl bed, fitted net, ceiling fan, screened windows, built-in safe, flatscreen DSTV, Wi-Fi & en-suite hot shower. There's also 1 non en-suite sgl. *US$65/80/105 B&B sgl/dbl/twin. US$30 sgl using shared bathroom.* **$$$**

🏠 **Reinah Tourist Hotel** (20 rooms) Cnr Kasese/Malibo Rd; ☎ 039 2175974; e info@reinahtouristhotel.co.ug. This characterless but rather slick multi-storey hotel has a useful location close to the taxi park & main bus termini, but rooms facing the road can also be quite noisy. Spacious rooms have queen-sized beds with walk-in net, flatscreen DSTV, writing desk, fridge, balcony & en-suite hot tub & shower. Rack rates are bit overpriced but negotiable. *US$63 B&B dbl.* **$$$**

Budget

✳ 🏠 **Daj Guesthouse** (6 rooms) Mugurusi Rd; ☎ 039 3176279; m 0781 584366. This smashing little hotel occupies an old Asian residence with a small green garden close to Stanbic bank. Large brightly coloured rooms come with fitted nets, DSTV & en-suite hot shower. It is popular & space is limited, so book ahead. *US$20/23 B&B sgl/dbl.* **$$**

🏠 **Delhi Garden Guesthouse** [map, page 379] (18 rooms) Government Rd; m 0716 010195. Beneficiary, one suspects, of a bulk sell-off of purple paint, this guesthouse's quirky feel is furthered by its courtyard being shaded by the rickety stilted wooden platform of the eponymous Indian restaurant. Pleasant clean rooms come with fitted nets, fan, flatscreen DSTV & en-suite hot shower. Good value, assuming you can live with the uniform interior & exterior colour scheme! *US$10/13/17 B&B sgl/dbl/twin.* **$**

🏠 **West End Motel** (15 rooms) m 0700 713833; e motel.westend@gmail.com. Tucked away on a quiet back street connecting to the main Kamwenge Rd, this pleasant 2-storey hotel has small but clean en-suite rooms with net, DSTV & hot shower set around a leafy courtyard. Good value. *US$17/20/24 B&B sgl/dbl/twin.* **$$**

🏠 **Rwenzori Travellers Inn** (22 rooms) Kasese Rd; ☎ 048 3422075; m 0712 400570/0774 504020; e reservations@rwenzoritravellersinn. com; www.rwenzoritravellersinn.com. This popular & sensibly-priced 3-storey block has comfortable en-suite rooms, a covered terrace restaurant where simple but tasty mains cost US$4–6, & a suspended orchid garden in the 1st-/2nd-floor atrium. You'll sleep most soundly in rooms as far as possible from the road & lively 1st-floor bar. *US$17/22/25 standard sgl/twin/dbl, US$33/40 superior twin/dbl. All rates B&B.* **$$**

🏠 **Saaka Motel** (18 rooms) Rukidi III Rd; m 0751 500413. This comfortable central hotel has clean & well-maintained en-suite rooms with net set around a 1st-floor courtyard. Fair value. *US$12/14/17 B&B sgl/dbl/twin.* **$$**

🏠 **Leba Guesthouse** [map, page 379] (3 rooms) 22 Njara Rd; m 0777 635333/0772 451662/0712 446304. Situated about 700m south of the main entrance to Toro Botanical Gardens, this homestay, run by a charming retired Ugandan couple, enjoys a lovely view towards the golf course & the Rwenzori. Advance booking is necessary. A large b/fast is provided but other meals are only by prior arrangement. *US$23pp B&B sgl/dbl.* **$$**

Shoestring

✳ 🏠 **YES Hostel** [map, page 379] (1 room & 10 dorms) Lower Kakiiza Rd; m 0772 780350 e yesuganda@gmail.com; http://caroladamsministry.com/yes_hostel.html. A Fort Portal NGO, which supports orphans Youth Encouragement Services (YES) runs a popular hostel set in a green garden that faces a delightful pastoral setting with mountain views north of the town centre. Accommodation is mostly in 4- or 6-bed dorms using common showers, but singles & couples will usually be given private use of a room unless the hostel is too full. All beds have a net. Other facilities include free Wi-Fi, solar-powered lighting & hot water, & a common room with seating & table tennis. A full b/fast costs US$3, while other mains are in the US$2–3 range. It's about 2km from the town centre; a boda should cost around US$0.30. *US$6pp in rooms, US$3pp camping.* **$**

🏠 **Morning Star Guesthouse** (8 rooms) Malibo Rd; m 0780 757097/0756 735150. Bright clean rooms with ¾ bed & net using common showers only 100m from the taxi park. *US$5 sgl.* **$**

🏠 **Mesh's Inn** (19 rooms) Malibo Rd; ☎ 0392 176281. Clean & pleasant rooms with net & hot shower, plus a ground-floor restaurant serving affordable local meals. *US$5 sgl using common shower, US$10 en-suite dbl.* **$**

15

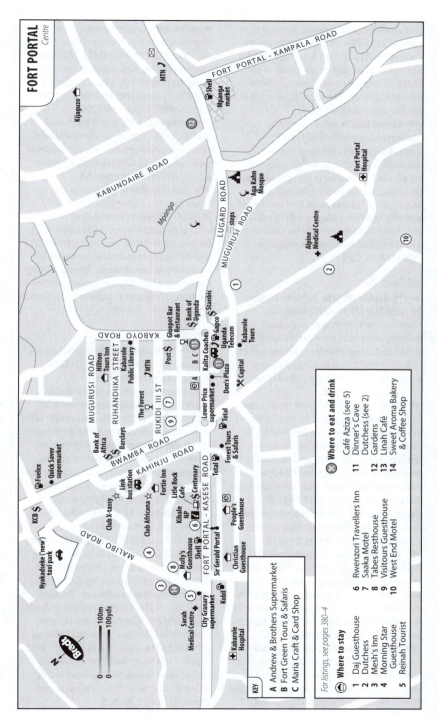

FORT PORTAL
Centre

Where to stay

A Andrew & Brothers Supermarket
B Fort Green Tours & Safaris
C Maria Craft & Card Shop

For listings, see pages 380–4

1 Daj Guesthouse
2 Dutchess
3 Mesh's Inn
4 Morning Star Guesthouse
5 Reinah Tourist

6 Rwenzori Travellers Inn
7 Saaka Motel
8 Tabes Resthouse
9 Visitours Guesthouse
10 West End Motel

Where to eat and drink

Café Aziza (see 5)
Dinner's Cave
Dutchess (see 2)
Gardens
Linah Café
Sweet Aroma Bakery & Coffee Shop

11
12
13
14

KEY

Fort Portal Hospital

Alpine Medical Centre

Aga Kahn Mosque

Mpanga market

Shell

FORT PORTAL – KAMPALA ROAD

Kijaguzo

KABUNDAIRE ROAD

Mpanga

LUGARD ROAD

MUGURUSI ROAD

Bank of Uganda

Stanbic

Gapco

Uganda Telecom

Kabarole Tours

Capital

Gluepot Bar & Restaurant

Post

Kalita Coaches

Don's Plaza

Lower Price supermarket

Total

Kabarole Public Library

Hillton Tours Inn

MTN

KABOYO ROAD

RUHANDIIKA STREET

The Forest

RUKIDI III ST

Barclays

Bank of Africa

BWAMBA ROAD

Forest Tours & Safaris

KAHINJU ROAD

Link bus station

Fortie Inn

Club Africana

Little Rock Café

Centenary

Kibale NP

People's Guesthouse

Guesthouse Shell

Christian Guesthouse

Sir Gerald Portal

FORT PORTAL – KASESE ROAD

Molly's Guesthouse

MALIBO ROAD

Nyakadseke (new) taxi park

KCB

Fuelex

Quick Saver supermarket

Club X-tassy

MUGURUSI ROAD

Kobil

City Granary supermarket

Sarah Medical Centre

Kabarole Hospital

MTN

Fort Portal Hospital

Total

N

0   100m
0   100yds

🏠 **Tabes Resthouse** (16 rooms) Malibo Rd; m 0714 775620. The town's best cheapie offers clean, tiled 1st-floor rooms with nets above a grim courtyard. A balcony even provides Rwenzori views. *US$5 sgl with common facilities. US$7/8 en-suite sgl/dbl.* $

🏠 **Visitours Guesthouse** (39 rooms) Lugard Rd; m 0772 927063. Located on the corner of Bwamba Rd, adjacent to, but better value than, the Continental. *US$5 sgl with shared facilities, US$10 en-suite dbl.* $

Camping
🏕 **Garden of Eden** [map, page 379] Off Kabundaire Rd; m 0783 343108. Tucked away at the back of what passes as the town's industrial area, this new campsite occupies a lush meadow close to the Mpanga River. You'll find a bar & restaurant, a butterfly & chameleon garden, cycad nursery & a resident woodcarver. *Camping US$5pp.* $

🏕 **RA Bistro Palm Gardens** [map, page 379] Kasese Rd; m 0772 339340; https://palmgardensp.wordpress.com. Set in 7ha of terraced gardens complete with patches of natural forest (plenty of monkeys & birds) & a canal used to breed tilapia (canoeing & fishing permitted), this quaint family-run campsite is only 1km from the bustle of the town centre but it feels like another world. Facilities are limited to an ablution block with cold showers. *Camping US$5pp.* $

🍴 **WHERE TO EAT AND DRINK** *Map, page 382, unless otherwise stated*
In addition to the restaurants listed below, the covered terrace facing the manicured gardens at the Mountains of the Moon Hotel is a fabulous spot for a relaxed outdoor meal, though the food is a touch pricey and service is variable. Another very pleasant spot for a meal or drink is the Koi Koi Village out along the Kasese Road (page 380). See also the entry for Lake Kyaninga on page 395.

Moderate to expensive
✴ 🍴 **Dutchess Restaurant** Mugurusi St; m 0704 879474/0718 746 211; www.dutchessuganda.com; ⏱ 07.00–23.00 daily. This brightly decorated Dutch-owned &-managed deli & restaurant is generally rated the best in Fort Portal. It offers the choice of indoor, terrace or garden seating, with views to the Rwenzori peaks on a clear day. An innovative & varied menu, with light meals & mains, includes pizzas, salads & sandwiches, while specialties include crocodile burgers, porterhouse steak & chicken cordon bleu. The best coffee in town is complemented by a good wine list. There's fast but not free Wi-Fi throughout & an internet café is attached. Self-caterers will appreciate the range of cheeses, breads & salamis. *Mains in the US$4–9 range.*

✴ 🍴 **Linah Café** Lugard Rd; m 0701 711347; ⏱ 07.00–22.00 daily. This highly regarded recent addition to Fort Portal's culinary scene occupies the same building that used to house the Gluepot Bar, but with more grace & style. The wood-&-cane furniture lends the fan-cooled interior a contemporary feel, while a cosmopolitan menu includes gourmet burgers, imaginative salads, wrap, stews & grills. No alcohol is served, but the blended juices are delicious, & it also serves good coffee, shakes & smoothies. *Meals in the US$5–7 range.*

🍴 **Gardens Restaurant** Junction Lugard Rd & Kabundaire Rd; ☎ 048 3422090; ⏱ 07.00–22.30 daily. The wide & shady terrace here is Fort Portal's favourite rendezvous spot, set a few hundred metres downhill from the town centre opposite the Mpanga River bridge & junction for Kampala Rd. The excellent lunchtime buffet is a favourite with tour groups on the go, & decent value at US$5. Pizzas are the à la carte specialty, but it also does good burgers & grills, including a great pork escalope. There's also a well-stocked bar & great coffee, juices & smoothies. *Most mains cost around US$4–8.*

Cheap to moderate
✴ 🍴 **Dinner's Cave** Off Lugard Rd; m 0751 790657; e dinnerscave@hotmail.com; ⏱ 07.00–22.00 Mon–Sat. Popular with budget-conscious volunteers & locals alike, this small restaurant has an indifferent ambience & obscure location along a small alley, but the food produced by the Kenyan chef scores highly when it comes to both quality & value for money. Pepper steak with mash is the specialty, but it serves a range of other grills & pastas. *Most dishes around US$3–4, salads US$1.*

✴ 🖥 **Sweet Aroma Bakery & Coffee Shop** Malibo Rd; m 0790 916151; ⏱ 08.00–19.00 Mon–Sat. Delicious fresh cakes & biscuits,

15

& a good selection of teas & coffees are served at this cosy & inexpensive café with terracotta tiling, cane furniture & free Wi-Fi. It's currently owned & managed by an American philanthropist with a long-term plan to have locals take over once it is properly up & running. *Most items less than US$1.*

�excafe **Delhi Garden Restaurant** [map, page 379] Government Rd; m 0716 010195; �clock 08.00–23.00 daily. This Indian-owned restaurant, set on a sparsely-furnished & oddly lopsided wooden platform, serves very good Indian food, as well as a few Ugandan selections for those who prefer it low on spice. *Meat dishes around US$4, vegetarian selections US$3, & naan or rice will add another US$1.*

✗ **Café Avizia** Cnr Kasese/Malibo Rd; m 0781 015497; e cafeazivia@gmail.com; ⏰ 24hrs daily. Set on the ground floor of the Reinah Tourist Hotel (page 381), this smart modern eatery has a massively varied menu embracing Chinese & Indian cuisine, as well as pizzas, grills, burgers & salads. Beverages include fresh coffee, juices, milkshakes & smoothies. *Mains in the US$5–7 range.*

BARS AND NIGHTLIFE

🍷**Gluepot Bar & Restaurant** Lugard Rd; m 0777 661919. Fort Portal's longest-serving & most popular drinking hole has been lubricating throats since the 1950s, with Wed initially being busiest, as expats trundled into town to meet the weekly tilapia truck from Lake George. Today, despite the name, it's closer to being a disco than a bar or restaurant, having relocated upstairs to a thatched dance floor whose large-screen TVs & even larger speakers would doubtless have caused the original colonial clientele to flee straight back to from whence they came. Great fun, with an inclusive atmosphere, especially on Fri & Sat nights, when it kicks into full action late & keeps going into the early morning.

🍷**The Forest Bar** Rukidi III St; m 0772 912349. Slightly more sedate than the Gluepot, this popular & well-stocked garden-style bar is a good place for a not-too-quiet evening drink, to watch football & other sporting action on large screens, or to play a game of pool.

☆ **Club Africana** Off Bwamba Rd. This down-to-earth bar & club behind the Link bus terminal has terrace seating where you can cool off between dances.

☆ **Club X-tassy** Off Bwamba Rd. Also adjoining the Link terminal, this relatively classy nightclub keeps going until the early morning over weekends. If you're still going at dusk, the Café Avizia, right around the corner & open 24/7, will be a welcome sight.

☆ **Jerusalem Paradise** Toro Rd; m 0775 619557; ▆ fb.me/JerusalemParadiseFort. This quirky set-up, sandwiched between the golf course & Toro Botanical Garden, is convenient for those staying in the northern suburbs. The garish indoor bar is complemented by a large garden, while a bewilderingly large selection of fruit & vegetable cocktails (complete with some unexpected New-Age hype about their benefits) shares menu space with a more conventional selection of alcoholic drinks & bar snacks.

SHOPPING The best general store is **Andrew & Brothers Supermarket** (*Lugard Rd; m 0772 55 4602*), which stocks a good range of local and imported food and drinks. For fresh brown bread, your best bet is the **Dutchess Restaurant**, which also has a deli selling cheese and other goodies. The large **Mpanga Market** opposite Gardens Restaurant is the place to buy fresh produce and much else besides. The **Maria Craft and Card Shop** on Lugard Road sells high-quality cards, clothes and other handicrafts made by a church-affiliated vocational training centre near Fort Portal.

OTHER PRACTICALITIES

Foreign exchange Stanbic and Barclays banks provide their usual ranges of forex and ATM services.

Internet The fastest internet and Wi-Fi is at Dutchess Restaurant. Several other internet cafés are dotted around the town centre.

Swimming The Mountains of the Moon Hotel charges US$5 for non-residents to use its swimming pool.

Sports Kyaninga Lodge organises an annual triathlon in April (*www.kyaningatriathlon.com*) and marathon/half-marathon in November (*www.runningtheriftmarathon.com*) to raise money for children living with disabilities.

TOURIST INFORMATION

Kibale National Park Office Lugard Rd; ☏ 039 2175976; e knp@ugandawildlife.org; ⏰ 08.00–17.00 Mon–Fri & 08.00–14.00 Sat. This helpful information office allows you to book chimp tracking & habituation permits on the spot, assuming availability, but payments must be made at the park headquarters at Isunga (page 399). It also sells a range of books & maps, & is a good source of up-to-date information about activities & facilities at the underused Sebitoli sector.

TOUR OPERATORS

Kabarole Tours Molidina St; m 0774 057390; e ktours@infocom.co.ug; f fb.me/KabaroleTours; ⏰ 08.00–18.00 Mon–Sat, 10.00–16.00 Sun. This commendable setup, operated by the same hands-on owner-manager since it opened in 1992, has a positive attitude to budget travellers complemented by its active role in the development & support of community ecotourism projects around Fort Portal. Its office is plastered with flyers, maps & information sheets about regional tourist attractions, so it effectively doubles as a tourist information office. Although it has now expanded its services to include countrywide tours, it remains very active locally & can arrange a variety of reasonably priced day or overnight driving excursions to the likes of Kibale National Park & nearby crater lakes, the Semliki Valley or Queen Elizabeth National Park.

Forest Tours & Safaris Lugard Rd; m 0792 909604/0788 652575; e foresttoursandsafaris@gmail.com; www.foresttoursandsafaris.com. This new operator next to the Total filling station is committed to helping tourists interact with local people & experience local food, music, crafts & traditional medicine, etc. In addition to offering community walks, it also arranges tours to Kibale, Queen Elizabeth & Semliki national parks.

Fort Green Tours & Safaris Lugard Rd; m 0788 651535/0777 638415; e fortgreentours@gmail.com; f fb.me/FortGreenToursAndSafaris. This new company has been recommended for offering a range of affordable day & overnight tours out of Fort Portal.

WHAT TO SEE AND DO The section below covers most sites of interest within or close to Fort Portal, but it excludes several popular day trips detailed elsewhere in this chapter under the headers *Toro Crater Lakes* and *Kibale National Park* (pages 388 and 397). Fort Portal is the sole road gateway to the Semliki Valley, the subject of *Chapter 16*, and the usual starting point for the Northern Rwenzori mini-hike between Kazingo and Bundibugyo detailed in *Chapter 17*.

Northern suburbs Both the sites listed below lie a short walk north of the town centre, amidst the green administrative suburbs that also house the Mountains of the Moon Hotel, Ruwenzori View Guesthouse and YES Hostel.

Fort Gerry and the Toro Club The short-lived 1891 construction after which Fort Portal is named once stood on a hill about 1km north of the modern town centre. All that survives of it is a defensive trench that now partially encloses the Toro Club, where a bronze plaque commemorating Fort Gerry is still displayed. The focal point of the Toro Club (m *0772 479492*) is the lovely nine-hole Fort Portal Golf Course, which was laid out across 3ha of well-wooded land back in 1914.

Non-members pay US$10 to play a round, and caddies are available along with clubs for hire. The sociable clubhouse bar is reliably busy on weekend evenings.

Toro Botanical Gardens (e *tooboga@yahoo.com*; ⊕ *08.00–17.00 Mon–Sat, 09.00–16.00 Sun; entry US$3*). Founded in 2001 with the objective of conserving and promoting awareness of the Albertine Rift flora, this commendable garden occupies around 50ha of forested valley between the Mountains of the Moon Hotel and the golf course. It contains demonstration gardens of medicinal plants, herbs and spices, fruits, flowers and trees, and the entrance fee includes an optional guided tour. It is also a good place to look for typical woodland and forest birds, including great blue turaco, Ross's turaco and black-and-white flycatcher, and birding guides are available for US$7. The main entrance is on Njara Road opposite the Mountains of the Moon Hotel, but if you're coming from the town centre, it's quicker to walk out to the second entrance 1km along the Kampala Road. Organised birding tours can be booked through the Ruwenzori View Guesthouse.

Kasese Road The attractions listed below lie alongside the Kasese Road as it runs southwest from Fort Portal, and can easily be reached by boda or matatu.

Toro Palace (⊕ *0.64716, 30.26848; www.torokingdom.org*) Perched on Kabarole Hill immediately south of the town centre, Toro Palace is an imposing but rather charmless two-storey circular monolith constructed in 1963 for Omukama Rukidi III. Looted in the wake of the abolition of the old kingdoms under Obote, the palace had been reduced to little more than a concrete shell by the time Omukama Oyo was crowned in 1995, but it was fully restored in 2001, at considerable expense to royal benefactor President Gaddafi of Libya. It's worth walking or driving up Kabarole Hill for the panoramic view over the town and surrounding countryside, and there's some talk of eventually opening a proper museum within its crowning palace. For the time being, however, the palace remains unoccupied, casual visitors are forbidden from entering it, and those who approach too closely might be asked to pay the caretaker an 'entrance fee' equivalent to US$5 for being informed of this fact.

Koi Koi Village Cultural Centre (⊕ *0.63383, 30.2652; m 0751 744239/ 569569; e koikoivillage@gmail.com; ☐ fb.me/Koikoivillage; ⊕ 09.00–23.00 daily*) The brainchild of an NGO called Ensi Women (*www.ensiwomen.org*), this stylish new tourist 'one-stop shop' is set in lush gardens looking towards the Rwenzori, 2km out of town along the Kasese Road. In addition to good accommodation, it incorporates a quality handicraft shop, a gallery of contemporary paintings by locally based artists, a museum displaying traditional items from Toro and elsewhere in Uganda, and a modern restaurant with indoor and terrace seating and a varied menu that includes whole tilapia, pepper steak, grilled half chicken, burgers and pasta, mostly in the US$4–6 range. The biggest draw, however, is the charismatic music and dance performances of the 16-strong cultural troupe Angabu Za Toro (*Tradition of Toro; http://engabuzatooro.blogspot.co.za*), which performs in the garden every Sunday from 13.00 to 21.00, when a small entrance fee (less than US$1) is levied.

Karambi Tombs (⊕ *0.6342, 30.24553; m 0779 357646; ⊕ 08.00–18.00 daily; entry US$3*) Situated 3km southwest of Toro Palace as the crow flies, the Karambi Tombs comprises a thatched construction housing the graves of three former Toro kings – Kasagama (died 1928), Rukidi II (died 1965) and Rukidi III (died 1995) – along with

an open-air cemetery where several lesser members of the royal family are buried. Plans to renovate the tombs and develop them as a tourism attraction were announced in November 2015, and include the eventual construction of a museum, restaurant, bar and swimming pool. For the time being, the friendly and softly spoken caretaker – grandson of the original guardian appointed after the death of Omukama Kasagama – will happily show visitors inside the tombs, which are decorated with various royal paraphernalia. The unsignposted tombs lie 150m off the Kasese Road and can be reached by following it out of Fort Portal for 5.5km to the village of Karambi, then turning right 50m before a large whitewashed mosque on the left.

Rubona Basket Weavers Association (*RUBOWA;* m *0782 562640*) Situated on the west side of the Kasese Road in the village of Rubona 22km from Fort Portal, the Rubona Basket Weavers Association is a cooperative of more than 200 women that produce *ekibo*-style baskets – colourful, flattish and circular – using raffia palm fibre and organic pigments made from *Rubia* roots and other indigenous plants. The intricately patterned baskets make wonderful wall hangings, and while most are sold to international markets or through outlets in Kampala, a good selection is available to be bought directly from RUBOWA for up to US$10 apiece.

Mugusu and Rwimi markets The colourful weekly markets at Mugusu (✪ *0.61229, 30.21278*) and Rwimi (✪ *0.37734, 30.2171*), which lie along the Kasese Road below the Rwenzori peaks, are important social events, and well worth visiting if you're in town on the right day. The Wednesday market at Mugusu, 10km south of Fort Portal, is mostly concerned with second-hand clothing, attracting buyers from as far afield as Kampala. The more conventional Friday vegetable and food market at Rwimi, about 45km south of Fort Portal, is very large and colourful, with a spectacular setting.

Rwagimba hot springs This little-visited site is set in the deep Rwimi River Valley in the shadow of the Rwenzori, 12.5km west of the Kasese Road. Don't expect too much from the actual springs – this is not Iceland or Yellowstone – but rather go for the walk there, which provides a great opportunity to stretch your legs in superb mountain scenery with no national park entry fees. The actual springs comprise a pair of excavated pools beside the Rwimi River, one for women, the other for men. Despite the calm and contented expressions of the folk sitting in the pool, the water is hot! And the possibility of a temperature-related incident is not limited to the pools. Paddle in the adjacent river and shuffle your feet down into its sandy bed, and you'll experience confusingly contrasting sensations as your ankles numb in the glacial meltwaters while the soles of your feet heat up to the point of pain. To get there, first head to Kibito, roughly 30km south of Fort Portal on the Kasese Road, then drive or catch a boda west for 6km to the village of Rwagimba. From here, the up-and-down 6km hike to the springs takes around 2–3 hours, culminating in a particularly steep and rocky decent to the narrow rocky floodplain of the Rwimi River. Rather than trying to find your own way, we suggest you hire John (m *0784 690018*), an experienced former employee of Kabarole Tours whose home, indicated by a roadside 'Tourist Guide' signpost beside a set of speed bumps, lies on the northern end of Kibito near Yeriya School. There is no fee to visit the springs but John charges US$7 per person for his guiding services.

Semliki Viewpoint The rift escarpment near Harugongo, about 10km north of Fort Portal, offers some spectacular views over the Semliki Valley to Lake Albert

almost 1,000m below. To get there follow Toro Road north out past the Mountains of the Moon Hotel for about 8km until you reach Harugongo trading centre, then continue north for 500m to a T-junction (⊕ *0.73846, 30.27895*), where you need to turn right. After 1.2km, you'll pass Harugongo Sub-County Headquarters, then after another 1km, you'll see St Raphael Catholic Church signposted to the left (⊕ *0.74583, 30.2965*). Take this left turn and continue for about 2.5km to the main viewpoint (⊕ *0.76472, 30.29277*). Using public transport, you could catch a matatu to Harugongo, then walk the last 5km, or take a boda all the way from Fort Portal. Kyaninga Lodge organises guided day hikes to the viewpoint for its guests.

TORO CRATER LAKES

A scenic highlight of Toro subregion is the concentration of jewel-like crater lakes that runs between Fort Portal and Kibale National Park, providing the setting for some wonderfully sited upmarket and budget lodges from which to explore the fertile countryside or track Kibale's chimps. A total of more than three-dozen permanent crater lakes can be found in Toro, scattered across a 10km-wide longitudinal band that runs parallel to the western boundary of Kibale National Park from Fort Portal south to Kasenda. Geographically, there are two main groups of lakes: an isolated quintet set in the hilly countryside immediately north of Fort Portal, and a much larger and more sprawling cluster that starts about 15km from Fort Portal as the crow flies. For logistical regions, however, we have divided the southern lakes into three further subgroups. These are: the Rweetera cluster of three lakes on the west side of the main road between Fort Portal and Kibale Forest; the Rwaihamba cluster of about ten lakes focussed around Nkuruba, Rwaihamba and Kabata; and the Kasenda cluster of about 20 lakes sprawling in all directions from Kasenda trading centre. Set below a majestic Rwenzori backdrop and offering easy access to Kibale National Park, this fertile lakes region is dominated by lush cultivation, but it also supports many relict pockets of indigenous forest and swamp, together with a profusion of birds, monkeys and butterflies, providing almost limitless opportunities for casual exploration.

GEOLOGY, FLORA AND FAUNA The Toro Crater Lakes are the most northerly component in a vast field of volcanic calderas that runs south from Fort Portal via Queen Elizabeth National Park to the Rift Valley Escarpment around Bunyaruguru. Legend has it that these fertile craters, overshadowed by the glacial peaks of the Rwenzori, and numbering more than 100 in total, are the bountiful handiwork of Ndahura, the first Bachwezi king. Geologically, the craters – many of which formed within the last 10,000 years and host small freshwater or saline lakes – provide a graphic reminder of the immense volcanic forces that have moulded the landscapes of western Uganda.

The fertile volcanic soils and high annual rainfall of the lakes region ensures it supports a lush mosaic of verdant tropical cultivation, forest, grassland and swamp. While the region lacks the biodiversity of neighbouring Kibale National Park, the relict forest patches associated with the steep-sided calderas wherein the lakes are nestled are often conspicuously inhabited by monkeys and forest-associated turacos, hornbills, barbets and sunbirds. For wildlife enthusiasts, the highlight of the region is probably the communally-managed Lake Nkuruba Nature Reserve, but the grounds of upmarket lodges such as Ndali and Kyaninga are also very rewarding.

GETTING THERE AND AWAY All lodges and places of interest associated with the Rweetera, Rwaihamba and Kasenda clusters can be approached from Fort Portal

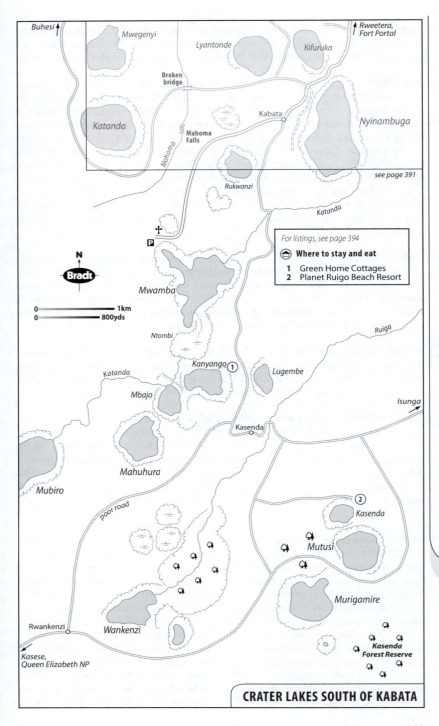

Buhesi

Mwegenyi

Lyantonde

Kifuruka

↑ Rweetera,
Fort Portal

Broken
bridge

Kabata

Nyinambuga

Katanda

Mahoma
Falls

see page 391

Rukwanzi

Katanda

N

Bradt

For listings, see page 394

⊕ **Where to stay and eat**

1   Green Home Cottages
2   Planet Ruigo Beach Resort

Mwamba

Ruiga

0 ――――――― 1km
0 ――――――― 800yds

Ntombi

Kanyango ①

Lugembe

Katanda

Mbajo

Kasenda

Isunga

②
Kasenda

Mahuhura

poor road

Mutusi

Mubiro

Murigamire

Rwankenzi

Kasenda
Forest Reserve

Wankenzi

Kasese,
Queen Elizabeth NP

CRATER LAKES SOUTH OF KABATA

along the route described below. Exceptions are Rujuna Hilltop Lodge, Kluge's Guest Farm and Bella Vista, which are most easily accessed from the Kasese Road, and Kyaninga Lodge to the north of Fort Portal (see individual entries for more details).

Self-drive Heading from central Fort Portal to any of the crater lakes south of here, you follow Lugard Road north for a few hundred metres, then turn right on to the Bigodi Road immediately before the Mpanga River Bridge. After 12km, the road forks at Kasisi (⊕ *0.57552, 30.31015*). Heading to the Rwaihamba or Kasenda clusters, take the right fork at Kasisi, and continue along a fair dirt road that arrives at Lake Nkuruba, Rwaihamba, Kabata/Ndali Lodge and Kasenda after 8km, 10km, 13km and 18km respectively. To get to the Rweetera cluster, bear left at Kasisi (as if heading to Kibale National Park) and you'll reach the lodges associated with lakes Nyinabulitwa and Nyabikere after another 8–11km.

Coming from Queen Elizabeth National Park or Kasisi, an unsurfaced short cut to Kasenda and Rwaihamba branches east from the Kasese–Fort Portal Road about 1.5km north of Rwimi.

Public transport A few matatus run daily from Fort Portal to both Rwaihamba and Kasenda, along a road that tends to be busiest on Rwaihamba's market days (Mon and Thu). They leave Fort Portal from a stand close to Mpanga Bridge, and can drop you anywhere *en route* (*US$2.50; 1hr*). If you are heading to a lodge in the Rweetera cluster, you need a matatu for Bigodi (page 399). It is also possible to charter a boda from Fort Portal to any of the lakes.

 WHERE TO STAY In addition to the lodges and camps listed on the following pages, any hotel in Fort Portal can be used as a base for exploring the Toro Crater Lakes. Equally, most lodges associated with the crater lakes are well placed for chimp tracking in Kibale National Park, assuming you have private transport.

The Fort Portal cluster and Kasese Road *Map, page 374*
Of the four lodges listed below, Kyaninga Lodge lies on the rim of the eponymous crater lake a few kilometres north of Fort Portal, while the other three all lie alongside or a short distance east of the main Kasese Road. Kyaninga Lodge and Kluge's Guest Farm rank among the most popular upmarket bases from which to track Kibale's chimps, while Bella Vista is uniquely well-positioned as a base from which to explore both Kibale and Queen Elizabeth national parks.

Exclusive

* 🏠 **Kyaninga Lodge** (8 cottages) m 0772 999750; e info@kyaningalodge. com; www.kyaningalodge.com; see ad, 4th colour section. This monumental masterpiece of imaginative engineering took 7 years to construct using massive eucalyptus logs. It comprises a central dining/reception area & 8 spacious luxury cottages (all with king-sized bed, walk-in net, en-suite hot shower & well-appointed private balcony) connected by tall timber catwalks & flights of wooden steps. It is perched on the eastern rim of the stunning 220m-deep Kyaninga Crater Lake, which lies 4km north of Fort Portal as the crow flies, & offers a view across startlingly blue waters hemmed in by forested cliffs to the rolling green hills of Toro & (weather permitting) snow-capped Rwenzori peaks. A 2.4m deep swimming pool overlooks the lake, while the 60ha grounds incorporate a grass tennis, badminton & croquet court, as well as a vegetable garden & orchard providing organic produce to the kitchen. Activities include a 3-hour forest walk (good for colobus monkeys & birds) & a 90-minute walk around the crater rim, while a footpath also leads down to the shore of the bilharzia-free lake, where you can swim or explore on a canoe. To get to Kyaninga, head 2km out of town along the Kampala Rd, then turn left up the Kijura Rd, then left again

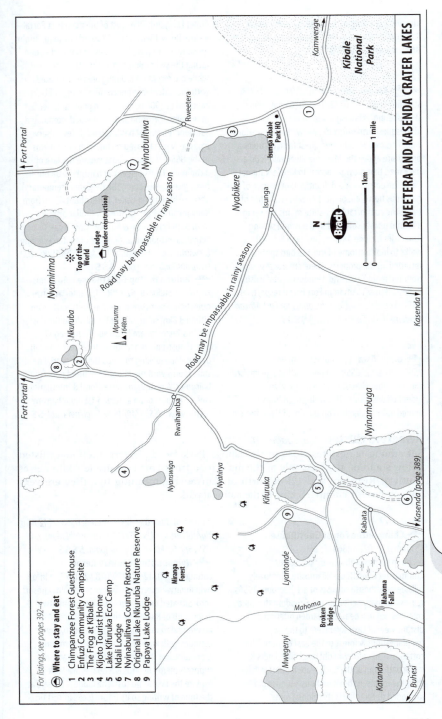

RWEETERA AND KASENDA CRATER LAKES

Kibale National Park

N

Bradt

0   1km
0   1 mile

Kamwenge

Fort Portal

Rweetera

Nyinabulitwa

Isunga Kibale Park HQ

Nyabikere

Isunga

Kasenda

Road may be impassable in rainy season

Top of the World

Lodge (under construction)

Nyamirima

Nkuruba

Mpurumu
▲ 1648m

Fort Portal

Road may be impassable in rainy season

Rwaihamba

Nyanswiga

Nyahirya

Kifuruka

Nyinambuga

Kasenda (page 389)

Kabata

Lyantonde

Miranga Forest

Mahoma

Broken bridge

Mahoma Falls

Mwegenyi

Katanda

Buhesi

For listings, see pages 392–4

ⓘ **Where to stay and eat**
1 Chimpanzee Forest Guesthouse
2 Enfuzi Community Campsite
3 The Frog at Kibale
4 Kijoto Tourist Home
5 Lake Kifuruka Eco Camp
6 Ndali Lodge
7 Nyinabulitwa Country Resort
8 Original Lake Nkuruba Nature Reserve
9 Papaya Lake Lodge

15

after 2km at a signposted turning & carry on for 4.5km. *US$360/485 sgl/dbl FB, discounts for East Africa residents.* $$$$$

Upmarket

✳ 🏠 **Kluges Guest Farm** (10 rooms & 7 standing tents) m 0772/0755/0701 440099; e marketing@klugesguestfarm.com or klugesguestfarm@gmx.de; www.klugesguestfarm. com. This owner-managed guest farm occupies a pretty site above the Mahoma River Valley, on a back road that provides access to Kibale National Park. The entrance is a delight: a 1km avenue of gorgeous flowering plants beneath twin lines of trees. The comfortable en-suite rooms are set in a formal terrace softened by a pastoral setting. Amenities include a swimming pool & forest walks to look for some of the 175 bird species recorded on the property. There are 2 access roads from the main Kasese Rd, signposted at Kasusu & Buhesi, 3km & 15km from Fort Portal respectively. *US$135/165 B&B sgl/dbl, discounts for East African residents. US$15pp camping.* $$$$

Moderate

🏠 **Bella Vista** (10 rooms) m 0794 756577/0794 756558; e booking@lodgebellavista. com or lodgebellavista@gmail.com; www. lodgebellavista.com. This well-priced Italian-owned lodge is perched on the rim of Nyamiteza

Crater Lake, only 2km east of the main Fort Portal–Kasese Rd, & 13km west of Kasenda by road. Bright en-suite rooms have balconies on both sides, one facing the swimming pool & the other the lake, while the reception & dining area is decorated with eye-catching monochrome images of Uganda captured in 1906 by the Italian photographer & mountaineer Vittorio Sella. The wood-dominated 1st-floor restaurant has a splendid view & serves a pasta- & pizza-based menu, with most mains in the US$4–7 range. Negatives are the lack of a communal outside deck or balcony, & on our most recent inspection, the (hopefully temporary) absence of running water. It lies about 40km from Kanyanchu Visitors' Centre & a similar distance from both Fort Portal & Kasese. More local activities include mountain bike or motorcycle hire & swimming or boating at the lake. *US$65/85/100 twin/dbl/king-sized B&B.* $$$

🏠 **Rujuna Hilltop Guesthouse** (10 rooms) m 0772 930608/0752 930608; e info@rujuna-guesthouse.com; www.rujuna-guesthouse.com. Situated 8km south of Fort Portal along the Kasese Rd, this 2-storey family-owned & -managed guesthouse enjoys a fabulous location on a high grassy slope looking towards the Rwenzori. En-suite rooms with tiled floor have fitted nets & balconies. A restaurant serves local & international cuisine indoors or on a shaded 1st-floor balcony with a view. *US$35/40/45 B&B sgl/twin/dbl.* $$

Rweetera cluster *Map, page 391*

Set among tea estates close to the Isunga Park Headquarters, the lodges listed below stand on the west side of the main road from Fort Portal, a few kilometres south of Rweetera and 12km north of Kanyanchu, meaning that they are very convenient for chimp tracking in the national park.

Upmarket

🏠 **Chimpanzee Forest Guesthouse** (7 rooms) m 0772 486415; e chimpgueste@yahoo.com; 🔲 fb.me/ ChimpanzeeGuestHouseNCampsite. This lovely hillside guesthouse consists of a 2-bedroom 1950s tea-estate manager's house & 5 modern thatched cottages, set in a beautiful garden offering a distant view of Lake Nyabikere to the north, & tea plantations & forest to the east & south. The cottages – all with twin dbl beds, fitted nets & stone bathroom at the back – are far better value than the rooms in the main house, whose old-fashioned décor reflects its colonial roots.

A range of guided walks is offered. *US$83/142 B&B sgl/dbl cottage, US$77/118 B&B sgl/dbl room. Add US$25pp for FB. US$7pp camping.* $$$$

🏠 **Nyinabulitwa Country Resort** (5 cottages) m 0712 984929/0782 291577; e info@ nyinabulitwaresort.com; www.nyinabulitwaresort. com. Situated on the rim of Lake Nyinabulitwa 3km south of Rweetera, this lodge offers accommodation in spacious thatched luxury cottages with walk-in nets, wooden furniture & en-suite hot showers. The forested crater rim supports plenty of birds & a boat is available to explore the lake at no cost. The lodge is for sale at the time of writing so its future looks uncertain.

US$70/120 sgl/dbl B&B. Add US$10pp for a cottage with terrace, US$10 for lunch, & US$15 for dinner. Camping costs US$15pp. **$$$$**

Budget & camping

🏠 **The Frog at Kibale** (8 rooms) m 0780 176166; e thefrogatkibale@gmail.com; www. thefrogatkibale.com. Formerly Crater Valley Kibale Resort, this long-serving & perennially rundown budget lodge has an idyllic position on the forested rim of Lake Nyabikere. Red-tailed monkey &

black-&-white colobus are resident in the lushly vegetated grounds, & the birdlife is excellent, with more than 100 species recorded. Said somewhat improbably to be 400m deep, Nyabikere means 'lake of frogs' & you'll usually hear plenty of these croaking through the night. Accommodation is provided in pleasant (but currently quite overpriced) en-suite bandas that are likely to be renovated under the dynamic new management. Meals cost around US$7. *US$33/43/53 sgl/dbl/ twin. US$10pp camping. All rates B&B.* **$$**

Rwaihamba cluster *Map, page 391*

The main cluster of accommodation associated with the Toro Crater Lakes lies along the 5km stretch of road running south from Lake Nkuruba to the junction village of Kabata. It includes two top-notch exclusive options in the form of Ndali Lodge and the newer Papaya Lake, along with one of our favourite community ecotourism ventures anywhere in Uganda, i.e. the budget-friendly original, Lake Nkuruba Nature Reserve. With private transport, all these lodges are conveniently based for chimp tracking, whether you follow the main road back through Kasisi, or take one of two 4x4-only short cuts – an 8.5km dirt track between Rwaihamba and Isunga, or a 5km dirt track between Lake Nkuruba and Rweetera – that are sometimes impassable after rain.

Exclusive

☀ 🏠 **Ndali Lodge** (8 cottages) m 0772 221309; e info@ndalilodge.com; www.ndalilodge. com; see ad, 4th colour section. Situated 1km south of Kabata along a narrow private road, owner-managed Ndali Lodge has ranked among Uganda's most highly regarded lodges since 1996, when it opened on a tea estate founded in the 1920s by the same family that owns it today. Set in colourful gardens on the rim of the beautiful Lake Nyinambuga, the lodge has an English country-house ambience offset by the fine western panorama across rolling hills & crater lakes towards the Rwenzori Peaks. Spacious & stylishly decorated thatch cottages come with walk-in nets, en-suite hot baths, solar bedside lights & private verandas. Other amenities include a swimming pool, an airy lounge decorated with etchings of flora & fauna, an excellent library & superb candlelit 5-course dinners & b/fasts served with silver cutlery. Kibale Forest is the main draw, but guests should be sure to explore the local lakes & trot down the hill to visit the estate farm, which supplies organic vanilla to several British supermarkets. *US$535/720 sgl/dbl cottages FB, discounts for East African residents.* **$$$$$**

☀ 🏠 **Papaya Lake Lodge** (8 cottages) m 0793 388277; e info@papayalakelodge.com;

www.papayalakelodge.com; see ad, 4th colour section. Opened in 2015, this Polish-owned & -managed lodge sprawls across the forested inner slope of the crater that encloses the beautiful Lake Lyantonde. The secluded cottages, with wooden floor & tall thatched ceiling, are spacious, airy & cleanly decorated in contemporary classic style. They come with 1 dbl & 1 sgl wood & wrought-iron bed, both with walk-in nets, balcony with lake view, & large en-suite hot shower. A magnificent dining area adorned with ethnic artefacts overlooks the lake, & there's a lovely elevated swimming pool area behind the main lodge. Birds & monkeys are plentiful. *Rates by application.* **$$$$$**

Moderate

🏠 **Kitojo Tourist Home** (4 rooms) m 0772 469333; e info@kitojotouristhome.com. Attractively sited on a small hill 2.5km west of Rwaihamba, this homely development enjoys good regional views & access to the crater lakes. Profits support the Kitojo Integrated Development Association, a local NGO that provides medical, financial & agricultural services to HIV/AIDS-infected community members. En-suite cottage accommodation available but no alcohol. *US$30pp B&B, US$40pp FB.* **$$$**

Budget, shoestring & camping

✳ 🏠 **Original Lake Nkuruba Nature Reserve** (9 cottages) m 0773 266067/0782 141880; e lake_nkuruba@yahoo.com; www. nkuruba.com. Protecting a jungle-fringed crater lake 2km north of Rwaihamba, this well-maintained & laidback community-run reserve & rest camp (proceeds fund a local primary school) is a perfect budget base from which to explore the crater lakes. The self-explanatory Rwenzori view bandas come with net & paraffin lamp, while the solitary lakeside cottage & en-suite hilltop bandas also have electric lighting. Decent meals are available for US$3–7, & beers & sodas are also sold on site. Amenities include mountain-bike hire & a short hiking trail from where you are likely to see red colobus, black-&-white colobus & red-tailed monkey along with a good variety of forest birds. Guided walks to Mahoma Falls, Top of the World, etc, are also offered. *US$25 en-suite dbl or twin, US$20 dbl lakeside cottage, US$12/18 sgl/dbl banda with shared bathroom, US$3pp camping.* **$$**

🏠 **Lake Kifuruka Eco Camp** (4 rooms) m 0772 562513/0773 640655; e info@ecolodge-uganda.com; www.ecolodge-uganda.com. This basic facility overlooks Kifuruka Crater Lake only 100m from Kabata junction. The site is rather bare & exposed, but the cottages are tucked below the crater rim & enjoy a good view over the lake. Guided walks on offer at US$15pp include a 3-hour round trip to Mahoma Falls & a 6-hour circuit taking in 9 crater lakes. *US$7/14pp with shared/ en-suite bathrooms, US$3pp camping.* **$$**

🏠 **Enfuzi Community Campsite** (5 rooms) m 0782 972756/779910; e pastorbosco@yahoo.com; www.enfuzicommunitycampsite.com. Set on the southern rim of Lake Nkuruba, this newer camp is inferior to the Original Lake Nkuruba Nature Reserve is most respects & its claim to be a community-based project is rather spurious, but the musty cottages are a lot cheaper. Be aware that local boda & matatu drivers have, in the past, been incentivised to drop travellers asking to stay at Lake Nkuruba here instead of at the Original Nature Reserve next door. *US$5pp for a room, or US$3pp to camp.* **$**

Kasenda Lakes cluster *Map, page 389*

The two accommodation facilities listed below are somewhat isolated and remote, which is part of their charm. They could be used as chimp-tracking bases, but realistically only by travellers with private transport.

Budget, shoestring & camping

🏠 **Planet Ruigo Beach Resort** (24 rooms) m 0754 509717. So remote that you might as well be in outer space, the most southerly lodge in the crater lake region lies almost 3km from Kasenda trading centre & is reached via a 1.5km track through lovely forest that terminates inside a small crater containing the pretty Lake Kasenda. A variety of bandas, some en suite, is dotted around the sprawling resort, & there are plenty of opportunities for guided & unguided walks in the forest to the immediate north & other crater lakes to the south. A good range of forest & water birds can be seen on site, along with 4 monkey species, & swimming is reputedly safe. Usually it is very quiet, but it is occasionally taken over by large groups of Spanish tourists, so you might

want to call ahead to check. Meals cost around US$8 & there's a well-stocked bar. It lies beyond the reach of public transport, so those without their own car will need to walk the last 3km, or hire a boda from Fort Portal (expect to pay US$5–7). *US$12/20 dbl with common/en-suite shower. US$3 camping.* **$$**

🏠 **Green Home Cottages** (4 cottages) m 0772 333203; e aphia.barungi@gmail.com or 4greencottages@gmail.com. This serene retreat lies about 1km north of Kasenda village on the west side of the road back to Kabata. The wood-&-concrete cottages lie in the rim of Lake Kanyangi, which is nestled in a steep crater surrounded by lushly vegetated cliffs. Several other crater lakes lie within 1km of the lodge. *US$45/50/60 B&B sgl/ dbl/family cottage.* **$$$**

WHAT TO SEE AND DO As with accommodation, the activities described on the following pages are grouped together under the four main crater lake clusters: Fort Portal, Rweetera, Rwaihamba and Kasenda. The lodges serving the crater lakes are also regularly used as bases for chimp tracking in Kibale National Park and the swamp walk in Bigodi.

Fort Portal cluster The sites listed below are associated with the small group of crater lakes that lies immediately north of Fort Portal. They all make straightforward targets for a day trip out of the town.

Lake Kyaninga The most spectacular of the crater lakes north of Fort Portal is also the site of Kyaninga Lodge (pages 390–2), which offers a superb view across the emerald-green water and forested cliffs of the twin calderas to the Rwenzori Peaks. When the lodge isn't too busy, day visitors are usually welcome to enjoy a two- or three-course lunch (*US$18/22*) or dinner (*US$20/23*) – a thoroughly enjoyable and rather decadent outing, but booking is absolutely essential, and availability depends on overnight occupancy. Lunch and dinner guests are also welcome to swim in the lake and explore the trails on the lodge property. More ambitiously, Ruwenzori View Guesthouse (page 380) can organise a guided 8km hike from Fort Portal to the Kyaninga, culminating in lunch or dinner, though once again this depends on how busy the lodge is.

Amabere Caves and Lake Kigere Situated 5km west of Fort Portal as the crow flies, the small cave known as Amabere (⊕ *0.67602, 30.22594;* m *0785 352193;* ◷ *07.00–18.00 daily; entry US$10*) is notable less perhaps for its visual impact than for its cultural significance as the reputed birthplace of the founding Bachwezi king Ndahura (see box, page 396). The main cave is very small, really more of an exaggerated overhang, though it is supported by several pillar-like formations of connected stalactites and stalagmites. Alongside it, you can stand on the moss-covered rocks behind a powerful small waterfall and watch the ice-cold water plunge down right in front of you, kicking spray back into your face. It's said to be safe to swim in the pool below the falls, though the water is very chilly. The riparian forest around the waterfall is rattling with birds, and it supports a few black-and-white colobus monkeys. From Amabere, 10–15-minutes' walk northeast leads you to Kigere Crater Lake, which is surrounded by dense stands of plantains and palms, and is reportedly safe for swimming.

Amabere used to be a popular goal for a day hike out of Fort Portal, but following a recent threefold increase in the entrance fee, it gets mixed reviews, since many people feel it is a bit too low-key to justify the cost. To get there by car or boda, follow the Bundibugyo Road out of Fort Portal for 6km to a signposted junction to the right (⊕ *0.66331, 30.22881*), from where it's another 2km to the school, turning right halfway, immediately before the entrance to Nyakasura School (founded by an eccentric Scotsman in 1926 and whose male students still wear kilts).

Lake Saka The largest water body in the immediate vicinity of Fort Portal, Saka is not strictly speaking a crater lake, but rather a flooded valley dammed by a crater. It is one of the few lakes in the area to support fish large enough for commercial harvesting, and it is reputedly safe to swim in. It's possible to walk there directly from Fort Portal over 1½ to 2 hours. Coming from the town centre, follow Lugard Road downhill for a few hundred metres until you cross the bridge over the Mpanga River, then (just before Gardens Restaurant) turn left into the small industrial area, curving to the right after 500m, then bearing left after another 500m, where it becomes Saka Road. From here, continue straight for about 5km, then just after you pass a small col to the left, turn left (⊕ *0.69193, 30.25318*) on to a 1km track that leads to the eastern lakeshore. On the way back, you might want to climb the above-mentioned col, actually a pair of adjoining craters, one with a lushly forested

floor and the other nesting a tiny lake. Alternatively, if your legs are up for it, you could loop back to Fort Portal via the Amabere Caves, which lie about 2km to the southwest of Lake Saka, passing by Lake Kigere on the way.

Rweetera cluster The most popular activity here is a circular walking trail that follows the rim of Lake Nyabikere from the Frog at Kibale. There is no charge for walking this trail, nor is any guide required. Black-and-white colobus and other monkeys are often encountered, while a varied selection of resident birds includes Ross's turaco, great blue turaco, pygmy goose, little bittern and black-crowned night heron. More energetically, you could continue on foot to Nyinabulitwa and Nyamirima, both of which lie on the west side of the Fort Portal Road, respectively 1.5km and 2.5km north of the Frog at Kibale. Another attractive walk follows the driveable track from Rweetera to emerge on the Kasenda Road a few hundred metres south of Lake Nkuruba. There are great views over the three crater lakes from Mpurumu Hill to the south of this track.

Rwaihamba cluster The activities below can all be undertaken independently, but they can also be organised as guided outings through Go Swamp Walk and Vanilla Tours (m *0778 125903;* e *goswampwalkandvanillatours@gmail.com*), a Rwaihamba-based community project that offers nature walks, crater-lake exploration, village tours, birding, swamp walks and cultural visits.

Lake Nkuruba Nature Reserve Known mainly for the great budget camp on its rim (page 394), Lake Nkuruba, though small, is also very beautiful, and well worth a visit even if you are staying elsewhere. The lake is enclosed by a steep forest-lined crater in which red-tailed monkey, red colobus and black-and-white colobus are resident, while at least 100 species of bird might be seen on the limited network of walking trails near the lake (a regularly updated checklist is pinned up in the office). The water is

considered to be free of bilharzia, which if true means there's no obstacle to swimming. A nominal entrance fee is charged to day visitors but not to overnight guests.

Lake Nyahirya From Lake Nkuruba, the tiny forest-fringed Lake Nyahirya can be reached by walking south along the road to Kabata, passing through Rwaihamba trading centre after 2km, then continuing 1km further to a sharp westward kink in the road. The lake lies 500m west of this kink – if you're uncertain, ask in Rwaihamba for directions. A second crater lake, Nyanswiga, lies 1km directly to the north of Nyahirya. Rwaihamba hosts a large, colourful market on Mondays and Thursdays.

Around Kabata This small junction village, 5km south of Lake Nkuruba by road, is the site of Ndali Lodge and Lake Kifuruka Eco Camp. On the left side of the road as you approach Kabata, the relatively large Lake Nyinambuga, named for its mildly saline water, is enclosed by steep cliffs on which stands Ndali Lodge (a view, incidentally, that appears on the Ush20,000 banknote). To the right, the smaller forest-fringed Lake Kifuruka is a good place to look for black-and-white colobus as well as Ross's turaco, great blue turaco, African grey parrot, yellow-billed duck and pygmy goose. Only 1km west of Kabata, Lake Lyantonde is set in a thickly vegetated crater that also now houses Papaya Lake Lodge. Also accessible from Kabata, Mahoma Falls (*entry fee US$5, payable at Lake Kifuruka Eco Camp, optional guide US$10 per person*) surges with more than a little conviction over a series of large boulders into a forested valley. Below the waterfall, you can swim in the river – it flows at a velocity that should negate any fears about bilharzia, and the crisp water is a welcome treat after a sweaty walk.

Kasenda cluster Three further crater lakes can easily be seen from the 6km road running south from Kabata to Kasenda trading centre. About 1.5km past the main junction in Kabata, Lake Rukwanzi lies only 100m to the right of the road, but is invisible from it. Another 1.5km further, also on the right, the much larger Lake Mwamba has an irregular outline suggesting that it fills several different collapsed calderas. Finally, another 1.5km towards Murukomba, and again on the right, the stunning Lake Kanyangi, overlooked by Green Home Cottages, lies within 200m of the road, also hidden by a cliff. Directly opposite Kanyangi, Lake Lugembe lies at the base of a very deep and sheer-sided steep crater, no more than 25m left of the road, but also invisible from it.

Several more crater lakes can be found to the south of Kasenda. The only one that's developed for tourism is the lushly forested Lake Kasenda, site of the Planet Ruigo Beach Resort (page 394), a friendly set-up that's also your best source of information about exploring the area further.

KIBALE NATIONAL PARK

Uganda's premier chimpanzee-tracking destination, Kibale National Park protects 766km^2 of predominantly forested habitat that extends more than 50km south from the main Kampala–Fort Portal Road to the northeast border of Queen Elizabeth National Park. Originally gazetted as a forest reserve in 1932, Kibale was upgraded to national park status, and extended southward to form a contiguous block with the Queen Elizabeth National Park, in 1993. The trailhead for chimp tracking and main centre of tourist activity within the park is the Kanyanchu Visitors' Centre, which lies 35km south of Fort Portal along a soon-to-be-surfaced road continuing south to Kamwenge. Chimps aside, Kanyanchu offers some superb forest birding

and monkey viewing, with the community-run Bigodi Wetland Sanctuary, only 5km away immediately outside the park boundary, being a particular highlight in this respect. While Kibale National Park and Kanyanchu are practically synonymous so far as most visitors are concerned, a lesser-known secondary point of entry – no chimp tracking offered, but good for forest walks – can be found at the northerly Sebitoli Sector, 15km east of Fort Portal along the Kampala Road.

FLORA AND FAUNA Kibale National Park is dominated by rainforest, but this is interspersed with tracts of grassland and swamp. Spanning altitudes of 1,100–1,590m, Kibale boasts a floral composition transitional to typical eastern Afro-montane and western lowland forest with more than 200 tree species recorded in total. Unlike Budongo Forest to its north, Kibale wasn't logged commercially until the 1950s, when it became an important source of timber for the Kilembe Copper Mine near Kasese, and logging was discontinued during the civil war. As a result, areas of mature forest are still liberally endowed with large-buttressed mahoganies, tall fruiting figs, and other hardwood trees whose canopy is up to 60m above the ground. It also supports a dense tangle of lianas and epiphytes, while the thick undergrowth includes wild Robusta coffee.

At least 60 mammal species are present in Kibale National Park. It is particularly rich in **primates**, with 13 species recorded, the highest total for any Ugandan national park. Kibale Forest is the most important stronghold of Ugandan red colobus, but it supports eight other diurnal primate species: vervet, red-tailed, L'Hoest's and blue monkeys; Uganda mangabey; black-and-white colobus; olive baboon; and chimpanzee. It also supports four species of nocturnal prosimian including the sloth-like potto.

While Kibale Forest offers superlative primate viewing, it is not an easy place to see other large **mammals** – this is despite an impressive checklist which includes lion, leopard, elephant, buffalo, hippo, warthog, giant forest hog, bushpig, bushbuck, sitatunga, and Peter's, red and blue duikers. The elephants found in Kibale Forest belong to the forest race, which is smaller and hairier than the more familiar savannah elephant. Elephants frequently move into the Kanyanchu area during the wet season, but they are not often seen by tourists.

Roughly 335 **bird** species have been recorded in Kibale, including four species not recorded in any other national park: Nahan's francolin, Cassin's spinetail, blue-headed bee-eater and masked apalis. Otherwise, the checklist for Kibale includes a similar range of forest birds to Semliki National Park, with the exclusion of the 40-odd Semliki 'specials' and the inclusion of a greater variety of water and grassland species. A recent first sighting of a green-breasted pitta caused some excitement in Ugandan ornithological circles, while the truly optimistic might want to look out for the Kibale ground-thrush, a presumably endemic species or race collected by Alexandre Prigogine in 1978 and yet to be seen again. The most productive birding spots are generally Bigodi Wetland Sanctuary and the stretch of main road running either side of Kanyanchu Tourist Centre.

FURTHER INFORMATION A very useful and inexpensive 60-page UWA-produced booklet on Kibale National Park can be bought at Kanyanchu. Uganda Maps Sheet 7 *Fort Portal and the Kibale Forest* (*www.east-africa-maps.com*) shows the national park and crater lake area in great detail.

FEES The entrance fee to Kibale National Park is US$40/30 non-resident/resident per 24 hours. This fee is not charged to people who are simply staying overnight at

one of the two accommodation facilities set within the national park (eg: Kibale Primate Lodge and Sebitoli Camp), nor for driving along the sections of the Fort Portal–Bigodi or Fort Portal–Kampala Road that bisect it, nor – more obviously – for staying at any lodge or undertaking any activity outside its boundaries.

Per person activity fees applicable to Kibale National Park are: US$150/100 non-resident/resident for chimp tracking (dropping to US$100/75 in April, May and November); US$220/150 for the full-day chimp habituation experience; US$40/20 for night walks; US$30/15 for daytime forest walks; and US$30 (irrespective of residence status) for guided birding. The park entrance fee is included in the activity fees for chimp tracking and habituation, but excluded from the cost of other activities. This means that anyone already paying for a chimp-related activity will not need to pay an additional entrance fee on any other activities they undertake within the same 24-hour period.

Since Kibale National Park is on the new card system (*www.ugandawildlife.org/wildlife-card*), it seems that entrance and activity fees for Kanyanchu (including chimp-tracking permits) can be paid only at the UWA reservations office in Kampala or at the Isunga Park Headquarters (near Chimpanzee Forest Guesthouse, 11km back along the Fort Portal Road). Local information suggests that by 2017, Kanyanchu will be the beneficiary of a new entrance gate where fees can be paid. Visitors to Sebitoli can pay entrance and activity fees on the spot.

KANYANCHU AND BIGODI The Kanyanchu Visitors' Centre and village of Bigodi, situated only 5km apart on the main road to Kamwenge, form the focal point of most tourist visits to the Fort Portal area. A common itinerary for rushed tour parties is to track chimps from Kanyanchu in the morning, then – assuming they still have the energy – to do the Bigodi Swamp Walk (outside the national park) in the afternoon. For those able to take a more leisurely approach, we would recommend against doing Bigodi Swamp Walk in the afternoon, mainly because the birding is far better in the morning. Note, too, that because the national park entrance fee of US$40 is included in the chimp-tracking fee, you could do another activity in the park within the same 24-hour period without having to pay an entrance fee.

Getting there and away Kanyanchu Visitors' Centre and Bigodi respectively lie 35km and 40km south of Fort Portal on the road to Kamwenge. Currently a dirt road, the stretch between Fort Portal and Bigodi was in the process of being widened in 2015, and should be fully surfaced within the lifespan of this edition. Note that you'll pass Isunga Park Headquarters (where any outstanding national park fees must be paid) about 23km out of Fort Portal.

Two alternative road approaches to Kanyanchu could be considered. The first, coming from Ankole, is the newly surfaced road from Mbarara to Bigodi via Ibanda and Kamwenge. The other, coming from Queen Elizabeth National Park and Kasese, is the unsurfaced short cut branching east from the Kasese-Fort Portal road about 1.5km north of Rwimi.

Matatus between Fort Portal and Bigodi (*US$2.50; 1hr*) run throughout the day, leaving Fort Portal from close to Mpanga Bridge. A few matatus also run daily between Fort Portal and Mbarara via Bigodi, Kamwenge and Ibanda. These typically leave Fort Portal at 08.00, arrive in Bigodi at around 09.00, and get to Mbarara by 13.00, then start the return trip from Mbarara at around 14.00, passing through Bigodi between 17.00 and 18.00, and reaching Fort Portal an hour later. If you miss the direct matatus, plenty of more localised public transport runs along the surfaced

road from Mbarara to Bigodi, but you may need to change vehicles at Ibanda or Kamwenge. Larger buses are likely to start using this road between between Mbarara and Fort Portal once the stretch north of Bigodi is surfaced.

Where to stay *Map, page 374*

Spanning everything from budget homestays to upmarket bush lodges, the accommodation described below is focussed on Bigodi, a small village straddling the main road 5km south of the chimp-tracking trailhead at Kanyanchu Visitors' Centre. It also includes Kibale Primate Lodge, which is situated right next to Kanyanchu and is the only private accommodation set within the national park.

Upmarket

Kibale Primate Lodge (16 rooms) ✆ 0.43735, 30.39498; 0414 267153; m 0701 426368/0776 411316; e info@ugandalodges. com; www.ugandalodges.com. Situated less than 5mins' walk from the chimp-tracking trailhead, this atmospheric lodge in the heart of the jungle is alive with mysterious rustles & bird calls during the day, & washed over by a white noise of cicadas & other insects after dark. Rebuilt & upgraded in 2015, the luxurious new thatched cottages come with stylishly earthy décor, timber floor, king-sized bed with walk-in net, indoor seating, private balcony, large glass windows & spacious en-suite hot shower. The older cottages have been refurbished to semi-luxury standards. For adventurous travellers, an isolated budget treehouse overlooks a scenic elephant wallow 10mins' walk from the main camp. *US$266/414 cottages FB, US$144/198 sgl/dbl tents FB, US$49/64 treehouse B&B, US$14pp camping (meals excl). For those not on FB, meals are in the US$14–19 range.* **$$$–$$$$**

Kibale Forest Camp (17 tents) ✆ 0.3903, 30.40486; 031 2294894, m 0779 820695; e booking@naturelodges.biz; www.naturelodges.biz. This long-serving tented camp, set in a pretty forest patch 2km south of Bigodi, is now managed by Nature Lodges, who spruced up the rooms & slashed the prices to make it a contender for the best value facility in the vicinity of Kibale Forest. Classic en-suite safari tents have slate floors & bright ethnic décor, & there are also some cheaper & more basic tents using common showers on a slope leading down to a lily-covered river. Monkeys & birds are plentiful around the camp, which is centred on a 2-storey wood-&-thatch restaurant/bar. *US$90/115 en-suite sgl/dbl, US$30/45 sgl/dbl with common shower. All rates B&B. Add US$10/15pp for lunch/dinner.* **$$–$$$**

Chimps' Nest (14 rooms) ✆ 0.40331, 30.38348; m 0774 669107; e info@chimpsnest. com; www.chimpsnest.com. This rustic setup, reached via a 3km feeder road branching west from Nkingo (between Kanyanchu & Bigodi), provides reasonably priced accommodation in a forest setting in the Dura River Valley on the edge of Kibale National Park. The small characterful stilted en-suite cottages are set in regenerating farmland & face a hillside of pristine forest across the river. A gorgeous tract of onsite swamp forest drips with palms, climbers, orchids & tree ferns, with plenty of birds & monkeys, while chimps & elephants are often heard. Budget cottages also available. *US$90/210 sgl/ dbl cottage B&B. US$25 budget dbl (bed only). Add US$18/30 for HB/FB.* **$$$$**

Kibale Guest Cottages (10 rooms) ✆ 0.42051, 30.40155; m 0785 726101/0702 839376; e reservations@kibaleguestcottages. co.ug; www.kibaleguestcottages.co.ug. Set in a neat garden of lawn & hedges leading down to the forested national park boundary, this place feels more 'country' than 'bush'. The thatched en-suite rooms are spacious & attractively furnished with wrought-iron beds, fitted nets, hot tub/shower & small private balcony. Fair value. *US$118/177/266 sgl/dbl/trpl FB.* **$$$$**

Kibale Safari Lodge (10 rooms) ✆ 0.41975, 30.39963; 031 2277304; m 0772 515672; e reservations@kibalesafarilodge.com; www.kibalesafarilodge.com. Functional but unremarkable accommodation in large twin or dbl standing tents set on stilted platforms & carved into a forest clearing. Overpriced. *US$150/300 sgl/ dbl FB.* **$$$$$**

Moderate/budget

The best moderate to budget options are the cheaper tents & rooms at Kibale Forest Camp & Chimps' Nest, as listed above.

Shoestring & camping

☀ 🏠 **Tinka's Homestay** (2 rooms)
⊕ 0.40505, 30.40879; m 0772 468113;
e comm-tour@infocom.co.ug. Owned by an
articulate & engaging local conservationist who
helped set up the nearby Bigodi Swamp Walk,
this homestay offers visitors the chance to share
local meals with the family, assist with food
preparation, & plant or harvest crops in the garden.
The tiled twin rooms are en suite & clean but have
no nets. *US$17pp FB.* **$$**

🏠 **Bigodi Community Lodge** (11 rooms)
⊕ 0.40616, 30.40846; m 0772 997289.
Conveniently located opposite the office for Bigodi
Swamp Walk, this misleadingly named private

lodge is owned by a former national park guide
& has co-community links. Simple rooms with
¾ beds & nets, & use of common cold showers.
Overpriced but negotiable. *US$10 per room, sgl or
dbl occupancy.* **$**

🏠 **Safari Hotel** (7 rooms) ⊕ 0.42053,
30.4016; m 0772 468113; e comm-tour@
infocom.co.ug. Now under the same management
as Tinka's Homestay, the stalwart Safari Hotel in
Nkingo is the closest budget option to Kanyanchu,
situated only 3km further south along the road
to Bigodi. Local meals cost around US$3. Rooms
are not en suite, but clean pit toilet & warm basin
showers are provided. Overpriced. *US$13pp.
US$3pp camping.* **$$**

✖ Where to eat and drink *Map, page 374*

Most people will eat at their lodge or camp, but two standalone eateries aimed at
tourists can be found in Bigodi close to the office for the swamp walk.

✖ **Ecoburrito** m 0780 142926; e ecoburrito.
uganda@gmail.com, www.ecoburrito.com. Situated
right next to the Bigodi Swamp Walk office, this
new community-run outdoor eatery serves delicious
vegetarian burritos & tortilla chips with guacamole.
Cheaper snacks are also served, along with beers,
sodas & coffee. *Mains around US$3 per plate.*

✖ **Tinka's Homestay** m 0772 468113. Perhaps
200m from the Bigodi Swamp Walk office, this
place offers filling buffets, eaten barefoot on floor
mats, of various traditional meat & vegetarian
dishes. It's a popular diversion for safari groups, but
needs to be arranged in advance. *US$5pp.*

What to see and do

Chimp tracking and habituation A highlight of any visit to Kibale National
Park will be the chimp-tracking excursions that leave twice-daily from Kanyanchu, at
08.00 and 14.00. Chimp sightings are not guaranteed on these walks, but the odds of
encountering them now stand at well above 90%. The chimpanzee community whose
territory centres on Kanyanchu is well habituated, with the result that visitors can
often approach to within 8–10m of individuals feeding or grooming on the ground,
though it is more difficult to get close or clear sighting when the chimps are on the
move or feeding high in the trees. Standard tracking excursions usually take up to 3
hours, including the maximum period of 1 hour with the chimps. A good alternative
for those who think they'll want to spend longer with the chimps is the habituation
experience, which allows you to hang around all day while researchers take notes.

Chimp-tracking permits cost US$150/100 non-resident/resident, while the
habituation experience costs US$220/150. Ideally, permits should be booked in
advance, as only 72 can be issued for any given day (36 each in the morning and
afternoon). If permits are still available on the day, they can be issued on the spot,
but this is unlikely to happen in season, especially over January, February, August
and September. Last-minute availability can be checked at the national park office
in Fort Portal or at Kanyanchu, but permits can be issued and paid for only at the
UWA booking office in Kampala or at the Isunga park headquarters. The easiest
months to get permits at short notice (though nothing can be guaranteed) are April,
May and November, when arrivals are so low that UWA drops the tracking fee to
US$100/75 FNR/FR.

Most likely you'll hear them before you see them. An excited hoot from somewhere deep in the forest; just one voice at first, then several, rising in volume and tempo and pitch to a frenzied unified crescendo, before it stops abruptly or fades away. Jane Goodall called it the 'pant-hoot' call, a kind of bonding ritual that enables any chimpanzees within earshot of each other to identify exactly who is around at any given moment, through the individual's unique vocal stylisation. To the human listener, this eruptive crescendo is one of the most spine-chilling and exciting sounds of the rainforest, and a strong indicator that visual contact with man's closest genetic relative is imminent.

It is, in large part, our close evolutionary kinship with chimpanzees that makes these sociable black-coated apes of the forest so enduringly fascinating. Though different DNA studies have yielded different percentages, it is universally agreed that humans, chimpanzees and bonobos (also known as pygmy chimpanzees) are more closely related to each other than to any other living creature, gorillas included. A few superficial differences notwithstanding, the similarities between humans and chimps are consistently striking, not only with regard to the skeletal and skull structure, but also the nervous system, the immune system, and many behaviours – bonobos, for instance, are the only animals other than humans to copulate in the missionary position.

Unlike most other primates, chimpanzees don't live in troops, but instead form extended communities of up to 100 individuals, which roam the forest in small, socially mobile subgroups that often revolve around a few close family members such as brothers or a mother and daughter. Male chimps normally spend their entire life within the community into which they were born, whereas females often migrate into a neighbouring community after reaching adolescence. A high-ranking male will occasionally attempt to monopolise a female in oestrus, but the more normal state of sexual affairs is non-hierarchical promiscuity. A young female in oestrus will generally mate with any male chimp that takes her fancy, while older females tend to form close bonds with a few specific males, sometimes allowing themselves to be monopolised by a favoured suitor for a period, but never pairing off exclusively in the long term.

Within each community, one alpha male is normally recognised – though coalitions between two males, often a dominant and a submissive sibling – have often been recorded. The role of the alpha male, not fully understood, is evidently quite benevolent – chairman of the board rather than crusty tyrant. This is probably influenced by the alpha male's relatively limited reproductive advantages over his potential rivals, most of whom he will have known for his entire life. Other males in the community are generally supportive rather than competitive towards the alpha male, except for when a rival consciously contests the alpha position, which is far from being an everyday occurrence. One male in Tanzania's Mahale Mountains maintained an alpha status within his community for more than 15 years between 1979 and 1995!

Little was known about chimpanzee behaviour until the early 1960s, when three separate pioneering studies – all still active today – were established in East Africa. Best known is the behavioural study established by Jane Goodall in Tanzania's Gombe Stream National Park in 1960, but other projects were founded in 1962 in Uganda's Budongo Forest by Prof Vernon Reynolds and in 1965 in Tanzania's Mahale Mountains National Park by Prof Toshisada Nishida.

The longstanding assumption that chimps are strictly vegetarian was rocked when Jane Goodall witnessed her subjects hunting down a red colobus monkey

in Gombe Stream. Such behaviour has since been discovered to be common and widespread, particularly during the dry season when other food sources are depleted. An average of 20 kills is recorded in Gombe annually, with monkeys being the prey on more than half of these occasions, though young bushbuck, young bushpig and even infant chimps have also been victimised and eaten. Closer to home, researchers in Uganda's Kalinzu Forest have observed blue monkeys and red-tailed monkeys being eaten by chimps, as well as unsuccessful attempts to hunt black-and-white colobus. The normal *modus operandi* is for four or five adult chimps to slowly encircle a monkey troop, then for another chimp to act as a decoy, creating deliberate confusion in the hope that it will drive the monkeys into the trap, or cause a mother to drop her baby.

Chimp communities are by-and-large stable and peaceful entities, but intensive warfare has been known to erupt within the several habituated communities. In Mahale, one of the two communities originally habituated by researchers in 1967 had exterminated the other by 1982. A similar thing happened in Gombe Stream in the 1970s, when the Kasekela community, originally habituated by Goodall, divided into two discrete communities. The Kasekela and breakaway Kahama community coexisted alongside each other for some years. Then in 1974, Goodall returned to Gombe Stream after a break to discover that the Kasekela males were methodically persecuting their former community mates, isolating the Kahama males one by one, and tearing into them until they were dead or terminally wounded. By 1977, the Kahama community had vanished entirely.

Chimpanzees are essentially inhabitants of the western rainforest, but their range does extend into the extreme west of Tanzania, Rwanda and Uganda, which have a combined population of perhaps 7,000 individuals. These are concentrated in Tanzania's Mahale and Gombe national parks, Rwanda's Nyungwe Forest, and about 20 Ugandan national parks and other reserves, most notably Budongo, Kibale, Semliki, Maramagambo and Bwindi. Although East Africa's chimps represent less than 3% of the global population, much of what is known about wild chimpanzee society and behaviour stems from the region's many ongoing research projects.

An interesting pattern that emerged from the parallel research projects in Gombe Stream and Mahale Mountain, which lie little more than 100km apart on the shore of Lake Tanganyika, is a wide variety of social and behavioural differences between the two populations. Of the plant species common to both national parks, for instance, as many as 40% of those utilised as a food source by chimps in the one reserve are not eaten by chimps in the other.

In Gombe Stream, chimps appear to regard the palm-nut as something of a delicacy, but, while the same plants grow profusely in Mahale, the chimps there have yet to be recorded eating them. Likewise, the 'termite-fishing' behaviour first recorded by Jane Goodall at Gombe Stream in the 1960s has a parallel in Mahale, where the chimps are often seen 'fishing' for carpenter ants in the trees. But the Mahale chimps have never been recorded fishing for termites, while the Gombe chimps are not known to fish for carpenter ants. Mahale's chimps routinely groom each other with one hand while holding their other hands together above their heads – once again, behaviour that has never been noted at Gombe. More than any structural similarity, more even than any single quirk of chimpanzee behaviour, it's such striking cultural differences – the influence of nurture over nature if you like – that bring home our close genetic kinship with chimpanzees.

Other forest walks Unguided walking is no longer permitted in Kibale National Park, except within the immediate vicinity of Kanyanchu Visitors' Centre, where dedicated birders should look out for the localised red-chested paradise flycatcher (a stunning bird that's easy to locate by call), as well as various robin-chats, weavers and greenbuls. Daytime guided walks into the forest are available out of Kanyanchu, and offer a good chance of spotting several types of monkey, including the endemic Uganda mangabey, but at a cost of US$30/15 excluding park entrance, they seem like poor value compared to the guided trail at Bigodi. Rather more alluring are spotlighted night walks (*US$40/20 excluding park entrance*), which run from 19.30 to 22.00 daily, and offer a good chance of sighting nocturnal creatures such as galagos, various small predators, and the peculiar potto. Serious birdwatchers might also consider a birding walk (*US$30 excluding park entrance*), since the forest proper has a very different species composition to Bigodi. The most rewarding option for first-time birders in Kibale is the forest-flanked section of the Fort Portal Road that runs for several kilometres north of Kanyanchu. This area often throws up the likes of Sabine's spinetail, blue-breasted kingfisher and Afep pigeon, as well as butterflies in their hundreds and a decent selection of monkeys. It remains to be seen whether the planned surfacing of this road will make it less attractive to birders. Note that, as with chimp tracking, these activity fees must be paid at Isunga park headquarters.

Bigodi Swamp Walk Offering some of the finest birding and monkey-viewing in Uganda, the swamp walk through Bigodi Wetland Sanctuary is also an admirable example of conservation and tourism having a direct mutual benefit at grassroots level. The award-winning programme is run by the Kibale Association for Rural and Environmental Development (KAFRED), and all profits are used to support education-related and other such projects in Bigodi trading centre. The fee of US$17/13 per non-resident/resident, inclusive of a knowledgeable guide, also makes Bigodi a far more affordable prospect than a guided walk in the national park, particularly as the guides know the terrain intimately and can usually identify even the most troublesome species by sight or call.

The sanctuary's main ornithological virtue is quality rather than quantity. You'd be lucky to identify more than 40 species in one walk, but most will be forest-fringe and swamp specials, and a good number will be West African species at the eastern limit of their range. A spectacular bird strongly associated with the swamp is the great blue turaco, which will be seen by most visitors. Another more elusive speciality is the papyrus gonolek, which is most frequently encountered from the wooden walkway about halfway along the trail. Other regularly observed birds include: grey-throated, yellow-billed, yellow-spotted and double-toothed barbets; speckled, yellow-rumped and yellow-throated tinker-barbets; yellow-bill; brown-eared woodpecker; blue-throated roller; grey parrot; bronze sunbird; black-crowned waxbill; grey-headed Negro-finch; swamp flycatcher; red-capped and snowy-headed robin-chats; grosbeak and northern brown-throated weavers; and black-and-white casqued hornbill. The most common monkey is red colobus, but red-tailed monkey, L'Hoest's monkey, black-and-white colobus and Uganda mangabey are also regularly sighted. If you are extremely fortunate, you might see chimpanzees, which occasionally visit the swamp to forage for fruit, or the shy sitatunga antelope.

The 4.5km circular trail starts in Bigodi trading centre at the Bigodi Swamp Walk office (✤ *0.4061, 30.40871;* m *0772 468113;* e *comm-tour@infocom.co.ug; www.bigodi-tourism.org;* ⏱ *07.30–17.00 daily*), where serious birdwatchers should

mention their special interest, since some guides are better at identification than others. Walks technically start at 07.30 and 15.00, and generally take around 3 hours, but dedicated birders will require longer. For general monkey viewing, it doesn't matter greatly whether you go in the morning or afternoon, but birders should definitely aim to do the morning walk. For morning walks, it is worth getting to the office as early as you can, or possibly even arranging a dawn start a day in advance. For afternoon walks, it's advisable to get going an hour earlier than the scheduled departure. Be warned that the trail is very muddy in parts, so if you don't have good walking shoes, then you'd do well to hire gumboots from the KAFRED office – this costs less than US$2.

Bigodi Cultural Centre (m *0782 541164; entry US$10*) Situated right opposite the Bigodi Swamp Walk office, this small museum displaying traditional clothes, grinding stones, musical instruments and other such artefacts offers a sedate alternative for those who don't feel like doing the walk. A private venture, it is the brainchild of an experienced and articulate national park guide whose lengthy explanation of the various exhibits is probably more interesting than the artefacts themselves.

Mpanga Falls This impressive waterfall is formed by the Mpanga River as it tumbles over the rim of the 1,200m Mount Karubaguma some 15km before emptying into Lake George. Estimated to be about 50m high, the waterfall is enclosed by a steep gorge and supports a lush cover of spray forest. A remarkable feature of the gorge's vegetation is one of Africa's largest cycad colonies, comprised entirely of the so-called Uganda Giant Cycad (*Encephalartos whitelockii*), a critically endangered species endemic to this single location. Perhaps the closest thing among trees to living fossils, the cycads are relics of an ancient order of coniferous plants that flourished some 300 to 200 million years ago, with the aptly prehistoric appearance of an overgrown tree fern perched on top of a palm stem up to 10m tall. Like *E. whitelockii*, many modern cycad species are classified as endangered, due to their extremely localised distribution and very slow life cycle.

The outside world caught up with *E. whitelockii* in 2008 when a controversial hydro-power scheme for the gorge was pushed through. Many cycads were bulldozed before a public outcry led to mitigation measures, including the establishment of local nurseries to grow more cycads, and recent reports suggest the colony remains substantially intact. What remains of the Mpanga Falls can be reached with reasonable ease as a day trip from Kibale Forest or as a diversion from the newly surfaced main road between Kamwenge and Ibanda. Kamwenge is well served by public transport from both directions. From there, you'll need a special hire or boda to cover the 22km from town to the gorge. Mpanga Gorge lies in the remotest corner of Queen Elizabeth National Park, so technically you'll need to clear this with the park authority in Kebuko village, 18km from Kamwenge.

SEBITOLI SECTOR An extension of Kibale National Park that opened in 2002 to help ease tourist pressure on Kanyanchu, Sebitoli has never really caught on with travellers, despite its convenient location a few hundred metres off the main Fort Portal–Kampala Road. Partly this is because no chimp tracking is offered, but it doesn't help that Sebitoli has received little publicity, nor that activities are relatively costly since they attract full national park fees. Outside the national park, by contrast, guided walks in the Kihingami Wetlands, only 1km from Sebitoli, are very good value, and make for a thoroughly worthwhile budget outing from Fort Portal.

Getting there and away Coming from Fort Portal, Sebitoli Camp is signposted to the right 16km along the Kampala Road, some 1.5km before a bridge across the Mpanga River. Using public transport, any matatu between Fort Portal and Kyenjojo can drop you at the junction, from where it's a 5-minute walk to the camp, though you may need to pay full fare (*US$1.50*). To get to Jacaranda Hilltop Guesthouse, continue east along the Kampala Road for about 5.5km past Sebitoli Camp, then turn right at the signposted junction and continue south for another 6km to the guesthouse. Using public transport, ask to be dropped at Kasunga stage, from where you can walk the last 6km or catch a boda to the guesthouse.

Where to stay and eat Accommodation is limited to two excellent budget options, both with campsites.

Sebitoli Camp (5 rooms) ⊕ 0.64381, 30.38491; 039 2175976; e knp@ugandawildlife. org. Set in a forest clearing only 600m south of the main road to Kampala, this very reasonably priced UWA facility lies at the northern tip of Kibale National Forest. Plenty of monkeys & birds can be seen in the camp. En-suite rooms have electricity & a canteen serves simple meals. No entrance fee is charged unless you do activities within the national park. *US$14 dbl, US$5pp camping.* **$**

Jacaranda Hilltop Guesthouse (6 rooms) ⊕ 0.61593, 30.44113; m 0774 057390/0703 291263. This former estate manager's house south of the Kampala Rd has been converted to a cosy guesthouse set amidst the tea plantations that abut the eastern boundary of Kibale National Park's Sebitoli sector. Self-guided walking trails have been cut through 2 small forest patches that lie outside the park but support both species of colobus monkey, as well as many birds. Other activities include cycling, tea-estate tours & visits to Sebitoli & the Kihingami Wetlands. Rooms all have nets & some are en suite. Meals are available. *US$15/21 sgl/dbl B&B using common shower, US$25 B&B en-suite dbl. US$4pp camping.* **$$**

What to see and do

Sebitoli Forest Hikes Several short guided hikes are available. The prosaically named 6–8-Hour-Long Hike starts at Sebitoli Camp at 08.00 and exits the national park near the Jacaranda Hilltop Guesthouse. It offers a good chance of seeing red colobus, black-and-white colobus, Uganda mangabey, red-tailed monkey and blue monkey, as well as a wide range of bird species. Chimpanzees are often heard but seldom seen, while elephants are occasionally encountered close to the Mpanga River. All hikes cost US$30 per person, plus US$40 park entrance per 24 hours. For those without transport to meet them at Jacaranda Hilltop Guesthouse, you could either walk the 6km back to the main road and pick up a matatu there, or ask the rangers or guesthouse to call you a boda. At night, Sebitoli is reportedly a superb site for spotlighting for nocturnal creatures such as galagos and potto. The Kibale National Park office in Fort Portal is a good source of up-to-date information about Sebitoli.

Kihingami Wetlands (⊕ 0.64378, 30.37751; m 0774 057390; e ktours@infocom. co.ug) Protected as part of a community project, the 13km² Kihingami Wetlands border Kibale National Park on the north side of the Kampala Road about 15km out of Fort Portal and 1km from Sebitoli. Home to more than 230 bird species, it is best known as a refuge for the localised white-spotted flufftail, an elusive and largely nocturnal swamp-dweller that is very difficult to see despite its often persistent calling. Other alluring species associated with the forest fringes and

swamp are great blue turaco, papyrus gonolek, masked apalis, white-winged warbler, black-faced rufous warbler, Jameson's wattle-eye, Holub's golden weaver, grey-winged robin-chat and blue-shouldered robin-chat. Guided bird-watching tours leave at 07.30 and 15.00 daily (*US$7pp; 3–4hrs*), with morning generally being most productive. Guided forest walks leave at 08.00 and 15.00 daily (*US$7pp*), and come with a good chance of spotting red colobus, black-and-white colobus and red-tailed monkeys. Other activities are tea plantation tours (*US$7*) and push-bike hire (*US$3 per day*). The wetlands office is clearly signposted at Sebitoli village, and easily reached from Fort Portal by matatu, but transport out there can also be arranged through Kabarole Tours (page 385).

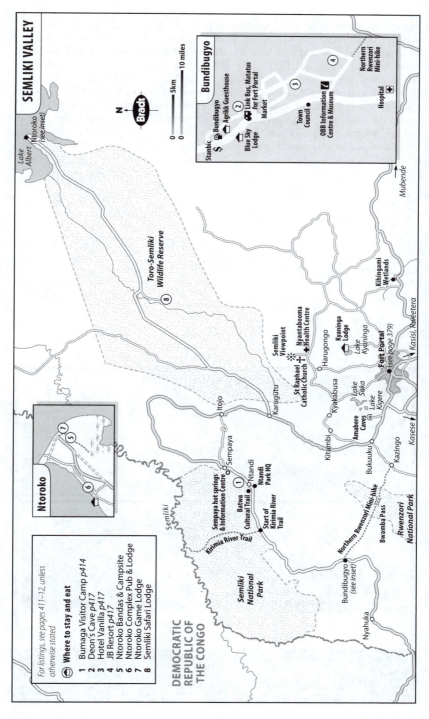

SEMLIKI VALLEY

BUNDIBUGYO

Stanbic
Bundibugyo
Agrikk Guesthouse
Link Bus, Matatus for Fort Portal
Blue Sky Lodge
Market
Town Council
OBB Information Centre & Museum
Northern Rwenzori Mini-hike
Hospital

Mubende

Lake Albert
Ntoroko (see inset)

Toro-Semliki Wildlife Reserve

N

Bradt

0   5km
0   10 miles

Semliki Viewpoint
St Raphael Catholic Church
Nyantabooma Health Centre
Harugongo
Kyaninga Lodge
Lake Kyaninga
Kihingami Wetlands

Itojo

Karugutu

Kitumbi
Kyakabusa
Amabere Caves
Lake Soka
Lake Kigere
Bukuuku
Kazingo

Fort Portal
(see page 379)

Kasisi, Kaveetera
Kasese

Ntoroko

Semliki

Sempaya
Ntandi
Ntandi Park HQ

Sempaya hot springs & Information Centre
Batwa Cultural Trail
Start of Kirimia River Trail

Kirimia River Trail

Semliki National Park

Northern Rwenzori Mini-hike

Bwamba Pass

Rwenzori National Park

Bundibugyo (see inset)

Nyahuka

DEMOCRATIC REPUBLIC OF THE CONGO

For listings, see pages 411–12, unless otherwise stated

Where to stay and eat

1 Bumaga Visitor Camp p414
2 Deon's Cave p417
3 Hotel Vanilla p417
4 JB Resort p417
5 Ntoroko Bandas & Campsite
6 Ntoroko Complex Pub & Lodge
7 Ntoroko Game Lodge
8 Semliki Safari Lodge

408

16

The Semliki Valley

Set at the base of the Albertine Rift west of Fort Portal, the spectacular but little-visited Semliki Valley is hemmed in by Lake Albert to the north and by the Semliki River along the Congolese border, while the Rwenzori foothills protrude into it from the south to create two geographically discrete and ecologically divergent sectors. Northeast of the Rwenzori, the Toro-Semliki Wildlife Reserve protects a tract of moist woodland running towards the marshy southern shores of Lake Albert. By contrast, the northwest Rwenzori footslopes give way to the steamy lowland jungle of Semliki National Park, whose affinities with the contiguous Congolese rainforest are reflected by the presence of dozens of birds and other creatures found nowhere else in Uganda.

Foreigners who make it to Semliki generally fall into one of three categories: either upmarket tourists headed to the wildlife reserve's excellent lodge for an off-the-beaten-track safari; dedicated birders in search of the national park's many avian rarities; or backpackers doing the Rwenzori mini-hike (page 437). But, even if you're none of the above, the new surfaced 85km road that rounds the Rwenzori foothills between Fort Portal and Bundibugyo (the region's largest town) is one of the most breathtaking in Uganda.

FURTHER INFORMATION

The Semliki Valley area is covered by Sheet 7 in the 'Uganda Maps' series, *Fort Portal & Kibale Forest*.

TORO-SEMLIKI WILDLIFE RESERVE

Uganda's oldest wildlife reserve was originally gazetted in 1932 as the Toro Game Reserve. Extending over 543km², it runs northeast of the Bundibugyo Road to Ntoroko, a sprawling fishing village and district administrative centre set on the southern shore of Lake Albert. The reserve itself is topographically unremarkable, set at a relatively low altitude of around 600–700m above sea level, but on a clear day the setting is truly awesome, with the sheer Rift Valley Escarpment rising sharply from the eastern shore of Lake Albert, the 2,500m-high Congolese Blue Mountains on the western horizon, and the glacial peaks of the Rwenzori visible to the southwest. The reserve's touristic centrepiece is the isolated and rather wonderful Semliki Safari Lodge, which offers all-inclusive packages to tourists seeking a holistic wilderness experience rather than wall-to-wall game viewing. Ntoroko is now the centre of more low-key tourist developments including a mid-range lakeshore lodge and affordable UWA camping and banda site.

FLORA AND FAUNA The dominant vegetation of Toro-Semliki is open Acacia-Combretum woodland and grassy savannah, interspersed with patches of borassus

One of the first Europeans to enter the Semliki Valley was Dr Albert Cook, who visited it on foot in 1898, an experience he would later describe vividly in his memoir *Ugandan Memories*:

The ground descended abruptly at our feet, and we looked out over a vast plain. Beneath us the Semliki River twisted in and out across the plain like a large snake. Beyond to the west was the commencement of Stanley's Great Forest. It looked like a dark green carpet, stretching away until it was lost in the haze ... After a short rest, we began to descend from the summit of the pass into the Semliki Valley. Down, down, down for seven thousand feet, we had to leap like goats from rock to rock, and it was with bleeding fingers that we reached the bottom, for there were plenty of thorns.

At the bottom ... was a village of the Bwamba, hill tribes who inhabit the western slopes of the Rwenzori. The village was composed of little beehive shaped huts, each with its own porch. The people were splendid specimens ... stalking about with spears in their hands ... They file their front teeth to a point, and dress their hair very carefully, frizzing it into long curls like a poodle dog. They wear brass rings on their arms and legs [and] nothing but a wisp of cloth passed between the legs and secured by a girdle.

In the afternoon we went to the celebrated hot springs ... Emerging from the long grass we suddenly came on a belt of rich tropical foliage ... paved with slabs of rock. From these, great sheets of steam were rising ... all along the upper edge were springs of boiling water, bubbling furiously ... in front were clouds of steam. In some of the holes, we boiled plantains, in other potatoes, and in a third we stuck our kettle.

palm forest, significant belts of riparian woodland along the main watercourses, and extensive swamps towards Lake Albert. In its pre-Amin heyday, the vast geographic scale of Toro-Semliki Wildlife Reserve was complemented by some of East Africa's most prolific plains game. More than 10,000 Ugandan kob were resident, together with large herds of Jackson's hartebeest, Defassa waterbuck, elephant and buffalo. As for predators, the hunter Brian Herne wrote: 'The area is famous for the number of massive maned lions that live there. I have never seen so many big lions in other parts of Africa ... Leopard were numerous throughout ... None of the cats in Semliki had to work very hard for their dinner; they could simply lie in the grass and throw out a paw, for some animal or another was always about.' Isolated from similar habitats by various mountain ranges, Toro-Semliki was also at one point mooted as the site of a bizarre scheme to introduce commercial tiger hunting to Uganda – indeed, six pairs of tiger made it as far as Entebbe before the scheme was abandoned as potentially detrimental to indigenous predators.

Wildlife has partially recovered from the poaching that took a heavy toll during the civil war. The Ugandan kob population, which plummeted below 1,000 in the early 1990s, today totals several thousand. More than 1,000 buffalo are resident, up from about 50 in the early 1990s, and elephant and waterbuck numbers are growing, too. Leopards are still common, while lions – at one point poached to local extinction – are gradually re-colonising the area. Primates are well represented, with black-and-white colobus, olive baboon and red-tailed and vervet monkey all conspicuous in suitable habitats, while a community of perhaps 70 chimpanzees is resident in the Mugiri River Forest. The reserve is highly alluring to birdwatchers: some 462 species have been recorded and it is one of the best places in Uganda to see shoebill.

FEES The entrance fee is US$35/25 for FNR/FR per 24 hours. No fee applies to using the public road from Karugutu to Ntoroko, nor to using accommodation at Ntoroko. The fee is levied to guests staying at Semliki Safari Lodge, and for any guided walks, boat trips or other activities undertaken out of Ntoroko. Note that the fee does not cover Semliki National Park, so if you were to visit the national park as a day trip from Semliki Safari Lodge, you'll end up paying two sets of entrance fees.

GETTING THERE AND AWAY

By air Scheduled flights to Semliki Airstrip, 1.5km south of Semliki Safari Lodge, must be booked in advance. The Fly Uganda flight is scheduled to leave Kajjansi Airstrip for Entebbe at 09.30 (*US$290 one-way; 40mins*) and requires a minimum of 2 passengers. Aerolink Uganda flies from Entebbe at 07.45 or 12.45 (*US$303/505 one-way/return; 2hrs*), sometimes stopping at other airstrips on the way, and a minimum of 4 passengers is needed.

By road The drive from Fort Portal to Toro-Semliki takes around 90 minutes in a private vehicle. Follow the surfaced Bundibugyo Road for 30km to Karugutu (⊕ *0.78903, 30.22645*), where a signposted turn-off to the right leads on to a fair 40km dirt road that terminates at Ntoroko. If you are headed to Semliki Safari Lodge, look out for the signposted junction (⊕ *0.92979, 30.36787*) to the right after about 25km, shortly after crossing the Wasa River bridge. It's 3km from this junction to the lodge.

Using public transport, a few matatus (*US$5; 2–3hrs*) run directly between Fort Portal and Ntoroko, usually leaving in the early morning. Alternatively, any vehicle heading to Bundibugyo can drop you at Karugutu, from where matatus to Ntoroko (*US$2.50; 90mins*) run throughout the day.

By boat Overloaded passenger boats travel erratically along the lakeshore between Ntoroko, Butiaba and Wanseko, but fatal accidents are commonplace, especially in squally weather.

WHERE TO STAY AND EAT *Map, page 408*
A growing number of accommodation options can be found at Ntoroko, a sprawling and fantastically scruffy peninsula-bound fishing village enclaved within the wildlife reserve. The most upmarket place to stay anywhere in the Semliki Valley is Semliki Safari Lodge, which has a wonderfully isolated setting on the site of an older hunting lodge halfway between Karugutu and Ntoroko.

Exclusive

✳ 🏠 **Semliki Safari Lodge** (8 tents)
⊕ 0.9091, 30.35583; 📞 041 4251182; m 0772 489497; e info@wildplacesafrica.com; www. wildplacesafrica.com. Built in 1996, Semliki Safari Lodge is Uganda's oldest upmarket tented camp & it still rates as one of the best, boasting a truly remote bush setting overlooking a stretch of riparian woodland teeming with birds & monkeys. Large thatched tents have wooden floors, walk-in nets, stylish ethnic décor & en-suite hot showers, while the main lodge is built of stone, log & thatch & decorated in a manner that emphasises its earthy open-air feel. Facilities include a large swimming pool area overlooking a stretch of riverine forest inhabited by black-&-white colobus & vervet monkeys. Guided activities include game drives, night drives & birdwatching walks in the adjacent forest (included in the price), all of which emphasise a holistic wilderness experience rather than ticking off wildlife. Chimp tracking, boat trips on Lake Albert & day trips to Semliki National Park are charged extra. *US$455/700 sgl/dbl Dec–Feb & Jun–Sep, US$385/590 other months, with discount for East African residents. Rates inc all meals, most drinks & 2 activities per day.* **$$$$$**

Upmarket

☗ **Ntoroko Game Lodge** (5 tents)
✪ 1.05721, 30.54543; ☏ 031 2503065; m 0756
000598; e info@ntorokogamelodge.com; www.
ntorokogamelodge.com. This new lodge has a
lovely setting in a shady copse on the sandy shore
of Lake Albert about 3km by road from Ntoroko
village. Well-appointed & spacious standing tents
are set on wooden platforms & come with twin or
queen-sized bed with fitted nets & en-suite tub
& shower. The screened restaurant/bar also has
a lake view, as well as DTSV, & it serves 4-course
meals for US$17 or standalone mains for US$10.
The lack of management presence makes it feel
somewhat less than the sum of its parts, & a touch
overpriced. *US$200/300 B&B sgl/dbl. Camping
US$7pp.* **$$$$$**

Budget, shoestring & camping

☗ **Ntoroko Bandas & Campsite** (4 rooms)
✪ 1.05666, 30.54448; m 0784 923707. This underpublicised gem of a UWA camp, set only 50m from
Lake Albert right next to Ntoroko Game Lodge, has
1 en-suite dbl banda & 3 dbl bandas using common
showers, all clean & adequately comfortable with
2 ¾ beds & fitted nets. There's also a campsite &
pleasant canteen & bar selling local-style meat-
based dishes for US$3 & vegetarian meals for
US$1.50. It's about 1km from the matatu as the crow
flies, & further by road, so you might want to charter
a boda out. *US$13/17 dbl with common/en-suite
showers. US$5pp camping.* **$$**

☗ **Ntoroko Complex Pub & Lodge** (12
rooms) ✪ 1.05395, 30.53816; ☏ 039 2582184;
m 0772 996391. Only 100m from the matatus
stand, this looks about the best of Ntoroko's
handful of very basic lodges. If nothing else, it's
very cheap. *US$2 sgl using common shower.* **$**

WHAT TO SEE AND DO Two activities daily are included in the rate for Semliki Safari Lodge, though chimp tracking and boat trips on Lake Albert are billed as extras. Visitors staying in or around Ntoroko can organise activities through the helpful UWA staff at Ntoroko Bandas and Campsite.

Game drives For self-drivers, game drive options are more or less limited to the main road between Karugutu and Ntoroko, which runs through the reserve for most of its length. Game viewing along this road is rather hit-and-miss, but taken slowly it can be quite rewarding, especially if you've an interest in birds. Guests at Semliki Safari Lodge are offered guided day and night drives in open 4x4s, which can explore tracks and off-road areas closed to less robust vehicles. Either way, look out for black-and-white colobus monkey in areas of gallery forest, and olive baboon and vervet monkey in lighter woodland. Small herds of Ugandan kob and waterbuck inhabit the grassy plains, along with shyer pairs of common reedbuck and family parties of warthog.

Elephant, buffalo and giant forest hog are also around, but are not seen on an everyday basis and they tend to be rather skittish when approached by a vehicle. Leopard and even lion are very occasionally seen, most usually on night drives. Birding is excellent. The open grassland hosts Abyssinian ground hornbill and a variety of raptors, while areas of rank vegetation are good for marsh tchagra and African crake. The Mugiri River Forest is regarded to be the best site in Uganda for the elusive leaf-love, and it also hosts a variety of other localised forest species. Night drives are good for owls, as well as the improbable pennant-winged and standard-winged nightjars.

Boat trips Boat trips on scenic Lake Albert are a highlight of any visit to the wildlife reserve. For birdwatchers, this is one of the most reliable sites in Uganda to see shoebill, often at closer quarters than is usually the case in Murchison Falls. A profusion of more common waterbirds are also present, and the dazzling red-throated bee-eater forms large breeding colonies on sandbanks near Ntoroko

between December and March. Less ornithologically minded visitors are usually boated to the base of the impressive Nkusi Falls, which – like a smaller replica of Murchison Falls – explode through a cleft in the Rift Valley Escarpment before tumbling noisily into the lake. Boat rides arranged through UWA cost US$30pp (exclusive of park entrance fees), while the boat charter will work out at around US$60 per party. Guests at Semliki Safari Lodge can arrange boat trips directly through the lodge for US$225 per party.

Walks You can walk freely in the immediate vicinity of Ntoroko, where the lake shallows are teeming with birdlife. Guided nature walks out of Ntoroko Bandas & Campsite cost US$30pp (exclusive of park entrance fees) and focus mainly on birds, though you might see a few antelopes. Far more alluring at the same price are guided primate walks through the Mugiri River Forest (US$30pp exclusive of park entrance fees), near Semliki Safari Lodge, where an isolated community of 70 chimpanzees has been partially habituated by students from the University of Indiana. Chimp sightings are far from guaranteed in Mugiri, and most individuals are quite shy, but you should also see a variety of smaller forest primates.

SEMLIKI NATIONAL PARK

Gazetted in 1993, Semliki National Park – previously known as Bwamba Forest, a name that often crops up in old ornithological literature – protects a practically unspoilt 220km² tract of rainforest bounded to the northwest by the Semliki River as it runs along the Congolese border into Lake Albert, and to the southeast by the surfaced main road connecting Fort Portal to Bundibugyo. The tropical lowland forest of Semliki, set at an average altitude of 700m, forms an ecological continuum with the Ituri Forest, which extends eastward for more than 500km to the Congo River, and it supports a wealth of wildlife unknown from elsewhere in East Africa, including more than 35 bird species. Despite this, the park is seldom visited, even by ornithological tours. To some extent, this is because access north of the main Bundibugyo Road is limited to a few little-used hiking trails through the sweltering rainforest. But it doesn't help that the one attraction readily accessible to casual visitors, a short walking trail to the Sempaya Hot Springs, attracts a combination of park entrance and guide fees that feels disproportionately high for what it is.

FEES The entrance fee is US$35/25 for FNR/FR per 24 hours. No fee is charged for driving or walking along the main road to Bundibugyo, which falls just outside the park's southeastern boundary, or for staying overnight at Bumaga Visitors Camp. All formal activities in the park, including birding walks and the hike to Sempaya Hot Springs, attract a guide fee of US$30 per person, over and above the entrance fee. Note that the fee is separate from the one for Toro-Semliki National Park, so if you visit both reserves in the same 24-hour period, you must pay two sets of entrance fees.

FLORA AND FAUNA Seated at the juncture of several ecological zones, Semliki National Park has an exceptionally diverse flora. The dominant tree is the Uganda ironwood (*Cynometra alexandri*), but the forest also contains several Congolese species at the easternmost extent of their range. A checklist of 60 **mammal** species includes 11 that occur nowhere else in Uganda, among them the pygmy antelope, two types of flying squirrel and six types of bat. Semliki National Park is also the only East African stronghold of the oddball water chevrotain (or fanged deer), a superficially duiker-like relic of an ancient ungulate family that shares several

16

structural features with pigs and is regarded to be ancestral to all modern-day antelopes, deer, cows and giraffes. Eight diurnal primates have been recorded: red-tailed monkey; vervet monkey; blue and De Brazza's monkeys; grey-cheeked mangabey; olive baboon; black-and-white colobus and chimpanzee. Other large mammals include elephant, bushpig, buffalo, sitatunga and white-bellied duiker. Hippos are common along the Semliki River, as are crocodiles. More than 300 species of butterfly have been identified, including 46 species of forest swallowtail, together with 235 moth species.

Over 435 **bird** species have been recorded in Semliki National Park. The checklist includes a full 35 Guinea–Congo forest biome bird species unknown from elsewhere in East Africa. These are spot-breasted ibis, Hartlaub's duck, Congo serpent eagle, chestnut-flanked goshawk, red-thighed sparrowhawk, long-tailed hawk, Nkulengu rail, black-throated coucal, chestnut owlet, Bates's nightjar, black-wattled hornbill, white-crested hornbill, black dwarf hornbill, red-billed dwarf hornbill, red-rumped tinkerbird, spotted honeyguide, lyre-tailed honeyguide, Zenker's honeyguide, African piculet, Gabon woodpecker, white-throated blue swallow, palm swamp greenbul, simple greenbul, eastern bearded greenbul, Sassi's olive greenbul, yellow-throated nicator, northern bearded scrub-robin, lowland akalat, grey ground thrush, fiery-breasted bush-shrike, red-eyed puffback, black-winged oriole, Maxwell's black weaver, blue-billed malimbe and Grant's bluebill. Furthermore, another 12 species with an extremely limited distribution in East Africa are reasonably likely to be seen by visitors spending a few days in Semliki National Park. These are western bronze-naped pigeon, yellow-throated cuckoo, piping hornbill, red-sided broadbill, Xavier's greenbul, Capuchin babbler, yellow longbill, blue-headed flycatcher, red-billed helmet-shrike, crested malimbe, pale-fronted antpecker and chestnut-breasted negro-finch.

For amateur ornithologists, Semliki is not only certain to throw up a clutch of 'lifers' – it also offers a faint but real possibility of a brand-new East African record. Indeed, three of the seven 'recent records' depicted in Stevenson and Fanshawe's 2002 *Field Guide to the Birds of East Africa* – namely Congo serpent-eagle, grey-throated rail and black-throated coucal – were discovered in Semliki during the 1990s.

GETTING THERE AND AWAY The gateway to the park is Sempaya Information Office (❂ *0.8359, 30.16721*), which is signposted alongside the right side of the new Bundibugyo Road, 60km from Fort Portal, only 300m past the intersection with the old road. The drive from Fort Portal shouldn't take longer than 1 hour. Any public transport heading between Fort Portal and Bundibugyo can drop you there.

🏠 WHERE TO STAY AND EAT   *Map, page 408*
If you don't fancy staying at the bandas listed below, the park could also be visited as a day trip from Toro-Semliki Wildlife Reserve (allow about 90 minutes each way), Fort Portal or Bundibugyo.

🏠 **Bumaga Visitor Camp** (6 rooms)
❂ 0.82203, 30.15924. Situated alongside the Bundibugyo Road 2km past Sempaya, this self-catering camp is set on the edge of the forest & offers good birding possibilities. Take insect repellent to discourage midges, which can also be repelled by wearing long-sleeved shirts buttoned at the cuff & long trousers tucked into socks. *US$17/27pp dbl/twin, US$5pp camping.* **$$**

WHAT TO SEE AND DO Note that all the guided walks described below cost US$30 per person, excluding the non-resident/resident park entrance fee of US$35/25.

Scenic drive Even if you opt not to enter Semliki National Park, it's worth taking a day drive to Sempaya, especially now that the new and old road combine to form a scenic loop around the northern Rwenzori. If the weather looks clear, you can turn off the new surfaced road about 10km beyond Karugutu (⊕ *0.84051, 30.2273*) signposted to Itojo, and follow the rough 14km old road up to the rocky Buranga Pass until it reconnects with the new road at Sempaya (⊕ *0.8388, 30.16788*) following a long and tightly winding descent that offers fantastic views across the Rift Valley towards Congo. The 5km stretch of the Bundibugyo Road running south from the junction at Sempaya is fringed by forest but lies outside the national park, so no park fee or guide is required to drive along it or stop to look for monkeys and birds. The patch of fig and palm forest about halfway between Sempaya and Ntandi is worth scanning carefully for the likes of swamp greenbul and various forest hornbills. You can then return to Sempaya and use the new tarmac road back to Fort Portal.

Sempaya and surrounds The most popular attraction in Semliki National Park is the cluster of hot springs at Sempaya, which can be reached via a short guided walking trail (no more than 500m) from the Sempaya Information Office. Ringed by forest and palm trees, and veiled in a cloud of steam, these springs are a primeval, evocative sight: the largest geyser spouts up to 2m into the air from an opening in a low salt sculpture. Take care: the emerging water has a temperature of more than 100°C and the surrounding pools are hot! The trail to the springs leads through a patch of forest where red-tailed monkey, grey-cheeked mangabey and black-and-white colobus are common. Among the more interesting birds regularly seen here are various forest hornbills, blue-breasted kingfisher, red-rumped and yellow-throated tinkerbird, Frasier's ant-thrush and honeyguide greenbul. Another spring, more of a broad steaming pool than a geyser, lies on the far side of the swampy clearing reached by a boardwalk. Rather than retracing your steps to Sempaya, you might ask whether the UWA has finally reopened an old trail that creates an attractive loop, passing through forest and a lovely tract of swamp/grassland.

Red Monkey Trail Following the eastern margin of the national park to the Semliki River, this wilderness trail takes at least 3 hours in either direction, but offers exposure to a far greater variety of localised birds than the trail to the springs. It can be undertaken as a day trip, or, if you carry your own tent and food, as an overnight trip camping on the bank of the river. In addition to birds, you can expect to see a variety of monkeys, hippos and crocodiles on the river, and possibly even buffalo and elephant.

Kirimia River Trail Highly recommended to birdwatchers, this 15km trail runs north from Kirimia (⊕ *0.79606, 30.09608*) on the main Bundibugyo Road to the banks of the Semliki River, crossing the Kirimia River twice, as well as passing a succession of forest-fringed oxbow lakes. The first 4km, as far as the first crossing of the Kirimia River, can be undertaken as a guided day hike, and passes through secondary and riparian forest where African piculet, long-tailed hawk, red-sided broadbill, black-faced rufous warbler and lemon-bellied crombec are resident. The full round hike offers birders the best opportunity to see a good selection of Semliki 'specials', but realistically it can only be undertaken as a two- to four-night self-sufficient camping expedition. Among the 20–30 bird species associated with the oxbow lakes and their environs, but unlikely to be seen in the vicinity of the main road or elsewhere in Uganda, are spot-breasted ibis, Nkulengu rail, black-throated

16

A community of roughly 40 Bambuti Pygmies live at Bundimasoli (✆ *0.80596, 30.13866, look out for the sign reading Batwa Cultural Trail*) on the Bundibugyo Road about 5km past Sempaya and 500m from the park headquarters at Ntandi. They are more closely affiliated to the Basua Pygmies of the Congolese Basin than to the Batwa of Kigezi and Rwanda. I first encountered them in the early 1990s, an occasion described in previous editions of this book as follows:

One of the most depressing experiences I've had in Africa. Far from offering an insight into another lifestyle and culture, the Ntandi Pygmies are basically a bunch of shorter-than-average people who spend the day hanging around their banana-leaf huts, smoking dope, drinking and waiting for the next bunch of tourists to arrive. I've yet to meet anyone who left these people without feeling disturbed.

Many visitors who followed in my footsteps weren't merely disturbed, but also hassled, ripped off or stolen from, culminating in an incident in the mid-1990s in which an aid worker from Fort Portal was stabbed in the hand.

What I didn't realise then is that this aggression towards tourists was a manifestation of a deeper resentment against the sort of prejudice discussed in the box on Batwa Pygmies (see pages 486–7). Among their neighbours, the Bambuti are regarded to be dirty ne'er-do-wells, stigmatised by such unacceptable customs as eating snakes and monkeys, growing and smoking marijuana, and the women walking around topless. Until recently, tourist fees supposedly paid to the Ntandi community were regularly confiscated by non-Bambuti guides and the Bambuti, like the Batwa of Kigezi, were forbidden to use their traditional hunting grounds after Semliki National Park was gazetted in 1993.

Today, the Bambuti live outside the forest in a cluster of basic shacks on the edge of Bundimasoli village, ten minutes' walk from the Semliki National Park headquarters. There has been some progress and under the guidance of the self-styled 'king' of the Ugandan Bambuti, Geoffrey Nzito, and a local

coucal, yellow-throated cuckoo, lyre-tailed honeyguide, grey ground thrush, blue-billed malimbe, Maxwell's black weaver and Grant's bluebill, while Hartlaub's duck and white-throated blue swallow are resident on the Semliki River.

BUNDIBUGYO

This pretty, rather remote little town, situated only 10km from the Congolese border, lies some 25km west of Fort Portal as the crow flies, but more than three times that distance by road, thanks to the intervention of the northern Rwenzori. It is the largest town in the Semliki Valley, supporting a population of around 20,000, as well as being the western terminus of the Rwenzori mini-hike (page 437) and a relatively comfortable base from which motorised travellers can explore Semliki National Park. The town itself is rather short on tourist attractions, though the new museum is worth a quick look. Bundibugyo District was practically off-limits to travel in the late 1990s following several brutal attacks by the Congo-based Allied Democratic Forces (ADF), and while this situation has long resolved itself, you might want to check the situation before heading this way. Amenities are limited but include a decent hospital and one bank with an ATM.

primary school teacher, several Bambuti have learned enough English to deal directly with tourists rather than through the medium of crooked guides. The Bambuti's relationship with the national park has also improved greatly following a concession allowing them limited rights to fish and hunt within its boundaries (the main restriction being against hunting larger mammals such as elephant, buffalo and chimps) and to barter the forest produce with other local communities. According to the king, they are also the only people in Uganda who are legally permitted to grow and smoke marijuana. The latter they do constantly and with great enthusiasm, through bubble pipes, especially – and somewhat incredibly – before they go hunting.

It's not all roses for the Bambuti by any means. Batwa women are regularly impregnated by outsiders, partially due to the belief that sleeping with one cures certain diseases, and Batwa men have little hope of finding a partner outside their own community on account of their unacceptable customs. Interbreeding means that the genetic stock of Uganda's most ancient inhabitants is rapidly being diluted – the average height of its teenagers far exceeds that of the adults. Historically, their main sources of income are digging on local farms and entertaining tourists. One is hardly a key to advancement, while opportunities for the other are increasingly rare. Few visitors find their way to Bundimasoli these days, and many who do must feel that the experience veers uncomfortably close to a freak-show exhibit – look at the short people, shake their hand, snap a photograph, and off we go. It would, I think, be more edifying for all parties were the community to be facilitated to offer guided walks into the national park and to show off their consummate knowledge and mastery of the forest setting. As it stands, after haggling a fee, you'll get some semblance of a traditional dance and the opportunity to buy a selection of crafts, mostly dope pipes. It might not be the most edifying of encounters, but it's also true that the Bambuti of Bundimasoli, caught in limbo between their hunter-gathering heritage and an uncertain future in the modern world, need the money more than most.

GETTING THERE AND AWAY The scenic drive from Fort Portal to Bundibugyo via Semliki National Park once followed one of the roughest roads anywhere in Uganda, but it is now surfaced in its entirety and the 85km drive should take no longer than 90 minutes. Using public transport, Link Bus (m *0787 336278*) operates two buses daily in either direction between Kampala and Bundibugyo via Fort Portal. These leave Kampala at 09.00 and 11.00 and Bundibugyo at 07.00 and 09.00 (*US$8; 5–6hrs*). There are also regular matatus between Fort Portal and Bundibugyo (*US$3*).

WHERE TO STAY AND EAT   *Map, page 408*

Deon's Cave   (8 rooms) m 0783 300612. This has clean en-suite rooms with nets set around a neat green courtyard. Good value. *US$7 dbl.* **$**

JB Resort   (7 rooms) m 0772 954040/396096. Set in quiet green gardens a few hundred metres south of the town centre, this place has clean en-suite rooms with net & fan. There's a bar but no restaurant. *US$12 dbl.* **$**

Hotel Vanilla   (27 rooms) m 0772 912110; e hotelvanilla@gmail.com. This long-serving 2-storey hotel has clean tiled en-suite rooms with net & fan. The courtyard is about as good as it gets in Bundibugyo, serving basic local meals for around US$3. A 1st-floor balcony at the front enjoys mountain views. *US$8 dbl using common shower, US$12/23 en-suite sgl/twin. All rates B&B.* **$$**

16

WHAT TO SEE AND DO
OBB Information Centre & Museum (m *0772 966094;* ⊕ *08.00–16.30 Mon–Fri; entry US$3*). Opened in 2014, this rather underwhelming museum displays basketwork, household and farm utensils, fish traps and other traditional artefacts associated with the region's three main cultural groups, the Bamba, Babwisi and Bavanuma.

Nyahuka This little-visited trading centre 20 minutes' drive from Bundibugyo offers marvellous views of the Rwenzori peaks, a bustling Saturday market, and access to the 100m-high Ngite Falls and smaller Nyahuka Falls on the Rwenzori foothills. Once there, it would be a shame not to enjoy the pretty, 10km drive to the border where a large concrete bridge over the River Lamia leads to the Congolese bank. Do note, however, that the bridge represents the end of the road in Ugandan terms, since it is forbidden to cross in to Congo here for security reasons.

17

The Rwenzori Mountains and Kasese

Often associated with Ptolemy's legendary *Mountains of the Moon*, the majestic Rwenzori Mountains – a UNESCO World Heritage Site since 1994 – are protected in a 996km² national park that runs along the Congolese border between Semliki Valley and Queen Elizabeth National Park. The range's upper slopes constitute an aptly lunar landscape of bare black rocks and tussocked moorland studded with surreal giant lobelias and groundsels, while the lower contours are swathed in a tangled jungle inhabited by shy forest elephants and chimpanzees, as well as a wealth of forest monkeys and birds including several Albertine Rift endemics. Above all this, towering to a maximum altitude of 5,109m, a series of craggy black peaks is coated in permanent equatorial snow and ice. Now served by two different hiking circuits, both of which offer more experienced climbers access to the glacial peaks, Rwenzori Mountains National Park is the most popular hiking destination in Uganda, less iconic perhaps than Kilimanjaro in neighbouring Tanzania, but offering far more of a wilderness experience, as well as being significantly more affordable.

KASESE

The gateway town to the Rwenzori, Kasese lies at an altitude of 950m on the open plains that separate the ice-capped mountains from Lake George and Queen Elizabeth National Park. Unexpectedly hot and humid, Kasese isn't the most prepossessing of Ugandan towns, and its rather pokey feel contrasts oddly with a potentially attractive setting at the base of one of Africa's largest mountain ranges. For many years, Kasese's economic wellspring was the nearby Kilembe Copper Mine, a Canadian venture that started up in 1950 and led to the town becoming the railhead of a line connecting western Uganda to the Kenyan coast via Kampala in 1956. The mine was sold to the Ugandan Government in 1975 and ceased operations seven years later, though it looks set to reopen in the near future under a recent new agreement granting extraction rights of its four million tonnes of copper (and untold cobalt reserves) to the Chinese-owned Tibet Hima Mining Company. Even after the mine collapsed, the Kasese's railhead status ensured it remained a popular springboard for independent travel in western Uganda, but it fell off the travel map somewhat after 1995, when passenger services from Kampala were suspended. Now the ninth-largest town in Uganda with a population of 108,000, Kasese is a convenient place to stay overnight and shop for provisions prior to a Rwenzori hike, and it could also be used as a cheap base for visits to Queen Elizabeth National Park, but in most respects it has far less going for it than Fort Portal, only 75km to the north.

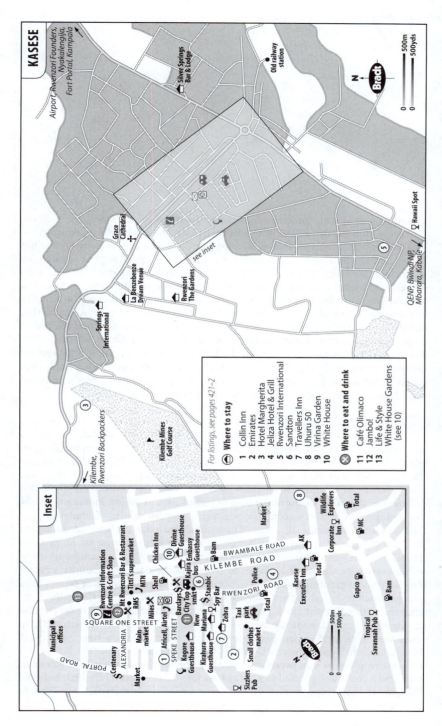

KASESE

Airport, Rwenzori Founders, Nyakalengija, Fort Portal, Kampala

Silver Springs Bar & lodge

Grace Cathedral

La Benzebenze Dream Venue

Rwenzori The Gardens

Springs International

Kilembe, Rwenzori Backpackers

Kilembe Mines Golf Course

Old railway station

see inset

QENP, Bwindi NP, Mbarara, Kabale

Hawaii Spot

N

Bradt

0   500m
0   500yds

Inset

Municipal offices

PORTAL ROAD

Centenary

Market

ALEXANDRIA

Rwenzori Information Centre & Craft Shop

Mt Rwenzori Bar & Restaurant

Titti's supermarket

Main market

Kogore Guesthouse

Africeli, Airtel

MTN

Shell

Chicken Inn

Divine Guesthouse

Embassy Guesthouse

Tajira bus

Bam

Market

Wildlife Explorers

Total

SQUARE ONE STREET

SPEKE STREET

Miles

RMS

Bardays

City Top smkt

Stanbic

New

Mariana

Kirahura Guesthouse

Spy Bar

Zebra

Taxi park

Police

AK

Corporate Inn

MC

BWAMBALE ROAD

KILEMBE ROAD

RWENZORI ROAD

Kasese Executive Inn

Total

Total

Gapco

Bam

Small clothes market

Sizzlers Pub

Tropical Savannah Pub

Bradt

N

0   500m
0   500yds

GETTING THERE AND AWAY Coming directly from Kampala, the best route is the well-maintained 370km surfaced road through Fort Portal, which can be covered in 5–6 hours (there's also a more southerly route via Mbarara, but it's 50km longer and parts are heavily potholed). Distances to other key locations in the southwest are: 35km/60 minutes on the potholed road to Katunguru (for Queen Elizabeth National Park); 75km/90 minutes to Fort Portal; 155km/2–3 hours to Mbarara; 170km/3 hours to Buhoma (Bwindi National Park) via the Ishasha Road;and 220km/4 hours to Kabale along the newly surfaced direct road between Ishaka and Ntungamo.

Plenty of matatus connect Kasese to Katunguru, Mbarara, Kabale and Fort Portal. Link and Kalita buses between Kampala and Kasese via Fort Portal run throughout the day in both directions (*US$8; 6hrs*).

WHERE TO STAY *Map, opposite*
Kasese has a decent selection of accommodation at the lower end of the price scale, but if you are looking for something more upmarket, you're better off in Queen Elizabeth National Park, Fort Portal or even Nyakalengija.

Upmarket

Hotel Margherita (38 rooms)
✪ 0.18627, 30.06115; ✆ 041 4232183; m 0772 695808; e info@hotel-margherita.com; www. hotel-margherita.com. Situated 3km from the town centre along the Kilembe Rd, this former government hotel nudges into the upmarket bracket on the basis of price more than quality. Still, the spacious & comfortable rooms have nets, DSTV, optional AC & en-suite tub/shower, there's a commanding view of the Rwenzori at the front, some birdlife in the flowering rear garden & a restaurant serving an unimaginative menu of grills & stews in the US$7–8 range. Despite the institutional architecture & fuddy-duddy décor, this is the most tranquil & appealing option in Kasese, at least if you have the funds (& there seems to be leeway for negotiation). *US$70/95 sgl/dbl without AC, US$95/107 with AC. All rates B&B.* **$$$**

Moderate

Rwenzori International Hotel (36 rooms) Mbogo Rd; ✪ 0.16051, 30.07573; ✆ 048 3444148; m 0782 282008; e info@ rwenzoriinternationalhotel.com; www. rwenzoriinternationalhotel.com. Set in a quiet suburban garden off the Mbarara Rd 2km south of the main roundabout, this pleasant hotel has clean rooms with nets, AC, private balcony & en-suite hot shower. A restaurant/bar with garden seating serves mains in the US$3–5 range & amenities include sauna, massage & Wi-Fi. Very good value. *US$24/27/32 sgl/dbl/twin B&B.* **$$**

Sandton Hotel (50 rooms) Rwenzori Av; ✆ 048 3445307; m 0705 763655/0750 780560; e info@sandtonhotelkasese.net; www. sandtonhotelkasese.net. This large & centrally located hotel is easily the smartest option in the town centre. It has a good AC restaurant with mains in the US$5–7 range. The modern rooms all have net, fan, AC, DSTV & en-suite tub or shower. There's Wi-Fi throughout. *US$35/52/61 sgl/dbl/ twin.* **$$$**

Budget

Uhuru 50 Hotel (14 rooms) m 0784 414632/0755 994085; e reservations@ uhuruhotelkasese.com; www.uhuruhotelkasese. com. This well-managed new 2-storey hotel 300m north of Kilembe Rd has small but comfortable rooms with net, en-suite hot shower & in some cases private balcony. A 1st-floor restaurant serves a fair selection of mains for around US$3 & there's a ground-floor bar. Good value. *US$14/18 sgl/dbl B&B.* **$$**

Virina Garden Hotel (50 rooms) Square One St; m 0751 805838/ 0772 588161; e info@ virinahotels.com; www.virinahotels.com, 🅕 fb.me/Virina-Garden-HOTEL. This well-established central hotel offers the option of conventional rooms in the main building or thatched mock-traditional cottage in the garden. All rooms have nets, DSTV & fan. Maybe a touch overpriced. *US$17/23 sgl/dbl, or US$33 dbl with AC.* **$$**

Collin Inn (24 rooms) Margherita St; m 0781 987730. This adequate hotel with distinctive frontage lies at the far end of the main street. Small but clean rooms come with net, fan, DSTV & en-suite cold shower. *US$12/13 sgl/dbl, or US$20 superior 1st-floor dbl.* **$**

Shoestring

White House Hotel (27 rooms) Off Kilembe Rd; m 0782 536263; e whitehse_hotel@yahoo.co.uk. This long-serving backpackers' favourite has small but clean rooms with fitted nets, fan & DSTV, & a reasonable restaurant is attached (see below). Good value. *US$7/12 sgl/twin with common showers; US$13 en-suite dbl with hot water. All rates B&B.* **$**

Travellers Inn (10 rooms) m 0776 812981/0754 329909. Situated just 200m from the taxi park, this annex of the White House has clean sgl rooms with ¾ bed, fitted net & en-suite hot shower. Great value. *US$8 sgl.* **$**

Emirates Hotel (10 rooms) m 0756 359973. Just a few doors up from the Travellers Inn, & similarly good value, this clean lodge has spacious rooms with fitted net, fan, DSTV & hot shower. *US$8/12 dbl or twin with common/en-suite shower.* **$**

Jeliza Hotel & Grill (30 rooms) Rwenzori Rd. This 3-storey hotel 100m from the main taxi park isn't as smart as the exterior might lead you to expect, but the en-suite rooms with DSTV are fine at the price (though some lack a fan) & a decent restaurant is attached. *US$10/13 dbl with cold/hot shower.* **$**

✕ WHERE TO EAT AND DRINK *Map, page 420*

The standout in terms of location is the restaurant at the out-of-town Margherita Hotel, though the food here doesn't quite match up to the daunting montane backdrop. The Sandton Hotel has the best continental menu in the town centre, while cheap drinks and snacks can be found at any number of unpretentious bars and roadside barbecues on Stanley Road.

✳ ✕ **Jambo!** Alexander St; m 0774 552266/0751 662844; ▮ fb.me/Jambocafekasese; ⏱ 08.00–19.30 daily. Run by 3 local women, this chilled-out church-affiliated cooperative serves good locally sourced coffee, smoothies & juices, light meals (fajitas, filled pancakes, pizza, salads) & cakes geared towards the palates of volunteers & travellers. It also sells a range of local handicrafts, & has secondhand books to buy or swap. *Most drinks under US$1.50 & meals under US$3.*

✳ ✕ **White House Gardens** Off Kilembe Rd; m 0782 536263; ⏱ 07.00–23.00 daily. This open-air restaurant opposite the eponymous guesthouse

has a long, varied & well-priced menu embracing Indian & Ugandan dishes, pasta & excellent whole grilled tilapia. It's also the greenest spot in town for a drink. *Mains in the US$1.50–3.50 range.*

✕ **Café Olimaco** Stanley St; m 0772 480580; ⏱ 08.00–22.30 daily. This pleasant café with terrace seating serves fresh coffee & a very limited selection of snacks.

✕ **Life & Style Restaurant** Rwenzori Rd; ⏱ 07.30–21.30 Sun-Fri. This clean & friendly local eatery serves filling meat & vegetarian dishes. *Meals under US$3.*

SHOPPING For groceries, try the well-stocked Rwenzori Supermarket on Margherita Street, or the Titti's and City Top supermarkets on Rwenzori Road. For handicrafts, your best bet is the Rwenzori Information Centre and Craft Shop or Jambo! – the latter also has a few secondhand novels for sale.

OTHER PRACTICALITIES

Foreign exchange The usual services are provided by the Stanbic and Barclays banks, both of which have ATMs.

Internet Internet facilities include Kasese Computer Solutions on Margherita Road, and the White House Hotel.

Swimming A kidney-shaped swimming pool can be found at the otherwise rather moribund and difficult-to-recommend Spring International Hotel, which

lies about 1km along the Kilembe Road and is easily recognised by a broken-tusked elephant statue at the entrance. Swimming costs US$1.50.

TOURIST INFORMATION AND OPERATORS

Rwenzori Information Centre & Craft Shop Square One St. Situated next to the Virina Garden Hotel, this once helpful source of travel information still stocks a few brochures, but it seems to be more craft shop than information office these days.

Rwenzori Mountaineering Services Rwenzori Rd; m 0784 327841; e rwenzorims@yahoo.co.uk; www.rwenzorims.com. The sole operator on Rwenzori's Central Circuit maintains an information & booking office in Kasese.

Wildlife Explorers Sebwe Rd; 048 3444053, m 0703 857266; e info@wildlife-explorers.com; www.wildlife-explorers.com. This Kasese-based operator can arrange trips into nearby Queen Elizabeth National Park.

WHAT TO SEE AND DO Kasese is the sort-of springboard for day and overnight hikes in Rwenzori National Park, though in truth there is no need to stop in town if you'll be exploring the central circuit out of Nyakalengija, while those doing the southern circuit could continue directly to the trailhead at Kilembe. Budget conscious self-drivers might settle on Kasese as a base for visits to Queen Elizabeth National Park.

Kilembe Mines Golf Club (m 0706 593059; e kilembeminesgolfclub@gmail.com).

This recently revived 18-hole golf course, one of the most beautiful and reputedly the most challenging in Uganda, was founded in 1960 at the foot of the Rwenzori Mountains, 3km out of Kasese close to the Margherita Hotel. A round costs US$13 and caddies and clubs are available to hire.

Kilembe Situated on the Rwenzori footslopes about 8km west of Kasese, the small

town of Kilembe was established in 1950 to service the adjoining copper mine of the same name. It remains a strangely time-warped place, dotted with 1950s-style buildings, most of which survived being damaged by boulders washed down in 2013 by the flooded river Nyamwamba. How long Kilembe will retain its late-colonial era aura is an open question, given that the mine is set to reopen under new Chinese management in 2016, but as things stand it's an intriguing albeit inessential diversion from Kasese.

Rwenzori Art Gallery, Sculpture Centre and Coffee Bar Set on a 60ha tract

of bush owned by Rwenzori Founders (⊕ 0.25728, 30.10788; m 0782 238036; e rfkasese@yahoo.com; www.rwenzorifounders.com; see ad, 4th colour section), this gallery displays the bronze work of 15 Ugandan sculptors, several of whom were trained in the lengthy lost-wax casting process in the UK in 2008. Permanent exhibits include a series of more than 30 magnificent bronzes representing the different clan totems of Uganda, as well as soapstone and marble carvings made by local artists. The land on which the gallery stands has been rehabilitated as a private nature sanctuary through the extensive replanting of indigenous trees, and the checklist now includes 150-plus bird species, as well as various small mammals and reptiles. A guided tour of the foundry costs US$5, and there is also a gallery with items for sale (at very reasonable prices by international standards), and a coffee shop serving hot drinks, biscuits and snacks. To get to there from Kasese, follow the Fort Portal road out of town for 10km to Makumlana (also known as Kyemihoko) trading centre (⊕ 0.24941, 30.11631), then turn left on to the signposted feeder road and follow it for 1.5km. The management requires all visitors to call in advance.

17

RWENZORI MOUNTAINS NATIONAL PARK

Gazetted in 1991, the 996km² Rwenzori Mountains National Park protects the upper slopes and glacial peaks of the immense 5,109m-high mountain range that runs along the Congolese border for a full 120km south of Lake Albert and north of Lake Edward. Rwenzori is Uganda's most alluring hiking destination, traversed by two discrete six- to nine-day trail circuits, one starting at Kilembe in the south and the other at Nyakalengija about 20km further north. These trails

pass through a fascinating succession of altitudinally-defined vegetation zones, ranging from montane rainforest to Afro-alpine moorland, and the scenery can be breathtaking. Be warned, however, that the upper Rwenzori is widely regarded to present tougher hiking conditions than the ascents of Mount Kilimanjaro or Kenya, largely due to the mud, which can be knee-deep in places after rain, and as such it requires above-average fitness and stamina. Unlike on Kilimanjaro, normal Rwenzori hikes stick below the snowline (around 4,500m), which reduces the risk of altitude-related illness, but the glacial peaks are accessible to

The advent of colonial rule robbed the Bakonjo of Uganda of much of their former independence, since their territory was placed under the indirect rule of the Toro monarchy, to which they were forced to pay hut taxes and other tributes. Widespread dissatisfaction with this state of affairs led to the Bakonjo Uprising of 1919, which endured for two years before its leader, Chief Tibamwenda, and his two leading spiritual advisers, were captured by the authorities and executed. But the strong resentment against Toro that still existed amongst the Bakonjo and their Bwamba neighbours resurfaced 40 years later, during the build-up to independence.

In 1961, the Bakonjo and Bwamba, frustrated by Toro's unwillingness to grant them equal status within the kingdom, demanded that they be given their own federal district of Ruwenzururu (Land of the Snow), to be governed independently of Toro. This request was refused. In August 1962, two months before Uganda was to gain independence, the Bakonjo took up arms in the Ruwenzururu Rebellion, attacking several Toro officials and resulting in a number of riots and fatalities. In February 1963, the central government declared a local State of Emergency in affected parts of Toro, and the Bakonjo were invited to elect their own government agents to replace the local representatives of Toro. Instead, the Bakonjo and Bwamba unofficially but effectively ceded from Uganda, by establishing their own Ruwenzururu kingdom, ruled by King Mukirania, and placing border posts and immigration officers at all entry points.

In 1967, the researcher Kirstin Alnaes, who had made several previous study trips to the region, noted that:

'The difference ... from 1960 was marked ... Earlier ... spirit possession rituals were performed surreptitiously. Now people sported houses and shrines for the spirits, and were more than willing to talk about it. It was as if the establishment of their own territory in the mountains had released a belief in themselves and their cultural identity [formerly] suppressed not only by government regulations and missionary influence, but also by their own fear of seeming 'backward', 'uncivilised', 'monkeys' and the many other epithets the Batoro had showered upon them.'

The situation in Ruwenzururu deteriorated after 1967, as government troops made repeated forays into the breakaway montane kingdom to capture or kill the rebel ringleaders. Ironically, it was only under Amin, who came to power in 1971, that the right to self-determination among the Bakonjo and Bwamba was finally accorded official recognition, with the creation of Rwenzori and Semliki districts, which correspond to the modern districts of Kasese and Bundibugyo. Even so, clan elders must still today obtain a permit from the authorities before they may visit centuries-old sacrificial shrines to the various mountain spirits situated within the national park.

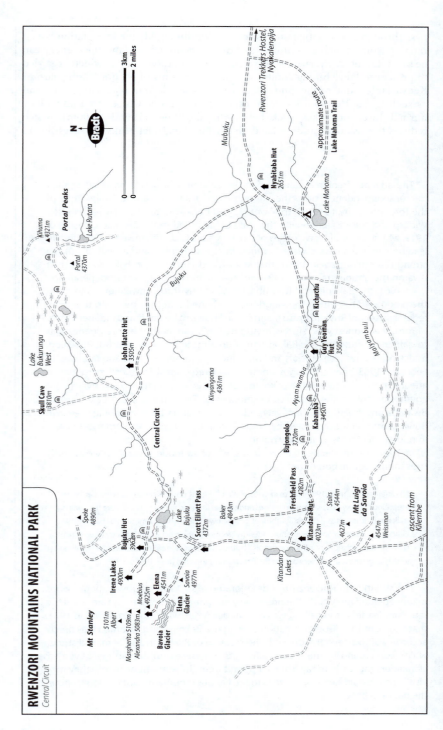

RWENZORI MOUNTAINS NATIONAL PARK

Central Circuit

Central Circuit

Mt Stanley

5101m
Albert ▲

Margherita 5109m ▲
Alexandra 5083m ▲

Bavoia
Glacier

Elena
Glacier

Moebius ▲

Elena
4541m

Savoia
4977m

Irene Lakes
4900m

Bujuku Hut
3962m

Speke ▲
4890m

Lake
Bujuku

Scott Elliott Pass
4372m

Kitandara Hut
4023m

Kitandara
Lakes

Baker ▲
4843m

Freshfield Pass
4282m

Stairs ▲
4544m

Mt Luigi
da Savoia

4627m ▲

4547m ▲
Weissman

*ascent from
Kilembe*

Bujongolo
3720m

Kabamba
3450m

Guy Yeoman
Hut
3505m

Kichuchu

Mayambuli

Nyamwamba

Kinyangoma ▲
4361m

Bujuku

Central Circuit

Skull Cave
3810m

Lake
Bukurungu
West

John Matte Hut
3505m

Mubuku

Kihuma ▲
4321m

Portal Peaks

Portal ▲
4370m

Lake Rutara

Nyabitaba Hut
2651m

Lake Mahoma

approximate route

Lake Mahoma Trail

*Rwenzori Trekkers' Hostel,
Nyakalengija*

N

Bradt

3km

2 miles

0

0

experienced technical climbers. At the other end of the commitment scale, those with with limited time, money or stamina can choose from a number of day or short overnight hikes through the forested slopes above Kilembe or Nyakalengija, or head up to Fort Portal and follow the Northern Rwenzori mini-hike between nearby Kazingo and Bundibugyo.

GEOLOGY AND HISTORY Rising from the western base of the Albertine Rift, the ancient gneissic, quartzite and other crystalline rocks of the Rwenzori peaks were uplifted to their present altitude about three million years ago, during the same tectonic upheaval responsible for the creation of lakes Albert, Edward and George more than 4,000m below. Roughly 120km long and 65km wide, the range incorporates six main massifs, the tallest being Mount Stanley, whose loftiest peaks are Margherita (5,109m) and Alexandra (5,083m). Margherita is exceeded in altitude elsewhere in Africa only by the free-standing volcanic cones of Kilimanjaro and Kenya, meaning that the Rwenzori is the highest proper mountain range anywhere on the continent. There are four other glacial peaks – Speke (4,890m), Emin (4,791m), Gessi (4,715m) and Luigi da Savoia (4,627m) – but global climate change has caused the combined extent of glacial coverage to retreat from 7.5km² in 1906 to a mere 1.5km² today.

Habitually obscured by clouds, the Rwenzori, though obviously well known to the local Bakonjo people (see box, pages 424–5), eluded European geographers until as recently as 1889, when the peaks were observed by Arthur Jephson and Thomas Parke, members of Henry Morton Stanley's cross-continental expedition to rescue Emin Pasha. Stanley's second in command, William Stairs, ascended the slopes as high as the 3,250m contour, followed in 1895 by the geologist George Scott Elliot and in 1900 by the biologist JES Moore, both of whom managed to reach the 4,500m snowline. Margherita was summited for the first time in 1906, when Duke Luigi di Savoia's expedition – comprising more than 150 porters, a miscellany of scientists and the photographer Vittorio Sella – undertook a pioneering cartographic and biological survey of the Rwenzori, conquering all the major peaks in the process.

Ever since the Stanley expedition observed its distant glacial peaks in 1889, Rwenzori has been popularly identified as the snow-capped 'Montes Lunae' (Mountains of the Moon) which Ptolemy's *Geography*, written circa AD150, cited as the primary source of the Nile. According to Ptolemy, the existence of the Mountains of the Moon was based on a report by a Greek merchant named Diogenes, who followed a waterway inland from a port called Rhapta for 25 days to reach their base. Some modern geographers speculate that Diogenes's story is pure fabrication, and that the existence of several snow-capped ranges in equatorial Africa is mere coincidence. But even if Diogenes's account is true, it seems most likely that the mountain he saw was either Kilimanjaro or Kenya – both of which lie far closer to the coast, are reachable from it along rivers, and have more frequently visible snow caps – and that its supposed connection with the Nile was based on hearsay or extrapolation.

FLORA AND FAUNA As is the case with other comparably lofty East African mountains, the vegetation of the Rwenzori can be divided into several altitude zones, each with its own distinct microclimate, flora and fauna. The Afro-montane forest zone, which starts at 1,800m, has the most varied fauna. Above 2,500m, closed canopy forest starts to give way to dense bamboo stands. Higher still, spanning altitudes of 3,000m to 4,500m, the open vegetation of the heather and alpine zones has an otherworldly quality, with forests of giant heather trees throughout, and

the striking 10m high *Lobelia wollanstonii* and giant groundsel (*Senecio admiralis*) most common above 3,800m.

The diverse fauna of the Rwenzori includes 70 mammal and 177 bird species, several of the latter being Albertine Rift endemics. It is the only national park in Uganda where the Angola colobus has been recorded, though identification of this localised monkey will require careful examination as the similar and more widespread black-and-white colobus also occurs on the mountain. The only other mammal you're likely to see in the forest is the blue monkey, but elephant, buffalo, golden cat, servalline genet, chimpanzee, yellow-backed duiker and giant forest hog are all present. At night, the forest resounds with the distinctive and eerie call of the southern tree hyrax. Mammals are scarce above the forest zone.

Birds of the forest zone include Rwenzori turaco, barred long-tailed cuckoo, long-eared owl, handsome francolin, cinnamon-chested bee-eater, Archer's ground robin, white-starred forest robin, Rwenzori batis, montane sooty boubou, Lagden's bush shrike, slender-billed starling, blue-headed sunbird, golden-winged sunbird, strange weaver, and several varieties of barbet, greenbul, apalis, illadopsis, flycatcher and crimson-wing. At higher altitudes, look out for lammergeyer (bearded vulture) and black eagle soaring overhead, as well as alpine and scarce swifts, and the stunning scarlet-tufted malachite sunbird.

CLOTHING AND EQUIPMENT Wet conditions and sub-zero temperatures are normal, so it is essential you are properly prepared. Bring plenty of layered warm clothing for the nights. Rain is to be expected at all times of year (even the relatively dry months from late December to early March and late June to early September), so pack a decent waterproof jacket and trousers which you've tried on before the climb, and take plenty of plastic bags, both to keep clean clothes dry and to quarantine wet or dirty garments. Some paths are incredibly muddy after rain (knee-deep in parts), so while you'll need hiking boots if scaling any peaks, you'll be happier wearing locally bought gumboots elsewhere above the forest and bamboo zone.

Rwenzori Trekking Services includes all meals in its package rates, but Rwenzori Mountaineering Services gives you the option of feeding yourself. If you decide to self-cater, you'll need to plan meals and quantities for a week or more. Vegetables and dried foods – noodles, rice, packet soups, posho, groundnut flour, etc – are available in Kasese and Fort Portal. You'll also need to bring or hire a camping stove (*US$50*) and utensils. At altitude, eating can be a bit of a chore so do what you can to generate an appetite by varying meals. Whichever you choose, take a few snacks – chocolate and the like – and include some for the poor chap who's carrying your luggage!

If you intend to climb one of the glacial peaks, bring climbing boots and equipment such as ropes, ice-axes, harnesses, crampons and walking sticks, or hire gear from your mountain operator. Make sure they are aware of your requirements and allow plenty of time so that shoes, etc, can be sized, fitted and paid for, ideally the day before departure to avoid misunderstandings and other delays. Snow goggles, a compass and an altimeter will also be useful.

MOUNTAIN HEALTH Do not attempt to climb the Rwenzori unless you are reasonably fit, or if you have heart or lung problems (asthma sufferers should be all right). Once above 3,000m, hikers may not feel hungry, but they should try to eat. Carbohydrates and fruit are recommended, whilst rich or fatty foods are harder to digest. Dehydration is one of the most common reasons for failing to complete the climb. Drink at least three litres of liquid daily, and bring enough water bottles to carry

this. If you dress in layers, you can take off clothes before you sweat too much, thereby reducing water loss.

Altitude-related illness is not a major concern below the snowline. That said, few people climb above 3,500m without feeling minor symptoms such as headaches, nausea, fatigue, breathlessness, sleeplessness and swelling of the hands and feet. You can reduce these by allowing yourself time to acclimatise by taking an extra day over the ascent, eating and drinking properly, and trying not to push yourself. If you walk slowly and steadily, you will tire less quickly than if you try to rush each day's walk. Acetazolamide (Diamox) also helps speed acclimatisation. Take 250mg twice a day for five days, starting two or three days before reaching 3,500m. Be warned that the side-effects of Acetazolamide may resemble altitude sickness, so best try the medication for a couple of days about two weeks before the trip to check it suits you.

The risk of developing full-blown altitude sickness is greatest if you ascend the peaks. But at any altitude, should symptoms become severe or suddenly get worse, you may be developing pulmonary or cerebral oedema, both of which can be fatal. Symptoms of pulmonary oedema include shortness of breath even when at rest, and coughing up frothy spit or blood. Symptoms of cerebral oedema are headaches, poor co-ordination, staggering, disorientation, poor judgement and even hallucinations. Sleeping high with significant symptoms of altitude sickness is dangerous, and the only treatment is to descend as quickly as possible; even going down 500m is enough to start recovery. Sufferers often don't realise how sick they are, and may argue against descending. Fortunately, guides are trained to recognise altitude-related symptoms, and will force their clients to turn back immediately if they feel it is unsafe to continue.

Hypothermia is a lowering of body temperature usually caused by a combination of cold and wet. Mild cases usually manifest themselves as uncontrollable shivering. Put on dry, warm clothes and get into a sleeping bag; this will normally raise your body temperature sufficiently. Severe hypothermia is potentially fatal: symptoms include disorientation, lethargy, mental confusion (including an inappropriate feeling of well-being and warmth!) and coma. In severe cases the rescue team should be summoned.

BOOKS AND MAPS The definitive written guide is the revised 2006 edition of the late Henry Osmaston's self-published *Guide to the Rwenzori*, which is now out of print but can be tracked down through the usual online outlets. Andrew Wielochowski's excellent *Rwenzori Map and Guide* shows contours and new routes, has plenty of practical and background information on the reverse side, and can be ordered online from www.ewpnet.com. Also useful for the peak area is the Department of Lands and Surveys' 1:25,000 *Central Rwenzori* contour map.

HIKING ROUTES Two main hiking circuits traverse Rwenzori Mountains National Park. The longer and newer **Southern Circuit**, which starts near Kilembe near Kasese, then ascends to the upper moorland via the Nyamwamba Valley, is operated exclusively by Rwenzori Trekking Services (*RTS*; m *0774 199022*; e *rwenzoritrekking@ gmail.com*; *www.rwenzoritrekking.com*), an offshoot of the Australian-managed Kampala Backpackers. The more established (and until recently only) option is the **Central Circuit**, which ascends to the peak area from Nyakalengija via the Mubuku and Bujuku valleys, and is in theory operated exclusively by Rwenzori Mountaineering Services (*RMS*; m *0784 327841/308425*; e *rwenzorims@yahoo. co.uk*; *www.rwenzorims.com*), a community tourism group established in the 1990s to provide local Bakonjo people with the opportunity to benefit from tourism on the

Though RMS guides are generally able to lead hikes around the Central Circuit Trail, the consensus over several years of reader feedback is that few, if any, are competent to lead climbers above the snowline. Unless you have experience in alpine climbing conditions and carry your own map, compass and GPS, it's highly questionable whether you will be safe above the snowline with this organisation. Here's an extract from a letter from a British climber which remains as relevant today as it was when it was written in 2002.

'The guides vary enormously in terms of quality and experience. We had two guides, one of whom spoke no English and was utterly useless from start to finish. He had no cold-weather equipment and became a serious liability on the summit day because he had only thin cotton trousers, a light anorak and no hat. He also wore gumboots, which cannot realistically take crampons, all the way to the summit. On the glacier stages we had to continually stop in cold and windy weather while he tried in vain to get his crampons to stay on.

'Our second guide at least spoke English and had a basic idea of the plants and animals of the mountains. He was a nice guy and meant well. But his technical skills were extremely rusty and on the summit day he became alarmingly confused about how to rope up and how to set up a belay. His climbing calls were all wrong, he gave no instruction to the team, and on a particularly steep and exposed rock face below the summit he was essentially hauling us up with brute strength from a non-belayed position – until we as a team made clear our climbing knowledge and insisted on better protection.

'On the Stanley Plateau we got lost in thick mist and the guides became stubborn and silent when we insisted that we stop and assess our situation. As a group we had carried a map, a compass and a GPS, so knew exactly where we were and which way we should proceed. Meanwhile the guides had no such aids and were going on memory alone. It was only our team's skill that averted a disaster. Even when we located cairns and flags that marked the summit route, the guides still maintained the pretence that we were not going the right way, apparently to protect their own pride. All in all, quite frightening and unprofessional.'

mountain. Recently, hikes on the Central Circuit, and minor variations thereof, have also been offered by Rwenzori Ranges Hikers Association (*RRHA;* m *0750 767973;* e *rwenzorihikers@gmail.com; www.rwenzorihikers.com)*, a breakaway outfit with reputable backers that aims to offer better quality services than RMS, and might well do as and when it obtains a UWA mandate to operate on the mountain, but has to be considered a bit dodgy until that happens.

Comparing the two routes, the main advantages of the established Central Circuit are that it is shorter and slightly cheaper. The ascendant Southern Route is rapidly gaining greater popularity, however, for the very simple reason that RMS, for all its ostensible worthiness, has a dismal record by comparison to RTS when it comes to quality of guides, safety and rescue procedures, transparency with clients, environmental practices, and pretty much every other organisational facet of a successful trek.

A third option, suited to time- or budget-conscious travellers who just want to spend a day on the mountain, is the **Northern Rwenzori mini-hike** connecting Kazingo (13km from Fort Portal) to Bundibugyo. This is operated by the dedicated guides'

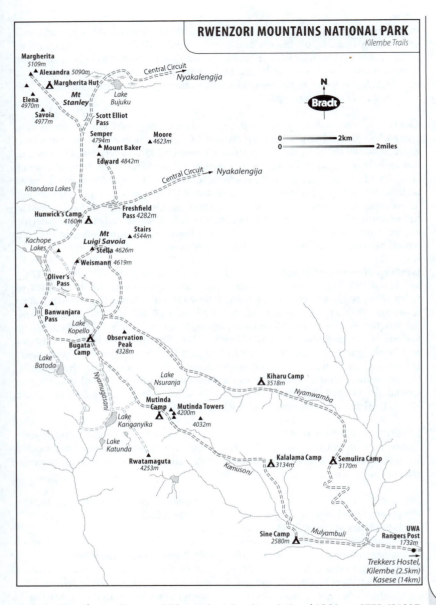

RWENZORI MOUNTAINS NATIONAL PARK
Kilembe Trails

Margherita
5109m
Alexandra *5090m*
Margherita Hut
Elena
4970m
Mt Stanley
Lake Bujuku
Central Circuit
Nyakalengija
Savoia
4977m
Scott Elliot Pass
Semper
4794m
Moore
4623m
Mount Baker
Edward *4842m*
Kitandara Lakes
Central Circuit → *Nyakalengija*
Hunwick's Camp
4160m
Freshfield Pass *4282m*
Stairs
4544m
Kachope Lakes
Mt Luigi Savoia
Stella *4626m*
Weismann *4619m*
Oliver's Pass
Banwanjara Pass
Lake Kopello
Observation Peak
4328m
Bugata Camp
Lake Batoda
Lake Nsuranja
Kiharu Camp
3518m
Nyamwamba
Nyamugasani
Mutinda Camp
Mutinda Towers
4200m
4032m
Lake Kanganyika
Lake Katunda
Rwatamaguta
4253m
Kamusoni
Kalalama Camp
3134m
Semulira Camp
3170m
Sine Camp
2580m
Mulyambuli
UWA Rangers Post
1732m
Trekkers Hostel,
Kilembe (2.5km)
Kasese (14km)

N

Bradt

0 — 2km
0 — 2miles

17

organisation Abanya-Rwenzori Mountaineering Association (*AMA;* m *0772 621397;* e *abanya_rwenzori@yahoo.com; https://sites.google.com/site/abanyarwenzori*).

Inexpensive day hikes outside the national park boundary can be arranged through the Ruboni Community Camp near Nyakalengija.

Nyakalengija and the Central Circuit
For many years the only trail network in Rwenzori Mountains National Park, the Central Circuit ascends from Nyakalengija trailhead, which lies off the Fort Portal Road about 25km northwest

of Kasese. Although hikes on this circuit can be booked through any tour operator in Uganda, on-the-ground arrangements are the exclusive domain of RMS, which maintains offices in Kampala and Kasese, as well as at Nyakalengija. The standard circuit is six days and five nights, but extra nights are required to ascend Margherita or any other peaks, while other options include day hikes into the forest around Nyakalengija.

Costs The standard six- or seven-day guided hike along the Central Circuit loop costs US$500/580 per person (slightly less for groups of five or more), to which must be added the national park entrance fee of US$35/25 FNR/FR per 24 hours. An eight-day package including the ascent of Margherita or Mount Stanley costs an additional US$200 per person. If you want RMS to feed you, you'll pay an additional US$20 per party per day for a cook and US$20 per person per day for food. These rates include one porter per client, carrying a maximum of 25kg, as well as hut accommodation, guide and park entrance fees. They exclude mountaineering equipment such as climbing boots, sleeping bags, ropes, crampons and the like, which can be rented from RMS at US$25 per item.

Getting there and away The Nyakalengija trailhead (✪ 0.35538, 30.02741) lies about 25km northwest of Kasese and takes approximately 40 minutes to reach in a private vehicle. To get there, follow the Fort Portal Road north out of town for 10km to the junction village of Nkenda (✪ 0.25423, 30.11683), where the junction for Rwenzori Mountains National Park is signposted to the left. The various accommodation options below lie alongside the road between Nkenda and Nyakalengija. Matatus between Kasese and Fort Portal can drop passengers at Nkenda, and there are also matatus to Ibanda, about 6km before Nyakalengija, but no further. Most travellers charter a boda from Kasese (*US$5–8*) or arrange a special hire (*US$15–25*). Transport from Kasese (or indeed Kampala, or anywhere else in Uganda) can be arranged with RMS.

🏠 **Where to stay and eat** Many people overnight in Kasese immediately before and after their ascent, but there are also several prettier and pricier accommodation options in the Mubuku Valley alongside the main road between Nkenda and Nyakalengija.

Upmarket

🏠 **Equator Snow Lodge** (4 cottages)
✪ 0.35456, 30.02814; ☎ 041 4258273; m 0703 723274; e reservations@geolodgesafrica.com; www.geolodgesafrica.com. Situated less than 1km from Nyakalengija trailhead, this smart lodge is set at a chilly altitude of 1,600m in a lovely forest patch bisected by the babbling Mubuku River & inhabited by Rwenzori duiker, giant forest hog, various monkeys & at least 110 species of forest bird. The spacious stone cottages all have 1 dbl & 2 sgl beds, skylight, a sitting area with fireplace, wood-&-stone finishes offset by bright ethnic fabrics, balcony with a view through the forest to the river & large ensuite bathroom with hot water. A lovely & reasonably priced forest retreat even if you've no intention of hiking higher. *US$132/242 sgl/dbl FB.* **$$$$**

Moderate

🏠 **Rwenzori Base Camp Holiday Inn** (15 rooms) ✪ 0.3325, 30.07163; m 0772 482248/0752 796445; e cobwa@yahoo.co.uk. Situated in Ibanda 10km from Nkenda along the Nyakalengija road, this agreeable hotel is set in pretty green garden rooms on the edge of the village. The spacious & clean en-suite rooms come with net, DSTV, seating & hot shower, while a restaurant with garden seating serves meals in the US$5–6 range. Expensive compared to similar accommodation in Kasese. *US$50/55/60 sgl/dbl/ twin B&B.* **$$$**

Budget

⌂ **Ruboni Community Camp** (6 rooms)
⌖ 0.35023, 30.03007; m 0773 650049; e info@
rubonicamp.com; www.rubonicamp.com. This
worthy community project is perched on the
western slopes of the Mubuku River Valley, 2km
beyond Ruboni trading centre. It has a lovely
hillside location & great mountain views, & is only
about 1km from Nyakalengija trailhead. Guided
morning or afternoon walks through the local
Bakonjo communities cost US$15pp. Simple meals
cost US$3–6. Coming from Nkenda, make sure
you aren't deposited at the office, also confusingly

signposted for Ruboni Community Camp,
about 3km before the camp itself. Again, pricey
compared to similar accommodation in Kasese.
*US$20/25pp B&B room with common/en-suite
showers, US$5 camping.* **$$**
⌂ **Rwenzori Turaco View Camp** (3 rooms)
⌖ 0.3458, 30.03471; m 0772 855318/0781
758826; e mbakaniazave@gmail.com. Located
in a pretty meadow about 600m before Ruboni
Camp, this friendly, community-run set up offers
accommodation in basic but clean & relatively
inexpensive bandas using shared facilities.
US$10/15 sgl/twin. **$**

Hiking and walking routes The Central Circuit, described stage-by-stage below, takes six or seven days, depending on whether you break up the final ascent over one or two days. This circuit sticks below the snow line, so an additional extra one or two days is required to tackle the peaks. In addition to the Central Circuit, Nyakalengija is also the starting point for the newer three-day Lake Mahoma Trail, and a number of day trails.

The Central Circuit For many years, this circuit out of Nyakalengija provided the only available access to the Upper Rwenzori. Issues with RMS notwithstanding, it remains an exciting and superbly scenic experience. Note that the ascent of Margherita or Mount Stanley each require an additional one day, slotting in between days three and four of the circuit described below. Mount Speke is reached from Bujuku Hut, where you will need to spend one extra night to allow you a full day to summit and return. To ascend the 5,109m Margherita Peak, the Rwenzori's highest point, you need spend a night at Elena Hut (4,541m), 2km off the Central Circuit Trail, and 3–4 hours on foot from either Bujuku or Kitandara Huts.

Day One: Nyakalengija (1,615m) to Nyabitaba Hut (2,651m) (*5hrs; altitude gain: 1,036m*) From the trailhead at Nyakalengija, it's a 10km ascent to Nyabitaba Hut, passing first through cultivation then through forest. There's a piped water supply at the hut.

Day Two: Nyabitaba Hut (2,651m) to John Matte Hut (3,505m) (*7hrs; altitude gain: 854m*) This is the longest and most strenuous day's walk. From Nyabitaba Hut, the path descends through forest for a short time before it crosses the Bujuku River at the Kurt Schafer Bridge (built in 1989). Between the bridge and Nyamileju Hut, the path is good for the first couple of hours, but it becomes steeper and very rocky as you enter the moorland zone, where heather plants are prolific. After about 5 hours you will emerge at Nyamileju, where the little-used hut is supplemented by a rock shelter, making for a good lunch stop. From Nyamileju, the path passes a giant heather forest and follows the Bujuku River for 2 hours to John Matte Hut, which is in good condition and stands about 200m from the Bujuku River, where water can be collected.

Day Three: John Matte Hut (3,505m) to Bujuku Hut (3,962m) (*5hrs; altitude gain: 457m*) This stage takes up to 5 hours, depending on the condition of the two Bigo Bogs, which are often knee-deep in mud, though a boardwalk has now been constructed across

part of it. On the way, Lake Bujuku has a magnificent setting between mounts Stanley, Speke and Baker.

Day Four: Bujuku Hut (3,962m) to Kitandara Hut (4,023m) (*3–4 hrs; altitude gain: 61m*) From Bujuku Hut you will ascend to Scott Elliot Pass (4,372m), which is the highest point on the Central Circuit Trail, before descending to the two Kitandara lakes. The hut is next to the second lake.

Day Five: Kitandara Hut (4,023m) to Guy Yeoman Hut (3,505m) (*5hrs; descent: 518m*) This stage starts with a steep ascent to Freshfield Pass (4,282m) then a descent to Bujongolo Cave (3,720m), which formed the base of Duke Luigi di Savoia's 1906 expedition. Further along the trail, there is an attractive waterfall and rock shelter at Kabamba Cave (3,450m), where you can overnight as an alternative to Guy Yeoman Hut.

Day Six: Guy Yeoman Hut (3,505m) to Nyakalengija (*5hrs; descent: 1,890m*) It's a 5-hour descent from Guy Yeoman Hut to Nyabitaba Hut (a descent of 851m). You can stay overnight at the hut, but most people continue to the trailhead at Nyakalengija, which will take a further three hours and increases the total descent to 1,890m.

Lake Mahoma Day Trail This new one- to three-day route opened in late 2012 as a shorter and more wildlife-oriented alternative to the Central Circuit. The shortest variation, a day hike out of Nyakalengija (*up to 6hrs; US$65pp*), involves a reasonably gentle climb to an altitude of 2,088m, and offers a good opportunity to see forest monkeys and birds, occasionally even elephants. The full three-day route climbs from Nyakalengija trailhead into the bamboo forest zone, where the glacial Lake Mahoma offers fine views towards the high peaks, weather permitting. Nights are spent at Omu'ka Kizza Camp (2,977m) and Lake Mahoma Camp (3,515m), neither of which offer hutted accommodation, but are geared to wilderness camping only. It's debatable, however, whether the rewards associated with the three-day hike justify the exertion of what is probably the stiffest bit of legwork on the whole Central Circuit – having willed yourself that far, it would be a shame not to see some Afro-montane vegetation. A far better three-day option is the first two days (then one day to return) of the Kilembe Trail, which is equally tough on the first day, but gets you up with the giant heathers, lobelias and groundsels on the second.

Kilembe and the Southern Circuit Based out of Kilembe (or more accurately the village of Kyanjuki) 14km west of Kasese, the southerly Kilembe Circuit follows a combination of trails along (and between) the Nyamugasani, Kamusoni and Nyamwamba river valleys to reach the peaks area. This route was first used by Professor Scott Elliot in 1895, 11 years before Luigi di Savoia pioneered the more direct route from Nyakalengija via the Bujuku Valley. Coming from the Kilembe trailhead, the hiking distance to the peaks is significantly longer than on the established Central Circuit, and the ascent of Margherita will push the full duration of the excursion to nine days unless you are very fit. On the plus side, the trails run through some pristine and astonishingly beautiful landscapes, most of which had been unvisited by hikers for decades prior to the trail opening. All hikes on this route are operated by RTS, which has a top reputation when it comes to guiding and safety standards.

Costs The cost of the six-day hike to Mount Luigi di Savoia is US$790 per person for one or two people, or US$$710 for three or more. The nine-day trek

to Margherita costs US$1,280 per person for one or two people, or US$1,150 for three or more. A more rapidly paced eight-day variation on the Margherita Climb, suited only to very fit hikers, costs US$1,150 per person for one or two people, or US$1,050 for three or more. Day hikes are priced at US$40 per person (or US$35 for more than three people), while two-/three-day hikes work out at US$190/330 per person for one or two people, or US$160/290 for three or more.

In all cases, these prices includes porters, meals and accommodation whilst on the mountain, but they exclude VAT, which is charged at 18%, and the national park entrance fee of US$35/25 FNR/FR per day.

Getting there and away The base camp for the Kilembe Trail is Rwenzori Backpackers in Kyanjuki, a tiny village situated in the Nyamwamba Valley 3.5km past Kilembe's small town centre coming from Kasese. A boda from Kasese costs US$1.50–3 and a special hire around US$10.

Where to stay and eat If the only accommodation in Kyanjuki is too basic for your tastes, it is perfectly possible to stay overnight in Kasese and head up to trailhead on the day of departure.

🏠 **Rwenzori Backpackers** (6 rooms & 4 dorms) ✆ 0.21748, 30.00049; m 0774 199022; e rwenzoritrekking@gmail.com; www.rwenzoritrekking.com. Run by RTS, this hostel is set at an altitude of 1,450m in an old mine-associated building overlooking the deep Nyamwamba Valley & offering enticing (or daunting!) views of the high Rwenzori. Simple but clean rooms and 5-/6-/7-bed dorms all have nets but use common hot showers & flush toilets. Services include massages (*US$25pp*) & meals in the US$3–6 range. *US$12/20 sgl/dbl rooms, US$8 dorm bed, US$5 camping.* **$$**

Hiking and walking routes The most popular option, requiring no technical climbing ability or equipment, is a six-day loop trail summiting the 4,620m Weisman's Peak and 4,627m Stella Peak on Mount Luigi di Savoia. A longer variation on this is the nine-day loop trail incorporating a summit of Mount Stanley's 5,109m Margherita Peak. Even longer variations taking in both these peaks, and possibly other, can be arranged, too.

Six-day hike to Mount Luigi di Savoia
Day One: Kyambogho Trailhead (1,450m) to Sine Hut (2,590m) (*altitude gain: 1,140m*) This day involves the greatest altitude gain. Starting at the main trailhead 2km past Rwenzori Backpackers, the route runs along the side of the Nyamwamba River Valley for 3km before entering the park for a long, steady climb through montane forest, followed by a stiff ascent through bamboo to reach the Sine Hut in the heather zone. Strong climbers can push on to Kalalama Camp, which lies at 3,147m, and allows longer to acclimatise before continuing to Mutinda the next day.

Day Two: Sine (2,590m) to Mutinda (3,810m) (*altitude gain: 644m*) After a stiff climb through bamboo to Kalalama Camp, the route follows the Kamusoni River Valley up to Mutinda. The overnight camp enjoys a particularly pretty setting among giant groundsels and moss-draped Erica at the foot of the 4,200m multi-pronged Mutinda Towers.

Day Three: Mutinda (3,810m) to Bugata Camp (4,060m) (*altitude gain: 250m*) From Mutinda, the landscape becomes bleaker and more dramatic as the trail traverses open moorland between the Kamusoni and Nyamugasani valleys. The third night's

campsite, set on a high rocky bluff above the Nyamugasani, enjoys a terrific, map-like view of Lake Bugata far below (one of eight glacial lakes in this valley) and north towards Duke Luigi di Savoia.

Day Four: Climb Duke Luigi di Savoia (4,627m) and return to Bugata Camp (*5–6hrs; altitude gain and loss: 567m*) Spend another night at Bugata Camp in order to climb to the two main peaks of Mount Louis di Savoia. This day hike through superb Afro-montane vegetation provides the possibility (weather permitting, of course) of viewing the high peaks to the north and encountering patches of equatorial snow. The climb is not normally technical, but ropes may be required when the rock is snowy or icy.

Day Five: Bugata Camp (4,060m) to Kiharu Camp (3,520m) (*altitude loss: 542m*) This lovely hike back towards Kilembe follows a different route through a valley to an area of evergreen forest where tree hyrax can be heard at night, and monkeys and Rwenzori turacos call by day. It is possible to continue further downhill to Samalira Camp (3,170m), which makes for a shorter and less knee-crunching Day Six.

Day Six: Kiharu Camp (3,520m) to Kyambogho Trailhead (1,450m) (*altitude loss: 2,070m*) The trail descends along a long ridge through bamboo and montane forest to the hostel at Kilembe.

Nine-day hike to Mount Stanley (Margherita Peak)
Days One–Three Same as for the six-day hike to Mount Luigi di Savoia (page 435).

Day Four: Bugata Camp (4,060m) to Hunwick's Camp (3,974m) (*altitude loss: 15m*) Though this day ends with a net descent of 86m, it involves several ups and downs through magnificent scenery. The trail starts with a short but stiff climb to Bamwanjara Pass (4,450m) before a long descent through groundsel forest to the Kachope lakes. The route flanks Mount Savoia before climbing on to a moraine ridge to find the camp. This faces Mount Baker and overlooks the Butawu Valley which drains on to the Rift Valley floor – visible in clear conditions – in the DRC.

Day Five: Hunwick's Camp (3,974m) to Margherita Hut (4,485m) (*altitude gain: 511m*) A great day, this one. The route passes the two lovely Kitandara lakes before ascending the great glacier-carved chasm between mounts Stanley and Baker to Scott Elliot Pass. Hopefully you'll be able to see Lake Bujuku, far below in the classic, U-shaped, vast Bujuku Valley on the eastern side of the pass, before turning up on to Mount Stanley where you'll find Margherita Hut just below RMS's Elena Hut.

Day Six: Climb Margherita Peak (5,109) and return to Hunwick's Camp (3,974m) (*altitude gain: 624m; altitude loss: 1,135m*) An early start is required to ascend Mount Stanley before cloud obscures the views. The route then descends to Hunwick's Camp.

Days Seven–Nine Descend to Bugata Camp, then as Day Five and Six of the six-day hike to Mount Luigi di Savoia (see above).

Shorter variations A good option for birders and wildlife lovers, the **Munyamubuli River Trail** is a 6–7-hour day hike passing through pristine Afro-montane forest rich in plants, primates and birds. A two-night variation of this follows the same valley further, before climbing a steep ridge to sleep in Omusitha Camp (2,792m). Better for scenery but less wildlife-oriented, the two-night **Samalira**

Trail leads over 5–6 hours to the eponymous camp, set at an altitude of 3,140 metres, and offers the option of climbing a bit higher for better views over Lake George and Queen Elizabeth National Park. The three-day **Kalevala Loop Trail** passes through the Munyamubuli before climbing a heavily forested ridge where black-and-white colobus, blue monkey and L'Hoest's monkey are often seen. Overnight stops are at Samalira Camp, then at Kalalama Camp, which stands at an altitude of 3,134m in an area characterised by giant heather forest.

Kazingo and the Northern Rwenzori mini-hike

This long day hike crosses from the trading centre of Kazingo (13km from Fort Portal) to Bundibugyo via the northern tip of the Rwenzori Mountains National Park using the Bwamba Pass, which once served as the only access route between Fort Portal and the Semliki Valley. Despite being relatively strenuous, and taking 6–8 hours from the trailhead at Kazingo, the mini-hike has become popular with travellers reluctant to pay the high fees asked for longer Rwenzori hikes based out of Kasese. From the 1,650m trailhead at Kazingo, a choice of routes traverses the range, ascending through farmland/grassland, forest and bamboo forest to the medial ridge before descending to Bundibugyo. It's hard going, especially if your trail takes in the 3,012m Mount Karangora. Consolation for the leg strain is provided by excellent regional views (weather permitting) and the chance to spot four monkey species, including Angola colobus.

Guided hikes out of Fort Portal can be arranged through Kabarole Tours (page 385) or the Rwenzori View Hotel. Alternatively, you can make arrangements directly with the Abanya-Rwenzori Mountaineering Association, which charges US$90 per person inclusive of UWA fees for any day route that crosses through the national park, or US$25 for any routes that bypass it. The main AMA office is in Kazingo, set at an altitude of 1,675m close to the eastern trailhead, but it has a second one in Bundibugyo near the Stanbic Bank. To get to Kazingo in a private vehicle, follow the Bundibugyo Road out of Fort Portal for 9.5km as far as Bukuuku, then turn left at a junction (⊕ 0.67437, 30.19814) signposted for Rwenzori Mountains National Park, and continue for another 3.5km. Using public transport, occasional matatus run from Fort Portal to Kazingo (US$3), or you could catch one of the more regular matatus to Bukuuku (US$2), then walk or use a boda from there. Inexpensive bandas, camping facilities and basic meals are available at the Rwenzori Unique Campsite, 2km from the Kazingo trailhead.

UGANDA UPDATES WEBSITE

Go to www.bradtupdates.com/uganda for the latest on-the-ground travel news, trip reports and factual updates. Keep up to date with the latest posts by following Philip on Twitter (🐦 @philipbriggs) and via Facebook: 📘 fb.me/pb.travel.updates. And, if you have any comments, queries, grumbles, insights, news or other feedback, you're invited to post them directly on the website, or to email them to Philip (📧 philip.briggs@bradtguides. com) for inclusion.

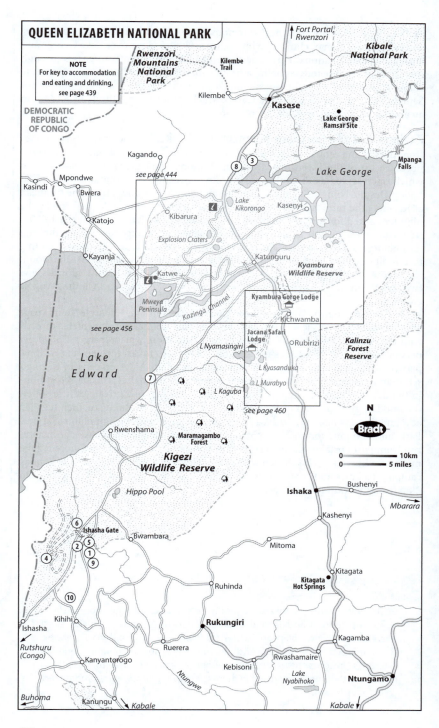

QUEEN ELIZABETH NATIONAL PARK

NOTE
For key to accommodation and eating and drinking, see page 439

Fort Portal, Rwenzori

Rwenzori Mountains National Park

Kilembe Trail

Kibale National Park

Kilembe

Kasese

Lake George Ramsar Site

DEMOCRATIC REPUBLIC OF CONGO

Kagando

Lake George

Mpanga Falls

Mpondwe

Kasindi

Bwera

Katojo

Kayanja

8

3

see page 444

Kibarura

Lake Kikorongo

Kasenyi

Explosion Craters

Katunguru

Kyambura Wildlife Reserve

Katwe

Mweya Peninsula

Kazinga channel

Kyambura Gorge Lodge

Kichwamba

Kalinzu Forest Reserve

see page 456

Jacana Safari Lodge

Rubirizi

L Nyamasingiri

L Kyasanduka

L Murabyo

see page 460

Lake Edward

7

L Kaguba

N

Bradt

Rwenshama

Maramagambo Forest

Kigezi Wildlife Reserve

0   10km
0   5 miles

Hippo Pool

Ishaka

Bushenyi

Kashenyi

Mbarara

6

Ishasha Gate

Bwambara

Mitoma

2   5

1

9

4

Kitagata

Kitagata Hot Springs

10

Ruhinda

Kihihi

Ishasha

Rukungiri

Ruerera

Kagamba

Rutshuru (Congo)

Kanyantorogo

Kebisoni

Rwashamaire

Lake Nyabihoko

Ntungamo

Buhoma

Kanungu

Kabale

Ntungwe

Kabale

18

Queen Elizabeth National Park

Uganda's second-largest, joint-oldest and most biodiverse national park is set in the low-lying Rift Valley where it crosses the equator south of the lofty Rwenzori Mountains and north of the Kigezi Highlands. Protected as a wildlife reserve since the late 1920s, it was gazetted under the name Kazinga National Park in 1952, but renamed two years later to commemorate the first visit to Uganda by Queen Elizabeth II and Prince Philip. Extending over 1,978km², Queen Elizabeth National Park (QENP) protects a fabulously diverse landscape of tropical habitats: rolling grassland, moist acacia woodland, tropical rainforest, sheer-sided volcanic calderas, and a variety of wetland habitats including the open waters and swampy shores of Edward and George, the 40km-long Kazinga Channel that connects them, and several freshwater and saline crater lakes.

Uganda's busiest safari destination, QENP makes for a convenient stopover *en route* between Kibale and Bwindi Impenetrable national parks. The park's most popular attraction is a scenic boat trip that runs out of the Mweya Peninsula along the Kazinga Channel past large herds of elephant, buffalo and hippo. But there are plenty of other potential highlights: game drives on the Kasenyi Plains; chimp tracking at Kyambura Gorge (inside the park) or Kalinzu Ecotourism Site (outside it); birding and monkey-viewing in Maramagambo Forest; exploring the Katwe or Bunyaruguru crater lakes; and – last but emphatically not least – heading off in search of the legendary tree-climbing lions that inhabit the remote Ishasha Plains.

GENERAL INFORMATION

GEOLOGY Set on the floor of Albertine Rift, Queen Elizabeth National Park broadly took its present geological shape around three million years ago, when the uplifting of the Rwenzori Mountains split the paleo-lake Obweruka – then similar in extent to present-day Lake Tanganyika – into what are now lakes Albert, Edward and George. The entire Ugandan shore of Lake Edward now lies within QENP, as do the northern and western shores of Lake George, and the connecting Kazinga Channel. Despite their common origin and identical surface altitude of 913m, lakes Edward and George could scarcely be more different in character. Elongated Lake Edward, extending over almost 2,000km² and up to 120m deep, is the smallest of a quartet of major freshwater bodies that arc through the base of the Albertine Rift floor, a broadly north–south orientation, to form the

QUEEN ELIZABETH NP
For listings, see pages 470–1, unless otherwise stated

Where to stay and eat
1. At The River
2. Enjojo Lodge
3. Ihamba Lakeside Safari Lodge *p445*
4. Ishasha campsites & bandas
5. Ishasha Jungle Lodge
6. Ishasha Wilderness Camp
7. Kisenyi Lake Retreat
8. Little Elephant Camp *p445*
9. Ntungwe Tree Lion Safari Lodge
10. Savannah Resort

Congolese border with Uganda, Rwanda, Burundi and Tanzania. The 250km² Lake George, by contrast, is essentially an extension of Lake Edward fed by the Kazinga Channel: roughly circular in shape, nowhere more than 3.5m deep, and bordered by extensive marshes. Although geologically calm in recent millennia, the area around lakes Edward and George has been subject to massive tectonic upheaval over the past 500,000 years, as evidenced by a total of at least 35 crater lakes and numerous dry volcanic calderas within 20km of the Kazinga Channel. Fecund as QENP is today, the geological and archaeological records indicate that only 7,000 years ago, the area was temporarily denuded of practically its entire fauna and flora as a result of a particularly violent bout of volcanic activity.

FLORA AND FAUNA Most of QENP comprises open grassland and savannah, which tends to be moister and woodier in the west than in the east. A variety of thorny acacias predominate in savannah habitats, though a striking feature of the park is its high concentrations of the candelabra shrub *Euphorbia candelabrum*, a cactus-like succulent that grows to tree-like dimensions along the Kazinga Channel and on the Kasenyi Plains. The park also incorporates substantial areas of papyrus swamp around Lake George, which is listed as a Ramsar Wetland, as well the extensive rainforest of Maramagambo Forest and riparian woodland in the Kyambura Gorge (bordering Kyambura Game Reserve) and the Ishasha and various tributary rivers in the southwest.

QENP supports at least 95 **mammal** species, the highest for any Ugandan national park. Ten primate species are present, including chimpanzee, vervet, blue, red-tailed

RETURN OF THE CROCODILES

An enduring casualty of the most recent volcanic cataclysms in what is now QENP was the Nile crocodile which occurs naturally in almost all suitable aquatic habitats south of the Sahara, but vanished from the local archaeological record some 7,000 years ago, and was absent from Lake Edward, Lake George and the Kazinga Channel until recent historical times. This anomaly was a subject of considerable debate during the colonial era. Some biologists attributed the absence to a physical or chemical factor in the water, a theory that had little grounding in fact, since crocodiles elsewhere are tolerant of more extreme water temperatures, higher levels of alkalinity and more toxic chemical dilutes than are presented by either of the lakes in question. As a Cambridge scientific expedition to Uganda in 1931 noted, 'Lake Edward seems to be an ideal habitat for crocodiles; there are plenty of quiet beaches and swamps and an abundance of fish and other food.'

The other prevalent notion was that the crocodiles, having been wiped out by volcanic activity 7,000 years ago, were unable to recolonise QENP due to their inability to navigate the rapids and gorges along the Semliki River, the only major associated waterway they still inhabited. Implausible as this may sound, subsequent events suggest it was at least halfway correct. However, it was probably not the rapids or gorges per se that inhibited the crocodiles' movement, but the obstacle they presented in tandem with the surrounding rainforest. As a result, deforestation along the Semliki Gorge in the 1980s led to crocodiles making an unexpected reappearance on Lake Edward towards the end of that decade. Since then numbers have proliferated. Large crocodiles are frequently observed on Kazinga launch trips, while local fishermen now regard them as a hazard in the reedy shallows of Lake George.

and L'Hoest's monkeys, black-and-white colobus and olive baboon. A checklist of around 20 carnivores is headed by lion and leopard, but spotted hyena and side-striped jackal are also quite common, and a habituated banded mongoose troop is conspicuous on the Mweya Peninsula. The most common antelope is Ugandan kob, some 20,000 of which are resident in the park, but bushbuck, topi and Defassa waterbuck are also locally common, while the elusive semi-aquatic sitatunga occurs in papyrus swamps around Lake George, and four duiker species are primarily confined to the Maramagambo Forest. Buffaloes are common and often reddish in colour due to interbreeding with the redder forest buffalo of the Congolese rainforest. The park's elephants are also sometimes said to display affinities with the smaller and slightly hairier forest-dwelling race of elephant found in the DRC. Among other ungulates, notable absentees include rhino, giraffe and zebra, but more than 5,000 hippos inhabit the park's waterways, warthogs are very common, and the Kasenyi Channel is one of the few non-forested places in Africa where giant forest hog are regularly seen.

Although it now ranks as Uganda's most popular safari destination, QENP suffered an alarming loss of wildlife during the years of instability that followed Amin's 1971 coup. The elephant population, for instance, dropped from a high of 4,000 in the 1960s to perhaps 150 in 1980, and buffalo numbers were reduced from 18,000 to 8,000. Over the past 30 years, however, the situation has improved greatly. An aerial survey undertaken in May 2015 estimated that almost 3,000 elephants – about 60% of the national population – inhabit QENP, while the buffalo population now stands at above 15,000. The national park is an important stronghold for lions, which had become very uncommon and elusive in the 1980s, but are thought to number at least 200, concentrated on the Kasenyi Plains and around Ishasha and Mweya.

Some 610 **bird** species have been recorded in QENP, a remarkable figure for what is a relatively small national park by continental standards (to place this in some perspective, that's more birds than have ever been seen in the Serengeti or Kruger national parks, fine birding destinations that are seven- and ten-times larger than QENP respectively). In addition to 54 raptors, the checklist includes virtually every waterbird species resident in Uganda, and a variety of woodland and forest birds, the latter largely confined to the Maramagambo Forest. Birding anywhere in the park is good, but the Mweya stands out for the myriad waterbirds on the Kazinga Channel, while the riparian forest at Ishasha is a good place to see certain more unusual species.

ORIENTATION QENP is a park of many parts – and, it might be said, one adorned with an above average quota of appendages, in the form of tourist sites that technically lie outside its boundaries but are most often visited in conjunction with it, for instance the Kalinzu Forest, Lake Katwe, Kyambura Wildlife Reserve and Kasenyi fishing village.

The park might simplistically be broken up into five main sectors, starting in the north as follows:

Lake George Ramsar Wetland
The most northerly part of QENP comprises an all-but-inaccessible expanse of papyrus swamp that divides Lake George from Kasese and Kibale National Park.

Northern Plains and Kazinga Channel
Historically, the Kazinga Channel and plains running for about 10km to its north form QENP's main focus of tourist development. The area incorporates the Mweya Peninsula, Kasenyi Plains, the western shore of Lake George, the northeast shore of Lake Edward, and the Katwe Crater Lakes.

Between Kazinga and Maramagambo Bounded by Maramagambo Forest in the south, the part of QENP immediately south of the Kazinga Channel is largely undeveloped for tourism, one notable exception being the chimp-tracking site at Kyambura Gorge. It is, however, integrated with several of the aforementioned appendages, including the Bunyaruguru Crater Lakes, Kyambura Wildlife Reserve, a chimp-tracking site at Kalinzu Eco-Tourism Project, and a cluster of lodges perched the Kichwamba Escarpment above the QENP's eastern boundary.

Maramagambo Forest This vast tract of medium altitude rainforest is largely inaccessible, bar a limited number of tourist developments in the vicinity of Lake Nyamasingiri in the far northeast.

Ishasha Sector This small but wildlife-rich area of savannah running along the Congolese border south of Lake Edward is now well-developed for tourism and a popular overnight stop *en route* to or from Bwindi Impenetrable National Park.

The circuits In practice, QENP and environs can be split up into two distinct but very unequal tourist circuits. The larger of these, and the more loosely defined, is North-Central QENP, which comprises the first four sectors listed above, and is serviced by more than 30 lodges and guesthouses centred on half-a-dozen nuclei, eg: Kikorongo, Kasenyi, Katunguru, Katwe, Mweya and the Kichwamba Escarpment. The smaller circuit, flanking the murram road to Bwindi Impenetrable National Park some 2 hours' drive southwest of North-Central QENP, consists of the isolated Ishasha Sector, which is serviced by around five lodges and offers just one game-viewing circuit.

Logistically, the common thread linking the lodges and sites associated with North-Central QENP is a 50km stretch of the surfaced Kasese–Ishaka Road that runs between Kikorongo in the north and the Kalinzu Eco-Tourism Project in the south, crossing the Kazinga Channel *en route* at Katunguru Bridge. Almost all lodges and sites of interest in North-Central QENP lie alongside this road, or are connected to it by a short (up to 20km) feeder road, which means that (with a few extreme exceptions) you can drive between almost any of the circuit's lodges and main attractions in under an hour.

FEES The entrance fee for QENP is US$40/30 FNR/FR per 24 hours. The standard vehicle entrance fees are also charged (see box, page 32), but only once per entry. No fee is charged for driving along the surfaced Mbarara–Kasese Road, the main dirt roads to Katwe and Kasenyi villages, the dirt road between Katunguru and the Ishasha border post, or any other public roads that run through the park. Since the introduction of the new card system (*www.ugandawildlife.org/wildlife-card*), the idea is that all entrance and activity fees for QENP must be paid either at the UWA reservations office in Kampala, or else at Katunguru Park Headquarters 3km south of Katunguru Bridge (page 451). This rule seems to be imposed erratically: it definitely applies to chimpanzee tracking at Kyambura Gorge, and to entrance fees for the northern and southeast sectors, but it appears that all charges relating to accommodation, camping and activities at Mweya must be paid for at the visitors' centre there, while entrance fees for the southwest sector can be paid directly at Ishasha Gate.

Although it is not mandatory to take a ranger/guide on private game drives, it is strongly recommended, at least until you get to know your way around the park, and it will greatly improve your odds of seeing lions and leopards. The fee for a guide is US$20 per vehicle.

Fees for individual activities are given under the relevant section later in the chapter.

FURTHER READING Andrew Roberts's QENP guidebook describes the national park and contains checklists for mammals and birds. Sheet 6 in the 'Uganda Maps' series covers QENP. Both are available at the park entrance gates.

NORTH-CENTRAL QENP AND THE KASESE–ISHAKA ROAD

This main developed part of QENP incorporates a remarkable diversity and number of tourist attractions and amenities in a relatively compact area. Prime activities are the boat trip out of the Mweya Peninsula and game drives on the Kasenyi Plains, but North-Central QENP and its immediate environs also include two chimpanzee-tracking sites, a couple of dozen crater lakes, scenic lakes George and Edward, a variety of worthwhile community projects – not to mention around three dozen lodges and other accommodation facilities. Despite this diversity, almost everything covered in this section lies within 10km of the Kazinga Channel as the crow flies, and with private transport, most sites of interest can be visited as a day trip from any of the lodges.

GETTING THERE AND AWAY

By air   There is a small airstrip on Mweya Peninsula, a few hundred metres west of the Mweya Safari Lodge. Fly Uganda (*www.flyuganda.com*) and Aerolink (*www.aerolinkuganda.com*) flights from Entebbe to Kihihi (page 469) can divert there by prior arrangement.

By road   The stretch of the Kasese–Ishaka Road between Kikorongo and Kichwamba bisects North-Central QENP, crossing the Kazinga Channel at Katunguru Bridge. The park lies about 400km by road from Kampala and self-drivers travelling directly between the two can choose between two more-or-less equidistant routes. The northern route via Fort Portal and Kasese is generally quicker – bank on around 6 hours – as there is less traffic than on the southern route through Mbarara and Ishaka. Driving from elsewhere in Uganda, Katunguru Bridge lies about 40km/45 minutes from Kasese, 115km/90 minutes from Fort Portal, 115km/90 minutes from Mbarara, 73km/2 hours from Ishasha Entrance Gate, 135km/4 hours from Buhoma (Bwindi National Park) and 182km/4 hours from Kabale via Ishaka. Directions for individual sites within North-Central QENP are included under the relevant heading later in the chapter.

Self-drivers might take note that while Kasese and Ishaka both have several brand filling stations, opportunities to fuel up along the 95km road between them are limited. Diesel and petrol are available from the Shell filling station on the Mweya Peninsula. This charges the same prices as Kasese, but can be quite time-consuming as you need to pay at the lodge, get a receipt, then locate the (sometimes elusive) attendant. There are also a couple of filling stations at Kiburara on the Mpondwe Road about 15km west of Kikorongo.

Using public transport, Katunguru village (on the north side of the bridge) is the most useful goal for travellers wanting to organise budget game drives in the Kasenyi sector, or to take a special hire to Mweya. Katwe, with its well-organised and affordable community tourism project, is another good option for shoestring travellers. Both are accessible on public transport as detailed under the relevant heading later in the chapter.

KIKORONGO AND SURROUNDS   Only 22km south of Kasese, the village of Kikorongo lies on the Ishaka Road immediately outside the northern boundary of QENP, at the junction of a little-used surfaced road running west towards the

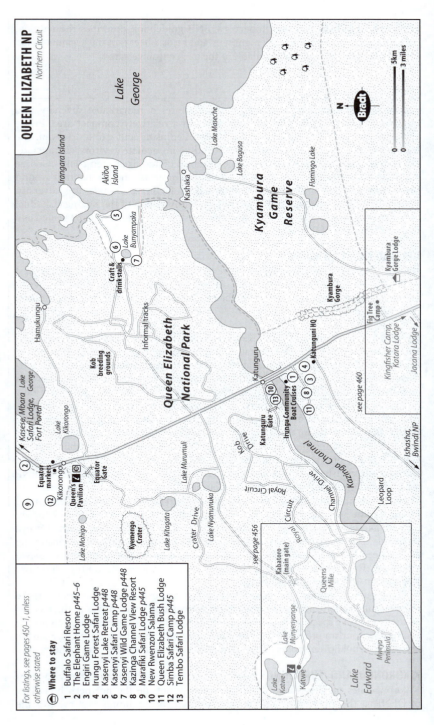

QUEEN ELIZABETH NP
Northern Circuit

Lake George

Irangara Island

Akiba Island

Kashaka

Lake Moseche

Lake Bagusa

Kyambura Game Reserve

Flamingo Lake

Lake Bunyampaka

Craft & drink stalls

⑤ ⑥ ⑦

Kyambura Gorge

Kyambura Gorge Lodge

Kyambura HQ

Fig Tree Camp

Kingfisher Camp, Katara Lodge

Jacana Lodge

see page 460

Katunguni HQ

① ④ ③
⑧
⑪

Irungu Community Boat Cruises

⑬ ⑩

Katunguru Gate

Katunguru

Ishasha, Bwindi NP

Kazinga Channel

Leopard Loop

Channel Drive

Kob Drive

Royal Circuit

Lake Nyamunuka

Lake Murumuli

see page 456

Kabatoro (main gate)

Royal Circuit

Queens Mile

Lake Munyenyange

Lake Katwe

Katwe

Mweya Peninsula

Lake Edward

Lake Kitagata

Kyemengo Crater

Lake Mohigo

Crater Drive

Queen's Pavilion

⑫

Equator markets

Kikorongo

⑨

Equator Gate

Lake Kikorongo

② *Kasese, Mbara Lake Safari Lodge, Fort Portal*

Kob breeding grounds

Informal tracks

Hamukungu

Queen Elizabeth National Park

For listings, see pages 450–1, unless otherwise stated

ⓘ Where to stay

1　Buffalo Safari Resort
2　The Elephant Home *p445–6*
3　Engiri Game Lodge
4　Irungu Forest Safari Lodge
5　Kasenyi Lake Retreat *p448*
6　Kasenyi Safari Camp *p448*
7　Kasenyi Wild Game Lodge *p448*
8　Kazinga Channel View Resort
9　Marafiki Safari Lodge *p445*
10　New Rwenzori Salama
11　Queen Elizabeth Bush Lodge
12　Simba Safari Camp *p445*
13　Tembo Safari Lodge

N

Bradt

0　5km
0　3 miles

444

Congolese border town of Mpondwe. Kikorongo is a blink-and-you'll-miss-it kind of place, distinguished mainly by its hemisphere-straddling location (although the equator officially crosses the Ishaka Road at a signposted lay-by 400m further south, a gradual northward drift means it now more-or-less runs through the village) and proximity to the crater lake for which it is named (about 1km to the southeast). A number of relatively new lodges scattered in the vicinity of Kikorongo are well positioned for game drives on the Kasenyi Plains and boat trips out of Mweya. Other possible activities include birding in the vicinity of nearby Lake George, drives into the Rwenzori foothills around Kyarumba, and a more far-flung excursion to the backpacker-friendly Pan-Afrique Hippo Resort on the shores of Lake Edward.

Getting there and away The drive from Kasese to Kikorongo takes 15 minutes on a good surfaced road. Any matatu heading south from Kasese can drop you there, or at the Elephant Centre 1km to the north. Directions to other lodges are given under the individual listing.

Where to stay *Map, page 444, unless otherwise stated*

Upmarket
Ihamba Lakeside Safari Lodge
[map, page 438] (7 rooms) ✪ 0.0617, 30.05251; 📞031 2513675; m 0700 903882; e info@ ihambasafarilodge.com; www.ihambasafarilodge. com. Situated 1.5km east of a signposted junction on the Kasese Rd 9km north of Kikorongo, this isolated lodge boasts an attractive location on the western shore of Lake George. The neat euphorbia-studded gardens are centred on a swimming pool & are grazed by hippos at night, while birdlife is plentiful. The spacious thatched dbl or twin bandas have walk-in nets, stylish ethnic décor, sofa, desk, big funky bathrooms with tub & shower, large windows & a private balcony (if possible, ask for one of the 3 that offer an uninterrupted view). Great value. *US$190/220 sgl/dbl FB.* **$$$$**

Marafiki Safari Lodge (9 rooms) ✪ 0.00586, 29.99253; m 0775 941189/0784 056831; e info@marafikisafaris.com; www. marafikisafaris.com. This attractive new hillside lodge offers fabulous views to Lake George, & a choice of spacious canvas-sided dbl cottages set on wooden platforms or smaller 4-bed cabins, all with en-suite open-air showers. The food comes highly praised. From Kikorongo, follow the Mpondwe Rd west for 2km, then turn right on to a signposted dirt road that leads to the lodge after another 1km. *US$120/200 sgl/dbl cottage; US$65pp cabin. All rates FB.* **$$$$**

Moderate
Simba Safari Camp (12 rooms & 1 dorm) ✪ 0.00135, 29.98901; 📞0414 267153;

m 0701 426368/0776 411316; e info@ ugandalodges.com; www.ugandalodges.com. This unpretentious lodge 1.5km along the Mpondwe Rd has pleasant bandas with fitted nets, fan, private balcony & en-suite hot shower, as well as a dorm using common showers. Attractively priced & well placed for early morning game drives to the Kasenyi Plains, it is responding to the recent surfacing of the Mpondwe Rd & resultant increase in noisy truck traffic by relocating the bandas further uphill from the road to a site overlooking Lake Kikorongo. *US$71/94/138 sgl/dbl/trpl B&B, US$26pp dorm bed, US$9pp camping. Add US$15pp for dinner & US$13 for lunch.* **$$$$**

Little Elephant Camp [map, page 438] (4 tents) ✪ 0.04385, 30.02681; m 0787 722355; www.littleelephantcamp.com. This brand new, self-catering tented camp lies right on the edge of the park at Muhokya, midway between Kasese & the Crater Drive Gate at Kikorongo. The en-suite tents are each provided with a private dining/ kitchen tent with BBQ, coolbox & utensils. *U$75 sgl/dbl.* **$$$**

Budget & camping
The Elephant Home (3 rooms) ✪ 0.01041, 29.99996; m 0706 581477/0773 426748; e info@ theelephanthome.com; www.theelephanthome. com. Situated in large cultivated gardens on the west side of the Kasese Rd 1km north of Kikorongo, this new community project comprises 3 en-suite twin rooms, 5 camping sites & a small restaurant that serves local meals in the US$3–5 range that doubles as an art gallery & gift shop selling locally

18

made handicrafts, paintings & cards. It further engages local community members by arranging traditional dances (*US$50 per party*), basket weaving workshops (*US$2pp*), cotton-growing tours (*US7$pp*) and hill climbs (*US$10pp*). *Rooms cost US$25pp B&B, camping US$7pp.* **$$**

What to see and do The lodges listed above are all less than 30 minutes' drive from the Kasenyi Plains and no more than an hour away from the Mweya Peninsula, making them very useful bases for general exploration of northern QENP.

Queen's Pavilion This bandstand-like pavilion, set on a low ridge above the west side of the Kasese–Ishaka Road 1km south of the official equator lay-by, was built in 1958 to receive the British Queen Mother and Omukama Rukidi III of Toro. Offering a great view across the main road to the circular Kikorongo Crater Lake, the site was also visited by Queen Elizabeth II and Prince Philip in 1954 and again in 2007, and it has hosted a great many picnicking tour groups over the years. Today, it is home to the Queen's Pavilion Coffee Shop and Tele-centre (✪ *-0.01033, 30.00199;* m *0774 408124;* e *info@ctph.org; www.ctph.org*), a community project operated by the NGO Conservation Through Public Health. The advertised internet café isn't available, but it's an agreeable place for a coffee, snack or light meal (prepared to order from scratch, so expect a wait). The coffee shop lies just outside QENP's northern entrance gate, so no fees are payable unless you enter the park to follow the Katwe Explosion Craters Track (page 454) southwest through towards Mweya. Another option out of Queen's Pavilion is a guided walk across the road to circle around the 1.5km^2 Lake Kikorongo.

Lake George Ramsar Site Extending across 150km^2 of swampland to the northwest of Lake George, Uganda's oldest Ramsar Wetland, listed in 1988, falls almost entirely within the expansive but inaccessible northern sector of QENP. It has the highest avian diversity of any Ugandan wetland, with 491 bird species recorded, including 167 wetland specialists and nine listed as globally threatened. The papyrus swamps of the Lake George Ramsar Site support one of Uganda's most substantial breeding populations of the elusive shoebill. Other residents include papyrus endemics such as white-winged warbler, papyrus gonolek, papyrus canary and papyrus yellow warbler, while large concentrations of migrant waders and waterfowl aggregate in the area during the northern hemisphere winter. The localised sitatunga antelope is also resident. You can approach the southern tip of the wetland along a 10km dirt road that runs east from the Kasese–Ishaka Road, leaving at a junction (✪ *-0.01337, 30.0032*) 200m south of Queen's Pavilion, to the fishing village of Hamukungu on the eastern shore of Lake George. To reach the swamp proper, however, you'll need to enquire about a ranger/guide at Mweya Visitors' Centre or the Katunguru Park Headquarters.

Southern Rwenzori foothills If you've had your fill of lakes and savannah, and have some time at your disposal, the little-visited southern Rwenzori foothills to the west of Kikorongo are worth exploring. Some 40km west of Kikorongo and linked to it by regular matatus, the twin towns of Mpondwe and Bwera support a population of around 52,000 and – situated less than 5km east of the Congolese border – are also regarded to be the busiest centre of trade between the two countries. The most worthwhile time to visit is on Tuesday or Friday, when the daily market in Mpondwe, 2km beyond Bwera, is at its busiest and most colourful. If you want to spend the night, the Islander Guest House has en-suite rooms with DSTV, and a garden bar and restaurant.

On other days, travellers with access to a vehicle could follow a lovely road loop to the village of Kyarumba, by striking north from the Mpondwe Road at the small town of Kiburara (✪ *0.00936, 29.89679*), 12.5km west of Kikorongo.

If you fancy delaying, there's an affordable guesthouse at the Kagando Mission Hospital (✪ *0.06313, 29.89816;* m *0772 425150*) about 7km north of Kiburara, or slightly more commodious accommodation at the Farmland Guesthouse, set on a working farm halfway between the two.

Pan-Afrique Hippo Resort (✪ *-0.0931, 29.76291;* m *0779 592561/0788 115628;* e *afriquehitours@gmail.com;* f *fb.me/PanafriqueHippoResortBeach*) Set in Kayanja fishing village on the northern shore of Lake Edward, the quirky Pan-Afrique Hippo Resort comes across like a throwback to what passed for a beach resort elsewhere in Uganda in the 1980s. The massive grassy compound, cropped by hippos at night, leads to a rickety but breezy and well-shaded wooden lakeside platform ideally placed to enjoy a chilled beer while the sun sets over the Congolese shore, before partaking from a deceptively lengthy menu that usually boils down to the choice of goat or fish and accompanying starch for US$5–8. For day trippers, the main attraction is boat trips on the lake, which cost US$33 per party, and come with a near certainty of seeing hippos and water birds, and an outside chance of elephants. If you fancy overnighting, basic en-suite rooms with nets and cold water cost US$13 per person, or you can brave the hippos and pitch a tent for a negotiable fee.

To get there, follow the Mpondwe Road out of Kikorongo for 27.5km to Katojo (✪ *-0.0177, 29.76856*), where you need to turn left on to a conspicuously signposted dirt road, then right after another 900m at a junction (✪ *-0.02441, 29.77383*) signposted for Kayanja but not for the resort. From here, it's 8km along a rough dirt road to Kayanja and the Pan-Afrique Hippo Resort. Using public transport, any Mpondwe-bound matatus can drop you at Katojo, but you'll need to charter a boda from there. Note that the Pan-Afrique Hippo Resort can also be reached from Katwe (page 452) by following a good dirt road that runs northeast to Kitojo, passing the junction for Kayanja junction after about 19km.

KASENYI AND SURROUNDS

QENP's most popular game-drive circuit traverses the bushy plains running east from the Kasese–Ishaka Road to the rundown fishing village of Kasenyi on the western shore of Lake George. If lions are your sole measure of quality, Kasenyi also probably ranks as Uganda's best game-viewing spot anywhere, especially if you're there shortly after sunrise, accompanied by a guide who knows the areas currently favoured by the plains' resident prides. That said, aside from lions and the conspicuous herds of buffalo and kob whereupon they prey, the Kasenyi circuit does tend to be rather lacking in mammalian variety, though the eponymous village is a reliable spot for hippos and waterbirds. An interesting feature of the plains, only 2km west of Kasenyi village, is the scenic Bunyampaka Crater Lake, overlooked by a cluster of kiosks selling handicrafts and chilled drinks, and still active as a traditional salt extraction site. Logistically, the Kasenyi Plains are easily accessed from most lodges covered in this chapter, the main exception being those listed under Ishasha, but there's no better base for locating lions in the early morning – when they tend to be most active, and before the traffic from further afield starts trickling in – than the two upmarket lodges overlooking Bunyampaka Crater Lake or their budget counterpart in Kasenyi village.

Getting there and away Access to the Kasenyi Plains is from a public dirt road that runs east from the Kasese–Ishaka Road to terminate on the Lake George shore at Kasenyi village after 16km. The signposted junction, sometimes referred to as Kasenyi Crossroads (✪ *-0.08187, 30.03027*), is 10km south of Kikorongo, 5km north of Katunguru, and directly opposite the public road west to Katwe and Mweya.

Coming from Kasenyi Crossroads, the southern and northern game-viewing circuits both depart from the public road after 1.2km, where the rather superfluous Kasenyi Gate (✪ -0.07403, 30.03821) stands on the left side of the road. Those making a beeline for prime lion territory would be better off following the public road for another 7km, where they have the choice of turning south at the junction signposted 'Janet Track' (✪ -0.03851, 30.08118), or north at an unsignposted junction (✪ -0.03933, 30.08239) 150m past this. Bunyampaka Crater Lake and the two associated lodges both lie 5km past the junction for Janet Track.

Park entrance fees need not be paid to use the public road to Kasenyi, nor to visit or to stay at Bunyampaka Crater Lake or Kasenyi village (both these sites fall within community land enclaved by the national park on three sides). It is mandatory, however, to pay park entrance fees in advance (either at the UWA office in Kampala or at Katunguru park headquarters) if you plan to leave the public road on a game drive.

⌂ Where to stay   *Map, page 444*

Upmarket

✴ ⌂ **Kasenyi Safari Camp** (4 rooms, 4 more under construction) ✪ -0.03346, 30.12609; m 0756 992038/0791 992038; e info@kasenyisafaricamp.com; www.kasenyisafaricamp.com. This owner-managed tented camp is set on a 20ha tract of uncleared indigenous bush on the rim of Bunyampaka Crater Lake outside the national park but bordering right on it. The large & stylishly decorated standing tents have king-sized beds with walk-in nets, spacious bathrooms with high-quality fittings & a large deck overlooking the lake & any passing wildlife. In addition to lying in prime lion territory, the lodge offers night drives around the crater rim (good chance of hippo, genet, leopard, spotted hyena & more occasionally aardvark) & a day hike in the Rwenzori foothills. The 5-course dinners are exceptional. *US$240/325/385 sgl/dbl/trpl B&B, US$315/385/495 sgl/dbl/trpl inc all meals, sodas, beers & house wine.* **$$$$$**

⌂ **Kasenyi Wild Game Lodge** (8 cottages) ✪ -0.04168, 30.12239; m 0752 652861/0772 583108; e bookings@kasenyigamelodge.com; www.kasenyigamelodge.com. One of the best value lodges anywhere in the vicinity of QENP, this place stands on the bushy rim of Bunyampaka Crater Lake adjacent to Kasenyi Safari Camp. Stilted circular cottages have a cool & airy interior, twin ¾ or dbl beds in a fitted net, en-suite shower, & elevated wooden deck with a view over the lake. *US$80/140 sgl/dbl B&B, plus US$20pp FB.* **$$$$**

Budget & camping

⌂ **Kasenyi Lake Retreat** (4 rooms) ✪ -0.04158, 30.15202; m 0774 768090/0701 536197; e info@ugandalodge.com; www.ugandalodge.com/lake-retreat. Set on the Lake George shore 1km south of Kasenyi fishing village, this new budget lodge stands just outside the national park on 50ha of private land frequently passed through by hippo, buffalo & various antelope, & more occasionally visited by elephants, lions & leopards. Accommodation is in simple but spacious twin bandas that currently share a toilet block but will soon have en-suite facilities added. Birding is exceptional & the staff can arrange local boats to go out & look for shoebills in the papyrus swamps verging Lake George. A proportion of proceeds goes towards community projects in Kasenyi, & funding orphan education. Camping permitted. *US$50pp B&B, US$10pp camping.* **$$$**

What to see and do

Kasenyi Plains Criss-crossed by a labyrinthine network of game viewing roads, the plains running east from the Kasese–Ishaka Road to Kasenyi cover a moist short-grass savannah interspersed with solitary euphorbia trees and low clumps of bushy thicket. The area is an important breeding ground for Ugandan kob – thousands congregate here at times – and it is also frequented by numerous buffalo and fewer and more skittish pairs of bushbuck. The main attraction for most visitors, however, is the trio of lion prides that lurk around the main kob breeding

grounds, picking off the occasional unwary antelope or buffalo for dinner. The open habitat of Kasenyi means that its super-habituated lions are unusually easy to locate, particularly in the first hour or two after sunset, when they are usually still active (and the cubs are often very playful) and the heat has yet to drive them into the shade of thicker bush. If you can't locate the lions directly by sight or sound, pay attention to the male kobs, whose high whistling alarm call may warn of a predator lurking in a nearby thicket. Vultures – most commonly white-backed and white-headed – either circling or perched purposefully in a tree may indicate a kill, with lions possibly still in attendance. Such bush craft may actually be necessary in prime lion viewing hours, from sunrise to around 07.00, when the main morning influx of 4x4s starts rolling up. At other times of day, it may be more effective to watch where safari vehicles are congregating and tag along. Hiring a UWA guide – they generally have a good idea where to look – could also help provide you with a more exclusive sighting. Lion, kob and buffalo aside, you're unlikely to see too many other large mammals on the Kasenyi Plains, but an interesting selection of grassland birds includes grey crowned crane, red-throated spurfowl and yellow-throated longclaw.

Bunyampaka Crater Lake An interesting spot to take a break after the morning's first intense burst of lion-seeking, circular Lake Bunyampaka lies at the base of a steep but small crater whose rim is covered in thick natural bush. It is one of only two crater lakes in this part of Uganda that supports a salt-extraction industry, albeit it on a far smaller scale than the better-known Lake Katwe. A mosaic of small individual plots worked by villagers from nearby Kasenyi encloses the lake's green open water on three sides, accounting for roughly half its total surface area of 40ha. Water birds are also prolific, with large flocks of flamingos and pelicans often congregating on the unmined southern shore, particularly in the early evening. Most safari groups stop at the northwest crater rim viewpoint (⊕ -0.03818, 30.12311), where there's a cluster of kiosks selling chilled drinks and curios, but it is also possible to breakfast or lunch at Kasenyi Safari Camp by prior arrangement. To see the salt workings or lakeshore birdlife up close, you can follow a rough motorable track past Kasenyi Safari Camp to a parking spot on the northern shore (⊕ -0.03638, 30.12891).

Kasenyi fishing village Having come this far, it's worth continuing the last couple of kilometres to Kasenyi, a small and scruffy but friendly fishing village where hippos can reliably be seen basking a few metres from the shore. There are lots of birds around too, most strikingly the marabou storks that scavenge around a fishing beach lined with small local boats and nets. If you are thinking of chartering a boat to look for shoebills, or whatever else, it is best to talk to the helpful staff at Kasenyi Lake Retreat, 12km south of the village.

KATUNGURU AND THE EASTERN KAZINGA CHANNEL
It may not be much to look at in itself, but the small town of Katunguru could scarcely have a wilder or more strategic location, straddling the Kasese–Ishaka Road in the heart of QENP immediately north of the only bridge across the Kazinga Channel. Katunguru is the established springboard for backpackers looking to set up a budget safari into QENP, and the small town and its immediate environs offers a fair selection of no-frills shoestring accommodation. By contrast, the south shore of the Kazinga Channel facing Katunguru is lined with a few mid-range lodges favoured by budget-conscious group safaris. Don't be fooled by Katunguru's paper-thin urban veneer: hippos are plentiful in the nearby channel, while buffalo, elephant and the like regularly pass within a few hundred metres of town, and the birdlife in and around the channel is fantastic.

Getting there and away Flanking the Kasese–Ishaka Road 40km south of Kasese and 55km north of Ishaka, Katunguru is easy to reach and difficult to miss in a private vehicle. Coming directly from Kampala on public transport, Kalita and Link operate buses to Kasese via Mbarara and Katunguru (*US$8; 7–8hrs*) but do make sure you get on the right vehicle, as they also operate a service to Kasese via Fort Portal. More locally, any matatu heading between Fort Portal or Kasese and Ishaka or Mbarara can drop you at Katunguru, though you may be asked to pay full fare. It is also easy enough to pick up transport out of Katunguru in either direction along the main Kasese–Ishaka Road. The south bank lodges are reached along a 2km dirt road that runs west from the Kasese–Ishaka Road at a clearly signposted junction (✦ *-0.13206, 30.05485*) 1km south of Katunguru Bridge.

Where to stay *Map, page 444*

All the lodges listed below lie within the Katunguru enclave, surrounded by QENP but technically outside it. This means no park fees are charged just for staying overnight at any of these lodges. They are also centrally located for game drives on the Kasenyi Plains (18km to the north), boat trips on the Mweya Peninsula (25km to the west) and chimp tracking in Kyambura Gorge (8km to the south).

Moderate

✳ Queen Elizabeth Bush Lodge (12 cottages & 13 tents) ✦ -0.13726, 30.04141; ☎031 2294894; e booking@naturelodges. biz; www.naturelodges.biz. This popular & reasonably priced camp is set in dense bush verging the south bank of the Kazinga Channel 2km west of the Kasese–Ishaka Road. There's the choice of canvas-sided cottages with wooden floor, queen-sized bed, fitted net, eco-toilet, private outside shower, & small balcony, or more basic standing tents using a shared ablution block. The dining tent faces the channel, & the grounds are bristling with chattering birdlife & honking hippos. *US$95/140 sgl/dbl cottage, US$30/60 sgl/dbl tent. All rates B&B, add US$20–30pp FB.* **$$$–$$$$**

Buffalo Safari Resort (8 cottages) ✦ -0.13694, 30.04925; ☎041 4693085; m 0755 994409; e info@buffalosafariresort. co.ug or buffalosafariresort@yahoo.com; www. buffalosafariresort.co.ug. Among the better offerings in this range, this comfortable resort on the south bank 1km west of the Kasese–Ishaka Road lacks a direct channel view but the thatched restaurant does overlook 'Lake Rubirizi', a small & muddy natural waterhole regularly visited in daylight hours by elephant, buffalo, kob & giant forest hog. Spacious & cool thatched cottages all come with 2 dbl beds, fitted nets, nice private balcony & en-suite hot shower. *US$100/120 sgl/dbl B&B, plus US$20pp FB.* **$$$**

Irungu Forest Safari Lodge (5 rooms) ✦ -0.13706, 30.05611; m 0703 128677/0774 392047; e info@irunguforestsafarilodge.com; www.irunguforestsafarilodge.com. Set in compact wooded gardens on the west side of the Ishaka Rd 1.5km south of Katunguru Bridge, this place is conveniently located for those using public transport, but it's also potentially noisy & lacks any scenic merit. The thatch-&-canvas en-suite bandas are set on a wooden platform & the comfortable restaurant/bar has DSTV & a varied menu of meat & vegetarian mains (*US$10*) as well as salads & sandwiches (*US$4–5*). A good contact for boat trips & game drives. *US$70/90/120 sgl/dbl/trpl B&B. Camping US$15pp.* **$$$**

Engiri Game Lodge (5 cottages) ✦ -0.13935, 30.05171; m 0772 503994; ▮ fb.me/ engirigamelodge. Set in a rather nondescript patch of bush 800m south of the channel, this rather overpriced lodge offers accommodation in rickety stilted wood-&-canvas huts with twin ¾ beds, fitted nets & en-suite cold tubs. Elephants, buffalos & other wildlife regularly pass through. *US$80pp B&B, plus US$20pp FB.* **$$$$**

Budget

Kazinga Channel View Resort (26 rooms) ✦ -0.138, 30.04638; ☎041 4580968; m 0705 717132; e info@kazingachannelviewresort.com; www.kazingachannelviewresort.com. Boasting all the character of a little-used small-town conference facility, the most peculiar of the south

bank lodges has clean & well-maintained en-suite rooms with net, a restaurant serving adequate meals in the US$5–7 range, & excellent in-house game-viewing potential thanks to its location on an open slope 300m from the channel. *US$40/60 sgl/dbl room or USD$100 dbl banda, but half the price if paid in shillings. All rates B&B.* **$$$**

Shoestring & camping

🏠 **Tembo Safari Lodge** (5 rooms) ✪ -0.12475, 30.04615; m 0705 338778/0772 423037. Perched on the north bank of the Kazinga Channel immediately west of Katunguru (but 1km

away by road), this no-frills facility gets full marks for its waterside setting. The musty & tired-looking rooms aren't up to much, but they do at least have hot showers & nets. You can watch fishing boats, see kids jumping off the road bridge & scan the shoreline for birds & other wildlife from the attached bar/canteen, which serves local meals for around US$5. *US$18/22 sgl/dbl B&B. US$5pp camping.* **$$**

🏠 **New Rwenzori Salama Hotel** (8 rooms) ✪ -0.12171, 30.04791. The pick of a few very basic lodges in Katunguru village has scruffy en-suite rooms with net & cold water. *US$10/13 sgl/dbl.* **$**

Tourist information and operators
Katunguru is the most common and accessible base for backpackers wanting to do a day safari into QENP. Prices quoted below include car, fuel, driver/guide and vehicle entrance fees, but exclude individual entrance fees and any boat trip costs.

🛈 **Katunguru Park Headquarters** ✪ -0.14916, 30.06394; ☎ 039 2700694; m 0782 387805; e queenelizabethnp@yahoo. co.uk. Situated just off the Ishasha Rd 3km south of Katunguru Bridge, the ticket office at QENP's headquarters is where visitors are required to pay all entrance fees for gates other than Ishasha. **Kazinga Channel Safaris** m 0772 608614; e kcsafari@yahoo.com. This reliable, responsive & well-established small operator has been recommended by the owners of Fort Portal's Ruwenzori View Guesthouse & several readers. It charges US$50 per group for a 3-hour game drive in Kasenyi and transfer to Mweya for the boat trip. Add another US$30 for a full-day package

including an evening game drive. It also offers full-day safaris to Ishasha for around US$105 per party. **Irungu Forest Safari Lodge** See page 450. This well-organised lodge offers game drives to Kasenyi for US$60 (1–2 people) or US$80 (up to 7 people). It is also the agent for channel boat trips out of Katunguru village. **Queen Elizabeth Tourism Guides & Drivers Association** ✪ -0.12091, 30.04791; m 0774 300018/0772 380044/0704 614668. This recently formed association has an office on the main road through Katunguru a few doors up from the Unity Pub & Lodge. It gets mixed reviews & seems to charge higher rates than the two companies listed above.

What to see and do
Katunguru is entrenched as the best place for backpackers to arrange budget day safaris into the park (page 442). Boat trips on the adjacent stretch of the Kazinga Channel can be arranged indirectly through most of the lodges listed above, or directly with Irungu Community Boat Cruises (✪ *-0.1313, 30.04994; US$50/60/75/100 for 1/2/3/5 passengers*), which maintains an (often unmanned) office on the south bank 400m west of the Ishaka Road immediately south of Katunguru Bridge. Assuming that you won't be entering the national park, the advantage over boat trips out of Mweya is that no fees need to be paid. But if you will be entering the park anyway, you are better off doing a boat trip out of Mweya, as the scenery is more interesting and the wildlife at that end of the channel is far more habituated to boats.

KATWE AND THE NORTHERN CRATER LAKES Lined with rundown, partially boarded-up buildings that give it the aura of a recently resettled ghost town, the small but sprawling settlement of Katwe occupies an odd urban enclave within QENP, enclosed by park boundaries on three sides, and lapped by the waters of Lake

18

Edward to the south. A potentially interesting goal for backpackers who cannot afford a full-scale safari into QENP, Katwe is named after and owes its existence to a bordering crater lake that has formed one of Uganda's most important sources of coarse salt for at least 500 years. Munyenyange Crater Lake, also bordering Katwe, is seasonally good for flamingos, while the nearby Lake Edward shoreline is a reliable location for elephant, hippo, warthog, waterbuck and an abundance of waterbirds (though, for obvious reasons, it should be explored on foot only with considerable caution – indeed, a small area of shore has now been fenced off to allow townsfolk to collect water without being taken by crocodiles or attacked by hippos).

History The first written report of Lake Katwe was penned by Speke, who heard second-hand about a legendarily wealthy source of salt close to the base of the Mountains of the Moon. By that time, the lake had been mined for at least 400 years, and with salt being regarded as more valuable than precious metal in pre-colonial Uganda, control of this prized possession regularly shifted between the region's different kingdoms. Indeed, when Speke visited Uganda in 1862, Lake Katwe had for some years been part of Toro, but in the late 1870s it was recaptured by Omukama Kabalega, a coup that led to the first military confrontation between Bunyoro and a combined British-Toro expedition led by Captain Frederick Lugard.

Lugard arrived at Katwe in 1890 and recorded that: 'Everywhere were piles of salt, in heaps covered with grass, some beautifully white and clean. On our right was the Salt Lake, about three-quarters of a mile [1.2km] in diameter, at the bottom of a deep crater-like depression with banks some 200ft [61m] high. The water was of a claret red, with a white fringe of crystallised salt about its margin. A narrow neck, only some 40 yards [36m] across at the top, and perhaps 300 yards [274m] at its base, divided the Salt Lake from [Lake] Edward.' Lugard and his Toro entourage had little difficulty claiming the site – the resident Banyoro were not soldiers but miners and businessmen, and evidently they subscribed to the view that discretion forms the better part of valour – and built there a small fort, of which little trace remains today, before continuing northwards to Fort Portal.

Today, you'd be fortunate to encounter Lake Katwe in the rich claret incarnation encountered by Lugard and other early European visitors. This seems to happen only when the level of salt in the water approaches a certain concentration. However, this phenomenon is frequently seen in individual salt pans when they are almost ready to be 'harvested'. Particularly in the harsh midday light, however, Lake Katwe still retains the vaguely foreboding atmosphere described by E J Wayland: 'stifling and malodorous … a fiend-made meeting place for the Devil and his friends'. Commercial salt extraction from the lake peaked in the early 1970s when the faded plant that dominates Katwe village briefly pumped out an annual 2,000 tonnes before breaking down owing to corrosion of the pipework. Extraction of the lake's characteristic pink-hued coarse salt remains the main source of local income – though judging by the state of the village, it's not quite so lucrative an activity as it was in Katwe's heyday. However, a recent university study suggests that the lake holds more than 20 million tonnes of crystalline salts, enough to support commercial extraction of 40,000 tonnes per annum for longer than 30 years, and plans are afoot to build a new factory.

Getting there and away A well-maintained 18km dirt road runs west from a clearly signposted junction (✪ *-0.08187, 30.03027*) on the Kasese–Ishaka Road, 5km north of Katunguru and 8km south of Kikorongo. The road passes Kabatoro Entrance Gate (only 6km from the Mweya Peninsula) to the south about

4km before it enters Katwe. Coming from the north, Katwe can also be reached via the Explosion Crater Track that leaves the main road at Queens Pavilion (see page 446). A few matatus run back and forth between Kasese and Katwe daily.

 Where to stay and eat *Map, page 456*

All the lodges listed below lie within the Katwe enclave or along the main road, so no park fees are charged just for staying overnight. Katwe is also a useful base for game drives on the Kasenyi Plains (15–20km to the east) and boat trips on the Mweya Peninsula (6–10km to the south).

Moderate
Hippo Hill Safari Lodge (10 tents)
-0.13756, 29.89301; **m** 0782 399235;
e kitanda@infocom.co.ug; www.hippohilllodge. com. This grid of en-suite tented cottages lies above Katwe town, & enjoys good views over Lake Edward & (with a short stroll) Lake Munyenyange. Official rates are on the high side, but there's scope for negotiation. *US$150/200 sgl/dbl FB.* **$$$$**

Budget
Njovu Park Lodge (7 rooms) -0.13598, 29.89542; **m** 0752 992551; **e** njovuparklodge@ yahoo.com; **f** fb.me/njovuparklodgeug. Situated on the same hill as Hippo Hill, this new good-value lodge 500m north of Katwe has neat, clean en-suite rooms with nets & a pleasant terrace restaurant/bar. Hippos & elephants come past regularly, and it's only 300m from the rim of Lake Munyenyange. *US$20/33 sgl/dbl B&B or US$25/47 FB.* **$$**

Katwe Tourism Guesthouse (2 rooms, more under construction) -0.14251, 29.88239; **m** 0772 397354/0752 618265; **e** katic.org@gmail. com. In the same compound & under the same management as the Katwe Tourism Information Centre, this new USAID-funded guesthouse is already looking at bit rundown but it would

make a useful budget base for exploring Katwe & environs. *US$20 en-suite dbl.* **$$**

Shoestring
Kabatoro Guesthouse (6 rooms)
-0.13713, 29.9246; **m** 0782 082731/0772 415571; **e** info.kabatoro@gmail.com; www. kabatoro.co.nr. This unique guesthouse 400m west of Kabatoro Entrance Gate occupies the only inhabited building in the otherwise abandoned colonial-era village of Kabatoro. The time-warped façade & sleepy veranda, which could be transplanted from any medium-sized Ugandan town, feel rather surreal in this bush environment, thrillingly so on the regular occasions when elephants stroll past! The en-suite dbl rooms have nets & hot water, while a restaurant serves a limited selection of meals for around US$4. A fabulous shoestring safari destination in its own right & an ideal base for hitching into the park (or elsewhere). *US$17 dbl B&B.* **$$**

Excellent Lodge (12 rooms) **m** 0752 501905. Excellent overstates the case, but this just-about-acceptable shoestring lodge – the finest in downtown Katwe – is better than the flaking frontage might suggest. *US$8 en-suite dbl, US$3/7 sgl/twin with shared bathroom.* **$**

Tourist information
Katwe Tourism Information Centre
-0.14251, 29.88239; **m** 0772 397354/0753 393450; **e** katic.org@gmail.com; www.katwe-council.com; 08.00–19.00 daily. Located just west of what passes for downtown Katwe, this community-based organisation charges US$10pp

for a variety of guided activities including salt lake tours, birding excursions, boat trips on Lake Edward & cultural tours to the bustling Thu & Sat market at Mpondwe. A heritage museum is scheduled to open on the site at some indeterminate point.

What to see and do
Katwe Bay The 30km² bay separating Katwe from the Mweya Peninsula isn't technically part of QENP, but the surrounding shore is, and it hosts plenty of wildlife, including elephant, buffalo, kob and warthog. Hippos are resident in the

18

offshore shallows, and the aquatic birdlife is prodigious. The more enjoyable way to explore the bay is on a boat trip arranged through the Katwe Tourism Information Centre, which costs US$10 per person, and forms a good budget alternative to the launch trip from the Mweya Peninsula.

Lake Katwe Separated from the northern shore of Lake Edward by its 400m-wide rim, the 2.5km² hyper-saline Lake Katwe occupies the base of a volcanic caldera that last erupted between 6,000 and 10,000 years ago. It is one of the oldest and most productive sources of coarse salt anywhere in Uganda (page 452), and the view from the rim – with a honeycomb of individually-worked extraction plots running around the shore – is quite stunning. If you are interested in seeing the salt extraction process up close, there's nothing stopping you from driving or walking down the short road that leads out of town to the lakeshore. However, you'll get far more from the experience, as will the local salt miners toiling away in the sun, by arranging a tour with the Katwe Tourism Information Centre. This costs US$10 per person and enables you to see (and photograph) the various mining processes in the company of well-informed and articulate local guides.

Lake Munyenyange Even closer to town than Lake Katwe, but hidden from view by an enclosing caldera, the small and shallow Lake Munyenyange is known for the large numbers of lesser (and sometimes greater) flamingos that gather there when conditions are right, most usually from September to March. It also usually supports an interesting selection of resident (and, seasonally, migrant) waders. You can watch the birds from the road that skirts the lake's rim, but if you want to head closer to the water, you need to make arrangements with Katwe Tourism Information Centre, which charges US$10 per person whether you visit independently or are guided by its informative flamingo expert.

Other crater lakes Between Katwe and the Kasese Road, the landscape is studded by several dozen volcanic explosion craters, variously filled with water, grassland, acacia woodland and forest. A viewpoint on the Katwe Road (⊕ -0.09713, 29.98894), 5km from the junction with the Kasese–Ishaka Road, overlooks the near-circular **Lake Nyamunyuka** (literally, 'rotting meat'), an impressive body whose green and odorous waters are often attended by herds of buffalo.

With a solid 4x4 and at least 2 hours to spare, it's also worth exploring the rough, rocky and occasionally vertiginous 27km **Katwe Explosion Craters Track**, which runs northeast from opposite Kabatoro Entrance Gate to the Queen's Pavilion (page 446). This track offers some splendid views over Lake Kyemengo as well as a number of other deep craters, each with its own microhabitat – some lushly forested from rim to rim, others supporting a floor of practically treeless savannah. Although more notable for its scenic qualities than its game viewing, the hilly country traversed by this road is frequently haunted by large elephant herds in the dry season, and the thick woodland is the best place in QENP for acacia-associated birds (and, be warned, for tsetse flies).

Pelican Point Immediately west of Katwe, the Pelican Point sector of QENP was suggested as the location for the park's first lodge in the 1950s, but Mweya was selected owing to its more central location. Despite its proximity to Katwe, this sector has a remote, unspoiled flavour, and although wildlife volumes are relatively low, the likes of buffalo, kob, warthog, hippo and lion are all present. The main attractions are excellent views across Lake Edward and the opportunity to explore

off-road. There are currently no facilities in the area, not even tracks, but the QENP management plan proposes that a basic campsite will be cleared in the near future.

MWEYA PENINSULA Historically, the main tourist focus in QENP is the 10km² Mweya Peninsula, an elevated arrowhead of bushy land connected to the northern mainland by a natural isthmus little wider than the road that traverses it. Protruding between Lake Edward and the Kazinga Channel, immediately north of where the two waters merge, the peninsula has an inspirational setting, overlooking an archetypal equatorial African riverbank scene, with elephant and buffalo milling around the opposite shore, subverted by occasional glimpses of the snowy Rwenzori peaks (at least when they're not blanketed in cloud). Logistically, Mweya remains a popular base for exploring QENP, since it houses the park's oldest and arguably swankiest lodge, along with several budget-friendly UWA-managed guesthouses, and lies less than 45 minutes' drive from the game-viewing circuit on the Kasenyi Plains. While the peninsula may no longer be the be-all and end-all when it comes to tourist development in QENP, it remains the launch point for the park's most iconic activity – boat excursions on the Kazinga Channel.

Getting there and away Mweya lies 20km west of the Kasese–Ishaka Road. Coming from the south, the most direct route runs from just north of Katunguru Bridge via Katunguru Gate (⊕ -0.12801, 30.03428) and Channel Track. Coming from the north, follow the Katwe Road for 14km until you reach Kabatoro Gate (⊕ -0.13546, 29.92814), then turn left, and it's 8km to Mweya. Using public transport, the easiest option is to bus or matatu to Katunguru, from where a special-hire taxi to Mweya should cost US$10–15 one-way. Alternatively, catch a matatu from Kasese to Katwe, and ask to be dropped at Kabatoro Entrance Gate, where the rangers will usually help you find a lift (and you have the shoestring Kabatoro Guesthouse, 400m to the west, as a fall-back). When you're ready to leave Mweya, wait for a lift with outgoing lodge or park staff at the barrier guarding the entrance to the peninsula.

Where to stay   *Map, page 456*

Upmarket
✳ 🏠 **Mweya Safari Lodge** (54 rooms)
⊕ -0.18882, 29.90011; 📞 031 2260260/041 4340054; e reservations@marasa.net; www.
mweyalodge.com. Aptly described by both admirers & detractors as a 'Sheraton in the Bush', this plush lodge lacks the intimate wilderness associated with smaller tented camps, but this is more than compensated for by the fabulous location, proximity to QENP's main attractions, good food & excellent service, while the knock-the-dirt-off pressure showers will be welcome after a few days under canvas. On a clear day, the Rwenzori Mountains provide an incomparable backdrop while the dining veranda enjoys a grandstand view of the opposite bank of the Kazinga Channel, which routinely attracts large herds of buffalo & elephant. The lodge gardens rustle with animal life, ranging from warthogs & banded mongoose to slender-billed weavers & marsh flycatchers that approach the veranda so closely you can practically touch them. The standard en-suite rooms with fitted net & fan are more than adequate (ask for one facing the channel as opposed to the drive) but pale in comparison with the palatial new safari tents. Facilities & activities include daily game drives, balloon safaris, boat trips on the channel, a discreet TV lounge with DSTV, a good craft shop & a foreign-exchange facility. *US$209/354 standard sgl/dbl, US$403 deluxe dbl with AC, US$446 dbl luxury tent with AC. All rates B&B. Add US$24pp for FB.* **$$$$$**

Budget & shoestring
🏠 **Mweya Hostel, Lower Camp & UWA guesthouses** (42 rooms) m 0782 387805. Situated a few hundred metres west of Mweya Safari Lodge, these UWA-managed facilities are on the basic side, but clean, comfortable & very reasonably priced. The hostel has dbl rooms using common showers, while Lower Camp offers a

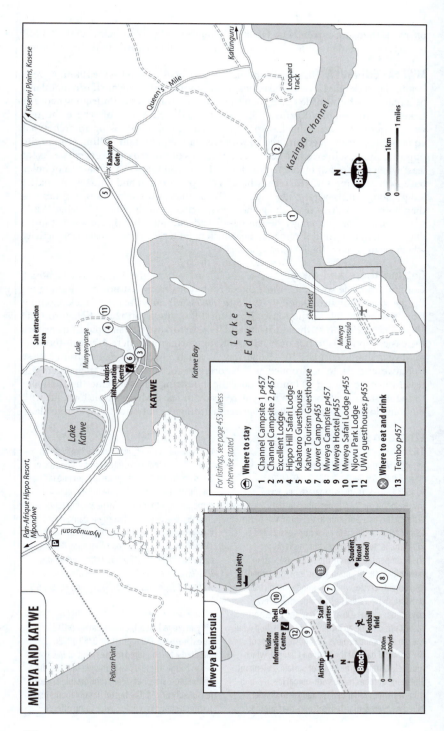

MWEYA AND KATWE

Kisenyi Plains, Kasese

Queen's Mile

Katunguru

Leopard track

Kabatoro Gate

Kazinga Channel

Salt extraction area

Lake Munyenyange

Tourist Information Centre

Lake Katwe

KATWE

Katwe Bay

Lake Edward

see inset

Mweya Peninsula

Pan-Afrique Hippo Resort, Mpondwe

Nyamugasani

Pelican Point

N

Bradt

0   1km
0   1 miles

For listings, see page 453 unless otherwise stated

Where to stay

1   Channel Campsite 1 *p457*
2   Channel Campsite 2 *p457*
3   Excellent Lodge
4   Hippo Hill Safari Lodge
5   Kabatoro Guesthouse
6   Katwe Tourism Guesthouse
7   Lower Camp *p455*
8   Mweya Campsite *p457*
9   Mweya Hostel *p455*
10   Mweya Safari Lodge *p455*
11   Njovu Park Lodge
12   UWA guesthouses *p455*

Where to eat and drink

13   Tembo *p457*

Mweya Peninsula

Launch jetty

Shell

Visitor Information Centre

Staff quarters

Student Hostel (closed)

Football field

Airstrip

N

Bradt

0   200m
0   200yds

range from sgl, dbl & twin rooms, some en suite, & the 3 guesthouses comprise 3- or 4-bedroom former staff houses with 1 en-suite room, a shared bathroom for the other rooms, & a kitchen with gas cooker. *US$7/10pp room using common showers in Lower Camp/Mweya Hostel; US$17/27 en-suite sgl/dbl Lower Camp; US$85/100 3-/4-bedroom guesthouse (sleeping 6/8).* **$$–$$$**

Camping

⚐ Mweya Campsite ⊕ -0.19625, 29.90173. This fabulously located campsite on the southern end of the peninsula has few facilities & is passed through by hippo *en masse* nightly & lions with some regularity, making it potentially dangerous after dark if you don't have a vehicle. If you

intend cooking for yourself, bring your own food. Alternatively, you could brave the hippos & wander up to the Tembo Restaurant for a meal, but be careful after dark, & don't even think about it without a good torch. *US$5pp.* **$**

⚐ Channel Campsites 1 & 2 ⊕ -0.17839, 29.91791 & -0.17492, 29.93383. If you have your own vehicle & are self-sufficient in food & water, you might prefer to camp at one of the secluded exclusive campsites that lie along Channel Drive about 5km from Mweya. Camping here is relatively expensive, but nocturnal encounters with large mammals are thrown in for free. Campsite No 2 has a good reputation for leopard sightings, but do seek advice about security in advance. *US$30pp.* **$$**

✕ Where to eat and drink *Map, opposite*

✳ ✕ Tembo Restaurant ⊕ -0.19276, 29.90193; **m** 0776 376955; ⊕ 07.00–22.00 daily. Situated about 300m south of the entrance to Mweya Safari Lodge & sharing its more illustrious neighbour's fabulous view over a stretch of channel

frequented by buffalo, elephant & hippos, this unpretentious canteen with indoor, terrace & garden seating & a well-stocked bar serves a fair range of tasty meat & vegetable dishes. *Meals in the US$6–7 range.*

Tourist information

ℹ Mweya Visitor Information Centre ⊕ -0.19008, 29.89845; **m** 0782 387805; ⊕ 06.30–18.00 daily. Near Kabatoro Guesthouse. This purpose-built facility 100m west of Mweya Safari Lodge contains clear & concise (though now somewhat weathered) interpretive exhibits including a topographic model, complete with buttons & flashing lights to identify landscape features, illustrating QENP's setting within the dramatic Albertine Rift Valley. Outside, a covered

timber deck faces the dramatic panorama across Lake Edward towards the Semliki Valley & the Rwenzori. Although park entrance fees cannot be paid at this office, it does handle bookings & payments for all UWA-managed accommodation on the Mweya Peninsula, UWA-operated boat trips on the Kazinga Channel, the lion- or leopard-tracking experience with the Queen Elizabeth Predator Project, & ranger-guides for game drives out of Mweya.

What to see and do In addition to the activities listed below, organised game drives along Channel Drive to look for the lions that inhabit the Kasenyi Plains are offered by Mweya Safari Lodge. The rate is US$200 for up to three people and US$220/240/280 for four/five/six.

Around the peninsula Plenty of wildlife can be seen on or from Mweya Peninsula, and there is no restriction on walking around the developed area between Mweya Safari Lodge, the airstrip and the campsite, though you should be cautious of any wildlife, and hippos in particular. Herds of buffalo and elephant routinely gather to drink on the channel shore facing Mweya Safari Lodge and Tembo Restaurant, while Defassa waterbuck, hippo and warthog are often seen milling along the peninsula's road. Giant forest hogs sometimes emerge on to the airstrip towards dusk, a family of habituated banded mongooses lives in the lodge grounds, and lion and spotted hyena are heard – and seen – with a frequency that might unnerve solitary campers! Birdlife is prolific, too. Marabou storks regularly roost on a bare tree between the

18

lodge and restaurant, while the exquisite red-throated sunbird, black-headed gonolek and a variety of weavers are among the more common residents of the lodge grounds. It's also well worth taking a bottle of beer down to the end of the peninsula airstrip to watch the sun set behind the DRC mountains – but ask which track to use, as driving down the airstrip itself is prohibited for obvious reasons.

Kazinga Channel boat trips The most popular activity at Mweya is the 2-hour boat trip from a jetty below the lodge to the mouth of the Kazinga Channel. Although not as spectacular as the equivalent boat trip in Murchison Falls, this is a great excursion, and wildlife viewing is excellent. Elephant, buffalo, waterbuck, Ugandan kob and large hippo pods are seen on a daily basis, while giant forest hog, leopard and lion are observed with unexpected frequency. Keep an eye open for the enormous water monitor lizard, which is common in the riverine scrub, as well as crocodiles, seen with increasing regularity since first colonising the area in the early 1990s. Waterbirds are plentiful, in particular water thick-knee, yellow-billed stork and various plovers, while pink-backed pelicans and white-bellied cormorants often flock on a sandbank near the channel mouth. One smaller bird to look out for is the black-headed gonolek, a member of the shrike family with a dazzling red chest.

Boat trips are operated by UWA (*US$30pp*), and by Mweya Safari Lodge, which asks slightly less (*US$28*) and has more comfortable boats. UWA trips leave daily at 09.00, 11.00, 13.00, 15.00 and 17.00, while the lodge boats leave at 11.00, 14.00 and 16.15, as well as at 07.00 and 09.00 by special request for groups. The 15.00 and 14.00 departures are most likely to yield good elephant sightings, particularly on hot days, when these thirsty creatures generally gravitate towards water from midday onwards, sometimes bathing in the channel. The odds of seeing predators and other nocturnal creatures coming to drink are highest in the late afternoon. In theory, departures are subject to minimum numbers, which used to be a concern for single travellers and couples, but these days the tourist volume through Mweya is so high that you can be confident there will be several departures daily. The trip lasts about 2 hours.

Balloon safaris Based in Mweya Safari Lodge, a new company called Uganda Balloon Safaris (m *0759 002552/4*; e *info@ugandaballoonsafari.com; www. ugandaballoonsafari.com*) now runs daily flights over the Kasenyi Plains, subject to weather conditions and demand. They leave from Mweya at 05.00, meet any guests coming from other lodges at Kasenyi Crossroads at 05.45, then launch about 15 minutes' drive further east. The 7–10km flight takes about 1 hour, and offers a chance to see lions and other wildlife from close to the ground, as well as going up high for views of the lanes, channel and (clouds permitting) Rwenzori peaks. It is followed by a champagne bush breakfast. The trip costs US$380 per person, with a minimum group size of two, and space for up to 16.

Lion and leopard tracking The Queen Elizabeth Predator Project, overseen by Dr Ludwig Siefert, now monitors the activities of several lion prides and a few individual leopards living to the north of the Kazinga Channel. At least one member of each research pride has been fitted with a radio collar, as have all the leopards under study, which makes it is easy to locate them at any time of day. A limited number of tourists is permitted to join the research team as part of an Experiential Predator Tourism activity offered twice-daily by the Mweya Visitor Information Centre. Lion sightings are all but certain, and close-up leopard encounters are also very likely. The excursion leaves at 06.30 or 16.00, takes up to 3 hours, and costs US$60, of which US$10 goes directly to local communities.

Channel Drive circuit Running roughly parallel to the Kazinga Channel's northern shore, Channel Drive now serves mainly as a through route between Katunguru Bridge and the Mweya Peninsula. However, the compact network of tracks that emanates from the main road can provide some excellent game viewing, albeit a little more hit and miss than the Kasenyi Plains due to its dense cover of euphorbia trees protruding above the tangled scrubby thickets. The most common large mammals in the area are warthog, bushbuck and waterbuck, but elephants often cross through from midday onwards, heading to or from the water. Leopard Track and the short side road to Campsite No 2 (page 457) are the best places to look for the – unusually habituated – leopards that frequent the area, while lions are seen fairly regularly, and it is also a good place to look for the localised giant forest hog. Because it lies so close to Mweya and consists of several interconnecting tracks, the circuit can easily be explored from the lodge over 2 hours. Potentially rewarding night drives are also permitted provided you take a guide/ranger, which costs US$30 per person and can be arranged at Mweya Visitor Information Centre.

KYAMBURA, MARAMAGAMBO AND THE KICHWAMBA ESCARPMENT

Relatively undeveloped for tourism compared to the plains north of the Kazinga Channel, southeastern QENP is dominated by the 750km² Maramagambo Forest, some 60% of which lies within the park boundaries, while the remainder is divided between the abutting Kalinzu Forest Reserve and Kigezi Wildlife Reserve. Maramagambo is regarded to be one of the most biodiverse forests anywhere in East Africa, with strong faunal affinities to the Congo Basin, and it can be explored on a network of guided trails emanating from a pair of jungle-bound crater lakes called Nyamasingiri and Kyasanduka. A popular tourist activity in this part of QENP is chimp tracking in the Kyambura River Gorge, a forested ravine carved into the surrounding flat savannah along the border with Kyambura Wildlife Reserve, a little-visited tract of savannah notable for the waterbirds – in particular flamingos – attracted to its lovely crater lakes. Although Maramagambo Forest is serviced by a solitary upmarket lodge and a couple of low-key campsites, the stretch of the Rift Valley wall that overlooks it, known as the Kichwamba Escarpment, supports an ever-growing proliferation of lodges used by mid-range safaris primarily as a base for day trips to Mweya, Kasenyi and elsewhere north of the Kazinga Channel. A short distance further south, the affordable chimp-tracking experience offered by the Kalinzu Eco-Tourism Project in the eponymous forest reserve is rapidly becoming a firm favourite with budget-minded travellers. Another attraction for birders, keen walkers and others on a budget is the Bunyaruguru Crater Lakes, many of which are within easy striking distance of the Ishaka Road.

Getting there and away

All the sites described under this heading are accessed from the Kasese–Ishaka Road as it runs south from Katunguru Bridge. Plenty of public transport runs along this main road, but most sites lying off it are accessible only in a private vehicle, on foot, or by special hire or boda from Kichwamba trading centre, 13km south of Katunguru Bridge. Directions to individual lodges and sites are included as required in the descriptions below.

Where to stay *Map, page 460*

Except where noted, the lodges listed below lie alongside or within 1.5km of the main Kasese–Ishaka Road. With the exception of Jacana Safari Lodge, they all sit outside the national park boundary, so no park fees are charged simply for staying

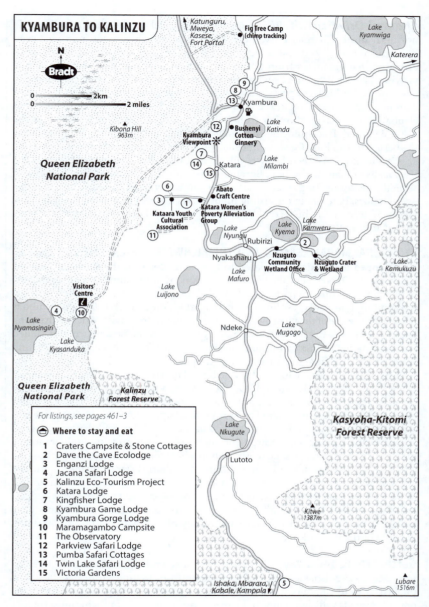

KYAMBURA TO KALINZU

N

Bradt

0 _____ 2km
0 _____ 2 miles

*Katunguru,
Mweya,
Kasese,
Fort Portal*

Fig Tree Camp
(chimp tracking)

*Lake
Kyamwiga*

Katerera

⑨
⑧ ⑬ Kyambura

⑫

Bushenyi
Cotton
Ginnery

*Lake
Katinda*

Kyambura
Viewpoint ✳

⑦
⑭
⑮ Katara

*Lake
Milambi*

Queen Elizabeth
National Park

▲ *Kibona Hill
963m*

⑥

Abato
● Craft Centre

③ ① Katara Women's
Poverty Alleviation
Group

Kataara Youth
Cultural
Association

⑪

*Lake
Nyungu*

Rubirizi

*Lake
Kyema*

*Lake
Kamweru*

*Lake
Kamukuzu*

Nyakasharu

Nzuguto
Community
Wetland Office

Nzuguto Crater
& Wetland ②

*Lake
Mafuro*

Visitors'
Centre ℹ

④
⑩

*Lake
Luijono*

Ndeke

*Lake
Mugogo*

*Lake
Nyamasingiri*

*Lake
Kyasanduka*

Queen Elizabeth
National Park

*Kalinzu
Forest Reserve*

*Lake
Nkugute*

Lutoto

**Kasyoha-Kitomi
Forest Reserve**

▲ *Kitwe
1387m*

For listings, see pages 461–3

🛏 **Where to stay and eat**

1 Craters Campsite & Stone Cottages
2 Dave the Cave Ecolodge
3 Enganzi Lodge
4 Jacana Safari Lodge
5 Kalinzu Eco-Tourism Project
6 Katara Lodge
7 Kingfisher Lodge
8 Kyambura Game Lodge
9 Kyambura Gorge Lodge
10 Maramagambo Campsite
11 The Observatory
12 Parkview Safari Lodge
13 Pumba Safari Cottages
14 Twin Lake Safari Lodge
15 Victoria Gardens

*Ishaka, Mbarara,
Kabale, Kampala* ⑤

▲ *Lubare
1516m*

there. Many are strung along the Kichwamba Escarpment, where they enjoy a terrific view north across the plains of QENP to the Kazinga Channel as it zigzags between lakes George and Edward, stretching all the way to the Rwenzori peaks on a clear day. Conveniently located for visits to Maramagambo Forest, or for chimp tracking in Kyambura Gorge or Kalinzu Forest Reserve, these lodges also offer good access to the Kasenyi Plains (20km north of Kichwamba trading centre) and Mweya Peninsula (35km northwest).

Exclusive

⌂ **Kyambura Gorge Lodge** (6 cottages)
✣ -0.20698, 30.10333; ☎ 041 4346464; m 0772 741718; e salesug@volcanoessafaris.com; www.volcanoessafaris.com. Overlooking the south end of Kyambura Gorge about 1km north of Kichwamba trading centre, this architecturally innovative lodge consists of a main building converted from an abandoned coffee shed & a half-dozen spacious cottages whose eclectic 'African bric-a-brac chic' décor is influenced by local building styles — your bedside table might be a ramshackle stand created from a village payphone (still crudely painted with networks & rates) or a converted old cable drum. This contemporary vernacular feel extends to the nocturnal soundscape — trucks rattle along the highway, villagers sing into the night & mosque calls provide an early morning wake up— but the large beds with walk-in nets, cosy sofa areas, bathrooms, communal lodge areas, swimming pool, etc, are all unashamedly luxurious. Rooms in the gorge wing have better views & stand further from the road. *US$336/560 sgl/dbl inclusive of all meals, drinks, laundry & complimentary massage. Rates drop by around 10% in the low season.* **$$$$$**

Upmarket

⌂ **Kyambura Game Lodge** (8 cottages)
✣ -0.20873, 30.10078; ☎ 041 4322789; m 0703 614337; e reservations@kyamburalodge.com; www.kyamburalodge.com. Carved into the bush above the south end of Kyambura Gorge 500m north of Kichwamba trading centre, this recently reconstructed lodge offers accommodation in lovely canvas-fronted cottages with beds made from logs & protected by walk-in nets, screed floor, bright ethnic décor, a wooden balcony with a view to a hill & a large bathroom with tub & shower. The swimming pool & restaurant both enjoy a nice view. A good choice at the price. *US$209/364 sgl/dbl FB.* **$$$$**

⌂ **Jacana Safari Lodge** (12 cottages)
✣ -0.28422, 30.04159; ☎ 041 4258273; e reservations@geolodgesafrica.com; www.geolodgesafrica.com. The only accommodation set within Maramagambo Forest, this attractive wooden construction stands beside the jungle-fringed Lake Nyamasingiri, 15km southwest of the main road. Wooden suites with a private veranda & bathrooms all overlook the lake. The open-sided bar & restaurant are suspended over the shore,

& there's a lakeshore swimming pool. Primates & birds are plentiful (though chimps are more often heard than seen) & activities include boat trips on the lake. It's a bit of a drive back to the main road, but the secluded jungle setting compensates. *US$210/320 sgl/dbl FB.* **$$$$$**

⌂ **Katara Lodge** (8 cottages) ✣ -0.24116, 30.07803; m 0773 011648/0712 812560; e info@kataralodge.com; www.kataralodge.com. Scenically perched on the escarpment edge overlooking the rolling plains of QENP, this highly rated lodge offers accommodation in thatched wood-&-canvas cottages all with 1 dbl & 1 ¾ bed, fitted nets, safe, large bathroom with tub & shower, & private balcony where you can sleep under the stars if you so choose. There's a swimming pool, good wine list & cocktail menu. *US$250/400 sgl/dbl FB, discounts for East African residents & children.* **$$$$$**

⌂ **Enganzi Lodge** (9 cottages) ✣ -0.24375, 30.07701; m 0756 702583/0712 810388; e info@enganzilodge.com; www.enganzilodge.com. This blatant copy of the adjacent Katara Lodge barely merits a separate description, but it is just as attractive & scenically located as its neighbour, with more pocket-friendly rack rates. *US$160/270 sgl/dbl FB.* **$$$$$**

Moderate

☀ ⌂ **Twin Lake Safari Lodge** (14 units)
✣ -0.2314, 30.08911; m 0772 892866/348509; e info@twinlakesafari.com. Situated on the lip of the escarpment 500m west of the Ishaka Rd, this owner-managed lodge is centred around a wooden chalet erected by the engineers who built Katunguru Bridge in 1948. The name refers to crater lakes Katinda & Milambi, which are on the opposite side of the main road & invisible from the lodge, but the location is nonetheless glorious & offers great views over the plains below. The large wood-&-canvas cottages have a wood-framed queen-sized bed with fitted net, en-suite bathroom with tub & shower, & a balcony that makes the most of the view. Above average value. *US$150/200 sgl/dbl FB.* **$$$$**

⌂ **Parkview Safari Lodge** (7 rooms)
✣ -0.21963, 30.09461; m 0703 623063/0772 377954; e reservations@parkviewsafarilodge.com; www.parkviewsafarilodge.com. Opened in 2015 & still experiencing a few teething pains when we dropped by, this potentially stunning lodge 500m

west of the main road is centred upon an impressive 2-storey thatched bar/restaurant whose view is compromised by a foreground of overly fussy lawns, pine plantations & cottage roofs. The spacious & airy circular thatched cottages, individually named after past & present African heads of state, have terracotta tile floors, attractively contemporary African décor, walk-in nets, large bathroom with tub & shower, & private balcony. Good value. *US$140/200 sgl/dbl FB.* **$$$$**

🏠 **The Observatory** (4 rooms) ✆ -0.2577, 30.07333; ☎041 4258273; m 0782 424250; e reservations@geolodgesafrica.com; www.geolodgesafrica.com. Perched high on the edge of the Kichwamba Escarpment, this self-catering wooden house sleeping up to 10 stands on a small coffee plantation, 2.5km southeast of the main road. The views to the Kazinga Channel & Rwenzori are peerless, & it is also very attractively decorated. Facilities include a well-equipped kitchen, sitting room with games & books, solar & generator power, jacuzzi & fabulous balcony aimed to catch the sunset. Guests must bring their own food but a cook can be provided by prior arrangement. Good value & ideal for family parties. *US$80/55 adult/child.* **$$$$**

🏠 **Kingfisher Lodge** (20 rooms) ✆ -0.23026, 30.08988; m 0753 367980/0774 159579; e kingfisher-kichwamba@gmx.net; www.kingfisher-uganda.net. This is the oldest lodge on the Kichwamba Escarpment & it shows. The views are excellent, & the whitewashed Swahili-style cottages with banana-leaf roof & crenulated verandas are appealingly suggestive of a fortified mountain village (complete with swimming pool). But rooms feel a bit cramped & tired by comparison to the competition. *US$125/230 B&B.* **$$$$**

Budget

🏠 **Dave the Cave Ecolodge** (4 rooms & 1 4-bed dorm) ✆ -0.261, 30.12255; m 0706 825615/0772 863399; e nyanzibiriecotour@gmail.com; http://mirtheboerdijk.wix.com/dave-the-cave. Set in lush gardens on the southwest rim of Kamweru Crater Lake 2km east of Nyakasharu (on the main Kasese–Ishaka Road), this rustic owner-managed lodge has no shortage of character, comprising wooden Tarzan-style huts with lake views, twin or dbl bed, nets, & en-suite semi-outdoor eco-toilets. Camping is also permitted. Room rates are a little steep by standards

elsewhere in Uganda, but seem more reasonable when you consider its proximity to Kichwamba & QENP, & that they include meals & free access to Izoguto Cave & the boardwalk around Kamweru. *US$25/40/50pp FB camping/dorm/private room.* **$$$**

🏠 **Pumba Safari Cottages** (3 cottages & 1 standing tent) ✆ -0.21013, 30.10055; m 0772 482462; e info@mamalandsafaris.com; www.pumbasafaricottages.n.nu. This rustic & unpretentious cluster of basic en-suite cottages, situated right next to Kyambura Game Lodge a few hundred metres north of Kichwamba trading centre, fills an otherwise empty niche at the upper end of the budget range. The cottages are all built in traditional style, but have hot water & nets, as well as a great view over the plains, & the friendly staff go out of their way to generate a home-away-from-home mood. It would feel overpriced in any other context, but it's fair value for QENP. *US$80/100/150 sgl/dbl/trpl B&B. Add US$10pp FB.* **$$$**

Shoestring & camping

🏠 **Craters Campsite & Stone Cottages** (4 tents, 2 rooms under construction) ✆ -0.24563, 30.08429; m 0701 504900/0757 869503; 📘 fb.me/campsitecraters.kichwamba. Set in large grassy gardens 1km west of the main road (a boda from the junction costs around US$0.60), this friendly new campsite lies 5mins' walk downhill from the rim of the forested Kyemengo Crater. Simple standing tents with bed & bedding are available, & you can camp in your own tent, but the stone cottages should be complete by the time you read this. Meals cost US$5, as does a 3-hour guided walk to the green Nyungu Crater Lake. The staff can also arrange ½-day safaris to the Kasenyi Plains or Mweya Peninsula for US$100, inclusive of driver/guide & fuel, for a group of up to 4. *US$20pp standing tent, US$10pp camping.* **$$**

🏠 **Victoria Gardens** (2 rooms, more under construction) ✆ -0.23626, 30.09338; m 0772 463443/0779 285102; 📘 fb.me/victoriagardensandsafaris. Only 200m from the main road, this low-key guesthouse stands in green gardens on the rim of the cultivated Kyangabi Crater. The en-suite rooms have cold showers & fitted nets, & there's also a local restaurant/bar with pool table. *US$27/33 sgl/dbl.* **$$**

⛺ Kalinzu Eco-Tourism Project
✆ -0.37565, 30.11526; ☎ 041 4230365/6; m 0772
568168/0702 032312; www.nfa.org.ug. Although
long-term plans exist to build accommodation at
Kalinzu, the only on-the-spot overnight option at
present is a simple campsite with a toilet & shower
on the west side of the Ishaka Rd right next to the
chimp-tracking office. There's no restaurant, so
campers should ideally be self sufficient, but basic
supplies can be purchased at a nearby trading
centre. US$5pp. **$**

⛺ Maramagambo Campsite Rustic campsite
cut into a forest glade close to (but not in sight
of) Lake Kyasanduka. Facilities are limited to cold
showers & firewood but it's possible (at a price) to
eat at Jacana Lodge, 1km away (page 461). The
birdlife around the campsite is superb, & monkeys
are everywhere. US$5pp. **$**

What to see and do The sites below are described in the sequence you'd
encounter them – or the primary junction for the associated access road – driving
from north to south between Katunguru and Ishaka.

Kyambura Gorge chimp tracking The only habituated chimpanzee
community in QENP inhabits an isolated strip of riparian forest in the 100m-deep
Kyambura River Gorge, which runs for 16km on the park's eastern boundary with
Kyambura Wildlife Reserve. The confined nature of the forested gorge makes it
quite easy to locate the chimps by sound, and once you've found them, they can
usually be approached quite closely. Black-and-white colobus, vervet monkey and
olive baboon are also regularly observed in the gorge, while less visible residents
include red-tailed monkey and giant forest hog. For birdwatchers, Kyambura Gorge
is one of the best places in Uganda for black bee-eater and blue-bellied kingfisher,
both of which might be seen from the rim.

Guided chimp-tracking excursions depart twice-daily from Fig Tree Camp on
the gorge's western rim. Permits cost US$50, inclusive of the guide but excluding
the park entrance fee, and must be booked and paid for at the Katunguru park
headquarters 8km to the north. Up to 16 permits are issued for any given day, with
trackers leaving in two groups of up to four people each at 08.00 or 13.00. The
excursion typically takes about 3 hours but this depends greatly on whether you
locate the chimps, and how quickly. A few years ago, Kyambura was one of the most
reliable chimp-tracking sites in Uganda, with a success rate of 85%, but this has
dropped to around 50% in recent years, which makes Kalinzu Eco-Tourism Project
(see above), only 28km further south, a better prospect in many respects.

The chimp-tracking trailhead at Fig Tree Camp (✆ -0.1885, 30.10085) lies 2.5km
east of the Ishaka Road. The junction (✆ -0.19579, 30.08567) is 9km south of
Katunguru Bridge.

Maramagambo Forest The immense Maramagambo Forest, which runs west
from the Katunguru–Ishaka Road almost as far as the shore of Lake Edward, is largely
inaccessible to tourists, the only exception being the northeastern tip around the
crater lakes Nyamasingiri and Kyasanduka. The vastness of this forest is alluded to in
its name, which derives from a local phrase meaning 'the end of words' and refers to
a legend about a group of young people who got lost there many years ago, and took
so long to find their way out there they were unable to speak when they returned home. A
medium-altitude rainforest with strong affiliations to its counterparts on the opposite
side of the Congolese border, Maramagambo supports a rich selection of birds, along
with forest mammals such as chimpanzee, red-tailed and L'Hoest's monkeys, potto,
giant forest hog, yellow-backed duiker, pygmy antelope and giant elephant shrew

The main tourist development in northeast Maramagambo is Jacana Safari Lodge,
which lies on the shore of Lake Nyamasingiri. In addition, a nearby visitors' centre and

18

campsite stand close to the shore of the smaller Lake Kyasanduka. The 1km stretch of road between the visitors' centre and Jacana Safari Lodge passes through lush primary forest and can be walked unguided at no charge other than the standard entrance fees. Plenty of monkeys are likely to be seen – most commonly black-and-white colobus, red-tailed and vervet – and there's a slimmer chance of encountering the lovely L'Hoest's monkey, chimpanzees and even leopard. Birdwatchers could pace up and down here several times without exhausting the opportunities to identify a confusing assembly of forest greenbuls, sunbirds, woodpeckers and other more elusive species.

Three different **guided walks** can be undertaken from the visitors' centre at a cost of US$30 per person per activity. The most straightforward trail loops around the forested shore of Lake Kyasanduka, and shouldn't take much longer than an hour, depending on how interested you are in the prolific birdlife. For dedicated birdwatchers, the most rewarding walk is likely to be the half day around the back of Lake Nyamasingiri, which comprises five interlocking craters and extends over 4km². The forest here hosts rarities such as scaly-breasted illadopsis, snowy-headed robin-chat and chestnut wattle-eye, while the lake itself is a good site for African finfoot. A third hike, roughly 90 minutes in duration, leads to a large cave that hosts a massive colony of bats, as well as a few rock pythons that feed on them. The cave is viewed from a platform 15m away, a precaution imposed after a visitor died of Marburg fever contracted through contact with a bat inside the cave.

The feeder road to Jacana Safari Lodge departs from the west side of the Ishaka Road (⊕ -0.21623, 30.09302), 2.5km south of the junction for Kyambura Gorge and 1km before Kichwamba trading centre. The road reaches the visitors' centre and campsite after 14km, then terminates at Jacana Safari Lodge after another 1km.

Kyambura Wildlife Reserve (entry US$10/5 FNR/FR) Characterised by wooded savannah, the little-visited 157km² Kyambura Wildlife Reserve is a contiguous extension of QENP bordered by the Kyambura Gorge in the west and Kazinga Channel in the north. Though it supports a similar selection of wildlife to the Kasenyi Plains, it cannot be regarded as prime game-viewing territory, if only because of a lack of suitable tracks. The main point of interest is a cluster of seven scenic crater lakes, three of which are accessible from a public road that connects Kyambura trading centre to Kashaka, a fishing village sited at the confluence of the Kazinga Channel and Lake George.

About 10km out of Kyambura village, the bumpy track to Kashaka runs along the northern rim of Lake Chibwera, offering the opportunity to alight from the car and scan the surface for waterbirds such as little grebe and various ducks. About 3km further on, it offers distant views over the aptly entitled Flamingo Lake, where concentrations of several thousand greater and lesser flamingos gather when conditions are conducive. The 1km track leading down from the crater rim to the

inner wall of Flamingo Lake is just about motorable, but a safer bet would be to head down on foot. Some 6km further the Kashaka road skirts Lake Bagusa, then passes a breached crater connected to Lake George immediately before it arrives at the fishing village. A small side turning along the southern edge of this breached crater leads to Lake Maseche, where flamingos are also sometimes seen.

The Kashaka Road runs northeast from Kichwamba trading centre, 13km south of the Katunguru Bridge, and after passing Kyambura Game Lodge and Kyambura Gorge Lodge to the left, it enters the reserve after 4km. Although the track isn't in great condition, you'll have no problems in a 4x4, and it is traversed by a steady trickle of shared taxis connecting Kichwamba to Kashaka.

Kyambura Viewpoint and lakes Katinda and Milambi Set on the west side of the Ishaka Road about 1.5km south of Kichwamba trading centre, the Kyambura Viewpoint (⊕ *-0.22515, 30.09418*), set on the escarpment overlooking QENP and the Kazinga Channel, is a scenic spot to stop for a cold drink. There's a well-stocked handicraft shop, and it also sells good locally produced honey. The viewpoint is the home of the Bunyaruguru Community-Based Tourism Association (*BUCOBATA*; m *0772 873542/0754 206569*), which offers guided hikes to the twin 'love lakes', Katinda (vaguely heart-shaped) and Milambi (vaguely egg-shaped) 1km to the east. The scenic walk takes about an hour, and also includes visits to a local coffee plantation and beer brewery, which seems like a fair return for the guide fee of US$7 per person.

Kataara Women's Poverty Alleviation Group (*KWPAG*; ⊕ *-0.24481, 30.08948*; m *0774 373794/0758 151362*; e *katarawomens@gmail.com*; *https://kwpag.wordpress.com*) Operating out of a handicraft centre situated 300m west of the Ishaka Road towards Katara Lodge, this community-based NGO specialises in making paper from dried elephant dung collected in and around the borders of QENP. It's an innovative and laudable way to create local support for animals that are frequently destructive to subsistence farms bordering the park. Elephant dung is bought from locals who collect it at a rate of US$3 per basin, and the project also provides partial employment to 30 (mostly female) craftspeople, while profits are used to help support orphans or to finance a local savings and credit scheme. Visitors are welcome to watch the paper being manufactured at the back of the shop, or to shop for the reasonably priced products, which include elephant-dung cards, notebooks, beads and purses, as well as some basketwork and engraved calabashes.

Kataara Youth Cultural Association (⊕ *-0.24445, 30.07941*; m *0704 489204/0782 698528*; e *kyoca2013@gmail.com*) Situated more or less opposite Katara Lodge, the Kataara Youth Cultural Association offers 2-hour community walks taking in everything from local coffee farms and weavers to traditional healers for US$15 per person.

Nzuguto Community Wetland The Nzuguto Environmental Conservation Association (*NECA*; ⊕ *-0.26238, 30.1139*; m *0703 630944*; e *ugandapal@gmail.com*; *www.luxuryecotours.com/index.php/blog*) was established in 2012 to save a 56ha wetland nestled within Nzuguto Crater, an important water source and wildlife refuge that had been degraded as a result of pollution. The main activity offered by NECA is a guided 1.6km walk (*US$10pp*), incorporating a 600m boardwalk, through the papyrus swamp. The sitatunga antelope, once resident, is now extinct, but more than 130 bird species have been recorded, with grey crowned crane, Ross's turaco, marsh tchagra, black-capped yellow warbler, white-collared olive-back and red headed bluebill ranking among the more interesting regulars.

THE FORMATION OF LAKE KAMWERU

Kamweru translates as 'fertile place', and legend has it that the crater in which the lake now nestles had a dry floor that was covered in agriculture until about 100 years ago. Back then, it was Nzuguto Crater that hosted a lake, one whose secretive spirit guardian served as an oracle to a local king called Heru. One day, when Heru was away on safari, his wife had sex with another man, and revealed the secret of the lake's spirit to her lover. This indiscretion so incensed the spirit that he lured the king's eldest son into the lake's waters, and pulled him under to drown. When Heru returned home, he in turn was angry at the sprit, and told it to leave the lake, threatening never to leave it another sacrifice. The next day, when Heru woke up, the spirit had indeed vanished. But so had the lake itself, as the spirit caused its water to flow through the subterranean river that passes through Izoguto Cave into Kamweru Crater, which has hosted a lake ever since.

NECA also offers a 5km guided walk around the rim of Lake Kyema (*US$10pp*), which is nestled in a deep steep crater about 500m to the east. On a clear day, the highest point on the Kyema rim offers views over QENP to the Rwenzori. A small group of hippos is reputedly resident in the lake.

The NECA office lies 1km east of the Ishaka Road. The junction is at Nyakasharu trading centre (✪ *-0.26593, 30.10685*), just south of the larger settlement of Rubirizi. Any transport running along the main road can drop you at Nyakasharu, from where a boda to NECA (or on to Dave the Cave) shouldn't cost more than US$1.

Lake Kamweru Accessible through the grounds of Dave the Cave Ecolodge (page 462), this small crater lake is best known as the site of the large but low Izoguto Cave (*entry US$3pp*), which has been carved by a subterranean river that originates in the Nzuguto Wetlands and empties into the lake. Dave the Cave also offers guided walks around the lake, which supports more than 100 bird species, incorporating a visit to the cave (*US$15pp*), and canoe trips on the lake (*US$15/hr*).

Kasyoha-Kitomi Forest Reserve (m *0772 568168; www.nfa.org.ug*) A southern extension of QENP's Maramagambo Forest, Kasyoha-Kitomi is a 400km² tract of medium-altitude evergreen forest that harbours a varied fauna, including an estimated 300 elephants, 350 chimpanzees and an abundance of monkeys. The forest is of particular interest to birders, with more than 300 species recorded, including African grey parrot, red-chested owlet, black bee-eater, chocolate-backed kingfisher and equatorial akalat. Kasyoha-Kitomi is poorly developed for tourists at present, but NECA does offer guided day hikes to Kamukuzu Crater Lake (*US$10pp*), a pretty body of transparent water bordering the forest reserve. The lake is safe for swimming, and wildlife likely to be seen includes black-and-white colobus, red-tailed and L'Hoest's monkey, giant kingfisher and great blue turaco. To get to the forest reserve from the NECA office, you need to drive for 30 minutes to the trailhead, or catch a boda, then it's a 1-hour walk in either direction. Future plans include the construction of a community-run campsite next to the lake, and the introduction of canoeing. There is also talk of starting up chimpanzee tracking and constructing a canopy walk in the forest.

Kalinzu Chimp Tracking and Eco-Tourism Project The highly accessible Kalinzu Eco-Tourism Project (✪ *-0.37565, 30.11526;* ☎ *041 4230365/6;* m *0772*

568168/0702 032312; www.nfa.org.ug), set alongside the Kasese–Ishaka Road 35km south of Katunguru, now ranks as Uganda's most reliable chimpanzee-tracking option for budget-conscious travellers. The project is centred on the 137km² Kalinzu Forest Reserve, an eastern extension of QENP's Maramagambo Forest that comprises more than 400 tree species and supports a similar range of forest wildlife than its better-known neighbour. The main draw of this medium-altitude forest is chimpanzees, but five other diurnal primate species are present, namely olive baboon, black-and-white colobus and red-tailed, blue and L'Hoest's monkeys, along with the nocturnal potto and two varieties of galago. Kalinzu also provides refuge to the rare pygmy antelope. Other wildlife includes 378 bird, 262 butterfly and 97 moth species.

Kalinzu harbours an estimated 300–400 chimpanzees, including a 40-strong community habituated for tourist visits, and a slightly larger one reserved for researchers. Chimp tracking (*US$40pp*) now comes with a 95% success rate, making the site almost as reliable as Kibale Forest, and recent reports suggest the quality of sightings is usually very good. There is no fixed departure time, tracking can start from 07.30 until around 14.00, but an early start offers the best chance of a good sighting. The walk from the project to the habituated troop's territory is around 3–4km and the round trip usually takes up to 4 hours. Because it lies outside the national park system, no park fees are charged.

Also on offer are 3–4-hour general forest walks (*US$20pp*), which provide an opportunity to see a variety of primates, notably the localised L'Hoest's monkeys, as well alluring forest birds such as great blue turaco, black bee-eater and African pygmy kingfisher. Travellers with a specialised interest in birds or butterflies should specify this before they set out.

Any public transport heading along the main road between Kasese and Mbarara can drop you at Kalinzu's clearly signposted office, trailhead and campsite, which stand on the west side of the road 22km south of Rubirizi. Camping is permitted (page 463), or you could overnight in Ishaka, only 20km to the south, and come through by boda, which shouldn't cost more than US$5 one way.

ISHAKA AND BUSHENYI Now arguably the most important route focus in southwest Uganda, the junction town of Ishaka is where travellers coming from QENP or Kasese must choose between heading east via Mbarara towards Kampala, south via Ntungamo to Kabale, or southwest via Rukungiri to Buhoma (Bwindi Impenetrable National Park). Ishaka, like Bushenyi less than 5km further east, is now half of the rapidly-growing Bushenyi-Ishaka Metropolitan Area, which supports a combined population of 41,000. Ishaka is also home to the Kampala International University's Western Campus, a medical college that attracts students from all around East Africa, and it has a few decent hotels that make an ideal base for tracking chimps at the nearby Kalinzu Eco-Tourism Project.

Getting there and away Ishaka lies at the three-way junction of the main road between Fort Portal and Mbarara, and a newly surfaced road running south to Kabale via Kitagata and Ntungamo. Distances and approximate driving times are 55km/45–60 minutes to Katunguru (QENP), 95km/90–100 minutes to Kasese, 175km/3 hours to Fort Portal, 60km/45 minutes to Mbarara, 330km/4½–6 hours to Kampala, and 100km/2 hours to Kabale.

Using public transport, those coming directly from Kampala are best off trying to catch a bus to Kasese via Mbarara (as opposed to via Fort Portal) and hopping off in Ishaka. Alternatively, take a bus to Mbarara and pick up an onward matatu there. More locally, regular matatus connect Ishaka to Kasese (*US$2.50*), Fort Portal

18

(*US$4*), Mbarara (*US$2.50*) and Kabale (*US$3*). There is no taxi park as such; matatus out of Ishaka all leave from within 100m or so of the main central junction, on the left side of the appropriate road.

Where to stay and eat In addition to the two budget standouts listed below, a few indifferent shoestring guesthouses line the main road through Ishaka and Bushenyi.

Cielo Country Inn (15 rooms) ⊕ -0.5321, 30.12378; m 0703 082597/0772 934697. This welcoming owner-managed hotel is set in pleasant gardens alongside the Kasese Rd, 2.5km northwest of the main central junction. En-suite rooms are clean & comfortable, but choose one set back from the main road. Facilities include a good restaurant with garden seating, fast Wi-Fi & back-up generator. *US$24/28/30 B&B sgl/dbl/twin.* **$$**

Crane Resort Hotel (19 rooms) ⊕ -0.54145, 30.13108; m 0757 317910; e craneresorthotelishaka@gmail.com; f fb.me/ craneresorthotel. The larger & more ostentatious & impersonal Crane Resort Hotel, abutting the Kasese Rd 2.5km northwest of the main central junction, offers a great view over the green hills to the west, & has functional modern rooms with DSTV, Wi-Fi & access to a sauna & steam bath. A restaurant serves tasty Ugandan fare in the US$4–7 range. *US$20 sgl with shared bath, US$24/27/31 en-suite sgl/dbl/twin. All rates B&B.* **$$**

What to see and do Ishaka is the closest town to the Kalinzu Eco-Tourism Project and, with private transport, its budget hotels would also make an affordable base for a day trip into QENP. The only other attraction in the area is the Kitagata Hot Springs, which lies along the recently surfaced and upgraded direct road to Kabale via Ntungamo.

Kitagata Hot Springs (⊕ *-0.6782, 30.1603; no entrance fee*) Situated 16km south of Ishaka and 1.5km south of Kitagata trading centre, these sulphuric hot springs hold few mysteries for linguists – Kitagata translates somewhat prosaically as 'boiling water' – and it could be argued that they are also of limited visual interest, bubbling as they do into a clear, shallow, steaming pool about 200m west of the Kabale Road. Kitagata has long been believed to possess therapeutic qualities (and so probably does, should you be suffering from creaky joints or aching muscles, though it's doubtful it would do much to cure malaria or several other ailments as it claims) and the surrounding rocks are generally draped in a couple of dozen half-naked bathers who, needless to say, will be less than enamoured of any passing tourist who pulls out a camera. Facilities are limited to the communal hot bath created naturally by the springs. South of Kitagata, the road to Ntungamo passes through some impressively scenic hills, and follows a papyrus-fringed river for several kilometres, offering excellent views over patches of swamp that might potentially prove to be excellent for papyrus endemics.

ISHASHA SECTOR

Somewhat removed from the rest of QENP, the remote Ishasha Sector, which runs south from Lake Edward flanked by the Ishasha River (also the Congolese border) to the west and the Ntungwe River to the east, ranks among the most alluring game-viewing areas anywhere in the country. Its best-known attraction is a population of tree-climbing lions, comprising around 40 individuals split across three prides, but the plains also support large herds of buffalo and kob, smaller family groups of topi and waterbuck, and the like of elephant, warthog and various monkeys. Ishasha retains

a relatively untrammelled wilderness character, one best appreciated by spending a night or two within the sector, or at one of the flurry of lodges constructed a short distance outside it. However, those intent on seeing lions up trees, which most often happens in the heat of the day, could think about visiting as a (long) day trip from one of the lodges listed elsewhere in this chapter, or (better) as a diversion *en route* between other sectors of QENP and Bwindi Impenetrable National Park.

The funnel for all southerly approaches to Ishasha, only 22km away by road, is the small but jacked-up town of Kihihi, where amenities include a Stanbic Bank providing the usual financial services, a filling station, a few supermarkets, and several modest guesthouses. Clustered together on the road towards Ishasha only 4km from Kihihi are the upmarket Savannah Resort Hotel, the Guraga Golf Course, and an airstrip connected to Entebbe and Kampala by daily flights.

GETTING THERE AND AWAY

By air   Subject to demand, **Fly Uganda** (*www.flyuganda.com*) and **Aerolink** (*www.aerolinkuganda.com*) both fly daily to Kihihi, the former from Kajjansi Airfield near Kampala, the latter from Entebbe. The flight takes about 90 minutes. The Savannah Resort Hotel, right next to Kihihi Airport, is a popular base for exploring Ishasha in tandem with Bwindi Impenetrable National Park.

By road   Ishasha is most normally approached in one of two directions: from the northeast, via Katunguru on the main Kasese–Ishaka Road; or from Kabale and Bwindi National Park in the south via Kihihi. It is thus easily visited *en route* between central QENP and Bwindi, though road conditions are such that the game-viewing tracks can be explored thoroughly only on an overnight stay.

To/from Katunguru   Ishasha Entrance Gate (✪ *-0.58543, 29.71733*) lies 70km southwest of the Kasese–Ishaka Road along a fair dirt road that starts 4km south of Katunguru Bridge and continues to the Congolese border at Ishasha Town. The gate is clearly signposted 1km beyond the Ntungwe River bridge, and 17km before the border post. The drive between Katunguru and Ishasha Entrance Gate shouldn't take more than 2 hours, but the road tends to deteriorate during the wet season, so ask local advice before using it. A 4x4 is recommended, though any robust saloon car should get through with ease in normal conditions. If you don't have private transport, hitching along the main road is a possibility, but the only realistic way of exploring deeper into the park would be as a day trip from Katunguru, where Kazinga Channel Safaris can arrange a full-day tour to Ishasha for around US$105 per party.

To/from Kabale/Bwindi/Kampala via Kihihi   In a private vehicle, the 60km drive between Buhoma and Ishasha via Butogota, Kanyantorogo and Kihihi takes about 90 minutes on decent dirt roads. From Kabale, the best route is through Hamurwa, Kanungu and Kihihi, connecting with the road from Buhoma at Kanyantorogo, a distance of around 120km on mostly dirt that should take at least 4 hours (but best to allow longer). Coming from elsewhere in Bwindi, it's an 85km/4-hour drive from the Ruhija area, connecting with the road from Buhoma at Butogota, while the best route from the Rushaga or Ntungamo areas entails returning to the surfaced Kisoro–Kabale Road, driving northwest to Hamurwa, then using the same route (via Kanungu and Kihihi) as you would from Kabale. If coming directly from Kampala, follow the main road to Kabale as far as Ntungamo, then turn right on to the new 45km tarmac road to Rukungiri. Beyond Rukungiri, 70km of murram roads lead to Ishasha via Kihihi.

Using public transport, a daily bus runs between Kampala and Kihihi, which is also connected to Butogota, Kanungu and Rukungiri by regular matatus. Matatus between Buhoma and Kihihi cost around US$3.50. From Kihihi, you'd need to charter a special hire or boda to Ishasha, where the most useful budget base is At The River Lodge, which can arrange game drives into the park. You could also ask around at the taxi park for a special hire to take you on a full-day game drive to Ishasha – expect to pay around US$70 inclusive of fuel and the driver's entrance fee.

⌂ WHERE TO STAY AND EAT   *Map, page 438*

Exclusive

✳ ⌂ **Ishasha Wilderness Camp**   (10 tents) ✪ 0.54908, 29.72112; ☏ 041 4321479; m 0772 721155; e reservations@ugandaexclusivecamps. com; www.ugandaexclusivecamps.com; see ad, page 407. Arguably the only true wilderness facility in Uganda, & the only lodge actually set within the park's Ishasha sector, this excellent camp is carved into the riparian forest along the Ntungwe River & located in the thick of the wildlife action. Elephant regularly cross the river within view of camp, lion & leopard are often found close by, while colobus monkeys emit their guttural croak in the trees overhead. The place is alive with birds, including African finfoot & Pel's fishing owl. The en-suite canvas-sided cottages with fitted nets & river-facing balconies are comfortable & beautifully appointed, with large mesh windows to bring the river views indoors. Tasty, ample & beautifully presented 4-course dinners demonstrate that isolation is no excuse for mediocre catering. Excellent in every respect. *US$475/720 sgl/dbl FB, discounts available for East African residents.* **$$$$$**

Upmarket

✳ ⌂ **Enjojo Lodge**   (3 cottages & 3 huts) ✪ -0.59403, 29.72267; ☏ 041 4669487; m 0782 803518; info@enjojolodge.com; www.enjojolodge.com. This characterful new lodge 3km from the entrance gate is set in a steamy jungle-like stand of fever trees & palms overlooking a lake on the national park border. Upmarket thatched & stilted cottages, reached via wooden walkways, come with walk-in net & outdoor shower, & are decorated with colourful local fabrics & geometric Rwandan paintings. There is also a separate campsite with more basic bamboo huts using common showers. *US$110/180 sgl/dbl cottage, US$50/70 sgl/ dbl hut, US$15pp camping. All rates B&B, add US$30pp FB.* **$$$–$$$$**

⌂ **Savannah Resort Hotel**   (46 rooms) ✪ -0.71726, 29.69381; ☏ 038 2280330; m 0751 382916; e reservations@savannahresorthotel. com; www.savannahresorthotel.com. Set in large park-like grounds & boasting an attractive 'country club' façade, this rather suburban-feeling hotel stands adjacent to Kihihi airstrip & the Guraga golf course, some 4km south of Kihihi Town, & represents a lone oasis of comfort between Bwindi (Buhoma, 1hr) & Ishasha Gate (30mins). Facilities include a swimming pool, steam/sauna & good restaurant. A popular lunch spot for safari groups, it's good value & infinitely smarter than anything in Kihihi, but the cottage accommodation is still unremarkable. *US$120/165 sgl/dbl B&B, or US$150/225 FB.* **$$$$**

⌂ **Ishasha Jungle Lodge**   (6 cottages) ✪ -0.59101, 29.73002; ☏ 041 4232754; e info@ugandajunglelodges.com; www. ugandajunglelodges.com; see ad, page 503. Situated about 3km from Ishasha Gate in densely wooded gardens some 200m from the Ntungwe River, this agreeable lodge offers accommodation in neat thatched cottages with 1 dbl & 1sgl bed, walk-in nets, & private wooden balcony. *US$95pp B&B or US$170/272/382 sgl/dbl/trpl FB.* **$$$$**

⌂ **Ntungwe Tree Lion Safari Lodge** (4 rooms) ✪ -0.59128, 29.73296; m 0772 602205. The en-suite stilted tents at this small camp are starting to look quite rundown, & set back from the meandering Ntungwe, they lack a sense of place. Hefty price tag for what it is. *US$180/200 FB.* **$$$$**

Moderate

⌂ **At The River**   (12 rooms) ✪ -0.59894, 29.73478; m 0787 005888; e bookings@ attheriverishasha.com; www.attheriverishasha. com. Set alongside the meandering Ntungwe River 5km outside the park entrance gate, this relatively modestly priced lodge comprises a raised thatch bar overlooking the river (& the birdlife & monkeys in

the riparian forest beyond) as well as stilted en-suite cabins with nets & hot water, & simple 'lazy camping' in standing tents with bedding. It also offers game drives in the park for US$25pp (minimum group size 3) including driver/guide & fuel, but not entrance fees. *US$125/160 sgl/dbl en-suite cabin, US$90/140 cabin using common showers, US$60pp lazy camping. All rates FB.* **$$$$**

Budget & camping
Aside from the options listed below, budget huts are available at Enjojo Lodge, as listed above. Basic local lodgings in Kihihi include the no-frills Westland Guesthouse (US$3.50 sgl with shared amenities).

✳ **Ⱥ Ishasha campsites & bandas** 2 lovely UWA-run campsites (⊕ -0.6161, 29.65791 & -0.61388, 29.65711) flanked by the Ishasha River a few hundred metres north of the UWA offices. Set in riverine forest, these provide guaranteed views of (& sometimes encounters with) hippos. There are showers & flush toilets, & bottled drinks & simple meals are available in a canteen at the park offices. A couple of simple bandas (⊕ -0.61877, 29.65987) are also available close to the park offices. *US$12/14 sgl/dbl bandas, US$5pp camping.* **$**

🏠 **Kisenyi Lake Retreat** ⊕ -0.31076, 29.86705; m 0774 768090/0701 536197, info@ ugandalodge.com, www.ugandalodge.com/lake-retreat. Not to be confused with its near namesake on Lake George, Kisenyi is a pretty forest-fringed fishing village set on the southern Lake Edward shore just north of the Nyamweru River about 1km northwest of, & halfway along, the road between Katunguru & Ishasha. This lakeshore campsite, set on 2.5ha of private land & affiliated to Kasenyi Lake Retreat, has a modern toilet & shower block, & can provide meals by advance arrangement. It's also a nice place to stop for lunch between Katunguru & Ishasha. Rooms are planned. *US$10pp.* **$$**

WHAT TO SEE AND DO
Game drives Two main game circuits run out of Ishasha, the northern and southern loops, both roughly 20km in length. The southern circuit is the more productive for lion sightings, since it passes through the main kob breeding grounds – as in Kasenyi, the predators often stick close to their prey, and their presence is often revealed by the antelope's alarm calls. This area is also better provided with the trees favoured by lions. Navigating the **South Circuit** is a tricky task, being confused by side tracks leading to lion trees and diversions to bypass boggy sections. Though the 'Uganda Maps' QENP sheet makes a good stab at making sense of all this, it's a good idea to take a guide. The simpler **North Circuit** is better for general game viewing while the open landscape and boundless horizons on the northwestern

ISHASHA'S TREE-CLIMBING LIONS

As a rule, lions are strictly terrestrial. Indeed, Ishasha is one of a handful of places anywhere in Africa where these regal predators regularly take to the trees (the others being Lake Manyara National Park and parts of the Serengeti, both in Tanzania), and it is probably the most reliable site of the lot. The explanation for this localised behaviour is open to conjecture. Limited studies undertaken in Lake Manyara indicate that the custom of ascending trees is culturally ingrained rather than a response to any immediate external stimuli, though it may well have been initiated to escape the attention of biting flies during an epidemic of these irksome creatures. In Ishasha, sycamore fig and to a lesser extent Albezias are favoured over other trees, with around 20 specific individual trees being favoured – which makes it quite easy to locate the lions when they are up in the canopy. The behaviour might be observed throughout the year but it is most frequent during the rainy seasons. Ishasha's lions are most likely to be seen in arboreal action in the heat of the day, between 11.00 and 15.00, and they invariably descend back to the ground well before dusk.

part of the loop represents some of the finest wilderness in southwestern Uganda, even though it's actually only 4km from the main road to Katunguru. This section of the North Circuit also overlooks the Ntungwe River floodplain, a long low trough punctuated by pools and wallows enjoyed by buffalo; look out here for redder animals related to the forest buffalo of the Congo.

At the northern part of the loop, the boggy wallows described above develop into a full-blown wetland where birdwatchers might look out for black coucal, compact weaver, fan-tailed widow and other water-associated birds. A cairn in this area marks an 8km track extending north towards the marshy Lake Edward Flats. This papyrus-fringed site is good for waterbirds, including various herons, storks and plovers, and shoebills are quite often seen too, though that is far from definite. They also often harbour decent concentrations of elephant, buffalo, kob, topi and waterbuck. Road conditions are erratic, however, so seek advice from the rangers before striking out alone, particularly after rain, when getting stuck is a very real risk!

The Ishasha River, which can be explored on foot from the campsites along its bank, supports a healthy hippo population, most easily observed from Campsite 2. The fringing riparian forest harbours good numbers of bushbuck and black-and-white colobus monkey, and an interesting variety of birds including black bee-eater, broad-billed roller and the localised Cassin's grey flycatcher. Away from the river, light acacia woodland and savannah support large herds of Uganda kob, topi and buffalo, while elephants are seasonally common.

Ishasha Community Uplift Group (e *reservations@ugandaexclusivehomes. com, ishashacommunityupliftgroup@gmail.com*) Ishasha's wildlife might be popular with tourists but it has few fans when it strays into the farming communities that live along the protected area boundary at Bukorwe village. This fascinating community tour shows how Deo, a typical local farmer, copes. This really is life on the front line – Deo and co even use a 20km-long trench in their daily battle to defend their crops. Dug with support from the Uganda Conservation Foundation, this is one of various strategies employed by park-edge communities to keep hungry elephants out of the crops. Bukorwe is 1km off the road to Kihihi, just outside the Kigezi Wildlife Reserve boundary. A second visit, to Agartha in nearby Kazinga trading centre, 2km along the main road towards Kihihi, demonstrates the day-to-day life of Bakiga women.

Uganda's most breathtaking lodge

KYANINGA LODGE

Fort Portal, Western Uganda
+256 772 999750 | +256 794 304211
info@kyaningalodge.com | www.kyaningalodge.com

EXPERIENCE
Uganda's
WILD SIDE

Great Lakes Safaris, voted 'Best Tour Operator' at the Uganda Tourism Board's Tourism Excellence Awards 2015, is one of the leading safari companies in Uganda and Rwanda.

Under our Uganda Lodges brand, we also own 3 Safari Lodges i.e. Primate Lodge Kibale in Kibale Forest NP, Budongo Eco Lodge in Murchison Falls NP and Simba Safari Camp, bordering Queen Elizabeth NP.

We provide high quality and personalized services of international standards.

The only real Uganda Specialist!

MATOKE TOURS

The Africa Experience!

RWENZORI FOUNDERS

**Art Centre
Sculpture Gallery
Bronze Foundry
Coffee Bar**

please ring ahead:
+256 (0)782 238036
+256 (0)702 858556

rfkasese@yahoo.com

www.rwenzorifounders.com

On the way between QE
National Park and Fort Portal
11km from Kasese

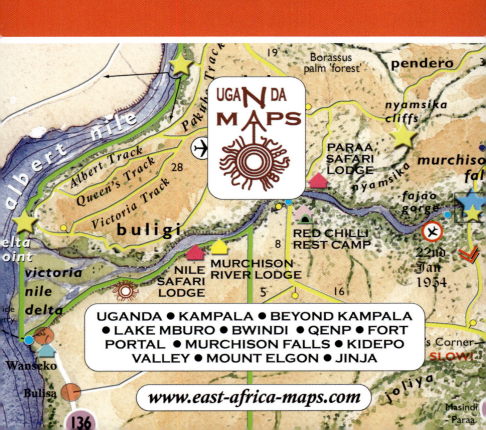

Travel the world from your armchair

Bradt's travel literature features true-life tales of adventure, discovery and danger, ranging from the plains of Africa to the streets of Mexico.

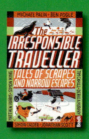

For discount offers on all our books, visit our website.

www.bradtguides.com

 BradtTravelGuides   @BradtGuides   @BradtGuides   bradtguides

19

Kabale and Kisoro Districts

Nudged up against the Rwandan and Congolese borders in Kigezi subregion, Uganda's two most southwesterly administrative districts form the southern gateway to Bwindi Impenetrable National Park and its habituated mountain gorillas. But Kabale and Kisoro, named after the small towns that serve as their administrative capitals, have plenty to offer travellers in their own right. The highlands of Kigezi rank as the most fertile and arguably most scenic part of Uganda, a kind of equatorial counterpart to Switzerland, where steep slopes covered in terraced cultivation frame expansive blue lakes that sparkle tantalisingly in the tropical sun. The scenic highlight is the Virunga Mountains, a magnificent cross-border range of eight dormant and active volcanoes whose highest peak tops 4,500m. The verdant Ugandan slopes of the Virungas, protected in the underrated Mgahinga National Park, are home to one group of habituated gorillas, while other activities include organised guided forest walks and day hikes to the volcanic peaks of mounts Muhabura, Sabyinyo and Gahinga. The region's main tourist focus, set within walking distance of Kabale town, is scenic Lake Bunyonyi, whose eastern shore and islands are studded with hotels and resorts. Several other lakes in Kigezi now also support lodges, most notably Mutanda and Mulehe, which are sufficiently close to the trailheads at Rushaga and Nkuringo to be used as overnight bases for gorilla tracking in Bwindi.

FURTHER INFORMATION

A superb resource for Kabale and Kisoro Districts, as well as for Bwindi Impenetrable National Park, is the marvellously comprehensive interactive e-book, *Gorilla Highlands: Travel Guide to Southwestern Uganda* compiled by the management of Edirisa. The full book is available from the Apple iTunes Store for US$14.99, or you can download a smaller pocket guide from its website www.gorillahighlands.com, which also contains plenty of useful information, not to mention a new video map with footage of 30-odd sites of interest in the region. More conventionally, Sheet 5 in the 'Uganda Maps' series, *Bwindi and the Kigezi Highlands*, illustrates the regional topography, main tourist routes and hotspots, viewpoints and gorilla ranges derived from the 2011–12 gorilla census.

KABALE

Set at a refreshing altitude of 1,800m some 400km southwest of Kampala, Kabale is one of the largest towns in western Uganda, with a population of around 50,000. It was founded in 1913, when the British government station at Ikumba was relocated to Makanga Hill, which rises northeast from the present-day town centre and was then known as Kabaare after a trough-like depression at its

summit. Today, the original hilltop site houses an expansive green golf course, a few old government buildings, and a handful of relatively smart hotels, all shaded by eucalyptus trees planted in the 1920s as part of a swamp-clearance and malaria-control programme. A few years back, Kabale was a crucial overnight springboard for budget travellers heading on to Bwindi or the Virungas to track gorillas. Its significance has since declined as a result of several factors – the closure of its UWA gorilla-permit booking office, the improved accessibility of Kisoro, and the proliferation of superior accommodation on nearby Lake Bunyonyi. Indeed, despite its pretty natural setting, Kibale has of late acquired a rather scruffy and moribund aura, a situation that wasn't helped by the temporary gutting of its main road in 2015 in order to install a new drainage system to reduce the impact of heavy rainfall on the town centre.

GETTING THERE AND AWAY The 400km surfaced road that connects Kampala to Kabale via Mbarara should take about 6 hours in a private vehicle. Coming from Kasese (or Fort Portal or North-Central QENP), the best option is the 220km 3–4-hour route taking in the newly surfaced road between Ishaka and Ntungamo. Directions for Kisoro, the various gorilla-tracking trailheads at Bwindi and other relatively local sites are included in the relevant sections.

Buses from Kampala cost US$8–10 and take 7–9 hours. The pick of the operators is Jaguar Executive Coaches (m *0782 811128 (Kampala)* or *0777 763491 (Kabale))*, which operates five executive buses to Kisoro or Kigali (Rwanda) daily, all passing through Kabale, from its terminal on Namirembe Road about 500m west of the Qualicell Bus Park. Also recommended is the Rwandan company Trinity Coaches, which runs about five coaches daily to Kigali via Kabale, leaving Kampala from practically next door to Jaguar. A slower but still reliable option is the Post Bus that leaves Kampala from the rear of the main post office at 08.00 daily except Sundays. Other buses to Kabale leave Kampala from in and around Qualicell Bus Park throughout the morning, generally stopping at Mbarara *en route*.

Regular matatus connect Kabale to Kisoro (*US$5; 90mins*) and more locally to Muko and Rutinda (Lake Bunyonyi), leaving from a small taxi park at the north end of town near the Highland Inn. Coming from or heading to Katunguru (QENP), Kasese or Fort Portal, you need to change vehicles at Mbarara (*US$5; 2–3hrs*), matatus to which leave from the main taxi park. Shared taxis run to Rukingiri and to Katuna on the border with Rwanda.

WHERE TO STAY Map, *opposite*
The overall low standard of hotels in Kabale reflects the recent downturn in overnight tourist traffic. Far better out-of-town accommodation is available at Lake Bunyonyi, though prices there tend to be higher.

Moderate

White Horse Inn (42 rooms) \ 048 6426010; m 0772 444921; e whitehorseinnkle@ yahoo.com; http://whitehorseinn.wix.com/ whitehorseinn. Easily the smartest option in Kabale, this former government hotel on Makanga Hill is set in large green grounds adjacent to the golf course & overlooking the town centre. The small carpeted en-suite rooms feel a bit institutional but come with queen-sized bed, net,

DSTV & en-suite hot shower, while the cosy bar is lit by a log fire on cooler nights, & the restaurant with a choice of indoor or terrace seating, serves decent international mains for around US$7. *US$34/48/52 sgl/dbl/twin old wing, US$130–200 dbl new wing. All rates B&B.* **$$–$$$**

Green Hills Hotel (23 rooms) \ 031 2275369; m 0772 327830; e info@greenhills-hotel.com; www.greenhills-hotel.com. This rather uninspiring but well-run multi-storey hotel has a

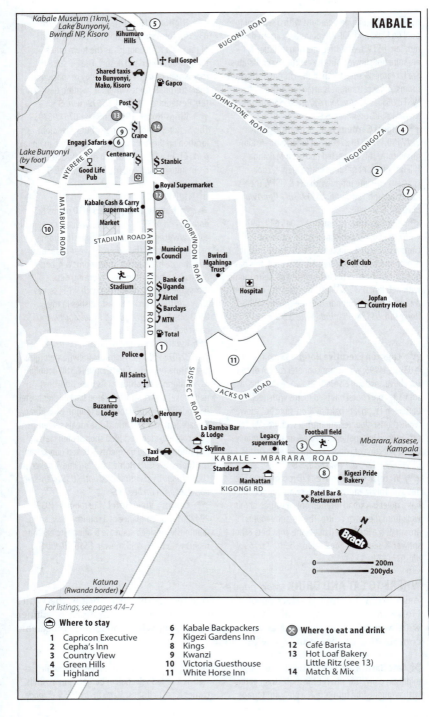

KABALE

Kabale Museum (1km),
Lake Bunyonyi,
Bwindi NP, Kisoro

Kihumuro Hills

(5)

BUGONJI ROAD

Full Gospel

Shared taxis
to Bunyonyi,
Mako, Kisoro

Gapco

JOHNSTONE ROAD

Post $

(13)

Crane

(9) (6)
Engagi Safaris

Centenary

Lake Bunyonyi
(by foot)

NYERERE RD

Good Life Pub

(14)

Stanbic

Royal Supermarket

(12)

Kabale Cash & Carry
supermarket

Market

MATABUKA ROAD

STADIUM ROAD

KABALE - KISORO ROAD

(10)

Stadium

NGORONGOZA

(4)

(2)

(7)

CORYNDON ROAD

Municipal Council

Bwindi Mgahinga Trust

Golf club

Bank of Uganda

Airtel

Barclays

MTN

Total

(1)

Hospital

Jopfan
Country Hotel

Police

(11)

All Saints

SUSPECT ROAD

JACKSON ROAD

Buzaniro Lodge

Market

Heronry

La Bamba Bar
& Lodge

Skyline

Legacy
supermarket

Football field

(3)

Mbarara, Kasese,
Kampala

Taxi stand

KABALE - MBARARA ROAD

Standard

Manhattan

KIGONGI RD

(8)

Kigezi Pride
Bakery

Patel Bar &
Restaurant

N

Brack

0 —————— 200m
0 —————— 200yds

Katuna
(Rwanda border)

For listings, see pages 474–7

Where to stay

1 Capricon Executive
2 Cepha's Inn
3 Country View
4 Green Hills
5 Highland

6 Kabale Backpackers
7 Kigezi Gardens Inn
8 Kings
9 Kwanzi
10 Victoria Guesthouse
11 White Horse Inn

Where to eat and drink

12 Café Barista
13 Hot Loaf Bakery
    Little Ritz (see 13)
14 Match & Mix

quiet location in green gardens with a swimming pool on Makanga Hill. All rooms are carpeted with net, fan, DSTV, tea-/coffee-making facilities & en-suite hot shower, but the executive semi-suites are far larger & smarter than the cramped standard rooms. A fair restaurant is attached & there's free Wi-Fi. *US$30/43 standard sgl/dbl, US$50/60 sgl/dbl executive. All rates B&B.* **$$**

🏠 **Kigezi Gardens Inn** (8 rooms) 📞038 2277100; m 0779 870999; e kigezigardensinn@ gmail.com. This converted house on Makanga Hill has pleasant gardens with a view & cool spacious en-suite rooms with net & DSTV. There's no restaurant. Fair value. *US$17/30/33 sgl/twin/ dbl B&B.* **$$**

🏠 **Cepha's Inn** (22 rooms) 📞048 6422097; m 0772 240946; e birungicephas@yahoo. com; www.cephasinn.com. Set in a large green compound with sauna & swimming pool, this has good views & attractively furnished en-suite rooms with net, fan, DSTV & Wi-Fi. Sgls are very cramped & dbls are pricey compared to the superior White Horse Inn. *US$28/60 sgl/dbl B&B.* **$$$**

Budget

🏠 **Capricon Executive Hotel** (38 rooms) 📞039 2944996; www.capriconhotel.com. A distinct cut above anything else in the town centre, this smart 3-storey hotel has tiled rooms with nets, flatscreen TV, private balcony & en-suite hot shower, while the 1st-floor restaurant/bar with free Wi-Fi serves good international meals & an uncommonly varied selection of wines & spirits. Excellent value. *US$17/23/33 sgl/dbl/twin B&B.* **$$**

🏠 **Victoria Guesthouse** (20 rooms) m 0772 389030. This friendly & long-serving budget hotel has a quiet backroad location only a couple of mins' walk from the town centre. The en-suite rooms are small & a little dated but come with nets & hot shower, & seem like good value. *US$10/13/15 sgl/ dbl/twin B&B.* **$**

🏠 **Highland Hotel** (30 rooms) m 0778 639513. This venerable hotel at the north end of the main road doubles as the town office for Bunyonyi Overland Resort. The en-suite rooms aren't exactly slick but they're spacious & characterful, & come with nets, writing desk & hot tub. Restaurant attached. *US$12 twin.* **$**

🏠 **Kings Hotel** (51 rooms) m 0751 983939. This 5-storey hotel has a noisy but convenient location on the main road 500m from the main taxi park. Clean rooms come with nets, flatscreen DSTV & en-suite hot shower. *US$11/12 sgl/dbl.* **$**

Shoestring

✳️ 🏠 **Kabale Backpackers** (10 rooms & 2 dorms) m 0782 421519; e engagisafaris@gmail. com; www.engagiexperience.com. The home of Engagi Safaris, this popular owner-managed guesthouse has neat en-suite rooms & 4-bed dorms with fitted nets plus a writing desk. A cosy garden restaurant/bar with Wi-Fi serves tasty stir-fries, curries & pasta dishes in the US$3.50–4 range. *US$8/12/13 sgl/dbl/twin, US$5 dorm bed.* **$**

🏠 **Kwanzi** (5 rooms & 1 dorm) m 0774 789782/0775 855445; e info@anewhomeforgirls. org. Formerly Edirisa Guesthouse (& still doubling as an information office for its Lake Bunyonyi namesake) this centrally located backpacker hostel has individually sized rooms, a lounge with library, an excellent menu of affordable meals served on a cool elevated deck, & a shop selling crafts, beautifully tailored garments & baked goods from the Grace Villa Girls Home tailoring line & bakery. *US$7/10 sgl/twin with shared bath, US$16 en-suite dbl, US$5pp dorm bed.* **$$**

🏠 **Country View Hotel** (10 rooms) 📞039 2947241. No semblance of a country view, a fabulously lopsided staircase & adequate en-suite rooms with net & cold shower. *US$6.50 dbl.* **$**

✕ WHERE TO EAT AND DRINK *Map, page 475*

Aside from the limited selection of standalone restaurants listed below, the White Horse Inn on Makanga Hill is the place to head for an al fresco lunch or dinner with a view, while the central café at Kabale Backpackers offers an unbeatable combination of choice and value for money.

✕ **Café Barista** m 0780 828668; 🕘 07.00– midnight daily. This smart little high-street eatery with wrought-iron furniture & a pleasant terrace serves good & inexpensive coffee & smoothies, as well as a varied selection of burgers, pizzas, grills, curries & pasta dishes. *Meals in the US$5–7 range.*

✕ Little Ritz This 1st-floor bar & restaurant with balcony seating serves a limited selection of mains including good chicken masala. There's DSTV in the bar & a warming log fire in chilly weather. *Mains US$5.*

✕ Hot Loaf Bakery Once a mandatory stop with overland trucks, this long-serving bakery used to serve a wide variety of freshly-baked cakes, pies & pastries, but these days it seems to limit its output to white bread.

🍷 Match & Mix This large multi-roomed bar on the main street is a lively place to drink & watch Premier League football on large flatscreen TVs. Open until late.

SHOPPING There are a couple of good supermarkets in Kabale, notably the **Royal Supermarket** next to Café Barista.

OTHER PRACTICALITIES

Foreign exchange Stanbic, Crane and Barclays all have foreign exchange facilities and ATMs.

Internet A few internet cafés line the main road, while free Wi-Fi is available at the café in Kabale Backpackers and most of the smarter hotels on Makanga Hill.

TOUR OPERATORS Any of the operators listed below can arrange transport to the gorilla-tracking trailheads, as well as other local excursions.

Amagara Travel m 0752 296197; e info@ amagaratours.com; www.amagaratours.com
Edirisa m 0752 558222; e info@edirisa.org; www.edirisa.org. This local cultural organisation offers tours to QENP, as well as extended canoe/ camping trips on Lake Bunyonyi.
Engagi Safaris m 0782 421519; e engagisafaris@gmail.com; www. engagiexperience.com

Gatatu Safaris ℡ 0392 591262; m 0704874217; e gorillatours@gatatusafaris.com; www. gatatusafaris.com
Safari 2 Gorilla Tours Above Royal Supermarket; m 0774 608916/0784 889008; e info@ safari2gorilla.com; www.safari2gorilla.com

WHAT TO SEE AND DO The most popular tourist attraction in the immediate vicinity of Kabale is Lake Bunyonyi, covered later in this chapter, and the town also makes a possible base for gorilla tracking at Ruhija, 55km to the north (pages 521–6).

Kwanzi Cultural Centre

A non-profit organisation that strives to promote and preserve Bakiga culture, this centre was started several years ago by a Bakiga elder concerned at the erosion of his local culture. It is the site of the town's only cultural museum, featuring a traditional Bakiga compound complete with a fenced hut, and a range of artefacts such as musical instruments, weapons, utensils, furniture, attire and even a local granary. Guided tours cost US$3 per person.

Kabale Museum

(⊕ -1.24522, 29.97276; m 0752 500435; ⏱ 10.00–17.30 daily)
The new out-of-town Kabale Museum is still a work in progress, but it has some interesting displays relating to Kigezi's four main ethnic groups: the Bakiga of Kabale; the Mpororo of Rukingiri; the Bafumbira of Kisoro; and the Kinkizi of Kanungu. Traditional artefacts on display, some evidently very old, include musical instruments, jewellery, weapons, pots and iron-smelting equipment. It isn't formally open yet, but the friendly and articulate curator is happy to show visitors around; no entrance fee but a tip would be appropriate. The museum is situated off the Kisoro Road along the junction to Lake Bunyonyi about 1.5km northwest of Kabale town centre.

Kisiizi Waterfall This 30m-high waterfall lies on the Rushoma River a few hundred metres from the Kisiizi Hospital, which was founded by the Church of Uganda in 1958, some 65km north of Kabale by road. The waterfall is a very pretty and peaceful spot, with plenty of birdlife around including Ross's turaco and double-toothed barbet, and the surrounding forests and quiet roads offer some pleasant rambling possibilities. The waterfall is used to provide hydro-electric power to the hospital – in Uganda's darker days, Kisiizi was one of the few places countrywide that had a reliable 24-hour electricity supply and functional street lamps. The gorge below the waterfall is also now spanned by a zip wire, access to which can be arranged through John Nshabomwe (m *0772 854650*) for around US$3–4 per person.

The tranquil atmosphere around the waterfall belies its macabre historical association with the local custom described somewhat euphemistically by one

FISHY TALES

According to the late Paul Ngologoza, an eminent Kigezi politician and historian, Lake Bunyonyi harboured 'no fish at all, just *encere*, which are edible frogs' prior to 1919. While this claim seems rather unlikely, several other sources do imply that Bunyonyi naturally harbours very low fish densities. Presumably, this is because the lake slopes underwater too sharply and deeply from the shoreline to provide suitable habitat for shallow-water species such as tilapia and Nile perch, which would have lived in the river before Bunyonyi became a lake.

Whatever the situation before 1919, great efforts were made to stock Lake Bunyonyi during the colonial era. The most valiant of these was initiated in 1927 by District Commissioner Trewin, who arranged for a volume of fish to be relayed manually from Lake Edward to Lake Bunyonyi. 'This was a very involved task,' writes Ngologoza, 'because of the difficulty created by fish dying in transit. Many people [were] divided into groups ... The first group brought fish from a place called Katwe ... This group raced at great speed to hand over the fish to the second group, who raced to hand over to the third group, and so on, putting in fresh water, pouring out the old water, and finally bringing them to Lake Bunyonyi. It took a day and a night to cover the distance of about 80 miles [120km].'

Initially, the introduced fish flourished, as did commercial fishing, and the rapidly multiplying schools were used to restock several other lakes in the region. Then, in the early 1950s, for reasons that remain unclear, they died out *en masse*, so that 'one might see the whole lake full of floating bodies of dead fish'. Following this disaster, Ngologoza himself experimented with digging a shallow pool next to the lake and stocking it with 50 fish, which rapidly reproduced, allowing him to distribute 4,500 fish to local fishermen, to be bred in the same way.

The only fish to thrive in the lake today is *Claria mozambicus*, known locally as *evale*, which forms an important component of the local subsistence diet. Bunyonyi is also well known for its small freshwater crayfish, a delicacy served in curries at most of the tourist resorts along the shore.

Quotes extracted from the late Paul Ngologoza's excellent and often amusing introduction to the history and culture of Kigezi entitled Kigezi and its People, *first published in 1967, reprinted by Fountain Publishers in 1998 and still widely available.*

Ugandan source as 'damping'. In traditional Bakiga society, virginity was a highly prized asset and an unmarried girl who fell pregnant could, at best, hope to be a social outcast for the rest of her days. More often, however, the offender would be mortally punished: tied to a tree and left at the mercy of wild animals, thrown from a cliff, or abandoned to starve on an island. Many disgraced girls were 'damped' at Kisiizi: tossed over the waterfall, arms and legs tightly bound, to drown in the pool below.

Several roads connect Kabale to Kisiizi, but the best option is to follow the surfaced Kampala Road for 32km as far as Muhanga, from where a 33km dirt road leads north to the hospital and waterfall. The drive should take less than 2 hours in a private vehicle. Using public transport, regular matutus between Kabale and Muhanga cost around US$1, as does a berth in one of the pick-up trucks that bump their way up to Kisiizi a few times daily. Kisiizi Hospital's Rose Cottage Guest House (✪ -0.99824, 29.94392; ☏ 039 2700806; e kisiizihospital@yahoo.com; www. kisiizihospital.org.ug; US$20pp) can provide comfortable accommodation.

Nshenyi Cultural Village (e winlinksEA@gmail.com; www.nshenyi.com) This secluded cultural retreat lies in the Mirama Hills, about 115km from Kabale and 35km south of the main road running northeast to Ntungamo, Mbarara and Kampala. Situated on a traditional Ankole farm close to the village of Kitwe and only 10km from the borders with Rwanda and Tanzania, the centre offers a variety of accommodation ranging from a basic grass-thatched or clay-and-brick hut to a room in a modern farmhouse, as well as traditional meals and a wide range of activities that encourage direct interaction with the local community. These include milking the long-horned Ankole cattle, joining the pastoralists as they graze the cattle, a market-day experience, nature walks and birdwatching on the undulating hills that overlook the village or along the Kagera River (the border with Tanzania), tribal encounters, visits to rock art and historical sites, traditional cooking, and cultural singing and dancing. Rates are US$100 per person inclusive of all meals, plus an additional US$50 per group for all activities.

LAKE BUNYONYI

Serpentine Lake Bunyonyi, as its shape suggests, comprises a flooded river valley that extends northwards for 25km, following the steep contours of the hills separating Kabale from Kisoro, but is nowhere more than 5km wide. The lake formed about 8,000 years ago, when a lava flow blocked off the Ndego River at present-day Muko to create a natural dam. The 60km² lake stands at the core of a larger wetland incorporating the Ruhuma Swamp and several other permanent marshes. Set at an altitude of 1,950m, it is encircled by steep terraced hills that rise to above 2,500m, and although estimates of its depth vary wildly, it is probably nowhere more than 45m deep. Bunyonyi translates as 'place of little birds', presumably in reference to the weaver colonies that proliferate on the shore, but larger birds are also represented by the likes of grey crowned crane and a variety of herons and egrets. The spotted-necked otter is unusually common and visible at Bunyonyi, presumably due to the lack of competition from larger aquatic carnivores such as crocodiles.

Over the last couple of decades, Bunyonyi has come to supersede Lake Victoria's Ssese Islands as Uganda's most popular waterfront chill-out venue. In part this is because Bunyonyi is more accessible than the islands, and is easily visited in tandem with the gorilla-tracking trailheads of Bwindi and the Virungas. Further

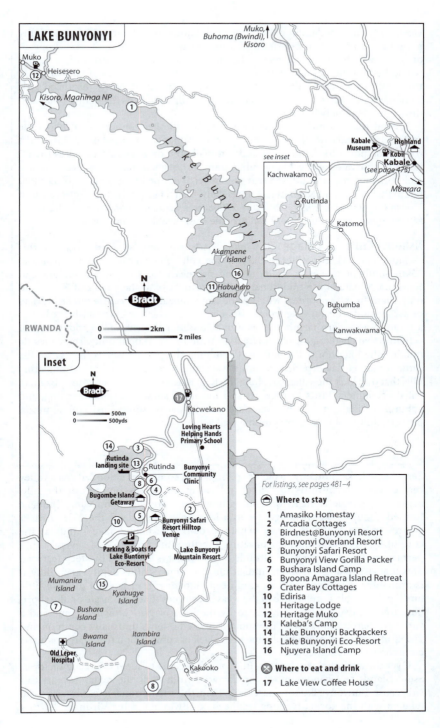

LAKE BUNYONYI

Muko,
Buhoma (Bwindi),
Kisoro

Muko
Heisesero
(12)

Kisoro, Mgahinga NP
(1)

Lake Bunyonyi

Kabale
Museum
Kobil
Kabale
(see page 475)

Highland

see inset

Kachwakamo

Rutinda

Mbarara

Katomo

Akampene
Island
(16)

N

Bradt

(11) Habuharo
Island

Buhumba

Kanwakwama

RWANDA

0   2km
0   2 miles

Inset

N

Bradt

0   500m
0   500yds

(17)
Kacwekano

Loving Hearts
Helping Hands
Primary School

(14) (3)
Rutinda
landing site (13) Rutinda
(8) (6)
(4)

Bunyonyi
Community
Clinic

Bugombe Island
Getaway

(2)

(10) (5)

Bunyonyi Safari
Resort Hilltop
Venue

Lake Bunyonyi
Mountain Resort

Parking & boats for
Lake Buntonyi
Eco-Resort

Mumanira
Island

(15)

Kyahugye
Island

(7)
Bushara
Island

Bwama
Island

Itambira
Island

Old Leper
Hospital

Kakooko

(8)

For listings, see pages 481–4

🛏 **Where to stay**

1   Amasiko Homestay
2   Arcadia Cottages
3   Birdnest@Bunyonyi Resort
4   Bunyonyi Overland Resort
5   Bunyonyi Safari Resort
6   Bunyonyi View Gorilla Packer
7   Bushara Island Camp
8   Byoona Amagara Island Retreat
9   Crater Bay Cottages
10 Edirisa
11 Heritage Lodge
12 Heritage Muko
13 Kaleba's Camp
14 Lake Bunyonyi Backpackers
15 Lake Bunyonyi Eco-Resort
16 Njuyera Island Camp

✖ **Where to eat and drink**

17 Lake View Coffee House

in Bunyonyi's favour, its greater elevation ensures a more temperate climate and lower prevalence of malaria, while swimming is more-or-less hazard-free due to the absence of hippos and crocodiles (by most accounts, the lake is also free of bilharzia, though occasional localised outbreaks cannot be ruled out entirely). Tourist development is focused on Rutinda, a fishing village that stands on a pretty bay halfway along the eastern shore, only 8km from Kabale by road. Close on a dozen different resorts and hotels are clustered in and around Rutinda, whose jetty is also the best place to pick up a boat to the lake's 29 small islands, several of which also support rustic retreats.

GETTING THERE AND AWAY An 8km all-weather dirt road connects Kabale to Rutinda. Self-drivers should follow the Kisoro Road out of town for 1.5km, then turn left at an easily recognised junction (✪ -1.24479, 29.97408) signposted for the various lakeshore resorts. After about 5km, the road reaches the summit of the hill overlooking Lake Bunyonyi at the five-way junction village of Kacwekano (✪ -1.25861, 29.94471). The track to the left leads to Arcadia Cottages, while the road on the right follows a lovely (but narrow) 20km route along the lakeshore to Muko on the main Kabale–Kisoro Road. Otherwise, keep going straight ahead for the 2km descent to Rutinda.

Regular matatus run between Kabale and Rutinda (*US$3; 30mins*), with market days (Monday and Friday) being busiest. A special hire should cost less than US$8 and a boda around US$3. Alternatively, it's possible to walk from Kabale in around 2 hours. Either follow the road described above, with a slight chance of hitching a lift, or take the quieter and more scenic direct route, which involves following Butambuka Road west out of the town centre then using local footpaths (there are plenty of villagers around to point the way). Either way, the walk out is a delight, passing by traditional homesteads and patches of forest rustling with birdlife, though it does involve a very stiff ascent as you approach the summit above the lake. One thing you don't want to do, unless you're supremely fit, is hire a bicycle – you'll spend more time pushing it up steep hills than you will actually cycling.

If you'll be staying on one of the islands, head to Rutinda Landing Site (✪ -1.26916, 29.93648), where those without pre-arranged transfers can expect to pay a negotiable fare of US$8 per party for a short one-way motorboat transfer, or US$2 per person for a 30- to 45-minute transfer in a dugout canoe. Motorists should find safe overland parking in a compound provided by their intended destination, but failing that they can leave their vehicle at Lake Bunyonyi Overland Camp for a small charge.

 WHERE TO STAY *Map, opposite*
Rutinda & surrounds
Upmarket

✱ 🏠 **Birdnest@Bunyonyi Resort**
(25 rooms) m 0754 252560/0776 252560; e reservations@birdnestresort.com; www.birdnestatbunyonyi.com. This plush 4-storey hotel, set on a quiet bay 500m north of Rutinda village, opened in 1965 as the 4-bedroom Bunyonyi Lake View Resort, but stood derelict for decades after 1972, when its owner, the Kigezi-born politician Frank Kalimuzo, was abducted & killed by Amin's soldiers. Still owned by the Kalimuzo family but restored & extended by Belgian investors, it is now the chicest lodge on the shore of Bunyonyi, with a funky dining room leading out on to a deck offering splendid views over the lake, & spacious rooms whose modernist lines & contemporary country décor – rough wood floor, slate-tiled lake-facing balcony, cheerful fabrics – is complemented by a fabulous cave-lake bathroom at the back. A cosmopolitan menu includes vegetarian dishes, with mains in the US$12–15 range & 3-course set menus at around US$20. Amenities include a swimming pool & free Wi-Fi. *US$169/190/210 sgl/dbl/trpl B&B.* **$$$$**

🔆 🏠 Arcadia Cottages (11 cottages, 8 more under construction) m 0772 727995/0701 999912; e arcadiacottages123@gmail.com; ⓕ fb.me/ArcadiaCottagesUganda. The sensational view from this ridge-top lodge, an almost map-like panorama of Lake Bunyonyi & its myriad islands, must surely appear in some top 50 list of panoramas to see before you die. The lodge itself doesn't quite live up to the view – few would! – but the octagonal cottages, complete with domed reed ceiling & thatch roof, wooden furniture & modern en-suite bathroom with hot shower, are very pleasant indeed, as are the large well-tended gardens & earthy high-roofed main building leading out to a wooden deck ideally located for breakfast above the lake. Coming from Kabale, turn left at Kacwekano's 5-way junction, then continue south for about 2km. Activities include jet-skiing & quad-biking. *US$135/200 sgl/dbl B&B, plus US$35pp FB.* **$$$$**

Moderate

🏠 Bunyonyi Safari Resort (45 rooms) ☎041 4547460; m 0772 119852/0782 187892; e sales@ bunyonyisafaris.com; www.bunyonyisafarisresort. com. Set on an isolated stretch of lakeshore about 750m south of Rutinda, this 3-storey hotel has large open-plan public areas with a contemporary African feel, but limited lake views & no outdoor seating. The spacious parquet-floored en-suite rooms in the main building are attractively furnished, but the garden cottages make more of the setting by having private balconies. A restaurant is attached. A touch institutional, & more like a city hotel than a beach resort, but decent value at the asking price. *US$50/80 sgl/dbl room, US$60/100 sgl/dbl cottage.* **$$$**

Budget

🔆 🏠 Bunyonyi Overland Resort (44 rooms & 2 dorms) m 0793 930006; e resort@ bunyonyioverland.com; www.bunyonyioverland. com. This vast, long-serving & justifiably popular resort sprawls down a terraced green slope to a lovely papyrus-fringed bay immediately south of Rutinda. Facilities include a sociable open-sided restaurant/bar that has a pool table, DSTV & good meals in the US$7–10 range. Other amenities include a small curio shop, inexpensive canoe & mountain-bike hire, volleyball, badminton & indoor games, & a good private swimming beach.

Away from the main camping area are several rows of comfortable en-suite chalets, smaller twin rooms using common showers & furnished tents. It's a truly excellent setup, & even though several overland trucks might congregate there on a busy night, the grounds are spacious enough that it won't disturb people staying in rooms. *US$50/70 sgl/dbl cottage, US$40/55 sgl/dbl rooms using common showers, US$35/50 sgl/dbl furnished tent, all B&B. US$15pp dorm bed, US$8pp camping.* **$$$**

🏠 Crater Bay Cottages (22 units) ☎048 6426255; m 0772 643996; e clairek22@yahoo. com; www.craterbaycottageslakebunyonyi.com. Situated within Rutinda, this owner-managed lodge comprises a row of clean & comfortably furnished round cottages with nets & en-suite hot showers, as well as smaller rooms & furnished standing tents using common showers, & space for pitching a tent, all set in compact flowering grounds that drop down to the lake. Friendly, quiet, uncrowded & decent value. *US$50/60 sgl/dbl B&B cottage, US$20/30 sgl/dbl room, US$20/25 sgl/ dbl tent, US$5pp camping.* **$$–$$$**

🏠 Kaleba's Camp (6 rooms) m 0772 907892; e kalebasbunyonyi@yahoo.com; ⓕ fb.me/ Kalebasbunyonyicampsite. Set on pretty lakeshore gardens in the heart of Rutinda, this unpretentious backpacker-oriented lodge (formerly Karibuni) offers the choice of clean en-suite rooms with hot shower & balcony, standing tents using common showers, or camping in your own tent. A restaurant serves a fair selection of meals in the US$7–8 range. A little rough at the edges, but fine at the price. *US$20/40 sgl/dbl room, USS$20 dbl tent, US$5pp camping.* **$$**

🏠 Bunyonyi View Gorilla Packer (9 rooms & 1 dorm) m 0772 660331; e info@www.lovingheartsuganda.com; www. lovingheartsuganda.com. Situated at the south end of Rutinda on the opposite side of the road to the lake, this friendly new lodge, proceeds from which go towards the NGO Loving Hearts Uganda, has cool, comfortable & agreeably decorated en-suite rooms with hot shower & balcony offering what would be a great lake view were it not for an intrusive corrugated-iron roof in the foreground. The restaurant/bar has an uninterrupted view, however. Fair value. *US$30/35 sgl/dbl, US$13pp dorm bed. All rates B&B, add US$12–22pp for FB.* **$$**

Shoestring

🏠 **Edirisa** (2 rooms & 2 dorms) m 0752 558222; e home@edirisa.org; www.edirisa.org. Home to the social enterprise Edirisa & its canoe trekking operation (see page 485), this isolated Robinson Crusoe-style camp sprawls across a wooded peninsula 2km south of Rutinda on foot or by car (you could also cross from the landing site by dugout). Accommodation is in clean traditional huts: a dbl with net, writing table & chairs, 2 4-bed dorms with nets, & a dbl room in the manager's house. The camp also serves as a base for volunteers involved in Edirisa's award-winning ecotourism-related multimedia productions. Activities include free canoeing & swimming in a submerged pool in the lake. Solar power is supplemented by grid electricity & there's free Wi-Fi. Meals cost under US$5 with specialities being fresh bread, pizzas & meatloaf from the firewood oven, as well as crayfish & giant samosas. *US$24 dbl, US$8pp dorm bed, US$6pp camping in Edirisa's tent, US$4pp camping in your own tent.* **$$**

🏠 **Lake Bunyonyi Backpackers** (3 rooms, 1 6-bed dorm) m 0778 107950; e goldenmutatina@yahoo.com. This new budget backpackers lies on the mainland shore directly opposite Rutinda & about 10mins away by canoe. Lighting is solar-powered, there's a restaurant & bar, & access to the self-catering kitchen costs around US$1.50pp. It can also arrange transport to Bwindi & Mgahinga to track gorillas. *US$13/16 sgl/dbl, US$6.50pp dorm bed or US$3pp to camp.* **$**

Camping

The most popular & in most respects best place to pitch a tent at Rutinda is the Lake Bunyonyi Overland Resort, though nearby Kaleba's & Crater Bay are cheaper & quiet, while the more remote Edirisa Camp is cheaper still.

Island retreats

The lodges listed below are all set on one or other of the lake's 29 islands &, except where otherwise stated, are usually accessed by motorboat or canoe transfer from Rutinda landing jetty.

Upmarket

✳ 🏠 **Lake Bunyonyi Eco-Resort** (8 rooms) ☎ 041 4372067; m 0776 280344; e info@bunyonyiecoresort.com, www.bunyonyiecoresort.

com. Set on the elevated west side of wooded Kyahugye Island, this excellent & well-managed new retreat offers accommodation in rustically stylish wooden cabins with nets & en-suite bathrooms. In addition to birding & canoe trips, the island is stocked with zebra, waterbuck, kob, & impala translocated from Lake Mburo National Park. It lies 500m south of the same peninsula that houses Edirisa Camp, 2km south of Rutinda, & is usually accessed from a landing & parking site (⊕ *-1.27857, 29.93654*) on the left side of the road to Edirisa. *US$110/160 sgl/dbl FB.* **$$$$**

🏠 **Heritage Lodge** (7 tents, 1 family cottage) m 0789 966696/0703 606114; e www.heritagelodgesuganda.com. Situated on secluded, heart-shaped Habuharo Island on the western side of the lake 6km from Rutinda, this comfortable tented camp enjoys a lovely garden setting of lawns & flowering plants beneath mature trees sloping down to the lake from an open-sided lounge & dining area tastefully decorated with local artefacts. Free motorboat transfers for guests. *US$100/145 sgl/dbl B&B, or US$140/190 FB.* **$$$$**

Budget

✳ 🏠 **Byoona Amagara Island Retreat** (9 rooms & 2 dorms) m 0752 652788; e bookings@lakebunyonyi.net; www.lakebunyonyi.net. This popular & very chilled backpackers' haunt stands on the south side of Itambira Island, about 3km south of Rutinda. A range of accommodation is available, the most popular option being the 'geodomes', fresh-air arrangements consisting of a round thatched roof & a rear wall over twin or dbl beds (nets provided). *US$72 Family Cottage (sleeps 5), US$28pp for en-suite Wood Cabin (sleeps 5), US$15/20pp basic/luxury geodome, US$7–9 dorm bed, US$4 camping.* **$$**

🏠 **Bushara Island Camp** (10 units) m 0772 464585; e busharaisland@africaonline.co.ug; www.busharaislandcamp.com. The community resort on the medium-sized island of Bushara, 2.5km southwest of Rutinda by motorboat, has come a long way since its rickety 1993 incarnation. Today, a selection of en-suite furnished tents, cottages & a 'treehouse' (a slightly elevated wooden cabin) are offered. Accommodation set in secondary vegetation along the southern side of the island is preferable to that located within the eucalyptus forest on the northern slopes. Amenities include a checklist of

the 100-plus bird species recorded on the island, free transfers for overnight guests from Rutinda, & Wi-Fi. *US$35/40 sgl/dbl bed only or US$60pp FB, US$10pp dorm bed, US$6pp camping.* **$$**

🏠 **Njuyera Island Camp** (8 units) m 0773 149752/0774 087809; e samunva@yahoo.com or sharpsisnjuyera@yahoo.com. Also known as Sharp's Island Camp, this pleasant, low-key retreat, operated in partnership with the Church of Uganda, occupies the island home of Dr Leonard Sharp, who established the leper colony on nearby Bwama Island in 1929. The refurbished house – not the original, but quite old all the same – stands in a pretty garden containing aged flowering trees & younger ones planted by the doctor's grandson in 2008. An interesting history is displayed, with a terrific map of the lake drawn in *Swallows & Amazons*-style by the doctor's children. *US$22/40/50 sgl/dbl/trpl, US$4pp camping.* **$$**

Northern lakeshore
The 2 very different resorts listed below both have isolated locations on the lakeshore north of Rutinda.

✳ 🏠 **Amasiko Homestay** (4 bandas) m 0782 583815/077654; e info@amasiko.org; www.amasiko.org. This small Dutch-run enterprise – whose name means 'Hope' – is committed to developing grassroots education through the affiliated Amasiko Green School in the village of Hamukaka & to developing permaculture & other sustainable agricultural practices. Accommodation is in rustic, solar-lit earth-bag or wooden constructions set in a quiet lakeshore compound with communal showers & compost toilets, & rates include simple but tasty local meals eaten communally with other guests & management. Activities include swimming, boating, a 2½hr hike to the Echuya Forest & village visits to Hamukaka. Amasiko lies on the back road along the northeast Bunyonyi shore about 5km south of Muko & 15km north of Kacwekano. An enjoyable, unique & worthy set-up. Good value. *US$30pp FB.* **$$$**

🏠 **Heritage Muko** (2 rooms) m 0784 451268. Set at the most northerly point on the lake, overlooking its marshy outflow alongside the surfaced road between Kabale & Kisoro, this consists of 2 furnished en-suite tents placed unappealingly close to the main road. *US$60/100 sgl/dbl FB. Camping US$10 per tent.* **$$$**

✖ WHERE TO EAT AND DRINK *Map, page 480*
All the lodges listed above provide food. Staying at Rutinda, Birdnest@Bunyonyi is hard to beat for a stylish no-expense-spared night out, while Lake Bunyonyi Overland Resort is a good mid-priced option.

✖ **Lake View Coffee House** m 0775 925848; ⏱ 08.00–17.00 daily. This Bangladeshi-owned restaurant in the junction village of Kacwekano, 2km from Rutinda, offers fantastic views over the lake from its wooden deck, though you can also eat indoors in windy or wet weather. The menu is dominated by Indian-style fare, but there are also pizzas & Uganda dishes. Great for a lazy lunch with a view, a chilled afternoon beer, or a freshly brewed coffee *en route* between Kabale & the lake. *Dishes in the US$4–6 range.*

WHAT TO SEE AND DO Lake Bunyonyi is a great place to chill out, but it also caters well to more active travellers, with canoes, kayaks and mountain bikes available for hire, and enough potential excursions to keep you busy for days. Visits to most of the places of interest described on the following pages can be arranged through any lakeshore resorts and hotels, and it's also possible to reach some sites using public transport and/or dugout canoes chartered at a negotiable rate from the jetty at Rutinda.

The lakeshore near Rutinda Rutinda itself, though rather small, is considerably enlivened on Mondays and Fridays, when dozens of canoes arrive in the early morning from all around the lake, carrying local farmers and their produce to a

colourful market on the main jetty. A pleasant **short stroll** out of town, roughly 1.5km in either direction, leads south past Bunyonyi Safari Resort then to the left and uphill to the same resort's Hilltop Venue (✪ *-1.27625, 29.93988*), which is open to the public and offers fabulous views over the lake.

A **longer circuit** entails following the Kabale Road north out of Rutinda, past the smart Birdnest@Bunyonyi, before it begins the steep ascent to the summit above the lake. Just before the ascent, the road skirts a patch of papyrus swamp where various colourful bishop- and widow-birds breed, and a few pairs of the peculiar thick-billed weaver construct their distinctive neat nests. From here, more energetic travellers could ascend via a series of switchbacks to ridge-top Kacwekano, where you might consider a refreshment stop at the Lake View Coffee House. Turn right here, and after about 2km you'll reach Arcadia Cottages, with its stunning view over the lake and islands. Using local footpaths, it's possible to descend directly from Arcadia to the lakeshore about 1km south of Rutinda, but the paths are very steep and probably best avoided after rain.

For those with private transport, a lovely **drive** out of Rutinda runs north from the five-way junction at Kacwekano along a 20km back road that offers some fantastic views over the northern part of the lake before connecting with the surfaced main road between Kabale and Kisoro at Muko.

Canoe trekking The social enterprise **Edirisa Canoe Trekking** (m *0752 558222*; e *home@edirisa.org; www.canoetrekking.com*) specialises in canoeing and trekking excursions based out of its lakeshore camp, 2km south of Rutinda. Shorter options include the 2-hour Touch of Bunyonyi (*from US$15pp*), the 5-hour Culture on the Crest Tour (*from US$40pp*) taking in the peaks of Kyabahinga for superb views, a nursery and a herbalist, and the full-day Islands of Miracles (*from US$90pp*) which extends the latter to include visits to three special islands. Two- and three-day expeditions (*US$180/230pp*) include tented accommodation at pretty lakeshore and island campsites (upgrades available), all food, and visits to a group of Batwa Pygmies.

The islands Several of the 20-plus islands on Bunyonyi are worth a visit, with the most accessible being the half-dozen or so situated in the central part of the lake close to Rutinda. Aside from Bushara Island, which uses its own motorboat for transfers, the best way to reach most of the islands is by dugout canoe. This is easily arranged through any lakeshore lodge or with local fishermen at Rutinda landing site. Rates are negotiable but expect to pay around US$25–30 per person for a trip taking in up to three islands.

Bwama Island The largest island on Lake Bunyonyi and the site of a well-known mission, school and handicraft centre for the disabled. Most of the buildings on Bwama date to 1929, when Leonard Sharp, a British doctor with several years' medical experience in southwest Uganda, established a leper colony on the island. Leprosy was a serious problem in Kigezi at that time, and for longer than three decades the island provided refuge for up to 100 victims of the disease. Leprosy was eradicated from Kigezi in the 1960s and the colony ceased operating in 1969. The island remains of interest for its scenery, architecture and handicraft shop.

Bushara Island Immediately north of Bwama, Bushara is well developed for tourism, and although the accommodation is highly recommended, day trips are also encouraged. The ideal would be to go to the island for a lingering lunch, then

> We have always lived in the forest. Like my father and grandfathers, I lived from hunting and collecting in this mountain. Then the Bahutu came. They cut the forest to cultivate the land. They carried on cutting and planting until they had encircled our forest with their fields. Today, they come right up to our huts. Instead of forest, now we are surrounded by Irish potatoes!
>
> *Gahut Gahuliro, a Mutwa born 100 years*
> *earlier on the slopes of the Virungas, talking in 1999*

The most ancient inhabitants of inter-lacustrine Africa, the Batwa (singular Mutwa) are a Pygmoid people easily distinguished from other Ugandans by their short stature – an adult male seldom exceeds 1.5m in height – and paler, more bronzed complexion. Semi-nomadic by inclination, small egalitarian communities of Batwa kin traditionally live in impermanent encampments of flimsy leaf huts, set in a forest clearing, which they up and leave when food becomes scarce locally, or upon the death of a community member, or when the whim takes them. Traditionally, the Batwa lifestyle is based around hunting, which is undertaken as a team effort by the male members of a community, usually using nets or poisoned arrows. Batwa men also gather wild honey, while the women gather edible plants to supplement the meat. In times past, the Batwa wore only a drape of animal hide or barkcloth, and had little desire to accumulate possessions – a few cooking pots, some hunting gear, and that was about it.

According to a recent survey, around 3,500 Batwa live in Uganda, mostly concentrated in Kigezi. Only 2,000 years ago, however, east and southern Africa were populated almost solely by Batwa and related hunter-gatherers, whose lifestyle differed little from that of our earliest common human ancestors. Since then, agriculturist and pastoralist settlers, through persecution or assimilation, have marginalised the number to a few small and mostly degraded communities living in habitats unsuitable to agriculture or pasture, such as rainforest interiors and deserts.

The initial incursions into Batwa territory were made when the Bantu-speaking farmers settled in Kigezi, sometime before the 16th century, and set about clearing small tracts of forest for subsistence agriculture and pasture. This process of deforestation was greatly accelerated in the early 20th century: by 1930 the last three substantial tracts of forest remaining in Kigezi were gazetted as the Impenetrable and Echuya forest reserves and Gorilla Game Sanctuary by the colonial authorities. In one sense, this move to protect the forests was of direct benefit to the Batwa, since it ensured that what little remained of them would not be lost to agriculture. But the legal status of the Batwa was altered to their detriment – true, they were still permitted to hunt and forage within the reserves, but where formerly these forests had been recognised as Batwa communal land, they were now government property.

Only some three generations later would the Batwa be faced with the full ramifications of having lost all legal entitlement to their ancestral lands. In 1991, the Gorilla Game Sanctuary and Impenetrable Forest Reserve were re-gazetted to become Mgahinga and Bwindi national parks, a move backed by international donors who stipulated that all persons resident within the national parks were to be evicted, and that hunting and other forest harvesting should cease. Good news for gorillas, perhaps, but what about those Batwa communities that had dwelt within the forest reserves for centuries? Overnight, they were reduced in status to illegal squatters whose traditional subsistence lifestyle had been criminalised. Adding insult to injury, while some compensation was awarded to non-Batwa

farmers who had settled within the forest since the 1930s and illegally cleared it for cultivation, the evicted Batwa received compensation only if they had destroyed part of the forest reserve in a similar manner.

Today, more than 80% of Uganda's Batwa are officially landless, and none has legal access to the forest on which their traditional livelihood depends. Locally, the Batwa are viewed not with sympathy, but rather as objects of ridicule, subject to regular unprovoked attacks that occasionally lead to fatalities. The extent of local prejudice against the Batwa can be garnered from a set of interviews posted on the website www.edirisa.org. The Batwa, report some of their Bakiga neighbours, 'smoke marijuana … like alcohol … drink too much … make noise all night long … eat too much food … cannot grow their own food and crops … depend on hunting and begging … don't care about their children … the man makes love to his wife while the children sleep on their side' – a collection of circumstantially induced half-truths and outright fallacies that make the Batwa come across as the debauched survivors of a dysfunctional hippie commune!

Prejudice against the Batwa is not confined to their immediate neighbours. Richard Nzita's otherwise commendable *Peoples and Cultures of Uganda*, for instance, contrives, in the space of two pages, to characterise the Pygmoid peoples of Uganda as beggars, crop raiders and pottery thieves – even cannibals! Conservationists and the Western media, meanwhile, persistently stigmatise the Batwa as gorilla hunters and poachers – this despite the strong taboo against killing or eating apes that informs every known Batwa community. Almost certainly, any gorilla hunting that might be undertaken by the Batwa today will have been instigated by outsiders.

This much is incontestable: Batwa and their hunter-gatherer ancestors have in all probability inhabited the forests of Kigezi for some half-a-million years. Their traditional lifestyle, which places no rigorous demands on the forest, could be cited as a model of that professed holy grail of modern conservationists: the sustainable use of natural resources. The Batwa were not major participants in the deforestation of Kigezi, but they have certainly been the main human victims of this loss. And Batwa and gorillas cohabited in the same forests for many millennia prior to their futures both being imperilled by identical external causes in the 20th century. As Jerome Lewis writes: 'They and their way of life are entitled to as much consideration and respect as other ways of life. There was and is nothing to be condemned in forest nomadism … The Batwa … used the environment without destroying or seriously damaging it. It is only through their long-term custody of the area that later comers have good land to use'.

Travellers to Kigezi might well be approached by self-styled guides offering to take them to a local Batwa community. The answer to this query should be no. Unofficial encounters set up by street guides are almost invariably dodgy or exploitative. If you want to meet Batwa in a culturally sensitive environment, the best places to do so are at Mgahinga National Park, at a few sites listed in the Bwindi chapter, or through Edirisa, which arranges visits to Echuya Forest from Lake Bunyonyi. Should you witness any incident where Batwa are exploited or victimised, contact the Forest Peoples Project (*www.forestpeoples.org*), a UK-based charity that works with the Batwa of Uganda to help them determine their own future, control the use of their lands, and carry out sustainable use of the forest resources.

For further information, Karsten Tadie's fascinating self-published book *The Batwa of Uganda: A Forgotten People* (2010) can be bought at Crater Bay Cottages for around US$13. Also check out the website: www.minorityrights.org.

either arrange to take a dugout canoe around its circumference or else to walk the self-guided trail along the shore – both options cost day visitors US$2–3.

Akampene Island Shaded by a solitary tree, the tiny 'Island of Punishment' is visible both from the north shore of Bwama and the east shore of Bushara. Like Kisizi Falls, this island is traditionally associated with the Bakiga taboo against pre-marital sex. In times gone by, unmarried girls who became pregnant would be exiled to Akampene, where they faced one of two possible fates. Any man who did not own sufficient cows to pay for an untainted bride was permitted to fetch the disgraced girl from the island and make her his wife. Failing that, the girl would usually starve to death.

Akabucuranuka Island A rather fanciful legend is attached to this island whose name literally means 'upside down'. Many years ago, it is said, a group of male revellers on Akabucuranuka refused to share their abundant stock of beer with an old lady who had disembarked from her canoe to join them. Unfortunately for the drinking party, the woman was a sorceress. She returned to her canoe, paddled a safe distance away, and then used her magical powers to overturn the island – drowning everybody in the party – and then flip it back the right way up as if nothing had happened.

Kyahugye Island This medium-sized island only 500m from the mainland is the site of Lake Bunyonyi Eco-Resort (page 483), and day visitors are charged an entrance fee of US$3 to wander around in the company of its introduced populations of zebra, impala, waterbuck and kob antelope. A solitary De Brazza's monkey of unknown provenance also inhabits the island.

Muko and the Ruhuma Swamp
The small trading centre of Muko, situated 45km from Kabale along the main road to Kisoro Road, is where the Ndego River flows out of Bunyonyi's northern tip to form the vast Ruhuma (or Kigeyu) Swamp, which meanders river-like north and then west to skirt Bwindi National Park before entering Lake Mutanda, and forms one of the best places in Uganda to see the likes of papyrus gonolek and papyrus yellow warbler. A good access point to the swamp is a rough motorable track that leads north from the tar road to Kabale about 10km northeast of Muko. Fred Hodgson, who visited the area in 2015, recorded 'white-winged warbler, fan-tailed widowbird and papyrus canary as well as two mysterious weaver species that are currently before the East African Rarities Committee'.

Any vehicle heading along the main road between Kabale and Kisoro can drop you at Muko, and one elevated stretch of this road also affords good views over the swamps. Self-drivers could also follow the 20km back road between Rutinda and Muko via Kacwekano and Hamukaka. Bushara Island Camp (pages 483–4) charges US$25 for a motorboat to Muko, or you could charter a dugout canoe from Rutinda. The only accommodation at Muko is the overpriced Heritage Lodge (page 483), whose grounds also host an interesting selection of water birds.

Batwa Pygmies Kigezi once supported a large population of Batwa, ancient Pygmoid hunter-gatherers (see box, pages 486–7) who have been evacuated from traditional forest haunts such as Echuya Forest Reserve and Bwindi Impenetrable National Park in modern times. Batwa visits around Bunyonyi usually occur at

Rubanga on the other side of the lake from Rutinda. It is pointless making your own way there as they live on the higher slopes bordering Echuya Forest Reserve, and only descend to Ruhanga by arrangement. These are best made with Edirisa (page 485), who charge around US$30 per person and will ensure that the community sees a proper benefit. Ethical Batwa visits are also possible at Mgahinga Gorilla National Park and Bwindi Impenetrable Park (pages 502 and 520).

KISORO

Set at an altitude of 1,900m within 10km of the Rwandan and Congolese borders, Kisoro is an inherently unremarkable small town with an utterly stupendous setting in an area of rolling green hills at the base of the Virunga Volcanoes. A few years back, Kisoro came across as a scruffy and amorphous backwater, set on something of a limb in terms of Kigezi's main tourist circuit, and even today it is only one-third the size of Kabale, with a population estimated at 18,000. But Kisoro of late has acquired an altogether more modern and economically vibrant feel, as reflected in its newly sealed main road and freshly painted shopfronts, a rash of new construction activity, and its overdue upgrade to municipal status in August 2015. It has also taken over from Kabale as Kigezi's busiest urban tourist hub, partly as a result of improved access following the surfacing of the main road to Kampala, but also thanks to the opening of gorilla-tracking trailheads at Nkuringo and Rushaga in southern Bwindi, and of several lodges on nearby Lake Mutanda. Kisoro's most striking feature, at least in clear weather, is its stupendous Virunga backdrop, in particular the 4,127m peak of Muhabura, which stands only 10km to the south. The town is a potential base for gorilla tracking not only in southern Bwindi, but also in Mgahinga National Park or across the border in Rwanda's Volcanoes National Park and the Congolese Virunga National Park, both of which are accorded full chapters in the companion Bradt guide to Rwanda (see www.bradtguides.com/rwanda).

GETTING THERE AND AWAY Kisoro is connected to Kabale by what is now a good and very scenic 75km surfaced road via Hamurwa, Muko and the Echuya Forest Reserve. Crossing through Echuya, do stop at the lofty Kanaba Gap, where on a clear day you'll see all the Virunga volcanoes laid out in front of you, from Muhabura in the east to the tempestuous Congolese twins Nyiragongo and Nyamuragira. The drive takes up to 90 minutes, or 2 hours allowing for a few scenic stops. About 10km shorter, but no quicker unless you are coming from Rutinda as opposed to Kabale, is the back road between Kabale and Muko via Kacwekano and the northeast shore of Lake Bunyonyi.

Several **buses** run daily between Kampala and Kisoro (*around US$8; 10hrs*). The priciest and most upmarket service is the overnight Trinity Coach (m *0772 422451*), which charges US$13 for a wide and comfortable reclining seat, and leaves Kampala at 21.00 and Kisoro at 20.00 daily. Best of the rest is Jaguar Executive Coaches (m *0782 811128 (Kampala) or 0777 763491 (Kisoro)*), which operates two buses in either direction daily, leaving Kampala from its terminal on Namirembe Road about 500m west of the Qualicell Bus Park at 08.00 and 21.00, and from Kisoro at 07.30 and 20.30. A more conservative choice is the Post Bus, though with numerous stops along the way, it is far from being the fastest. More locally, **matatus** between Kabale and Kisoro (*US$5; 90mins*) run back and forth throughout the day. Bodas are available for those continuing to the Rwandan border at Cyanika (aka Kyanika) or Congolese border at Bunagana.

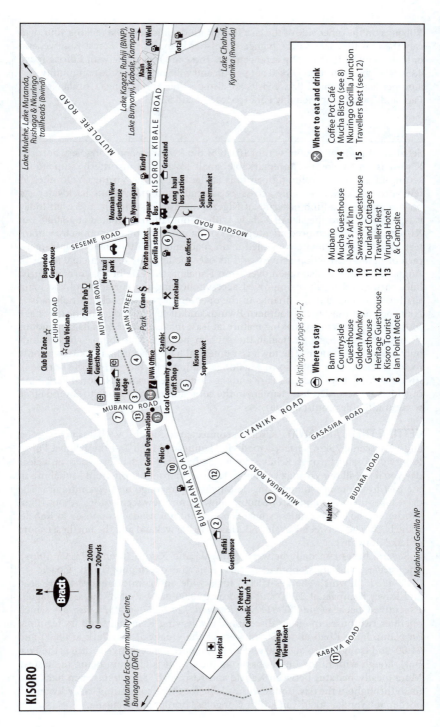

KISORO

Lake Mulehe, Lake Mutanda,
Rushaga & Nkuringo
trailheads (Bwindi)

Lake Kagezi, Ruhiji (BINP),
Lake Bunyonyi, Kabale, Kampala

Lake Chahafi,
Kyanika (Rwanda)

MUTOLERE ROAD

KISORO - KIBALE ROAD

MOSQUE ROAD

SESEME ROAD

CHUHO ROAD

MUTANDA ROAD

MAIN STREET

MUBANO ROAD

CYANIKA ROAD

GASASIRA ROAD

MUHABURA ROAD

BUDARA ROAD

BUNAGANA ROAD

KABAYA ROAD

Mutanda Eco-Community Centre,
Bunagana (DRC)

Mgahinga Gorilla NP

Main
market

Oil Well

Total

Kindly

Graceland

Jaguar
Bus

Long haul
bus station

Selina
Supermarket

Mounain View
Guesthouse

Nyamagana

Potato market

Gorilla statue

Bus offices

Bugondo
Guesthouse

New taxi
park

Zebra Pub

Crane

Park

Terraceland

Club DE Zone

Club Volcano

Mirembe
Guesthouse

Hill Base
Lodge

UWA Office

Stanbic

Kisoro
Supermarket

Local Community
Craft Shop

The Gorilla Organisation

Police

Rafiki
Guesthouse

St Peter's
Catholic Church

Hospital

Mgahinga
View Resort

Market

Where to stay For listings, see pages 491–2

1 Bam
2 Countryside
   Guesthouse
3 Golden Monkey
   Guesthouse
4 Heritage Guesthouse
5 Kisoro Tourist
6 Ian Point Motel
7 Mubano
8 Mucha Guesthouse
9 Noah's Ark Inn
10 Sawasawa Guesthouse
11 Tourland Cottages
12 Travellers Rest
13 Virunga Hotel
   & Campsite

Where to eat and drink

   Coffee Pot Café
   Mucha Bistro (see 8)
14 Nkuringo Gorilla Junction
15 Travellers Rest (see 12)

N

Bradt

0   200m
0   200yds

WHERE TO STAY *Map, opposite*

Kisoro is well supplied with budget hotels, though they tend to be costlier than in other similarly sized Ugandan towns, and it's one of those places where places recommended by guidebooks tend to have the most inflated rates. Better upmarket options are available at the gate of Mgahinga National Park and around Lake Mutanda. Use water sparingly as Kisoro suffers from a chronic shortage due to the porous nature of the underlying volcanic rock.

Moderate

Travellers Rest Hotel (11 rooms) m 0772 533029; e postmaster@gorillatours. com; www.gorillatours.com. Opened by gorilla enthusiast Walter Baumgärtel in the 1950s, Kisoro's oldest hotel hosted such eminent personages as George Schaller & Dian Fossey prior to being nationalised under Idi Amin. Privatised & restored in the late 1990s, it still has plenty of period character, & the well-tended & largely indigenous gardens offer great in-house birding. The small rooms, though slightly lacking in privacy, are attractively decorated in ethnic style, & come with nets & en-suite hot showers. The hotel is located at the turn-off to Mgahinga National Park. Meals, taken indoors or on the courtyard terrace, cost around US$5. Good value. *US$77/95 sgl/dbl B&B.* **$$$**

Kisoro Tourist Hotel (6 rooms) \048 6430135; m 0712 540527; e kisorotouristhotel@ gmail.com. The Travellers Rest's closest competitor is a smart, centrally-located & comparatively boring 2-storey block where large & airy rooms come with nets, tiled floors, DSTV & en-suite hot showers. An acceptable fall back. *US$100 dbl.* **$$$**

Tourland Cottages (13 rooms) \048 6430369; m 0772 439245. Boasting a quiet location in large gardens on a backroad west of the town centre, this potentially nice hotel has adequate rooms with fitted net & flatscreen DSTV, but they are rather small & it is all undermined by the tacky décor. Sub-par value. *US$33/50 sgl/dbl B&B.* **$$$**

Budget

Mucha Guesthouse (9 rooms) m 0784 478605/479520; e bistro@hotel-mucha. com; www.hotel-mucha.com. The neat & brightly decorated rooms at this funky high street guesthouse come with nets & en-suite hot shower & are set around a courtyard behind the popular Mucha Bistro. Breakfast costs US$3 & there's free Wi-Fi. *US$12/22 sgl/dbl.* **$$**

Sawasawa Guesthouse (9 rooms) m 0774 472926; booking@sawasawaguesthouse. com; www.sawasawaguesthouse.com. Owned by the assistant manager of the nearby Travellers Rest, this clean & friendly guesthouse has been getting plenty of good feedback from travellers. Rooms all have nets & walls adorned with African art, & some are en suite with hot showers. A small restaurant/bar is attached & it's also a good contact for locating guides or car transfers to Bwindi or Mgahinga. *US$10/28 en-suite sgl/dbl, US$10/15 sgl/dbl using common shower. All rates B&B.* **$$**

Noah's Ark Inn (5 rooms) m 0772 826061. Situated in leafy suburban gardens around the corner from the Travellers Rest, this small & agreeable owner-managed lodge has old-fashioned but spacious suite-like rooms with net, sitting area & en-suite hot shower. Good value for Kisoro. *US$27 dbl.* **$$**

Heritage Guesthouse (8 rooms) \048 6430126; m 0772 517416. Set around a quiet courtyard, the clean & pleasant rooms at this central hotel come with net, wood ceiling, DSTV & en-suite hot shower. A terrace restaurant serves typical Ugandan fare for around US$4. *US$10/20/22 sgl/twin/dbl B&B.* **$$**

Countryside Guesthouse (10 rooms) m 0706 212496. Set in a small garden on the western edge of town, this place has clean en-suite rooms with nets & a restaurant. *US$12/18/20 en-suite sgl/dbl/twin.* **$$**

Bam Hotel (28 rooms) m 0756 565665; e bamkisoro@gmail.com. This 3-storey hotel opposite a mosque is conveniently located for the early morning buses. En-suite rooms have DSTV & hot water. Secure compound parking. *US$13/20 sgl/dbl.* **$$**

Golden Monkey Guesthouse (7 rooms & 1 6-bed dorm) m 0772 435148; e info@goldenmonkeyguesthouse.com; www. goldenmonkeyguesthouse.com. This friendly & service-oriented lodge has long been a favourite with backpackers, but unfortunately it is now one

19

of Kisoro's worst offenders on the silly pricing front. Rooms are small & scruffy, & inferior to several places charging half as much. Free Wi-Fi in the bar. *US$25/35 sgl/dbl. US$10 dorm bed. B/fast an additional US$5pp.* **$$**

⌂ **Virunga Hotel & Campsite** (18 rooms) m 0782 360820; e virungahotelcampsite@gmail. com. This long-established budget favourite is past its prime & seems overpriced. There are tiled rooms with net, flatscreen DSTV, Wi-Fi & en-suite hot shower in the new block, & more basic rooms with ¾ bed in the old block. The attached restaurant keeps short hours. *US$40 dbl B&B in new block. US$20 sgl B&B in old block. US$7pp camping.* **$$**

Shoestring

⌂ **Mubano Hotel** (15 rooms) m 0773 337511. This solid-looking hotel, set in large quiet gardens at the west end of the town centre, has adequate en-suite rooms with cold showers (hot water supplied in buckets by request) & a restaurant serving inexpensive local fare. Outstanding value. *US$10 dbl with sitting room. US$7 twin.* **$**

⌂ **Ian Point Motel** (9 rooms) m 0789 261685. Centrally located close to the main bus depots, this adequate cheapie has small & rather shabby but well-equipped & affordable en-suite rooms with net, fridge, DSTV & hot shower. An inexpensive local restaurant is attached. *US$12 dbl.* **$**

✗ **WHERE TO EAT AND DRINK** *Map, page 490*
If you're looking for a break from urban settings, the top pick in terms of aesthetics is undoubtedly the garden terrace at the **Travellers Rest Hotel**, whose continental-style mains are also very reasonably priced at around US$5. In pure culinary terms, however, the more central restaurants listed below are more interesting.

✗ **Coffee Pot Café** m 0772 625493; www. coffee-pot-cafe.com; ⊕ 08.30–22.00 Mon–Sat. Sprawling out on to the shaded terrace of the corner plot next to the UWA office, Kisoro's most perennially popular country style eatery serves everything from meatballs or chilli con carne to pizzas or fish & chips. There's also superfast Wi-Fi at US$1 per 30 mins, delicious coffee & juice, packed lunches for hikers at US$5, a good selection of second-hand novels to buy (*US$2*) or swap (*US$1*), & a well-stocked craft shop. *Most mains in the US$4–5 range.*

✗ **Nkuringo Gorilla Junction** m 0774 535236; ⊕ 07.00–22.00 daily. Offering the choice of eating indoors or on a shady green terrace, this chilled eatery specialises in fresh plunger coffee & delicious smoothies & juices, but the menu also includes soups, salads, pasta & other relatively healthy snacks. *Dishes in the US$2.50–5 range.*

✗ **Mucha Bistro** m 0784 478605/479520; e bistro@hotel-mucha.com; www.hotel-mucha. com. Attached to the eponymous guesthouse, this high street bistro opposite the central park has indoor & pavement seating & a tempting menu with the likes of ratatouille, meatballs & various burgers & sandwiches. Freshly brewed coffee, juices, beer & a selection of wines are available, too. *Meals in the US$4–6 range.*

NIGHTLIFE **Club Volcano** and **Club DE Zone** can both get lively at night.

SHOPPING For groceries, try the **Selina Supermarket** next to the Ian Point Motel or the **Kisoro Supermarket** on the main road opposite the park. The main market – busiest on Mondays and Thursdays – is a short distance along the Kabale Road opposite the California Inn. For crafts, the Local Community Craft Shop next to the Kisoro Supermarket is recommended, and a good selection is also on sale at the Coffee Pot and Nkuringo Gorilla Junction restaurants. A wide selection of 'antique' Congolese carvings and masks decorate the foyer of the Travellers Rest Hotel. Secondhand books can be bought or swapped at the Coffee Pot Café.

OTHER PRACTICALITIES Branches of Crane and Stanbic banks offer the usual forex services. Several internet cafés are dotted around town, and there's free Wi-Fi at Mucha Bistro or inexpensive and faster Wi-Fi at the Coffee Pot Café.

TOURIST INFORMATION, OPERATORS AND GUIDES If you need a guide, ask for a recommendation at your hotel or the Coffee Pot Café rather than engaging a self-styled tourist guide off the street (and be warned that the UWA office will often suggest the same chaps who accost travellers in the street).

Uganda Wildlife Authority Office
⊕ 08.00–18.00 daily. Situated at the western end of the town centre next to the Coffee Pot, this helpful UWA office provides information about the Mgahinga National Park & southern Bwindi, as well as other tourist attractions in the region. Depending on availability, gorilla-tracking permits for Mgahinga, Nkuringo & Rushaga can all be bought here up until the evening prior to departure, as can permits for all other activities. Even if you've pre-bought gorilla-tracking permits for Mgahinga you should pop in here the day before to check which of the two trailheads will be used.
Virunga Adventure Tours
m 0772 435148/0785 799766; e info@

virungaadventuretours.com; www. virungaadventuretours.com. Based out of the Golden Monkey Guesthouse, this local operator offers a variety of tours in & around Kisoro, as well as same-day return transfers to the Nkuringo and Rushaga gorilla-tracking trailheads in Bwindi for US$100.
Nkuringo Adventure Safaris 039 2176327; m 0774 805580; e info@nkuringowalkingsafaris. com; www.nkuringowalkingsafaris.com. Though it's based in Kampala, this excellent small operator specialises in hikes in the Kisoro, including volcano climbs in Mgahinga National Park & the 2-day Nkuringo overnight hike via Mutanda, with a possible day extension through Bwindi Impenetrable National Park to Buhoma.

WHAT TO SEE AND DO Kisoro is the main springboard for gorilla tracking and other hikes in Mgahinga National Park, while the surrounding hills host several pretty lakes, of which the largest and best-developed for tourism is Mutanda, whose southernmost shore is only 5km from the town centre. Kisoro also lies within striking distance of the two southern gorilla-tracking trailheads detailed in the chapter on Bwindi Impenetrable National Park.

Around town There's not much to see in the town centre. The small central park serves as a roost for large numbers of black-headed and other herons, while the central 'Irish potato' market, where the region's main crop is sold to traders from Kampala and elsewhere, can be a hive of economic activity in season. Also of interest is the enormous Monday and Thursday market out along the Kabale Road. For a more rigorous leg stretch, try hiking up the insular and distinctively terraced volcanic hill that lies about 1.5km south of Kisoro overlooking the right side of the road to Mgahinga National Park. A small but perfectly formed dry crater lies within the rim, which also offers terrific views of the surrounding region.

Nkuringo overnight hike Operated by Nkuringo Adventure Safaris (see above), this ridiculously scenic two-day excursion connects Kisoro to Nkuringo Gorilla Camp (near the Nkuringo gorilla-tracking trailhead) by means of a dugout-canoe voyage across Lake Mutanda and footpaths leading through the Kigezi Hills. The option of continuing through a lovely section of Bwindi Forest to Buhoma is also highly recommended. A two-day excursion with overnight accommodation at Nkuringo Gorilla Camp (pages 530–1; lazy camping on full-board arrangement) costs from US$485 for one person and drops to US$230 per person for groups of four.

Lakes Mutanda and Mulehe Following the 1,800m contour of the steep-sided hills that separate Kisoro from Bwindi National Park, the pretty 22km² Lake Mutanda, like larger Bunyonyi, is a narrow flooded valley system that formed

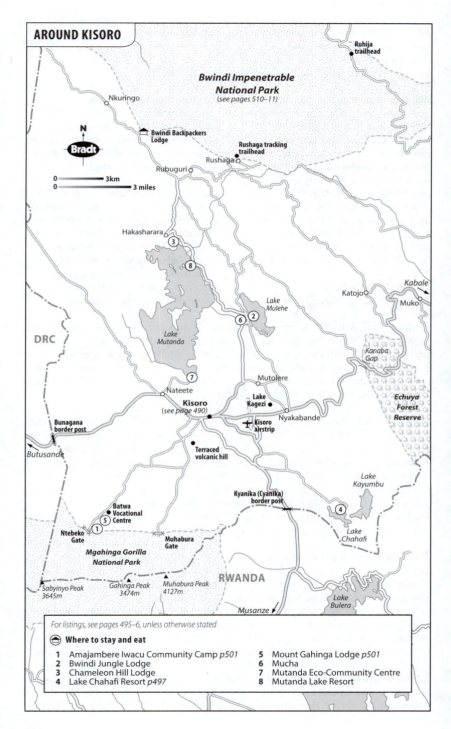

AROUND KISORO

Bwindi Impenetrable National Park
(see pages 510–11)

Ruhija trailhead

Nkuringo

Bradt

N

Bwindi Backpackers Lodge

Rushaga tracking trailhead

0   3km
0   3 miles

Rubuguri   Rushaga

Hakasharara   ③

          ⑧

          Lake Mulehe

          ⑥ ②

Katojo   Kabale

          Muko

DRC

Lake Mutanda

          Kanaba Gap

          ⑦

Nateete   Mutolere

Kisoro
(see page 490)   Lake Kagezi

Bunagana border post   Kisoro airstrip   Nyakabande

          Echuya Forest Reserve

~Butusande

          Terraced volcanic hill

          Lake Kayumbu

          Kyanika (Cyanika) border post   ④

          Lake Chahafi

Batwa Vocational Centre

⑤   Lake Kayumbu

①
Ntebeko Gate   Muhabura Gate

Mgahinga Gorilla National Park   **RWANDA**

Sabyinyo Peak 3645m   Gahinga Peak 3474m   Muhabura Peak 4127m

          Musanze   Lake Bulera

For listings, see pages 495–6, unless otherwise stated

◯ **Where to stay and eat**

1	Amajambere Iwacu Community Camp *p501*	5	Mount Gahinga Lodge *p501*
2	Bwindi Jungle Lodge	6	Mucha
3	Chameleon Hill Lodge	7	Mutanda Eco-Community Centre
4	Lake Chahafi Resort *p497*	8	Mutanda Lake Resort

several thousand years ago when the Rutshuru River, its main effluent, was dammed by a lava flow. About 3km east of Mutanda lies the relatively shallow but equally pretty Lake Mulehe, which extends across 9km² at a slightly lower altitude. Recent years have seen the emergence of several tourist developments around the lakes, which are conveniently located *en route* from Kisoro to the gorilla-tracking trailheads at Rushaga and Nkuringo. Aimed mainly at gorilla trackers, there are now four upmarket lodges in the vicinity of the two lakes. Of greater interest to budget travellers (and to day trippers out of Kisoro) is the **Mutanda Eco-Community Centre** (*www.lakemutandacamp.com/ecotourism.html*), which lies at the south end of the lake, off the Bunagana Road and within walking distance of town. In addition to offering budget accommodation, the centre operates guided boat trips on to the island-studded lake, which is home to plenty of otters and a wide variety of birds. These range from full-day boat outings at US$40 per person to shorter tours and dedicated birding excursions in the US$10–20 per person range.

Getting there and away Mutanda Eco-Community Centre lies on the marshy southern lakeshore, about 2.5km southeast of where the Rutshuru River flows out, and a similar distance north of Kisoro as the crow flies. In a car, the best way to get there from Kisoro is to follow the Bunagana Road for 3km west out of town to Nateete, then turn right at the signposted junction (⊕ *-1.26856, 29.6647*) and follow for another 3.5km to the lakeshore. You could also walk out along the road in about 90 minutes, or try to make your way via a maze of footpaths running north out of town. A boda will cost around US$1.50.

To get from Kisoro to any of the four upmarket lodges in the vicinity of the lakes, you need to follow the soon-to-be-surfaced road to Nkuringo that leads northeast from the main Kabale Road next to the Kindly Filling Station (⊕ *-1.2823, 29.69693*). After 8km, the road passes the Mucha Hotel to the left, then after another 100m it arrives at a three-way junction (⊕ *-1.2235, 29.71628*). Turn right here, and you'll reach Bwindi Jungle Lodge after about 500m. Bear left, and you'll reach the Mutanda Lake Resort after another 8km, and Chameleon Hill 3km past that.

 Where to stay and eat *Map, opposite*

Exclusive

✴ 🏠 **Chameleon Hill Lodge** (10 cottages) m 0772 721818; e welcome@chameleonhill. com, www.chameleonhill.com. Set on a high hill offering a panoramic view across the island-studded northeast corner of the lake to the Virungas, this refreshingly different lodge is distinguished by its boldly painted turreted exteriors, whose use of primary colours makes it look like a fairytale castle from a children's colouring-in book, & spacious stylish interiors decorated with mosaic & contemporary African art. The cottages all have dbl or twin beds with walk-in net, en-suite hot shower with imported fittings & a private lake-facing balcony & garden. Mainly used as a base for gorilla tracking in southern Bwindi, the lodge also arranges village walks, coffee-farm visits, boat trips on the lake & canoeing.

US$330/460 sgl/dbl B&B. Add US$20pp for FB. Low season discounts available. $$$$$

Upmarket

✴ 🏠 **Mutanda Lake Resort** (13 cottages) m 078 9951943; e info@mutandalakeresort. com; www.mutandalakeresort.com; see ad, 3rd colour section. Set on a peninsula 45mins' drive from Kisoro, this lodge enjoys a stupendous southerly outlook across peaceful island-studded waters towards the Virunga volcanoes, so insist on a cottage facing in this direction. The cosy stilted rooms have wooden floors, canvas sides, thatched roof, fitted nets, en-suite hot shower & private lake-facing balcony, but be warned that they are quite cramped together so noise does travel between rooms. Set menus are eaten in a lovely stilted wooden restaurant/bar, also with

lake views, & packed lunches can be provided. It's a justifiably popular base for gorilla tracking in southern Bwindi, & very reasonably priced. *US$130/170 sgl/dbl B&B, or an additional US$25pp FB.* $$$$

🏠 **Mucha Hotel** (10 rooms) m 0784 478605/479520; e bistro@hotel-mucha.com; www.hotel-mucha.com. This upmarket relative of the namesake guesthouse & bistro in Kisoro lies on the south bank of the Mucha River about 8km north of town. The spacious & uncluttered rooms are simply but stylishly furnished, & have fitted nets & en-suite hot showers. A highly rated restaurant serves à la carte meals for around US$7. It's a slightly odd location, nestled between the rural shambas, & there's not much of a view, but it's well priced & conveniently located for gorilla tracking in southern Bwindi. *US$80/120 sgl/dbl B&B. Add US$25pp FB.* $$$

🏠 **Bwindi Jungle Lodge** (4 cottages) ☎041 4232754; e info@ugandajunglelodges. com; www.ugandajunglelodges.com; see ad, page 503. This new lodge overlooks the western shore of Lake Mulehe, 8km north of Kisoro along the road to the gorilla-tracking trailheads at Rushaga & Nkuringo. The en-suite cottages are very spacious & cosy, with stone floor & walls & wood-&-cane furniture offset by a rather garish colour scheme. Nice enough, but the disingenuity of the name grates (it's neither in Bwindi nor in a jungle) & it also seems a bit overpriced. *US$210/340 sgl/dbl FB.* $$$$$

see ad, page 503.

Budget

🏠 **Mutanda Eco-Community Centre** (4 rooms) m 0785 799766/0782 306973; e info@ lakemutandacamp.com; www.lakemutandacamp. com. Set on the papyrus-fringed southern lake shore, this community-oriented development offers accommodation in stilted wooden cabins with fitted nets & private balconies. A restaurant serves a fair selection of meals in the US$3–4 range. The location is fantastic, but rooms seem steeply priced for what they are. *US$50 en-suite dbl, US$30/40 sgl/dbl using common shower. US$10pp dorm bed.* $$

Lake Kagezi Kigezi subregion is named after Uganda's most southwesterly colonial-era district, whose name is in turn bastardised from that of the region's first British government station, established by Captain Coote in 1910. The site chosen by Coote stood next to a lake called Kagezi, and though the station was abandoned two years later in favour of Ikumba (on the Kabale Road near the junction to Ruhija), the name endured. For those who are interested, the site of Coote's short-lived station is easy enough to reach, situated as it is only 800m from the Kabale Road along a rough track leading north from alongside a conspicuous church, 1km east of Kisoro airstrip. The lake itself, rather disappointingly, is little more than a grassy seasonal swamp set in what appears to be an old volcanic caldera no more than 200m in diameter. No trace of any former government building remains.

Lake Chahafi This small lake, 12km southeast of Kisoro, lies in a wedge of Ugandan land surrounded by Rwandan territory to the southeast and southwest. Fringed with papyrus and covered in water lilies, it's a pretty spot, particularly on clear days with Muhabura towering above the western horizon, and it supports plenty of otters and birds. The setting wasn't always so tranquil. On 1 January 1915, German forces attacked an Anglo–Belgian outpost positioned on nearby Murora Hill, where some remnants of trenches remain. Then a few days later, according to an account in the *Uganda Journal*, '1,500 natives attacked the base in a fighting that took six hours, claiming that they had come to pay taxes but armed with spears'. A 10-minute walk east from Chahafi leads to the slightly larger Lake Kayumbu.

Getting there and away To get to Lake Chahafi from Kisoro, follow the surfaced Kabale Road east out of town for 500m, then turn right on to the signposted Cyanika Road and follow it for 4km to a signposted junction to the left (✛ -1.305, 29.72468). From here it is about 8km along a maze of dirt roads to the lakeside resort.

Where to stay and eat *Map, page 494*

Lake Chahafi Resort (3 rooms & 1 dorm) m 0782 754496/0793 330974; e info@lakechahafiresort.com; www.lakechahafiresort.com. Something of a work in progress, this pretty lakeshore resort offers accommodation in large but sparsely furnished standing tents with wooden floors, tiled bathrooms & nets. Facilities include a swimming pier, a boat, & a restaurant/bar. *US$50/70 sgl/dbl, US$20 dorm bed, US$12 camping. All rates B&B.* **$$$**

Shozi Crater and caves Shozi Crater, reaching an altitude of 2,000m, is a relic of the volcanic activity that shaped this mountainous corner of Uganda. Close by is a 400m-long cave, formed by a petrified lava flow, which houses a colony of thousands upon thousands of bats. The crater and cave are located near the trading centre of Mutolere (✪ -1.26312, 29.72249), off the road to Mutanda about 5km northeast of Kisoro.

Echuya Forest Reserve Extending over 35km² of hilly terrain between Lake Bunyonyi and Kisoro, Echuya Forest Reserve is one of Uganda's least-visited and most under-researched protected areas, yet it still ranks among the top six sites in the country in terms of forest biodiversity. With an altitude span of 2,200m to 2,600m, the reserve protects a range of montane habitats including evergreen and bamboo forest, while the adjacent Muchuya Swamp is one of the most extensive perennial high-altitude wetlands in East Africa, harbouring the largest-known population of the globally endangered Grauer's swamp warbler. Little information is available about the reserve's non-avian fauna, but it is likely to be similar to the forest belt of nearby Mgahinga National Park and includes at least four small mammal species endemic to the Albertine Rift. Until recent times, Echuya was permanently inhabited by Batwa Pygmies (see box, pages 486–7). Several Pygmy communities living on the verge of the forest still derive their livelihood from bamboo and other resources extracted from within the reserve.

A surprisingly low bird checklist of 100 species suggests that scientific knowledge of Echuya is far from complete, but even so 12 Albertine Rift endemics have been recorded, and it is the only locality outside the national park system where a comparable selection of these sought-after specialities is resident. The easiest way to explore the reserve is along the 5km of the main Kisoro–Kabale Road that passes through it. Birding here was easier, or at least a lot more more peaceful, before the road was surfaced, but Fred Hogdson, who made several visits to the site in 2014 and 2015, reports that it is perfectly safe, despite the traffic, and the birding is excellent. Among the commoner birds noted by Fred were the following: regal sunbird, strange weaver, white-starred robin, mountain masked apalis, long-tailed barred cuckoo, Shelley's greenbul, chestnut-throated apalis, Rwenzori batis and red-throated alethe. Fred also notes that African black duck and cinnamon bracken-warbler were seen at the swampy area where a stream crosses under the road in the summit area at Kanaba Gap.

A welcome new development is the recent formation of the community-run **Echuya Eco-Tourism Association** (✆ 039 2584982; m 0750 084211; e echuyaforest@gmail.com) which offers guided hikes into the forest for US$10–20 per person. Two trails are currently available, one of which crosses the forest, while the other descends to Muchuya Swamp (water levels permitting) via hardwood forest and bamboo forest. Also on offer are cultural visits to surrounding Batwa, Bakiga and Bafumbira communities. Self-sufficient camping is currently available (*US$7pp*) on the east side of the forest reserve, where it is crossed by the Kabale–Kisoro Road. The campsite also serves as the base for hikes, and it has handicrafts and drinks for sale. Future plans include a dorm, homestay opportunities and a campground on the western side of the reserve as well as additional activities.

Straddling the borders of Uganda, Rwanda and the DRC, the Virungas are not a mountain range as such, but a chain of isolated free-standing volcanic cones strung along a fault line associated with the same geological process that formed the Rift Valley. Sometimes also referred to as the Birunga or Bufumbira Mountains, the chain comprises six inactive and two active volcanoes, all of which exceed 3,000m in altitude – the tallest being Karisimbi (4,507m), Mikeno (4,437m) and Muhabura (also known as Muhavura, 4,127m). Three of the eight mountains lie partially within Uganda: Muhabura and Gahinga (3,475m) straddle the Rwandan border, while Sabyinyo (3,669m) stands at the junction of the three national borders.

The names of the individual mountains in the Virunga chain reflect local perceptions. Sabyinyo translates as 'old man's teeth' in reference to the jagged rim of what is probably the most ancient and weathered of the eight volcanoes. The lofty Muhabura is 'the guide', and anecdotes collected by the first Europeans to visit the area suggest that its perfect cone, topped today by a small crater lake, still glowed at night as recently as the early 19th century. The stumpier Gahinga translates as 'small pile of stones', a name that becomes clear when you see local people tidying the rocks that clutter their fields into heaps named *gahingas*. Of the volcanoes that lie outside Uganda, Karisimbi – which occasionally sports a small cap of snow – is named for the colour of a cowrie shell, while Bisoke simply means 'watering hole', in reference to the crater lake near its peak.

The vegetation zones of the Virungas correspond closely with those of other large East African mountains, albeit that much of the Afro-montane forest below the 2,500m contour has been sacrificed to cultivation. Between 2,500m and 3,500m, where an average annual rainfall of 2,000mm is typical, bamboo forest is interspersed with stands of tall *hagenia* woodland. At higher altitudes, the cover of Afro-alpine moorland, grassland and marsh is studded with giant lobelia and other outsized plants similar to those found on Kilimanjaro and the Rwenzori.

The most famous denizen of the Virungas is the mountain gorilla, which inhabits the forested slopes of all six of the inactive volcanoes, but not – for obvious reasons – the denuded slopes of their more temperamental kin. The Virungas also form the main stronghold for the endangered golden monkey and support relic populations of elephant and buffalo along with typical highland forest species such as yellow-backed duiker and giant forest hog. The mountains' avifauna is comparatively poorly known, but some 150 species are recorded including about 20 Albertine Rift endemics.

Still in their geological infancy, none of the present Virunga Mountains is more than two million years old, and two of the cones remain highly active. However, eruptions of earlier Virunga volcanoes ten to 12 million years ago marked the start of the tectonic processes that have formed the western Rift Valley. The most dramatic volcanic explosion of historical times was the 1977 eruption of the

MGAHINGA GORILLA NATIONAL PARK

Comprising the Ugandan portion of the Virungas, the 34km² Mgahinga Gorilla National Park (MGNP) is the smallest component in a 430km² cross-border system of protected areas that incorporates the Rwandan and Congolese sectors of the same volcanic mountain range. Established in 1930 as the Gorilla Game Sanctuary,

3,470m Mount Nyiragongo in the DRC, about 20km north of the Lake Kivu port of Goma. During this eruption, a lava lake that had formed in the volcano's main crater back in 1894 drained in less than one hour, emitting streams of molten lava that flowed at a rate of up to 60km/h, killing an estimated 2,000 people and terminating only 500m from Goma Airport.

In 1994, a new lake of lava started to accumulate within the main crater of Nyiragongo, leading to another highly destructive eruption on 17 January 2002. Lava flowed down the southern and eastern flanks of the volcano into Goma itself, killing at least 50 people. Goma was evacuated, and an estimated 450,000 people crossed into the nearby Rwandan towns of Rubavu (Gisenyi) and Musanze (Ruhengeri) for temporary refuge. Three days later, when the first evacuees returned, it transpired that about a quarter of the town – including large parts of the commercial and residential centre – had been engulfed by the lava, leaving 12,000 families homeless. The 50m-diamater lava lake in the crater of Nyiragongo crater remains active, and although there has been no major eruption since 2002, a minor one did occur in 2011.

Only 15km northwest of Nyiragongo stands the 3,058m Mount Nyamuragira, which also erupted in January 2002. Nyamuragira is probably the most active volcano on the African mainland, with 34 eruptions recorded since 1882, though only the 1912–13 incident resulted in any fatalities. Nyamuragira most recently blew its top on 7 November 2011, emitting a 400-metre high column of lava – its largest eruption in 100 years – that destroyed large tracts of cultivated land and forest. In mid 2014, a new lava lake appeared in Nyamuragira for the first time since the last one was emptied in a 1938 eruption. Thought to be 500 metres deep and still growing, the lake has caused locally-based volcanologists to study the possibility of evacuating Goma once again.

It is perhaps worth noting that these temperamental Congolese volcanoes pose no threat to visitors to Uganda. The three cones shared by Uganda are all long inactive – indeed, while plumes from the Congolese volcanoes might well be seen around Kisoro at night, no active lava flow has touched Ugandan soil in recorded history. That might change one day: there is a tradition among the Bafumbira people of the Ugandan Virungas that the fiery sprits inhabiting the crater of Nyamuragira will eventually relocate to Muhabura, reducing both the mountain and its surrounds to ash.

Another Bafumbira custom has it that the crater lake atop Mount Muhabura is inhabited by a powerful snake spirit called Indyoka, which only needs to raise its head to bring rain to the surrounding countryside. It is said that Indyoka lives on a bed of gold and protects various other artefacts made of precious metal, and that it can extend itself as far as Lake Mutanda to a lakeshore sacrificial shrine at Mushungero. An indication of its presence at the lake and associated shrine is the inundation of the seasonal Gitundwe Swamp near Lake Mutanda.

MGNP was gazetted in 1991, when more than 2,000 people were relocated from within its boundaries. Small it might be, but this is arguably the most scenic park in Uganda, offering panoramic views that stretch northward to Bwindi, and a southern skyline dominated by the steep volcanic cones of the Virungas, surely one of the most memorable and stirring sights in East Africa. MGNP's main attraction, as its name suggests, is gorilla tracking, though it harbours only one habituated group as

opposed to Bwindi's dozen. Permits at Mgahinga are seldom booked by operators due to the gorillas' (now slightly unfair) reputation for vanishing across the border into Rwanda for months on end, which makes it a good place for independent travellers to try for last-minute permits in the high season. Other activities, aimed mainly at keen hikers and walkers, include a challenging day hike to the peaks of Muhabura, Gahinga and Sabyinyo volcanoes, as well as golden monkey-tracking, a Batwa cultural trail, caving, and forest walks.

WILDLIFE A checklist of 76 mammal species includes mountain gorilla, black-and-white colobus, leopard, elephant, giant forest hog, bushpig, buffalo, bushbuck, black-fronted duiker, several varieties of rodents, bats and small predators, and the charismatic golden monkey (an Albertine Rift Endemic whose range is now more-or-less restricted to the Virungas). A surprisingly small bird checklist of 115 species might be influenced by the park's small size, but it also suggests that further species await discovery. Even so, MGNP is still of great interest to birdwatchers, as several of the species recorded are localised forest specialists, and 12 are Albertine Rift Endemics.

FEES The park entrance fee is US$40/30 FNR/FR per 24 hours. For some reason, this entrance fee is incorporated into the per person activity fee for gorilla tracking (*US$600/500 FNR/FR*), volcano climbs (*US$80*) and the Batwa Experience (*US$80*), but excluded from the per person activity fee for golden monkey tracking (*US$50*) and the Sabyinyo Gorge hike (*US$30/15 FNR/FR*). No entrance fee is applied for simply staying overnight at the community campsite or lodge at the park gate. All activities can be booked and paid for at the UWA headquarters in Kampala, the UWA office in Kisoro, or the new visitors' centre 100m inside Ntebeko Entrance Gate.

GETTING THERE AND AWAY There are two points of entry: the westerly Ntebeko Gate (⊕ *-1.3541, 29.61905*) 14km from Kisoro; and the easterly Muhabura Gate (⊕ *-1.35496, 29.66157*) 9km from Kisoro. Ntebeko Gate is the site of the lodge, community campsite and visitors' centre, as well as being the trailhead for golden monkey tracking and hikes to Gahinga Peak, Sabyinyo Peak, Sabyinyo Gorge and the short version of the Batwa Trail. Muhabura Gate is the trailhead for hikes to Muhabura Peak and the long version of the Batwa Trail. The habituated gorillas move between the two gates so it is advisable to check which will be used as a trailhead the day before you track (this can be done at the office in Kisoro or the visitors' centre at Ntebeko).

Both gates are reached along a rough and seasonally slippery dirt road that leaves Kisoro next to the Travellers Rest Hotel. Allow an hour for the journey, and be warned that a 4x4 may be necessary after heavy rain. If you are driving yourself, 2km out of Kisoro you'll reach a junction (⊕ *-1.29672, 29.67824*) where you need to fork to the left, then after another 2km a second junction (⊕ *-1.3147, 29.67848*) where you need to fork right for Ntebeko and left for Muhabura Entrance Gate.

If you don't have a vehicle, the UWA office in Kisoro will know whether any official vehicles are heading out to the appropriate entrance gate. Failing that, a boda costs US$5–7 one-way and is best arranged through the UWA office in Kisoro.

WHERE TO STAY AND EAT *Map, page 494*
It's perfectly possible to visit Mgahinga on a day trip from a lodge in Kisoro or Lake Mutanda, but the accommodation at Ntebeko Entrance Gate is difficult to beat scenically, and it has the advantage of placing you right on the spot for those early-starting hikes.

Upmarket

🏠 Mount Gahinga Lodge (9 cottages)
📞041 4346464; e salesug@volcanoessafaris.
com; www.volcanoessafaris.com. This wonderful
lodge a few hundred metres from the entrance
gate offers accommodation in recently refurbished
stone cottages with papyrus roof, en-suite solar
hot shower & private terrace facing the volcanoes.
Plenty of birdlife passes through the grounds &
amenities include free Wi-Fi & laundry. Good value.
*US$216/360 sgl/dbl including all meals & drinks.
Low season discount offered.* **$$$$$**

Budget & camping

**🏠 Amajambere Iwacu Community
Camp** (6 rooms) m 0772 954956/0782
306973; e info@amajamberecamp.com; www.
amajamberecamp.com. The community campsite
just outside the entrance gate to Mgahinga has a
truly magnificent setting, with Muhabura, Gahinga
& Sabyinyo peaks forming an arc to the south,
& a grandstand view over Lake Mutanda & the
rolling hills of Bwindi to the north. Simple meals
cost about US$4–7, & there is a bar, too. Simple
but reasonably priced accommodation includes
en-suite bandas & a 6-bed dorm. Camping is
permitted (though chilly). *US$30/40 twin/dbl
banda, US$10 dorm bed. US$5pp camping.* **$$**

WHAT TO SEE AND DO Activities described below can usually be arranged at the visitor's centre at Ntebeko Gate, but it is advisable to drop into the UWA office in Kisoro before heading out there. Most activities start at Ntebeko Gate, though the hike to Muhabura Peak starts at Muhabura Gate, and gorilla tracks might start from either gate, depending on the expected location of the habituated group.

Gorilla tracking Eight permits are issued daily to track the Nyakagazi Group, which currently comprises five silverbacks, two adult females and three youngsters. Frustratingly, this group spent most of its time in Rwanda's Volcanoes National Park between 2004, when it was chased across the border by a belligerent lone silverback, and November 2012, since when it has maintained a permanent presence in MGNP. For this historical reason, tour operators tend to shun Mgahinga in favour of Bwindi as a gorilla-tracking destination, which means that permits for the Nyakagazi Group are usually available at short notice, even in peak season. Permits cost US$600/500 FNR/FR, dropping to US$450/400 in April, May and November, and include all park entrance and guiding fees. They are sold at the UWA office in Kisoro but can also be bought at the gate. In the unlikely event that the gorillas cross the border into Rwanda between the time of booking and the time of tracking, UWA will transfer the permit to Bwindi, or refund the cost. The Nyakagazi Group's territory lies between the Ntebeko and Muhabura entrance gates, so check a day in advance which trailhead will be used the next morning.

Mountain hikes Guided day hikes to each of the three volcanic peaks in MGNP leave on demand daily at 07.00–07.30, at a cost of US$80 per person, inclusive of park entrance and guiding fees. A reasonable level of fitness is required for these hikes, all of which take between 7 and 9 hours, while good boots, raingear and warm clothes are recommended. The least-demanding hike, the 1,100m climb from Ntebeko Gate up Mount Gahinga, offers a good chance of seeing various forest birds in the bamboo zone, while duikers and bushbuck inhabit the marshy crater at the peak. The tougher 1,300m ascent from Ntebeko Gate to Sabyinyo, a round trip that takes at least 8 hours, passes through montane forest and moorland, and culminates in three challenging ladder climbs up rock faces that will sorely test anyone with a poor head for heights.

Less vertiginously challenging but far more of an uphill slog, the hike to the park's highest point, the 4,127m Muhabura Peak, involves a 1,793m ascent from the

19

trailhead at Muhabura Gate, which means that hikers may well feel mild altitude-related symptoms near the peak. The open moorland that characterises Muhabura offers great views in all directions, though unless you're lucky this will be reduced by haze by the time you reach the top. Look out for Afro-alpine endemics such as the beautiful scarlet-tufted malachite sunbird. A small crater lake at the top of Muhabura is encircled by giant lobelias.

Golden monkey tracking The next-best thing to seeing the mountain gorilla is the chance to track the golden monkey (*Cercopithecus kandti*), a little-known bamboo-associated primate listed as Endangered by the IUCN. Endemic to the Albertine Rift, the golden monkey is characterised by a bright orange-gold body, cheeks and tail, contrasting with its black limbs, crown and tail end. As a result of deforestation elsewhere in the region, the Virungas now harbour the only remaining viable breeding population of the golden monkey, which is the numerically dominant primate within this restricted range – indeed a 2003 survey estimated a population of 3,000–4,000 in MGNP alone. Golden monkey-tracking excursions leave from Ntebeko at 08.30–09.00 daily, cost US$50 exclusive of park entrance fees, and involve an easy 90-minute walk in either direction to the habituated troop's home range. Ordinary trackers are allocated a maximum of one hour with the monkeys, but those who opt for the habituation experience (US$100 exclusive of park entrance fees) can spend all day with them.

Sabyinyo Gorge Trail (*US$30/15 FNR/FR*) Of particular interest to birders, this half-day nature trail ascends from Ntebeko Gate through the heath into a stand of bamboo forest, then follows a small stream through the lushly forested Sabyinyo Gorge. The bamboo forest is a good place to see golden monkey, as well as handsome francolin, Kivu ground thrush and regal sunbird. The evergreen forest harbours such localised birds as Rwenzori turaco, western green tinkerbird, olive woodpecker, African hill babbler, Archer's ground robin, Rwenzori batis, montane sooty boubou, Lagden's bush-shrike and strange weaver, several of which are Albertine Rift endemics.

The Batwa Trail (*Book through UWA;* \ *041 4355000;* e *info@thebatwatrail. com; www.ugandawildlife.org*) A welcome alternative to the usual tawdry visits to impoverished Batwa/Pygmy communities, this initiative provides a genuine opportunity to experience something of traditional Batwa forest culture. The event follows a trail along the lower slopes of the Virungas to Garama Cave, and involves Batwa guides demonstrating a range of practical traditional skills such as lighting a fire by rubbing together sticks, bivouac building, target practice with a bow and arrow (meat must have been a rare dish indeed!) and food gathering. The trail culminates with a memorable performance of Batwa song and music in the council chamber of Garama Cave, a dramatic setting with powerful acoustics. Importantly, the Batwa Trail is no 'pretty Pygmy' celebration; the day should include a discussion of the current plight of the Batwa, who have been reduced to squatting in bivouacs on Bakiga-owned farmland along the forest margins. The activity costs US$80 per person (including park entrance), and the fee is split approximately 50–50 between UWA and the Batwa. Two variations are possible, both leaving at 08.30–09.00 and culminating in a visit to Garama Cave. The short trail leaves from Ntebeko Gate and takes around 3 hours while the longer trail leaves from Muhabura Gate and takes up to 7 hours.

19

20

Bwindi Impenetrable National Park

Uganda's single most important tourist hotspot is the 331km² Bwindi Impenetrable National Park (BINP), which protects a rugged landscape of steep hills and valleys abutting the Congolese border south of Ishasha and north of Kisoro. Rolling eastward from the Albertine Rift Escarpment, the tangled forested slopes of Bwindi provide shelter to one of Africa's most diverse mammalian faunas, including 45% of the global mountain gorilla population. Unsurprisingly, the main tourist activity in BIMP is gorilla tracking, which was first established at the Buhoma park headquarters in 1993, but now operates out of four trailheads – the others being Ruhija, Nkuringo and Rushaga – all of which are serviced by a selection of tourist lodges. Today, 11 habituated (and three semi-habituated) gorilla groups can be tracked in Bwindi, a thrilling but costly venture regarded by most who have undertaken it to be a true once-in-a-lifetime experience. BINP is also one of the finest birding destinations in Uganda, thanks in part to the presence of 23 Albertine Rift Endemics, while other attractions include forest walks in search of smaller primates such as black-and-white colobus and L'Hoest's monkey. There are also a few reputable cultural programmes that offer the opportunity to interact with the Batwa Pygmies who were evicted from the forest interior following the gazetting of the national park.

GENERAL INFORMATION

FLORA AND FAUNA Bwindi is one of Africa's most biodiverse forests, due to its altitudinal span of 1,160m to 2,607m and an antiquity of more than 25,000 years, and its **flora** includes 160 tree and more than 100 fern species. It formed part of a much larger forest belt that stretched south to the slopes of the Virunga Mountains until about 500 years ago, when agriculturists started planting crops in the Kisoro area. The area was first accorded protection in 1932 with the creation of the Kayonza and Kasatora Crown Forest, which had a combined area of 207km². In 1964, the protected area was extended to its present-day size, renamed the Impenetrable Central Forest Reserve, and designated as a gorilla and wildlife sanctuary. Gazetted as a national park in 1991, it protects a true rainforest that receives an average annual rainfall of almost 1,500mm, and a vital catchment area at the source of five major rivers that flow into Lake Edward. The park was listed as a UNESCO World Heritage Site in 1994 on account of its biodiversity and wealth of International Union for Conservation of Nature (IUCN) red-listed wildlife.

BINP harbours at least 120 **mammal** species, more than any national park except Queen Elizabeth. Its most famous residents are the mountain gorillas, which number around 400 individuals split across 25–30 troops according to the most recent survey, undertaken in 2012. Another ten primate species are present, a list

that includes a healthy population of (unhabituated) chimpanzees, and substantial numbers of olive baboon, black-and-white colobus, L'Hoest's monkey, red-tailed monkey and blue monkey. Of the so-called 'big five', only elephants are present, though the herd of 30 animals in the southeast of the park – assigned to the forest race – is very seldom seen by tourists. Buffaloes and leopards were present until recent times, but they are thought to have been hunted to extinction. Six antelope species occur in the park: bushbuck and five types of forest duiker. Small mammals such as rodents and bats are well represented, too.

A total of 350 **bird** species has been recorded in Bwindi, a remarkably high figure when you consider that it includes very few water-associated birds. Of particular interest to birders are 23 species endemic to the Albertine Rift, and at least 14 species recorded nowhere else in Uganda, among them the African green broadbill, white-tailed blue flycatcher, brown-necked parrot, white-bellied robin chat and Frazer's eagle owl. In addition to its extensive bird checklist, Bwindi is also home to at least 200 **butterfly** species, including eight Albertine Rift Endemics, and dedicated butterfly watchers might hope to identify more than 50 varieties in one day. Bwindi is also home to many **reptiles and amphibians**, notably the Rwenzori three-horned chameleon (*Trioceros johnstoni*), a spectacularly colourful foot-long Albertine Rift Endemic.

ORIENTATION Tourism to BINP focuses on four separate locations: Buhoma in the northwest; Ruhija in the east; Nkuringo in the southwest; and Rushaga in the southwest. Each of these four destinations functions as a self-standing gorilla-tracking destination, insofar as it has its own habituated gorilla groups, is serviced by its own set of accommodation options, and is reached by a different approach road to the other locations. For this reason, coverage of the park is divided up into four sections corresponding to the four above-mentioned locations, which are dealt with in a clockwise direction, starting with Buhoma, which is the oldest trailhead, and remains the most popular and the most directly accessible from Kampala. Common information about subjects such as gorilla tracking and behaviour is scattered around the chapter in prominent grey boxes.

FEES The park entrance fee is US$40/30 FNR/FR per 24 hours, which is incorporated into the activity fee for gorilla tracking (*US$600/500 FNR/FR, dropping to US$450/400 in Apr, May & Nov*). Nature walks cost US$30/15 FNR/FR, exclusive of park entrance fee, unless the walk is undertaken on the same day as gorilla tracking in which no additional entrance fee is charged. No entrance fee is applied for simply staying overnight at community campsites or lodges inside a park gate.

FURTHER INFORMATION The UWA offices in Kampala (page 154) and Kisoro (page 493) can give up-to-date information on gorilla tracking and other travel practicalities in Bwindi and Mgahinga. The 96-page booklet *Mgahinga Gorilla & Bwindi Impenetrable National Parks*, written by David Bygott and Jeannette Hanby, and published by UWA in 1998, remains a useful but in parts quite dated introduction to the park. A full checklist of the birds recorded in Bwindi can be bought for a nominal price at the park headquarters. The 'Uganda Maps' sheet for Bwindi shows the ranges of the habituated gorillas as established by the 2010–11 census. The comprehensive e-book, *Gorilla Highlands: Travel Guide to Southwestern Uganda* is available from the Apple iTunes Store for US$14.99, or you can download a smaller pocket guide at www.gorillahighlands.com.

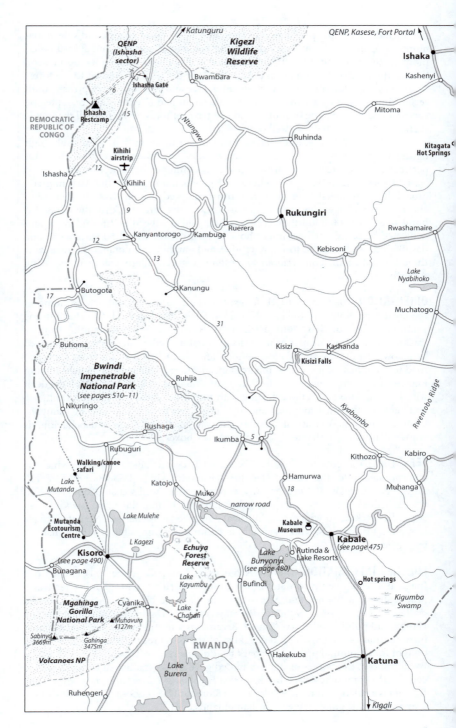

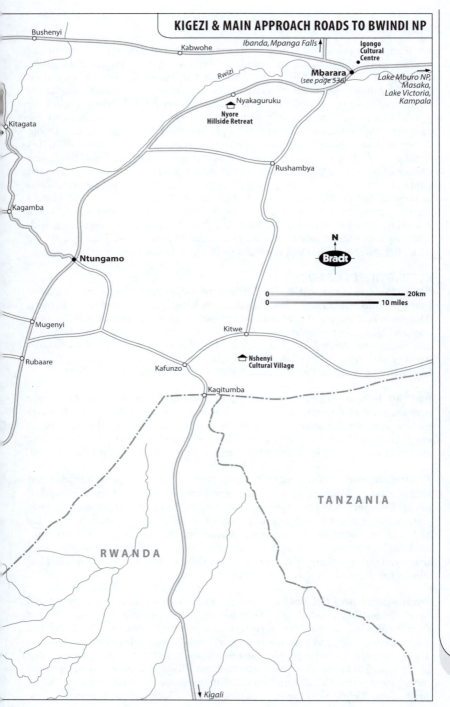

KIGEZI & MAIN APPROACH ROADS TO BWINDI NP

Bushenyi

Kabwohe

Ibanda, Mpanga Falls

Igongo
Cultural
Centre

Mbarara
(see page 536)

*Lake Mburo NP,
Masaka,
Lake Victoria,
Kampala*

Rwizi

Nyakaguruku

**Nyore
Hillside Retreat**

Kitagata

Rushambya

N

Bradt

Kagamba

Ntungamo

0   20km
0   10 miles

Mugenyi

Kitwe

Rubaare

**Nshenyi
Cultural Village**

Kafunzo

Kagitumba

TANZANIA

RWANDA

Kigali

For many years practically synonymous with Bwindi, Buhoma, set at an altitude of 1,500m on the park's northern boundary, is where Uganda first launched gorilla tracking back in 1993, and for 11 years after that, it remained the only trailhead for an activity that accounts for 99% of tourist visits to the national park. Despite the opening of three other gorilla-tracking trailheads since 2004, Buhoma remains the park's busiest tourist focus, partly perhaps as a matter of convention, but also due to its excellent selection of upmarket lodges and the relative ease of access from Kampala. And although 24 tracking permits are advisable for Buhoma daily, it is usually the first of the trailheads to be booked solid, and thus offers the lowest chance of picking up a last-minute permit on any given day – indeed, such is the demand for permits in the high season that many upmarket tours base themselves at Buhoma but do their tracking at Ruhija, about 45km to the southeast. Gorilla tracking aside, Buhoma is also the site of Bwindi's park headquarters, and a rewarding base for birdwatchers. Indeed, 190 bird species, most associated with relatively low-altitude forest, have been recorded in and around Buhoma, among then 10 listed in the *Red Data Book* and/or endemic to the Albertine Rift.

GETTING THERE AND AWAY

By air Subject to demand, Fly Uganda (*www.flyuganda.com*) and Aerolink (*www.aerolinkuganda.com*) both fly daily to Kihihi, the former from Kajjansi Airfield near Kampala, the latter from Entebbe. Flights cost around US$275 one-way and take about 90 minutes. Kihihi Airport lies 40km from Buhoma on the Ishasha Road so you will need to arrange a transfer with your hotel. The savannah Resort Hotel, right next to Kihihi Airport, is a possible base for exploring Bwindi Impenetrable National Park in tandem with the Ishasha Sector of QENP.

By road Buhoma can be approached along several different routes that converge near the town of Butogota, 17km north of the park entrance. All approach routes involve some driving along dirt roads that may become slippery after rain, so an early start is advised. Best carry all the fuel you need but, if you run short, there are filling stations in Kihihi, roughly 20km north of Butogota on the Ishasha Road.

From Kampala and the east Buhoma is about 465km west of Kampala and 190km west of Mbarara by road. The best route entails following the surfaced Kabale Road for 60km past Mbarara to Ntungamo, then turning right on to a newly surfaced 45km road to Rukungiri. A number of different dirt roads through the highlands of northeast Kigezi connect Rukungiri, the most direct of which runs for 85km in a roughly westerly direction via Kambuga and Kanungu, but you could also travel through Kambuga and Kihihi. The drive usually takes up to 8 hours but allow a full day and aim for an early start.

From Kasese and the north Two main routes connect Kasese, Fort Portal and North-Central QENP to Buhoma. The more direct and interesting route branches west from the Mbarara Road at Katunguru, then runs past the Ishasha sector of QENP and north through Kihihi and Butogota. From Kasese, this 170km route takes around 5 hours driving non-stop, but most people divert to Ishasha to look for its tree-climbing lions (see box, page 471). The alternative route via Ishaka, Kagamba and Rukungiri is longer coming from north of Katunguru (about 210km from Kasese) but as good as equidistant and probably slightly faster coming from the vicinity of Kichwamba Escarpment.

From Kabale and the south The 108km drive from Kabale to Buhoma follows dirt roads most of the way, and typically takes about 3 hours. Follow the Kisoro Road out of Kabale for 18km to Hamurwa, then turn right at the turn-off signposted for Buhoma and continue for 60km via Kanungu to Kanyantorogo, where you turn left to Butogota. A far more scenic but slightly slower alternative is to travel through Ruhija (page 521), taking the signposted shortcut left turn 5km before Butogota.

By public transport Reaching Buhoma on public transport used to be complicated, but these days three companies operate direct **buses** from Kampala via Mbarara and Butogota (*US$12; 12–13hrs*). The Highway Bus (m *0774 608325/0705 144119*), which leaves Kampala from Kasenyi bus park at 06.30 and at Buhoma at 16.00, is recommended. Other options are the Muhabura and Al Marline buses, which leave Kampala Qualicell at around 05.30–06.30. With a US$600 gorilla-tracking permit at stake, be sure to book your ticket a day ahead, and to allow a spare day in case of breakdowns.

Coming from elsewhere, you'll be dependent on **matatus**. From the north or east, your first goal will most likely be Rukingiri, a substantial but unremarkable town now connected by good surfaced roads and plenty of matatus to Ishaka (on the Kasese–Mbarara Road) and Ntungamo (on the Mbarara–Kabale Road). Coming from the south, your first goal will be Kanungu, which is connected to Kabale by regular matatus. You won't have any problem finding transport from Rukingiri or Kanungu to Butogota, a small town with several hotels only 17km from Buhoma. From Butogota, you could either wait for one of the buses coming from Kampala, or – more convenient – engage a special hire taxi (*US$15–20*) or a boda (*US$4*).

On foot The most unusual and perhaps exciting way to get to or from Buhoma is the day hiking trail that runs through the national park to the southwestern trailhead of Nkuringo. The hike is not particularly steep and takes up to 5 hours, with a good chance of spotting black-and-white colobus, L'Hoest's monkey and red-tailed monkey, as well as forest birds. Like other nature walks, it costs US$30/15 FNR/FR, plus the usual national park entrance fee. If you are on an organised safari, you can arrange for your driver to drop you at the one trailhead and meet you at the other, though bear in mind that he might actually take longer to drive between Nkuringo and Buhoma, since the two are 130km apart by road, mostly on dirt. The hike can be arranged at either trailhead a day in advance, but it can also can be extended to a (pricier) three-day hiking and boat excursion involving a canoe trip across Lake Mutanda to Kisoro with Nkuringo Walking Adventure Safaris (page 493).

 WHERE TO STAY The camps and lodges servicing Buhoma are spread along the steeply sloping, well-wooded and rather damp Munyaga River Valley. Most enjoy a memorable view of the wall of misty forest covering the opposite side of the valley, but getting around the site tends to involve negotiating an inordinate number of steps as they move around each site. Due to high demand, accommodation at Buhoma tends to cost considerably more than comparable facilities elsewhere in Uganda.

Exclusive

✳ 🏠 Gorilla Forest Camp [510 A7] (8 tents) \041 4340290; e reservations.kenya@ sanctuaryretreats.com; www.sanctuaryretreats.com. This long-serving tented camp remains the absolute top place to stay at Buhoma, thanks to its superb location in a forest glade at the top of a 91-step staircase 500m inside the park entrance. It's worth the climb to sleep in a large, individually secluded en-suite tent with twin queen-sized beds, fitted nets, a large bathroom with hot tub & shower, & comfortable private balcony. The forest here takes on a tangible presence, with plenty of monkeys passing through, even the occasional gorilla, while great

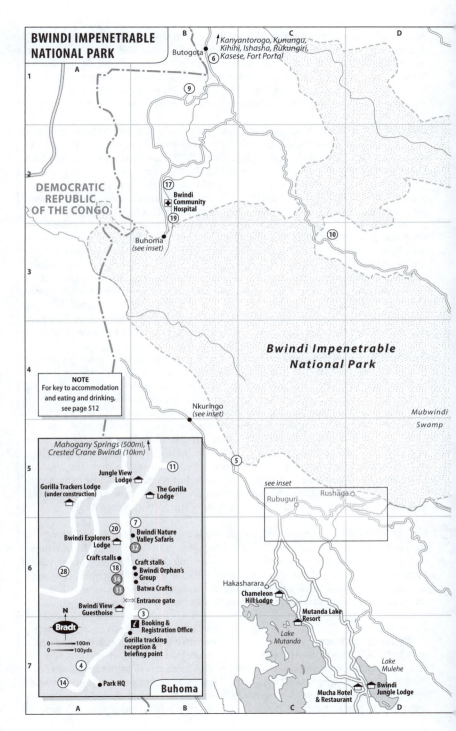

BWINDI IMPENETRABLE NATIONAL PARK

↑ Kanyantorogo, Kunungu, Kihihi, Ishasha, Rukungiri, Kasese, Fort Portal

Butogota

DEMOCRATIC REPUBLIC OF THE CONGO

Bwindi Community Hospital

Buhoma *(see inset)*

Bwindi Impenetrable National Park

Mubwindi Swamp

NOTE
For key to accommodation and eating and drinking, see page 512

Nkuringo *(see inset)*

Mahogany Springs (500m), Crested Crane Bwindi (10km) ↑

Jungle View Lodge

Gorilla Trackers Lodge (under construction)

The Gorilla Lodge

see inset

Rubuguri   Rushaga

Bwindi Nature Valley Safaris

Bwindi Explorers Lodge

Craft stalls

Craft stalls

Bwindi Orphan's Group

Batwa Crafts

Entrance gate

Bwindi View Guesthoise

Hakasharara

Chameleon Hill Lodge

Mutanda Lake Resort

Lake Mutanda

Booking & Registration Office

Gorilla tracking reception & briefing point

0   100m
0   100yds

Park HQ

Buhoma

Lake Mulehe

Mucha Hotel & Restaurant

Bwindi Jungle Lodge

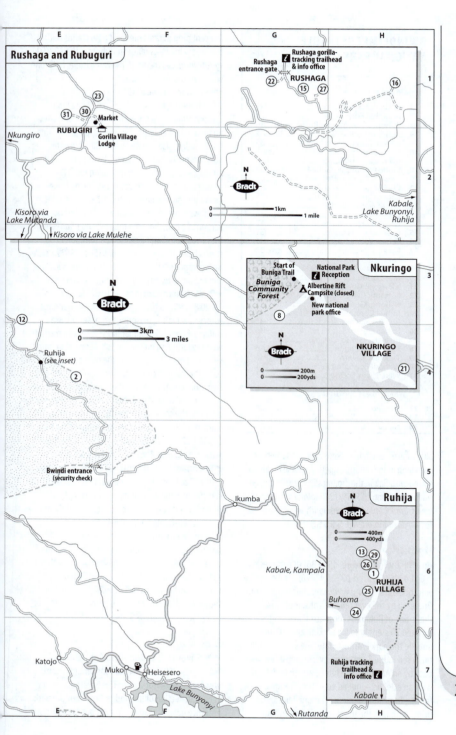

Rushaga and Rubuguri

㉓
㉛ ㉚ **Market**
RUBUGIRI
**Gorilla Village
Lodge**

Nkungiro

*Kisoro via
Lake Mutanda*

Kisoro via Lake Mulehe

**Rushaga
entrance gate**
**Rushaga gorilla-
tracking trailhead
& info office**
㉒ **RUSHAGA**
⑮ ㉗
⑯

*Kabale,
Lake Bunyonyi,
Ruhija*

Bradt

N

0
0 ————— 1km
————— 1 mile

**Start of
Buniga Trail**
*Buniga
Community
Forest*
**National Park
Reception**
⛺ **Albertine Rift
Campsite (closed)**
**New national
park office**
⑧

Nkuringo

**NKURINGO
VILLAGE**
㉑

Bradt
N
0 ——— 200m
0 ——— 200yds

⑫

Bradt
N
0 ——————— 3km
0 ——————— 3 miles

*Ruhija
(see inset)*
②

**Bwindi entrance
(security check)**

Ikumba

Kabale, Kampala

Ruhija

Bradt
N
0 ——— 400m
0 ——— 400yds

⑬ ㉙
㉖ ①
**RUHIJA
VILLAGE**
㉕

Buhoma
㉔

**Ruhija tracking
trailhead &
info office**

Kabale

Katojo
Muko Heisesero

Lake Bunyonyi

Rutanda

	BWINDI IMPENETRABLE NATIONAL PARK

BWINDI IMPENETRABLE NATIONAL PARK
For listings, see pages 509–13, 524–5, 528 & 530–1

🛏 **Where to stay**

1	Bakiga Lodge	H6
2	Broadbill Forest Camp	E4
3	Buhoma Community Rest Camp	B6
4	Buhoma Lodge	A7
5	Bwindi Backpackers Lodge	B5
6	Bwindi Forest Safari Resort	B1
7	Bwindi Lodge	B6
8	Clouds Mountain Gorilla Lodge	G3
9	Crested Crane Hotel Bwindi	B1
10	Cuckooland Tented Camp	C3
11	Engagi Tented Camp	B5
12	Gift of Nature Lodge	E3
13	Gorilla Mist Camp	H6
14	Gorilla Forest Camp	A7
15	Gorilla Safari Lodge	G1
16	Gorilla Valley Lodge	H1
17	Green Tree	B2
18	Lake Kitandara Bwindi Camp	A6
19	Mahogany Springs	B2
20	Mist Lodge	A6
21	Nkuringo Gorilla Camp	H4
22	Nshongi Camp	G1
23	Nshongi Gorilla Resort	E1
24	Ruhija Community Rest Camp	H6
25	Ruhija Gorillas Friends Resort	H6
26	Ruhija Gorilla Safari Lodge	H6
27	Rushaga Gorilla Camp	G1
28	Silverback Lodge	A6
29	Trekkers Tavern	H6
30	Wagtail Eco Safari Park	E1
31	Wild Olives Lodge	E1

✕ **Where to eat and drink**

32	Blessed	B6
33	Bwindi Gorilla Coffee Cup	A6
34	Nadia's	A6

blue turacos, emerald cuckoos & tinker barbets call from high in the canopy. Superb 3-course meals are served with flair in the organically-decorated open-sided restaurant. *US$930/1240 sgl/dbl inclusive of all meals, drinks, laundry & community walk. Huge low season discounts offered.* **$$$$$**

Upmarket

✱ 🏠 **Bwindi Lodge** [510 B6] (8 cottages)
📞 041 4346464/5; m 0772 741720; e salesug@volcanoessafaris.com; www.volcanoessafaris.com. Operated by the ever reliable Volcanoes Safaris, this is one of Buhoma's most attractive lodges, situated 70 steps below a parking area 300m outside the park entrance gate. The spacious half-timbered lodge & cottages, overhauled a few years back by an Australian architect, are quite delightful with an eclectic – indeed eccentric – range of fabrics, furnishings, colours & framed botanical prints within, & the usual forest view without.

A recent drop in rates means it now stands out as the best value in its range at Buhoma. *US$300/500 sgl/dbl including meals, drinks & massage, with low season discounts.* **$$$$$**

🏠 **Buhoma Lodge** [510 A7]
(10 cottages) 📞041 4321479; m 0772 721155; e reservations@ugandaexclusivecamps.com; www.ugandaexclusivecamps.com; see ad, page 407. This terrific lodge, also situated inside the park gates 100m from Gorilla Forest Camp, has a particularly atmospheric 1st-floor lounge-dining room & comfortable stilted cottages with wide balconies facing the forest & en-suite hot tub & shower. Mesh windows & gumpole-&-plaster walls (a lightweight version of a half-timbered medieval building) ensure they avoid the clinging dampness common to tropical forest accommodation. *US$445/660 en-suite cottages sgl/dbl FB, with significant discounts in the low season, or for East African residents.* **$$$$$**

🏠 **Mahogany Springs** [510 B2] (8 cottages)
📞 020 8736 0713 (UK); e info@mahoganysprings.com; www.mahoganysprings.com; see ad, 3rd colour section. This popular lodge is set in a tract of wooded farmland on the northern edge of Buhoma village, about 1.5km outside the park entrance gate. The lodge & cottages, all with king-sized or twin dbl beds, present a rather modernistic take on the usual safari style & if this results in some austere interiors, the scales are tipped the other way by the warmth of the service & the excellence of the food. *US$382/574 sgl/dbl FB, with discounts in the low season, or for East African residents.* **$$$$$**

🏠 **Engagi Tented Camp** [510 B5] (8 cottages)
📞041 4320152; e info@kimbla-mantanauganda.com; www.kimbla-mantanauganda.com. This recently overhauled camp on the edge of Buhoma has an open-fronted, wooden-floored dining & lounge area with lounge chairs & fireplace, fascinating historical prints, a library, bar, veranda & the usual great forest view. These priorities within a structure of local stone, timber & thatch brings to mind the home of a (very wealthy) colonial-era settler. *US$330/470 sgl/dbl FB, discount available for East African residents.* **$$$$$**

Moderate

🏠 **Silverback Lodge** [510 A6] (12 rooms)
📞031 2660260/1; e reservations@marasa.com; www.silverbacklodge.com. This isolated & rather suburban-feeling hilltop lodge 1km from the park entrance gate by road lies in neat but rather fussy

gardens that seem far removed from the tangled forest over which it offers stunning views. The tiled rooms, though not large, have a modern feel, & come with nets, en-suite hot shower & private balcony. If nothing else, it represents Buhoma's best deal for comfort-conscious travellers on a mid-range budget. *US$192/252 B&B, add US$24pp FB. Good low season discounts.* **$$$$**

Crested Crane Hotel Bwindi [510 B1] (10 rooms) ✪ -0.90975, 29.62711; 📞039 2176063; m 0753 176063/0792 200380; e reservations@thecrestedcranebwindi.com; www.thecrestedcranebwindi.com. Set on a grassy green hill overlooking rolling farmland 10km north of Buhoma alongside the road to Butogota, this rather institutional-looking complex of round bandas lacks the character of the upmarket options close to the national park, but it is also far more competitively priced. Rooms all have nets, DTSV, Wi-Fi, balcony & en-suite hot shower, & a restaurant with a fine view towards the forest serves tasty meals. Flocks of several dozen crowned crane are semi-resident. Despite (or perhaps because of) its remoteness, a good-value base for gorilla tracking. *US$100/120 sgl/dbl B&B, add US$20pp FB.* **$$$$**

Lake Kitandara Bwindi Camp [510 A6] (20 tents) 📞031 2277304; m 0782 399235; e kitanda@infocom.co.ug; www.kitandarabwindicamp.com. Located just outside the park gate, this long-serving camp was looking quite abandoned on last inspection & the basic en-suite tents seem overpriced. *US$180/250 sgl/dbl FB.* **$$$$$**

Budget

Buhoma Community Rest Camp [510 B6] (11 rooms & 1 dorm) m 0772 384965; e buhomacommunity@yahoo.com; www.buhomacommunity.com. Located just inside the park gate, this popular camp has a great jungle setting & considerably lower rates than almost anywhere else in the vicinity, but still it feels quite pricey given the lack of frills, even allowing for the contribution they make to local community development. There's the choice of pleasant but simple en-suite bandas & smaller bandas using common showers, or you pitch a tent. *US$85/106 en-suite sgl/dbl, US$60 dbl with common shower, US$30pp dorm bed, US$12 camping. All rates bed only. Meals cost US$10–13 a pop.* **$$$–$$$$**

Bwindi Forest Safari Resort [510 B1] (9 rooms) ✪ -0.89186, 29.63823; m 0784 049398; e bwindiforestsafariresoer@yahoo.co.za. Situated in Butogota town, this friendly but otherwise unexceptional hotel is a lot more urban in feel than the name suggests. Nevertheless, the large & rather spartan rooms with nets & en-suite hot shower are pretty good value if you don't mind being based in town & have wheels to get to the gorilla tracking trailhead in time. *US$15/25 bed only.* **$$**

Shoestring

☀ **Mist Lodge** [510 A6] (8 rooms) 0788 656310/0786 532480; e mistlodgebuhoma@gmail.com. This friendly, clean & unpretentious set-up in the heart of Buhoma village is no more than a slightly superior variation on your standard shoestring Ugandan guesthouse, but it's still a refreshingly affordable alternative to anything else within 5 mins' walking distance of the entrance gate. Rooms have a ¾ bed with net, & showers are hot. *US$10/17 sgl with common/en-suite shower.* **$$**

Green Tree Hotel [510 B2] (10 rooms) ✪ -0.9572, 29.61489; 📞0392 950110; m 0772 830878; e greentreehotelbwindi@gmail.com. Popular with drivers, this small local hotel 3km from the entrance gate has clean en-suite rooms with net & hot shower. *US$17 dbl.* **$$**

✖ WHERE TO EAT AND DRINK
Most visitors eat at their lodge or camp, but there are a few eateries in Buhoma village, as listed below.

✖ **Nadia's Restaurant** [510 A6] m 0782 783491; ⏰ 07.00–21.00 daily. Named after its friendly owner/chef, Nadia's serves typical local dishes. *Around US$3 per plate.*

✖ **Bwindi Gorilla Coffee Cup** [510 A6] m 0772 399224. Set right outside the park entrance, this neat café with outdoor seating serves fresh coffee & chilled beers throughout the day, but meals must be ordered in advance.

✖ **Blessed Restaurant** [510 B6] Situated opposite Mist Lodge, this place serves cheap local eats such as matoke, rice or chapati with various stews. *Around US$2 per meal.*

The largest living primates, gorillas are widespread residents of the equatorial African rainforest, with a global population of around 100,000 concentrated mainly in the Congo Basin. Until 2001, all gorillas were assigned to the species *Gorilla gorilla*, split into three races: the western lowland gorilla (*G. g. gorilla*) of the western Congo Basin; the eastern lowland gorilla (*G. g. graueri*) in the eastern DRC; and the mountain gorilla (*G. g. beringei*), which lives in highland forest on the eastern side of the Albertine Rift. The western race was formally described in 1847, but the mountain gorilla remained unknown to zoologists until 1903, when the German army officer Captain Friedrich Robert von Beringe shot the first two documented individuals on the Rwandan slopes of Mount Sabyinyo, and the eastern lowland gorilla remained undescribed until 1914.

Post-millennial advances in DNA testing and fresh morphological studies have forced the revision of this conventional taxonomic classification. It seems that the western and eastern populations, whose ranges lie more than 1,000km apart, diverged at least 250,000 years ago and should be treated as two species, usually referred to as the western gorilla (*G. gorilla*) and eastern gorilla (*G. beringei*).

The status of the other western race (*G. g. gorilla*) is relatively secure, with a global population estimated at 80,000–90,000 spanning half a dozen countries. Furthermore, the Cross River race *G. g. dielhi* is IUCN-listed as 'Critically Endangered', since it lives in five fragmented populations in the Cameroon–Nigeria border region, with a combined total of fewer than 300 individuals, making it one of the world's most threatened primate taxa. Elsewhere, numbers of western gorilla are still in decline, largely due to hunting for bush meat and the lethal Ebola virus.

The fate of the eastern gorilla – still split into a lowland and mountain race – is more precarious still. As recently as the mid 1990s, an estimated 17,000 eastern lowland gorillas remained in the wild, but it is thought that the population has since dropped below 5,000 largely as a result of ongoing civil war in the DRC. Rarer still, but more numerically stable, is the mountain gorilla, with a global population of fewer than 900 individuals split between the border-straddling Virunga Volcanoes and Uganda's Bwindi Impenetrable National Park.

The first study of mountain gorilla behaviour was undertaken in the 1950s by George Schaller, whose pioneering work formed the starting point for the better publicised research initiated by Dian Fossey in the 1960s. The brutal – and still unsolved – murder of Fossey at her Rwandan research centre in December 1985 is generally thought to have been the handiwork of one of the many poachers with whom she crossed swords in the Virungas. Fossey's acclaimed book *Gorillas in the Mist* remains perhaps the accessible starting point for anybody who wants to know more about mountain gorilla behaviour, while the eponymous movie, a posthumous account of Fossey's life, drew global attention to the plight of the mountain gorilla.

The mountain gorilla is distinguished from its lowland counterparts by several adaptations to its high-altitude home, most visibly a longer and more luxuriant coat. It is on average bulkier than other races, with the heaviest individual gorilla on record (of any race) being Guhondo, the 220kg dominant silverback in

SHOPPING While most lodges contain some sort of sales area, take the time to browse through the roadside craft shops in Buhoma village. The outlet below is particularly recommended.

Rwanda's Sabyinyo Group. The mountain gorilla is a highly sociable creature, living in defined groups of anything from five to 50 animals. A group typically consists of one dominant silverback male (the male's back turns silver when he reaches sexual maturity at about 13 years old) and sometimes one or more subordinate silverbacks, as well as a harem of three or four mature females, and several young animals. Unusually for mammals, it is the male who forms the focal point of gorilla society; when a silverback dies, his troop normally disintegrates. A silverback will start to acquire his harem at about 15 years of age, most normally by attracting a young sexually mature female from another troop. He may continue to lead a troop well into his 40s.

A female gorilla reaches sexual maturity at the age of eight, after which she will often move between different troops several times. Once a female has successfully given birth, however, she normally stays loyal to the same silverback until he dies, and she will even help defend him against other males. (When a male takes over a troop, he generally kills all nursing infants to bring the mothers into oestrus more quickly, a strong motive for a female to help preserve the status quo.) A female gorilla has a gestation period similar to that of a human, and if she reaches old age she will typically have raised up to six offspring to sexual maturity. A female's status within a troop is based on the length of time she has been with a silverback: the alpha female is normally the longest-serving member of the harem.

The mountain gorilla is primarily vegetarian. Its dietary mainstay is bamboo shoots, but it has been recorded eating the leaves, shoots, stems or other parts of more than 140 different plant species. About 2% of its diet is made up of insects and other invertebrates, with ants being the most favoured protein supplement. A gorilla troop will spend most of its waking hours on the ground, but climbs into the trees at night, when each group member builds its own temporary nest. Gorillas are surprisingly sedentary creatures, typically moving less than 1km in a day, which makes tracking them on a day-to-day basis relatively easy for experienced guides. A group will generally only move a long distance after a stressful incident, for instance an aggressive encounter with other gorillas. But this is quite rare, as gorillas are fundamentally peaceable animals. They have few natural enemies and often live for up to 50 years in the wild, but their long-term survival is critically threatened by poaching, deforestation and exposure to human-borne diseases.

It was previously thought that the Virunga and Bwindi gorilla populations were racially identical, not an unreasonable assumption given that a corridor of mid-altitude forest linked the two mountain ranges until about 500 years ago. But recent DNA tests show sufficient genetic differences to suggest that the two breeding populations have been mutually isolated for many millennia. Based on this, some taxonomists now propose the 'mountain gorilla' be split into discrete Bwindi and Virunga races, the former endemic to Uganda and the latter to within a few kilometres of the tripartite border of Uganda, Rwanda and the DRC. Neither of these proposed races numbers more than 500 in the wild, nor have they ever bred successfully in captivity, and both meet several criteria for an IUCN classification of 'Critically Endangered'.

Batwa Crafts [510 B6] m 0773 342963; ⏲ 08.00–18.30 Mon–Sat, noon–18.30 Sun. Affiliated to the highly regarded Batwa Development Programme, this small shop outside the national park entrance sells a variety of handicrafts made by local Batwa communities.

Tracking mountain gorillas in the Virungas or Bwindi ranks among the absolute highlights of African travel. The exhilaration attached to first setting eyes on a wild mountain gorilla is difficult to describe. These are enormous animals: up to three times as bulky as the average man, their size exaggerated by a shaggily luxuriant coat. Yet despite their fearsome appearance, gorillas are remarkably peaceable creatures – tracking them would be a considerably more dangerous pursuit were they possessed of the aggressive temperament of, say, vervet monkeys or baboons, or for that matter human beings.

More impressive even than the gorillas' size and bearing is their unfathomable attitude to people, which differs greatly from that of any other wild animal I've encountered. Anthropomorphic as it might sound, almost everybody who visits the gorillas experiences an almost mystical sense of recognition. Often, one of the gentle giants will break off from the business of chomping on bamboo to study a human visitor, soft brown eyes staring deeply into theirs as if seeking a connection – a spine-tingling wildlife experience without peer.

Gorilla tracking should not present a serious physical challenge to any reasonably fit adult whatever their age, but the hike can be tough going. Exactly how tough varies greatly, and the main determining factor is basically down to luck, specifically how close the gorillas are to the trailhead on the day you trek (1–2 hours is typical, anything from 15 minutes to 6 hours possible). Another variable is how recently it has rained, which affects conditions underfoot – June to August are the driest months and March to May are the wettest.

The effects of altitude should not be underestimated. Tracking in Bwindi usually takes place at around 1,400–2,000m above sea level, but in the Virungas the gorillas are often encountered closer to 3,000m – sufficient to knock the breath out of anybody who just flew in from low altitude. For this reason, travellers might want to leave gorilla tracking until they've been in the region for a week and are reasonably acclimatised – most of Uganda lies above 1,000m.

Trackers must meet at the relevant trailhead at 08.00 and will be given a short briefing about what to expect before they depart into the forest. It is no longer the case that permits specify which gorilla group you will track. At trailheads servicing more than one habituated group, however, the rangers usually do their best to allocate older or relatively unfit looking trackers to whichever group they expect to be easiest to reach on the day, so if you need special consideration, best get there a bit early. Take advantage when the guides offer you a walking staff before the walk; this will be invaluable to help you keep your balance on steep hillsides. Once on the trail, don't be afraid to ask to stop for a few minutes whenever you feel tired, or to ask the guides to create a makeshift walking stick from a branch. Drink plenty of water, and do carry some quick calories such as biscuits or chocolate.

OTHER PRACTICALITIES There are no banking or foreign exchange facilities in Buhoma; the closest town with banks and ATMs is Kihihi, 40km along the Ishasha Road. Several lodges have Wi-Fi and internet access is available at the Bwindi Community Hospital [510 B2], 4km from Buhoma.

TOURIST INFORMATION AND TOUR OPERATORS

National Park Booking & Reception Office [510 B7] m 0772 438323/0787 273370.

This helpful office stands on the left side of the road 100m inside the entrance gate, just before the

The good news is that in 99% of cases, whatever exhaustion you might feel on the way up will vanish with the adrenalin charge that follows the first sighting of a silverback gorilla!

Put on your sturdiest walking shoes for the trek, and wear thick trousers and long sleeves as protection against vicious nettles. It's often cold at the outset, so bring a sweatshirt or jersey. The gorillas are used to people, and it makes no difference whether you wear bright or muted colours. Whatever clothes you wear are likely to get very dirty, so if you have pre-muddied clothes, use them! During the rainy season, a poncho or raincoat might be a worthy addition to your daypack, while sunscreen, sunglasses and a hat are a good idea at any time of year, as are gloves to protect against nettles.

In all reserves, ordinary trackers are permitted to spend no longer than one hour with the gorillas (people who sign on for the habituation experience can stay for up to four hours). It is forbidden to eat, smoke, urinate or defecate in the vicinity of a gorilla group. Gorillas are susceptible to many human diseases, and it has long been feared by researchers that one ill tourist might infect a gorilla, resulting in the possible death of the whole troop should no immunity exist. For this reason, people who know they are harbouring a potentially airborne infection such as a flu or cold should not track gorillas (the permit fee will be refunded). Once in the forest, trackers should not approach the gorillas more closely than 7m (a rule that is often contravened by curious youngsters and sometimes adults approaching their human visitors) and should turn their head away if they need to sneeze.

As for photography, our advice, unless you're a professional or serious amateur, is to run off a few quick snapshots, then put the camera away, enjoy the moment, and buy a postcard or coffee-table book later. Gorillas are tricky photographic subjects, on account of their sunken eyes, the gloomy habitat in which they are often found, and a jet-black skin that tends to distort light readings. Flash photography is forbidden, so carrying a tripod or monopod will help you to get sharper results. It is also worth pre-programming your camera to a relatively high ISO (around 800), and pushing it even higher if conditions demand it. Make sure, too, that your camera gear is well protected – if your bag isn't waterproof, seal your camera in a plastic bag.

Above all, do bear in mind that gorillas are still wild animals, despite the 'gentle giant' reputation that has superseded the old King Kong image. An adult gorilla is much stronger than a person and will act in accordance with its own social codes when provoked or surprised. Accidents are rare, but still it is important to listen to your guide at all times regarding the correct protocol in the presence of gorillas.

gorilla-tracking reception and briefing point. It is the place to enquire about & pay for all activities out of Buhoma, including last-minute gorilla-tracking permits, & it also sells booklets about the park & other memorabilia.
Buhoma Mukono Community Development Association (BMCDA) [510 B6] m 0772 384965; e buhomacommunity@yahoo.com;

www.buhomacommunity.com. Based out of the community rest camp just inside the park gate (page 513), the BMCDA can organise a variety of community-based activities outside the park.
Bwindi Nature Valley Safaris [510 B6] m 0772 973841/0773 828351. This small private operator in Buhoma village offers 2- to 4-hour birding, river & community walks outside the park for US$30–65pp.

WHAT TO SEE AND DO

Gorilla tracking Buhoma is the trailhead for tracking three habituated gorilla groups, all of which currently have one silverback. These are the Mubare Group (13 individuals), Habinyanja Group (18) and Rushegura Group (14), which are often referred to locally as the M, H and R Group. The Mubare Group, named after the hills where it was first observed, was the first to be habituated for tourism in Uganda, a process that started in October 1991 and culminated with the first tourist visit exactly two years later. Habituation of the then 30-strong Habinyanja Group started in 1997 and tourist visits commenced in 1999. Following the death of Habinyanja dominant silverback Mukurusi, a territorial dispute between his two sons Rwansigazi and Mwirima led to the latter splintering off to lead the Rushegura Group, which was already habituated to tourism at the time of its formation in February 2002.

Eight permits are available for each of these groups, bringing the daily total to 24. These are often booked up months in advance, especially during the high season, but if any are available at the last minute, they can be bought at the booking office 100m inside the entrance gate. Trackers must be at the reception and briefing point next to the booking office by 08.00, and will leave after a short briefing. The round trip might take anything from 3 to 10 hours, depending on the proximity of the gorillas and how easily they are located. The success rate is as good as 100%, though it

GORILLA-TRACKING PERMITS AND LOGISTICS

When gorilla tracking was introduced to Uganda in 1993, it was limited to a single habituated group at Buhoma. Today, by contrast, 11 fully habituated groups can be tracked from four different sites in Bwindi (three from Buhoma, two from Ruhija, five from Rushaga and one from Nkuringo), while another habituated group can be tracked in Mgahinga Gorilla National Park (pages 498–502). This means that 96 gorilla-tracking permits are available daily, 88 for Bwindi and eight for Mgahinga. Furthermore, another 24 tracking or habituation permits can be allocated for three further splinter groups, one each at Ruhija, Rushaga and Nkuringo, that are now more-or-less habituated to tourists.

Two types of permit are available. The vast majority of visitors buy a standard permit, which costs US$600/500 FNR/FR, dropping to US$450/400 in April, May and November, and includes all park entrance and guiding fees. The alternative, applicable only to the sixth group that is currently under habituation at Rushaga, is a habituation permit, which allows you 4 hours with the gorillas. This costs US$1,500 per person, however, and is reserved for one group of up to six people daily. In all cases, the permit includes park entrance fees, guides and trackers, but not a porter if one is required.

In addition to this primary cost, other financial considerations must be taken into account. One is the cost of transport. Mountain gorillas inhabit remote areas some way from tarmac highways and major bus routes, so most of the trailheads (Buhoma being the most obvious exception) are accessible only on basic public transport or by chartering a boda or special hire. When you finally reach the trailhead, you'll find the cost of accommodation to be on the high side – plenty of opportunities to splash out US$500-plus per night on an upmarket lodge or tented camp – but each of the tracking trailheads also has at least one more affordable (but still relatively overpriced) budget option.

If you're tracking gorillas as part of an organised tour, you can safely assume that your operator will have booked permits in advance and will make all the necessary

may sometimes depend on the age, fitness and determination of individual permit-holders, who will occasionally turn back before reaching the gorillas because they are too tired to continue.

If you are concerned about your age or fitness, let the rangers know, and they will probably allocate you to the group they expect to be easiest to locate based on its location the day before. Mubare is probably the most reliably physically undemanding group to track, since it generally sticks close to the park's northern boundary, and often strays outside it. Rushegura, whose territory incorporates Buhoma, occasionally passes through lodge and camp grounds within the park boundary, and is often very quickly located close to the trailhead, but it also sometimes moves deeper into the forest. Habinyanja has the largest territory, and is usually the most remote from Buhoma, so the hike can be quite taxing, and trackers are often driven to an isolated trailhead along the Ruhija Road before the hike starts.

Nature walks from Buhoma Several guided nature walks, ranging from 30 minutes to 8 hours in duration, lead from Buhoma, offering the opportunity to enjoy the tranquillity and broader biodiversity of the forest, and to see a variety of monkeys and birds. For monkeys and general scenery, the best of the guided walks is probably the 3-hour **Waterfall Trail**, which leads for 2km along an abandoned road before ascending through a beautiful area of forest to a 33m-high waterfall

arrangements to get you there and find you a comfortable bed. Independent travellers, on the other hand, will generally need to make their own booking, often at relatively short notice. A few years back, when relatively few groups were habituated, the highly coveted permits were often booked up months in advance by tour operators, and there was little point in heading to southwest Uganda hoping to see gorillas unless you had pre-booked a permit. Things are a lot more flexible and straightforward now. For one, the itinerant reputation of the Nyakagazi Group (page 501) means that gorilla-tracking permits for Mgahinga are usually available at short notice. Even at Bwindi, while the 24 permits for Buhoma and eight at Nkuringo are still highly coveted and hard to come by in peak season, it is usually possible to obtain unsold permits at the other Bwindi trailheads on the day of tracking (the full rate applies), though you might want to check availability in advance from the UWA headquarters in Kampala. In the slowest months of April, May and November, permits are now in such oversupply that UWA has discounted the standard permit fee to US$450/400 FNR/FR to in order to encourage more off-season visits.

OBTAINING A PERMIT To book a gorilla permit, visit the UWA headquarters on Kiira Road in Kampala (041 4355000; www.ugandawildlife.org). If booking privately from abroad, write to UWA at e info@ugandawildlife.org. Payment is currently made by bank transfer, though UWA reputedly has plans to establish an online credit card payment mechanism. Alternatively, most tour agents and backpacker hostels can sort you out for a commission of around 10%. You might also check out the Kampala-based online booking website www.gorilla-permits.com (US$60 commission). If you buy a permit during the discounted months of April, May and November, check that you get the discounted price – we've heard of some intermediaries charging their clients the full price plus commission during these times, which is naughty!

on the Munyaga River. The **Mazubijiro Loop Trail** and **Rushara Hill Trail**, each of which takes about 3 hours, offer good views across to the Virunga Mountains. The 8-hour **Ivo River Walk**, which leads to the Ivo River on the southern boundary of the park, offers a good opportunity for seeing monkeys, duikers and a variety of birds. Guided nature walks cost US$30/15 FNR/FR, exclusive of the US$40/30 park entrance fee, which is waived on walks undertaken on the same day as gorilla tracking. Tipping the guide is not mandatory but it is customary, bearing in mind that the rangers are very poorly paid.

Birdwatching Birders with a limited amount of time in Buhoma are strongly urged to stick to the Munyaga River Trail, which starts on the edge of the park behind the gorilla-tracking trailhead, and follows the same old road through the forest south of Buhoma as the Waterfall Trail. The open road provides better birding opportunities than a narrow forest path and on a good morning you could hope to see around 40–50 species, a high proportion of which are more easily seen here than in any similarly accessible part of Uganda. Among the great many remarkable birds commonly seen along this road, some of the more readily identifiable include the great blue turaco, black-billed turaco, barred long-tailed cuckoos, bar-tailed trogon, black bee-eater, grey-throated barbet, Petit's cuckoo-shrike, Elliot's woodpecker, red-tailed bulbul, white-bellied robin-chat, white-tailed ant-thrush, rusty-faced warbler, white-browed crombec, yellow-eyed black flycatcher, white-tailed blue flycatcher, white-tailed crested monarch, narrow-tailed starling, McKinnon's grey shrike, Doherty's bush-shrikes, black-headed waxbill mountain and icterine and yellow-whiskered greenbuls. In addition to the outstanding birding, this road supports a dazzling array of colourful butterflies, and the lovely L'Hoest's monkey is often encountered. Birders who specify their area of interest when they book a walk could ask for one of several UWA guides with above average birding skills, but note that while non-residents pay US$30 either way, residents who ask specifically to go on a birding walk will be charged a fee of US$30 instead of US$15.

Village walk This 3-hour stroll through Buhoma and its margins immerses visitors in the customs and practices of the Bakiga and Batwa people. The tour takes in varied activities such as farming, brewing local beer, dispensing traditional medicines and concludes with dancing displays by members of the Batwa community. The walk is organised through the BMCDA (page 517) and costs US$15 per person.

Batwa visits The most authentic and best regulated Batwa visit is provided by the Batwa Experience (ℓ 039 2888700; m 0772 901628; e info@batwaexperience. com; www.batwaexperience.com), a day-long encounter that takes place in a patch of private forest contiguous with the national park and provides a fascinating insight into the traditional forest life and lore of this hunter-gatherer culture. The experience is organised by the well-regarded Batwa Development Programme and can be arranged through their sales outlet at Batwa Crafts. The outing costs US$85/70/60 per person for groups of one/two or three/four or more. Volunteers get a discount and film crews are charged more.

Dance performances Situated behind Batwa Crafts, the Bwindi Orphan's Group [510 B6], affiliated to the NGO Educate Bwindi (m 0773 132457; educatebwindi@ gmail.com; www.educatebwindi.org), dedicated to helping educate orphaned and disadvantaged Bakiga and Bagisu children living in and around Buhoma.

The name Bwindi derives from the local phrase 'Mubwindi bwa Nyinamukari', which most probably originally referred to the Mubwindi Swamp, near Ruhija in the southeast of the park, rather than to the forest itself. The story behind this name goes back to about a century ago, when, it is said, a family migrating northwards from the Kisoro area found themselves standing at the southern end of a seemingly impenetrable swamp. The parents asked the swamp spirits for guidance, and were told that only if they sacrificed their most beautiful daughter, Nyinamukari, would the rest of the family cross without mishap. After two days of deliberation, the family decided that they could not turn back south, and so they threw the girl into the water to drown, and went on their way safely to the other side. When news of the sacrifice spread, people began to avoid the swamp, calling it 'Mubwindi bwa Nyinamukari' – 'Dark Place of Nyinamukari'.

The forest was proclaimed as the Impenetrable Forest Reserve in 1932, and this remained its official name until 1991 when it was gazetted as a national park and renamed Bwindi. Realising that this local name has less allure to tourists than the colonial name (though the two words are close in meaning), UWA subsequently expanded the name to Bwindi Impenetrable National Park. Today, most people refer to the park as plain Bwindi, though the murderous swamp is still known by the more correct name of Mubwindi.

Traditional dances, supplemented by rather contrived but enjoyable 'gorilla dances', can be arranged on site or at any if the nearby lodges. There is no fixed charge but a significant donation will be welcomed.

RUHIJA

Bwindi's highest and arguably most beautiful gorilla-tracking trailhead, sited at an altitude of 2,340m in the hills abutting the park's eastern boundary, affords fabulous southerly views over forested ridge after forested ridge to the distant Virunga Volcanoes. Equally panoramic views towards the western Rift Valley are offered from sections of the road leading beyond Ruhija towards Buhoma, as well as from the hill a short distance beyond the main cluster of lodges (pages 524–5). Prior to the opening of the Bitakura gorilla group for tracking in 2008, Ruhija was accessible only by very rough roads, and tourist activity was limited to the odd visiting birdwatcher in search of the super-localised green broadbill and various other high-altitude Albertine Rift endemics associated with the area. Recently, however, this backwater status has changed. Three gorilla groups can now be tracked out of Ruhija, which handles a lot of overspill from the upmarket lodges at Buhoma during the peak tourist season. In addition, several mid-range and budget lodges are scattered in and around Ruhija, while the road there from Buhoma or Kabale – though hardly pristine – is sufficiently improved that it is usually negotiable by saloon cars.

GETTING THERE AND AWAY Coming directly from Kampala, the best option is through Kabale, where you'll probably need to spend a night before continuing to Ruhija.

Over the two decades following the European discovery of mountain gorillas, at least 50 individuals were captured or killed in the Virungas, prompting the Belgian government to create the Albert National Park in 1925. This protected what are now the Congolese and Rwandan portions of the Virunga Mountains, and was managed as a cohesive conservation unit.

The gorilla population of the Virungas is thought to have been reasonably stable in 1960, when a census undertaken by George Schaller indicated that some 450 individuals lived in the range. By 1971–73, however, the population had plummeted to an estimated 250. This decline was attributed to several factors, including the post-colonial division of the Albert National Park into its Rwandan and Congolese components, the ongoing fighting between the Hutu and Tutsi of Rwanda, and a grisly tourist trade in poached gorilla heads and hands – the latter used by some sad individuals as ashtrays! Most devastating of all perhaps was the irreversible loss of almost half of the gorillas' habitat between 1957 and 1968 to local farmers and a European-funded agricultural scheme.

In 1979, Amy Vedder and Bill Webber initiated the first gorilla tourism project in Rwanda's Volcanoes National Park, integrating tourism, local education and anti-poaching measures with remarkable success. Initially, the project was aimed mainly at overland trucks, who paid US$20 per person – paltry by today's standards – to track gorillas. Even so, gorilla tourism was raising up to ten million US dollars annually by the mid 1980s, making it Rwanda's third-highest earner of foreign revenue. The mountain gorilla had practically become the national emblem, and was officially regarded to be the country's most important renewable natural resource. To ordinary Rwandans, gorillas became a source of great national pride: living gorillas ultimately created far more work and money than poaching them had ever done. As a result, a census undertaken in 1989 indicated that the local mountain gorilla population had increased by almost 30% to 320 animals.

Despite the success of ecotourism, there are still several threats to the ongoing survival of mountain gorillas in the wild. For the Virunga population, the major threat is undoubtedly political. In 1991, the long-standing ethnic tension between Rwanda's Hutu and Tutsi populations erupted into a civil war that culminated in the genocide of 1994. In context, the fate of a few gorillas does seem a rather trivial concern, even if you take into account the important role that gorilla tourism is playing in rebuilding Rwanda's post-war economy, and the fact that the integrated conservation of their habitat will also protect a watershed that supplies 10% of the country with water.

Nevertheless, the Rwandan conflict had several repercussions in the Virungas. Researchers and park rangers were twice forced to evacuate the Volcanoes National Park, leaving the gorillas unguarded. Tourism to Rwanda practically ceased in 1991, and although gorilla tracking has been available since 1999, tourist arrivals have yet to approach the level of the 1980s. Remarkably, however, when researchers were finally able to return to the Volcanoes National Park in the late 1990s, only four gorillas were unaccounted for. Two were old females who most probably died of natural causes. The other two might have been shot, but could just as easily have succumbed to disease.

But in this most unstable part of Africa, little can be taken for granted. Just as Rwanda started to stabilise politically, the DRC descended into anarchy. For

years, eastern Congolese officials, who lived far from the capital, received no formal salary and were forced to devise their own ways of securing a living, leading to a level of corruption second to none in the region. At least 20 gorillas were killed in the DRC between 1995 and 2007, during most of which time the Congolese Virunga National Park was effectively closed to tourists and researchers alike. Under the circumstances, it is remarkable to learn that the latest Virunga-wide gorilla count, undertaken in 2010, showed a further increase to at least 480 individuals – almost double the number recorded in the early 1970s. The Bwindi population has also increased by around 20% since 1997, with the 2010–11 census returning an estimate of 408 individuals. These figures also suggest that longstanding fears about the vulnerability of habituated gorillas to poachers are far outweighed by the positive effects of the revenue inflow generated by tourism, and the support it has generated among local communities, who receive 10% of tracking permit fees, and also operate community campsites and other grassroots projects outside the national parks.

A more tangible risk associated with tourism is that humans and gorillas are genetically close enough for there to be a real risk of passing a viral or bacterial infection on to a gorilla. To reduce this risk, there is a restriction on the number of people allowed to visit a troop on any given day, and visitors are now forced to wear surgical masks and asked to keep a few metres' distance between themselves and the animals. It is up to individual tourists to forgo their gorilla-tracking permit if they are unwell – easier said than done when you've already spent a small fortune to get all the way to Uganda, but perhaps not if you imagine the consequences if even one individual were to be infected by a contagious disease to which gorillas have no acquired resistance.

Nevertheless, so long as gorilla tourism generates local revenue and employment opportunities, neighbouring communities are more likely to perceive the survival of the gorillas as being in their long-term interest. Without tourism, why would they give a damn? The benefits also extend much further afield: gorilla tracking is the cornerstone of Uganda's (and also Rwanda's) national tourist industry, and the majority of people who come for the gorillas will end up spending money elsewhere in the country, consequently generating foreign revenue and creating employment beyond the immediate vicinities of the mountain gorilla reserves. The end result is a symbiotic situation whereby a far greater number of people, both nationally and internationally, are motivated to take an active interest in the protection of the gorillas than would otherwise be the case.

FRIEND-A-GORILLA (*www.friendagorilla.org*) It's now possible to get involved in gorilla conservation and have fun (a word that doesn't really describe the rewards of tracking them). In 2009, UWA launched the Friend-a-Gorilla initiative which, for a consideration of US$1, enables interested individuals to befriend a mountain gorilla and, through regular online updates, learn more about this animal, its character, family group and interactions. A Geo-Trek link on the website enables you to establish your friend's whereabouts in Bwindi using GPS technology. You can also apply your gorilla friend's thumbnail photo to your Facebook profile (and similar sites).

From Kabale and the southwest Driving from anywhere in southern Kigezi, first head to the village of Ikumba, on the surfaced Kisoro Road 26km out of Kabale, then turn right at the clearly signposted junction (⊕ *-1.12301, 29.87668*) for Ruhija and Buhoma. After 12km, you'll pass through a park entrance gate (security check but no fees payable), from where the road continues through lush forest to reach the Ruhija tracking trailhead and park information office (⊕ *-1.05161, 29.77815*) after another 13km. About 800m past this, a junction to the right (⊕ *-1.04695, 29.77535*) leads outside the park and straight into Ruhija village – site of most of the accommodation servicing the area – after another 500m or so. The road between Ikumba and Ruhija is currently well maintained, but allow 2 hours coming from Kabale, and be aware there are some rocky sections that might deteriorate during rainy season, so if you are setting off in a saloon car, ask for an update first.

A few matatus run back and forth between Kabale and Ruhija on week days (*US$3; 2hrs*). The matatus all overnight in Ruhija, then set off for Kabale in the early morning (typically around 05.00) arriving in time for breakfast. They then spend the morning in Kabale before starting the return trip in the early afternoon, between 13.00 and 16.00. There are no matatus on Saturday, Sunday or public holidays. Alternatively, a special hire is likely to cost around US$70–100, depending on whether it has 4x4, while a boda costs around US$20. Some travellers opt to overnight in Kabale before they go gorilla tracking at Ruhija, but this enforces a very early start and leaves no margin for error in the event of a breakdown or delay.

From Buhoma and the north It's a straightforward 50km, 2-hour drive from Buhoma to Ruhija, passing through the park and some lovely scenery for much of the way, and ideally using the shortcut that avoids Butogota and cuts about 6km from the route passing through that town. Quite a lot of organised tours now use Buhoma as a base for gorilla tracking in Ruhija, in which case a 05.00 start is advisable. Coming from QENP, Kasese, Fort Portal or other sites to the northwest, directions are as for Buhoma, except that when you reach the last junction (⊕ *-0.90618, 29.64535*) 1.5km past Butogota, you need to continue straight towards Ruhija rather than turning right for Buhoma. No public transport runs to Ruhija from the north, but you could presumably arrange a special hire or boda from Butogota.

WHERE TO STAY Lodges at Ruhija are typically more down-to-earth than Buhoma's finest, but rates tend to be far more grounded, too. Except where noted, the places listed below are accessed from a dusty/muddy track that runs through scenically located Ruhija village from a turn-off marked by a cluster of signposts 800m northwest of the Ruhija tracking trailhead. Most of these camps and lodges enjoy terrific views over the forest and adjacent terraced hills, but get chilly at night. Ruhija has a serious water shortage: when it doesn't fall from the sky, it has to be fetched from a valley stream spring located a parachute-worthy distance below the ridge. Consequently, in place of the usual grass thatch, you'll find roofs covered by tiles or corrugated sheets to maximise the potential for rainwater harvesting.

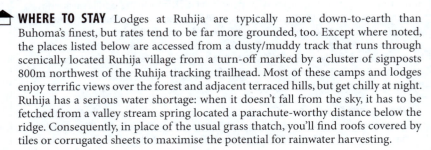

Upmarket

✳ 🏠 Cuckooland Tented Camp [510 C3] (4 tents) ⊕ -1.00084, 29.70796; m 0793 399046; e info@cuckooland.com; www.bwindicuckooland. com. This small tented camp, 10mins' walk from the Buhoma Rd some 15km northeast of

Ruhija, lies in an area of regenerating forest that looks directly into the part of BINP roamed by the Oruzogo Group & is regularly frequented by chimpanzee, black-&-white colobus, red-tailed monkey & L'Hoest's monkey. On-site birdlife is exceptional, while amenities include a natural

swimming pool with aquatic marginal plants & a gym using engine blocks, differential housings, etc, as weights. The prices of the comfortable en-suite standing tents are refreshingly sane. *US$100/136 sgl/dbl B&B, add US$25pp FB.* **$$$$**

☀ 🏠 **Gorilla Mist Camp** [511 H6] (8 rooms) m 0772 563577; e info@gorillamistcamp.com; www.gorillamistcamp.com. This agreeable lodge set in manicured gardens at the north end of Ruhija village is distinguished by its on-the-ball staff & sensible rates. Stilted half-timbered cottages & furnished tents are all en suite with hot water & balconies offering a really fantastic view over the hills. Fair value. *US$137/208 sgl/dbl FB.* **$$$$**

🏠 **Ruhija Gorilla Safari Lodge** [511 H6] (14 rooms) m 0712 187411; e info@asyanuttours-safaris.com; www.asyanuttours-safaris.com. The smartest lodge in Ruhija is set on a hillside that enjoys a terrific view across the forest towards the Virungas & the Rift Valley. The spacious rooms are in semi-detached cottages, some of which have a welcome fireplace. *From US$80/116 standard sgl/dbl room to US$226/374 'superior' cabins. All rates B&B, add US$40pp FB.* **$$$$**

🏠 **Bakiga Lodge** [511 H6] (4 units) m 0774 518421; e info@bakigalodge.org; www.bakigalodge.org. A flagship for the Bakiga Community Project, this super-friendly non-profit lodge in Ruhija village offers the choice of 2 attractively furnished twin tents or 2 open-plan family cabins, all en suite with hot water & a view. *US$160/200 sgl/dbl tent or US$180/250 sgl/dbl cabin. All rates FB.* **$$$$**

Moderate

🏠 **Broadbill Forest Camp** [511 E4] (5 tents) ✪ -1.05781, 29.79623; m 0754 134875; e enquiries@broadbillforest.com; www.broadbillforest.com; see ad, 3rd colour section. This new, likeable tented camp has an isolated location on private land bordering the park & forest about 7km southeast of Ruhija tracking trailhead. Accommodation is in simple but comfortable

en-suite furnished tents whose balconies offer great views into the forest canopy & a glade sometimes visited by Bwindi's elusive elephants. The hands-on owner-manager is a superb naturalist & adept at locating Rwenzori three-horned chameleons as well as some of the rarer birds associated with the Ruhija area. Good value. *US$65/120 sgl/dbl FB.* **$$$**

🏠 **Trekkers Tavern** [511 H6] (5 cottages) m 0772 455423; e accessug@utlonline.co.ug; www.trekkerstavern.com. Set in a patch of woodland beyond Ruhija village, this small lodge offers inferior but correspondingly cheaper copies of the upmarket cottages at Ndali Lodge. The pedigree of the chef ensures a culinary standard. Fair value. *US$100/150 sgl/dbl FB.* **$$$$**

🏠 **Gift of Nature Lodge** [511 E3] (10 rooms) ✪ -1.02936, 29.76755; m 0756 731767. This residential house with rising damp in Mburameizi village 3km from the Ruhija trailhead feels like a standard shoestring guesthouse but at ten times the price. Friendly enough but delusionally overpriced. *US$100/150 sgl/dbl FB.* **$$$$**

Budget & camping

☀ 🏠 **Ruhija Community Rest Camp** [511 H6] (10 rooms) m 0771 846635; e ruhija@gmail.com. Offering an absolutely stunning view over the forest, this community-run camp helps fund local development problems. Very basic but clean en-suite rooms are accessed through a pretty flowering garden in Ruhija village. A restaurant serves meals in the US$5–7 range. Fair value. *US$25/30pp room/cabin, US$10pp camping, all rates B&B.* **$$**

🏠 **Ruhija Gorilla Friends Resort** [511 H6] (13 units) m 0784 905112/0752 619725. This low-key campsite occupies a compact site offering a splendid view over cultivated hills (as opposed to forest) behind Ruhija village. Simple furnished tents have shared facilities but some of the rooms are en suite. *US$30pp tent, US$25/50pp room using common/en-suite shower. All rates B&B, add US$20pp FB.* **$$**

OTHER PRACTICALITIES
There are no banks or internet cafés in Ruhija, but several craft shops line the main road through the village.

TOURIST INFORMATION
ℹ **National Park Reception** m 0785 799901. Situated on the west side of the main road to Kabale 1.3km south of Ruhija village, the Ruhija

tracking trailhead & park information office is the best place to enquire about & pay for all activities out of Ruhija, including gorilla tracking.

WHAT TO SEE AND DO

Gorilla tracking Ruhija opened up as a gorilla-tracking destination in October 2008 following the habituation of the Bitukura Group, which ranges across the steep mountainside between the roadside trailhead on Ruhija Ridge and the Mubwindi Swamp several hundred metres below. Named after a river that runs through its territory, this is an unusual group in two respects: firstly, insofar as four of its 14 members are silverbacks; and secondly, possibly related, in that it split into two separate groups that lived 10km apart in early 2011, only to reunite four months later. Two other habituated groups can now be tracked from Ruhija. The Oruzogo Group, comprising 17 individuals including two silverbacks, opened to tourist visits in 2012 and inhabits the forest running north from Ruhija towards Bwindi Neck. The 19-strong Kyaguliro Group, which was in a state of flux in 2015 following the death of its established silverback and a tussle for power between another silverback and near-silverback, is habituated primarily as a research group, but tracking permits are issued to tourists in peak seasons.

Eight permits are available for each group. These are usually booked solid over June–August and December, but the odds of last-minute availability are good at other times of year. Permits can be booked at the national park offices in Kampala or Kisoro, but are also sold on the spot subject to availability. Trackers must be at the trailhead by 08.00. As with Buhoma, the success rate is practically 100%, but tracking conditions are generally slightly tougher due to the higher altitude and steep slopes.

Forest walks and drives It is permitted to walk or drive unguided along the public road through Ruhija sector, which offers good monkey viewing, with black-and-white colobus particularly common. It's also the part of the park where Bwindi's elephants – occasionally known to rock vehicles – are resident, so caution is required. Because it lies at a higher altitude than Buhoma, the tree composition is more characteristic of Afro-montane than lowland forest, and it supports a significantly different avifauna, making it an essential destination for enthusiasts. It is one of the few places where you stand a chance of seeing all four crimson-wings recorded in Uganda, and other specialities include a variety of apalis species, Lagden's bush-shrike and handsome francolin. The only Ugandan record for yellow-crested helmet-shrike is an unconfirmed sighting at Ruhija.

Guided nature walks out of Ruhija cost US$30/15 FNR/FR. Unlike at Buhoma, it is not really feasible to do any of these hikes on the same day as you track gorillas, so you will also need to pay the US$40/30 park entrance fee. For peak-baggers, the 6-hour **Bamboo Trail** leads to the 2,607m Rwamunyoni Peak, which is the highest point in the park, and notable for good birding. But Ruhija's top birding walk has to be the **Mubwindi Swamp Trail**, which descends several hundred metres from the trailhead to a swampy area that harbours 20 bird species listed in the IUCN *Red Data Book* and/or endemic to the Albertine Rift, notably the extremely localised African green broadbill and Grauer's rush warbler. Technically, it is a 3-hour walk, but dedicated twitchers are likely to take more than twice as long as they stop to look for rarities.

RUSHAGA

Situated at an altitude of 1,900m near the southern tip of BINP, Rushaga became Uganda's newest gorilla tracking site in October 2009, following an unusually high-profile launch wherein a brat pack of American film stars including

Jason Biggs was flown in to make positive statements about the experience. Although Rushaga is less well-known and quieter than Buhoma and Ruhija, and accommodation facilities are generally more low key, there are five habituated gorilla groups in the area, meaning that 40 permits are available daily, while up to six permits are currently available daily for the 'habituation experience' with a sixth group. Scenically, unlike some parts of Bwindi, where you can't see the forest for the proverbial trees, Rushaga offers terrific views across deep jungle-clad valleys as well as glimpses of the Virunga Volcanoes, and there's plenty to attract birders including the localised Rwenzori turaco and Shelley's crimsonwing. All of which means Rushaga is set to grow in popularity, not only with tour operators as a peak-season alternative to gorilla-tracking at Buhoma and Ruhija, but also with independent travellers, overland truck groups and regional expatriates seeking a last-minute permit. Rushaga is also the most accessible of the four trailheads for visitors who opt to track gorillas as a day trip out of Kisoro or Lake Mutanda.

GETTING THERE AND AWAY

By air Rushaga is just 90 minutes' drive from the Cyanika border with Rwanda, and about 3 hours by road from the Rwandan capital Kigali, meaning that catching an international flight to Kigali to track gorillas here is perfectly feasible.

By road Road access to Rushaga is from the south only, via two murram link roads to the main surfaced strip between Kabale and Kisoro. Coming **from Kabale** (or indeed, from anywhere else to the north or east), you need to follow the Kisoro Road for 43km to a signposted junction to the right (✛ *-1.20511, 29.80237*) some 4.5km past the northern tip of Lake Bunyonyi and 3km past Muko. From the junction, it's 24km on dirt to the gorilla tracking trailhead and office at Rushaga (✛ *-1.11643, 29.71009*), culminating in a long and winding descent into the Ruhezanyenda Valley via Rushaga Village.

Approaching **from Kisoro**, it's only 35km to Rushaga via the small town of Rubuguri, and word is that this murram road is soon to be surfaced. Follow the road running northeast towards lakes Mutanda and Mulehe from next to the Kindly filling station (✛ *-1.2823, 29.69693*). After 8km, you'll arrive at a three-way junction (✛ *-1.2235, 29.71628*) where you need to turn right if you want to use the direct route via Rubuguri and stick to the left if you want to follow the more scenic but rougher and slightly (2km) longer route via Lake Mutanda and Hakasharara.

The main focal point of **public transport**, such as it exists, is the small town of Rubuguri, which lies 10km from Rushaga along the road to Kisoro. A few pick-up trucks run between Kisoro and Rubuguri on Monday and Thursday (*US$1; 90mins*) and between Kabale and Rubuguri on Tuesday and Saturday (*US$3; 3hrs*). Transport from Kabale passes within 2km of Rushaga, so if you want to stay there, ask to be dropped at the junction for Rushaga. Coming from Kisoro, you'll need to catch a boda to Rushaga, which costs around US$1.50–2.50 one-way. Alternatively, with a pre-booked permit, you could stay in Rubuguri, and catch a boda through for the day, which costs US$10–15 return.

If pick-ups and bodas don't appeal, then Nshongi Camp can arrange a transfer from Kisoro/Kabale for around US$30/45 for a party of up to five. If you prefer to travel from Kisoro on the day of tracking, a special hire should cost around US$50 and a boda around US$15, and it's advisable to make these arrangements through the national park booking office there.

WHERE TO STAY The main accommodation clusters serving Rushaga are in the village of the same name, which lies immediately outside the entrance gate no more than 15 minutes' walk from the tracking trailhead, and Rubuguri town 10km back along the road to Kisoro. If you're prepared to make an early start, it's also possible to stay in Kisoro or at Lake Mutanda – indeed, the two lodges at the northern end of this lake now function primarily as bases for gorilla tracking at Rushaga. The exclusive Clouds Lodge at Nkuringo, 45 minutes' drive to the west, is also commonly used as a base for tracking at Rushaga.

Upmarket

Gorilla Safari Lodge [511 G1] (11 rooms) 041 4346463; m 0772 470260; e info@ crystalsafaris.com; www.gorillasafarilodge. com. This gem of a lodge stands on a hillside facing the forest only 1km from the Rushaga trailhead. The en-suite cottages are attractively & colourfully decorated in ethnic style, & spread across a pretty garden site surrounded by scattered local homesteads. Good, but is also a touch overpriced. *US$271/424 standard sgl/ dbl, US$295/472 deluxe, all rates FB. Low season discounts & promotions for East African residents available.* **$$$$$**

Moderate

Rushaga Gorilla Camp [511 G1] (11 rooms) m 0774 633331/0752 409510; e info@rushaga.com; www.rushaga.com. This new camp about 1km from the tracking trailhead is under the same management as the ever popular Bunyonyi Overland Camp. It offers the choice of luxury rooms with canvas sides, glass fronts, stone bathrooms & wooden decks with seating & forest views, or a log cabin-like row of smaller en-suite budget rooms with private balcony looking over a eucalyptus plantation. Excellent value. *US$80/120 sgl/dbl B&B luxury, US$40/70 B&B budget, US$10pp camping. Additional meals US$10 each.* **$$$**

Gorilla Valley Lodge [511 H1] (12 cottages) 041 4200221; m 0777 820071; e postmaster@gorillatours.com; www. naturelodges.biz. This latest offering from Nature Lodges has an isolated position on the park boundary 1.5km east of the tracking trailhead as the crow flies, but more like 5km by road. Sprawling across a hillside, the comfortable en-suite cottages all offer views towards the nearby forest canopy. Decent value. *US$95/101 sgl/dbl B&B, add US$25pp FB.* **$$$**

Budget

Nshongi Gorilla Resort [511 E1] (10 rooms) m 0773 127086; e nshongiresort@ yahoo.com; www.nshongigorillaresort.com. This church-built set-up on the northern edge of Rubuguri town has undergone a rather slipshod conversion to accommodate gorilla trackers. There's nothing to admire in the way of location or artisanship & it feels very pricey for what it is. *US$70/100pp B&B/FB.* **$$$**

Wagtail Eco Safari Park [511 E1] (4 rooms & 2 tents) m 0787 719136. This unpretentious facility offers en-suite cottages & furnished tents in a shady compound just off the main road in Rubugeri. *US$40pp B&B, US$10pp camping, meals US$5–10.* **$$$**

Shoestring

Nshongi Camp [511 G1] (4 cottages) m 0774 231913; e nshongicamp@gmail.com; http://nshongicamp.altervista.org. This wonderful budget lodge is set in lush grounds next to a stream bordering the forest & national park, only 5mins' walk downhill from Rushaga village & 15mins' walk from the tracking trailhead. There's great onsite birding & monkey viewing, & even gorillas pass through from time to time. Basic wood-&-mud cottages are lit by kerosene lamp (there's no electricity), & camping is permitted. The friendly staff can arrange reasonably priced transfers from Kabale or Kisoro. *US$34/48 sgl/ dbl B&B, or 48/76 FB, US$4/27pp camping B&B/ FB.* **$$**

Wild Olives Lodge [511 E1] (9 rooms) 039 2591262; e info@wildoliveslodge.com; www.wildoliveslodge.com. This friendly family-run set-up in Rubuguri offers clean en-suite rooms with hot shower & net, set around a courtyard in the style of a typical small-town guesthouse, which is basically what it is. *US$30/50 sgl/dbl bed only. Meals are around US$10 each.* **$$**

TOURIST INFORMATION

National Park Reception m 0782 35420. Situated just inside the eponymous park entrance about 500m from Rushaga village, the Rushaga tracking trailhead and park information office is the best place to enquire about & pay for all activities out of Rushaga, including gorilla tracking.

WHAT TO SEE AND DO

Gorilla tracking When gorilla tracking started up at Rushaga, the habituated Nshongi Group was the largest in Bwindi, comprising 34 individuals including three silverbacks, six blackbacks and eight infants. Since then, the Nshongi Group has split into three groups, while the more recently habituated Businge Group split into two, which means there are five habituated groups at Rushaga, and a total of 40 daily permits. These are Nshongi, Mishaya and Businge (all 10 individuals, one silverback) and the larger Bweza (12 individuals, two silverbacks) and Kahungye (20 individuals, three silverbacks) groups. This means that 40 standard gorilla-tracking permits are available at Rushaga daily. In addition, the Bikingi Group of around 16 individuals is currently being habituated and up to six people daily can join it for the all-day habituation experience, which costs US$1,500 per person.

These 46 permits are more often than not booked up on any given day over June to August, but even in peak season, odds of obtaining a last-minute permit are better than anywhere else in Bwindi. At other times, permits are nearly always available at short notice. They can be bought in the national park office in Kisoro, or on site at the Rushaga tracking trailhead and park information office. Trackers must be at the trailhead by 08.00, and will leave after a short briefing. The success rate is better than 99%, but trackers who are concerned about their age or fitness should let the rangers know, and they will allocate you to the group they expect to be easiest to reach. Usually this will be the Bweza and Nshongi Groups, which are typically less than 2 hours' walk away on relatively easy terrain. Reaching the other three groups usually entails a longer walk of up to 3 hours on steeper terrain.

Nature walks Nature walks are offered at the same fees as elsewhere in Bwindi. Birdlife is broadly similar to Buhoma, and L'Hoest's, blue and red-tailed monkey are often seen, along with black-and-white colobus, while chimpanzees have a large vocal presence but are seldom observed. The 3–4-hour **Waterfall Trail** descends into a steep valley dripping with giant tree ferns, then climbs upwards through a narrow, stream-filled fissure in the cliff face to reach a towering, rock-walled atrium containing a cascade of more than 30m. Outside the park, a candidate for further exploration would seem to be the dramatic and deeply incised Ruhezanyenda River Valley.

NKURINGO

Chronologically Bwindi's second gorilla-tracking trailhead, Nkuringo, which opened in 2004, lies at an altitude of 2,100m on the park's southwestern border north of Kisoro. The surrounding hills are densely settled by farming communities, but have a remote and undeveloped feel, on account of the location on a dead-end road ending at the nearby Congolese border. It is a very scenic area, set along the Nteko Ridge, which provides grandstand views across the Kashasha River Valley into BINP and the forest which cloaks the valley's northern slopes. 'Nkuringo' means 'round stone' and refers to a knoll-like forested hill that's set beside the river, but is dwarfed by loftier ridges above it. To the south and west, superb panoramas include the entire length of the Virunga volcanic range. The International Gorilla Conservation Programme has purchased a 10km-long

20

by 400m-wide strip of public land along the river as a buffer zone for the growth of crops that are not appealing to gorillas and will encourage them to remain in the park.

GETTING THERE AND AWAY

By road Nkuringo trailhead lies in the small village of Ntungamo, which lies 40km/90 minutes north of Kisoro by road, and 90km/3 hours from Kabale via Rubuguri. Coming **from Kisoro**, directions are the same as for Rushaga (page 527), except that you need to turn left at a junction 1km before Rubuguri (✤ *-1.13183, 29.67314*) then continue driving northeast for about 8km to Ntungamo. Coming **from Kabale**, directions are also the same as for Rushaga, except that you need to continue past the last junction for Rushaga for about 10km and turn right 1km past Rubuguri. The dirt sections of these routes are generally in reasonable condition, but a 4x4 vehicle driven at a sensible speed is recommended in wet conditions.

Nkuringo is poorly suited to independent travellers without private transport, since permit availability is often problematic, accommodation is on the pricey side, and public transport, such as it exists, amounts to a few pick-up trucks that run between Kisoro and Rubuguri on Monday and Thursday (*US$1; 90mins*). It would also be possible to pick up public transport to Rubugeri and take a boda from there. Otherwise the only reliable way to reach Ntungamo from Kisoro is by special hire (*US$20–30 one-way*) or boda (*US$5–7*).

On foot/boat The wonderful day-hike from Nkuringo described under the *Getting there and away* section for Buhoma (page 509) can also be walked in reverse. Another option are the two-day canoe and walking safaris from Kisoro via Lake Mutanda organised by Nkuringo Adventure Safaris (page 493).

WHERE TO STAY
Though accommodation in the vicinity of Nkuringo is limited, you'll find additional lodgings in Rubuguri (30–45 minutes distant), Lake Mutanda (45–60 minutes) or Kisoro (60–90 minutes). It's feasible to spend the night in any of these locations and then travel up to Ntungamo in the early morning. Like Ruhija, Ntungamo is located on a lofty ridge and water must be collected as rain or transported from streams in distant valleys. Do bear this in mind when you open a tap or flush a loo.

Exclusive

✱ ⌂ Clouds Mountain Gorilla Lodge
[511 G3] (8 cottages) ☏ 041 4251182; m 0772 489497; e info@wildplacesafrica.com; www. wildplacesafrica.com. This absolutely stunning lodge stands on Nteko Ridge a few mins' walk from the Nkuringo trailhead. It enjoys unparalleled views of the Virunga chain & the western Rift Valley by day & the glowing cone of the active Nyiragongo Volcano by night. Spacious (80m²) cottages incorporate a 2-sofa lounge & bedroom with interconnected fireplace, & bathroom with piping-hot shower. Each is decorated with work by an individual Ugandan artist. The comfort of guests in the main lodge building, a large & airy stone building with massive timber roof beams, is also assured, not least through a generous ratio of 1:8 armchair/sofa spaces per guest. The food is superb, too. *US$795/1220 sgl/dbl including all meals & drinks, with significant low season discounts.* **$$$$$**

Moderate

⌂ **Nkuringo Gorilla Camp** [511 H4] (18 units) m 0774 805580; e nkuringo@ gorillacamp.com; www.nkuringocampsite.com. The old Nkuringo community campground is unrecognisable in its new privately run incarnation as a borderline upmarket lodge whose rooms have generous dimensions, vibrant décor & the

homely atmosphere of a budget hostel. It was rather lacking of any management presence when we dropped by in 2015, but it remains a stunning site with views north across Bwindi towards Buhoma village, Lake Edward & the Rwenzori, & the Virungas to the south. *US$300/418 sgl/dbl cottages, US$200/250 sgl/dbl room with shared bathroom, all rates FB.* $$$$$

Budget
✳ 🏠 **Bwindi Backpackers Lodge**
[511 B5] m 0772 661854; e info@

bwindibackpackerslodge.com; www. bwindibackpackerslodge.com. This appealing roadside set-up 5km before Nkuringo trailhead has a storeyed, half-timbered structure with rooms at the bottom, & a restaurant & stunning forest view above. It's quite smart for an ostensible backpacker lodge, but the vibe is friendly & rates are very reasonable. *US$45/80 B&B en-suite sgl/dbl, US$30/50 B&B sgl/dbl with shared bathrooms, US$15pp dorm bed, US$10pp camping. Additional meals US$5–10.* $$$

TOURIST INFORMATION
ℹ **National Park Reception** m 0773 570094/0772 590018. This is currently on the east side of the road as you enter Nkuringo village, opposite Clouds, but a new building was under construction on the west side next to Clouds in 2015. It is the best place to enquire about & pay for all activities out of Nkuringo, including gorilla tracking.

WHAT TO SEE AND DO
Gorilla tracking One habituated group of gorillas can be tracked at Nkuringo. Until a few years back it comprised 21 individuals, but the two dominant silverbacks went their own ways in 2014, so the original Nkuringo Group now consists of 12 individuals including three silverbacks, while the splinter Bushaho Group contains nine individuals and just one silverback. The latter was being habituated at the time of research and should open to tourism towards the end of 2016, which will bump up the number of permits available from 8 to 16. The Nkuringo Group ranges over a 10km section of the Kashasha River Valley along the boundary of the national park, and though it is usually encountered in the forest, it often ventures out into public lands on the southern slopes of the valley to eat crops. You need to check in at 08.00. Last-minute permit availability is rare at Nkuringo, but this may change once the Bushaho Group opens to tourist visits.

Nkuringo is the most physically challenging of all gorilla-tracking locations. Unlike existing tracking sites at Buhoma and Mgahinga, there is no vehicle access from the Nteko Ridge to the park boundary which follows the Kashasha River. The closest road is the Rubuguri–Nkuringo–Nteko Road on the ridge 600m above the river. Trackers face a steep 1-hour descent simply in order to cross the river and enter the forest. After the arduous but rewarding business of gorilla tracking, you'll face a 1- to 2-hour climb back up to the ridge. This is not a problem for the fit, but Nkuringo is definitely not for the unfit or faint-hearted, though a number of routes have been improved by the addition of steps and gentler switchback turns.

Buniga Community Forest With the tagline, 'Meet the Batwa, then and now', this 3km² patch of regenerating forest (⊕ -1.08016, 29.6268) on the outskirts of Nkuringo village is owned by the local Batwa community and inhabited by a variety of monkeys and birds. A 2–3-hour guided trail through the forest gives you the chance to see it through Batwa eyes, and is usually followed by a visit to the contemporary settlement of Sanuriio, where 150 of the former hunter-gatherers have been resettled about 4km from Nkuringo. Batwa guides demonstrate aspects of their traditional forest life – creating shelter, firing bows and arrows, making fire, identifying medicinal herbs, etc. The enjoyable and informative guided walk

costs US$25 per person (no park fees or UWA guide fees are involved) and can be arranged through Clouds Lodge or Nkuringo Gorilla Camp (pages 530–1), as well as at the NCCDP office (m *0780 846881*) right opposite the forest. Ideally, make arrangements a day in advance.

Hiking Nature walks into the national park can be arranged at the usual UWA rates, but the steep nature of the descent (and ascent) makes it a less-appealing prospect than at the other trailheads. That said, Nkuringo is a superbly scenic area with great potential for hiking outside the forest, though the possibilities for haphazard exploration are pretty limited. The steep nature of Nteko Ridge means that the main alternatives for a pleasant stroll are either west along the ridge-top road towards DRC or east towards Rubugeri. Bear in mind that Ntungamo lies about 8km from the Congolese border and it is a sensitive area. Tourism development has been subject to all manner of evaluations to ensure visitor safety and it's most unlikely that you'd wander off into the DRC, or indeed be allowed to.

Nkuringo community walk This community-run activity provides insights into Bakiga life and culture, with visits to a traditional healer, blacksmith, brewer and homestead in the vicinity of Nkuringo village. The walk costs US$30 per person and can be arranged through Clouds Lodge or Nkuringo Gorilla Camp (pages 530–1).

21

Ankole and Lake Mburo

The modern administrative subregion of Ankole, which lies to the west of Buganda and east of Kigezi, has its roots in an eponymous kingdom established more than 500 years ago. The subregion is administered from Mbarara, a bustling and rapidly growing town – soon to be city – that holds little of interest to tourists, but now ranks as the country's most populous urban area outside the immediate vicinity of Kampala. The main tourist attraction in Ankole is Lake Mburo National Park, a fine savannah reserve whose acacia woodland supports substantial herds of zebra and various antelope, along with an increasingly visible population of leopards and recently introduced giraffes. Lake Mburo makes for a great overnight stop between the far southwest and Kampala, and it's also the only place in Uganda to offer horseback safaris. The most worthwhile cultural site in Ankole, the fine museum at the Igongo Cultural Centre, 15km east of Mbarara, is a popular place to stop for lunch and a leg stretch *en route* to or from Kampala.

HISTORY

The ancient kingdom of Ankole (also known as Nkore) was founded c1500 in the power vacuum created by the demise of the Bachwezi. Although Ankole was a centralised polity like Buganda or Bunyoro, its social structure differed from the other pre-colonial kingdoms of present-day Uganda insofar as it recognised two rigidly stratified but interdependent castes: the pastoralist Bahima nobility and the agriculturist Bairu peasantry. Ankole was ruled by a hereditary king, called the *omugabe*, a role reserved for prominent members of the Bahinda clan of the Bahima. The omugabe was served by an appointed *enganzi* (prime minister) and a number of local chiefs.

Ankole rose to regional prominence in roughly 1700, after Omugabe Ntare IV Kiitabanyoro, the 11th in the dynasty, defeated the Banyoro army (Kiitabanyoro means 'Killer of the Banyoro'). By the mid 19th century, the kingdom, bounded by the Katonga River in the north and the Kagera River in the south, extended from east of Lake Mburo to the shores of Lake Albert. After 1875, however, Ankole went into decline, attributable partly to a combination of disease and drought, but primarily to the rejuvenation of Bunyoro under Kabalega, who might well have co-opted Ankole into his realm were it not for outside intervention.

In 1898, the 21-year-old Omugabe Kahaya II, then just three years into a troubled five-decade reign, decided that the only way to safeguard his kingdom against Bunyoro was to enter into an alliance with the British administration in Buganda. Three years later, the kingdom was incorporated into the British Protectorate of Uganda on 25 October 1901 with the signing of the Ankole agreement. The Ankole royalty became increasingly irrelevant and powerless during the course of the colonial era, and it was abolished by President Obote in 1967. Unlike the other traditional monarchies of Uganda, it has never been restored (see box, page 541).

Situated 260km southwest of Kampala at the junction of the main roads running south to Kabale and Bwindi and north to QENP and Kasese, Mbarara is a rapidly growing town that now ranks as Uganda's largest urban centre outside the environs of greater Kampala. It hasn't always been this way. In 1955, when Alan Forward arrived here to serve as the new district officer, he found himself 'choking in the dust' of what 'seemed to have the atmosphere of a one-horse town'. Even as recently as 1992, when the first edition of this guidebook was researched, Mbarara was a sleepy and nondescript kind of place, its moribund infrastructure still visibly scarred by the Tanzanian invasion during the Amin era. By contrast, post-millennial Mbarara has evolved into what is surely the only urban centre in western Uganda to which the adjectives 'modern' or 'vibrant' could be applied without any hint of facetiousness. Yet, paradoxically, while it boasts a selection of business hotels and well-stocked shops as good as any in western Uganda, the former are aimed mostly at the conference market, and the town lacks for any genuinely scintillating sightseeing. That said, Mbarara does posses a certain contemporary urban buzz, particularly along its hectic High Street, that makes refreshingly few concessions to tourism. For adrenalin junkies, meanwhile, there's the prospect of interacting with Uganda's most psychotic drivers as they do their best to curb Mbarara's rapidly growing population by mowing down any pedestrian or boda that ventures close to their line of trajectory. More sedately, and less centrally, the museum at the Igongo Cultural Centre is worth an hour of your time, while the Nkokonjeru Tombs are the burial place of the last two kings of Ankole.

HISTORY In 1898, John Macallister, a former railway engineer, was dispatched westward from Buganda to establish a British government station and fort in the Kingdom of Ankole. In January 1899, Macallister settled on a site called Muti, which had served as the capital of Omugabe Ntare V Rugingiza a few years earlier, when Captain Lugard visited Ankole. Muti had been abandoned in the interim, thanks to a smallpox epidemic that claimed the lives of several prominent citizens and one of Ntare V's sons, but Macallister was impressed at the site's eminent defendability and the presence of perennial water supply in the form of the Rwizi River. That the station built at Muti was called Mbarara evidently stemmed from some confusion on the part of Macallister. Mbarara (or more correctly Mburara, after a type of grass that grows locally) was actually the name of the site of another of Ntare's short-lived capitals, situated a few kilometres from the abandoned Muti.

Whatever other merits it possessed, the site selected by Macallister had one serious drawback. 'The more one journeys about', wrote the missionary J J Willis, 'the more one is impressed with the fact that [Mbarara] is the one spot in all Ankole where you have to march a whole day or two days before you come on any cultivation worth the name.' The scarcity of food around Mbarara was rooted less in the area's geography than in local cultural attitudes – the Bahima, like so many other African pastoralists, had no tradition of cultivation. The British administration, supported by Enganzi Mbaguta, did much to encourage the growth of agriculture in Ankole during the early years of the 20th century. In 1905, Mbaguta remarked that, following the establishment of Mbarara, the annual famines were 'becoming yearly less severe'. Within a few years, the new capital of Ankole, accorded township status in 1906, would be practically self-sufficient in food, and its future role as the main centre of trade in Ankole secure.

Mbarara grew slowly during the colonial era. Indeed, following a census undertaken in the late 1950s, it was too small to be ranked among 12 towns countrywide whose

On 19 May 1905, Harry St George Galt, stabbed to death on the veranda of the government resthouse at Katooma in northern Ankole, earned the unwanted distinction of becoming the only British administrative officer in Uganda ever to be murdered. The circumstances of Galt's death have never been satisfactorily explained. The killer was identified, somewhat tenuously, as a local man called Rutaraka, said to have been acting strangely prior to the murder, and found dead shortly afterwards in circumstances that may or may not have implicated suicide. If Rutaraka did kill Galt, it is widely believed somebody in authority enlisted his services, but nobody knows exactly who: a local Saza chief, tried and convicted for conspiracy in Galt's murder at a court in Kampala, later succeeded in having the ruling overturned on the basis of tainted evidence. Whatever else, as famous last words go, those uttered by the unfortunate Galt surely deserve greater recognition. According to an article by H F Morris in the *Uganda Journal* of 1960, the mortally wounded officer 'called for his cook, said 'Look, cook, a savage has speared me', and thereupon fell down dead'.

Katooma, the site of the murder, lies about 75km north of Mbarara and only 3km from Ibanda, a substantial junction town on the soon to be asphalted road north to Fort Portal via Kamwenge. A 3m-tall cairn-like memorial of piled stones was erected a few days after the event at Katooma, which lies along the Kagongo Road coming from Ibanda. Recent reports suggest the pyramidal memorial fell into disrepair a few years back, but the Ibanda Town Clerk recently resolved to renovate and beautify the site and to promote it as a tourist attraction.

population exceeded 4,000. It remained something of a one-horse town in the 1990s, but by the turn of the millennium it had grown to become one of the ten largest towns in Uganda, with a population of almost 70,000 in 2002. Mbarara has developed rapidly since then, partly due to its strategic importance as a regional transport hub at the junction of roads connecting Kampala to Rwanda, Burundi, Tanzania and the DRC, but also as a result of increased industrialisation and government investment. Surprisingly, Mbarara now ranks as Uganda's third-largest urban area (or second, if you count Kira as a satellite of Kampala), supporting a population of 195,000 according to the 2014 census. In 2015, central government approved its application for city status, an upgrade that should come to pass in 2017.

GETTING THERE AND AWAY Mbarara is a major route focus, situated at the junction of the surfaced roads east to Kampala via Masaka, southwest to Kabale and Kisoro, and northwest to Fort Portal via QENP and Kasese. Distances and approximate driving times in a private vehicle are 50km/1 hour to Lake Mburo National Park (Sanga Gate), 140km/2 hours to Masaka, 270km/4–5 hours to Kampala, 115km/1½–2 hours to Katunguru (QENP), 145km/2–3 hours to Kasese, 235km/4 hours to Fort Portal, 140km/2½ hours to Kabale, and 180km/3–4 hours to Buhoma (Bwindi).

Using **public transport**, Swift Safaris (m *0702 529663/230160;* f *fb.me/swift. safaris.1*) runs a reliable and comfortable coach service between Kampala's Sisenyi Bus Terminus and Mbarara's central taxi park. These buses leave every 30 minutes in either direction between 05.30 and 20.30, and come with five (as opposed to the usual six) seats per aisle, as well as Wi-Fi and charging points (*US$5; 4–5hrs*). The central

Ankole and Lake Mburo MBARARA

21

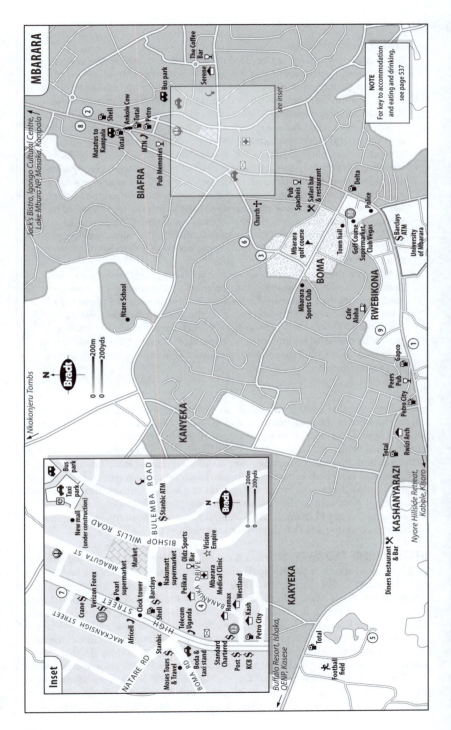

MBARARA

NOTE For key to accommodation and eating and drinking, see page 537

Jack's Bistro, Igongo Cultural Centre, Lake Mburo NP, Masaka, Kampala

Nkokonjeru Tombs

The Coffee Bar

Serene

Bus park

Ankole Cow

Total Petro

Matatus to Kampala

Shell

Total

MTN

Pub Memories

BIAFRA

See inset

Church

Pub Spacheis

Safari bar & restaurant

Delta

Police

Mbarara golf course

Town hall

Golf Course Supermarket, Club Vegas

Barclays ATM

University of Mbarara

BOMA

Mbarara Sports Club

Cafe Aloha

RWEBIKONA

Sapco

Peers Pub

Petro City

Rwizi Arch

Total

KANYEKA

Ntare School

KASHANYARAZI

Diners Restaurant & Bar

Nyore Hillside Retreat, Kabale, Kisoro

KAKYEKA

Total

Football field

Buffalo Resort, Ishaka, QENP, Kasese

Inset

Bus park

Taxi park

New mall (under construction)

Mackansigh Street

Crane

Verizon Forex

HIGH STREET

Stanbic

Africell

Clock tower

Shell

Pearl supermarket

Barclays

MBAGUTA ST

Telecom Uganda

Market

Nakumatt supermarket

Pelikan

Oldz Sports Bar

BISHOP WILLIS ROAD

BULEMBA ROAD

Stanbic ATM

Vision Empire

Mbarara Medical Clinic

BANANUKA DRIVE

Westland

Romax

Kash

Petro City

Standard Chartered

Post

KCB

Moses Tours & Travel

BOMA RD

NATARE RD

Boda boda & taxi stand

taxi park is also the place to pick up matatus to Ishaka (*US$2.50*), Ibanda (*US$3.30*), Kasese via Katunguru (*US$5*), Kabale (*US$5*) and Kisoro (*US$10*).

WHERE TO STAY   *Map, opposite*

Mbarara boasts an extraordinary number of hotels, most of them falling at the superior end of the budget range and catering mainly to the conference market, but which are also perfectly adequate for unfussy tourists. The main central cluster, strung along Bananuka Drive, comprises about half-a-dozen similarly priced hotels of which the pick is the **Hotel Oxford Inn** (*35 rooms;* \ *048 5661167;* m *0783 821880; US$26.70/28.30/33/50 B&B sgl/twin/dbl/suite,* **$$**). The smartest lodge in the vicinity of Mbarara is the Igongo Country Hotel at Biharwe, 15km along the Masaka Road (page 540). The listings below are highly selective.

Upmarket

Lake View Resort Hotel (80 rooms)
\ 048 5422112; m 0772 367972;
e info@lakeviewresorthotel.co.ug; www.
lakeviewresorthotel.co.ug. Mbarara's largest hotel lies in expansive green grounds set around a papyrus-lined manmade lake off the Fort Portal Road, some 2km northwest of the town centre. It's a definite notch down from the Igongo Country Hotel in terms of quality, but it's also substantially cheaper & more central, & facilities include specious well-equipped rooms, free Wi-Fi, swimming pool, gym & sauna. *US$65/80/120 B&B sgl/dbl/suite.* **$$$**

Moderate

 Nyore Hillside Retreat (4 cottages)
✪ -0.6805, 30.44176; m 0791 738746/0783 356142; e info@nyoreretreat.com; www.

nyoreretreat.com. Aimed more at people heading on Kigezi than as a base for exploring Mbarara, this wonderful owner-managed lodge is set in a flowering hillside garden near the village of Nyakaguruka, 25km along the Kabale Rd. The bright stone-&-thatch en-suite cottages are individually decorated, & there is also a campsite with the option of hiring a tent. The restaurant, earthily decorated with stone, wood & cane, serves tasty grills, stews & salads in the US$6–7 range, & gives a commanding view of the surrounding steep terraced slopes, which offer plenty of walking possibilities & are teeming with birds & butterflies. The retreat lies 2km south of Nyakaguruka along a dirt road, and the junction (✪ -0.66735, 30.44556) is clearly signposted. *From US$40/67/100 B&B sgl/dbl/family cottage. Camping US$6 per tent, or US$11.50/16.50 to rent a sgl/dbl tent.* **$$$**

Acacia Hotel (40 rooms) 7 High St; \ 039 2916391; m 0779 494447; e acaciahotel@live. com; www.skyblue-hotels.com. This relatively smart & central hotel has spacious modern rooms with queen-sized bed, net, fan, flatscreen DSTV & Wi-Fi. There's ample secure parking & a decent restaurant with garden seating serving grills, pasta, Indian & local dishes in the US$5–8 range. *US$30/43 B&B sgl/dbl.* **$$**

Agip Motel (13 rooms) Masaka Rd;
\ 048 5421615; m 790 916739;
e reservations@agipmotelmbarara.co.ug; www. agipmotelmbarara.co.ug. Once the top hotel in Mbarara & still a well-known landmark on the Kampala side of town, the Agip really has seen better days; the small carpeted rooms with fan, DSTV & en-suite hot shower are in pressing need of refurbishment to justify the relatively high asking price. *US$39/59/79 B&B sgl/dbl/suite.* **$$$**

Budget

✳ 🏠 **Little Woods Inn** (16 rooms) Muti Rd; ☎ 039 2175573; m 0752 459618; e info@littlewoodsinn.com; www.littlewoodsinn.com. Set in quiet green suburban grounds less than 500m from the main road, this well-managed & professionally staffed new inn is the closest thing in Mbarara to a boutique hotel, though it's perhaps a little too downmarket to quite fit that label. Bright, clean, tastefully furnished rooms come with ¾ or twin beds, fitted net, writing desk, flatscreen DSTV, quality fittings & modern bathroom with hot shower. A highly rated restaurant with cane-&-wood furniture & garden seating serves a cosmopolitan selection of salads & grills (the whole fish & burgers are particularly recommended) in the US$4.50–6.50 range, & it also has a varied selection of desserts & espresso machine. Other facilities include safe parking, free Wi-Fi, book swap & back-up generator. Exceptional value. *US$27/31 B&B sgl/twin.* **$$**

🏠 **University Inn** (20 rooms) High St; ☎ 040 5420334; m 0784 839194. Built in 1933, this fabulously outmoded but nonetheless likeable hotel lies in magnificent wooded grounds that shield the traffic noise from the main road. Rooms are variable in size & quality, & looking quite rundown as things stand, but extensive refurbishment is planned in the near future. There's a bar & restaurant with garden seating in thatched summer houses. Camping is permitted. *US$14/21/24 B&B sgl/dbl/twin.* **$$**

🏠 **Ruhanga Uganda Lodge** (20 bandas) m 0701 536197/0774 768090; e info@ugandalodge.com; www.ugandalodge.com. Situated in Ruhanga on the Kabale Rd 50km past Mbarara, this guesthouse operates as a social enterprise whose profits go towards helping the local community. It accommodates both passing visitors & long- or short-term volunteers in 1–4 bed bandas, all with bedding, nets, hot showers & electric power points. Meals are freshly cooked on a help-yourself basis. Set near the eastern limit of the Kigezi Highlands, the lodge offers plenty of scope to explore the surrounding hills & visit markets, lakes & hot springs. Volunteer accommodation & projects are available. *US$22pp FB.* **$$**

🏠 **New Classic Hotel** (24 rooms) High St; m 0772 666107. Centrally located & close to the main taxi park, this otherwise unexceptional hotel has clean rooms with fan, net, DSTV, Wi-Fi & en-suite hot tub/shower. *US$25/32 B&B sgl/dbl.* **$$**

Shoestring

🏠 **Tobiz Guesthouse** (20 rooms) Masaka Rd; m 0782 872418. The spotless, spacious & well-equipped rooms at this well-priced multi-storey lodge opposite the Agip all come with fan, DSTV & en-suite hot shower. *US$8.50/13.50/17 sgl/dbl/king size.* **$**

🏠 **Hotel Boma** (15 rooms) Johnstone Rd; ☎ 048 5421210; m 0779 491097. Boasting a quiet location in large gardens opposite the golf course 500m southwest of the town centre, this timeworn hotel is one of Mbarara's most agreeable shoestring options. The en-suite rooms, though a little threadbare, are clean & have nets & hot showers. Indian food can be prepared by request. *US$5.30/7.30/10 sgl/dbl/twin.* **$**

✖ WHERE TO EAT AND DRINK *Map, page 536*

In addition to the places listed below, several of the hotels recommended above have good restaurants, with the Little Woods Inn and Lake View Regency Hotel being the picks of the more central options. In addition, for those passing through Mbarara *en route* to Kabale, the out-of-town Nyore Hillside Retreat makes for a scenic lunch stop, but safest to call ahead with your order.

Numerous bars and *muchomo* (meat) joints come to life at night in the Wrebekona market area just up the Fort Portal Road. They serve cheap drinks and barbecue tilapia, pork, chicken and goat with matoke, cabbage and the like.

✖ **Ark Café** Lower Circular Rd; ☎ 048 5443046; m 0702 612282; e info@cafeark.co.ug; www.cafeark.co.ug; ⏰ 07.30–midnight daily. This excellent 1st-floor restaurant opposite the golf course has a long & varied menu embracing salads, soups, burgers, pasta, grills, Indian dishes & several vegetarian selections. There's also free Wi-Fi, comfortable leather seating indoors, a terrace, excellent fresh coffee & ice-cream, & a disco from 21.00 over weekends. *Most mains in the US$5–7 range.*

Jack's Bistro ✦ -0.59181, 30.66838; 📱 0758 966903; 🕐 09.00–midnight daily. Despite the rather off-putting setting above a filling station 1km out of town along the Masaka Rd, this modern 1st-floor bistro is an attractive place to dine, with a backdrop of contemporary Western music &/or DSTV, & the choice of indoor & balcony seating. The long & varied menu serves sandwiches, burgers, pizza, pasta, Indian dishes, steak & Chinese-style sizzlers. *Meals in US$6–7 range.*

Ben's Organic Restaurant High St; 🕐 07.00–20.00 Mon–Sat. Tucked away in an alley next to Verizon Forex, this popular local eatery prides itself on serving traditional steamed foods rather than the fried fare than has increasingly come to dominate local menus. Great value, too. *Around US$2.50 for a filling main.*

Buffalo Resort ✦ -0.60241, 30.61855; 📞 039 2829250; 📱 0777 188418; 🕐 08.00–23.00 daily. Situated about 4km out of town on the north side of the Fort Portal Rd, this thatched restaurant set in pleasant gardens serves an excellent buffet lunch complete with soup & fruits. *US$4.30pp.*

Tuwezera Confectionary Shop Bananuka Dr; 🕐 07.00–21.00 daily. Centrally located around the corner from the Standard Chartered Bank, this snack-friendly bakery sells a selection of sweet & savoury pies, cakes, donuts, samosas & mini-pizzas. *Most under US$1.*

BARS AND NIGHTSPOTS

☆ **Club Vegas** Lower Circular Rd; www.cafeark.co.ug, 🕐 15.00–late. Set on the 2nd floor of the same building as Ark Café, & under the same management, this rooftop cocktail bar is an attractive sundowner spot that transforms into a pumping music venue late at night.

🍷 **The Coffee Bar** Bulemba Rd; 📞 039 2080805; 📱 0702 162444; 🗗 fb.me/coffeebarmbarara; 🕐 08.00–01.00 daily. More sports bar than coffee shop in feel, this is a popular place to watch Premier League football & knock back a few beers at weekends, & it also hosts occasional live music. A good selection of hot & iced coffees, mostly at around US$2 a shot, is supplemented by excellent ice-cream & a varied snack menu.

🍷 **Pub Spacheis** High St; 📱 0776 907890/0706412042; 🗗 fb.me/spacheis; 🕐 24hrs daily. This brightly decorated & well-stocked bar on the main road has indoor & terrace seating.

🍷 **Peers Pub** High St. Set on a roadside terrace 200m before the turn-off to Kasese, this pub with indoor & outdoor seating is a smart place for drinks & BBQ snacks.

☆ **Vision Empire** Bananuka Dr; 📱 0791 532473; 🕐 24hrs daily. Mbarara's top nightclub is dark & noisy but has a more exclusive upstairs area to which one can escape.

SHOPPING

Lack of parking opportunities makes shopping in the busy town centre a frustrating experience, though those should improve once the new bypass opens to divert passing traffic that is currently forced to use the main road through town. Nevertheless, it's worth a little hassle to visit the Mbarara branch of **Nakumatt** (*Bulemba Rd; www.nakumatt.netl* 🕐 *08.30–22.00 Mon–Sat, 10.00–22.00 Sun*), which is surely the country's best supermarket outside Kampala. Alternatively, and less of a headache for parking, the **Golf Course Supermarket** (*Lower Circular Rd;* 📞 *0702 974729;* 🗗 *fb.me/GolfCourseSupermarket;* 🕐 *24hrs daily*), in the same building as the Ark Café, is very well stocked, especially when it comes to imported packaged goods, wines and spirits.

OTHER PRACTICALITIES

Foreign exchange and banking

Most of the major banks, including Stanbic, Standard Chartered and Barclays, are represented, and have foreign exchange facilities and 24-hour ATMs that accept international cards. Private bureaux de changes include Verizon Forex on the High Street.

Internet

There are several internet cafés along the High Street.

Swimming Day visitors can use the swimming pool at the Lake View Resort Hotel (page 537) for a small fee.

TOUR OPERATORS

Moses Tours & Travel Room No 19A, URA Bldg (next to Stanbic Bank), Boma Rd; m 0772 422825/0752 422825. Mbarara's 1st choice for tours & vehicle hire.

WHAT TO SEE AND DO The main tourist attractions in the vicinity of Mbarara are the Igongo Cultural Centre and Lake Mburo National Park, both covered under separate headings later in the chapter.

Nkokonjeru Tombs The last two kings of Ankole, Omugabe Edward Solomon Kahaya II, who died in 1944, and Omugabe Sir Charles Godfrey Rutahaba Gasyonga II, who ruled from 1944 until 1967 and died in 1982, were buried at Nkokonjeru 3km northwest of central Mbarara. Unfortunately, by comparison to the impressive and lovingly tended royal tombs at Kasubi and Mparo, Nkokonjeru is utterly anticlimactic: two bland concrete slabs protected within a rundown colonial-style tiled house. To get there, follow Ntare Road out of town for 1.5km, then just after it curves sharply to the left, take a right turn and continue for another 800m to a three-way junction whose central fork leads to the tomb after 500m.

IGONGO CULTURAL CENTRE

Set in neat gardens abutting the Masaka Road 15km east of Mbarara, this smart new multi-faceted development has quickly become a popular lunch stop *en route* between sites further west and Kampala. The centre incorporates a modern and well-organised museum that achieves its goal of preserving and promoting the history and culture of the dormant Ankole Kingdom with far greater success than any similar installation associated with Uganda's officially recognised kingdoms. Other facilities include the most upmarket hotel in the vicinity of Mbarara, as well as a good restaurant that serves a top-notch buffet lunch, a well-stocked craft and book shop, and clean toilets. Something of an annex to the centre is the Biharwe Eclipse Monument, which stands conspicuously on the opposite hill having been unveiled by President Museveni in August 2014.

GETTING THERE AND AWAY Prominently signposted, Igongo (⊕ -0.52183, 30.73998) stands on the north side of the Masaka Road in a village called Biharwe. For those without private transport, any matatu running east from Mbarara can drop you at the entrance, or you could take a boda.

WHERE TO STAY Most visitors to Igongo just stop there for an hour or two in passing, but the centre now also boasts its own upmarket hotel.

Igongo Country Hotel (52 rooms) 039 2722828/9; e reservations@igongo.co.ug; www.igongo.co.ug. Situated in Biharwe 15km out of town along the Kampala Rd, this new hotel in the Igongo Cultural Centre is comfortably the swankiest in the vicinity of Mbarara. The ostentatious lobby, complete with instrumental muzak & AC, leads through to an attractively decorated restaurant, while the stylish rooms – split between the main building & a cluster of garden cottages – all come with colourful fabrics, dark-wood furniture, large flatscreen DSTV, fridge, queen-sized bed, writing desk & a spacious modern bathroom. *From US$100/120 B&B sgl/dbl.* **$$$$**

The untended state of the Nkokonjeru Tombs is symptomatic of a popular ambivalence to the Ankole royalty that stretches back to the early years of independence. In 1967, the constitutional abolition of the monarchies under Obote was hotly protested in Buganda, Bunyoro and Toro. In Ankole, by contrast, the reaction was closer to muted indifference. In 1971, Idi Amin opened a short-lived debate with regard to reinstating all the ancient monarchies, a notion that garnered strong support in Buganda and elsewhere. Not so in Ankole, where a committee of elders signed a memorandum stating that the matter 'should not be raised or even discussed', since it would 'revive political divisions and factionalism' and stand in the way of the 'march forward to our stated goal of freedom and progress'.

The widespread anti-royalist sentiment in Ankole is so fundamentally at odds with popular attitudes in the other kingdoms of Uganda that it requires explanation. Two main factors can be cited. The first is that the traditional social structure of Ankole, like that of pre-colonial Rwanda but not of Buganda or Bunyoro, was informed by a rigid caste system. For the majority of Banyankole – who are of Bairu descent – reinstating the Bahima monarchy would smack of retrogression to that obsolete caste system. Secondly, Ankole, as it was delineated from the early colonial era until post-independence, was an artificial entity, one that encompassed several formerly independent kingdoms – Igara, Sheema, Bweju and parts of Mpororo – that had no prior historical affiliation or loyalty to the omugabe.

Ankole is the only one of the ancient Ugandan kingdoms that was not officially restored by Museveni in 1993. And although the recognised heir to the throne John Patrick Barigye was clandestinely crowned as Omugabe Ntare VI in November of that year, Museveni annulled the ceremony immediately afterwards. Following Barigye's death in October 2011, his 21-year-old son Charles Aryaija Rwebishengye was installed as crown prince of Ankole, and vowed to continue lobbying for the restoration of the kingdom, but it seems unlikely anything of the sort will happen in the foreseeable future.

✖ WHERE TO EAT AND DRINK

✖ **Kaahwa Kanuzire Restaurant** m 0705 867027/0782 553564; www.igongo.co.ug; ⏱ 10.00–23.00 daily. This smart garden restaurant is well known for its daily lunchtime buffet (⏱ *noon–15.30*), which is very popular with tour groups. An à la carte menu of Ankole & continental dishes is available at other times. *Buffet US$8.30, main menu dishes in the US$5–7 range.*

WHAT TO SEE AND DO

Igongo Museum (m *0704 629921;* e *museum@igongo.co.ug; www.igongo.co.ug;* ⏱ *07.00–20.00 daily; entry US$6.70/1.70 foreigners/East African residents*) Arguably the finest museum anywhere in Uganda, Igongo houses a number of detailed and well-annotated displays covering everything from the development of currency in Uganda to traditional Ankole and Bakiga dress, drums and other musical instruments, agricultural practices and herbal medicine. There are also plenty of informative displays relating to the foundation and history of the Ankole and Bakiga Kingdom and its rulers, and to the 18th-century warrior queen Kitami kya Nyawera, whose murder by a rival king presaged a series of local disasters and led to the establishment of the Nyabingi cult at her shrine in

the vicinity of Lake Bunyonyi. All in all, it's is a veritable treasure trove for those with the time and interest.

Biharwe Eclipse Monument (*Make arrangements with the museum ticket office at Igongo; US$6.70/1.70 foreigners/East African residents*) This striking hilltop monument – comprising a golden orb supported by a trio of pillars representing the three kings of Bunyoro, Ankole and Buganda – commemorates a historic solar eclipse associated with the emergence of the Ankole Kingdom. Oral history holds that the collapse of Bachwezi in the 15th century led to the formation of several smaller polities of which Bunyoro initially emerged as the most powerful. In the early 16th century, Omukama Olimi I of Bunyoro took advantage of his prowess by orchestrating a series of cattle raids that depopulated what are now Buganda and Ankole of livestock, and led to a devastating famine. The tide of events turned when one day the sky fell ominously dark during daylight hours, prompting the terrified omukama to flee back to Bunyoro, leaving behind a large number of stolen cattle, from which the Ankole people were able to start breeding new herds. This incident is now regarded to be the only accurately datable event in the region's early history, since the ominous darkening of the sky witnessed by the omukama was almost certainly the solar eclipse of AD1520.

LAKE MBURO NATIONAL PARK

Extending over 260km² of undulating territory in southern Ankole, Lake Mburo National Park (LMNP) is an underrated gem dominated scenically by the eponymous lake, whose forest-fringed shores hemmed in by rolling green hills recall Kenya's more celebrated Lake Naivasha. Until recently, LMNP, despite its relative accessibility, was bypassed by the majority of safaris and independent travellers due to its low 'big five' count, in particular the lack of elephant and infrequent presence of lion. These days, however, the park is an increasingly popular overnight stop *en route* between Bwindi or QENP and Kampala, as well as being a popular weekend break from the capital. In part, this is because it offers some excellent game viewing, despite the absence of the aforementioned heavyweights. Indeed, visitors are now likely to see as many different large mammal species over the course of a day as they would in any Ugandan national park. LMNP is also a great interest to birders for its wealth of acacia-associated and aquatic species, while more active travellers have the opportunity to view wildlife on horseback, on foot, or from a mountain bike.

FEES Entrance to Lake Mburo National Park costs US$30/40 FR/FNR per 24 hours. The standard vehicle entrance fees are also charged (see box, page 32), but only once per entry. Since the introduction of the new card system (*www.ugandawildlife.org/wildlife-card*), entrance fees can theoretically be paid only at the UWA reservations office in Kampala or at Sanga Entrance Gate, though in practice it seems that Nshaara Gate also takes cash payments for fees. Activity fees can be paid for in cash at the office in Rwonyo.

GEOGRAPHY AND VEGETATION Spanning altitudes of 1,220m to 1,828m, LMNP is a hilly park underlaid by pre-Cambrian granitic rocks and sandy soils. Although the park has a relatively low average annual rainfall of around 800mm, some 20% of its surface area consists of wetland habitats. The most important of these is Lake Mburo, which extends over some 13km² and is fringed by lush riparian woodland and significant areas of papyrus swamp. Mburo is the largest of five lakes that lie within

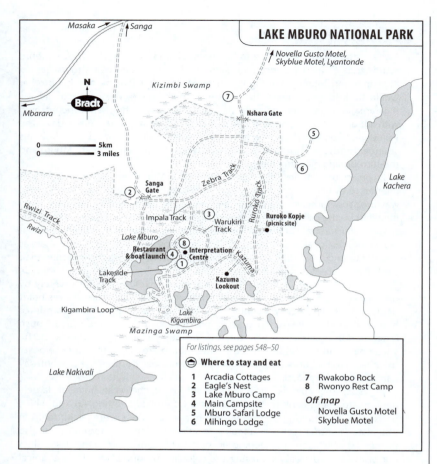

LAKE MBURO NATIONAL PARK

Kizimbi Swamp

Nshara Gate

↑ Novella Gusto Motel,
Skyblue Motel, Lyantonde

Masaka ↗ ↑ Sanga

← Mbarara

N
Bradt

0 ———— 5km
0 ———— 3 miles

Lake Kachera

Zebra Track

Sanga Gate

Rwizi Track

Rwizi

Impala Track

Warukiri Track

Ruroko Kopje (picnic site)

Lake Mburo
Restaurant & boat launch

Interpretation Centre

Lakeside Track

Kazuma Lookout

Kigambira Loop

Lake Kigambira

Mazinga Swamp

Lake Nakivali

For listings, see pages 548–50

Where to stay and eat

1 Arcadia Cottages
2 Eagle's Nest
3 Lake Mburo Camp
4 Main Campsite
5 Mburo Safari Lodge
6 Mihingo Lodge
7 Rwakobo Rock
8 Rwonyo Rest Camp

Off map
Novella Gusto Motel
Skyblue Motel

the park boundaries, and the second-most westerly component in a chain of 16 lakes and connecting swamps fed by the Rwizi River on its course from Mbarara to Lake Victoria. The remainder of LMNP supports a cover of open savannah and woodland dominated by thorny acacia trees such as *Vachellia hockii*, *V. gerrardii*, *V. sieberiana* and *Senegalia polyacantha*. It is thought that the absence of elephant in recent decades has contributed to the transformation of many areas of savannah to thicket. The park's western savannah is interspersed with rocky ridges and forested gorges.

WILDLIFE LMNP harbours several **mammal** species not easily observed elsewhere in the country. It supports Uganda's only remaining population of impala, the handsome antelope for which Kampala is named, and is one of only two national parks where Burchell's zebra occurs. Other antelope species likely to be seen by casual visitors are topi, common duiker, oribi, Defassa waterbuck, Bohor reedbuck and bushbuck – the latter, rather unusually, often seen standing sentinel on top of thicketed termite mounds. The sitatunga antelope is confined to swamp interiors, while the rock-loving klipspringer is occasionally observed on hills, notably in the grounds of Mihingo Lodge. The roan antelope, once common, is now locally extinct, but large herds of the majestic eland still move seasonally through parts of the park.

21

Many centuries ago, according to oral tradition, the valley in which Lake Mburo stands today was dry agricultural land, worked by a pair of brothers named Kigarama and Mburo. One night, Kigarama dreamed that he and his brother would be in danger unless they moved to higher land. The next morning, as Kigarama prepared to relocate to the surrounding hills, he shared the warning with Mburo, who shrugged it off and decided to stay put. Within days, the valley was submerged, and Kigarama watched on helplessly from the hills as his younger brother drowned. The lake was named for the unfortunate Mburo and the surrounding hills after Kigarama.

In pre-colonial times, the area around Lake Mburo, known as Nshara and referred to by Bahima pastoralists as Karo Karungyi (literally 'good grazing land'), was probably rather thinly populated. Pastoralist settlement would have been inhibited by the periodic prevalence of *Glossina morsitans*, a species of tsetse fly that transmits a strain of trypanosome harmless to wild animals and humans, but fatal to domestic cattle. Furthermore, the Omugabe of Ankole favoured Nshara as a royal hunting ground, and forbade the Bahima from grazing and watering their cattle there except during times of drought.

In the early 1890s, Mburo – like the rest of Ankole – was hit severely by the rinderpest epidemic that swept through East Africa, and the resultant depletion of livestock precipitated a famine that claimed thousands of human lives. The decreased grazing pressure also led to widespread bush regeneration, paving the way for a devastating tsetse fly outbreak c1910. Those pastoralists who had resettled the Mburo area were forced to relocate their herds to the more arid savannah of Nyabushozi, north of the present-day Kampala–Mbarara road.

In 1935, the colonial government set aside the vast tract of largely depopulated land centred on Mburo as a Controlled Hunting Area in which both regulated hunting and traditional human activities were permitted. Ten years later, another tsetse outbreak – this time not only *G. morsitans*, but also *G. palpalis*, which spreads sleeping sickness to humans – forced the pastoralists out of the Mburo area. As a result, the colonial authorities instituted a radical programme to eradicate the tsetse from Ankole in the 1950s – its premise being that if every last wild animal in the area were killed, then the bloodsucking tsetse would surely be starved to extinction.

Brian Herne includes a scathing account of this first phase of the anti-tsetse campaign in his book *African Safaris*:

> They employed vast teams of African hunters with shot-bolt rifles … with orders to shoot every single animal, irrespective of age or sex. Everything was to be exterminated. We watched in horror and anger. They did slaughter everything they could … anything and everything that crossed their gunsights. The wildlife was decimated almost out of existence … after the grass fires in July, the plains were richly scattered with bleached skeletons and gaunt sun-dried carcasses.

> According to Herne, the 'wondrous final solution had proved a disastrous and expensive bloodbath … It is of course almost possible to kill off entire populations but some stock always survives, especially of more elusive animals like duiker and bushbuck. Of course, some did survive – enough to ensure the survival of the tsetse fly!'

The authorities reasoned that if it was not possible to starve the tsetse to death, then the only solution was to eradicate the shady bushes and trees around which it lived. Hundreds of square kilometres of bush around Mburo were stripped, cut and/ or burned, until barely any trees were left. After the first rains fell, however, a dense cover of secondary undergrowth quickly established itself, offering adequate cover for tsetse flies to survive, Herne wrote, 'voracious and hungry and as indiscriminate in their hunger as ever'. Over the next season, the authorities implemented a new campaign, aimed directly at the tsetse, employing teams of locals to spray every inch of Ankole with insecticide. This final phase did result in the virtual elimination of the tsetse, but at considerable ecological cost, since it also took its toll on almost every other insect species, as well as insectivorous birds and small mammals.

In the early 1960s, with tsetse-borne diseases all but eradicated, Bahima pastoralists flocked back to the controlled hunting area. It soon became clear that, were any wildlife to survive, the resettlement of Mburo would need to be regulated. In 1964, the first Obote government de-gazetted a large portion of the controlled hunting area to make way for subsistence farmers and herders, while the remainder was upgraded to become the Lake Mburo Game Reserve. Pastoralists were granted transit and dry-season watering rights to the newly gazetted reserve, but were forbidden from residing within it.

This stasis was undermined in the 1970s, after some 650km^2 of gazetted land were excised to become a state cattle ranch. Conservation activities in what remained of the game reserve practically ceased, allowing for considerable human encroachment along the borders. The volume of wildlife, largely recovered from the anti-tsetse slaughter 20 years earlier, was again severely depleted, this time as a result of subsistence poaching. The park's lions – unpopular with local herders not only because they occasionally hunted cattle, but also for their long-standing reputation as man-eaters (one particularly voracious male reputedly accounted for more than 80 human lives in the 1960s) – were hunted to local extinction.

In 1983, the second Obote government gazetted Lake Mburo as a national park, following the boundaries of the original game reserve and forcibly evicting some 4,500 families without compensation. As a result, local communities tended to view the park somewhat negatively – a waste of an important traditional resource from which they had been wrongly excluded. As the civil war reached its peak in 1986, Lake Mburo was almost wholly resettled, its facilities and infrastructure were destroyed, and subsistence poaching once again reached critical levels. In 1987, the Museveni government agreed to reduce the area of the national park by 60%, and it allowed a limited number of people to live within the park and fish on the lake, but still tensions between the park and surrounding communities remained high.

The turning point in Mburo's fractious history came in 1991, with the creation of a pioneering Mburo Community Conservation Unit, established with the assistance of the Africa Wildlife Foundation. A community representative was appointed for each of the neighbouring parishes, to be consulted with regard to decisions affecting the future of the park, and to air any local grievances directly with the park management. Between 1991 and 1997, the remaining inhabitants of the park were relocated outside its borders and awarded a negotiated sum as compensation. Since 1995, 20% of the revenue raised by park entrance fees has been used to fund the construction of local clinics and schools, and for other community projects.

The lake and its lush fringing vegetation also support healthy populations of buffalo, warthog, bushpig and hippopotamus. Some 15 Rothschild's giraffe from Murchison Falls were introduced to LMNP in mid 1995; all but one individual survived the translocation and the herd has settled well into the savannah northeast of Lake Mburo, where it is often seen on game drives.

Only two diurnal primate species are present, namely vervet monkey and olive baboon, but Lake Mburo is one of the very few places in Uganda where the greater galago has been recorded. Up to eight of these cat-sized nocturnal primates make a nightly appearance at a feeding table at Mihingo Lodge, and the jet-black coloration of most individuals suggests they belong to a little-known and taxonomically controversial population of silvery greater galago restricted to woodland habitats in the Lake Victoria basin, and designated as *Otolemur monteiri argentatus* by some authorities.

As for predators, the lions for which LMNP was once famed had been hunted to local extinction by the late 1970s, but the odd individual still finds its way there: indeed, a solitary male has been seen regularly since it first showed up in 2008, and we also heard a recent unsubstantiated report of three females. Leopards are abundant and quite commonly seen, especially on night drives out of Mihingo Lodge, which has identified a dozen different individuals over the past few years based on photographs taken in the northeast of the park. The eerie, rising, nocturnal call of the spotted hyena is often heard from the camps, and individuals are also observed crossing the road at night or shortly after dawn with increasing frequency. Side-striped jackal and

ANKOLE CATTLE

From mountain gorillas to lions, from elephants to shoebills, Uganda is blessed with more than its fair share of impressive wild beasties. But it is also the major stronghold for what is unquestionably the most imposing of Africa's domestic creatures: the remarkable long-horned breed of cattle associated with various pastoralist peoples of the Ugandan–Tanzanian–Rwandan border area, but most specifically with the Bahima of Ankole.

Ankole cattle come in several colours, ranging from uniform rusty-yellow to blotched black-and-white, but they always have a long head, short neck, deep dewlap and narrow chest, and the male often sports a large thoracic hump. What most distinguish the Ankole cattle from any familiar breed, however, are their preposterous, monstrous horns, which grow out from either side of the head like inverted elephant tusks and, in exceptional instances, reach dimensions unseen on any Ugandan tusker since the commercial ivory poaching outbreak of the 1980s.

The ancestry of the Ankole cattle has been traced back to Eurasia as early as 15,000BC, but the precursors of the modern long-horned variety were introduced to northern Uganda only in late medieval times. Hardy, and capable of subsisting on limited water and poor grazing, these introduced cattle were ideally suited to harsh African conditions, except that they had no immunity to tsetse-borne diseases, which forced the pastoralists who tended them to keep drifting southward. The outsized horns of the modern Ankole cattle are probably a result of selective breeding subsequent to their ancestors' arrival in southern Uganda about 500 years ago. The Bahima value cows less for their individual productivity than as status symbols: the wealth of a man would be measured by the size and quality of his herd, and the worth of an individual cow by her horn size and, to a lesser extent, her coloration.

Traditionally, Bahima culture was as deeply bound up with its almost mystical relationship to cattle as the lifestyle of the Maasai is today. Like Eskimos and

various smaller predators are also present, most visibly white-tailed mongoose (at dusk and dawn) and three otter species resident in the lakes.

Some 315 species of **bird** have been recorded in Lake Mburo National Park, and it is probably the best place in Uganda to see acacia-associated birds. Rwonyo Camp is as good a place as any to look for the likes of mosque swallow, black-bellied bustard, bare-faced go-away bird and Rüppell's starling. A handful of birds recorded at Lake Mburo are essentially southern species at the very northern limit of their range, for instance the southern ground hornbill, black-collared and black-throated barbets, and green-capped eremomela. Of special interest to birders are the swamps, in which six papyrus endemics are resident, including the brilliantly coloured papyrus gonolek, the striking blue-headed coucal, and the highly localised white-winged warbler and papyrus yellow warbler, the last recorded nowhere else in Uganda. Lake Mburo itself is known as a reliable site for the elusive African finfoot.

FURTHER INFORMATION The informative new *Lake Mburo National Park Information Guide*, written by Mark Jordhal and published by UWA in 2014, is well worth a look. Sheet 5 in the 'Uganda Maps' series covers Lake Mburo National Park and includes lists of wildlife and birding highlights.

GETTING THERE AND AWAY Four dirt access roads run south from the surfaced Masaka-Mbarara road to Lake Mburo National Park. The most westerly, longest,

their physical landscape, the abiding mental preoccupation of the Bahima is reflected in the 30 variations in hide coloration that are recognised linguistically – the most valued being the uniform dark-brown *bihogo* – along with at least a dozen peculiarities of horn shape and size. The Bahima day is traditionally divided up into 20 periods, of which all but one of the daylight phases is named after an associated cattle-related activity. And, like the Maasai, the Bahima traditionally regarded any activity other than cattle herding as beneath contempt. They also declined to hunt game for meat, with the exception of buffalo and eland, which were sufficiently bovine in appearance for acceptable eating.

In times past, the Bahima diet did not, as might be expected, centre on meat, but rather on blood tapped from a vein of a living cow, combined with the relatively meagre yield of milk from the small udders that characterise the Ankole breed. The Bahima viewed their cattle as something close to family, so that slaughtering a fertile cow for meat was regarded as akin to cannibalism. It was customary, however, for infertile cows and surplus bullocks to be killed for meat on special occasions, while the flesh of any cow that died of natural causes would be eaten or bartered with the agriculturist Bairu for millet beer and fresh produce. No part of the cow would go to waste: the hide would be used to make clothing, mats and drums, the dung used to plaster huts and dried to light fires, while the horns could be customised as musical instruments.

The Ankole region is not as defiantly traditionalist as, say, Ethiopia's Omo Valley or Maasailand, and most rural Bahima today supplement their herds of livestock by practising mixed agriculture of subsistence and cash crops. But the Ankole cattle and their extraordinary horns, common in several parts of Uganda but most prevalent in the vicinity of Mbarara and Lake Mburo, pay living tribute to the bovine preoccupations of Ankole past.

roughest and least-used route leads south from Biharwe (⊕ -0.52188, 30.74215), only 200m east of Igongo Cultural Centre, and passes through Katengyeto Gate before emerging at Rwonyo after about 50km. A far better approach coming from the west is the 10km road to Sanga Gate that branches south at Sanga (⊕ -0.49823, 30.90681), 35km east of Mbarara. Coming from Kampala or Masaka, you're better off using the 8km road to Nshaara Gate that branches south at a junction (⊕ -0.46966, 31.02603) about 1.5km west of the village of Akegeti. All three of these approach roads are signposted, and conditions are variable, so a 4x4 vehicle is recommended, particularly during the rainy season or if you opt for the Biharwe route.

The fourth and most· easterly approach is unsignposted and in relatively poor condition, but there's plenty of game along the way and it is worth considering if you are heading to either Mihingo Lodge or Mburo Safari Lodge in a sturdy 4x4, and want to avoid paying park fees just to transit. Approaching from Lyantonde, you need to turn right at Akagate trading centre and continue for 14km to Akashensero village. From here, it's a challenging road that traverses several swampy valleys and there are numerous diversions around wet or boggy sections, so best hire a boda to guide you through the maze.

There is no public transport along any of the approach roads, but it is possible to charter a special hire from Sanga (*around US$30 one-way*) or pick up a boda (*around US$8–10*).

WHERE TO STAY   *Map, page 543*

A good selection of small, mid-range and upmarket camps and lodges serves LMNP. The only budget option within the park is Rwonyo Rest Camp, but there are plenty of cheap hotels in Lyantonde, a small town that straddles the Masaka Road about 16km east of the junction for Nshaara Gate.

Upmarket

✳ ⌂ Mihingo Lodge (12 tents) ⊕ -0.60298, 31.0484; m 0752 410509; e reservations@ mihingolodge.com; www.mihingolodge.com; see ad, 3rd colour section. One of the best lodges associated with any Ugandan national park, Mihingo is superbly positioned atop an extensive kopje (rock outcrop) within a private 97ha wilderness area abutting the eastern boundary of LMNP & offering views eastward to Lake Kacheera. The privately positioned luxury tents all enjoy outward views from a veranda & spacious bathroom, with 6 units dramatically placed on the summit of the kopje with others along less giddy contours around the flanks. Attention to detail is evident throughout; from the loo handles to the organic thatched lounge/dining shelter supported by gnarled olive-wood branches. The setting for excellent 3-course dinners is perfectly positioned (as is an adjacent rock-sided swimming pool) to enjoy the breeze, sunsets & the wildlife visiting a salt lick in the valley below. Visitors with walking difficulties or small children should note that some tents are accessed by varying numbers of rough

stone steps. Mihingo is the only base for horseback safaris in & around the national park (page 550), & it also offers mountain biking excursions outside the park, guided walks, night drives & cultural visits to a nearby village. It is a good place to see klipspringers by day & the little-known silvery greater galago by night. Mihingo Lodge reinvests a portion of its income in community & ecological projects, notably by supporting the local school & by compensating locals for livestock killed by leopard & hyena, which has enabled the populations of these predators to recover. *US$370/520 FB sgl/dbl non-residents, discounts available for East African residents.* **$$$$$**

⌂ Lake Mburo Camp (8 tents) ⊕ -0.61805, 30.98085; ☎ 041 4320152; m 0772 401391; e info@kimbla-mantanauganda.com; www. kimbla-mantanauganda.com. Also sometimes referred to as Kimbla-Mantana after the company that runs it, this classic luxury tented camp offers a genuine bush experience in secluded & fully furnished en-suite tents, all with solar lighting, eco-friendly toilet & private veranda. The camp runs along a lightly wooded ridge, which is rattling with

birds, lizards & other small animals. If the views towards Lake Mburo are impressive from the new thatched dining/lounge shelter, they are even more memorable from the sundowner fireplace on the summit just above the camp. The tented camp lies off Impala Track & is clearly signposted about 7km from Sanga Gate. *US$330/440 sgl/dbl FB, discount available for East African residents.* **$$$$$**

Moderate

✳ 🏠 **Rwakobo Rock** (9 cottages, 5 rooms, 3 tents) ✛ -0.52825, 31.00011; **m** 0755 211771; **e** info@rwakoborock.com; www.rwakoborock.com; see ad, 3rd colour section. Like Mihingo, this newer lodge 1.5km outside Nshaara Gate is spread across a rock outcrop looking into the national park. The simple but comfortable & meticulously constructed en-suite cottages are individually positioned in secluded sites across the kopje. Though each has a view, don't miss the 360° regional panorama from the top of the kopje. En-suite rooms are also available within the new Hornbill House, & there are safari tents. The new swimming pool should be complete by the time you read this. Can arrange mountain bike tours. *Cottages US$150/125 FB sgl/sharing, rooms US$100/80 sgl/sharing, tents US$50pp, discounts for tour operators & those with a Ugandan work permit.* **$$$**

🏠 **Eagle's Nest** (10 tents) ✛ -0.6014, 30.91981; ☎ 041 4200221; **m** 0777 820071; **e** postmaster@gorillatours.com; www. gorillatours.com. Perched on a cliff just outside Sanga Gate, this sensibly priced bush camp offers accommodation in large standing twin tents with en-suite eco-toilet & bush shower, solar lights, & private balconies offering a splendid view over the plains below. *US$60/70/100 B&B sgl/dbl/trpl, plus US$12pp dinner & US$10pp lunch.* **$$$**

🏠 **Mburo Safari Lodge** (15 cottages) ✛ -0.58575, 31.05468; ☎ 0414 577997; **m** 0712 433744; **e** info@mburosafarilodge.com; www. mburosafarilodge.com. This hilltop lodge is located just outside the park's eastern boundary 2km from Mihingo Lodge. Accommodation is in en-suite wooden chalets with king-sized beds. Facilities include a swimming pool & 2-storey thatched restaurant with a great view. *US$120/180/240/270 FB sgl/dbl/twin/trpl.* **$$$$**

🏠 **Arcadia Cottages** (8 cottages) ✛ -0.64151, 30.95343; **m** 0701 999910/0773 142561; **e** info@ arcadialodges.com; www.arcadialodges.com.

Located 2km south of Rwonyo, this offshoot of its namesake at Bunyonyi accommodates guests in stuffy cement cabins with a wooden floor, fitted nets, en-suite hot showers & private balcony. The lodge's best feature is the 2-storey wooden restaurant, whose 1st-floor canopy offers views across the tree canopy to the lake. Rates seem rather steep for what you get. *US$145/265/440 FB sgl/dbl/trpl.* **$$$$$**

Budget

✳ 🏠 **Rwonyo Rest Camp** (7 tents, 4 bandas) ✛ -0.63388, 30.96506; ☎ 041 4355000; **m** 0751 048904; info@ugandawildlife.org; www. ugandawildlife.org. Perched on a hillside 1km from the lakeshore, this stalwart national park rest camp offers the choice of rather exposed bandas & a more discreetly placed group of standing tents, most of which use communal showers & toilets. It's a pleasant enough site, though not the most imaginative choice given the proximity of the lovely Lake Mburo shoreline & panoramic Rwonyo hilltop. You can cook for yourself, eat at the nearby Lakeside Restaurant (travellers without transport will need to be walked there by a ranger). Waterbuck, warthog & even the occasional bushpig wander through at night, & if you sit quietly they will often come very close. True, facilities are a bit rundown, but more to the point, this rustic camp offers budget travellers a genuine bush experience at a bargain price. *US$12/14/20 sgl/dbl/trpl bandas, US$10/13 sgl/dbl tents.* **$**

🏠 **Skyblue Motel** (13 rooms) ✛ -0.4101, 31.14046; **m** 0772 487559; skybluehotels@live. com; www.skyblue-hotels.com. Situated 500m west of Lyantonde town only 40 mins' drive from Nshaara Gate, this affiliated branch of Mbarara's Acacia Hotel has comfortable tiled en-suite rooms with nets, DSTV & hot shower, & there's a decent restaurant attached. *US$35/50 sgl/dbl B&B.* **$$**

🏠 **Novella Gusto Motel** (13 rooms) ✛ -0.40418, 31.15771; **m** 0750 118230. The pick of half-a-dozen budget hotels in the centre of Lyantonde, this new place has spacious clean rooms with fitted nets, DSTV & en-suite hot shower. The restaurant serves typical Ugandan fare in the US$2.50–3.50 range. *US$20 B&B dbl.* **$$**

🏠 **Leopard Tail Rest Camp** **m** 0782 862088/0757 731641; **e** info@ explorerbikingsafaris.com. As we went to print, we received news about this new budget camp set to

open outside Nshara Gate in late 2016. It will offer a choice of dorms, lazy camping, rooms & safari tents, as well as a great range of activities including day & night game drives, biking & walking safaris, & nature & community walks. *Expect rates to be around US$30/55 dbl/trpl rooms, US$35 dbl safari tent, US$15pp dorm bed, US$25pp lazy camping or US$10pp camping in your own tent.* **$$$**

Camping

⋀ Main Campsite ✪ -0.63754, 30.95308. This lakeshore campsite 1.5km from Rwonyo is serviced by a clean ablution block & the Lakeside Restaurant. Birdlife is plentiful & hippos come ashore at night to keep the lawns cropped short. If you have your own transport & provisions, & aren't too fussed by tsetse flies, lakeshore camping is also possible at a second campsite 5km further south. *US$5pp.* **$**

WHAT TO SEE AND DO

Game drives The part of the national park to the east of Lake Mburo is traversed by a network of game tracks. The quality of game viewing in particular locations is influenced by the season as well as long-term vegetative changes. Overall, though, the best game viewing is in the park-like savannah north and east of Rwonyo along the Research, Zebra, Impala and Warukiri tracks, an area that usually hosts substantial concentrations of impala, zebra, waterbuck, topi and buffalo. The relatively open savannah along the Kazuma and Ruroko tracks is also good for game viewing, passing through a landscape interspersed with rocky hills where pairs of klipspringer are frequently observed. The recently introduced giraffe are most commonly seen in the vicinity of Kazuma and Research tracks. You should also park up and walk to the top of Kazuma Hill for the southern panorama over four of the park's lakes.

Historically, during the dry season, when animals congregate around the swamps and lakes, the best game viewing was often along the stretch of Lakeside Track south of the junction with Kazuma Track, together with the more southerly Kigambira Loop. These days, however, the increasingly dense bush cover near the lake has complicated game viewing (unless you're searching specifically for bush-dwelling birds, or hoping to spot a leopard), and it is also often infested with tsetse flies. The 360° panorama from the once-grassy summit of Kigambira Hill has been all but obscured by scrub.

To the west of Rwonyo, starting near Sanga Gate, the Rwizi Track leads through an area of light acacia savannah where impala, eland and Burchell's zebra are common. After 12km, the track approaches the Rwizi River and fringing swamps, before veering west to follow the wooded watercourse for 33km to Bisheshe Gate. This road is particularly rewarding for birds but tsetse flies can be a problem.

Horseback safaris Mihingo Lodge (page 548) has introduced horseback safaris in the east of the park, a first in a Ugandan protected area, and a great opportunity to get close to animals such as zebra and buffalo, which are far more relaxed around horses than around cars. Rides are tailored to individual experience and requirements. Kids can be led on good-natured ponies while (at the other extreme) experienced riders can help a couple of retired racehorses burn off some calories. Day rates vary from US$40/60 per person for a 30–60-minute taster in the grassy valley floor below the lodge (an area habitually filled with game) to US$300 for a full-day hack to various hilltop viewpoints with a picnic breakfast and bush lunch. Guests staying at Mihingo get a substantial discount (*US$25/40 for 30/60mins or US$200 for a full day*). Overnight, two-day and three-day rides are also available. Further details and rates are posted at www.mihingo-lodge.com.

Guided night drives The success of Mihingo Lodge's compensation scheme for locals whose livestock is killed by leopards or hyenas means that numbers of these once elusive nocturnal predators have increased greatly in recent years, particularly in the

northeast of the park. Night drives out of Mihingo now come with a 30–40% chance of seeing leopards, which are often quite relaxed around vehicles, while packs of up to 20 hyena are regularly observed. The cost is US$30 per person in your own vehicle, or for those without a vehicle, Mihingo Lodge can provide one for US$60 per group.

Boat trips (*US$60 for up to 4 people, then US$15pp for every additional passenger*) Motorboat trips on Lake Mburo leave from the jetty at the main campsite 1km from Rwonyo Camp. In addition to the attractive scenery and simple pleasure attached to being out on the water, the boat trip reliably produces good sightings of hippo, crocodile, buffalo, waterbuck and bushbuck, and it's also worth looking out for the three species of resident otter. Among the more conspicuous waterbirds are African fish eagle, marabou stork, pied kingfisher and various egrets and herons, while Ross's turaco and Narina trogon are frequently seen in lakeside thickets. Lake Mburo is possibly the easiest place in Uganda to see the African finfoot, which is generally associated with still water below overhanging branches. The excursions last 90 minutes and leave every 2 hours from 08.00 to 16.00 as well as at 17.30.

Guided walks (*US$15/30pp FR/FNR*) Visitors are permitted to walk anywhere in LMNP in the company of an armed ranger. Near to the camp, the road to the jetty remains a good place to walk, rich in birds and regularly visited by hippos. An even better target is a viewing platform that overlooks a salt lick about 2km from the camp – an excellent place to see a wide variety of animals. Of particular interest to walkers and birders is the **Rubanga Forest,** which lies off the Rwizi Track and can only be visited with the permission of the warden, who will provide you with an armed ranger.

Appendix 1

LANGUAGE

Although 33 local languages are spoken in Uganda, the official language is English, spoken widely by most urban Ugandans, and certainly by anybody with more than a moderate education level and/or who works in the tourist industry. It is not uncommon to come across Ugandans from different parts of the country using English to communicate, and most English-speaking visitors to the country will have no problem getting around. Of several indigenous languages, the most widely spoken is Luganda, which to some extent serves as a lingua franca for the uneducated. So, too, does Swahili, a coastal Bantu language that is no more indigenous to Uganda than is English.

LUGANDA Luganda is the first language of Buganda and most widely spoken of the languages indigenous to Uganda. Pronunciation is very similar to Swahili. Some words and phrases follow. A detailed phrasebook and dictionary can be viewed online at www.buganda.com.

Greetings

Hello (informal)	*Ki kati*	Thank you	
How are you?	*Oli otya?*	(very much)	*Webale (Nyo)*
I am OK	*Gyendi*	Excuse me	*Owange*
Have a nice day	*Siba bulungi*	Sorry	*Nsonyiwa*
Goodnight	*Sula bulungi*	Sir	*Ssebo*
Farewell	*Weraba*	Come here	*Jangu wano*
See you later	*Tunalabagana*	Madam	*Nnyabo*
Please	*Mwattu*	Mr	*Mwami*
		Mrs	*Mukyala*

Useful phrases

Where are you from?	*Ova mukitundu ki?*
I am from England	*Nva mu England*
Where have you come from?	*Ovude wa?*
I have come from Kampala	*Nvude Kampala*
Where are you going?	*Ogenda wa?*
I am going to Mbale	*Ngenda Mbale*
How can I get to Mbale?	*Ngenda ntya okutuka e Mbale?*
Does this bus go to Kampala?	*Eno baasi egenda e Kampala?*
Which bus goes to Kampala?	*Baasi ki egenda e Kampala?*
What time does the bus leave?	*Baasi egenda sawa meka?*
Where can I buy a bus ticket?	*Tikiti ya baasi nyinza kugigula wa?*
What time does the bus arrive?	*Baasi etuka ku sawa meka?*

Where is the road to Kampala?	*Olugudo lwe Kampala luliwa?*
Where is this taxi going?	*Eno taxi eraga wa?*
Where is it?	*Kiriwa?*
How far is it?	*Kiri wala wa?*
Is it far?	*Kiri wala?*
Is it near?	*Kiri kumpi?*
How much does it cost?	*Sente meka?*
Do you speak English?	*Oyogera oluzungu?*
Do you have any …?	*Olinayo ko …?*
I would like …	*Njagalayo …*
I want a room	*Njagala kisenge*
There is	*Waliwo*
There is not	*Tewali*
What is this called?	*Kino kiyitibwa kitya?*
What is your name?	*Amanya go gw'ani?*
My name is Philip	*Nze Philip*

Words

big	*kinene*	OK	*ye*
come (here)	*jangu (wano)*	please	*bambi*
good	*kirungi*	possible	*kisoboka*
here	*wano*	slow down	*genda mpola*
hurry up	*yanguwa*	small	*katono*
later	*edda*	today	*lero*
many	*bingi*	toilet	*toileti*
me	*nze*	tomorrow	*enkya*
morning	*kumakya*	water	*mazi*
no	*neda*	yes	*ye*
not possible	*tekisoboka*	yesterday	*jjo*
now	*kati*	you	*gwe*

Foodstuffs

avocado	*kedo*	melon	*wuju*
banana (green)	*matooke*	onion	*katungulu*
banana (sweet)	*menvu*	orange	*mucungwa*
beans	*bijanjalo*	pawpaw	*paapaali*
beef	*nte*	peanuts	*binyebwa*
cabbage	*mboga*	pepper	*kaamulali*
carrot	*kalati*	pineapple	*naanansi*
cassava	*muwogo*	pork	*mbizi*
chicken	*nkoko*	potato	*lumonde*
corn	*kasooli*	rice	*muceere*
fish	*kyenyanja*	salt	*munnyo*
goat meat	*mbuzi*	sugar	*sukali*
lamb/mutton	*ndiga*	sugarcane	*kikajo*
mango	*muyembe*	sweet potato	*lumonde*
meat	*nyama*	tomato	*nyanya*

AFRICAN ENGLISH Although a high proportion of Ugandans speak English as a second language, not all do so regularly, and as a result they are less fluent as they could be. Furthermore, pronunciation of a second language tends to retain the vocal inflections

of the person's first language, and people often also use sentence structures derived from their home tongue. In other words, most Ugandans, to a greater or lesser extent, speak a version of English infused with Bantu inflections and grammar.

It could even be said that African English – like American English, or Australian English – is a distinct linguistic entity with a unique rhythm and pronunciation that visitors would do well to familiarise themselves with. In which context, the following points may prove to be useful:

- Greet simply, using easily understood phrases such as the ubiquitous sing-song 'How-are-you! – I am fine'. In Uganda it is customary to greet a stranger before you ask directions or any other question.
- Speak slowly and clearly. There is no need to take this too far, as if you are talking to a three-year old. Just speak naturally, but try not to rush or clip phrases.
- Phrase questions simply, with an ear towards Bantu inflections. 'This bus goes to Mbale?' might be more easily understood than 'Could you tell me whether this bus is going to Mbale?' and 'You have a room?' is better than 'Is there a vacant room?' Try to avoid unusual words – such as 'vacant' – that might obstruct easy understanding.
- Listen to how people talk to you, and learn from it. Vowel sounds are often pronounced as in the local language, so that 'bin', for instance, might sound more like 'been'. Many words, too, will be pronounced with the customary Bantu stress on the second-last syllable.
- Most African languages contain few words with compound consonant sounds, or that end in consonants. This can result in the clipping of soft consonant sounds such as 'r' (important as eem-POT-ant) or the insertion of a random vowel sound between running consonants (so that pen-pal becomes pen-i-pal and sounds almost indistinguishable from pineapple). It is commonplace, as well, to append a random vowel to the end of a word, in the process shifting the stress to what would ordinarily be the last syllable (eg: pen-i-PAL-i).
- The 'l' and 'r' sounds are sometimes used interchangeably. Rubaga Hill in Kampala, for instance, is sometimes spelt Lubaga. The same is to a lesser extent true of 'b' and 'v' (Virunga versus Birunga), 'ky' and 'ch' (Kyambura is pronounced 'Chambura') and, very occasionally, 'f' and 'p'.
- Some English words are in wide use. Other similar words are not. A request for a 'hotel' or 'guesthouse', is more likely to be understood than one for 'accommodation', as is 'taxi' (or better 'special hire') for 'cab', or 'the balance' for 'change'.
- Avoid the use of dialect-specific expressions, slang and jargon such as 'feeling crook', 'pear-shaped' or 'user-friendly'.
- Avoid meaningless interjections. If somebody is struggling to follow you, appending a word such as 'mate' to every other phrase is only likely to further confuse them.
- Try to avoid asking questions that can be answered with a yes or no. People may well agree with you simply to be polite or to avoid embarrassment.
- Keep calm. No-one is at their best when they arrive at a crowded bus station after an all-day bus ride. It is easy to be short-tempered when someone cannot understand you. Be patient and polite; it's you who doesn't speak the language.
- It can be useful to know that the Ugandan phrase for urinating is 'short call'. Useful, because often you will be caught short somewhere with no toilet, and if you ask for a toilet will simply be told there is none. By contrast, if you tell somebody you need a 'short call', you'll be pointed to wherever locals take theirs!
- Last but not least, do gauge the extent to which the above rules might apply to any given individual. It would be patently ridiculous to address a university lecturer or an experienced tour guide in broken English, equally inappropriate to babble away without making any allowances when talking to a villager who clearly has a limited English vocabulary.

Appendix 2

acacia woodland	any woodland dominated by thorn trees of the acacia family
Albertine Rift	western Rift Valley between Lake Albert and northern Lake Tanganyika
Amin, Idi	dictatorial President of Uganda 1971–79
Ankole	extant medieval kingdom centred on modern-day Mbarara
askari	security guard
Bachwezi	legendary medieval kingdom, centred on present-day Mubende
Baker, Lady Florence	wife and travel companion to Sir Samuel
Baker, Sir Samuel	first European to Lake Albert, Murchison Falls 1864, Governor of Equatoria 1872–73
balance	change (for a payment)
banda	any detached accommodation such as a hut or chalet
barkcloth	traditional material made from the bark of the fig tree
Batembuzi	legendary medieval kingdom, possibly centred on present-day Ntusi
Bell, Sir Henry Hesketh	Commissioner to Uganda 1905–09 after whom Port Bell (and thus Bell Beer) is named
Besigye, Kizza	Leader of the Forum for Democratic Change (FDC) who unsuccessfully contested the four presidential elections between 2001 and 2016
boda	short for boda-boda; motorbike, scooter or occasionally bicycle taxi
boma	colonial administrative office
Buganda	extant kingdom for which Uganda is named, centred on modern-day Kampala
Bunyoro	extant kingdom centred on modern-day Hoima
Bwana	Mister (polite Swahili term of address, sometimes used in Uganda)
chai	tea
Colville, Colonel	led the attack on Mparo that drove Kabalega into hiding, 1894
cowrie	small white shell used as currency in pre-colonial times
Daudi Chwa, Kabaka	crowned King of Buganda at age one in 1897, ruled until death in 1939
DSTV	South African multi-channel satellite television service
duka	stall or kiosk
endemic	unique to a specific area
exotic	not indigenous, for instance pine plantations
forest	wooded area with closed canopy
forex bureau	bureau de change
fundi	expert (especially mechanic)

Grant, Captain James	accompanied Speke on journey to source of the Nile, 1862
guesthouse	cheap local hotel
Hannington, Bishop James	missionary killed on Mwanga's instructions *en route* to Buganda in 1885
hoteli	local restaurant
indigenous	occurring in a place naturally
Interlacustrine Region	area between Lake Victoria and Albertine Rift Lakes: Rwanda, Burundi, south Uganda, northwest Tanzania
Isuza	legendary Batembuzi ruler
Kabaka	King of Buganda
Kabalega, Omukama	King of Bunyoro from 1870, exiled to Seychelles by the British 1897, died there 1923
Kaggwa, Sir Apollo	Katikiro of Buganda 1889–1926, and copious chronicler of Kiganda folklore and history
Kakunguru, Semei	Muganda leader who conquered east Uganda for the British in the 1890s and founded Kumi and Mbale
Kamurasi, Omukama	powerful Bunyoro King, ruled c1852–69, met by Speke and Baker
Katikiro	'Prime Minister' of Buganda
Kiganda	relating to the culture or religions of Buganda
Kiira	Luganda name for the Victoria Nile
Kintu	legendary founder of Buganda
Kony, Joseph	leader of the LRA
kopje/koppie	small, often rocky hill (from Afrikaans meaning 'little head')
Kyebambe III, Omukama	King of Bunyoro c1786–1835
LRA	Lord's Resistance Army
Lubaale (plural Balubaale)	important Kiganda spirit
Luganda	language of Buganda
Lugard, Captain Frederick	Representative of the Imperial British East Africa Company who signed a provisional treaty with Mwanga in 1890
mandazi	fried doughnut-like pastry
matatu	minibus used as a shared taxi carrying ten to 13 passengers
matoke	staple made from cooking plantains (bananas)
mbugo	barkcloth (traditional dress of Buganda)
minibus-taxi	see *matutu*
mishkaki	meat (usually beef) kebab
mobile	mobile satellite phone
MTN	main satellite-phone provider in Uganda
Muganda	citizen of Buganda kingdom (plural: Baganda)
murram	dirt road built with laterite soil
Museveni, Yoweri	President of Uganda 1986–present
Mutesa I, Kabaka	King of Buganda 1857–84, hosted Speke 1862
Mutesa II, Edward Kabaka	King of Buganda 1939–66, President of Uganda 1962–66, died in exile 1969
mazungu	white person
Mwanga, Kabaka	King of Buganda 1884–93, exiled to Seychelles 1897, died there 1903
Namasole	'Queen mother' or more accurately mother of the Kabaka of Buganda
Ndahura	legendary founder of Bacwezi dynasty, son of Isuza

netting	mosquito net
NRM	National Resistance Movement (governing part of Uganda)
Nyerere, Julius	President of Tanzania who initiated the war that ousted Amin in 1979
Obote, Milton	dictatorial President of Uganda, 1962–71 and 1981–85
Okello, Tito	military President of Uganda, July 1985–January 1986
Omukama	King of Bunyoro/Toro
Omugabe	King of Ankole
Owen, Roderick	companion of Portal in 1893 for whom Owen Falls at the source of the Nile is named
panga	local equivalent of a machete
Pasha, Emin	Governor of Equatoria 1878 until 'rescued' by Stanley 1889
pesa	money
pombe	local beer
Portal, Sir Gerald	Governor of Zanzibar, visited Uganda 1893, Fort Portal named in his honour
QENP	Queen Elizabeth National Park (often called QE or QENP)
riparian/riverine	strip of forest or lush woodland following a watercourse, often woodland rich in fig trees
Ruhanga	legendary king of the underworld and founder of the Batembuzi dynasty
Runyoro	language of Bunyoro
safari	Swahili word for journey, now widely used to refer to game-viewing trip
savannah	grassland with some trees
Saza chief	ruler of a County (Saza) of Buganda, answerable to the kabaka
shamba	small subsistence farm
short call	urinate
soda	fizzy drink such as Fanta or Coca-Cola
special hire	taxi
Speke, John Hanning	first European to visit Buganda, Bunyoro and the source of the Nile, 1862
Ssemogorere, Paul	one-time prime minister under Museveni, stood in the 1996 presidential election
Stanley, Henry Morton	explorer to Uganda in 1875–76 and 1889, discovering Rwenzoris on latter trip
surfaced (road)	road sealed with asphalt or similar
tented camp	rustic but generally upmarket small camp offering canvassed accommodation
Thomson, Joseph	in 1883, became the first European to enter present-day Uganda from the east
Toro	extant 19th-century kingdom centred on modern-day Fort Portal
tot packet	sachet of whisky or waragi
track	motorable minor road or path
trading centre	small town or village where local villagers would go to shop
ugali	staple porridge made from maize (corn) meal
UPDF	Uganda People's Defence Force
UWA	Uganda Wildlife Authority
Wamala	legendary Bacwezi ruler, son of Ndahura
Waragi	local brand of gin
wazungu	plural of Mazungu
woodland	wooded area lacking closed canopy

Appendix 3

Readers with a particular interest in Arua and West Nile will enjoy *Oh Uganda, may God uphold thee*, a new memoir by John Haden and John Ondoma. The two men were teachers in West Nile when Idi Amin took power. As the story unfolds, and Uganda starts to unravel, you appreciate how the book's title, borrowed from the first line of the national anthem, must have assumed equal significance as a prayer. (*The book costs £12.99 + P&P from www. barnybooks.biz while the Kindle e-book costs £6.55 from Amazon.*)

BOOKS
History and background
In addition to the books listed below, an excellent overview of literature about the Amin years, put together by reader Gavin Parnaby, is posted on www.bradtupdates.com/uganda (click on the category 'books').

Apuuli, K *A Thousand Years of Bunyoro-Kitara* Fountain, 1994. Inexpensive and compact locally published book that ranks close to being essential reading on pre-colonial events, despite being riddled with internal contradictions.

Behrend, Heike *Alice Lakwena & The Holy Spirits* James Currey, 1999. The bizarre and disturbing story of the emergence of the spirit medium in northern Uganda in 1986, which laid the foundation for the present-day Lord's Resistance Army and its brutal leader Joseph Kony.

Bussman, Jane *The Worst Date Ever* Macmillan, 2009. Readable investigation into the LRA war by a British comedienne/journalist and first-time visitor to Africa. Against a subplot of a supposed romantic agenda, Bussman combines a sharp wit and purported naivety whilst stumbling through murkier issues to raise some reasonable questions concerning the failure of government and the international community to end the conflict.

Carruthers, John *Mrs Carruthers is Black* Book Guild Publishing, 2005. An autobiographical account by a Scottish insurance chairman of his marriage to a Ugandan during the days when mixed-race marriages were something of an eyebrow raiser. An entertaining read, liberally seasoned with salacious tales in which names have been changed to protect the guilty.

Chrétien, Jean-Pierre *The Great Lakes of Africa: Two Thousand Years of History* Zone Books, 2006. Probably the most comprehensive one-volume history of a region centred on Rwanda and Uganda, with details of Bachwezi legends as well as more modern events.

Green, Matthew *The Wizard of the Nile* Portobello, 2008. This investigative travelogue tackles the war in northern Uganda and does much to explain the complex, internecine baggage behind this apparently futile conflict. Highly recommended.

Jagielski, Wojciech *The Night Wanderers: Uganda's Children and the Lord's Resistance Army* Old Street Publishing, 2012. A harrowing award-nominated exploration of the lives led by children captured by the LRA during and after their reign of terror in northern Uganda.

Jeal, Tim *Stanley: The Impossible Life of Africa's Greatest Explorer* Faber and Faber, 2007. A readable biography that delves beneath the standard image of Stanley as an imperialist bully to paint a more nuanced portrait of Africa's most successful explorer.

Karugire, S *A Political History of Uganda* Heinemann, 1980. The most concise introduction to Ugandan history on the market, highly readable, with a useful chapter covering precolonial events and razor-sharp commentary on the colonial period.

Miller, Charles *The Lunatic Express* 1971, reprinted Penguin Classics, 2001. Eminently readable account of the building of the Uganda Railway with an excellent history of the events in Uganda that brought about the project.

Moorehead, Alan *The White Nile* Hamilton, 1960. Classic example of the history-as-adventure-yarn genre, detailing the race to discover the source of the Nile and its leading characters.

Museveni, Yoweri *Sowing the Mustard Seed* Macmillan, 1997. The acclaimed autobiography of Uganda's president, mostly devoted to his wilderness years fighting the Amin and Obote regimes but with good coverage of post-1986 reconstruction. Inevitable bias notwithstanding, a frank and insightful read.

Nzita, Richard *Peoples and Cultures of Uganda* Fountain, 1993, 3rd edition 1997. Useful introduction to the various ethnic groupings of Uganda, and the monochrome photos make for an interesting browse.

O' Connor, Kevin *Uganda Society Observed* Fountain, 2006. A collection of light-hearted (sometimes exploring serious themes) articles written for *The Monitor* newspaper by an expat columnist.

Packenham, Thomas *The Scramble for Africa* Weidenfeld & Nicolson, 1991. Gripping and erudite 600-page account of the decade that turned Africa on its head – a 'must read', aptly described by one reviewer as 'Heart of Darkness with the lights switched on'.

Reader, John *Africa: A Biography of the Continent* Penguin, 1997. Bulky, and working the broadest canvas, this excellent introduction to Africa past and present has met with universal praise as perhaps the most readable and accurate book to capture the sweep of African history for the general reader.

Reid, Richard *Political Power in Pre-colonial Buganda* James Currey, 2002. Accessible and clearly written introduction to the kingdom that lies at the heart of Uganda.

Rice, Andrew *The Teeth May Smile But The Heart Does Not Forget* Picador, 2010. Compelling journalistic account of Duncan Laki's four-year investigation into the murder of his father at the hands of Amin's henchmen, and attempt to bring the killers to justice.

Speke, John *Journal of the Discovery of the Source of the Nile*, 1863, reprinted Dover Press, 1996. In this classic account of Victorian exploration, John Hanning Speke displays a wonderful ability to capture the flavour of local cultures, nowhere more so than in a series of chapters about the Buganda court under Mutesa. An enjoyable, instructive and occasionally mind-boggling read!

Twaddle, Michael *Kakungulu and the Creation of Uganda* James Currey, 1993. Excellent and readable biography of the enigmatic and controversial Semei Kakunguru, a Muganda who started his career as a British expansionist and ended it as the founder of a bizarre Judaic sect that still thrives in the Mbale area to this day. Essential stuff!

Nature and wildlife
General
Briggs, Philip and Van Zandbergen, Ariadne *East African Wildlife* Bradt Travel Guides, 2015. A handy and lavishly illustrated one-stop handbook to the fauna of East Africa, with detailed sections on the region's main habitats, varied mammals, birds, reptiles and insects. It's the ideal companion for first-time visitors whose interest in wildlife extends beyond the Big Five but who don't want to carry a library of reference books.

Mammals

Erickson Wilson, Sandra *Bird and Mammal Checklists for Ten National Parks in Uganda* European Commission, 1995. Increasingly difficult-to-locate 88-page booklet containing a complete checklist of all mammals and birds known in Uganda, and in which national parks, if any, each species has been recorded. Hundreds of copies are available at the office in Kidepo National Park.

Estes, Richard *The Safari Companion* Green Books UK, Chelsea Green USA, Russell Friedman Books South Africa, 1992. Not a field guide in the conventional sense so much as a guide to mammalian behaviour, this superb book is very well organised and highly informative, but rather bulky perhaps for casual safari-goers.

Fossey, Dian *Gorillas in the Mist* Hodder and Stoughton, 1983. Thirty-plus years after its original publication, this seminal work remains the best introduction to gorilla behaviour in print.

Goodall, Jane *In the Shadow of Man* Collins, 1971. Classic on chimp behaviour based on Goodall's acclaimed research in Tanzania's Gombe Stream National Park.

Kingdon, Jonathan *Field Guide to African Mammals* Academic Press, 1997. The definitive field guide of its type, with immense detail on all large mammals, as well as a gold mine of information about the evolutionary relationships of modern species, and good coverage of bats, rodents and other small mammals. Excellent illustrations, too. Arguably too pricey and heavy for casual safari-goers, but an essential reference for anybody with a strong interest in Africa's mammals.

Schaller, George *The Year of the Gorilla* Chicago University Press, 1963. Subsequently overshadowed, at least in popular perception, by *Gorillas in the Mist*, this formative behavioural study of gorillas in the Virungas did much to dispel their violent image on publication in 1963, and it remains a genuine classic (with the somewhat parochial advantage over later gorilla books in that most of the action takes place in Uganda rather than Rwanda).

Stuart, Chris and Tilde *Mammals of Southern and East Africa* Struik Publishers, 2002. Compact and well-organised field guide to all the larger mammals likely to be seen in Uganda.

Birds

Russouw, Jonathan and Sacchi, Marco *Where to Watch Birds in Uganda* Uganda Tourist Board, 1998. This excellent little book is out of print and hard to find these days so if you see a copy snap it up! It contains detailed descriptions and advice for all key birding sites in Uganda, with special reference to local rarities and specials, as well as an up-to-date national checklist referencing all the bird species recorded at each of 15 locations in Uganda. The ideal companion to a good field guide.

Meunier, Quentin and McKelvie, Sherry *Birds of Uganda* Self-published, 2015. Attractive coffee-table type book containing more than 900 photographs depicting about a quarter of Uganda's bird species in a variety of plumages. A kindle version is available from Amazon.

Stevenson, Terry and Fanshawe, John *Field Guide to the Birds of East Africa* T & A D Poyser, 2002. The best bird field guide, with useful field descriptions and accurate plates and distribution maps covering every species recorded in Uganda as well as Kenya, Tanzania, Rwanda and Burundi. No other book will suffice for serious birdwatchers, but it is much bulkier and pricier than Van Perlo's competing title.

Butterflies

Carter, Nanny and Tindimubona, Laura *Butterflies of Uganda* Uganda Society, 2002. Very useful albeit non-comprehensive field guide illustrating and describing roughly 200 of the more common butterfly species in Uganda.

Health Self-prescribing has its hazards so if you are going anywhere very remote consider taking a health book. For adults there is *Bugs, Bites & Bowels* by Dr Jane Wilson-

Howarth, published by Cadogan (2009); if travelling with the family look at *Your Child: A Travel Health Guide* by Dr Jane Wilson-Howarth and Dr Matthew Ellis, published by Bradt Travel Guides (2014).

Coffee-table books

Gonget, Barbara, et al *Imagine Uganda*. Excellent and reasonably priced pocket-sized compilation of images by four Ugandan and expatriate photographers: an eclectic representation of landscapes, activities, people, wildlife, etc. Available locally.

Guadalupi, Gianni *Discovery of the Source of the Nile* Stewart, Tabori and Chang, 1997. This hefty and expensive-looking volume contains superb and lavish illustrated spreads of maps and coloured engravings from the age of exploration. The text (translated from the Italian) includes explorers usually omitted from the standard Anglophonic accounts of the search for the Nile's origins. The original hefty price tag notwithstanding, copies can be found for a few pounds on Amazon.

Kampala Attractively produced photo book with a difference. Instead of notable buildings and standard panoramas, *Kampala* depicts the reality of Uganda's hectic capital. Ugandans have complained that that reality does not present their city in a very complimentary light!

Michel, Kiguli, Pluth and Didek *Eye of the Storm: A Photographer's Journey across Uganda* Camerapix, 2002. Sumptuous book, which boldly contrasts evocative scenic and wildlife photography with more gritty urban and rural images reflecting the realities of day-to-day life in Uganda.

Fiction

Foden, Giles *The Last King of Scotland* Faber and Faber, 1998. The Whitbread Prize-winning fictional account of a young Scots doctor working in the service of Idi Amin.

Kingsolver, Barbara *The Poisonwood Bible* HarperCollins, 2000. Set in the Belgian Congo rather than Uganda, this is still a highly insightful novel, particularly about religion in Africa.

Isegawa, Moses *The Abyssinian Chronicles* Vintage, 2001 Uganda's best-known work of modern fiction (set in Uganda in the 1970s and 80s, not as the title suggests Ethiopia) has drawn comparisons to Salman Rushdie's *Midnight's Children* and Gabriel Garcia Marquez's *One Hundred Years of Solitude*.

Okorot, Mary Karooro *The Invisible Weevil* FemRite, 1993. Written by a Ugandan MP, this readable novel provides an insight into the many problems (notably men) that Ugandan women must endure.

Other Africa guides For a full list of Bradt's Africa guides, see www.bradtguides.com.

Briggs, Philip and McIntyre, Chris *Northern Tanzania* Bradt Travel Guides, 2013.
Briggs, Philip and Booth, Janice *Rwanda* Bradt Travel Guides, 2015.
Briggs, Philip and McIntyre, Chris *Tanzania Safari Guide* Bradt Travel Guides, 2013.
Gibbons, Bob and Pritchard-Jones, Sian *Africa Overland* Bradt Travel Guides, 2014.
Lovell-Hoare, Sophie and Lovell-Hoare, Max *South Sudan* Bradt Travel Guides, 2013.
Rorison, Sean *Congo* Bradt Travel Guides, 2012.

MAPS A decent countrywide map can be a great asset. The 1:800,000 map of Uganda published by International Travel Maps (ITMB) of Vancouver is the smallest-scale map available for the whole country, and more accurate than most (one major error in some editions being a displacement of latitudinal lines, causing the Equator, for instance, to be marked as 1°N, etc). Other options are Nelles's 1:700,000 map and the excellent German-produced 1:600,000 Uganda sheet (*www.reise-know-how.de*).

More illustrative maps are available in the popular 'Uganda Maps' series at around US$5 apiece. The current range covers Uganda, Jinja and the Nile, Kampala, Fort Portal and the Rwenzori, and Murchison Falls, Kidepo Valley, Mount Elgon, Lake Mburo, Queen Elizabeth and Bwindi national parks (m *0772 462646;* e *info@east-africa-maps.com; www. east-africa-maps.com*).

TRAVEL MAGAZINES For readers with a broad interest in Africa, an excellent magazine dedicated to tourism throughout Africa is *Travel Africa*, which can be visited online at www.travelafricamag.com.

UGANDA ONLINE The internet is an increasingly valuable tool when it comes to researching most aspects of a trip to Uganda or elsewhere in Africa, though it is advisable to be somewhat circumspect when it comes to heeding advice on personal websites. Do also be aware that the internet is clogged up with sites constructed but never maintained and thus prone to be rather out of date. Websites for individual hotels, lodges, tour operators and other institutions are included alongside the relevant entries elsewhere in this guide. What follows is a list of more generic websites that might prove useful to travellers planning a trip in Uganda.

Uganda-specific sites

www.africatravelresource.com/africa/uganda Superb website operated by a high-end safari company containing reviews and hundreds of excellent pictures of Uganda's best tourist accommodation.

http://birdinguganda.blogspot.com Run by Derek Kverno, this is a superb free resource for independent travellers with the birding bug.

www.buganda.com Detailed historical and cultural essays about the Buganda kingdom past and present.

www.diaryofamuzungu.com Award-winning travel blog by Ugandan resident Charlotte Beauvoisin, covering 'adventure travel, birdwatching, conservation and cultural (mis) observations'.

www.monitor.co.ug News, generally with a more independent stance than the government-backed *New Vision*.

www.newvision.co.ug News, travel features, etc, posted by the country's most established English-language newspaper.

www.traveluganda.co.ug The most useful site for independent travellers also has numerous links for tour companies and community-based tourism sites.

www.ugandawildlife.org The recently revamped website of the Uganda Wildlife Authority has the latest on gorilla-tracking permits and other fees and facilities in the national parks and wildlife reserves.

www.visituganda.com The official website of Tourism Uganda (aka Uganda Tourist Board) has some stunning photographs as section headers and a few useful links.

General sites

www.fco.gov.uk/travel British Foreign & Commonwealth Office site, containing up-to-date, generally rather conservative information on trouble spots and places to avoid.

www.bradtupdates.com/uganda Travel update service for Bradt readers sourced from and aimed at travellers, volunteers and service providers in Uganda.

www.travelafricamag.com Site for the quarterly magazine *Travel Africa* – good news section, travel archives and subscriptions.

http://travel.state.gov/content/passports/en/country/uganda.html US State Department equivalent to FCO.

www.openstreetmap.org Free online maps of countries and major towns.

Index

Page numbers in **bold** indicate main entries; those in *italics* indicate maps

INDEX OF ADVERTISERS

PHOTOGRAPHS AND ILLUSTRATIONS

Photographs Ariadne Van Zandbergen (AVZ); AWL Images: Nigel Pavitt (NP/AWL);
Dreamstime: Erica Schroeder (ES/D), Oleg Znamenskiy (OZ/S), Sergey Uryadnikov (SU/D)
IMAGEBROKER, ROLF SCHULTEN/Imagebroker/FLPA (FLPA); Matoke Tours (MT);
Nalubale Rafting (NR); Shutterstock: Kubica Boleslaw (S/KB), Pecold (S/P), Sergey Uryadnikov
(S/SU); SuperStock (SS)

Front cover De Brazza's monkey (AVZ)
Back cover Northern carmine bee-eater (AVZ); Sipi Falls (AVZ)
Title page Women of the Karamoja (AVZ); Shoebill (AVZ); Sipi Falls (S/P)
Part openers Page 95: Kampala (ES/D); Page 281: Murchison Falls (OZ/D); Page 371: Gorilla,
Bwindi Impenetrable National Park (SU/D)

Illustrations Annabel Milne, Mike Unwin

above   Horseback safaris are a great opportunity to get close to animals in Lake Mburo National Park, as they are far more relaxed around horses than cars (AVZ) page 550

left   Budongo Forest Reserve is one of Uganda's key birdwatching destinations, with over 360 species recorded (AVZ) pages 341–4

below   A boat trip along the Victoria Nile is one of the highlights of a visit to Murchison Falls National Park (AVZ) pages 362–4

above Thanks to fertile soils, ample sunshine and abundant water, you'll see colourful displays of fresh market produce all year round (SS)

right Brightly coloured stools for sale at a stall along the Mbarara Road (AVZ)

below Circumcision ceremonies are still carried out by the Bagisu, a Bantu-speaking people from the western slopes of Mount Elgon (AVZ)

pages 260–1

Uganda in colour

above left   Dugout canoes provide the simplest route to market for farmers living around Lake Bunyonyi (AVZ) pages 479–89

above right   Towering above the plains of eastern Uganda, Mount Kadam marks the gateway into the vast and undeveloped region of Karamoja (AVZ) pages 304–5

below   On the vast, semi-arid plains of Karamoja, hundreds of families still live in traditional *manyattas* (MT) pages 302–8

Tree-climbing lions

The unusual tree-climbing behaviour of Ishasha's lion prides makes these felines unusually easy to spot
(AVZ) page 471

Mountain-gorilla tracking

Few visitors are unmoved by the magical hour spent in the presence of a group of mountain gorillas
(AVZ) pages 516–17

Murchison Falls

At Murchison Falls, the Nile explodes through a 6m-wide gorge to form the most dramatic feature along its 6,650km course
(SS) page 361

Uganda
Don't
miss...

White-water rafting
Every year, thousands of
adventure seekers enjoy
thrills and spills on the
turbulent headwaters of
the Nile near Jinja
(NR) pages 242–3

Fort Portal region
Between the Rwenzori and the
forest of Kibale National Park, the
landscape is one of lush vegetation
(AVZ) pages 375–407

SUDAN

Kidepo Valley National Park

Apoka

Kaabong

Kitgum

Kotido

Matheniko Wildlife Reserve

Patonga

Moroto

Mount Moroto 3084m

Lira

Bokora Wildlife Reserve

Orungo

Napak 2537m

Kadam 3068m

KENYA

Lake Bisina

Soroti

Pian Upe Wildlife Reserve

Lake Kyoga

Kumi

Kapchorwa

Sipi Falls

Nakasongola

Mt Elgon 4321m

Mount Elgon National Park

Mbale

Kamuli

Tororo

Nairobi, Eldoret

Luwero

Mabira Forest Reserve

Iganga

Busia

Mukono

Nairobi, Kisumu

Jinja

KAMPALA

Kajjansi airport

Buvuma

Equator

Entebbe

Kome

Ise Islands

Lake Victoria

TANZANIA

Travel north to the magnificent, mountain-ringed plains of Kidepo Valley National Park, an unforgettable tract of true African wilderness
pages 308–12

Shake off the dust and relax on the slopes of Mount Elgon around Sipi Falls
pages 268–70

Raft and kayak the turbulent headwaters of the mighty Nile
pages 242–3

Tap your feet to a thrilling performance of traditional dances from all corners of Uganda by the Ndere Troupe
pages 151–2

Bradt

0   80km
0   50 miles

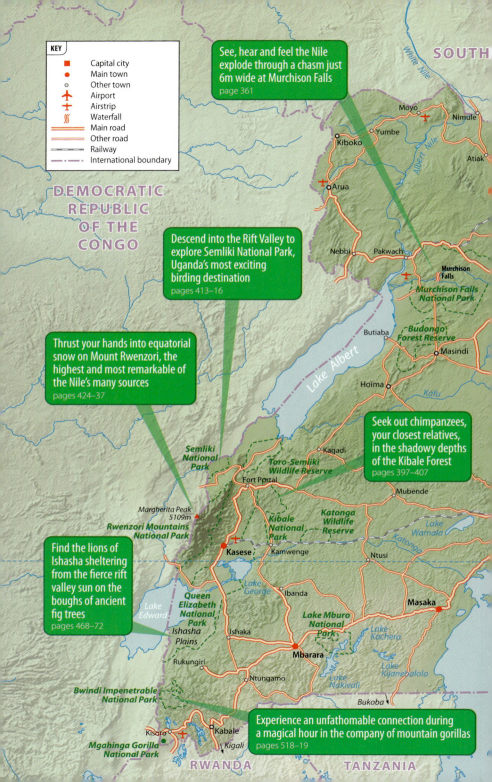

KEY

- 🟥 Capital city
- 🔴 Main town
- ⚬ Other town
- ✈ Airport
- ✛ Airstrip
- 〰 Waterfall
- ═══ Main road
- ─── Other road
- ▦▦▦ Railway
- ·—·— International boundary

SOUTH

See, hear and feel the Nile explode through a chasm just 6m wide at Murchison Falls
page 361

Moyo
Nimule
Kiboko
Yumbe
Atiak

Albert Nile

White Nile

Arua

Nebbi
Pakwach

DEMOCRATIC REPUBLIC OF THE CONGO

Descend into the Rift Valley to explore Semliki National Park, Uganda's most exciting birding destination
pages 413–16

Murchison Falls

Murchison Falls National Park

Butiaba

Budongo Forest Reserve

Masindi

Thrust your hands into equatorial snow on Mount Rwenzori, the highest and most remarkable of the Nile's many sources
pages 424–37

Lake Albert

Hoima

Kafu

Semliki National Park

Kagadi

Seek out chimpanzees, your closest relatives, in the shadowy depths of the Kibale Forest
pages 397–407

Toro-Semliki Wildlife Reserve

Fort Portal

Mubende

Margherita Peak 5109m ▲

Rwenzori Mountains National Park

Kibale National Park

Katonga Wildlife Reserve

Lake Wamala

Kasese

Kamwenge

Ntusi

Katonga

Find the lions of Ishasha sheltering from the fierce rift valley sun on the boughs of ancient fig trees
pages 468–72

Lake George

Ibanda

Lake Edward

Queen Elizabeth National Park

Ishasha Plains

Ishaka

Lake Mburo National Park

Masaka

Lake Kachera

Mbarara

Lake Kijanebalola

Rukungiri

Lake Nakivali

Bwindi Impenetrable National Park

Ntungamo

Bukoba

Experience an unfathomable connection during a magical hour in the company of mountain gorillas
pages 518–19

Kisoro

Kabale

Mgahinga Gorilla National Park

Kigali

RWANDA

TANZANIA

Uganda

the Bradt Travel Guide

Philip Briggs

with Andrew Roberts

edition
8

www.bradtguides.com

Bradt Travel Guides Ltd, UK
The Globe Pequot Press Inc, USA